Also by Robert Kimball

Cole (editor)

Reminiscing with Sissle and Blake (co-author)

The Gershwins (co-author)

The Unpublished Cole Porter (editor)

The Complete Lyrics of Cole Porter (editor)

The Complete Lyrics of Lorenz Hart (editor)

Catalog of the American Musical (co-author)

THE COMPLETE LYRICS OF IRA GERSHWIN

THE COMPLETE LYRICS
OF IRA GERSHWIN

First published in Great Britain in 1994 by
PAVILION BOOKS LIMITED
26 Upper Ground, London SE1 9PD

A CIP catalogue record for this book is available
from the British Library

ISBN 1 85793 248 X

Printed and bound in the USA
2 4 6 8 10 9 7 5 3 1

This book may be ordered by post direct from the
publisher. Please contact the Marketing Department.
But try your bookshop first.

In memory of Leonore Gershwin

(1900–1991)

who wanted this book "for Ira"

CONTENTS

Introduction   xi

Chronology   xxi

Acknowledgments   xxvii

1917–1920   3

You May Throw All the Rice You Desire · Beautiful Bird · The Real American Folk Song (Is a Rag) · Kitchenette · There's Magic in the Air · If You Only Knew · When There's a Chance to Dance · Waiting for the Sun to Come Out · For No Reason at All · Back Home

PICCADILLY TO BROADWAY, 1920 Who's Who with You? · Mr. and Mrs. · Something Peculiar · Piccadilly's Not a Bit Like Broadway · Pick Yo' Partner! (Get Ready for the Raggy Blues)

Somehow I Knew · Bambino · Gondolier

A DANGEROUS MAID, 1921
TWO LITTLE GIRLS IN BLUE, 1921   11

A DANGEROUS MAID, 1921 Anything for You · Just to Know You Are Mine · Boy Wanted · The Simple Life · The Sirens · Dancing Shoes · Some Rain Must Fall · Every Girl Has a Method of Her Own

TWO LITTLE GIRLS IN BLUE, 1921 We're Off on a Wonderful Trip · Wonderful U.S.A. · When I'm with the Girls · Two Little Girls in Blue · The Silly Season · Oh Me! Oh My! · You Started Something · We're Off to India · Here, Steward · Dolly · Just Like You · There's Something About Me They Like · Rice and Shoes · Finale, Act II · Honeymoon · I'm Tickled Silly · Utopia · Happy Ending · Little Bag of Tricks · Make the Best of It · Summertime

1921–1923   23

Phoebe · Peacock Alley · Molly on the Shore · The Piccadilly Walk

FOR GOODNESS SAKE, 1922 Someone · Tra-La-La · French Pastry Walk

Fascination · What I Care! · A New Step Every Day [and] (I'll Build a) Stairway to Paradise · What Can I Do? · When All Your Castles Come Tumbling Down · Mischa, Jascha, Toscha, Sascha · Mary-Louise

UNPRODUCED CHOPIN SHOW, 1923 Someday You'll Realize · Man, the Master · On the Wings of Romance · My All

Bittersweet · Hubby · The Sunshine Trail · Little Rhythm, Go 'Way · The Nevada · Tell Me in the Gloaming · Singing in the Rain · Honorable Moon · Baby Me Blues · I Won't Say I Will, But I Won't Say I Won't · Fabric of Dreams · Hot Hindoo · The Hurdy-Gurdy Man

MISCELLANEOUS, 1924
BE YOURSELF, 1924
PRIMROSE, 1924   35

Imagine Me Without My You · Turn to the Dreams Ahead

BE YOURSELF, 1924 I Came Here · My Heart Is Yours · The Wrong Thing at the Right Time · Uh-Uh · Money Doesn't Mean a Thing · What *of* It? · They Don't Make 'Em That Way Anymore

All of Them Was Friends of Mine · 'Atta Girl! · Cheerio! · Don't You Remember? · Not So Long Ago · Opening—Crazy Quilt · The Whole World's Turning Blue · At 11 P.M. · Dear Old Correspondence School · Kiss Me, That's All

PRIMROSE, 1924 Isn't It Wonderful · Some Faraway Someone · Wait a Bit, Susie · Naughty Baby

The Voice of Love (Cellini's Love Song) · You Must Come Over Blues

LADY, BE GOOD!, 1924   46

Hang On to Me · A Wonderful Party · End of a String · We're Here Because · Fascinating Rhythm · So Am I · Oh, Lady, Be Good! · Finale, Act I · Linger in the Lobby · The Half of It, Dearie, Blues · Juanita · Little Jazz Bird · Swiss Miss · Seeing Dickie Home · The Man I Love · Weatherman [and] Rainy-Afternoon Girls · The Bad, Bad Men · Evening Star · Singin' Pete · Will You Remember Me? · Little Theatre

TELL ME MORE, 1925
MISCELLANEOUS, 1925   58

TELL ME MORE, 1925 Tell Me More · Shopgirls and Mannequins · Mr. and Mrs. Sipkin · When the Debbies Go By · Three Times a Day · Why Do I Love You? · How Can I Win You Now? · Kickin' the Clouds Away · Love Is in the Air ·

My Fair Lady · In Sardinia · Baby! · Finaletto, Act II, Scene 1 · Ukulele Lorelei · Once · I'm Somethin' on Avenue A · The He-Man · Gushing

MISCELLANEOUS, 1925 I Want a Yes-Man · I Know Somebody (Who Loves You)

TIP-TOES, 1925
AMERICANA, 1926   67

TIP-TOES, 1925 Waiting for the Train · Nice Baby · Looking for a Boy · Lady Luck · When Do We Dance? · These Charming People · That Certain Feeling · Sweet and Low-Down · Finale, Act I · Our Little Captain · It's a Great Little World! · Nightie-Night! · Tip-Toes · Harlem River Chanty · Harbor of Dreams · Gather Ye Rosebuds · Weaken a Bit · Life's Too Short to Be Blue · We

AMERICANA, 1926 Sunny Disposish · That Lost Barber Shop Chord · Blowing the Blues Away

OH, KAY!, 1926   78

The Woman's Touch · Don't Ask! · Guess Who? · Dear Little Girl · Maybe · Clap Yo' Hands · Do, Do, Do · Finale, Act I · Bride and Groom · Someone to Watch over Me · Fidgety Feet · Heaven on Earth · Finaletto, Act II, Scene 1 · Oh, Kay! · The Moon Is on the Sea · Show Me the Town · Ain't It Romantic? · Bring On the Ding Dong Dell · Stepping with Baby · What's the Use? · When Our Ship Comes Sailing In

STRIKE UP THE BAND, 1927   89

Fletcher's American Cheese Choral Society · 17 and 21 · Typical Self-Made American · Meadow Serenade · The Unofficial Spokesman · Patriotic Rally · The Man I Love · Yankee Doodle Rhythm · Finaletto, Act I · Strike Up the Band · Oh, This Is Such a Lovely War · Hoping That Someday You'd Care · Military Dancing Drill · How About a Man? · Jim, Consider What You Are Doing! · Homeward Bound · The War That Ended War · Come-Look-at-the-War Choral Society · Nursie, Nursie

FUNNY FACE, 1927   101

Birthday Party · Funny Face · High Hat · 'S Wonderful · Let's Kiss and Make Up · Come! Come! Come Closer! · Finale, Act I · In the Swim · He Loves and She Loves · Tell the Doc · My One and Only · The Babbitt and the Bromide ·

CONTENTS

Blue Hullabaloo · Aviator · When You're Single · Your Eyes! Your Smile! · How Long Has This Been Going On? · The World Is Mine · Finest of the Finest · Dance Alone with You · Acrobats · Bluebeard · Invalid Entrance · When the Right One Comes Along

ROSALIE, 1928
THAT'S A GOOD GIRL, 1928   113

ROSALIE, 1928   Show Me the Town · Hussar March · Say So! · Let Me Be a Friend to You · Oh Gee! Oh Joy! · What Could I Do? · Finale, Act I · New York Serenade · The King Can Do No Wrong · Ev'rybody Knows I Love Somebody · Follow the Drum · At the Ex-Kings' Club · Beautiful Gypsy · Rosalie · I Forgot What I Started to Say · Now That the Dance Is Over · Glad Tidings in the Air · Two Hearts Will Blend as One · Enjoy Today · True to Them All · You Know How It Is · Under the Furlough Moon · When Cadets Parade · Cadet Song

THAT'S A GOOD GIRL, 1928   Let Yourself Go! · Whoopee · Chirp-Chirp · Weekend · The One I'm Looking For · Sweet So-and-So · Before We Were Married · Day After Day · There I'd Settle Down · Why Be Good?

TREASURE GIRL, 1928   127

Skull and Bones · I've Got a Crush on You · According to Mr. Grimes · A-Hunting We Will Go · Place in the Country · K-ra-zy for You · I Don't Think I'll Fall in Love Today · Got a Rainbow · Feeling I'm Falling · Finale, Act I · Treasure Island · What Causes That? · What Are We Here For? · Where's the Boy? Here's the Girl! · Oh, So Nice! · Good-bye to the Old Love · I Want to Marry a Marionette · Dead Men Tell No Tales · This Particular Party

EAST IS WEST, 1928–1929
SHOW GIRL, 1929   137

EAST IS WEST, 1928–1929   In the Mandarin's Orchid Garden · Yellow Blues · Lady of the Moon · Under the Cinnamon Tree · Awake, Children, Awake · Sing-Song Girl · We Are Visitors Here · I Speak English Now · East Is West

SHOW GIRL, 1929   Happy Birthday · My Sunday Fella · How Could I Forget? · Finaletto, Act I, Scene 1 · Magnolia Finale · Lolita, My Love · Do What You Do! · One Man · So Are You! · I Must Be Home by Twelve O'Clock · Harlem Serenade · Home Blues · Follow the Minstrel Band · Liza · Feeling Sentimental · Stage Door Scene ·

I Just Looked at You · Minstrel Show · Tonight's the Night · At Mrs. Simpkin's Finishing School · Adored One · Somebody Stole My Heart Away · I'm Just a Bundle of Sunshine · Someone's Always Calling a Rehearsal · I'm Out for No Good Reason Tonight · Home-Lovin' Gal · Home-Lovin' Man · Casanova, Romeo, and Don Juan

STRIKE UP THE BAND, 1930   149

Fletcher's American Chocolate Choral Society · I Mean to Say · Typical Self-Made American · Soon · A Man of High Degree [and] The Unofficial Spokesman · Three Cheers for the Union [and] This Could Go On for Years · If I Became the President · Hangin' Around with You · He Knows Milk · In the Rattle of the Battle [and] Military Dancing Drill · Mademoiselle in New Rochelle · How About a Boy? · Official Résumé · Ring-a-Ding-a-Ding-Dong Dell · There Never Was Such a Charming War · I Want to Be a War Bride · Thanks to You · Finaletto, Act II, Scene I

GIRL CRAZY, 1930   160

Bidin' My Time · The Lonesome Cowboy · Could You Use Me? · Bronco Busters · Barbary Coast · Embraceable You · Goldfarb, That's I'm! · Sam and Delilah · I Got Rhythm · Finale, Act I · Entr'acte · Land of the Gay Caballero · But Not for Me · Treat Me Rough · Boy! What Love Has Done to Me! · Cactus Time in Arizona · And I Have You · The Gambler of the West · You Can't Unscramble Scrambled Eggs · Are You Dancing? · You've Got What Gets Me

DELICIOUS, 1931   171

Delishious · Dream Sequence · Somebody from Somewhere · Katinkitschka · Blah, Blah, Blah · You Started It

OF THEE I SING, 1931   175

Wintergreen for President · Who Is the Lucky Girl to Be? [and] The Dimple on My Knee [and] Because, Because · Exit, Atlantic City Scene · As the Chairman of the Committee [and] How Beautiful [and] Never Was There a Girl So Fair [and] Some Girls Can Bake a Pie · Love Is Sweeping the Country · Adlai's Sweeping the Country · Of Thee I Sing · Finale, Act I, including Entrance of Supreme Court Judges [and] A Kiss for Cinderella [and] I Was the Most Beautiful Blossom [and] Some Girls Can Bake a Pie—Reprise [and] Of Thee I Sing—Reprise [and] Zwei Hertzen · Hello, Good Morning · Who Cares? ·

Garçon, S'il Vous Plaît [and] Entrance of French Ambassador [and] The Illegitimate Daughter [and] Because, Because—Reprise [and] We'll Impeach Him [and] Who Cares?—Reprise · The Senatorial Roll Call · Impeachment Proceeding [and] Garçon, S'il Vous Plaît—Reprise [and] The Illegitimate Daughter—Reprise [and] Jilted [and] Senatorial Roll Call—Continued [and] I'm About to Be a Mother [and] Posterity Is Just Around the Corner · Trumpeter, Blow Your Golden Horn · On That Matter, No One Budges · Entrance of Wintergreen and Mary · While We're Waiting for the Baby [and] Opportunity Has Beckoned [and] Strike the Loud-Resounding Zither [and] You'll Pardon Me If I Reveal

PARDON MY ENGLISH, 1933   192

In Three-Quarter Time · The Lorelei · Pardon My English · Dancing in the Streets · So What? · Isn't It a Pity? · My Cousin in Milwaukee · Hail the Happy Couple · The Dresden Northwest Mounted · Luckiest Man in the World · What Sort of Wedding Is This? · Tonight · Where You Go, I Go · I've Got to Be There · Finaletto, Act II, Scene 4 · He's Not Himself · Fatherland, Mother of the Band · Freud and Jung and Adler [and] He's Oversexed! · Watch Your Head · Together at Last · Opening, Act II

LET 'EM EAT CAKE, 1933   205

Tweedledee for President · Union Square [and] Down with Everyone Who's Up · Store Scene, including Shirts by Millions [and] Comes the Revolution [and] Mine · Climb Up the Social Ladder · The Union League [and] Comes the Revolution—Reprise · On and On and On · Finale, Act I, including I've Brush My Teeth [and] The Double Dummy Drill [and] On and On and On—Reprise [and] The General's Gone to a Party [and] All the Mothers of the Nation [and] Yes, He's a Bachelor [and] There's Something We're Worried About [and] What's the Proletariat? [and] Let 'Em Eat Cake · Opening, Act II, including Blue, Blue, Blue [and] Who's the Greatest? · League of Nations Finale, including No *Comprenez*, No *Capish*, No *Versteh*! [and] Why Speak of Money? [and] Who's the Greatest?—Reprise · Baseball Scene, including Play Ball! [and] Nine Supreme Ball Players [and] No Better Way to Start a Case [and] The Whole Truth [and] Up and At 'Em, On to Victory · Oyez, Oyez, Oyez! · The Trial of Throttlebottom, including That's What He Did! [and] I Know a Foul Ball [and] Throttle Throttlebottom · The Trial of Wintergreen, including A Hell of a Hole [and] Down with Everyone Who's Up—Reprise [and]

CONTENTS

It Isn't What You Did [and] Mine—Reprise · Hanging Throttlebottom in the Morning · First Lady and First Gent · Fashion Show [and] Finale Ultimo

LIFE BEGINS AT 8:40, 1934
MISCELLANEOUS, 1930–1934   221

LIFE BEGINS AT 8:40, 1934   Life Begins · Spring Fever · You're a Builder-Upper · My Paramount-Publix-Roxy Rose · Shoein' the Mare · Quartet Erotica · Fun to Be Fooled · C'est la Vie · What Can You Say in a Love Song? · Let's Take a Walk Around the Block · Things! · All the Elks and Masons · I Couldn't Hold My Man · A Weekend Cruise · It Was Long Ago · I'm Not Myself · Life Begins at City Hall · I Knew Him When · I'm a Collector of Moonbeams

MISCELLANEOUS, 1930–1934   Ask Me Again · That Well-Known Smile · I Am Only Human After All · Cheerful Little Earful · In the Merry Month of Maybe · The Key to My Heart · Till Then

PORGY AND BESS, 1935   235

I Got Plenty o' Nuthin' · Bess, You Is My Woman Now · Oh, I Can't Sit Down! · It Ain't Necessarily So · I Loves You, Porgy · A Redheaded Woman · Oh, Heav'nly Father · There's a Boat Dat's Leavin' Soon for New York · Oh, Bess, Oh Where's My Bess?

ZIEGFELD FOLLIES OF 1936   242

Time Marches On! · He Hasn't a Thing Except Me · My Red-Letter Day · Island in the West Indies · Words Without Music · The Economic Situation · Fancy! Fancy! · Maharanee · Trailer for *The 1936 Broadway Gold Diggers* [and] The Gazooka [and] It's a Different World · That Moment of Moments · Sentimental Weather · Five A.M. · I Can't Get Started · Modernistic Moe · Dancing to the Score · Does a Duck Love Water? · The Last of the Cabbies · The Ballad of Baby Face McGinty · Please Send My Daddy Back to Mother · The Knife Thrower's Wife · I'm Sharing My Wealth · Wishing Tree of Harlem · Why Save for That Rainy Day? · Hot Number · Sunday Tan · Oh, Bring Back the Ballet Again · The Better Half Knows Better · I Used to Be Above Love

SHALL WE DANCE, 1937   263

Slap That Bass · (I've Got) Beginner's Luck · They All Laughed · Let's Call the Whole Thing Off · They Can't Take That Away from Me · Shall We Dance? · Hi-Ho! · Wake Up, Brother, and Dance

A DAMSEL IN DISTRESS, 1937   268

I Can't Be Bothered Now · The Jolly Tar and the Milkmaid · Put Me to the Test · Stiff Upper Lip · Things Are Looking Up · Sing of Spring · A Foggy Day · Nice Work If You Can Get It · Pay Some Attention to Me

THE GOLDWYN FOLLIES, 1938
MISCELLANEOUS, 1935–1939   274

THE GOLDWYN FOLLIES, 1938   Love Walked In · I Was Doing All Right · Love Is Here to Stay · Spring Again · Night of Nights · I Love to Rhyme · Just Another Rhumba · I'm Not Complaining · Exposition

MISCELLANEOUS, 1935–1939   By Strauss · Dawn of a New Day · Baby, You're News · No Question in My Heart · Once There Were Two of Us · Now That We Are One · People from Missouri · I've Turned the Corner · I Was Naïve · Something's Wrong · Hard to Replace · Let It Rain! Let It Pour!

LADY IN THE DARK, 1941   283

GLAMOUR DREAM: Oh, Fabulous One, Huxley, One Life to Live, Girl of the Moment, It Looks Like Liza, Girl of the Moment—Reprise · WEDDING DREAM: Mapleton High Chorale, This Is New, The Princess of Pure Delight, The Woman at the Altar · CIRCUS DREAM: The Greatest Show on Earth, The Best Years of His Life, Tchaikowsky, The Saga of Jenny · My Ship · It's Never Too Late to Mendelssohn · Bats About You · Unforgettable · MINSTREL DREAM: A Trial Combined with Circus [and] The Unspoken Law [and] No Matter Under What Star You're Born [and] Song of the Zodiac · HOLLYWOOD DAYDREAM: The Boss Is Bringing Home a Bride, Home in San Fernando Valley, Party Parlando

THE NORTH STAR, 1943   303

No Village Like Mine · Village Scene Jingles · Younger Generation · Song of the Guerrillas · Song of the Fatherland · Collective Loading-Time Song · Wagon Song · Unite, You Workers of All Nations

COVER GIRL, 1944
MISCELLANEOUS, 1940–1944   307

COVER GIRL, 1944   The Show Must Go On · Who's Complaining? · Sure Thing · Make Way for Tomorrow · Put Me to the Test · Long Ago · Midnight Music · Midnight Madness · Any Moment Now · Cover Girl · Time: The Present · That's the Best of All · Tropical Night

MISCELLANEOUS, 1940–1944   Honorable Moon · If That's Propaganda · Women of America · Don't Let's Be Beastly to the Germans · Let's Show 'Em How This Country Goes to Town

WHERE DO WE GO FROM HERE?,
1945   316

All at Once · Morale [and] Dancing with Lucilla · If Love Remains · Song of the Rhineland · The *Nina*, the *Pinta*, the *Santa Maria* · That's How It Is [and] Telephone Passage · It Could Have Happened to Anyone · Woo, Woo, Woo, Woo, Manhattan

THE FIREBRAND OF FLORENCE,
1945   323

Song of the Hangman [and] Civic Song—"Come to Florence" [and] Aria—"My Lords and Ladies" [and] Farewell Song—"There Was Life, There Was Love, There Was Laughter" · Duet—"Our Master Is Free Again" · Arietta—"I Had Just Been Pardoned" · Love Song—"You're Far Too Near Me" · The Duke's Song—"Alessandro the Wise" · Finaletto—"I Am Happy Here" · Duchess's Entrance · The Duchess's Song—"Sing Me Not a Ballad" · Madrigal—"When the Duchess Is Away" · Love Song—"There'll Be Life, Love, and Laughter" · Trio—"I Know Where There's a Cozy Nook" · Night Music—"The Nighttime Is No Time for Thinking" [and] Tarantella—"Dizzily, Busily" [and] This Night in Florence · Cavatina—"The Little Naked Boy" · Letter Song—"My Dear Benvenuto" · March of the Soldiers of the Duchy—"Just in Case" · Ode—"A Rhyme for Angela" · Procession—"Souvenirs," "Hear Ye, Hear Ye" [and] Chant of Law and Order—"The World Is Full of Villains" [and] Trial by Music—"You Have to Do What You Do Do" · Arietta—"How Wonderfully Fortunate" [and] Duet—"Love Is My Enemy" [and] Reprise—"The Little Naked Boy" · Civic Song—"Come to Paris"

PARK AVENUE, 1946   337

Tomorrow Is the Time · For the Life of Me · The Dew Was on the Rose · Don't Be a Woman If You Can · Sweet Nevada · There's No Holding Me · There's Nothing Like Marriage for People · Hope for the Best · My Son-in-law · The Land of Opportunitee · Good-bye to All That · Stay as We Are · Remind Me Not to Leave the Town · Heavenly Day · The Future Mrs. Coleman

THE SHOCKING MISS PILGRIM,
1947   350

Sweet Packard · Changing My Tune · Stand Up and Fight · March of the Suffragettes · Aren't You

Kind of Glad We Did? · The Back Bay Polka · One, Two, Three · Demon Rum · For You, for Me, for Evermore · Tour of the Town · Welcome Song

THE BARKLEYS OF BROADWAY, 1949　357

Swing Trot · You'd Be Hard to Replace · My One and Only Highland Fling · Weekend in the Country · Shoes with Wings On · Manhattan Downbeat · Natchez on the Mississip' · The Courtin' of Elmer and Ella · The Well-Known Skies of Blue · The Poetry of Motion · Taking No Chances on You · There Is No Music · These Days · Call On Us Again · Second Fiddle to a Harp · Minstrels on Parade

GIVE A GIRL A BREAK, 1953　366

Give a Girl a Break · Nothing Is Impossible · In Our United State · It Happens Ev'ry Time · Applause, Applause · Dreamworld · Ach, Du Lieber Oom-Pah-Pah · Woman, There Is No Living with You

A STAR IS BORN, 1954　372

Gotta Have Me Go with You · The Man That Got Away · The TV Commercial · Here's What I'm Here For · It's a New World · Someone at Last · Lose That Long Face · I'm Off the Downbeat · Green Light Ahead · Dancing Partner

THE COUNTRY GIRL, 1954　378

The Pitchman [and] It's Mine, It's Yours · Commercials · The Search Is Through · The Land Around Us · Dissertation on the State of Bliss

KISS ME, STUPID, 1964　382

Sophia · I'm a Poached Egg · All the Livelong Day

EPILOGUE　387

Doubting Thomas · I Won't Give Up · Saying My Say

Index　391

INTRODUCTION

Ten thousand steamboats hootin'—
A million taxis tootin'—
What a song! What a song!
That dear old New York Serenade!
Just hear those rivets rattling—
And hear that traffic battling—
Come along, come along and hear it played.

George and Ira Gershwin, musical laureates of the Jazz Age, wrote "New York Serenade" in 1927, at the height of Broadway's glory years—a time when nightlife was at its gaudiest, materialism was running riot, the talkies were just arriving, and skyscrapers were soaring ever upward in relentless profusion—a time when the American theatre was at its most varied and abundant. At the peak of their own productivity, they wrote it for Florenz Ziegfeld's majestic *Rosalie*, a colossal combination of musical comedy, operetta, and extravaganza that served as a sumptuous salute to the Main Stem's most radiant star, Marilyn Miller. It was an opulent entertainment that critic Gilbert Gabriel, in the New York *Evening Sun,* called "11 scenes of girls glorified and tunes rarified and romance in fine feathers and gold and ermine all over everything from the curtain to the plot." It was precisely this sort of show that the Irish playwright, novelist, and drama critic St. John Ervine had in mind when he wrote that "when the historian seeks a symbol of our time, he will find it in musical comedy, which is our equivalent of the Roman arena. In this large, costly and extraordinarily popular form of entertainment the spirit of our age appears to be expressed."

The "gold and ermine," as well as *Rosalie*'s brown, blue, scarlet, and silver, were the work of Ziegfeld's master builder, the protean Austrian-born architect-designer Joseph Urban. The plot was by veteran librettists Guy Bolton and William Anthony McGuire; the "romance in fine feathers" was supplied by operetta's chief minstrel, Sigmund Romberg, who shared composition of the "tunes rarified" with the Gershwins and P. G. Wodehouse. The girls, of course, were chosen by the great Ziegfeld.

When *Rosalie* opened on January 10, 1928, it quickly vied for top box-office honors with Ziegfeld's *Show Boat*, which had bowed to hosannas during Broadway's record-breaking Christmas week, 1927, when twenty offerings premiered during a seven-night period, eleven on the evening of December 26. *Show Boat* was closely pursued by several other high-grossing attractions, including Ziegfeld's *Rio Rita;* Kalmar and Ruby's *The 5 O'Clock Girl*; DeSylva, Brown, and Henderson's *Good News* (composer Burton Lane was present when George and Ira Gershwin's mother said to George, "Why can't you write hits like DeSylva, Brown, and Henderson?"); the Gershwin's own *Funny Face,* which starred Fred and Adele Astaire and had inaugurated the Alvin Theatre on November 22, 1927; and a return engagement of the Gershwins' 1926 hit *Oh, Kay!* Had *Strike Up the Band,* the groundbreaking political satire written with George S. Kaufman, made it safely out of Philadelphia's Shubert Theatre in September, the Gershwins would have had four shows running concurrently on the Great White Way in January 1928.

*

Ira Gershwin was born December 6, 1896, in a building that still stands on the corner of Hester and Eldridge streets on the Lower East Side of Manhattan. He was the first of four children born to Russian immigrants Morris Gershovitz and the former Rose Bruskin from St. Petersburg. When George was born (September 26, 1898), the family lived at 242 Snediker Avenue in the East New York section of Brooklyn on a block that is now a weed-covered wasteland (the house of George's birth was vandalized several years ago and later leveled) in an area that is currently zoned for light industry. When brother Arthur (born March 14, 1900) and sister Frances (born ten years to the day after Ira) arrived, the family was back in Manhattan.

It was amazing, Ira later recalled, that before he was twenty years old his family had had twenty-eight different residences, twenty-five in Manhattan and three in Brooklyn. As Ira told George's first biographer, Isaac Goldberg, this was due "to the fact that the head of the house of Gershwin liked to live within walking distance of his place of business, and it seemed that every six months he had a new business. . . . My father engaged in various activities: restaurants, Russian and Turkish baths, bakeries, a cigar store and pool parlor on the 42nd Street side of what is now Grand Central Station, bookmaking at the Brighton Beach racetrack for three exciting but disastrous weeks." Another reason for the peripatetic life, which Ira described to me as "full of surprises but often bewildering and fatiguing," was that landlords "knew that my mother could be encouraged to move by the offer of a free month's rent." He also said that "George seemed to adapt to the changes much better than I did. He was constantly absorbing new experiences. When I bought this house [in early 1941] next door to the house—1019 North Roxbury Drive in Beverly Hills, now Rosemary Clooney's home—where George, my wife, Lee, and I had lived during George's last year in Hollywood, I decided I never wanted to move again." In fact, "this house" was not sold until the fall of 1992, a year after Leonore Gershwin's death.

"My introduction to the literary life," Ira explained, "came from Paul Potter, a playwright, who used to come to the Lafayette Baths, where I worked as a cashier. He gave me magazines to read (I was already keeping scrapbooks with clippings of columns from the newspapers by F.P.A., C. L. Edson, and others, which often featured guest contributions) and encouraged me to send a short story I had written—"The Shrine"—to the *Smart Set*, which was edited by George Jean Nathan." That was in 1917—three years after Ira's first contribution to a New York newspaper had appeared in the New York *Mail*.

Ira was always a reader. He immersed himself in nickel-and-dime novels—adventure stories—and was a frequenter of public libraries. In 1909, the year of his thirteenth birthday, he began keeping a record of the books he'd read, and soon noted his completion of works by Alexandre Dumas *père (The Count of Monte Cristo)*, James Fenimore Cooper *(The Pathfinder)*, Jules Verne *(The Mysterious Island* and *20,000 Leagues Under the Sea)*, Anna Sewell *(Black Beauty)*, Harriet Beecher Stowe *(Uncle Tom's Cabin)*, and Arthur Conan Doyle *(Micah Clarke* and the *Adventures of Sherlock Holmes)*. By 1912 he was devouring more than a book a week, adding Arnold Bennett, John Galsworthy, and the humorist John Kendrick Bangs to his list of literary favorites.

By 1915 he had become a lover of Ibsen, Barrie, Gilbert and Sullivan (he had begun to savor and love the Savoyard works when he and George were small boys), and Shaw. Most important, he discovered P. G. Wodehouse, and read *Something New* (in England it was called *Something Fresh)*, the first of the "Blandings Castle" novels, in the year of its initial publication.

In 1916, the same year that Ira began to keep a record of his visits to the theatre, Wodehouse commenced a theatrical partnership with librettist Guy Bolton and composer Jerome Kern. The small-scale, high-spirited Bolton–Wodehouse–Kern "Princess Theatre" shows (so-called after the 299-seat playhouse that housed several of them) attracted discerning audiences who longed for stylish, urbane lyrics, suave melodies, and coherent librettos that drew their humor more from situations than from gags and one-liners. These shows were, in size and spirit, far away from the extravaganzas that played such commodious palaces as the Century, the Winter Garden, and the Hippodrome. Ira Gershwin patronized these big shows, but in 1917 and 1918 he also saw many of the Bolton–Wodehouse–Kern offerings. Ira told me he especially loved one of Wodehouse's happy couplets from *Oh, Lady! Lady!!,* which he charmingly recalled ("Whenever he dances / His partner takes chances"). Not surprisingly, one of George and Ira's earliest songs was titled "When There's a Chance to Dance."

Much as Wodehouse was Ira's mentor, George looked to Kern as a musical model; many of George's first theatre songs show Kern's influence. Ira remembered that Kern said to George, whose great talent Kern was quick to appreciate, "When I leave the business, you can have all my shows." Ira chuckled when he told me, "George showed promise, and Kern promised shows."

Sitting Pretty (1924) was the last Bolton–Wodehouse–Kern collaboration. The Gershwins, who would work frequently with Bolton, inherited the "Princess" collaborators' mantle, and later in 1924, with *Lady, Be Good!,* offered the first in a series of lighthearted, "smart" shows that, while larger scaled than the Princess productions, sought to duplicate their infectious spirit. Initially, the Gershwins did little to change the traditional song forms of the musical. There were the obligatory "icebreakers" (opening choruses), rhythm songs, comedic offerings, and ballads, including the occasional "unrequited" love song (love was seldom unrequited for long in musical comedy). Yet, in each of these genres, the mating of the brothers' pulsating music and deft, colloquial lyrics achieved magical results.

With *Lady, Be Good!* (1924), *Tell Me More* (1925), *Tip-Toes* (1925), *Oh, Kay!* (1926), *Funny Face* (1927), *Treasure Girl* (1928), *Show Girl* (1929), and *Girl Crazy* (1930), the Gershwin brothers achieved a high level of songwriting craftsmanship and excellence that powerfully influenced the future of the musical stage. In addition, the Gershwin scores were the smart, exuberant, and utterly beguiling foundations for some of the best-remembered performances on both sides of the Atlantic by Gertrude Lawrence and Fred and Adele Astaire, and for the spectacular debut of Ethel Merman.

Never content to rest on their accomplishments, the Gershwins teamed with playwright George S. Kaufman to bring American political satire to the lyric stage and carry on the tradition of Gilbert and Sullivan. Their first musical satire, *Strike Up the Band,* fashioned in the spring and summer of 1927, was a brilliant antiwar musical that drew critical plaudits during its pre-Broadway tryout. Yet audiences stayed away and it closed after two weeks in Philadelphia. Revised, with many new musical numbers and a new, milder libretto by Morrie Ryskind, the second *Strike Up the Band* was a solid success when it opened in New York on January 14, 1930. Less than two years later, *Of Thee I Sing,* by Kaufman, Ryskind, and the Gershwins, opened in triumph, providing the Gershwins with the longest-running Broadway success of their careers and earning for all of its creators—except George Gershwin!—the Pulitzer Prize, the first ever given to a musical. The ambitious sequel, *Let 'Em Eat Cake* (1933), satirized revolution, drawing its plot from the Great Depression and the rise of Nazi Germany; it lasted only ninety performances. It followed the more conventional though musically impressive *Pardon My English* (1933) and proved, except for the folk opera *Porgy and Bess* (1935), to be the last Gershwin musical show. Had

George survived his illness and been able to continue working, there would have been another Gershwin political satire in late 1937 or early 1938—with a book by Kaufman and Moss Hart.

The Gilbertian strain remained a potent influence on Ira. He was well versed in the *Bab Ballads* and the entire G&S canon (biographer Deena Rosenberg writes that Ira recalled reading *Trial by Jury* during the week Gilbert died in May 1911). Readers of this volume will note how often a trial or impeachment occurs—the Circus Dream in *Lady in the Dark*, Cellini's trial in *The Firebrand of Florence*, as well as the Impeachment Proceeding in *Of Thee I Sing* and the trials of Throttlebottom and Wintergreen in *Let 'Em Eat Cake*.

One often-overlooked aspect of Ira's career was his contribution as a sketch writer for the revues *Life Begins at 8:40* (1934) and *Ziegfeld Follies of 1936*. For the former he collaborated with his close friend and colleague E. Y. Harburg on the song-surroundings for "C'est la Vie," and for the latter he worked with David Freedman on the more ambitious materials for "Fancy! Fancy!" and both versions of "The Gazooka." He had the opportunity to work on these shows because at that time George was writing *Porgy and Bess*.

In the mid-1980s, when Irving Berlin learned that I was working on Ira Gershwin's complete lyrics, he exhorted me to remember and mention that "no one wrote greater songs than George and Ira did during the last year of George's life." Their three film scores (for *Shall We Dance*, *A Damsel in Distress*, and *The Goldwyn Follies*) boasted some incredible riches, including "They Can't Take That Away from Me," "They All Laughed," "Things Are Looking Up," "A Foggy Day," "Nice Work If You Can Get It," "I Was Doing All Right," "Love Walked In," and their last song, "Love Is Here to Stay." And, Berlin added, "No one will ever know how much Ira suffered when George died."

Some time after Ira struggled to finish the songs for *The Goldwyn Follies*, which he did with the assistance of Vernon Duke, he persuaded himself that he would have to overcome his grief, shake off his deep state of despondency, and return to work. Ira recalled that "days and nights passed in a blur. Then one afternoon I got to the record player and somehow found myself putting on the Fred Astaire–Johnny Green recordings of the *Shall We Dance* score, most of which had been written in that very room less than a year before. In a few minutes the room was filled with gaiety and rhythm, and I felt that George, smiling and approving, was there listening with me—and grief vanished." Ira told me, "One reason I did my first work after George died with Kern was that it took me back to when we started in the theatre, when Kern was our musical god and George was frequently his rehearsal pianist."

Soon after came *Lady in the Dark*, written with Kurt Weill and Moss Hart, and that success proved that Ira had not lost his touch and could work with others—just as he had before he cast aside his pseudonym "Arthur Francis" in 1924 to team with George on a regular basis. Ira remained active as a lyric writer until 1954, and his collaborations with Vernon Duke, Kurt Weill, Aaron Copland, Jerome Kern, Arthur Schwartz, Kay Swift, Harry Warren, Burton Lane, and Harold Arlen confirmed his status as one of the American musical's finest lyricists. When Ira's book, *Lyrics on Several Occasions*, arguably the best book ever on lyrics and lyric writing, appeared in 1959, his friend and hero P. G. Wodehouse described it as "absolutely terrific. . . . You are the best of the whole bunch . . . the greatest lyrist of them all."

It is an early afternoon in August 1972, and Ira Gershwin's second-floor bedroom is almost as warm as the steam room of the sort of Turkish bath that he had worked in, read in, and wrote in as a young man. His seventy-fifth birthday is behind him, and he says he will give no more formal interviews because he is afraid he "will say something that will offend someone." He has just been recalling for his guest the exquisite verse to the song "Delishious," which he and his brother George created for Janet Gaynor and Charles Farrell for a film of the early 1930s. Over the intercom in his room, we hear Lee Gershwin saying, "It's Oscar, dear," referring to the curmudgeonly pianist-raconteur—and the Gershwins' neighbor—Oscar Levant. "He said you should turn on *The Mike Douglas Show*." The television set is quickly tuned and adjusted, and there is Benny Goodman performing "Oh, Lady, Be Good!" on his clarinet. Ira listens in rapt attention to the legendary bandleader, who had been in the pit orchestra—along with Glenn Miller, Gene Krupa, and other future titans of the Swing Era—for the Gershwins' *Girl Crazy*. Here was Goodman caressing the Jazz Age anthem that had been a theme song for a generation and had even found its way into the literary offerings of such diverse writers as John Galsworthy, who mentioned it in his 1926 play *Escape*, and Ezra Pound, who mocked it cleverly in his "Canto LXXIV." When Goodman finished, Ira noted wistfully, "George and I wrote that song in 1924. I can't believe that it is still being played today."

Such modesty and humility had always been characteristic of the affable scholar-lyricist (his library in the room next to his bedroom contained over 2,500 volumes of literature, history, and reference) who, along with his beloved brother, helped shape and define our popular culture. When Alfred Simon, longtime Gershwin friend and rehearsal pianist in 1931 for *Of Thee I Sing*, and I began talking with Ira about a book we had been asked to write on the Gershwins, Ira took us aside and said, "Please make this a book entirely about George." Gently and politely, we turned down his request.

We had many happy hours working with Ira. One day he brought down a copy of *Variety* and, after noting the current grosses, began musing on how many newspaper critics there had been when he and George were writing for Broadway. He tolled the names of the scribes as if he were reciting the roster of American presidents— "Percy Hammond, Heywood Broun, Gilbert Gabriel, John Anderson, Alan Dale, Richard Lockridge, Alexander Woollcott, Walter Winchell, Burns Mantle, Kelcey Allen, Arthur Pollock, John Mason Brown, Richard Watts." He went on and on and then stopped and said, "No, I didn't forget J. Brooks Atkinson of the *Times*. I just wanted to point out the many critics we had and how no single aisle-sitter could close a show."

On another day he said, "Boys, I hope I am not interrupting you, but I wanted to ask you, Al, if you still remember the score to *Of Thee I Sing*? Would you play it for me? I want to see if I can still recall the lyrics." We went upstairs to the living room, adorned with paintings, some of which George had purchased, by Modigliani, Rouault, Pascin, Vlaminck, and others. Al sat at George's piano; Ira, sitting in a club chair, closed his eyes, and with his arms making elipses in the air began to sing in a kind of cantorial wail. By the time he reached "A Kiss for Cinderella," we were all having a hard time keeping our feelings from interrupting the music. By the second act's "Senatorial Roll Call," it was evident that Ira, recalling every word, was having a very satisfying afternoon.

Later, Ira asked whether Al had ever been to George's penthouse on Riverside Drive. Al said, "I was writing songs, and my brother Dick [George and Ira's friend Richard Simon, cofounder of Simon and Schuster] arranged for me to play some of my numbers for George. I remember that before we started, George took me out on the roof and said, 'On a clear day you can almost see Yonkers.' George was wonderful. When I finished one number, he sat next to me at the piano and made several suggestions on how I could improve the release. It was like getting a batting lesson from Babe Ruth."

On another occasion, I asked Ira and Al whether they believed that the image most people had of George was accurate. "Not entirely" was their answer. They concurred that George was neither as aggressive nor as brash as he was often depicted. He was gentler, more soft-spoken, Al noted: "I know it is hard for people to believe, but as energetic as he was, he was not a driven person, in a hurry to make time, fearful that his days were numbered."

Almost everyone who knew the Gershwins spoke fervently about the closeness of their collaboration. Leonore Gershwin said, "I never saw a greater love than the love George and Ira had for each other." This love was reflected in the special quality of their working relationship. Ira believed that their songs were indivisible. "The song is the important thing," he told George's biographer Isaac Goldberg, "not the words or music as separate entities."

"We worked best under deadlines and we worked mostly at night," Ira recalled to Alfred Simon and me. "I might have been home reading a book," he noted, "when George returned from a party, and, depending on where we lived at the time, he would call me up or say to me, 'Let's get to work.' But first we would go the kitchen and have ice cream and figure out what we had to do. George's mind and his notebooks were full of tunes. There were times when melodies would pour out so quickly and naturally that he would have several ideas in a day. Usually, if we were happy with something he had written, I would memorize it and try to find a title or idea for it. The title, the idea, and the last line of the refrain were most important for me. Of course, when we wrote the political satires, which called for more extended numbers, we worked somewhat differently."

"Good lyrics," Ira told Isaac Goldberg, "should be simple, colloquial, rhymed conversational lines." He later said to me that throughout his career he had tried "to capture the ways people spoke to each other—their slang, their clichés, their catchphrases."

The Gershwins imbued each of musical comedy's song genres with words and music of remarkable distinction. Some of their most characteristic and best-remembered songs were written for what Ira described as "the not impossible he" category. Best known are "The Man I Love," "Looking for a Boy," "Someone to Watch Over Me," and "Where's the Boy? Here's the Girl!" Others include "One Man," "Somebody from Somewhere," "My Son-in-law," "Sure Thing," and "Someone at Last."

They are equally esteemed for the almost gymnastic skill of their exuberant rhythm numbers, including such gems as "Fascinating Rhythm" (heavily influenced by Ira's earlier "Little Rhythm, Go 'Way"), "Kickin' the Clouds Away," "Sweet and Low-Down," "Clap Yo' Hands," "My One and Only," "K-ra-zy for You," "Harlem Serenade," and "I Got Rhythm."

Although he is renowned for treating the love song with a naturalness and a contemporaneity of speech and for creating civilized lyrics about young people finding the road to love a little bumpy, he, by his own admission, often found that ballads gave him no end of difficulty. It was in love songs that his tireless quest for perfection was most frequently tested. "If I wanted to upset Ira," Harold Arlen noted, "I would tell him that we had just received an offer from a studio to write a film score with five ballads." Ira told me that "Kern was so impatient when I had trouble coming up with a satisfactory, at least to me, setting of the melody that became 'Long Ago (and Far Away)' that he sent me his own dummy lyric. It began, 'Watching little Nelly P.' "

One of the most thankless tasks in musical comedy is writing opening choruses and other customary icebreakers. Yet here the Gershwins were especially accomplished. Whether the setting was a party on a splendid estate at the height of Prohibition, a frolic by the seaside, or some other leisure-oriented escapade showcasing the yearnings of romantic innocents, the Gershwins usually responded with delectable conceptions. "The Woman's Touch," "Birthday Party," "Waiting for the Train," "In the Swim," and "Love Is in the Air" are just a few of their salient successes in this realm.

In Hollywood, Ira and Leonore held a continuous open house for their friends, complete with epic battles at the pool table, sing-alongs with such close friends as Judy Garland, Humphrey Bogart, Lauren Bacall, Betty Comden, and Adolph Green, and regular poker games that continued, in later years organized by Angie Dickinson, until the last months of Leonore's life. All who ever knew Ira spoke of his erudition, but emphasized that he always wore it lightly. To give merely a couple of examples of the richness of his literary references, consider how he invoked the words of the seventeenth-century poet Robert Herrick—"Whenas in silks my Julia goes, / Then, then, methinks, how sweetly flows / That liquefaction of her clothes" (*Hesperides*—"Upon Julia's Clothes")— which Ira transformed almost directly into lines in *Lady in the Dark*'s "Oh, Fabulous One." Sixteen years earlier, Ira had drawn on Herrick's most famous phrase—"Gather ye rosebuds while ye may"—for a song for *Tip-Toes*, one of the finest of the previously unpublished Gershwin songs.

Proud as he was of the sound devices he used in "Uh-uh," "Sunny Disposish," "'S Wonderful," and "Delishious," he was prouder by far of his hard-won successes in writing comedy songs that captured something of the charm and wit of his beloved mentor, P. G. Wodehouse. Arguably, Ira's first successes in this area were "The Silly Season" and "Mischa, Jascha, Toscha, Sascha," but he did not feel he had passed muster until "These Charming People" in *Tip-Toes*. As he further developed his craft and built on his experience, he was to write some of the wittiest of all comic love songs—"Let's Take a Walk Around the Block" (with Harold Arlen and E. Y. Harburg), "I Can't Get Started" (with Vernon Duke), and "They All Laughed" (written with George).

Finally, it is not surprising that Ira and his collaborators wrote dozens of songs about music or dance. From his first songs with George to some of his last work as a lyricist, long after he had moved "from the Island of Manhattan to the Coast of Gold" to write primarily for the movies, often with the composers whom he and George had encouraged so warmly at the start of their careers in the late 1920s and early '30s, he kept responding to the spirit of Orpheus and Terpsichore and to the talent that had made him one of this century's most admired lyricists.

There are more than seven hundred lyrics in this compilation, and they are arranged, for the most part, chronologically and under the titles of the shows and films for which they were first written, and in the sequence in which they were first performed. Nearly four hundred of the lyrics are being published for the first time. Most of the previously published lyrics were first printed in the sheet music for individual songs; others were published in the piano-vocal scores and selections that usually accompanied a show's original run or a film's first release.

Each major Ira Gershwin production is introduced with information on that production (creative credits, length of run, tryout data, etc.), and each lyric is prefaced with a headnote that includes the publication date or the month and year in which the piece was first registered for copyright as an unpublished song, alternate or earlier titles, the names of the artists who introduced the song, as well as the role those artists played in the show or film in which the song was first heard. I also have noted if the music for a lyric is not known to survive.

Over one hundred of the lyrics in this compilation appeared in *Lyrics on Several Occasions*, in which Ira frequently accompanied his lyrics with witty, scholarly commentary. Much of Ira's commentary follows the headnotes for the lyrics in this volume. In addition, I have drawn on other notes he prepared for lyrics that were at one time intended for but did not ultimately appear in his book.

The sources for lyrics in this compilation are manuscripts, typed lyric sheets, sheet music and piano-vocal scores, scripts, cast recordings, sound tracks, and private acetates, most of which were preserved by Ira Gershwin in the voluminous files he maintained at his home in Beverly Hills or in the Gershwin Collection in the Music Division of the Library of Congress in Washington, D.C. Established in 1939 by Ira and his mother, Rose Gershwin, the Gershwin Collection has been the chief repository for all works and memorabilia of George and Ira Gershwin. Other important sources are the Tams-Witmark Music Library (dramatic agent for most of the Gershwin shows), the Shubert Archive, and the Library for the Performing Arts at Lincoln Center—all in New York.

Through the years, many dedicated individuals assisted Ira and Leonore Gershwin in preserving George and Ira's works. They include Lawrence D. Stewart, Edgar Carter, Walter Reilly, Michael Feinstein, Mark Trent Goldberg, and Tommy Krasker. These people's contributions, direct and indirect, to this collection are incalculable.

Plans for this compilation were formulated after Ira Gershwin's death in 1983 by Leonore Gershwin, Ira and Leonore's attorney, Ronald L. Blanc, and myself, as artistic adviser to Ira Gershwin's estate. While all of us were aware that Ira would have had some reservations about publication of his entire surviving output (Ira did not save all of his early work), we, especially Leonore, were convinced that such a compilation was commensurate with his place as one of the American musical's greatest lyricists, and that the availability of his less distinguished offerings would in no way diminish his finest work and would, in large measure, contribute to a deeper appreciation of such work. I also view this project—and I told Ira so on the one occasion I discussed such an undertaking with him—as an important step toward achieving one of his own most cherished goals: the publication of his brother George's complete works.

Ira Gershwin was a saver and constant reviser. Often, when he examined a lyric in his extensive files, he would feel compelled to tinker with it. Sometimes, of course, he would receive requests for a male version of a song first written for a woman (or vice versa) or for a duet to be made of a solo, and he would happily oblige with the needed changes. Whenever one of his shows was revived, he carefully scrutinized his lyrics to see if references needed to be revised or updated.

It is not widely known, but Ira played a pivotal role in the amazing rediscovery in early 1982 of thousands of scores and manuscripts by himself and George, Jerome Kern, Cole Porter, Vincent Youmans, Richard Rodgers, Lorenz Hart, and many others in the Secaucus, New Jersey, warehouse of Warner Bros. Music (now Warner-Chappell), the foremost music publisher for the Broadway musical from before World War I until the mid-1930s. It was only after Ira had given his blessing to a search through the Secaucus materials and had dispatched his musical assistant, Michael Feinstein, to help in the search that Warner executives were willing to permit an extensive examination and inventory of the materials that had been rediscovered. The cache turned out, to everyone's astonishment, especially Ira's, to include nearly ninety Gershwin manuscripts, including those of some of George and Ira's most famous songs, such as "The Man I Love," "Fascinating Rhythm," "But Not for Me" and "I Got Rhythm," along with many original lyric sheets. The Gershwin Secaucus material is now in the Gershwin Collection in the Music Division of the Library of Congress.

Late in 1987, Leonore Gershwin decided to donate to the Library of Congress all of the George and Ira manuscripts that were still housed at 1021 North Roxbury Drive, as well as the balance of the massive song and show files that Ira had preserved so diligently over the years. This important gift also included the George and Ira Gershwin Special Numbered Song File that Ira Gershwin and Kay Swift had carefully assembled in the mid-1940s as they began their collaboration on the score, utilizing unused music completed before George's death, for the 1947 film *The Shocking Miss Pilgrim*. Over the years, Kay, an outstanding composer in her own right, was responsible for the preservation of several Gershwin songs, including "Meadow Serenade," "Comes the Revolution," "The Union League," and "Freud and Jung and Adler."

Only a few months before her death at age ninety in August 1991, Leonore Gershwin invited Librarian of Congress James Billington to her home to present to him, on behalf of the Library, George Gershwin's earliest surviving notebook, which she had purchased in November 1987 at Christie's in New York City for what was and remains the highest price ever paid for an American music manuscript. This purchase was only one of many efforts on behalf of George and Ira that Leonore undertook during her eight-year stewardship of Ira's estate. Her generosity helped make possible the 1986 concert performances and subsequent recording by conductor Michael Tilson Thomas of the political satires *Of Thee I Sing* and *Let 'Em Eat Cake*. She traveled to Minneapolis to support *Hang On to Me*, director Peter Sellars's mating of Gershwin songs to Maxim Gorky's play *Summerfolk*. (Sellars had captivated Lee and Ira Gershwin, and convinced Ira that a lighthearted spoof of American capitalism in the 1920s was an intriguing way to revive *Funny Face*. What ended up as the more commercial *My One and Only* was only possible because of Sellars's iconoclastic vision.) Her visits to England's Glyndebourne Festival Opera and her strong backing of director Trevor Nunn and conductor Simon Rattle were major boosts to what became a hugely acclaimed and subsequently filmed production of *Porgy and Bess*. Again and again she came to the aid of beleaguered Gershwin concerts, and her numerous purchases of manuscripts for the Library of Congress and her decision to leave a large portion of her and Ira's estate to the Library have made her one of the foremost benefactors ever to the Library's Music Division. Finally, in partnership with the Library of Congress and Elektra Entertainment, she created, funded, and shaped Roxbury Recordings to preserve George and Ira's extraordinary musical legacy. Already issued are faithful re-creations of *Girl Crazy*, the 1927 *Strike Up the Band*, *Lady, Be Good!*, and *Pardon My English*; others are yet to come.

—ROBERT KIMBALL

CHRONOLOGY

1896

DECEMBER 6   Israel Gershovitz born in New York City, in a building at the corner of Hester and Eldridge streets on the Lower East Side of Manhattan, to the former Rose Bruskin and Morris Gershovitz (married July 21, 1895). The family name will be changed to Gershwine, then Gershvin, then Gershwin; Israel will become Ira.

1898

SEPTEMBER 26   Jacob Gershwine (later George Gershwin), younger brother of Ira, born in Brooklyn, New York; the family lives at this time at 242 Snediker Avenue in the East New York section of Brooklyn.

1900

MARCH 14   Arthur, the youngest Gershwin son, born in New York City; the family now lives at 91 Second Avenue, Manhattan.

1906

DECEMBER 6   Frances Gershwin born in New York City, ten years to the day after the birth of her oldest brother, Ira.

1909

Ira Gershwin begins keeping a record of the books he reads.

1913

NOVEMBER   Ira Gershwin and his friend Isadore Hochberg (later E. Y. Harburg) begin their "Much Ado" column for the *Academic Herald*—the Townsend Harris Hall literary magazine. Ira continues his contributions to this column until June 1914.

1914

MAY   George Gershwin begins work as a song plugger for Jerome H. Remick & Company.

SEPTEMBER 26   Earliest known Ira Gershwin contribution to a New York newspaper ("Tramp jokes, writes Gersh, are bum comedy"). This item appeared in C. L. Edson's column, "Always in Good Humor," in the New York *Mail*. Ira makes other contributions to the *Mail* in late 1914 and early 1915.

NOVEMBER 11   Ira Gershwin makes his first contribution to *The Campus*, a weekly journal of the City College

of New York. Other Ira Gershwin contributions appear in *The Campus* in late 1915 and early 1916 in a column that he prepared and wrote with E. Y. Harburg titled "Gargoyle Gargles."

1915

MAY 12   "Aunt Prudella," a short poem by Ira Gershwin, is included in "The Sun Dial," Don Marquis's column in the New York *Evening Sun*. This is the first of several Ira Gershwin contributions to this column.

OCTOBER 26   Ira Gershwin's poem "I Remember!" is published in the City College monthly, *College Mercury*.

1916

MARCH   Ira Gershwin begins keeping a private record, which he calls "The Theatre," of the plays and musical shows he attends.

APRIL 11   An Ira Gershwin contribution, his first, appears in Franklin Pierce Adams's *Evening Mail* column, "The Conning Tower."

JUNE   Ira Gershwin contributions appear in *Cap and Bells*, a City College publication.

AUGUST   The St. Nicholas Baths open and Ira Gershwin begins work there as a cashier.

SEPTEMBER 5   Ira Gershwin begins a diary, which he titles "Every Man His Own Boswell." At this time, the Gershwin family lives at 108 West 111th Street, Manhattan. Ira attends night classes at City College and works days at the baths.

DECEMBER   The Wolpin and Gershwin families take over the Lafayette Baths and Hotel in Greenwich Village. Ira works there until July 2, 1917—at fifteen dollars, then seventeen dollars, a week.

1917

MARCH 17   George Gershwin gives up his job at Jerome H. Remick & Company.

APRIL 22   Rose Gershwin's father dies in New York City.

MAY 17   Ira Gershwin writes a short story titled "The Shrine."

MAY 23   Ira Gershwin writes his first song lyric—"You May Throw All the Rice You Desire." It is published in Don Marquis's column in the New York *Evening Sun*.

MAY 27   Ira Gershwin meets Lou Paley and Emily Strunsky. Lou Paley will become an early collaborator of George Gershwin's; Emily Strunsky's sister Leonore will marry Ira Gershwin in 1926.

JULY 2   Lafayette Baths placed in receivership.

SEPTEMBER 25   Ira Gershwin takes a job at B. Altman & Co.—in the receiving department—at fifteen dollars a week.

SEPTEMBER 28   The Gershwin family moves to 520 West 144th Street in Manhattan.

OCTOBER   George Gershwin is working at the Century Theatre as a rehearsal pianist.

NOVEMBER   Morris Gershwin opens Gershwin's Restaurant at 3508 Broadway in Manhattan.

NOVEMBER 14   Ira Gershwin's short story "The Shrine" is accepted by the literary magazine *Smart Set*.

NOVEMBER 22   Ira Gershwin writes his first vaudeville review for the New York *Clipper*, a trade paper. It appears on November 28. Ira continues as an occasional vaudeville reviewer for the *Clipper* until February 1918.

DECEMBER   Ira Gershwin writes a lyric titled "You Are Not the Girl" for a George Gershwin melody. It is his first collaboration with his composer brother (the song has not survived). Ira writes other songs with George, who is also collaborating with Lou Paley, Irving Caesar, and Leonard Praskins.

1918

FEBRUARY   George Gershwin joins the staff of the music publisher T. B. Harms—at thirty-five dollars a week. Ira Gershwin's short story "The Shrine" appears in *Smart Set*. George, Ira, and Lou Paley collaborate on a song titled "Beautiful Bird." It is the oldest surviving George and Ira Gershwin song collaboration.

MARCH   Ira Gershwin quits his job at B. Altman & Co. and returns to work at the St. Nicholas Baths. Morris Gershwin closes Gershwin's Restaurant.

MAY 26   Ira Gershwin writes the lyric for "The Real American Folk Song (Is a Rag)." It is sung by Nora Bayes and then by Hal Ford in the musical *Ladies First*. It is the first George and Ira Gershwin song to be performed in a Broadway show.

DECEMBER 9   *Half Past Eight*, with music by George Gershwin, begins a pre-Broadway tryout in Syracuse, New York. It closes out of town—less than a week later.

1919

MAY 26 *La-La-Lucille!*, with music by George Gershwin, opens at the Henry Miller Theatre, New York City. It runs for 104 performances.

SUMMER Ira Gershwin works as treasurer for Colonel Lagg's Greater Empire Shows.

OCTOBER 24 "Swanee" (music by George Gershwin, lyrics by Irving Caesar) is introduced in the Capitol Theatre revue *Demi-Tasse*. By early 1920, Al Jolson has interpolated it into the post-Broadway tour of his show *Sinbad*. Jolson also records "Swanee" and quickly establishes it as George Gershwin's first great hit song.

1920

FEBRUARY 2 *Dere Mable*, with George and Ira Gershwin's song "Back Home," begins a pre-Broadway tryout in Baltimore. It closes out of town.

APRIL "Waiting for the Sun to Come Out" is the first George and Ira Gershwin song to be published. It is introduced on Broadway (August 31, 1920) in *The Sweetheart Shop*.

SEPTEMBER 27 *Piccadilly to Broadway*, with music by George Gershwin, Vincent Youmans, William Daly, and others, and lyrics by Arthur Francis (pseudonym for Ira Gershwin), E. Ray Goetz, and others, begins a pre-Broadway tryout at the Globe Theatre, Atlantic City. The show tours extensively but does not reach New York City.

1921

MARCH 21 First performance of *A Dangerous Maid* at Nixon's Apollo Theatre, Atlantic City. It closes out of town after performances in Wilmington, Washington, D.C., and Pittsburgh.

APRIL 11 First performance of *Two Little Girls in Blue* at the Colonial Theatre, Boston.

MAY 3 *Two Little Girls in Blue* opens at the George M. Cohan Theatre, New York City; 135 performances.

DECEMBER Ira Gershwin, as Arthur Francis, writes lyrics for the theme song (music by Louis Silvers) of the Mae Murray film *Peacock Alley*.

1922

FEBRUARY 1 *Pins and Needles*, with the song "The Piccadilly Walk," opens at the Shubert Theatre, New York City; 46 performances.

FEBRUARY 22 *For Goodness Sake*, with lyrics to three numbers by Arthur Francis, opens at the Lyric Theatre, New York City; 103 performances.

APRIL Mae Murray's film *Fascination* is released; the lyrics for the film's theme song (music by Louis Silver) are by Arthur Francis and Schuyler Greene.

JULY Arthur Francis and B. G. DeSylva write lyrics to George Gershwin's music for the song "(I'll Build a) Stairway to Paradise," which is introduced in *George White's Scandals of 1922*—Globe Theatre, New York City, August 28, 1922; 88 performances.

SEPTEMBER 1 "When All Your Castles Come Tumbling Down" is introduced in *Molly Darling*, Liberty Theatre, New York City; 101 performances.

SEPTEMBER 2 "Mischa, Jascha, Toscha, Sascha," a party song by George Gershwin and Arthur Francis, written June–July 1922, is registered for copyright as an unpublished song.

1923

MARCH George Gershwin and Arthur Francis write the theme song for Thomas H. Ince's film *The Sunshine Trail*.

MARCH–APRIL Arthur Francis writes lyrics for an unproduced show to William Daly's adaptation of Chopin piano pieces.

MAY Arthur Francis writes lyrics to "Little Rhythm, Go 'Way" (music by William Daly and Joseph Meyer). This lyric contains many phrases and ideas that Ira will use later in "Fascinating Rhythm."

AUGUST 28 *Little Miss Bluebeard*, in which star Irene Bordoni sings "I Won't Say I Will, But I Won't Say I Won't," opens at the Lyceum Theatre, New York City; 175 performances.

SEPTEMBER 5 *Nifties of 1923*, with the song "Fabric of Dreams," opens at the Fulton Theatre, New York City; 47 performances.

1924

FEBRUARY 12 George Gershwin's *Rhapsody in Blue* for Jazz Band and Piano receives its world premiere at Aeolian Hall, New York City, with Paul Whiteman conducting his Palais Royal Orchestra; George Gershwin, piano soloist.

MAY "Imagine Me Without My You" (music by Lewis E. Gensler, lyrics by Ira Gershwin and Robert Russell Bennett) is the first song published with lyrics attributed to Ira (who is credited here as "Ira B. Gershwin").

SEPTEMBER 3 *Be Yourself* opens at the Sam H. Harris Theatre, New York City; 93 performances.

SEPTEMBER 11 *Primrose* opens at the Winter Garden, London; 255 performances.

NOVEMBER 17 First performance of *Lady, Be Good!* at the Forrest Theatre, Philadelphia.

DECEMBER 1 *Lady, Be Good!* opens at the Liberty Theatre, New York City; 330 performances.

1925

The Gershwins move to 316 West 103rd Street, New York City.

APRIL 6 First performance of *Tell Me More* at Nixon's Apollo Theatre, Atlantic City.

APRIL 13 *Tell Me More* opens at the Gaiety Theatre, New York City; 100 performances.

MAY 26 *Tell Me More* opens at the Winter Garden, London; 264 performances.

NOVEMBER 24 First performance of *Tip-Toes* at the National Theatre, Washington, D.C. Additional tryouts take place in Newark, Philadelphia, and Baltimore.

DECEMBER 3 World premiere of George Gershwin's *Concerto in F* for Piano and Orchestra at Carnegie Hall, New York City, by the New York Symphony Society conducted by Walter Damrosch; George Gershwin, piano soloist.

DECEMBER 28 *Tip-Toes* opens at the Liberty Theatre, New York City; 194 performances.

1926

APRIL 14 *Lady, Be Good!* opens at the Empire Theatre, London; 325 performances.

JULY 26 *Americana*, with three lyrics by Ira Gershwin, opens at the Belmont Theatre, New York City; 224 performances.

AUGUST 31 *Tip-Toes* opens at the Winter Garden, London; 181 performances.

SEPTEMBER 14 Ira Gershwin marries Leonore (Lee) Strunsky (b. October 3, 1900) in New York City.

OCTOBER 18 First performance of *Oh, Kay!* at the Shubert Theatre, Philadelphia.

NOVEMBER 8 *Oh, Kay!* opens at the Imperial Theatre, New York City; 256 performances.

1927

APRIL The Gershwins rent Chumleigh Farm, Ossining, New York, for the spring and summer.

AUGUST 29 First performance of *Strike Up the Band* at Reade's Broadway Theatre, Long Branch, New Jersey. Subsequent pre-Broadway performances at the Shubert Theatre, Philadelphia, begin September 5, 1927. The show closes out of town.

SEPTEMBER 21 *Oh, Kay!* opens at His Majesty's Theatre, London; 215 performances.

OCTOBER 11 First performance of *Smarty* (the interim title for the musical originated as and eventually retitled *Funny Face*) at the Shubert Theatre, Philadelphia. Pre-Broadway tryout continues with weeks in Washington, D.C. (October 31), Atlantic City (November 7), and Wilmington (November 14).

NOVEMBER 22 *Funny Face* opens at the Alvin Theatre, New York City; 244 performances. It is the first attraction at the newly built theatre, renamed, years later, the Neil Simon.

DECEMBER 5 First performance of *Rosalie* at the Colonial Theatre, Boston.

1928

JANUARY 10 *Rosalie* opens at the New Amsterdam Theatre, New York City; 325 performances.

FEBRUARY 6 First performance of *That's a Good Girl* at the Empire Theatre, Cardiff, Wales.

MARCH 10 George, Lee, Ira, and Frances Gershwin sail from New York City to Europe on the S.S. *Majestic*. It is Ira's first trip abroad.

MARCH 16 The Gershwins arrive in London.

MARCH 26 The Gershwins arrive in Paris, where George works on the orchestral tone poem that becomes *An American in Paris*.

APRIL 23 The Gershwins arrive in Berlin after a train trip from Paris.

APRIL 28 The Gershwins arrive in Vienna after an overnight train trip from Berlin.

MAY 6 George and Frances Gershwin return to Paris, where George accompanies Frances's opening-night performance (May 10) in Cole Porter's show *La Revue des Ambassadeurs*. Lee and Ira Gershwin sail down the Danube from Vienna to Budapest. On May 8 they return to Vienna and on May 11 they arrive in Nice; two days later they begin a stay in Antibes, returning to Paris on May 22.

JUNE 5 *That's a Good Girl* opens at the London Hippodrome; 365 performances.

JUNE 13 The four Gershwins sail from Southampton, England, on the SS *Majestic*.

JUNE 18 The Gershwins arrive in New York.

SEPTEMBER 24 *Funny Face* begins its English tryout at the Empire Theatre, Liverpool.

OCTOBER 15 First performance of *Treasure Girl* at the Shubert Theatre, Philadelphia.

NOVEMBER 8 *Funny Face* opens at Princes Theatre, London; 267 performances. *Treasure Girl* opens at the Alvin Theatre, New York City; 68 performances.

DECEMBER 13 *An American in Paris* is given its world premiere at Carnegie Hall, New York City, by the Philharmonic-Symphony Society of New York conducted by Walter Damrosch.

1929

George and Ira Gershwin take penthouse apartments at 33 Riverside Drive, New York City. They abandon work on *East Is West*, also known as *Ming Toy*, a Ziegfeld show for which they had written some songs in 1928.

JUNE 24 First performance of *Show Girl* at the Colonial Theatre, Boston.

JULY 2 *Show Girl* opens at the Ziegfeld Theatre, New York City; 111 performances.

DECEMBER 25 First performance of revised version of *Strike Up the Band* at the Shubert Theatre, Boston. Subsequent tryout engagement at the Shubert Theatre, New Haven, January 6, 1930.

1930

JANUARY 14 *Strike Up the Band* opens at the Times Square Theatre, New York City; 191 performances.

SEPTEMBER 29 First performance of *Girl Crazy* at the Shubert Theatre, Philadelphia.

OCTOBER 14 *Girl Crazy* opens at the Alvin Theatre, New York City; 272 performances.

NOVEMBER 2 Frances Gershwin marries Leopold Godowsky, Jr., in New York City.

NOVEMBER 5 George, Ira, and Lee Gershwin leave New York City by train for California, where George and Ira are to begin work on the film score for *Delicious*.

1931

FEBRUARY 22 George, Ira, and Lee Gershwin return from California by train to New York City.

DECEMBER *Delicious* is released.

DECEMBER 8 First performance of *Of Thee I Sing* at the Majestic Theatre, Boston.

DECEMBER 26 *Of Thee I Sing* opens at the Music Box Theatre, New York City; 441 performances.

1932

JANUARY 29 *Second Rhapsody* for Orchestra with Piano, by George Gershwin, receives its world premiere at Symphony Hall, Boston, by the Boston Symphony Orchestra conducted by Serge Koussevitzky; George Gershwin, piano soloist.

MAY Ira Gershwin, along with librettists George S. Kaufman and Morrie Ryskind, is awarded the Pulitzer Prize for *Of Thee I Sing*—the first musical to receive the Pulitzer Prize for drama. George Gershwin is not cited by the Pulitzer committee.

MAY 14 Morris Gershwin dies.

AUGUST 16 *Cuban Overture* (originally *Rumba*) for Orchestra, by George Gershwin, receives its world premiere at Lewisohn Stadium, New York City, by the New York Philharmonic-Symphony Orchestra conducted by Albert Coates.

SEPTEMBER Publication of *George Gershwin's Song-Book*, which includes his piano transcriptions of eighteen of his songs and the original sheet-music arrangements. A special limited edition of three hundred copies had been published in May.

DECEMBER 2 First performance of *Pardon My English* at the Garrick Theatre, Philadelphia. Pre-Broadway tryout continues with weeks in Brooklyn (December 26), Newark (January 2, 1933), and Boston (January 9, 1933).

1933

George Gershwin moves to a duplex apartment at 132 East Seventy-second Street; Lee and Ira Gershwin take an apartment across the street at 125 East Seventy-second Street.

JANUARY 20 *Pardon My English* opens at the Majestic Theatre, New York City; 46 performances.

OCTOBER 2 First performance of *Let 'Em Eat Cake* at the Shubert Theatre, Boston.

OCTOBER 21 *Let 'Em Eat Cake* opens at the Imperial Theatre, New York City; 90 performances.

1934

JANUARY 14 George Gershwin's *Variations on "I Got Rhythm"* for Orchestra and Piano Solo receives its world premiere at Symphony Hall, Boston, by the Leo Reisman Symphonic Orchestra conducted by Charles Previn; George Gershwin, piano soloist. This is the first stop in a twenty-eight-concert tour of North America that concludes on February 10.

FEBRUARY 19 George Gershwin's first performance in a series of radio programs sponsored by Feen-A-Mint, devoted to his and others' music. The broadcasts run twice a week until May 31, then once a week from September 23 to December 23.

AUGUST 6 First performance of *Life Begins at 8:40* at the Shubert Theatre, Boston.

AUGUST 27   *Life Begins at 8:40* opens at the Winter Garden, New York City; 237 performances.

1935

SEPTEMBER 30   First performance of *Porgy and Bess* at the Colonial Theatre, Boston.

OCTOBER 10   *Porgy and Bess* opens at the Alvin Theatre, New York City; 124 performances.

DECEMBER 30   First performance of *Ziegfeld Follies of 1936* at the Boston Opera House. Tryout also includes performances in Philadelphia.

1936

JANUARY 30   *Ziegfeld Follies of 1936* opens at the Winter Garden, New York City; 115 performances (initial edition), 112 performances (second, revised edition).

AUGUST 8   George, Ira, and Lee Gershwin fly from Newark to Los Angeles to begin writing film scores for RKO. They take a house at 1019 North Roxbury Drive in Beverly Hills.

1937

MAY   *Shall We Dance*, the brothers' first RKO film, is released.

JULY 11   George Gershwin dies at the age of thirty-eight of a brain tumor in Cedars of Lebanon Hospital, Los Angeles.

JULY 15   Funeral service for George Gershwin at Temple Emanu-El in New York City. He is buried at Westchester Hills Cemetery, New York.

NOVEMBER   *A Damsel in Distress*, the brothers' second RKO film, is released.

1938

FEBRUARY   The film *The Goldwyn Follies* is released. During this year Ira collaborates on a number of songs with composer Jerome Kern.

1940

FEBRUARY   Ira Gershwin begins collaboration with composer Kurt Weill and librettist Moss Hart on a theatre piece that becomes *Lady in the Dark*.

DECEMBER 30   First performance of *Lady in the Dark* at the Colonial Theatre, Boston.

1941

JANUARY 23   *Lady in the Dark* opens at the Alvin Theatre, New York City; 467 performances.

FEBRUARY   Lee and Ira Gershwin purchase house at 1021 North Roxbury Drive, Beverly Hills, next door to the house they had lived in with George during the last months of his life.

1943

Ira Gershwin works with Aaron Copland on the score for RKO's *The North Star* and with Jerome Kern on songs for the Columbia Pictures musical *Cover Girl*.

OCTOBER   *The North Star* is released.

NOVEMBER   Ira Gershwin begins work with Kurt Weill on songs for the film *Where Do We Go from Here?*

1944

APRIL   *Cover Girl* is released.

JULY   Ira Gershwin begins work with Kurt Weill on the score for an adaptation of Edwin Justus Mayer's play *The Firebrand*, tentatively titled "Much Ado About Love."

1945

FEBRUARY 23   First performance of *Much Ado about Love* (eventually retitled *The Firebrand of Florence*) at the Colonial Theatre, Boston.

MARCH 22   *The Firebrand of Florence* opens at the Alvin Theatre, New York City; 43 performances.

MAY   *Where Do We Go from Here?* is released.

SEPTEMBER   *Rhapsody in Blue*, a film biography of George and Ira Gershwin, is released.

1946

SEPTEMBER 23   First performance of *Park Avenue* at the Colonial Theatre, Boston. Tryout continues in Philadelphia (October 7) and New Haven (October 21).

NOVEMBER 4   *Park Avenue* opens at the Shubert Theatre, New York; 72 performances. It is to be Ira Gershwin's last "new" Broadway score.

1947

JANUARY   Film musical *The Shocking Miss Pilgrim* (music by George Gershwin [posthumous], lyrics by Ira Gershwin) is released by 20th Century Fox.

1948

Ira Gershwin at work with composer Harry Warren on the songs for the Metro-Goldwyn-Mayer film *The Barkleys of Broadway*.

DECEMBER 15   Rose Gershwin dies.

1949

MAY   *The Barkleys of Broadway* is released.

1950

AUGUST   Production begins on the Metro-Goldwyn-Mayer film *An American in Paris*.

1951

NOVEMBER   *An American in Paris*, with songs by George and Ira Gershwin, is released. It subsequently wins the Academy Award as Best Picture of 1951.

1952

Ira Gershwin at work with composer Burton Lane on the songs for the Metro-Goldwyn-Mayer film *Give a Girl a Break*.

MAY 5   *Of Thee I Sing*, with some revised lyrics by Ira Gershwin, is revived at the Ziegfeld Theatre, New York City; 72 performances.

1953

DECEMBER   *Give a Girl a Break* is released.

1954

SEPTEMBER   The Warner Bros. film *A Star Is Born* is released.

DECEMBER   The Paramount film *The Country Girl* is released.

1959

SEPTEMBER   Ira Gershwin's *Lyrics on Several Occasions* is published by Alfred A. Knopf.

1964

DECEMBER   The United Artists film *Kiss Me, Stupid* (music by George Gershwin [posthumous], lyrics by Ira Gershwin) is released.

1981

NOVEMBER 20 Arthur Gershwin dies.

1983

MAY 1 *My One and Only*, the last project on which Ira Gershwin works, opens at the St. James Theatre, New York City; 762 performances.

AUGUST 17 Ira Gershwin dies at home in Beverly Hills at the age of eighty-six.

1991

AUGUST 20 Leonore Gershwin dies at home in Beverly Hills at the age of ninety.

1992

FEBRUARY 19 *Crazy for You*, with songs by George and Ira Gershwin, opens at the Shubert Theatre, New York City. It receives the Tony Award as the best musical of the 1991–1992 season.

ACKNOWLEDGMENTS

The editor acknowledges with deep gratitude and appreciation the extensive help he has received over many years in the compilation and annotation of the lyrics of Ira Gershwin. Thanks, first and foremost, to Leonore and Ira Gershwin, and to Michael S. Strunsky, Trustee of the Ira and Leonore Gershwin Trusts. The editor also wishes to thank Tommy Krasker, archivist for the Ira and Leonore Gershwin Trusts, for his careful reading of the manuscript and his cogent editorial suggestions. Many others have assisted, directly and indirectly, in large ways and small, in the preparation and completion of this book. They include Frances Gershwin Godowsky, Emily Paley, Lucy and English Strunsky, Rosamund Walling Tirana, Leopold Godowsky III, Marc George Gershwin, Jean Strunsky, Elaine Godowsky, Vicky Gershwin, and other members of George and Ira Gershwin's families. The editor also extends his thanks to Mark Trent Goldberg (who compiled the extensive copyright notices which appear in the index) and Camille Kuznetz of the Ira and Leonore Gershwin Trusts; Donald S. Passman, Hermione Brown, Lisa Thomas, James A. Reuben, and Ronald L. Blanc for legal assistance and help on song copyrights; Mabel Schirmer, Kay Swift, Henry Botkin, Kay Halle, Emil Mosbacher, Kitty Carlisle Hart, Edgar Carter, Walter Reilly, June Levant, Tom Monjack, Marlene Stepanic, and other friends of Ira and Leonore Gershwin's; James H. Billington, Librarian of Congress, James W. Pruett, Chief of the Music Division of the Library of Congress, and their colleagues John Newsom, Elizabeth H. Auman, Raymond White, Kate Rivers, Florence Barber, Wayne Shirley, and Helen Dalrymple; Lewis H. Aborn, Sargent Aborn, and Dale Kugel of Tams-Witmark Music Library; Leslie Bider, Jay Morganstern, Frank Military, and Al Kohn of Warner-Chappell Music; biographers and scholars on the life and work of George and Ira Gershwin, including Edward Jablonski, Lawrence D. Stewart, Deena Rosenberg, Philip Furia, Walter Rimler, Isaac Goldberg, Merle Armitage, and my collaborator Alfred E. Simon; Michael Feinstein and Miles Kreuger, for their constant help and encouragement; the institutions that preserve the legacy of the American musical: the Library of Congress, the New York Public Library for the Performing Arts, the Institute of the American Musical, the Harvard University Library, the Free Library of Philadelphia, the Kurt Weill Foundation, the Yale University Library, the Shubert Archive, the Museum of the City of New York, and the Theatre Museum, London; Harold Arlen, Fred Astaire, George Balanchine, Irving Berlin, Mario Braggiotti, Anne W. Brown, John W. Bubbles, Irving Caesar, Virginia Christiansen, Todd Duncan, John Green, E. Y. Harburg, Eva Jessye, Tessa Kosta, Burton Lane, Lotte Lenya, Oscar Levant, Ethel Merman, Barbara Newberry, Aileen Pringle, Richard Rodgers, Ginger Rogers, Arthur Schwartz, and other artists who worked with Ira Gershwin; and to many, many more, including William W. Appleton, Paulette Attie, Robert Baral, Robert L. Barlow, Sharma Bennett, Roderick Bladel, Ken Bloom, William Bolcom, Daniel J. Boorstin, Gerald Bordman, Steven D. Bowen, Richard M. Buck, Maryann Chach, Allen Churchill, Henry Cohen, Ceciley Youmans Collins, Jon Allen Conrad, Nancy Cotton, Mary Corliss, Lee Davis, Geraldine Duclow, Lehman Engel, David Farneth, Hugh Fordin, Donald Fowle, James J. Fulch, Kurt Ganzl, Charles Gaynor, Herbert G. Goldman, Stanley Green, Charles Hamm, Mary Henderson, Ernie Harburg, James H.

Heineman, Tony Holmes, Barbara Horgan, Mary Ann Jensen, Catherine J. Johnson, Joseph Keller, James Kendrick, Abigail, Philip, and Miranda Kimball, Andrew Kirk, Kim Kowalke, Glenn Loney, Robert Marx, John McGlinn, Brooks McNamara, Max Morath, Ethan Mordden, Larry Moore, John Mueller, Jeanne T. Newlin, Brian O'Connell, Donald Oliver, Vivian Perlis, Jack Raymond, Joshua Robison, Albert Rocha, Donald Rose, Evan Ross, Brian Rust, Karyn Saroka, Judith M. Schiff, Daniel Shigo, Leida Snow, Richard Stoddard, Richard M. Sudhalter, Michael S. Sukin, Steven Suskin, Robert Taylor, Richard Traubner, Richard Wall, Richard Warren, Jr., Katherine Weber, and Max Wilk. And thanks to Robert Cornfield, to Benjamin Dreyer, Donald M. Marshman, Jr., and Tony Davis, and to my friends at Alfred A. Knopf who guided this book through its many stages: Robert A. Gottlieb, Martha Kaplan, Katherine Hourigan, Nancy Clements, Cassandra Pappas, Andy Hughes, William Koshland, Karen Latuchie, Mona West, Jennifer Bernstein, and Sonny Mehta.

THE COMPLETE LYRICS OF IRA GERSHWIN

OPPOSITE: *George and Ira Gershwin*

1917–1920

YOU MAY THROW ALL THE RICE YOU DESIRE

Ira Gershwin's diary entry: May 24, 1917.
> "5/24/17 Thurs. Wrote a song yesterday called—
> Title
> You may throw all the rice you desire—
> Subtitle
> But please, friends, throw no shoes."

Years later, Ira Gershwin noted: "In the first lyric of mine ever printed, the words came first—they had to come first as it was never intended that any tune be composed for them. It was written as a spoof and sent to Don Marquis, the brilliant poet, playwright, and columnist, and it appeared as a letter and lyric in his New York *Evening Sun* column, 'The Sun Dial,' May 1917":

THERE IS NOTHING THE MATTER: IT'S PERFECT

Mr. Marquis, *Dear Sir:* I have sent the following lyric to six different publishers and they all sent it back. Maybe you or some of your readers can tell me what is the matter with it as I am a young fellow and want to give the public what it wants. It goes as follows . . .

Maybe it is a little old-fashioned, but I don't know, the old songs are the best, they say, and it points a moral. If any reader likes it and can write music to it, I will go fifty-fifty with him.

Respectfully yours,
I. B. Gershwin

Ira Gershwin's last word on the subject:
"I never met Mr. Marquis and so I never found out whether he thought my letter and lyric were to be taken seriously or not."

VERSE 1

The ceremony was over,
And all was happy and gay.
The blushing bride and her lover
To the steps did wend their way.
Their young friends them had preceded
And had formed a merry plot;
Although the older folks pleaded,
The younger folks heeded them not.
But the bridegroom knew all about it,
And he stood with his haughty head,
He lifted his hand (you may doubt it,
But 'tis true), these words he said:

REFRAIN

"You may throw all the rice you desire,
But please, friends, throw no shoes.
For 'twill surely arouse my ire,
If you cause my wife one bruise.
Should you heed these words and don't fire,
Then my friendship you won't lose.
You may throw all the rice you desire,
But please, friends, throw no shoes."

VERSE 2

A thrill o'er that throng so motley
Went like a flash so quick;
And many young faces flamed hotly,
Their consciences made them sick.
Many a spirit so reckless
Was beginning to meditate.
Persons with souls not so fleckless
Their wrongdoings vowed to abate.
As the decades rolled by, they never
Forgot that brave husband's part.
They behaved thereafter, forever,
Like they knew, as follows, by heart:

REPEAT REFRAIN

BEAUTIFUL BIRD

During 1917, Ira sold his first story, "The Shrine," to *Smart Set;* he received one dollar for his contribution. The story appeared in the February 1918 issue. He also began writing vaudeville reviews for the New York *Clipper.* On December 18, 1917, he noted in his diary: "I wrote a chorus for a melody of Geo's. 'You Are Not the Girl.' " The song does not survive. On December 30, Ira noted: "Geo is writing songs at present with Lou Paley + [Irving] Caesar + myself (a couple), and [Leonard] Praskins also."

On February 10, 1918, he wrote: "Geo has been placed on the staff of T. B. Harms Co. He gets $35 a week for this connection, then $50 advance + 3 cents royalty on each song of his they accept. This entails no other efforts on his part than the composing, they not requiring any of his leisure for 'plugging' nor for piano-playing. Some snap . . . Lou and Geo have about 10 splendid numbers, which with the addition of say half a dozen more could score and lyricize a M.C. [musical comedy] book, as artistically and entertaining as any M.C. book I have seen. . . . 'Beautiful Bird' is a number that Geo, Lou + I are working on. Hope it turns out to be a 2nd 'Poor Butterfly.' "

Music by George Gershwin. Lyrics by Lou Paley and Ira Gershwin. No. 98 in the George and Ira Gershwin Special Numbered Song File, which was prepared in the mid-1940s by Ira Gershwin and Kay Swift.

VERSE

I have been haunted by a sound that I heard
Deep in a forest one day.
I heard the piping of a beautiful bird
Telling its love in that way.
I know that chance
Had brought me near to a springtime romance.

REFRAIN

Beautiful Bird,
Your plaintive piping I've heard.
No bird can sing me a sweeter
Melodious meter than you.
Your trilling lay
Intrigues my senses.
My love commences
Anew each day.
Your throbbing throat
So sweetly swelling
In every note a love tale telling
You love me.
Whene'er you start
You send a dart
And it pierces my heart
With [*Whistle*].

ADDITIONAL LINES

"Will' Oo? Will' Oo?"
His plaintive "Will' Oo? Will' Oo?"
His mate so softly replying
Sent all my thoughts flying to you.
"Will' Oo? Will' Oo?"
A strain so thrilling
My heart is filling with love anew.
Will you be true with love that none can undo?
When I'm cooing—"Will' Oo?"

With love his message was filling me;
His image was thrilling me through.

THE REAL AMERICAN FOLK SONG (IS A RAG)

Diary entry: May 21, 1918.

Am still at the St. Nicholas [the bathhouse in which Ira worked]. Have done nothing in the way of writing except ideas for a couple of songs.
1. It's Such a Lovely Day (for Love) (Thunderstorm outside).
2. If You Only Knew What I Thought of You, You'd Think a Little More of Me.

3. I've Got a Lot to Tell You.
4. You're A Treasure I Treasure, etc.
5. Bird Song.

[Lyrics for "If You Only Knew" and "Bird Song" are the only ones of the above to survive.]

Diary entry: Sunday night, May 26, 1918.

Writing songs for musical comedy consumption (embryo M. comedies, that is) certainly gives me remarkable practice in applied penmanship. I had an idea that 'American Folk Song' might be suitably developed to be classed in that category we'll call m.c. songs, awright. Well & good & proper unspeakably, ineffably nice. So I started on the chorus. I wrote one. Discarded it. Wrote another. Started a third. Wastebasketed all. Finally after several sporadic starts came to some agreement with myself somewhat on this fashion:

The Great American Folk Song is a rag—
A mental jag.
Captures you with a pure melodic strain
Its aboriginal odd refrain
Has been inoculated with an ultra-syncopated
Rhythm and with 'im,
There's a happy, snappy, don't-care-a-rappy sort of
I don't know what to call it.
But it makes you think of Kingdom Come
You jazz it, as it makes you hum.
Concert singers say that they despise it
Hoary critics never eulogize it.
Still—It's our national, irrational
Folk song—It's a masterstroke song
It's a rag.

Not good, not bad. Passable with a good rag refrain. Geo liked it. So we sat down on (at, rather) the piano & Geo started something. Something sounded good so we kept it. It was a strain for the 1st 2 lines. That in our possession we went along and Geo developed the strain along legitimate or illegitimate (if you prefer) rag lines and with a little editing here & there the chorus, musical, stood forth in all its glory. But unhappily the musical lines were of different lengths from the lyric, so after having sweated & toiled & moiled over 20 or so different versions, it now devolves upon me to start an entirely new one keeping the 1st 2 lines as a memento of a tussle strenuous and an intimation of a struggle heroic to materialize.

Three months later, Nora Bayes was singing the song in *Ladies First*.

Published June 1958. The printed song included the following note: "Written in the spring of 1918, 'The Real American Folk Song' was introduced in *Ladies First*, starring Nora Bayes, at the Broadhurst Theatre on October 24, 1918." This was Ira Gershwin's first lyric to be performed in any show.

VERSE 1

Near Barcelona the peasant croons
The old traditional Spanish tunes;
The Neapolitan Street Song sighs—
You think of Italian skies.
Each nation has a creative vein
Originating a native strain,
With folk songs plaintive and others gay
In their own peculiar way.
American folk songs, I feel,
Have a much stronger appeal.

REFRAIN

The real American folk song is a rag—
A mental jag—
A rhythmic tonic for the chronic blues.
The critics called it a joke song, but now
They've changed their tune
And they like it somehow.
For it's inoculated
With a syncopated
Sort of meter,
Sweeter
Than a classic strain;
Boy! You can't remain
Still and quiet—
For it's a riot!
The real American folk song
Is like a Fountain of Youth:
You taste, and it elates you,
And then invigorates you.
The real American folk song—
A masterstroke song—
IS A RAG!

VERSE 2

You may dislike or you may adore
The native songs from a foreign shore;
They may be songs that you can't forget,
They may be distinctive, yet—
They lack a something: a certain snap,
The tempo ticklish that makes you tap,
The invitation to agitate—
And leave the rest to Fate.
A raggy refrain anytime
Sends me a message sublime.

REPEAT REFRAIN

KITCHENETTE

Music by George Gershwin. Lyrics by Ira Gershwin and B. G. DeSylva. Ira completed the first draft of the lyric in August 1918. He and DeSylva then revised the lyric for inclusion in *La-La-Lucille!* (1919). As "Our Little Kitchenette," the song was introduced during the pre-Broadway tryout of La-La-Lucille! by Lorin Raker (Britton) and Helen Clark (Peggy), and ensemble, but was dropped prior to the New York opening. DeSylva later revised the lyric again for *Sweet Little Devil* (1924), but the song was deleted prior to the pre-Broadway tryout. What follows here is the version from *La-La-Lucille!*

VERSE 1

I am looking forward to the day
When in a little nookery,
We can practice cookery sublime.
When we say good-bye to dining out,
We'll cater to our wishes, dear,
Preparing all our dishes, dear,
On time.
We'll learn to cook and fry and bake,
And then, some day, we'll undertake
A pie o'er which the whole world will start raving.
And then think of the heavy tips
We needn't hand their waiterships,
And all the hatcheck ransom we'll be saving.

REFRAIN 1

Oh, when we get our little kitchenette,
We'll make of it our pride and pet.
You'll preside o'er both the pot and pan
And watch me while I'm wrestling with a salmon can.
Life will seem so pleasant and serene,
When I grind the coffee bean.
On no bills of fare we'll gamble,
And from home we needn't ramble,
When the eggs we learn to scramble
In our cozy little kitchenette.

VERSE 2

I will practice day and night and learn
To wield a wicked frying pan,
Most anything, by trying, man can do.
I will learn to make the complicated dish
That's known as succotash;
And then we'll try our luck at hash
And stew.
Ah, hash will be delicious,
But you're really too ambitious—

Yes, I realize that it would take us too long;
We'd have to take a lot of looks,
In many diff'rent cooking books,
Before we'd get the knack of brewing oolong.

REFRAIN 2

Oh, when we get our little kitchenette,
'Twill be our joy, our pride and pet.
We'll have onions, if for them you pine,
But when it comes to garlic, dear, I draw the
    line.
Some fine day, undaunted, unafraid,
We'll concoct some lemonade.
As a chef I'll be no Jonah.
We will tame the wild bologna—
Ah! the rapture when we own a
Cute and cozy little kitchenette.

THERE'S MAGIC IN THE AIR

According to a note by Ira Gershwin, it was written on October 10, 1918. Music by George Gershwin. Sung in the show *Half Past Eight* at the Empire Theatre, Syracuse, New York (opened December 9, 1918). Later, George used its melody for "It's Great to Be in Love" (with new lyrics by B. G. DeSylva and Arthur J. Jackson) in *La-La-Lucille!* (1919).

VERSE

Wise men all have come to this conclusion,
Magic is a fanciful delusion.
But with them I can't agree,
For anyone can plainly see
You could put their notions in confusion.

REFRAIN

For there is magic in the air
When you're around.
In you a vision fair
I know I've found.
Your charm is so appealing,
It sets my mind a-reeling,
And makes my heart begin to jump and bound.
Of gloom I'm not aware
When you're around.
I lose my every care
Where'er you're near, dear.
It's clear, dear,
There's magic in the air.

IF YOU ONLY KNEW

Completed December 1918. Music by George Gershwin. The melody of the verse was subsequently reused in "Tee-Oodle-Um-Bum-Bo," a song in *La-La-Lucille!* (1919).

VERSE

Wonderful maid, I can't evade
Falling more and more in love with you
Each day.
And when you learn how much I yearn,
That's the time my dreams will all come true.
I must say:

REFRAIN

You'd think a little more of me
If you only knew
What I thought of you.
How very happy I should be
If my thoughts you could see,
For words can never quite explain, dear,
Your hold upon my heart and brain.
Dan Cupid and his dart
Would surely find your heart
If you only knew,
If you only knew.

WHEN THERE'S A CHANCE TO DANCE

Written c. 1919. Music probably by George Gershwin. No music is known to survive.

When there's a chance for me to dance,
I always embrace the opportunity.
The whole community
Knows, that in my clothes,
You'll find a prancing personality,
Whose dancing quality
Kills dull care!
Away with all despair,
I like to walk on air—
That's why I dance.
A rhythmic tonic for the blues
I always choose.
The ticklish tempo tempting heart and soul
Until I lose control—

Arcady my only goal.
Come, let's go—For tomorrow
May bring woe—may bring sorrow.
So—I'm never slow
When there's a chance to dance.

WAITING FOR THE SUN TO COME OUT

Published April 1920. Music by George Gershwin. Lyrics by Arthur Francis. Introduced by Helen Ford, Joseph Lertora, and ensemble in *The Sweetheart Shop*, which, after a long tour, opened in New York on August 31, 1920.

VERSE

When the clouds, the skies, are filling,
And the songbirds stop their trilling,
Don't take it to heart,
Let worry depart,
Soon the sunshine will say "Howdy."
Skies are not forever cloudy.
Just learn to sing and never mope,
There is a thing that's known as hope.

REFRAIN

Weary are the flowers,
Dreary are the hours,
Waiting for the sun to come out.
Yet while clouds are crying,
I smile, never sighing,
For I know that presently,
The sun will come and smile on me.
Gray skies will be clearing,
Gay skies soon appearing,
Chasing ev'ry worry and doubt.
There's no use in having sorrow about
While waiting for the sun to come out.

*P*seudonym. Early in 1920 in Chicago there was a successful show called *The Sweetheart Shop*. One day, some weeks before this musical was to make its New York debut, George learned that its management wanted a new song for ingénue Helen Ford. So, hopefully, that night, in a period when the musical-comedy cycle called for at least one Pollyanna song in a show, we wrote something called "Waiting for the Sun to Come Out."

Next day George got in touch with producer Edgar MacGregor, who was in New York and was willing to listen. For fear that if MacGregor learned the song was a sibling collaboration he might listen to it skeptically, I suggested that the lyricist be called Arthur Francis—a combination of the prenames of our younger brother, Arthur, and our sister, Frances. MacGregor liked the song, then asked: "Who's Arthur Francis?" "Oh, he's a clever college boy with lots of talent," said George (as he later told me). The asking price of $250 for the song was agreeable to MacGregor. A couple of weeks later the song went in, was rehearsed, and was mentioned in all the reviews.

The acclaim given the show in the Loop—it ran three months there—wasn't repeated on Broadway. During its third week in New York, when MacGregor was reminded of the as yet unpaid $250, he confided that business was very bad and it looked as though the show would close in two or three weeks. "I'm working, so I don't mind not being paid myself if things are that tough," said George, "but the college boy really needs the money." Whereupon a most welcome check for $125 was made out to Arthur Francis. "Waiting for the Sun" was my first published song. The $125, plus, within the year, earnings of $723.40 from sheet music and $445.02 from phonograph records, kept the "college boy" going for some time.

(As Arthur Francis I did the lyrics for *Two Little Girls in Blue*, with composers [Vincent] Youmans and [Paul] Lannin; *A Dangerous Maid*, with my brother; and a dozen or so songs, interpolated in various revues, with composers Lewis Gensler, Raymond Hubbell, Milton Schwarzwald, and one or two others. In 1924 I dropped Arthur Francis. He was beginning to be confused with lyricist Arthur Jackson; also I'd been made aware that there was an English lyricist named Arthur Francis. Besides, all who knew me knew me as a Gershwin anyway.)

—from *Lyrics on Several Occasions*

FOR NO REASON AT ALL

Probably written in early 1920. Composer is unknown, but probably George Gershwin. Lyrics by Arthur Francis and B. G. DeSylva.

VERSE

A rhyming dictionary isn't all that it should be
As you'll discover should you look one through.
Tho' oftentimes you find that rhymes have
    reason, I'll agree,
Your reason tells you lots of rhymes won't do.
A word like "kiss" should rhyme with "bliss";
That's rhyming as it *should* be.
But common sense and experience
Show some as bad as *could* be.

REFRAIN

Just take a word like "hubby";
The rhyme for that is "clubby"
For no reason at all.
Then there's the movie actor;
He rhymes with "benefactor"
For no reason at all.
I can get the sense when "whiskey"*
Makes a rhyme for "frisky"
For there's some connection there as I recall,
But when then our subway traction
Rhymes with "satisfaction"
There's no reason at all.

BACK HOME

Written in early 1920. Music by George Gershwin. Lyrics by Arthur Francis. Probably written for *Dere Mable*, which opened at the Academy of Music in Baltimore, February 2, 1920, and closed without a New York engagement. No music is known to survive. Introduced by Hattie Burks (Mable). Show programs incorrectly attributed the lyric to Irving Caesar.

VERSE

All the flowers are in bloom, back home,
And all the birds sing.
There's no room for gloom, back home,
For it is spring.
Yet our hearts would be lighter,
Dear, and life would seem brighter,
If we knew that you too
Were back home.

REFRAIN

We all are yearning back home
For your returning back home.
It's been so lonely
Wanting you only;
No more I hope you'll roam.
Here where the lights are aglow,
Back home may seem to be slow;
But where the skies are bluer,
You'll find that cares are fewer,
And I know that

*Alternate version of refrain, lines 7–9:
I agree a word like "ladies"
Finds a perfect rhyme in "Hades"
For they've always raised the devil since man's fall.

Hearts are friendlier and truer, dear,
Away back home.

PICCADILLY TO BROADWAY, 1920

Tryout: Globe Theatre, Atlantic City, September 27, 1920. Tryout continued through December 1920 and included stops in Baltimore, Detroit, Providence, and Boston, but the show did not reach New York. (Some of its material eventually reached Broadway in *Snapshots of 1921*, June 2, 1921.) Book and some songs by Glen MacDonough and E. Ray Goetz. Additional music by William Daly, George Gershwin, Vincent Youmans, and George W. Meyer. Additional lyrics (uncredited in program) by Arthur Francis. Produced by E. Ray Goetz. Staged by George Marion and Julian Alfred. Orchestra under the direction of William Daly. The cast, headed by Johnny Dooley, Anna Wheaton, Clifton Webb, and Morris Harvey, included Mai Bacon, Helen Broderick, Ray Cochrane, Lester Crawford, Vivian Gilbert, Gina Gray, and Violet Strathmore. By Boston, where the show was titled *Vogues and Vanities* (it was also known for a time as *Here and There*), the stage director was Ned Wayburn, and the cast featured Johnny Dooley, Anna Wheaton, William Kent, Clifton Webb, Helen Broderick, Robert Emmet Keane, Lester Crawford, Maurice Diamond, Evelyn Law, and Edith Hallor.

WHO'S WHO WITH YOU?

Written in 1920. Published April 1921. Music by Vincent Youmans. Lyrics by Arthur Francis. Introduced by Clifton Webb, Anna Wheaton, and ensemble. Introduced in *Two Little Girls in Blue* (1921) by Oscar Shaw (Bobby) and Marion Fairbanks (Polly). An earlier version had been intended for Fred Santley (Jerry) and Madeline Fairbanks (Dolly). We do not know which if either of these versions was introduced in *Piccadilly to Broadway* (1920).

First Version

VERSE 1

JERRY: Ev'ry day my love keeps grow-
Ing, darling, I'm all for you.
But with Bobby 'round I'm woe-
Ful, dear, when I call for you.
You're so wonderful, I know;
He can't help but fall for you;
So don't you see
What worries me?

REFRAIN 1

Who's who with you?
Please tell me, do!
What lucky chap
Can make you hap-
Py when you're blue?
Who makes you sigh
As he goes by?
Who thrills you with his call?
Who is your one and all?
I wish I knew
Who's who with you?

VERSE 2

DOLLY: Since we met I've been inclined
To like your society.
But there's something on my mind
That gives me anxiety.
I'm afraid that you're the kind
Who likes his variety.
So you can see
What worries me.

REFRAIN 2

Who's who with you?
Oh, tell me, do!
What girly's kiss-
Ing are you miss-
Ing when you're blue?
Whose winning voice
Makes you rejoice?
I lose my sleep at night
Just wond'ring who's in right.
Who is that who?
JERRY: You know it's you!

Second Version (Published)

VERSE 1

BOBBY: Ev'ry day my love keeps grow-
Ing, darling, I long for you.
If you learn to care, I know
I'll make life a song for you.

But there's Jerry 'round and Oh!
I know he is strong for you.
So don't you see
What worries me?

REFRAIN 1

Who's who with you?
Please tell me, do!
What lucky chap
Can make you hap-
Py when you're blue?
Who makes you sigh
As he goes by?
Who thrills you with his call?
Who is your one and all?
I wish I knew
Who's who with you?

VERSE 2

POLLY: Since we met there's much I find
In life to be glad about.
But there's something on my mind
That I am quite sad about.
I'm afraid that you're the kind
Who always will gad about.
So you can see
What worries me.

REFRAIN 2

Who's who with you?
Oh, tell me, do!
Who knits your ties
To match your eyes
Of baby blue?
Whose winning voice
Makes you rejoice?
I lose my sleep at night
Just wond'ring who's in right.
Who is that who?
BOBBY: You know it's you!

MR. AND MRS.

Written in 1920. Music by Vincent Youmans. Lyrics by Arthur Francis. Introduced by Helen Broderick and Clifton Webb, also by Mai Bacon and Clifton Webb. Programs list the song title as "Now That We're Mr. and Mrs." Later, sung in the Boston tryout of *Two Little Girls in Blue* (April 1921) by Fred Santley, Madeline Fairbanks, and ladies of the ensemble. It was the seventh number in the first act. Dropped before the New York opening, it was replaced with "You Started Something."

Orchestra parts survive. The song is No. 34 in the Vincent Youmans Collection.

VERSE 1

Ev'ry jokesmith 'neath the sun*
Seems to keep on poking fun
At the marriage knot.
It won't stand the acid test,
Say the skeptics and the rest,
But I know that's rot.
So why listen to what critics tell us?
Happiness like ours would make them
jealous.
We could show them all they're wrong.
We could make of married life a song.

REFRAIN 1

If we were Mr. and Mrs.,
We'd know what real bliss is.
With such a lovable spouse, dear,
I'd hate leaving the house, dear;
I'd want you near me night and day.
Our little home would be rosy,
So comfy and cozy,
A love nest ever bright and gay.
There would be no armistices
For hugs and for kisses,
If we were Mr. and Mrs.

VERSE 2

Can't you picture—can't you see—
What a loving pair we'd be
In a two by four?
We should be such perfect mates!
Ev'ry time you'd wipe the plates,
I could sweep the floor.
When you'd start to bake or cook, I'd pitch
in,
Prove a handy man around a kitchen.
SHE: You work fast, I must confess.
HE: I keep hoping someday you'll say yes.

REFRAIN 2

If we were Mr. and Mrs.,
"Oh boy!" we'd say, "this is
The one and only existence;
Gloom in all its persistence
Would never stand a chance with us."
I'm sure that soon you'd discover

---

*Alternate version of verse 1, lines 1–2:
There isn't a jokesmith 'neath the sun
Who doesn't keep on poking fun

A husband as lover
Could make earth seem like heaven plus.
For you I'd strain ev'ry muscle,
I'd toil and hustle,
If we were Mr. and Mrs.

SOMETHING PECULIAR

Probably written in 1920 for *Piccadilly to Broadway*. Music by George Gershwin. Lyrics by Arthur Francis. Later considered for *Lady, Be Good!* (1924) and *Girl Crazy* (1930). This is likely the song listed in *Piccadilly to Broadway* programs as "There Is Something Peculiar," introduced by Anna Wheaton, Morris Harvey, and Johnny Dooley.

VERSE

Once in a music hall
I hear the jazz band,
And right away I fall
For jazzy jazz band.
When they begin to play
Their bingo bango,
Then right away I say,
"To hell with tango."
Now when lover want to show
How much love he have for me,
He must play the vo-de-o
'Neath the balcony! For

REFRAIN

There is something peculiar
About the jazz time of America—
Ola! Ola! la, la!
This funny jazz musique
It make me cry,
"Come on and kiss me queek,
Or else I die!"
It make me act so indiscreet,
From my head down to my feet;
In the sky I kick a hole;
Of my heart I lose control.
Oh, there is something peculiar
About the jazz time of America—
Ola! la! la!

TRIO

Las chiquitas están borrachas
Con la música de los Yankees;
Señoritas, pepitas, muchachas
Todititas están feliz!

Girl Crazy version (unused)

VERSE

PATSY: It sets me all aglow—
The tempo Spanish—
Suppressed desires go—
Commandments vanish.
SLICK: Just listen to my heart
Go bingo bango!
Don't stop me if I start
To do the tango!
PATSY: Passionate and sweet and low—
It's a musical caress.
SLICK: From my head down to my toe
Everything is yes!

REFRAIN

BOTH: For there is something peculiar
About the music of la Mexico.
Ola! Ola! la! la!
This passionate musique
It make me sigh,
"Come on and kiss me queek,
Or else I die!"
I make the motion indiscreet
From my head down to my feet;
In the sky I kick a hole;
Of my heart I lose control.
For there is something peculiar
About the music of la Mexico.
Ola! la! la!

PICCADILLY'S NOT A BIT LIKE BROADWAY

Written in 1920. Music by Vincent Youmans. Lyrics by Arthur Francis. Intended for *Piccadilly to Broadway* (1920), but there is no evidence that this Prohibition-themed song was ever performed in the show. No music is known to survive.

VERSE

Not long ago, wine used to flow
In ev'ry bright café along Broadway.
But now the drink comes from the sink;
The Gay White Way is dull and gray today.
Poor Broadway! Poor Broadway!
Your bacchanalian days are over now.
No H_2O can give the glow
That makes a dreary heart forget its woe.
Here's how.

REFRAIN

I'll say Piccadilly's not a bit like Broadway;
They drink 'er down in London Town.
Good old Piccadilly's an oasis today;
That's why I say I'm here to stay.
I miss the lights of Broadway nights
But I'm content to pay the rent
Over here, Over here.
I'll say Piccadilly is the one place for me.
Good old Piccadilly's like Broadway used to be.

PICK YO' PARTNER! (GET READY FOR THE RAGGY BLUES)

Written in 1920. Music by Vincent Youmans. Lyrics by Arthur Francis. Possibly intended for *Piccadilly to Broadway* (1920). No music is known to survive.

REFRAIN 1

Pick yo' partner!
Get ready for the raggy blues.
They're gonna play it soon,
A draggy southern tune
The kind you love to croon.
Pick yo' partner!
And tie the laces on yo' shoes.
You're gonna walk on air,
Feel like a millionaire,
Forgettin' ev'ry care.

PATTER

You're gonna start a-reeling
On the polished floor;
You'll find it so appealing
That you'll cry fo' more.
For when they syncopate those blues,
It's like the bestest sort of news.
When it commences,
You lose yo' senses.
You find there's magic in yo' shoes.
Oh! Hallelujah!

REFRAIN 2

Pick yo' partner!
Oh, take yo' lady by the hand.
Soon you'll be going some,
Yes, when they start to strum,
You'll think of Kingdom Come.

Pick yo' partner!
And try to make her understand,
It's not a lullaby—
She's got to step on high—
The limit is the sky.

SOMEHOW I KNEW

Written in 1920. Music by Vincent Youmans. Lyrics by Arthur Francis and Lou Paley. No music is known to survive.

VERSE 1

I used to laugh at—
I used to chaff at—
The sort of fellow who
Believed that love at sight would
Be found forever true.
But my conclusions
On love's delusions
Have met their Waterloo.
I cannot hide it—
I must confide it—
The very moment that I met you.

REFRAIN

Somehow—somehow I knew
I could always be true,
Though you merely gave me a smile.
Something clearly
Told me I would love you dearly;
My heart started to dance.
It was love at a glance.
That no other
Girl I'd ever take to mother,
Somehow—somehow I knew.

VERSE 2

Oh, I've been learning
A lot concerning
The way a heart is won.
This love at sight idea
I thought was overdone.
The first who said it

Deserves the credit;
He knew a thing or two.
For that's how really,
I say it freely,
I fell in love with you.

Earlier Version of Verse 2

I've heard it stated
That it is fated
That love must come to all.
And yet I always doubted
That I would ever fall.
But I've been learning
A lot concerning
The way a heart is won.
I cannot hide it—*
I must confide it—
I really felt the same as you.

Verse to Different Music

I've heard a lot about predestination
And of lovers who love at first sight,
But thought them all the fanciful creation
Of the poets and others who write.
But now I find I've changed my mind
    completely;
Every trace of doubt vanished fleetly;
When first I looked in your eyes.

BAMBINO

Written in 1920. Music by Vincent Youmans. Lyrics by Arthur Francis. No music is known to survive.

VERSE

When you and me first meet-a,
My heart he lose a beat.
For, Oh! You look so sweet-a,
You drive me off my feet.

*Alternate version of earlier verse 2, lines 9–11:
For very soon, dear—
I've changed my tune, dear—
Right after I met you.

I say, "Pasqual',
For you here's the only gal."
Into my heart you creep-a,
Now no more I can eat or sleep-a.

REFRAIN

Oh, say that you love me, Bambino,
You're my queen-o, sweet Bambino.
See, I buy-a this new mandolino
Jus' to sing-a my love to you.
Oh, please-a don't treat-a me mean-o.
Maraschino, I'll be true.
The love moon is bright,
So let's make-a da hay.*
Come make-a with me monkey business till day.
For I must have love, sweet Bambino,
And no other girl will do.

GONDOLIER

Written in 1920. Music probably by Vincent Youmans. Lyrics by Arthur Francis. No music is known to survive.

VERSE

Cares of day will fade away
While all the world is asleep.
Moon so bright our course will light
Until the sun starts to peep.

REFRAIN

Gondolier, take me far away
To some mystic shore
Where lovers' hearts are light.
Gently steer, while the moonbeams play
And the zephyrs murmur softly
Through the night.
Drift along with a simple song,
One you know from long ago.
Gondolier, on the silv'ry streams,
We'll go floating through the land of dreams.

*Alternate version of refrain, lines 7–8:
I'll climb to your window like in da romance.
I no give a rap if I rip-a da pants.

A DANGEROUS MAID
TWO LITTLE GIRLS IN BLUE
1921

A DANGEROUS MAID, 1921

Tryout: Nixon's Apollo Theatre, Atlantic City, March 21–23, 1921; The Playhouse, Wilmington, March 24–26, 1921; Ford's Theatre, Baltimore, March 28–April 2, 1921; National Theatre, Washington, D.C., April 4–9, 1921; Nixon Theatre, Pittsburgh, April 11–16, 1921. Closed out of town. Music by George Gershwin. Lyrics by Arthur Francis. Produced by Edgar MacGregor. Book by Charles W. Bell, based on his 1919 play, *The Dislocated Honeymoon*. Directed by Julian Alfred. Cast featured Juliette Day (replaced with Vivienne Segal) (Elsie), Amelia Bingham (Mrs. Hammond), Ada Meade (Anne), Juanita Fletcher (Margery), Creighton Hale (Harry), Vinton Freedley (Blakely), Arthur Shaw (Alfie), Frederic Burt (Philip), and William Cameron (Parker).

Lyrics are missing for "True Love" and "Pidgie Woo."

ANYTHING FOR YOU

Introduced by Vinton Freedley (Blakely) and Juanita Fletcher (Margery). A sketch for the music was in George Gershwin's earliest tune book, which was donated to the Library of Congress in 1991, but no piano-vocal score or lyrics were known to survive until a copyist score came to light in New Hampshire in some papers that had belonged to a daughter of Vinton Freedley's.

VERSE

I've one aim in life,
And that is winning you.
If you'll be my wife,
There's nothing I won't do
To bring you joy, dear.
Yes, I'm the boy, dear,
Who'd do the darndest all he
Could to be your Walter Raleigh.

REFRAIN 1

Just tell me what to do;
I'll more than see it through.
Dear, I'll do anything for you.
I'll buy insurance from your brother;
I'll even learn to like your mother.

With you I'll always brave
The bargain sales you crave;
I'll be your everlasting slave.
And if the cook should get too frisky,
Although the task is rather risky,
You'll find that I, myself,
Will tell her she is through.
Dear, I'll do anything for you.

REFRAIN 2

I'll let you choose my hats
And pick out my cravats;
You'll be my connoisseur of spats.
I'll even smoke cigars you buy me
And always pay your bills when they eye me.
You'll order all you see;
You'll charge it C.O.D.
And never hear a word from me.
Then what is more, dear, for good measure,
All your father's jokes I'll treasure.
I'm going to laugh at them
Until I'm black-and-blue.
Dear, I'll do anything for you.

JUST TO KNOW YOU ARE MINE

Published April 1921. Introduced by Juliette Day (Elsie), then by her replacement, Vivienne Segal.

VERSE

All gloom and sorrow ended
When I knew you loved me;
Two hearts in one were blended
For all eternity;
We'll live a wonderful dream,
Happiness reigning supreme,
For there can be no sighing
When love, dear, is undying.

REFRAIN

Just to know that you are mine
In all your splendor
Brings a feeling that's divine,
So true and tender;
Shadows disappear,
When I know you're near;
Just to hear your voice makes me rejoice.

When I feel your fond caress,
Then life is sweet, dear,
With the greatest happiness I've ever known;
It makes living complete, dear,
Just to know that you are mine alone.

TAG

Just to know that you are mine alone,
Just to know, just to know,
You are mine, mine, alone.

BOY WANTED

Published April 1921 and September 1924. Introduced by ladies of the ensemble (listed in the program as "The Girls from the Glowworm"), led by Lorna Sanderson (Teddy), Virginia Clark (Toots), Mary Woodyatt (Babe), and Mae Carmen (Bunny). With a revised lyric by Ira Gershwin and Desmond Carter, used in *Primrose* (1924), introduced by Heather Thatcher (Pinkie Peach) and ensemble.

Original Version

VERSE

I've just finished writing an
advertisement
Calling for a boy.
No halfhearted Romeo or flirt is meant;
That's the kind I'd not employ.
Though anybody interested can apply,
He must know a thing to qualify.
For instance:

REFRAIN 1

TEDDY: He must be able to dance.
He must make life a romance.
I said a boy wanted,
One who can smile;
Boy wanted,
Lovable style.
He must be tender and true.
And he must know how to woo.
I know we'll get acquainted mighty soon,
Out in a garden 'neath a harvest moon;
And if he proves to be the right little
laddie,
I'll make him glad
He'll answer my ad!

REFRAIN 2

TOOTS: To be the boy of my choice,
He needn't own a Rolls-Royce.
The kind of boy wanted*
Needn't have gold;
Boy wanted,
Mustn't be cold.
If he has oodles of charm,
I'll even live on a farm.
If he fits in my picture of a home,
I'll be so nice he'll never have to roam.†
Yes, if he proves to be the right little
    laddie,
I'll make him glad
He answered my ad!

REFRAIN 3

BABE: He must like musical shows,
And he must wear snappy clothes.
Yes, that is my story,
And to it I'll stick;
There's no glory
In having a hick.
He must know how to say "Yes!"‡
When I look at a new dress.
Oh, I'll be ready when the right one
    calls,
And I'll start vamping him until he
    falls;
And if he subsidizes me, oh, sweet
    daddy!
I'll make him glad
He answered my ad!

REFRAIN 4

BUNNY: The movies he must avoid,
He'll know his Nietzsche and Freud.
I said a boy wanted,
One who knows books;
Boy wanted,
Needn't have looks.
He mustn't be such a saint,
But, Oh! He dassent say "ain't."
I don't care if his bankroll totals naught,
For we can live on love and food for
    thought.

Alternate version of this line:
    The sort of boy wanted
†*Alternate version of this line:*
    I'll be so nice he'll never care to roam.
‡*Alternate version of refrain 3, lines 7–8:*
    And so his boots mustn't squeak;
    And he must love like a sheik.

If he's a scholar, when I see him I'll
    holler,
"My lad, I'm glad
You answered my ad!"

Primrose Version

VERSE

I've just finished writing an advertisement
Calling for a boy.
No halfhearted Romeo or flirt is meant;
That's the kind I won't employ.
Though anybody interested can apply,
He must know a thing to qualify.
For instance:

REFRAIN 1

To have a ghost of a chance,
He must be able to dance.
The sort of boy wanted
Must have a smile;
Boy wanted,
Lovable style.
He must be tender and true,
And if he knows what to do,
I think I'll learn to love him very soon;
I'll want him morning, night, and afternoon.
So if you know of one who's wanting
    employment,
Just tell him that
I'm wanting a boy!

REFRAIN 2

To be the boy of my choice,
He's got to own a Rolls-Royce.
He must be quite reckless
Buying me things:
Pearl necklace,
Diamond rings.
He must be ready to pay
A dozen bills ev'ry day.
I'd simply smother him with tender care
If I could find a multimillionaire.
So if you see one dining at the Savoy-oh!
Just tell him that
I'm wanting a boy!

REFRAIN 3

I won't have anyone small,
He must be handsome and tall.
I said a boy wanted,
Beautifully dressed;
Boy wanted,

Trousers well pressed.
He must have wonderful eyes;
He must wear wonderful ties.
I want a boy who'll always look as though
He's only just come out of Savile Row.
So if some Paris wants a Helen of Troy-oh!
Just tell him that
I'm wanting a boy!

Version for Ella Fitzgerald

VERSE

[*Same as in original*]

REFRAIN 1

He must be able to dance.
He must make life a romance.
I said, a boy wanted,
One who can smile;
Boy wanted,
Lovable style.
He must know how to say "Yes!"
When I look at a new dress.
Oh, I'll be ready when the right one calls,
And I'll start vamping him until he falls.
Yes, if he proves to be the right little laddie,
I'll make him glad
He answered my ad!

REFRAIN 2

He must like musical shows,
And he must wear snappy clothes.
Yes, that is my story,
And to it I'll stick;
No glory
In having a hick.
He needn't be such a saint.
But, Oh! He dassent say "ain't."
I don't care if his bankroll totals naught,
For we can live on love and food for thought.
If he's a scholar, when I see him I'll holler,
"My lad, I'm glad
You answered my ad!"

THE SIMPLE LIFE

Published April 1921. According to programs, introduced by Juliette Day (Elsie), then by her replacement, Vivienne Segal. As written, however, the song is a duet for Elsie and Blakely (Vinton Freedley).

VERSE 1

ELSIE: I've been all along the Gay White Way.
There I often turned the night to day.
So when coming to the country, I
Was sure I'd find
It would be an awful bore, but, my!
I've changed my mind.
With the gay and giddy whirl I'm
    through;
I would rather be a Simple Sue.

REFRAIN 1

I love the simple life.
I'm here to stay.
Away from care and strife,
I'm making hay.

I love the humming of the bees;
I love the birdies;
I'll say it's great to be
Away from hurdy-gurdies.

Beside a babbling brook,
I love to sit
And read my cooking book,
Or else I knit.

The life of Riley
Was praised very highly,
But the simple life for me.

VERSE 2

BLAKELY: If ev'rything you say is really so,
I will leave the town where subways
    grow.
I am ready now to say good-bye
To hectic nights
And to leave without a single sigh.
Electric lights,
Rector's, Healey's, with you all I'm
    through;
And that goes for Greenwich Village,
    too.

REFRAIN 2

I love the simple life.
I'm here to stay.
Away from care and strife,
I'm making hay.

I love to chase the butterflies
And watch them flutter.
I think the greatest exercise
Is churning butter.

And when the day is done,
I love to rest
And watch the golden sun
Sink in the west.

The life of Riley
Was praised very highly,
But the simple life for me.

THE SIRENS

Introduced by ladies of ensemble (listed in the program as "The Girls from the Glowworm") led by Mary Wood-yatt (Babe), Lorna Sanderson (Teddy), Mae Carmen (Bunny), and Virginia Clark (Toots). Later, slightly revised, used in *Primrose* (1924) under the title "Four Little Sirens" and introduced by ensemble. Published in December 1924 as part of *Primrose*'s complete vocal score.

Four little sirens, we,
Making the mermen fall for us.
We never go in the sea,
But we work as well as any sirens of
    mythology.
Four little sirens, we,
Making the mermen call for us.
We never swim in the sea,
Still we get along quite swimmingly.
It's bad to pun,*†
It isn't being done,
But still we get along quite swimmingly.
If you should come along the beach,
If you should come within our reach.
Take care! Beware!
For though your fingers may be crossed,
Your heart soon tells you that you're
    lost;
Poor John! You're gone!

For we are beautiful,
We're tutti-frutti-ful;
With charm perpetual,
We get you all.
We get you one and all.
We're grace personified;‡

Alternate version of line 9:
    It's wrong to pun!
†*Alternate version of lines 9–10:*
    Our hearts are set
    On never getting wet
‡*Alternate version of lines 23–24:*
    We'll fool each one of you,
    Each mother's son of you,

Our forms are bona fide.*
So you who linger on the shore
Fall by the score
Without a fuss.
And when the waves grow very wild,
You find they're mild
Compared to us.

Each one of us works a diff'rent plan
To catch the poor fish known as man.

BABE: The men all follow me;†
My popularity
Depends on something stronger than tea.
[*Shows whiskey flask*]

TEDDY: My method, I'll confess,
Has brought me great success—
It's simply knowing how to say yes.

BUNNY: When I see a big wave coming,
I just murmur, "Oh, sir!
I'm afraid, so won't you cuddle closer?"

TOOTS: My work is never rough;
No Theda Bara stuff.‡
I find a baby stare is enough.

Four little sirens, we,
Making the mermen fall for us,
Making the mermen call for us,
Making them say they're all for us;
Four little fly little sly little sirens, we.

DANCING SHOES

Published April 1921. Introduced by Vinton Freedley (Blakely), Juliette Day (Elsie), then her replacement Vivienne Segal, and ensemble.

Alternate version of line 24:
    Our figures bona fide,
†*Alternate version of lines 33–44:*
BABE: My method I'll confess
    Has brought me great success.
    It's simply knowing how to say yes.
TEDDY: My ways are never rough;
    No Theda Bara stuff.
    I find a baby stare is enough.
BUNNY: When I see a big wave coming,
    I just murmur, "Oh, sir!
    I'm afraid, so come a little closer."
TOOTS: I find I can't go wrong;
    To bring the men along
    I sing this sort of Sullivan song.
‡*Alternate version of line 43:*
    No Mrs. Potiphar stuff,

VERSE

Dancing shoes make you treasure ev'ry measure
Of a raggy strain;
Dancing shoes bring a gladness and a madness
That go to your brain.
They will make you frolic,
Lose the diabolic,
Weary melancholic blues.
If the world's "agin" you,
Show there's something in you.
Try a pair of dancing shoes
And

REFRAIN

You'll start to sway in a gay sort of way;
In a trance, you'll dance
And lose the doggone blues.
Oh boy! Then joy fills the air.
Not a care, anywhere,
For there's magic in a pair of dancing shoes.

SOME RAIN MUST FALL

Published April 1921. Introduced by Juliette Day (Elsie), then by her replacement, Vivienne Segal.

VERSE

I recited once when I was small,
"Into ev'ry life some rain must fall."
I was a little child of ten
Whose days were never gloomy,
My life was filled with sunshine then,
And sorrow never knew me.
So the thought meant nothing then to me.
Older, wiser, now, I plainly see:

REFRAIN

Some rain must fall
For one and all,
Sending all our dreams astray.
They fly away
When skies are gray,
Though all the while
We try to smile.
As the poet stated,
It is fated:
Some rain must fall.

EVERY GIRL HAS A METHOD OF HER OWN

Intended for Vinton Freedley (Blakely) and ensemble. Unused. Alternate title: "Every Girl Has a Way." No music is known to survive.

VERSE

BLAKELY: The maid of long ago
Was oh so very slow
Whene'er she tried to win a beau.
She'd never wink her eye;
She acted coy and shy—
That was her one and only plan
To try and win a man.
GIRLS: But girlies nowadays
All work in diff'rent ways.

REFRAIN

Some girls woo you with a smile.
Some girls with a dashing style.
Others bill and coo you with a song.
When they start singing,
A message of love they're bringing:
In the subtle art of wooing
You will find they stand alone.
If you're a great, great lover,
You'll discover
Ev'ry girlie has a method of her own—
Of her own—
Ev'ry girlie has a method of her own.

INTERLUDE

With voice so sweet, so tender, so true,
A message of love she brings you.

TWO LITTLE GIRLS IN BLUE, 1921

Tryout: Colonial Theatre, Boston, April 11, 1921. New York run: George M. Cohan Theatre, opened May 3, 1921. 135 performances. Post-Broadway tour included Baltimore and Philadelphia. Music by Vincent Youmans and Paul Lannin. Lyrics mostly by Arthur Francis. Produced by A. L. Erlanger. Book by Fred Jackson. Directed by Ned Wayburn. Orchestra under the direction of Charles Previn. Orchestrations by Maurice B. De Packh, Stephen O. Jones, and others. New York opening cast, starring Madeline Fairbanks (Dolly), Marion Fairbanks (Polly), Oscar Shaw (Bobby), Fred Santley (Jerry), Olin Howland (Atwell), and Virginia Earle (Hariette), also featured Julia Kelety (Ninon), Stanley Jessup (Captain), Jack Tomson (Jennings), Tommy Tomson (Kennedy), Vanda Hoff (Cecile and Maid o' the Mist), Edith Decker (Mary Bird), Evelyn Law (Margie), and Patricia Clarke (Ophelia). Lyrics for "The Gypsy Trial" and "Orienta" are not by Arthur Francis.

WE'RE OFF ON A WONDERFUL TRIP

Music by Vincent Youmans. Lyrics by Arthur Francis. Alternate titles: "Opening, Act I" and "A Wonderful Trip." Introduced by Stanley Jessup (Captain), Jack (Jennings) and Tommy (Kennedy) Tomson (the Tomson Twins), and ensemble. Stanley Jessup was replaced with George Mack within three weeks of the New York opening. The original orchestration, the only musical manuscript known to survive, is No. 71 in the Vincent Youmans Collection.

CAPTAIN: All hands are aboard,
MATES: The cargo is stored;
We're ready to get under way.
The hour is near
For leaving the pier,
And soon we'll be gliding off;
Soon we'll be riding off.
We have said good-bye to all
Our ladyloves on shore.
All in all, we had to call
Upon a score or more.
And now that we're through,
We've nothing to do
Excepting to get under way.

GIRLS: What have I forgotten?
Well, now, let me see.
It's very clear
My purse is here,
But with my feminine memory,
I cannot be too careful.
So I'll look once more,
For it's too late
To investigate
When the ship leaves shore.

BOYS: Have you lost your senses?
Why this awful fuss?

GIRLS: We want to find
What's left behind.

BOYS: But, oh, why worry?
Just look at us—
We've left our bills behind us,
IOUs galore,
Yet you can bet
We will never fret
When the ship leaves shore.

ALL: The weather is fine
For crossing the brine.
We're off on a wonderful trip.
There's no place like home,
But life on the foam
Will always appeal to us.
Romance is real to us.
When the angry waves appear
And tell in awful tones
That we're oh so very near
The home of Davy Jones.
Excitement galore
For us is in store:
We're off on a wonderful trip.

WONDERFUL U.S.A.

Music by Paul Lannin. Lyrics by Arthur Francis.
Introduced by Olin Howland (Atwell) and ensemble. Alternate title: "Your Wonderful U.S.A." Replaced "Utopia" during the pre-Broadway tryout. Less than two months after the New York opening, it, too, was dropped from the score. No music is known to survive.

VERSE 1

Your institutions all are meritorious;
They're glorious—I think.
I've not a thing to say that is censorious
Except on the question of drink,
Except on the question of drink.

REFRAIN 1

I've taken a fancy to the U.S.A,
Despite the fact the Volstead Act
Is driving me away.
A pitcher of H$_2$O fills me with woe;
And sarsaparilla and ginger ale

And lemonade all seem to fail.
You keep on drinking to no avail
In your wonderful U.S.A.

VERSE 2

Your girls are all exceedingly imperial,
Imperial to see.
Besides them all the others look funereal;
To my heart they've all won the key.
They're all just as sweet as can be.

REFRAIN 2

I've taken a fancy to the U.S.A.
I can't forget the girls I met,
So charming and so gay.
And if I could have my way, I'd like to stay.
But I'm afraid it can never be,
For far away, across the sea,
My twenty wives are expecting me
From your wonderful U.S.A.

WHEN I'M WITH THE GIRLS

Music by Vincent Youmans. Lyrics by Arthur Francis.
Introduced by Oscar Shaw (Bobby) and ensemble. Replaced "Win Some Winsome Girl" during the pre-Broadway tryout. The original orchestration, the only musical manuscript known to survive, is No. 74 in the Vincent Youmans Collection.

VERSE 1

It makes no diff'rence if I roam
To Madagascar or to Nome;
In foreign parts or on the foam,
With girls around me, I'm at home.

REFRAIN 1

For I'm at my prime with the girls,
Flirting all the time with the girls.
All the slim ones,
Full-of-vim ones,
Even prim ones
Make living sublime.
Ev'ry girl I see I adore,
And there's always room for one more.
I don't hesitate
To let business wait,
Ev'ry time that I'm with the girls.

REFRAIN 2

For I'm at my prime with the girls,
Flirting all the time with the girls.
Bold or shy ones,
Tame or spry ones,
Even fly ones
Make living sublime.*
If the world's a stage, as they say,
I play Romeo night and day.
I don't care a jot
If school keeps or not,
Ev'ry time that I'm with the girls.

TWO LITTLE GIRLS IN BLUE

Music by Vincent Youmans. Lyrics by Arthur Francis.
Introduced by Madeline (Dolly) and Marion (Polly) Fairbanks (the Fairbanks Twins). Replaced "Happy Ending" during the pre-Broadway tryout. The original orchestration, the only musical manuscript known to survive, is No. 72 in the Vincent Youmans Collection.

N ed Wayburn, director of my first show, *Two Little Girls in Blue*, had his own notion of an ideal musical setup.

At an early conference with the composers, Vincent Youmans and Paul Lannin, and myself, Wayburn handed us slips of paper indicating what he thought the tentative musical spots in the script called for. I wish I had kept the memo. All I can recall is that there were eighteen or twenty items, with no mention of possible subject matter or type of melody or mood. What we were given was along these lines:

Act I

1. Opening
2. 2/4
3. 4/4
4. 6/8
5. Finaletto
6. "Oh, Me, Oh, My, Oh, You" [one of two songs already written and spotted]
7. 3/4
8. Finale

And similar fractions for Acts II and III. Obviously, to Wayburn neither the play nor the numbers played were the thing—with his dancing-school proprietorship, tempo alone mattered.

—from *Lyrics on Several Occasions*

*Alternate version of refrain 2, line 6:
I fall for them all.

VERSE 1

DOLLY: It seems as if this trip
Would take forever and a day,
But where there is a will,
You know, there has to be a way.

POLLY: I know a million reasons now
Why we should turn and run,
But really, I'm so frightened
That I can't remember one.

REFRAIN 1

BOTH: With an Irish cook and a wild-man crew
And a mate who is Portuguese and six
feet two
Ooh! ooh! I wonder what they'd do
If they ever knew—if they ever knew—
We were two little girls in blue,
Not one—
But two little girls in blue.

VERSE 2

POLLY: With you along, I know
I won't be *very* terrified;
But dear, you know a trunk's
An awful place in which to hide.

DOLLY: Now be a Pollyana, Polly,
And I'm sure you'll find
The trunk as comfy as the two
By four we left behind.

REFRAIN 2

BOTH: We can fool the cook and the wild-man
crew
For we fooled our mother and our father
too,
Ooh! ooh! When we made our debut
And the old stork flew—and before they
knew—
There were two little girls in blue,
Not one—
But *two* little girls in blue.

THE SILLY SEASON

Music probably by Vincent Youmans. Lyrics by Arthur Francis. Introduced by Virginia Earle (Hariette Neville), Oscar Shaw (Bobby), Fred Santley (Jerry), Evelyn Law (Margie), possibly Patricia Clarke (Ophelia), and ensemble. Ira Gershwin's typed lyric sheet indicates that the song was conceived originally as a trio for "Bobby, Jerry,

and Miss Neville." During the pre-Broadway tryout, the part of Hariette Neville was played by Emma Janvier. In his biography of Youmans *(Days to Be Happy, Years to Be Sad)*, Gerald Bordman writes that "a character named Olive is listed as singing 'The Silly Season' in *Two Little Girls in Blue*, but no such name appears in any list of the cast of characters for the show I have seen." Perhaps "Olive" is "Ophelia," Patricia Clarke's role. No music is known to survive for this number.

VERSE

In the springtime you discover
That you want to bill and coo.
Yes, you want to play the lover,
And most any girl will do.
It's the season of flirtation
And of puppy-love romance.
Ev'ry heart fills with elation.
It's the time when Cupid likes to take a chance.

REFRAIN

The silly season—
Ev'ry April, May, and June,
You lose your reason—
Underneath a yellow moon,
You give the girl your heart and your frat pin,
And in return she gives you her hat pin.
You act so moony
Call her "darling popsy-wop."
When you get spoony—
Neighbors want to call a cop.
It's so enthralling
When she starts calling
You "dear—oh ducky dear!"
Whenever she is near
You start reciting tender verse.
Your friends begin to fear
You need a doctor and a nurse.
You just go loco—
Loving phrases fill the air;
Right off your coco—
Two are comfy on a chair,*
For it's the Jack-and-Jilly,
Oh so silly part of the year.

OH ME! OH MY!

Published April 1921. Music by Vincent Youmans. Lyrics by Arthur Francis. Introduced by Oscar Shaw

In the script, this line is:
Two are comfy in a chair,

(Bobby) and Marion Fairbanks (Polly). Alternate title: "Oh Me, Oh My, Oh You." This was the first song with lyrics by Arthur Francis to be a major commercial success.

VERSE 1

HE: Little girly,
Late and early,
You'll be on my mind.
For you're just the kind
I tried so long to find.
When you're near me,
When you cheer me,
I can plainly see,
Love is everything that
It's cracked up to be.

REFRAIN 1

Oh me! Oh my! Oh you!
No other girl will do.
Cares would be forever ended,
And this world would be so splendid.
If you cared enough, dear,
To be true.
Oh me! Oh my! Oh you!
Those lips! Those eyes of blue!
You're so lovely; you're so sweet;
You simply lift me off my feet.
Oh me! Oh my! Oh you-oo!

VERSE 2

SHE: In replying,
I am trying
To be shy and coy,
But, oh, wonder boy,*
I can't restrain my joy.
Something tells me
And compels me
To say you were right
In believing love may
Often come at sight.

REFRAIN 2

Oh me! Oh my! Oh you!
What can a girly do!
I find you so fascinating
That my heart keeps palpitating
In a way that thrills me
Through and through.
Oh me! Oh my! Oh you!

Alternate version of verse 2, line 4:
But, with you, dear boy,

I'm sure I could be true.
You're so splendid, so ideal,
That I keep wondr'ing if you're real.*
Oh me! Oh my! Oh you-oo!

YOU STARTED SOMETHING

Published June 1921. Music by Vincent Youmans. Lyrics by Arthur Francis. Alternate title: "You Started Something When You Came Along." Introduced by Fred Santley (Jerry) and Madeline Fairbanks (Dolly). It replaced "Mr. and Mrs." (which had been performed previously in *Piccadilly to Broadway*) during the pre-Broadway tryout. When Youmans was writing the score for *No, No, Nanette* a few years later, he outfitted "You Started Something" with an entirely new lyric ("I'm Waiting for You," by Otto Harbach). It was sung in *No, No, Nanette* by Louise Groody (Nanette) and Jack Barker (Tom). As "Waiting for You," it was sung in the 1971 Broadway revival of *Nanette* by Susan Watson and Roger Rathburn.

VERSE

I've not been entangled in romances,
Never played the gay Lothario,
Never seemed to care to make advances,
But now it's diff'rent, I know.

REFRAIN

You started something
When you came along,
For when I saw you I knew
There could really never be another,
You're the girl I'd like to take to mother.
You've brought the sunshine
So long overdue,
Turning the gray skies to blue.
So you see you started something
When you came along,
And I'll see that I'll see it through.

WE'RE OFF TO INDIA

Music by Vincent Youmans. Lyrics by Arthur Francis. Introduced by Madeline Fairbanks (Dolly), Oscar Shaw (Bobby), Stanley Jessup (Captain), and ensemble. Alter-

Alternate version of refrain 2, line 9:
I really can't believe you're real.

nate title: "Finale, Act I." This number introduced the "Maid o' the Mist" Ballet. The "I'm so elated" section was set to music from "The Silly Season." The "We're off to India" portion seems to fit the music for the dropped number "Win Some Winsome Girl." The "So long, so long" material accompanies new music. A section of the original orchestration survives. The song is No. 113 in the Vincent Youmans Collection.

DOLLY: I'm so elated.
GIRLS: (Soon the whistles all will say:)
DOLLY: For this I've waited.
GIRLS: ("Let's be on our merry way.")
DOLLY: I never knew a trip so romantic,
Soon we'll be far across the Atlantic.
GIRLS: We're so elated.
(Yet we hate to say good-bye.)
For this we waited.
(Shall we laugh or shall we cry?)
Our hearts are beating, madly
repeating,
"Let's go! It's time to go!"
BOBBY: To me it's clear that I'll
Enjoy this Oriental trip,
For I'll be near the smile
Of some sweet someone on the ship.
CAPTAIN:
[*spoken*]
All ashore that's going ashore.
[*Whistles, etc.*]
ALL: We're off to India, to far-off India,
Across the bay, they say, from
Mandalay.
We've read old Mr. Kipling, so our
wish is
To see those educated flying fishes.
A land mysterious
Will never weary us.
In each romantic village we will stray.
And with our hearts a-flutter,
We'll invade Calcutta,
And with greetings we will bomb
Bombay.
[*Fog on. Foghorns, whistles, etc.*]
So long, so long,
City of lights.
So long, so long,
Wonderful nights.
Little old New York, we know that
we'll miss you,
But we're all here to kiss you
Good-bye.
Sailing, sailing,
Over the blue;
Sailing, sailing,
We'll think of you.
Father Knickerbocker,

You'll find none of us a knocker,
We'll be true
To you.

HERE, STEWARD

Music probably by Vincent Youmans. Lyrics by Arthur Francis. Introduced by Jack (Jennings) and Tommy (Kennedy) Tomson, Patricia Clarke (Ophelia), and ensemble. Alternate titles: "Stewards" and "Opening, Act II." No music is known to survive.

We have to serve six meals a day
And serve 'em piping hot.
To do our best we try, says I.
Aye! aye! [*salute*]
But passengers are all a howling
Scowling, growling lot.
They're hard to satisfy, says I.
Aye! aye! [*salute*]
Some ask for hummingbird,
Some ask for whale.
If we could have our way,
We'd give 'em jail.

REFRAIN

For it is "Steward, here, steward, I say;
Bring this or that right away."
Busy from early morn right through the dinner,
They're growing stouter while we're growing
thinner.
We've got to yes 'em and dress 'em all day.
There's not a moment we're free.
For you're a sailor, a nurse, and a tailor,
When you're a steward at sea.

DOLLY

Published April 1921. Music by Vincent Youmans. Lyrics by Arthur Francis and Schuyler Greene. Introduced by Oscar Shaw (Bobby) and Fred Santley (Jerry). Alternate title: "Dolly Dear."

VERSE

Little lady of my dreams,
Since the day we met,
Ev'ry other girly seems

Easy to forget.
On this heart of mine
I have placed a sign:
"No room to let."
With your sweet and winning smiles
And your tender eyes,
You have brought me miles and miles
Nearer paradise.
Ev'ry joy I know
Here on earth below,
I know I owe to you, dear—

REFRAIN

Dolly, Dolly, sad or gay,
There is something charming about you;
Something sweet that seems to say
Life would be empty for me without you.
Dolly, Dolly, when you're near,
Clouds and shadows all disappear,
And the stars above you
Spell the words "I love you,
Dolly, Dolly dear."

VERSE 2

All the songbirds night and day
Set my heart aflame
As your wondrous beauty they
Merrily proclaim.
Ev'ry gentle breeze
Floating through the trees
Whispers your name.
All the flowers that I see
Wear their fairest hue.
That's their way of telling me
Dreams have all come true.
And the lovely theme
Of each lovely dream,
Darling, is you, just you, oh—

REPEAT REFRAIN

JUST LIKE YOU

Published April 1921. Music by Paul Lannin. Lyrics by
Arthur Francis. Introduced by Fred Santley (Jerry),
Madeline Fairbanks (Dolly), Edith Decker (Mary Bird),
Vanda Hoff (Cecile), and Jack (Jennings) and Tommy
(Kennedy) Tomson.

VERSE

JERRY: Though they say love is blind,
In dreams I have pictured the one girl.
Deep in my heart enshrined,
She's been the one kind
I have wanted to find.
Mem'ries come thronging
Of years filled with longing,
For though we'd not met,
I was not fancy-free.
DOLLY: If she's to enter
Your heart's very center,
Then what sort of maid
Is this "one girl" to be?
JERRY: I'll tell my secret to you;
Yes, I'll describe her.
DOLLY: Please do!

REFRAIN

JERRY: Someone I can care for;
Someone whose heart I'll possess;
Someone I can dare for;
Someone to hold and caress.
Tender, slender—
She'll make life start anew.
I'll surrender
If that someone is just like you.
[*Dance interlude*]
If that someone is just like you.

THERE'S SOMETHING ABOUT ME THEY LIKE

Music by Vincent Youmans. Lyrics by Fred Jackson and
Arthur Francis. Introduced by Olin Howland (Atwell),
Evelyn Law (Margie), and ensemble. No music is known
to survive.

VERSE

I'm not what you'd call irresistibly handsome,
Nor wealthy enough to be held up for ransom;
Yet somehow the ladies all say they are for me,
And often quite shamelessly show they adore me.
I cast a wicked spell.
Just why I cannot tell.

REFRAIN

There's something about me they like.
With me they never are on strike.

Boston girls are chilly,
I have been advised,
But with me they, well, I won't say
But you'd be surprised.
Whenever they get me alone,
They want the number of my phone.
No matter where I go, they chase me,
And if I try to hide, they trace me.
With pouting lips they always face me.
There's something about me they like.

RICE AND SHOES

Published June 1921. Music by Vincent Youmans. Lyrics by Schuyler Greene and Arthur Francis. Introduced
by Oscar Shaw (Bobby), Fred Santley (Jerry), and ensemble. Original title: "Sweetest Girl."

VERSE 1

I've met the one and only one.
Heigh ho! Heigh ho!
Folly at last with you I'm done.
Heigh ho! Heigh ho!
To me who sampled the peaches,
Wherever wild peaches grew,
My heart this sermon preaches:
"You're through."

REFRAIN

Bring on the rice and shoes
And roses from the rambler vine.
Tell ev'ryone the news—
She's promised to be mine!
I see two happy dreamers
With satin streamers
Walk side by side.
I hear the organ playing
As all are saying,
"Here comes the bride."
Bring on her gay bouquet,
And all the friends of auld lang syne.
Bring on the happy day
With wedding bells divine.
And tell them all the rarest pearl,
The sweetest girl,
In all this great big world
Has promised to be mine.

VERSE 2

I know a hundred times or more.
Heigh ho! Heigh ho!

I've said the same of girls before.
Heigh ho! Heigh ho!
I told them all I was certain
My love would always endure.
This time I mean it, this time
I'm sure.

REPEAT REFRAIN

FINALE, ACT II

Music by Vincent Youmans. Lyrics by Arthur Francis.
Introduced by ensemble. Alternate title: "She's Innocent." No music is known to survive.

NINON: I can tell you where the jewels are.
CAPTAIN: If you know, then tell us where.
ATWELL: She is just suspicious;
    She's not certain.
NINON: But I know the jewels are in there!
ALL: What!
NINON: When you search her cabin,
    Then you will find I'm right.
ATWELL: But the girl is so demure and shy—
NINON: I wouldn't trust her out of sight.
JERRY: No one shall accuse her
    While I am here to befriend her.
BOBBY: No one shall abuse her
    While I am here to defend her.
NINON: I insist that the cabin be searched!
ALL: But she's innocent!
NINON: I insist that her cabin be searched!
ALL: But she's innocent!
BOYS: How can you suspect the girl?
    It is very unfair to her.
NINON: Nonsense—She's deceived you!
ALL: Come! Let us open the door and—

HONEYMOON

Published April 1921. Music by Paul Lannin. Lyrics by
Arthur Francis. Introduced by Julia Kelety (Ninon),
Fred Santley (Jerry), and ensemble; specialty dance by
Evelyn Law. Alternate titles: "Honeymoon, When Will
You Shine for Me?" and "Honeymoon (When Will You
Shine on Me?)."

VERSE

Honeymoon, I never have seen you shine.
Honeymoon, sorrow fills this heart of mine.
Ev'rywhere fond hearts are glowing;
Lovers' eyes the love-light showing.
Honeymoon, all alone I sit and pine.

REFRAIN

When night is falling,
I miss you, Honeymoon;
Love sings no golden tune to me.
No voice enthralling
Fills me with happiness;
No lover smiles on me caressingly.
My heart keeps calling
And so I turn to you;
Oh, won't you listen to my plea?
Dear Honeymoon, till you send love to me,
My poor heart will be gloomy.
Tell me, when will you shine on me?*

I'M TICKLED SILLY

Music by Paul Lannin. Lyrics by Arthur Francis. Introduced by Olin Howland (Atwell), Oscar Shaw (Bobby),
and Fred Santley (Jerry). Original title: "Slapstick." No
music is known to survive.

VERSE

When the lastest film by Sennett
Or by Fox is mentioned, then it
Is my one and burning wish
To get a seat for it.
All the highbrows call 'em frightful,
But for my part they're delightful,
So I comb the town and look
On ev'ry street for it.
I'm a gent, and I'm a scholar,
Yet I'd part with my last dollar
Just to see a slapstick artist frolic.
Though there's nothing that's dramatic
In his actions acrobatic,
There's an end to all that's melancholic.

REFRAIN 1

I'm tickled silly
When there is a scene

Where a chap gets a rap
On the bean;
When, willy-nilly,
A brick or a pie
Comes to rest on his chest
Or his eye.
Life is complete
When I gaze at his feet
As they gambol all over the street.
Off goes a gun,
And I chortle with glee,
When, on the run,
They all fall in the sea.
I laugh when they soak 'em,
I roar when they choke 'em,
The old movie hokum for me.

VERSE 2

When you see a film by Chaplin,
Though your name be Smith or Kaplan,
I am very sure you're bound to be hilarious;
With young Lloyd or Keaton clowning
(Though you know your Keats and Browning),
You'll say slapstick hath a charm
That's multifarious.
When a fav'rite movie idol
Does a stunt that's suicidal,
Bookworms all declare it's not aesthetic.
Yet when he's hit by a wagon
Or he gets an awful jag on,
Who cares if the scene is not poetic?

REFRAIN 2

I'm tickled silly
And I've got to roar
When they all start to fall
Through the floor;
When, willy-nilly,
A club or a mop
Finds a home on the dome
Of a cop.
My heart's aglow
When they find things are slow
And they start slinging pastry and dough.
Scenes on the beach
Make me holler with glee;
When there's a peach
Losing her dignity;
Whenever they grill 'em,
Whenever they kill 'em,
Oh, that is the "fillem" for me!

*Originally and in the published version:
Tell me, when will you shine for me?

UTOPIA

Music by Vincent Youmans. Lyric by Arthur Francis. Introduced during the Boston tryout by Olin Howland (Atwell), Julia Kelety (Ninon), and Edward Begley (Dudley). (Begley's role was eliminated before the New York opening.) It was the second song in Act I. Dropped before the New York opening. Replaced with "Wonderful U.S.A." No music is known to survive.

VERSE 1

I often feel I'd like to get away
To a golden land
That I have planned.
Yes, there I'd like to hike
This very day.
No dream was ever so enthralling;
Utopia, I hear you calling.

REFRAIN 1

I'd have no roughneck taxi drivers there.
Ticket speculators all would get the air.
There you'd find no politicians
And no jumping jazz musicians.
Of the blue laws not a sign
In that land divine.
You can bet I'd make it my one mission
To prohibit Prohibition
In that dream Utopia of mine.

VERSE 2

It isn't on the map of land or sea.
Just the same, I'm king
'N' ev'rything.
And I'd live in the lap
Of luxury
And have a new queen ev'ry day there.
Oh, please don't wake me while I stray there.

REFRAIN 2

Oh, it would be an earthly paradise.
Summertime, no one would raise the price of
ice.
And there'd be no hatcheck pirate
In hotels to make you irate.
There the sun would always shine
And no heart would pine;
For the girls would be a bunch of dollies
All imported from the Follies
In that dream Utopia of mine.

REFRAIN 3

The stocks you buy will go up ev'ry day.
And no income tax you'll ever have to pay.
No police will be officious
When your motor gets ambitious.
You'll have music everywhere,
Floating through the air,
But you'll hear no songs about that Mammy
Way down south in Alabammy
In that dream Utopia of mine.

HAPPY ENDING

Music by Paul Lannin. Lyrics by Arthur Francis. Introduced during the Boston tryout by Madeline (Dolly) and Marion (Polly) Fairbanks. It was the fourth song in Act I. Dropped before the New York opening. Replaced with "Two Little Girls in Blue." No music is known to survive.

VERSE

We must try to make the best of it
When trouble comes along;
Never sigh, though everything seems wrong.
Though we feel
Our lot is terrible,
It is real-
Ly not unbearable;
What is more,
Let's keep on smiling; for—

REFRAIN

Somehow I feel there's bound to be
A happy ending;
So no matter what may happen,
Let's look trouble in the eye.
Although at present fate seems
Fearful and unbending,
Something tells me that to ev'ry sorrow
Soon we'll say good-bye.
So let's be cheerful, while we may;
Never tearful, ever gay.
Just forget that now the skies are gray.
Let's smile and keep on waiting for
The happy ending,
For it is on the way;
And some fine day,
It will come to stay.

LITTLE BAG OF TRICKS

Music probably by Paul Lannin. Lyrics by Arthur Francis. Introduced during the Boston tryout by Olin Howland (Atwell), Madeline (Dolly) and Marion (Polly) Fairbanks, and Jack (Jennings) and Tommy (Kennedy) Tomson. It was the third number in Act III. Dropped before the New York opening. No music is known to survive.

VERSE

As a prestidigitator,
I'm as great or even greater
Than the best there is;
The rest come after me.
I may as well admit,
In magic I am "it."
If you think that Mr. Kellar
Was a tricky sort of feller,
I'm a double-barreled "heller."
Watch and see.

REFRAIN

Presto! The rest, oh! You never will detect.
Mumbo jumbo! Little rabbits have habits
You'd never suspect.
Roses with ease I can squeeze
From wooden sticks.
Hocus-pocus! I can puzzle all the hicks
With my little bag of tricks;
With my little bag of tricks!

MAKE THE BEST OF IT

Music by Vincent Youmans. Lyrics by Arthur Francis. Intended for Madeline (Dolly) and Marion (Polly) Fairbanks. Dropped during rehearsals. The original orchestration, the only musical manuscript known to survive, is No. 73 in the Vincent Youmans Collection.

VERSE

Though our troubles may to us seem endless,
I am certain quite
They will soon take flight
If we bravely fight.
Though we're all alone today and friendless
In this sorry plight,
We can surely win by hoping;
Nothing's ever gained by moping.

REFRAIN

We must make the best of it
Till our journey's through;
And smile through all the rest of it
Though luck is overdue.
We must make a jest of it
Though our purse is flat.
When all our castles tumble down
And fortune seems to frown,
We must make the best of it
And let it go at that.

SUMMERTIME

Music by Paul Lannin. Lyrics by Arthur Francis. Intended for *Two Little Girls in Blue*. Dropped during rehearsals. No music is known to survive.

VERSE

When flowers are blooming, perfuming the air
In Summertime—
There's no room for care or for gloom anywhere
In Summertime.
The birds are a-flutter as ever they sing
And trill and call.
A message of love they are trying to bring
To one and all.

REFRAIN

Love is at its highlight
In the Summer twilight
When the zephyrs blow o'er the heather
And all the world's in rhyme.
Lovers cling together
In the balmy weather;
Fond hearts are lighter,
Eyes shine the brighter,
In the Summertime.

OPPOSITE: *Irene Bordoni*

1921–1923

PHOEBE

Written in August 1921. Music by George Gershwin. Lyrics by Lou Paley and Arthur Francis. The music to the verse was later used for the verse of "All the Livelong Day" in *Kiss Me, Stupid* (1964). No. 89 in the George and Ira Gershwin Special Numbered Song File.

VERSE 1

Oh, how I love you—
I meant to tell you—
I should have told you before.
I'm through delaying;
I'll just keep saying, "I do."
I'll always love you;
How can I help it
When you were made to adore?
I've made my mind up
I should be signed up with you.

REFRAIN

Phoebe—
Oh, Phoebe!
Let me be your boy;
For your smile so true
Makes me feel I must have you.
The daisies all say
That love is coming my way,
So Phoebe,
Sweet Phoebe!
Let me be your boy.

VERSE 2

I have no phrases
To sing your praises;
I simply love you, that's all.
While I'm existing,
I'll keep insisting I do.
At ev'ry meeting
My heart stops beating;
Oh, baby! Oh, how I fall!*
And then I've paid for
A cottage made for just two.

REPEAT REFRAIN

Earlier version of verse 2, lines 8–10:
It means I'm going to fall.
When your eyes light up,
I must move right up to you.

PEACOCK ALLEY

Published in late 1921, exact month unknown. Music by Louis Silvers. Lyrics by Arthur Francis, although the sheet music inexplicably omits his name. Theme song for the film *Peacock Alley*, starring Mae Murray, which was released in December 1921–January 1922.

VERSE

There's a place that never knows dull care;
Laughter always seems to fill the air
There; soon after twilight,
Life is at its highlight,
Birds of plumage ev'rywhere.

REFRAIN

In Peacock Alley
The rounders rally
'Round Flo and Sally
The whole night through.
The band is playing,
And forms are swaying;
It really seems
A land of dreams.
The lights are white there
And faces bright there;
Each heart seems light there
And ever gay.
But all are weary,
And life is dreary,
In Peacock Alley,
At break of day.

MOLLY ON THE SHORE

Written January 1922. Music by George Gershwin. Lyrics by Arthur Francis. No. 54 in the George and Ira Gershwin Special Numbered Song File.

VERSE

Oh, I've met your fine lassies in Dublin,
And it's true they are charmers of men;
But for me, I will never be troublin'
To be going there once again.
I found someone at last who's my true love,
And I found her beside the sea.
Molly's my latest, my new love,
But it's lasting love this time for me.

REFRAIN 1

I love to stroll along with Molly on the shore.
And when the moon is shining, who could ask
for more?
I've traveled far and wide, but never a maid I've
seen
Sweet as my darling colleen.
Her lips are redder than the sunset on the wave.
Sure! They are always causing mine to
misbehave;
That's why the moonlight always finds me
waiting for
My Molly on the shore.

REFRAIN 2

I love to stroll along with Molly on the shore.
And when the moon is shining, who could ask
for more?
We both believed that Paradise had come to stay
Till I had to sail away.
I see her sitting there beside a restless sea,
And I keep dreaming all her thoughts are just of
me.
For some fine day my heart knows I'll be
sending for
My Molly on the shore.

THE PICCADILLY WALK

Written in 1920. Published February 1922. Music by Edward A. Horan. Lyrics by Arthur Francis and Arthur Riscoe. Introduced in *Pins and Needles* (1922), probably by Harry Pilcer.

VERSE

All the town is falling
For the latest dancing craze.
It has made a hit;
Yes, ev'rybody sings its praise.*
Though it's just a simple walk
That's causing all the talk;
Once you try it—you'll find
A riot—designed
To leave dull care behind.

Alternate version of verse, lines 3–4:
It has made a hit; the town is all ablaze.

REFRAIN

The Piccadilly Walk—
The Pic– Pic– Piccadilly Walk—
It's all the talk.
It's just a simple step,
Yet you will find it full of pep.
You walk up to some winsome little maidie,
Then remember, "Faint heart never won
Fair lady."
Introduce yourself;
Just put convention on the shelf.
Have no alarm;
Just take her by the arm
And walk along
Amid the throng;
Say you're fancy-free
But very lonely;
Ask her if she'll be
Your one and only.
Once you've got the girl,
You've got the Piccadilly Walk.

FOR GOODNESS SAKE, 1922

SOMEONE

Published March 1922. Music by George Gershwin. Lyrics by Arthur Francis. Introduced in *For Goodness Sake* by Helen Ford (Marjorie), Vinton Freedley (Jeff), and ensemble.

VERSE

SHE: When I take a husband, I shall want one
         that will last.
HE: I'm here to say you're looking at him now.
SHE: Don't you think that you are working just a
         trifle fast?
HE: It's just because you're different somehow.
     I must find a way, dear, to compel you
     To believe the things I'm going to tell you:

REFRAIN

If someone like you
Loved someone like me,
Then life would be one long, sweet song.
We would smile all the while.
Why can't you see
That someone like me
Could make your dreams all come true
And could bring gladness to
Someone like me?

VERSE 2

SHE: You're the most convincing speaker that
         has come my way.
HE: I'm sure I haven't told you all I feel.
SHE: But they tell me lawyers often don't mean
         all they say.
HE: Now please don't tease, you know my love
         is real.
SHE: Well, your speech was great, it's hard to
         beat it;
         Let me see, sir, if you can repeat it:

REPEAT REFRAIN

TRA-LA-LA

Published March 1922. Music by George Gershwin. Lyrics by Arthur Francis. Introduced in *For Goodness Sake* by Marjorie Gateson (Vivian) and John E. Hazzard (Perry). Lyric revised by Ira Gershwin for the film *An American in Paris* (1951), in which it was reintroduced by Gene Kelly and Oscar Levant.

Original Version

VERSE

Let me introduce you to Tra-la-la;
For it's time that you all knew Tra-la-la.
It's a silly strain, it's true—Tra-la-la.
But it's guaranteed to cure
Ev'ry sort of blues, and you're
Going to like it, I am sure—
Tra-la-la.

REFRAIN

Just learn this little song:
Tra-la-la-la;
Won't take you very long:
Tra-la-la-la.

It has the cutest swing—
Tell me, Papa,
Isn't it a cunning thing?
Tra-la-la-la-la.
Makes ev'rybody's heart
Go pit-a-pat;
Your troubles will depart.
They'll go like that;
Hum it, strum it, sing and drum it;
You'll get worlds of pleasure from it:
Tra-la-la, Tra-la-la-la.

An American in Paris Version
Subtitled "This Time It's Really Love"

VERSE

Am I happy? Am I proud? Tra-la-la!
Am I floating on a cloud? Tra-la-la!
Let me sing it clear and loud—Tra-la-la!
That I finally have met
One I always hoped to get
And the day of days is set—
Tra-la-la!

REFRAIN 1

This time it's really love:
Tra-la-la-la!
I'm in that blue above:
Tra-la-la-la!
She fills me full of joy—
Tell me, Papa,
Am I not a lucky boy?
Tra-la-la-la-la!
Just listen to my heart
Go pit-a-pat.
It started from the start—
I fell like that!
Hum it, strum it, sing it, drum it;
What a thrill I'm getting from it!
Tra-la-la, Tra-la-la, la!

REFRAIN 2

He's like a breath of spring,
Tra-la-la-la!
He's got but ev'rything,
Tra-la-la-la.
This thing that we've begun—
Tell me, Mama,
Am I not the lucky one?
Tra-la-la-la-la!
Into a daze I go
When he appears.
This daze I want to know
All through the years.
Hum it, strum it, sing it, drum it!

Finally I've reached the summit!
Tra-la-la, Tra-la-la, la!

FRENCH PASTRY WALK

Published March 1922. Music by William Daly and Paul Lannin. Lyrics by Arthur Jackson and Arthur Francis. Introduced in *For Goodness Sake* by Charles Judels (Count), Fred Astaire (Teddy), Vinton Freedley (Jeff), and ensemble.

VERSE

Over in Paris they show
A dance ev'ryone ought to know—
Invented by a certain chef
When he needed the dough.
Known as the French Pastry King,
He really started the thing;
It's simply taking the steps in baking.
See! See! Here's the recipe:

REFRAIN

Start it with a little bit of ginger;
Throw in a little spice.
I'm sure a dash of this will never injure;
A dash of that will make it very nice.
Next thing is to mix it all together;
Sweeten with tender talk.
And then you'll be dancing to the recipe
For the French Pastry Walk.

FASCINATION

Published in 1922, exact month unknown. Music by Louis Silvers. Lyrics by Arthur Francis and Schuyler Greene. Theme song for the film *Fascination*, released in April 1922. The song was dedicated to Mae Murray, the star of the picture.

VERSE

When you meet girls most attractive
And your heart does not grow active,
You may think for none of them you'll yearn.
You have almost made your mind up
That you never will be signed up
Till you meet a certain one and find—

REFRAIN

There's a wondrous fascination
In the lovely eyes that glance
With the mystic invitation
To the realm of fair romance.
There's a deeper fascination
In the sweet anticipation
Of kissing lips that are tender—
Lips that surrender—
Lips that speak of love.
There's a flood of animation
When you hold her little hand,
And a feeling of elation
That you cannot understand.
And then before you can tell,
You find you're under a spell
Of that magic fascination
That's known as love.

WHAT I CARE!

Written June 1922. Music by Vincent Youmans. Lyrics by Schuyler Greene and Arthur Francis. No music is known to survive.

VERSE

When I am sad and grave,
Some good advice that mother gave
Comes flashing through my mind.
"Put on your sweetest smile,"
She said. "Just wear it all the while,
And leave your frowns behind.
For you can make the future brighter,
Your burden lighter,
If you'll but try."
So when I chance to meet
Old Trouble walking down the street,
I simply pass him by.
For after all, our journey's far too short
To give to rainy days a second thought—
To waste our time on people of his sort.

REFRAIN

Though life to me just seems to be
A stretch of miles where sunny smiles
Are few—What I care!
Though neighbors say I'm somewhat gay
And rather like a Lucky Strike
Or two—What I care!
Though jealous wives delight to tell of
The wicked spell of my baby stare—
While I have you or someone who
Can make me glad when I am sad
And blue—What I care!

A NEW STEP EVERY DAY and (I'LL BUILD A) STAIRWAY TO PARADISE

"A New Step Every Day" was written c. 1919. Music by George Gershwin. Lyrics by Ira Gershwin. No music is known to survive. It led—three years later—to "(I'll Build a) Stairway to Paradise," which was written in July 1922. Published August 1922. Music by George Gershwin. Lyrics by B. G. DeSylva and Arthur Francis. Introduced by the principals of *George White's Scandals of 1922*: Winnie Lightner, Pearl Regay, Coletta Ryan, Olive Vaughn, George White, Jack McGowan, Richard Bold, Newton Alexander, and ensemble, with Paul Whiteman's Orchestra. It was the Act I finale.

A New Step Every Day

VERSE

I can dance the old gavotte;
I can shimmy, I can trot.
I can even do the Scot-
Tish Highland Fling.
Jig and minuet appeal
And the old Virginia Reel
Oh! I dance them all with zeal.
It's joy they bring.
Ev'ry dancing step I've heard of I have got
down pat;
Yet I keep on being so wild about dancing
that—

REFRAIN

I want to learn a new step ev'ry day.
I want to do the two-step a different way.
The old-fashioned waltz entrances—
And I love all the modern dances.
And yet I want to learn a new step ev'ry day,
For nothing makes me half so gay,
I'll build a staircase to Paradise,
With a new step ev'ry day.

One day lyricist B. G. (Buddy) DeSylva said to me: "I've been thinking about a song you and George wrote, that 'New Step Every Day.' Anything particular in mind for it?" I said No—it was just a song, and not much of one. He then told me: "I think the last line has an idea for a production number. If you like, we could write it up and I *think* it could be used in the *Scandals*."

Naturally I was tickled to be able to collaborate on something for the *Scandals*. The next night George and I had dinner in DeSylva's Greenwich Village apartment, and about nine p.m. we started on the new song. About two a.m. it was completed, verse included. Outside of the line DeSylva liked, the result was totally different from the simple ditty "A New Step Every Day"—and even "staircase" had become "stairway." The new song had a complicated, for those days, twenty-four-bar verse, replete with sixteenth notes and thick chords, plus a refrain with key changes. I agreed with Buddy and George that it sounded like a good first-act production-finale, but figured my returns would be program credit and nothing else; the song seemed too difficult for popular publication.

Honestly surprised to learn just before the out-of-town opening that the song was to be one of the show's seven published numbers, I was pleased—but who would buy it? Especially as the boys had written an out-and-out commercial song they weren't too proud of: "I Found a Four-Leaf Clover (And the Next Day I Found You)"— an obvious concession to the popular ear, a song with so pronounced a Sousa march quality and the soldiers' "Tipperary"-like beat that it inevitably must sweep the country. (My father, when referring to it, kept saying: "Play me that war song.")

Well, I was wrong. The bands around town and some record companies played up "Stairway to Paradise" more than anything else in the show, and it became a hit—that is, for a revue. (Most hit songs from the stage emerge from musicals rather than revues.) "Four-Leaf Clover" attracted little attention, while my one third of "Stairway"'s royalties amounted to thirty-five hundred dollars, enough to support me for a year.

—from *Lyrics on Several Occasions*

(I'll Build a) Stairway to Paradise

VERSE

All you preachers
Who delight in panning the dancing teachers,
Let me tell you there are a lot of features
Of the dance that carry you through
The Gates of Heaven.

It's madness
To be always sitting around in sadness,
When you could be learning the Steps of
    Gladness.
(You'll be happy when you can do
Just six or seven.)

Begin today. You'll find it nice:
The quickest way to Paradise.
When you practice,

Here's the thing to do—*
Simply say as you go:

REFRAIN

I'll build a Stairway to Paradise,
With a new Step ev'ry day.
I'm going to get there at any price;
Stand aside, I'm on my way!
I got the blues,
And up above it's so fair;
Shoes,
Go on and carry me there!
I'll build a Stairway to Paradise
With a new Step ev'ry day.

I forgot to mention that there was a patter attached to "Stairway," which we added some days later. It was a week's Dance Diet.

PATTER

On Monday—happy as a lark,
You'll be getting started
When you learn to Toe the Mark.

[*Demonstrate step*] That's Toe the Mark.

On Tuesday—then you ought to show
Both your little Regals
How to do the Heel and Toe.

[*Demonstrate step*] That's Heel and Toe.

On Wednesday—walk around the block
And at ev'ry corner stop and do the Eagle Rock.

[*Demonstrate step*] That's the Eagle Rock.

On Thursday—whistle as you go
On a little journey with the Off to Buffalo.

[*Demonstrate step*] Off to Buffalo.

On Friday—take a little stroll
Up and down the beach
And learn the Oceana Roll.

[*Demonstrate step*] Oceana Roll.

On Saturday—then you let 'er go.
All your troubles vanish
When you do the Toadalo.

[*Demonstrate step*] That's the Toadalo.

On Sunday—I will guarantee
Happiness will claim you
If you will do the Shivaree.

*In Lyrics on Several Occasions, *changed to:*
Here's the thing to know—

[*Demonstrate step*] That's the Shivaree.

So people—Follow my advice
Learn a step a day and you will get to Paradise.
There's Paradise.

P.S. Even though a newly revised rhyming dictionary (Burgess Johnson's) lists "feature" with "teacher," I doubt that I'd rhyme them today.

WHAT CAN I DO?

Written in August 1922 to the tune of "Avec le Sourire" by Maurice Yvain. Lyrics by Arthur Francis and Schuyler Greene. Intended for Irene Bordoni.

VERSE

Ev'ry widow is a flirt, they say,
But they are wrong.
For example, take myself: I'm rarely indiscreet.
Holding to the straight and narrow way,
I stroll along,
Frowning on each gay Lothario
I chance to meet.
Ev'ry entrance to my heart I shut,
Shunning sentimental dangers—but—

REFRAIN 1

When two arms steal around me,
What can I do?
Just let my conscience be my guide?
Why should I sink or swim
If squeezing pleases him?
I just keep drifting along the tide.
When two eyes bend above me,
Tender and true,
Sending this message: "I'm so blue";
I really can't insist
That I was never kissed;
I'm only human—
What can I do?

REFRAIN 2

So many men are handsome;
What can I do?
When they are near I'm not the same,
I've not a trace of guile;
So if they take my smile
For something stirring—I'm not to blame.
I'm for the straight and narrow,

Nighttime and day.
I never really want to stray.*
So when I meet a lad
Who looks just like an ad
For Arrow Collars—
What can I do?

WHEN ALL YOUR CASTLES COME TUMBLING DOWN

Published September 1922. Music by Milton Schwarzwald. Lyrics by Arthur Francis. Introduced in *Molly
Darling* (1922) by Mary Millburn.

VERSE 1

The whole world's always building
Castles in Spain;
When sunshine is streaming,
Then ev'ryone's dreaming, scheming.
When you find that you have
Builded in vain,
There's one thing to do:
Start building anew.

REFRAIN 1

There's no use sighing,
There's no use crying,
When all your castles come tumbling down.
But just remember,
From day to day,
That after bleak December,
There's sunny May.
When fears assail you
And friends all fail you,
Just dare to smile and hide your frown.
There's no use sighing,
There's no use crying,
When all your castles come tumbling down.

VERSE 2

The Pollyanna way of thinking
Is, oh
So easy to swallow,

Alternate version of refrain 2, lines 9–13:
But nature likes to have her way.
So when some Romeo
Turns all the lights down low,
I've got to let him—
What can I do?

But terribly hard to follow.
When they call the castle mortgage,
You know,
That even in spring,
One hardly can sing.

REPEAT REFRAIN

MISCHA, JASCHA, TOSCHA, SASCHA

Written June–July 1922. Registered for copyright as an
unpublished song September 1922. Published 1932.

Party Song. I liked the sound—*circa* 1921—of the
given names of four internationally renowned vio-
linists then living in New York. As a consequence this
song, written merely for our own amusement—no vehicle in mind.

Popular with musicians and instrumentalists at infor-
mal musicales, this opus surely must have been one of
the best-known unpublished and non-commercial hits of
the Twenties. Especially was it called for when any one
of the four Russian-born—all American citizens now—
was present: Mischa Elman, born in Talnoe; Jascha
Heiftz, Vilna; Toscha Seidel, Odessa; and Sascha Jacob-
sen, Finland—at that time part of Russia.

When Random House in 1932 was preparing a three-
hundred-copy, signed, de luxe edition of *George Gershwin's Song-Book* (eighteen songs plus rather tricky
piano transcriptions), they decided a novel item could be
added to their twenty-dollar issue by a cover-insert of
something as yet unpublished. And that's how a party
song, "Mischa, &c.," which was really never intended to
see print, achieved publication.
                    —from *Lyrics on Several Occasions*

VERSE 1

We really think you ought to know*
That we were born right in the middle
Of Darkest Russia.
When we were three years old or so,
We all began to play the fiddle
In Darkest Russia.
When we began,
Our notes were sour—

Original version of verse 1, lines 1–2:
Amid the ice, amid the snow,
We all were born right in the middle

Until a man
(Professor Auer)
Set out to show us, one and all,
How we could pack them in,
In Carnegie Hall.

REFRAIN 1

Temp'ramental Oriental Gentlemen are we:
Mischa, Jascha, Toscha, Sascha—
Fiddle-lee, diddle-lee, dee.
Shakespeare says, "What's in a name?"
With him we disagree.
Names like Sammy, Max or Moe
Never bring the heavy dough
Like Mischa, Jascha, Toscha, Sascha—
Fiddle-lee, diddle-lee, dee.

VERSE 2

Though born in Russia, sure enough,
We're glad that we became relations
Of Uncle Sammy.
For though we play the high-brow stuff,
We also like the syncopations
Of Uncle Sammy.
Our magic bow
Plays Liszt and Schumann;
But then you know
We're only human
And like to shake a leg to jazz.
(Don't think we've not the feelings
Everyone has.)

REFRAIN 2

Temp'ramental Oriental Gentlemen are we:
Mischa, Jascha, Toscha, Sascha—
Fiddle-lee, diddle-lee, dee.
High-brow He-brow may play low-brow
In his privacy.
But when concert halls are packed,
Watch us stiffen up and act
Like Mischa, Jascha, Toscha, Sascha—
Fiddle-lee, diddle-lee, dee.

VERSE 3

You find our pictures ev'rywhere.*
They show you we're artistic persons
Who play the fiddle.
When critics hear us, they declare
The rest are all so many worse 'uns
Who play the fiddle.
We're from the best;

Alternate version of verse 3, line 1:
You see our pictures ev'rywhere.

The critics said it—
But to the rest
We still give credit.
And so we want it understood
We think that Paganini also was good.

REFRAIN 3

Temp'ramental Oriental Gentlemen are we:
Mischa, Jascha, Toscha, Sascha—
Fiddle-lee, diddle-lee, dee.
We give credit when it's due—
But then you must agree
That outside of dear old Fritz,
All the fiddle-concert hits
Are Mischa, Jascha, Toscha, Sascha—
Fiddle-lee, diddle-lee, dee.

Earlier Version of Refrain 2

Temp'ramental Oriental Gentlemen are we:
Mischa, Jascha, Toscha, Sascha—
Fiddle-lee, diddle-lee, dee.
We're not high-brows, we're not low-brows,
Anyone can see.
You don't have to use a chart
To see we're He-brows from the start.
Just Mischa, Jascha, Toscha, Sascha—
Fiddle-lee, diddle-lee, dee.

Additional Refrains

Temp'ramental Oriental Gentlemen are we:
Mischa, Jascha, Toscha, Sascha—
Fiddle-lee, diddle-lee, dee.
"Art for art's sake" is our motto,
Anyone can see.
But oh! What joy when we have played
To know the fiddler must be paid
With dollars, sterling, yen and franc notes—
Fiddle-lee, diddle-lee, dee.

Temp'ramental Oriental Gentlemen are we:
Mischa, Jascha, Toscha, Sascha—
Fiddle-lee, diddle-lee, dee.
Here's a secret, we were born
On Broome Street, N.Y.C.
Papa, seeing his mistake,
Changed our names from Max and Jake
To Mischa, Jascha, Toscha, Sascha—
Fiddle-lee, diddle-lee, dee.

Temp'ramental Oriental Gentlemen are we:
Mischa, Jascha, Toscha, Sascha—
Fiddle-lee, diddle-lee, dee.
Other fiddlers are just piddlers,*

Alternate version of line 4 of the above refrain:
Magic lingers in our fingers

Anyone can see.
For no matter what their claims,
They've no music like the names
Of Mischa, Jascha, Toscha, Sascha.
Fiddle-lee, diddle-lee, dee.

MARY-LOUISE

Written December 1922. Music by Richard Myers. Lyrics by Arthur Francis. No music is known to survive.

VERSE

Ev'ry single time I hear your name,
Seems to me my heart's a ball of flame.
Can't you read it in my eyes?
You're the girl I idolize.
Won't you treat me other than a brother?

REFRAIN

Mary-Louise, oh, lovely Mary-Louise,
Don't make me think you're a tease
All of the time.
Oh, can't you see
That you have pierced my armor, little charmer?
Say you've learned to care a little for me.
I never knew that I could care as I do,
All day and all the night through.
Oh, how I pine.
Tell me you care
And I'll climb a steeple,
Yelling from there
To the green-eyed people,
"Mary-Louise, Mary-Louise is mine."

UNPRODUCED CHOPIN SHOW, 1923

In 1921, the Shuberts presented *Blossom Time*, a musical biography of Franz Schubert that transformed the composer's melodies into operetta numbers. It was a fabulous success and inspired many similar offerings using the music of famous composers. In 1923, William

Daly and Ira Gershwin (as Arthur Francis) tried their hands at a Chopin show, adapting and lyricizing the great Polish composer's themes, but this project was never completed. Eventually, in 1928, the Shuberts brought Chopin to Broadway in *White Lilacs*, but William Daly and Ira Gershwin were not part of that enterprise.

SOMEDAY YOU'LL REALIZE

Act I, No. 2. (Act I, No. 1, does not survive.) Intended for Gaston and Delphine. Music by Frédéric Chopin, arranged by William Daly. Music for the verse was drawn from the Mazurka in A-flat, Op. 50, No. 2; music for the refrain was drawn from the Waltz in A-flat, Op. 34, No. 1 ("Valse brillante").

VERSE 1

GASTON: Pray tell me how much longer must
    my poor heart suffer;
    Though I'm no genius, still you know
    I'm not a duffer.
    No one alive could measure up to
    your ideal man;
    Why waste your time in dreams, when
    here you have a real man?

REFRAIN 1

Someday, someday you'll realize
Daydreams are gay dreams that
    seldom come true;
Someday, someday you'll realize
I am the lover who's slated for you.
Sleeping Beauty, wake from the spell
    of dreams—
True love you're abusing;
See the time we're losing!
Someday, someday you will realize
With a heart that's glad—
I'm not so bad.

VERSE 2

DELPHINE: Sir, you're a paragon—I know your
    ev'ry virtue;
    And if you think you need me, I will
    not desert you.
    True friendship is platonic, but if that
    won't do you,
    Then only this remains—I'll be a
    sister to you.

REFRAIN 2

Someday, someday you'll realize
That I'm in love with a golden ideal.
Someday, someday you'll realize
Visions Elysian may seem to be real.
Find some blue-eyed nurse for your
    breaking heart;
Soon you'll get the feeling
It is quickly healing.
Someday, someday you will realize
No one else will do;
She's meant for you.

MAN, THE MASTER

Act I, No. 3. Intended for "[George] Sand (and Ladies)."
Music by Frédéric Chopin, arranged by William Daly.

VERSE

Ever since the world began,
We've merely been Man's chattel.
We are playthings in his plan—
He likes to hear us prattle.
I'm a rebel!—Tyrant Man,
I've drawn the sword of battle.
Woman's day is on the way,
And when we have our say, then believe me,
When he walks, he'll never strut;
We'll show him he's no hero.
After all, he's nothing but
A zero or a Nero.

REFRAIN

Man, the master, courts disaster
When he tries to master me!
I defy him, fiercely eye him—
I have rights as well as he.
I'm his match,
For I can scratch!
Man, the master, courts disaster
Trying to master me!

CODA

Man, ever tyrannical,
I throw off your manacle!
Man, the master, courts disaster
Trying to master me.

ON THE WINGS OF ROMANCE

Act I, No. 4. Intended for Dubusson and Sand. Music by
Frédéric Chopin, arranged by William Daly.

VERSE

DUBUSSON: Into the center
Of my heart you enter;
Ah! fair tormentor,
Tell me you'll be mine.
I'll spend my treasure
On you without measure;
Your whims my pleasure—
How can you decline?
SAND: Curb your rare devotion,
Lachrymose emotion,
Or you'll start an ocean
Made of tearful brine.
DUBUSSON: What hidden joys we'll unravel!
There will be no gravel
On the roads we travel
When our souls entwine.

REFRAIN 1

Love, let us go flying
On the wings of romance.
Why be so denying?
Give your true love a chance.
Though women keep sighing,
At no other I'll glance.
Love is blind,
But we will find
Paradise on the wings of romance.

REFRAIN 2

SAND: Sir, I would go flying
On the wings of romance.
Sir, I'm not denying
My heart's longing to dance.
I've dreamed of a dream home
Where no sorrow would chance—
Just for two,
But not with you—
You will not do for wings of romance.

MY ALL

Act I, No. 5. Intended for Chopin and Sand. Music by
Frédéric Chopin, arranged by William Daly. Refrain
adapted from Etude in E Major, Op. 10, No. 3.

VERSE

In your eyes I see
All eternity;
From your smile I feel
That somehow you are real.
I've known sorrow from
Fear you'd never come.
Here you are at last;
The past is but the past.
Through years serene,
Naught shall intervene.
Love will lead us on
Till breath is gone,
Where'er we wander.

REFRAIN

You are my all,
Holding me in thrall;
Sunshine floods the shadows
When I hear you call.
Lovely and rare,
Fairest of the fair,
Tell me how to prove to you
How much I care.
Trembling madly, gladly,
My heart told me,
You alone were meant for me—
Enfold me, hold me.
You are my all,
Holding me in thrall;
Fate has sent me you in answer to my call.

BITTERSWEET

Probably written in 1923. Music by William Daly or
Lewis E. Gensler. Lyrics by Arthur Francis. Possibly
intended for unproduced Chopin show.

VERSE

Life as it goes is no bed of red roses.
But troubles that happen along
Always depart, so don't take it to heart so

If something has turned out all wrong.
Happiness never is quite complete
All things are made up of bittersweet.

REFRAIN

Bittersweet the days we spend;
Bittersweet until the end.
Ev'ry hope hides a fear;
Ev'ry smile knows a tear.
Wise the maiden who forgets
When the bitter brings regrets.
Just recall that one and all
Must taste the bittersweet.

HUBBY

Written in 1923. Music by William Daly. Lyrics by Arthur Francis. No music is known to survive.

VERSE

It seems to be the right thing now
To overlook the marriage vow.
It's out of date to love your mate.*
But I'm afraid that I'm designed
To be a quaint, old-fashioned kind.
So come what may
I'll honor and obey.

REFRAIN 1

Hubby, oh, darling hubby,
Let's be as clubby as we can be.
I'm going to scorn convention
And pay attention to hubby-hubby.
Hold me, oh, please enfold me,
The world would scold me
If it but knew.
But oh! I cannot hide it,
I must confide it,
Dear, I'm in love with you.

REFRAIN 2

Hubby, oh, darling hubby,
Let's be as clubby as we can be.

Alternate version of verse, lines 3–7:
Each one can choose whose is whose.
The hearts that beat for one alone
Are seldom beating for their own.
In me you find
A quaint, old-fashioned kind.

While others go to Reno,
I'll play casino with hubby-hubby.
Press me, and always "Yes" me,
Oh, dear, caress me
My whole life through.
Please start right in and practice,
For oh! the fact is
That I'm in love with you.

THE SUNSHINE TRAIL

Published March 1923 in conjunction with Thomas H. Ince's film *The Sunshine Trail*, starring Douglas MacLean. Music by George Gershwin. Lyrics by Arthur Francis.

VERSE

When you lend a helping hand to others,
Scattering the sunbeams night and day,
Making all your fellow men your brothers;
You are on The Sunshine Trail to stay.

REFRAIN

You'll find true happiness along
The Sunshine Trail.
That's where the bluebird begins his song—
The Sunshine Trail.
I cannot guide you there,
But seek it while you may;
Your heart will tell you where
To find the way.
If you can start with a sunny smile,
A song of cheer,
You'll realize in a little while,
The trail is near.
No matter where you are,
It's never very far;
And once you find it you'll never stray
From The Sunshine Trail.

LITTLE RHYTHM, GO 'WAY

Written in May 1923. Music by William Daly and Joseph Meyer. Lyrics by Arthur Francis. This lyric was the precursor to "Fascinating Rhythm" (see *Lady, Be Good!*—1924). No music is known to survive.

VERSE

I've got a rhythm—a raggedy rhythm—and oh!
I've got it bad.
It's so persistent the day isn't distant, I know,
When I'll go mad.
Enters my room in the morning;
Follows wherever I go.
I'll have to sneak up right on it and speak up
Someday—Here's what I'll say:

REFRAIN

Little rhythm, go 'way.
You'll be turning me gray
If you lengthen your stay.
I got up with the sun;
There was work to be done,
But I haven't begun.
Won't you give up your beating,
Heating up my weary brain?
All my senses are blazing
While you're raising Cain.
From the moment I wake,
Must I quiver and quake
Like a flivver a-shake?
Little rhythm, go 'way!
Little rhythm, come some other day.

PATTER
(sung as a countermelody to the refrain)

Oh! Rhythm, slow rhythm,
You made me what I am today.
I hope you're satisfied.
Mad rhythm, bad rhythm,
Why do you follow me this way?
Say, haven't you any pride?
I'm up a tree—Tell me, why
Pick on me? Passersby
Wink an eye, and they cry,
"Is he dizzy,
Busy bouncing like an old Tin Lizzie?"
Your meter was sweeter once.
All that I do now is moan and sigh,
Crying, "Oh! Set me free!
Oh! Please let me be.
Go to someone who's lonely,
Only let me be."

THE NEVADA

Written in May 1923. Music by Joseph Meyer and William Daly. Lyrics by Arthur Francis. No music is known to survive.

VERSE

If your mate, you find, is out of date,
Then don't you hesitate;
Just come this way.
If your partner isn't in your heart,
And if your sky has start-
Ed turning gray—
Then I am sure I've got a cure that will endure.
It comes from Reno; it's a dance.
Come on and take your chance,
For everybody's prancing
It today.

REFRAIN

Dance along with me;
Come and do the step they call Nevada.
(Change your partner.)
Let's go on a spree;
Come and get the pep they call Nevada.
(Change your partner.)
Look around until you find a new love
Who'll be a true love,
Who has the smile that you love—
Maybe Baby—
Go to blue-eyed Baby;
Ask her when will the day be.
If she's full of charm,
Show her you're a wonderful romancer.
(Make it snappy.)
Take her by the arm!
Never take a "No, sir!" for an answer.
(You'll be happy.)
But if she is cold and tries to chill you,
Just dance until you
Find somebody who can thrill you.
If you want to be*
Gay and fancy-free,
Do the Nevada with me.

*Alternate version of refrain, lines 22–24:
Let's go on a spree.
Let's be fancy-free.
Do the Nevada with me.

TELL ME IN THE GLOAMING

Written in May 1923. Music by Niclas Kempner. Lyrics by Irving Caesar and Arthur Francis. No music is known to survive.

Tell me in the gloaming,
In the quiet gloaming,
When the birds are weary of their roaming;
When the whippoorwill
From his nest upon the hill
Tells the rover it is time for homing;
Love is ever tender,
Eager to surrender.
When the sun goes down in crimson splendor—
When the moon is in the blue—
When the stars come stealing through—
I want you.

Tell me
Oh! that wonderful story
That has brought me the glory
Of a love that is ever true, ever new.
Tell me
You will always caress me,
You will tenderly press me,
When the gloaming brings me love and you.

SINGING IN THE RAIN

Written in May 1923. Music by Joseph Meyer. Lyrics by Arthur Francis. Ira Gershwin was not enamored of this lyric (especially since "Singin' in the Rain," bearing a lyric by Ira's close friend and pool-playing partner Arthur Freed, is vastly more famous), so Michael Feinstein used to play and sing it during the last two years of Ira's life—to make him laugh.

VERSE 1

Even though the wind is roaring
And the torrent keeps on pouring,
Somewhere you can always hear a robin singing.
He knows, though the skies are cloudy,
Soon the sunshine will say "Howdy";
He has always found it so.
Dear, let's learn from him—
Let's go on

REFRAIN 1

Singing, singing in the rain.
Don't mind the patter on the windowpane;
For if the robin sings on, so can we.
You see, the thing to do is
Dry that tear up—Smile and cheer up.
There's a rainbow overdue;
Why let a rainstorm be a Waterloo?
Just cuddle close and we'll go
Helter-skelter to our shelter,
Singing in the rain.

VERSE 2

I was frightened for a minute;
But if you've a song, begin it—
I'll be brave and try to string along with you,
    dear.
And if I'm no Tetrazzini
Singing tunes by G. Puccini
Still, I'll do my best, I know,
And I promise that
I'll go on

REFRAIN 2

Singing, singing in the rain,
Nor mind the pitter-patter on the pane;
For if the robin sings on, so can we.
With you beside me, I'll be
Ever cheerful, never tearful.
You will see, I'll not complain;
I'll show the bird his song is not in vain.
Just hold me tight and we'll go
Hurry-scurry, not a worry,
Singing in the rain.

HONORABLE MOON

Written in June 1923. Music by William Daly. Lyrics by B. G. DeSylva and Arthur Francis. No music is known to survive. Ira Gershwin wrote at the bottom of the typed lyric sheet: "Do this in revue. Japanese girl singing 1 + 1 [verse and refrain] seriously. Chorus of American sailors comes on. Each loves her. She has 2 babies." In 1941, Ira Gershwin and E. Y. Harburg wrote the lyrics for a new song with this title (see page 314).

VERSE

Far away in old Japan, a little maid is sad;
Tears arise in her eyes.
It's the same old story—

How a handsome Yankee lad
Loved a day—sailed away.
Patiently she waits, hoping to discover
Honorable boat that took her lover.
Always when the moon appears,
She hopes the news is glad
That it brings; so she sings:

REFRAIN

Honorable Moon, I look to you,
Honorable Moon, as lovers do.
Make a silver path across the sea,
So my love'll find his way to me.
Must I wither like a flower without sunshine,
    without rain?
Must my weary nights of waiting be in vain?
Honorable Moon, oh, hear my plea,
Tell me he will soon come back to me.

BABY ME BLUES

Written August 1923. Music by Vincent Youmans. Lyrics by Arthur Francis. No music is known to survive.

VERSE

Success has only made me more lonely;
My days are lonesome affairs.
In that connection I crave affection,
But there is no one who cares.
There is not a soul I have mentioned this to;
You alone now know my secret.
I cannot hide it; I must confide it to you.

REFRAIN

I'm lonesome all through the day,
Forever getting those Baby Me Blues.
(I want some petting.)
They tell me hugging has charms
Well, I've a lap, and two arms I could use.
(That's why I'm fretting.)
And I'm just realizing now, dear,
When your sweet smile I see,
There's no one else in all the world
I'd rather have baby me.
And so I hope and pray
You'll make me lose all those Baby Me Blues.
(I need a mamma.)

I WON'T SAY I WILL, BUT I WON'T SAY I WON'T

Published September 1923. Music by George Gershwin. Lyrics by B. G. DeSylva and Arthur Francis. Introduced by Irene Bordoni in *Little Miss Bluebeard*, which opened in New York at the Lyceum Theatre on August 28, 1923; 175 performances.

VERSE

You're a very naughty boy;
When you ask me for a kiss,
I'm dismayed—
A little bit afraid.
Now, holding hands is quite a joy
For a truly modest miss;
It should do
Just as well for you.
I am not refusing you, dear;
Let me make this perfectly clear:

REFRAIN 1

I won't say I will, but I won't say I won't!
I don't say I do, but I don't say I don't!
Kissing of any kind
Never was on my mind.
Maybe I can arrange it—
It's *my* mind, and I can change it.
I might say I might, but modesty forbids;
That's the reason why I don't!
So you mustn't be cross at a little delay:
You ought to know Rome wasn't built in a day!
I won't say I will, but I won't say I won't!

REFRAIN 2

I won't say I will, but I won't say I won't!
I don't say I do, but I don't say I don't!
Maybe it's just my way;
Maybe I'm cold—but, say!
Although my glance like ice is—
How I warm up in a crisis!
I might say I might, but modesty forbids;
That's the reason why I don't!
You'd have *taken* your kiss if you had any
    cheek—
Maybe I'd scream, but my voice is so weak!
I won't say I will, but I won't say I won't!

REFRAIN 3

I won't say I will, but I won't say I won't!
I don't say I do, but I don't say I don't!

Kissing has seemed to me
Vulgar as it can be.
Mentally I'm much higher.
(Don't believe me—I'm a liar!)
I might say I might, but modesty forbids;
That's the reason why I don't!
A virtue like mine is a hard thing to find,
But it's lucky for me that you can't read my
    mind!
I won't say I will, but I won't say I won't!

REFRAIN 4

I won't say I will, but I won't say I won't!
I don't say I do, but I don't say I don't!
That is the stand I take
Just for convention's sake.
Though I frown like a deacon,
Coax me more—perhaps I'll weaken!
I might say I might, but modesty forbids;
That's the reason why I don't!
Though I have to say "No"—if a chappie is
    wise,
He can read "Yes" in the light of my eyes!
I won't say I will, but I won't say I won't!

REFRAIN 5

I won't say I will, but I won't say I won't!
I don't say I do, but I don't say I don't!
Stealing a kiss is theft—
But, sir, if you are deft,
Letting no fears assail you,
I'm sure no cop would ever jail you.
I might say I might, but modesty forbids;
That's the reason why I don't!
But supposing you kissed me, now, isn't it true:
My lips would be sealed—tell me, what could I
    do?
I won't say I will, but I won't say I won't!

REFRAIN 6

I won't say I will, but I won't say I won't!
I don't say I do, but I don't say I don't!
When you ask for a kiss,
I know the rhyme is bliss;
But, dear, if I agreed to,
No one knows what it might lead to.
I might say I might, but modesty forbids;
That's the reason why I don't!
My affection for you, darling, keeps me in check,
For once I got started, you'd soon be a wreck.
I won't say I will, but I won't say I won't!

FABRIC OF DREAMS

Written in August 1923. Published September 1923. Music by Raymond Hubbell. Lyrics by B. G. DeSylva and Arthur Francis. Introduced by Joe Schenck and Hazel Dawn in *Nifties of 1923*, which opened in New York at the Fulton Theatre on September 25, 1923.

VERSE 1

I sing of a dress for my lady;
Orpheus gave me the theme.
I dreamed of a dress for my lady;
Morpheus lent me the dream.
The Muses have lent me the rhyme;
The fancy's completed, and I'm

REFRAIN

Weaving a dress for my lady
Out of the fabric of dreams;
Fashioned of twilight,
Sewn with the shy light
Of stars and the moon's fragile beams;
Clasped with a girdle of dawning,
Rainbows to cover the seams,
Brightened with kisses,
Ladylove, this is
Your gown from my fabric of dreams!

VERSE 2

My lady's cheek wears a dimple;
My lady's lips wear a smile.
No gown of gossamer simple
With them would quite be in style.
In gardens where fantasies bloom,
I sit at the sunset, my loom.

REPEAT REFRAIN

HOT HINDOO

Published September 1923. Music by Lewis E. Gensler. Lyrics by Arthur Francis. Written for *Greenwich Village Follies of 1923*, which opened in New York at the Winter Garden Theatre on September 20, 1923, the song was apparently dropped before the show's New York opening.

VERSE

Back in the land where Buddha is all supreme,
There's a sweet nautch girl who can dance like a dream.
When she is dressed up, wearing a string of pearls,
Give her a tom-tom rhythm, and off she twirls.
Listen to all the natives begin to cheer.
If you could translate, this is what you would hear:

REFRAIN 1

Hot Hindoo,
Show what you kin do,
And go right into your dance.
Hot Hindoo,
Shake all your skin, do!
We get a thrill in advance.
Come on, do your stuff;
We can't get enough;
Make it rough!
Hot! Hot! Hot Hindoo,
Won't you begin, do!
Go right into your dance.

REFRAIN 2

Hot Hindoo,
Show what you kin do,
And go right into your dance.
Hot Hindoo,
Shake all your skin, do!
We get a thrill in advance.
Start your dizzy whirl,
Like a top a-twirl;

Atta girl!
Hot! Hot! Hot Hindoo,
Won't you begin, do!
Go right into your dance.

THE HURDY-GURDY MAN

About 1918, George Gershwin (music) and Lou Paley (lyrics) wrote a song titled "A Corner of Heaven with You." No. 99 in the George and Ira Gershwin Special Numbered Song File. A few years later, probably 1923, Lou Paley and Ira Gershwin wrote a new lyric to the tune, itself revised somewhat, titled "The Hurdy-Gurdy Man." Music by George Gershwin. Lyrics credited to Lou Paley and Arthur Francis.

VERSE

If you've wondered where the good songs go
After they've had their day,
You'll be glad to meet a man I know,
Wrinkled and old and gray.
He collects the tunes that time has thrown
    aside—
Puts them under lock and key;
For a penny he is glad to set them free.

REFRAIN

When the hurdy-gurdy man is here,
There's a magic in the atmosphere
That seems to drive away
All the cares of the day.
As he ambles up and down the street,
All the kids begin to move their feet;
No music can compete with the hurdy-gurdy.
All his melodies are spun of gold—
Tender recollections they unfold;
He'll bring you joy untold.
Follow him when you can,
For while he's grinding, you're finding
The daydreams of old
In the sentimental melodies of the hurdy-gurdy
    man.

OPPOSITE: Primrose, *Finale, Act I. Leslie Henson (Toby), hat in hand, faces the swooning Heather Thatcher (Pinkie), being held by Percy Heming (Hilary).*

MISCELLANEOUS | BE YOURSELF

IMAGINE ME WITHOUT MY YOU

Published May 1924. Music by Lewis E. Gensler. Lyrics by Ira Gershwin (credited as "Ira B. Gershwin") and Robert Russell Bennett; Bennett's name does not appear in the published sheet music. Written for but not used in *Top-Hole* (opened in New York on September 1, 1924, Fulton Theatre—104 performances). Intended for the characters of Marcia and Bob, portrayed by Clare Stratton and Ernest Glendinning. This is the first published song for which Ira Gershwin, discarding "Arthur Francis," took credit. For a time in 1924, he used his middle initial—*B* for "Bruskin."

VERSE 1

MARCIA: Maybe in the face of stormy weather,
Love would depart
Out of your heart.
BOB: We were simply meant to be together;
We are a team
Like cornflakes and cream!

REFRAIN 1

Imagine me without my you
And you without your me!
You dear, you, when near you, I'm in
the clouds;
And that is no blarney
From Killarney!
Just to know how very slow
A place this world could be,
Imagine me without my you
And you without your me!

VERSE 2

BOB: That's a sentiment I hope you cared for;
Give me a clue—
Say that you do!
MARCIA: This is something I was unprepared for;
Maybe someday
I also will say:

REFRAIN 2

"Imagine me without my you
And you without your me!"
For, dearie, how dreary this life would
be

If you'd let some Venus
Come between us.
Like a ship without a skipper,
I'd be all at sea.
Imagine me without my you
And you without your me!

TURN TO THE DREAMS AHEAD

Written June 1924. Music by Morris Hamilton. No music is known to survive.

VERSE

Voices are singing—sorrow is winging
When the sun begins to smile;
But when it's raining, people, complaining,
Frown in a little while.
The skies are crying—There'll be no sighing
If you follow out my plan.
Don't let old trouble grieve you.
Take this advice and
He will be nice and leave you—

REFRAIN

Turn to the dreams that are lying before you.
Think of someone who will come one fine day to
adore you.
Don't borrow sorrow or let trouble floor you.*
Just learn to turn to the dreams that lie ahead.

*Alternate version of refrain, line 3:
If you should find trouble trying to floor you,

BE YOURSELF, 1924

I CAME HERE

Published September 1924. Music by Lewis E. Gensler. Lyrics by Marc Connelly, George S. Kaufman, and Ira Gershwin. Introduced in *Be Yourself* (opened in New York on September 3, 1924, Sam H. Harrie Theatre—93 performances) by Barrett Greenwood (David), Dorothy Whitmore (Marjorie), and ensemble. During the New York run, Whitmore was replaced with Norma Terris.

VERSE 1

HE: Ev'ry man can find some consolation,
When fate has picked him
To be her victim.
There are courts of law throughout the
nation
Where reparation
Can be obtained.
You are my judge and jury and defendant,
And as all my future is dependent
On your verdict, please let no decision
Becloud your vision
Till I've explained—

REFRAIN 1

I came here; I saw you;
I liked you; I love you.
My fancy no longer is free.
And I should like to remark now to the
jury
You're guilty as guilty can be.
My nerves are all in tatters;
My heart doesn't beat.
I don't say that it matters;
I merely repeat:
I came here; I saw you;
I liked you; I love you!
So bring in a verdict for me.

VERSE 2

SHE: I'll admit the way you plead is splendid;
You skip the ways-es
Of legal phrases.
But in spite of all that you've contended,
The trial is ended,
If you don't mind.
That is what I've set my hand and seal to;
There is no higher court you can appeal to;
Now that I observe our present status
Must separate us,
I am resigned.

REFRAIN 2

You came here; I saw you;
I heard you; I liked you.
But now I've a new point of view.
You'll notice I am in no mood to examine
A plaintiff as skillful as you.
I might hear pleas from you till
I could not resist.
So arguments are futile;
The case is dismissed.
You came here; I saw you;
I liked you; I hate you!
There's nothing a jury can do.

MY HEART IS YOURS

"I Came Here" evolved from an earlier, unfinished Arthur Francis lyric, which is marked with the title "My Heart Is Yours."

VERSE

From the very first I made my mind up
That we would wind up
By being signed up.
When from dreams of you Big Ben awakes me
He only takes me
To dreams of you.
Crossword puzzles take up no more time now;
Find I must express myself in rhyme now
That's the way I feel—I cannot hide it;
I must confide it—It's time you knew:

REFRAIN [*Outline*]

I came here, saw, like, love, tell—yours.
It's fated, it's slated, that we should be mated,
For you're all that my heart adores.

And it's more than merely a mild flirtation;
Dear, to me it's clearly predestination.
I came, etc.

THE WRONG THING AT THE RIGHT TIME

Written in 1924. Published April 1925. Music by Milton Schwarzwald. Lyrics by George S. Kaufman, Marc Connelly, and Ira Gershwin. Introduced in *Be Yourself* (1924) by Queenie Smith (Tony). Later in the New York run, it was sung by Queenie Smith and Teddy Hudson.

VERSE 1

Tho' I always laugh and frolic,
I feel somewhat melancholic
And can use a lot of sympathy.
In my heart I know I mean well,
But when I come on the scene, well,
Getting in wrong is my specialty.
So I'm always ruing
The fact I'm always doing

REFRAIN

The wrong thing at the right time,
Right thing at the wrong time.
Wide awake at nighttime,
Dreaming by day.
People all assure me
Nobody can cure me;
They may just endure me
While they say:
"She's so young and pretty;
Oh, what a pity."
Something
Tells me I'm no dumb thing,
But I do the "rum" thing
As I go 'long;
So I have a high time
Spending all of my time
Picking out the right time
To do what's wrong.

VERSE 2

If Mah-Jongg should be the fashion,
Then Old Maid becomes my passion;*

Alternate version of verse 2, line 2:
Pinochle becomes my passion.

Ev'rything I ever do is wrong.
If I call a baby "Tillie,"
I'm informed the name is "Willie";
Seems to me that I just don't belong.
So I'm always rueing
The fact I'm always doing

REPEAT REFRAIN

Earlier Version

VERSE

Tho' I'm not the least bit willful,
Seems to me I'm only skillful
Doing things that get me in a jam.
Tho' I'm not a little sinner,
If a rabbi came to dinner,
I'd forget and offer him some ham.
I could weep, decrying
The fates that keep me trying

REFRAIN

The wrong thing at the right time,
Right thing at the wrong time.
Keep awake the nighttime,
Dreaming all day.
Learning ev'ry minute
When I start to chin, it
Seems my foot is in it;
Find I'm saying,
"Good-bye, old fellow,"
When I mean "Hello!"
Something
Tells me I'm no dumb thing,
But I do the "rum" thing
As I go 'long.
Life could be a bright thing,
A cupful-of-delight thing,
If I did the right thing,
But I do the wrong.

UH-UH

Published September 1924. Music by Milton Schwarzwald. Lyrics by Marc Connelly, George S. Kaufman, and Ira Gershwin. Introduced in *Be Yourself* (1924) by Queenie Smith (Tony) and Jack Donahue (Matt).

In *Be Yourself*, a piece for which I did some lyrics in collaboration with Kaufman and Connelly, Milton Schwarzwald came up with a rhythmic, jerky tune for which I had an idea that Kaufman and Connelly approved. When I was traveling with a carnival show in the Midwest some years before, I had heard for the first time the sound *Uh-uh* for *No*. In the East, I'd always known and used *mm-hmmm* for yes or agreement, but hadn't known the antonymic sound, which naturally intrigued me. The result was a song for Jack Donahue and Queenie Smith, where he protested that she was always "uh-uhing" him and wherein he wondered when the miraculous day would occur that he'd hear *mm-hmmm* from her (also the sounds *tch-tch, tch-tch,* for "too bad," and *tut-tut, tut-tut,* for "Take it easy" or "No use worrying," were used, employed, sung, tongued). The last line of the male chorus was:

"You'd better change your 'Uh-uh, uh-uh, uh-uh'
To 'Mm-hmm.'"

And of the female was:
"Sometimes a girlie's 'Uh-uh, uh-uh, uh-uh'
Means 'Hm-hm.'"

—Ira Gershwin
(written for but not included in
Lyrics on Several Occasions)

VERSE 1

MATT: Like Mother Goose's Mary,*
You're always so contrary;
So life is not as airy
As it could be.
I'm not a waxen dummy,
So each time you "Uh-uh" me—
I don't think you're as chummy
As you should be.
The stand you take with other men
Gives me no great concern,
But when it comes to me,
You've got to learn—
Altho' you show a firm will,
Remember that the worm will turn.

REFRAIN 1

It's always "Uh-uh! uh-uh! uh-uh! uh-uh!"
when I come closer;
It's always "Uh-uh! uh-uh! uh-uh!" at the
least caress.

Earlier version of verse 1, lines 1–8:
Like Mother Goose's Mary,
You never seem to vary
From being more contrary
Than you should be.
I'm not a waxen dummy,
So each time you "uh-uh" me—
I don't think you're as chummy
As you could be.

All that I ever can get from you is "How
dare you!" or "No, Sir!"
It makes me wonder if you've ever heard
of the word "yes."
I realize I'm a very lucky dog now that
I've found you,
And you have made a whale of a hit with
me, I confess;
But if you like the idea of my always
hanging around you,
You'd better change your "Uh-uh! uh-uh!
uh-uh!" to "Hm-hm!"
(Said yes!)

VERSE 2

TONY: The atmosphere is clearing;
Your words sound most endearing;
It may be I am hearing
My Prince Charming.
Your argument's succeeding;
For you my heart is bleeding;
I must admit your pleading
Is disarming.
If you have suffered, as you say,
Then you deserve reward;
If I've been cold,
Excuse it, please, my lord;
I feel apologetic—
You've struck a sympathetic chord.

REFRAIN 2

It's just too tch-tch, tch-tch, tch-tch,
tch-tch, too bad about you;
I may have carried that "Uh-uh! uh-uh!" a
bit too far.
But after all, you're a stranger, so how
can I help but doubt you
Until I know just exactly what your
intentions are?
However, if I were you, I'd never take
"No!" for an answer,
But just say "Tut-tut! tut-tut!" when I say
"Uh-uh! Uh-uh!"
Because you'll learn from the novels
written by any romancer,
Sometimes a girlie's "Uh-uh! uh-uh!
uh-uh!" means "Hm-hm!"
(Said yes!)

MONEY DOESN'T MEAN A THING

Written in 1924. Music probably by Lewis E. Gensler. Introduced in *Be Yourself* (1924) by Queenie Smith

(Tony), Jack Donahue (Matt), Barrett Greenwood (David), Dorothy Whitmore (Marjorie), and ensemble. Dropped soon after the New York opening. Only a portion of the lyric survives. No music is known to survive.

VERSE 2

GIRLS: After all is said and done,
Once the mating is begun,
Two can live as cheap as one;
They can, can, can, can.
BOYS: When Cupid makes a fellow fall,
The overhead should not appall;
The thing to do is leave it all
To Dan, Dan, Dan, Dan.
When the troth is plighted
Through his magic touch,
Two hearts united
Don't need much.

REFRAIN

Just a little block of U.S. Steel,
Just enough to pay the rent.

[*Manuscript of lyric breaks off at this point*]

WHAT OF IT?

Written in 1924. Music by Lewis E. Gensler. Intended for Dorothy Whitmore (Marjorie) in *Be Yourself* (1924). Dropped before the New York opening. No music is known to survive.

VERSE

Being somewhat older,
I've learned, when things go flat,
It's best to shrug a shoulder
And murmur, "That's that."
Doesn't pay to change things;
Stand by through thick and thin.
No one can arrange things
To suit What Might Have Been.

REFRAIN

When a heart is bruised a bit,
It's great if one can say, "What *of* it?"
Though it's been abused a bit,
No need to pine away—What *of* it?
If the thing they call man
Seems today to bring you cares and sorrow,
Don't forget the alman-

Ac will guarantee that there's
Another day tomorrow.
Though your castles tumble,
And though clouds are thickly spread—What *of*
  it?
Passing from the jumble,
There are dreams that lie ahead—So, what *of* it?
You see, there's really no use letting
The days go by in vain regretting.
Sad or cheerful,
Gay or tearful,
Time keeps flying just the same.

THEY DON'T MAKE 'EM THAT WAY ANYMORE

Written in 1924. Music by Lewis E. Gensler. Intended for G. P. Huntley (Prescott) and Georgia Caine (Grandma Brennan) in *Be Yourself*. Dropped before the New York opening. No music is known to survive.

VERSE 1

PRESCOTT: The future of this nation, with the
    present generation,
    You must admit is nothing but a joke.
GRANDMA: You now find human zeros, where in
    my day we had heroes,
PRESCOTT: Who were men of brain and brawn
    and hearts of oak.
GRANDMA: I spent my childhood days astride a
    bronco in the West.
PRESCOTT: I trailed the cunning redskin and I
    fought him in his nest.
GRANDMA: With men of mighty muscle, we were
    set for any tussle.
PRESCOTT: Why, even as a baby, I had hair upon
    my chest.

REFRAIN 1

BOTH: But they don't make 'em that way
    anymore.
    Like Davy Crockett in the days of
    yore.
PRESCOTT: He was a chap who had the goods;
    He tracked the Injuns through the
    woods—
    And how they bit the dust when he
    got sore.
GRANDMA: He had no time to moon and
    turtledove.

PRESCOTT: But just would sock a girl to show his
    love.
    His shirt contained a torso
    Like Hercules' and more so—
BOTH: But they don't make 'em that way
    anymore.

VERSE 2

PRESCOTT: Back in the open spaces, the men had
    honest faces;
    The women all were beautiful, of
    course.
GRANDMA: Not only were we cutelike, but if we
    couldn't shoot like
    Annie Oakleys, there was good
    grounds for divorce.
PRESCOTT: When roaming on the Western
    prairies or the desert sands,
GRANDMA: Though rattlesnakes abounded so they
    traveled 'round in bands,
PRESCOTT: We couldn't waste a rifle shot on such
    a little trifle;
    Convention, then, demanded that we
    choke 'em with our hands.

REFRAIN 2

BOTH: But they don't make 'em that way
    anymore,
    Like Daniel Boone or Buffalo Bill of
    yore.
GRANDMA: Our mornings we would while away
    By shooting cards a mile away
PRESCOTT: And wrestling with a bear was just a
    bore.
GRANDMA: When day was over, we put on no
    silk—
PRESCOTT: But in the kitchen we'd uncow the
    milk.
BOTH: Those were the days of he-men
    When to live, men had to *be* men—
    But they don't make 'em that way
    anymore.

ALL OF THEM WAS FRIENDS OF MINE

Written in 1924. Music by Lewis E. Gensler. No music is known to survive.

VERSE 1

Though the old Bartenders' Union don't come
  'round no more for dues
And has kind of disappeared since times got
  hard,
I've a souvenir that cheers me up each time I
  get the blues—
I'm referring to my good old union card.
Ev'ry evening when I've said my prayers and
  crawled into my bed,
I read that card until I fall asleep;
And I dream about the friends I knew in days
  that now has fled;
And I often find I break right down and weep.
I got this when I worked on Fourteenth Street.
Oh, the lovely customers I used to meet.

REFRAIN 1

Mr. Porter and Mr. Ferguson
And Mr. McIntyre and Mr. Stein;
Messrs. Duffy and O'Malley
And occasionally
State Senator Milton Klein.
I can see them like it was yesterday,
As before the bar they neatly stood in line.
Good fellowship was always there unless
  someone got sore,
And then, of course, there'd be a face upon the
  barroom floor
Of Porter, Duffy, McIntyre,
Or Ferguson or Klein—
All of them was friends of mine.

VERSE 2

There was mottos on the ceiling; there was
  sawdust on the floor;
There was works of art the visitor could see.
With that bar of pure mahogany! That lovely
  swinging door!
Oh, the place was really home, sweet home, to
  me.
Not a customer was worried he'd be greeted
  with a punch
Though he got home to wifey 'way after three;
All he had to say was he'd been down to
  Schultze's with the bunch,
And she knew that he'd been in good company.
Oh, when I think of days that now are gone,
I wonder, Does it pay to carry on?

REFRAIN 2

Mr. Silver and Mr. Robinson;
Messrs. Denowitz and Valentine.
Also District Leader Coffen

Used to come in often
With Alderman David Fein.
For a nickel, you got a schooner there,
And on pretzels and on pickles you could dine.
When they got through discussing what was
    what at Tam'ny Hall,
They'd stand and watch the picture of the lady
    on the wall,
Did Denowitz and Silver, Robinson and
    Valentine—
All of them good friends of mine.

'ATTA GIRL!

Written in 1924. Music by Lewis E. Gensler. No music
is known to survive.

VERSE

Oh, I'm afraid
That with a maid
I have no gift of gab.
I simply can't routine
The thoughts within my bean.
I'll never show*
Up Romeo—
My lingo's very drab.
But I know one good phrase
For someone I would praise:

REFRAIN

When I look at a girl, at a girl like you,
I'm no fool, yet I don't know what to say
To a Juliet I could love and obey—
'Cept a phrase, just a phrase that I think'll do—
" 'Atta Girl"—which means I think you're
    hot—
" 'Atta Girl"—Take everything I've got—
When I look at a girl—'Atta Girl—like you

CHEERIO!

Probably written in 1924. Music by Lewis E. Gensler. No
music is known to survive.

Alternate version of verse, lines 6–7:
Just like a sheik
I'll never speak.

VERSE

Though you've read about Old King Cole,
The merry soul, who ruled in Britain—
Up to now the cause of the joy
Of that old boy was never written.
Well, he used a magic phrase when days were
    blue;
I deciphered it, and you can use it, too.
So now if trouble happens along,
Just greet it with a song. It's

REFRAIN

"Cheerio! Cheerio!
Tweedle-dee-dum-dum!
Cheerio! Cheerio!"
That's what he would hum.
You can smile all the while
When a cloud appears.
For you know it'll go
If you're singing:
"Cheerio! Cheerio!"—
Makes December May;
It'll keep, it'll sweep
Trouble far away.
Old Man Gloom will meet his doom
With "Cheerio! Cheerio!
Tweedle-dee-dum-dum!"

DON'T YOU REMEMBER?

Written in 1924. Music by Lewis E. Gensler. No music
is known to survive.

VERSE 1

HE: Really, I'm not trying to be flirtatious
    When I say that we have met before.
    Please don't look at me that way, my
        gracious!
    Why, we've met a dozen times or more.
    Always I have worshiped and enshrined
        you;
    I can't see how you can be in doubt.
    If you're really puzzled, I'll remind you
    When and how and what it's all about.

REFRAIN 1

Don't you remember? When I was Paris—
    You were Helen of Troy.
Don't you remember? When you were
    Juliet—

I was that Montague boy.
When you were Cleo, I was the 'Tony
Who used to see you to your door.
Don't you remember, or *won't* you
    remember
That we've met before?

VERSE 2

SHE: Pardon me, I thought you had a dizziness;
    When you spoke, I thought your mind was
        gone.
    But I recollect that tadpole business
    And the well-known queen of Babylon.
    I can see the shore to which you're drifting;
    Think I understand your point of view;
    And discover, since the fog is lifting,
    You resemble someone that I knew.

REFRAIN 2

Now I remember, when you were
    Bluebeard,
I was one of your wives.
You were Henry, the good king Henry,
And chopped off one of my lives.
When you were Nero, you were the hero,
Who pushed me through the lions' door.
Now I remember, Oh, *how* I remember!
That we've met before.

NOT SO LONG AGO

Written in 1924. Music by Lewis E. Gensler.

VERSE 1

My simple notions will cause no commotions;
You'll think me old-fashioned, I'm sure.
Into some kitchen I'm longing to pitch in;
From city life let me detour.
I'd have a garden where flowers unfurl:
Just like my mother's, when she was a girl.

REFRAIN

Take me, take me
Back to the quiet of not so long ago.
Make me, make me
Live in a dollhouse and dress in plain calico.
Never roaming, I'll know the charms
Of each gloaming, waiting for arms
To take me, take me
Back to the quiet of not so long ago.

VERSE 2

If you want my angle on the love triangle,
I'm for no front-headline stunts.
I hope to discover a husband and lover,
But both in the same man at once.
When I am married, I hope it will last;
I know of cases that did in the past.

REPEAT REFRAIN

OPENING—CRAZY QUILT

Probably written in 1924, around the time of *Be Yourself*. Music by Lewis E. Gensler. Lyrics by Morrie Ryskind and Ira Gershwin. This appears to be the opening number of a revue (it is not, however, related to Billy Rose's 1931 revue, *Crazy Quilt*). No music is known to survive.

Howda do, Papa—Howda do, Mamma—
Howda do, customers.
We're here to know you; we're here to show
     you—
Howda do, customers.
Shout from the housetops and let 'em know
We can't be beat;
We have the greatest and finest show
On Fifty-second Street.
Howda do, Hammond, Howda do, Benchley—
Howda do, "Round the Town."
Howda do, Woollcott, Howda do, Corbin—
Howda do, Heywood Broun.
If you like us as we like you
Please tell the *World*, the *Telegram*, too,
Tell it to Papa, Tell it to Mamma,
Tell it to Sweeney, too.

[*Dance 32 bars*]
[*New girls enter:*]

Just in case you want to know
How we came to do this show;
We'll be big and openhearted—
Let you in on how it started:
One—I found a dime
Two—I found a gag
Three—I found a rhyme
Four—I found a flag
Five—I found a tune
Six—I found a step
Seven—I found a moon
Eight—I found some pep.

When we put them all
Together they spelled "Mother"—
That's the sweetest name of all.

[*Repeat "I found a dime"—Chorus: "She found a dime"; etc.*]
Sewing, sewing, sewing on our Crazy Quilt—
Singing crazy lyrics with a crazy lilt—
Pulling nifty humor which is bound to have you
     all
Sewing, sewing, sewing on our Crazy Quilt in
     stitches;
For we love to do designing in sunny silver
     lining.

[*16-bar dance to "Sewing"*]

[*Repeat "Howda do" chorus*]
Seeyagain, Papa—Seeyagain, Mamma—
Seeyagain, customers.
Having said which we exit laughingly.

THE WHOLE WORLD'S TURNING BLUE

Written in 1924. Music by Lewis E. Gensler. Lyrics by Morrie Ryskind and Ira Gershwin. Possibly intended for *Be Yourself* (1924).

VERSE

Once the highbrows, when they heard the blues,
Lifted eyebrows—but they've changed their
     views.
The years advance; we keep advancing with 'em;
And now we dance to that entrancing rhythm.
It is taking all the world by storm—
It is shaking ev'ry human form—
And you will be doing it, too.

REFRAIN 1

You'll find the whole world's turning blue,
From the Himalayas to Peru.
Ev'rybody struts—It's the only thing to do.
They say that every foreign Tom, Dick, and
     Jerry can
Sing tunes distinctly American.
They're hot—All the world is mad;
They've got the fever bad.
I know a guy who lived pretty high;
In England, they called him a baronet.
He joined the mob—He gave up his job
To play in a band on a clarinet.
Why, ev'ry name that's in *Who's Who*
Does a shimmy just like me and you—
Because the twirling, whirling world is turning
     blue.

REFRAIN 2

You'll find the whole world's turning blue,
From the Himalayas to Peru.
Ev'rybody struts—it's the only thing to do.
Someday they'll send the best trombone-playin'
     resident
To Washington to be president—
Hey! Hey! Hotsy-totsy too!
Dey! Dey! Red, white, and blue!
I know a state that's not up to date,
Where even the emperor lacks a phone;
But he's not so lax; he put through a tax
That got him enough for a saxophone.
Of course, you know the goings on
Of that little fellow—Roger Kahn.
You'll find this twirling, whirling world is
     turning blue.

AT 11 P.M.

Composer unknown. Lyric credited to "I. B. Gershwin." No music is known to survive. The lyric seems to have been written in the early months of 1924.

VERSE

There's one hour of the night
When virtue reigns supreme;
When ev'rything turns out all right
And all is peaches and cream.
You'd think that life was staged in heaven
By the way we see it at eleven.

REFRAIN 1

True sweethearts are again united;
True lovers clutched in fond embrace.
Her future no longer will be blighted
Because she owned a winning face.
The mortgage they find can be extended.
They've foiled the villain's stratagem.
And it's too bad that virtue's reign is ended
When the curtain falls at eleven P.M.
(And on matinées at five).

REFRAIN 2

The man with the silk hat is an oilcan;
His past is just dripping with gore.
They find that a self-respecting goil can
Be trusted with that scoundrel no more.
All night, he's been cutting dirty capers.
As a villain, he sure was a gem.
Thank God! that the hero's found the papers!
When the curtain falls at eleven P.M.
(And on matinées at five).

REFRAIN 3

That vampire was such a deadly sinner!
We're glad when she gets it in the neck.
She's skinny—but soon she'll get much thinner:
In prison, she'll soon become a wreck.
The hero has foiled the strong banditti;
An ending we could never condemn—
Ah! Virtue *always* wins in this big city,
When the curtain falls at eleven P.M.
(And on matinées at five).

DEAR OLD CORRESPONDENCE SCHOOL

Composer unknown. Probably written in 1924. No music is known to survive.

VERSE

I've often wanted a class reunion
Where I could cheer and play the fool.
And here we are in glad communion,
Alumni of a grand old school.
Though I've never seen my little old college
Somewhere back in Scranton, P A. Ah!
Compared to it I am forced to acknowledge
All the other schools are blah!

REFRAIN 1

Dear old correspondence alma mater—
No seat of learning ever was so clear.
We could learn to write like Walter Pater
Or else become a radio engineer.

We were taught a lot of things unknown to Yale
    men;
Detective courses taught us how to trail men.

Oh, the thrill when we were summoned by the
    mailmen
In the dear old correspondence school.

REFRAIN 2

[*Repeat first 7 lines of refrain 1*]
In our dear but not so very expensive school.

Additional endings:

After four years we went to the postal station.
The tears were falling; we felt great elation;
We were celebrating final graduation
From our dear old correspondence school.

There were no flighty coeds there to vamp us.
You could tell we were in earnest when you'd
    lamp us.
In my kitchen, I would walk along the campus
Of my dear old correspondence school.

KISS ME, THAT'S ALL

Music by Philip Charig. Since the only typescript of this lyric attributes it to "Ira B. Gershwin," it was written in 1924 or earlier. 1919, the last prior year when he wrote under the name Ira B. Gershwin, would seem too early since Charig, born in 1902, would have been only seventeen.

VERSE

I know the way
To make life gay.
I am the joy—
Bringing boy.
My specialty
Fills you with glee.
You'll say it's great
When I demonstrate.

REFRAIN

Girls, I've studied osculation,
In most every modern nation;
Your lips are my avocation,
Don't waste 'em
I taste 'em.
Try a sample of my kisses
Oh, you lovely maids and misses
If you want to know what bliss is,
Just kiss me, that's all.

PRIMROSE, 1924

Tryout: no information. London run: Winter Garden, opened September 11, 1924. 255 performances. Music by George Gershwin. Lyrics by Desmond Carter and Ira Gershwin. Produced by George Grossmith and J.A.E. Malone. Book by George Grossmith and Guy Bolton. Book staged by George Grossmith and Charles A. Maynard. Dances and ensembles by Laddie Cliff and Carl Hyson. Orchestra under the direction of John Ansell. Orchestrations by George Gershwin, Frank Saddler, and, possibly, John Ansell. Cast, starring Heather Thatcher (Pinkie Peach—Mme. Frazeline), Percy Heming (Hilary Vane), Margery Hicklin (Joan), and Leslie Henson (Toby Mopham), featured Claude Hulbert (Freddie Falls), Vera Lennox (May Rooker), Guy Fare (Sir Benjamin Falls), Thomas Weguelin (Michael), Ernest Graham (Jason), Ruth Taylor (Mrs. Warrender), Muriel Barnby (Lady Sophia Mopham), and Sylvia Hawkes (Pritchard).

For the lyrics to "Boy Wanted" and "Four Little Sirens" (also known as "The Sirens"), see *A Dangerous Maid* (1921). All other lyrics for *Primrose*, except those that follow, are by Desmond Carter alone.

ISN'T IT WONDERFUL

Published September 1924. Lyrics by Ira Gershwin and Desmond Carter. Introduced by Margery Hicklin (Joan) and ensemble. Original title: "Once There Were Two of Us (Now We're Only One)." The version performed in *Primrose* was based on an earlier lyric of Ira's alone; the published version contained additional alterations.

Original Version

VERSE 1

HE: Just before Dan Cupid knew of us,*
    Honeybunch, you can't deny
    That you were simply you of us,
    And that I was only I.
    So you see that there were two of us
    In the lonesome days gone by.

---

*Alternate version of verse 1, lines 1–5:
    Before Dan Cupid knew of us,
    My dear, you can't deny
    That you were simply you of us,
    And I was only I.
    Yes, there were really two of us

Darling, now at ev'ry meeting
I can hear my heart repeating:

REFRAIN

Isn't it wonderful!
Once there were two of us—
Now we're only one.
The stormy weather has passed,
And we're together at last.
Before our meeting we only existed;*
Now living has really begun.
Heaven, dear, knew of us,
When there were two of us,
So now we're only one.

VERSE 2

SHE: Darling, we are one for evermore;
    And my heart's no longer free.
    And I vow that never, nevermore,
    Any other man there'll be.
    Ev'ry day, dear, I'll endeavor more
    To bring happiness, you'll see.
    We will share the joys and sorrows
    Brought by all the new tomorrows.

REPEAT REFRAIN

Primrose Version

VERSE 1

JOAN: Any man who would appeal to me
    Must appeal in ev'ry way,
    Like the man my dreams reveal to me;
    I can see him ev'ry day.
    Oh, it all seems very real to me,
    And I know what he would say;
    For he seems so near my heart stops
        beating
    When I hear his voice repeating:

REFRAIN 1
[Same as in original version]

INTERLUDE

That's what he'll have to say to me.
I know he'll come someday to me.
No other man can wake my heart.
He'll take my heart, I know.

Alternate version of refrain, lines 6–7:
    Though we existed before we were married,
    Life has just really begun.

VERSE 2

MEN: We would steal your heart forevermore,
    If the way we only knew.
    Ev'ry day we would endeavor more
    To bring happiness to you.
    For we know that never, nevermore
    Shall we find a heart so true.
JOAN: But my heart will never go a-straying
    Till I hear the right one saying:

REFRAIN 2

MEN: Isn't it wonderful!
    Once there were two of us—
    Now we're only one.
    The stormy weather has passed,
    And we're together at last.
    But while you're waiting and hoping to
        find him,
    With others you might have begun.
    Why not a few of us?
    Just one or two of us?
JOAN: No, I want only one.

Published Version

VERSE 2

He will steal my heart forevermore,
Though today that heart is free.
And I vow that never, nevermore
Any other man there'll be.
Ev'ry day he will endeavour more
To bring happiness to me;
But my heart will never go a-straying
Till I hear the right one saying:

SOME FARAWAY SOMEONE

Published September 1924. Lyrics by Ira Gershwin and
B. G. DeSylva. Introduced in *Primrose* by Percy Heming (Hilary) and Margery Hicklin (Joan). Alternate title:
"Some Sweet Faraway Someone." The music had originally been used for the song "At Half Past Seven" (lyrics
by B. G. DeSylva) in the revue *Nifties of 1923*.

VERSE 1

HILARY: It is never too late for man to mend;
    And though at times, no doubt,
    We pick the wrong ones out,
    To discover the right one I intend.

She may be far away;
She may turn up today;
But I've made up my mind to find her
    in the end.

REFRAIN 1

There's some sweet faraway someone
Who'll soon be nearer to me,
And when we meet I'll show my new
    love
What true love
Can be.
I'll lose my heart to no other.
The one I'm waiting to see
Is that sweet faraway someone who
Will soon be nearer to me.

VERSE 2

JOAN: That's a dangerous thing for you to say.
    To find her you may try
    And yet may pass her by.
    You've known dozens of girls before
        today,
    And why should you suppose
    She wasn't one of those?
    You may have met her and have let her
        go away.

REFRAIN 2

HILARY: There's some sweet faraway someone
    Who'll soon be nearer to me.
    And when we meet I'll show my new
        love
    What true love
    Can be.
    I always flirt with each new one*
    To make quite certain that she
    Is *not* that faraway someone who
    Will soon be nearer to—
JOAN: Soon be dearer to—
BOTH: Soon be nearer to me.

Alternate version of refrain 2, lines 6–9:
    I know I'm going to find her;
    I almost fancy I see
    That some sweet faraway someone who
    Will soon be nearer to me.

WAIT A BIT, SUSIE

Published September 1924. Lyrics by Desmond Carter and Ira Gershwin. Introduced by Percy Heming (Hilary), Margery Hicklin (Joan), and ensemble. The same music was used later for "Beautiful Gypsy," intended for but not used in *Rosalie* (1928).

VERSE 1

HILARY: Susie wasn't mad about
A dozen men or so.
She was only sad about
Just one—'cause he was slow.
Susie said to her mother,
"He's in love with some other."
But her mother said, "My dear,
Don't lose your little head, my dear.
Those tears you needn't shed, my dear,
I know."

REFRAIN

Wait a bit, Susie.
Wait a bit, Susie.
There is someone who
Some fine day
Will come and say
He loves you.
Someone who's lonely,
Someone who only
Wonders what to do;
Watching, waiting,
Hesitating,
Too.
He doesn't say much when you're
there
But he's a bit shy.
Doesn't know yet if he dare—
But he's going to try.
Wait a bit, Susie.
Wait a bit, Susie.
If you only knew
Someone's set
His heart on getting
You.

VERSE 2

JOAN: Though she didn't care about
The other men she met,
She was in despair about
The one she couldn't get—
Wished that something
Would wake him,
Felt she wanted to shake him.

Life looked very gray to her;
Each hour was like a day to her;
But something seemed to say to her,
"Don't fret."

REPEAT REFRAIN

NAUGHTY BABY

Published September 1924, but probably written at least one year earlier. Lyrics by Ira Gershwin and Desmond Carter (based on an earlier lyric by Ira alone). Introduced by Margery Hicklin (Joan) and ensemble.

Original Version

VERSE

Always find you at the Ritz or Plaza;
Tell me, won't you ever settle down?
Honestly, I think there never was a
Girl so naughty in this town.
Don't you think it's time
You thought of someone
Who keeps thinking there's no one like you?
One who loves you dearly—yours sincerely—

REFRAIN

Naughty baby, naughty baby, hold me closer.
Naughty baby, naughty baby, don't say "No,
sir!"
You're the cutest little winner
That I know.
You could make a saint a sinner—
You're so sweet! Oh!
Won't you take me, dear, and make me glad
I found you?
Let the others be your brothers when they're
'round you.
If you're looking for a daddy,
Can't you see
That there's no laddie
Who could daddy you like me?

Primrose Version

VERSE 1

JOAN: If you want a girl who's sentimental,
One who'll never set you in a whirl,
One who will be always sweet and gentle,
I am not that sort of girl.

But if you prefer a rather swift one,
If you think you'd like to run around
With a bright one,
I am just the right one.

REFRAIN 1

Naughty baby, naughty baby, who will
tease you.
I can show the way and know the way to
please you.
If you're wanting a beginner,
I shan't do.
I can make a saint a sinner
When I want to.
If you find the simple kind are rather
slow, dear,
Then you ought to try a naughty one, you
know, dear
But you'll never meet another who will be
A naughty baby, naughty baby, just like
me.

VERSE 2

I'm the sort of girl you might expect to
Flirt with ev'ry fellow that she knew;
Just the sort your mother would object to
If she saw me out with you.
But I always do the things I want to.
Ev'ryone will tell you that I show
Too much stocking;
I am simply shocking.

REFRAIN 2

MEN: Naughty baby, naughty baby, we adore
you.
Say you'll stay and let us lay our hearts
before you.
We're not wanting a beginner:
You'll just do.
Let us take you out to dinner:
We should love to.
We're depressed because the rest are
rather slow, dear.
You're not shy and that is why we love
you so, dear.
Ev'ryone of us is longing to pursue
A naughty baby, naughty baby, just like
you.

LYRIC FOR COUNTERMELODY TO REFRAIN

MEN: Naughty baby, we love you.
Though you may be bad, it's true.
Please don't go;
For though we've been warned about you,

You must know
That we want you so.
Can't you see that
We'd be glad to keep you here?
We're all mad to have you near.
We'd pursue
The whole day through
A naughty baby, naughty baby, just like
you.

THE VOICE OF LOVE
(CELLINI'S LOVE SONG)

Published December 1924. Music by Robert Russell Bennett and Maurice Nitke. Written for the New York production of Edwin Justus Mayer's *The Firebrand*, which opened on October 15, 1924. More than twenty years later, Ira wrote lyrics for *The Firebrand of Florence* (1945), a musical version of the play.

VERSE

Day is done and the sun descends in red
  splendor;
Ev'ry rose now is dozing in sweet surrender.
Through the murmur of the trees,
Hear the linnet singing
Soft and silver music as homeward he is
  winging,
Echoing tender yearnings to the breeze.
But hearken all else above
To the voice of love.

REFRAIN

Hark, fairest maid,
To my plaintive serenade;
The voice of love is calling,
Calling to you
To brighten up our rendezvous
While the dusk is falling;
Bidding you make the night enthralling
Is the voice of love.

YOU MUST COME OVER
BLUES

Published September 1925. Music by Lewis E. Gensler. Intended for *Be Yourself* (1924) but not used in that

show. In 1925, the song was added to the score of *Captain Jinks* (opened in New York on September 8, 1925—107 performances), in which it was introduced by Arthur West and Marion Sunshine. In the published version, only one verse and one refrain of the lyric were included, and they were incorrectly credited to B. G. DeSylva. When the mistake was found, the proofs were changed (an additional verse and refrain of the lyrics were typeset, and Ira was properly credited), but Ira, writing in 1956, expressed his doubt that the corrected version had ever been actually published. On February 16, 1978, Michael Feinstein noted on a sheet accompanying Ira Gershwin's file copy of the song that "the corrected proof was never released."

VERSE 1

There are some dames who, lamping men,
Are all intent on vamping men,
And I am here to warn you of the same.
Singing their little song for you,
They tell you they are strong for you—
"You must come over, dearie!" they exclaim.
For instance, Mrs. Potiphar—
Can you imagine what if her
Maneuvering had ever won the day!
We'd put up no security
For Joseph and his purity—
But Joe was hep and didn't want to play.

REFRAIN 1

She had the *You*-must-come-over,
You-*must*-come-over,
You-*must*-come-over blues.
She was the sort of weaker vessel,
Who always wants to wrestle.
Take my advice, and let 'em alone;
Always think twice whenever they moan:
"I've got the *You*-must-come-over,
You-*must*-come-over,
You-*must*-come-over blues!"

VERSE 2

Really, it's simply scandalous
How some of them manhandle us;
That dame Delilah is Exhibit Two.
She didn't care for writing men—
But she was hot for fighting men—
So did her stuff when Samson came in view.
She said, "Come out Delilah way—
The evening we will while away—
I've got a case of hootch for you and me."
History tells how Sam came out—
A lion went in, and a lamb came out;
No more was he the man he used to be.

REFRAIN 2

She had the *You*-must-come-over,
You-*must*-come-over,
You-*must*-come-over blues.
When first he met her he was virile,
But soon he changed his name to Cyril.
Sailor, beware! The moral is this—
Always take care whenever they hiss:
"I've got the *You*-must-come-over,
You-*must*-come-over,
You-*must*-come-over blues!"

VERSE 3

There was a Jane in Italy,
Who did things rather prettily—
Lucretia Borgia is the gal I mean.
She was born high—a royal dame,
But she was not a loyal dame—
Oh, what a vamp she'd make upon the screen!*
Her victims were so numerous,
It got to be quite humorous;
With her a noble knight would last a day.
After she'd feed him certain drops—†
Upon his life the curtain drops—
And if you wonder how he got that way:

REFRAIN 3

She had the *You*-must-come-over,
You-*must*-come-over,
You-*must*-come-over blues!
She used to love to call the boys in‡
And hand them cocktails made of poison.
Don't be a chump—Boy! Let 'em alone!§
Hop, skip, and jump whenever they groan:
"I've got the *You*-must-come-over,
You-*must*-come-over,
You-*must*-come-over blues!"

Alternate version of verse 3, line 6:
Oh, what a screen vamp Lucy would have been!
†*Alternate version of verse 3, lines 10–11:*
If he ate what she'd feed to him,
The funeral pray'r they'd read to him.
‡*Alternate version of refrain 3, line 3:*
She used to love to lead the boys on
§*Alternate version of refrain 3, lines 5–6:*
Sailor, beware—Avast and belay!
Always take care—whenever they say:

OVERLEAF: *Adele and Fred Astaire*

LADY, BE GOOD!
1924

Tryout: Forrest Theatre, Philadelphia, November 17, 1924. New York run: Liberty Theatre, opened December 1, 1924. 330 performances. Music by George Gershwin. Lyrics almost entirely by Ira Gershwin. Produced by Alex A. Aarons and Vinton Freedley. Book by Guy Bolton and Fred Thompson. Book staged by Felix Edwardes. Dances staged by Sammy Lee. Orchestra under the direction of Paul Lannin. Orchestrations by Robert Russell Bennett, Charles N. Grant, Paul Lannin, Stephen O. Jones, Max Steiner, and William Daly. Cast, starring Fred Astaire (Dick Trevor) and Adele Astaire (Susie Trevor), featured Walter Catlett (J. Watterson "Watty" Watkins), Cliff "Ukulele Ike" Edwards (Jeff), Alan Edwards (Jack Robinson), Gerald Oliver Smith (Bertie Bassett), Kathlene Martyn (Shirley Vernon), Patricia Clarke (Daisy Parke), Jayne Auburn (Josephine Vanderwater), and James Bradbury (Rufus Parke). Victor Arden and Phil Ohman at the pianos.

London run: Empire Theatre, opened April 14, 1926. 325 performances. Produced by Alfred Butt with Alex A. Aarons and Vinton Freedley. Staged by Felix Edwardes and Max Scheck. Orchestra conducted by Jacques Heuvel. Cast, starring Fred Astaire (Dick Trevor) and Adele Astaire (Susie Trevor), featured William Kent (J. Watterson Watkins), Buddy Lee (Jeff), George Vollaire (Jack Robinson), Ewart Scott (Bertie Bassett), Irene Russell (Shirley Vernon), Glori Beaumont (Daisy Parke), Sylvia Leslie (Josephine Vanderwater), and Denier Warren (Rufus Parke).

The following lyrics are missing: "Leave It to Love" and "Laddie Daddie."

HANG ON TO ME

Published December 1924. Introduced by Fred and Adele Astaire (Dick and Susie Trevor).

VERSE

Trouble may hound us,
Shadow surround us—
Never mind, my dear.
Don't be downhearted;
When we get started,
They will disappear.
Listen to brother:
While we've each other,
There's no need to fear;
For like Hansel and Gretel,
We will prove our mettle.

REFRAIN

If you hang on to me
While I hang on to you,
We'll dance into the sunshine, out of the rain
(Forever and a day).
Don't sigh—we'll get along;
Just try humming a song,
And my! Soon we shall hear the bluebird again.
That's right! Hold tight!
We're on our way!
Uphill until
We lose the shadows.
If you hang on to me,
While I hang on to you,
We'll dance into the sunshine, out of the rain.
(Forever and a day,
We'll make December May—
That's all I have to say.)

A WONDERFUL PARTY

Introduced by ensemble. Added during the pre-Broadway tryout. In London programs, titled "Oh, What a Lovely Party."

GUESTS: Oh, what a lovely party
This is going to be!
This sort of party
Always appeals to me.

I'm looking forward to
A night of pleasure,
As we go dancing through
Each raggy measure.

Oh, what a lovely party!
Everyone will be there!
They say this party
Is to be some affair.

MAN: [to flunky]
Good evening, tell us, do—
Is this the way in?
FLUNKY: Good evening, sir, to you—
This is the way in.
GUESTS: Sounds like our entrance cue—
Let's start to stray in.

GUESTS: [exiting]
Oh, what a lovely party
This is going to be!
This sort of party
Always appeals to me.

END OF A STRING

Introduced by ensemble.

GIRLS: Love is a gamble
If you scramble
For the very first man who comes along.
Don't be a-flutter;
Bread your butter;
He may be the worst man who comes
along.
A chance for romance is meager
When a maiden is too eager;
She may lose the one big leaguer,
Falling for the first man who comes
along.
The proper angle
Is to let them dangle—
Is to let them dangle on a string;
And have aplenty—
Really, ten or twenty—
Really, ten or twenty is the thing.

But here tonight, with the moon so bright
And the music in the air,
I very much fear, the first cavalier
Can win this lady fair.

But here tonight, with the moon so bright
And the music in the air,
I very much fear, the first cavalier
Can win this lady fair.

BOYS: Love is a gamble
If you scramble,
But we'll take the first girl who comes
along.
We'll do our duty
To each cutie,
And we'll take the first girl who comes
along.
On with the dancing,
Flirting and romancing,
Flirting and romancing so sublime.
Let's throw all care off
And begin to pair off,
And begin to pair off—Now's the time.

BOTH: Someone waits for me,
Wonder who he (she) will be,
On the end of a string.
Maybe Fred or Ned, Teddy or Jed,
(Maybe Chloe or Jo, Floey or Zoe,)
On the end of a string.
If full of pep, he'll find a peppy partner
in me;
I want to step and step until it's way after
three;

Oh! Someone waits for me, wonder who
   he (she) will be,
On the end of my string.

WE'RE HERE BECAUSE

Introduced by Patricia Clarke (Daisy Parke), Gerald Oliver Smith (Bertie Bassett), and ensemble. Clarke replaced Cecil Bruner during the pre-Broadway tryout. Introduced in London by Glori Beaumont, Ewart Scott, and ensemble.

VERSE 1

Philosophers the whole world over often put this
   query:
"Why are we here?"
But none of them has found the answer to the
   question, dearie:
"Why are we here?"
And so, why others occupy this planet I've not
   learned;
But oh! My heart informs me that where we're
   concerned—

REFRAIN 1

We're here, we're here, we're here because
I love you and because you love me.
It's plain to see, it's clear as can be,
We're here because, we're here because,
My dear, my dear, my dear, because I'm made
   for you
And you're made for me.
Ev'ry time we are together,
This is the thought that thrills me through—
We're here, we're here, we're here because
You love me and because I love you.

VERSE 2

Now, though you know that I agree with you,
   dear, on your viewpoint:
Why we are here;
There's something I should like to add—It's just
   another new point:
Why we are here.
I'm not a bit old-fashioned, so I would be
   overjoyed*
To psychoanalyze the question à la Freud.

*Original scripts read:
And so if you'll permit me, darling, I'd be overjoyed

REFRAIN 2

We're here, we're here, we're here because
I love you and because you love me.
We're here because there's nobody near,
And so you know there's naught to fear
If you should try to cuddle close
And maybe steal a kiss—or maybe two.
When you're obeying that impulse,
Tell me, my dear, don't you agree,
We're here, we're here, we're here because
I love you and because you love me?

FASCINATING RHYTHM

Published December 1924. Introduced by Fred and Adele Astaire (Dick and Susie Trevor) and Cliff Edwards (Jeff). Introduced in London by Fred and Adele Astaire and Buddy Lee. Earlier title: "Syncopated City." (A George Gershwin pencil manuscript of a musical verse, refrain, and interlude discovered in 1982 at the Warner Bros. Music warehouse in Secaucus, New Jersey, bears the title "Syncopated City." No lyric for this title survives.) The British edition of the sheet music contains additional lyrics (for a second verse) that are probably not by Ira Gershwin. See also "Little Rhythm, Go 'Way" (page 31).

> My first eight bars were composed in London, when I was there putting on a show [*Primrose*]. . . . When I returned to New York, I played this theme for my brother Ira. He mulled it over for a while and then came through with a perfect title for the theme. However, it wasn't all as easy as that, for the title covered part of the first bar only, and there was many a hot argument between us as to where the accent should fall in the rest of the words. You see, the theme repeated itself, but each time on a new accent. . . . If you saw the show, you remember that "Ukulele Ike" [Cliff Edwards] sang the verse and chorus, followed by a miraculous dance by Fred and Adele Astaire. The song was played by an orchestra which featured Ohman and Arden in the pit—so—who could ask for anything more?
> —George Gershwin, 1934

The following note is excerpted from Isaac Goldberg's *George Gershwin* (Simon and Schuster, 1931):

" 'When George was in London doing *Primrose*,' Ira relates, 'he wrote the first eight bars of what afterwards became Fascinating Rhythm. Alex Aarons, who was with him, and who is one of the keenest judges of a smart tune among the managers, told him to develop it for the next show. George didn't finish the tune until weeks later in New York. It was a tricky rhythm for those days, and it took me several days to decide on the rhyme scheme. I didn't think I had *the* brilliant title in Fascinating Rhythm but A, it *did* sing smoothly, and B,—I couldn't think of a better. The rhyme scheme was a, b, a, c,—a, b, a, c. When I got to the 8th line I showed the lyric to George. His comment was that the 4th and 8th lines should have a double (or two-syllable) rhyme where I had rhymed them with single syllables. I protested and, by singing, showed him the last note in both lines had the same strength as the note preceding. To me the last two notes in these lines formed a spondee; the easiest way out was arbitrarily to put the accent on the last note. But this George couldn't see, and so, on and off, we argued for days. Finally I had to capitulate and write the lines as they are today:

4th line: I'm all a-*quiv*er.
8th line: —Just like a *fliv*ver,

after George proved to me that I had better use the double rhyme; because, whereas in singing, the notes might be considered even, in conducting the music, the downbeat came on the penultimate note.' "

My father was not unmusical, but sometimes he couldn't recall the title of a song as clearly as he could the melody. To him this one frequently was "Fashion on the River."
   —from *Lyrics on Several Occasions*

VERSE

Got a little rhythm, a rhythm, a rhythm
That pit-a-pats through my brain;
So darn persistent,
The day isn't distant
When it'll drive me insane.
Comes in the morning
Without any warning,
And hangs around me all day.
I'll have to sneak up to it
Someday, and speak up to it.
I hope it listens when I say:

REFRAIN

Fascinating Rhythm,
You've got me on the go!
Fascinating Rhythm,
I'm all a-quiver.

What a mess you're making!
The neighbors want to know
Why I'm always shaking
Just like a flivver.

Each morning I get up with the sun—
Start a-hopping,
Never stopping—
To find at night no work has been done.

I know that
Once it didn't matter—
But now you're doing wrong;
When you start to patter
I'm so unhappy.

Won't you take a day off?
Decide to run along
Somewhere far away off—
And make it snappy!

Oh, how I long to be the man I used to be!
Fascinating Rhythm,
Oh, won't you stop picking on me?

Version Sung in "Finale Ultimo"

WATTY: [*to Josephine*] Fascinating wedding,
    Say, that appeals to me.
    Fascinating wedding,
    I hear you calling.

BERTIE: [*to Daisy*] Why not make it double?
    Oh, say that you agree.
    Save a lot of trouble—

DAISY: It sounds enthralling.

DICK: [*to Shirley*] And now that my
        engagement is through,
    I'm a chappie
    Who is happy.
    What's to stop me from marrying you?

SUSIE: [*to Jack*] You told me of a señorita—
    You said that you were wed
    To this señorita;
    Now how about it?

JACK: [*to Susie*] Well, I meant Juanita;
    I looked a bit ahead.
    You're that señorita
    And don't you doubt it.

MEN: Oh, what a busy day in church
    There's going to be.
    Fascinating wedding,
    You're calling my lady and me.

In preparing *Lyrics on Several Occasions*, Ira Gershwin revised the "Finale Ultimo" lyrics for inclusion as follows:

"*F*inale Ultimo" Note. In the Twenties it was almost *de rigueur* in the finale of a show to wind up the plot and relationships by setting new lyrics to one of the principal songs. For example: In *Lady, Be Good!* four couples, each formerly at odds, reunited at eleven p.m. each evening to "Fascinating Rhythm." After a cue such as "How about our getting hitched?" the first couple sang:

Fascinating wedding,
That sure appeals to me.
Fascinating wedding,
I hear you calling.

Second pair:
Why not make it double?
Please say that you agree.
Saves a lot of trouble
And sounds enthralling.

Third set:
Now that misunderstanding is through,
Aren't we silly
Being chilly?
What's to stop me from marrying you?

In the next eight bars the fourth couple decided they too would merge, and in the last eight the four suddenly engaged men, *unisono*, wound up with:

Oh, what a busy day in church
There's going to be.
Fascinating wedding,
You're calling my lady and me.

1940s Revision

VERSE

It's like our nation,*
A conglomeration;
It isn't any one thing.
Somehow you can't confine it,
And no one could define it.
It's just a rhythm that you sing:

REFRAIN

Fascinating Rhythm,
Oh! Never let it stop!
That Manhattan rhythm—
The joint is jumping.

What an orchestration
Of classic and of bop!
Fills you with elation;
Your cares you're dumping!

The taxi horns and planes up above
(Riff and bop it—
Never stop it!)
Join in that symphony that I love.

The nightclubs
Turn you topsy-turvy.
The girls are pure delight.
Ev'ry one so curvy,
You can't resist 'em.

These lines would replace verse, lines 6–12.

Broadway and its chatter
To music day and night
And to subway clatter,
Oh! How I've missed 'em.

It sends your spirits flying high, won't let you
    down!
Fascinating Rhythm,
The rhythm of Old New York Town.

SO AM I

Published January 1925. Introduced by Alan Edwards (Jack Robinson) and Adele Astaire (Susie Trevor). It replaced "Will You Remember Me?" during rehearsals. Introduced in the London production by George Vollaire and Adele Astaire. The British edition of the sheet music contains additional lyrics (for a second verse) that are probably not by Ira Gershwin.

Show Version

VERSE

JACK: Just before I go, I'd like to know
    If maybe now and then you'll give a
        thought to me.
SUSIE: Yes, I think I can—In fact, I plan
    To keep you in a corner of my memory.
    It won't be hard to think of you each day;
    But I'm afraid when you are far away,
    Maybe you'll grow fond
    Of something blonde.
JACK: No, that will never, never be!

REFRAIN 1

JACK: Leaving you—
    Me oh my! I am blue—
SUSIE: So am I.
JACK: When I leave—
SUSIE: Will you sigh?
JACK: I shall grieve—
SUSIE: So shall I.
BOTH: Isn't it just wonderful how we agree!
    Plain to see it's not a case of you for
        you—me for me.
JACK: Hope we meet by and by—
SUSIE: Funny thing—So do I.

REFRAIN 2

JACK: I am poor—Me oh my!
SUSIE: That's all right—So am I.

JACK: Cross my heart, hope to die—Feel a
thrill—
SUSIE: So do I.
BOTH: Isn't it just wonderful how we agree!
Makes me think that maybe I was meant
for you—you for me.
JACK: How I hate this good-bye!
SUSIE: Funny thing—So do I.

REFRAIN 3

JACK: Leaving you—Me oh my! I am blue.
SUSIE: So am I.
[Dance]
JACK: I'm in love, how I sigh!
SUSIE: Don't be sil'—So am I.

ENCORE REFRAIN

JACK: Know a girl: nice as pie, sweet as sugar—
SUSIE: So am I.
JACK: Must confess, can't deny, I love her—
SUSIE: So do I.
BOTH: Isn't it just wonderful how we agree!
Feel that all the world's in tune with such
divine harmony.
JACK: I've lots to say, but I'm shy. Guess I'm
scared—
SUSIE: [Throwing arms around him] So am I.

ENCORE REFRAIN 2

JACK: This can't be—Me oh my! I'm just a
bum—
SUSIE: So am—[He stops her]
[Dance, then—]
JACK: Well, good-bye.
SUSIE: Well, good-bye.
JACK: Well, good-bye.
SUSIE: Well, good-bye.

ACT II REPRISE

SUSIE: He was grand, how I sigh, what a man!
JACK: So am I.
SUSIE: He was kind, sweet as pie, he could love!
JACK: So can I!
I'm sure I could double for him easily.
Seems to me that I am just like him,
And he, just like me.
SUSIE: He was smart, me oh my, he was wise!
JACK: So am I!

Published Version

VERSE 1

JACK: Just before I go, I'd like to know
If maybe now and then you'll give a
thought to me.
SUSIE: Yes, I think I can—In fact, I plan
To keep you in a corner of my memory.
It won't be hard to think of you each day;
But I'm afraid when you are far away,
Maybe you'll grow fond
Of something blonde.
JACK: No, that will never, never be!

REFRAIN 1

JACK: Leaving you—
Me oh my! I am blue—
SUSIE: So am I.
JACK: When I leave—
SUSIE: Will you sigh?
JACK: I shall grieve—
SUSIE: So shall I.
BOTH: Isn't it just wonderful how we agree!
Plain to see it's not a case of you for
you—me for me.
JACK: Hope we meet by and by—
SUSIE: Funny thing—So do I.

REFRAIN 2

JACK: Cross my heart, hope to die—Feel a
thrill—
SUSIE: So do I.
JACK: But I'm poor—
SUSIE: Me oh my! That's all right—So am I.
BOTH: Isn't it just wonderful how we agree!
Makes me think that maybe I was meant
for you—you for me.
JACK: I'm in love, how I sigh!
SUSIE: Don't be sil'—So am I.

OH, LADY, BE GOOD!

Published December 1924. Introduced by Walter Catlett (Watty) and ladies of the ensemble. Or as Ira Gershwin wrote in *Lyrics on Several Occasions:* by "Walter
Catlett, as breezy lawyer J. Watterson Watkins, to a flock
of flappers." Introduced in London by William Kent
and ladies of the ensemble. In *Lyrics on Several Occasions*, Ira Gershwin also noted, " 'Oh, Lady, Be Good!'
was written for a show whose working title was *Black-*

Eyed Susan. At one of our pre-rehearsal conferences,
when librettists Bolton and Thompson heard this song,
they decided to jilt *Susan* and to call the show *Lady, Be
Good!*"

Show Version

VERSE 1

What a killing we could make;
Oh, lady, oh, please come through!
Susie, oh, for goodness' sake;
It isn't so hard to do.
In this moment of distress
Hear my S.O.S.
All my future is at stake,
And, Susie, it's up to you.
So—

REFRAIN 1

Oh, sweet and lovely lady, be good.
Oh, Susie, be good to me!
I am so awf'ly misunderstood,
So, Susie, be good to me.
Oh, please have some pity—
I'm all alone in this big city.
I tell you
I'm just a lonesome babe in the wood,
So, Susie, be good to me.

VERSE 2

Listen to my tale of woe,
It's terribly sad, but true:
All dressed up, no place to go,
Each ev'ning I'm awf'ly blue.
I must win some winsome miss;
Can't go on like this.
I could blossom out, I know,
With somebody just like you.
So—

REFRAIN 2

Oh, sweet and lovely lady, be good.
Oh, lady, be good to me!
I am so awf'ly misunderstood,
So, lady, be good to me.
This is tulip weather;
So let's put two and two together.
I tell you
I'm just a lonesome babe in the wood,
So, lady, be good to me.

ACT II REPRISE (JACK)

Oh, sweet and lovely wifey, be good.
Oh, wifey, be good to me!
I've put an end to your widowhood
So, wifey, be good to me.
We should be more clubby—
I hope you're glad to see your hubby.
Or else, dear,
I'll be a lonesome babe in the wood,
Oh, wifey, be good to me.

Published Version

VERSE 1

Listen to my tale of woe,
It's terribly sad, but true:
All dressed up, no place to go,
Each ev'ning I'm awf'ly blue.
I must win some winsome miss;
Can't go on like this.
I could blossom out, I know,
With somebody just like you.
So—

REFRAIN 1

Oh, sweet and lovely lady, be good.
Oh, lady, be good to me!
I am so awf'ly misunderstood,
So, lady, be good to me.
Oh, please have some pity—
I'm all alone in this big city.
I tell you
I'm just a lonesome babe in the wood,
So, lady, be good to me.

VERSE 2

Auburn and brunette and blonde:
I love 'em all, tall or small.
But somehow they don't grow fond;
They stagger but never fall.
Winter's gone, and now it's spring!
Love! where is thy sting?
If somebody won't respond,
I'm going to end it all.
So—

REFRAIN 2

Oh, sweet and lovely lady, be good.
Oh lady, be good to me!
I am so awf'ly misunderstood,
So, lady, be good to me.
This is tulip weather—

So let's put two and two together.
I tell you
I'm just a lonesome babe in the wood,
So, lady, be good to me.

Unused Version for Watty and Susie

VERSE

WATTY: What a killing we could make;
  Oh, lady, oh, please come through!
  You could cut yourself a cake!
  With plenty of icing, too.
SUSIE: I would do it if I dared,
  Watty, but I'm scared.
WATTY: But my future is at stake,
  And, Susie, it's up to you.

REFRAIN

WATTY: Oh, sweet and lovely lady, be good.
  Oh, lady be good to me!
  Things haven't gone as well as they
    should;
  So, lady, be good to me.
SUSIE: Hear me, bad and bold man—
  All I can say is "So's your old man!"
WATTY: Have pity!
  I'm just a lonesome babe in the wood,
  So, lady, be good to me.

Unused Version for Jack

VERSE

Lady, I was always classed
As one who was fancy-free;
But I'm falling, falling fast—
No other girl there can be.
You turned nighttime into day
When you came my way.
Won't you please forget the past
And concentrate just on me?
And—

REFRAIN

Oh, sweet and lovely lady, be good.
Oh, lady, be good to me!
I am so awf'ly misunderstood,
So, lady, be good to me.
Stars above have stated*
That you and I, dear, should be mated.

Alternate version of Jack's refrain, lines 5–6:
This world that we live in
Will be just heaven if you give in.

Have pity!
I'm just a lonesome babe in the wood
Oh, lady, be good to me.

Unused Version for Dick

VERSE

Oh, how I need cheering up,
And, lady, it's up to you.
Sorrow seems to fill my cup—
There's something that you can do.
You can chase away my blues;
Say you won't refuse.
All you have to do, you see,
Is show me some sympathy.
And—

REFRAIN

Oh, sweet and lovely lady, be good.
Oh, lady, be good to me!
Things haven't gone as well as they should,
So, lady, be good to me.
This is tulip weather—
So let's put two and two together.
I tell you
I'm just a lonesome babe in the wood,
So, lady, be good to me.

FINALE, ACT I

Introduced by Adele Astaire (Susie Trevor), Walter Catlett (Watty), and ensemble.

ENSEMBLE: Ting-a-ling, the wedding bells will
    jing-a-ling-a-ling
  For the groom, our Dickie, and his
    bride, our Josephine;
  Ting-a-ling, the wedding bells will
    sing-a-ling-a-ling,
  Wishing them a future that is happy
    and serene.

  Make it soon, and take the month that
    makes a rhyme with "spoon";
  That's the month when newlyweds
    should take their honeymoon.
  Make it soon, and take the month that
    makes a rhyme with "croon";
  That's the month when everybody
    feels the world's in tune.

SUSIE: If you hang on to me,
While I hang on to you,
We'll dance into the sunshine out of
the rain.

WATTY: Sweet little Sue, I knew that you
could—
I knew that you would for me.

LINGER IN THE LOBBY

Introduced by ensemble. Replaced the linked numbers "Weatherman" and "Rainy-Afternoon Girls" during the pre-Broadway tryout. Alternate title: "Opening, Act II."

New York may have its Plaza and Ambassador
and Ritz,
But we in Eastern Harbor have the Robinson;
And there is not a dweller in this city but
admits
That there is no hotel just like the Robinson.
Though adjectives are spilt more
About Manhattan's Biltmore.
With this hotel, we all are satisfied.
New York can keep its Plaza and Ambassador
and Ritz,
As long as Eastern Harbor has its Robinson.

New England laws are blue,*
Permitting no amusement;
With not a thing to do,
We all knew what the blues meant.
But they were chased away
When this hotel was finished—
At last there came a day
When dreariness diminished.

When we've the time to spare,
We linger in the lobby.
In fact, we must declare
It's grown to be a hobby.
The reason should be clear—
You'll understand our passion—
We get the scandal here
And see the latest fashion.

If you want to know what's what, here's the
spot—
You must linger in the lobby of the Robinson
Hotel.
If you want to see *Who's Who* come in view—

This stanza was deleted during the run of the show.

You must linger in the lobby of the Robinson
Hotel.
Foreigners from every clime;
Something doing all the time;
If you want to dish the dirt, want to flirt,
You must linger in the lobby of the Robinson
Hotel.

THE HALF OF IT, DEARIE, BLUES

Published December 1924. Introduced by Kathlene Martyn (Shirley Vernon) and Fred Astaire (Dick Trevor). Martyn replaced Brenda Bond during the pre-Broadway tryout. Introduced in London by Irene Russell and Fred Astaire.

Show Version

VERSE 1

DICK: Each time you trill a song with Bill
Or look at Will, I get a chill—
I'm gloomy.
I won't recall the names of all
The men who fall—It's all appall-
Ing to me.
Of course, I really cannot blame them a
bit,
For you're a hit wherever you flit.
I know it's so, but, dearie, oh!
You'll never know the blues that go
Right through me.

REFRAIN 1

I've got the You-Don't-Know-the-Half-
of-It-Dearie Blues.
The trouble is you have so many from
whom to choose.
If you should marry
Tom, Dick, or Harry,
Life would be the bunk—
I'd become a monk.
I've got the You-Don't-Know-the-Half-
of-It-Dearie Blues!

VERSE 2

SHIRLEY: To Bill and Ben I'd pay atten-
Tion now and then, but really, men
Would bore me.

When I'd begun to think I'd run
And be a nun, I met the one
Man for me.
And now just when the sun is starting
to beam—*
You get engaged—Zip! goes a dream!
What will I do away from you?
I feel the future will be blue
And stormy.

REFRAIN 2

I've got the You-Don't-Know-the-Half-
of-It-Dearie Blues.
It may be my heart isn't broken, but
there's a bruise.
Through you I've known some
Days that were lonesome—
Though you say that I'm
Flirting all the time.
I've got the You-Don't-Know-the-Half-
of-It-Dearie Blues!

REFRAIN 3

I've got the You-Don't-Know-the-Half-
of-It-Dearie Blues.
Although I know that love's a gamble,
I hate to lose.
Life will be duller—
Will have no color;
Jill without a Jack
Makes the future black.
I've got the You-Don't-Know-the-Half-
of-It-Dearie Blues!

REFRAIN 4

JACK: I've got the You-Don't-Know-the-Half-
of-It-Dearie Blues.
Will I walk up the aisle or only watch
from the pews?
With your permission,
My one ambition
Was to go through life
Saying, "Meet the wife."
I've got the You-Don't-Know-the-Half-
of-it-Dearie Blues!

Verse 2, lines 7–12, as revised for Ella Fitzgerald:
I felt a glow—The sun was starting to beam—
Seems I was wrong—Zip! goes a dream.
You're just a guy who makes me cry,
And lately my unclouded sky
Is stormy.

Alternate (Published) Female Version

VERSE

SHIRLEY: You dare assert that you were hurt
Each time I'd flirt with Bill or Bert—
You brute, you!
Well, I'm repaid: I felt betrayed
When any maid whom you surveyed
Would suit you.
Compared to you, I've been as good as
could be;
Yet here you are—lecturing me!
You're just a guy who makes me cry;
Yet though I try to "cut" you, I
Salute you.

REFRAIN

I've got the You-Don't-Know-the-Half-
of-It-Dearie Blues.
Oh, how I wish you'd drop an anchor
and end your cruise.
You're just a duffer
Who makes me suffer;
All the younger set
Says your heart's to let.
I've got the You-Don't-Know-the-Half-
of-It-Dearie Blues!

Additional (Unused) Refrains

I've got the You-Don't-Know-the-Half-of-It-
Dearie Blues.
Each time I try to kiss my baby I get bad news.
She takes new dresses
But no caresses;
Though I come across
It's a total loss—
I've got the You-Don't-Know-the-Half-of-It-
Dearie Blues!

I've got the You-Don't-Know-the-Half-of-It-
Dearie Blues.
You tell me that I have so many from whom to
choose—
The rest mean nothing;
They don't mean *a* thing.
Now that we must part,
Way down in my heart,
I've got the You-Don't-Know-the-Half-of-It-
Dearie Blues!

Patter (Unused)

DICK: I used to be prouder than a chowder
that contains a clam;
But now as a lover, I discover

I am just a ham.
You've started me wond'ring: Are we
blund'ring?
Have we lost the track?
My life is much duller, has no color,
Excepting black.
SHIRLEY: With men I'd go dancing, not
romancing,
Then I'd leave them flat;
They didn't mean *a* thing, really
nothing;
So you see, that's that!
BOTH: I don't want to blame you, all the
same, you
Know you've hurt my pride.
You made me what I am today;
I hope you're satisfied.

JUANITA

Introduced by Adele Astaire (Susie Trevor) and "boys."

VERSE

Tell us, señorita, do they grow
Any more like you
Down in Mexico?
That is something we should like to know;
For, in case they do,
There we'll have to go.
Though love in Spanish,
We can't discuss;
Please don't be clannish
With us.
Hearken to our plaintive serenade,
Fascinating maid:

REFRAIN

Wonderful Juanita,
Dark-eyed señorita,
Blushing tropic rose, so divine,
Could you learn to be a clinging vine?
Never was so sweet a
Maid as you, Juanita.
My heart beating,
Keeps repeating,
"When will Juanita be mine?"

LITTLE JAZZ BIRD

Published December 1924. Introduced by Cliff Edwards (Jeff). Not performed in the London production. The British edition of the sheet music contains additional lyrics (for a second verse) that are probably not by Ira Gershwin.

VERSE 1

Into a cabaret, one fatal day,
A little songbird flew;
Found it so very gay, he thought he'd stay,
Just to get a bird's-eye view.
When he heard the jazz band playing,
He was happy as a lark.
To each measure he kept swaying,
And he stayed till after dark.
Then back to the land he knew, thrilled through
and through,
He sailed on in the air.
Called all the other birds, and in these words
Started gurgling then and there:*

REFRAIN

I'm a little jazz bird,
And I'm telling you to be one, too.
For a little jazz bird
Is in Heaven when it's singing "blue."
I say it with regret,
But you're out of date;
You ain't heard nothin' yet,
Till you syncopate.
When the going is rough,
You will find your troubles all have flown,
If you warble your stuff
Like the moaning of a saxophone.
Just try my recipe,
And I'm sure you'll agree
That a little jazz bird
Is the only kind of bird to be.

SWISS MISS

Lyrics by Arthur Jackson and Ira Gershwin. Introduced by Adele and Fred Astaire (Susie and Dick Trevor).

*I.G.'s lyric sheets read "singing" instead of "gurgling."

Up on the top of a snow-covered mountain
There lived an Alpine miss,
And oh! What a sweet little miss was this.
We mean this little Swiss miss.
While down in the valley below-ho-ho,
Lived a boy who loved her so-ho-ho.
He loved her with all his might;
He loved her day and night.

And ev'ry night just to see this miss
He used to risk his scalp,
For the house where she lived was away up high,
And the poor guy didn't know how to fly.
So he jumped from Alp to Alp.
What a chump—to jump from Alp to Alp!

And then beneath her balcony,
He used to stand around and try to make a hit
    with her.
And he would yodel, "O-lay-o-lee!"
That's the Swiss idea of melody.
And oh! What a yodeling fool was he—
He shook a wicked yodel.

And one night as he stood there,*
The lights were very dim;
While leaning out a bit too far across her
    balcony,
She fell for him.
He sat with his arms around her, until the night
    was gone,
And here's the way they carried on:

He said: "Dear, I think you're just as sweet as
    you can be,
You're like a cake of sweet Swiss chocolate to
    me."
She said: "Oh, my loving one, your talk I can't
    resist;
I hope you're steady as the Swiss watch ticking
    on your wrist."
He said: "How I yearn for you and burn for
    you—I do! I do!
Oh, lady, oh, I swear it on my knees:
My love for you is just as strong
As a piece of Switzer cheese."

*Alternate (script) version:
And one night as she stood there,
The lights were very dim;
While leaning out of the balcony,
She fell for him.

SEEING DICKIE HOME

Introduced during the pre-Broadway tryout by gentlemen of ensemble, it was the original opening number of Act I. Dropped from the show before the New York opening.

Rolling along,
Never a care;
Laughter and song
Filling the air;
Never a frown
As through the town we roam;
Painting it red,
Maybe when we
Tossing in bed
Should be—
But we're seeing Dickie home.

Can't go wrong
When there is wine and song—
So we have found the night
Quite a bit of all right.
Fill the cup!
Let's have it bottoms up!
For we're seeing Dickie home.

Half a percent
Never was meant
For any gent
Holiday bent;
Trouble we drown
As through the town we roam;
Painting it red,
Maybe when we
Tossing in bed
Should be—
But we're seeing Dickie home.

THE MAN I LOVE

Published December 1924 and September 1927. Introduced in the pre-Broadway tryout by Adele Astaire (Susie Trevor), it was the second number of Act I. Reprised in Act II by Adele Astaire, Alan Edwards (Jack Robinson), and "guests." Dropped before the New York opening. Not used in the London production. Introduced by Vivian Hart and Roger Pryor, and reprised by Morton Downey with new lyrics as "The Girl I Love," in *Strike Up the Band* (1927), which closed out of town. Intended for Marilyn Miller in *Rosalie* (1928) but not used. Became a major commercial success in 1928. An early version of the song, with a different verse and no

lyric, was found in 1982 at the Warner Bros. Music warehouse in Secaucus, New Jersey. See also *Strike Up the Band* (1927). The story of "The Man I Love" is told by Ira Gershwin in *Lyrics on Several Occasions:*

*M*uch Ado about "The Man I Love"; or, 3 Strikes and Out. In the spring of 1924 when I finished the lyric to the body of a song—the words and tune of which I cannot recall—a verse was in order. My brother composed a possibility we both liked, but I never got around to writing it up as a verse. It was a definite and insistent melody—so much so that we soon felt it wasn't light and introductory enough, as it tended to overshadow the refrain and to demand individual attention. So this overweighty strain, not quite in tune as a verse, was, with slight modification, upped in importance to the status of a refrain. I gave it a simple set of words, then it had to acquire its own verse; and "The Man I Love" resulted.

As an originally intended verse it appears, undated, in George's early 1924 notebook between pieces dated April 4 and 24. It consists of the familiar eight-bar theme which repeats itself and is followed by a "vest" (songwriter jargon for the ending of a verse, usually two lines, leading to the refrain or chorus). This vest was somewhat expanded to become the "release"—or "middle" or "bridge"—and then the opening theme was repeated again for the last eight bars. Clear? Confusing? Anyway, that's what was done.

When *Lady, Be Good!* was being prepared, Maecenas Otto H. Kahn was approached as a potential investor. He listened to the set-up, said it sounded like a success; therefore he wasn't interested. He helped financially only those shows, ballets, and other artistic ventures which were worth doing but which inevitably reach the point of no returns. Then either George or producer [Alex A.] Aarons happened to mention that "The Man I Love"—which Kahn had heard some time before at a party—would be in the new show. "Well," reflected Kahn, "that's worth something. All right, put me down for ten thousand." (The following year when he got back not only his money but a dividend greater than his investment, he wrote Aarons and Freedley thanking them for a unique experience—the first time he had ever received any return from a theatrical venture.)

When the show opened in Philadelphia, Adele Astaire, solo, sang the song charmingly and to an appreciative hand. But sweetness and simplicity in style do not make for the vociferous applause given dancing duets and novelty numbers. So, after a week, "The Man I Love" was withdrawn. Actually the show was in good shape and the elimination required no replacement, as the show was a bit long anyway.

In New York somewhat later, Lady Mountbatten asked George for an autographed copy of the published song. (In those days the music publisher thought nothing of putting out five to seven numbers for the out-of-town theater-lobby sales. Today scarcely any sheet music is sold that way; in its stead a brisk business seems to have arisen in souvenir programs.) On her return to London, Lady Mountbatten had her favorite band, the Berkeley Square Orchestra, make a special arrangement for their concerts. Soon other London bands were playing it more or less correctly by ear, since the published song hadn't been released there. And from London it spread to Paris, where it was played frequently by several Negro combinations. So, some performance and no sales over there, while much less happened over here.

Three years later, Edgar Selwyn, for whom we were doing *Strike Up the Band*, insisted the song be introduced in the score of that otherwise satirical operetta. So in late August 1927, "The Man I Love" again was havened between footlights and backdrops. But this first version of *Strike Up the Band*, after a half-week in Long Branch, New Jersey (there were any number of tryout theaters and towns before the movies talked), and two weeks in Philadelphia, had to close because of lack of business. ("Awful!" said a man sitting behind me in Long Branch. "Father, I think it's just wonderful!" said his daughter.) Once more was this hapless song orphaned.

It was a busy year. Not only had we musicalized *S.U.T.B.* but also *Funny Face*. Sometime in October, while we were day-and-nighting it on the road doing a plastic job on the latter, we finally agreed to join forces as soon as possible with [composer Sigmund] Romberg and [lyricist P. G.] Wodehouse on the rush-job score of *Rosalie* for Ziegfeld. Actually we'd been approached about this project before and had blocked out two or three numbers for it, in case.

And *again* "The Man I Love." Suddenly Ziegfeld wanted it in *Rosalie* for Marilyn Miller. We informed him this would be up to Selwyn, who still wasn't unsold on *S.U.T.B.* and expected to put it on again one day. On October 28, 1927, this telegram: "GEORGE GERSHWIN ROOM 705 SYLVANIA HOTEL PHILADELPHIA PENN—FEEL SENTIMENTAL ABOUT THE MAN I LOVE AS IT WAS RESPONSIBLE FOR DOING MUSICAL SHOW STOP WOULD HATE TO LOSE IT BUT IF YOU FEEL KEENLY ABOUT IT WILL DO ANYTHING TO PLEASE YOU STOP REGARDS EDGAR SELWYN." Ziegfeld must have worked on Selwyn, because we really weren't *that* keen about the number. Personally, by this time I was bored with it as a possible show song. However, Marilyn Miller was Broadway's biggest musical star; fine—maybe she could do something with it.

After *Funny Face* opened successfully, we went immediately on to *Rosalie*, already in rehearsal. It was a hectic period for two librettists, [Guy] Bolton and [William Anthony] McGuire; two composers, Romberg and Gershwin; and two lyricists, Wodehouse and myself. But somehow this show—based on mythical-kingdom royalty visiting the U.S., in turn based on the recent visit of Marie, Queen of Rumania—managed to make its sched-

uled Boston opening on time—and even became a big hit.

"The Man I Love"? Keeping the title, I rewrote most of it—twice, I think—to fit possible plot cues for Miss Miller. And? Well, it certainly wasn't in the show opening night. For that matter, there were so many switches in the score that I can't recall Miss Miller ever even rehearsing it.

But Max Dreyfus, our publisher, still had faith in it and felt it oughtn't remain so comatose. He told us that if we cut our sheet-music royalty a cent each (production sheet music generally paid six cents: three cents each for music and lyric) some money could be afforded for exploitation. We cut, he exploited, and the song began to be heard quite a bit and sold fairly well—within six months about one hundred thousand copies, plus several good recordings.

That, however, wasn't the end. The thrice-orphaned song was adopted by Helen Morgan and sister singers who kept on vocalizing whatever virtues it had; and it has since led a fairly active and respectable life for over thirty years, thanks also to dozens of recordings and uses in motion pictures.

Mildly Ironic Addendum. In December 1929, *Strike Up the Band*, after a major job of rewriting by Morrie Ryskind and ourselves, was produced by Edgar Selwyn to critical acclaim. But the song he loved wasn't in it. Its popularity by this time precluded any possible use in the score—and a probable fourth ousting.

VERSE

When the mellow moon begins to beam,
Ev'ry night I dream a little dream;
And of course Prince Charming is the theme:
The he
For me.
Although I realize as well as you
It is seldom that a dream comes true,
To me it's clear
That he'll appear.

REFRAIN

Some day he'll come along,
The man I love;
And he'll be big and strong,
The man I love;
And when he comes my way,
I'll do my best to make him stay.

He'll look at me and smile—
I'll understand;
And in a little while
He'll take my hand;
And though it seems absurd,
I know we both won't say a word.

Maybe I shall meet him Sunday,
Maybe Monday—maybe not;
Still I'm sure to meet him one day—
Maybe Tuesday
Will be my good news day.

He'll build a little home
Just meant for two;
From which I'll never roam—
Who would? Would you?
And so, all else above,
I'm waiting for the man I love.

WEATHERMAN and RAINY-AFTERNOON GIRLS

Introduced by ensemble. Together, these linked numbers were the original "Opening, Act II." Dropped soon after the New York opening and replaced with "Linger in the Lobby." Alternate title of "Rainy-Afternoon Girls": "Six Little Rainy-Afternoon Girls." Not performed in the London production.

"Weatherman"

Wondering whether this thundering weather will
    clear up soon—
Weatherman, weatherman, please tell us whether
    it will—
But cut out the fiction, the sort of prediction
You gave us for this afternoon.
Oh, you misinformer,
You said, "Fair and warmer."
Terribly boring, this awful downpouring that
    never stops;
May be all right for potatoes, tomatoes, and
    hops—
But for a chappy who's longing for happiness
This sort of thing is a pain!
Weatherman, weatherman, we want the sunshine
    again.

"Rainy-Afternoon Girls"

GIRLS: Six little rainy-afternoon girls
    With nothing at all to do;
    You can't blame us if we're blue—
    We've nothing at all to do.
BOYS: Six little rainy-afternoon boys
    With nothing at all to do;
    We're in the same boat as you.
    So let's drift along together,
    Never giving any thought to the weather.

So let's drift along together,
Never giving any thought,
GIRLS: Never giving any thought,
Never giving any thought
BOTH: To the weather.

BOYS: It's much too menacing for golf or
tennis-ing—
GIRLS: Today the bridle path an idle path must
be.
There's really naught to do.
BOYS: Then what you ought to do
It just to listen to a fellow
Whose heart is feeling mellow;
Come along, girls, and say hello to love!
GIRLS: Love?
BOYS: L O V E Love!
GIRLS: [to each other] It's much too menacing
for golf or tennis-ing—
There's really naught to do we thought to
do, you see.
BOYS: Come on, let's loaf a while
Upon a sofa. While
Outside the elements are roaring,
You'll find us most adoring.
GIRLS: [to each other] Well, we can't go on
ignoring their love—
Love—L O V E Love!
BOYS: Pitter-patter, pitter-patter, pitter-patter,
pitter-patter.
GIRLS: Six little rainy-afternoon girls, we're
leaving it all to you;
Now show us what you can do; we're
leaving it all to you.
BOYS: Six little brainy afternoon boys;
The rainbow has come in view;
The silver lining is you.
BOTH: It's very lovely weather; now we're alone
together, let it rain!
GIRLS: Six little rainy—
BOYS: Six little brainy—
BOTH: Afternoon girls and boys.
Six little rainy—six little
brainy—afternoon girls and boys.

THE BAD, BAD MEN

Introduced during Act II of the pre-Broadway tryout by
Walter Catlett (Watty), Fred Astaire (Dick), and Cliff
Edwards (Jeff). Dropped before the New York opening.
No. 86 in the George and Ira Gershwin Special Num-
bered Song File. In 1921, this lyric had been set to music
by Vincent Youmans.

VERSE 1

WATTY: In reading my *Britannica*,
I've learned enough to panic a
Desire to be good and kind and gracious.
DICK: Compare the life that Nero led
To the one that any hero led—
You find the life of sin the more
vivacious.
JEFF: Now I admire the good men,
The Masons and the Woodmen,
But *they* don't make a victim walk the
plank.
WATTY: And when I read that women all
Fall for the man who's criminal,
I know someday I'm going to rob a
bank.

REFRAIN 1

Oh, I think I'd love to lead a life of
crime,
For the bad, bad men have such a good
time.
It really must be wonderful
To lead a life so plunderful,
And not work seventeen hours for a
dime.
While honest men were sweating,
Jesse James would think of fun;
He did a lot of petting,
And he made a lot of "mon."
Oh, I think I'll go right out and buy
myself a little gun
Like the revelish, devilish,
Not-on-the-levelish
Bad, bad men.

VERSE 2

WATTY: Why be a lot of Babbitts who
Are only frightened rabbits who
Think riding in the subway is romantic?
DICK: Let's lead the life unlawful, then!
WATTY: My boy, you said a jawful, then!
JEFF: Let's get a ship and sweep the broad
Atlantic.
ALL: The thing that they call virtue
Will never, never hurt you—
But also never get you anywhere.
JEFF: And then you know the good die young;
WATTY: Where I'm concerned, they *should* die
young—
Teetotalers are more than I can bear.

REFRAIN 2

Oh, I know I'd love to lead a life of
crime,
For the bad, bad men have such a good
time.
How lovingly the buccaneer
Would slit a throat or pluck an ear!
The life of Captain Kidd I call sublime.
A girly he would shanghai,
If he thought she was a pip;
Her feller's neck would hang high,
If he started any lip.
If I only had a bottle of rum, I'd get
myself a ship
Like the rollicking, frolicking,
Wood-alcoholicking
Bad, bad men.

VERSE 3

WATTY: I'm hotter than Vesuvius
When Fairbanks starts to movie us,
And shows us Robin Hood in all his
glory.
JEFF: Though Robin Hood lived by his wits,
He wouldn't stoop to try his wits
At cracking ribs or doing second-story.
DICK: But leaping through a transom,
He'd hold a king for ransom,
While with the queen he'd hold a
tête-à-tête.
WATTY: So why the straight-and-narrow path,
When there's a bow-and-arrow path
That's lined with rubies and with silver
plate?

REFRAIN 3

Oh, I'm sure I'd love to lead a life of
crime,
For the bad, bad men have such a good
time.
I know that we're the very men
For Robin and his merry men,
For just like him on castles I long to
climb.
As playful as a kitten,
He would visit the royal ball;
He'd kid the lords of Britain,
Then he'd make a princely haul.
I must get me a bow and arrow for I'm
throbbing to the call
Of those wonderful, plunderful,
Red-blood-and-thunderful
Bad, bad men.

EVENING STAR

Intended for Kathlene Martyn (Shirley Vernon). Unused. No. 88 in the George and Ira Gershwin Special Numbered Song File.

VERSE

When the little pinholes start peeping through
    the blue,
Ev'ry night when twilight is here,
Evening Star, I'm watching, I'm waiting just for
    you;
I am blue until you appear.
Nobody else is aware
Of all the secrets we share;
And tonight of all nights, in you I must confide;
There is something you must decide.

REFRAIN

Tell me, tell me, do!—my Evening Star,
If his heart is true, my Evening Star.
Can it be he really wants me?
He—the only theme of ev'ry dream
That haunts me.
I have always known how wise you are;
Now that we're alone, my Evening Star—
Tell me, what shall I believe?
I look to you, my Evening Star.

SINGIN' PETE

Intended for Cliff Edwards (Jeff). Dropped during rehearsals.

VERSE

If you ever take a trip
Down to dear old Mississip',
There's a chap you ought to meet, called Singin'
    Pete.
When he starts to throw his voice,
Baby, you ain't got no choice—
You gotta listen to the pipes of Singin' Pete.
He sings anything that's catchy,
From a low-down blues
To a thing like *Pagliacci*—
Anything you choose.
If you ever take that trip,
And you've nothin' on the hip—
You can get a kick from Pete—Boy! He's a treat!

REFRAIN

Singin' Pete, singin' sweet.
He's the reason for shufflin' feet—
Oh, baby! What a voice he's got—
I'll say he's hot.
He looks like a yokel,
But when he gets vocal
He can capture any maid
With a jazzy serenade.
Singin' high—Singin' low—
Singin' fast and then singin' slow—
The John McCormack of sweet and low-down.
When he croons, I bet my hat
He gets the key to any flat—
Women sigh for—babies cry for
Sweet Singin' Pete.

WILL YOU REMEMBER ME?

Intended for Alan Edwards (Jack Robinson) and Adele Astaire (Susie Trevor). Dropped during rehearsals. Replaced with "So Am I." No. 91 in the George and Ira Gershwin Special Numbered Song File.

VERSE 1

JACK: Now that I am starting,
    I cannot deny
    I'd prefer a "See you later" to a mere
      "Good-bye."
    But before departing—
    Do I hope in vain?
    Something makes me wonder whether
    You'll forget me altogether,
    If we never meet again.

REFRAIN 1

When I go my way,
Along some highway,
Will you remember me?
When you are lonesome,
I'd like to own some
Place in your memory.
I know that you'll play a part
In my heart when I start;
That's something I can guarantee.
But when I stray off,
Somewhere away off—
Will you remember me?

VERSE 2

SUSIE: There's a cozy section
    Of my memory

I shall set aside for you now that I've
    heard your plea.
But upon reflection—
What's a girl to do?
There's a saying since creation:
"Ev'ry traveler meets temptation"—
And it may apply to you.

REFRAIN 2

When you go your way
Out through my doorway,
Will you remember me?
You may grow fonder
Of something blonder;
Your heart no longer free.
If I thought you'd not forget
That we'd met—You can bet
A very flattered girl I'd be.
But at the mercy
Of some sweet Circe—
Will you remember me?

LITTLE THEATRE

A notation of "Catlett + Girls" on Ira Gershwin's manuscript of this lyric suggests that it may have been intended for *Lady, Be Good!* No music is known to survive.

VERSE

Leading lady, I have an improvement
On the well-known little-theatre movement
Where I know we never will be baffled
When we find the house is only half-filled.
I mean a theatre so small
That there will be no audience at all.

REFRAIN

We'll build a little theatre of our own,
So small that we will always be alone.
Where I will be your Barrymore,
The handsomest of mimes.
And you'll be Francine Larrimore
Because it rhymes.
I'll write a play with oh-so-many charms,
Where always you'll be nesting in my arms.
I've a suspicion
There'll be no intermission
In that little theatre of our own.

OVERLEAF: *Lou Holtz and Florence Auer in* Tell Me More

TELL ME MORE
MISCELLANEOUS
1925

TELL ME MORE, 1925

Tryout: Nixon's Apollo Theatre, Atlantic City, April 6, 1925. New York run: Gaiety Theatre, opened April 13, 1925. 100 performances. Music almost entirely by George Gershwin. Lyrics by B. G. DeSylva and Ira Gershwin. Produced by Alfred E. Aarons. Book by Fred Thompson and William K. Wells. Book staged by John Harwood. Dances staged by Sammy Lee. Orchestra under the direction of Max Steiner. Cast included Phyllis Cleveland (Peggy Van de Leur), Alexander Gray (Kenneth Dennison), Lou Holtz (Monty Sipkin), Emma Haig (Bonnie Reeves), Esther Howard (Jane Wallace), and Andrew Tombes (Billy Smith). Specialty dancers: Dorothy Wilson, Mary Jane, and Vivian Glenn. Portland Hoffa (Mrs. Fred Allen) was one of the chorus girls.

London run: Winter Garden Theatre, opened May 26, 1925. 264 performances. Produced by George Grossmith and J.A.E. Malone (by arrangement with Alfred E. Aarons). Book staged by Felix Edwardes and Charles A. Maynard. Dances staged by Sammy Lee. Orchestra under the direction of John Ansell. Cast included Elsa Macfarlane (Peggy Van de Leur), Arthur Margetson (Kenneth Dennison), Leslie Henson (Monty Sipkin), Vera Lennox (Bonnie Reeves), Heather Thatcher (Jane Wallace), and Claude Hulbert (Billy Smith).

Except where noted all *Tell Me More* lyrics are by B. G. DeSylva and Ira Gershwin.

TELL ME MORE

Published April 1925. Introduced by Alexander Gray (Kenneth) and Phyllis Cleveland (Peggy). Introduced in London by Elsa Macfarlane and Arthur Margetson.

VERSE

KENNETH: All night long I've waited,
Feeling it was fated
I would meet wonderful you.
PEGGY: I have heard that dangers
Lurk in meeting strangers;
That's what one never should do.
KENNETH: Don't you care to know me, then?
PEGGY: I'll explain it all again:

REFRAIN 1

PEGGY: I came in—thought I'd been here before.
KENNETH: Tell me more, tell me more, tell me more!
PEGGY: Heard a sound—looked around—finding you.
It was chance and not romance that brought me to you.
Now you know, I must go—
KENNETH: I implore
You to stay, don't go 'way—Tell me more!
PEGGY: Though I'm leaving now, I wish somehow
That we had met before—
KENNETH: That's a start—Have a heart! Tell me more!

REFRAIN 2

KENNETH: I believe now that we've met before
PEGGY: Well, if you're *very* sure, tell me more.
KENNETH: You were mine in divine days of yore
When I used to fight the other cavemen for you.
[*Peg laughs*]
That's not half—Please, don't laugh—I implore.
PEGGY: I don't mind—I'm resigned—Tell me more.
KENNETH: And I knew you right away tonight
When you came through that door—
PEGGY: I despise all your lies! Tell me more!

REFRAIN 3

KENNETH: I'm afraid you're the maid I adore.
PEGGY: Tell me more, tell me more, tell me more!
KENNETH: You have eyes like the skies when they're blue.
PEGGY: And believe me, those two eyes can see right through you.
KENNETH: Though we part, you are leaving behind
All the grace of your face in my mind.
PEGGY: Though I'm sure that you have told this to
A dozen girls before—
Tell me more! Tell me more! Tell me more!

ACT II REPRISE

KENNETH: You're the girl I will always adore
PEGGY: Tell me more, tell me more, tell me more!
KENNETH: I am sure you were sent from above.
PEGGY: Well, I'm glad that I was sent here if you love me.
KENNETH: You've been mine, dear, for years, in my dreams.
If I wrote, I could write reams and reams,
And could sing your praise for days and days,
But maybe it would bore—
PEGGY: Don't be sil'! It's a thrill—Tell me more!

Additional (Unused) Refrains

BOYS: I'm afraid you're the maid I adore.
GIRLS: Tell me more, tell me more, tell me more!
BOYS: You have eyes like the skies when they're blue.
GIRLS: Now, you don't believe I'll fall for that, now, do you?
BOYS: You're above what my love would demand;
As a start, take my heart and my hand!
GIRLS: Though I'm sure that you have told this to
A dozen girls before—
Tell me more! Tell me more! Tell me more!

KENNETH: Was I bold when I told you before?
PEGGY: Yes, you were! Just the same, tell me more!
KENNETH: There's a heap I must keep in my heart.
PEGGY: Please don't keep too much from me now that you've started.
KENNETH: That you're sweet, I'll repeat o'er and o'er!
PEGGY: That is trite, sir, you might tell me more!
KENNETH: I could sing your praise for days and days
But maybe it would bore—
PEGGY: Don't be sil'! It's a thrill—Tell me more!

SHOPGIRLS AND MANNEQUINS

Introduced by ensemble. Alternate titles: "Opening, Act I" and "Opening Ensemble."

GIRLS: From nine to five, half-alive,
All we do is try to please!
Nine to five, in this hive,
We are busier than bees!
What a life, oh me!
What a life, oh my!
What a life, oh, you must come over!
It's not the cat's selling hats
To a lot of fussy dames!
Fitting boots, trying suits,
On a lot of dumpy frames!
What a life, oh me!
What a life, oh my!
What a life, oh, you'll never know the half!
Really it's a laugh,
How we stand the gaff!
Up till the dawning,
We had a night of laughter;
That's why we're yawning—
This is the morning after.
For we were all at a ball
Where we danced and romanced.
Oh what a night of delight!
Oh, what a night. (So we're feeling rocky!)
Now back to business (We cannot tread a measure.)
What right has business to interfere with pleasure?
When full of synthetic gin,
We were gay—But to-day—
Oh, what a head! Nearly dead!
What'll we do in case the boss should see us?
Where's the Lincoln who will free us?
[Interlude—Mannequins enter]
Well, fancy that! fancy that!
Look! The mannequins are here!
MANNEQUINS: How-de-do? How are you?
GIRLS: Did you finally appear?
What a life of ease—
What a life of ease—
Doing as they please!
Don't you love it?

MANNEQUINS: Now that we're here—Give a cheer—
You can open up the store.
GIRLS: What a break! What a break!
MANNEQUINS: You're not what we're waiting for.
Never mind the sauce.
Tell us, where's the boss?
GIRLS: He's a total loss.
Monty's late today.
MANNEQUINS: When the cat's away
How the mice will play!

MR. AND MRS. SIPKIN

Introduced by Lou Holtz (Monty) and female ensemble. ntroduced in London by Leslie Henson and female ensemble. Alternate title: "Monty! Their Only Child!"

VERSE

MONTY: That I'm the talk of Broadway isn't doubtful;
I'm Heaven's gift to girlies who are blue.
My book of dates is more than just about full—
For I'm the boy the social lights pursue.
Though I dislike the parties that I go to,
I feel I have to give the folks a treat;
I owe it to my public—don't you know—to
Be everywhere that charming people meet.
The day that I was born in Scranton Hollows,
My parents issued cards that read as follows:

REFRAIN

Mr. and Mrs. Sipkin have the honor to present—
GIRLS: Monty!
MONTY: Their only child!
Mr. and Mrs. Sipkin offer you the perfect gent—
GIRLS: Jaunty!
MONTY: But undefiled!
How I love to mingle with the swellest swells!
GIRLS: He's met all the bouncers at the best hotels!
MONTY: Right!

Mr. and Mrs. Sipkin have the honor to present you to
Monty! Their favorite child!

INTERLUDE

My suits are all from London;
That's where I have each one done;
With ties from Brooks
To help my looks,
My rivals are in tears.
A perfect male production
For feminine destruction—
I must admit
I've been a hit
For twenty-seven years. Oh!

Repeat Refrain with the Following Catch Lines:

MONTY: I've a grand apartment—full of tasty bits.
GIRLS: Linen by the Astor—Silver by the Ritz.
MONTY: How d'ya like my diamond? Don't you think it's trim?
GIRLS: Fifty weekly payments—It'll belong to him.

INTERLUDE 2

MONTY: I smoke the best of Cubans,
My meals are all by Reuben's
And it's the boast
Of Mrs. Post
My manners have no flaw.
My line of conversation
Delights an eager nation,
For it is styled
On Oscar Wilde
And Mr. Bernard Shaw. Oh!

Repeat Refrain with the Following Catch Lines:

MONTY: I spoke to the Prince of Wales just the other day.
GIRLS: And what do you think the prince said?
He said, "Get out of the way!" Oh!
Mr. and Mrs. Sipkin have the honor to present you to
Monty!
MONTY: Their favorite child!

WHEN THE DEBBIES GO BY

Listed in the Atlantic City program as "We Are the Debs." Introduced by Esther Howard (Jane) and ensemble. Introduced in London by Heather Thatcher and ensemble.

VERSE

A charity bazaar
Could not get very far
Unless the debutantes were there
To make it popular.
Attention they engage;
They seem to hold the stage;
In Sunday rotogravure sections
They're on ev'ry page.
Int'rest never ebbs
In the lovely debs.

REFRAIN 1

When the debbies go by
With their noses held high,
They make a business of looking seraphic
In case they meet any cameramen
From the *News* or *Graphic*.
When they smile at a cop,
Traffic comes to a stop.
Oh, show me the man
Who doesn't straighten his tie
When the debbies go by.

REFRAIN 2

When the debbies go by
With their noses held high—
Although their clothes are a blow to a pastor,
They make a whale of a hit with a sheik
Or a riding master.
Each, a smart little rogue
From the pages of *Vogue*—
So show me the man who isn't risking an eye
When the debbies go by.

THREE TIMES A DAY

Published April 1925. Introduced by Alexander Gray (Kenneth) and Phyllis Cleveland (Peggy). Introduced in London by Arthur Margetson and Elsa Macfarlane.

VERSE 1

KENNETH: If I had my way,
I'd trail you night and day;
For I so crave your company,
I'd be in it
Ev'ry minute!
But, upon my soul,
I'll exercise control;
In case it be that you should see
More than just enough of me.

REFRAIN

I'll call round about
Three times a day;
Maybe I could make it four!
You may throw me out
Three times a day,
But I'll come right back for more!
When the sky
Falls into the ocean blue,
That's when I
Will stop proposing to you.
For I long to see
Your smiling face across the table,
  dear,
Three times a day!

VERSE 2

PEGGY: Yes, I realize
That you are very wise
In limiting our rendezvous;
Such a stand'll
Cause no scandal.
Just three times a day
Is quite enough, I'd say;
But if your calls are more than three
Folks might think you fond of me!

REPEAT REFRAIN

WHY DO I LOVE YOU?

Published April 1925. Introduced by Esther Howard (Jane), Lou Holtz (Monty), and ensemble. Introduced in London by Heather Thatcher, Leslie Henson, and ensemble.

VERSE 1

JANE: Once I was so willing
To believe that love is thrilling;
But, of late, a doubt is filling my mind.
You say you adore me.
That should be sufficient for me;
But the path of love is stormy, I find.
When love gets you,
It upsets you.
All day long I phone you,
'Cause I'm never sure I own you;
Darling, ever since I've known you,
I've pined. Oh,

REFRAIN 1

Why do I love you, love you, love you?
My! How I love you, love you, love you!
When we met, it's true,
I never knew
That love could do this to me.
No time for sleepin', sleepin', sleepin';
Just time for weepin', weepin', weepin'.
Blue the whole night through—
Oh, tell me, why do I love you?

VERSE 2

MONTY: Dear, it is my duty
To announce 'twas not your beauty
That convinced me you're the cutie to
  woo.
Lately, more's the pity,
I have noticed in the city
Many girlies twice as pretty as you.
Though they thrill me,
Gal, you kill me!
You're a loving bandit
And to you I've got to hand it;
But I cannot understand it,
It's true. Oh,

REPEAT REFRAIN

COUNTERMELODY FOR CHORUS (UNUSED)

Love, we think, should be unlawful,
For it hits you something awful—
Just entangles you and says you're
Not to have a moment's pleasure.
Your day is done—
Good-bye to fun—
When you find one
Whom you treasure.
But the wise men all assure us

There is something that can cure us—
Cupid starts to droop and falter
When you stand before the altar.
So, ducky dear,
The road is clear—
Let's be heading for that wedding day.

HOW CAN I WIN YOU NOW?

Introduced by Emma Haig (Bonnie) and Andrew Tombes (Billy). Added during the pre-Broadway tryout, replacing "I'm Somethin' on Avenue A." Replaced soon after the New York opening with "Once." Introduced in London by Vera Lennox and Claude Hulbert.

VERSE 1

BILLY: Since the world began,
   I have been your man.
   You have always brought me Paradise.
BONNIE: In our former lives,
   I was all your wives.
BILLY: So I ask your advice.

REFRAIN 1

   How can I win you now?
   I've got to have you once more!
BONNIE: I really don't know how—
   Although you've done it before.
BILLY: Back in the Stone Age, all I did was hit
      you
   Right on the dome;
   And when you fainted, darling, by your
      hair
   I dragged you home.
BONNIE: And back in Nero's days,
   Somehow I seem to recall,
   With honeyed words of praise
   You made me fall.
BILLY: I overcame your resistance
   In ev'ry former life—
   But how can I win you now?

VERSE 2

BILLY: Just as sure as fate,
   Lady, you're my mate.
   You were mine the moment that we met.
BONNIE: Maybe it was so
   In the long ago.
   Now I'm harder to get.

REFRAIN 2

BILLY: How can I win you now?
   I've got to have you once more!
BONNIE: I really don't know how—
   Although you've done it before.
BILLY: Back in Beau Brummell's day, I dolled
      up and
   Was awfully cute,
   And it wasn't hard to win you when
   I pressed my suit.
BONNIE: In 1300, sir,
   Those days when you were a knight,
   I fell because you were
   So darn polite.
BILLY: I overcame your resistance
   In ev'ry former life—
   But how can I win you now?

KICKIN' THE CLOUDS AWAY

Published April 1925. Introduced by Phyllis Cleveland (Peggy), Esther Howard (Jane), Lou Holtz (Monty), and female ensemble. Introduced in London by Elsa Macfarlane, Heather Thatcher, Leslie Henson, and female ensemble.

VERSE

I just heard a spiritual,*
One that ev'ry phonograph should own;
I know when you hear it you will
Find that all your troubles have flown.
When the sky looks cloudy to you—
When the blue is turning gray—
It'll make the sun say "Howdy!" to you—
It'll drive your cares away.
Get all set and up on your toes,
This is the way it goes:

REFRAIN

Come on along! You can't go wrong!
Kickin' the clouds away.
Keep makin' hay,
Kickin' the clouds away.
Be wise and take it to heart,
And you will laugh from the start
To the end of a perfect day.

*Alternate version of verse, line 1:
There's a southern spiritual,

Get in the swing! Give it a fling!
Kickin' the clouds away.
Live while you may,
Shoutin' a big "Hey! Hey!"
It's not so easy to do—
What of it?
For, when you're through,
You'll love it!
Follow the dancin' crowds
And kick the clouds away!

LOVE IS IN THE AIR

Introduced by ensemble. Alternate title: "Opening, Act II."

VERSE

Summer is the season
When for no good reason
Love pays you a call.
You become a lover
Only to discover
Summer caused it all.
But what can you do,
It's not up to you, for

REFRAIN

Love is in the air
Beside a summer sea.
There's a big affair
Awaiting you and me.
Something in the weather
Calls to ev'ry heart,
"Time to get together
With a new love,
Swearing true love."
Ripples hug the shore
And kiss the burning sand;
Nature is implor-
Ing you to take a hand.
So if you are fancy-free,
This is where you ought to be,
For love is in the air
Beside a summer sea.

MY FAIR LADY

Published April 1925. Introduced by Phyllis Cleveland (Peggy), Esther Howard (Jane), and male ensemble. In London, the song was reassigned and introduced by Heather Thatcher (Jane) and male ensemble. Alternate title: "Lady Fair."

VERSE

BOYS: Listen, fair one, I'm in love!
PEGGY: Why should that int'rest me?
BOYS: You're the one I'm thinking of.
PEGGY: To ev'ry mister
　　　I'll be a sister;
　　　Though I'm not fancy-free,
　　　I'm curious to hear your plea.

REFRAIN

BOYS: You're as fair as you can be—
　　　My fair lady!
　　　Won't you please be fair with me?
　　　My fair lady!
　　　Give me just an afternoon
　　　Where the lanes are shady.
　　　Then we'll make a date for June—
　　　My fair lady!

INTERLUDE

PEGGY: Though I should like to heed the call of
　　　you,
　　　My heart is given just to one.
　　　So, boys, I can't be fair to all of you;
　　　And I'm resisting!
BOYS: And we're insisting—

REPEAT REFRAIN

IN SARDINIA

Introduced by Lou Holtz (Monty) and female ensemble. Dropped during New York run. Not used in the London production. Alternate title: "Where the Delicatessen Flows." A spoof of Jerome Kern, P. G. Wodehouse, and Clifford Grey's "The Schnitza-Kommisski" from *Sally* (1920). The music of the refrain for "In Sardinia" was published in the piano selection from the New York production of *Tell Me More* under the title "Where the Delicatessen Flows."

VERSE 1

MONTY: Near Michael Arlen's Armenia*
　　　Lies my estate in Sardinia.
GIRLS: That is important, if true.
MONTY: Country so quaintly suburban
　　　Might have been painted by Urban.
GIRLS: We'll have to take it from you.
MONTY: Tourists who pass'll be charmed by a
　　　castle†
　　　With plenty of gilt on the dome.
　　　That's where I colicked, and later I
　　　frolicked,
　　　For that was my ancestral home.
　　　Close by a river whose name is‡
　　　Long and as wide as its fame is—
GIRLS: Tell us the name of it, do!

REFRAIN 1

MONTY: In Sardinia on the Delicatessen—
　　　That river 'way back home—
　　　Where the breezes are spicy and balmy,
　　　You can stroll through the fields of
　　　salami.
　　　All the folks there in their mayonnaise
　　　dressin'
　　　Are free of earthly woes.
　　　Oh! To live and to die
　　　While the caviar swim by,§
　　　Where the Delicatessen flows.

REFRAIN 2

　　　In Sardinia on the Delicatessen—
　　　That river 'way back home—
　　　Get a farm and you'll never go broke,
　　　for
　　　All the bushes are laden with Roquefort.
　　　All is peaceful; there's no subway to
　　　lessen
　　　The quiet and repose.
　　　That's where friendship abounds
　　　On the old Coffee Grounds,
　　　Where the Delicatessen flows.

REFRAIN 3

　　　In Sardinia on the Delicatessen—
　　　That river 'way back home—
　　　All the sporting events there are tony,
　　　Such as trapping the vicious baloney.
　　　With no business for a person to mess
　　　in,
　　　All day there people doze;*
　　　Or in bathing they flock,
　　　For the water's *geschmack*,
　　　Where the Delicatessen flows.

VERSE 2

MONTY: If on my breeding I'm touchy—†
　　　I'm from the old Sipkin duchy!
GIRLS: Gee! But you've got it down pat!
MONTY: I, from the Bourbons descended,
　　　Sprang from a line that was splendid—
GIRLS: Sounds like a Keith acrobat!
MONTY: If I should speak of
　　　The titles we reek of,
　　　I'm sure you'd accuse me of swank.
　　　Dukes and marquises,
　　　We're quite the big cheeses—
　　　There's no fam'ly there quite so rank.
　　　So troubles here never down me,
　　　For there, they are waiting to crown me!
GIRLS: We are in favor of that!

REFRAIN 4

MONTY: In Sardinia on the Delicatessen—
　　　That river 'way back home—
　　　Though with Shakespeare the folks
　　　aren't taken,‡
　　　They are certainly mad about Bacon.
　　　There's no int'rest, as you'll probably
　　　guess, in
　　　Cafés or radios;
　　　For the country's not dry,
　　　And the bread's full of rye,
　　　Where the Delicatessen flows.

Alternate version of verse 1, lines 1–3:
MONTY: Not many miles from Armenia
　　　Lies my old homeland, Sardinia.
GIRLS: We think that you're lying, too.
†*Alternate version of verse 1, line 7:*
　　　Trav'lers who pass'll be charmed by a castle
‡*Alternate version of verse 1, lines 11–12:*
　　　Close to a river whose name is
　　　Wide and as long as its fame is—
§*Alternate version of refrain 1, line 8:*
　　　While the herring swim by,

Alternate version of refrain 3, lines 6–8:
　　　All day there you can doze;
　　　You can loaf all you wish
　　　Catching gefilte fish,
†*Alternate version of verse 2, lines 1–3:*
MONTY: From a Sardinia duchy—
　　　On my breeding I'm touchy!
GIRLS: You need a two-gallon hat!
‡*Alternate version of refrain 4, lines 3–4:*
　　　Any man is a prince among princes
　　　Who can corner the market in blintzes.

BABY!

Published April 1925. Introduced by Emma Haig (Bonnie), Andrew Tombes (Billy), and ensemble. The "Baby!" music was originally joined with a Clifford Grey lyric titled "Sweetheart" and intended for the unproduced 1922 musical *Flying Island*. "Sweetheart" was eventually used in the 1923 Gershwin/Grey London revue *The Rainbow* and was published with that show's sheet music. Ira Gershwin and B. G. DeSylva's "Baby!" lyric was matched with the "Sweetheart" music for the New York production of *Tell Me More!*, though when the show played London, George Gershwin set the "Baby!" lyric to new music (as London audiences had already heard the tune). The second "Baby!" was introduced in London by Vera Lennox, Claude Hulbert, and ensemble.

VERSE

BONNIE: Baby, heed me,
Listen when I say
That you need me,
Need me night and day;
I'm just the girly
Who, late and early,
Will protect you
So no trouble can affect you.

REFRAIN 1

You're as cute as you can be, Baby!
But you need someone like me, Baby!
Just take it from a
Little girl who knows.
You need a mamma
Who will make the future rosy!
If you'll promise not to cry, Baby,
I will kiss you by-and-by—Maybe!
Though you're six feet three,
You will always be
Nothing but a Baby, dear, to me.

REFRAIN 2

BILLY: I'm so glad that I am your Baby.
Save a lot of loving for Baby.
You mustn't throttle
Me if I should cry.
Give me a bottle—
Fill it up with rock and rye—
And I will be a very good Baby,
Doing ev'rything I should—Maybe!

If you will agree
To mamma only me,
Mamma, what a Baby I will be!

FINALETTO, ACT II, SCENE 1

Introduced by Phyllis Cleveland (Peggy), Esther Howard (Jane), and ensemble. Introduced in London by Elsa Macfarlane, Heather Thatcher, and ensemble. Alternate title: "Kenneth Won the Yachting Race."

PEGGY: Why do I love you, love you, love you?
My! How I love you, love you, love you!
Though you've made me blue,
I only know that I love you.

[*Exit Peggy. Enter girls*]
GIRLS: Kenneth won the yachting race.
Oh, isn't it wonderful!
Isn't it marvelous!
All of us picked the winner.
He led them a merry chase.
Oh, isn't he wonderful!
If he were here, we would give him a cheer.

[*Jane enters*]
JANE: Girls! I'm so upset!
GIRLS: How do you get that way?
You shouldn't bet that way!
JANE: Don't be sil'! My father's here,
And I must interview him.
GIRLS: What's the reason for your fear?
JANE: You wouldn't ask me that if you knew him.
GIRLS: Tell us more! Tell us more! Tell us more!
JANE: That I intend to marry
I must inform him;
And somehow I've an inkling
That the knowledge will not warm him.
GIRLS: Tell us more! Tell us more! Tell us more!
We'd like to know the reason, Jane.
JANE: The reason, girls, I can't explain:
A secret for a while it must remain.

UKULELE LORELEI

Introduced by Emma Haig (Bonnie) and female ensemble. Introduced in London by Heather Thatcher and ensemble.

VERSE

Ev'ry time the Lorelei of long ago would play,
She won all the sailormen who came along her way;
Legend tells of her success, and even if it's true—
I am here to state that she could not compare with you.
Beggar man and duke,
Butter men from Dubuque,
Ev'ryone surrenders when you play your uke.

REFRAIN

Hum a little tune,
Ukulele Lorelei;
Strum a little tune,
Ukulele Lorelei.
In my heart, when you start, there's a warm glow.
What you do to me you never will know.
Shake a little hip—
You'll be hypnotizing me.
You're a little pip—
One I'd walk a mile to see.
Make the men young again—
Throw 'er in high—
Ukulele Lorelei.

ONCE

Music by William Daly. Lyrics by Ira Gershwin. Introduced by Emma Haig (Bonnie) and Andrew Tombes (Billy). Replaced "How Can I Win You Now?" soon after the New York opening. George Gershwin later reset this lyric for *Funny Face* (1927), in which it was introduced by William Kent (Dugsie), Betty Compton (Dora), and ensemble. Replaced in the London production of *Funny Face* by "Look at the Damn Thing Now."

VERSE

In the very first dream that I ever had,
Darling, I dreamed about you;

So I've really loved you since I was a lad—
No other girlie would do.
Others don't as quickly find their true affinity—
Look at the records and see:

REFRAIN 1

Once Rockefeller didn't have a nickel;
Once Henry didn't have a Ford.
Once Mr. Heinz had never met a pickle—
Dobbs, a hat—or Ruth, a bat.
Once Mr. Childs had never seen a wheat cake;
Regal didn't know about a shoe.
But I'm here to assever,
My dear, there was never
A time I didn't know about you.

REFRAIN 2

Once Mr. Armour didn't know a mutton;
Once Peggy Hopkins had no mate.
Once Kuppenheimer didn't have a button;
Hearst, a press—Lucille, a dress.
Once Ringling didn't know about a circus;
Brunswick didn't know about a cue.*
But I'm here to assever,
My dear, there was never
A time I didn't know about you.

I'M SOMETHIN' ON AVENUE A

Introduced during the pre-Broadway tryout by Emma Haig (Bonnie). Replaced before the New York opening with "How Can I Win You Now?" No music is known to survive.

VERSE

There's a part of Manhattan
That's Jewish and Latin—
My neighborhood, Avenue A.
Where all Irish Roses have Abies,
And our biggest product is babies.
Though gunmen may roam there,
I'm proud of my home there—
No matter what people may say.
If someone gets fresh from uptown,
This is how I call 'em down:

Alternate version of refrain 2, line 6:
Georgie White about a big revue.

REFRAIN 1

I may be nothin' on Fift' Avenue,
But I'm somethin' on Avenue A.
Down there at least, I got my pals—
Way over East—where gals is gals.
There where a sweater's the fashion,
I am the queen of the May.
Though I'm not the berries
At Ciro's or Sherry's
I'm somethin' on Avenue A.

REFRAIN 2

I may be nothin' on Fift' Avenue,
But I'm somethin' on Avenue A.
Saturday nights at Kelly's Hall,
I am the belle of ev'ry ball.
There where Elizas are Lizzies—
Ev'ryone's speech is okay;
Where ersters are berled,
And life is unsperled,
I'm somethin' on Avenue A.

THE HE-MAN

Introduced during the pre-Broadway tryout by Esther Howard (Jane) and ensemble. Dropped before the New York opening.

VERSE

If we girls all should 'fess up why
We take such pains to dress up, why,
The answer is: to please the other sex.
We spend our days in dropping in-
To stores to do our shopping in.
We buy and buy until we're nervous wrecks.
But, tell me, is it worth the while
To decorate this earth the while
The men are so unworthy of our zeal?
No more the days of heroes now—
The men are only zeros now—
A sex without the slightest sex appeal.

REFRAIN 1

The he-man ain't the man he used to be.
Instead of gulping rye, he's sipping tea.
The only thing that Lancelot
Can do today is dance a lot,
And oh! my God! The difference to me!
Oh, where's the man who has a lot of "go"—
Who won't believe me when I tell him "No!"

No more the man of muscle
Who'll scratch and bite and tussle!
The he-man ain't the man he used to be.

REFRAIN 2

The he-man ain't the man he used to be.
From armor he has sunk to B.V.D.
The master of the Amazon
Made love with tin pajamas on—
And you know what pajamas mean to me.
The only man who'll make me say "Uh-huh!"
Must overwhelm me with a lot of "UH!"
Today the men you meet with
Just use their hands to eat with.
The he-man ain't the man he used to be!

GUSHING

Written in the early 1920s. Lyrics by Ira Gershwin and, possibly, Brian Hooker. Alternate titles: "Gush-Gush-Gushing" and "When My Oil Well Starts Gush-Gush-Gushing." Intended at one time for *Tell Me More!* Unused. Later considered for Jack Donahue (Bill) and Bobbe Arnst (Mary) in *Rosalie* (1928), but again unused. No. 84 in the George and Ira Gershwin Special Numbered Song File.

VERSE 1

HE: Very soon my troubles will be over.
SHE: That's good.
HE: Knock wood!
SHE: Oh, I bet you found a four-leaf clover.
     That right?
HE: Not quite.
     But I bought some oil stock from a chap
       the other day;
     Though they have no wells yet and no
       dividends to pay—
     Something tells me when they drill, the
       wells will start to play.
SHE: What bliss!
HE: Get this:

REFRAIN 1

When my oil well starts
  gush-gush-gushing,
Golly, gosh! Gosh! Gosh! What a day!
We can settle down in
  Flush-Flush-Flushing, dear,
Or anywhere you say.

In a Rolls-Royce we'll be
    rush-rush-rushing—
Nevermore the subway way.
When that oil well starts
    gush-gush-gushing
Down in Oklahoma someday.

VERSE 2

SHE: What a life we'll lead when Heaven sends
    wells.
    Hot stuff!
HE: Sure 'nough!
    Didn't Shakespeare say, "Oil's well that
    ends wells"?
    No joke.
SHE: You spoke.
    We could have a place in Newport for a
    summer home—
    Fill it full of trinkets from the Orient and
    Rome.
HE: For a house in town I think I'll get the
    Hippodrome.
SHE: You're hot!
HE: That's what!

REFRAIN 2

BOTH: When my oil well starts
    gush-gush-gushing,
    Golly, gosh! Gosh! Gosh! What a day!
    At our breakfast no more
    mush-mush-mushing—
    Ham and eggs will come to stay.
    With society we'll be
    brush-brush-brushing
    Elbows at some swell soirée,
    When my my oil well starts
    gush-gush-gushing
    Down in Oh-oh-kla-ah-homa someday.

Alternate Version of Verse 2

SHE: We will both devote our lives to pleasure.
HE: O.K!
SHE: I'll say!
HE: Lobster à la Newburg without measure.
    Oh joy!
SHE: My boy!
    At Number One on Easy Street we'll build
    a little home.
    Will we be presented at St. James and
    maybe Rome?
HE: Sure! We'll show up all those muckamucks
    from Teapot Dome.
SHE: You're hot!
HE: That's what!

MISCELLA-NEOUS, 1925

I WANT A YES-MAN

Published September 1925. Music by Vincent Youmans. Lyrics by Clifford Grey, Irving Caesar, and Ira Gershwin. Intended for *A Night Out*, which tried out at the Shubert Theatre, Philadelphia, in September 1925 but closed before reaching New York.

VERSE

SHE: Nobody knows how happy I'd be to find
    someone—
    Somebody nice who really would
    understand;
HE: Lady, I'm here, I'm willing to be that kind
    someone.
SHE: For my heart and hand,
    Here's what I'm demanding:

REFRAIN

I want a Yes-Man,
Kiss-and-Caress Man;
I want a Yes-Romeo,
Someone who will never say "No."
If he will pet me,
Never forget me;
Then at the altar, I guess,
It'll be my turn to say "Yes."
If any man I call mine
Proves he is all mine,
I'm sure he'll find me just as loving as can
    be.
I want a Yes-Man.
Take my address, man,
If you will always agree
To be a sweet Yes-Man to me.

I KNOW SOMEBODY (WHO LOVES YOU)

Music probably by George Gershwin. The editor tentatively dates this lyric to 1925 or 1926—around the time of *Tip-Toes* and *Oh, Kay!* No music is known to survive.

VERSE 1

BOY: I know a boy who is very much in love.
GIRL: I know a girl with the same affliction.
BOY: I'd like to know whom you are thinking
    of.
GIRL: "You'd be surprised" is my firm
    conviction.
BOY: Is that somebody in love with me?
    Am I the only one whom she can "see"?
GIRL: Oh, charming, modest youth.
    It's time you had the truth.

REFRAIN 1

I know somebody who loves you
Far more than you'll ever know.
This certain someone who loves you
Will always follow you wherever you go.
For her there can be no other;
For her the rest are taboo.
Why don't you fly to her?
You're earth and sky to her.
BOY: Who is it? Tell me, do!
GIRL: Your mother.*

VERSE 2

BOY: Still, I repeat, there's someone in love with
    you:
    Someone who loves you madly, yet
    genteelly.
GIRL: All right, I'll bite. Kind sir, if this be true,
    You're among friends, so you can speak
    freely.
    Really, I'm curious to know.
    I can feel my heart begin to glow.
BOY: For many years I've yearned.
    I think it's time you learned.

REFRAIN 2

I know somebody who loves you:
A ball of passionate flame.
This certain someone who loves you
Is up in Heaven when they mention your
    name.
This someone thinks you're a wonder
And also the crème de la crème.
I wonder if you've guessed
Who is it loves you best.
GIRL: Who is it? Tell me, do!
BOY: You, yourself, dear!

*Alternate version of refrain 1, line 10:
It's Fido.

OPPOSITE: *Gertrude McDonald, Andrew Tombes, and Lovey Lee doing "Sweet and Low-Down" in* Tip-Toes

TIP-TOES | 1925
AMERICANA | 1926

TIP-TOES, 1925

Tryout: National Theatre, Washington, D.C., November 24, 1925; Shubert Theatre, Newark, November 30, 1925; Forrest Theatre, Philadelphia, December 7, 1925; Ford's Theatre, Baltimore, December 21, 1925. New York run: Liberty Theatre, opened December 28, 1925. 194 performances. Music by George Gershwin. Produced by Alex A. Aarons and Vinton Freedley. Book by Guy Bolton and Fred Thompson. Book staged by John Harwood. Dances staged by Sammy Lee. Orchestra under the direction of William Daly. Cast, starring Queenie Smith (Tip-Toes Kaye) and Allen Kearns (Steve Burton), featured Andrew Tombes (Al Kaye), Harry Watson, Jr. (Hen Kaye), Jeanette MacDonald (Sylvia Metcalf), Robert Halliday (Rollo Metcalf), Amy Revere (Peggy Schuyler), Gertrude McDonald (Binnie Oakland), Lovey Lee (Denise Marshall), and Victor Arden and Phil Ohman at the pianos. A number titled "Dancing Hour," dropped during the pre-Broadway tryout, was almost certainly an ensemble specialty that included no new music or lyrics.

London run: Produced by Musical Plays Ltd. (by arrangement with Alex A. Aarons and Vinton Freedley) at the Winter Garden Theatre, London, opened August 31, 1926. 181 performances. Book staged by William Ritter. Dances staged by Sammy Lee. Orchestra under the direction of I. A. de Orellana. Cast, starring Dorothy Dickson (Tip-Toes Kaye), Laddie Cliff (Al Kaye), and Allen Kearns (Steve Burton), featured John Kirby (Hen Kaye), Vera Bryer (Sylvia Metcalf), Evan Thomas (Rollo Metcalf), Eileen Stack (Peggy Schuyler), Peggy Beaty (Binnie Brighton), Lovey Lee (Denise Miller), and Jack Clarke and George Myddleton at the pianos.

WAITING FOR THE TRAIN

Introduced by ensemble. Alternate titles: "Florida" and "Opening, Act I." By the time of the post-Broadway tour, most programs listed the title as "Florida." A portion of the music for this number was published in the piano selection from the New York production. In many versions of the score and script, the lyric begins with "Oh, look at what we've got," indicating that the first three stanzas were deleted in rehearsal.

GROUP A: Oh, when it starts to blow
And it feels like snow
'Way up in the North—

Then we sally forth to Florida—
We sally forth to Florida.

Gee! What a place to see!
We will guarantee—
If you've got the price—
Earthly paradise is Florida.
Yes, paradise is Florida.

Bring all your metal here,
For you ought to settle here,
And get yourself a home.
Flowers are blooming here,
And values are booming here,
So get yourself a home!

Oh, look at what we've got—
Option on a lot—
Cutest little plot—
We advise you to grab this little parcel
While it's hot!

[Enter Group B]
GROUP B: We've come down to meet the train;
Hurried here to beat the train.
It would be a crime
To find that we are late.

GROUP A: No, the train is not in yet—
Really hasn't got in yet—
You have lots of time
To buy some real estate.

GROUP B: We can show no interest
In a home for winter rest.
We are brokers, too—
Just the same as you.

ALL: Ev'rybody's doing it!
Ev'ryone pursuing it!
Trading all the time
In this sunny clime.
[Train noises]

Oh! Listen to the train!
What a glad refrain!
Pleasant music when
Bringing back our men to Florida—
They're coming back to Florida!

[During the next five lines, half the girls ad-lib: "Oh, there's George!" "Look at Harry," etc.]
Oh! when your love is near—
Then it's very clear—
Needn't tell you twice—
Paradise, paradise, paradise
On earth is Florida!
[Dance]

NICE BABY

Published December 1925. Introduced by Robert Halliday (Rollo), Jeanette MacDonald (Sylvia), and ensemble. Introduced in London by Evan Thomas, Vera Bryer, and ensemble. Alternate title: "Nice Baby! Come to Papa!"

VERSE 1

ROLLO: When I look at you, I have to own up:
I've been lucky since my wedding day.
Seems to me that you have never grown up—
But I mean that in the nicest way.
Just a sweet and charming little baby—
And as Shakespeare said, "I don't mean maybe!"*
You have all the other girlies shown up.
None of them will ever hear me say:

REFRAIN 1

Nice baby! Come to Papa! Don't be shy!
Nice baby! Come to Papa! Or you'll make him cry.
If you like candy,
Come hold my handie.
When we go bye-bye,
You'll like the things that I buy.
Nice baby! Be nice, baby!
And your papa will be nice to you—
Said, your papa will be nice to you.

VERSE 2

SYLVIA: I'm afraid your views are somewhat twisted;
And I'm sorry I must disagree.
You may be a he-man, double-fisted,
To outsiders, dear, but not to me.
In my arms I always want to hold you,
Even when I know I ought to scold you;
For the feeling always has persisted
You're the baby of the family.

REFRAIN 2

Nice baby! Come to Mamma! Don't be shy!
Nice baby! Come to Mamma! Or you'll make her cry.

*The original script reads "Ziegfeld" instead of "Shakespeare."

If you'll let my chair
Become your high chair,
I'll tell a story
Or sing you "Annie Laurie."
Nice baby! Be nice, baby!
And your mamma will be nice to you—
Said, your mamma will be nice to you!

LOOKING FOR A BOY

Published December 1925. Introduced by "Queenie Smith as 'Tip-Toes' Kaye in 'one'—i.e., downstage while the set was being changed behind the drop" (Ira Gershwin—*Lyrics on Several Occasions*). Introduced in London by Dorothy Dickson. The British edition of the sheet music contains additional lyrics (for a second verse) that are probably not by Ira Greshwin.

I notice that in her yearned-for's requirements the vocalist mentions merely desired height: " 'bout five foot six or seven." Matters not background, earning capacity, taste in breakfast foods, or even the color of his eyes. Obviously a damsel easily pleased. But about the only rhymes I could use for "Heaven" were "seven" and "eleven"; hence preoccupation with height. ("Devon" was geographically out-of-bounds; Laborite E. Bevin was probably already married; and what could one do with "replevin"?)

Luckily, talented Queenie Smith was tiny, and Allen Kearns, who played opposite her, was a couple of mites taller.

I thought I knew most of the terms for the classification of rhyme: masculine, feminine, double, triple, near, eye, assonantal, internal, &c. But Babette Deutsch's recent and scholarly *Poetry Handbook* reveals half a dozen I'm sure I'd never come across before. One term especially intrigues me: "Apocopated rhyme, so called because the end of one rhyming word is cut off." Examples given are: "Say" to rhyme with the first syllable of "crazy"; "Spain" with the first of "gainless."

Why titillated at this late stage? Because I am suddenly made aware that long, long ago in the last two verse lines of "Looking for a Boy" the music made me rhyme, apocopatedly, "way" with "saying"; and I now feel one with Molière's M. Jourdain the day he learned he'd been speaking prose for over forty years.

     —from Lyrics on Several Occasions

VERSE

If it's true that love affairs
Are all arranged in Heaven,

My Guardian Angel's holding out on me.
So, I'm looking for a boy
'Bout five foot six or seven,
And won't be happy till I'm on his knee.
I'll be blue until he comes my way;
Hope he takes the cue when I am saying:

REFRAIN

I am just a little girl
Who's looking for a little boy
Who's looking for a girl to love.

Tell me, please, where can he be,
The loving he who'll bring to me
The harmony I'm dreaming of?

It'll be good-bye, I know,
To my tale of woe
When he says, "Hello!"

So,
I am just a little girl
Who's looking for a little boy
Who's looking for a girl to love.

Act II—Reprise

VERSE

STEVE: If it's true that love affairs
    Are all arranged in Heaven,
    My Guardian Angel has been good to
    me.
TIP-TOES: I have found my little boy
    'Bout five foot six or seven,
    And I think I'm lucky as could be.
BOTH: I was blue until you came my way;
    But from now on, you will hear me
    saying:*

REFRAIN

STEVE: I have found my little girl.
TIP-TOES: And I have found my little boy.
BOTH: And we have found the thing called
    love.

TIP-TOES: Now that you have come to me
    There's sure to be, eternally,
    The harmony I'm dreaming of.

STEVE: It has been good-bye, I know,
    To my tale of woe,
    Since you said, "Hello!"

    Oh!
    I have found my little girl.

Script version: But from now on, always I'll be saying:

TIP-TOES: And I have found my little boy.
BOTH: And we have found the thing called
    love.

Unused Act II Reprise

ROLLO: I am just a little boy
    Who's wild about a little girl.
    And strange to say, I mean my wife.

SYLVIA: Here and there, I'm telling you
    The thing to do is to be true,
    And we'll be happy all through life.

ROLLO: It will be good-bye to all
    [*in* The other girls I know.
harmony
  with]
SYLVIA: It must be good-bye to all
    The other girls you know.
BOTH: That's what I call love.

    Just me for you
    And you for me—
SYLVIA: Just two—
ROLLO: Not three—
BOTH: And there will be the harmony
    We're dreaming of.

LADY LUCK

Introduced by ensemble. Alternate title: "Opening, Act I, Scene 2." The middle section of the number ("Watch the little wheel spin . . . Come back just the same!") was deleted during the run of the show.

We always make a scramble for
The rooms where one can gamble, for
It's often very hard to get a place.
You find high and near society—
'Most every variety—
Examples of the so-called Human Race.
It's no wonder that we tingle here;
You're privileged to mingle here
With dowagers and titles, in the flesh;
And at times, what lovely men you see—
Though ev'ry now and then, you see
Some butter-and-egg man who is strictly fresh.

Watch the little wheel spin
With a real spin—
See our fingers crossed!
If it stops at zero,
Then we fear—Oh!—

That our money's lost.
We importune Mistress Fortune
Not to let us lose;
Not to slumber when a number
Finally we choose.
Oh! The fascination—
All creation
Loves to play the game;
You lose all you borrow,
Then, tomorrow,
Come back just the same!

Lady Luck, listen to me!
Lady Luck, answer my plea!
It would be so thrilling
To make a killing—
Is this the beginning
Of my lucky inning?
Lady Luck, shall I play red?
Or will black butter my bread?
If you get me a bankful
Of notes, I'll be thankful—
Oh, Lady, be good to me!

WHEN DO WE DANCE?

Published December 1925. Introduced by Allen Kearns (Steve), Gertrude McDonald (Binnie), Lovey Lee (Denise), and ensemble. Introduced in London by Allen Kearns, Peggy Beaty, Lovey Lee, and ensemble. (Soon after the London opening, Kearns and Lee were replaced with Charles Lawrence and Rita McLean.)

VERSE

I'm fed up with discussions
About the music of Russians,
And I'm most unhappy when you talk about art.
Conversation so highbrow
Is much too heavy for my brow;
Teacher, darling teacher, won't you please have
　a heart?
Then our day is done,*
And we'll have to go;
But there's really one
Thing I want to know:

REFRAIN

When do we dance? When do we dance?
Teacher dear, when do we dance?

*Alternate line (in sheet music and script):
Then our work is done,

Let's take a chance, I'm in a trance,
Getting a thrill in advance.
Just can't help swaying—I must begin
When they are playing Kern or Berlin.
I want to slide, I want to glide,
With a sweet thing at my side.
You'll walk on air, lose ev'ry care,
If you'll let me be your guide.
There's too much sadness here below;
Come on, my dear, let's go!
When do we dance?
Teacher dear, when do we dance?

THESE CHARMING PEOPLE

Published December 1925. "The Kayes, two uncles and a niece, a vaudeville trio stranded in Palm Beach. Influenced by the environment, they decide to go posh" (Ira Gershwin—Lyrics on Several Occasions). Introduced by Queenie Smith (Tip-Toes), Andrew Tombes (Al), and Harry Watson, Jr. (Hen). Introduced in London by Dorothy Dickson, Laddie Cliff, and John Kirby. The British edition of the sheet music contains additional lyrics (for a second verse) that are probably not by Ira Gershwin.

I was scared stiff when tackling my first Broadway show, Two Little Girls in Blue (not that I ever learned to relax any time later on a job, whether a complete score or a single interpolation). However, I managed to survive and turn out a passable set of lyrics to the lively music of Vincent Youmans, with one song, "Oh, Me, Oh, My, Oh, You," becoming quite popular. (I kept hoping, though, no listener would particularly notice that among the various lyrics there were three uses of the "tender—surrender" rhyme.)

For about three years after that I worked with half a dozen composers and was able to have ten or twelve numbers interpolated in about as many shows and revues. Only two of these songs earned anything to speak of or deposit: "When All Your Castles Come Tumbling Down" (music by Milton Schwarzwald) and "Stairway to Paradise."

Then came Lady, Be Good!, a hit show with a generally admired score. Delighted of course with its success and the $300 or so royalty each week, I was still not completely satisfied with my contribution. I had adequately fitted some sparkling tunes, and several singable love songs and rhythm numbers had resulted. Yet I was a bit bothered by there being no lyric I considered comic.

A year later, with Tip-Toes, I chose to believe there had been some development in craftsmanship. Tip-Toes

contained longer openings, many of the songs had crisp lines, and the first-act finale carried plot action for four or five minutes. And I liked the trio "These Charming People," which seemed to amuse the audience. Up to then I'd often wondered if I could do a comedy trio like the ones P. G. Wodehouse came up with—"Bongo on the Congo" from Sitting Pretty, for instance.

A Small Summing Up. Given a fondness for music, a feeling for rhyme, a sense of whimsy and humor, an eye for the balanced sentence, an ear for the current phrase, and the ability to imagine oneself a performer trying to put over the number in progress—given all this, I still would say it takes four or five years collaborating with knowledgeable composers to become a well-rounded lyricist. I could be wrong about the time element—there no doubt have been lyricists who knew their business from the start—but time and experiment and experience help.

　　　　　　　　—from Lyrics on Several Occasions

VERSE 1

HEN: We must make it our ambition
　　　To live up to our position
　　　As we take our places in society.
AL: When those million-dollar blokes pass,
　　I will never make a faux pas;
　　I will show them I am full of pedigree.
TIP-TOES: And the lady isn't born yet
　　　　Who can beat me at a lorgnette,
　　　　When I'm honoring the op'ra at the
　　　　　Met.
ALL: So if you're not social winners,
　　Don't invite us to your dinners—
　　We must warn you we'll be awful hard
　　　to get.

REFRAIN 1

We'll be like These Charming People,
Putting on the ritz,
Acting as befits
These charming people:
Very debonair,
Full of savoir-faire.
I hear that Mrs. Whoozis
Created quite a stir:
She built a little love nest
For her and her chauffeur.
If these people can be charming,
Then we can be charming, too!

VERSE 2

HEN: Please recall, if you've forgotten,
　　　That my father was in cotton,
　　　And my family is truly F.F.V.

AL: Merely social climbing varmints!
Ours was made in undergarments,
So you see before you one who's
   B.V.D.
TIP-TOES: If that's pedigree, enjoy it!
My old man came from Detroit,
So I'll have you know that I am F.O.B.
ALL: In our veins there runs the true blood!
When we mingle with the blue blood,
The Four Hundred will become Four
   Hundred Three.

REFRAIN 2

We'll be like These Charming People,
Putting on the ritz,
Acting as befits
These charming people:
Very debonair,
Full of savoir-faire.
It seems that Mr. Smythe-Smythe
Had no children, till
Some twenty-seven turned up
To listen to the will.
If these people can be charming,
Then we can be charming, too!

Alternate Versions of Refrain 2, Lines 7–10

Sheet-Music Version

I hear that Mr. You-Know
Has made up with his wife—
Since each allows the other
To lead a double life.

Script Version

I hear that Mrs. You-Know
Is riding for a fall;
It seems that when her child was born
She wasn't there at all.

Earlier Manuscript Version

I hear that Mrs. You-Know
Is out to make a fuss—
Found backstage at the Follies,
Her husband thus-and-thus!

Other Versions (unused)

It's nice of Mr. Blank-Blank
To lead a moral life.
He's keeping three apartments
And one is for his wife.

You've heard of Mr. Yiff-Niff—
He's quite a social light.

To keep up his position
He gets lit up ev'ry night.

I hear that Mrs. You-Know
Is starting quite a fuss.
It seems there was a blonde
And her husband thus-and-thus.

THAT CERTAIN FEELING

Published December 1925. Introduced by Queenie Smith (Tip-Toes) and Allen Kearns (Steve). Introduced in London by Dorothy Dickson and Allen Kearns.

There are some vocal recordings of this song wherein the singer misses the rhythmic point of the tune by giving equal value to the first three notes and words of such lines as:

The first time I met you.
I could not forget you.
I've got what they call love, &c.

which should be heard as:

(Beat) *Thefirst* time I met you
(Beat) *Icould* not forget you
(Beat) *I'vegot* what they call love, &c.
   —from *Lyrics on Several Occasions*

VERSE 1

STEVE: Knew it from the start—
Love would play a part.
Felt that feeling come a-stealing
In my lonesome heart.
TIP-TOES: It would be ideal
If that's the way you feel.
But tell me, is it really real?
STEVE: You gave me

REFRAIN 1

That certain feeling—
The first time I met you.
I hit the ceiling;
I could not forget you.
You were completely sweet;
Oh, what could I do?
I wanted phrases
To sing your praises.
That certain feeling—
The one that they all love—
No use concealing,
I've got what they call love.

Now we're together,
Let's find out whether
You're feeling that feeling too.

VERSE 2

TIP-TOES: I have symptoms too,
Just the same as you.
When they centered, when they
   entered
In my heart, I knew.
Brighter is the day
Since you've come my way.
Believe it when you hear me say:
You gave me

REFRAIN 2

That certain feeling—
The first time I met you.
I hit the ceiling,*
I could not forget you.
I felt it happen
Just as you came in view.
Grew sort of dizzy;
Thought, "Gee, who *is* he?"
That certain feeling—
I'm here to confess, it
Is so appealing
No words can express it.
I cannot hide it,
I must confide it:
I'm feeling that feeling too.

Finale—Act II

STEVE: I've had my lesson.
I thought it was money
That you put stress on.
Forgive me, my honey.
If you'll say "Yes," we'll see
A preacher today.
TIP-TOES: That seems to be a
Darn good idea.
ROLLO: I've got a feeling
That I'll be true to you.
TIP-TOES: You keep that feeling,
And I'll bill and coo you.
AL AND HEN: Our trouble's over;
We'll be in clover.
ALL: We're feeling that feeling, too!

---

*In Lyrics on Several Occasions, *I.G.* changed this line to:*

That certain feeling—

Unused Act II Reprise

STEVE: That certain feeling—
    Dear, when you confided
    You felt a feeling,
    The same sort that I did.
TIP-TOES: From now on ev'ry other
    Man is taboo;
    Love is in season—
    And you're the reason!
STEVE: June bells will tingle
    For me and my someone.
TIP-TOES: I'm all a-tingle;
    Two hearts will become one.
    No one can hold me,
    Dear, since you told me
    You're feeling that feeling too.

SWEET AND LOW-DOWN

Published December 1925. "Sung, kazooed, tromboned, and danced by Andrew Tombes [Al], Lovey Lee [Denise], Gertrude McDonald [Binnie], and ensemble at a party, Palm Beach" (Ira Gershwin—*Lyrics on Several Occasions*). As "Blow That Sweet and Low-Down," introduced in London by Laddie Cliff, Lovey Lee, and Peggy Beaty.

B efore Ukulele Ike in *Lady, Be Good!* accepted our "Little Jazz Bird" for his specialty spot, he had rejected something we'd concocted called "Singin' Pete"—"the reason for shufflin' feet." (We didn't particularly fancy "Singin' Pete" but thought Ike would.) A year later I remembered from this discarded attempt at something patently popular one line I liked: "He's the John McCormack of the sweet and low-down." So I salvaged for a title the portmanteau phrase, arrived at from "sweet and low" and "low-down."

It makes for small philological honor, but one is pleased to note that invented phrases like "sweet and low-down" and *Of Thee I Sing*'s "with a hey, nonny nonny and a ha cha cha!" are included in *The American Thesaurus of Slang*.

As for "portmanteau" in its application to words and phrases rather than luggage, credit Lewis Carroll. In *Through the Looking Glass*, Humpty-Dumpty explains to Alice the meaning of some of the words in "Jabberwocky." After "brillig," he analyzes "slithy": "Well, *slithy* means 'lithe and slimy.' You can see it's like a portmanteau—there are two meanings packed in one word."

(Re this contraction device—in *The American Language: Supplement One*, Mencken evidences a preference for "blends" to "portmanteau-words." And others,

since Carroll, prefer other coinages, such as "telescope-words," "amalgams," &c. But enough of Carrollinguistics.)

—from *Lyrics on Several Occasions*

VERSE

There's a cabaret in *this* city
I can recommend to you;*
Peps you up like electricity
When the band is blowing blue.
They play nothing classic, oh no! down there;
They crave nothing else but the low-down there.
If you need a tonic,
And the need is chronic—
If you're in a crisis,
My advice is:

REFRAIN

Grab a cab and go down
To where the band is playing;
Where milk and honey flow down;
Where ev'ry one is saying,
"Blow that Sweet and Low-Down!"

Busy as a beaver,
You'll dance until you totter;
You're sure to get the fever
For nothing could be hotter—
Oh, that Sweet and Low-Down!

Philosopher or deacon,
You simply have to weaken.
Hear those shuffling feet—
You can't keep your seat—
Professor, start your beat!

Come along, get in it—
You'll love the syncopation!
The minute they begin it,
You're shouting to the nation:
"Blow that Sweet and Low-Down!"

FINALE, ACT I

Introduced by ensemble. The number is a blend of song and spoken dialogue.

ENSEMBLE: Oh, what was that noise?
    I heard a scream.

*In the script, this line is:
I have heard about it, too;

Who can it be?
I'm very sure that someone has been
    hurt. If so,
Maybe it's someone we know.
[*Tip-Toes is carried in and placed on settee*]
ENSEMBLE: Poor little girl, I wonder if she is
    hurt,
    If she is hurt badly.
[*After much dialogue, Act I ends with a reprise of the refrain of "Sweet and Low-Down"*]

OUR LITTLE CAPTAIN

Introduced by Queenie Smith (Tip-Toes) and "the boys." Introduced in London by Dorothy Dickson and "the boys." Originally, this number was part of the encore to "Harlem River Chanty." When "Harlem River Chanty" was dropped during the pre-Broadway tryout, the "Our Little Captain" section was retained as the opening number of Act II.

BOYS: Here comes our little captain!
    Give her a hip-hip-hip—Hurray!
    Welcome, dear little captain,
    To our ship-ship-ship—today!
TIP-TOES: Yo-Ho, I'm glad to be here with you;
    Yo-Ho, to share the good cheer with
    you;
    Yo-Ho, I'm tickled to death to say
    That I'll be your little captain!
BOYS: Give her a hip-hip-hip—Hurray!

IT'S A GREAT LITTLE WORLD!

Published February 1926. Introduced by Allen Kearns (Steve), Jeanette MacDonald (Sylvia), Andrew Tombes (Al), Gertrude McDonald (Binnie), Lovey Lee (Denise), and ensemble. As "Give In" (later changed back to "It's a Great Little World"), introduced in London by Vera Bryer, Laddie Cliff, Lovey Lee, and ensemble. Some copies of the British sheet music contain lyrics for a second verse and refrain that are probably not by Ira Gershwin.

VERSE

The world is so full of a number of things;
I'm sure we should all be as happy as kings.
Make it all a big party!
Fill the cup with us and drink hearty!
When you realize that this life is so short,
The wise thing to do is to be a good sport.
Why take time out for sorrow?
If your day is blue,
We're telling you:*

REFRAIN

Give in!
For it's a great little world we live in—
Live while you may!
Laughter
Is something ev'ryone should be after—
Find it today!
Don't be shy! Why, oh, why stay on the shelf?
Clear the stage! Act your age! Just be yourself!
Oh, give in!
For it's a great little world we live in today!

NIGHTIE-NIGHT!

Published December 1925. Introduced by Queenie Smith (Tip-Toes) and Allen Kearns (Steve). As "Nighty-Night!" introduced in London by Dorothy Dickson and Allen Kearns.

Show Version†

VERSE 1

TIP-TOES: It isn't good for one to stay up late, and so,
I think you'd better go, don't you?
STEVE: I know it isn't good for one to stay up late.
But, Gee! I'll bet it's great for two.
TIP-TOES: Tomorrow morning you must start to work and win.
And nothing, dear, must interfere.
STEVE: Well, if you think that it is really for the best—
I'll try to get some rest, my dear.
TIP-TOES: If you count up to a thousand sheep,
I am certain you will fall asleep.

Sheet-music version:
I'm telling you!
†*Only Refrain 1 was actually performed.*

REFRAIN 1

Nightie-night! Little boy, good night!
STEVE: Nightie-night! Little girl, sleep tight!
A million sheep I'll count.
TIP-TOES: That's quite a great amount.
STEVE: Will I sleep? No! I'll keep on pining.
All the night I'll be weeping like a willow.
All the night I'll be envying your pillow.
TIP-TOES: Nightie-night! Till the sun is shining.
BOTH: Goody, goody, good night! Sleep tight!

VERSE 2

STEVE: The future looks to me like one eternal spring,
If she means ev'rything she said.
But, Gee! I promised her I'd get some sleep, and so
I guess I'd better go to bed.
Although I realize I'll only toss and roll
And keep awake the whole night through;
For when she's near me all the world is filled with dreams
And somehow, now, it seems I'm blue.
What a happy chappy I should be
If I thought that she would dream of me.

REFRAIN 2

TIP-TOES: Nightie-night! Little boy, good night!
STEVE: Nightie-night! Little girl, sleep tight.
TIP-TOES: I hope you're comfy now!
STEVE: You've made me so, and how!
TIP-TOES: Try to sleep, or you'll have me pining!
Little boy, all my dreams you'll be adorning.
But how I'll thrill to hear you say, "Good morning!"
Nightie-night! Till the sun is shining.
Goody, goody, goody night!
STEVE: Goody, goody, good night!
BOTH: Goody, goody, good night! Sleep tight!

Published Version

VERSE 1

TIP-TOES: It's time for little boys like you to be in bed.
The dawn is just ahead, you know.
STEVE: I think I'll hang around till night is at an end,

Just watching out for friend or foe.
TIP-TOES: That's awf'ly sweet; but then, if trouble comes at all,
You bet you'll hear me calling you.
STEVE: If I should leave you now, I'd only toss and roll,
And keep awake the whole night through.
TIP-TOES: If you try to count a thousand sheep,
I am certain you will fall asleep.

REFRAIN 1

STEVE: Nightie-night! Little girl, good night!
TIP-TOES: Nightie-night! Little boy, sleep tight.
STEVE: A million sheep I'll count—
TIP-TOES: That's quite a great amount.
STEVE: Will I sleep? No! I'll keep on pining.
All the night, I'll be weeping like a willow.
All the night, I'll be envying your pillow.
TIP-TOES: Nightie-night! Till the sun is shining.
BOTH: Goody, goody, good night! Sleep tight.

VERSE 2

TIP-TOES: They say the night air isn't good for one, and so
I think you'd better go, don't you?
STEVE: Night air is very bad for one. You have it straight,
But, lady, it is great for two.
TIP-TOES: No, I'm afraid that I'll be acting like a loon,
For there's a gorgeous moon above.
STEVE: But I'll be glad to show you Jupiter and Mars,
And lots of little stars you'll love.
TIP-TOES: All that I can do for you, it seems,
Is to wish you lots of pleasant dreams.

REFRAIN 2

STEVE: Nightie-night! Little girl, good night!
TIP-TOES: Nightie-night! Little boy, sleep tight.
STEVE: I guess I'd better go.
TIP-TOES: Don't think that I'll say "No!"
STEVE: Will I sleep? No! I'll keep on pining.
TIP-TOES: Little boy, all my dreams you'll be adorning.
But how I'll thrill to hear you say, "Good morning!"
STEVE: Nightie-night! Till the sun is shining.
BOTH: Goody, goody, good night! Sleep tight.

TIP-TOES

Introduced by Queenie Smith (Tip-Toes) and ensemble. Introduced in London by Dorothy Dickson and ensemble.

VERSE

There's a treat in store for you,
Right here on the floor for you.
There's a dancer of renown
Who is honoring the town.
Tip-Toes is the charmer's name;
She'll make you exclaim:

REFRAIN

Tip-Toes, tip, tip your hat to Tip-Toes;
Dear little Tip-Toes tops them all.
Tip-Toes, you'll pit-a-pat when Tip-Toes'
Tap, tap-a-tapping, to your call.
"On with the dance!"—
You'll shout it willingly;
She'll bring romance
And bring it thrillingly.
Tip-Toes, tip, tip your hat to Tip-Toes;
Dear little Tip-Toes tops them all!

HARLEM RIVER CHANTY

Published November 1968 in a choral arrangement. Lyrics first published in Ira Gershwin's *Lyrics on Several Occasions* (1959). Introduced in the pre-Broadway tryout by Harry Watson, Jr. (Hen), and ensemble. Dropped before the New York opening. Originally the opening number of Act II, it was replaced with "Our Little Captain," which had been part of its encore.

S ince the first four lines of the introduction were rendered slowly, and the latter four in accelerated tempo, the line "*Allegro* and *andante*" should be, if ordered sense prevailed, "*Andante* and *allegro*." Obviously the reason for reversal is that "*andante*" was easier to rhyme.

The tribute to soft drink (outside of Bevo, a beverage permitted to have a tiny alcoholic content) was an attempt at irony in a Prohibition Era when bathtub gin and flavored alcohol flooded the country, and pocket-flask manufacture was at its peak. (Personally, I prefer soft drinks, but of course had to have a bootlegger or else be a social pariah.)

I note that "sass' " (shortened from "sarsaparilla")

makes two appearances to rhyme with "glass." This is unusual in that I ordinarily try not to use the same rhyme twice in a refrain. But I was stuck because even today I can dig up only a non-alcoholic, distasteful "Seltzer gas"; "Bass," an ale; and the Russian beer, "*kvass.*"
—from *Lyrics on Several Occasions*

VERSE

SAILORS: When our supply of pieces of eight
Is getting rather scanty,
And we are all unable to spend
The night at penny ante,
'Tis then we burst into a refrain—
Allegro and *andante*—
And sing that rollicking, frolicking strain,
The Harlem River Chanty:

REFRAIN

SOLO: It's great to be a sailor,
No life is quite so free;
And the right boat
Is the night boat
Heading for Albany.
SAILORS: He's glad to be a sailor,
His life is gay and free;
And the right boat
Is the night boat
Heading for Albany.

Yo-ho-ho, and a bottle of milk shake,
Yo-ho-ho, and a bottle of sass',
Yo-ho-ho, with a celery tonic—
Yo-ho-ho, fill up the glass!

REFRAIN 2

SOLO: Heave to! Me precious hearties!
The sea life I adore.
I've so much affection
In that direction—
I always hug the shore.
SAILORS: He's glad to be a sailor—
The sea life to adore.
With so much affection
In that direction—
He always hugs the shore!

Yo-ho-ho, and a bottle of Bevo,
Yo-ho-ho, and a demitasse,
Yo-ho-ho, with a frosted coffee—
Yo-ho-ho, fill up the glass!

REFRAIN 3

SOLO: Oh, how I love a schooner!
Oh, how I love the foam!

But cash or credit,
Try and get it!
Back in home sweet home!*
SAILORS: Oh, how he loves a schooner!
Oh, how he loves the foam!
But cash or credit,
Try and get it!
Back in home sweet home.

Yo-ho-ho, and a bottle of Pluto,
Yo-ho-ho, for the drugstore lass,
Yo-ho-ho, with a Coca-Cola—
Yo-ho-ho, fill up the glass!

ENCORE REFRAIN

SOLO: I've been aboard a whaler
And every sort of bark,
But there is no boat
Like a rowboat
Out on Central Park.
SAILORS: He's been aboard a whaler
And every sort of bark,
But there is no boat
Like a rowboat
Out on Central Park.

Yo-ho-ho, with a chocolate frosted,†
Yo-ho-ho, and a bottle of sass',
Yo-ho-ho, with a bottle of ketchup—‡
Yo-ho-ho, fill up the glass!

OFFICER: [*spoken*]Stand by! Here come the ladies!
SAILORS: Stand by! Here come the ladies—
The ladies we adore.
We've so much affection
In that direction—
We hate to leave the shore!

ALL: Yo-ho-ho, for a wonderful party,
Yo-ho-ho, for a night of romance,
Yo-ho-ho, for the music and moonlight—
Yo-ho-ho, when do we dance?
[*At this point the number segued into "Our Little Captain"*]

*I.G. also considered the line
"In the saloon back home!"
†*Alternate version:*
Yo-ho-ho, with a pineapple phosphate,
‡*Alternate version:*
Yo-ho-ho, with a choc'late malted—

HARBOR OF DREAMS

Introduced during the pre-Broadway tryout by Queenie Smith (Tip-Toes), Gertrude McDonald (Binnie), Lovey Lee (Denise), and ensemble. Dropped before the New York opening. No music is known to survive.

VERSE

TIP-TOES: There's a haven meant for you and me
When your ship is tossing on a stormy
sea.
If you ever go there,
Beggar or banker,
You'll drop your anchor,
For it's as peaceful as can be.
GIRLS: But how can we get a lift there?
We'd like to drift there.
Can we get there today?
TIP-TOES: No need to travel—
It isn't far away.

REFRAIN

You'll find the bluebird, the rainbow,
the silver lining, too,
When your ship is in the harbor of
dreams.
No day is gray there, it's gay there, the
skies are always blue,
When your ship is in the harbor of
dreams.
By those who know, it's highly
recommended—
There ev'ry care is ended
And ev'ry lonely heart befriended.
You'll find the rainbow, the bluebird,
the silver lining, too,
When your ship is in the harbor of
dreams.

VERSE

Puritans there are who say:
"It is sinful to be gay."
But I cannot share that view—
Life's too short to be blue.
There's no one can stand the gaff
'Less they learn the way to laugh.
I'm for the poet who said one day,
"Gather ye rosebuds while ye may."

REFRAIN 1

The thing to do from ev'ry Monday to Sunday
Is to make of ev'ry one day a fun day.
What's the use of taking time out for sorrow?
You're here today and gone tomorrow.
Why turn down the sun and watchfully wait for
The well-known rainy day?
Rather—Gather rosebuds while ye may.

PATTER

Now Lincoln liked to have his little joke.
And Grant was never seen without a smoke.
When Bobbie Burns and Edgar Allan Poe
Were asked to have a drink, did they say "No"?
You'll find that famous men from A to Z
Were somehow always ready for a spree.
These names have never faded
And anything that they did,
I'm here to tell the world,
Is good enough for me.

REFRAIN 2

This world, I find, is very pleasant to live in
When you learn the thing to do is give in.
Have pajamas made of silk—not of cotton—
For when you're gone, you're soon forgotten.
Why turn down the blue to watchfully wait for
Those well-known skies of gray?
Rather—Gather rosebuds while ye may.

VERSE 1

Puritans often say:
"It's a sin to be gay."
But I don't hold that view.
Life's too short to be blue.
Guided by one that I recommend quite highly,
I, in brief, took a leaf from the Life of Riley.

REFRAIN 1

You will find
That it's a great life only
When you weaken a bit.
Leave the grind;
Forget your worries—
Let your fancy flit.
Ev'ry day, I'm at my best if I
Stay away from work, I'll testify.
It's a great life only
When you weaken just a bit.

VERSE 2

Bobbie Burns, Eddie Poe,
Found that drink made them glow.
Bonaparte danced at court.
Byron was one good sport.
Grant would smoke, Lincoln joke—We have
proof that's ample.
Great men, they, so I say, Follow their example.

REFRAIN 2

You will find
That it's a great life only
When you weaken a bit.
Never mind
The straight and narrow—
That's no path to hit.
Happy-faced, I'd feel much worse if I'd
Not embraced the life diversified.
It's a great life only
When you weaken just a bit.

GATHER YE ROSEBUDS

Introduced by Allen Kearns (Steve) and ensemble during the pre-Broadway tryout. Dropped before the New York opening and replaced with "Life's Too Short to Be Blue," which, in turn, was replaced with "It's a Great Little World." In March 1980, Ira Gershwin made some revisions in the lyric, and he and Michael Feinstein prepared this definitive version. No. 107 in the George and Ira Gershwin Special Numbered Song File.

WEAKEN A BIT

Dropped during rehearsals. This number was a forerunner of "Gather Ye Rosebuds." Note that line 4 of verse 1, retained in "Gather Ye Rosebuds," provided the title for "Life's Too Short to Be Blue." No music is known to survive.

LIFE'S TOO SHORT TO BE BLUE

Introduced by Allen Kearns (Steve) and ensemble during the pre-Broadway tryout. Replaced "Gather Ye Rosebuds." But it, too, was replaced before the New York opening, this time with "It's a Great Little World." No music is known to survive.

VERSE

People! People! I'm here to state:
I'm feeling great,
And here's the reason:
Nothing matters—All's applesauce!
Worry's a total loss!
Come and join my party;
Come and have a drink!
We'll put all our cares on the blink!
People! People! Don't hesitate!
Tomorrow may be too late!

REFRAIN

Life's too short to be blue—
I'm telling you—
Take a tip, take a tip, take a tip from me!
Be the sort of a lad
Who's never sad—
Take a sip, take a sip, take a sip with me!
Oh! Oh! Oh! Oh! Hear that music play—play!
So, so, so, so let's start making hay! Hey!
Life's too short to be blue—
I'm telling you—
Take a tip, take a tip, take a tip from me!

WE

Intended for Robert Halliday (Rollo) and Jeanette Mac-
Donald (Sylvia). Dropped during rehearsals. No music
is known to survive.

VERSE 1

ROLLO: Let's be seasoning
Love with reasoning.
Can't you see it at all?
If we're in for a squall,
We, divided, must fall.
Shouldn't hurt a bit
If I flirt a bit—
You have nothing to fear.
To the wedding tie
I am faithful, my dear.

REFRAIN 1

We—spelt W E—
Should be pally
Genera*ll*y.
For I—am going to try
Hard to please you,
Never tease you;

But you—must say you'll be true—
Never doubt me,
Never flout me—
And you'll see I can be
The perfect lover.
She means nothing to me!
As you can see—
Just a fancy!
But thou—wilt make me somehow
Climb a steeple,
Telling people
That he and she and they
Can say just what they may—
But we—
Oh, how happy we'll be!

VERSE 2

SYLVIA: Oh, if you're sincere,
Really more sincere
Than you've been in the past,
I am here to forecast
That the union will last.
All your Loreleis
With immoral eyes
You must promise to quit.
Darling, if you do,
I'll be saying, to wit:

REFRAIN 2

We—I'm glad you agree—
Should be pally
Genera*ll*y.
For I—could never deny
That I need you.
And I'll heed you.
But you—must say you'll be true—
Now and all time,
Spring and fall time—
For I grieve when you leave
The straight and narrow.
He—means nothing to me!
Just a dancer,
That's my answer!
But thou wilt never know how
I adore you;
I live for you!
And he and she and they
Can say just what they may—
But we—
Oh, how happy we'll be!

AMERICANA, 1926

SUNNY DISPOSISH

Published August 1926. Music by Philip Charig. Introduced in the revue *Americana*, which opened in New
York on July 26, 1926, by Arline and Edgar Gardiner.
(As Julian English, the protagonist of John O'Hara's
1934 novel *Appointment in Samarra*, drinks his way to
self-destruction, he plays three of his favorite phonograph records—one is bandleader Jean Goldkette's version of "Sunny Disposish.")

VERSE 1

Anytime the thunder starts to rumble down,
Don't let hope tumble down
Or castles crumble down.
If the blues appear, just make the best of them;
Just make a jest of them;
Don't be possessed of them.
At the risk of sounding rather platitudinous—
Here's what I believe should be the attitude in
us:

REFRAIN

A sunny disposish
Will always see you through—
When up above the skies are blah
'Stead of being blue.
Mister Trouble makes our faces grow long,
But a smile will have him saying, "So long!"
It really doesn't pay
To be a gloomy pill—
It's absolutely most ridic',
Positively sil'.
The rain may pitter-patter—
It really doesn't matter—
For life can be delish
With a sunny disposish.

VERSE 2

Must confess I like your way of viewing it—
No use in ruing it
When gloom is blueing it.
Taking your advice, the sad and weary'll
Have no material

To be funereal.
It's a thought that they should be swallowing,
    my dear,
Look at me, already you've a following, my dear.

REPEAT REFRAIN

THAT LOST BARBER SHOP CHORD

Published August 1926. Music by George Gershwin. Introduced in *Americana* (1926) by Louis Lazarin and "The Pan-American Quartet" (Charles H. Downy, Joseph E. Loomis, John W. Turner, and Walter Hilliard). Alternate title: "Lost Barbershop Chord."

This, like "Sweet and Low-Down," has a portmanteau title. The derivation is of course from "The Lost Chord," Sullivan's setting of the Adelaide Proctor poem, and "Play That Barber Shop Chord," by McDonald, Tracey, and Muir. (Incid., checking in the anthologies, I find that the Proctor poem is called "A Lost Chord." Whoever—Sir Arthur?—changed the indefinite to the definite article in the title did the song no harm. An 1893 quote: " 'The Lost Chord,' perhaps the most successful song of modern times. . . ." [Willeby: *Masters of English Music*.] And a 1928 quote: "It has been computed that 'The Lost Chord' is one of the six most popular songs ever written." [Isaac Goldberg: *The Story of Gilbert and Sullivan*.] Sorry, Goldberg doesn't state all the five others, only two: Nevin's "The Rosary" and Faure's *"Les Rameaux."* As for the 1910 "Play That Barber Shop Chord"—it isn't one of The Six, but it certainly is one of the best ragtime songs ever written.)

Our song, "That Lost Barber Shop Chord," got lost pronto 11:15 p.m. closing night of *Americana*, and remains to this day a six-page sheet-music nonentity. But it had its day—one or two days anyway. The critics more than liked it. Here's how Charles Pike Sawyer in the *New York Evening Post* reviewed it, 7/27/26: "that wonderfully beautiful 'Lost Barber Shop Chord' . . . is Gershwin at his best, which is saying a lot. Full of beautiful melody and swinging rhythm, it was a perfect joy, and right well was it sung by Louis Lazarin and a Negro

quartet with delightful voices." And on 7/31/26 he insisted: "What a joy is George Gershwin's 'Lost Barber Shop Chord' . . . and fully the equal of anything this great American composer has written, even in that gloriously beautiful tone poem—he called it a piano concerto, which it wasn't—played last season by Walter Damrosch's New York Symphony Orchestra." Stephen Rathbun, *New York Evening Sun*, 7/27/26: "The music of the revue is quite as attractive as the humor. The high mark is George Gershwin's ambitious 'Lost Barber Shop Chord.' " And Others.

Possibly these judgments were to some degree correct at the time. Me, I haven't heard the song sung anywhere in over thirty years.

—from *Lyrics on Several Occasions*

VERSE

Seated one day at the barber's,
A place up in Harlem that harbors
Four barbers who certainly could harmonize,
I listened to them in amazement—
Not caring what minutes or days meant—
For Lordy! They certainly could vocalize.
Suddenly I heard them strike a chord,
Felt my miseries go overboard,
Seemed as if I heard the angels hum,
Seemed as if I were in Kingdom Come.
"Oh, sing it again!" I entreated,
But oh! It was never repeated.
I cried out and cried out,
But it died out.

REFRAIN

I'm looking for that lost barber shop chord—
Where can it be?
I'm looking for that lost barber shop chord—
Come back to me!
I'm growing gray,
Searching nighttime and day;
When is it coming to stay?
I'm looking for that lost barber shop chord—
Sweet misery!—
For it will bring eternal jubilee.
I'm looking high,
I'm looking low,
Before I die
I want to know

What happened to that heaven'ly lost barber
    shop chord.
Where can it be, where can it,
Where can it be?
Where can it be?
Where can it, where can it be?

BLOWING THE BLUES AWAY

Published August 1926. Music by Philip Charig. Alternate title: "Blowin' The Blues Away." Introduced in *Americana* (1926) by Lew Brice, Betty Compton, Helen Morgan, Evelyn Bennett, Gay Nell, and Elizabeth Morgan.

VERSE

There's an aggregation down South,
Playing syncopation down South.
It will never snow there,
When the blues they blow there.
If you're at that station down South,
For your information down South,
Every local yokel calls you aside,
Starts in getting vocal, tells you with pride:

REFRAIN

Come on and listen, think what you're missin;
Now that you're here, you'll stay.
Wait'll you hear 'em Blowin' the Blues Away.
If they get hotter, you'll need a blotter;
Say, when they start to play,
Neighbor, you'll cheer 'em Blowin' the Blues
    Away.
I bet your clothes'll burn up
When they turn up
And they "Hey! Hey!" you.
I'm shoutin', they will thrill you;
They will kill you;
Baby, they'll slay you!
Wait'll they give it—hot as a rivet—
Brother, I bet you'll say,
"Heaven is nearer, Blowin' the Blues Away!"

OVERLEAF: *Inset: Gertrude Lawrence singing "Someone to Watch Over Me"*

OH, KAY! | 1926

Tryout: Shubert Theatre, Philadelphia, October 18, 1926. New York run: Imperial Theatre, opened November 8, 1926. 256 performances. Music by George Gershwin. Lyrics by Ira Gershwin. Additional lyrics by Howard Dietz. Produced by Alex A. Aarons and Vinton Freedley. Book by Guy Bolton and P. G. Wodehouse. Book staged by John Harwood. Dances staged by Sammy Lee. Orchestra under the direction of William Daly. Orchestrations by Hilding Anderson. Cast, starring Gertrude Lawrence (Kay), Oscar Shaw (Jimmy Winter), and Victor Moore ("Shorty" McGee), featured Harland Dixon (Larry Potter), Marion Fairbanks (Phil Ruxton), Madeline Fairbanks (Dolly Ruxton), Gerald Oliver Smith (The Duke), Sascha Beaumont (Constance Appleton), Harry T. Shannon (Revenue Officer Jansen), Betty Compton (Molly Morse), Constance Carpenter (Mae), Paulette Winston (Daisy), Frank Gardiner (Judge Appleton), Janette Gilmore (Peggy), and Phil Ohman and Victor Arden at the pianos.

London run: Produced by Musical Plays Ltd. in conjunction with Alex A. Aarons and Vinton Freedley at His Majesty's Theatre, London, opened September 21, 1927. 215 performances. Staged by William Ritter, Sammy Lee, and Elsie Neal. Orchestra under the direction of Arthur Wood. Cast, starring Gertrude Lawrence (Kay), featured Harold French (Jimmy Winter), John Kirby ("Shorty" McGee), Claude Hulbert (The Duke), Beth Dodge (Dolly Ruxton), Betty Dodge (Phil Ruxton), Eric Coxon (Larry Potter), April Harmon (Constance Appleton), Percy Parsons (Revenue Officer Jansen), Rita McLean (Molly), Cecile Maule-Cole (Peggy), Charles Cautley (Judge Appleton), and Phyllis Dawn (Daisy).

THE WOMAN'S TOUCH

Published July 1984 in the *Oh, Kay!* vocal selections. Registered for copyright as an unpublished composition in June 1958. Introduced by Betty Compton (Molly), Constance Carpenter (Mae), and ensemble. During the pre-Broadway tryout, it opened Act I, Scene 3. Introduced in London by Rita McLean (Molly), Cecile Maule-Cole (Peggy), and ensemble.

Oh, my goodness! What a mess this place is!
Dust upon our faces!
It needs a woman's touch.

Oh! The atmosphere is sad and ghostly.
What is needed mostly
Is the woman's touch.

What a sight this room is!
Tell me where a broom is!
Find a can of Gold Dust
And we'll chase the old dust.
Plain to see it needs the woman's touch.

Jimmy's coming, so we want to clean up,
Brighten all the scene up
With the woman's touch.
Color, charm, and such
Need the woman's touch.

Whoop it up! Tonight is the night!
For dear old Jimmy's coming home!
Jimmy's coming home!

We must get
Ev'rything all set
For tonight, there's a party!
Shout, "Hey! Hey!"
Throw your cares away—
For tonight, there's a party!
But work must be done
By ev'ryone—
Clear the floor!
For Jimmy's a pal
That ev'ry gal
Must adore!
And so we'll get
Ev'rything all set
By the time that Jim gets home.

DON'T ASK!

Published July 1984 in the *Oh, Kay!* vocal selections. Previously registered for copyright as an unpublished composition in June 1958. Introduced by Harland Dixon (Larry), Marion Fairbanks (Phil), and Madeline Fairbanks (Dolly). Introduced in London by Claude Hulbert (The Duke), Betty Dodge (Phil), and Beth Dodge (Dolly). Also see "Guess Who?," the lyric which follows.

VERSE 1

LARRY: If you're looking for a playmate,
There's a chap whose praises I'd sing.
You will find that he's a gay mate,
If you care for that sort of thing.
You'll be feeling dizzy when you've kissed him,
And you'll murmur, "Oh, is this a system!"

REFRAIN 1

Who is the guy—
Oh me, oh my—
Thinks you're peaches and pie?
Don't ask!
Who is the chap?
Who is the sap?
Love all over his map?
Don't ask!
Moon and stars, stars and moon, heaven above—
Lady, lady, someone's in love. Oh!
Who is the sheik
Who'd make you weak
With his parlor technique?
Don't ask!

VERSE 2

GIRLS: Are you sure he won't mislead us?
LARRY: Maybe it'll pay to take a chance.
GIRLS: Is satisfaction guaranteed us?
LARRY: You can count on that in advance.
He's the sort of chap to set your cap for.
He's the kind of bird the flappers flap for.

REFRAIN 2

BOYS: Who is the miss
Who'd like a kiss?
GIRLS: If you have to know this,
Don't ask!
BOYS: Is there a Jill
Who'd like a thrill?
GIRLS: Be yourself! Don't be sil'!
Don't ask!
But, oh my, she is shy, what'll she do?
Laddie, laddie, it's up to you.
BOYS: Say, no use to sigh;
Come on and try.
GIRLS: But will he satisfy?
BOYS: Don't ask!

GUESS WHO?

An earlier lyric setting to the music that was eventually used for "Don't Ask!" Intended for Gerald Oliver Smith (Duke), Betty Compton (Molly), Constance Carpenter (Mae), and ensemble. Unused. Replaced with "Don't Ask!" (In 1960, Guy Bolton and P. G. Wodehouse reset the "Guess Who?"/"Don't Ask!" music with a new lyric, titled "Home," for a revival of *Oh, Kay!*)

VERSE 1

DUKE: Though you know I'm rather
British,
Please don't think that my heart
is cold.
If I'm acting rather skittish—
Ladies, on your beauty I'm sold.
Just one look at you—Pip-pip,
and What ho!
Somehow I feel absolutely
blotto!

REFRAIN 1

Who is the chap—
Love on his map—
Who wants you on his lap?
Guess who?
Whose love is hot,
Hot and whatnot,
And all that sort of rot—
Guess who?
Moon and stars, stars and moon,
heaven above—
Lady, lady, someone's in love.
Oh!
Who is the sheik
Who'd make you weak
With his parlor technique?
Guess who?

VERSE 2

MOLLY AND MAE: We should say, if you are
English—
It's a wicked line that you swing.
DUKE: Yes, my heart is feeling tinglish,
If you care for that sort of thing.
Could you take a fancy to a
Briton
Who is somehow positively
smitten?

REFRAIN 2

BOYS: Who is the miss
Who'd steal a kiss?
GIRLS: All we can say is this:
Guess who?
BOYS: Is there a Jill
Who'd like a thrill?
GIRLS: Be yourself, don't be sil'!
Guess who?
But, Oh my, if you're shy, what
can she do?
Laddie, laddie, it's up to you; so

Please be a man!
Time you began!
BOYS: Now I know that I can—
Guess who?

DEAR LITTLE GIRL

Published August 1969 separately and in the vocal score
for the film biography of Gertrude Lawrence, "Star!"
Also published July 1984 in the *Oh, Kay!* vocal selections. Added to the score of *Oh, Kay!* during the pre-
Broadway tryout. Introduced by Oscar Shaw (Jimmy)
and girls. Introduced in London by Harold French and
girls. Earlier title: "I Hope You've Missed Me."

VERSE 1

JIMMY: It's good to see familiar faces—
Rosie, Posie, Josie, Polly, Molly,
May.
I've thought of you in far-off
places—
Hilda, Gilda, Tilda, Billie, Lily, Fay.
Without you, dear old pals, I've
known some
Days that were awf'ly lonesome.

REFRAIN 1

I hope you've missed me as I missed
you,
Dear little girl.
I was lonesome; were you lonesome,
too,
Dear little girl?
Now that I am here again,
I could jump for joy;
With such friends, it's clear again
I'm a lucky boy.
Make me happy, tell me this is true,
Dear little girl;
Say you missed me much as I
missed you,
Dear little girl.

VERSE 2

SIX GIRLS: Oh, how we've missed you! Take the
word of
SIX OTHERS: Rosie, Posie, Josie, Polly, Molly,
May.
SIX OTHERS: With loyalty that is unheard of—

SIX OTHERS: Hilda, Gilda, Tilda, Billie, Lily, Fay.
ALL: To show our sentiment unspoken
Please take this little token.
[*presentation and speech*]

REFRAIN 2

GIRLS: I hope you've missed me as I missed
you,
Dear little boy.
I was lonesome; were you lonesome,
too,
Dear little boy?
Now that you are here again,
My head's in a whirl.
Dear old pal, it's clear again
I'm a lucky girl.
Make me happy, tell me this is true,
Dear little boy;
Say you missed me much as I
missed you,
Dear little boy.

MAYBE

Published November 1926. Introduced by Gertrude
Lawrence (Kay) and Oscar Shaw (Jimmy). Introduced in
London by Gertrude Lawrence and Harold French.

VERSE 1

JIMMY: Though today is a blue day,
Still, tomorrow is near;
And perhaps with the new day,
Cares will all disappear.
Though happiness is late,
And we must wait,
There's no need to be nervous.
There are dreams at your service.

REFRAIN 1

Soon or late—maybe—
If you wait—maybe—
Some kind fate—maybe—
Will help you discover
Where to find your lover.
You will hear "Yoo-Hoo."
He'll be near you-oo.
Paradise will open its gate—
Maybe soon—maybe late.

VERSE 2

KAY: Though I'm patiently waiting,
He is long overdue.
If he keeps hesitating,
Tell me, what can I do?
Someday he will appear—
Perhaps he's near.
I'm not going to worry,
But I do wish he'd hurry.

REFRAIN 2

Soon or late—maybe—
If I wait—maybe—
Some kind fate—maybe—
Will help me discover
Where to find my lover.
JIMMY: You will hear "Yoo-Hoo."
He'll be near you-oo.
BOTH: Paradise will open its gate
Maybe soon—maybe late.

CLAP YO' HANDS

Published November 1926. Introduced by Harland Dixon (Larry), Betty Compton (Molly), Paulette Winston (Daisy), Constance Carpenter (Mae), Janette Gilmore (Peggy), and ensemble. Introduced in London by Claude Hulbert (The Duke), Rita McLean (Molly), Cecile Maule-Cole (Peggy), Beth Dodge (Dolly), Betty Dodge (Phil), and ensemble. Alternate title: "Clap-a Yo' Hand."

Two Matters: The First, Unimportant; The Second, Longer.

1. Looking over some old worksheets, I noticed that the original and logical title for this song was "Clap-a Yo' Hand," a phrase occurring three times in the refrain. Today, thirty-three years later—sue me, third-degree me—I've no idea why I thought a better title for sheet-music publication was "Clap Yo' Hands," a phrase which doesn't appear in the song at all.

2. In "Clap Yo' Hands" the words of the refrain's first section are repeated in the last. There is no attempt to wind up the lyric with a verbal twist or variation. That's because "Clap Yo' Hands" is basically a stage tune for dancing, vocally carrying a one-minded invitation to Join the Jubilee. So the better part of lyric valor was to avoid any verbal change which might impede the song's exhortatory momentum before the dance.

Usually, though, when possible, a verbal twist or turn is striven for. A simple one, for example, is an ending of "But Not for Me":

> When ev'ry happy plot
> Ends with the marriage knot—
> And there's no knot for me.

Somewhat more elaborate is the wind-up of "Let's Call the Whole Thing Off," when the disagreeing pair decide the separation might be too great a dose of sweet sorrow, and switch to: "Better call the calling-off off, /Let's call the *whole* thing off."

What I have just been vaguely informative about is, shall we say, a minor form of the trick or surprise ending, a structural device I have always liked. When I was very young I admired O. Henry, then later Maupassant (as in "The Necklace"), and others like Bierce and John Collier. Also, in my late teens I fooled around with French verse forms, such as the triolet, villanelle, and especially the rondeau—with its opening phrase taking on new meanings when repeated. I even sold one to the New York *Sun*, for which I received three dollars:

RONDEAU TO ROSIE

My Rosie knows the places where
One goes to lose all trace of care.
The ultra swagger cabaret . . .
The crystal chandeliered café . . .

And oh, she knows the waiters there.
Her wink will fetch from magic lair
A bottle of a vintage rare . . .
And potent beer? Hot dog! I'll say
My Rosie knows!

Without my Rosie, I declare
I'd plumb the depths of dark despair.
To her I dedicate this lay;
To her I owe my spirits gay,
My smiling mien, my cheerful air,
My rosy nose.

Whether it was worth three dollars or not, Buddy De-Sylva liked it and thought it was an idea for us to collaborate on for a song lyric. But we never got around to it. Probably just as well.

(*Special Note for Those Who Wonder Why Rosie Had to Wink:* Prohibition was in effect.)
—from *Lyrics on Several Occasions*

VERSE

Come on, you children, gather around—
Gather around, you children.
And we will lose that evil spirit
Called the Voodoo.

Nothin' but trouble, if he has found,
If he has found you, children—

But you can chase the Hoodoo
With the dance that you do.

Let me lead the way.
Jubilee today! Say!
He'll never hound you;
Stamp on the ground, you children!
Come on!

REFRAIN

Clap-a yo' hand! Slap-a yo' thigh!
Halleluyah! Halleluyah!
Ev'rybody come along and join the Jubilee!

Clap-a yo' hand! Slap-a yo' thigh!
Don't you lose time! Don't you lose time!
Come along—it's Shake Yo' Shoes Time
Now for you and me!

On the sands of time
You are only a pebble;
Remember, trouble must be treated
Just like a rebel;
Send him to the Debble!

Clap-a yo' hand! Slap-a yo' thigh!
Halleluyah! Halleluyah!
Everybody come along and join the Jubilee!

DO, DO, DO

Published November 1926. Introduced by Gertrude Lawrence (Kay) and Oscar Shaw (Jimmy). Introduced in London by Gertrude Lawrence and Harold French.

An hour before dinner one evening at our house on 103rd Street I told George that maybe we could do something with the sounds of "do, do" and "done, done." We went up to his studio on the top floor and in half an hour wrote the refrain of the song. (I am certain of the time it took because just as we started to work, my bride-to-be telephoned that she *could* make it for dinner with us; and when she arrived, taxiing in half an hour—less, she says—from Eighth Street, we were able to play her a complete refrain.)

The lyric isn't much to look at, but its sounds of triply repeated syllables were effective over the footlights. The duet was sung with a somewhat faster and steadier beat than would be done today, and came over to the audience with the intended result, a catchy song about a kiss—and nothing else.

I stress this point because the first essay in Sigmund Spaeth's *The Facts of Life in Popular Song* is concerned with suggestive songs, musical-comedy "smart smut," and many songs palpably prurient. In that book musicologist Spaeth turns lyricologist and has made an excellent and frequently amusing study of not only songs of questionable taste, but many other popular-song matters, such as grammar and bad rhymes. Among the suggestive songs he lists "Do, Do, Do," based apparently on this finding: "In the language of Popular Song it is understood that such words as 'hug' and 'kiss' may represent any stage of procreative activity. . . ." If the overtones—and undertones—of a "do, do" and a "done, done" sound-effect effort gave Mr. Spaeth a feeling that some stage of procreative activity was implied, I'm sorry. Whatever may have been hinted at or outspokenly stated in other songs of mine, "Do, Do, Do" was written for its face, not body, value.

(Despite this disclaimer, "Do, Do, Do" can of course be suggestive, if leeringly inflected in husky tones by anyone sexy. But this can be true of anything vocalized in that manner—from the alphabet to the telephone directory to national anthems.)

—from *Lyrics on Several Occasions*

From "Marginalia on Most of the Songs" by Ira Gershwin in *The George and Ira Gershwin Song Book:*

Do, Do, Do. Writing and rewriting a song (mostly the lyric, that is) usually took two days to three weeks before a "That's that!" could be sighed in relief. The refrain of this song (the verse came later), including both the words and the music, was a notable exception, as "Do, Do, Do" was done in about half an hour. (A bow to my restraint: the last sentence could easily have ended with "as 'Do, Do, Do' was done, done, done in about half an hour.")

VERSE 1

JIMMY: I remember the bliss
Of that wonderful kiss.
I know that a boy
Could never have more joy
From any little miss.
KAY: I remember it quite;
'Twas a wonderful night.
JIMMY: Oh, how I'd adore it
If you would encore it. Oh—

REFRAIN 1

Do, do, do
What you've done, done, done
Before, Baby.
Do, do, do
What I do, do, do
Adore, Baby

Let's try again,
Sigh again,

Fly again to heaven.
Baby, see
It's A B C—
I love you and you love me.

I know, know, know
What a beau, beau, beau
Should do, Baby;
So, don't, don't, don't
Say it won't, won't, won't
Come true, Baby.

My heart begins to hum—
Dum de dum de dum-dum-dum,*
So do, do, do,
What you've done, done, done
Before.

VERSE 2

KAY: Sweets we've tasted before
Cannot stand an encore.
You know that a miss
Who always gives a kiss
Would soon become a bore.
JIMMY: I can't see that at all;
True love never should pall.
KAY: I was only teasing;
What you did was pleasing. Oh—

REFRAIN 2

Do, do, do
What you've done, done, done
Before, Baby.
Do, do, do
What I do, do, do
Adore, Baby.

Let's try again,
Sigh again,
Fly again to heaven.
Baby, see
It's A B C—
I love you and you love me.

JIMMY: You dear, dear, dear
Little dear, dear, dear,
Come here, snappy!
And see, see, see
Little me, me, me
Make you happy.

KAY: My heart begins to sigh—
Di de di de di-di-di,

In Lyrics on Several Occasions, *Ira Gershwin substituted an earlier version of this line:*
"Hum de dum de dum-dum-dum."

So do, do, do
What you've done, done, done
Before.

FINALE, ACT I

Introduced by principals and ensemble. Alternate title: "Isn't It Grand." Includes some sung material and much dialogue. Most of the latter is omitted here.

GIRLS: [*Sing*] Oh, isn't that thrilling!
Oh, it's perfectly grand!
He's won her heart and her hand.
Don't they make a lovely pair?
Our best wishes to you—
Take our blessing. Oh, do!
Lots of happiness we hope you'll
share.
[*Music continues*]
CONSTANCE: [*spoken*] What's that noise?
JIMMY: I didn't hear anything.
CONSTANCE: Who is in that room?
PHIL: We heard it when we were here
before.
DOLLY: Jimmy says it's a ghost.
GIRL: [*at door*] I distinctly hear footsteps.
CHORUS: [*Sings*] Yes, we heard a noise like
someone softly creeping.
JIMMY: If you heard a noise, it's just my
butler sweeping.
CHORUS: There was a noise like someone
creeping.
But he says it's just his butler
sweeping.
[*Enter Shorty, carrying tray*]
SHORTY: [*spoken*] I ain't sure about one of
these eggs. It acted kind of tired
when I busted it in the pan.
JUDGE: Are you Mr. Winter's butler?
SHORTY: Yes, ma'am.
CONSTANCE: Then *who* is in there?
[*Jimmy tries to explain*]
CHORUS: [*Sings*] Yes, yes, who can it be?
This looks funny to me.
It is odd, you must agree.
[*Kay appears*]
KAY: [*spoken*] Did you call, sir?
JIMMY: Ah, Jane—my maid.
[*Sings*] It was Jane—
KAY: Yes, sir.
CHORUS: What a very pretty maid!
JIMMY: Simply Jane—
KAY: Yes, sir.

CHORUS: What a very pretty maid!
Now the myst'ry we can explain.
It was Jane—merely Jane.
CHORUS: Isn't it grand! Clap-a yo' hand!
Halleluyah! Halleluyah!
Ev'rybody's feeling gay—
It's Jimmy's wedding day.
Isn't it grand! Clap-a yo' hand!
Halleluyah! Halleluyah!
Now we'll hear them vow to love
And honor and obey!
Bach'lor days and ways for our
Jimmy are ended;
And if the bach'lor days and ways of
Jimmy are mended—
Ev'rything is splendid!
Isn't it grand! Clap-a yo' hand!
Halleluyah! Halleluyah!
Ev'rybody come along,
It's Jimmy's wedding day!

BRIDE AND GROOM

Published July 1984 in the *Oh, Kay!* vocal selections. Previously registered for copyright as an unpublished composition in June 1958. Introduced by Sascha Beaumont (Constance), Oscar Shaw (Jimmy), Frank Gardiner (Judge Appleton), and ensemble. Introduced in London by April Harmon, Harold French, Charles Cautley, and ensemble. Alternate titles: "Opening, Act II" and "Never Too Late to Mendelssohn." The "Mendelssohn—Journey's Endelssohn" and "Lohengrin and bear it" lines were used again in *Lady in the Dark* (1941).

ENSEMBLE: It's never too late to Mendelssohn;
It doesn't matter how long you have
tarried.
Two hearts are at Journey's
Endelssohn—
And we're invited here to see them
married.
Two fond hearts will always
blendelssohn—
At least, we're all expecting them to
swear it.
A gay honeymoon they'll
spendelssohn;
We hope they Lohengrin and bear
it.
[*Enter Constance, Jimmy, and Judge Appleton*]
JIMMY: This is my wedding day—
CONSTANCE: And it is mine, too!

JIMMY
AND JUDGE: This is her wedding day!
CONSTANCE: And it's divine, too!
ENSEMBLE: This is their wedding day—
Which will combine two!
GIRLS: Don't you just adore it!
BOYS: They've a nice day for it!
ENSEMBLE: Bachelor boy and bachelor
girl—good-bye!

We'd love
To take a picture of
The happy bride and groom.
Let's "shoot"
Them while they're looking cute—
The happy bride and groom.
Be gay!
This is your wedding day—
Oh, happy bride and groom.
It's wrong
To wear your faces long—
Be happy! Happy, happy bride and
groom!

Get ready now, for we're
To take your photo.
The wedding, it is clear,
Is one of note. Oh!
Your picture may appear
In Sunday's roto!

Watch the little birdie!
Smile and stand the gaff!
Watch the little birdie!
Watch the little birdie!
Watch the little birdie
Taking your photograph.
[*Picture is taken*]
[*Dance*]

SOMEONE TO WATCH OVER ME

Published November 1926. Introduced by Gertrude Lawrence (Kay). During the pre-Broadway tryout, it was the third number in Act I. "A Long Island drawing-room. Gertrude Lawrence, alone on stage, meditates musically. Stooping to conquer, she has disguised herself as a housemaid. Actually, she is the sister of a duke—all this a not unusual involvement in the Jazz Age" (Ira Gershwin—*Lyrics on Several Occasions*). The British edition of the sheet music contains additional lyrics (for a second verse) that are probably not by Ira Gershwin.

The Tune. As originally conceived by the composer, this tune would probably not be around much today. At the piano in its early existence it was fast and jazzy, and undoubtedly I would have written it up as another dance-and-ensemble number. One day, for no particular reason and hardly aware of what he was at, George started and continued it in a comparatively slow tempo; and half of it hadn't been sounded when both of us had the same reaction: this was really no rhythm tune but rather a wistful and warm one—to be held out until the proper stage occasion arose for it.

The Title. Here and there among the notes in this book are a number of references to, and experiences and experiments with, song titles—matters such as their importance, their elusiveness, their non-copyrightability, the use of the colloquial phrase (or its paraphrase), the dummy title, the title-song, &c. And one will gather that suitable titles are usually not easily come by, especially when a lyric is to be imposed on music already set. The following, however, will be a paraphrase on "The Easiest Way to a Song Title."

George and I were well along with the score for *Oh, Kay!* when one morning at six a.m. I was rushed to Mt. Sinai Hospital for an emergency appendectomy. I was there six weeks—this was long before the antibiotics shortened stays. When, after great insistence ("They're waiting for me to finish the lyrics!"), exit was finally permitted, I was still weak but able to work afternoons. Then, with rehearsals nearing, and myself a bit behind schedule, a friend and many-faceted talent, Howard Dietz, showed up one day and offered to help out, and did. We collaborated on two lyrics and he was helpful on a couple of others. Also, one day when he heard the slowed-up ex-jazz tune he ad-libbed several titles, one of which stuck with me and which, some days later, I decided to write up. And that's how it happens that this song is titled "Someone to Watch over Me." And that's: "The Easiest Way to a Song Title."

—from *Lyrics on Several Occasions*

VERSE

There's a saying old
Says that love is blind.
Still, we're often told
"Seek and ye shall find."
So I'm going to seek a certain lad I've had in
mind.
Looking ev'rywhere,
Haven't found him yet;
He's the big affair
I cannot forget—
Only man I ever think of with regret.
I'd like to add his initial to my monogram.
Tell me, where is the shepherd for this lost
lamb?

REFRAIN

There's a somebody I'm longing to see:
I hope that he
Turns out to be
Someone who'll watch over me.

I'm a little lamb who's lost in the wood;
I know I could
Always be good
To one who'll watch over me.

Although he may not be the man some
Girls think of as handsome,
To my heart he'll carry the key.

Won't you tell him, please, to put on some
  speed,
Follow my lead?
Oh, how I need
Someone to watch over me.

Male Version

REFRAIN

There's a somebody I've wanted to see:
I hope that she
Turns out to be
Someone who'll watch over me.

I'm a little lamb who's lost in the wood;
I know I could
Always be good
To one who'll watch over me.

She may be far;
She may be nearby;
I'm promising hereby,
To my heart she'll carry the key.

And this world would be like heaven if she'd
Follow my lead.
Oh, how I need
Someone to watch over me.

FIDGETY FEET

Published November 1926. Introduced by Harland
Dixon (Larry), Marion Fairbanks (Phil), and ensemble.
Introduced in London by Claude Hulbert (The Duke),
Beth Dodge (Dolly), Betty Dodge (Phil), and ensemble.
Shortly after the New York opening, "Fidgety Feet" and
"Someone to Watch Over Me" switched places in Act II.

VERSE

LARRY: Something is the matter with me.
    Oh, but it's chronic!
PHIL: Do you need a tonic?
LARRY: Oh, can't you see
    A dumb thing is the matter with me?
    I'm in condition—
    I need no physician.
PHIL: What can it be?
LARRY: You can help me out.
PHIL: What's it all about?

REFRAIN

LARRY: I've got fidgety feet, fidgety feet, fidgety
    feet!
    Oh, what fidgety feet, fidgety feet, fidgety
    feet!
    Say, mate, come and be my sway mate;
    How can anyone resist that rhythmical
    beat?
    You will never go wrong, never go
    wrong, never go wrong
    If you toddle along, toddle along, toddle
    along.
    All I need's a partner to make my life
    complete—
    Two more fidgety, fidgety feet.

HEAVEN ON EARTH

Published November 1926. Lyrics by Ira Gershwin and
Howard Dietz. Introduced by Oscar Shaw (Jimmy),
Betty Compton (Molly), Constance Carpenter (Mae),
and ensemble. Introduced in London by Harold French
(Jimmy), Rita McLean (Molly), Cecile Maule-Cole
(Peggy), and ensemble.

VERSE

At a very early age I decided
That worry doesn't get you anywhere;
And it's very lucky for me that I did,
For of trouble I've had much more than my
  share.
If you give in when breaks are bad, you're gone;
Here's the only way to carry on:

REFRAIN

Reach up high—Pull down the sky—
Make this a heaven on earth.
Can't go wrong singing a song—

Make this a heaven on earth.
This is the advice I'm giving:
Start loving and living
For all that you're worth.
Oh, reach up high—Pull down the sky—
Make this a heaven on earth!

FINALETTO, ACT II, SCENE 1

Introduced by principals and ensemble during the pre-
Broadway tryout. Possibly dropped before the New
York opening. Reinstated for the London production.
Alternate title: "On Single Life Today."

[*Jimmy reprises "Someone to Watch over Me"*]
[*Dolly, Phil, and girls enter to music. Sing:*]
    On single life today
    The curtain's falling:
    And oh! We've got to say
    It's most enthralling.
    They'll honeymoon away—
    Niag'ra's calling.
    Don't you just adore it!
    They've a nice day for it!
    Bachelor boy and bachelor
      girl—good-bye!

[*Dialogue*]
[*Enter Constance and bridesmaids*]
BRIDESMAIDS: It's never too late to
    Mendelssohn
    It doesn't matter how long you
    have tarried.
    Two hearts are at Journey's
    Endelssohn
    And we have all come here to see
    them married.

ENSEMBLE: And now
    We'll hear them take their vow—
    The happy bride and groom.
    They're through
    When they have said "I do!"—
    The happy bride and groom.
    One thing!
    Please don't forget the ring—
    Oh, happy bride and groom.
    Be gay—
    This is your wedding day—
    Be happy! Happy, happy bride
    and groom!

[*Dialogue*]

ENSEMBLE: Soon or late—maybe—
If you wait—maybe—
Some kind fate—maybe—
Will make all your troubles
Vanish just like bubbles.
Joy will be nearing.
Skies will be clearing.
Paradise will open its gate.

JIMMY AND KAY: Maybe soon—maybe late.

OH, KAY!

Published November 1926. Lyrics by Ira Gershwin and Howard Dietz. Introduced by Gertrude Lawrence (Kay) and boys.

VERSE 1

BOYS: You've a charm that is all your own—
Makes 'em all stare.
You've a style you can call your own;
Lady, you are there!

KAY: I can't see what you see in me;
It must be rare.
But I'd like to hear a little more;
Speak right up, boys, you can have the floor.

REFRAIN 1

BOYS: Oh, Kay! You're O.K. with me!
You're a dear!
Oh, Kay! You're O.K. with me!
Listen here:
Venus couldn't compare—
'Tween us, you've her charms and
Two good arms, and
You're like a beautiful pome, it is clear;
You could break up any home. Say,
Since you've shown up,
I must own up
I'm up a tree. Say,
Oh, Kay! You're O.K. with me!

VERSE 2

KAY: If my heart were a free-for-all—
Me for all you.
But my heart has no key for all;
So what can I do?
Entre nous, there's a laddie to
Whom I am true.

Though you cannot have my heart and hand,
I will tell the world I think you're grand.

REFRAIN 2

Hey-hey! You're O.K. with Kay!
Listen here:
Hey-hey! You're O.K. with Kay!
Never fear!
Hear me—if I were free—
Dear me! Nothing to it!
You're so cu-it!
You've got that *je- ne- sais- quoi*, little boy,
That makes the others look blah. Say,
I'm another's,
But if brothers
You care to be—
Oh, that would be O.K. with me!

THE MOON IS ON THE SEA

Introduced by the ensemble during the first week of the Philadelphia tryout. It was the original opening number of Act I. Replaced with "The Woman's Touch." A portion of the music, fitted with an almost entirely new lyric, became "In the Swim" in *Funny Face* (1927). Some authorities have said that an alternate title for this number is "The Sun Is on the Sea," but that does not seem likely.

The moon is on the sea.
The sea is where we'd be.
The darkness is no menace—
It's as though you were in Venice.
Oh, we hope the water's warm
When we go to perform.
You need no sunburn lotion
For a lovely midnight ocean,
So for moonlight bathing each night we appear;
And there's another reason why we're here:

You see, the fact is
We're keeping in trim.
We are out here for practice.
We'd be in the swim.
There's a test we'd go through
Like the rest wanting to
Swim the Channel—
That's what we'd do!

We're going over
To show 'em some speed,

Swimming Gris-Nez to Dover;
And if we succeed,
Then we'll be sitting pretty—
Getting the key to the city—
Oh boy! What a thrill!

The moon is on the sea.
The sea is where we'd be.
The water may be fishy
But it peps you up like Vichy.
Bring along your valentine,
And join us in the brine;
Come on, the water's fine!

Bathing underneath the moon
Beats the morn or afternoon.
There's no crowd a-cluttering the sand;
You will find the solitude is grand.
Water-sporting in the dark—
What cavorting! What a lark!
So won't you step out with us some midnight soon,
And do your bathing 'neath the moon?

SHOW ME THE TOWN

Published November 1926. One of the first four songs printed from the score. Introduced during the pre-Broadway tryout by Oscar Shaw (Jimmy), Marion Fairbanks (Phil), and Madeline Fairbanks (Dolly). Replaced with "Dear Little Girl." Revived (with a different verse) for *Rosalie* (1928), in which it was introduced by Bobbe Arnst and ensemble.

VERSE

JIMMY: Boy! It's simply grand to have the gang around.*
The moment you appeared, my troubles got the gate.
Don't you leave; I want you all to hang around.
Tonight's the night for a blowout—
Let's step out! Let's go out!
And where the bright lights shine, we'll celebrate.

GIRLS: That's a suggestion! Leave it to you!
But here's a question: What'll we do?

Original version of verse, line 1:
Gee! It's simply grand to have the gang around.

REFRAIN

JIMMY: Hey! How about a dance?
Say! Let's go out and take a chance!
Show me, show me, come and show me
the town!
Drink! Let's fill up the glass!
Clink! While we're stepping on the gas!
Let's go where the wets go—
Show me the town!
Woof! Want to raise the roof!
Said! Want to paint the whole town red!
Wow! Let me show you how to throw a
party.
Shout! Tell the world that I'm
Out looking for a dizzy time.
Show me, show me, come and show me
the town!

AIN'T IT ROMANTIC?

Introduced by Gertrude Lawrence (Kay) and Victor Moore (Shorty) in Act II during the first week of the Philadelphia tryout. Dropped before the second week in Philadelphia. No. 44 in the George and Ira Gershwin Special Numbered Song File.

VERSE

KAY: Listen to a dream—
Came to me
With a lovely theme,
As you'll see;
Made me very happy;
In it was a chappie
Who was handsome as could be.
Girls along the way
Used to sigh;
But he wouldn't play—
He'd pass them by.
Their glances all were futile;
Love he never knew till
One fine day I caught his eye.

REFRAIN 1

I met him and he met me—
Oh gosh, oh gee!
SHORTY: Ain't it romantic?
KAY: He was shy and so was I—
Oh me, oh my!
SHORTY: Ain't it romantic?
KAY: I began to blush;
He began to flush.

All the noisy world was a-hush.
Then he grabbed me. Oh, what
charms
Were in his arms!
SHORTY: Ain't it romantic?
KAY: Very soon the month of June—
A wedding tune—
SHORTY: Ain't it romantic?
KAY: Then a little cottage fair—
Everything so lovely there!
But my castles went up in smoke
At the moment that I awoke.
I was nearly frantic—
BOTH: Yes, but ain't it romantic, dear?

ENCORE REFRAIN

POLICEMAN: Oh, how happy we shall be!
MAID: Oh gosh, oh gee!
Ain't it romantic?
POLICEMAN: We'll be wealthy, too, says I.
MAID: Oh me, oh my!
Ain't it romantic?
POLICEMAN: You shall be a queen
Whose like was never seen.
MAID: Can I have a sewing machine?
POLICEMAN: You'll be through with broom and
sink,
And you'll wear mink.
MAID: Ain't it romantic?
POLICEMAN: Lots of pinkish underthings
And di'mond rings.
MAID: Ain't it romantic?
POLICEMAN: Then we'll have a private yacht
Seven castles and whatnot.
[He disappears]
MAID: But my castles went up in smoke
At the moment that I awoke.
I was nearly frantic—
Oh, but ain't it romantic, dear?

BRING ON THE DING DONG DELL

Introduced during the first week of the pre-Broadway tryout (Philadelphia—October 18–23) by Gertrude Lawrence (Kay), Oscar Shaw (Jimmy), Harland Dixon (Larry), Marion Fairbanks (Phil), Gerald Oliver Smith (The Duke), and Madeline Fairbanks (Dolly). Dropped before the second week of the tryout. Revised for the 1930 *Strike Up the Band* as "Ring-a-Ding-a-Ding-Dong Dell." Alternate title of *Oh, Kay!* version: "Ding-Dong-Dell."

VERSE

BOYS: Let the wedding bells ring on!
Let the world know the news!
GIRLS: While our dearest friends bring on
Tons of rice and old shoes.
BOYS: Clear the way! Make room
For the very happy bride and groom.

REFRAIN

When the bells in the belfry go
ding-dong,
They'll be ringing for you and for me.
GIRLS: "Be gay today," they're singing.
ALL: For girl and boy, a message of joy
They're bringing.
GIRLS: Sweet is the beat of the ding-dong.
BOYS: What a glorious story they tell:
ALL: The news they're spreading—
There's going to be a wedding—
Bring on the ding dong dell.

STEPPING WITH BABY

Intended for Harland Dixon (Larry), Madeline Fairbanks (Dolly), and Marion Fairbanks (Phil). Dropped during rehearsals. May have been replaced with "Don't Ask." No music is known to survive.

VERSE 1

LARRY: I'm no Apollo, I'm granting you that.
Yet women follow me by the score.
DOLLY AND
PHIL: What makes them flutter? It's not
your cravat.
Why do they clutter up your door?
LARRY: This is how I win my baby:
Take her to a dancing floor.

REFRAIN 1

When I'm stepping with baby—
Step, step, stepping with baby—
Ev'rywhere people come to stare;
And if I may say it—Lady, I'm there!
Oh, what rapture I'll bring you!
Say the word and I'll swing you!
Take a step in the right direction and
you'll be
Step, step, stepping with me!

VERSE 2

DOLLY AND
    PHIL: You have no title or castle or yacht—
         And that is vital, you must agree.
  LARRY: Why be a duchess, and that sort of
         rot
         When you can have such as me?
         What's the use of social climbing
         When a-stepping you might be?

REFRAIN 2

Won't you step with me, baby?
Step, step, step with me, baby.
If you do, if you take the cue,
I know I'll be bringing
Heaven to you.
In our dancing you'll glory,
So I stick to my story:
Take a step in the right direction and
   you'll be
Step, step, stepping with me!

WHAT'S THE USE?

Intended for Oscar Shaw (Jimmy) and girls. Dropped during rehearsals. No music is known to survive.

VERSE

We never seem to realize
The sex that we idealize
Will always get us in wrong.

Marc Antony, a cheerful guy,
Became a gloomy, tearful guy
When Cleo happened along.

When somebody's daughter
Leads you to the slaughter
That's the time a feller needs a friend.

It does no good to run away—
You're only putting one away—
Another one'll get you in the end.

REFRAIN 1

You lose your heart, and you start
Right in taking abuse—
Oh, what's the use?
Right there, you swear you don't care—
They can go to the deuce—
But what's the use?

When you're through and you're filled with
   regret,
When your lawyer pays off that brunette,
Soon you grow fond of a blonde
That Anita let loose—
Oh, what's the use?

REFRAIN 2

You lose your heart, and you start
Right in taking abuse—
Oh, what's the use?
Right there, you swear you don't care—
They can go to the deuce—
But what's the use?
You may think you're a hard-boiled egg,
Then you meet a neat ankle or leg.
That does the trick; soon some chick-
En is cooking your goose—
Oh, what's the use?

WHEN OUR SHIP COMES SAILING IN

Lyric by Ira Gershwin and Howard Dietz. Intended for Gerald Oliver Smith (Duke), Victor Moore (Shorty), and Harland Dixon (Larry). Dropped during rehearsals. No. 82 in the George and Ira Gershwin Special Numbered Song File. Introduced on Broadway in producer David Merrick's 1990 revival of *Oh, Kay!* by Stanley Wayne Mathis (Duke), Helmar Augustus Cooper (Shorty), and male ensemble, and in the "new" 1991 version of the Merrick *Oh, Kay!* by Gregg Burge (Billy), Helmar Augustus Cooper (Shorty), and male ensemble.

VERSE 1

  DUKE: When you find your friends have
         tricked you,
         And calamity has kicked you;
         When your luck has never smiled again,
         it seems.
SHORTY: Don't consider it a crisis;
         Don't you worry. Our advice is
         Just start waiting for your golden ship
         of dreams.
  LARRY: Though the waiting often may become a
         bore,
         Still, it's surely worthwhile waiting for.
    ALL: Look at us, we're waiting for a ship
         right now;
         Waiting now—and how!

REFRAIN 1

When our ship comes sailing in,
We will shout our joy
With a "Ship ahoy!"
Then our glad days will begin
When we start unloading the gin.
Our guilty conscience we will try to
   smother;
We'll hail each Prohibitionist a brother,
And sell a dozen cases to his mother!
When our ship comes sailing in—
Full of Haig and Haig and gin!

VERSE 2

  DUKE: Just imagine our position.
         Think of all the competition
         That we've got along the whole Atlantic
         shore.
SHORTY: From Southampton to Miami;
         Coast patrols of Uncle Sammy
         On our business are declaring open war.
  LARRY: You would think that what we're doing
         was a crime—
         Helping you to have a decent time.
    ALL: Congressmen and senators kick up a
         fuss—
         Then they buy from us!

REFRAIN 2

When our ship comes sailing in—
When our ship of dreams
Through the harbor steams,
Then our glad days will begin—
Mr. Volstead, pardon our sin.
There's champagne in our cargo that
   will please ya;
Just give your girl a case and she will
   squeeze ya!
(She needn't know we mixed it with
   magnesia!)
When our ship comes sailing in—
Full of Haig and Haig and gin!

VERSE 3

We stand watching the horizon,
Casting anxious eager eyes on
All the little ships as they go passing
   by.
How we're hoping, how we're yearning,
For a safe and sound returning.
Are we soon to see our ship against the
   sky?
Anyone who's ever waited on a pier
Will appreciate our feeling here.

What a tender welcome we will give our
   friends
As their journey ends.

REFRAIN 3

When our ship comes sailing in—
Ev'ry worry gone—

How we'll carry on!
Boy! It's great when dreams come
   true
And you see your ship on the blue.
But, Oh, the risk! It's paining us to tell
   of it!
The money that we get is not all
   vel-e-vit;

The cops take our profits—That's the
   hell of it!
When our ship comes sailing
   in—
Full of Haig and Haig and gin!

STRIKE UP THE BAND !

EDGAR SELWYN
presents
The Gershwin Kaufman
MUSICAL PLAY

STRIKE UP THE BAND

Military Dancing Drill
Seventeen And Twenty-one
Yankee Doodle Rhythm
Strike Up The Band!
The Man I Love

BOOK BY
GEORGE S. KAUFMAN

LYRICS BY
IRA GERSHWIN

MUSIC BY
GEORGE GERSHWIN

STAGED BY
R. H. BURNSIDE

DANCES BY
JOHN BOYLE

NEW WORLD MUSIC
CORPORATION
HARMS
INCORPORATED
NEW YORK

MADE IN U. S. A.

STRIKE UP THE BAND | 1927

roadway Theatre, Long Branch, New
1927; Shubert Theatre, Philadelphia,
. Closed without reaching New York.
Gershwin. Produced by Edgar Selwyn.
S. Kaufman. Book staged by R. H.
staged by John Boyle. Orchestra
n of William Daly. Orchestrations by
t featured Herbert Corthell (Horace J.
Hart (Joan Fletcher), Roger Pryor
Edna May Oliver (Mrs. Draper), Doro-
Draper), Max Hoffman, Jr. (Timothy
rn (Colonel Holmes), Robert Bentley
Jimmy Savo (George Spelvin), Ruth
le), Beth Meakins (Mary), Clementine
John Uppman (Marine Guard), Rich-
geant), Morton Downey (Soldier), and
ra (Local Band).

sion of *Strike Up the Band*, see pages

'S AMERICAN
CHORAL SOCIETY

lax Hoffman, Jr. (Timothy), Robert
Herbert Corthell (Fletcher), and en-
w altered lyrics, this number was in-
0 revision of *Strike Up the Band* as
ican Chocolate Choral Society" and
piano-vocal score for the show.

ging, singing ev'ry morning
en the clock is striking eight—
at's a duty that we never shirk.
love singing ev'ry morning,
we're never, never late
en we start our daily work.
are Fletcher's American Cheese
Choral Society,
cher's American Cheese Choral
Society.

ppy, happy workers, we
ging, singing merrily.
love our vocal exercising.
ce efficiency's the thing,
ey encourage us to sing
d start the day by vocalizing.
la la la la la—if we're happy,
la la la la la—work is snappy.
if we seem rather gay
we're working through the day—
u needn't find it too surprising.

Tra la la la, good morning, Mr.
Foreman!

TIMOTHY: Good morning!
From office boy to doorman,
Ev'ryone agrees
That I'm the finest foreman
Working for Fletcher's Cheese.
Our product, as represented,
Never fails to please;
We've cows that are contented
Working for Fletcher's Cheese.

WORKERS: We're glad to know the cows are so
contented!
Tra la la la, good morning, Mr.
Manager!

SLOANE: Good morning!
Work, work, work—
That's all that I'm asking of you!
Never shirk, shirk, shirk—
But show me just what you can do!
On Saturday we pay off
The help in our employ;
On Sunday there's a day off
For ev'ry girl and boy;
Unless I am away off,
This job should be a joy.
I am telling you
There's little to do
But work, work, work!

WORKERS: With Sunday free we all should be
contented.
And now our fav'rite boss you see—
An American institution!
The finest type of man is he—
Three cheers for evolution!
Fletcher! Fletcher! Fletcher!
Tra la la la, good morning, Mr.
Fletcher!

FLETCHER: Good morning!
My product is so nourishing
The factory is flourishing.

TIMOTHY
AND SLOANE: When Fletcher first began it, he
Was working for humanity.

WORKERS: His product is so nourishing
The factory is flourishing!
When Fletcher first began it, he
Was working for humanity.

FLETCHER: Like Listerine and Woolworth,
Lux and B.V.D.s,
The public gets its full worth,
Purchasing Fletcher's Cheese.

WORKERS: Oh, sing its praises loudly—
It's known on seven seas;

We'll tell the world we'
Working for Fletcher's

FLETCHER: Let's start the day
In the usual way
With a program that's
Before we part,
Suppose we start
To do the daily ritual:
I firmly believe—

WORKERS: I firmly believe—
FLETCHER: That Fletcher's Americ
WORKERS: That Fletcher's Americ
FLETCHER: Makes bigger and bette
WORKERS: Makes bigger and bette
FLETCHER: For the U.S.A.!
WORKERS: For the U.S.A.!

Tra la la la la la—while
working,
Tra la la la la la—neve
So if at machines you s
Labor singing merrily,
You needn't find it too

We are Fletcher's Ame
Choral Society—
Fletcher's American Ch
Society!

Tra la la la, we're off to
Tra la la la, we're off to

17 AND 21

Published September 1927. Introduce
James (Anne), Max Hoffman, Jr. (Timot
ble. The reprise for Edna May Oliver (M
Herbert Corthell (Fletcher) was dropped
als. Alternate title: "Seventeen and Twe

VERSE 1

TIMOTHY: Age was creeping on me
I had just turned twenty-c
You then dawned upon m
And a new day was begur

ANNE: I was getting wrinkled—
I had just turned seventee
Then my bright star twin
As it brought you on the

TIMOTHY: All the day and night tim
It was true love that I cra
You came at the right tim
And a lonely soul was sav

ANNE: Oh, love was late in reaching me!
I never had been kissed—
And from what you've been teaching
me—
Oh dear, how much I've missed!

REFRAIN 1

ANNE: I had to wait till I was seventeen;
TIMOTHY: And I, in turn, till I was twenty-one.
When we met, I asked myself
quizzically,
"Do you only love this girl
physically?"
But bigger, better, finer, your appeal—
My heart soon told me that my love
was real.
Oh why, oh why, oh why did
I have to wait as I did—
And mope along till I was twenty-one?
Heigh ho! Heigh ho!
Oh, what a blow!
I had to wait till twenty-one!

VERSE 2

ANNE: At the age of seven,
In the days of long ago,
I'd have thought it Heaven
If you'd been my gigolo.
TIMOTHY: If I'd only caught you
When my blood was young and hot,
Then, when others sought you,
I'd have shot them on the spot!
ANNE: Let us grin and bear it,
Though it be a bitter pill;
We cannot repair it—
Time alone cures ev'ry ill.
TIMOTHY: There still is love, and plenty, too!
And plainly to be seen:
Think! I might have been twenty-two,
While you'd have been eighteen.

REFRAIN 2

ANNE: I had to wait till I was seventeen;
TIMOTHY: And I, in turn, till I was twenty-one.
ANNE: Years and years I moped and
sat—tragically;
You appeared—I changed like
that!—magically.
It's you who caused my sleeping heart
to wake.
When you came 'round I really got a
break.
You've made life gay and fresher;
You gave me high blood pressure—
Why did I have to wait till seventeen?

Oh me, oh my!
To think that I
Was forced to wait till seventeen!

Reprise

MRS. DRAPER: I had to wait till I was—how d'ya
do?
To find a charming Romeo like
you.
When we met, I asked myself
quizzically,
"Do I only love this man
physically?"
FLETCHER: If you are asking me, dear, to
propose,
I'd rather take a good sock on the
nose.
MRS. DRAPER: Svengali, here's your Trilby.
A loving maid I will be.
Why did I have to wait till—
(Now, let me see. Anne is twelve,
and I was married when I was
ten)—
Twenty-two!
BOTH: Heigh ho! Heigh ho!
Oh, what a blow!
I/You had to wait till twenty-two!

TYPICAL SELF-MADE AMERICAN

Introduced by Herbert Corthell (Fletcher), Roger Pryor
(Jim), and ensemble. With a few altered lyrics, this number was included in the 1930 revision and published in
that show's piano-vocal score.

INTRODUCTION

FLETCHER: While other lads were trying out the
bicycle
Or pitching pennies on the parlor
floor,
Their pleasures left me colder than an
icicle,
For I knew what I was predestined
for.
CHORUS: Yes, he knew what he was predestined
for!
FLETCHER: I got a job and worked both day and
night at it;
I watched the cheese but never
watched the clock.

The big boss thought I was so very
bright at it
That when he died he left me all the
stock.
I was there when opportunity came to
knock!

VERSE 1

JIM: Like the hero in an Alger novel
He was born and brought up in a
hovel;
FLETCHER: Though I often had to face disaster,
I would always prove myself the
master!
CHORUS: He would always prove himself the
master!
FLETCHER: I'm a man of very quick decision,
For I always had the gift of vision.
JIM: He upholds the country's
Constitution,
And he hates the Russian Revolution!
CHORUS: How he hates the Russian Revolution!
He upholds the country's laws
Because, because, because, because:

REFRAIN 1

FLETCHER: I am a typical self-made American;
I've been a go-getter ever since life
began.
In a modest way, I feel
I am basically sound—
With my shoulder to the wheel
And my two feet on the ground!
ALL: I am/He is a typical, typical, typical
self-made American!

VERSE 2

FLETCHER: From the lowest of the ranks I've
risen!
JIM: Now both honor and success are his'n!
FLETCHER: Always fighting for the small
consumer—
JIM: And now tell 'em of your sense of
humor—
CHORUS: Of your devastating sense of humor!
FLETCHER: I'm a Mason and an Elk and
Woodman—
JIM: Which unquestionably shows a good
man!
FLETCHER: I've been very good to dear old
Mother—
CHORUS: So we'll never work for any other;
We don't care to work for any other!
And we give him our applause
Because, because, because, because:

REFRAIN 2

He is a typical self-made American.
FLETCHER: With wheat cakes for breakfast,
    cornflakes and lots of bran!
I'm as good a man, I feel,
As a ruler who is crowned—
With my shoulder to the wheel
And my two feet on the ground!
ALL: I am/He is a typical, typical, typical
    self-made American!

MEADOW SERENADE

Introduced by Roger Pryor (Jim) and Vivian Hart (Joan). The music to the refrain, which had been lost, was reconstructed from memory by Kay Swift. George Gershwin's music to the verse was never recovered, so Burton Lane composed new music for it in late 1990 for the Roxbury/Library of Congress recording of the complete score. The lyrics of an earlier (perhaps 1919) "Meadow Serenade" survive. Its verse is different, but the refrain is similar to the 1927 version. The music is not known to have survived.

VERSE 1

JIM: Though my voice is just a singsong,
I must burst into a spring song:
Hey! Nonny, nonny—piminy miminy mo!
Fondest mem'ries seem to waken—
To my boyhood days I'm taken—
Hey! Nonny, nonny—piminy miminy mo!
In that dearest section
Of my recollection,
Back to fields of clover I'm conveyed.
In that charming locale,
Nature must get vocal—
Listen to the meadow serenade!

REFRAIN

I hear the rustle of the trees
From the nearby thickets,
Where the oriole is calling,
And the bobolink is falling
For his mate.
I hear the sighing of the breeze
And the chirping crickets
Where the whippoorwill is wooing
And the katydid is cooing
To his Kate.
And I can hear the cowbell chorus
That's now being played;

Hummingbirds humming for us
From deep in the shade.
There's music in my heart as my thoughts
    go winging
Where the spring is ever singing
That meadow serenade.

VERSE 2

JOAN: In that meadow now there lodges
A garage for Buicks and Dodges—
Hey! Nonny, nonny—piminy miminy mo!
You had Prince and Rover. What dogs!
Now you'll find them there as hot dogs—
Hey! Nonny nonny—piminy miminy mo!
"Get your Coca-Cola!"
"Buy a new Victrola!"
Through the scene the billboards are
    displayed.
You can fill your car there,
Even find a bar there;
BOTH: Give me back the meadow serenade!

REPEAT REFRAIN

Earlier Version

VERSE

With a heart as light as the thistledown
Floating o'er the grass,
From my attic room, I would whistle down
When I saw you pass.
Soon, along the lane,
Past the fields of grain,
Hand in hand we strayed
To the meadow serenade.

REFRAIN

We heard the rustle of the trees
From the nearby thickets,
Where the oriole was calling
To his mate.
We heard the sighing of the breeze
And the chirping crickets,
While the katydid was falling
For his Kate.
The bullfrog started his song;
The bees were buzzing;
The cowbells jingled along
Deep in the shade.
And I'd rejoice to hear your voice
In an old-time greeting,
For it seemed to be completing
That meadow serenade.

THE UNOFFICIAL SPOKESMAN

Introduced by Herbert Corthell (Fletcher), Lew Hearn (Holmes), and ensemble. "The Wizard of the Age" section was not included in the 1930 Strike Up the Band's version of this number (see page 152). The remainder of these lyrics differ somewhat from those published in the 1930 piano-vocal score.

FLETCHER: The man you are about to see
Will live on hist'ry's page;
He's a man of very high degree,
And the unofficial wizard of the age!
ALL: Unofficial wizard of the age!
Unofficial wizard of the age!
Unofficial wizard of the age!

FLETCHER: He is no ordinary gent—
This confidential sage;
He's right behind the president
Is the unofficial wizard of the age!

ALL: He is no ordinary gent—
This confidential sage;
He's right behind the president
Is the unofficial wizard of the age!
Unofficial wizard of the age!
Unofficial wizard of the age!
Unofficial wizard of the age!

[Bugle call. Holmes enters, accompanied by marines]
ALL: Tra la la la, Good morning, Mr.
    Colonel!
HOLMES: Good morning!

FLETCHER: He's joined so many diff'rent societies
He has degrees of ninety-nine
    varieties!

FLETCHER: He's an F.F.V.
HOLMES: And an E-S-Q.
FLETCHER: He's a Z.B.T.
HOLMES: And he's O.K., too.
ALL: He's an L.L.D.
And a G.O.P.,
Which emphatically shows
That no matter where he goes,
From A B C
To X Y Z,
He's a man of very high degree—
He's a man of very high degree!
Very high, not low—
Very high, not low degree!

FLETCHER: We all know he was picked by Fate
    initially

To be a famous man, though
    unofficially!

He's an E-L-K
HOLMES: And an R.I.P.
FLETCHER: And an F.P.A.
HOLMES: And a K.C.B.
    ALL: With his P's and Q's
And his I.O.U.s,
He emphatically shows
That no matter where he goes,
From A B C
To X Y Z,
He's a man of very high degree—
He's a man of very high degree!
WOMEN: Very high!
    MEN: Not low!
WOMEN: Very high!
    MEN: Not low!
WOMEN: High!
    MEN: Low!
WOMEN: High!
    MEN: Low!
WOMEN: High!
    MEN: Low!
    ALL: Degree!

VERSE

HOLMES: When I was born into this universe
    (By a process which I do not care to
      mention),
I never once said "Goo-goo!" to my
    nurse,
Which was quite beyond the lady's
    comprehension.
I found I drew attention being silent;
And that is how my rise to fame
    occurred.
Great dignity to politics soon I lent
By never, never uttering a word.
    ALL: He never said a thing that was absurd,
Because, you see, he never said a
    word.

REFRAIN

HOLMES: I'm the unofficial, unofficial
Spokesman of the U.S.A.
Though to interview me, interview
    me,
All reporters do essay,
If I tell 'em nothing, tell 'em nothing,
How can I be blundering?
And I find it helpful, very helpful
Just to keep 'em wondering.
Like a Massachusetts, Massachusetts
    resident

Who once became a, once became a
    president,
I never, never, never, never say a
    word!

    ALL: He's the unofficial, unoffical
Spokesman of the U.S.A.
Though to interview him, interview
    him,
All reporters do essay,
If he tells 'em nothing, tells 'em
    nothing,
How can he be blundering?
And he finds it helpful, very helpful
Just to keep 'em wondering.
Like a Massachusetts, Massachusetts
    resident
Who once became a, once became a
    president,
He never, never, never, never says a
    word!

FLETCHER: Some matters have come up today,
Important as can be—
So won't you kindly step this way
To a confidential conference with me?

    ALL: Some matters have come up today
Some matters, dark and grim—
So won't you kindly step this way
To a confidential conference with
    him—
Confidential conference with him—
Confidential conference with him—
Confidential conference with him?

[*As Holmes and Fletcher walk downstage, all
sing either "He's an F.F.V. . . ." etc. "He's the
unofficial, unofficial . . ." etc.*]

PATRIOTIC RALLY

Introduced by ensemble. Included in the 1930 revision,
although the music to the patter section ("Land of
Washington and Lincoln . . .") was entirely rewritten.
Published with a few revised lyrics in the 1930 piano-
vocal score. Includes "Three Cheers for the Union" and
"This Could Go On for Years."

CHORUS: We are Fletcher's Get-Ready-for-War
    Choral Society,
Fletcher's Get-Ready-for-War Choral
    Society.

"Three Cheers for the Union"

We're all here for a rally,
So, patriots, get pally—
Three cheers for the Union!
Siss for the Swiss!
Oh, isn't it exciting!
There may be lots of fighting.
Three cheers for the Union!
Siss for the Swiss!
Oh, isn't it grand! This wonderful land
Will show 'em the stuff it's made of;
We're ready to go to prove to the foe
There's nobody we're afraid of!
We're all here for a rally,
So, patriots, get pally—
Three cheers for the Union!
Siss for the Swiss!
Three cheers for the Union!
Siss for the Swiss!

"This Could Go On For Years"

Land of Washington and Lincoln, Henry Ford
    and Morris Gest,
Land of Franklin, land of Coolidge—
Men who stood the test!
Land of Jefferson and Adams,
Dempsey and Ben Turpin, too,
Andrew Jackson, Woodrow Wilson—
All red, white, and blue!
Francis Bushman, Charlotte Cushman,
And old Edwin Booth,
Admiral Dewey, "Lefty" Louie,
And "Bambino" Ruth.
We could go on naming great men, but we have
    our fears—
This could go on for years!

Land of Ginsberg and O'Reilly,
Fazio and Abie Cohn,
Leffingwell and Fenevessi—
How this land has grown!
Land of Schmaltz and Guggenheimer,
Rufus Rastus Jackson, too,
Land of Big Chief Muddy Waters—
Patriots all through!
Land of Minsky and Rumshinsky,
Land of Donahue—
Land of Johnson and Yon Yonson,
Land of Ching Ling Foo.
We could go on naming Americans, but we have
    our fears—
This could go on for years!

We're all here for a rally,
So, patriots, get pally—
Three cheers for the Union!
Siss for the Swiss!

Three cheers for the Union!
Siss for the Swiss!

THE MAN I LOVE

Introduced by Vivian Hart (Joan) and Roger Pryor (Jim). Reprised in Act II as "The Girl I Love" by Morton Downey (Soldier). For more detailed information, see the entry for "The Man I Love" in *Lady, Be Good!* (1924), pages 54–55.

VERSE

JOAN: When the mellow moon begins to beam,
Ev'ry night I dream a little dream;
And of course Prince Charming is the
     theme:
The he
For me.
Although I realize as well as you
It is seldom that a dream comes true,
To me it's clear
That he'll appear.

REFRAIN

Some day he'll come along,
The man I love;
And he'll be big and strong,
The man I love;
And when he comes my way,
I'll do my best to make him stay.

He'll look at me and smile—
I'll understand;
And in a little while
He'll take my hand;
And though it seems absurd,
I know we both won't say a word.

Maybe I shall meet him Sunday,
Maybe Monday—maybe not;
Still I'm sure to meet him one day—
Maybe Tuesday
Will be my good news day.

He'll build a little home
Just meant for two;
From which I'll never roam—
Who would? Would you?
And so, all else above,
I'm waiting for the man I love.

JIM: Some day she'll come along,
The girl I love;

Her smile will be a song,
The girl I love;
And when she comes my way,
I'll do my best to make her stay.

I'll look at her and smile—
She'll understand;
And in a little while
I'll take her hand;
And though it seems absurd,
I know we both won't say a word.

Maybe I will meet her Sunday,
Maybe Monday—maybe not;
Still I'm sure to meet her one day—
Maybe Tuesday
Will be my good news day.

For her I'll do and dare
As ne'er before;
Our hopes and fears we'll share—
For evermore;
And so, all else above,
I'm waiting for the girl I love.

YANKEE DOODLE RHYTHM

Published September 1927. Introduced by Jimmy Savo (Spelvin), Ruth Wilcox (Miss Meade), Max Hoffman, Jr. (Timothy), and Dorothea James (Anne). Later intended for *Rosalie* (1928) as an Act II duet for Oliver McLennan (Bill) and Bobbe Arnst (Mary).

VERSE

Talk about the music of the Sirens
And the Pipes of Pan.
Talk about the music of the Minstrel
And Pied Piper Man.
Well, sir, their day is through now,
For ev'rything is blue now!
Listen to the piping of the Jazzbo!
Real American! Oh,

REFRAIN

Yankee Doodle Rhythm is in demand
In ev'ry land upon the map;
Yankee Doodle Rhythm, they love it so—
The Eskimo, the Greek and Jap.
It's an insidious rhythm
Making the universe dance—
Carrying ev'rything with 'im!
Ev'ry gringo
Speaks the lingo!

It'll start a riot of stamping feet—
It's got a beat that brings good news;
It's the daily diet of ev'ry band
In this land of blues.
Dancing that tick-l-ish tempo,
Everything else is passé;
Yankee Doodle Rhythm, it wins the cup—
It's burning up the world today!

FINALETTO, ACT I

Introduced by Roger Pryor (Jim), Herbert Corthell (Fletcher), Robert Bentley (Sloane), Lew Hearn (Holmes), Vivian Hart (Joan), Max Hoffman, Jr. (Timothy), and ensemble. Alternate title: "Ensemble." Revised and included in the 1930 *Strike Up the Band* under the title "He Knows Milk," and published in the piano-vocal score for that show. The melody of one four-bar phrase ("Jim, how could you do such a thing? . . .") became the basis for "Soon," the principal love song of the 1930 *Strike Up the Band*. Music is missing for the section beginning "Though Jingos wave the flag . . ." and ending "allegiance to our flag!"

JIM: Stop! What is this mischief you're
     doing?
Stop! Reflect, consider, and pause!
Can't you see this trouble you're
     brewing
Won't be in a worthy cause?

FLETCHER: Be careful of a trick!
SLOANE: He's just a Bolshevik!

CHORUS: We will fight for all we hold dear,
     sir!
JIM: But I say this war is a fake!
FLETCHER: Why the hell must you interfere,
     sir?
CHORUS: Fletcher's reputation is at stake!

JIM: Fellow countrymen, lend me your
     ears for a minute.
MEN: If you have anything important to
     say, better begin it.

JIM: Folks, I was born
     Down on a farm—
     There 'midst the corn,
     Far from all harm—
     I learned about
     Cows and their ilk,
     So, my friends, I know milk!
CHORUS: He knows milk!
JIM: Some men are butchers;

Some men are bakers;
Some specialize as
Candlestick makers—
Some, cloaks and suits—
Some men know silk—
I, my friends, I know milk.

CHORUS: He knows milk!
You may know milk, but tell us
more!
What the devil has that got to do
with war?
What the devil has that got to do
with war?

JIM: I'd go to war
For cheese I could trust,
But never for
A cause so unjust—
For I'm afraid—
Oh, can't you see?—
This cheese is made,
Fletcher's Cheese is made
Of milk—Grade B!

CHORUS: Not A?
JIM: No. B!
CHORUS: Not A?
JIM: No. B!
Oh, my friends, I know milk!
CHORUS: He still knows milk!

FLETCHER,
SLOANE,
AND
HOLMES: No, no! Nay, nay!
We're here to say
It is Grade A.
We always use the best ingredients!

JIM: Here today
You hear me say
It's not Grade A!
You're using Grade B for expedience!

MEN: He says they do not use the best
ingredients,
But that they're using Grade B for
expedience;
And Fletcher told us that when he
began it, he
Was only making cheese to help
humanity!

WOMEN: He says they do not use the best
ingredients,
But that they're using Grade B for
expedience;
And Fletcher told us that when he
began it, he
Was only making cheese to help
humanity!

CHORUS: Maybe he is telling us the truth!
Maybe he is telling us the truth!

JOAN: Jim, how could you do such a
thing?
Oh, Jim, unworthy of you, such a
thing!
Just look at my father and see
He'd never use Grade B.

[*Joan repeats, while:*]
JIM: Joan, I had to do such a thing—
Oh, Joan—the moment I knew such
a thing!
My conscience and I both agree
The milk is still Grade B.

FLETCHER: To me the whole thing is simply
ridiculous—
My honor has been struck an awful
blow.
The populace knows I am too
meticulous.
I'd never stoop to do a thing so low!

HOLMES
AND SLOANE: He'd never stoop to do a thing so
low!
TIMOTHY: He'd never stoop to do a thing so
low!
FLETCHER: And you're a dirty so-and-so-and-so!
CHORUS: A very dirty so-and-so-and-so, while
He is a typical self-made American.
JIM: He is a true, profiteering American.
FLETCHER: I've made a pure product ever since
I began.
JIM: He'll get us all into war if he works
his plan.
CHORUS: In 'most ev'ry way, we feel,
He is basically sound—
With his shoulder to the wheel
And his two feet on the ground.
He is a typical, typical, typical
self-made American!

JIM: Though jingos wave the flag to win
applause,
My friends, again I'm asking you to
pause—
My countrymen, you're all asleep;
Why don't you look before you
leap?
I say you haven't got a worthy
cause.

[*Jim repeats, while:*]
CHORUS: My country, right or wrong—
That's our battle song.
Till we die
We shall cry:
My country, right or wrong.

JIM: Why fight for cheese I know to be
inferior
While masquerading as a cheese
superior?

CHORUS: We're sure that it contains the best
material;
And then we hate the
Swiss—they're too imperial!
So we pledge allegiance to our flag!

JOAN: Alas! Alackaday! Unlucky me!
My hero and my father can't agree.
FLETCHER: I think this fellow is a spy!
SLOANE: Well, if he is, he'll have to die,
For we must all protect our liberty.

CHORUS: Yes, yes, we say,
He'll have to pay!
He's in the way!
With propaganda he's been fillin' us!
He's a fake—
And no mistake;
His neck we'll break!
Whoever heard of one so villainous?

He says that we use Grade B for
expedience!
We'll teach him soon the meaning
of obedience!
We're all crusading for a cause
that's glorious,
And who the hell is he to be
censorious?

[*Repeat last four lines*]

[*Music rises to climax—Yells, shouts, "Get
him!" etc. Red lights*]
JOAN: Jim, how could you do such a thing?
Oh, Jim, unworthy of you, such a
thing!
JIM: My conscience and I both agree
The milk is still Grade B.

[*Jim taken off*]

TIMOTHY: Now ev'ry man get into uniform,
And for those foreigners we'll make
it warm!
MEN: Those sons o' guns will never scoff—
We'll show them all where they get
off!
We're out to take the enemy by
storm!
CHORUS: Around the flag we'll rally—
Come, patriots get pally!
Three cheers for the union!
Siss for the Swiss!
Three cheers for the Union!
Siss for the Swiss!

STRIKE UP THE BAND

Published September 1927, December 1929, May 1930 (in the complete piano-vocal score), and many times thereafter. Introduced by Max Hoffman, Jr. (Timothy), and ensemble. Introduced in the 1930 revision of *Strike Up the Band* by Jerry Goff (Jim) and ensemble, with Red Nichols and his band. "Strike Up the Band for U.C.L.A." was published in October 1936.

The Fifth Try. Late one weekend night in the spring of 1927, I got to my hotel room with the Sunday papers. I looked for a slit of light under the door of the adjoining room—but no light, so I figured my brother was asleep. (We were in Atlantic City for *Strike Up the Band* discussions with producer Edgar Selwyn.) I hadn't finished the paper's first section when the lights went up in the next room; its door opened and my pajamaed brother appeared. "I thought you were asleep," I said. "No, I've been lying in bed thinking, and I think I've got it." "Got what?" I asked. "Why, the march, of course. I think I've finally got it. Come on in." It was off-season and, with no guests to disturb within ten rooms of us, the hotel had sent up a piano. I sat down near the upright and said: "I hope you've *really* finally made up your mind." He played the refrain of the march practically as it is known today. Did I like it? Certainly I liked it, but—"But what?" "Are you sure you won't change your mind again?" "Yes, I'm pretty sure this time." "That's good. Don't forget it." By this last remark I meant not only the new tune but also an implied guarantee that he wouldn't try for another.

The reason I wanted assurance was that over the weeks he had written four different marches and on each occasion I had responded with "That's fine. Just right. O.K., I'll write it up." And each time I had received the same answer: "Not bad, but not yet. Don't worry. I'll remember it; but it's for an important spot, and maybe I'll get something better."

This fifth try turned out to be it. Interestingly enough, the earlier four had been written at the piano; the fifth and final came to him while lying in bed. . . .

—from *Lyrics on Several Occasions*

VERSE

We fought in 1917,
Rum-ta-ta tum-tum-tum!
And drove the tyrant from the scene,
Rum-ta-ta tum-tum-tum!

We're in a bigger, better war
For your patriotic pastime.

We don't know what we're fighting for—
But we didn't know the last time!

So load the cannon! Draw the blade!
Rum-ta-ta tum-tum-tum!
Come on, and join the Big Parade!
Rum-ta-ta tum-tum,
Rum-ta-ta tum-tum,
Rum-ta-ta tum-tum-tum!

REFRAIN 1

Let the drums roll out!
(Boom-boom-boom!)
Let the trumpet call!
(Ta-ta-ra-ta-ta-ta-ta!)
While the people shout—
(Hooray!)
Strike up the band!

Hear the cymbals ring!
(Tszing-tszing-tszing!)
Calling one and all
(Ta-ta-ra-ta-ta-ta-ta!)
To the martial swing,
(Left, right!)
Strike up the band!

There is work to be done, to be done—
There's a war to be won, to be won—
Come, you son of a son of a gun—
Take your stand!

Fall in line, yea bo—
Come along, let's go!
Hey, leader, strike up the band!

REFRAIN 2

[*First 14 lines are same as in refrain 1*]
Yankee doo doodle-oo doodle-oo,
We'll come through, doodle-oo doodle-oo,
For the red, white and blue doodle-oo,
Lend a hand.

With our flag unfurled,
We can lick the world!*
Hey, leader, strike up the band!

*The 1927 verse] was written in a comparatively peaceful period when there was much talk and some action among nations about disarmament.

Thirteen years later (1940), with another World War in the offing, it would have been unpatriotic not to have

*Alternate version of refrain 2, line 20:
For a brave, new world!*

changed the sentiment of the "pastime—last time" quatrain; so an edition was published with these lines.

We hope there'll be no other war,
But if we are forced into one—
The flag that we'll be fighting for
Is the Red and White and Blue one!

(The standard version today.)
Two years later (1942), after we had been forced into World War II, this became:

Again the Hun is at the gate
For his customary pastime;
Again he sings his Hymn of Hate—
But we'll make this time the last time!

(This version is out of print now—I hope.)

Another version was published between the 1927 and 1940 ones—this, with a completely rewritten lyric called "Strike Up the Band for U.C.L.A." In 1936 I was asked to adapt "Strike Up" so that it could be included among the college songs of the University of California at Los Angeles, to be used particularly at football games. And for over twenty years I have been the recipient annually of a rather unusual song royalty or dividend: two season passes to the home football games.

—from *Lyrics on Several Occasions*

"Strike Up the Band for U.C.L.A."

VERSE

We stand undaunted in the fray,
Rum-ta-ta tum-tum-tum!
And sing of old U.C.L.A.,
Rum-ta-ta tum-tum-tum!

We're Sons and Daughters of the Bear,
We're the California Bruins;
We fight the foe and do and dare,
And the foe is left in ruins!

We're standing firm! Our line will hold!
Rum-ta-ta tum-tum-tum!
Strike up the band for Blue and Gold!
Rum-ta-ta tum-tum,
Rum-ta-ta tum-tum,
Rum-ta-ta tum-tum-tum!

REFRAIN

Let the drums roll out!
(Boom-boom-boom!)
Let the trumpets call!
(Ra-ta-ta-ta-ta-ta!)
Let the whole world shout—
(Hooray!)
U.C.L.A.!

With our battle cry—
(Grrrah! Grrrah! Grrrah!)—
Bruin! Conquer all!
(Ta-ta-ra-ta-ta-ta-ta!)
We will do or die!
(Hooray!)
U.C.L.A.!

There's a game to be won, to be won!
Put the foe on the run, on the run!
And it's got to be done, to be done,
Here today!

With our flag unfurled
(Boom-boom-boom!)
We can lick the world!
You see, we're U.C.L.A.!

OH, THIS IS SUCH A LOVELY WAR

Introduced by ensemble. Alternate title: "Opening, Act II." Includes "The Knitting Song." No. 92 in the George and Ira Gershwin Special Numbered Song File. See also "Nursie, Nursie," page 100.

SOLDIERS: Sitting, sitting,
Busy with our knitting
As the day goes flitting by
Comfy, cozy,
Life is never prosy
Underneath a rosy sky.
This war's so delightful, it isn't
quite rightful
That we shouldn't think of those
way back home;
And what could be better than
knitting a sweater
For those sad ones who have to stay
back home?

Stitching, stitching,
Handiwork bewitching—
That's what we've been itching for.
We assever
We could stay forever
And the place would never bore.
Oh, ev'rything's luscious—with
work they don't rush us;
We only know one disappointment
here:
Until there's a treaty we can't send
for sweetie—

Oh, that's the one fly in the
ointment here!

[*Swiss girls enter*]

SWISS GIRLS: Listen and lend us an ear, soldier!
Why should a war interfere, soldier?
Swiss hospitality's here, soldier—
What is there that we can do?

How can you say that you miss
cuties
When you can entertain Swiss
cuties?
And if you're longing to kiss cuties,
We can arrange it for you.

[*Dance*]

SOLDIERS: Oh, this is such a lovely war!
Whoops! What a lovely war!
Whoops! What a lovely war!
It keeps you out in the open air.
Oh, this is such a lovely war!
Whoops! What a lovely war!
Whoops! What a lovely war!
We're glad that we're over here over
there!

Oh boy! We get three meals a day
and all our clothing free;
And ev'ry month they pay us
dollars up to thirty-three;*
We can't be fired because we've got
a two-year guarantee—
Oh, isn't this a lovely war!

Oh, this is such a charming war!
Whoops! What a charming war!
Whoops! What a charming war!
It keeps you out in the open air.
Oh, this is such a charming war!
Whoops! What a charming war!
Whoops! What a charming war!
We're glad that we're over here over
there!

We sleep in downy feather
beds—We never see a cot;
Our contract calls for ice-cream
sodas when the weather's hot;
And very good publicity if ever we
get shot!
Oh, isn't this a charming war!

---

*Alternate line:

At five o'clock, the sergeant comes and
takes us out for tea;

HOPING THAT SOMEDAY YOU'D CARE

Introduced by Roger Pryor (Jim) and Vivian Hart (Joan). The music to the verse was used for the verse of "Soon" in the 1930 revision of *Strike Up the Band*. No. 93 in the George and Ira Gershwin Special Numbered Song File.

VERSE

JIM: If ever fortune had an unlucky victim,
Surely she picked him in me.
My cares do not diminish;
Oh, what will the finish be?

JOAN: If ever happiness for us was intended,
Now it is ended, I see.

BOTH: How were we to know
How the wind would blow?

REFRAIN 1

JIM: You were enthralling, how could I help
falling
And hoping that someday you'd care?
My star was twinkling, for I had no
inkling
Of heartaches that I'd have to bear.
Oh, I thought that your love would
waken;
But no! I see how badly I was mistaken!
Oh, how this duffer is learning to suffer
For hoping that someday you'd care!

REFRAIN 2

JOAN: My heart was beaming, for I, too, was
dreaming
And hoping that someday you'd care.
I thought it fated that we two be mated
All gladness and sorrow to share.
Though I see our castle divided,
I know that once again I would do as I
did.
This woeful maiden, her heart
heavy-laden,
Was hoping that someday you'd care.

MILITARY DANCING DRILL

Published September 1927. Introduced by Max Hoffman, Jr. (Timothy), Dorothea James (Anne), and ensemble. The refrain, added to an entirely different verse, was later performed in the revision of *Strike Up the Band*, pages 155–56, and included in the 1930 published piano-vocal score.

VERSE

TIMOTHY: The military man
Doesn't find much time for fighting!
ANNE: There are things much more inviting
In the governmental plan.
You never see a trench—*
TIMOTHY: No, we have to do our homework;
Night and day we make the dome
work
Learning etiquette and French.
And in our spare time, dancing
masters reach us;
I'll demonstrate the method that they
teach us:

REFRAIN

Soldier, advance!
Then heave a sigh.
Here comes romance—
Never say die!
Ding, ding-a-derry,
That military
Dancing drill!
If she is cute,
If she appeals—
Soldier, salute!—
Clicking the heels.
She'll love it, oh boy!
Doing the doughboy
Dancing drill!
Throw out your chest,
Try to look at your best—
Full of splendor;
Ev'ry mother's daughter,
If you're looking as you oughter,
Will surrender.
Properly done,
Right from the start—
Soldier, you've won:
You've captured her heart!

---

*Published version of verse, lines 5–6:
We never see a trench,
For we have to do our homework;

Doing the very
Gay, military
Dancing drill!

HOW ABOUT A MAN?

Introduced by Herbert Corthell (Fletcher), Lew Hearn (Holmes), and Edna May Oliver (Mrs. Draper). See also "How About a Boy?," pages 156–57, in the 1930 revision of *Strike Up the Band*.

VERSE

FLETCHER AND
HOLMES: Lady, Lady Bountiful,
How happy you could make me!
MRS. DRAPER: But there are a county full
Of men all glad to take me.
They are brave and gallant;
All of them have talent.
What have you to offer
If my hand I proffer?
FLETCHER AND
HOLMES: Lady, Lady Bountiful,
I do not like to boast,
But I am sure that my talents offer
most.

REFRAIN 1

HOLMES: How about a man who can fill you
with romance?
FLETCHER: How about a man who can lead
you in the dance?
HOLMES: How about a man who's strong as
steel?
FLETCHER: How about a man with sex appeal?
How can you refuse me?
HOLMES: Surely you can use me.
How about a man who is full of
tenderness?*
FLETCHER: How about a man who can button
up a dress?
BOTH: Lady, lovely lady, here's your cue:
How about a man like me for you?

---

*Earlier version of refrain 1, lines 7–8:
FLETCHER: How about a man who is full of
sentiment?
HOLMES: How about a man who's behind the
president?

REFRAIN 2

FLETCHER: How about a man can recite like
Edwin Booth?*
HOLMES: How about a man sang soprano in
his youth?
FLETCHER: How about a man who's six feet
tall?
HOLMES: How about a man who's five feet
small?
FLETCHER: Why remain a widow?
HOLMES: Kiss me quick, old kiddo!
FLETCHER: How about a man who can whistle
like a lark?
HOLMES: How about a man who can row
you in the park?
BOTH: Lady, lovely lady, here's your cue:
How about a man like me for you?

JIM, CONSIDER WHAT YOU ARE DOING!

Introduced by Vivian Hart (Joan), Lew Hearn (Holmes), Robert Bentley (Sloane), Herbert Corthell (Fletcher), Roger Pryor (Jim), Jimmy Savo (Spelvin), and ensemble. Alternate titles: "Finaletto, Act II" and "Finaletto, Act II, Scene 1."

JOAN: Jim, consider what you are doing!
Jim, his reputation's at stake!
[*Points to Sloane*]
HOLMES: What is all this mess that you're
brewing?
SLOANE: He's a troublemaker we must break!
FLETCHER: Take him to the guardhouse—this
impetuous youth!
JIM: I say you'll be sorry when you learn
the truth—
All about the buttons and the
milk—that's cut.
FLETCHER: Take him to the guardhouse—He's a
Grade B nut.

---

*Earlier version of refrain 2, lines 1–4:
FLETCHER: How about a man who can kick above
his head?
HOLMES: How about a man who'll be famous
when he's dead?
FLETCHER: How about a man who likes to play?
HOLMES: How about a man who's always gay?

ALL: Crazy talk of buttons and of
    milk—Grade B!
    Just a traitor to the U.S.A. is he.
[*A yodel offstage, followed by the sound of gunfire*]

    What's that? What's that?
    A wheel gone flat?
    What's that? What's that?
    It sounds like shooting grand and
      glorious!
    What the deuce!
    If hell breaks loose—
    We'll cook their goose!
    America must stand victorious.
    It sounds like cannon shooting grand
      and glorious—
    Well, if it is we're sure to be
      victorious!
    We know that when our boys begin
      admonishing,
    They get results that really are
      astonishing.
    It sounds like cannon shooting grand
      and glorious—
[*Interrupted by Spelvin and soldiers marching in*]
SOLDIERS: Yankee doo doodle-oo doodle-oo,
    We've come through, doodle-oo,
      doodle-oo,
    For the red, white and blue doodle-oo,
    What a land!

SPELVIN: We met the enemy and we are
    theirs—They are ours!

ALL: Hooray! Hooray! Hooray!
    Tell us how you did it.

SPELVIN: There were we, way up in an Alp!
SOLDIERS: Up in an Alp, up in an Alp!
SPELVIN: Out to get the enemy scalp!
SOLDIERS: Get the enemy scalp!
SPELVIN: I told my men to hide—
SOLDIERS: We scattered far and wide—
SPELVIN: Soon as I saw I was alone—
SOLDIERS: He was alone, he was alone—
SPELVIN: I cleared my throat, tightened my belt,
    Pointed my gun, and let out a yodel:
    Oh-le-oh-layee!
    And then I waited—
    The Swiss, you see, thought it must
      be *their* general.
    They came running to me.
    But my men were on the job.
    The Swiss were surrounded.
    A yodel won the war! Oh-le-oh-layee!
[*General hurrah*]
ALL: He's won the day—
    Hip, hip, hooray!

He's won the day—
Hip, hip, hooray!

SPELVIN: My friends, if from the bonds of war
    we're free,
    Please do not give the credit all to
      me.
    There was a mastermind who planned
    The strategy that saved our land.
    And oh, my friends, the mastermind
      is—he!
[*Points to Jim*]

ALL: What? How ridiculous!
    Ha ha, we laugh,
    Ho ho, you chaff,
    The fatted calf
    Will never go to one so villainous.
    How you jest—
    He's just a pest—
    A prison guest.
    Please stop your joking, you are
      killin' us.

SPELVIN: The man who told me how to win
    is—he!
[*This time, they rush to Jim*]

ALL: He won the war!
    Hip, hip, hooray!
SPELVIN: Now an encore!
    Hip, hip, hooray!

FLETCHER: To me the whole thing is
    incomprehensible—
SLOANE: They'd start to string him up, if they
    were sensible.

ALL: He won the war! Hip, hip, hooray!
    A hero! A hero! Hurrah!
    Speech, speech!
[*He is carried off in triumph to:*]
ALL: Let the drums roll out!
    (Boom-boom-boom!)
    Let the trumpet call!
    (Ta-ta-ra-ta-ta-ta-ta!)
    While the people shout
    (Hooray!)
    Strike up the band!
    Hear the cymbals ring!
    (Tszing-tszing-tszing!)
    Calling one and all
    (Ta-ta-ra-ta-ta-ta-ta!)
    To the martial swing,
    (Left, right!)
    Strike up the band!
[*All off but principals—Dialogue—Then:*]

JOAN: I knew he'd come along,
    The one I love;

Though ev'rything went wrong
With one I love;
I'll still keep dreaming of
The one and only man I love.

HOMEWARD BOUND

Introduced by Morton Downey (a soldier) and ensemble.

SOLDIERS: Gee! But it's great to get up in the
    morning
    When you're on the trail that's
      winding
    To your little gray home in the West.

VERSE

A SOLDIER: Once again the golden sun is shining
    For the lonesome soldier boy;
    And the heavy heart that knew but
      pining
    Beats again a song of joy.
    Soon we'll be in our native land once
      more—
    There to greet all the dear ones we
      adore.*

REFRAIN

Homeward bound—
On the way!
Homeward bound—
Home to stay!
What a thrill!
Jack and Jill
Will soon be deep in clover—
Trouble's over
For me!
Me, oh my!
Misery—
Say good-bye!
Can't go wrong—
Won't be long!
Boy! You're lucky when you're
    homeward bound!

Alternate version of verse, line 6:
    There to greet all the loved ones we adore.

THE WAR THAT ENDED WAR

Introduced by ensemble. The piano-vocal version is titled "Opening, Act II, Scene Three."

VERSE

WOMEN: Ev'ry girl is dressed
In her very best;
All the world's in tune,
For we know that soon
The boyfriends are coming home!

Banners here and there;
Music in the air;
Ev'rywhere the flag;
Patriotic jag;
The boyfriends are coming home!

Tommy, Dick, and Frank,
Percival and Hank,
Isidor and Gus—
What a thrill for us!
The boyfriends are coming home!

Happiness arrives
In our lonely lives;
Soon we'll know the charms
Of their brawny arms;
The boyfriends are coming home!

REFRAIN

Civilization is improving—
This war ends all war!
Higher and higher we are moving—
This war ends all war!
Fighting is through, for Fletcher has
said it!

Fletcher deserves the credit!
So give three cheers
And then give one cheer more
For the war that ended war!

COME-LOOK-AT-THE-WAR CHORAL SOCIETY

The lyric of this probably unused number intended for Act II, Scene 1, is set to music from "Fletcher's American Cheese Choral Society" and "Patriotic Rally."

WOMEN: We are Fletcher's Come-Look-at-the-War
Choral Society,
Fletcher's Come-Look-at-the-War Choral
Society.
We're here to see the fighting—
That's what we adore!
Oh, isn't it exciting
Visiting Fletcher's War!

We're here to cheer the boys on
Through the cannon's roar—
We hate the Swiss like poison,
Fighting in Fletcher's War.

Oh, isn't it grand! Our wonderful land
Will show 'em the stuff we're made of.
We're ready to go to prove to the foe
There's nobody we're afraid of!

We're here to see the fighting—
That's what we adore!
Oh, isn't it exciting
Visiting Fletcher's War!

NURSIE, NURSIE

At one time, a section of the Act II opening. Intended for ensemble. Dropped during rehearsals. Much of the music is missing.

NURSES: [demurely] We are the red, white, and
blue nurses—
Willing-to-dare-and-to-do nurses!
For your fevers and your chills,
We've prepared some lovely pills.
We're over here just to cure soldiers,
But we find healthy and pure soldiers.
We would like to do our stuff,
But alas! No one is sick enough.

We are the red, white, and blue
nurses—
Willing-to-dare-and-to-do nurses!
But this war is not so hot—
There's nobody getting shot.
Listen to us, all you brave heroes,
Though we are here just to save heroes,
Things are quiet, so we beg,
Won't somebody kindly break a leg?
Won't somebody kindly break a leg?

SOLDIERS: Nursie, nursie,
Lovely little nursie,
Show me a little mercy—do!
I keep aching
When asleep or waking,
And my heart is breaking, too!
My head is sad, my knee is bad,
My tongue is like a piece of plaid—
But there's no use in tonics you may
pick for me.
A pill or two will never do—
The cure is really up to you:
A little love will surely do the trick for
me!

OPPOSITE: *Fred Astaire and ensemble in "High Hat." Inset: Betty Compton, Adele Astaire, Gertrude McDonald, and Fred Astaire*

FUNNY FACE | 1927

Tryout: Under the titles *Smarty* and *Funny Face*, at the Shubert Theatre, Philadelphia, October 11, 1927; as *Funny Face*, at Poli's Theatre, Washington, D.C., October 31, 1927; Nixon's Apollo Theatre, Atlantic City, November 7, 1927; Playhouse, Wilmington, November 14, 1927. New York run: Alvin Theatre (first show in that theatre), opened November 22, 1927. 244 performances. Music by George Gershwin. Produced by Alex A. Aarons and Vinton Freedley. Book by Fred Thompson and Paul Gerard Smith (*Smarty* book credited to Fred Thompson and Robert Benchley). Book staged by Edgar MacGregor. Dances staged by Bobby Connolly. Orchestra under the direction of Alfred Newman. Cast, starring Fred Astaire (Jimmy Reeve) and Adele Astaire (Frankie), featured Victor Moore (Herbert), William Kent (Dugsie Gibbs), Allen Kearns (Peter Thurston), Betty Compton (Dora), Gertrude McDonald (June), Earl Hampton (Chester), the Ritz Quartette, and Victor Arden and Phil Ohman at the pianos.

English tryout: Empire Theatre, Liverpool, September 24, 1928. London run: Produced by Alfred Butt and Lee Ephraim with Alex A. Aarons and Vinton Freedley at Princes Theatre, opened November 8, 1928. 267 performances. Book staged by Felix Edwardes. Dances staged by Bobby Connolly. Orchestra under the direction of Julian Jones. Cast, starring Fred Astaire (Jimmy Reeve), Adele Astaire (Frankie), and Leslie Henson (Dugsie Gibbs), featured Bernard Clifton (Peter Thurston), Sydney Howard (Herbert), Rita Page (Dora), Renee Godd (June), John McNally (Chester), D'Arcy's Quartette, and Jacques Fray and Mario Braggiotti at the pianos.

For the lyric to "Once," see *Tell Me More*. "Sing a Little Song," listed in the New York programs, is really only a specialty number consisting of reprises. It includes no new lyrics. "Dancing Hour," dropped during the pre-Broadway tryout, was a specialty number for the ensemble and, almost certainly, included no new music or lyrics.

BIRTHDAY PARTY

Introduced by Betty Compton (Dora), Gertrude McDonald (June), and ensemble. At the start of the Philadelphia tryout, it was the fourth number of Act I. By the week of October 24, 1927, it had become the show's opening number. During part of the tryout, it was sung by Gertrude McDonald (June) and Maxine Carson (Olive); Olive's role was eliminated before the New York opening. Introduced in London by Rita Page, Renee Godd, and ensemble.

GUESTS: Here's a bit of all right:
Birthday party tonight.
How can we keep quiet?
We know, by and by, it
Will be one long riot.
Ting-a-ling-ting-a-ling-ting!

Birthday presents we've bought—
Cost us more than they ought;
But the cost, we're thinking,
We'll make up by drinking,
When the butler we've caught.

[*Enter Dora and June*]

DORA
AND JUNE: Hello, everybody!
GUESTS: Hello, girls, hello!
Where's the man whose birthday we acclaim?
DORA
AND JUNE: Jimmy—our guardian, our guardian, our guardian—will shortly appear.
GUESTS: Oh, why must he keep us waiting?
DORA
AND JUNE: Jimmy—our guardian, our guardian, our guardian—is nervous, we fear.
GUESTS: Why should he be hesitating?
Isn't he aware that ev'ry birthday
Ought to be a very special mirth day?
Jimmy—your guardian, your guardian, your guardian—He may be a dear,
But we're hungry, we are stating,
And we'd like the party to begin!
ALL: Let the band start playing!
What's a party for?
Let's begin a-swaying
On the polished floor.
And when Jimmy comes, let's give a cheer—
Show him how glad we are to be here.

Let the curtain ring up!
Let's start filling the cup!
How can we keep quiet?
We know, by and by, it
Will be one long riot.
Ting-a-ling-ting-a-ling-ting!

Let the party begin!
Holding out is a sin!
The cake we'd be slicing;
Just look at that icing!
Now's the time to give in!

FUNNY FACE

Published December 1927. Introduced by Adele Astaire (Frankie) and Fred Astaire (Jimmy). Added to the score during the Atlantic City week (November 7–12) of the tryout. In Atlantic City, it was the next-to-last number of Act I.

VERSE 1

JIMMY: Frankie, dear, your birthday gift reveals to me
That at heart you're really not so bad.
If I add, your funny face appeals to me,
Please don't think I've suddenly gone mad.
You have all the qualities of Peter Pan;
I'd go far before I'd find a sweeter pan.
And yet

REFRAIN 1

I love your funny face,
Your sunny, funny face;
For you're a cutie
With more than beauty;
You've got a lot
Of personality N.T.
A thousand laughs I've found
In having you around.
Though you're no Gloria Swanson,
For worlds I'd not replace
Your sunny, funny face.

VERSE 2

FRANKIE: Needn't tell me that I'm not so pretty, dear,
When my looking glass and I agree.
In the contest at Atlantic City, dear,
Miss America I'd never be.
Truth to tell, though, you're not such a lot yourself;
As a Paul Swan, you are not so hot yourself.
And yet

REFRAIN 2

I love your funny face,
Your sunny, funny face.
You can't repair it,
So I declare it
Is quite all right—
JIMMY: Like Ronald Colman?

FRANKIE: So's your ol' man!
   Yet it's very clear,
   I'm glad when you are near.
   Though you're no Handsome Harry
   For worlds I'd not replace
   Your sunny, funny face.

REFRAIN 3

FRANKIE: I love that funny face,
   That sunny, funny face.
   Though it upsets one,
   In time, it gets one—
   That's true, for you
   Have personality for two.
   Those eyes! Those nose! Those cheek!
   Won't make a movie sheik,
   But though you're no patootie,
   For worlds I'd not replace
   Your sunny, funny face.

EXTRA CHORUS

FRANKIE: [*to dog*] I love your funny face,
   Your sunny, funny face.
   You never bother
   About your father.
   Have you no shame?
   You're just a mutt and nothing but!
   Yet when you wag your tail,
   You'll never be for sale.
   Though you're no Rin Tin Tin, dear,
   For worlds I'd not replace
   Your sunny, funny face.

Version sung in "Finale Ultimo"

PETER: I love your funny face—
FRANKIE: Your sunny, funny face—
PETER: The news I'm spreading
   About our wedding—
[*Enter Dugsie and Dora*]
DUGSIE: My heart's enlarged.
   I'll buy a home and have it charged.
[*Enter Jimmy and June*]
JIMMY: Trouble takes the air;
   We'll be a happy pair.
[*Enter Chester and Herbert*]
HERBERT: We thank you for our freedom.
   You've saved us from disgrace.
   We love your funny face.

Earlier Version of "Finale Ultimo"

PETER: I love your funny face—
FRANKIE: Your sunny, funny face—
PETER: The news I'm spreading
   About our wedding—

[*Enter Dugsie and Dora*]
DUGSIE: I feel so tinglish,
   I'll even overlook your English.
[*Enter Jimmy and June*]
JIMMY: Trouble takes the air;
   We'll be a happy pair.
[*Enter Chester and other crook*]
CHESTER: For twenty years at Sing Sing,
   My cell I'll have to pace
   And love your funny face.

HIGH HAT

Published December 1927. Introduced by Fred Astaire (Jimmy) and "boys" (in London, billed as "Fred Astaire and men").

VERSE

JIMMY: When a fellow feels he's got to win a
   girlie's handie,
   He will send her loads of flowers, books,
   and tons of candy.
BOYS: The overhead is big;
   Oh, how they make us dig!
JIMMY: No use stepping out that way—The thing
   to do is lay low.
   You can't win by treating her as if she
   wore a halo.
BOYS: What is your solution?
   Tell us if you can.
JIMMY: Here's my contribution
   To Man:

REFRAIN

   High hat!
   You've got to treat them high hat!
   Don't let them know that you care;
   But act like a Frigidaire.
   You'll win them like that!
   Stand pat!
   Put on your gayest cravat,
   But keep your feet on the ground.
   Oh boy! How they'll come around!
   Just treat them high hat!

'S WONDERFUL

Published October 1927. Introduced by Adele Astaire (Frankie) and Allen Kearns (Peter). (During most of the tryout, Peter was played by Stanley Ridges.) Introduced in London by Adele Astaire and Bernard Clifton.

The principal reason for writing this lyric was to feature the sibilant sound effect deleting the "it" of "it's" and slurring the leftover "s" with the first syllable of the following word. So I'm frequently baffled by what some singers have in mind and throat when they formalize the phrases to "*It's* wonderful," "*It's* marvelous," "*It's* Paradise," &c.

Re "fash," "pash," "emosh," and "devosh" in the second verse: I had heard comedian Walter Catlett in *Lady, Be Good!* clipping syllables from some favored words, so thought it would be novel to adopt this device in a song. I used it first in "Sunny Disposish," written with composer Phil Charig for *Americana*. (A few years later I came across some light verse by England's Captain Harry Graham to discover that he had specialized in this lopping-off device long before me.)

The Proper Twenties. In Philadelphia, where *Funny Face* opened, one of the town's top critics saw me one afternoon in the lobby of the Shubert Theatre (a rehearsal was going on inside) and stopped to ask how the changes in the show were coming along. He then wondered if I had done anything about "'S Wonderful," which, it developed, he thought contained an obscene phrase. I don't know what he would think about it these Freedom-of-Four-Letter-Speech days, but at that time he felt that "feeling amorous" was something better scrawled in chalk than sung from a stage.

   —from *Lyrics on Several Occasions*

VERSE 1

PETER: Life has just begun:
   Jack has found his Jill.
   Don't know what you've done,
   But I'm all a-thrill.
   How can words express
   Your divine appeal?
   You could never guess
   All the love I feel.
   From now on, lady, I insist,
   For me no other girls exist.

REFRAIN 1

   'S wonderful! 'S marvelous—
   You should care for me!
   'S awful nice! 'S Paradise—
   'S what I love to see!

You've made my life so glamorous,
You can't blame me for feeling
    amorous.
Oh, 's wonderful! 'S marvelous—
That you should care for me!

VERSE 2

FRANKIE: Don't mind telling you
In my humble fash
That you thrill me through
With a tender pash.
When you said you care,
'Magine my emosh;
I swore, then and there,
Permanent devosh.
You made all other boys seem blah;
Just you alone filled me with AAH!

REFRAIN 2

'S wonderful! 'S marvelous—
You should care for me!
'S awful nice! 'S Paradise—
'S what I love to see!
My dear, it's four-leaf-clover time;
From now on my heart's working
    overtime.
Oh, 's wonderful! 'S marvelous—
That you should care for me!

Version sung in "Finale Ultimo"

FRANKIE: 'S wonderful!
PETER: 'S marvelous!
BOTH: City hall's in view.
FRANKIE: 'S marriage license.
PETER: 'S Niag'ra Falls.
BOTH: 'S 'appiness for two!
DUGSIE: You've made my life so ting-a-lish;
I'll even overlook your Eng-a-lish.
JIMMY: Oh, wedding bells fill the air
Now that I know you care.

Unused Stanzas

VERSE 3

PETER: How can I refuse
Damsel in distress?
FRANKIE: There's no time to lose
On this awful mess.
PETER: If danger you behold,
Please do not be blue.
FRANKIE: Like a knight of old,
I know you'd come through.
PETER: I'm at your beck and call, you see,
A Boy Scout once I used to be.

REFRAIN 3

'S wonderful! 'S marvelous—
Fate sent me to you.
Chivalry 'peals to me;
Your troubles I'll undo.
Fair maid, your smile will lead me on;
And your rescue I will speed me on.
Oh, 's wonderful! 'S marvelous—
Meeting someone like you.

VERSE 4

FRANKIE: If I'm in a daze,
I am not to blame.
Having heard your praise,
I'll never be the same.
When at last fate brings
Someone you adore,
And he tells you things—
Who could ask for more?
There really is a Santa Claus!
My dear, I'm sure there is, because

REFRAIN 4
[*same as refrain 2*]

VERSE 5

PETER: You are very young;
Shouldn't talk that way.
You're too highly strung
To know what you say.
Someday there'll appear
Your ideal, no doubt;
I am only here
Just to help you out.
There will be hundreds, by and by,
Who'll be far worthier than I.

REFRAIN 5

'S wonderful! 'S marvelous—
All that you've told me
'S awful nice! 'S Paradise—
To that I must agree.
But oh, what's all this dizziness?
I thought that I came here on business.
Oh, 's wonderful! 'S marvelous!
But why must you pick on me?

REFRAIN 6

'S *magnifique!* 'S what I seek—
You should care for me!
'S *élégant!* 'S what I want!
'S what I love to see!

You've made my life so ting-a-lish;
I'll even overlook your Eng-a-lish.
'S *exceptionnel!* 'S no bagatelle—
That you should care for me!

LET'S KISS AND MAKE UP

Published October 1927. Introduced by Adele Astaire
(Frankie), Fred Astaire (Jimmy), and ensemble. During
the pre-Broadway tryout, the Ritz Quartette joined the
Astaires and the ensemble in this number. Also see
"Come! Come! Come Closer!," which follows. The Brit-
ish edition of the sheet music contains additional lyrics
(for a second verse) that are probably not by Ira
Gershwin.

VERSE

I didn't mean to
Start any scene to
Make you sigh.
Hope to die!
It's most immoral
For us to quarrel.
Why can't we
Both agree?
Don't you know Ben Franklin wrote about this
    thing at length—
On the proposition that in union there is
    strength?
Why raise a storm up?
If we just warm up,
The blues will slumber;
We'll have their number!

REFRAIN 1

Let's kiss and make up;
Come on! Let's wake up,
For I need you and you need me.
Let's kiss and make up;
No use to break up
When we can live in harmony.
I'll give you your way,
You give me my way,
And out the doorway,
Our cares will fly 'way.
If we'd be happy, the way is clear:
Let's kiss and make up;
No use to break up;
We need each other, dear!

REFRAIN 2

Let's kiss and make up—*
No cares to rake up—
For I need you and you need me.
No reprimanding;
Full understanding
That we can live in harmony.
The world is prosy
When we are fighting;
Let's make it rosy
By reuniting.
Two heads are better than one, I hear;
So, kiss and make up;
No use to break up;
We need each other, dear!

COME! COME! COME CLOSER!

An early lyric set to the music that was eventually used for "Let's Kiss and Make Up." Intended for Fred Astaire (Jimmy) and Adele Astaire (Frankie). Unused. Replaced with "Let's Kiss and Make Up."

VERSE

Let's kiss and make up.
We mustn't break up—
You and I.
I didn't mean to
Start any scene to
Make you cry.
Dry that tear up;
Show some ambition;
Skies will clear up—
So will your disposition.
I can assure you,
I have a cure you
Ought to try:
Let's take a chance on
Putting a dance on—
Swinging—clinging—

—————————
Earlier version of refrain 2, lines 1–6:
Let's kiss and make up—
No use to shake up—
Why should we make our faces grow long?
No reprimanding;
Just understanding
To ev'ry quarrel we'll say, "So long!"

REFRAIN

Come! Come! Come closer!
Don't say "No, no, sir!"
And we will dance away our troubles.
Come! Come! Let's do it!
Snap! Snap! Into it!
And we will float along like bubbles.
Come! Come! And pull yourself together—
Why raise a storm up?
Let's change the weather—
Warm up!
Come! Come! Start dancing, and you will see
The blues will slumber—
We've got their number—
Come! Come! Come closer to me!

FINALE, ACT I

Introduced by principals and ensemble. Alternate title: "Come Along, Let's Gamble." Includes dialogue as well as song. Most of this number was deleted during the pre-Broadway tryout: only the last eight lines (beginning "Good heavens! They're gone!") were actually performed in New York and London.

ENSEMBLE: Come along, let's gamble,
        Gamble on the wheel.
        Losing, winning,
        When it's spinning,
        What a thrill you feel!

        Come along, let's gamble,
        Get yourself a stack.
        Ev'ry sinner
        Wants a winner
        On the red or black.

GIRLS: Very good idea—
       Why play games of chance?
       Let's upset the
       Game and get the
       Boys away to dance.

BOYS: Though we'd like to gamble,
      There is not a chance.
      One who knows girls
      Won't oppose girls
      When they want to dance.

ENSEMBLE: What are they here for?
        Certainly queer, for
        Each is a perfect stranger!
        What are they doing?

Something is brewing!
Maybe we're all in danger!

ENSEMBLE: How did they get here?
        We're all upset here;
        Wonder, Were they invited?
        What can they gain here?
        Lots to explain here!
        Makes us a bit excited!

ENSEMBLE: Good heavens! They're gone!
        Good heavens! They're gone!
        What an awful mess
        Make 'em both confess!
        Judging by their looks,
        They must be the crooks!
        Call the police!
        Call the police!

IN THE SWIM

Published 1983 in the *My One and Only* vocal selections. Introduced in *Funny Face*, by female ensemble. Alternate titles: "If You Will Take Our Tip" and "Opening, Act II." A portion of the music and a few of the lyric lines had been used in the discarded *Oh, Kay!* number "The Moon Is on the Sea."

GIRLS: If you will take our tip,
       You'll join us in a dip;
       We're all set to go dashing
       To the lake and start splashing.
       Oh, we hope the water's warm
       When we go to perform.
       We'll give our skin a tanning;
       That is one thing we are planning.
       And we think that maybe we'll try getting
         drowned
       (If we chance to see a handsome guard
         around).

       One thing we lack here
       When we're on the beach,
       And that thing is known as Man.
       Can't find his track here;
       He's not within reach—
       Won't you help us if you can?

       The sun is on the lake,
       And ev'rything is jake.
       The water may be fishy,
       But it peps you up like Vichy.
       All we need's a valentine
       To make the day divine—
       Come on, the water's fine!

Swimming, swimming, what a sport!
Keep your golf, your tennis court.
Once you're in the water you are set,
And you'll say the other sports are wet.
Whitecaps far as you can see;
Nightcaps when it's time for tea.
If you want that feeling full of pep and
vim,
Come on and join us in the swim!

HE LOVES AND SHE LOVES

Published December 1927. Introduced by Adele Astaire (Frankie) and Allen Kearns (Peter). Added to the score in the last week of the tryout. Replaced in the London production with Joseph Meyer and Roger Wolfe Kahn's song "Imagination."

VERSE 1

PETER: Now that I have found you,
I must hang around you.
Though you may refuse me,
You will never lose me.
If the human race is
Full of happy faces—
FRANKIE: It's because they all love
That wondrous thing they call love.

REFRAIN

PETER: He loves and she loves and they love,
so why can't
You love and I love, too?
FRANKIE: Birds love and bees love and
whispering trees love,
And that's what we both should do.
PETER: Oh, I always knew some-
Day you'd come along;
FRANKIE: We'll make a twosome
That just can't go wrong. Hear me—
PETER: He loves and she loves and they love,
so won't you
Love me as I love you?

VERSE 2

FRANKIE: Feel a funny feeling
In my heart a-stealing;
If it's love, I'm for it.
Gosh! How I adore it!
You're the silver lining
For which I've been pining.

PETER: Lonesome days are over;
From now on, we're in clover.

REPEAT REFRAIN

TELL THE DOC

Published December 1928 as a vocal arrangement only. Introduced by William Kent (Dugsie) and ensemble. Introduced in London by Leslie Henson and ensemble.

VERSE 1

DUGSIE: I'm a physician whose mission you
know—
Deals with the subject of dreams.
I'll burst your troubles like bubbles,
for Oh!
No dream is just what it seems.
Bring your dreams to me and I assure
you
I'll interpret them—That's how I'll
cure you.

REFRAIN

If happiness is failing you—Tell the
doc!
If you've no sweetie trailing you—Tell
the doc!
If Mr. Gloom is hailing you—Tell the
doc!
No matter what is wrong, come along,
Tell it to the doctor!
I don't know much of medicine, but I
say
I'm just as smart as Edison—in my
way.
So if you care to take happiness out of
hock,
Come and tell your troubles to the
doc!

VERSE 2

1ST GIRL: I dream of princes.
2ND GIRL: And I dream of tramps.
3RD GIRL: I dream of library lamps.
4TH GIRL: I dream of music.
5TH GIRL: And I dream of birds.
6TH GIRL: I dream of cross-puzzle words.
DUGSIE: To explain each dream I will contrive
it;

But come in my office, where it's
private.

REPEAT REFRAIN

MY ONE AND ONLY

Published October 1927 as "What Am I Gonna Do?," the title under which it was listed in most programs during the show's original run. Introduced by Fred Astaire (Jimmy), Gertrude McDonald (June), Betty Compton (Dora), and girls. Introduced in London by Fred Astaire (Jimmy), Renee Godd (June), and girls; reprised by Rita Page (Dora), Renee Godd (June), and girls. The British edition of the sheet music contains additional lyrics (for a second verse) that are probably not by Ira Gershwin.

VERSE 1

JIMMY: To show affection
In your direction,
You know I'm fit and able.
I more than merely
Love you sincerely;
My cards are on the table.
There must be lots of other men you
hypnotize.
All of a sudden, I've begun to realize—
As follows:

REFRAIN

My one and only—
What am I gonna do if you turn me
down,
When I'm so crazy over you?
I'd be so lonely—
Where am I gonna go if you turn me
down?
Why blacken all my skies of blue?
I tell you I'm not asking any miracle;
It can be done! It can be done!
I know a clergyman who will grow
lyrical—
And make us one! And make us one!
So, my one and only—
There isn't a reason why you should turn
me down,
When I'm so crazy over you.

VERSE 2

JUNE: It's time you woke up—
It's time you spoke up—
My praise you've never chanted.
Though we're not strangers,
You see the dangers
Of taking me for granted.
And if you cared, you should have told
me long ago;
Dear, otherwise how in the world was I
to know?
JIMMY: Well, listen:

REPEAT REFRAIN

THE BABBITT AND THE BROMIDE

Published December 1927. Introduced by Adele Astaire (Frankie) and Fred Astaire (Jimmy). Added to the score during the last week of the tryout, it replaced Fred Astaire's "Nut Dance," performed to a George Gershwin instrumental.

I t needs work" unquestionably applied to *Funny Face* when it opened in Philadelphia and looked like a failure. We were on the road six weeks, and everyone concerned with the show worked day and night, recasting, rewriting, rehearsing, recriminating—of rejoicing, there was none. "The Babbitt and the Bromide" was the final change. It went in on a Thursday or Friday night in Wilmington, when the audience consisted of no more than two hundred—mostly pretty and young and pregnant Du Pont matrons (my wife's observation). The number was introduced at 10:50 and concluded with Fred and Adele doing their famous "run-around"—to show-stopping applause—and suddenly, with all the other changes, the show looked possible. The week's business in Wilmington totaled $6,000. The following week we opened the new Alvin Theatre in New York and grossed $44,000.

Although our conception for performance of "Babbitt-Bromide" was that all the lines be sung in unison by Fred and Adele (as a dead-pan conversation carried on with neither listening to the other), they immediately felt it would be more effective nonsense to offer the phrases by turns:

FRED: Hello!
ADELE: How are you?
FRED: Howza folks?
ADELE: What's new? &c.

Which presentation too was fine with us.

Fred and Vinton (Vinton Freedley, co-producer) won't recall this, but I made a mental note at the time: The day my brother and I demonstrated the song, Fred took me aside and said: "I know what a Babbitt is, but what is a Bromide?" Just about an hour later, in the Wilmington Hotel elevator, Vinton said to me: "I was brought up on Gelett Burgess and the Goops, so I know what a Bromide is—but what's a Babbitt?"
—from *Lyrics on Several Occasions*

VERSE 1

A Babbitt met a Bromide on the avenue one
day.
They held a conversation in their own peculiar
way.
They both were solid citizens—They both had
been around.
And as they spoke you clearly saw their feet
were on the ground:

REFRAIN 1

Hello! How are you?
Howza folks? What's new?
I'm great! That's good!
Ha! Ha! Knock wood!
Well! Well! What say?
Howya been? Nice day!
How's tricks? What's new?
That's fine! How are you?
Nice weather we are having but it gives me such
a pain:
I've taken my umbrella, so of course it doesn't
rain.
Heigh ho! That's life!
What's new? Howza wife?
Gotta run! Oh, my!
Ta! Ta! Olive oil! Good-bye!

VERSE 2

Ten years went quickly by for both these
sub-sti-an-tial men,
Then history records one day they chanced to
meet again.*
That they had both developed in ten years there
was no doubt,
And so of course they had an awful lot to talk
about:

Sheet-music version:
And then it happened that one day they chanced to meet
again.

REFRAIN 2

[*Repeat first 8 lines of refrain 1*]
I'm sure I know your face, but I just can't recall
your name;
Well, how've you been, old boy? You're looking
just about the same.

[*Repeat last 4 lines of refrain 1*]

VERSE 3

Before they met again some twenty years they
had to wait.
This time it happened up above, inside St.
Peter's gate.
A harp each one was carrying and both were
wearing wings,
And this is what they sang as they kept
strumming on the strings:

REFRAIN 3

[*Repeat first 8 lines of refrain 1*]

You've grown a little stouter since I saw you
last, I think.
Come up and see me sometime and we'll have a
little drink.

[*Repeat last 4 lines of refrain 1*]

BLUE HULLABALOO

Introduced by Betty Compton (Dora), Gertrude McDonald (June), and ensemble. Added late in the tryout (in Atlantic City, it was sung by Lillian Roth, who had replaced Maxine Carson as Olive before the role was written out altogether), "Blue Hullabaloo" was dropped soon after the New York opening, and was not used in London.

VERSE

Friends, Romans, and fellow men,
If you are blue,
I'll change you to mellow men
With something new.
If you want to romp around—
If you care to stomp around—
Tune in on a new rhythm
Meant for us, one and all.
(Though I know they won't approve it
In Carnegie Hall.)

REFRAIN

Girls and boys, come and try it;
Make a noise that's a riot!
Learn to do the Blue Hullabaloo. Blue! Blue!
  Blue!
You can dance—you can sing it;
What a chance when you spring it.
Here's your cue: the Blue Hullabaloo.
You'll make no blunder—
This seventh wonder,
Melodic thunder,
Will drive your troubles from you.
Hits the spot—Come on, give it!
It's as hot as a rivet!
Do the Blue Hullabaloo!

AVIATOR

Introduced by ensemble ("Girls and Reporters") during
the first two weeks of the tryout, this was the show's
original opening number. The entire opening scene was
then dropped, including its three songs: "Aviator,"
"When You're Single," and "Your Eyes! Your Smile!"
As a result, "Birthday Party," previously the fourth
song in the show, assumed the Act I, number one, spot.
Alternate titles: "We're All A-Worry, All Agog," "Flying Fete," and "Opening, Act I."

GIRLS: We're all a-worry, all agog!
    We're all a-flurry—in a fog!
    Poor Peter's in a trial flight,
    And sad to say, he's not in sight!
[*They scan the skies*]
    Poor little feller,
    'Way up there—
    If his propeller
    Needs repair,
    Or if, perchance, he's out of gas—
    Oh dear! Alackaday! Alas!

    Boo-hoo! Boo-hoo!
    There's nothing we can do!
    Boo-hoo! Boo-hoo!
    Oh, Peter! Please come through!
    Although for flying
    You've a knack,
    Our hearts are crying:
    "Please come back!"
    Though no one in the air is fleeter,
    Please come down, for the love of
      Peter!
[*Reporters coming on*]

    You may have talent
    For the air,
    But you're not gallant,
    Staying there!

REPORTERS: Good morning! Good morning!
    We're gentlemen—
GIRLS: Yes, gentlemen?
REPORTERS: Gentlemen of the press!
ALL: Gentlemen of the press!

1ST 4 BOYS: Who is it who can tell you who is
    who and who is whose?
BOY A: The *Graphic*—
BOY B: The *Journal*—
BOY C: The *Mirror*—
BOY D: The *News!*
2ND 4 BOYS: Where can you get the lastest dope
    on these and foreign climes?
BOY E: The *Tribune*—
BOY F: The *World and*—
BOY G: The *Telegram*—
BOY H: The *Times!*
3RD 4 BOYS: Whom will you find right on the job
    when dirty work is done?
BOY I: The *American*—
BOY J: *Staats-Zeitung*—
BOY K: The *Wahrheit*—
BOY L: The *Sun!*
ALL
REPORTERS: Without us the country could never
    be run!

REPORTERS: And now that you know
    Who we are,
    We're aiming to know:
    Where's the star?—
    The shooting star whose name is Pete.
    Our public wants the news complete.

GIRLS: Boo-hoo! Boo-hoo!
    Poor Pete and his machine!
    Boo-hoo! Boo-hoo!
    They haven't yet been seen!

REPORTERS: What! What! What!
[*taking notes or pointing to imaginary
headlines*]
    FLIER NOT YET FOUND!
    IS HE IN THE AIR?
    IS HE ON THE GROUND?
    FRIENDS ARE IN DESPAIR!
    Gee! We see a front-page story
      there!
GIRLS:
[*at same time*]
    Ought to see a front-page story
      there!
REPORTERS: Thanks, thanks, thanks for the
    information!

    Now we've got to run along and find
      a telephone station!
GIRLS:
[*at same time*]
    So long! So long! So long!
    Good-bye! Good-bye! Good-bye!
[*Reporters run off*]

    Aviator!
    You're just a traitor!
    Why don't you cater
    To us?
    No mistaking
    The hearts you're breaking;
    That's why we're making
    This fuss.
    If you ever want us to know mirth
      again,
    You must come down to earth again.
    We keep sighing,
    The while we're crying,
    "Come off your flying
    Bus."

WHEN YOU'RE SINGLE

Introduced by William Kent (Dugsie) and girls during
the first week of the tryout (Oct. 11–15), when it was the
second number in Act I. Dropped.

VERSE

DUGSIE: I've often been a best man
    But never a groom;
    So I'm not a distressed man—
    I blossom and bloom.
    Each bride in white looks splendid—so
    Dressed up—but oh, alack!
    The groom knows all is ended, so
    You see him dressed in black.
    Oh, he can have the thrills
    Of wedding bells and bills.

REFRAIN 1

    Boy! But it's grand when you're single—
    You're in demand when you're single.
    Pardon my enthusiasm,
    But a single chappie has 'em.
    You needn't be an Apollo,
    Just crook your finger and they will
      follow.
    With blonde, brunette, henna,

One plays around when a
Chap leads the single life.

REFRAIN 2

Boy! But it's grand when you're single—
You're in demand when you're single.
GIRLS: Please excuse our girlish laughter—
But we get what we go after.
Some night out on a veranda,
You'll fall for some baby's propaganda.
Next day you'll be lined up
Waiting to be signed up—
Good-bye to single life!

YOUR EYES! YOUR SMILE!

Introduced by Stanley Ridges (who originated the role of
Peter but was replaced with Allen Kearns) and Adele
Astaire (Frankie) during the first two weeks of the tryout, when it was the third number in Act I. Dropped.
Alternate title: "Those Eyes" (as it was listed in the
Philadelphia *Smarty* programs). No. 108 in the George
and Ira Gershwin Special Numbered Song File. The
music to the verse was later used in the verse of "You
Started It," intended for both *Girl Crazy* (1930) and the
film *Delicious* (1931); the music to the release became
the release of "You've Got What Gets Me," written for
and used in the first film version of *Girl Crazy* (1932).

VERSE 1

PETER: It gave me joy to be a Boy Scout many
years ago;
And if I add, Sir Galahad was my ideal,
you'll know
That surely I will always try your
troubles to undo.
Fair lady, who would not come through
for lady fair as you?

REFRAIN 1

I'd do a lot for
Your eyes! Your smile!
I'd start a plot for
Your hair! Your style!
Oh, lady, listen, do!
Let's begin an alliance;
I'll start protecting you
From your dragons and giants.
Where did you get them?
Those eyes? Those nose?
I'm glad I met them—

Those cheeks! Those those!
Oh, you can count on me, knowing,
lady, that I'll
Always do a lot for
Your eyes! Your smile!

VERSE 2

FRANKIE: Forsooth, my lad, my Galahad, it thrills
this little maid
To think that she's to be the reason for
a new crusade.
I'm just a clinging vine, old thing, but
should your plans go wrong,
I must confide that at your side I'd like
to help along.

REFRAIN 2

What a collection!
Those eyes! Those nose!
They need your protection!
Those hair! Those clothes!
You know, for you're not dumb,
Lots of women raise Hades;
I want to save you from
Those insidious ladies.
I'd go in hock for
That tie! That cheek!
Jump off a dock for
That strong physique!
Oh, you can count on me any way the
wind blows.
Gosh! I'd do a lot for
Those eyes! Those nose!

HOW LONG HAS THIS BEEN GOING ON?

Published October 1927. Introduced by Stanley Ridges
(the original Peter) and Adele Astaire (Frankie) during
the tryout. It was the second number in Act II. Replaced
before the New York opening with "He Loves and She
Loves." With a slightly revised lyric, introduced by
Bobbe Arnst (Mary) in *Rosalie* (1928).

Blue Pencil Out of the Blue. As if we didn't have
enough on our minds in Philadelphia after *Funny
Face* opened (cf. note to "Babbitt and Bromide"): I was
at work in my room at the Ritz-Carlton when the telephone rang. The caller was the then professional manager of Shapiro Bernstein & Co., one of the three or four

most important popular-music houses. He said: "I saw
your show last night. Not very good." I agreed that we
needed fixing. He: "You've got a number called 'How
Long Has This Been Going On?' " Myself: "Yes, what
about it?" He: "Doesn't mean a thing." I couldn't agree
to that extent, but did concede its reception had been
lukewarm; still, why his interest in this particular number? He: "Well, we bought a song with the same title and
we're about to publish it. Yours is getting you nowhere,
so how about taking it out of the show?"

This was as gratuitous a request as ever I heard. However, wanting a little further insistence from him, I explained that eliminating a song from a book show wasn't
a one-man job; that it would take some days before
conferences reached the spot; that then, if decision
called for elimination, a new song would have to be
written, learned, staged, and orchestrated. So it was
beyond me to help him out at the moment. I concluded
by wishing him good luck on his song.

Well, he had *his* wish. A couple of weeks later on
the road (either in Atlantic City or Washington) "How
Long . . ." was out, replaced by "He Loves and She
Loves" (not as good a song as the former, but one that
managed to get over). *My* wish (good luck), though,
apparently didn't help, for even if the other "How
Long . . ." was published, I've never heard it or of it.

Two months later the eliminated song, because Ziegfeld
liked it, found itself in *Rosalie*. There being no spot in
the show for it as a duet, it became—with a few line
changes—a solo for the soubrette, played by Bobbe
Arnst.

—from *Lyrics on Several Occasions*

VERSE 1

PETER: As a tot,
When I trot-
Ted in little velvet panties,
I was kissed
By my sist-
Ers, my cousins, and my aunties.
Sad to tell,
It was hell—
An Inferno worse than Dante's.
So, my dear, I swore,
"Never, nevermore!"
On my list,*
I insist-

*In Rosalie's solo female version, lines 12–17 of
verse 1 were:*

Then a boy
Brought me joy
From the moment that I knew him.
Oh, what bliss!
Billy's kiss
Made me say directly to him:

Ed that kissing must be crossed out.
Now I find
I was blind,
And—Oh, lady—how I've lost out!

REFRAIN 1

I could cry
Salty tears;
Where have I
Been all these years?
Little wow,
Tell me now:
How long has this been going on?
There were chills
Up my spine,
And some thrills
I can't define.
Listen, sweet,
I repeat:
How long has this been going on?
Oh, I feel that I could melt;
Into heaven I'm hurled.
I know how Columbus felt
Finding another world.
Kiss me once,
Then once more.
What a dunce
I was before!
What a break—
For heaven's sake!
How long has this been going on?

VERSE 2

FRANKIE: 'Neath the stars,
At bazaars,
Often I've had to caress men.
Five or ten
Dollars, then,
I'd collect from all those yes-men.
Don't be sad;
I must add
That they meant no more than
    chessmen.
Darling, can't you see—
'Twas for charity?
Though these lips
Have made slips,
I was never really serious.
Who'd 'a' thought
I'd be brought
To a state that's so delirious?

REFRAIN 2

I could cry
Salty tears;
Where have I
Been all these years?
Listen, you—
Tell me, do:
How long has this been going on?
What a kick—
How I buzz!
Boy, you click
As no one does!
Hear me, sweet,
I repeat:
How long has this been going on?
Dear, when in your arms I creep—
That divine rendezvous—
Don't wake me if I'm asleep,
Let me dream that it's true.
Kiss me twice,
Then once more—
That makes thrice;
Let's make it four!
What a break—
For heaven's sake!
How long has this been going on?

REPRISE

Dear, oh dear!
Is that nice!
Listen here,
I smell a mice!
What's the mess?
Come, confess!
How long has this been going on?
Goodness' sake!
My, what brass!
Just a big snake
In the grass!
I must know,
You so-and-so,
How long has this been going on?

THE WORLD IS MINE

Published October 1927. Introduced by Fred Astaire (Jimmy), Gertrude McDonald (June), Betty Compton (Dora), and ensemble during the tryout, when it was the eighth number in Act I. Later performed during the tryout by Lillian Roth (Olive) and ensemble, also in Act I. Dropped before the New York opening. As "Toddlin'

Along," introduced by Nan Blackstone in the *9:15 Revue*, which opened in New York at the George M. Cohan Theatre on February 11, 1930.

VERSE

JIMMY: I'm not as rich as Henry Ford is,
    But that doesn't mean a thing!
    Ev'ry rich man often bored is,
    While I'm happy as a king!
    I've not the fame of Mr. Tunney
    Nor the looks of Barrymore,
    Yet to me the world is sunny
    As it never was before.
    Friends like you are dear to me—
    Make me feel content;
    Yes, sir, it is clear to me,
    I'm a lucky gent!

REFRAIN

Toddling along,
Making hay,
Whistling a song
Through the day—
Certainly is fine!
The world is mine!
How can I complain?
Skies are blue.
Haven't lived in vain—
Friends are true—
Certainly a sign
The world is mine!
It's a grand and glorious feeling to be
    living;
Ev'ry day's that holiday they call
    Thanksgiving.
Oh, toddling along,
Here and there,
Whistling a song—
Not a care!
Certainly is fine!
The world is mine!

FINEST OF THE FINEST

Introduced by ensemble ("Policemen") during the tryout. It was the third number in Act II. Dropped before the New York opening.

VERSE

Crooks and dips, you'd better beware!
Thieves and gyps, you'd better take care!
We're here to state: We're the State Police.
Gunmen, you had better look out!
Burglars, too, there isn't a doubt
You'll meet your fate with the State Police.
You've been told just what a Texas Ranger is;
Compared to us, he doesn't know what danger
  is.
O do-de, O de-ay!
O do-de, O de-ay!
You've got to believe us when we say:

REFRAIN

We're the finest of the finest of the finest;
We're the grandest of the grandest of the grand!
Days we while away
Shooting crooks a mile away;
We're never, never bored
Galloping in a Ford.
We're the strongest of the strongest of the
  strongest!
Better beware! Better take care! You burglar
  band!
We can truly say without exaggeration,
We're the finest and the grandest in the land!

DANCE ALONE WITH YOU

Published October 1927. Introduced by Adele Astaire
(Frankie) and Fred Astaire (Jimmy) during the tryout
late in Act I. Dropped before the New York opening.
Alternate title: "Why Does Ev'rybody Have to Cut In?"
The music was revived for "Ev'rybody Knows I Love
Somebody" in *Rosalie* (1928).

REFRAIN 1

JIMMY: Why does ev'rybody have to cut in
         When I want to be alone with you?
         What's the big idea when they butt in;
         Why won't they leave me alone with
           you?
         Hear me!
         Someday my temper's going to snap!
FRANKIE: Dear me!
         I'll help you push them off the map!
JIMMY: Oh, why does ev'rybody have to strut
         in
         When I want to be alone with you?

VERSE

There are lots of fellows at ev'ry dance
  Who take a chance,
  Chaps who love to cut in the whole
    night through.
FRANKIE: You and I are dancing—We're going
           strong—
         Stepping along.
JIMMY: Then some darn collegiate comes into
           view.
         He's just a gag line
         Out of the stag line,
         But he wants to dance—What can I
           do?
         He nabs you;
         Quickly he grabs you.
         As away you fly,
         I'm sighing:

REFRAIN 2

Why does ev'rybody have to cut in
When I want to dance alone with you?
What's the big idea when they butt in
When I want a chance alone with you?
Hear me!
I'm sure the judge and jury will
Clear me
If any one of them I kill.
Oh, why does ev'rybody have to strut
  in
When I want to be alone with you?

ACROBATS

Written for the pier scene in Act II. Probably intended
for Adele and Fred Astaire. Unused. No. 109 in the
George and Ira Gershwin Special Numbered Song File.

VERSE

When we were little tots, our brains would
  always go a-tingling
Watching acrobats who used to work for Mr.
  Ringling.
There was a brother team that never failed to
  win the house.
Despite the fact that they were known as
  Schmerzenheim and Schlaus.
We asked them just how one becomes an
  ath-a-lectic actor,

But sad to tell, they said we lacked the most
  important factor.
"May all your children be acrobats!" someone
  said to their mother.
That's how it came about that they could juggle
  each the other.
But nobody ever wished that on our parents,
  so—Oh gee!
We never can be the acrobats that once we
  hoped to be.
Allez-oop! Hoop-la!

REFRAIN

Acrobats!
We envy the acrobats!
Those wonderful pouncing, bouncing, jouncing,
  flouncing acrobats!

See them fly—
So high up they reach the sky!
Those marvelous clinging, swinging, singing
  acrobats!

Oh, you can keep your op'ra singers and your
  comics;
The greatest thrill of all is bouncing on your
  stomics.

Oh, rum-tum tiddle-liddle um-tum-tum-tum,
Rum-tum tiddle-liddle um-tum-tum-tum—
Acrobats for mine!

BLUEBEARD

Intended for Adele Astaire (Frankie), Fred Astaire
(Jimmy), and William Kent (Dugsie). Unused. No music
is known to survive.

VERSE

FRANKIE: I sing the praise of good old days
           When gentlemen had romance
           And knew just how to act to-wards a
             lady.
DUGSIE
AND
JIMMY: But how about that good old scout
           That gentleman born in France,
           Who lived about the sixteenth century
             A.D.?
DUGSIE: His name was Bluebeard and he knew
           just how to handle women;

FRANKIE: No flapper ever fooled him and no gold
        digger took him in.
JIMMY: If any dame suggested that his beaver
        needed trimmin'—
ALL: Oh, he just laid down the law
        With a good sock on the jaw.

REFRAIN

Bluebeard, Bluebeard—
He was a wonderful chap!
His methods were so criminal,
And yet, we read, the women all
Would fight to sit on his lap.
He'd give a midnight frolic
With highballs of carbolic,
And feed his wives a lot of T.N.T.
Of life he would relieve 'em;
He'd love 'em—then he'd cleave 'em;
Bluebeard, Bluebeard—
There was a man for me!

INVALID ENTRANCE

Intended for Adele Astaire (Frankie) and William Kent
(Dugsie). Unused. No music is known to survive.

[*Peter wheeled on by Dugsie and Frankie*]

FRANKIE
  AND
DUGSIE: [*to girls*]
    Hush! Hush! Hush!
    Pss! Pss! Pss!
FRANKIE: [*in a whisper*]
    His temperature is a hundred and five;
    We're wondering how he can still be
      alive.
DUGSIE: [*at the top of his voice*]
    IF YOU'RE NOT QUIET, HE'LL
      NEVER SURVIVE!
FRANKIE
  AND
DUGSIE: Hush! Hush! Hush!
    Pss! Pss! Pss!
FRANKIE: A most unfortunate patient is he;
    He's just a little bit cuckoo, you see!
DUGSIE: [*loudly*]
    So please be QUIET AS QUIET CAN
      BE!
FRANKIE
  AND
DUGSIE: Hush! Hush! Hush!
    Pss! Pss! Pss!

WHEN THE RIGHT ONE COMES ALONG

Intended for Act I of *Funny Face*—it's not certain for
whom. Dropped during rehearsals. The music was later
used for the refrain of "Say So!" in *Rosalie* (1928). Ira
Gershwin later employed the "romantic mountain—
soda fountain" couplet in "Where's the Boy? Here's the
Girl!" in *Treasure Girl* (1928). The "Somewhere there's
a someone" line resurfaced years later in "Someone at
Last," in *A Star Is Born* (1954).

Girlie, late and early,
Shedding pearly little tears—
You'll know when the right one comes along.

Somewhere there's a someone
Who will somehow calm your fears—
Someday when the right one comes along.

Maybe you'll meet him on some romantic
    mountain.
Maybe he'll greet you soon at some soda
    fountain.

He'll floor you, he'll adore you,
He's been for you all these years.
You'll know when the right one comes along.

ROSALIE
THAT'S A GOOD GIRL
1928

ROSALIE, 1928

Tryout: Colonial Theatre, Boston, December 5, 1927. New York run: New Amsterdam Theatre, opened January 10, 1928. 335 performances. Music by George Gershwin and Sigmund Romberg. Lyrics by P. G. Wodehouse and Ira Gershwin. Produced by Florenz Ziegfeld. Book by William Anthony McGuire and Guy Bolton. Staged by Florenz Ziegfeld, Seymour Felix, and William Anthony McGuire. Orchestra under the direction of Oscar Bradley. Orchestrations by Hans Spialek, Emil Gerstenberger, Max Steiner, Maurice B. De Packh, William Daly, and Hilding Anderson. Cast, starring Marilyn Miller (Princess Rosalie) and Jack Donahue (Bill Delroy), featured Frank Morgan (King Cyril), Bobbe Arnst (Mary O'Brien), Margaret Dale (the Queen), Oliver McLennan (Lieutenant Dick Fay), Clay Clement (Captain Banner), Charles Gotthold (Ship Steward and West Point Superintendent), and A. P. Kaye (Prince Rabisco). For the lyric to "How Long Has This Been Going?," see *Funny Face*, pages 109–10.

SHOW ME THE TOWN

Published 1926 with other sheet music from *Oh, Kay!* for which it was originally intended. Music by George Gershwin. This version (the verses are new; the chorus is virtually unchanged) was introduced by Bobbe Arnst (Mary) and ensemble.

VERSE 1

MARY: Looking for a good time, I've come
here to get some action;
I'll take ev'rything you've got to give.
Prohibition and the blue laws drive me
to distraction;
After all, I've just one life to live.
Come and show me what you've got
here;
How about a spree?
If you've anything that's hot here,
Serve it up to me:

REFRAIN

Hey! How about a dance?
Say! Let's go out and take a chance!
Show me! Show me! Come on, show me
the town!

Drink! Let's fill up the glass!
Clink! While we're stepping on the gas;
Let's go where the wets go—
Show me the town!

Woof! want to raise the roof!
Said! Want to paint the whole town red!
Wow! let me show you how to throw a
party.

Shout! Tell the world that I'm
Out looking for a dizzy time!
Show me! Show me! Come on, show me
the town!

VERSE 2

NATIVES: Though we have no cabarets, no skating
rinks, or movies,
We can step out when we get the
chance.
When the concertina plays, each native
loves to prove he's
Just about the last word in the dance.
Jazz may make the Yankee tingle;
He gets hot, but—Ah!
When we hear our native jingle,
We get HOT ZA-ZA!

REPEAT REFRAIN

Earlier Version of Verse 1 (Discarded)

MARY: Ev'ryone's asleep by nine o'clock since I
have been here;
Nothing ever happens after dark.
In a nice way, friends, I ask, when does
the fun begin here?
Where do all the Good-Time Charlies
park?
'Way back home, no evening passes
But that I go out;
When I'm through with demitasses,
You can hear me shout:

HUSSAR MARCH

Published December 1927. Music by Sigmund Romberg. Lyrics by P. G. Wodehouse (verse) and Ira Gershwin (refrain). Introduced by Marilyn Miller (Rosalie) and men. Most sources, including the original sheet music, incorrectly attribute the entire lyric to Wodehouse.

VERSE

ROSALIE: I lead a regiment bold—
Each man like those knights of old
Of whom the poets tell.

In moonlight parties
Or when out on the dancing floor,
They cast a magic spell.

MEN: But though they're fine at cotillions
And quite outshine all civilians—

ROSALIE: Don't think these gentlemen
Are mere ornamental men;
They're made for use as well.

REFRAIN

ROSALIE: For when they hear the war drum
sound:
MEN: Rat-a-plan! Rat-a-plan!
ROSALIE: On guard and at his post is found
MEN: Ev'ry man! Ev'ry man!
ROSALIE: Yes, clustered, keener than mustard
You'll find them there—
Prepared to do and dare.
And though they know when fights
grow warm—
MEN: Rat-a-tat! Rat-a-tat!
ROSALIE: One's apt to crease one's uniform.
MEN: What of that? What of that?
ROSALIE: If, fighting for old Romanza,
Their boots chance to lose their shine,
They don't repine, these soldiers fine
Of mine.

Refrain (Original Version, Discarded)

ROSALIE: For when they hear the war drum
sound—
MEN: We're a very lucky band,
With a princess in command.
ROSALIE: On guard and at his post is found—
MEN: Ev'ry regimental man—
Ev'ry member of your clan.
ROSALIE: Yes, clustered, keener than mustard,
You'll find them there—
Prepared to do and dare.
And though they know when fights
grow warm—
MEN: It's a pleasure fighting for
A commander we adore.
ROSALIE: One's apt to crease one's uniform.
MEN: Though the crease we don't retain,
Your Hussars will not complain.
ROSALIE: If, fighting for old Romanza,
Their boots chance to lose their shine,

They don't repine, these soldiers fine
Of mine.

SAY SO!

Published January 1928. Music by George Gershwin.
Lyrics by Ira Gershwin and P. G. Wodehouse. Introduced by Marilyn Miller (Rosalie) and Oliver McLennan
(Dick). Reprised by Jack Donahue (Bill) and, later, by
ensemble. Replaced "Beautiful Gypsy" during the pre-
Broadway tryout. The music of "Say So!" had earlier
been joined with the lyric of "When the Right One
Comes Along," intended for but not used in *Funny Face*
(1927).

VERSE

DICK: When your eyes look into mine,
There's something they would say:
Is it "no" or "yes"?
ROSALIE: Surely you can guess?
Look again, and quickly, then,
Your doubts will fly away.
DICK: If their secret you'd tell,
Words are needed as well.

REFRAIN

Say so!
Say you love me;
None above me
In your heart.
Pining—I'll be pining till you do!

ROSALIE: Say so!
Don't resist me;
Say you've missed me
From the start.
Say so, for I pray so that it's true.

BOTH: There are just three little words I sigh
for—
Crazy about them;
Three little words I'd die for—
Can't live without them.

ROSALIE: Say so!
Change the gray sky
To a gay sky
Ever blue.

DICK: Say so! I should say so! I love you.

Act II Reprise

VERSE

CADETS
AND
GIRLS: While the silver furlough moon
Is rising up above,
Breezes whisper low,
Stealing to and fro.
Hear the message that they bring
To all young men in love:
"Time is flying away;
Why should lovers delay?"

REPEAT REFRAIN

LET ME BE A FRIEND TO YOU

Music by George Gershwin. Introduced by Marilyn
Miller (Rosalie) and Jack Donahue (Bill). Alternate title:
"The Kind of Friend." No music is known to survive.

VERSE

BILL: If ever you could get in trouble,
I'll double for you.
I'll be a dozen Texas Rangers
When danger's in view.
ROSALIE: It's great to have a friend around one,
I've found one, I see;
And likewise I'll be there when you
call,
So do call on me.

REFRAIN

BOTH: Oh, let me be a friend to you—
The kind I'd like for you to be to me;
The sort of pal who, when you're
feeling blue,
A perfect cure can always guarantee.
BILL: I'll hold your hand
Like Mother did;
You understand—
ROSALIE: I gotcha, kid!
BOTH: It's great to be the kind of friend to
you—
The kind I'd like for you to be to me!

OH GEE! OH JOY!

Published January 1928. Music by George Gershwin.
Lyrics by Ira Gershwin and P. G. Wodehouse. Introduced by Marilyn Miller (Rosalie) and Jack Donahue
(Bill). Added to the show during the pre-Broadway tryout. Also see "What Could I Do?," which follows.

VERSE

BILL: Yea bo, but isn't love great! Gee whiz!
ROSALIE: Heigh-ho! I'm willing to state, it is!
BOTH: Don't know the chap was who first
began it,
But it's the only thing on this planet.

REFRAIN 1

Oh gee! Oh joy! The birds are singing.
Because why? Because I am in love!
Oh gee! Oh joy! The bells are ringing.
Because why? Because I am in love!
ROSALIE: And all the while I seem in a dream;
I never was so happy!
BILL: Folks complain I'm insane,
Because I act so sappy.
BOTH: Oh gee! Oh joy! The birds are singing.
Because why? Because I am in love!

REFRAIN 2

BOTH: Oh gee! Oh joy! The birds are singing.
Because why? Because I am in love!
Oh gee! Oh joy! The bells are ringing.
Because why? Because I am in love.
ROSALIE: You shouldn't act that way, though I
say
I hate to be contrary.
BILL: My mistake! What a break!
I thought you were my Mary!
BOTH: Oh gee! Oh joy! The birds are singing.
Because why? Because I am in love!

WHAT COULD I DO?

Music by George Gershwin. An early version of the song
that became "Oh Gee! Oh Joy!" Intended for Marilyn
Miller (Rosalie) and Jack Donahue (Bill). The two songs
share the same music. It is quite possible that "What
Could I Do?" was merely a dummy for "Oh Gee! Oh
Joy!" (For further discussion of dummy lyrics, see Ira

Gershwin's comments accompanying "I Got Rhythm," *Girl Crazy*—1930.)

REFRAIN

ROSALIE: What could I do?
True love had beckoned,
And that was—
And that was
All I knew.

BILL: What could I do?
She smiled, by heck, and
I knew that—
I knew that
I was through.

ROSALIE: My heart began to beat.
Life was sweet.
And, oh, I felt so happy!

BILL: Same with me.
I said, "Gee!"
And started acting sappy!

BOTH: What could I do?
True love had beckoned,
And so what—
And so what
Could I do?

FINALE, ACT I

Music by Sigmund Romberg. Introduced by ensemble, this was the opening sequence of the Act I finale and was followed by reprises of "Say So!" and "Why Must We Always Be Dreaming?" (a Romberg-Wodehouse song). Under the title "West Point Bugle," this lyric was originally part of the Act II opening, but was moved during the tryout. Only its last four lines were included in the *Rosalie* piano-vocal score. Another number titled "West Point Bugle" (by Romberg and Wodehouse) was eventually placed into Act I.

Oh, when it's nighttime here at West Point,
And twinkling stars are in the blue,
Life is really at its best point
For with the cares of day we're through.
We leave the music that is martial
For the music of the dance;
Yes, to the nighttime we are partial
Because it brings romance.

NEW YORK SERENADE

Music by George Gershwin. Introduced by Bobbe Arnst (Mary) and ensemble. Added to the show during the pre-Broadway tryout.

VERSE

Since I came from Romanza,
I've heard many a serenade.
Fellows there sing a stanza
When they're wooing a pretty maid.
But there's one that's better far
Than any old tune on an old guitar;
It's the serenade you hear
When you land on a New York pier.

REFRAIN

Ten thousand steamboats hootin'—
A million taxis tootin'—
What a song! What a song!
That dear old New York Serenade!
Just hear those rivets rattling—
And hear that traffic battling—
Come along, come along and hear it played.
Ev'ry corner has bands moaning—
Jazz bands groaning all night long.
Even though your nerves they shatter
With their clatter,
It really doesn't matter, matter, matter, matter,
matter! matter!
So keep your peace and quiet—
Give me that good old riot!
Come along and hear that New York Serenade!

THE KING CAN DO NO WRONG

Music by Sigmund Romberg. Lyrics by Ira Gershwin and, probably, P. G. Wodehouse. Introduced by Frank Morgan (King Cyril) and girls. There is some possibility that the lyric to the earlier version is by P. G. Wodehouse.

VERSE

Though the cares of state are ever so
troublesome,
Yet my spirits manage to bubble some,
For I make up when I take up

Women, wine, and song.
Doesn't matter what I do, ev'rything is right;
There's a law says: Always, a king is right.
Let me stress it and impress it:
I am diff'rent from the throng—
For the king can do no wrong.

REFRAIN 1

If a maid I chance to dandle,
She must not fly off the handle—
Just remember that the king can do no wrong.
Never criticize His Highness—
Give him plus and never minus.
If with you I go a-Maying,
And by chance my arm is straying—
Please recall that splendid saying:
That the king—that the king—that the king can
do no wrong!

REFRAIN 2

He's at liberty to squeeze a
Girl in his Hispano-Suiza—
For remember that the king can do no wrong.
Though a girl who with a boy rides
Often walks home from her joyrides,
When the kingly arms enfold her,
She grows warmer—never colder,
For her mother's often told her
That the king—that the king—that the king can
do no wrong!

REFRAIN 3

Although Mrs. Grundy eyes him,
She may never criticize him—
Please remember that the king can do no wrong.
If a husband, without warning,
Comes home early in the morning,
Wifey says, "Don't fret, because it
Was the *king* inside that closet!"
And the husband says, "Oh, *was* it?
Well, the king—well, the king—well, the king
can do no wrong!"

Encore Refrain

Though his conduct may seem sprightly,
You must not condemn him lightly—
Just remember that the king can do no wrong.
If you come upon him creeping
Up the stairs when all are sleeping,
Bear in mind that it is treason
To inquire what business *he's* on
(Though he's only B.V.D.'s on);
For the king—for the king—for the king can do
no wrong.

Verse 2 (Unused)

I'm a king who feels that it doesn't hurt a bit
If I fool 'round and maybe flirt a bit;
So I call for—and I'm all for
Women, wine, and song.
'Way back home I always have all the gang
   around,
So I'm asking you girls to hang around.
Please come closer—Don't say "No, Sir!"
Don't be shy—but come along—
For the king can do no wrong.

Earlier Version (Unused)

VERSE 1

There's just one thing about a king that makes
   his job worth trying
And separates him from the common throng—
And that's the ancient legend, which has shown
   no signs of dying,
That the king can do no wrong.
Oh, it helps him get along.

For though persons staid and steady
There may be around him *who* wish
That he wasn't quite so ready
With a story that is blueish;
Though he may shock Mrs. Grundy
With behavior of a pattern
Which is criticized each Sunday
By the Reverend Doctor Stratton—

REFRAIN 1

Still, the king can do no wrong!
No, the king can do no wrong!
And he finds the fact consoling
When he starts the ball a-rolling
With women, wine, and song—
For if husbands, without warning,
Come home early in the morning,
He need never worry long;
Wives say, "Do not fret, because it
Was the *king* inside that closet!"
And the husband says, "Oh *was* it?"
For the king can do no wrong.

VERSE 2

A king's existence nowadays, there's no denying,
   is hard.
It's not so pleasant as it used to be.
He never knows when somebody won't bump
   him in the gizzard
With a charge of T.N.T.
It's a wearing life, you see.

For although it's no use whining,
Still, he *does* feel rather shaken
When he finds a bomb reclining
In his morning eggs and bacon;
And remorse and agitation
Like a dagger seem to strike him
When he gets the information
That Bill Thompson doesn't like him—

REFRAIN 2

Still, the king can do no wrong!
No, the king can do no wrong!
He's at liberty to squeeze a
Girl in his Hispano-Suiza—
And squeeze her good and strong.
Though a girl who with a boy rides
Often walks home from her joyrides
On a road that's rough and long;
When a monarch's arms enfold her
She just nestles on his shoulder,
For she knows that Mother told her
That the king can do no wrong.

EV'RYBODY KNOWS I LOVE SOMEBODY

Published December 1927. Music by George Gershwin. Introduced by Jack Donahue (Bill) and Bobbe Arnst (Mary). This song's music was previously used for "Dance Alone With You," which was cut from *Funny Face* (1927) during its tryout.

VERSE 1

BILL: When you kiss your dad, I've nothing to
    say;
    I'm big that way.
    But when you kiss others—Well, fun is
    fun.

MARY: Don't be sil'! You've no right picking on
    me!
    What can it be?
    Wish you'd tell me just what it is I've
    done.

BILL: You say you love me,
    No one above me.
    How am I to know
    It's really so?

    All that I have is your say-so.
    How do I know it will stay so?

REFRAIN 1

Ev'rybody knows I love somebody.
Does that somebody—Oh, gee!—love me?
Ev'ry heartbeat shows I love somebody.
Does that certain she—Oh, gee!—love
   me?
Save me! This little feller needs a friend.
Crave me! Or in the river I will end!
Oh! Ev'rybody knows I love somebody.
Does that somebody—Oh, gee!—love me?

VERSE 2

MARY: In Romanza, ev'ry maid you would meet
    You'd always greet.
    Why, you hardly knew that I was alive.

BILL: All I've said to them was "How do you
    do?"
MARY: I've heard that you
    Flirted till the minute that I'd arrive.

    Oh, I've been checking
    Up on your necking.
    You're the baby who
    Isn't so true.

    And it has started me wond'ring
    If in loving you I'm blund'ring.

REFRAIN 2

Ev'rybody knows I love somebody.
Does that somebody—Oh, gee!—love me?
Ev'ry heartbeat shows I love somebody.
Does that certain he—Oh, gee!—love me?
Hear me! I knew my lecture couldn't last.
Dear me! I'll gladly overlook the past.
Oh, ev'rybody knows I love somebody.
Does that somebody—Oh, gee!—love me?

FOLLOW THE DRUM

The refrain (music only) was printed March 1928 in the *Rosalie* piano selection. Music by George Gershwin. Added after the New York opening. Introduced by Marilyn Miller (Rosalie) and ensemble.

VERSE

When cadets are on parade
And a march is being played,
There's a rhythmic beat
And a rhythmic treat
That you simply cannot evade.

When your feet just won't keep still
And you shout against your will,
And a martial air
Fills the thoroughfare—
It's the drum that gives you the thrill.
It'll set you all aglow;
It'll make you shout, "Let's go!"

REFRAIN

Follow the drum—Boom!
Follow the drum—Boom!
Follow the drum!
It calls you,
Enthralls you—
The greeting
It's beating.
Follow the fellow who beats the drum!
Ra-ta-ta-tum—Boom!
Ra-ta-ta-tum—Boom!
Ra-ta-ta-tum!
It thrills you—
It chills you.
Excites you—
Invites you.
Follow the fellow who beats the drum!
Seems to cast a magic spell
That'll make you feel like *that!*
Troubles all can go to hell
When the drums go "Ra-tat-tat!"

You can't go wrong—Boom!
Follow the throng—Boom!
Come on along!
Come on and follow the drum!

Earlier Version (Discarded)

VERSE

Oh, the gay trombone
Has a charm, we own,
And the fife and trumpet may appeal to some,
But when we parade
And a march is played,
Oh, it doesn't mean a thing without a drum.
To music martial
That's got a swing
If you are partial,
The drum's the thing.
And when down the street
Come the marching feet,
It's needed to make the thing complete.

Tara boom—tara boom—tara
    boom—boom—boom!
Tara boom—tara boom—tara
    boom—boom—boom!

Tara tara tara boom—tara tara tara boom—
Tara boom—boom—boom—boom—boom!

REFRAIN

Follow the drum—drum—drum
Booming away;
Ra-ta-ta-tum—tum—tum!
You must obey
Its rhythmic greeting!
Dull care defeating!
With heart a-beating
You hear it play!

Follow the drum—drum—drum
Thundering clear;
Who could be glum—glum—glum
When it is near?
"Oh, hurry—Come—Come—come!"
It is repeating.
Be quick and come—
Follow the drum!
Follow the drum!

AT THE EX-KINGS' CLUB

Music by George Gershwin. Introduced by A. P. Kaye (Prince Rabisco) and gentlemen of the ensemble. Alternate title: "Ex-Kings' Number."

There's always something doing
At the Ex-Kings' Club,
When pleasure they're pursuing
At the Ex-Kings' Club.

Tonight is ladies' night and we're a-tingle;
Ev'ry ex-king'll
With ladies mingle.

There's pleasure without measure
At the Ex-Kings' Club;
We serve the best of wine and grub.

And kings who still
Are on the throne
And love a thrill
Are heard to moan—
They wish that there would be a revolution.
So they could join the Ex-Kings' Club.

BEAUTIFUL GYPSY

Published December 1927. Music by George Gershwin. Introduced during the tryout by Marilyn Miller (Rosalie) and Oliver McLennan (Dick). According to the Boston program for December 5, 1927, the number was "arranged" (choreographed, presumably) by Fred Astaire. Dropped before the New York opening and replaced with "Say So!" The music of "Beautiful Gypsy" had previously been used for the George and Ira Gershwin–Desmond Carter song "Wait a Bit, Susie" in *Primrose* (1924).

VERSE

DICK: Always I'll recall the night
         My heart began to stir;
         Gazing at you all the night,
         I wondered who you were.

ROSALIE: It was all I could do to
         Keep from gazing at you, too.

DICK: So—I've come to see again
         The one with whom I'd be again;
         Oh! Smile your smile at me again,
         Please do!

REFRAIN 1

         Beautiful gypsy, beautiful gypsy,
         What's a man to do
         When he's always dreaming of your
             blue eyes?
         Couldn't forget you
         Once I had met you,
         Sought you ev'rywhere:
         Hither, thither, yonder, here, and there.
         Ev'ry sweet smile, ev'ry movement sets
             me aglow,
         And in my dreams how much you've
             meant you'll never know.
         Beautiful gypsy, driving me tipsy,
         Read my hand and see
         If my little gypsy girl loves me.

REFRAIN 2

ROSALIE: Wonderful Yankee, handsome and
             lanky,
         From across the sea—
         Oh, I'm glad that you've been seeking
             me; I
         Couldn't forget you
         Once I had met you—
         Ev'ry now and then,
         I'd been wond'ring if we'd meet again.

DICK: Ev'ry sweet smile, ev'ry movement sets
    me aglow,
    And in my dreams how much you've
    meant you'll never know.
ROSALIE: Wonderful Yankee, handsome and
    lanky,
    Yes, I know it's true—
[reading his palm]
    That your little gypsy girl loves you!

ROSALIE

Published December 1927. Music by George Gershwin. Introduced during the tryout by Marilyn Miller (Rosalie) and Oliver McLennan (Dick). Dropped before the New York opening. Replaced by "Oh Gee! Oh Joy!"

Published Version

VERSE 1

DICK: In my dreams you've always played the
    leading part,
    And I've held you fast in my
    remembrance.
    There's a vision of you ever in my
    heart,
    Dearer to me than a thousand
    Rembrandts.
    I must tell you
    Of the spell you
    Cast when you're around;
    Cannot hide it—
    Must confide it—
    Paradise I've found.

REFRAIN 1

Rosalie,
Loveliest of names to me,
Hear my plea—
Pretty Rosalie!
Prosily,
All the world was drifting by,
Rosalie,
Till I caught your eye.
I just had to surrender
To all the splendor
Of you.
How I hurried to find you
Just to remind you
That I love you!
Rain or shine,
To my heart you've won the key;

Say you're mine,
Little Rosalie!

VERSE 2

ROSALIE: Though the birds were all proclaiming,
    "It is spring!"
    When you left, the world was like
    December.
    Dreams that I'd been dreaming all were
    on the wing,
    For I thought you'd not care to
    remember.
    Though I tried my
    Best to hide my
    Tears, so none could learn—
    My heart, beating,
    Kept repeating,
    "When will he return?"

REFRAIN 2

Rosalie,
Say again that you adore
Rosalie;
Won't you tell her more?
Cozily,
Snuggled in those two strong arms,
Rosalie
Finds a lot of charms.
When you smiled at her sweetly,
Thrills went completely
Through her;
In a world that was futile,
She had been blue till
You came to her.
One and all,
Ev'ryone will envy me
When you call
Little Rosalie.

Earlier Version

VERSE

ROSALIE: When I crossed the ocean,
    I had not a notion
    You would greet this little girl
    With such a great big hand.
    You are all so handsome,
    Quite a kingly ransom
    I would give if I could live
    Forever in this land.
BOYS: Please become a citizen!
    We all feel that it is an
    Excellent idea that you have planned.

REFRAIN

Rosalie, Rosalie, hear us:
Smiling through, somehow you cheer
    us;
Always want Rosalie near us—
We have learned to love you more and
    more.
Now you know the way here,
We hope you will stay here.
Oh, Rosalie, Rosalie, hear us:
You're the ray of sunshine we adore.

Earlier Version (Finale Reprise)

ALL: Happy hearts, happy hearts mingling—
    All the world, all the world tingling—
    Wedding bells, wedding bells jingling.
    With dull care forever you are through.
    We're all so excited—
    Two hearts are united.
    Wedding bells, wedding bells jingling—
    Everlasting happiness to you.

PRINCE:
[simultaneously with last two lines]
    Rosalie, Rosalie, hear me:
    Smiling through, Princess, you cheer
    me;
ALL: Always want Rosalie near me,
    For I've learned to love you more and
    more.
    Oh, I'm so excited;
    Two hearts are united.
    Oh, Rosalie, Rosalie, hear me;
    You're the ray of sunshine I adore.

I FORGOT WHAT I STARTED TO SAY

Music by George Gershwin. Introduced by Jack Donahue (Bill) during the tryout. Dropped before the New York opening. Alternate title: "What I Started to Say."

VERSE 1

If I'm a guy who doesn't seem so merry,
It's just because I'm so misunderstood.
When I was young I ate a dictionary,
And that did not do me a bit of good.
For I've absorbed so many words and phrases—
They drive me dizzy when I want to speak.
I start explaining but each person gazes
As if I spoke in Latin or in Greek.
For instance:

REFRAIN 1

Last January—It was February—It was
    March—No, it was warmer—It was June—It
    was today—
I got a cable—a letter—a telegram—a
    summons—No, I'm wrong—'Twas a knock on
    my door—
I was sleeping—no, drowsing—I was
    walking—daily dozen—I was shaving—I'm
    funny that way—
I said, "Come in!"—She tripped in—She fell
    in—She staggered—She hopped in—She was
    there on the floor—
It was the collector—the landlady—She wanted
    rent—heavy pennies—the greenbacks—the
    cash—the dough—
I made up to her—tickled her—We were
    laughing—no, arguing—I socked her, but she
    didn't want to play—
She blew a whistle, and in rushed a detective—a
    bull—
He said, "You're intoxicated—You're
    cockeyed—You're full!"—
Gee, but it's funny how my thoughts can stray—
I forgot what I started to say!

VERSE 2

I went to Burbank with a solid notion
To cross a whale with a Long Island duck.
He loved it and he said with great emotion,
"Sir, as a man of science, you're no cluck."
He wanted just a day to think it over—
Oh, things were great as he showed me the
    door—
If I'd kept quiet, boy, I'd be in clover,
But like a sap I said, "Look here, what's more—
Now listen—

REFRAIN 2

Mussolini—Napoléon—I mean, Fairbanks—no,
    Lincoln—Just a minute—I mean, my dad—
Lives on Fifth Avenue—no, Sixth Avenue—It's
    Brooklyn—Swell neighborhood—Well, not so
    hot—It's pretty bad—
But he loves me—thinks I'm great—I'm his
    favorite—Why, only yesterday—He kicked
    me out—Boy! he gave me hell!—
So I'm with friends now—treat me
    royally—clean linen—They got a
    bathtub—They charge me two bits—It's the
    Mills Hotel—
I gotta make good—I got a sweetie—She's
    pretty—a little stout—a trifle obese—Boy!
    She's thick!—
I'm crazy for her—adore her—She follows

me—She's wonderful—She's my
    intended—She makes me sick—
So, Mr. Edison—Marconi—er, Burbank—you
    see"—
But, just then—those phrases—started
    working—on me—
Gee! But it's funny how my thoughts can
    stray—
I forgot what I started to say!

NOW THAT THE DANCE IS OVER

Composer uncertain—Sigmund Romberg or George
Gershwin. Alternate title: "Finale, Act I." One of many
intended components of the Act I finale, this was almost
certainly dropped during the tryout.

CADETS
AND GIRLS: Now that the dance is near,
    Dull care will disappear.
    When it's night at West Point,
    Life is at its best point.
    Come, join us, everyone—
    We're here to have some fun.
    Joy will reach its height
    Before the night is done.

CADETS: We are all good dancing men—
    Soft-and-tender-glancing men—
    The kind revealing
    A style appealing
    To ev'ry female heart.

    Yes, in that capacity,
    We say with veracity
    That when we guide you
    And swing and slide you
    We're a riot from the very start.

ALL: Now that the dance is near,
    Dull care will disappear.
    When it's night at West Point,
    Life is at its best point.
    Come, join us, ev'ryone—
    We're here to have some fun.
    Joy will reach its height
    Before the night is done.

GLAD TIDINGS IN THE AIR

Music by George Gershwin. Intended at one time for
inclusion in the Act I finale, this, too, was dropped
before the New York opening.

ENSEMBLE: Glad tidings in the air;
    Bells ringing ev'rywhere—
    Ev'ry heart rejoice—
    She has made her choice.

PRINCE: Rosalie,
    Loveliest of names to me—
    Rosalie,
    Happy we will be.

ENSEMBLE: Cozily,
    All the years will drift along—
    Rosalie—
    Life will be a song.

ROSALIE: My romance now is crumbling;
    My world is tumbling
    Madly.
    Ev'ry hope now has perished,
    Dreams that I cherished—
    Oh, so gladly.

ENSEMBLE: Rosalie,
    Loveliest of brides is she.
    Rosalie—
[Music breaks off as Dick speaks]

TWO HEARTS WILL BLEND AS ONE

Composer unknown—Sigmund Romberg or George
Gershwin. Another fragment of the Act I finale dropped
before the New York opening.

ENSEMBLE: Two hearts will blend as one;
    Their life has just begun.
    Joy will soon possess them;
    Nothing will distress them.
    Oh, there's no time to lose;
    We're all agog with news.
    Let's go find the price
    Of wedding rice and shoes.

ENJOY TODAY

Music probably by George Gershwin. At one time, part of the Act II opening. Replaced either in rehearsals or during the tryout by the Romberg-Wodehouse waltz "Like Eyes of Gold."

VERSE

There's nothing can attain the charms
Of waltzing in your lover's arms.
The waltz has a message for all—
Each lover hears the call:

REFRAIN

Enjoy today—
Live while you may—
Come, let us sway
Dreamily in the waltz.
With tender glance,
The night we'll dance—
There's true romance
Calling us in the waltz.

TRUE TO THEM ALL

Music probably by George Gershwin. Intended for Oliver McLennan (Dick) as part of the Act II opening. Cut before *Rosalie* arrived in New York. A note by Ira Gershwin on the typed lyric sheet indicates that this might have been the verse to a song called "Good-bye to the One Girl," which was dropped during the pre-Broadway tryout and which was probably not written by Ira Gershwin. No music is known to survive.

DICK: Today I was true to the one girl;
Tonight I am true to them all.
A carefree rover,
I'll look 'em over,
And make flirtation
My occupation.
I'm through being true to the one girl,
I'll answer the sirens who call;
The love of which I'll partake
Will never leave a heartache—
From now on I'm true to them all.

YOU KNOW HOW IT IS

Music by George Gershwin. Intended for Bobbe Arnst (Mary) and Jack Donahue (Bill). Dropped during rehearsals. Replaced with "Ev'rybody Knows I Love Somebody." No music is known to survive. The "poached egg" and "Philadelphia" lines later turned up in "It's Never Too Late to Mendelssohn," intended for but not used in *Lady in the Dark* (1941), and the "egg" lyric doubtless inspired Ira Gershwin years later when he wrote "I'm a Poached Egg" for the film *Kiss Me, Stupid* (1964).

VERSE 1

MARY: Comes a time in ev'ry life when love
starts calling.
BILL: Comes a time in my life now I feel I'm
falling.
I need you because
You can't change Nature's laws.
MARY: Living all alone makes any life appalling.
BILL: You said it!

REFRAIN 1

Ev'ry poached egg needs a piece of toast;
You know how it is.
Philadelphia needs the *Sat. Eve. Post;*
You know how it is.
I may be a dumb one,
But this much I know;
Each person needs someone,
And you can be
The one for me.
Ev'ry drugstore needs a little pill;
You know how it is.
Ev'ry Jack has got to have a Jill. Listen—
For me you're the one girl in My Country
'Tis,
So you see I really must have you—Know
how it is!

VERSE 2

MARY: You must buy me orchids if I'm to be
courted,
And I like my jewelry to be assorted.
BILL: Lady, fun is fun;
Where will I get the mon'?
MARY: Got to live the way I've always been
supported.
You know that

REFRAIN 2

Ev'ry girlie needs a sable coat;
You know how it is.
BILL: And the man has got to be the goat;
I know how it is.
I may be a dumb one,
But this much I know;
Each person needs someone,
And you can be
The one for me.
MARY: Ev'ry little Jill needs lots of jack;
You know how it is.
But for you I'd occupy a shack, darling.
BOTH: For me you're the one boy (girl) in My
Country 'Tis,
So you see I really must have you—Know
how it is!

UNDER THE FURLOUGH MOON

Music probably by Sigmund Romberg, although it is possible that George Gershwin collaborated. Intended for Oliver McLennan (Dick) and ensemble. Unused.

VERSE

DICK: When we get a furlough, do we rush away?
No! We get a girl-o and stay!
There's a great attraction for a cavalier;
Lonely hearts get action—right here.
Why should any soldier live nights back
home?
He can never find such delights back
home!

REFRAIN

Under the furlough moon,
You'll win your lady soon.
Love is there in all its glory
As you whisper your sweet story.
There can be no regretting
In such a perfect setting.
Two fond hearts will ever be singing in
tune
Under the furlough moon.

WHEN CADETS PARADE

Music by George Gershwin. Unused. Alternate title: "Cadets on Parade." The music for this number was originally matched with a Clifford Grey lyric titled "When the Mites Go By," written in 1922 for the unproduced musical *Flying Island*.

Original Version

Oh, the country's unafraid
When cadets are on parade;
There's a thrill for ev'ry maid
When cadets are on parade!
Just see them flash by!—
As a man they dash by!—
While the cymbals crash by
To the march that's played.
Ev'ry one's a man of steel
In his snappy uniform;
And you're confident that he'll
Take the enemy by storm.
In all things fearless,
As a band they're peerless!
What a thrill's conveyed
When cadets are on parade.

Revised Version

Oh, the country's unafraid
When cadets parade;
There's a thrill for ev'ry maid
When cadets parade!
Just see them flash by!—
As a man they dash by!—
While the cymbals crash by
To the march that's played.
Ev'ry heart goes pit-a-pat
As they swing along
To the drummer's rat-a-tat
And the bugler's song.
In all things fearless,
As a band they're peerless!
What a thrill's conveyed
When cadets parade.

CADET SONG

Composer uncertain—George Gershwin or Sigmund Romberg. Intended for Oliver McLennan (Dick) and "boys." Unused.

VERSE

DICK: When you roam
'Cross the plain or foam,
You will think of home—
Night and day!

I am keen
For the West Point scene;
That's the home I mean—
BOYS: Ev'ry way!

It's a place—you bet—
You can ne'er forget.

DICK: Things go wrong,
But the West Point song
Lives the years along
In your mem'ry.

REFRAIN

West Point—
You will ever be calling me;

West Point—
In my land or across the sea.

West Point—
Worthy of you I'll try to be
And fight the battle of freedom.

Lead me!
I am always at your command!

Speed me!
In the cause of my native land!

West Point—
As the years go by,
For you I live or die!

TRIO

Give a cheer for Alma Mater!
Let her praises fill the air!
Whoop it up! Don't be a traitor—
Show her that you care!
Come, cheer Alma Mater!
Show her that you care!

THAT'S A GOOD GIRL, 1928

Tryout: Empire Theatre, Cardiff, February 6, 1928, and other cities. London run: London Hippodrome, opened June 5, 1928. 365 performances. Music by Philip Charig and Joseph Meyer. Lyrics by Douglas Furber, Ira Gershwin, and Desmond Carter. Produced by Moss Empires Ltd. in conjunction with Jack Buchanan and United Producing Corporation Ltd. Book by Douglas Furber. Staged by Jack Buchanan. Orchestra under the direction of Leonard Hornsey. Orchestrations by Robert Russell Bennett. Cast, starring Jack Buchanan (Bill Barrow), featured Elsie Randolph (Joy Dean), Kate Cutler (Helen), Debroy Somers and his band, William Kendall (Timothy), Vera Pearce (Sunya Berata), Raymond Newell (Francis Moray), Maidie Andrews (Moya Malone), Dave Fitzgibbon (Specialty Dancer), and the Eight Tiller Girls.

The songs of *That's a Good Girl* seem to have been intended at one time for a never-finished show called *Katie Did*. Or, possibly, *Katie Did* was simply an early version of *That's a Good Girl*.

LET YOURSELF GO!

Published February 1928. Music by Philip Charig and Joseph Meyer. Introduced by Jack Buchanan (Bill) and ensemble. There are two somewhat different versions: Ira Gershwin's *Katie Did* lyric and the published *That's a Good Girl* version, credited to Douglas Furber and Ira Gershwin.

VERSE*

Listen, all of you,
I have read a few
Great physicians who say
If you'd be happy and gay,
Throw inhibitions away.
Dr. Freud is right—
Live with all your might.
Paint the town a bright red.
Let's go—Full speed ahead!
Here's the gospel that I spread:

REFRAIN 1

Come on, get in it—
Live ev'ry minute!
I say, begin it
And let yourself go!
Shake ev'ry rafter
With yells of laughter,
For what comes after
We never will know.
The fellow is dumb

*In *That's a Good Girl,* this was the second verse.*

Who'll never borrow
This bit of wisdom:
"You're here today and gone tomorrow."
So let's apply it;
Let's start a riot;
Come on and try it—
And let yourself go!

REFRAIN 2

Start in on Monday,
And right through Sunday,
Shake Mrs. Grundy
And let yourself go!
Let's give a volley
Of cheers for folly;
Send melancholy
To regions below.
The clever chappie
Is one who'll go forth
And have a snappy
Time with wine and song and so forth.
You'll find it thrilling;
You'll need no drilling;
The flesh is willing—
So let yourself go!

Verse (Published Version)

Hear me, ev'ryone,
If you'd have some fun,
Seek the sun ev'rywhere;
Make life a fun of the fair.
Just play the devil-may-care,
Though you're on the rocks.
Just pull up your socks;
Give a moment to mirth;
Struggle for all you're worth.
You'll feel you own the earth.

WHOOPEE

Music by Philip Charig and Joseph Meyer. Introduced by the Eight Tiller Girls (Esme Westhead, Marjorie Brown, Ivy Halstead, Dorothy Marlow, Molly Ellis, Mignon Harmon, Rene Forse, Vera Owen) and ensemble. Original title: "What to Do?"

BOYS: Now that we've finished dining,
It's time to start outlining
What to do—what to do.
We've guzzled all the brandy;
There's no more brandy handy—

What to do? What to do?
We might be playing billiards if we had a
    table here;
Or we might work the radio, but where's
    the engineer?
We might enjoy the theatre, but it's nine
    o'clock, old dear.
What to do? What to do?

GIRLS: You're each of you a dumb thing;
There certainly is something
You can do—you can do.
The first thing we can mention
Is: Pay us some attention—
There's your cue what to do.
If bridge and whist are boring, why not
    start the gramophone?
Put on a record that is hotter than the
    Tropic Zone,
And soon you'll find us quite the warmest
    partners who have shown
All of you what to do.

BOYS: You're right, we should have thought of
    that before;
Come on! Let's pull the carpet from the
    floor.

ALL: Whoopee! Hey-hey!
Let's go! Dey-dey!
Swinging the whole night long.
Go fly a kite!
We'll have the night
Ringing, with a snappy song.
We'll not adjourn;
We'll take a turn—
And one good turn deserves another.
Whoopee! Hey-hey!
Let's go! Dey-dey!
Clinging the whole night long.

CHIRP-CHIRP

Published February 1928. Music by Joseph Meyer and Philip Charig. Introduced by Elsie Randolph (Joy), specialty dancer Dave Fitzgibbon, and ensemble. Introduced on Broadway in *Shoot the Works* (Broadway Theatre, July 21, 1931, 87 performances) by Al Gold, Frances Dewey, and ensemble. In the programs, Philip Charig is listed as the sole composer.

VERSE 1

When Spring puts on her gay apparel
What is it the songbirds carol

Neatly,
So sweetly,
Tweet-tweetly?
Throughout the town with all its blasting,
It's a message they're broadcasting:
"Pitter,
Flit-flitter,
Twit-twitter."
The music of the air they're all usurping;
This is what they're saying when they're
    chirping:

REFRAIN

"Chirp-chirp! Get together!
It's the weather
Meant for love.
Chirp-chirp! Get right in it!"
Say the linnet
And the dove.
It's the mating season
For amorous birds;
You'll be held for treason
If you don't capture
Lovers' rapture.
"Chirp-chirp! Why be single?
There's a tingle
When you coo.
Chirp-chirp! People who coo
May be cuckoo—
Still they do.
We are little wise birds
Who always have found
Chirp-chirping makes the world go 'round."

VERSE 2

Though birds can hold their own at trilling,
Man and maid are just as willing.
Springtime
Means flingtime
P'raps ringtime.
And that's why men with anxious faces
Search the land for likely places,
Seeming
Half-dreaming
With scheming.
They're planning out a nest for some sweet girlie
When the birds sing good and early:

REPEAT REFRAIN

WEEKEND

Music by Joseph Meyer and Philip Charig. Introduced by ensemble. No music is known to survive.

We've traveled far
And here we are
At last! At last!
Now ev'ry guest
Can take his rest
At last! At last!
Flivvers have been taking us;
Oh, how they've been shaking us,
Breaking and earthquaking us,
Making us blue.
Oh boy! Somehow
It's over now—
We're here! Hear! Hear!
We'll have that old weekend at last.

Sat'day, Sunday—
Each one a fun day;
Maybe we'll take Monday, too.
How we treasure
Having this leisure,
Seeing ev'ry pleasure through.
We say that a liberal hostess
Is the person we like the mostes'.
Sat'day, Sunday—
Each one a fun day;
Maybe we'll take Monday, too.

We can't conceal
How happy we'll
Be starting this weekend.
With wine and song
We'll get along—
It won't be a bleak end.
We're not allowed to do thinking;
We're only here for heavy drinking!
No work to do—
Just sleep till two—
Thank the Lord for weekends!

THE ONE I'M LOOKING FOR

Published February 1928. Music by Joseph Meyer and Philip Charig. Lyrics by Douglas Furber and Ira Gershwin. Introduced by Jack Buchanan (Bill) and Elsie Randolph (Joy). The first version following is Ira Gershwin's own.

Original Version (Unused)

VERSE 1

BILL: I come highly recommended;
I am on the bargain shelf.
Surely any girlie can like a man like myself.
When you get the facts that witness my fitness, you'll see
You could really pick much wors'n a person like me.

REFRAIN 1

I'm six foot tall, my eyes are blue,
And you might call me good-looking, too;
I rather think I'm the one you're looking for.
I'm not a chap whose youth is gone;
I've got a lap you'd be sitting on
And never complain
That life was in vain.
I've lots of pash to thrill you through;
And as for cash, I've a pound or two;
And I'm a wizard on any dancing floor.
Not for worlds would I mislead you—
Satisfaction's guaranteed you;
Now, don't you think I'm the one you're looking for?

VERSE 2

JOY: I admit to your perfection—
That, of course, is nothing new.
Lots of girls would love to coddle a model like you.
Your appearance so disarming keeps charming the eye.
But to keep on living minus Your Highness I'll try.

REFRAIN 2

I hate to turn a good man down,
But I keep yearning for eyes of brown.
I don't think you're quite the one I'm looking for.
Your hand I touch, no thrill I feel—
I can't say much for your sex appeal;
But though you're no sheik,
I *do* like your cheek!
No use to talk—We can't agree,
For you like choc'late and I like tea;
And when you dance, I would never shout "Encore!"
I'd as lief be on my ownsome—
When you're near me, I'm still lonesome.
I don't think you're quite the one I'm looking for.

That's a Good Girl (Published) Version

VERSE 1

JOY: I come from the bargain basement—
Fallen off the half-price shelf.
Surely any fellow might like a sprite like myself.
When you get the facts to witness, my fitness you'll see;
You could really pick much wors'n a person like me.

REFRAIN 1

I'm five feet nowt- my eyes are brown:
And one looks up and the other looks down;
But still I think I'm the one you're looking for.
Your hand I touch—No thrill I feel—
Which don't say much for your sex appeal;
But though you're no sheik,
I do like your cheek!
I've lots of pash and savoir faire,
And as for cash, we can live on air;
For when I kiss, you will learn to shout "Encore!"
Not for worlds would I mislead you—
Satisfaction's guaranteed you;
Now, don't you think I'm the one you're looking for?

VERSE 2

BILL: You look like a bargain shuffle,
One that never was quite new;
Not a soul would want to coddle a model like you.
Why not stick a colored ribbon or squib on that hat?
Poets never weave their sonnets to bonnets like that.

REFRAIN 2

I hate to hand a frozen mitt,
But understand that I must have "It"—
I don't think you're quite the one I'm looking for.
Your hand I grip—It's like a dab—
I feel I've slipped on a marble slab;
Your face tells my brain
That life is in vain.
Your figure's gone; you look like sin.
What was pushed out has by now caved in
And when you dance, what you've lost has gone before.
I'd as lief be on my ownsome—
When you're near me, I'm still lonesome.

I don't think you're quite the one I'm
looking for.

SWEET SO-AND-SO

Published February 1928. Previously registered for
copyright as an unpublished composition March 1927.
Music by Joseph Meyer and Philip Charig. Lyrics cred-
ited to Douglas Furber and Ira Gershwin. Intended for
"Darry" and "Katie" in *Katie Did*. Introduced in
That's a Good Girl by Jack Buchanan (Bill) and ensem-
ble. Published again February 1931; lyrics credited to
Ira Gershwin alone. Introduced in the revue *Sweet and
Low*, which opened in New York at the 46th Street
Theatre on November 17, 1930, by Hannah Williams
and Jerry Norris. The version performed in *Sweet and
Low* used Ira Gershwin's original *Katie Did* lyric.

Katie Did Version

VERSE 1

DARRY: I knew, my dear, from the moment that
we met,
Deep in my heart I'd install you.
Hoping the love song would soon be a
duet,
I dreamed of pet names to call you.
I looked in my thesaurus
And there I found a few;
I'll sing a little chorus
Of pet names meant for you:

REFRAIN 1

You darling, you ducky, you sweet
so-and-so!
You sweet thing, you neat thing, you've
set me a-glow!
My heaven, my rapture, my sweet
this-and-that—
Without you my life would be flat.
Oh, I've a million more terms of
endearment,
If you'll agree that for each other we're
meant.
My Venus, my goddess, let me be your
beau,
And you'll be my sweet so-and-so.

VERSE 2

KATIE: All those impassioned avowals you have
made,

Those tender pet names you've chosen,
Have broken down my resistance, I'm
afraid;
You'd melt a heart that was frozen.
Oh, how could I be chilly?
You've thrilled me through and through;
Though pet names may be silly,
I've lots reserved for you:

REFRAIN 2

My brave man, my caveman, my sweet
so-and-so!
My mopsy, my popsy, my great Romeo!
My Pierrot, my hero, my sweet
this-and-that—
You're making my heart pit-a-pat.
I never knew you had such romance in
you;
You've got a sporting chance if you
continue.
Oh, laddie! Oh, daddy! In time I may
grow
To love you, you sweet so-and-so.

That's a Good Girl (Published Version)

VERSE 1

You fall in love with the modern Galahad,
Deep in his heart he'll install you;
But I am only a simple sort of lad,
I had no pet names to call you.
But now I've bought a thesaurus,
And there I found a few;
I'll sing a little chorus
Of pet names meant for you:

REFRAIN 1

You darling, you ducky, you sweet so-and-so!
You sweet thing, you neat thing, you set me
aglow!
My fond one, my blonde one, my sweet
this-and-that—
Without you my life would be flat.
I've lots of other names for your attention.
And one or two I dare not even mention.
My Venus, my goddess, let me be your beau,
And you'll be my sweet so-and-so.

VERSE 2

Henry the Eighth was the tough one of his time;
He stopped of nothing but murder.
Bluebeard would chortle some simple nurs'ry
rhyme,
Then hit his wife with a girder.

So when we start hobnobbing,
You'll soon learn what I mean;
A caveman's heart is throbbing
Beneath this Thermogene.

REFRAIN 2

My baby, my maybe, my sweet so-and-so!
My jazz queen, my has-been, you set me aglow!
Oh, Mammy! Oh, damme! Take care what you're
at—
You're making my heart pit-a-pat.
We'll join the noble army of smallholders
And build a love nest by the Green that
Golders.
Tallulah! Hallelujah! In time I may grow;
Let me be your sweet so-and-so.

BEFORE WE WERE MARRIED

Composers probably Joseph Meyer and Philip Charig.
Intended for "Hilary" and "Eloise" in *Katie Did*.
Unused. No music is known to survive.

VERSE 1

ELOISE: It's rumored by neighbors who have
seen us,
Our nation isn't what it used to be.
Of late, there is something come
between us—
And certainly, no one is blaming me.
Consider what you're doing—
Or else you'll find that there is trouble
brewing.

REFRAIN 1

Hist'ry discloses
That once you bought roses—
But that was before we were married.
You said that wedlock
Would not be a deadlock—
But somehow your plans have
miscarried.
I don't know what to blame,
But you've not been the same;
Please don't tell me it's all in fun.
Those were no dumb times,
You took me out sometimes—
But that was before we were one.

VERSE 2

HILARY: There always are two sides to an issue,
And now the other side will take the
floor.
Your notions, my dear, are thin as
tissue,
My evidence no jury would ignore.
I'll tell my story briefly;
The facts that I present to you are
chiefly:

REFRAIN 2

Once you would cheer me—
Alackaday! Dear me!—
Oh, that was before we were married.
You only had eyes for
The man you knit ties for
And never were Tom, Dick, and
Harry-ed.
There is just one thing more
Which I cannot ignore,
Showing what Father Time has done:
You were a glutton
For sewing a button—
But that was before we were one.

DAY AFTER DAY

Composers probably Joseph Meyer and Philip Charig.
Intended for "Eloise" and "Darry" in *Katie Did.*
Unused. No music is known to survive.

VERSE

Although I should know better
Than to send you this letter
Since the rendezvous already has been planned,
Still my yearnings insist you
Know how much I have missed you—
And so I take my pen in hand,
Hoping you will understand.

REFRAIN

Day after day, I keep patiently longing,
Day after day, just for you.
Night after night, tender mem'ries keep
thronging
Till early dawn comes in view.
But, darling, soon we'll be in clover;
Soon we'll see the sun;

Ev'ry worry over,
Two hearts will be one; and
Day after day, ev'ry joy bell ding-donging,
Dream after dream will come true.

THERE I'D SETTLE DOWN

Composers probably Joseph Meyer and Philip Charig. A
"schottische" intended for *Katie Did.* Unused. No
music is known to survive.

VERSE

I want to make my getaway
To a cottage set away
In the far-off hills.
I'm tired of the city folk,
Superficial witty folk,
And their social frills.
In an atmosphere bucolic
I would let my real self frolic.
When I think of skies of blue—
And perhaps two eyes of blue—
Somehow, I'm all thrills.

REFRAIN

I want to dally in a valley
With a pally sort of Sally,
Tried and true.
Where cowbells dingle, jingle-jingle,
Hearts would mingle, all a-tingle,
'Neath the blue.
We'd hear the wonderful song of robin;
We'd hear the thunderful neigh of Dobbin.
As we'd ramble, or we'd gambol,
All a-scramble, side by side, through the
bramble.
We would prattle tittle-tattle
Through the rattle of the cattle
Passing by;
Lose the creaking, noisy, squeaking,
Motor-shrieking, Babel-speaking
City cry.
I crave the scenery of the country
Where all the greenery's more than one tree—
There I dream of sett'ling down.
But try and make me leave the town!

WHY BE GOOD?

Composers probably Joseph Meyer and Philip Charig.
Intended for *Katie Did.* Unused. No music is known to
survive.

VERSE 1

Good little Susan stays at home—
She'll make a splendid wife;
While naughty Nellie loves to roam
And live what's known as "life."
Good Susan is respected;
She's noticed now and then.
But somehow, I've detected,
Naughty Nellie gets the men.

REFRAIN 1

So why be a good girl—
A Babe-in-the-Wood girl?
That doesn't get you a thing.
What's needed in my life
Is plenty of high life
Where I can have my fling.
When Pompadour would smile at Louie,
She made him feel so "Tea for Two"-y—
He gave her his castles—He wrapped her in
fur—
Oh, I want to be like her!

VERSE 2

I'll have a lot of gentlemen friends—
With passion over par.
I'll burn the candle at both ends
Like Mrs. Potiphar.
I'd live a life that's shady,
And homes I want to wreck.
The pleasure-loving lady
Rarely gets it in the neck.

REFRAIN 2

So why be a good girl—
A Babe-in-the-Wood girl?
That doesn't get you a thing.
Your picture's in papers
When you're cutting capers,
Making the welkin ring.
Lucretia Borgia called the boys in,
And those she didn't like she'd poison;
When she picked a lover, he'd never demur—
Oh, I want to be like her!

The Artist Visits "Treasure Girl" at the Shubert

WALTER CATLETT
as
LARRY HOPKINS

MARY HAY
as
POLLY TEES

CLIFTON WEBB
as
"NAT" McNALLY

PAUL FRAWLEY
as
NEIL FORRESTER

GERTRUDE
LAWRENCE
as
ANN WAINWRIGHT

RAY ROHN
SHUBERT THEATRE

TREASURE GIRL | 1928

Produced by Alex A. Aarons and Vinton Freedley. Book by Fred Thompson and Vincent Lawrence. Book staged by Bertram Harrison. Dances staged by Bobby Connolly. Orchestra under the direction of Alfred Newman. Orchestrations by William Daly. Cast, starring Gertrude Lawrence (Ann Wainwright), featured Walter Catlett (Larry Hopkins), Clifton Webb (Nat McNally), Paul Frawley (Neil Forrester), and Mary Hay (Polly Tees), and also included Ferris Hartman (Mortimer Grimes), Norman Curtis (Bunce), Gertrude McDonald (Mary), Charles Barron (Jack), Dorothy Jordan (Betty), Virginia Franck (Madge), Peggy O'Neill (Kitty), John Dunsmuir (First Mate), and Phil Ohman and Victor Arden at the pianos.

Treasure Girl's earlier titles were *Tally Ho* and *Run Across*.

SKULL AND BONES

Introduced by ensemble. Lines 35–38 ("On the Spanish Main . . ." through ". . . pirates of the foam") were cut from the number during the run of the show. No music is known to survive.

MEN: Rough and ready buccaneers are we!—
Salty and tough!
Ready and rough!
Naughty nautical specimens of the sea!—
Better beware!
Better take care!
Wave the Skull and Bones!
'Ray for Davy Jones!
On the Spanish Main we love to roam—
Pickled peppery pirates of the foam.

Oh, when we start to curse,
Our language couldn't be worse—
We make a hell of a hullabaloo,
A hell of a hullabaloo!
Our language would embarrass
The plays done by Jed Harris—
We make a hell of a hullabaloo,
A hell of a hullabaloo!

Ladies and gentlemen, we must insist
If Gilbert and Sullivan didn't exist,
We'd never have sung a song like this—

Naughty nautical specimens of the sea!

If you would like a trip to Shanghai,
Or if you'd like your neck to hang high,
We'll guarantee you satisfaction,
Will this rollicking, frolicking pirate crew!

Cutting a throat's a job we do like.
(You can have any choice cut you like.)
Any old time that you crave action,
Try this rollicking, frolicking pirate crew!
On the Spanish Main we love to roam—
Gaily we sweep
Over the deep!
Pickled peppery pirates of the foam.

And now while the world is sleeping,
And only the stars are peeping,
To our treasure we are creeping—
To our treasure we are creeping!

[*They advance to spot where one bottle is hidden*]

We've got a bottle of rum—
Don't you ask us where it's from!
We've got a bottle of rum—
Rum ta tum tum tum tum—
Rum ta tum tum tum!

We've got a bottle of rum—
Hallelujah! I'm a bum!
We've got a bottle of rum—
Rum ta tum tum tum—
Rum ta tum tum tum!

[*Girls come on*]

GIRLS: You've got a bottle of rum—
So we'll join you—We're not dumb!
You've got a bottle of rum—
Rum ta tum tum tum—
Rum ta tum tum tum!

ALL: Rum tum tum tum tum—
Rum—tum—tum—tum—tum!

GIRLS: Pirate, why look for treasure?
Pirate, look here!
Why waste the night?
Moonlight is bright,
And we're so lonesome.

MEN: Happy beyond all measure—
Whoopee! I've found my treasure!
For, lady, I'll be bound
Now that you've come 'round,
All my treasure's found!

Published February 1930. Introduced by Clifton Webb (Nat), Mary Hay (Polly), and ensemble. Replaced "Good-bye to the Old Love" during the tryout. Reused in *Strike Up the Band* (1930), introduced by Gordon Smith (Timothy) and Doris Carson (Anne). Also published May 1930 as part of the score for *Strike Up the Band*.

A *Wiley Change* or *Hot Tune into Ballad*. I can't recall now why *Treasure Girl*'s "Crush on You" was interpolated in the revised version of *Strike Up the Band*, since there were so much new material on hand for the latter. Anyway, although the song was a pleasant enough number in its original setting as done by Clifton Webb and Mary Hay, it was sung in *S.U.T.B.* at a faster tempo by Gordon Smith and Doris Carson—and then danced to by them at about the fastest 2/4 I ever heard. So for many years I thought of this song as one exceedingly hot. Then one day I bought a then new Lee Wiley album which included the first recording of this number. I listened awhile, and wondered what the girl was up to. Fast and furious "Crush" had become slow, sentimental, and ballady. After a third playing, though, I liked the new interpretation. And apparently so did many others, because I have yet to hear since a rendition other than the slowed-up, sentimental one.

—from *Lyrics on Several Occasions*

VERSE

NAT: How glad the many millions
Of Annabelles and Lillians
Would be
To capture me.
But you had such persistence*
You wore down my resistance;
I fell—
And it was swell.

POLLY: You're my big and brave and handsome
Romeo.
How I won you I shall never, never know.

NAT: It's not that you're attractive—
But oh, my heart grew active

Original version of verse, lines 5–8:
You've no idea how lucky

When you
Came into view.

REFRAIN 1

I've got a crush on you,
   Sweetie Pie.
All the day and nighttime
Hear me sigh.
I never had the least notion
That I could fall with so much emotion.

Could you coo,
Could you care
For a cunning cottage we could share?
The world will pardon my mush
'Cause I've got a crush,
My baby, on you.

REFRAIN 2

POLLY: I've got a crush on you,
   Sweetie Pie.
All the day and nighttime
Hear me sigh.
This isn't just a flirtation:
We're proving that there's
   predestination.

I could coo,
I could care
For that cunning cottage we could share.
Your mush I never shall shush
'Cause I've got a crush,
My baby, on you.

ACCORDING TO MR. GRIMES

Introduced by Ferris Hartman (Grimes) and ensemble. Originally, it was the fifth number in Act I. No music is known to survive.

GRIMES: Good evening, ladies fair and fellow
   pirates!
   A whim of mine tonight I'll
   crystallize.
   This evening it's my mission
   To announce a competition.

ENSEMBLE: Competition?

GRIMES: Competition for a prize!
   The contest, I may say, is a unique one;

Your int'rest for a time I'm sure 'twill
   hold.
I know you'll be delighted—

ENSEMBLE: Hurry up! We're all excited!

GRIMES: It's a treasure hunt!—

ENSEMBLE: A treasure hunt!—

GRIMES: For gold!
   There's lots of lucre for the lucky
    winner—
   In gold, in pearls, in diamonds, and
    such.
   I tell you it's worth seeking,
   In figures, roundly speaking,
   A hundred thousand dollars is not too
    much!

ENSEMBLE: Good God!
[Footman enters with charts]
GRIMES: Yes, somewhere there's a lot of
    hidden treasure
   Which I have taken lots of time to
    hide.
ENSEMBLE: Now, that's the place to visit!
   Come clean, old boy, where is it?
GRIMES: Your ingenuity has to be the guide.

   I've printed charts—It's up to you to
    solve them;
   At midnight the contest will begin.
   I'm through with my effusion;
   Just one word in conclusion—
   May the best man or the best girl win!

VOICE: What's the matter with Grimes?*

ENSEMBLE: He's all right!

A-HUNTING WE WILL GO

Introduced and reprised by ensemble. Alternate title: "Tally Ho." Only a portion of the song (lines 1–4 and 14–19) was being performed by the time the production reached New York. Not listed in the *Treasure Girl* programs.

A-hunting we will go—
Tally ho! Tally ho! Tally ho!
Like Captain Kidd and Co.

---

*Script reads:

   What's the matter with Morty Grimes?

Tally ho! Tally ho! Tally ho!
Yo ho! We're after a pot of gold!
After a pot of gold!
The lucky winner gets a lot of gold—
A pot of gold—
A pot of gold!

Oh, lucky star, please shine—
Tally ho! Tally ho! Tally ho!
And make the treasure mine—
Tally ho! Tally ho! Tally ho!
We'll search in manner that's passionate,
Because there's plenty of cash in it.
Tally ho!
A-hunting we will go!
Tantivy! Tantivy! Tantivy!
A-hunting we will go!

PLACE IN THE COUNTRY

Introduced by Paul Frawley (Neil), Norman Curtis (Bunce), and girls. Alternate title: "Opening, Act I, Scene 3."

GIRLS: We're looking for a place
   Somewhere in the country;
   In the open space
   Where there's more than one tree.
   What a scene,
   All dressed up in green!
   Nature's grand!
   Give the girl a hand!
   To the country's charm
   We are all succumbing;
   Even rent a farm
   If there's open plumbing.
   Say, say, say!
   We'll be making hay
   If we should rent a cottage today.

BUNCE: Ladies, what can I do for you?
   With me you needn't be distant;
   I'm Mr. Forrester's assistant.

GIRLS: Is Mr. Forrester in?
   Say, what do you say?
   Is Mr. Forrester in?
   We've come a long way.
   We'd like to go in conference—
   Important business, too!
   For he has such lovely eyes of blue!

BUNCE: Yes, Mr. Forrester's in;*
But sorry to say
Though Mr. Forrester's in
He's busy today.

GIRLS: We must consult with him at once—
Important business, too!
You, sir, will never, never do!
Oh, he has such lovely eyes of blue!

NEIL: Ladies, good morning. What can I do for
you?

GIRLS: Oh, isn't he grand?
Let's give him a hand!

NEIL: I'm yours to command.
[*The girls all speak at once*]
Ladies, ladies, please! One at a time so I
can understand.

GIRLS: We're looking for a place
Where the roses ramble;
Where it's no disgrace
If we start to gambol.
Something nice—
Never mind the price!
Can't you see?—
Neighbors we would be!

[*Neil opens portfolio*]
NEIL: I've some places here—
Shall I read them to you?
They have atmosphere;
Maybe they will do you.

GIRLS: If you please,
Show us some with trees—
With trees-es, breezes, birds-es, and bees!
[*During his next lines, they sing:*]
His eyes are lovely!

NEIL: Here's a very charming cottage that
perhaps will do;
Has no open plumbing but it has an
open view.

This is one that's really up-to-date, and
here's the proof:
Frigidaire and Duco paint and Anaconda
roof.

Here is one that's built for two and not a
person more;
But on a weekend you had best prepare
for forty-four.

---

*The script assigns four lines to the girls here:
Don't say he cannot be seen;
Don't think that we are fresh—
But we are terribly keen
To meet him in the flesh.

There are many others I should love to
have you see,
But today I fear that I'm not free.

Ladies, though I know
I should be beside you;
Though I ought to go,
Bunce will have to guide you.
Hope you find
The spot for which you've pined,
And thanks for having kept me in mind.
[*Exits*]
GIRLS:
[*to Bunce as they twirl him around*]
Summer is a bore
In the great big city;
That's the reason for
This research committee.
Understand!
We want something grand.
Something nice—
Never mind the price!
Hope you recommend
Something rather nifty.

BUNCE: How much would you spend?*

GIRLS: Nothing over fifty.
[*He throws up his hands in disgust and leaves*]

Moo! Moo! Moo!
And cockadoodle-doo!
We want a cottage under the blue!

K-RA-ZY FOR YOU

Published October 1928. Introduced by Clifton Webb
(Nat), Mary Hay (Polly), and ensemble. At one point in
the pre-Broadway tryout it was the second number in
Act II. This song inspired the title for the 1992 Gershwin
musical *Crazy for You*.

VERSE 1

NAT: When a guy like Byron
Would meet up with a siren,
In his dome
He'd find a poem [*"pome"*]
That made the girlie's skin burn.
I cannot spill passion
In highfalutin' fashion;
I'm afraid

---

*In the script, the girls have a line here:
And we'd like to spend

That with a maid
I'll never be a Swinburne.
But though I'm not the slightest bit
poetic,
In my own way you will find me
sympathetic.

REFRAIN 1

Let me give you the lowdown:
I'm k-ra-zy for you.
When it comes to a showdown,
I'm k-ra-zy for you.
And so, though love may not inspire my
lingo,
Still, it's making my heart go "Bango!
Bingo!"
Let me give you the lowdown:
I'm k-ra-zy for you.

VERSE 2

POLLY: Darling, I have never
Heard such a grand endeavor,
Though your bent
For sentiment
Is not exactly tony.
Though you sing my praises
In most peculiar phrases,
Yet I see
That you are free
From what is called baloney!
My dear, your kind of poetry will do me;
'F anybody doesn't like it, let him sue
me!

REFRAIN 2

I'm k-ra-zy to know that
You're k-ra-zy for me.
If you never outgrow that,
How ga-lad I shall be.
I really can't explain just what your
success is,
But I keep k-raving your sweet caresses.
I'm k-ra-zy to know that
You're k-ra-zy for me.

I DON'T THINK I'LL FALL IN LOVE TODAY

Published October 1928. Introduced by Gertrude Lawrence (Ann) and Paul Frawley (Neil).

T itle Adaptation. I doubt that the title of this duet would have come to me if at some time or other I hadn't read Chesterton's "A Ballade of Suicide" with its refrain of "I think I will not hang myself today." (Not that the other lines and content of the ballad and those of the duet have anything in common.) . . .

Treasure Girl's plot was concerned with a treasure hunt which took the proceedings to the Caribbean and, after a couple of months, took us all to Cain's Warehouse. There was some excellent dialogue by Vincent Lawrence and—if I may—the songs and dances, thanks to a brilliant cast headed by Miss Lawrence and Clifton Webb, were well—even rapturously—received. But, some songwriters to the contrary, numbers alone do not make a show.

—from *Lyrics on Several Occasions*

VERSE 1

ANN: Just think of what love leads to:
　　　Maybe to marriage—maybe divorce.
NEIL: Into a jam love speeds two;
　　　It may be Nature's course,
　　　But we mustn't be
　　　Like the other sheep.
ANN: Better far if we
　　　Look before we leap.
BOTH: Perhaps it's better after all
　　　If we don't answer Nature's call.

REFRAIN 1

NEIL: Who knows if we'd agree?
　　　You like you and I like me.
　　　I don't think I'll fall in love today.
ANN: When evening shadows creep,
　　　I like dancing—
NEIL: I like sleep.
　　　I don't think I'll fall in love today.
ANN: Still it might be fun to bring
　　　Your carpet slippers;
　　　When the dinner bell would ring,
　　　I'd serve a can of kippers.
NEIL: Don't you know how to cook?
ANN: I could look in a book.
NEIL: I don't think I'll fall in love today.

VERSE 2

NEIL: Love is a fever chronic;
　　　We can avoid it—Why take a chance?
ANN: Safer to be platonic;
　　　Why burn up with romance?
NEIL: Adam without Eve
　　　Happiness had known,
　　　So suppose we leave
　　　Well enough alone.

ANN: Imagine signing up for life,
　　　Then finding peas roll off his knife.

REFRAIN 2

NEIL: D'you sleep with window shut?
ANN: Window shut.
NEIL: Charming, but—
　　　I don't think I'll fall in love today.
ANN: Did you pick that cravat?
NEIL: I did that.
ANN: Here's your hat.
　　　I don't think I'll fall in love today.
BOTH: It's as clear as A B C
　　　We're not agreeing;
　　　Incompatability
　　　The judge would be decreeing.
　　　When all is said and done,
　　　Seems we two will never be one.
　　　Let's, oh, let's not fall in love today!

ENCORE REFRAIN

ANN: Do you play bridge or whist?
NEIL: I like pinochle.
ANN: I insist—
　　　I don't think I'll fall in love today.
NEIL: To what symphonies do you go?*
ANN: All I know
　　　Is "Vo-do-de-o!"
NEIL: I don't think I'll fall in love today.
　　　Is the combination wrong?
　　　I've wondered lately.
ANN: We should never get along—
　　　Not even companionately.
BOTH: When all is said and done,
　　　Dear, we two will never make one.
　　　Let's, oh, let's not fall in love today!

TAG

ANN: D'you wear pajamas, Neil?
NEIL: I wear nightshirts.
ANN: Then I feel—
　　　I don't think I'll fall in love today.

Before the presidential election of 1928, lines 5–8 of the encore refrain were:
ANN: For president, I like Smith.
NEIL: I'm for Hoover.
ANN: I like Smith.
　　　I don't think I'll fall in love today.

GOT A RAINBOW

Published October 1928. Introduced by Walter Catlett (Larry), Charles Barron (Jack), Gertrude McDonald (Mary), Dorothy Jordan (Betty), Virginia Franck (Madge), Peggy O'Neill (Kitty), and girls. Alternate title: "I've Got a Rainbow."

VERSE

Born on the thirteenth, on a Friday—
Somehow I've lived to tell the tale;
Every day is one blue-sky day,
Whether there's sunshine or a gale.
I've got a rainbow seeing me through,
Shining for me alone.
Why should you wait for rainbows when you
Can carry your own?

REFRAIN 1

What makes my misery fly
When clouds are dark in the sky?
Got a "Rainbow 'round my shoulder"!
The wolf who knocked at my door—
He doesn't knock anymore:
Got a "Rainbow 'round my shoulder"!
Oh, it may rain and it may thunder,
But I've got no reason to frown;
For with a rainbow in town,
A good man never is down!
So, blues get out of my way!
The joys are coming to stay,
With a rainbow always aroun'!

REFRAIN 2

If I should see a black cat,
I snap my fingers at that:
Got a "Rainbow 'round my shoulder"!
When under ladders I stroll,
I find it good for my soul:
Got a "Rainbow 'round my shoulder"!
I've broken sixty-seven mirrors
And spilt a barrel of salt;
Still, I've not come to a halt—
A good man never is down!
There's no blue Monday for me;
From heebie-jeebies I'm free,
With a rainbow always aroun'!

FEELING I'M FALLING

Published October 1928. Introduced by Gertrude Lawrence (Ann) and Paul Frawley (Neil).

VERSE 1

NEIL: Just a little while ago
You were a stranger—
My heart was free.
Suddenly you smile, and Oh!
My heart's in danger—
You own the key!

ANN: When
Love gets you, then
It gets you quicker than you've reckoned;
Fate
Hands you a mate
In just the twinkling of a second.

NEIL: Eeny, meeny, miny, mo!*
Fate has been kind
To me.

REFRAIN 1

No fooling, I'm feeling I'm falling, dear.
I felt it the moment I found you.
This failing I'm feeling keeps calling, dear.
It's fatal, can't wait'll I'm 'round you.
I'd like to tell you of the flame that makes
me flutter,
But it's so utterly impossible to utter.
I'm feeling I'm falling. When shall I see
Some feeling you're falling for me?

VERSE 2

ANN: Doctor, lawyer, Injun, thief—
Whom would I fancy?
I wondered who?
Now I sigh in great relief—
Darling, I can see
I fancy you.

NEIL: Who'd
'A' thought that you'd
Think you could love a real-estate man?

ANN: Well,
I think you're swell.
I'll sign your option any date, man.

*The script reads:
And I want the world to know.

And I'm telling you, in brief,
Nobody else will do.

REFRAIN 2

No fooling, I'm feeling I'm falling, dear.
I felt it the moment I found you.
This failing I'm feeling keeps calling, dear.
It's fatal, can't wait'll I'm 'round you.
Oh, if you feel you've found the one girl,
please enfold her,
And whisper things that no one yet has
ever told her.
You're feeling you're falling. I feel it, too:
A feeling I'm falling for you!

FINALE, ACT I

Introduced by Walter Catlett (Larry), Gertrude Lawrence (Ann), Clifton Webb (Nat), Paul Frawley (Neil), and ensemble. A blend of dialogue and song. No music is known to survive.

[Ensemble enters, singing and looking for treasure]

ENSEMBLE:
[Sings]
We're looking for the treasure,
The treasure Mr. Grimes has hidden.

LARRY:
[spoken]
Mr. Grimes . . . an old gentleman . . .
about so tall?
[Indicates]

ENSEMBLE:
[Sings]
That's the man! That's the man!

LARRY: A week ago, by chance,
I saw this very gent;
At me he didn't glance,
But straight ahead he went.

ENSEMBLE: Yes, yes, go on!
Yes, yes, go on!
Yes, yes, go on!

LARRY: I watched him like a fox;
I got behind a tree;
I saw him bury a box!
But what—was—that—to—me?

ENSEMBLE: Where is it? Where did he hide it?

LARRY: Way down yonder in the cornfield.

ENSEMBLE:
[Sings]
Congratulations, Ann!
Congratulations, Ann!
You've won it by a minute;
We'll bear it and we'll grin it.
Congratulations, Ann!

Now that you've found it, Ann, lucky
girl,
Let's gather round it, Ann, lucky girl

NAT:
[Takes parchment]
Hey! Everybody! Listen to this:
[Reads]
A message from the darkness to the
reader:
On Alligator Island there is light;
Contestants who will flock there
Will find a certain rock there—
A rock on which there is a cross of
white.

The latitude is thirty—forty—seven;
The longitude, geographers agree,
Is sixty—twelve and twenty.
You've information plenty;
The good treasure door is opened
with this key.

ENSEMBLE:
[singing as they exit]
To Alligator Island we've got to go.
The latitude and longitude we all
know.
Come on, we'd better hurry up,
ev'ryone!
And finish up the thing that we've
begun.

ANN:
[Calls]
Ne-il! Ne-il!
[Neil appears at the window. He closes it and
draws the shade. Ann shrugs her shoulders,
turns to audience, and sings:]
He likes his window shut—window
shut.
Charming, but—
I don't think I'll fall in love today!
[Ann walks upstage. Turns. Waves her hand
toward the window. Runs off]
[Curtain]

TREASURE ISLAND

Introduced by ensemble. Alternate title: "Opening, Act II." No music is known to survive.

Treasure Island—
Are you my land?
This is where we're told
There's a pot of gold.

What a myst'ry!
Maybe this tree—
Or it may be there!
We must look with care!

Is it hidden in a cave—
Or some catacombs?
Till we find it we'll behave
Just like Sherlock Holmes.

Softly, lightly,
Daily, nightly,
We've been on the quest
To find the treasure chest.

What's to be done? What's to be done?
We've got to finish up this thing that we've
    begun!

Lucky star,
Here we are;
Heed us!
Heavy dough
Waiting—So
Lead us!
To the right
Cross in white
Speed us;
Where the milk and honey flow.

We're wise and we're healthy;
Please help make us wealthy.

Lucky star,
Here we are;
Heed us!
Won't you tell us where to go?

WHAT CAUSES THAT?

Published June 1992 in the vocal selections from *Crazy for You*. Introduced in *Treasure Girl* (1928) by Clifton Webb (Nat), Mary Hay (Polly), and ensemble. During the first week of the pre-Broadway tryout, it was sung late in Act I. Performed in the 1992 Broadway show *Crazy for You* by Harry Groener (Bobby) and Bruce Adler (Zangler).

VERSE

NAT: You're so full of trickery—
    Life is bitter as chicory;
    Bitterness fills my cup.
POLLY: I'm sorry you brought that up.

NAT: Once I thought I'd search around
    For the Little Church Around
    The Corner. But now, I see
    It never was meant to be.

POLLY: Once you used to praise me—
    Why are you so high hat?
    Big boy, you amaze me!
    Tell me, what causes that?

REFRAIN 1

NAT: When I'm away from you, I start
        despairing—
    You ought to know by now what causes
        that!
    I'm growing balder from the hair I'm
        tearing—
    You ought to know by now what causes
        that!
    When some other chap takes you aside—
    Oh gosh, I'm all at sea!
    I go contemplating suicide—
    You're much too much for me!
    You're not so dumb that you don't know
        the answer:
    Loving you is what causes that!

REFRAIN 2

NAT: If I should climb the Brooklyn Bridge
        and jump off—
    Oh, I suppose you'd ask, "What causes
        that?"
    If I should get a gun and bump this
        chump off—
    Oh, I suppose you'd ask, "What causes
        that?"
POLLY: Really, you don't have to mope around
    And burn up as you do;
    There's a cannon and a rope around—
    There's lots of poison, too.
NAT: I'm very blue of late and there's a
        reason:
    Loving you is what causes that!

WHAT ARE WE HERE FOR?

Published October 1928. Introduced by Gertrude Lawrence (Ann), Clifton Webb (Nat), and ensemble.

VERSE

ANN: The sea is bright blue;
    The heavens, light blue;
NAT: Green things are growing;
    South wind is blowing;
BOTH: All nature's colors are unfurled.
ANN: Oh, see the sunbeams!
    How ev'ry one beams!
NAT: The crickets call us;
    The birds enthrall us;
BOTH: This is a pretty darn good world!
NAT: Never can understand
    People who reprimand
    You when they hear laughter.
ANN: Pity the Gloomy Gus,
    Speaking in manner thus:
    "You will suffer after!"

REFRAIN

BOTH: What are we here for?—
    What are we here for?—
    I'd like to know—
    If not to dance and to play?
    If not to laugh and be gay?
    What is the spring for?—
    What do birds sing for?—
    Down here below—
    If not to brighten the way
    As on we go?
    We all are actors in a gorgeous
        setting—
    It's full of magic;
    No use in getting
    Tragic.
    If we can't be full
    Of a joy gleeful
    All through the day,
    What are we here for
    Anyway?

WHERE'S THE BOY? HERE'S THE GIRL!

Published October 1928. Introduced by Gertrude Lawrence (Ann), pianists Phil Ohman and Victor Arden, and ensemble.

Show Version

VERSE

There is no doubt
About
The fact that life without
A lord and master
Is a disaster.

And there's a he
Who'd be
The world and all to me—
But who knows whether*
We'll get together?

There's just this man and it's high time
He came to take up my time.

I've swallowed pride,†
And cried,
"I want him at my side!"
Fate has assigned him;
When shall I find him?

REFRAIN

Where's the boy?
What's he waiting for?
Where's the boy?
Here's the girl!

What is he
Hesitating for?
Can't he see
Here's the girl!

There's no call for castles on romantic
mountains;‡

Earlier version of verse, lines 9–10:
But fate decided
We be divided.
†*Earlier version of verse, lines 13–17:*
Will he appear?
Oh dear!
Each day seems like a year.
But who knows whether
We'll get together?
‡*Refrain 2, lines 9–10:*
Will I hear the Wedding March in future hours?
All that I keep hearing now is "Hearts and Flowers."

With him I would share a straw at soda
fountains.

He'll bring me joy;
But what's he waiting for?
Where's the boy?
Here's the girl!

Published Version

VERSE

There is no doubt
About
The fact that life without
A lord and master
Is a disaster.

But I've not met
As yet
The man I'd like to get;
Of some I speak well,
But none's my equal.

There's just one man, and it's high time
He came to take up my time.

In dreams I see
This he
Who's all the world to me;
Though I've not met him,
I can't forget him.

REFRAIN

Where's the boy?
What's he waiting for?
Where's the boy?
Here's the girl!

What is he
Hesitating for?
Can't he see?—
Here's the girl!
Maybe we shall meet on some romantic
mountain;
Probably I'll meet him at a soda fountain.

He'll bring me joy,
But what's he waiting for?
Where's the boy?
Here's the girl!

Unused Reprise

BOYS:
[to Ann]
          You're the girl
          I've been waiting for;
          You're the girl—
          I'm the boy!

What are you
Hesitating for?
You're the girl
I adore.

You don't have to look far to find your
hero;
Little Columbine, in me you've found
your Pierrot.

I'll bring you joy;
What *are* you waiting for?
I'm the boy,
Little girl!

OH, SO NICE!

Published October 1928. Introduced by Gertrude Lawrence (Ann) and Paul Frawley (Neil). Dropped soon after the New York opening.

VERSE

ANN: Never thought I'd ever meet
A man like you,
Who could make my life complete—
My dreams come true.
The many men I'd known for years
All seemed the same;
They kept on boring me to tears—
And then you came.
I was taken off my feet;
What could I do?

REFRAIN 1

I was above love
Before,
But now I love love
Because you're
Oh, oh, so nice!
Awake or sleeping,
It seems
That you keep creeping
In my dreams,
And it's so nice!
When you are near me—
Oh my!
Oh dear! Oh dear me!
I just fly
To paradise.
I was above love
Before,
But now I love love

'Cause you're
Oh, oh, oh, so nice!

REFRAIN 2

NEIL: I was above love
Before,
But now I love love
Because you're
Oh, oh, so nice!
Awake or sleeping,
It seems
That you keep creeping
In my dreams,
And it's so nice!
I'm hoping maybe
You know
When will the day be
They will throw
Old shoes and rice.
Please make your mind up—
You'll see
That when we're signed up
'Twill be
Oh, oh, oh, so nice!

GOOD-BYE TO THE OLD LOVE

Introduced by Mary Hay (Polly), Gertrude McDonald (Mary), Clifton Webb (Nat), Charles Barron (Jack), and ensemble during the tryout—the second number in the first act. Dropped before the New York opening. Replaced with "I've Got a Crush on You." Alternate title: "Good-bye to the Old Love, Hello to the New."

VERSE

JACK
AND
NAT: I place my faith
In Henry Eighth,
And I'll do just as he did;
When a change is needed,
Pick out someone new.

MARY
AND
POLLY: When love is not
So very hot,
From now on I will carry
On just like Du Barry;
I'm for changing, too!

ALL: Though we may be shocking Mrs.
Grundy
Through and through,
Since your love is handy,
Ev'rything is dandy!

REFRAIN

Good-bye to the old love,
Hello to the new!
Do I love my new love?
Yes indeed, I do!
It's the only system—
Live while you're alive;
Doesn't pay to be conservative
[*pronounced "tyve"*].
Maine to Texas,
Both the sexes
Want the newer freedom;
When the old flame
Is a cold flame,
Then why *be* dumb?
When I looked in your eyes,
That gave me the cue:
"Off with the old love—
On with the new!"

I WANT TO MARRY A MARIONETTE

Introduced by Gertrude Lawrence (Ann) and boys during the tryout as the fourth number in Act I. Dropped before the New York opening.

VERSE

ANN: Men are so difficult to handle!
BOYS: You haven't met
The right one yet;
Haven't tried to get
The right one yet.
ANN: Kiss one and suddenly there's a scandal!
BOYS: Oh no! We never
Tell a thing.
Well, we hardly ever
Tell a thing.
On our bended knees-es,
We promise to be true!
ANN: I've heard those old wheezes;
Men will never do!

REFRAIN

I want to marry a marionette.
Then I'd have my say;
He'd do as I say.
I think I'll tarry until we have met.
He won't be moody;
I'll be his Judy.
If I should marry Dick or Harry, always
we'd be wrangling;
Why take chances on romances bound to
be entangling?
I want to marry a marionette,
So's I can keep him on a string.

DEAD MEN TELL NO TALES

Introduced by John Dunsmuir (First Mate) during the tryout. Dropped before the New York opening.

I trust no man but a dead man,
For dead men tell no tales.
I drift my way
With none to say
How I shall set my sails.
The mob will follow the headman
Whose courage never fails.
The man who knows me
Never, never dares oppose me;
Dead men tell no tales.

I trust no man but a dead man,
For dead men tell no tales.
Where I am boss
The double cross
Will find me harder than nails.
My gang will follow their headman
Through tempests and through gales.
We never quarrel
While my gun can point this moral:
"Dead men tell no tales!"

THIS PARTICULAR PARTY

Intended for ensemble as an Act I opening. Dropped during rehearsals. Replaced with "Skull and Bones." No music is known to survive.

BOYS: How dry I am!
Sweet Adeline!
How dry I am!
Sweet Adeline!

Liquor flows and worry goes
Whenever dear old Morty throws
A party.
Parties that he engineers
Have always made us give three cheers—
And hearty.
Just like Rockefeller, he saved his dimes;
Now he's spending them all on jolly
    times.

Whoop it up and let 'er rip!
This party's bound to be a pippin—
Thanks to Morty Grimes.

But what's the good of a party
Without some adorable party
Who is cute and charming and
    petite,
And can make the night complete?
This particular party
Wants a sweet, adorable party—
And if she's a party nice to me,
What a party this will be!

GIRLS: Here we are—the answer to your prayers.
BOYS: Oh, you lovable things!
GIRLS: Brighten up and throw away your cares.
BOYS: Now we're happy as kings!

ALL: Partner, let's raise the curtain!
Partner, let's go!
On with the show!
Let the music flow!
The sky the limit!
Partner, here's where romance is;
Oh, happiness is found
For this party hound—
Dear, when you're around!

OPPOSITE: Show Girl. *Top: Harriet Hoctor and ensemble in "An American in Paris" ballet. Bottom: Ruby Keeler with Eddie Jackson, Lou Clayton, and Jimmy Durante*

EAST IS
WEST
1928–1929

SHOW
GIRL
1929

EAST IS WEST, 1928–1929

East Is West, or *Ming Toy*, as it was also known, was an ultimately unproduced musical that Florenz Ziegfeld had hoped to present in 1929 with Ed Wynn as star and Oscar Shaw, Kathryn Hereford, Barbara Newberry, and Bobbe Arnst featured. (In *Lyrics on Several Occasions*, Ira Gershwin suggests that the stars were to have been Marilyn Miller, Bobby Clark, and Paul McCullough.) The book, to have been furnished by William Anthony McGuire, was planned as an adaptation of the play *East Is West* by Samuel Shipman and John B. Hymer. George and Ira Gershwin worked on several songs for this show, but the work, begun in 1928, was abandoned in 1929 when the project collapsed.

IN THE MANDARIN'S ORCHID GARDEN

Written 1929. Published February 1930.

Recitation. "Orchid Garden" was to be sung by a Sing-Song Girl at one side of the stage—as a vocal accompaniment to a Chinese ballet on full stage. When *East Is West* had to be abandoned by Ziegfeld, our music-publisher salvaged this unsung Sing-Song Girl lament and published it, feeling that some concert artists would take to it. But, so far as I know, only one used it—Eleanor Marum, in four or five recitals. A couple of years later, though, I found that it had an existence, however fleeting, in another form.

One night on our first trip to Hollywood we were dinner guests at the Bel-Air home of one of the studio's executives. After I was introduced by the gracious hostess, his wife, she took me aside and recited a few lines, starting with "Somehow by fate misguided, / A buttercup resided . . ." Vastly surprised, since the song had sold only a few copies, and wondering how it had traveled twenty-six hundred miles to Bel-Air, I said: "I didn't know anyone knew that song. How did you happen to learn it?" "Oh," she replied, "I can't play it—only recite it. You see, I take elocution lessons and my teacher gave me the words to learn."

Just then dinner was announced, and I never did find out who the elocution teacher was—nor why he, or she, had got hold of a copy to put it to this rather unlikely use.

—from *Lyrics on Several Occasions*

Somehow by fate misguided,
A buttercup resided
In The Mandarin's Orchid Garden—
A buttercup that did not grace
The loveliness of such a place.
And so it simply shriveled up
And begged each orchid's pardon.
Poor little buttercup
In The Orchid Garden.

The bees came buzzing daily
And kissed the orchids gaily
In The Mandarin's Orchid Garden.
The buttercup sighed longingly,
But love was not for such as she.
And so one day it shriveled up
And died, still begging pardon.
Poor lonely buttercup
In The Orchid Garden.

I, too, have been misguided.
Too long have I resided
In The Mandarin's Orchid Garden.
And though for friendliness I yearn,
I do not know which way to turn.
How long must I keep shriv'ling up
And beg each lady's pardon?
A lonely buttercup
In The Orchid Garden.

YELLOW BLUES

Written in 1928. No. 42 in the George and Ira Gershwin Special Numbered Song File. Years later, Ira Gershwin discarded the lyric and asked Kay Swift to prepare a piano arrangement, which William Bolcom recorded in 1973 as "Impromptu in Two Keys."

Life is never mellow
When you have got the yellow blues;
Most unlucky fellow
Is he who has the yellow blues.
People always cheat you*
Of happiness and beat you down.
Seems to be no doubt of
The fact they want you out of town.

Yellow man was king of many ages,
Left his magic on the sands of time;
Wrote his wisdom all through hist'ry's pages,
Yet he's treated like a plugged-up dime.

Alternate version of lines 5–6:
People always treat you
As if they'd like to beat you down.

Yellow seems a color
That gives to life a duller tone
And makes me moan:
"There's no good news
When you have got the yellow blues."

LADY OF THE MOON

This is the first lyric set to the tune that was next used for "I Just Looked At You," a song intended for but not used in *Show Girl* (1929), and ultimately became "Blah, Blah, Blah" in the film *Delicious* (1931).

REFRAIN 1

Lady of the Moon,
Drifting in the blue;
Lady of the Moon,
Let me drift with you.*
Waiting in the purple gloaming,
How I thrill when you appear, my dear.
I envy every star
Twinkling up above
Just because they are
'Neath the one I love.
We could drift to paradise
On a silver balloon.†
If you want me,
Lady of the Moon.

REFRAIN 2

Lady of the Moon,
Here I am below.
Lovelier you seem
Than the night before.

[*Manuscript breaks off here*]

UNDER THE CINNAMON TREE

A piano-vocal arrangement of this song is No. 85 in the George and Ira Gershwin Special Numbered Song File.

*Alternate line:
Are you lonely, too?
†Alternate line:
On your silver balloon.

VERSE

Somehow I feel much more sentimental
When the atmosphere is Oriental.
Scented trees and the balmy breeze
Seem to bring a fellow to his knees.
Tho' I'm fond of you, I could grow fonder
'Neath that cinnamon tree away down yonder.
Like as not,
That's the very spot
Where my lovely lotus petal
And her boyfriend ought to settle.

REFRAIN

I'll buy me some plottage
And build us a cottage
Right under the cinnamon tree.
We'll make a religion
Of dried fish and pigeon
And get all our laundry free.
We'll have a Chinese maid instead of Dinah.
What a thrill to listen to her broken china!
We'll eat of the scallion
And raise a battalion
Right under the cinnamon tree.

AWAKE, CHILDREN, AWAKE

The lyric is unfinished. No music is known to survive.

CHANG FOO: The world runs on,
But China slumbers;
Awake, children, awake.
The night is gone,
But China slumbers;
Awake, children, awake.
The patient implores,
Oh, Chinamen be men!
The world that once was yours
Can be your world again.
The spell of the dragon we'll break!
Awake, children, awake!

SING-SONG GIRL

Unfinished. A portion of the music survives in No. 77 of the George and Ira Gershwin Special Numbered Song File.

SOLO: Sing-Song Girl, no one beside you;
Sing-Song Girl, there's none to guide you.
The world grows colder
And men grow bolder;
You shrug your shoulder;
What can you do?
Skies are gray and full of sorrow;
True today and true tomorrow.
But keep on strumming
Of bright days coming—
Hoping 'twill come true.
Sing your song and no forgetting:
Dreams of love are idle dreams.
Drift along with no regretting;
Not for you are bridal dreams.
Though each day is like December,*
On your way you must remember
To sing your spring song
You're just a Sing-Song Girl.

SING-SONG
GIRLS: How sad it is to be a Sing-Song Girl.
Each season she must be a spring-song girl.
How sad it is to be a Sing-Song Girl.

Sing, Sing-Song Girl, sing;
Dry the tears that are falling
And dream your lover is calling.
Sing, Sing-Song Girl, sing;
Smile, Sing-Song Girl, smile.
The drooping flower
Lives but an hour.
Oh, sing, Sing-Song Girl, sing.
And one fine day†
The winter may
Give way to spring.

WE ARE VISITORS HERE

This seems to be a substantial, albeit fragmented, portion of an opening chorus. No music is known to survive.

*Alternate version of this and next three lines:
Don't you care if it's December.
Don't you care, but just remember
To sing your spring song
No wedding-ring song.
†Alternate version of this and next two lines:
Who knows but some-
Day there may come
The breath of spring.

We are visitors here;
We're tripping around the map.
With Mothersill's we've crossed the briny
To drink with Heinie
And now to study the heathen Chinee!
We are visitors here;
We're tripping around the map.
You'll find we travel quite deluxe
And read Baedeker books
And all by arrangement with
American Express and Cook's.

NATIVES: With faces full of vacancy,
They've come to see what they can see.
[Four men step out]

QUESTION: Where will we be when boat come?
ANSWER: We'll be there when love boat come.
QUESTION: Will we bid for Sing-Song Girl?
ANSWER: We shall bid for Sing-Song Girl.

1ST MAN: Keep your slender feminine gender;
I won't go near that one!
I am taken only by bacon;
I must have a fat one.

2ND MAN: I am weak one for the chic one—
High-tone baby—Class A.
If she drop sticks using chopsticks,
Then with me she's passé.

3RD MAN: Must be youthful, strong and toothful—
Then will she delight me.
I am smitten only when bitten;
Give me one who'll bite me.

4TH MAN: If she's hoity-toity-toity—
Home she'll have to fly back.
She must love it—not be above it
When she's scratching my back.

[Dance]

OLD HAG: How sad it is to be Sing-Song Girl.
Each season she must be a spring-song Girl
How sad it is to be a Sing-Song Girl.

Hi-yi! Hi-yi!
Smile down this day on everyone,
Most honorable sun.
Love boat today! Hi-yi!
Come buy yourself a dancing maid—
Some dainty little jade.
She's bought up by the mandarin
For some house he has planned her in.*

*Alternate line:
For some harem he has planned her in.

And for the price he pays he can't go
    wrong.
Oh me! You see—
The Sing-Song Girl he buys her for a
    song.

NATIVES: We make the day a holiday.
A jolly-fol-de-roliday—
A jolly-fol-de-roliday—
The day the dancing Sing-Song Girls
    appear.
Hi-yi! Come buy! Come make your
    offer to the auctioneer.
If one attracts you awfully,
You bargain for her lawfully,
And she is at your beck and call for
    life.
Hi-yi! Come buy
A most enchanting unofficial wife.

WOMEN: She lives a life of idle dreams;
But not for her are bridal dreams.

MEN: She's purchased by the mandarin
For some house he has planned her
    in.

WOMEN: And tho' she be delectable,
We fear she's not respectable.

[*Manuscript breaks off here*]

I SPEAK ENGLISH NOW

Unfinished. No music is known to survive.

Hotsy-totsy! Heebie-jeebie! Ev'rything is jake!
Gonna cut myself a piece of cake—
I speak English now.

Mammy! Mammy! Alabammy! Yea bo! Step on
    high!
Gonna tell the cockeyed world that I
Speakee English now.

Kiss me quick! Don't hold out!
Bimbo, don't be highbrow;
When I kiss, victim shout,
"Mosquitoes! Eyebrows!"

Big boy, listen—If you love me, I love you and
    how!
You will always be my cat's meow,
'Cause I speak English now.

EAST IS WEST

Some notes for a song that would probably have been
titled "East Is West." No music is known to survive.

MING TOY: Oh, east is west
And good is bad
And silver is gold.
And night will be day.
Heat turn to cold.
Moon will be sun—
And two will be one.
Devil—angels—
If he'll return to me—
If all these things could be—
Then possibly he could love me.

SHOW GIRL, 1929

Tryout: Colonial Theatre, Boston, June 24, 1929. New
York run: Ziegfeld Theatre, opened July 2, 1929. 111
performances. Music mostly by George Gershwin. Lyrics
mostly by Gus Kahn and Ira Gershwin. Produced by
Florenz Ziegfeld. Book by William Anthony McGuire,
based on the novel by J. P. McEvoy. Book directed by
William Anthony McGuire. Dances staged by Bobby
Connolly. Ballets by Albertina Rasch. Orchestra under
the direction of William Daly. Orchestrations by Mau-
rice B. De Packh and William Daly. Cast, starring Ruby
Keeler (billed as Ruby Keeler Jolson) (Dixie Dugan),
Lou Clayton (Gypsy and Carpenter), Eddie Jackson
(Deacon and Electrician), and Jimmy Durante (Somber
Eyes and Snozzle, the Property Man), featured Joseph
Macaulay (Alvarez Romano), Barbara Newberry (Vir-
ginia Witherby and Sunshine), Eddie Foy, Jr. (Denny),
Kathryn Hereford (Bobby), Frank McHugh (Jimmy),
Doris Carson (Raquel), Blaine Cordner (Steve), Austin
Fairman (John Milton), Noel Francis (Peggy), Harriet
Hoctor (Première Danseuse), Nick Lucas, Duke Elling-
ton's band, and the Albertina Rasch Dancers.

All of Ira Gershwin's *Show Girl* lyrics were written in
collaboration with Gus Kahn.

HAPPY BIRTHDAY

Introduced by ensemble. While programs for *Show Girl*
state the show had an "opening," they do not reveal
whether it was anything other than an overture. As far as
is known, "Happy Birthday" was the first sung number
in the show.

Happy birthday, Miss Virginia;
All good wishes for today.
May your life be bright and merry
As the birds in May.
Miss Virginia, Queen of May—
All good wishes for today.

Eighteen years ago this morning,
Miss Virginia made her bow;
And this tiny rosebud is a
Lovely lady now.

Miss Virginia, make your bow.
You're a lovely lady now!
Lady now! Lady now!
Miss Virginia is a lovely lady now!

Happy birthday, Miss Virginia;
Gallant knights from all the land
Soon will gather 'round you pleading
For your heart and hand.
All good wishes for today;
Miss Virginia, Queen of May.

Ev'ryone make way!
Here comes Virginia;
She's eighteen today—
Sweet Miss Virginia.
Eighteen tiny candles gleaming meaning
    eighteen years.
(My! How the time does fly!)
Eighteen years of youthful dreaming, happiness,
    and fears.
(Oh, how they've hurried by!)
In the years hereafter
May your joy and laughter
Always multiply.
Eighteen tiny candles gleaming meaning
    eighteen years.
(Each year a happy song!)
Eighteen years of youthful dreaming, happiness,
    and fears.
(Oh, how they've rushed along!)

Here's to skies of blue—
Sweet Miss Virginia.
Like your eyes of blue—
Sweet Miss Virginia.

Now blow the candles!
Out go the candles!
Blow!

MY SUNDAY FELLA

Introduced by Barbara Newberry (Virginia) and girls.

VERSE

Ev'ry Sunday
When I go to meeting,
How my heart keeps beating—
I'm all aglow!
There's a sermon,
But my heart's not in it—
Thinking of the minute
I'll see my beau.
While the parson rambles on and on,
I never hear him talk;
I can only keep my mind upon
That homeward walk!

REFRAIN

Strolling underneath my new umbrella—
My Sunday fella and me;
He's my Prince and I'm his Cinderella—
My Sunday fella and me!
I know the good in me says, "Only meet him
    Sunday";
But oh! The bad in me just makes us meet on
    Monday—
And
Tuesday, Wednesday, Thursday, Friday,
    Saturday—
My Sunday fella and me!

HOW COULD I FORGET?

Introduced by Blaine Cordner (Steve) and Barbara Newberry (Virginia) in the Boston tryout. Dropped as a separate number before the New York opening but apparently included in the "Finaletto, Act I, Scene 1."

How could I forget
Once our eyes had met?

Dear one, tell me,
How could I forget?
Ev'ry breeze that blew
Spoke to me of you—
How could I forget?
Ev'ry songbird seemed to me
To sing about you;
Ev'ry sunset seemed to be
An empty dream without you.
Years could not erase
Dreams of your embrace—
How could I forget?

FINALETTO, ACT 1, SCENE 1

Introduced by ensemble.

Tell me, what has happened?
Sounded like a gun!
Tell me, what has happened?
Shall we stay or run?
Someone has fallen there!
He must be hurt!
Stand back and give him air!

[*spoken*]
It's Robert!

MAGNOLIA FINALE

Possibly introduced by ensemble as part of the "Finaletto, Act I, Scene 1," although it does not receive a separate listing in the program and may have been dropped before the New York opening.

Oh, happy wedding day;
Joy bells are ringing.
Oh, happy wedding day;
Songbirds are singing:
"Here comes the bride,
The happy groom right by her side.
He's a lucky fellow!"

Oh, happy wedding day;
Joy bells are ringing.
Oh, happy wedding day;

Songbirds are singing:
"Life is beginning—
Somebody's winning
Happiness and joy today."

People congregating
From ev'rywhere;
Minister is waiting;
Time to declare:
"I will love her
Now and ever;
Leave her never!"

Oh, Mr. Mendelssohn,
All through your doing,
Two hearts will beat as one—
Billing and cooing.

Joy bells are ringing,
Ring-ting-a-linging:
"What a happy wedding,
What a happy wedding,
What a happy wedding day today!"

LOLITA, MY LOVE

Introduced by Joseph Macaulay (Alvarez). Dropped within three weeks of the New York opening. Alternate title: "Lolita."

VERSE

'Twas a silver summer night,
My sweet Lolita,
When we gave our hearts in sweet surrender.
Maybe you've forgotten quite,
My sweet Lolita,
But you may recall my song so tender:

REFRAIN

Lolita, my love—
The evening shadows fall;
Lolita, my love—
I listen for your call.
Why so afraid,
Loveliest maid?
My serenade
Is for no other.
I strum my guitar;
Oh, listen to the plea:
Wherever you are
Is where I want to be.
Throw me a rose!

Give me a sign,
Lolita, my love,
That you are mine!

DO WHAT YOU DO!

Published July 1929. Introduced by Ruby Keeler (Dixie) and Frank McHugh (Jimmy). When Keeler left the show, "Dixie" was played by Doris Carson during the weeks of July 22 and July 29, 1929, and by Dorothy Stone beginning the week of August 5, 1929, at which time Carson resumed her original role—"Raquel." Stone played "Dixie" through the end of the run.

VERSE

I never knew love was so nice;
I never kissed anyone twice.
I never wanted a beau;
Poor me! I just didn't know.
You came along—I got a thrill;
One kiss from you—I feel it still.
Now each time you look my way
You're gonna hear me say:

REFRAIN

Come on and do what you do!
It seems so new, what you do!
It thrills me through, what you do;
So do what you do some more!

You know I love what you do!
Keep dreaming of what you do!
Don't be above what you do;
But do what you do some more!

Can't get enough of the kisses you throw me;
I need a big supply.
Give me the kisses you owe me—
Oh, me! Oh, my!

Do I adore what you do?
More and more and more and more what you
do!
I'm crazy for what you do;
So do what you do some more!

ONE MAN

Introduced by Barbara Newberry (Sunshine) and girls. Beginning the week of July 22, the number was performed by Newberry, Jimmy Durante (Snozzle), and girls.

VERSE

SUNSHINE: When I marry, if I marry,
I don't want an ordinary
Fellow like the fellows I have met.
GIRLS: So what do you want, then?
SUNSHINE: You won't hear me holler, "Oh, boy!"
When I spy a heavy-dough boy,
Though I know that money's hard to
get.
GIRLS: So what do you want, then?
SUNSHINE: Though I'm very well aware he is hard
to find,
Here's the kind I've always had in
mind!

REFRAIN

One man—
A six-foot-type sort of man—
A Dunhill-pipe sort of man—
A true Apollo
The girls all follow!
Wise—
With most adorable eyes—
With brains and vim,
But still just dumb enough to think
That I'm the right little girl for him!

SO ARE YOU!

Published July 1929. Introduced by Eddie Foy, Jr. (Denny), Kathryn Hereford (Bobby), and girls.

VERSE

When a fella
Tries to tell a
Girl what's in his heart,
He'd save a lot of time
If he could only rhyme.

Ev'ry girl loves
Hearing her love
Speak with poet's art.

For the lover who's afraid,
Here's a love song ready-made.

Greeting cards never miss!
Send your sweetheart this:

REFRAIN

The rose is red,
Violets are blue,
Sugar's sweet—
Sweetie, so are you!

Punkin' pie,
Apple dumplings, too,
Catch my eye—
Sweetie, so do you!

This may be a silly way
To put my case before you.
What I really mean to say
Is "I adore you!"

The rose is red,
Violets are blue,
Sugar's sweet—
So are you!

I MUST BE HOME BY TWELVE O'CLOCK

Published July 1929. Introduced by Ruby Keeler (Dixie) and girls.

VERSE

There is one at ev'ry party,
A girl with one thought in her dome.
Fun is fun, but she's that party
Who just keeps on saying, "I gotta go home!"
She will dance till dawn is breaking;
But ev'ry chance, this speech she's making:

REFRAIN

I'll say I'm having a hot time.
I'd stay, but I haven't got time.
I must be home by twelve o'clock!
That band is wicked, but brother,
You know I promised my mother
I must be home by twelve o'clock!
Bup-a-rup-a-rup-pup!
What's the name of that song?
Hear the trumpet blowing!

Bup-a-rup-a-rup-pup!
I'll be getting in wrong,
I'm positively going!
Oh, good grief! It's three in the morning!
Once more I'm giving you warning,
I must be home by twelve o'clock!

HARLEM SERENADE

Published July 1929. Introduced by Ruby Keeler (Dixie) and girls.

VERSE

From the Congo jungle it came,
A rhythm setting Harlem aflame.
Hear it once, you're never the same;
I'm referring to the Harlem Serenade.
New kind o' music and new kind o' time,
New kind o' rhythm and new kind o' rhyme.
I have seen again and again
The sanest of men
Go daffydil when
It's played.

REFRAIN

Take a taxi and go there;
You'll meet people you know there;
Where the trumpeters blow their
Harlem Serenade.
Say! When you enter this new world,
This particular blue world,
You'll begin
Giving in—
All your cares are mislaid.
Oh, stop! Look! Listen to that
Uptown jungle wail!
Book your passage to that
Harlem Congo Trail
Where ev'rybody is saying,
"Mr. Leader, keep playing
Nothing but that Harlem Serenade!"

HOME BLUES

Introduced by Joseph Macaulay (Alvarez). The music for the refrain is based on the famous blues theme of the tone poem *An American in Paris*. The music to the

verse is missing, and so far, musical detectives have been unable to show that it, too, is based on material from *An American in Paris*. Alternate title: "Home."

VERSE

An American in Paris—
On a holiday.
An American in Paris—
Just a boy at play.
'Mid the magic of the city,
'Mid the scene so gay,
He hears a voice a-calling over the sea,
The voice of Homeland saying, "Come back to me!"
It haunts him—
His thoughts go flying;
It haunts him—
His lonely heart is sighing:

REFRAIN

Home—
That's where the sunshine learned to shine;
Home—
A place that love has made divine;
So my eyes are turning
To where I left this yearning
Heart of mine.
Blues—
I get the blues when I'm away;
Blues—
I hear them calling night and day.
Going back forever—
Oh, never, never, never more to roam—
Your wand'ring boy is coming home!

FOLLOW THE MINSTREL BAND

Introduced by Eddie Jackson and Duke Ellington's band. Dropped from the show after the New York opening.

VERSE

Hey, folks! Say, folks!
Come on and hear a minstrel band!
Young folks! Old folks!
You'll want to cheer that minstrel band!
Come and hear 'em play
Songs you used to know;

Taking you away—
Back to long ago.
Keep all your symphony halls
When any minstrel band calls.

REFRAIN

Come on, there, sister!
Let me take you by the hand!
'Cause we just must follow the minstrel band!
Just listen, mister,
And you're bound to understand
Why we just must follow the minstrel band!
Oh, don't those slide trombones
Send a shiver through ya!
Silv'ry tones
Keep a-calling to ya:
"Hallelujah!"
My puppies blister,
But I find the walking's grand
When I just must, just must follow the minstrel band!

LIZA

Published July 1929. Alternate title: "Liza (All the Clouds'll Roll Away)." According to the Boston program, it was to have been introduced by Ruby Keeler (Dixie) and girls. George Gershwin recalled what actually happened: "Mr. Ziegfeld said, 'I would like to have a minstrel number in the second act with one hundred beautiful girls seated on steps that cover the entire stage.' This minstrel number was to be sung and danced by Ruby Keeler. So we went to work on a minstrel number and wrote 'Liza.' The show opened in Boston—and I think the last scene was rehearsed on the train going up. The first act went along fine. The second act came, and the attractive and talented Ruby Keeler appeared to sing and dance 'Liza.' Imagine the audience's surprise and mine when without warning, Al Jolson, who was sitting in the third row on the aisle, jumped up and sang a chorus of 'Liza' to his bride! Miss Keeler and he had just been married. It caused a sensation, and it gave the song a great start!" When *Show Girl* opened in New York, Nick Lucas was supposed to join Keeler and the girls in presenting "Liza," but during the first several days of the run, more often than not it was Jolson who partnered her in the number. By July 22, Jimmy Durante had taken over for Lucas. Then it was Joseph Macaulay (Alvarez Romano), Doris Carson (who had replaced Keeler), and the girls. In the final weeks of the run, "Liza" was performed by Buddy Doyle and Dorothy Stone.

VERSE

Moon shinin' on the river—
Come along, my Liza!
Breeze singin' through the treetops—
Come along, my Liza!
Somethin' mighty sweet I want to whisper sweet
    and low,
That you ought to know, my Liza!
I get lonesome, honey,
When I'm all alone so long;
Don't make me wait;
Don't hesitate;
Come and hear my song:

REFRAIN

Liza, Liza, skies are gray,
But if you smile on me
All the clouds'll roll away.

Liza, Liza, don't delay,
Come, keep me company,
And the clouds'll roll away.

See the honeymoon a-shinin' down;
We should make a date with Parson Brown.

So, Liza, Liza, name the day
When you'll belong to me
And the clouds'll roll away.

FEELING SENTIMENTAL

Published July 1929. Introduced during the Boston tryout by Joseph Macaulay (Alvarez) and Ruby Keeler
(Dixie). Dropped before the New York opening.

VERSE

One time I was as gay as a king;
Sailed about like a bird on the wing;
Ev'ry day had the gladness of spring;
My heart was free.
I looked into your eyes, little dreaming
What the future would be.
Now your smile is the sun to me;
Lady, what have you done to me?
I'm

REFRAIN

Feeling sentimental—
It isn't accidental,

But all because of you.
My eyes must be revealing
That sentimental feeling—
So sweet, so dear, so new!
When the sun goes down and the stars come out
And the moonbeams kiss the blue,*
Then the thought comes stealing through
That I should be kissing you, dear.
Feeling sentimental—
I long to see
You feeling sentimental for me.

STAGE DOOR SCENE

Intended for Joseph Macaulay (Alvarez), Eddie Foy, Jr.
(Denny), Barbara Newberry (Sunshine), Austin Fairman
(Milton), Noel Francis (Peggy), Ruby Keeler (Dixie),
Frank McHugh (Jimmy), and ensemble, with specialty
contributions by Harriet Hoctor and the Albertina
Rasch Dancers, and the team of Lou Clayton, Eddie
Jackson, and Jimmy Durante. Consisting largely of mu-
sical reprises with new lyrics, this number was either the
show's intended finale or a number late in Act II—just
before the finale. Probably unused.

ENSEMBLE: Although we're only the chorus,
          They're throwing big parties for us;
          We must be there by twelve o'clock!
          Our dancing may be attractive,
          But we don't really get active
          Till we go out at twelve o'clock!
          Bup-a-rup-a-rup-pup!
          What's the name of that song?
          Never mind, let's hurry!
          Bup-a-rup-a-rup-pup!
          Did we sing it all wrong?
          We're not gonna worry.
          And though the critics forget us,
          There's someone waiting to pet us—
          We must be there by twelve o'clock!

ALVAREZ: [Half chorus "Home Blues"]
HOCTOR
AND RASCH
  GIRLS: [Finish "Home Blues"]
DENNY
   AND
SUNSHINE: The rose is red,
          Violets are blue,

*Original version of refrain, line 8:
And the moonbeams kiss the sea,

I'm in love—
Sweetie, so are you!
We could share
A little four by two;
I'll be there—
Sweetie, so will you!

MILTON
   AND
PEGGY: This is where I settle down
       And leave the stage behind me;
       In our little kitchenette
       You'll always find me.

ALL: The rose is red,
     Violets are blue,
     We love love—
[to audience]
     So do you!
[Clayton, Jackson, and Durante sing a half
chorus of "Liza"]

DIXIE
   AND
JIMMY: When I hear you say, "I do!"
       Then all my dreams will come true.
       Come on and do say, "I do!"
       And do what you do some more!

I JUST LOOKED AT YOU

Intended for Eddie Foy, Jr. (Denny), and Ruby Keeler
(Dixie). Unused. Matched with the Ira Gershwin lyric
"Lady of the Moon," the music to the refrain had been
composed for *East Is West* (1928–29). The music was
reset one last time to Ira's lyric "Blah, Blah, Blah,"
introduced in the film *Delicious* (1931) and published.

VERSE

DENNY: "Love comes once to ev'ryone"—
       That's what I always read on the greeting
         cards.
       I'm not saying this for fun;
       This really comes from the heart:
       You won me right from the start.

REFRAIN 1

       I just looked at you;
       You just looked at me.
       Then and there I knew,
       It just had to be.
       When you smiled at me so sweetly,

You just swept me off my feet
   completely.
I just looked at you;
You just looked at me.
In your eyes of blue,
I could plainly see
You across the table ordering breakfast
   for two,
While you looked at me
Looking at you.

REFRAIN 2

DENNY: I'll just look at you;
   You'll just look at me
   In our four by two
   On Flatbush Avenue
DIXIE: Will you help me with the dishes?
DENNY: No, but you'll have my good wishes,
   My darling.
DIXIE: I'll learn how to cook.
DENNY: I don't like sardines.
DIXIE: I read in a book
   How to warm baked beans.
DENNY: And there's one thing, dearie, that I will
     promise to do:
   If *you* throw plates at me,
   I'll *throw* them at you.

MINSTREL SHOW

Probably intended to come directly after "Follow the
Minstrel Band." Unused. No music is known to survive.

Ladies and gentlemen, ladies and
   gentlemen,
We're about to start our minstrel
   show!
Ladies and gentlemen, ladies and
   gentlemen,
We're about to start our minstrel
   show!

Are you there? We are here!
Are you there? We are here!
Are you there? We are here!
Let's go!

We're not going to start our minstrel
   show
With "Hello, hello, hello!"
Because ev'ry other minstrel show
Starts, "Hello, hello, hello!"

Even the Vitaphone's making a hit
With "Hello, hello, hello!"
So to be different we'll omit
"Hello, hello, hello!"

Hello! Hello!
How are you tonight?
How are all the folks-es?
We feel sure that when
You hear all our jokes-es,
You will call again.
Hello! Hello!
Is everything all right?
Greetings, everybody—Hello, hello,
   hello!

JONES: Mr. Bones, Mr. Bones,
   How do you feel this evening, Mr.
     Bones?
   Explain it to me fully.

BONES: Mr. Jones, Mr. Jones,
   I'll be tickled to death to tell you, Mr.
     Jones.
   I feel just like a piece of roast beef;
   In fact, I'm feeling bully.

ENSEMBLE: He feels just like a piece of roast beef.
   In fact, he's feeling bully.
   He says he's feeling bully.
   He must be feeling bully.

Absolutely, positively bully!
Positively, absolutely bully!

BONES: I'm telling you now,
   Like the husband of the cow,
   I feel bully, bully, bully, bully.

ENSEMBLE: Ha-ha—He's feeling bully.

He might have had bronchitis,
The measles, or the mumps,
Or even tonsilitis
Or maybe even dandruff.

It might be laryngitis
Or rheumatism, too.
Perhaps appendicitis
Or possibly a—hangnail.

BONES: But no, I'm feeling bully.

My mother was a lady—
For breakfast she gave me farina.
For luncheon she gave me farina.
For dinner she gave me farina.
But for dessert,
What do you think my mother gave
   me?
Farina!
And that's why I feel bully.

JONES: But Mr. Bones, Mr. Bones,
   You're looking rather pale, Mr.
     Bones.
BONES: Oh, no, I'm feeling bully.
JONES: But Mr. Bones, Mr. Bones,
   You seem to be much thinner, Mr.
     Bones.
BONES: Oh, no, I'm feeling bully.
[*Through the next lines, Mr. Bones gets weaker
and weaker until, finally, he collapses*]

JONES: But Mr. Bones, Mr. Bones,
   Your knees are all a-quiver, Mr.
     Bones.
   Perhaps it is your liver, Mr. Bones.
   You're starting in to shiver, Mr.
     Bones.
BONES: Oh, no, I'm feeling bully!

TONIGHT'S THE NIGHT

Published (refrain only) June 1992 in the vocal selec-
tions from *Crazy for You*. Intended for *Show Girl*.
Unused. A piano-vocal arrangement was discovered in
1982 in the Warner Bros. Music warehouse in Secaucus,
New Jersey. Introduced on Broadway by ensemble in
Crazy for You (1992).

VERSE

Never drink, never smoke,
Never tell a naughty joke;
That's what I've been hearing all these years.

Never neck, never pet,
That is all I ever get;
It's no wonder I've been bored to tears.

Just why I should
Be oh so good
I can't make out.

I feel that I'm
Just losing time;
I must break out.

REFRAIN

I've just got a feeling:
Tonight's the night!
Let's tear down the ceiling—
Tonight's the night!
Take the chain and ball off—
From now on I'm free;

This is where I fall off
The family tree.
There's no fun in being an angel child;
I hear the call of the wild.
If the worst should happen, it serves me right—
Tonight's the night!

AT MRS. SIMPKIN'S FINISHING SCHOOL

Unused.

VERSE

We are pupils
At Mrs. Simpkin's School for Perfect Ladies,
Learning all the scruples
Without which you cannot be perfect ladies.
Entering society
Is our only aim;
Studying propriety
Fits us for the same.

REFRAIN

We are taught to walk with downcast eye,
And to think about the Golden Rule;
We must never, never, never see a man go by—
At Mrs. Simpkin's Finishing School.
We are taught to shun all manner of frivolity;
Singing hymns must be our only form of jollity.
You are guaranteed a manner full of charm, if you'll
Attend Mrs. Simpkin's School
For Perfect Ladies.

ADORED ONE

Music by George Gershwin. No. 87 in the George and Ira Gershwin Special Numbered Song File. Probably intended for Joseph Macaulay (Alvarez). Unused.

VERSE

Hark to the song of the lover
Singing a sweet serenade;

Hark to the song and discover
How lovers capture a maid.
In my Costuragura where love is supreme,
Moonlight and music make life one sweet dream.
Dear one, if I were your lover,
I'd sing this serenade:

REFRAIN

Adored one,
When the sun goes to rest—
Adored one,
'Tis the time I love best,
For soon, dear, 'mid the roses we'll stray;
The moon, dear, gently lighting the way.
Adored one,
In the silvery light
Of the soft summer night,
I'll sing to you.
Adored one,
From your window above,
Come down and hear my tender tale of love.

SOMEBODY STOLE MY HEART AWAY

Unused.

VERSE

I should feel oh, so flurried—
But I don't!
I should be getting worried—
But I won't!
I guess you know what's happening to me;
I've told it once or twice.
It started when I happened to see
Somebody oh—
Somebody so—
Somebody oh, so nice!

REFRAIN

Somebody stole my heart away—away—away.
Somebody stole my heart away—away—away.
Still, I'll do no weeping;
It's in safekeeping
When I'm awake or sleeping.
Once I was oh, so fancy-free—so free—so free;
Somebody made those eyes at me—at me—at me.

I don't care what occurs;*
She got mine, but I got hers,
When somebody stole my heart away.

I'M JUST A BUNDLE OF SUNSHINE

Unused. No music is known to survive.

VERSE

The world is full of trouble—
The world is full of woe—
And so to make it better,
I travel to and fro.
I peddle happy greeting cards
By ones and tons and dozens,
To help you cheer your paws and maws
Your uncles, aunts, and cousins.

REFRAIN 1

I'm just a bundle of sunshine;
I'm just a bundle of cheer.
Your mother is your best friend, after all—
Oh me, oh my, oh dear!
Pal of my heart, are you lonesome?
Why did you leave me to roam?
Won't you be my valentine?
There's no place like home.

I could sail the waters of all the world—
Bitter and wild and blue—
And never I'd find a friend to love
Like the friend I've found in you.

Oh, I'm just a seller of sunshine
With pretty thoughts in my dome—
Good-bye, good luck, God bless you!
There's no place like home!

REFRAIN 2

[Repeat refrain 1, lines 1–8]

I could walk down the roads of all the world
And knock on the doors forever,

*Alternate version of this and the next line (for female singer):
What a world this world is—
He got mine, but I got his,

And never I'd find a friend like you—
Never! Never! Never!

[*Repeat refrain 1, lines 13–16*]

SOMEONE'S ALWAYS CALLING A REHEARSAL

An unused ensemble number. No music is known to survive.

It makes no difference who you are—
Dancing girl or great big star—
Someone's always calling a rehearsal.
The seats are sold. The show's a hit.
But what has that to do with it?
Someone's always calling a rehearsal.
The call is ten a.m. That's just for spite;
For ten a.m.'s the middle of the night.
All other pleasures we're denied;
We're busy being glorified—
Someone's always calling a rehearsal.

I'M OUT FOR NO GOOD REASON TONIGHT

Unused. Possibly replaced with "I Must Be Home By Twelve O'Clock." No music is known to survive.

VERSE

I never stayed up late
'Cause my mother wouldn't let me;
She told me, sure as fate,
That the boogeyman would get me.
Never knew until tonight
How other people live;
Now I'm gonna do things right
If I'm not too inquisitive.

REFRAIN

Strike up the music and turn on the pep;
Get out my slippers—I'm ready to step!
I'm out for no good reason tonight!
Take up the carpets and throw out the chairs;
Neighbors complaining—but nobody cares!

I'm out for no good reason tonight!
How did I get this way?
What will the old folks say?
My conscience tells me I'm not acting right—
Not quite—But
Strike up the music and turn on the pep;
Get out my slippers—I'm ready to step!
I'm out for no good reason tonight!

HOME-LOVIN' GAL

Unused. No music is known to survive.

VERSE

I'm so tired of going places, doing things
With someone diff'rent every night;
Thinking of the lonesomeness the morning
    brings—
It doesn't seem right.
Just a little lovin' ev'ry now and then
Used to be a lot of fun,
But I don't want to have a lot of men—
I want one.

REFRAIN

I'm just a home-lovin' gal
Looking for a home-lovin' man;
Home-lovin' gal—
Built upon that old-fashioned plan.
Can't live alone—
Nature didn't make me that way;
Man of my own,
Am I gonna meet him someday?

I'll mend his shirts
If he's for me;
I'll even scrub the floor.
Give till it hurts
If he's the he
That I've been looking for.

Oh, home-lovin' pal,
If you want to sign up a home-lovin' gal,
Where are you—
Where are you—
Home-lovin' man of mine?

HOME-LOVIN' MAN

Either intended as a companion piece to "Home-Lovin' Gal" or written previous to it. The lyric is typed on Colonial Theatre, Boston, stationery. Unused. No music is known to survive.

VERSE

I'm so tired of going places, doing things
With someone different every night;
Thinking of the lonesomeness the morning
    brings—
It doesn't seem right.
Once I thought that going out to paint the town
With a crowd was lots of fun;
But now I'm satisfied to settle down
With just one.

REFRAIN

I'm just a home-lovin' man
Looking for a home-lovin' gal.
Home-lovin' man—
Looking for an old-fashioned pal.
Can't live alone—
Nature didn't make me that way;
Gal of my own,
Am I gonna find you someday?

I wouldn't mind
If she were tall
Or only five foot two.
If I could find
The one to call
"My coodgee-coodgee-coo."

Oh, home-lovin' gal,
If you want to sign up a home-lovin' man,
Where are you—
Where are you—
Home-lovin' gal of mine?

CASANOVA, ROMEO, AND DON JUAN

Intended for Joseph Macaulay (Alvarez). Unused. No music is known to survive.

VERSE

People say the lover today
Is not the lover of the Middle Ages.
That's not so, for how should they know
That my affairs would fill a thousand pages?
My technique makes women grow weak,
For I am one of history's greatest lovers.
Lucky miss, the lady I kiss,
A new world she discovers.

REFRAIN

Casanova, Romeo, and Don Juan—
None of them had anything on me.
Princesses and duchesses are clamorous,
Begging me to grow a little amorous.
Lady, you don't know how much you're
    missing

Till you sit on Alvarez's knee.*
Of lovers, there've been many men,
But there were never any men
Like Casanova, Romeo, and Don Juan—and
    me.

Alternate line:
I am dynamite and T.N.T.

OPPOSITE: *Paul McCullough and Bobby Clark*

Tryout: Shubert Theatre, Boston, December 25, 1929; Shubert Theatre, New Haven, January 6, 1930. New York run: Times Square Theatre, opened January 14, 1930. 191 performances. Music by George Gershwin. Produced by Edgar Selwyn. Book by Morrie Ryskind, based on the 1927 *Strike Up the Band* libretto by George S. Kaufman. Book staged by Alexander Leftwich. Dances staged by George Hale. Orchestra under the direction of Hilding Anderson. Cast, starring Bobby Clark (Colonel Holmes) and Paul McCullough (Gideon), featured Blanche Ring (Mrs. Grace Draper), Jerry Goff (Jim Townsend), Doris Carson (Anne Draper), Dudley Clements (Horace J. Fletcher), Gordon Smith (Timothy Harper), Margaret Schilling (Joan Fletcher), Robert Bentley (Richard J. Sloane), Ethel Kenyon (Myra Meade), and Red Nichols and his orchestra.

For the lyric to "I've Got a Crush on You," which in *Strike Up the Band* (1930) followed "Mademoiselle in New Rochelle," see *Treasure Girl* (1928). For the lyric to "Strike Up the Band," which in *Strike Up the Band* (1930) followed "Finaletto, He Knows Milk," see *Strike Up the Band* (1927).

FLETCHER'S AMERICAN CHOCOLATE CHORAL SOCIETY

Published in the complete piano-vocal score May 1930. Alternate title: "Opening, Act I." Introduced by Gordon Smith (Timothy), Robert Bentley (Sloane), Dudley Clements (Fletcher), and ensemble. The number is erroneously listed in programs as "Fletcher's American Chocolate Choral Society Workers." With a slightly different lyric, introduced in the 1927 version of *Strike Up the Band* as "Fletcher's American Cheese Choral Society."

WORKERS: La, la, singing ev'ry morning
When the clock is striking eight—
That's a duty that we never shirk.
We love singing ev'ry morning,
So we're never, never late
When we start our daily work.
We are Fletcher's American Chocolate
Choral Society,
Fletcher's American Chocolate Choral
Society.

Happy, happy workers, we,
Singing, singing merrily.
We love our vocal exercising.
Since efficiency's the thing,

They encourage us to sing:
We start the day by vocalizing.
Tra la la la la la—if we're happy,
Oh, tra la la la la la—work is snappy.
So if we seem rather gay
As we're working through the day—
You needn't find it too surprising.
Tra la la la, good morning, Mr.
Foreman!

TIMOTHY: Good morning!
The office boy, the doorman,
Those who really know,
Say I'm the finest foreman
Working for Fletcher and Co.
Our product, as represented,
Sets my heart aglow;
We've cows that are contented
Working for Fletcher and Co.

WORKERS: We're glad to know the cows are so
contented!
Tra la la la, good morning, Mr.
Manager!

SLOANE: Good morning!
Work, work, work—
That's all that I'm asking of you!
Never shirk, shirk, shirk—
But show me just what you can do!
On Saturday we pay off
The help in our employ;
On Sunday there's a day off
For ev'ry girl and boy;
Unless I am away off,
This job should be a joy.
I am telling you
There's little to do
But work, work, work!

WORKERS: With Sunday free, we all should be
contented.
And now our favorite boss you see—
An American institution!
The finest type of man is he—
Three cheers for evolution!
Fletcher! Fletcher! Fletcher!
Tra la la la, good morning, Mr.
Fletcher!

FLETCHER: Good morning!
My product is so nourishing,
The factory is flourishing.

TIMOTHY
AND
SLOANE: When Fletcher first began it, he
Was working for humanity.

WORKERS: His product is so nourishing,
The factory is flourishing!

When Fletcher first began it, he
Was working for humanity.

FLETCHER: Like Listerine and Woolworth,
Lux and B.V.D.,
The public gets its full worth
When it'll buy from me.

WORKERS: We sing his praises loudly
Ev'rywhere we go;
We tell the world we're proudly
Working for Fletcher and Co.

FLETCHER: Let's start the day
In the usual way
With a program that's habitual.
Before we part,
Suppose we start
To do the daily ritual:
I firmly believe—
WORKERS: I firmly believe—
FLETCHER: That Fletcher's American Chocolate—
WORKERS: That Fletcher's American Chocolate—
FLETCHER: Makes bigger and better citizens—
WORKERS: Makes bigger and better citizens—
FLETCHER: For the U.S.A.!
WORKERS: For the U.S.A.!

Tra la la la, we're off to work—
Tra la la la, we're off to work.

I MEAN TO SAY

Published December 1929 and in the complete piano-vocal score May 1930. Introduced by Doris Carson (Anne) and Gordon Smith (Timothy).

VERSE

ANNE: Haven't you a lot of things to say to
me?
TIMOTHY: Feel a little dumb,
Words just will not come.
ANNE: Won't you make December seem like
May to me?
TIMOTHY: How can I impart
All that's in my heart?
ANNE: If you'd only make your feelings clear
to me.
TIMOTHY: Gosh, I'll do my darndest, lend an ear
to me:

REFRAIN

TIMOTHY: I mean to say,
I mean to say—

ANNE: You mean?

TIMOTHY: It's plainly seen,
My dear,
That I, that you,
That you, that I—

ANNE: That we?

TIMOTHY: Oh, I'm so green,
My dear.

Why, oh, why must I keep
Stuttering like this?
Muttering like this?

ANNE: Fluttering like this.

TIMOTHY: I mean to say—

ANNE: You mean
You love me?

TIMOTHY: That's it,
That's what I mean, my dear.

TYPICAL SELF-MADE AMERICAN

Published in the complete piano-vocal score May 1930.
Introduced by Dudley Clements (Fletcher), Jerry Goff
(Jim), and ensemble. A few lines were altered from the
version used in the 1927 *Strike Up the Band*, and the
encore is new.

INTRODUCTION

FLETCHER: While other lads were trying out the
bicycle
Or pitching pennies on the parlor
floor,
Their pleasures left me colder than an
icicle,
For I knew what I was predestined
for!

CHORUS: Yes, he knew what he was predestined
for!

FLETCHER: I got a job and worked both day and
night at it;
And all the day I never watched the
clock.
The big boss thought I was so very
bright at it
That when I poisoned him he left me
all the stock.
I was there when opportunity came to
knock!

VERSE 1

JIM: Like a hero in an Alger novel
He was born and brought up in a
hovel;

FLETCHER: Though I often had to face disaster,
I would always prove myself the
master.

CHORUS: He would always prove himself the
master!

FLETCHER: I'm a man of very quick decision,
For I always had the gift of vision.

JIM: He upholds the country's
Constitution,
And he hates the Russian Revolution!

CHORUS: How he hates the Russian Revolution!
He upholds the country's laws
Because, because, because, because:

REFRAIN 1

FLETCHER: I am a typical self-made American;
I've been a go-getter ever since life
began.
In a modest way, I feel
I am basically sound—
With my shoulder to the wheel
And my two feet on the ground!

ALL: I am/He is a typical, typical, typical
self-made American!

VERSE 2

FLETCHER: From the lowest of the ranks I've
risen!

JIM: Now both honor and success are his'n!

FLETCHER: Always fighting for the small
consumer—

JIM: And now tell 'em of your sense of
humor—

CHORUS: Of your devastating sense of humor.

FLETCHER: I'm a Mason, and an Elk, and
Woodman—

JIM: Which unquestionably shows a good
man!

FLETCHER: I've been very good to dear old
Mother.

CHORUS: So we'll never work for any other.
We don't care to work for any other!
And we give him our applause
Because, because, because, because:

REFRAIN 2

CHORUS: He is a typical self-made American!

FLETCHER: With wheat cakes for breakfast,
cornflakes and lots of bran.
I'm as good a man, I feel,

As a ruler who is crowned—
With my shoulder to the wheel
And my two feet on the ground!

ALL: I am/He is a typical, typical, typical
self-made American!

ENCORE VERSE

FLETCHER: Though my clothes from London are
imported—

JIM: And Italian cars alone he's sported—
Though he gets his liquor from
Bermuda—

FLETCHER: And my secretary's a Yehudah—

CHORUS: And his secretary's a Yehudah!

FLETCHER: Though they tell me that my nose is
Grecian—
And my drinking glasses are
Venetian—
Though I've ribbons from the king of
Siam—
What a patriotic Yankee I am!

CHORUS: What a patriotic Yank that guy am!
And his health we hereby toast;
We toast, we toast, and boast, and
boast:

ENCORE REFRAIN

He is a typical self-made American!
Where in the world could you show
us a nobler man?

FLETCHER: In a modest way, I feel
I'm as solid as a rock;
I made Mother my ideal,
And I never watched the clock.

ALL: I am/He is a typical, typical, typical
self-made American!

SOON

Published December 1929 and in the complete piano-
vocal score May 1930. Introduced and reprised by Jerry
Goff (Jim) and Margaret Schilling (Joan). The music to
the verse came from the verse of "Hoping that Someday
You'd Care" of the 1927 version of *Strike Up the Band*.
The music to the refrain originated in the 1927 show's
"Finaletto, Act I."

In the original version of *Strike Up the Band* there was
a longish Act I finale which wound up with the title
song, "Strike Up the Band." At one point in this fifteen-
minute musical sequence, Jim, our hero, publicly de-

nounced the use of Grade B milk in the manufacture of Fletcher's Chocolate Products.* Jim's girl friend, Joan Fletcher, denied the allegation about her father and, to a tune somewhat aria-like, sang:

Jim—how could you do such a thing?
Oh, Jim!—Unworthy of you such a thing!

This four-bar bit of melody intrigued some of our friends, who kept insisting this strain could be the basis of a song. We didn't disagree. So, for the new version of the show two and one half years later—"Soon."
—from *Lyrics on Several Occasions*

VERSE

JIM: I'm making up for all the years
That I waited;
I'm compensated
At last.
My heart is through with shirking;
Thanks to you it's working
Fast.
The many lonely nights and days
When this duffer
Just had to suffer
Are past.
JOAN: Life will be a dream song;
Love will be the theme song.

REFRAIN 1

JIM: Soon—the lonely nights will be ended;
Soon—two hearts as one will be blended.
I've found the happiness I've waited for:
The only girl that I was fated for.
Oh! Soon—a little cottage will find us
Safe, with all our cares far behind us.
The day you're mine this world will be in tune.
Let's make that day come soon.

REFRAIN 2

JOAN: Soon—my dear, you'll never be lonely;
Soon—you'll find I live for you only.
When I'm with you who cares what time it is,
Or what the place or what the climate is?
Oh! Soon—our little ship will come sailing
Home, through every storm, never failing.

*I.G. misremembered. The product in question in the 1927 show was cheese, not chocolate.

BOTH: The day you're mine this world will be in tune.
Let's make that day come soon.

A MAN OF HIGH DEGREE and THE UNOFFICIAL SPOKESMAN

These linked numbers published in the complete piano-vocal score May 1930. "A Man of High Degree," also titled "Entrance of Colonel Holmes," was introduced by Bobby Clark (Holmes), Dudley Clements (Fletcher), Paul McCullough (Gideon), and ensemble. "The Unofficial Spokesman" was introduced by Clark and ensemble. "Wizard of the Age," which bookended these numbers in the 1927 version of *Strike Up the Band*, was not used in 1930.

ALL: Tra la la la, Good morning, Mr. Colonel!
HOLMES: Good morning!

FLETCHER: He's joined so many diff'rent societies
He has degrees of ninety-nine varieties!

GIDEON: He's an E-L-K—
ALL: And an S-A-P—
GIDEON: And an F.P.A.
ALL: And a K.C.B.
HOLMES: With my P's and Q's
And my I.O.U.s—
ALL: He emphatically shows
That no matter where he goes,
From A B C
To X Y Z,
He's a man of very high degree—
He's a man of very high degree!
WOMEN: Very high!
MEN: Not low!
WOMEN: Very high!
MEN: Not low!
WOMEN: High!
MEN: Low!
WOMEN: High!
MEN: Low!
WOMEN: High!
MEN: Low!
ALL: Degree!

VERSE

HOLMES: When I was born into this universe
(By a process which I do not care to mention),
I never once said "Goo-goo!" to my nurse,
Which was quite beyond the lady's comprehension.
I found I drew attention being silent;
And that is how my rise to fame occurred.
Great dignity to politics soon I lent
By never, never uttering a word.
ALL: He never said a thing that was absurd,
Because, you see, he never said a word.

REFRAIN

HOLMES: I'm the unofficial, unofficial
Spokesman of the U.S.A.
Though to interview me, interview me,
All reporters do essay,
If I tell 'em nothing, tell 'em nothing,
How can I be blundering?
And I find it helpful, very helpful
Just to keep 'em wondering.
Like a Massachusetts, Massachusetts resident
Who once became a, once became a president,
I never, never, never, never say a word!

THREE CHEERS FOR THE UNION and THIS COULD GO ON FOR YEARS

Published in the complete piano-vocal score May 1930. These linked numbers comprise the "Patriotic Rally," also titled "Opening, Act I, Scene Three." Introduced by the ensemble. This lyric is taken, with only minor alterations, from the "Patriotic Rally" number of the 1927 *Strike Up the Band*.

ENSEMBLE: We're all here for a rally,
So, patriots, get pally—
Three cheers for the Union!
Siss for the Swiss!
Oh, isn't it exciting!
There may be lots of fighting.

Three cheers for the Union!
Siss for the Swiss!

Oh, isn't it grand! This wonderful
    land
Will show 'em the stuff it's made of;
We're ready to go to prove to the foe
There's nobody we're afraid of!
We're all here for a rally,
So, patriots, get pally—
Three cheers for the Union!
Siss for the Swiss!

Land of Washington and Lincoln,
    Henry Ford and Morris Gest,
Land of Franklin, land of
    Monroe—men who stood the test!
Land of Jefferson and Adams,
    Dempsey and Ben Turpin, too,
Andrew Jackson, Woodrow
    Wilson—all red, white, and blue!
Land of Cabot, land of Abbott,
Land of Edwin Booth,
Admiral Dewey, "Lefty" Louie,
And "Bambino" Ruth.
We could go on naming great men,
    but we have our fears—
This could go on for years!

Land of Ginsberg and O'Reilly, Fazio
    and Abie Cohn,
Leffingwell and Fenevessi—How this
    land has grown!
Land of Schmaltz and Guggenheimer,
    Rufus Rastus Jackson, too,
Land of Big Chief Muddy
    Waters—patriots all through!
Land of Minsky and Rumshinsky,
Land of Donahue—
Land of Johnson and Yon Yonson,
And of Ching Ling Foo.
We could go on naming Americans,
    but we have our fears—
This could go on for years!

IF I BECAME THE PRESIDENT

Published in the complete piano-vocal score May 1930. Introduced by Blanche Ring (Mrs. Draper) and Bobby Clark (Colonel Holmes). The Ira and Leonore Gershwin Trusts possess three pages of lyrics that Bobby Clark wrote and suggested as alternates.

The references to Prohibition and to newspaper mogul W. R. Hearst make this, from today's viewpoint, a period piece. I do like, though, going not so far afield as Tyler, Polk, or Gar-a-field. But there was more than appears above.

One day in the Boston tryout Bobby Clark, unfortunately for me, came up with four penciled pages of new lyrics (which I still have) he himself had written for possible encores. I shuddered when I saw them. No actor had ventured to change or add to my lyrics before this; besides, these were pretty terrible, with rhymes like "cellar—vanilla" (some weren't bad: "decorum—floor-um"). Since Bobby was one of the great comedians in an era when three or four top ones ruled the musical-comedy roost, management asked me to go along with him as far as possible. I was able to make some corrections and to cut the encores down to two; but unable to do anything with some lines he insisted on. My favorite couplet of his:

And just to show we're home-like
We'll bathe in the Potomac.

P.S. Imperfect rhymes or not, I am unhappy to report that his lines received as many chuckles as did mine.
—from *Lyrics on Several Occasions*

VERSE 1

MRS. DRAPER: If I made you the ruler
    Of this great democracy—
HOLMES: Then I'd make you First Lady,
    Which is reciprocity.
MRS. DRAPER: Imagine how delightful life
    Will be when we're on top.
HOLMES: Just think! No matter where we'd
    go
    They'd make the traffic stop.
BOTH: We'd beat King Solomon in all his
    glory.
    Oh, ev'rything would be just
    hunky-dory.

REFRAIN 1

HOLMES: If I became the President—
MRS. DRAPER: And I were the President's wife—
BOTH: We'd shake the hand of ev'ryone
    we'd see.
HOLMES: We could receive ambassadors—
MRS. DRAPER: The kind the upper class adores—
BOTH: And have the whole Supreme Court
    down for tea.
HOLMES: I'll talk on trade conditions—
MRS. DRAPER: We'll open expositions—
BOTH: And proudly march behind the
    drum and fife.
MRS. DRAPER: Oh, it thrills me just to tell of it!

HOLMES: We both would be on vel-a-vit—
    If I became the President—
MRS. DRAPER: And I were the President's wife.

VERSE 2

MRS. DRAPER: Dear, anytime that we'd need
    money
    We'd call up the Mint.
HOLMES: I'd tell them that I must try out
    The samples that they print.
MRS. DRAPER: Would you cut down your drinking
    When you're with the Ship of
    State?
HOLMES: I'd cut down on the water
    And I'd take my whiskey straight.
MRS. DRAPER: You mustn't chase around when
    you're the Prexy.
HOLMES: It's not my fault if women think
    I'm sexy.

REFRAIN 2

HOLMES: If I became the President—
MRS. DRAPER: And I were the President's wife—
BOTH: For four years down in Washington
    we'd camp.
MRS. DRAPER: The joys of domesticity
    Would bring us great publicity.
HOLMES: I'd have my picture on a postage
    stamp.
MRS. DRAPER: If Zanzibar grew tricky—
HOLMES: Or Russian Bolsheviki—
BOTH: There'd be no braver man in all the
    strife.
MRS. DRAPER: But to guard the Chief
    Executive—*
HOLMES: I'd get a big de-tec-a-tive,
    If I became the President—
MRS. DRAPER: And I were the President's wife.

REFRAIN 3

HOLMES: If I became the President—
MRS. DRAPER: And I were the President's wife—
    You'd flood the Senate with your
    orat'ry.
HOLMES: I'd make each politish-i-on
    Prohibit Prohibish-i-on—
BOTH: A hundred million drinkers would
    be free.

Alternate version of refrain 2, lines 10–13:
HOLMES: But I won't become your pappy till
    You get me in the cap-i-till,
    And I become the President—
MRS. DRAPER: And I am the President's wife.

HOLMES: I'd grow a beard, I'm thinkin'.
MRS. DRAPER: You'd be as great as Lincoln,
And Mister Hearst would surely
print your life.
HOLMES: But I'd never go so far afield
As Tyler, Polk, or Gar-a-field—
If I became the President—
MRS. DRAPER: And I were the President's wife.

HANGIN' AROUND WITH YOU

Published December 1929 and in the complete piano-vocal score May 1930. Introduced by Doris Carson (Anne) and Gordon Smith (Timothy). Alternate title: "What's the Use of Hangin' Around with You?"

VERSE 1

ANNE: Once you would hang around me,
Hang 'round me night and day;
I thought that love had found me
When we became that way.

Now it's a diff'rent story;
You're not a one-girl man;
I've heard you're in your glory
Playing the Dapper Dan.
You may tell me you're a saint
But listen to my complaint:

REFRAIN 1

What's the use of hanging around with
you,
Hanging around with you,
Hanging around with you, dearie?
I never know, I never know just where
I stand.

What's the use of banging around with
you,
Banging around with you,
Banging around with you, dearie?
You've got to give this little girl a
bigger hand.

You're not acting the beau
That I once used to know.
I'm beginning to see
That I'm likely to be
On the shelf.

If you want me hanging around with
you,

Hanging around with you,
Hanging around with you, dearie,
You've got to learn, you've got to learn
to be yourself.

VERSE 2

TIMOTHY: I simply must deny it;
I swear it isn't true.
My heart is on a diet,
Darling, except for you.

When I'm with the other damsels,
Really I don't go far;
I try to tell those mam'selles
Just what a peach you are.
Oh, I'm so misunderstood
Though I've tried to be so good.

REFRAIN 2

What's the use of hanging around with
you,
Hanging around with you,
Hanging around with you, dearie?
I never know, I never know just where
I'm at.

What's the use of banging around with
you,
Banging around with you,
Banging around with you, dearie?
Oh, I'm afraid you're forcing me to
leave you flat.

ANNE: Please don't be in a huff;
It was only a bluff.
Ev'rything is in vain
If you mean to remain
So upstage.

TIMOTHY: If you want me hanging around with
you,
Hanging around with you,
Hanging around with you, dearie,
You've got to learn, you've got to learn
to act your age.

Unused Reprise

TIMOTHY: What's the use of hanging around with
you,
Hanging around with you,
Hanging around with you, dearie?
Why must I wait till Mother gets
herself a man?

What's the use of banging around with
you,
Banging around with you,

Banging around with you, dearie?
I'm getting old—you know I'm not a
Peter Pan!

ANNE: Please don't be in a huff;
I've got troubles enough.
Though Mamma's in the way,
She's not likely to stay
On the shelf.

BOTH: If you want me hanging around with
you,
Hanging around with you,
Hanging around with you, dearie,
You've got to learn, you've got to learn
to be yourself.

HE KNOWS MILK

Published in the complete piano-vocal score May 1930. Introduced by Jerry Goff (Jim), Margaret Schilling (Joan), Robert Bentley (Sloane), Dudley Clements (Fletcher), Bobby Clark (Holmes), and ensemble. This number is virtually identical to the "Finaletto, Act I" of the 1927 version, with a few altered lyrics and one section deleted at the end.

JIM: Stop! What is this mischief you're
doing?
Stop! Reflect, consider, and pause!
Can't you see this trouble you're
brewing
Won't be in a worthy cause?

FLETCHER
AND
SLOANE: Be careful of a trick!
He's just a Bolshevik!

CHORUS: We will fight for all we hold dear, sir!
JIM: But I say this war is a fake!
FLETCHER: Why the hell must you interfere, sir?
CHORUS: Fletcher's reputation is at stake!

JIM: Fellow countrymen, lend me your ears
for a minute.
MEN: If you have anything important to say,
better begin it.

JIM: Folks, I was born
Down on a farm—
There 'midst the corn,
Far from all harm—
I learned about
Cows and their ilk,
So, my friends, I know milk!
CHORUS: He knows milk!

JIM: Some men are butchers;
Some men are bakers;
Some specialize as
Candlestick makers—
Some, cloaks and suits—
Some men know silk—
I, my friends, I know milk!

CHORUS: He knows milk!
You may know milk, but tell us more!
What the devil has that got to do with
war?
What the devil has that got to do with
war?

JIM: I'd go to war
For choc'late I could trust,
But never for
A cause so unjust—
For I'm afraid—
Listen to me!—
This choc'late's made,
Fletcher's Choc'late's made
Of milk—Grade B!

CHORUS: Not A?
JIM: No. B!
CHORUS: Not A?
JIM: No. B!
Oh, my friends, I know milk!
CHORUS: He still knows milk!

FLETCHER,
SLOANE,
AND
HOLMES: No, no! Nay, nay!
We're here to say
It is Grade A.
We always use the best ingredients!

JIM: Here today
You hear me say
It's not Grade A!
You're using Grade B for expedience!

CHORUS: He says they do not use the best
ingredients,
But that they're using Grade B for
expedience;
And Fletcher told us that when he
began it, he
Was making chocolate to help
humanity!
He says they do not use the best
ingredients,
But that they're using Grade B for
expedience;
And Fletcher told us that when he
began it, he
Was making chocolate to help
humanity!

Maybe he is telling us the truth!
Maybe he is telling us the truth!

JOAN: Jim, how could you do such a thing?
Oh, Jim, unworthy of you, such a
thing!
Just look at my father and see
He'd never use Grade B.

JIM: Joan, I had to do such a thing—
Oh, Joan—the moment I knew such a
thing!
My conscience and I both agree
The milk is still Grade B.

FLETCHER: To me the whole thing simply is
ridiculous—
My honor has been struck an awful
blow.
The populace knows I am too
meticulous.
I'd never stoop to do a thing so low!

CHORUS: He'd never stoop to do a thing so
low—
He'd never stoop to do a thing so
low—
And you're a very dirty so-and-so!
FLETCHER: A very dirty so-and-so-and-so!
CHORUS: While he is a typical self-made
American.
JIM: He is a true, profiteering American.
FLETCHER: I've made a pure product ever since I
began.
JIM: He'll get us all into war if he works
his plan.

CHORUS: In 'most ev'ry way, we feel,
He is basically sound—
With his shoulder to the wheel
And his two feet on the ground.
He is a typical, typical, typical
self-made American!

JOAN: Alas! Alackaday! Unlucky me!
My hero and my father can't agree.
Oh listen, all, I make it known
That I'm engaged to Mr. Sloane!
CHORUS: Hooray for you and Sloane and
liberty!

Yes, yes, we say,
He'll have to pay!
He's in the way!
With propaganda he's been fillin' us!
He's a fake—
And no mistake;
His neck we'll break!
Whoever heard of one so villainous?
He says that we use Grade B for
expedience!

We'll teach him soon the meaning of
obedience!
We're all crusading for a cause that's
glorious,
And who the hell is he to be
censorious?

IN THE RATTLE OF THE BATTLE and MILITARY DANCING DRILL

These linked numbers, whose collective alternate title is "Opening, Act II," were published in the complete piano-vocal score May 1930. "Military Dancing Drill" had been published separately in September 1927. Both numbers were introduced by the ensemble. Though the refrain of this version of "Military Dancing Drill" is identical to that of the 1927 song, the verse here is new.

SOLDIERS: Yankee doo doodle-oo doodle-oo,
We'll come through doodle-oo
doodle-oo,
For the red, white, and blue
doodle-oo,
Lend a hand!
With our flag unfurled,
We can lick the world!
Hey, leader!
Strike up the band!

In the rattle
Of the battle,
We will shoot them down like cattle
For their dirty tittle-tattle!
Yes, sir! All of 'em!

We are haters
Of dictators!
We are freeborn legislators!
Boy! We'll grab those foreign
traitors
And make small of 'em!

We will wreck 'em;
We'll henpeck 'em;
And with lilies we'll bedeck 'em!
We will do this just to check 'em
From atrocities.

When we've carted
Their departed,
And their land is brokenhearted,
They'll be sorry that they started
Animosities!

They'll be sorry that they started
Animosities!

VERSE

SWISS GIRLS: Soldier, soldier!
Listen, do!
We have been looking long for you.
Oh, show us, show us
If you will—
Your military dancing drill.

SOLDIERS: Ladies, ladies!
How-de-do!
We have been looking long for you.
Oh, please believe us,
It's a thrill
To show our military drill.

REFRAIN

Soldier, advance!
Then heave a sigh.
Here comes romance—
Never say die!
Ding, ding-a-derry,
That military
Dancing drill!
If she is cute,
If she appeals—
Soldier, salute!—
Clicking the heels!
She'll love it, oh boy!
Doing the doughboy
Dancing drill!
Throw out your chest,
Try to look at your best—
Full of splendor;
Ev'ry mother's daughter,
If you're looking as you oughter,
Will surrender.
Properly done,
Right from the start—
Soldier, you've won:
You've captured her heart!
Doing the very
Gay, military
Dancing drill!

MADEMOISELLE IN NEW ROCHELLE

Published January 1930 and in the complete piano-vocal
score May 1930. Introduced by Bobby Clark (Holmes),

Paul McCullough (Gideon), and ensemble. Alternate
title: "Mademoiselle from New Rochelle."

VERSE

HOLMES
AND
GIDEON: Little lady, as you stand before me,
You remind me
Of the little girl I left behind me.

Holding hands with you would never
bore me;
What a torso!
Like my gal in New Rochelle, but more
so!

GIRLS: Sir, where do you get this "you and
me" stuff?

HOLMES
AND
GIDEON: How about that "hands across the sea"
stuff?
Sweetness, if you think you could adore
me,
I'll forget about the gal back home.

REFRAIN 1

I left my mademoiselle in New Rochelle,
But what the hell!
You'll do as well.
I left my mademoiselle in New Rochelle,
But truth to tell,
You're twice as swell!
I love your lips!
Oh boy! What hips!
When I observe
Each lovely curve
Then I declare—
Yes, I can swear,
I'm glad I'm here "Over There."
Oh, lady, if you could learn to play
mammah
For zizz papah,
Then, what the hell!
I'll never go back again to New Rochelle!

REFRAIN 2

I left my mademoiselle in New Rochelle,
But what the hell!
You'll do as well.
I left my mademoiselle in New Rochelle,
But truth to tell,
You're twice as swell!
I love your knees!
I love your toes!
I love your these!

I love your those!
I'll say you're there,
Yes, I can swear,
I'm glad you're there over here.
A Wiener schnitzel if you can cook for
me—
And fricassee—
Then, what the hell!
I'll never go back again to New Rochelle!

HOW ABOUT A BOY?

Published in the complete piano-vocal score May 1930.
Introduced by Dudley Clements (Fletcher), Bobby
Clark (Holmes), Paul McCullough (Gideon), Blanche
Ring (Mrs. Draper), and ensemble. Alternate title: "How
About a Boy Like Me?" This song replaced "How About
a Man?" from the 1927 Strike Up the Band, and for a
time some of the additional refrains from the first "How
About" were used as patter-encore material for "How
About a Boy?" in Strike Up the Band (1930). Yet this is
an entirely different song.

VERSE

FLETCHER,
HOLMES,
AND GIDEON: Lady, look at me,
And you must agree
I'm the man for you.

MRS. DRAPER: Which one of the three
Shall my lover be?
MEN: I'm the man for you!

I've seen foreign beauties;
I've seen Follies cuties;
But when all is said and done,
There can be no other.
Will you be my mother
And my baby rolled in one?
Loving dreams of you I've always
carried;
Don't you think it's time that we
got married?

REFRAIN 1

MEN: How about a boy like me
For a girl like you?
Oh, how happy I could be
With a girl like you!

Give yourself a break;
Cut yourself a piece of wedding
cake!

How about a boy like me
For a girl like you?

REFRAIN 2

How about a boy like me
For a girl like you?
Oh, how happy I could be
With a girl like you!

You'll make no faux pas,
If you let me be your Sonny Bwah!
How about a boy like me
For a girl like you?

REFRAIN 3

[to Holmes]
MRS. DRAPER: I've been looking high and low
For a boy like you;
[to Gideon]
And I never could say no
To a boy like you.

Tho' I'm thirty-six,*
Still I have my little bag of tricks;
[to Fletcher]
I'd have left home long ago
For a boy like you.

REFRAIN 4

HOLMES: How about a man who could be a
cavalier
To a girl like you?
[Courtly gestures]
GIDEON: How about a man who can stand
upon his ear
For a girl like you?
[Tries it]
FLETCHER: How about a man who's six feet
tall?
[Stands on toes]
HOLMES: How about a man who's five feet
small?
[Crouches]
ALL: How about a man like me
For a girl like you?

REFRAIN 5

HOLMES: How about a man who'll recite like
Edwin Booth
For a girl like you?
[Shakespearean quotation]

*Alternate version of refrain 3, lines 5–6:
I am twenty-eight,
And it's time that I got me a mate.

GIDEON: How about a man sang soprano in
his youth
For a girl like you?
[Starts Pagliacci]
FLETCHER: How about a man who's strong as
steel?
[Tries to lift her]
HOLMES: How about a man with sox appeal?
[Shows sock and kicks Fletcher]
ALL: How about a man like me
For a girl like you?

REFRAIN 6

HOLMES: How about a man who can play the
piccolo
For a girl like you?
[Plays]
GIDEON: How about a man who can do the
"Heel and Toe"
For a girl like you?
[Dances]
FLETCHER: How about a man who's full of
pash?
[Tries to embrace her]
HOLMES: How about a man who wears a
mustache?
[Puts on false mustache]
ALL: How about a man like me
For a girl like you?

OFFICIAL RÉSUMÉ

Published in the complete piano-vocal score May 1930.
Introduced by ensemble.

WOMEN: Stop! We want a little attention!
Stop! Unless you want us to shout.
There are some things we'd like to
mention—
As, for instance, what this show's
about.

If you slept through our show, 'twill
only take a minute*
To tell you ev'rything that happened
in it.

First, there was Fletcher—
Chocolate he made;
The Swiss made it also

*In the published piano-vocal score, this line is:
If you follow us, 'twill only take a minute

So Fletcher was afraid.
Then there was Sloane—
The villain in the play—
Using milk Grade B
And calling it A.
PIT
ORCHESTRA: He knows milk.*
WOMEN: Fletcher raised the tariff;
Switzerland was sore.
One thing and another
Soon led to war.
Then there was Jim;
Then there was Joan. (Heigh ho.)
He liked milk
But he didn't like Sloane.
PIT
ORCHESTRA: He still knows milk.†
WOMEN: So here was Jim and there was Joan
And Fletcher and Sloane,
In complications rather curious.
Jim loved Joan and Fletcher trusted
Sloane,
And as we've shown,
There came a war in tempo furious.

You've seen how Fletcher won the
war—
A war that had no equal.
Be patient just a minute more
And see the happy sequel.

See Mr. Fletcher lose his heart;‡
See Anne now wed to Timmy;
And what was certain from the start—
Miss Joan give in to Jimmy.

And now we find we're very near
The end to which we're heading;
And so we want you all to hear
The theme song of the wedding:
Rum ta ta tum tum tum!

RING-A-DING-A-DING-DONG DELL

Published in the complete piano-vocal score May 1930.
Introduced by ensemble. Alternate title: "Ding-Dong."

*In the published piano-vocal score, this line is:
He lied about milk.
†In the published piano-vocal score, this line is:
He didn't like Sloane.
‡This and the next eight lines (through "Rum ta ta
tum tum tum!") are not in the published piano-vocal
score.

An earlier version, entitled "Bring on the Ding Dong Dell," was dropped from *Oh, Kay!* (1926).

REFRAIN

Hear the bells in the belfry go ding-dong;
They are ringing for Jim and for Joan.
"Be gay today," they're singing;
For girl and boy a message of joy they're
     bringing.
Sweet is the beat of the ding-dong;
What a glorious story they tell—
The news they're sending about that happy
     ending—
Oh, ring-a-ding-a-ding-dong dell!

INTERLUDE

Keep the trumpeter blowing,
Tell the world the good news,
While the people keep throwing
Tons of rice and old shoes.
Clear the way; make room
For the very happy bride and groom.

REPEAT REFRAIN

THERE NEVER WAS SUCH A CHARMING WAR

Introduced during the Boston engagement of the tryout by Jerry Goff (Jim) and female ensemble. Dropped before the New York opening. The lyric is adapted from the 1927 version's "Oh, This Is Such a Lovely War."

JIM: Oh, gather 'round me, ladies;
     I'll tell you about the war—

GIRLS: Oh, tell us about the war!

JIM: The war that's taken me over there.
     I'll tell you about the war—
     There never was such a charming war;
     It keeps me out in the open air!

     Oh boy! We get three meals a day and all
          our clothing free;
     At five o'clock the sergeant comes and
          takes us out for tea;
     We can't be fired because we've got a
          two-year guarantee!
     There never was such a lovely war!

Oh, gather 'round me, ladies—
[*Interruption by Joan*]

I WANT TO BE A WAR BRIDE

Published January 1930. Introduced during the tryout by Doris Carson (Anne), Gordon Smith (Timothy), and ensemble. Performed during the first weeks of the New York run by Ethel Kenyon (Myra Meade), then dropped.

Written for the revised *Strike Up the Band* which opened at the Shubert Theatre, Boston, late Dec. 1929. My recollection is that it was acceptably, if not excitingly, sung by a charming young woman who somehow, even after the Market crash, had access to enough money to become the principal backer of the show. Not in her ken, though, was that unwritten theatrical law: "The show must go on." During the second week of the New York run, she eloped with a Hollywood director without giving notice to the management. Neither she nor song ever returned (the song didn't carry the story line anyway), which is why when the complete vocal score of *Strike Up the Band* was published a couple of months later, "War Bride" wasn't included.
—Ira Gershwin, date unknown

VERSE

I grow all excited and tinglish
When thinking of brave Joan of Arc.
She rescued her land from the English
In days that looked dreary and dark.
Then hist'ry is certainly richer
If stories I've read all are true
Which tell of the brave Molly Pitcher
Who fought for the red, white and blue—
And that's just what I'd like to do.
Dear Uncle Sam,
Oh, here I am,
Willing to suffer for you.

REFRAIN

I've an i-de-a:
I want to be a
Blushing, blushing war bride.

Oh, to be rapt in
Love with a captain,
Mushing, mushing war bride.

If he's a colonel,
I'll promise love eternal;
To a major
I can wager
To be true.

Even a private
Still could contrive it
To make me a war bride, too.

THANKS TO YOU

Intended for Jerry Goff (Jim) and Margaret Schilling (Joan). Unused. Prepared for publication but never printed. The refrain is No. 38 in the George and Ira Gershwin Special Numbered Song File.

VERSE 1

JIM: If I say so, I was rather eligible;*
     Debutantes would chase me over town.
     But my answers were so unintelligible,
     Neither maids nor mothers pinned me
          down.
     Life was pretty dull, but I was strong
          enough,
     For I knew that if I waited long enough,
     Though the years of waiting would be
          terribly drear,
     Eventually I'd find love, my dear.

REFRAIN

     Thanks to you,
     All the blues have passed—
     Heigh ho!
     I'm in love at last!

     Thanks to you,
     Love has come to stay—
     Heigh ho!—
     In a great big way!

     My life was all jumbled—
     Castles tumbled—
     Till I stumbled
     Into your heart—
     Wasn't I smart?

Earlier version of verse 1, lines 1–4 (apparently intended for some other show):
JACK: Once upon a time they called me Little Boy
     Blue;
     I was blue and lonesome as could be.
JILL: Like poor Cinderella, I was downhearted, too;
     Felt there was no happiness for me.

Thanks to you,
Happiness came fast—
Heigh ho!
I'm in love at last!

VERSE 2

JOAN: Ev'ry day a string of beaux came calling,
    my dear;
    They'd insist on rushing me around.
    But I found the social whirl appalling, my
    dear—
    Found out that I was no party hound.
    I had crushes but they didn't mean a
    thing;
    I had beaux but knew I hadn't seen a
    thing;
    So for years I went on feeling something
    was wrong,
    And then, one lucky day you came along.

REPEAT REFRAIN

FINALETTO, ACT II, SCENE I

Intended for Dudley Clements (Fletcher), Blanche Ring (Mrs. Draper), Jerry Goff (Jim), Robert Bentley (Sloane), Margaret Schilling (Joan), and ensemble. Dropped during rehearsals. A revised lyric (now missing) was introduced in Act II during the Boston and New Haven tryouts but dropped before the New York opening. The early version—all that survives—is printed here.

FLETCHER,
MRS. DRAPER,
    AND
    GIRLS: Stop! What is this mischief you're
        brewing?
        Think—before you make your
        reply!

    JIM: Wait! I know just what I am
        doing—
        I insist this fellow is a spy!

SLOANE: If he's accusing me of treason—
    I caught him making love to
        Joan—And that's the reason!

JIM AND
    JOAN: Yes, love has come into our lives
        once more;
        I'll never leave the one whom I
        adore.

FLETCHER: Come, take this lunatic in hand;
    I've had as much as I can stand;
[spoken]   Arrest him!

    ALL: It's really just too bad, but war is
        war!

[to Joan]
    SLOANE: Do you believe the lies that he's
        been telling you?
        How can you stand the bluff that
        he's been selling you?

[Music changes to "Soon"]
    JOAN: [Speaks] He can tell me anything
        he likes and I'll believe him. As
        for you, Mr. Sloane, all I have to
        say is that the engagement is
        definitely broken.

[Goes to Jim]
    JIM AND
    JOAN: [Sing] The day you're mine this
        world will be in tune;
        Let's make that day come soon.

OVERLEAF: *Ethel Merman and ensemble*

GIRL CRAZY | 1930

Tryout: Shubert Theatre, Philadelphia, September 29, 1930. New York run: Alvin Theatre, opened October 14, 1930. 272 performances. Music by George Gershwin. Produced by Alex A. Aarons and Vinton Freedley. Book by Guy Bolton and John McGowan. Book staged by Alexander Leftwich. Dances staged by George Hale. Orchestra under the direction of Earl Busby. Orchestrations by Robert Russell Bennett. Cast, starring Willie Howard (Gieber Goldfarb), Ginger Rogers (Molly Gray), and Allen Kearns (Danny Churchill), featured Ethel Merman (Kate Fothergill), William Kent (Slick Fothergill), Carlton Macy (Lank Sanders), Donald Foster (Sam Mason), Eunice Healy (Flora James), Peggy O'Connor (Patsy West), Olive Brady (Tess Parker), The Foursome (Marshall Smith, Ray Johnson, Del Porter, and Dwight Snyder), Antonio and Renee De Marco, and Red Nichols and his orchestra.

The number "Something Peculiar," intended at one time for Act II, can be found among the numbers of *Piccadilly to Broadway* (1920), which closed during its pre-Broadway tryout.

BIDIN' MY TIME

Published October 1930. Introduced and reprised by The Foursome (Marshall Smith, Ray Johnson, Del Porter, and Dwight Snyder). During the tryout it was presented by Al Lydell (Wilbur) and The Foursome. Lydell's role was eliminated before the New York opening.

A *Title That Bided Its Time.* At Townsend Harris Hall, the high school then connected with CCNY, I was on the staff of *The Academic Herald* as one of its "Art Editors." As such, I drew some cartoons and department headings; and started a column called "Much Ado." (One semester, I think in 1913, was a prosperous one for the *Herald*, netting an unprecedented profit of almost a hundred dollars. The solution of what to do with this windfall was finally solved by the Editor-in-Chief. He had medals struck off for himself and four or five of the more important editors, and the balance of the money was spent on a spaghetti dinner at Guffanti's for the entire staff of eighteen. We felt rather devilish that night—Chianti was served, even cigars—but most of us were home by ten p.m.)

At City College I collaborated with E. Y. Harburg on a column called "Gargoyle Gargles" for the weekly *Campus;* too, I contributed to the monthly, *Cap and Bells.* Signed "Gersh," the following appeared in the June 1916 issue:

A desperate deed to do I crave,
Beyond all reason and rhyme:

Some day when I'm feeling especially brave,
I'm going to Bide My Time.

Fourteen years after quatrain, with *Girl Crazy* in work, I suggested that "Bidin' My Time" might make a good title for a song in lazy, lethargic mood. (Years earlier I had recollected the phrase and put it down as a possible title. Lyricists usually keep notebooks with titles jotted down from time to time. One day Buddy DeSylva told me that in an hour or two the night before he had put down twenty-two, of which he thought two were probable.) When "Bidin' " was completed, the result was a sixteen-bar verse and thirty-two-bar refrain. Later, in going over the song with my brother, I felt that the refrain was overlong and said: "Let's try cutting out the second eight measures." With the refrain A A B A construction becoming A B A, this version sounded a bit strange at first; but in a few days the eight-bar scissoring seemed to give the piece a more folksy validity.

"Bidin' " made for a novel quartet in two scenes of the show. Its performance was heightened by the cowboys' (The Foursome) now and then accompanying themselves on the lowly instruments of harmonica, jew's-harp, ocarina, and tin flute.

—from *Lyrics on Several Occasions*

VERSE 1

Some fellers love to Tip-Toe Through The
   Tulips;
Some fellers go on Singin' In The Rain;
Some fellers keep on Paintin' Skies With
   Sunshine;
Some fellers keep on Swingin' Down The
   Lane—
But—

REFRAIN 1

I'm Bidin' My Time,
'Cause that's the kinda guy I'm.
While other folks grow dizzy
I keep busy—
Bidin' My Time.

Next year, next year,
Somethin's bound to happen;
This year, this year,
I'll just keep on nappin'—

And—Bidin' My Time,
'Cause that's the kinda guy I'm.
There's no regrettin'
When I'm settin'—
Bidin' My Time.

VERSE 2

Some fellers love to Tell It To The Daisies;
Some Stroll Beneath The Honeysuckle Vines;
Some fellers when they've Climbed The Highest
   Mountain
Still keep a-Cryin' For The Carolines—
But—

REFRAIN 2

I'm Bidin' My Time,
'Cause that's the kinda guy I'm—
Beginnin' on a Mond'y
Right through Sund'y,
Bidin' My Time.

Give me, give me
A glass that's full of tinkle;
Let me, let me
Dream like Rip Van Winkle.

He Bided His Time,
And like that Winkle guy I'm.
Chasin' way flies,
How the day flies—
Bidin' My Time!

TAG

I'm Bidin' My Time,
'Cause that's the kinda guy I'm—
Stranger, so long,
I'll just go 'long
Bidin' My Time.

THE LONESOME COWBOY

Published May 1954 in the piano-vocal score. Introduced by gentlemen of the ensemble ("Cow Punchers"). Alternate title: "The Lonesome Cowboy Won't Be Lonesome Now."

VERSE

COWBOY: If you wonder why I am dressed up in
         my best,
      There's a gal that I'm a-dyin' for to
         see;
      I have bought the ring. Let the
         preacher do the rest.
      And I'll take her back to Rancho
         XYZ.
      Yes, sir, she'll return with me
      Back to Rancho XYZ.

REFRAIN 1

Oh, the lonesome cowboy won't be
    lonesome now,
'Cause I'm gonna go out and get
    myself a frau.
Say, for seven years I've saved up all
    my dough.

COWBOY
AND MALE
  CHORUS: With a yippy kiyi kiyi kiyi kiyi—Let's
      go!

COWBOY: Oh, I've gone and bought myself a
     brand-new suit,
    And I'm figgerin' that my gal will
     think I'm cute.
    So let's raise the deuce
    Till Hell breaks loose,
    'Cause the lonesome cowboy won't be
     lonesome now.

COWBOY
AND MALE
  CHORUS: Oh, the lonesome cowboy won't be
     lonesome now.

TRIO

MEN: Hee haw! Hee haw! Laugh, hyena,
    laugh!
  Hee haw! Hee haw! Gotta stand the
    gaff.
  Hee haw! Hee haw! When you get a
    wife,
  You have got a ball and chain—for
    life!

REFRAIN 2

Oh, he's gone and bought himself a
    brand-new suit,
And he's figgerin' that his gal will
    think he's cute.

COWBOY
AND MALE
  CHORUS: So let's raise the deuce
    Till Hell breaks loose,
    'Cause the lonesome cowboy won't be
     lonesome now.
    Oh, the lonesome cowboy won't be
     lonesome now.

Unused Act II Reprise

REFRAIN

GIRLS
AND BOYS: Oh, the lonesome cowboy won't be
     lonesome now;

He's decided he's got to get himself a
    frau.
Say, for seven years he's saved up all
    his dough.
With a yippy kiyi kiyi kiyi kiyi—Let's
    go!

BOYS: Through the nights I know I never
     will be bored,
    'Cause I'm getting myself a radio and
     Ford.

ALL: So to man and frau
   Let's drink! Here's how!
   Oh, the lonesome cowboy won't be
    lonesome now.
   Oh, the lonesome cowboy won't be
    lonesome now.

TRIO

Hee haw! Hee haw! Gonna take a wife.
Hee haw! Hee haw! Prisoner for life.
But the cowboy never will be bored
When he gets a radio and Ford.

COULD YOU USE ME?

Published October 1930. Introduced by Ginger Rogers
(Molly) and Allen Kearns (Danny).

Just as in films, where scenes are seldom shot in
sequence, so with work in progress on a musical:
songs are rarely written in the order the audience later
hears them. That is, a song for a situation in the second
act may be the first number completed, while an opening
for the show may be—and usually is—the last. The
attraction-repulsion duet "Could You Use Me?" was
written for an earlier meeting between characters Danny
and Molly. Several scenes later, now on a friendlier basis,
they sang "Embraceable You," a song which happened
to have been written two years before "Could You Use
Me?" . . .

           —from *Lyrics on Several Occasions*

VERSE 1

DANNY: Have some pity on an Easterner;
    Show a little sympathy.
    No one possibly could *be* sterner
    Than you have been with me.
    There's a job that I'm applying for—
    Let me tell it to you thus;

It's a partnership I'm dying for—
Mr. and Mrs. Us!
Before you file it on the shelf,
Let me tell you of myself:

REFRAIN 1

Oh, I'm the chappie
To make you happy:
I'll tie your shoes-ies
And chase your blues-ies;
Oh, lady, would you—
Oh, tell me, could you
Use me?

I'd shake the mat out
And put the cat out!
I'd clean the garret
And feed the parrot.
Oh, lady, would you—
Oh, tell me, could you
Use me?

Do you realize what a good man
You're getting in me?
I'm no Elk or Mason or Woodman
Who gets home at three.

The girls who see me
Grow soft and dreamy,
But I'm a gander
Who won't philander.
Oh, could you use me?
'Cause I certainly could use you!

VERSE 2

MOLLY: There's a chap I know in Mexico
    Who's as strong as he can be;
    Eating nails and drinking Texaco—
    He is the type for me.
    There is one in California,
    More romantic far than you.
    When he sings "Ha-Cha-Cha-Chornia,"
    I often think he'll do.
    But as for you, sir, I'm afraid
    You will never make the grade.

REFRAIN 2

For you're no cowboy;
You're soft—and how!—boy!
I feel no muscle
That's fit for tussle.
I must refuse you;
I cannot use you.
DANNY: 'Scuse me!

MOLLY: No nightlife for you,
The birds would bore you,
The cows won't know you,
A horse would throw you—
You silly man, you,
To ask me, "Can you
Use me?"

Though at love you may be a wizard,
I'm wanting to know:
Could you warm me up in a blizzard,
Say, forty below?

Your ties are freakish;
Your knees are weakish;
Go back to flappers
And highball lappers!
Though you can use me,
I most certainly can't use you!

ENCORE REFRAIN

DANNY: I'd love to rough it!
MOLLY: You'd only muff it!
You'd better track home;
You're safer back home.
DANNY: Oh, lady, would you—
Oh, tell me, could you
Use me?

If we've no butler,
I'll put the cutler-
Y on the table
As well's I'm able;
I'd slave as few could,
If only you could
Use me.

MOLLY: You don't even know how to lasso
A bull or a steer.
DANNY: When I speak to them in my basso,
They'll worry, don't fear!

I'd be no bother;
I'd make a father
Like no one other—
If you're the mother.
Oh, could you use me?
'Cause I certainly could use you!

Possible Act II Reprise

REFRAIN

MOLLY: The meals I'd serve us
Might make you nervous.
DANNY: It doesn't matter
What's on the platter.
I'll love the menu

If, as, and when you
Use me.

MOLLY: If we've no butler,
I'll put the cutler-
Y on the table
As well I'm able.
I'd slave as few could
If only you could
Use me.

Mother never gave me a lesson
At cooking, you see.
DANNY: I could thrive on delicatessen
If that has to be.

MOLLY: I'll make a mother
Like no one other,
If you could bother
To be the father.
Oh, could you use me?
'Cause I certainly could use you!

BRONCO BUSTERS

Published May 1954 in the piano-vocal score. Introduced by ensemble. Alternate titles: "We're Bronco Busters" and "Opening, Act I, Scene 3."

VERSE

DUDEENS: In town we used to fret away
Until we made our getaway
Out here, where there's no doubt that
men are men—
Where men are men!
We don't care if we don't go East
again.

It's wonderful to breeze around;
They seem to have real trees around;
And of the open spaces there's no
doubt—
No doubt! No doubt!—
This is the life that Riley told about.

Before we're at the ranch another
week,
We'll get the well-known roses in the
cheek;
We haven't missed old Broadway or
the white lights—
When the moon at night lights—
That's the best of bright lights.

This is the place to tarry at;
The chaps who throw the lariat
Can sling a line that does a girl no
good.
Knock wood! Knock wood!
They sling a line that does a girl no
good!

REFRAIN 1

COWBOYS: We're bronco busters; we bust the
broncos;
We never fear man or beast.
On Western prairies, we shoot the
fairies
Or send them back to the East.
Like the Rangers, we fear no dangers:
We are never fussed.
We're bronco busters; we bust the
broncos
Or else we bust!

REFRAIN 2

We're bronco busters; we bust the
broncos;
We never fear man or beast.
We pack a wallop—We never doll
up—
Our pants have never been creased.
If you trifle, we aim a rifle—
Bang! You bite the dust!
Oh! This is some burg! We'll sing à la
Romberg
Until we bust!

BARBARY COAST

Published May 1954 in the piano-vocal score. According to the opening-night New York program, it was introduced by Ginger Rogers (Molly), Olive Brady (Tess), and Eunice Healy (Flora). According to the published piano-vocal score, it was introduced by Peggy O'Connor (Patsy), Olive Brady (Tess), and ensemble, with a specialty dance by Eunice Healy (Flora) and the girls. During the Philadelphia tryout, programs suggest that it was presented by Olive Brady (Tess), Eunice Healy (Flora), and William Kent (Slick). Later New York programs show that Ginger Rogers (Molly) did not sing in this number.

VERSE

If you ask me what place
Is the hottest hot place,
Anywhere around—
Anywhere around—
Step up to the wicket,
Get yourself a ticket
San Francisco bound—
I said, Frisco bound!
Let me take you to a place
Where hummingbirds sing bass.

REFRAIN

Oh, the minute that you strike it,
You've got to like it—
The Barbary Coast—
Where baa, baa, black sheep baa, baa, baa the
    most.
If you like your music red-hot—
Yes, sir, I said *hot!*
You'd better run down
To hunky-dory, honky-tonky town!
Don't talk of other places,
Brother, if you don't mind;
This is the one oasis—
It's heaven and hell combined!
Ev'rything is open wide there;
Don't need a guide there—
The devil's your host—
At the bar-bar-barbarous
Bar-Bar-Barbary Coast!

EMBRACEABLE YOU

Published October 1930. Introduced and reprised by
Allen Kearns (Danny) and Ginger Rogers (Molly). Per
Ira Gershwin (*Lyrics on Several Occasions*): "Eastern
playboy Danny Churchill finally overcomes the preju-
dices of Custerville (Ariz.)'s young postmistress, Molly
Gray."

In the summer of 1928 my brother and I were busy on
an operetta version of *East Is West* for Ziegfeld. We
were most enthusiastic about this project, which was to
star Marilyn Miller and Clark and McCullough. Approximately one half of the score had been completed when,
alas, Mr. Ziegfeld read J. P. McEvoy's snappy *Show Girl*
(whose heroine was Dixie Dugan, a Ziegfeld Girl). In his
hypnotically persuasive manner (always great charm
until a contract was signed) Ziegfeld managed to have us

postpone the operetta and start on *Show Girl*. *Show Girl*
wasn't much—it cost much and lost much—and, unfortunately, *East Is West*, whose production would have
cost more, never happened. Most of the *East Is West*
music had Oriental overtones, but there were several
musical-comedy numbers: "Embraceable You" was one,
and we found a spot for it in *Girl Crazy*. Among other
salvable music were "Lady of the Moon," which was
later lyricized to "Blah, Blah, Blah" for the film *Delicious*; and "In the Mandarin's Orchid Garden," which
was published as a concert song.

"Embraceable" is rather unusual as a more or less
sentimental ballad in that some of its rhymes are four-
syllable ones: "embraceable you—irreplaceable you,"
and (in a reprise) "silk and laceable you"; "tipsy in
me—gypsy in me." Also, there is a trick four-syllable
one in: "glorify love—'Encore!' if I love."

Incidentally, the song was one of my father's favorites.
Whenever possible, with company present, his request
to George was: "Play that song about me." And when
the line "Come to papa—come to papa—do!" was sung,
he would thump his chest, look around the room, and
beam.

—from *Lyrics on Several Occasions*

VERSE 1

DANNY: Dozens of girls would storm up;
    I had to lock my door.
    Somehow I couldn't warm up
    To one before.
    What was it that controlled me?
    What kept my love life lean?
    My intuition told me
    You'd come on the scene.
    Lady, listen to the rhythm of my
        heartbeat,
    And you'll get just what I mean.

REFRAIN 1

    Embrace me,
    My sweet embraceable you.
    Embrace me,
    You irreplaceable you.
    Just one look at you—my heart grew
        tipsy in me;
    You and you alone bring out the gypsy
        in me.
    I love all
    The many charms about you;
    Above all,
    I want my arms about you.
    Don't be a naughty baby,
    Come to papa—come to papa—do!
    My sweet embraceable you.

VERSE 2

MOLLY: I went about reciting,
    "Here's one who'll never fall!"
    But I'm afraid the writing
    Is on the wall.
    My nose I used to turn up
    When you'd besiege my heart;
    Now I completely burn up
    When you're slow to start.
    I'm afraid you'll have to take the
        consequences;
    You upset the apple cart.

REFRAIN 2

    Embrace me,
    My sweet embraceable you.
    Embrace me,
    You irreplaceable you.
    In your arms I find love so delectable,
        dear,
    I'm afraid it isn't quite respectable, dear.
    But hang it!
    Come on, let's glorify love!
    Ding dang it!
    You'll shout "Encore!" if I love.
    Don't be a naughty papa,
    Come to baby—come to baby—do!
    My sweet embraceable you.

ENCORE REFRAIN

DANNY: Dear lady,
    My silk-and-lace-able you;
    Dear lady,
    Be my embraceable you.
    You're the only one I love, yes, verily
        so!
    But you're much too shy, unnecessarily
        so!
MOLLY: I'll try not
    To be so formal, my dear.
DANNY: Am I not
    A man who's normal, my dear?
    There's just one way to cheer me;
    Come to papa—come to papa—do!
    My sweet embraceable you.

UNUSED REFRAIN

MOLLY: You call me
    Your sweet embraceable you;
    You call me
    Your irreplaceable you.
    When you talk that way, it's so
        delectable, dear,

I'm afraid it isn't quite respectable, dear.
When you, sir,
Act so deliriously,
Then who, sir,
Could take you seriously?
There's no one I'm more fond of,
But I don't see any hurry to
Be your embraceable you.

GOLDFARB, THAT'S I'M!

Published May 1954 in the piano-vocal score. Alternate title: "Finaletto, Act I." Introduced by Willie Howard (Gieber), William Kent (Slick), and ensemble.

GIEBER: They needed a man who was brave and strong
To rid the town of crime!
ALL: Goldfarb!
GIEBER: That's I'm!
SLICK: They needed a man who would not take graft
Unless it was over a dime!
ALL: Goldfarb!
GIEBER: That's I'm!
ALL: Don't talk of General Custer!*
Don't talk of Buffalo Bill!
For Sheriff Goldfarb gives a bigger thrill!
GIEBER: They needed a man who knew the game
Through serving a lot of time!
ALL: Goldfarb!
GIEBER: That's I'm!
ALL: So vote for Gieber Goldfarb, he's all right!
So vote for Gieber Goldfarb, man of might!
They needed a man who knew the game
Through serving a lot of time!
Goldfarb!
GIEBER: That's I'm!

An "in one" reprise dropped either in rehearsal or during the tryout substituted these lines:
SLICK: Don't talk of Annie Oakley;
Don't talk of Diamond Lil!
For Sheriff Goldfarb gives a bigger thrill!

SAM AND DELILAH

Published October 1930. Introduced by Ethel Merman (Kate) and ensemble.

Acceptable pronunciation (and exigency) permit "passion" to rhyme with "cash in"; and "distressin' " with "lesson." What wasn't good lyric-writing, I see now, is the placing of "hooch" and "kootch" on long, full notes of a slow-blues tune. These words should be uttered quickly so that the listener hears them as monosyllables; not duo, as "hoo–ch" and "koo–tch." I got away with it, thanks to [Ethel] Merman's ability to sustain any note any human or humane length of time. Few singers could give you *koo* for seven beats (it runs into the next bar, like intermission people) and come through with a terrifically convincing *tch* at the end.

Brief Glossary for the Very Young: "Hooch" and "kootch" both entered our language in the 1890's. "Hooch" was a synonym for whisky in the Klondike, probably based on an intoxicating liquor developed earlier by the Hoochinoo Indians of Alaska; "kootch" from "hootchy-kootchy," a daring Oriental belly-dance viewed by the less respectable at the Chicago's World Fair in 1893.

—from *Lyrics on Several Occasions*

KATE: Delilah was a floozy;
She never gave a damn.
Delilah wasn't choosy
Till she fell
For a swell
Buckaroo whose name was Sam.

Delilah got in action;
Delilah did her kootch.
She gave him satisfaction,
And he fell
'Neath her spell
With the aid of love and hooch.

But one day—so they tell us—
His true wife he did crave.
Delilah, she got jealous
And she tracked him
And hacked him
And dug for Sam a grave.

It's always that way with passion,
So, cowboy, learn to behave,
Or else you're li'ble to cash in
With no tombstone on your grave.

KATE
AND
CHORUS: Delilah, oh, Delilah!
She's no babe in the wood;
Run, cowboy, run a mile-ah!
If you love
That kind of
Woman, she'll do you no good!

KATE: The sheriff got Delilah.
They swung her from a tree.
The records are on file-ah.
It's distressin'—
But the lesson
Is an easy one to see.

It's always that way with passion,
So, cowboy, learn to behave,
Or else you're li'ble to cash in
With no tombstone on your grave.

KATE
AND
CHORUS: Delilah, oh, Delilah!
She's no babe in the wood;
Run, cowboy, run a mile-ah!
If you love
That kind of
Woman, she'll do you no good!

I GOT RHYTHM

Published October 1930. Introduced by Ethel Merman (Kate) and The Foursome, and danced by Antonio and Renee De Marco. During the tryout, the specialty dance was performed by Kendall Capps.

Rhythm and Little Rhyme. Filling in the seventy-three syllables of the refrain wasn't as simple as it sounds. For over two weeks I kept fooling around with various titles and with sets of double rhymes for the trios of short two-foot lines. I'll ad lib a dummy to show what I was at: "Roly-Poly, / Eating solely / Ravioli, / Better watch your diet or bust. / / Lunch or dinner, / You're a sinner. / Please get thinner. / Losing all that fat is a must." Yet, no matter what series of double rhymes—even pretty good ones—I tried, the results were not quite satisfactory; they seemed at best to give a pleasant and jingly Mother Goose quality to a tune which should throw its weight around more. Getting nowhere, I then found myself not bothering with the rhyme scheme I'd considered necessary (aaab, cccb) and experimenting with non-rhyming lines like (dummy): Just go forward; / Don't look backward; / And you'll soon be / Winding up ahead of the game." This approach felt stronger, and finally I arrived at the present refrain (the rhymed verse came later), with only "more—door" and "mind him—

find him" the rhymes. Though there is nothing remarkable about all this, it was a bit daring for me who usually depended on rhyme insurance.

But what *is* singular about this lyric is that the phrase "Who could ask for anything more?" occurs four times—which, ordinarily and unquestionably, should make that phrase the title. Somehow the first line of the refrain sounded more arresting and provocative. Therefore, "I Got Rhythm." (Incidentally, although rejected for this song, "Who Could Ask For Anything More?" later did make it as a title—twice, in fact—when Kay Swift and Ethel Merman each at different times used it for their autobiographies.)

Got. In some entertainment reviews and on some disc labels this song is called "I've Got Rhythm." I appreciate the correctors' efforts to formalize the title, but I'm sticking with the more direct "I Got Rhythm" for this tune. Although "got" for some centuries has been accepted as a strengthener in "I've got" and "I have got"—and although "got" as the past of "get" generally means "acquired" or "achieved"—neither of these uses obtains here. In the title and refrain of this song (also in "I Got Plenty o' Nuthin' ") "got" is heard in its most colloquial form—the one used for the present tense instead of "have," and the one going back to my childhood: e.g., "I got a toothache" didn't mean "I had a toothache," but only "I have" one. Thumbing through many authorities on usage, style, and dialect, I find no discussion of "got" as a complete substitute for "have." This is somewhat surprising when one considers, say, how often and for how many years the spiritual "All o' God's Chillun Got Shoes" ("I got shoes, you got shoes") has been heard.

P.S. Obviously, I've got nothing against "I've got" since the verse ends with "Look at what I've got." The reason in this instance is that the musically less assertive and regularly rhymed verse seems to require the more conventional phrasing.

—from *Lyrics on Several Occasions.*

VERSE

Days can be sunny,
With never a sigh;
Don't need what money
Can buy.

Birds in the tree sing
Their dayful of song.
Why shouldn't we sing
Along?

I'm chipper all the day,
Happy with my lot.
How do I get that way?
Look at what I've got:

REFRAIN

I got rhythm,
I got music,
I got my man—
Who could ask for anything more?

I got daisies
In green pastures,
I got my man—
Who could ask for anything more?

Old Man Trouble,
I don't mind him—
You won't find him
'Round my door.

I got starlight,
I got sweet dreams,
I got my man—
Who could ask for anything more—
Who could ask for anything more?

FINALE, ACT I

Published May 1954 in the piano-vocal score. Introduced by Donald Foster (Sam), Ginger Rogers (Molly), Allen Kearns (Danny), Ethel Merman (Kate), and ensemble.

CHORUS: He's a bronco buster;
He busts the broncos;
He seems to be unafraid.
And now this caveman,
This big and brave man
Is out to capture a maid.

DANNY: I need you,
My sweet embraceable you.
I need you,
My irreplaceable you.
If you should ever leave me,
Really, I don't know what I would do,
My sweet embraceable you.

KATE: It's always that way with passion,
So, playboy, learn to behave,
Or else you're li'ble to cash in
With no tombstone on your grave.

ENTR'ACTE

Published May 1954 in the piano-vocal score. Authorship of the lyric is not certain. It might be Ira Gershwin's, or it might have been written by a member of the orchestra. Introduced by members of the orchestra. Alternate title: "Stop, Put That Stick Down."

Stop, put that stick down!
Here, take this cornet!
Don't play all that pretty music;
You'll have us all cryin' yet.
Play the notes that we play;
It's a number from the show.
Take it easy. Get the rhythm.
Play the cornet! Ready! Go!

LAND OF THE GAY CABALLERO

Published May 1954 in the piano-vocal score. Introduced by ensemble and danced by Antonio and Renee De Marco. Alternate title: "Opening, Act II."

Romantic land of the gay caballero;
Romantic land of guitar and sombrero;
The music charms you.
Love disarms you
In the land of the gay caballero;

Romantic land of the gay caballero;
No frantic country of worry and care-o!
Bolero, tango,
And fandango—
That's the land of the gay caballero!

BUT NOT FOR ME

Published October 1930. Introduced by Ginger Rogers (Molly) and Willie Howard (Gieber). Earlier title: "Not for Me." After Rogers's straightforward rendition, Howard's reprise had him imitating Maurice Chevalier, Al Jolson, and Eddie Cantor as Gieber attempts to cheer up the forlorn Molly.

Notes for Teenagers. Beatrice Fairfax was one of the earliest Advice-to-the-Lovelorn columnists. . . . Using "a feller need a friend" was a tangential tribute to the hundreds of nostalgic cartoons of boyhood by Clare Briggs (1875–1930), headed "When a Feller Needs a Friend." . . . The title of Eleanor H. Porter's 1913 novel, *Pollyanna*, is still with us as a term of excessive optimism. . . . "Bananas" as a pejorative term implying disbelief was one of many slang terms started by sports-writer and cartoonist Thomas Aloysius Dorgan (1877–1929), "Tad." . . . The "two by four" wasn't the hyphenated two-by-four piece of lumber. Rather, as sung here and elsewhere, it meant a dream house for two ("and baby makes three").

— from *Lyrics on Several Occasions*

VERSE

MOLLY: Old Man Sunshine—listen, you!
Never tell me Dreams Come True!
Just try it—
And I'll start a riot.
Beatrice Fairfax—don't you dare
Ever tell me he will care;
I'm certain
It's the Final Curtain.
I never want to hear
From any cheer-
Ful Pollyannas,
Who tell you Fate
Supplies a Mate—
It's all bananas!

REFRAIN 1

They're writing songs of love,
But not for me;
A lucky star's above,
But not for me.

With Love to Lead the Way,
I've found more Clouds of Gray
Than any Russian play
Could guarantee.

I was a fool to fall
And Get That Way;
Heigh ho! Alas! and al-
So Lackaday!

Love ain't done right by Nell;
However—what the hell!
I guess he's not for me.

REFRAIN 2

He's knocking on a door,
But not for me;

He'll plan a two by four,
But not for me.

I've heard that Love's a Game;*
I'm puzzled, just the same—
Was I the Moth or Flame . . . ?
I'm all at sea.

It started off so swell,†
This "Let's Pretend";
It all began so well;
But what an end!

The climax of a plot
Should be the marriage knot,
But there's no knot for me.

Reprise

GIEBER: They're writing songs of love,
But not for me;
A lucky star's above,
But not for me.

With Love to Lead the Way,
I've found more Skies of Gray
Than any Russian play
Could guarantee.

I was a fool to fall
And Get That Way;
Heigh ho! Alas! And al-
So Lackaday!

Although I can't dismiss
The mem'ry of her kiss—
I guess she's not for me.

TREAT ME ROUGH

Published June 1944. Introduced by William Kent (Slick) and ensemble. Ira Gershwin later revised the verse for Ella Fitzgerald.

*Alternate line:
I know that Love's a Game;
†Alternate version of refrain 2, lines 9–15.
It all began so well,
But what an end!
This is the time a Fell-
Er Needs a Friend:

When ev'ry happy plot
Ends with the marriage knot—
And there's no knot for me.

VERSE

When I was born, they found a silver spoon in
my mouth;
I had a barber just to curl my hair.
If winter came, the mater carried me to the
South;
The point is that I had the best of care.
Women and headwaiters fawned on me;
Life was just a bore till it dawned on me
That if I'd ever want to be a man among men,
I'd have to be manhandled now and then.
So

REFRAIN

Treat me rough,
Muss my hair,
Don't you dare to handle
Me with care.
I'm no innocent child, baby;
Make me woolly and wild.
Treat me rough,
Pinch my cheek,
Kiss and hug and squeeze me
Till I'm weak.
I've been pampered enough, baby,
Keep on treating me rough.

Verse for Ella Fitzgerald

When I was born, they found a silver spoon in
my mouth,
And so I always had the best of care.
When winter came up North, of course they
motored me South
Where I was princess in our villa there.
Tutors and headwaiters fawned on me;
Life was just a bore till it dawned on me
The cushy sheltered way of life was really no
fun!
From now on some manhandling must be done.

BOY! WHAT LOVE HAS DONE TO ME!

Published October 1930. Introduced by Ethel Merman (Kate). Listed in pre-Broadway and opening-night New York programs as "Look What Love Has Done for Me."

This was one of three *Girl Crazy* songs—the other two: "I Got Rhythm," "Sam and Delilah"—written for Frisco Kate, a role played by the dynamic Ethel Merman. Although this young woman was appearing for the first time on any stage,* her assurance, timing, and delivery, both as comedienne and singer—with a no-nonsense voice that could reach not only standees but ticket-takers in the lobby—convinced the opening-night audience that it was witnessing the discovery of a new star.

Girl Crazy was a lively show. Willie Howard was at his funniest as a New York taxi-driver become sheriff in a Western town; the dancing was novel; the score featured, in addition to the Merman songs, "Embraceable You," "Bidin' My Time," and "But Not for Me"; and I am told the hep pit orchestra, conducted by Red Nichols, included many instrumentalists who later became famous in the jazz world. All in all, this musical, which ran thirty-four weeks, was considered a hit. Thirty-four weeks, these days, wouldn't be considered much of a run; but for those depression days when the national income was about one tenth of what it is now, one couldn't complain.

Additional Note Written about a Year Later. As lyricist I had nothing to do with the pit orchestra except to listen and take for granted their excellence—concerned only that the playing wouldn't be too loud. (From an unfinished lyric: "When the orchestra drowns the singers / And the singers drown the words . . .") The musicians were usually selected—still are, I imagine—after discussions among composer, conductor, producer, and the union contractor. Recently I have been able to obtain the names of some of the *Girl Crazy* pitmen from the film producer Roger Edens, who was on-stage pianist for Miss Merman in the Western bar scene. Among them: Benny Goodman, Gene Krupa, Glenn Miller, Jack Teagarden, Jimmy Dorsey.

—from *Lyrics on Several Occasions*

VERSE

It happened down at the Golden Gate;
A fool there was and her name was Kate:
She went and found herself a mate
And she suffered ever after.
Of millionaires she had her pick,
But she played herself a dirty trick
When she chose that guy whose name was Slick.
She's a sap to love him so;
Listen to her tale of woe:

REFRAIN 1

I fetch his slippers,
Fill up the pipe he smokes;
I cook the kippers,

Actually, Merman had been appearing in night-clubs and vaudeville since 1928.

Laugh at his oldest jokes;
Yet here I anchor—
I might have had a banker—
Boy! What love has done to me!

His nature's funny—
Quarrelsome half the time;
And as for money,
He hasn't got a dime;
And here's the joker:
I might have had a broker.
Boy! What love has done to me!

When a guy looks my way,
Does he get emphatic?
Say, he gets dramatic!
I just want to fly 'way—
But if I left him I'd be all at sea.

I'm just a slavey;
Life is a funny thing.
He's got the gravy,
I got the wedding ring.
And still I love him,
There's nobody above him!
Boy! What love has done to me!

REFRAIN 2

His brains are minus,
Never a thought in sight—
And yet His Highness
Lectures me day and night;
Oh, where was my sense
To sign that wedding license?
Boy! What love has done to me!

My life he's wrecking;
Bet you could find him now
Out somewhere necking
Somebody else's frau.
You get to know life
When married to a lowlife—
Boy! What love has done to me!

I can't hold my head up:
The butcher, the baker,
All know he's a faker;
Brother, I am fed up—
But if I left him he'd be up a tree.

Where will I wind up?
I don't know where I'm at.
I make my mind up
I ought to leave him flat.
But I have grown so
I love the dirty so'n'so!
Boy! What love has done to me!

CACTUS TIME IN ARIZONA

Published May 1954 in the piano-vocal score. Introduced by Ginger Rogers (Molly) and ensemble. This may have been a late addition to the score; it was not listed in the pre-Broadway programs. Alternate title: "When It's Cactus Time in Arizona."

VERSE

New Mexico, I love you;
California, I love you, too;
Wyoming, I love you;
Oklahoma, I love you, too.
But of all the states in the West,
Dear, for us, there's one that's the best:

REFRAIN

When it's cactus time in Arizona,
I'll be waiting there for you.
I will serenade you with "Ramona"
'Neath the sunny skies of blue.
What a thrill, my darling, when we own a
Little rancho built for two;
When it's cactus time in Arizona,
I'll be waiting there for you.

AND I HAVE YOU

Introduced during the Philadelphia tryout by June Carr (Patsy) and Willie Howard (Gieber). Dropped before the New York opening. Listed in the Philadelphia programs as "I Have You." Carr was replaced with Peggy O'Connor. No music is known to survive.

VERSE 1

GIEBER: Once I cared for women, wine, and song;
That was just before you came along.
Lady, you're away off;
I'm still fancy-free,
So you'd better lay off
Chasing me!
Gal, why must you put me in a huff?
Don't you realize that life is tough
    enough?

REFRAIN 1

Ev'ry highball has its morning after;
Old Manhattan has a traffic zone;

Ev'ry golf course has lots of sand traps;
Rudy Vallee has a saxophone.
Mr. Julius Caesar had his Brutus;
And Napoleon his Waterloo;
Ev'ry garden has its poison ivy, dear—
And I have you!

VERSE 2

PATSY: When you talk that way, you darling
    boy,
I can see you're really shy and coy.
You have quite the oddest
Way of loving me;
But I know how modest
You can be.
Don't let anything stand in your
    way;
Keep it up and maybe I'll say "Yes"
    someday.

REFRAIN 2

Ev'ry fish, it seems, must have its
    parsley;
Ev'ry baby's got to have the croup;
Ev'ry trusting Frankie has her Johnnie;
Ev'ry Helen Kane her
    "Boop-a-doop-a-doop."
Ev'ry triangle must have a husband;
Life's no bowl of cherries, you'll agree.
But for you, my dear, this earth is
    paradise—
'Cause you have me!

REFRAIN 3

GIEBER: Once I had a case of laryngitis,
That was just before I had the flu,
Which was just before I had pneumonia;
At the same time I had measles, too.
PATSY: But today you're looking awf'ly healthy.
GIEBER: You may think so, but it isn't true;
For I just had Goldman Sachs at
    one-twelve,
And now I have you.

ADDITIONAL REFRAIN (UNUSED)

In the winter all the birds go
    southwards;
Coolidge has returned to old Vermont;
Christopher Columbus crossed the
    ocean;
Halliburton crossed the Hellespont.
There are folks who go to California;
There are some who visit Timbuktu.

Ev'ry other thing on earth can travel,
    dear,
So why can't you?

THE GAMBLER OF THE WEST

Introduced during the Philadelphia tryout by William Kent (Slick) and ensemble. Dropped before the New York opening.

REFRAIN 1

SLICK: I'm the Gambler of the West;
I have hair upon my chest.
I can lose a million at a poker session
Without a change of expression.

CHORUS: He's the Gambler of the West;
He has hair upon his chest!

SLICK: I'm a bad man—I'm a killer;
I'm an inside-straight-flush filler!

CHORUS: He's the Gambler, he's the Gambler,
He's the Gambler of the West!

REFRAIN 2

SLICK: I'm the Gambler of the West;
I am squarer than the rest!
I have never left a loser in a pickle—
For carfare he gets a nickel.

CHORUS: He's the Gambler of the West!
SLICK: I will bet my coat and vest—
[*Starts to remove them*]
    And by cracky! And by thunder!
    I will even bet my under—
[*All rush to stop him*]
CHORUS: He's the Gambler, he's the Gambler—
[*Flute solo*]
    —Of the West!

YOU CAN'T UNSCRAMBLE SCRAMBLED EGGS

Intended for Act I—after "Could You Use Me?" and before "Bronco Busters." No. 114 in the George and Ira Gershwin Special Numbered Song File. Not listed in the Philadelphia programs, though Ira Gershwin's list of

Girl Crazy's musical numbers suggests that it might have been performed there. Not in the show by the New York opening.

1

I have seen a movie show without a theme song.
I have seen a burlesque without the legs.
But there's one thing that you cannot do a thing
    with;
Brother, you cannot unscramble scrambled eggs.

Ding a derry, ching a roo!
They say drinkin' days are through.
But they're selling hops and kegs
'Cause you never can unscramble scrambled
    eggs.

2

When a city slicker thought he'd take up
    farming—
Farmer Brown, he was right there to pull the
    wool,
And he sold him fifty chickens and a milk
    cow—
But he didn't say the cow was Mr. Bull.

Ding a derry, ching a roo!
City slicker's face is blue.
Though the bull of milk he begs—
Oh, you never can unscramble scrambled eggs!

3

Farmer Jones, he took his daughter to the
    doctor,
And he said, "Find out the trouble if you can."
And it didn't take the doctor long to tell him
That the trouble was a traveling salesman.

Ding a derry, ching a roo!
Doctor, he said, "I am through!
I can straighten bandy legs
But I never can unscramble scrambled eggs!"

ARE YOU DANCING?

A duet intended for the characters of "June" and "Chesty." Dropped during rehearsals, as were "June" and "Chesty."

VERSE

JUNE: Let's pretend that I'm in love with you
and you with me.
CHESTY: I'll pretend, but don't forget, pretending
it must be.
JUNE: If I'm Juliet, you know you must be
Romeo.
CHESTY: Let's pretend that you're a queen and I
am just a slave;
Let's pretend, but do it quick, I've got
to get a shave.
JUNE: Let's pretend we give in to romance
While flirting at a dance.

REFRAIN 1

JUNE: Are you dancing?
CHESTY: Are you asking?
JUNE: I'm asking.
CHESTY: So I'm dancing.

JUNE: Do you like me?
CHESTY: Are you serious?
JUNE: I'm serious.
CHESTY: So I like you.

JUNE: You're big and brave—the kind I
crave;
I like you best so far.
CHESTY: If you don't mind, I'd like to
find
What your intentions are.

JUNE: Shall we marry?
CHESTY: Are you working?

JUNE: Not lately—
CHESTY: How've you been?

REFRAIN 2

JUNE: Are you drinking?
CHESTY: Is it analyzed?
JUNE: It's analyzed.
CHESTY: So I'm drinking.

JUNE: Are you hungry?
CHESTY: Am I hungry?
JUNE: Here's a ham sandwich.
CHESTY: I'm not hungry.

JUNE: Though love is blind, still we must find
A little flat for two.
CHESTY: Don't worry, please. My salary's
A little flat for two.

JUNE: Are you dancing?
CHESTY: Are you asking?
JUNE: I'm asking.
CHESTY: So I'm dancing.
[They dance off]

YOU'VE GOT WHAT GETS ME

Published March 1932. Written for the 1932 RKO film version of *Girl Crazy*. Introduced by Eddie Quillan and Arline Judge. The music for the release had previously been used for the release of "Your Eyes! Your Smile!," which was dropped from *Funny Face* (1927) during its pre-Broadway tryout.

VERSE

I've got a secret that I can conceal no longer,
And you're the one I simply must tell it to.
Seems ev'ry minute my love keeps on growing
stronger.
Somebody soft and sweet
Swept me right off my feet.
And when I say some sweet somebody,
I mean just you.

REFRAIN

You've got what gets me;
What gets me you've got.
You've got what gets me;
I don't know just what.

But when you smile on me,
I get prouder and prouder;
My heart goes on a spree,
Beating louder and louder.

You've got what gets me;
You're simply a wow!
Let's you and let's me
Sign up now.

This time I know it's love;
Here's the reason and rhyme.
You've got what gets me ev'rytime.

DELICIOUS | 1931

A film produced by Winfield Sheehan for Fox Film Corporation. Released in December 1931. Music by George Gershwin. Screenplay by Guy Bolton and Sonya Levien, adapted from an original story by Bolton. Directed by David Butler. Cast, starring Janet Gaynor (Heather Gordon) and Charles Farrell (Jerry Beaumont), featured El Brendel (Jansen), Raul Roulien (Sascha), Lawrence O'Sullivan (O'Flynn), Manya Roberti (Olga), Virginia Cherrill (Diana), Olive Tell (Mrs. Van Bergh), Mischa Auer (Mischa), and Marvine Manzel (Tosha).

DELISHIOUS

Published December 1931. Introduced by Raul Roulien (Sascha). Ira Gershwin wrote in *The George and Ira Gershwin Song Book:* "What occasioned the title was simply this: after a visit and dinner at my apartment, my father-in-law would invariably pronounce the meal 'De-lish-i-ous!' "

VERSE

What can I say
To sing my praise of you?
I must reveal
The things I feel.
What can I say?
Each lovely phase of you
Just seems to baffle my descriptive powers
Four-and-twenty hours of ev'ry day.
What can I say?
What is the thing
I'd love to sing?
I've said you're marvelous;
I've said you're wonderful;
And yet that's not it.
Now let me see;
I think I've got it!

REFRAIN

You're so delishious
And so caprishious;
I grow ambishious
To have you care for me.

In that connecshion,
You're my selecshion
For true affecshion
For all the time to be.

Oh, I've had one, two, three, four, five,
Six, seven, eight, nine, ten girls before;
But now there's one, and you're the one,
The one girl I adore.

'Cause you're delishious,
And so caprishious,
If I'm repetishious,
It's 'cause you're so delishious.

DREAM SEQUENCE

Introduced by Raul Roulien (Sascha), Marvine Manzel (Tosha), and ensemble. Alternate titles: "We're from the *Journal*, the *Wahrheit*, the *Telegram*, the *Times*" and "Welcome to the Melting Pot."

REPORTERS: We're from the *Journal*, the
  Wahrheit, the *Telegram*, the
  Times;
  We specialize in interviews and
  crimes.
  If we seem to pursue you,
  It's just to interview you—
  The *Journal*, the *Wahrheit*, the
  Telegram, the *Times*.

  We'd like to know what you think of
  America—
  ('S wonderful.)
  And what do you think of American
  women?
  (They're marvelous.)

  We thank you;
  You were splendid;
  The interview is ended—
  The *Journal*, the *Wahrheit*, the
  Telegram, the *Times*.

  We welcome all Hungarians,
  Australians, and Bavarians,
  The Chinee and the Heinie and the
  sons of Araby.
  We welcome all Mongolians,
  Brazilians, and Tyroleans,
  Each nation in creation to the Land
  of Liberty.

  We do not ask you who you are;
  We do not question what you are;
  We never ask you how much you
  have got.
  But be you Lithuanian, Italian, or
  Roumanian,
  We bid you welcome to the Melting
  Pot—
  The Melting Pot—
  We bid you welcome to the Melting
  Pot.

  We repeat and reiterate
  That you're welcome to the Land of
  Liberty.

SOLO: I'm Mister Ellis of Ellis Island
  And I offer you the freedom of the
  country.
  We offer hospitality of the very finest
  quality.
  We bid you welcome to the Melting
  Pot.

SOMEBODY FROM SOMEWHERE

Published December 1931. Introduced by Janet Gaynor (Heather).

VERSE

When a body knows nobody,
What's a body to do?
Shall she weep and sigh?
No, no! And I'll tell you why:
Someday there must be somebody
Bringing heaven in view—
And so her courage she must keep
As she sings herself to sleep.

REFRAIN

Somebody from somewhere
Will appear someday;
I don't know just from where,
But he's on his way.
I'll just keep on waiting,
Waiting till I see
Somebody from somewhere
For nobody but me.

KATINKITSCHKA

Published December 1931. Introduced by Mischa Auer (Mischa) and Manya Roberti (Olga).

VERSE 1

Katinkitschka, Katinkitschka,
Out all night long!

Katinkitschka, Katinkitschka,
Now, that was wrong!
We must find out just what you've done;
Were you out with the banker's son?
We waited up till after three;
We hope you weren't on a spree
With a soldier boy!
Oy!

REFRAIN 1

Popitschka, Momitschka,
Will not sleep a winkitschka.
Popitschka, Momitschka,
Will not sleep a winkitschka,
Thinking of Katink, Katink, Katink, Katink,
   Katinkitschka!

VERSE 2

Katinkitschka, Katinkitschka,
Oh, what a disgrace!
Katinkitschka, Katinkitschka,
Go, hide your face!
No more is she a model maid;
The worst has happened, I'm afraid.
Of you this house will soon be rid!
Confess and tell us what you did
With a soldier boy!
Oy!

REFRAIN 2

Popitschka, Momitschka,
Now can laugh and singitschka.
Popitschka, Momitschka,
Now can laugh and singitschka.
Since Katink, Katink, Katinka has a wedding
   ringitschka!

BLAH, BLAH, BLAH

Published December 1931. Introduced by El Brendel (Jansen). The "Russian" refrain was cut before the film was released. Also, see notes on "Lady of the Moon" from *East Is West* (1928–29) and "I Just Looked at You" from *Show Girl* (1929).

Another Palimpsest Melody. Although this song didn't have a history of as many lyrics rubbed out as did, say, "Long Ago and Far Away," it did take on three different sets of words in the course of three years.

The tune was composed in 1928 for the operetta *East*

Is West, and I wrote it up as a sort of Chinese invocation, titled "Lady of the Moon." But *East Is West* was called off "temporarily" by Ziegfeld and we were switched to *Show Girl*. For the new show Ziegfeld asked if I would mind collaborating with lyricist Gus Kahn, as he owed Gus a commitment. I welcomed the opportunity because *Show Girl* had to be done quickly to make a much too soon Boston opening date.

Including openings and finalettos and several songs written during rehearsal, George, Gus, and I wound up with twenty-seven musical items. Many of these were for imagined spots, as we were as vague about what most of the scenes would be as librettist William Anthony McGuire himself was. (We started rehearsals with the script for only the opening scene. Genial Bill McGuire apparently wasn't worrying much about a deadline on this one and loved listening to anything new we played him. And "You never can tell. Maybe I'll get a good idea for a scene from one of the songs.")

There was much musical entertainment in *Show Girl*. Of the twenty-seven items we wrote, fourteen were used. Then there was the ballet *An American in Paris*, which opened the second act and ran at least fifteen minutes. Then there was a scene in which Duke Ellington and his band played a couple of their numbers; and another in which Clayton, Jackson, and Durante contributed several of their own specialties. And I see by the program that singer-guitarist Nick Lucas did a few of the songs associated with him. Too, the finale of the show ("Stage-door Ziegfeld Theatre") reprised half a dozen of our numbers. Everything considered, I wouldn't be surprised if *Show Girl* set a record for spareness of dialogue in a musical.

One of the thirteen discarded numbers carried a new lyric to the tune of "Lady of the Moon." Sensing at the time that *East Is West* would never be produced (Ziegfeld's finances weren't what they'd been and the production costs of *East Is West* would be three times that of *Show Girl*), I salvaged the melody of the moon song, and Gus and I gave it a light ballad lyric called "I Just Looked at You." But since there was no particular use for this version either, I kept the tune in mind as a future possibility.

By 1930 the Hollywood "theme song" (usually a love song) was so much in the ascendance that I thought a mild spoof on the theme-song theme wouldn't be amiss. Needing a good ballady tune, I chose the present one, and as "Blah, Blah, Blah" it emerged for the third (and last) time as a song, when it was accepted for the film *Delicious*.

—from *Lyrics on Several Occasions*

VERSE

I've written you a song,
A beautiful routine.
(I hope you like it.)

My technique can't be wrong:
I learned it from the screen.
(I hope you like it.)
I studied all the rhymes that all the lovers sing;
Then just for you I wrote this little thing:

REFRAIN

Blah, blah, blah, blah, moon,
Blah, blah, blah, above;
Blah, blah, blah, blah, croon,
Blah, blah, blah, blah, love.
Tra la la la, tra la la la la, merry month of May;
Tra la la la, tra la la la la, 'neath the clouds of
   gray.
Blah, blah, blah, your hair,
Blah, blah, blah, your eyes;
Blah, blah, blah, blah, care,
Blah, blah, blah, blah, skies.
Tra la la la, tra la la la la, cottage for two—
Blah, blah, blah, blah, blah, darling, with you!

"Russian" Refrain

RUSSIANS: Tolstoy, Pushkin—
JANSEN: Love.
RUSSIANS: Lenin, Trotsky—
JANSEN: Croon.
RUSSIANS: Chaliapin—
JANSEN: Above.
RUSSIANS: Volga boatman—
JANSEN: Moon.
RUSSIANS: Korestchenko, Boris Godunoff—
JANSEN: Merry month of May.
RUSSIANS: Balalaika and Rachmaninoff—
JANSEN: 'Neath the clouds of gray.
RUSSIANS: Nevsky Prospect—
JANSEN: Hair.
RUSSIANS: P. Tschaikowsky—
JANSEN: Eyes.
RUSSIANS: Borscht and blintzes—
JANSEN: Care.
RUSSIANS: *Clug zu* Columbus—
JANSEN: Skies.
RUSSIANS: *Utch a chornia*, Rimsky-Korsakoff—
JANSEN: Cottage for two.
RUSSIANS: *Pinya miaspa russky*—
JANSEN: Darling, with you.

YOU STARTED IT

Lyric unused. The accompanying music was used in *Delicious* for background. The music for the verse originally was used for the verse of "Your Eyes! Your Smile!"

in *Funny Face* (1927). See page 109. No. 125 in the George and Ira Gershwin Special Numbered Song File.

VERSE

I traveled hither,
Yonder, thither—
Happy as a king.
One day I met love,
And I let love
Do that Fatal Thing.

I once was gayer
Than the mayor
Of New York—but now,
From dawn to sundown,
I am run-down
With the blues—and how!

REFRAIN

I know just how I got this way;
You started it.
Can't sleep at night and dream all day;
You started it.
With not a worry, all the years went by—
Then what happened?
I caught your eye!
Who is it keeps on raising Cain
And started it?
You'll pardon me if I complain;
You started it!
You've started something and you've got to see
　it through,
And love me as I love you!

OF THEE
I SING
1931

Tryout: Majestic Theatre, Boston, December 8, 1931. New York run: Music Box Theatre, opened December 26, 1931. 441 performances. Music by George Gershwin. Produced by Sam H. Harris. Book by George S. Kaufman and Morrie Ryskind. Book staged by George S. Kaufman. Dances staged by George Hale. Orchestra under the direction of Charles Previn. Orchestrations by Robert Russell Bennett, William Daly, and George Gershwin. Cast, starring William Gaxton (John P. Wintergreen), Lois Moran (Mary Turner), and Victor Moore (Alexander Throttlebottom), featured Grace Brinkley (Diana Devereaux), Florenz Ames (French Ambassador), George Murphy (Sam Jenkins), June O'Dea (Miss Benson), Ralph Riggs (Chief Justice), Dudley Clements (Matthew Arnold Fulton), George E. Mack (Senator Robert E. Lyons), Edward H. Robins (Senator Carver Jones), Sam Mann (Louis Lippman), and Harold Moffet (Francis X. Gilhooley).

WINTERGREEN FOR PRESIDENT

Published in the complete piano-vocal score April 1932. Introduced by ensemble. Per *Lyrics on Several Occasions:* "A city street across which marches a procession of torchlight campaigners."

For some years Strickland Gillilan's "On the Antiquity of Microbes":

Adam
Had 'em.

was considered the shortest poem extant. But this record fell when someone (Anon.) came up with "Lines on the Questionable Importance of the Individual":

I . . .
Why?

Compared with both of these, the words of "Wintergreen for President" almost equal the length of an Icelandic saga. I imagine, though, that in Songdom "Wintergreen" is one of the shortest lyrics ever.

Additional lines would have been supererogatory. During the four or five minutes of this torchlight-parade number, both title and couplet were repeated several times; but other than the first announcement, neither words nor music were heard—they were drowned out by gales of laughter from the audience when the marchers began showing their campaign banners. There were about twenty of these slogans (all by Kaufman and Ryskind), such as "Win with Wintergreen," "A Vote for Wintergreen Is a Vote for Wintergreen," "The Full Din-

ner Jacket," "Turn the Reformers Out," "Wintergreen—the Flavor Lasts," and a dozen others.

I once asked George Kaufman what the P. in John P. Wintergreen stood for. His answer: "Why, Peppermint, of course!" with a look that could only mean that any child knew *that*.

It was Oscar Hammerstein, I believe, who in an interview cited "Wintergreen" as an excellent example of words wedded to music. His point was that when one hears the title its music comes immediately to mind, and vice versa.

—from *Lyrics on Several Occasions*

Wintergreen for President!
Wintergreen for President!
He's the man the people choose;
Loves the Irish and the Jews.

WHO IS THE LUCKY GIRL TO BE? and THE DIMPLE ON MY KNEE and BECAUSE, BECAUSE

Published in the complete piano-vocal score April 1932. Together they comprise the opening of the Atlantic City scene ("Opening, Act I, Scene 3"). "Who Is the Lucky Girl to Be? (also known as "The President's Future Wife") was introduced by Grace Brinkley (Diana Devereaux) and ensemble. "The Dimple on My Knee" (also known as "Entrance of Photographers") was introduced by Brinkley, George Murphy (Sam Jenkins), and ensemble. "Because, Because," published separately in December 1931, was also introduced by Brinkley, Murphy, and ensemble.

"Who Is the Lucky Girl to Be?"

GIRLS: Who is the lucky girl to be?
Who is to leave the bourgeoisie?
Who is to be the blushing bride?
Who will sleep at the President's side?
Strike up the cymbals, drum, and fife!
One of us is the President's future wife!

FOUR
GIRLS: We're in Atlantic City
To meet with the committee.

FOUR
OTHERS: And when they've made their mind up
The winner will be signed up.

FOUR
OTHERS: The prize is consequential—
Presidential!
Our bodies will bear witness
To our fitness.

ALL: If a girl is sexy
She may be Mrs. Prexy!
One of us is the President's future wife!
[*The two sections are sung together. Photographers enter*]

"The Dimple on My Knee"

PHOTOG-
RAPHERS: More important than a photograph of
Parliament
Or a shipwreck on the sea—
What'll raise the circulation
Of our paper through the nation
Is the dimple on your knee.

More important than a photograph of
Parliament
Or a western spelling bee
Or the latest thing in science
For our pleasure-loving clients
Is the dimple on your knee.

What our readers love to see
Is the dimple on your knee;
What our readers love to see
Is the dimple on your knee.

GIRLS: More important than a photograph of
Parliament
Is the dimple on my knee.
But supposing I am losing
When the judges are a-choosing—
What will my poor future be?

Do I have to go back to the
cafeteria
With my lovely dimpled knee?
Does a girl who's so ambitious
Have to work at washing dishes?
I'm afraid that worries me.

Oh, what will the future be
Of my lovely dimpled knee?
Oh, what will the future be
Of my lovely dimpled knee?

"Because, Because"

PHOTOG-
RAPHERS: Don't worry, little girl,
For even if you lose the prize—
Don't worry, little girl,
Myself, I can't resist your eyes.

GIRLS: I'll worry, little boy,
Until you tell what's on your mind.

PHOTOG-
RAPHERS: Don't worry, little girl,
I've asked my heart and this is what I
find—
Don't worry, little girl;
Don't worry, little girl.

GIRLS: Why shouldn't I worry?

PHOTOG-
RAPHERS: Because, because, because, because,
Because you're in the money
With a smile that's sweet and sunny,
I could fall for you myself.

Because, because, because, because
Your looks are so appealing
They have given me a feeling
I could fall for you myself.

The thrills you're sending through me
All prove that you will do me;*
And so I'm giving you me—
If *they* don't want you, *I* want you!

Because, because, because, because,
Because your ways are simple
And your knee can show a dimple,
I could fall for you myself.

EXIT, ATLANTIC CITY SCENE

Published in the complete piano-vocal score April 1932.
Introduced by Grace Brinkley (Diana), William Gaxton
(Wintergreen), and ensemble. This sequence marks the
departure of Diana and the girls from the Atlantic City
hotel suite—Scene 4.

GIRLS: Who is the lucky girl to be?
Who is to leave the bourgeoisie?
DIANA: Bye-bye, Mister President—
I'm a-prayin'
I'm the little lady
You're obeyin'.
DIANA AND
GIRLS: Strike up the cymbal, drum, and
fife—
One of us is to be the President's
wife.

*Alternate version of this and the next line:
Are doing something to me;
The opposite of gloomy—

COMMITTEE: We'll get you Mrs. Wintergreen.
WINTERGREEN: Oh!
COMMITTEE: We'll get you Mrs. Wintergreen.
WINTERGREEN: Oh!
COMMITTEE: We'll present you with a bride.
She will be the nation's pride.
Ta ta ta ta ta ta ta.

AS THE CHAIRMAN OF THE COMMITTEE and HOW BEAUTIFUL and NEVER WAS THERE A GIRL SO FAIR and SOME GIRLS CAN BAKE A PIE

These four linked numbers, which comprise the finaletto
of the Atlantic City Hotel scene, were published in the
complete piano-vocal score in April 1932 (Finaletto, Act
I, Scene 4). "As the Chairman of the Committee" was
introduced by Dudley Clements (Fulton), Harold Moffet
(Gilhooley), George E. Mack (Senator Lyons), Sam
Mann (Lippman), Edward H. Robins (Senator Jones),
and ensemble. "How Beautiful" was introduced by the
ensemble. "Never Was There a Girl So Fair" was introduced by principals and ensemble, and "Some Girls Can
Bake a Pie" was introduced by William Gaxton (Wintergreen) and ensemble.

"As the Chairman of the Commitee"

[*Gong sounds. Music starts*]
FULTON: As the chairman of the committee,
I announce we've made our choice;
Ev'ry lover from Dubuque to Jersey
City
Should rejoice!
ALL: We rejoice!
When the angels up there designed her,
They designed a thoroughbred;
And on March the fourth the President
will find her
Worthy of his board and bed.
FULTON:
[*spoken*]
And now it thrills me to introduce the
rarest of American beauties, the
future First Lady of the land—a fit
consort for the ruler of 122 million
freeborn. Ladies and gentlemen—
Miss Diana Devereaux!

[*Diana appears with four other prize winners
holding train attached to her bathing suit*]

"How Beautiful"

ALL:
[*Sing*]
How beautiful, beautiful, beautiful!
How utterly, utterly so!
The charming, the gracious, the dutiful
Diana Devereaux.
FULTON:
[*spoken*]
The committee will now state its
reasons—with music!

"Never Was There a Girl So Fair"

COMMITTEE:
[*Sings*]
Never was there a girl so fair;
Never was there a form so rare;
DIANA:
[*spoken*]
Ah could throw mah arms right
around your neck!
COMMITTEE:
[*Sings*]
A voice so lyrical
Is given few;
Her eyes a miracle
Of Prussian blue;
Ruby lips and a foot so small;
As for hips—she has none at all!
GILHOOLEY: Did you ever see such footsies
Or a more enticing limb?
LIPPMAN: And the ankles of her tootsies
Are so slim!
LYONS: What a charming epiglottis!
What a lovely coat of tan!
Oh, the man who isn't hot is
Not a man!
COMMITTEE: She's a bargain to whom she's
wed;
More than worthy his board and
bed!
FULTON: Says the chairman of the
committee,
Let the newsmen now come in.
[*to Diana*]
For the sound reels you must look
your best, my pretty.
[*to guards*]
Have the interviews begin!
WINTERGREEN: Stop! No!
Though this may be a blow,

I simply cannot marry
Diana Devereaux!

COMMITTEE: What's this? What's this?

ALL: He says he cannot marry
Diana Devereaux!

COMMITTEE:
[to Wintergreen]
You mean you will not marry
Diana Devereaux!

WINTERGREEN: Please understand—It isn't that I
would jilt or spurn 'er;
It's just that I love someone else—

ALL: Who?

WINTERGREEN: Whom! Mary Turner.

COMMITTEE: The man is mad!
Or else a cad!
He'll have to take her—
He can't forsake her!

DIANA: This jilting me—
It cannot be!
This lousy action
Calls for retraction!

COMMITTEE: We must know why
You should prefer
Instead of Di
[pointing to Diana]
A girl like her.
[pointing to Mary]

ALL: Yes, tell us why
You should prefer
Instead of Di
A girl like her.

WINTERGREEN: All that I can say of Mary Turner
Is that I love Mary Turner.

COMMITTEE: What's to be done?
Though she has won,
[indicating Diana]
Though she is signed up,
He's made his mind up!
His love he'd ruther
Give to the other.
[indicating Mary]
What shall we do now?
What is our cue now?

DIANA:
[to Committee]
He will do nothing of the sort;
First we'll settle this thing in
court.
[to Wintergreen]
You seem to think Miss Turner
hits the spot;

But what has she got that I
haven't got?

ALL: Yes, what has she got
[pointing to Mary]
That she
[pointing to Diana]
hasn't got?

WINTERGREEN: My Mary makes corn muffins.
[to Diana]
Can you make corn muffins?

DIANA: I can't make corn muffins.

ALL: She can't make corn muffins!

WINTERGREEN: Well, there you are!

"Some Girls Can Bake a Pie"

Some girls can bake a pie
Made up of prunes and quinces;
Some make an oyster fry—
Others are good at blintzes.
Some lovely girls have done
Wonders with turkey stuffin's,
But I have found the one
Who can really make corn muffins.

DIANA: Who cares about corn muffins?
All I demand is justice.
[Wintergreen repeats "Some girls . . ." Mary
joins in, as Committee and Ensemble, sold on
the idea, sing obligato]

COMMITTEE
AND
ENSEMBLE: Corn muffins—
Though other girls are good at
turkey stuffin's,
She takes the cake—for she can
bake—corn muffins;
Corn muffins—
He's not to blame for falling if she's
able
To serve them at his table.
[Committee starts to sample muffins]
They should be happy night and
day;
They'll make a couple so delightful;
When two agree on corn muffins,
Their marriage is only rightful.

DIANA:
[against the above]
Don't surrender!
Don't be tender!
I'm the winner.
She is a little sinner.
Come! Make your mind up!
I, not she
Is the one who's really signed up!

COMMITTEE:
[holding up muffins]
Great, great!
It really must be fate!
We must declare these muffins
The best we ever ate!

There's none but Mary Turner
Could ever be his mate!

ALL: There's none but Mary Turner
Could ever be his mate!
[Half the voices keep repeating this, other half
sing:]
She can make corn muffins!
She can make corn muffins!

LOVE IS SWEEPING THE COUNTRY

Published December 1931 and as part of the complete
piano-vocal score April 1932. Introduced by George
Murphy (Jenkins), June O'Dea (Miss Benson), and ensemble.

Shortly after this song was completed I thought it
could stand a patter. George reflected a moment,
then: "Let's use the patter music from the *East Is West*
opening." (We'd written a quite elaborate opening for
that unproduced opus. At one stage in it, just before the
Love Boat arrived with its bevy of Sing-Song Girls to be
auctioned off, a quartet of mandarins sang their prefer-
ences.) And that's why the music to the present patter,
slightly changed from the original, sounds a touch
Chinese.

Although mandarins were supposedly highly educated, it seems that I slanged up their Mandarin a bit.
Here are a couple of qualifications required of the girls
on the block.

One Mandarin
I come here to seek
A high-tone baby, *Class* A;
Beautiful and chic,
And up-to-date, not *pass-é*.

Another
No say "Oh, you kid!"
To any thin or flat one;
I am here to bid—
But only for a fat one.
—from *Lyrics on Several Occasions*

VERSE

Why are people gay
All the night and day,
Feeling as they never felt before?
What is the thing
That makes them sing?

Rich man, poor man, thief,
Doctor, lawyer, chief,
Feel a feeling that they can't ignore;
It plays a part
In ev'ry heart,
And ev'ry heart is shouting "Encore!"

REFRAIN

Love is sweeping the country;
Waves are hugging the shore;
All the sexes
From Maine to Texas
Have never known such love before.

See them billing and cooing
Like the birdies above!
Each girl and boy alike,*†
Sharing joy alike,
Feels that passion'll
Soon be national.
Love is sweeping the country—
There never was so much love!

Patter (Original Version)

Spring is in the air—
Each mortal loves his neighbor.
Who's that loving pair?
That's Capital and Labor.

Chevrolet and Ford
Have felt this cosmic urging;
They, with one accord,
Have kissed and now are merging.

Florida and Cal-
Ifornia get together
In a festi*val*
Of oranges and weather.

Boston's upper zones
Are changing all their habits,
And I hear the Cohns
Are taking up the Cabots.

Alternate considered for refrain, lines 8–11:
It's overpowering;
Hearts are flowering,
Sure that passion'll
Soon be national
†Lyrics on Several Occasions *version:*
Girl and boy alike,

Taximen take dimes
And never curse the traffic,
While the New York *Times*
Adores the New York *Graphic*.

Patter (Revised Version)

Spring is in the air—
Each mortal loves his neighbor.
Who's that loving pair?
That's Capital and Labor.

Florida and Cal-
Ifornia get together
In a festi*val*
Of oranges and weather.

Boston's upper zones
Are changing social habits,
And I hear the Cohns
Are taking up the Cabots.

Cities are above
The quarrels that were hapless.
Look who's making love:
St. Paul and Minneap'lis!

ADLAI'S SWEEPING THE COUNTRY

In 1952, the year in which *Of Thee I Sing* was revived on Broadway, Ira Gershwin wrote a new lyric to the music of the refrain of "Love Is Sweeping the Country" in support of Adlai Stevenson's candidacy for president of the United States. (See also the special pro-Stevenson version of "It Ain't Necessarily So" in *Porgy and Bess,* 1935.)

Adlai's sweeping the country!
He will be the next Prez.
We'll be leaning
On words with meaning,
For he means every word he says.

What a man for our future!
Equal him if you can.
Fearless attitudes
With no platitudes;
Inspirational—
He's sensational!
Adlai's sweeping the country!
America—here's your man!

OF THEE I SING

Published December 1931 and as part of the complete piano-vocal score April 1932. Introduced by William Gaxton (Wintergreen), Lois Moran (Mary Turner), and ensemble. In the original New York production, the verse was not sung.

When we first played this sentimental political campaign song for those connected with the show, there were one or two strong objectors who thought that juxtaposing the dignified "of thee I sing" with a slangy "baby" was going a bit too far. Our response (a frequent one over the years) was that, naturally, we'd replace it with something else if the paying audience didn't take to it. This was one time we were pretty sure that they would; and they did. Opening night, and even weeks later, one could hear a continuous "Of thee I sing, *Baby!*" when friends and acquaintances greeted one another in the lobby at intermission time.
—from *Lyrics on Several Occasions*

VERSE

From the Island of Manhattan to the Coast of
    Gold,
From North to South, from East to West,
You are the love I love the best.
You're the dream girl of the sweetest story ever
    told;
A dream I've sought both night and day
For years through all the U.S.A.
The star I've hitched my wagon to
Is very obviously you.

REFRAIN

Of thee I sing, baby—
Summer, autumn, winter, spring, baby.
You're my silver lining,
You're my sky of blue;
There's a love-light shining
Just because of you.

Of thee I sing, baby—
You have got that certain thing, baby!
Shining star and inspiration,
Worthy of a mighty nation—
Of thee I sing!

FINALE, ACT I
including ENTRANCE OF SUPREME COURT JUDGES and A KISS FOR CINDERELLA and I WAS THE MOST BEAUTIFUL BLOSSOM and SOME GIRLS CAN BAKE A PIE (REPRISE) and OF THEE I SING (REPRISE) and ZWEI HERTZEN

These linked numbers, published in the complete piano-vocal score in April 1932 as "Finale, Act I," comprise the extended Inauguration Day sequence that concludes Act I. The "Entrance of the Supreme Court Judges," also titled "Nine Supreme Court Judges," was introduced by Ralph Riggs (Chief Justice) and ensemble. "A Kiss for Cinderella," also titled "Here's a Kiss for Cinderella," which had been published separately in December 1931, was introduced by William Gaxton (Wintergreen) and ensemble. The recitative "I Was the Most Beautiful Blossom" was introduced by Grace Brinkley (Diana), and the reprises of "Some Girls Can Bake a Pie" and "Of Thee I Sing" were introduced by the entire company. "Zwei Hertzen" was introduced during the Boston tryout by Gaxton, Brinkley, Lois Moran (Mary), and ensemble. It was dropped before the New York opening.

"Entrance of Supreme Court Judges"

[*Trumpet call. Boys and girls in military uniforms march on. Drill. Another fanfare. Judges enter*]

JUDGES: We're the one, two, three, four,
    five, six, seven, eight, nine
    Supreme Court Judges.
    As the super Solomons of this
    great nation
    We will supervise today's
    inauguration,
    And we'll sup'rintend the wedding
    celebration
    In a manner official and judicial.
    One, two, three, four, five, six,
    seven, eight, nine Supreme
    Court Judges!

    We have powers that are
    positively regal;

Only we can take a law and make
it legal.
ALL: They're (We're) the A.K.s who
    give the O.K.s!
    One, two, three, four, five, six,
    seven, eight, nine Supreme
    Court Judges!

[*Another fanfare*]

    Hail! Hail! The ruler of our
    gov'ment!
    Hail! Hail! The man who taught
    what love meant!
    Clear, clear the way
    For his inaugural and wedding
    day!

    Hail! Hail! The mighty ruler of
    love!
    Hail! Hail! The man who made us
    love love!
    Hip! Hip! Hooray!
    For his inaugural and wedding
    day!

[*Band marches on, followed by Wintergreen and Committee members*]

CHIEF JUSTICE:
[*spoken*]

    And, now, Mr. President, if you
    don't mind, we'd like your
    inaugural address.

WINTERGREEN:
[*Sings*]

    I have definite ideas about the
    Philippines*
    And the herring situation up in
    Bismarck;
    I have notions on the salaries of
    movie queens
    And the men who sign their
    signatures with *this* mark!

---

*This and the next seven lines were rewritten for the 1952 revival:

WINTERGREEN: I have definite ideas about the deficit;
    I have plans about our tonnage on the
    ocean.
    But before I grow statistical I'll
    preface it
    With a statement growing out of pure
    emotion.

ENSEMBLE: He has definite ideas about the deficit;
    He has plans about our tonnage on
    the ocean.
    But before he grows statistical, he'll
    preface it
    With a statement growing out of pure
    emotion.

[*Makes cross*]
ALL: He has definite ideas about the
    Philippines
    And the herring situation up in
    Bismarck;
    He has notions on the salaries of
    movie queens
    And the men who sign their
    signatures with *this* mark!

[*Make cross*]

"A Kiss for Cinderella"

WINTERGREEN: But on this glorious day I find
    I'm sentimentally inclined.
    And so—
    I sing this to the girls I used to
    know:

    Here's a kiss for Cinderella
    And a parting kiss for May;
    Toodle-oo, good-bye, this is my
    wedding day.

    Here's a parting smile for Della
    And the lady known as Lou;
    Toodle-oo, good-bye, with bach'lor
    days I'm through!

    Tho' I really never knew them,
    It's a rule I must obey;
    So I'm saying good-bye to them
    In the customary way.

    My regards to Arabella
    And to Emmaline and Kay!
    Toodle-oo, dear girls, good-bye!
    This is my wedding day.

[*Wintergreen repeats first six lines of above; all others sing against this:*]
ALL OTHERS: He is toodle-ooing all his lady
    loves,
    All the girls he didn't know so
    well,
    All the innocent and all the shady
    loves,
    Oh, ding-a-dong-a-dell!
    Bride and groom, their future
    should be glorious—
    What a happy story they will tell;
    Let the welkin now become
    uproarious,
    Oh, ding-a-dong-a-dell!
[*Enter Mary, escorted by Fulton*]
ALL: Clear the way!
    Hail the bride!
    Sweet and gay—
    Here comes the bride!

MARY: Is it true or am I dreaming?
Do I go to Heav'n to stay?
Never was a girl so happy on her
wedding day!

CHIEF JUSTICE:
[spoken]

Do you, John P. Wintergreen,
solemnly swear to uphold the
Constitution of the United
States of America and to love,
honor, and cherish this woman
so long as you two shall live?

WINTERGREEN: I do.

CHIEF JUSTICE: Do you, Mary Turner, promise to
love, honor, and cherish this
man so long as you two shall
live?

MARY: I do.

CHIEF JUSTICE: Therefore, by virtue of the power
that is vested in me as Chief
Justice, I hereby pronounce you
President of the United States,
man and wife.

WINTERGREEN: Mary!

MARY: John!

[They embrace]

BOTH:

[Sing]

Is it true or am I dreaming?
Do I go to Heav'n to stay?
Never was a girl (man) so happy
on her (his) wedding—

[Discord in orchestra. Diana appears]

DIANA: Stop! Halt! Pause! Wait!

ALL: Who is this intruder?
There's no one could be ruder!

[to Diana]

What's your silly notion
In causing this commotion?

"I Was the Most Beautiful Blossom"

DIANA: I was the most beautiful blossom
In all the Southland;
I was sent up North to enter the
contest
With the understanding that the
winner
Was to be the President's wife.
The Committee examined me.
My lily-white body fascinated
them.
I was chosen.
It was the happiest moment of my
life.

ENSEMBLE: Yes, yes, go on!
Yes, yes, go on!

DIANA: Suddenly, the sky fell.
Suddenly, for no reason at all,
No reason at all,
This man rejected me.

All my castles came tumbling
down.
And so I am serving him with a
summons*
For breach of promise!

ENSEMBLE: What! What!
The water's getting hot!
She says he made a promise,
A promise he forgot.

DIANA: It's true! It's true!

JUDGES: The day he's getting married,
You put him on the spot!
It's dirty work of Russia,†
A communistic plot!

WINTERGREEN: Please understand,
It wasn't that I would jilt or
spurn'er;
It just that there was someone
else.

ENSEMBLE: Whom?

WINTERGREEN: *Who!*
Mary Turner!

CHIEF JUSTICE: We're having fits!

ENSEMBLE: We're having fits!

CHIEF JUSTICE: The man admits . . .

ENSEMBLE: The man admits . . .

CHIEF JUSTICE: This little sinner . . .

ENSEMBLE: This little sinner . . .

CHIEF JUSTICE: Was really winner!

ENSEMBLE: Was really winner!

DIANA: I couldn't see . . .

ENSEMBLE: She couldn't see . . .

DIANA: His jilting me.

ENSEMBLE: His jilting she.

DIANA: And so I'm doing . . .

ENSEMBLE: And so I'm doing . . .

DIANA: A bit of suing.

ENSEMBLE: A bit of suing.

MEN: And if it's true she has a claim,
You should be called a dirty name!

GIRLS: Yes, if it's true she has a claim,
Then you're a dirty, dirty name!

---

*This and the next line were revised for the 1952
revival:*

He may be President—But he'll suffer
For having tricked me.

†1952 version:

She says that only she was
His true forget-me-not!

MARY: John, no matter what they do to
hurt you,
The one you love won't desert
you.

DIANA: I'm a queen who has lost her
king!
Why should she wear the wedding
ring?

"Some Girls Can Bake a Pie" (Reprise)

WINTERGREEN: Some girls can bake a pie
Made up of prunes and quinces;
Some make an oyster fry—
Others are good at blinzes.
Some lovely girls have done
Wonders with turkey stuffin's,
But I have found the one
Who can really make corn muffins

DIANA: Who cares about corn muffins?
All I demand is justice!

WINTERGREEN: Which is more important?
Corn muffins or justice?

ENSEMBLE: Which is more important?
Corn muffins or justice?

JUDGES: If you will wait a minute,
You'll have our decision.

[Judges go into huddle]

The decision of the Supreme Court
is—
Corn muffins!

ENSEMBLE: Great! Great!
It's written on the slate!*
There's none but Mary Turner
Could ever be his mate!

DIANA: It's I, not Mary Turner,
Who should have been his mate.
I'm off to tell my story
In ev'ry single state.

ENSEMBLE: Be off with you, young woman,
He's married to his mate.
There's none but Mary Turner
Could ever be his mate.

[Repeat these lines]

DIANA:

[spoken]

See you in court, y'all.

"Of Thee I Sing" (Reprise)

WINTERGREEN: Of thee I sing, baby—

ENSEMBLE: Summer, autumn, winter, spring,
baby!

---

*Alternate version:

It really must be fate!

Shining star and inspiration
Worthy of a mighty nation,
Of thee I sing!

[*Curtain*]

"Zwei Hertzen"

[*This section commenced toward the end of the "Beautiful Blossom" section, after the line "You're a dirty, dirty name"*]

MARY: John, the names they call you
mean nothing—
To me, it's love that is *the* thing!

WINTERGREEN:

[*to melody of "Some Girls Can Bake a Pie"*]
Call me whate'er you will—
Jack only did his duty
When he perceived his Jill
In this American Beauty.
Call me a gigolo!
Say I disgrace the Union!
But those who love must know
We're *zwei hertzen* in communion.

[*Mary and Wintergreen repeat this as the chorus counters:*]

GIRLS: And if it's true she has a claim,
You should be called a dirty name!
MEN: Yes, if it's true she has a claim,
You should be called a dirty name!

MARY: John, no matter what they do to
hurt you,
The one you love won't desert you.

DIANA: Listen, you, 'tis of thee I sing!
[*to crowd*]
Why should she wear the wedding
ring?
[*Scene resumes as above with "Some girls can bake . . ."*]

BOYS: And I'm feeling swell.
BOTH: It's great to be alive
And work from nine to five.
[*Enter two chief secretaries—Jenkins and Miss Benson*]
JENKINS
AND
BENSON: Hello, good morning!
GIRLS
AND
BOYS: Good morning, hello!
Isn't this a moment that's divine?
JENKINS
AND
BENSON: I see it's almost nine.
ALL: And we only have one minute more to
say:
Hello, good morning!
Isn't this a lovely day?
Isn't this a lovely day?

Oh, it's great to be a secret'ry
In the White House, D.C.
You get inside information on Algeria;
You know ev'ry move they're making in
Liberia.
You learn what's what and what is not
In the Land of the Free.
Ev'ry corner that you turn you meet a
notable
With a statement that is eminently
quotable.
Oh, it's great to be a secret'ry
In the White House, D.C.

[*Jenkins and Benson dance. At conclusion, all exit, arm in arm, singing:*]
So long, good morning!
Wasn't this a lovely day?
Wasn't this a lovely day?
[*They whistle as they exit*]

HELLO, GOOD MORNING

Published in the complete piano-vocal score April 1932 as "Opening Act II." Introduced by George Murphy (Jenkins), June O'Dea (Miss Benson), and ensemble. Added to the score late in the rehearsal period.

[*Secretaries enter, whistling*]
BOYS: Hello, good morning!
GIRLS: Good morning, hello!
BOYS: How are you this very lovely day?
GIRLS: I feel very well, sir.

WHO CARES?

Published December 1931 and as part of the complete piano-vocal score April 1932. Introduced by William Gaxton (Wintergreen), Lois Moran (Mary), and ensemble.

A *Change of Mood.* In any musical show, sometimes the same musical sequence can be repeated with lyrics changed either completely (for, say, new locales as in "Florence" and "Paris" [in *The Firebrand of Florence*]) or partially (in second refrains or in finales for new

or added sentiments). "Who Cares?," however, is an example of a refrain where, without a rewritten lyric, a musical offering sometimes can be reprised for a change of mood.

Styled "Brightly," this song was sung in that manner—even glibly—by President Wintergreen and the First Lady in their successful attempt to put the reporters off from further heckling about the girl Wintergreen jilted. In a later scene, when impeachment was threatened if he didn't divorce his wife to marry the jiltee, Wintergreen turned down the advice of his Cabinet and embraced his wife. The lights dimmed down, the music slowed up, and the tongue-in-cheek refrain was now sung with such sincerity that this moment became a quite sentimental, even a touching, one.

—from *Lyrics on Several Occasions*

REPORTERS: We don't want to know about the
moratorium,
Or how near we are to beer,
Or about the League of Nations,
Or the seventeen vacations
You have had since you've been
here.

Here's the one thing that the
people of America
Are beside themselves to know:
They would like to know what's
doing
On the lady who is suing
You—Diana Devereaux!

Ev'rybody wants to know:
What about Miss Devereaux?
From the highest to the low:
What about Miss Devereaux?

WINTERGREEN: It's a pleasant day—
That's all I can say!

MARY: Here's the one thing we'll
announce:
Love's the only thing that counts!

REPORTERS: People want to know:
What of Devereaux?

WINTERGREEN: When the one you love is near,
Nothing else can interfere.

ALL: When the one you love is near,
Nothing else can interfere.

VERSE

WINTERGREEN: Here's some information
I will gladly give the nation:
I am for the true love;
Here's the only girl I do love.

MARY: I love him and he loves me,
And that's how it will always be,
So what care we about Miss
Devereaux?

BOTH: Who cares what the public
chatters?
Love's the only thing that matters.

REFRAIN

Who cares
If the sky cares to fall in the sea?
Who cares what banks fail in
Yonkers,
Long as you've got a kiss that
conquers?
Why should I care?
Life is one long jubilee,
So long as I care for you—
And you care for me.

Published (Sheet Music) Verse

Let it rain and thunder!
Let a million firms go under!
I am not concerned with
Stocks and bonds that I've been burned with.

I love you and you love me,
And that's how it will always be.
And nothing else can ever mean a thing.

Who care what the public chatters?
Love's the only thing that matters.

When *Of Thee I Sing* was revived in 1952, Ira Gershwin, concerned that the "banks fail in Yonkers" reference was dated, decided to rewrite the "Yonker–conquers" couplet. Here are some of the many attempts:

Who cares what (if) headlines are shrieking,
Long as your kisses mine are seeking?
or
Long as we two are cheek-to-cheeking?

Who cares where hist'ry will place me,
Long as your lovely face will face me?

Who cares how history bills me,
Long as you've got a kiss that thrills me?

Who cares how history rates me,
Long as my wife appreciates me?
or
Long as your kisses dislocate me?
or
Long as your kiss just decimates me?
or

Long as your kiss just compensates me?
or
While your kiss incapacitates me?
or
Long as your kiss emancipates me?
or
Long as your kiss infatuates me?
or
While I know that your kiss awaits me?
or (*finally*) Ira's choice:
Long as your kiss intoxicates me?

GARÇON, S'IL VOUS PLAÎT and ENTRANCE OF FRENCH AMBASSADOR and THE ILLEGITIMATE DAUGHTER and BECAUSE, BECAUSE (REPRISE) and WE'LL IMPEACH HIM and WHO CARES? (REPRISE)

Together these numbers comprise the "Finaletto, Act II, Scene 1"—the scene in the President's office of the White House. Published in the complete piano-vocal score April 1932. "The Illegitimate Daughter" had been published separately in January 1932. "Garçon, S'il Vous Plaît" was introduced by the ensemble. "Entrance of French Ambassador" and "The Illegitimate Daughter" were introduced by Florenz Ames (French Ambassador) and ensemble. The "Because, Because" reprise was sung by Ames, Grace Brinkley (Diana), and ensemble. The "We'll Impeach Him" sequence was introduced by William Gaxton (Wintergreen), Dudley Clements (Fulton), George E. Mack (Senator Lyons), Harold Moffet (Gilhooley), and ensemble. The reprise of "Who Cares?" was sung by Gaxton and Lois Moran (Mary).

Genesis of the Illegitimacy. When we went to California for the film *Delicious* we had already had several discussions with Kaufman and Ryskind on *Of Thee I Sing*, which they were developing. Just before we made the trip they were able to give us a fourteen-page outline of the libretto. In Hollywood between the hours on the film we found time to do some work on the operetta and returned to New York with at least two notions in good shape. One was the anthemy campaign title song (later we changed it somewhat); the other was "The Illegitimate Daughter," as is.

Excerpt from page 11 of the scenario: "Throttlebottom also brings out the fact that there is a new angle to the Joan Devereaux matter. [Kaufman and Ryskind later gave Joan a new given name: Diana.] It turns out that she had a French father, so the French government is up in arms about the slight that has been inflicted on her."

"Joan" had to be born in the United States, otherwise couldn't have entered the contest for Mrs. First Lady. Obviously, though, it was more important to musicalize a French father for her. Should he be a baker in Lyons, or the prefect of police in Dijon, or what? More and more I kept thinking that his political or economic or social importance had to be important, else why France's fuss? Not wishing to use the names of any contemporary personages, I went historical. And, illegitimacy being not too socially disadvantageous among many broad-minded Europeans, I scribbled this possible genealogy for her on the margin of page 11: "She was an illegitimate daughter of an ill. nephew of Louie-Philippe (or Napoleon) so you can't inflict this indignity."

—from *Lyrics on Several Occasions*

"Garçon, S'il Vous Plaît"

[*Martial outburst. Six French soldiers march on*]
FRENCH
SOLDIERS: Garçon, s'il vous plaît,
Encore Chevrolet coupé;
Papah, pooh, pooh, pooh!
À vous tout dir vay à vous?
Garçon, qu'est-ce que c'est?
Tra la, Maurice Chevalier!
J'adore crêpes Suzette
Et aussi Lafayette!

[*They march, repeat this, come to attention*]
And now we give the meaning of this
song:
We're six of the fifty million and we
can't be wrong!

"Entrance of French Ambassador"

FRENCH
AMBASSADOR: I am the Ambassador of France,
And I've come here to see
A grievous wrong righted.
My country is deeply hurt.
Not since the days of Louis the
Seventh,
The Eighth, the Ninth, the Tenth,
And possibly the Eleventh,
Has such a thing happened.

ENSEMBLE: What's troubling you?
FRENCH
AMBASSADOR: You have done a great injustice
To a French descendant—
A lovely girl

Whose rights have been trampled
in the dust.

ENSEMBLE: Who is she? What's her name?

FRENCH
AMBASSADOR: Her name is Diana Devereaux.

ENSEMBLE: Diana Devereaux! Diana Devereaux!
Since when is she of French
descent?

FRENCH
AMBASSADOR: I've been looking up her family tree
And I have found a most important
pedigree!

"The Illegitimate Daughter"

She's the illegitimate daughter
Of an illegitimate son
Of an illegitimate nephew
Of Napoléon.

ENSEMBLE: Napoléon?

FRENCH
AMBASSADOR: She offers aristocracy
To this bizarre democracy,
Where naught is sacred but the
old simoleon!
I must know why
You crucify
My native country
With this effront'ry
To the illegitimate daughter
Of an illegitimate son
Of an illegitimate nephew
Of Napoléon!

ENSEMBLE: To the illegitimate daughter
Of an illegitimate son
Of an illegitimate nephew
Of Napoléon!

[Ensemble turns on Wintergreen]

ENSEMBLE: You so-and-so!
We didn't know
She had a tie-up
So very high up!
She's the illegitimate daughter
Of an illegitimate son
Of an illegitimate nephew
Of Napoléon!

DIANA: Ah!
I was the most beautiful blossom
In all the Southland.

MARY AND
WINTERGREEN: We know all that.

FRENCH
AMBASSADOR: You know all that,
But you *don't* know the misery
Of this poor little girl who has
suffered.
Because . . .

ENSEMBLE: Because?

MARY AND
WINTERGREEN: Because?

FRENCH
AMBASSADOR: Because . . .

"Because, Because" (Reprise)

DIANA: Because, because, because, because
I won the competition
But I got no recognition
And because he broke my heart!

Because, because, because, because
The man who ought to love me
Tried to make a monkey of me,
Double-crossing from the start!

I might have been First Lady,
But now my past is shady.
Oh, pity this poor maidie!

FRENCH
AMBASSADOR: And there's the man who ought to
pay!

ENSEMBLE: Because, because, because, because
She won the prize for beauty,
But he didn't do his duty;
He has broken her poor heart!

FRENCH
AMBASSADOR:
[to Wintergreen]
You see this poor girl has suffered.
And so, on behalf of France,
I demand that your marriage be
annulled
And that you marry Diana.

WINTERGREEN: Never, never!

FRENCH
AMBASSADOR: Then you will arouse the anger of
France,
And you must be prepared to face
the consequences!

[Soldiers line up with Ambassador and Diana.
They march off, singing]

FRENCH
SOLDIERS: Garçon, s'il vous plaît,
Encore Chevrolet coupé!
Papah, pooh, pooh, pooh,
À vous tout dir vay à vous?

FULTON: Jack, you've got to do something
about this.

WINTERGREEN: Leave Mary? Never!

FULTON: We are all in this together;
We are birdies of a feather.
And if you don't change your thesis
Then our party goes to pieces!

LYONS: All our jobs you'll be destroying
With your attitude annoying.

GILHOOLEY: You will get us all in trouble!
And in spades, sir, which is double!

WINTERGREEN: I will never leave my Mary!

LYONS: Since he's acting so contrary,
Send him off on a vacation.

GILHOOLEY: I suggest his resignation.

WINTERGREEN: Resignation?

ENSEMBLE: Resignation?

FULTON: You've got to face it—This is a
crisis!
To leave your Mary you may
decline;
But to save us, my good advice is:
You resign!

ENSEMBLE: Yes, resign.

WINTERGREEN: I assure you—though it's a crisis,
To leave my Mary I must decline,
And I don't care what your advice
is;
I decline to resign!

MARY: We decline to resign!

"We'll Impeach Him"

[to each other]

LYONS AND
GILHOOLEY: He is stubborn—We must teach
him;
I'm afraid we must impeach him!

ENSEMBLE: He is stubborn—We must teach
him;
He has forced us to impeach him!

COMMITTEE: You decline to resign.
So we'll teach you!
We'll impeach you!

SECRETARIES: You decline to resign—
We don't envy you at all!

COMMITTEE: You decline to resign.
So we'll teach you!
We'll impeach you!
You decline to resign—
Humpty Dumpty has to fall!

[They exit]

"Who Cares?" (Reprise)

MARY: Who cares
If the sky cares to fall in the sea?

WINTERGREEN: We two together can win out;*

*Earlier version of this and the next line:
Who cares if Congress is crummy?
They can never take my love from me!

MARY: Just remember to stick your chin out.

MARY: Why should we care?
Life is one long jubilee—

BOTH: So long as I care for you—
And you care for me!

THE SENATORIAL ROLL CALL

Published in the complete piano-vocal score April 1932 as "Opening, Act III, Scene 3." Introduced by Victor Moore (Throttlebottom) and ensemble. Alternate title: "The Senator from Minnesota."

[*At rise all the Senators are humming and swaying to tune*]

THROTTLE: The Senator from Minnesota?

SENATOR: Present.

THROTTLE: Check!
The Senator from North Dakota?

SENATOR: Present.

THROTTLE: Check!
The Senator from Louisiana?

SENATOR: Present.

THROTTLE: Check!
The Senator who's from Montana?

SENATOR: Present.

THROTTLE: Check!
The Senator who's from Nebraska?

SENATOR: Present.

THROTTLE: Check!
The Senator who's from Alaska?

SENATOR: Present.

THROTTLE: Check!
The Senators from other states will have to bide their time,
For I simply can't be bothered when the names don't rhyme!

ENSEMBLE: Oh, he simply can't be bothered when the names don't rhyme!
The Senators from other states will have to bide their time,
For he simply can't be bothered when the names don't rhyme!

THROTTLE: The country thinks it's got depression.

SENATORS: Ha! Ha! Ha!

THROTTLE: Just wait until we get in session!

SENATORS: Ha! Ha! Ha!

THROTTLE: The people want a lot of action.

SENATORS: Ho! Ho! Ho!

THROTTLE: We're here to give them satisfaction!

SENATORS: Ho! Ho! Ho!

THROTTLE: Today is really full of laughter.

SENATORS: Ha! Ha! Ha!

THROTTLE: Compared to what will follow after!

SENATORS: Ha! Ha! Ha!

THROTTLE: There's action ev'ry minute when this happy group convenes:

ALL: To get business into tangles
We can guarantee more angles
Than the town of Boston guarantees in beans!
If you think you've got depression,
Wait until we get in session,
And you'll find out what depression really means!
Ha! Ha! Ha!
Ha! Ha! Ha! Ha!
Ha! Ha! Ha! Ha! Ha!

Revised (1952) Version, Roll Call Conclusion

THROTTLE: The people think they've got taxation.

SENATORS: Ha! Ha! Ha!

THROTTLE: Just wait for further legislation.
Ha! Ha! Ha!

THROTTLE: Today is really full of laughter.

SENATORS: Ho! Ho! Ho!

THROTTLE: Compared to what will follow after.

SENATORS: Ho! Ho! Ho!

THROTTLE: With fury though you may be seething.

SENATORS: Ha! Ha! Ha!

THROTTLE: Just wait until we tax your breathing.

SENATORS: Ha! Ha! Ha!

THROTTLE: On taxes,
None relaxes
When this happy group convenes!

ALL: Be it payroll, be it income—
We are gathered here to sink 'em,
Till there's no one with a nickel in his jeans!
If you think you've got taxation,
Wait for further legislation,
And you'll find out what taxation really means!
Ha! Ha! Ha!
Ha! Ha! Ha! Ha!
Ha! Ha! Ha! Ha! Ha!

IMPEACHMENT PROCEEDING and GARÇON, S'IL VOUS PLAÎT (REPRISE) and THE ILLEGITIMATE DAUGHTER (REPRISE) and JILTED and SENATORIAL ROLL CALL (CONTINUED) and I'M ABOUT TO BE A MOTHER and POSTERITY IS JUST AROUND THE CORNER

Together these numbers make up the "Finaletto, Act II, Scene 3." Published in the complete piano-vocal score April 1932 as "The Senate." "Impeachment Proceeding" was introduced by Victor Moore (Throttlebottom), Dudley Clements (Fulton), Sam Mann (Lippman), Harold Moffet (Gilhooley), George E. Mack (Senator Lyons), Edward H. Robins (Senator Jones), Martin Leroy (Senate Clerk), and ensemble. The reprises of "Garçon, S'il Vous Plaît" and "The Illegitimate Daughter" were sung by Florenz Ames (French Ambassador) and ensemble. "Jilted" was introduced by Grace Brinkley (Diana) and ensemble. The continuation of the "Senatorial Roll Call" was sung by Moore, William Gaxton (Wintergreen), and ensemble. "I'm About to Be a Mother" (also titled "Who Could Ask For Anything More?") was introduced by Lois Moran (Mary) and ensemble. "Posterity Is Just Around the Corner" (also titled "Posterity") was introduced by Gaxton, Moran, and ensemble.

"Impeachment Proceeding"

CLERK: The next business before the Senate is the resolution on the impeachment of the President.

[*A fanfare of trumpets. Two pages enter*]

TWO PAGES: The President of the United States!

THROTTLE: Who?

CLERK: The President of the United States!

THROTTLE: Oh, Mr. President, won't you sit down while we kick you out?

FULTON, LIPPMAN, GILHOOLEY, AND LYONS: Whereas:

LYONS: At a meeting of the Senate at which a quorum was present a motion was made and it was proposed that—

FULTON, LIPPMAN, AND GILHOOLEY: Whereas:

LYONS: John P. Wintergreen has undertaken to marry the winner of a beauty contest held in Atlantic City—

FULTON, LIPPMAN, AND GILHOOLEY: Whereas:

LYONS: His refusal to marry the winner Diana Devereaux will lead to international complications—

FULTON, LIPPMAN, AND GILHOOLEY: Now therefore be it resolved that John P. Wintergreen be, and hereby is, impeached from the said office of President of these United States.

SENATOR JONES: I second the resolution.

FULTON: Our first witness—the French Ambassador!

"Garçon, S'il Vous Plaît" (Reprise)

FRENCH SOLDIERS: [marching in]

> Garçon, s'il vous plaît,
> Encore Chevrolet coupé,
> Papah, pooh, pooh, pooh!
> À vous tout dir vay à vous?

SENATORS: We say how-de-do—
Which means that we welcome you:
We're glad of the chance
To say hello to France.

[Enter French Ambassador]

FRENCH AMBASSADOR: You've dealt a lovely maid
A blow that is injurious;
A very dirty trick was played
And France is simply furious!

SENATORS: He says a lovely maid
Was dealt a blow injurious;
He says a dirty trick was played
And France is simply furious.

FULTON: Ambassador, please explain why France is so concerned about the plaintiff.

"The Illegitimate Daughter" (Reprise)

FRENCH AMBASSADOR: She's the illegitimate daughter
Of an illegitimate son
Of an illegitimate nephew
Of Napoléon.

SENATORS: Napoléon?

FRENCH AMBASSADOR: She's contemplating suicide
Because that man, he threw aside
A lady with the blue blood of Napoléon.
What sort of man
Is this who can
Insult my country
With his effront'ry.

SENATORS: To the illegitimate daughter
Of an illegitimate son
Of an illegitimate nephew
Of Napoléon?

FRENCH AMBASSADOR: The Atlantic City witnesses!

[Entrance of the Atlantic City bathing beauties and Diana Devereaux]

DIANA: I have come all ze way from France to bring ze greetings.

FRENCH AMBASSADOR: Tell your story, little one! Commencez, s'il vous plaît.

"Jilted"

DIANA: Jilted, jilted,
I'm a flow'r that's wilted;
Blighted, blighted,
Till the wrong is righted;

Broken, broken,
By a man soft-spoken;
Faded, faded—
Heaven knows why!

When men are deceivers, I'm afraid
'Tis sad to be a trusting maid.

Jilted, jilted, jilted am I.
Oh, what is there left but to die?

ENSEMBLE: Jilted, jilted,
She's a flower that's wilted;
Blighted, blighted,
Till the wrong is righted;

Broken, broken,
By a man soft-spoken;
Faded, faded—
Heaven knows why!

Just as in the Frankie and Johnny song,
He done her wrong, he done her wrong.

ENSEMBLE: Jilted, jilted, jilted is she!
Oh, what is there left but to dee?
Boo-hoo! Boo-hoo! Boo-hoo!

THROTTLE: And now, Mr. President, what have you to say for yourself?

WINTERGREEN: Impeach me! Fine me! Jail me! Sue me!
My Mary's love means much more to me!

THROTTLE: Enough! Enough! We want no preachment!
It's time to vote on his impeachment!

ALL: It's time to vote on his impeachment!

"Senatorial Roll Call" (Continued)

THROTTLE: The Senator from Minnesota?
SENATOR: Guilty!
THROTTLE: Check!
The Senator from North Dakota?
SENATOR: Guilty!
THROTTLE: Check!
The Senator from Louisiana?
SENATOR: Guilty!
THROTTLE: Check!
The Senator who's from Montana?

[Mary breaks into room]

MARY: Stop! Stop! Stop!
Before you go any further,
With your permission,
I must tell you of my husband's delicate condition.

ENSEMBLE: Delicate condition! What do you mean?

"I'm About to Be a Mother"

MARY: I'm about to be a mother;
He's about to be a father;
We're about to have a baby.
I must tell it;
These doings compel it!
Oh, I'm about to be a mother;
He's about to be a father;
We're about to have a baby.

ENSEMBLE: A baby!

MARY: A baby to love and adore—
Who could ask for anything more?

ENSEMBLE: She's about to be a mother;
He's about to be a father;
They're about to have a baby;
We can't bother
A budding young father!

WINTERGREEN:
[*spoken*]
Mary, is it true? Am I going to
have a baby?
MARY: It's true, John, it's true.
WINTERGREEN: Water!
[*He faints*]
ENSEMBLE:
[*Sings*]
They're about to have a baby, a
baby—

DIANA:
[*spoken*]
It eez a fine countree—I am
compromised and she has ze
baby!
THROTTLE: Gentlemen, gentlemen! This
country has never yet
impeached an expectant father.
What do you say?
SENATORS: Not guilty!
THROTTLE:
[*to Wintergreen*]
You can still be President and I'll
go back to Vice!
FRENCH
AMBASSADOR: Sacré! I go to the telegraph office
to cable my report;
This is American trickery of the
most reprehensible sort!

DIANA:
[*Sings*]
I was the most beautiful
blossom . . .
[*French Ambassador takes her by the hand,
leads her off*]
In all the Southland.
ATLANTIC CITY
GIRLS: Strike up the cymbals, drum, and
fife,
One of us was to be the
President's wife.
CHIEF JUSTICE:
[*spoken*]
Great work, Jack; you'll be
reinstated in the hearts of the
American people.
JONES: You're doing your duty by
posterity.
WINTERGREEN: Posterity—why, posterity is just
around the corner.

"Posterity Is Just Around the Corner"

WINTERGREEN: Posterity is just around the corner!
ALL: Posterity is just around the corner!
MARY: It really doesn't pay to be a
mourner.
ALL: Posterity is just around the corner!

WINTERGREEN: Posterity is here—I don't mean
maybe!
ALL: There's nothing guarantees it like
a baby!
MARY: Posterity is here and will continue!
ALL: We really didn't know you had it
in you!
Posterity is in its infancy!

WINTERGREEN: I sing to ev'ry citizen and
fore'gner
ALL: Posterity is just around the corner!
COMMITTEE: We'll soon be pulling plums like
Jackie Horner!
ALL: Posterity is just around the—
Oom-posterity, oom-posterity,
oom-pah, oom-pah,
oom-posterity!
Oom-posterity, oom-posterity,
oom-pah, oom-pah,
oom-posterity—
Is just around the corner!
Around the corner!

TRUMPETER, BLOW YOUR GOLDEN HORN

Published in the complete piano-vocal score April 1932.
Introduced by ensemble. Alternate title: "Trumpeter."
Earlier versions were titled "Gabriel, Gabriel, Blow
Your Golden Horn."

ALL: Oh, trumpeter, trumpeter, blow your
golden horn!
Oh, trumpeter, trumpeter, blow your
golden horn!
A White House baby will very soon
be born!
A White House baby will very soon
be born!
Blow your horn!
[*stiffly*]
FLUNKIES: With a hey-nonny-nonny and a
ha-cha-cha!

With a hey-nonny-nonny and a
ha-cha-cha!
ALL: There's something glorious
happening today
For all the citizens of the U.S.A.
A White House baby will very soon
be born!
Oh, trumpeter, blow your horn,
Oh, trumpeter, blow your horn,
Oh, trumpeter, blow your horn,
Your golden horn, your golden horn!
[*Doctor enters*]
Oh, doctor, doctor, what's the news,
we pray?
We've waited for your bulletin all
day.
DOCTOR: The baby of the President and Frau
Will be here almost any minute now.
FLUNKIES: With a hey-nonny-nonny and a
ha-cha-cha!
With a hey-nonny-nonny and a
ha-cha-cha!
ALL: Oh, doctor, here is the one thing we
must know—
We're all of us anxious and we've
got to know:
The baby, is it to be a girl or boy?
A baby girl or boy?
A nation's pride and joy!
We must know whether it's a girl or
boy,
A girl or boy!
DOCTOR: On that point, nobody budges,
For all matters of the sort
Are decided by the judges
Of the Supreme Court.
[*All repeat*]
CHIEF
FLUNKY: The Supreme Court!
JUDGES:
[*entering*]
We're the one, two, three, four, five,
six, seven, eight, nine Supreme
Court Judges!
FLUNKIES: With a hey-nonny-nonny and a
ha-cha-cha!
With a hey-nonny-nonny and a
ha-cha-cha!
ALL: About the baby—Will it be
A boy or girl—a he or she?
JUDGES: On that point nobody budges,
For all matters of the sort

Are decided by the judges
Of the Supreme Court.

[*All repeat*]

CHIEF
FLUNKY: The Secretary of Agriculture!

[*Music: "The Farmer in the Dell"*]

LIPPMAN:
[*entering*]

    The farmers in the dell,
    The farmers in the dell,
    They all keep a-asking me:
    A boy or a gel?

JUDGES: On that point nobody budges,
    For all matters of the sort
    Are decided by the judges
    Of the Supreme Court.

CHIEF
FLUNKY: The Secretary of the Navy.

[*Music: "Sailor's Hornpipe"*]

GILHOOLEY:
[*entering*]

    All the sailors in the Navy
    In these great United States,
    Do not eat their bowls of gravy,
    Nor the captains nor the mates.
    They refuse to jib an anchor,
    Strike a boom, or heave a sail,
    Till you've satisfied their hanker:
    Is it female or a male?

JUDGES: On that point nobody budges,
    For all matters of the sort
    Are decided by the judges
    Of the Supreme Court.

CHIEF
FLUNKY: Senator Carver Jones!

[*Music: "Come Be My Rainbow"*]

JONES:
[*entering*]

    Out on the prairie,
    The cowboys all keep asking of me:
    He or a she—
    She or a he?
    Out on the prairie,
    For baby boy or girl they are keen,
    But they want nothing in between.

JUDGES: On that point nobody budges,
    For all matters of the sort
    Are decided by the judges
    Of the Supreme Court.

CHIEF
FLUNKY: Senator Robert E. Lyons!

[*Music: "Swanee River"*]

LYONS:
[*entering*]

    Way down upon the Swanee River,

Folks are filled with joy;
But they want to know what will the
    stork deliver—
Will it be a girl or a boy?

JUDGES: On that point nobody budges,
    For all matters of the sort
    Are decided by the judges
    Of the Supreme Court.

ALL: There's something glorious
    happening today:
    A baby will be born!
    A baby will be born!
    Oh, trumpeter, trumpeter, blow your
    golden horn!

ON THAT MATTER, NO ONE BUDGES

Published in the complete piano-vocal score April 1932 as "Finale Ultimo." Introduced by the entire company.

CHIEF JUSTICE: Gentlemen, duty calls. We have to
    determine the sex of the infant.
WINTERGREEN: You decide?
CHIEF JUSTICE: We do.
JUDGES: On that matter, no one budges,
    For all cases of the sort
    Are decided by the judges
    Of the Supreme Court.

ENSEMBLE: Are decided by the judges
    Of the Supreme Court.
JUDGES: Whereas:
CHIEF JUSTICE: A child has been born to the
    President of the United States
    and his consort.
JUDGES: Whereas:
CHIEF JUSTICE: The judges of the Supreme Court
    have been sent to determine the
    sex of the aforesaid infant.
JUDGES: Whereas:
CHIEF JUSTICE: By a strict party vote it has been
    decided that—

[*spoken*]

    It's a boy.

JUDGES:
[*Sing*]

    On that matter, no one budges,
    For all cases of the sort
    Are decided by the judges
    Of the Supreme Court.

ENSEMBLE: Are decided by the judges
    Of the Supreme Court.

[*Fanfare*]

JUDGES: Whereas:
CHIEF JUSTICE: A child has been born to the
    President of the United States
    and his consort.

WINTERGREEN:
[*spoken*]

    Wait a minute; we've had all that.

CHIEF JUSTICE: Yes, but you're having it again.
    This time it's a girl.

JUDGES:
[*Sing*]

    On that matter, no one budges,
    For all cases of the sort
    Are decided by the judges
    Of the Supreme Court.

ENSEMBLE: Are decided by the judges
    Of the Supreme Court.

FRENCH
AMBASSADOR: Oh, I can stand no more;
    My temper's getting gingery;
    This certainly will lead to war!
    This insult added to injury!

ENSEMBLE: Oh, he can stand no more;
    His temper's getting gingery;
    He says that this will lead to war!
    This insult added to injury!

FRENCH
AMBASSADOR: Oh, my poor motherless child.
    Where is she? What is she doing?

[*Sings mournfully offstage to melody of "I Was the Most Beautiful Blossom"*]

DIANA: Ah!

[*Diana enters. Dialogue scene. War is averted and Diana is paired off with Vice President Throttlebottom*]

WINTERGREEN:
[*Sings*]

    Of thee I sing, baby,
    Summer, autumn, winter, spring,
    baby;
    You're my silver lining,
    You're my sky of blue;
    There's a love-light shining
    Just because of you.

ALL: Of thee I sing, baby,
    You have got that certain thing,
    baby!
    Shining star and inspiration
    Worthy of a mighty nation,
    Of thee I sing!

[*Curtain*]

ENTRANCE OF WINTERGREEN AND MARY

Intended for William Gaxton (Wintergreen), Lois Moran (Mary), and ensemble. Dropped before the tryout. Replaced with "Hello, Good Morning."

SECRETARIES: Hail! Hail! The rulers of our
 gov'ment!
 Hail! Hail! To those who taught
 what love meant!
 They'll soon be seen
 A-sitting down to start the day's
 routine.

 Hail! Hail! The mighty rulers of
 love!
 Hail! Hail! To those who made us
 love love!
 Clear, clear the way!
 A page of hist'ry will be made today!

WINTERGREEN
AND MARY: Good morning!
SECRETARIES: Good morning!

WHILE WE'RE WAITING FOR THE BABY and OPPORTUNITY HAS BECKONED and STRIKE THE LOUD-RESOUNDING ZITHER and YOU'LL PARDON ME IF I REVEAL

These numbers comprise a discarded version of most of the last scene. They are in an early draft of the script, a copy of which belonged to *Of Thee I Sing*'s set designer, Jo Mielziner (Ira Gershwin had donated his copy of this script to the Library of Congress). They were brought to the editor's attention by musical-theatre historian Steven Suskin. No music is known to survive, although some of the material became part of the final version of the sequence.

WOMEN:
[*variously*]
 Oh, here's the doctor!
 Here's the doctor!

 Is there any news?
 How is she?
DOCTOR: Splendid, splendid! The baby will be
 here very soon now.
WOMAN: Anything we can do?
DOCTOR: No, no. All we can do is wait.
ANOTHER
WOMAN: But can't we do something?
DOCTOR: Well, while we're waiting for the baby I
 suggest we have a dance.
[*This last line is half spoken, half sung. The others pick it up: "While we're waiting for the baby he suggests we have a dance." Into number*]

"While We're Waiting for the Baby"

ALL: When a child is ushered into
 Such a world as this of ours,
 We must straightaway begin to
 Arm against the foreign powers.
 It's a matter that embarrasses
 The diplomatic corps—
 For you can't deny that Paris is
 A-getting pretty sore.
 After this is over, maybe
 We will have a war with France—
 While we're waiting for the baby
 I suggest we have a dance.
[*Dance*]
 But like Irish Rose's Abie,
 We will fight for our romance—
 While we're waiting for the baby
 Let us have another dance.
[*More dancing*]
 Dark and gloomy though the way
 be,
 We must nonetheless advance—
 While we're waiting for the baby
 Let us have another dance.
[*More dancing*]
 Though we dearly love our neighby,
 We will kick him in the pants—
 While we're waiting for the baby
 Let us have another dance.
[*More dancing*]
WOMEN: Doctor, pray forgive the question,
 But you'd fill us all with joy
 If you gave us a suggestion
 Whether it's a girl or boy.
DOCTOR: Though admiring all of you here,
 Your enjoyment I must sperl,
 Re the infant that is due here—
 Whether it's a boy or girl.
 On that point, nobody budges,
 For all matters of the sort
 Are decided by the judges
 Of the Supreme Court.

WOMEN: The doctor is a sport,
 The doctor is a sport,
 He's going to leave the gender to
 The Supreme Court.
CHIEF
FLUNKY: The Supreme Court!
[*Enter the Chief Justice and the other Judges. Sing a chorus of "While We're Waiting for the Baby"*]
CHIEF
FLUNKY: The Secretary of Agriculture!
LIPPMAN:
[*entering*]
 The farmers in the dell,
 The farmers in the dell—
 They all keep a-asking me:
 A boy or a gel?
JUDGES: On that point, nobody budges,
 For all matters of the sort
 Are decided by the judges
 Of the Supreme Court.
[*All repeat this last*]
CHIEF
FLUNKY: The Secretary of the Navy!
GILHOOLEY:
[*entering*]
 All the sailors in the Navy
 In these great United States
 Do not eat their bowls of gravy,
 Nor the captains nor the mates.
 They refuse to jib an anchor,
 Strike a boom, or heave a sail,
 Till you've satisfied their hanker:
 Is it female or a male?
JUDGES: On that point, nobody budges,
 For all matters of the sort
 Are decided by the judges
 Of the Supreme Court.
CHIEF
FLUNKY: Senator Carver Jones!
JONES:
[*entering*]
 Speaking for Nevada's cowboys,
 And for both of the Dakotes;
 Speaking for Nebraska's plowboys,
 All of whom contribute votes;
 Since the West must be protected
 In this country of the free—
 Is the infant that's expected
 Gonna be a he or she?
JUDGES: On that point nobody budges,
 For all matters of the sort
 Are decided by the judges
 Of the Supreme Court.
CHIEF
FLUNKY: Senator Robert E. Lyons!

LYONS:
[entering]

Aunt Jemima, Uncle Joe,
Down on the levee—
Both the old folks want to know:
A niece or a nevee?

JUDGES: On that point nobody budges,
For all matters of the sort
Are decided by the judges
Of the Supreme Court.

[Fulton and Wintergreen enter]

FULTON:
[spoken]

Take it easy, Jack! Nothing can
happen to her.

WINTERGREEN: I know, but at a time like
this—Mary in there alone—

[The throng greets him]

Oh! Hello! Have to excuse the way
I look. I'm—anybody got a
drink?

[Every man brings out a flask. Wintergreen
takes Fulton's]

Thanks.

[Drinks]

I guess it's not going to be so hard
for her.

GILHOOLEY: Is there any news?

WINTERGREEN: Say, I haven't read a paper all
week.

GILHOOLEY: No, I mean about Mary.

[Dialogue continues. Entrance of French
Ambassador. Increased hostility. Then:]

NURSE:
[entering]

Oh, Mr. Wintergreen!

WINTERGREEN: Who said that?

[Sees the nurse]

Oh! Any news?

NURSE: The baby will be here at any
moment.

[Exits]

WINTERGREEN: My God! You hear that? What do
I do now?

[to the French Ambassador]

Got a drink?

FRENCH
AMBASSADOR:
[offering flask]

Permit me.

"Opportunity Has Beckoned"

JUDGES:
[Sing]

Opportunity has beckoned;
We must answer when it becks.

If you'll pardon us a second,
We will now decide the sex.
On that point, nobody budges,
For all matters of the sort
Are decided by the judges
Of the Supreme Court.

ALL: Comes a moment that is tender
In the nation's history;
They will now decide the gender
Of the baby that's to be.
Oh, there's nothing could be cuter
Than the judges when they vote.

WINTERGREEN: I'll take anything but neuter
From the Supreme Cou't.

ALL: He'll take anything but neuter
From the Supreme Cou't.

WINTERGREEN: Go then and decide the gender;
Make it masculine or tender.
If it's neuter I will shoot her
And the Supreme Cou't.

JUDGES: He wants no dilly-dallying;
He wants no shilly-shallying;
He wants the total tallying
When reading our report.
A girl with masculinity,
A boy with femininity,
Means hell in the vicinity
Of this here Court.

ALL: On that point, he never budges,
So bring in a true report,
Or he'll shoot up all the judges
Of the Supreme Court.

[Supreme Court Judges exit]

WINTERGREEN: They are men of legal vision,
Now preparing for to think;
While awaiting their decision,
Let us have another drink.

ALL: While awaiting their decision,
Let us have another drink.

[A trumpeter enters; blows trumpet. Supreme
Court Judges return]

"Strike the Loud-Resounding Zither"

JUDGES: Strike the loud-resounding zither!
Now there's nothing to perplex,
For we all have got togither
On the question of the sex.

For like greater men and lesser
(For example, Eddie Foy),
You are now the proud possessor
Of a bouncing baby boy.

WINTERGREEN: I am now the proud possessor
Of a bouncing baby boy.

ALL: He is now the proud possessor
Of a bouncing baby boy.

WINTERGREEN: Oh, there now is a successor
To the wealth that I enjoy—
I am now the proud possessor
Of a bouncing baby boy.

[Congratulations all around]

Gentlemen, my thanks are many.
May I write you out some checks?

CHIEF JUSTICE: Sir, we do not charge a penny
When the matter's one of sex.

JUDGES: No, we do not charge a penny
When the matter's one of sex.

[Judges exit]

FRENCH
AMBASSADOR: In the midst of this rejoicing
That goes up from every throat,
While you of your bouncing boy
sing,
France has wrote another note.

WINTERGREEN: In the midst of this rejoicing,
France has wrote another note?

FRENCH
AMBASSADOR: In the midst of this rejoicing,
France has wrote another note.
Down with all these conversations;
I am off to catch my boat!
We now sever our relations,
À la carte and table d'hôte!

ALL: He now severs all relations,
À la carte and table d'hôte!

WINTERGREEN: You now sever all relations,
Table d'hôte and à la carte?
What about the League of
Nations?
Sacré bleu, sir, have a heart!

ALL: What about the League of
Nations?
Sacré bleu, sir, have a heart!

FRENCH
AMBASSADOR:
[spoken]

Lafayette!

[Clicks his heels and salutes. Trumpeter enters
again, and again blows his trumpet. Instant
silence, as before, broken by just a low buzz
from the crowd. Enter the Supreme Court
Judges]

JUDGES: Strike again the zooming zither!
On this question of the sex
You could fell us with a fither—
We are in it to our necks.
For the first report was false, O—
There were two—one with a curl—

WINTERGREEN: So we're here to tell you also
You're the father of a girl.

WINTERGREEN: They are here to tell me also
I'm the father of a girl.

ALL: They are here to tell him also
He's the father of a girl.

[More congratulations]

WINTERGREEN: Ye gods, but there's a crew of
them!
First one, and now there's two of
them!
I'd like to have a view of them,
To make the matter short.

JUDGES: The boy has masculinity;
The girl has femininity;
So don't shoot in the vicinity
Of this here Court!

[Judges exit, singing]

WINTERGREEN: The girl has femininity;
The boy has masculinity,
And in another minute he
Can lick the Supreme Court.

ALL: He has too much masculinity
For that there Court!

FRENCH
AMBASSADOR: I'd like to offer my felicitations,
And at the same time sever our
relations.

ALL: He'd like to offer his felicitations,
And at the same time sever all
relations.

WINTERGREEN: Before you go away to catch your
boat,
I think that I have got an
antidote.

ALL: Before you go away to catch your
boat,
He thinks that he has got an
antidote.

WINTERGREEN: A method of renewing our
relations—

FRENCH
AMBASSADOR: If that is so, accept felicitations.

"You'll Pardon Me If I Reveal"

WINTERGREEN: You'll pardon me if I reveal
That, frankly, here's the way I
feel:
Squalling infants are a bother—

You'll admit that that is true.
Though I yearn to be a father,
It's to one and not to two.

ALL: Squalling infants are a bother—
You'll admit that that is true.
Though he yearns to be a father,
It's to one and not to two.

WINTERGREEN: Speaking frankly for the other
(Mrs. Wintergreen to you),
Though she yearns to be a mother,
It's to one and not to two.

ALL: Speaking frankly for the other
(Mrs. Wintergreen to you),
Though she yearns to be a mother,
It's to one and not to two.

WINTERGREEN: So I ask consideration
For a father and a mother;
Take one for your population
And let us retain the other.

ALL: So he asks consideration
For a father and a mother—
Take one for your population
And let them retain the other.

FRENCH
AMBASSADOR: By these friendly arbitrations
Mortal combat's been averted;
We resume all our relations
And nobody will get hurted.

ALL: By these friendly arbitrations
Mortal combat's been averted;
They resume all their relations,
And nobody will get hurted.

[They all shake hands; kiss each other. Enter
the trumpeter; again he blows his trumpet]
WINTERGREEN: Oh, my God!
[The Supreme Court Judges enter as the crowd
buzzes]
If you strike again that zither,
Tell my wife I'm finished with her!
Can those babies have another
Bouncing little baby brother?
If they have, then it's a nuisance
And I'll sell this one for two
cents!

JUDGES: Oh, President of Presidents,
Forgive that trumpet call;
There are no triple residents
To grace your banquet hall.
So we ask you throw no missile,
For the tally shows but two,
And we simply blew that whistle
To announce that she was through.

ALL: So we ask you throw no missile,
For the tally shows but two,
And they simply blew that whistle
To announce that she was through.

WINTERGREEN: Hooray! Hooroo!
I'm glad that she is through!

CHIEF
FLUNKY: Miss Diana Devereaux!
WINTERGREEN: Miss Diana Devereaux!
I will not see her ever-O.

ALL: It's Miss Diana Devereaux!
Yes, Devereaux! Yes, Devereaux!

[Diana enters]

DIANA: I come to offer my felicitations,
And at the same time ask
congratulations.

FULTON: Oh, you who very nearly caused
our ruin,
Pray tell us why you're here and
what you're doin'.

DIANA: Mr. President, I crave you,
Let us not be wooden-headed,
For this morning I forgave you
And this evening I was wedded.

ALL: Mr. President, we crave you,
Let your hatred be imbedded,
For this morning she forgave you
And this evening she was wedded.

WINTERGREEN: Thank the gods that came to save
me;
Let our hatred be imbedded.
I am glad that you forgave me,
But to whom, pray, are you
wedded?

ALL: Yes, to whom, pray, are you
wedded?

[Enter Throttlebottom]

DIANA: There he stands, the bold and
daring!
I the May and he December.
That's the man whose name I'm
bearing,
But a name I can't remember.

WINTERGREEN:
[to Throttlebottom]
Haven't I seen you before some
place?

THROTTLE: Oh, no! You don't pull that on me
again!

[His shirtfront lights up; on it is lettered "I am
Alexander Throttlebottom, Vice President."
Scene continues through finale]

OVERLEAF: *Jack Pearl and Lyda Roberti*

PARDON MY ENGLISH | 1933

Tryout: Garrick Theatre, Philadelphia, December 2, 1932; Majestic Theatre, Brooklyn, December 26, 1932; Broad Street Theatre, Newark, January 2, 1933; Colonial Theatre, Boston, January 9, 1933. New York run: Majestic Theatre, opened January 20, 1933. 46 performances. Music by George Gershwin. Produced by Alex A. Aarons and Vinton Freedley. Book by Herbert Fields, Morrie Ryskind, and uncredited others. Book staged by John McGowan and Vinton Freedley. Dances staged by George Hale. Orchestra under the direction of Earl Busby. Orchestrations by William Daly, Robert Russell Bennett, and Adolph Deutsch. Cast, starring Jack Pearl (Commissioner Bauer) and Lyda Roberti (Gita), featured George Givot (Michael Bramleigh/Golo), Josephine Huston (Ilse Bauer), Carl Randall (Johnny Stewart), Barbara Newberry (Gerry Martin), Gerald Oliver Smith (Dr. Richard Carter), Ruth Urban (Magda), John Cortez (Karl), and Cliff "Charlie" Hall (Schultz). The role of Blau (see pages 199 and 204) appears to have been changed during rehearsals to Karl. "Bauer's House," often listed as an unused song, is almost certainly a scene setting, not a song.

P ardon My English was a headache from start to finish. The Great Depression was at its deepest when we were asked to do the score for the show. Along with business, employment, and the stock market, the theater too was in terrible shape; and I felt we were lucky to be making a living from Of Thee I Sing. In addition, I disliked enormously the central notion of the project—duo-personality or schizophrenia or whatever the protagonist's aberration was supposed to be; so why toil and moil for six months on something we didn't want or need? However, loyalty to producer Aarons, who was broke and who told us if we didn't do the score his potential backers would back out, induced us to go ahead.

During the weeks we were on the road (Philadelphia, Boston, and even a week in Brooklyn), at least five or six librettists and play doctors were called in to work on the book. Herbert Fields was the only one brave enough to allow himself to be billed as librettist. Jack Buchanan, imported to play the duo-personality role (gentleman and gentleman-thief), was so unhappy in it that after a couple of weeks he insisted on buying himself out of the contract. (I heard it cost him twenty thousand dollars, but this is probably an exaggeration.) Whatever business we did, including one good week in Boston, was primarily due to our leading comic, Jack Pearl, whose Baron Munchhausen [sic] ("Vas you dere, Sharlie?") on the air attracted some of his radio audience to the theater. Opening night in New York, I stood among the few standees, but only for the first twenty minutes. A bad cold and a lukewarm audience had me home by nine thirty.

I've never known of any theatrical failure where, sooner or later, an author or the stage-manager or some of the backers or some member of the cast didn't reminisce to the effect that there were some pretty good things in it. So, I must add: there were a couple of pretty good songs, like "Isn't It a Pity?" and "My Cousin in Milwaukee," and a couple of pretty good comedy scenes in Pardon My English, olav hasholom.

—from Lyrics on Several Occasions

IN THREE-QUARTER TIME

Lyrics first published in Ira Gershwin's Lyrics on Several Occasions (1959). Introduced by John Cortez (Karl), Ruth Urban (Magda), and ensemble. Reprised by Jack Pearl (Bauer) and ensemble. Alternate title: "Three-Quarter Time." This number began the pre-Broadway tryout as the third of Act I.

VERSE

When Fred'rick the Great was at
    Potsdam
The French introduced the gavotte;
But Fred warned his henchmen
'Twas all right for Frenchmen—
But Germans? Oh, certainly not!
"With waltzes we've built up the
    Empire;
For waltzes," said Freddy, "I fight!"
So poet and peasant
From then to the present
Have waltzed from the morning till
    night.*
When a Musiker doesn't bring Strauss
    mit 'im,
He is no Musiker—'raus mit 'im!

REFRAIN 1

We laugh and we sing, Oom-pah-pah,
And we dance—in three-quarter time.
When having our fling, Oom-pah-pah,
We romance—in three-quarter time.
It makes us sentimental;
It makes the night sublime.
Our dogs, they have rabies;
Our women have babies
In three-quarter time
So—
Me for three-four time.

---

*Alternate version of verse, lines 10–11:
    Have waltzed all the day and the night.
    If a Musiker doesn't bring Strauss mit 'im,

REFRAIN 2

We laugh and we sing, Oom-pah-pah,
And we dance—in three-quarter time.
When having our fling, Oom-pah-pah,
We romance—in three-quarter time.
Way back in German hist'ry
When Man began to climb,
I'm certain that Adam
Made love to his madam
In three-quarter time,
So—
Me for three-four time.

REFRAIN 3

We laugh and we sing, Oom-pah-pah,
And we dance—in three-quarter time.
When having our fling, Oom-pah-pah,
We romance—in three-quarter time.
From Dusseldorf to Frankfurt,
From Lentz to Schnableheim,
The petticoat gender
Will always surrender
To three-quarter time
So—
Me for three-four,
Pooh for two-four,
Me for three-four time!

REPRISE

BAUER: I'm after the crooks—
POLICE: Oom-pah-pah.
BAUER: They'll get theirs—
POLICE: In three-quarter time.
BAUER: It's down on the books—
POLICE: Oom-pah-pah.
BAUER: 'Lectric chairs!
POLICE: In three-quarter time.
    We'll make those burglars suffer;
    They'll pay for ev'ry crime.
BAUER: The Dresden polices
    Will tear them to pieces—
ALL: In three-quarter time;
    So—
    Me for three-four time.

W ith new words, the music of the verse was reprised somewhere in Act II to introduce short specialty dances. Thus this oversimplified generalization about dance tempi:

The way we respond to the 3/4,
We're Germans, you tell at a glance;
Identification
Of many a nation
Is tied up with tempo in dance.

The Irishman's fond of the 6/8;
For 3/8 the Spaniard goes mad.
The Yankee goes more for
The ha-cha-cha 4/4;
With 5/4 the Russian is had.
And to make the point comprehensible,
A few steps are now indispensable.
(*business of various dances*)
—from *Lyrics on Several Occasions*

THE LORELEI

Published December 1932. Introduced during part of the pre-Broadway tryout by Lyda Roberti (Gita). Reassigned to Carl Randall (Johnny), Barbara Newberry (Gerry), and ensemble. Both versions follow. The Roberti version was published in the sheet music and in *Lyrics on Several Occasions*. The duet has never been published before.

First Version

VERSE

Back in the days of knights in armor,
There once lived a lovely charmer;
Swimming in the Rhine,
Her figure was divine.
She had a yen for all the sailors,
Fishermen, and gobs and whalers.
She had a most immoral eye;
They called her Lorelei.
She created quite a stir—
And I want to be like her.

REFRAIN

I want to be like that gal on the river
Who sang her songs to the ships passing by;
She had the goods and how she could deliver—
The Lorelei!

She used to love in a strange kind of fashion,
With lots of hey, ho-de-ho, hi-de-hi!
And I can guarantee I'm full of passion
Like the Lorelei.

I'm treacherous—*ja, ja!*
Oh, I just can't hold myself in check.
I'm lecherous—*ja, ja!*
I want to bite my initials on a sailor's neck.

Each affair had a kick and a wallop,
For what they craved she could always supply.
I want to be just like that other trollop—
The Lorelei.

Revised Version

VERSE

GERRY: Back in the days of knights in armor,
There once lived a lovely charmer.
JOHNNY: Swimming in the Rhine,
Her figure was divine.
GERRY: She had a yen for all the sailors,
Fishermen, and gobs and whalers.
JOHNNY: She had a most immoral eye—
They called her Lorelei.
BOTH: Hotter than a Minsky show,
Way back in the long ago.

REFRAIN

BOTH: I want to sing of that gal on the river
Who sang her song to the ships passing by;
She had the goods and how she could deliver—
The Lorelei!

She used to love in a strange kind of fashion
With lots of hey, ho-de-ho, hi-de-hi!
There never was a lady full of passion
Like the Lorelei!

GERRY: She'd make 'em all!
JOHNNY: *Ja! Ja!*
What a picture when she shook her frame!
GERRY: She'd take 'em all!
JOHNNY: *Ja! Ja!*
With ev'ry shake, forty battleships went up in flame!

BOTH: Those were days when romance packed a wallop,
But today we are left high and dry,
For the navy never found another trollop
Like the Lorelei!

PARDON MY ENGLISH

Introduced by Lyda Roberti (Gita) and George Givot (Michael/Golo), who was replaced during the brief Broadway run with Joseph Santley. (Givot himself had replaced Jack Buchanan in the latter part of the tryout.) Added to the score late in the pre-Broadway tryout. In February 1982, soon after the discovery of numerous Gershwin scores and manuscripts in the Warner Bros. Music warehouse in Secaucus, New Jersey, I telephoned Ira Gershwin to inform him of the find. When he heard we had located extensive material from *Pardon My English*, he said, "I hope you didn't find the lyric to the title song, because it is the worst lyric I ever wrote." We hadn't found it in Secaucus. Ira, of course, had a copy in his own extensive files. Much as he disliked it, he had not thrown it away.

VERSE

GOLO: I find you so attractive!
One-hundred-percent O.K.
GITA: My heart for you is active
In a great big Polish way.
GOLO: We're two birds of a feather.
That's why we're a perfect team.
GITA: We go as well together
As bananas go with cream.
GOLO: As a pal and partner,
Lady, you're supreme.

REFRAIN 1

You have got that certain something
Makes me sing of you till it hurts—
You'll pardon my English
But you're the nerts!

Once your laddie used to run 'round
But your laddie no longer flirts—
You'll pardon my English
But you're the nerts!

With your looks and my brains,
We ought to go far;
If we should have children,
They'd be above par.

You have won me so completely
I've forgotten all other skirts—
You'll pardon my English
But you're the nerts!

REFRAIN 2

GITA: I adore the way you wear clothes
And the monograms on your shirts—
You'll pardon my Polish
But you're the nerts!

I gave up my pie and ice cream
'Cause your lips make better desserts—
You'll pardon my Polish
But you're the nerts!

With my looks and my brains,
You ought to go far;
With my looks and my brains,
How lucky you are!

Never want another partner;
You must hang around till it hurts—

You'll pardon my Polish
But you're the nerts!

DANCING IN THE STREETS

Introduced during the pre-Broadway tryout by Joe Gerbei, Hans Kiendle, Mack Gassl, Alex Atzenback, Joe Wagner, and Max Seidl, billed as "The Schuhpladlers," and ensemble. Reassigned as an ensemble number.

ALL: There should be dancing in the streets!
Dancing in the streets!
It's Commissioner Bauer's birthday!
It's another-year-on-earth day;
It's a holiday, it's a mirth day
On the Dresden streets!

His birthday is July the third;
This is July the third!
Play the piccolo! Sound the cello!
You must pardon us while we bellow:
He's a jolly good German fellow!
Take us at our word!

GIRLS: We're telling you we've never met a
Man more deserving of your praise;
Ach! If this were an operetta
We'd sing of him for days!

MEN: Give a cheer for Bauer,
The man of the hour!
Give a cheer for Bauer—
His birthday's today!
[Last two stanzas sung together]

ALL: So let's have dancing in the streets!
Dancing in the streets!
Play the piccolo! Sound the cello!
You must pardon us while we bellow:
He's a jolly good German fellow!
His birthday ev'ryone greets
With dancing in the streets!

SO WHAT?

Published December 1932. Introduced by Jack Pearl (Bauer), Josephine Huston (Ilse), and ensemble. Huston replaced Roberta Robinson, who had, in turn, replaced Ona Munson during the tryout.

Show Version

VERSE

ILSE: Why should worry bother
You, my darling father?
You have been around—
You should know what it's all about.
BAUER: If the rain should patter—?
ILSE: Just say, "Does it matter?"
Hand yourself another plate of sausages
and 'kraut.
BAUER: When people tell me of their troubles—?
ILSE: You should always say,
"So well, so what? Perhaps tomorrow
Is your lucky day."
BAUER: That's what I should practice?
ILSE: If you do, the fact is
You'll be merry as the month of May.

REFRAIN 1

ILSE: You sigh—
So what?
Soon you're laughing—
So what?
So you might as well be laughing now.
You're blue—
So what?
So you worry—
So what?
So you get those wrinkles in your brow.
If you take philosophy, just what do you
find?*
Ev'ry rainbow has a bluebird silver-lined.
You cry—
So what?
Soon it's over—
So what?
So you might as well be happy now—
Might as well be happy now!

REFRAIN 2

ILSE: You sigh—
BAUER: So what?
ILSE: Soon you're laughing—
BAUER: So what?
BOTH: So we might as well be laughing now!
ILSE: You're blue—
BAUER: So what?
ILSE: So you worry—
BAUER: So what?
BOTH: So we get those wrinkles in the brow.

---

*Alternate version of refrain, lines 11–12:
"Why let trouble trouble you?" songwriters say;
"Why not rather gather rosebuds while you
may?"

If we take philosophy, just what do we
find?
Ev'ry rainbow has a bluebird silver-lined.
ILSE: You cry—
BAUER: So what?
ILSE: Soon it's over—
BAUER: So what?
BOTH: So we might as well be happy now—
Might as well be happy now!

Published Version

VERSE

I once had a father
Worry didn't bother;
He had been around—
He knew what it was all about.
When the rain would patter,
He'd say, "Does it matter?"
And he'd have another plate of sausages and
'kraut.
When people told him of their troubles,
He would always say,
"So, well? So what? Perhaps tomorrow
Is your lucky day."
If you'll act as he did,
Nothing else is needed;
You'll be merry as the month of May.

REFRAIN

[Same as show version, refrain 1]

ISN'T IT A PITY?

Published December 1932. Introduced during the tryout by Jack Buchanan (Michael/Golo), who was replaced with George Givot, who was replaced during the Broadway run with Joseph Santley; and Ona Munson (Ilse), who was replaced with Roberta Robinson, who was herself replaced before the New York opening with Josephine Huston.

VERSE 1

MICHAEL: Why did I wander
Here and there and yonder,
Wasting precious time
For no reason or rhyme?
Isn't it a pity?
Isn't it a crime?

My journey's ended;
Ev'rything is splendid.

Meeting you today
Has given me a
Wonderful idea;
Here I stay!

REFRAIN 1

It's a funny thing;
I look at you—
I get a thrill
I never knew;
Isn't it a pity
We never met before?

Here we are at last!
It's like a dream!
The two of us—
A perfect team!
Isn't it a pity
We never met before?

Imagine all the lonely years we've
wasted:
You, with the neighbors—
I, at silly labors;
What joys untasted!
You, reading Heine,
I, somewhere in China.

Happiest of men
I'm sure to be
If only you
Will say to me,
"It's an awful pity,
We never, never met before!"

VERSE 2

ILSE: While you were flitting,
         I was busy knitting.
MICHAEL: How did you survive
         Waiting till I'd arrive?
ILSE: All my Dresden boyfriends
         Were only half-alive.

Sleepy was Hermann,
Fritz was like a sermon,
Hans was such a bore!
MICHAEL: How well I planned it!
ILSE: I couldn't stand it
         Anymore!

REFRAIN 2

It's a funny thing;
I look at you—
I get a thrill
I never knew;
Isn't it a pity
We never met before?

Here we are at last!
It's like a dream!
The two of us—
A perfect team—
MICHAEL: For you're more than pretty,
         And I have charm galore!

ILSE: Imagine all the lonely years we've
         wasted:
         You, up in Norway—
         I, around my doorway.
         What joys untasted!
         If you'd been handy,
         'Twould have been just dandy!

Isn't it a shame
We had to wait?
MICHAEL: But thank the Lord
         It's not too late!
BOTH: Still, it's such a pity
         We never, never met before!

REFRAIN 3

ILSE: Love your funny smile,
         Your twinkling eye.
MICHAEL: That's very nice—
         For—so do I!
BOTH: Isn't it a pity
         We never met before?

MICHAEL: Put your hand in mine—
         A perfect fit!
         We never knew—
         Just think of it!
BOTH: Isn't it a pity
         We never met before?

MICHAEL: Imagine all the lonely years I've
         wasted:
         Fishing for salmon,
         Losing at backgammon.
ILSE: What joys untasted!
         My nights were sour
         Spent with Schopenhauer.

BOTH: Let's forget the past!
         Let's both agree
         That I'm for you
         And you're for me—
         And it's such a pity
         We never, never met before!

Act II Reprise

REFRAIN

ILSE: He's the only man
         Made life complete;
         My only love!

My bittersweet!
Isn't it a pity
We'll never meet again.*

That there'd be an end
I never feared,
But with the dawn
He disappeared—
Isn't it a pity
We'll never meet again?

It's like the well-known operetta curtain:
Lovers are parted—
She is brokenhearted.
But I am certain
Fate won't be sending
Me a happy ending!

He's the only love
I ever knew—
And—funny thing—
He looked—like—you!
Isn't it a pity
We'll never, never meet again?

MY COUSIN IN MILWAUKEE

Published December 1932. Introduced by Lyda Roberti (Gita) and ensemble. During part of the pre-Broadway tryout, it was the second number of Act II.

VERSE

Once I visited my cousin
In Milwaukee, U.S.A.
She got boyfriends by the dozen
When she sang in a low-down way.
She was a positive sensation;
The songs that she sang would never miss.
My cousin was my inspiration—
That's how I got like this!

REFRAIN 1

I got a cousin in Milwaukee;
She's got a voice so squawky;
And though she's tall and kind of gawky—
Oh, how she gets the men!

Her singing isn't operatic;
It's got a lot of static;

Alternate line:
    That Golo wasn't you?

But makes your heart get acrobatic—
Nine times out of ten.

When she sings hot, you can't be solemn;
It sends the shivers up and down your spinal
   column.
When she sings blue, the men shout, "What
   stuff!
That baby is hot stuff!"

So if you like the way I sing songs—
If you think that I'm a wow,
You can thank my squawky cousin from
   Milwaukee—
Because she taught me how!

REFRAIN 2 (RELEASE ONLY)

POLICE: When she sings hot, it makes you
            bubble!
   GITA: And how it helps a lady when she gets
            in trouble.
POLICE: When she sings blue, it makes you
            sizzle!
   GITA: And how you can chisel.

HAIL THE HAPPY COUPLE

Introduced by Carl Randall (Johnny), Barbara Newberry (Gerry), and ensemble. Alternate titles: "Bride
and Groom" and "Opening, Garden Scene." The music
to the refrain was taken from the refrain of the deleted
"Watch Your Head," and was later used for "Comes the
Revolution" in *Let 'Em Eat Cake* (1933).

VERSE 1

Soon the bells away up in the belfry will be
   ringing—
That's why we are singing!
(If you call it singing!)

Soon we'll hear the wedding march and pigeons
   will be winging—
That's why we are singing!
Let us call it singing!

Ilse and her Michael start their honeymoon today;
We help along
By bursting into song.
Ding dong, ding dong, ding dong dell!

REFRAIN

Hail the happy couple, hail the bride and groom,
Hail the apple blossoms, smiling as they bloom!

Soon we'll hear the words, "I do! I do!"
Soon there's paradise for two.
Hearts are uniting
As husband and frau;
Though later they'll be fighting,
They're happy now.
This is the time Cupid takes a bow;
A wedding is no time for gloom;
So we hail the happy bride and groom.

VERSE 2

Singing of a bride and groom is always most
   entrancing—
But we've shown we *can* sing,
So we'll start in dancing.

Soon it will be legal when the lovebirds are
   romancing—
That's why we are dancing!
(If you call it dancing!)

Ilse and her Michael start their honeymoon
   today;
We get a chance
To go into our dance.
Ding dong, ding dong, ding dong dell!

REPEAT REFRAIN

THE DRESDEN NORTHWEST MOUNTED

Introduced and reprised by Jack Pearl (Bauer) and ensemble. During part of the pre-Broadway tryout, it was
the third number in Act I.

VERSE

BAUER: All the crooks that I am after—
         They will never know from laughter
         When I really start to use this brain
            of mine.

      Let me tackle Dr. Jekyll;
      His life won't be worth a shekel!
      And that goes for Dracula and
         Frankenstein!

      As a bloodhound I'm a wizard—
      I'm as sneaky as a lizard
      When I'm after someone who should
         be in jail.

It is *Deutschland Uber Alles*!
It's as good as Edgar Wallace
When the Dresden cops are sniffing
   on the trail!

REFRAIN

ENSEMBLE: We're the Dresden Northwest
            Mounted
         And we always get our man—
         If we can!
         When our miracles are counted,
         Sherlock Holmes was just an also-ran!
  BAUER: Once I ran to catch a burglar, but I
            didn't have a chance
         Till I started breathing heavy and I
            caught him by the pants!
ENSEMBLE: We're the Dresden Northwest
            Mounted
         And we always get our man—
         If we can!

ADDITIONAL RELEASES

BAUER: Once a robber stole my staircase but
            it didn't hurt my rep,
         For I dressed up like a Russian and I
            caught him on the steppe.
         We're the Dresden Northwest
            Mounted (etc.)

      When they stole the Mona Lisa from
         the Louvre in Paree—
      I would like to have you tell me,
         What that has to do with me?
      We're the Dresden Northwest
         Mounted (etc.)

LUCKIEST MAN IN THE WORLD

Published February 1933. Introduced by George Givot
(Michael/Golo) and ensemble. An earlier version was
sung during part of the tryout by Jack Buchanan (Mi-
chael/Golo) and Lyda Roberti (Gita). At one time the
song was titled "Luckiest Boy in the World."

Published Version

VERSE

I'll never have the fame of Mussolini;
I'm sure I'll never win a Nobel Prize.
If I wrote music, I'd be no Puccini;

I'm a man whom you can criticize.
I'm always in the red at Monte Carlo,
And on the links I foozle when I drive;
Yet time will show
That there is no
Luckier man alive!

REFRAIN 1

I'm about the luckiest man in the world—
The girl I love loves me!
I've met that certain someone
And soon we shall become one.
I've known the stormy skies for years—
Now the sun appears!
Oh, I'm about the luckiest man in the world—
The girl I love loves me!
And that's the way it should be!

REFRAIN 2

I'm about the luckiest man in the world—
The girl I love loves me!
It's quite the perfect love tale;
In ev'ry way we dovetail.
For years I may have made mistakes—
Now I've got the breaks!
Oh, I'm about the luckiest man in the world—
The girl I love loves me!
And that's the way it should be!

Earlier Version

VERSE 1

GOLO: As soon as I have saved a little nest
    egg,
    I hope to ask you, "Dear, will you be
    mine?"
    The lovers you have had say you're the
    best egg;
    They repeat you're completely divine.
    I've heard of Pompadour and Cleopatra,
    But you are better than the two
    combined.
    How can it be
    You fancy me?
    Is it that love is blind?

REFRAIN 1

    I'm about the luckiest man in the world
    To have a girl like you.
    I'm told by Fritz and Peter:
    Your lips could not be sweeter.
    Oh, you must be a marvelous thing to
    delight
    The many men you do;

The secrets they confide
Have made me swell with pride.
We shall move to larger quarters
To make your boyfriends feel at home;
Your icemen and your cops and porters
Would fill the Hippodrome!
Oh, I'm about the luckiest man in the
    world
To have a girl like you!
GITA: You're very lucky to have a little girl like
    me!

REFRAIN 2

GOLO: I'm about the luckiest man in the world
    To have a girl like you.
    I'm proud because I can see
    You've struck the nation's fancy.
    Oh, you must have a marvelous gift to
    receive
    The many gifts you do;
    With sable coats and things
    Each time the doorbell rings.
    I have heard from Jack the plumber
    (A gentleman you may recall),
    When you were through with him last
    summer,
    He couldn't plumb at all!
    Oh, I'm about the luckiest man in the
    world
    To have a girl like you!
GITA: You're very lucky to have a little girl like
    me!

VERSE 2

    More precious than a clam inside a
    chowder—
    I wonder how I captured such a prize;
    With ev'ry meeting I keep growing
    prouder—
    You're a man no one can criticize.
    They talk of Romeo and Casanova,
    But you are better than the two
    combined.
BOTH: How can it be
    You fancy me?
    Is it that love is blind?

REFRAIN 3

GITA: I'm about the luckiest girl in the world
    To have a man like you.
    For I've been told by Hilda
    Your kisses almost kilda.
    You must be a marvelous man just to
    make

So many dreams come true;
    And ladies by the score
    Come knocking at your door.
    You have had affairs aplenty,
    So you must be plenty good;
    I stopped counting them at twenty—
GOLO: There were more—Knock wood!
GITA: Oh, I'm about the luckiest girl in the
    world
    To have a man like you!
GOLO: I guess you're lucky to have a loving man
    like me—
BOTH: To have a love like you!

WHAT SORT OF WEDDING IS THIS?

Introduced by Jack Pearl (Bauer), Ruth Urban (Magda), and ensemble. Alternate title: "Finale, Act I."

MAGDA:
[*recitative*]
    Commissioner Bauer! Commissioner
    Bauer! The wedding presents—
BAUER: Yes! Yes!
MAGDA: The wedding presents—
BAUER: *Ja! Ja!*
MAGDA: —have been stolen!
ALL:
[*Sing*]
    Oh, what sort of wedding is this?
    Oh, what sort of wedding is this?
    They shoot and then they steal;
    It makes our senses reel!
    Oh, what sort of wedding—
    Oh, what sort of wedding—
    Oh, what sort of wedding is this?
BAUER:
[*spoken*]
    Who stole the wedding presents?
    Who stole them?, I say! Where
    was I on the night of—Never
    mind!
[*A girl rushes in*]
GIRL:
[*recitative*]
    Commissioner Bauer! Commissioner
    Bauer! Michael and Ilse—
BAUER: Yes! Yes!
GIRL: —have taken a launch—
BAUER: *Ja! Ja!*

GIRL: —and eloped!

BAUER:
[*spoken*]

Eloped! My God! Can anything else
happen to me today?

ALL:
[*Sing*]

Oh, what sort of wedding is this?
Oh, what sort of wedding is this?
It's better than we hoped!
The bride and groom eloped!
Oh, what sort of wedding—
Oh, what sort of wedding—
Oh, what sort of wedding is this?

[*Blau steps forward*]

BLAU:
[*spoken*]

If they eloped, then there can't be
any wedding.

BAUER:
[*sarcastically*]

Not unless a few of you would like to
get married. The minister is all
paid for.

ANOTHER
GUEST: No wedding? After all the presents
we sent?

[*He beckons to the others. All get together in
consultation*]

BAUER:
[*to Magda*]

Call up the bakery and see if you can
get a refund on the wedding cake.

[*Blau steps forward*]

BLAU:
[*recitative*]

I am the speaker for these honest faces;
If you don't mind, I shall get down
to cases.

Your daughter, Ilse, met a man,
A man by Fate provided;
As soon as true romance began,
To marry they decided.

BAUER:
[*spoken*]

I'm dying and he's singing!

ALL:
[*recitative*]

To marry they decided!

BLAU: And to that wedding, as we hoped,
We all got invitations;
But suddenly they both eloped
To unknown destinations!

BAUER:
[*spoken*]

So what? So what?

ALL:
[*recitative*]

To unknown destinations!

BLAU: There was, so far as we're concerned,
No wedding of your daughter;
We want our wedding gifts
returned—
The presents that we brought 'er!

MAGDA:
[*to Bauer*]

They want their wedding gifts
returned—
The presents that they brought 'er!

BAUER:
[*spoken*]

Indian givers! That's what you are!
Indian givers!

ALL:
[*Sing*]

There was no wedding and things are
slack;
So we want our wedding presents back!
We want our wedding presents back!

MAGDA: Alas! Alack! they want their wedding
presents back!

BAUER:
[*spoken*]

Ha-ha-ha! Ha-ha-ha! Don't mind my
laughing. I'm only going crazy!

ALL:
[*Sing, mauling Bauer*]

But there was no wedding and things
are slack;
So we want our wedding presents back!
We want our wedding presents back!

[*A police whistle is heard. All let Bauer go as
Schultz enters with Gita in custody*]

SCHULTZ:
[*spoken*]

Caught her in a car trying to get off
the grounds.

GITA: You can't hold me! I didn't steal the
wedding presents! Search me!
Search me!

BAUER: That's the first good offer I got today!

GITA: If you want to find the robbers, look
for your new son-in-law. He stole
the wedding presents, the
double-crossing—

BAUER: How could a man steal his own
wedding presents?

GITA: Golo is so absentminded!

BAUER: Golo! Did Ilse marry Golo—the
thief?

GITA: Of course! A perfect son-in-law for
the police commissioner.

ALL:
[*Sing*]

Oh, what sort of wedding *is* this?
Oh, what sort of wedding *is* this?
It's quite beyond belief
That Ilse marry a thief!
Oh, what sort of wedding—
Oh, what sort of wedding—
Oh, what sort of wedding is this?

BAUER:
[*counting on his fingers*]

First—they steal the presents! Then,
my daughter elopes! Then, because
things are slack they want their
wedding presents back. Then, my
son-in-law is a crook! Where the
hell are my cops?

[*Blows whistle fiercely—Six cops walk on in
shorts*]

My God! They even stole the pants!

[*to policemen*]

Dummkopfs! Couldn't you lick a
handful of crooks?

POLICEMEN: Vas you dere, Sharlie?

[*Bauer collapses*]

ALL:
[*Sing*]

You sigh—
So what?
Soon you're laughing—
So what?
So you might as well be laughing
now—
Might as well be laughing now!

[*Curtain*]

TONIGHT

Music published November 1971 as "Two Waltzes in
C." Introduced during the tryout by Jack Buchanan
(Michael/Golo) and Ona Munson (Ilse). Buchanan's role
was assumed by George Givot and, then, Joseph Santley.
Munson was replaced with Roberta Robinson, who was
replaced with Josephine Huston. Originally the Act I
finale, the number was moved during the tryout to the
opening of Act II.

INNKEEPER: I wish that I were young again
When lovers embrace in the spring.
Fond memories make me sing.
I wish that I were young again.

GOLO: Dear one, it was fated
We've been living for

Tonight!
All the years I've waited
For the wonder of
Tonight!
Facing whatever
Morning may bring,
Love me tonight—or never!
Let the moonbeams find us
In each other's arms—
Tonight,
While we leave behind us
All the world's alarms—
Tonight!
You are love and love can lead the
way to heaven—
Lead me to heaven tonight!

ILSE: Deep in the heart of me—
Here, tonight!—
Love is more than a part of me—
Here, tonight!
Your kisses enthrall;
You are my all;
And though heaven fall,
I'm yours forever!
What is there to fear?
I'm with you!
Let my trembling disappear—
I'm with you!
The love star is bright!
Drink to love's delight!
I'm yours tonight!

WHERE YOU GO, I GO

Published February 1933. Introduced by Lyda Roberti (Gita) and Jack Pearl (Bauer). Added to the score during the tryout. For a time, it was titled "You Go Where I Go."

VERSE

BAUER: Lady, let me go!
I want to say good-bye.

GITA: My lover, don't you know
I'm yours until I die?

BAUER: If you leave me now,
It wouldn't be too soon!

GITA: But I have made a vow
We'll have a honeymoon.

BAUER: Can't you wait until tomorrow afternoon?

REFRAIN 1

GITA: Where you go, I go,
'Cause I wanna go where you go!
Ach! My honey!*
Love is so funny!
Where you flee, I flee,
'Cause I wanna fly where you flee!
I've got to follow when you call.
If you go to Mexico,
I want no excuses!
I must be there when we
Have our three papooses!
Where you go, I go,
'Cause I wanna go where you go!
You make me fall
In any old place at all!

REFRAIN 2

BAUER: Where you go, I go,
'Cause I gotta go where you go!
If you crave me,
No one can save me.
Where you flee, I flee,
'Cause I gotta fly where you flee—
I see the writing on the wall.
Since I know to let me go
I could never force you—
Hear my plea! Marry me!
So I can divorce you!
Where you go, I go,
'Cause I gotta go where you go!
You make me fall
In any old place at all!

I'VE GOT TO BE THERE

Published February 1933. Introduced by Carl Randall (Johnny), Barbara Newberry (Gerry), and girls. During part of the tryout it was sung by Jack Buchanan (Michael/Golo).

VERSE

When I keep seeing things and going places,
My life has color;
Without new songs, without new friends and
faces,
'Twould be much duller.

Whenever people step up
To say, "Let's step tonight,"

*Published version of refrain 1, line 3:
Oh! My honey!

If I've been low, I pep up;
Again the future's bright!
Whenever there's a party I can go to,
It makes the world seem right!

REFRAIN

When music is playing
And couples are swaying—
Say! I've got to be there!
I've got to be there!

When joy's in the making
And ceilings are shaking
And there's never a care—
I've got to be there!

Check my hat
And throw the stub away!
I'm a lamb
Who's gone astray!

When bottles are popping
And dignity's dropping
And the women are fair—
I've got to be there!

FINALETTO, ACT II, SCENE 4

Introduced by principals and ensemble.

COPS: Open in the name of the law!
GOLO:
[blowing pitch pipe]
Try it again!
COPS: Open in the name of the law!
GOLO: That's more like it!
BAUER: We'll give you one more chance to
come out—with your hands up!
KATZ: Wait a minute, Commissioner Bauer.
BAUER: Ja, ja.
KATZ: If you break in, we'll kill Michael
Bramleigh.
GOLO: Don't let him scare you—his nerve is
gone!
Come on, Bauer, come on!

MOB: If you don't save us from this jam,
We'll shoot you just like that!
Your life just won't be worth a damn,
You double-crossing rat!
With a rat-tat-tat-tat—tat-tat-tat—
You double-crossing, applesaucing,
double-crossing rat!

GOLO: Gentlemen, such language!

KATZ: Golo, prepare for the worst!
The minute they are in, you die first!

GITA: Stop! Wait!
Think of what you do!
If Golo must be shot,
Shoot me too!
[*Hands Golo a violin case*]
You can't do this to the man I adore.
Play, gypsy, as you've never played
before.
Play, gypsy!
[*Golo tunes violin and starts to play the
Mendelssohn "Spring Song"*]

COPS:
[*knocking on the door three times*]
Let us in! Let us in!
Let us in! Let us in!
Let us in! Let us in!

CROOKS: A remarkable fellow is Golo.
Though he's good at backgammon and
polo,
Who would ever believe, who would
ever conceive,
He could play us a violin solo?
A remarkable fellow is Golo.
Though he's good at backgammon and
polo,
Who would ever believe, who would
ever conceive,
He could play us a violin solo?
[*Golo opens the door and cops enter*]

BAUER: Ilse, where are you?

ILSE: Daddy!

GOLO: You can lose your heart, but better
watch your head.
[*Hits 1st Crook on head and walks eight
paces*]
Those are doctor's orders; that's what
they said.
[*Hits 2nd Crook on head and walks eight
paces*]
Here's another dirty crook for you.
One good sock and follow through.
[*Bauer hits Golo on the head*]

ILSE: But, Daddy, that was Michael!

BAUER: Why the hell didn't he say so?

COPS: We're the Dresden Northwest Mounted
And we always get our man—
If we can!
When our miracles are counted,
Sherlock Holmes was just an also-ran!
It has made us all so happy, catching
robbers in this den.
We may let them have their freedom,
just to catch them once again.

We're the Dresden Northwest Mounted
And we always get our man—
If we can!

In an earlier version of the scene, these lines followed
"... He could play us a violin solo?":

GOLO: Gentlemen, your pleasure is my
pleasure! What is your pleasure?

KATZ:
[*grimly*]
A funeral march!

OTHER
VOICES: "The Spring Song"!
"Humoresque"!
"Light Cavalry Overture"!

GOLO: I'm out of practice, I'm afraid,
But I'll try Schubert's "Serenade"!

ALL: What a man! He's not afraid
To tackle Schubert's "Serenade"!
[*Golo starts to play. Gang sighs, relaxes; some
sob. Cops beat an accompaniment on door. Door
breaks. Police enter. Confusion and fighting.
Golo rushes off to get Ilse*]

BAUER: [Ilse,] where are you?
[*Scene resumes as above*]

HE'S NOT HIMSELF

Introduced by principals and ensemble. Alternate titles:
"Poor Michael! Poor Golo!" and "Finale, Act II." This
is the only surviving version of the "Finale, Act II" lyric.
The original orchestra parts indicate that during the
pre-Broadway tryout, when the first version of "Luckiest
Man in the World" was deleted, Gita's reprise of this
number was replaced by a few measures of "Where You
Go, I Go." It is unclear which lyrics to "Where You Go,
I Go" were actually utilized. The part of Steiner, played
during the tryout by Royal Dana Tracy, was eliminated
before the New York opening.

ALL: He's not himself just now—
There is no doubt of it!
We're hoping that somehow
He'll soon come out of it!

GUESTS: Poor Michael!
GANG: Poor Golo!
GUESTS: Poor Michael!
GANG: Poor Golo!
GUESTS: Michael!
GANG: Golo!
GUESTS: Michael!
GANG: Golo!

GUESTS: Michael!
GANG: Golo!
ALL: Bah!

GUESTS:
[*to gang*]
If he should turn to you
It would be scandalous!

GANG:
[*to guests*]
Our leader will come through
Again to handle us!

GUESTS: Oh, Michael!
GANG: Oh, Golo!
GUESTS: Oh, Michael!
GANG: Oh, Golo!
GUESTS: Michael!
GANG: Golo!
GUESTS: Michael!
GANG: Golo!
GUESTS: Michael!
GANG: Golo!
ALL: Bah!

ILSE: When he finally comes to his senses,
I'm sure he'll commit no more
offenses!
He must be the Michael he used to be
To make an honest woman of me!

ALL: He must be the Michael he used to be
To make an honest woman of she!

GITA: When he's out of it, you will discover
My old gentleman crook and my lover!
He must be the Golo he used to be
To make an honest trollop of me!

ALL: He must be the Golo he used to be
To make an honest trollop of she!
[*They all march around the bed, singing their
argument once again*]

ALL: He's not himself just now—
There is no doubt of it!
We're hoping that somehow
He'll soon come out of it!

GUESTS: Poor Michael!
GANG: Poor Golo!
GUESTS: Poor Michael!
GANG: Poor Golo!
GUESTS: Michael!
GANG: Golo!
GUESTS: Michael!
GANG: Golo!
ALL: Bah!
GUESTS: Michael!
GANG: Golo!
[*Michael stirs*]

STEINER: Sh!

GOLO: Where am I?

STEINER: Don't you know me?

GOLO: No!

STEINER: Don't you know any of these people? [*Music plays—4 bars of "Isn't It A Pity?" Golo looks at Ilse, doesn't recognize her. Dramatic break in music. "Luckiest Man" music. Same business*]

STEINER: Try again.

ILSE: It's a funny thing;
I look at you—
I get a thrill
I never knew;
It'll be a pity
If you don't come right back—to me!

[*No recognition*]

GITA: I will be the luckiest girl in the
world—
If you come back to me!

MICHAEL:
[*Smiles*]
I'm told by Fritz and Peter:
Your lips could not be sweeter!

[*Goes to her*]

ILSE: You can't do this to me!

[*Hits him on head. They embrace*]

MICHAEL:
[*to Ilse*]
Let's forget the past!
Let's both agree
That I'm for you
And you're for me—

ALL: And it's such a pity
I/He didn't meet you long ago!

FATHERLAND, MOTHER OF THE BAND

Introduced during the tryout by ensemble. It was the original opening number of Act I. Deleted prior to New York premiere. No. 123 in the George and Ira Gershwin Special Numbered Song File. Alternate title: "Drink, Drink, Drink."

VERSE

We want to tell you to your face
That we're a music-loving race;
In ev'ry corner of our land
You'll always find at least one little band.

Their instruments are shiny,
Their music has a swing;
The patriotic Heinie
Must get right up and sing:

REFRAIN 1

Drink, drink, drink!
To the little German band—
Blowing our troubles away.
Drink, drink, drink!
To the little German band
Playing in ev'ry café.

When they finger
Meistersinger,
Mendelssohn, or Bach,
How we treasure
Ev'ry measure—
Ach, ach, ach!

Oh, drink, drink, drink!
To the dear old Fatherland:
Mother of the little German band!

REFRAIN 2

Drink, drink, drink!
To the little piccolo!
[*Piccolo solo*]
Drink, drink, drink!
When the tuba starts to blow!
[*Tuba solo*]

When they finger
Meistersinger,
Mendelssohn, or Bach,
How we treasure
Ev'ry measure—
Ach, ach, ach!

Oh, drink, drink, drink!
To the dear old Fatherland:
Mother of the little German—
The dear old Fatherland is
Mother of the little German band!

FREUD AND JUNG AND ADLER and HE'S OVERSEXED!

"Freud and Jung and Adler" introduced during the tryout by Jack Buchanan (Michael/Golo) and ensemble. "He's Oversexed" may have been introduced by the ensemble, although it is not listed in any program. Dropped before the New York opening. No. 55 in the George and Ira Gershwin Special Numbered Song File. According to the piano-vocal arrangement of "Freud and Jung and Adler" prepared by Kay Swift, "He's Oversexed!" was sung between the first and second re-

frains of "Freud and Jung and Adler." Alternate title of linked numbers: "Viennese Sextet."

"Freud and Jung and Adler"

VERSE

TWO
DOCTORS: If a person starts to quiver
Through cirrhosis of the liver,
We can't be bothered with that sort of
thing at all.

TWO
OTHERS: But how eagerly do we go
To an egg who has an ego
Or a brain that's scrambled 'way
beyond recall.

TWO
OTHERS: We don't cure appendicitis
Or the mumps or laryngitis—
That is not the kind of service that we
sell.

ALL: But we're always on location
When it's mental aberration,
For that pays twice as well.

NURSES: You must know that when a
Doctor's from Vienna—
That pays twice as well!

REFRAIN 1

DOCTORS: Doctor Freud and Jung and Adler,
Adler and Jung and Freud—
Six psychoanalysts, we!
Just let us make one diagnosis—
We'll know *was loss is*'!
Doctor Freud and Jung and Adler,
Adler and Jung and Freud.
Visiting hours, nine to three.
If you ever had the dream that Mrs.
Grundy's
Always keeping her eye on you on
Sund'ys,
And you suddenly find you're standing
in your undies—
We are positive that you had better see
Doctor Freud and Jung and Adler,
Adler and Jung and Freud—
Six sex psychos, we!

REFRAIN 2
[*Repeat refrain 1, lines 1–6*]

If you've any mental problem that
perplexes—

If there's anything that's wrong with
 your reflexes—
If you're really not certain as to which
 your sex is—
We are positive that you had better see
Doctor Freud and Jung and Adler,
 Adler and Jung and Freud—
Six sex psychos, we!

"He's Oversexed!"

A

DRS. ADLER: He's oversexed!
 DRS. JUNG: He's undersexed!
DRS. FREUD: He hasn't any sex at all!

 ALL: This sort of thing commences
 When children scribble on fences!

DRS. ADLER: He's oversexed!
 DRS. JUNG: He's undersexed!
DRS. FREUD: It happened when he was *that* small!

 ALL: His mind is in confusion;
 There's only one conclusion:
 He's oversexed,
 He's undersexed,
 He hasn't any sex at all!

B

DRS. ADLER: It's father love!
 DRS. JUNG: It's mother love!
DRS. FREUD: We're sure it isn't love at all!

 ALL: His thoughts, they should be purty,
 But they are probably dirty!

DRS. ADLER: It's father love!
 DRS. JUNG: It's mother love!
DRS. FREUD: It happened when he was *that* small!

 ALL: His head so badly cracked is,
 The analytical fact is:
 He's oversexed,
 He's undersexed,
 He hasn't any sex at all!

WATCH YOUR HEAD

Intended for Jack Buchanan (Michael/Golo) and ensemble (in this number, the hero seems to have been securely in his "Michael" personality). Probably unused. May have been part of the "Freud and Jung and Adler" sequence. The music of the refrain was subsequently

used for the refrain of "Hail the Happy Couple" and was later recycled for "Comes the Revolution" in *Let 'Em Eat Cake* (1933). A few measures of this number were also quoted in "Finaletto, Act II, Scene 4."

REFRAIN 1

NURSES: "You can lose your heart, but better
 watch your head!"
 Those are doctors' orders. That's what
 they said!

MICHAEL: What the devil is a chap to do
 When he meets a girl like you?

 NURSES: We give you warning:
 Cover up that head!
MICHAEL: I'll wear a hat each morning,
 Wear one in bed,
 But if my heart goes, my head goes,
 too!

 NURSES: Remember what the doctors said:
 "You can lose your heart, but watch
 your head!"

REFRAIN 2

MICHAEL: Thank you, Dr. Adler, Jung, and Dr.
 Freud.
 If you've really cured me, I am
 overjoyed.

DOCTORS: Mr. Bramleigh, you may rest assured:
 We are certain you are cured.

MICHAEL: I'll be all right now;
 I've been in a daze.
DOCTORS: Your future will be bright now—
 Honesty pays!
 We've taken care of your taking ways!

MICHAEL: I'm tickled pink that I've employed
 Dr. Adler, Jung, and Dr. Freud.

DOCTORS: Please remember also: Better watch
 your head.
 Those are doctors' orders. That's what
 we said.

TOGETHER AT LAST

Prepared for publication but never printed. Intended for Jack Buchanan (Michael/Golo). Dropped during the tryout. No. 71 in the George and Ira Gershwin Special Numbered Song File.

VERSE

You'll pardon me if I
Should sigh a manly sigh
And say I'm glad to be here.

Oh, time and time again,
I looked for you, and then,
My lucky star sent me here.

Oh, there's a lot to say, and now's the time to
 say it;
I've waited for this chance for years, so why
 delay it?

REFRAIN

Together at last!
Together at last!
My future looks much brighter than my past.
How can I conceal
The feeling I feel—
I never felt my heart beat quite so fast.
So, come what may,
I'm here to stay;
It's plain to see
That I'm for you
And you're for me.
It's never too late—
It's ordered by fate—
That we two be together at last!

OPENING, ACT II

Introduced during the tryout by Jack Pearl (Bauer), Ruth Urban (Magda), John Cortez (Karl), and ensemble. Alternate title: "No Tickee, No Washee." Dropped before the New York opening. Much of it was reworked into "What Sort of Wedding Is This?" During the rehearsals Lena's name was changed to Magda.

[*Bauer is seated, having breakfast, opening mail. Bell rings as commotion is heard*]

BAUER: Lena, go see who's making that din.
 If it's a magazine subscription working
 his way through college,
 Don't let him in.
[*Crowd enters, pushing Lena aside*]
 Good morning, my good friends, what is
 it?
 Why am I honored with this visit?
 Let me guess. It can't be my
 birthday—that's over!
CROWD: No!

203

BAUER: Perhaps you want me to run for mayor?

CROWD: No, no!

BAUER: That leaves me eighteen more questions.

CROWD: No, no, no, no!

[*Blau steps forward*]

BLAU: I am the speaker for these honest faces;
    If you don't mind I shall get down to
      cases:
    Your daughter, Frieda, met a man,*
    A man by Fate provided;
    As soon as true romance began,
    To marry they decided.

BAUER: *Ach so!*
    I know!

CROWD: To marry they decided!

BLAU: And to that wedding, as we hoped,
    We all got invitations;
    But suddenly they both eloped—
    To unknown destinations!

BAUER: Aha!
    Ja, ja!

CROWD: To unknown destinations!

BLAU: There was, so far as we're concerned,
    No wedding of your daughter;
    We want our wedding gifts returned—
    The presents that we brought 'er!

---

* *Frieda's name was changed to Ilse before the show began its tryout.*

LENA:

[*to Bauer*]

    They want their wedding gifts
      returned—
    The presents that they brought 'er!

BAUER: Indian givers! That's what you are!
    Indian givers!

CROWD: There was no wedding and things are
      slack;
    So we want our wedding presents back!
    We want our wedding presents back!

LENA: Alas! Alack!
    They want their wedding presents back!

BAUER: Ha, ha, ha, ha, ha, ha, ha!
    Your wedding presents were stolen by
      the robbers!

CROWD: It's none of our affair if they were
      stolen.
    There was no wedding and things are
      slack;
    So we want our wedding presents back!

BAUER: You cannot have your presents back!

LENA: Alas! Alack! The sky is black!
    They want their wedding presents back!

BAUER:

[*simultaneously*]

    Can't you see your gifts are gone?

CROWD: We gave her dishes,
    And we gave gold fishes,
    And we gave a smoking tray.

    We gave a cradle,
    And we gave a ladle,
    And we gave a load of hay!

    On other matters, you will find us
      pleasant;
    But we insist, if there's no
      wedding—there's no present!
    We want our dishes
    And we want our fishes
    And we want our cradles
    And we want our ladles—
    And we must have them right away!

[*Dance during which Bauer ad-libs—"But they were stolen! Mein Gott!" etc. Crowd pays no attention to him. They dismantle the room*]

    They took our dishes
    And they took our fishes
    And they took our cradles
    And they took our ladles—
    And it's up, sir, to you to pay!

    Remember, Herr Bauer, what we have to
      say:
    No wedding, no present!
    No tickee, no washee!
    No tickee, no washee!
    Good day!

OPPOSITE: *Top: Phillip Loeb and ensemble. Bottom: William Gaxton watches, Victor Moore waits.*

LET 'EM
EAT CAKE
1933

Tryout: Shubert Theatre, Boston, October 2, 1933. New York run: Imperial Theatre, opened October 21, 1933. 90 performances. Music by George Gershwin. Produced by Sam H. Harris. Book by George S. Kaufman and Morrie Ryskind. Book staged by George S. Kaufman. Dances staged by Von Grona and Ned McGurn. Orchestra under the direction of William Daly. Orchestrations by Edward Powell. Cast, starring William Gaxton (John P. Wintergreen), Lois Moran (Mary Wintergreen), and Victor Moore (Alexander Throttlebottom), featured Dudley Clements (Matthew Arnold Fulton), Philip Loeb (Kruger), Edward H. Robins (Senator Carver Jones), Florenz Ames (Gen. Adam Snookfield), Ralph Riggs (President of the Union League Club, Chief Justice), George E. Mack (Senator Robert E. Lyons), Harold Moffet (Francis X. Gilhooley), Grace Worth (Trixie Flynn), Consuelo Flowerton (Mrs. Lyons), George Kirk (Lieutenant), and Richard Temple (John P. Tweedledee). The lyrics to "Let 'Em Eat Caviar" are not known to survive.

I f *Strike Up the Band* was a satire on War, and *Of Thee I Sing* one on Politics, *Let 'Em Eat Cake* was a satire on Practically Everything. Straddling no fences, it trampled the Extreme Right one moment, the Extreme Left the next. Kaufman and Ryskind's libretto was at times wonderfully witty—at other times unrelentingly realistic in its criticism of the then American scene. Possibly the following short musical speech (unused) written for professional agitator Kruger gives an indication of what *Let 'Em Eat Cake* strove for:

Conditions as they were
Must nevermore recur.
Whatever is, shouldn't be;
Whatever isn't—should.
Whatever wasn't, will be;
And I'm arranging it all for your good.
　　　　　　—from *Lyrics on Several Occasions*

TWEEDLEDEE FOR PRESIDENT

Introduced by ensemble. Includes "Wintergreen for President," a brief section of the title song of *Of Thee I Sing* (1931) and a new number, "Tweedledee" (listed in programs as "Tweedledee for President"). Alternate title: "Wintergreen v. Tweedledee." The paraders' various "Ra ta"s are set to the melodies of "Stars and Stripes Forever," "Hail! Hail! The Gang's All Here!," "Hot Time in the Old Town Tonight," "Dixie," "The Battle Hymn of the Republic," and "Over There."

WINTERGREENERS: Ah——, Ah——
Wintergreen for President!
Wintergreen for President!
Give the man a second chance!
He has given us romance!
Ta ta ta ta ta ta ta!
Wintergreen for President!
Wintergreen for President!
Ta ta ta ta ta ta ta!
Ta ta ta ta.
Wintergreen for President!
Ta ta ta ta ta ta!
Wintergreen for President!
Ah——, Ah——
He's the man the people
　choose;
Loves the Irish and the Jews!
Ta ta ta ta ta ta ta ta ta
Ta ta ta ta ta ta ta,
Ta ta ta ta ta ta!

Of thee we sing, baby;
Wintergreen, you've got that
　thing, baby.
Shining star and inspiration,
Once again you'll rule the
　nation.
Of thee we sing!

[Wintergreen parade exits, and the Tweedledee parade enters]

TWEEDLEDEEITES: Tweedledee! Tweedledee!
Tweedledee! Tweedledee!
Tweedledee! Tweedledee!
He's O.K.
Tweedledee! Tweedledee
Leads the way.
"T" "W"
Double "E" "D" "L" "E"
　"D" double "E"—
That spells "Tweedledee."
Ra ta ta ta ta ta ta ta
Ra ta ra ta ta ta ta.
Yes, sir!
Tweedledee! Tweedledee!
He has guts!
Tweedledee! Tweedledee!
He's the nuts!
Ra ta ta ta ta ta ta
Ra ta ta ta ta.
Yankee Doodle needs that
　noodle.
Tweedledee! Tweedledee!
Ay!
Ra ta ta ta ta ta
Ta ta ta ta
Ra ta ta ta ta.
Yankee deedle-eedle
　Tweedledee,
Tweedledee, Tweedledee
Leads the way!
Tweedledee, Tweedledee,
He's O.K.
He's the man the country seeks!
Loves the Turks and Greeks!*
Ta ta ta!
Ta ta ta!
Ta ta ta ta ta ta ta ta ta!
Tweedledee, Tweedledee, ay!

[Wintergreen parade reenters. The two factions come face to face at last and sing simultaneously]

TWEEDLEDEEITES: Tweedledee! Tweedledee
Leads the way!
Tweedledee! Tweedledee!
He's O.K.
"T" "W"
Double "E" "D" "L" "E"
　"D" double "E"—
That spells "Tweedledee."
Ra ta ta ta ta ta ta ta
Ra ta ra ta ta ta ta.
Yes, sir!
Tweedledee! Tweedledee!
He has guts!
Tweedledee! Tweedledee!
He's the nuts!
Ra ta ta ta ta ta
Ra ta ta ta ta.
Yankee Doodle needs that
　noodle.
Tweedledee, Tweedledee!
Ay!
Ra ta ta ta ta ta
Ta ta ta ta
Ra ta ta ta ta.

WINTERGREENERS: Wintergreen for President!
Wintergreen for President!
He's the man the people choose;
Loves the Irish and the Jews!
Ta ta ta ta ta ta ta.
Wintergreen for President!
Wintergreen for President!
Ta ta ta! Ta ta ta!
Ta ta ta ta!
Wintergreen for President!
Ta ta ta ta ta ta!
Wintergreen for President!

TWEEDLEDEEITES: Yankee deedle-ee for
　Tweedledee.
Tweedledee! Tweedledee

Alternate version of this line and line 5 on next page:

　　　　Loves the wops and Greeks.

Leads the way!
Tweedledee! Tweedledee!
He's O.K.
He's the man the country seeks!
Loves the Turks and Greeks!
Ta ta ta ta ta ta
Ta ta ta ta ta ta ta ta
Tweedledee! Tweedledee!
We want Tweedledee!
  Tweedledee!
"T" "W"
Double "E" "D" "L" "E"
  "D" double "E"—
Ah, ah, ah!
Tweedledee! Tweedledee!
Tweedledee! Tweedledee!
This for Wintergreen!

[*Razz*]

Tweedledee!

WINTERGREENERS: Ah!——, Ah!——
He's the man the people choose;
Loves the Irish and the Jews!
Ta ta ta ta ta ta ta ta
Ta ta ta ta ta
Ta ta ta ta ta ta ta!
Wintergreen for President!
Wintergreen for President!
Ah!
Wintergreen for President
Ah! Ah! Ah!
Wintergreen! Wintergreen!
Wintergreen! Wintergreen!
This for Tweedledee!

[*Razz*]

Wintergreen!

[*They exit, singing*]

TWEEDLEDEEITES: Tweedledee! Tweedledee!
He has guts!
Tweedledee! Tweedledee!
He's the nuts!
Ah!——
WINTERGREENERS: Wintergreen for President!
Ah!——
Wintergreen for President!
Ah!——

UNION SQUARE and DOWN WITH EVERYONE WHO'S UP

These linked numbers were published October 1933 under the title "Union Square" ("Down With Everyone Who's Up" was printed as an interlude within "Union Square"). "Union Square" was introduced by ensemble. "Down With Everyone Who's Up" was introduced by Philip Loeb (Kruger) and ensemble.

"Union Square"

ENSEMBLE: Our hearts are in communion
When we gather down on Union
Square, heigh ho!
When whiskers are unshaven,
One can always find a haven
There, heigh ho!
Though some may prefer the
  charming Bronnix,
Though some sing of dainty Sutton
  Place,
'Tis here we discover all the tonics
That cure all the problems of the race.
Oh, on boxes they put soap in,
How we love it in the open
Air, heigh ho!
We may not fill our stomics,
But we're full of economics
Down on Union Square!
Down here on Union Square!

[*Agitators, led by Kruger, march on. Their tone is sharper, and grows more strident as the number continues*]

"Down with Everyone Who's Up"

KRUGER: Conditions as they are
Cannot go very far;
The world must move and we are
  here to move it!
The Brotherhood of Man
Is crying for a plan;
So here's my plan—I know you can't
  improve it!

ALL: Conditions as they are
Cannot go very far;
So, listen to his plan
For Man!

[*softly*]

Down, down, down, down,
Down, down, down, down.

KRUGER: Down with one and one make two!
Down with ev'rything in view!
Down with all majorities;
Likewise all minorities!
Down with you and you and you!

ALL: Down with one and one make three!
Down with all of us, says he.*

Alternate version of this line:
Down with ev'rything, says he.

KRUGER: Somehow I abominate
Anything you nominate!

ALL: Ev'rything from A, B, C to X, Y, Z!

KRUGER: That's the torch we're going to get
  the flame from!
If you don't like it, why don't you go
  back where you came from?

ALL: If you don't like it, why don't you go
  back where you came from!
If you don't like it, why don't you go
  back where you came from!

KRUGER: Let's tear down the House of Morgan!
ALL: House of Morgan!
KRUGER: Let's burn up the Roxy organ!
ALL: Roxy organ!

KRUGER: Down with Curry and McCooey!*
ALL: And McCooey!
KRUGER: Down with chow mein and chop suey!
ALL: And chop suey!

KRUGER: Down with music by Stravinsky!
ALL: By Stravinsky!
KRUGER: Down with shows except by Minsky!
ALL: Up with Minsky!

KRUGER: Happiness will fill our cup
When it's "Down with ev'rything
  that's up!"
ALL: When it's "Down with ev'rything
  that's up!"

KRUGER: Down with books by Dostoyevsky!
ALL: Dostoyevsky!
KRUGER: Down with Boris Thomashefsky!
ALL: Thomashefsky!
KRUGER: Down with Balzac! Down with Zola!
ALL: Down with Zola!
KRUGER: Down with pianists who play
  "Nola"!

[*Entire stage dances to "Nola"*]

KRUGER: Down with all the upper classes!
ALL: Upper classes!
KRUGER: Might as well include the masses!
  'Clude the masses!

KRUGER: Happiness will fill our cup
When it's "Down with ev'ryone who's
  up!"
ALL: When it's "Down with ev'ryone who's
  up!"

KRUGER: So down with this! And down with
  that!

Original version of this and the next line:
KRUGER: Down with Senators named Huey!
ALL: Down with Huey!

And down with ev'rything in view!
The hell with this! The hell with
  that!
The hell with you and you and
  you!

ONE
HALF OF
THE MOB: The hell with who?
KRUGER: The hell with you!
OTHER
HALF: The hell with whom?
KRUGER: The hell with youm!
ALL: The hell with you and you and
  you!

[*All square off. A free-for-all follows. They are struggling on the floor when a policeman enters, blows whistle. They get up, flick off the dust. All, including the policeman, saunter off, singing:*]

ENSEMBLE: Our hearts are in communion
  When we gather down on Union
    Square, heigh ho!
  When whiskers are unshaven,
  One can always find a haven
  There, heigh ho!
  Though some may prefer the
    charming Bronnix,
  Though some sing of dainty Sutton
    Place,
  'Tis here we discover all the tonics
  That cure all the problems of the
    race.
  Oh, on boxes they put soap in,
  How we love it in the open
  Air, heigh ho!
  We may not fill our stomics,
  But we're full of economics
  Down on Union Square!
  Down here on Union Square!

A mong some of the leftovers for "Union Square" I find:

Let's tear down the House and Senate!
Down with Joan and Connie Bennett!
Down with Russia, down with Stalin!
Down with four quarts to the gallon!
Down with Marx and those four brothers!
Down with plays by Rachel Crothers!
  —from *Lyrics on Several Occasions*

STORE SCENE including SHIRTS BY MILLIONS and COMES THE REVOLUTION and MINE

These linked numbers comprise the "Store Scene." "Shirts by Millions" (also titled "Orders, Orders!") was introduced by ensemble. "Comes the Revolution" was introduced by Victor Moore (Throttlebottom) and ensemble. "Mine" was introduced by William Gaxton (Wintergreen), Lois Moran (Mary), and ensemble. "Mine" was published separately in October 1933. "Comes the Revolution," which had been lost, was recalled and notated in 1973 by Kay Swift.

W ith only fifty-four notes to this stately refrain, and with a one-syllable title, "Mine," fitted in four times, the lyricist couldn't exactly be brilliant in setting the remaining fifty syllables. (I was lucky to get the phrase "never another valentine" to make up for the obvious "more than divine" line.) However, by the supplementing of the refrain with a lyricized counter-melody, then the prefacing of both with a verse more or less *recitativo*, the resultant complete "Mine" made interesting listening.

The use of counter-melody of course goes far back through the musical ages. We ourselves had used it several times before. In *Of Thee I Sing*, for instance, at one point protagonist Wintergreen sings "Some Girls Can Bake a Pie" while two groups, each to a different melodic line, concur with words and rhythms other than his—all the words, of course, lost in the vocal mixture, but three melodies do tickle the ear simultaneously.

The counter-melody of "Mine" was different. When the boys and girls came down to the footlights to point up the absolute togetherness of the Wintergreens, the happily married pair sang their refrain softly, and—most unusual for this sort of thing—the counter-lyric could be understood.
  —from *Lyrics on Several Occasions*

"Shirts by Millions"

WIVES: Orders, orders, orders by the
    thousands!
  Ev'rybody's buying, buying till it
    hurts;
  From Maine to Oklahoma,
  From Trenton to Tacoma,
  The country's growing conscious of
    our shirts!

GIRLS: The country's growing conscious of
    our shirts!
WIVES: Thank you, thank you, thank you,
    darling public!
  For a time, the bus'ness took it on
    the chin;
  But now that our civilians
  Are buying shirts by millions—
  Good God! How the money rolls in!
  Good God! How the money rolls in!
[*Wives look at wrist watches*]
  And now it's time to open up the
    store;
  Our clientele is clam'ring at the door.
[*Men march on*]
  MEN: Good morning!
  GIRLS: How do you do?
  MEN: We're here to try and maybe buy the
    Shirt of Blue.
  GIRLS:
[*to audience*]
  Bus'ness is booming, as you see.
  MEN: We've read you sell a shirt as cheap
    as dirt.
  GIRLS: We only charge a dollar.
  MEN: You only charge a dollar!
  Does it include the collar?
  GIRLS: Yes! Size, please?
[*Men make gesture of refusal*]
  What is it now?
  MEN: Oh my, oh my, we'd like to buy, but,
    lady, Oh—
  GIRLS: This is a shirt to set your heart
    aglow!
  MEN: This shirt looks very nice, but it's
    the price—
  Today a dollar is a helluva lot of
    dough!
  GIRLS: Oh!
  MEN: Dough!
  GIRLS: Oh! With ev'ry shirt, please
    understand,
  You're getting a revolution;
  You're really helping out your land
  With a dollar contribution.

  MEN: Great! Great! That's wonderful!*
  A dollar a shirt is cheap as dirt
  When you're getting a revolution;
  We're tickled we came to light the
    flame
  With a dollar contribution.
[*Dance*]
TWO GIRLS: Ladies, ladies, the floorwalker is
    coming!

*Alternate version of this line:
  Great! Great! That's diff'rent!

A man we all acclaim—
Alexander What's-his-name?
[Throttlebottom enters jauntily]

"Comes the Revolution"

THROTTLE: Comes the revolution,
Ev'rything is jake.
Comes the revolution,
We'll be eating cake.
Skies above are growing bright and
clear;
Happy days will soon be here.
The butcher and the baker—
Undertaker, too—
Thank their Lord and Maker
For the Shirt of Blue.
Comes the revolution, all is jake,
And soon we'll be eating cake.

ENSEMBLE: Comes the revolution,
Ev'rything is jake.
Comes the revolution,
We'll be eating cake.

THROTTLE: When the streets and rivers run
with red,
I'll be underneath the bed!
And after all their capers
Put the foe to rout,
I will buy the papers
To see how we came out!

[Throttlebottom gets in the way of the singers
and is shoved off]

ENSEMBLE: Comes the revolution, all is jake,
And soon we'll be eating cake.

[Mary and Wintergreen enter]

MARY AND
WINTERGREEN: Good morning!
ENSEMBLE: How do you do?
GIRLS:
[to men]

This is the team
Who dreamed a dream
And made it true!

MEN: Wonderful thing—the Shirt of
Blue!

MARY AND
WINTERGREEN: Say, we had no other choice;
We heard the Voice!
We heard a nation calling—
Calling to us to save 'em!
This is the thing we gave 'em!
ENSEMBLE: Hooray! Hooray!
Wintergreen again will save the
day!

"Mine"

WINTERGREEN: My good friends, don't praise me!
I owe it all to the little woman—
This little woman, my little
woman—
ENSEMBLE: His little woman!
WINTERGREEN: She's the reason for my success.
Why, when I think how we
suffered together—
MARY: Worried together, struggled
together—
WINTERGREEN: Stood together together!
I grow so sentimental, I'm afraid
I've got to burst into song.
ENSEMBLE: Please do!
We'd love to know how you feel
about her
And how she feels about you.

WINTERGREEN: Mine, love is mine,
Whether it rain or storm or shine.
Mine, you are mine,
Never another valentine.
And I am yours,
Tell me that I'm yours,
Show me that smile my heart
adores.
Mine, more than divine
To know that love like yours is
mine!

[Ensemble sings as Wintergreen and Mary
repeat "Mine" softly]
ENSEMBLE: The point they're making in the
song
Is that they more than get along;
And he is not ashamed to say
She made him what he is today.

It does a person good to see
Such happy domesticity;
The way they're making love,
you'd swear*
They're not a married pair.

He says, no matter what occurs,
Whatever he may have is hers;
The point that she is making is
Whatever she may have is his.

ALL: Mine, more than divine
To know that love like yours is
mine!

[Both melodies are sung together. At
conclusion, men pick up blue shirts, hold them
high, as all sing:]

---

*Original version of this and the next line:
For, after all is said and done,
For four years they've been one.

Mine, more than divine
To know the Shirt of Blue is mine!

CLIMB UP THE SOCIAL LADDER

Introduced by Lois Moran (Mary) and ensemble.
Dropped during the New York run. Alternate title:
"The New Blue D.A.R."

MARY: Though you have gentility
And respectability,
Though you have a social charm that
passes—
Girls, what are you but the middle
classes?

GIRLS: Sez you!
WIVES: It's true!

MARY: Let's cut out formality,
Get down to reality.
You're the kind the upper class looks
down on;
You're the sort Park Avenue will
frown on!

GIRLS: Sez you!
WIVES: It's true!

MARY
AND WIVES: Ladies, if you would advance
Socially, then here's your chance.
WIVES: Here's your chance to make a tie-up
Guaranteed to place you high up.

MARY: All you have to do
Is buy a Blouse of Blue,
And you become a member of the
new D.A.R.
WIVES: The Second Revolution and the Blue
D.A.R.

GIRLS: Purchasing a blouse, you say, is vital?
MARY: Ladies, it's like marrying a title!

WIVES: There's no one in the land can rise as
far
As members of the Second D.A.R.

MARY: Climb up the social ladder!
Join the Second D.A.R.!
What makes a woman gladder
Than to be a social star?
You'll be snubbing all the Abbots
And all the Cabots

And other Boston Babbitts!
You're high up on the ladder
When you join the new Blue D.A.R.!

ALL: We're on the social ladder
In the Second D.A.R.!
Each member's heart is gladder
Now that she's a social star!
We'll be snubbing all the Abbots
And all the Cabots
And other Boston Babbitts!
We're high up on the ladder
Now that we're the new Blue D.A.R.!

THE UNION LEAGUE and COMES THE REVOLUTION (REPRISE)

"The Union League" (lyrics first published in Ira Gershwin's *Lyrics on Several Occasions* [1959]) was introduced by Ralph Riggs (President of the Union League Club) and ensemble. Alternate titles: "Cloistered from the Noisy City" and "Members of the Union League." Much of this number was restored by Kay Swift.

"The Union League"

MEMBERS: We are members;
Our fathers were members;
Their fathers were members;
Our great-great-great-great-great-
Great-great-grandfathers were
members
Of the Union League,
Of the Un———ion League!

Cloistered from the noisy city,
Standing pat and sitting pretty,
We are they who represent
Safety first and five percent.

ATTENDANTS: Safety first and five percent!

MEMBERS: When we wake, which is infrequent,
We keep wond'ring where last week
went,
Then back to our chairs we creep,
And we go right back to sleep.

ATTENDANTS: And they go right back to sleep!

MEMBERS: "Don't swap horses in a river!"
"Watch your kidneys—Watch your
liver!"

That's the essence of our lives—
That, and New York Central Fives!

ATTENDANTS: That, and New York Central—
ALL: That, and New York Central Fives!

MEMBERS: Action would be suicidal.
Rip Van Winkle is our idol.
He's the one man does intrigue
ALL: The members of the Un———ion
League!

We are members;
Our fathers were members;

[*etc.*]
[*Members fall asleep*]

Once we had the old boys asleep . . . we had to let them lie. But the following was ready, in case:

Window gazing, nothing rankles
When we view the charming ankles
Of the lovely ladies who
Ramble down the avenue.

Too, the heartbeat in us quickens
When a new book's out by Dickens.
(Bulwer-Lytton's through and done.
Trollope is a name we shun.)

Yearly to the bar we bustle,
Drink a toast to Lil'ian Russell—
(Lil'ian, fairest of the fair!)—
Then we play at solitaire.

Finding this place to our liking,
We sent packing Lief the Viking.
"Sleep and rest shall ne'er fatigue
The members of the U-n-i-o-n League."
—from *Lyrics on Several Occasions*

"Comes the Revolution" (Reprise)

MEMBERS: Comes the revolution,
Ev'rything is jake!
Comes the revolution,
We'll be eating cake!
We are ready—Take us at our word!
We'll show up that George the Third!
Protecting our possessions,
We'll stir up a fuss!
The British and the Hessians
Won't get far with us!
Comes the revolution, all is jake,
And soon we'll be eating cake!

ON AND ON AND ON

Published October 1933. Introduced by William Gaxton (Wintergreen), Lois Moran (Mary), and ensemble.

BLUE SHIRTS: Left! Right! Left! Right!
Left! Right! Left! Right!
Marching, marching all the time.
Hep! Hep! Hep! Hep!
Through ev'ry kind of scenery
and—
Hep! Hep!—
Through ev'ry kind of clime.
Marching, marching, marching for a
dream,
We sing as we go marching,
And we've got a marching theme!
The theme is one that ev'ry army
sings
On its way to conquer cabbages and
kings!

On and on and on!
Hither and thither-and yon!
It seems to be the thing
For marching men to sing:
"On and on and on!"
So—
On and on and on!
Hither and thither-and yon!
For movements military,
There is no itinerary
Like
"On and on and on!"
On and on and on!

Additional Refrain (Unused)

On and on and on!
Hither and thither—and yon!
No matter what the time
Or scenery or clime!
"On and on and on!"
So—
On and on and on!
Crossing that ole Rubicon.
No sooner do we get there,
Than again this chansonnette there:
"On and on and on!"
On and on and on!

FINALE, ACT I, including I'VE BRUSHED MY TEETH and THE DOUBLE DUMMY DRILL and ON AND ON AND ON (REPRISE) and THE GENERAL'S GONE TO A PARTY and ALL THE MOTHERS OF THE NATION and YES, HE'S A BACHELOR and THERE'S SOMETHING WE'RE WORRIED ABOUT and WHAT'S THE PROLETERIAT? and LET 'EM EAT CAKE

Introduced by Florenz Ames (General Snookfield), Richard Temple (Tweedledee), Grace Worth (Trixie), William Gaxton (Wintergreen), George Kirk (Lieutenant), Lois Moran (Mary), Philip Loeb (Kruger), and ensemble. Alternate title for "I've Brushed My Teeth": "What More Can a General Do." Alternate title for "All the Mothers of the Nation": "Mothers of the Nation." The title number was published separately October 1933.

[*In front of the White House*]

"I've Brushed My Teeth"

4 DIGNITARIES: Tonight, July the fourth,
Nineteen hundred and um-tee-um,
Is the one hundred and
um-tee-umth birthday
Of our grand and glorious nation.
We celebrate it with the following
program:
Part A—General Snookfield will
review his troops in person;
Part B—President Tweedledee
will make an address,
After which finger bowls will be
served.
General Snookfield, are you ready?

GENERAL: Yes.
I've brushed my teeth, and I've
washed my face,
And I've had a fine shampoo;

What more can a general do
When his troops are on review?

4 DIGNITARIES: He's combed his hair, and he's
had a shave,
And his underwear is new;
What more, what more, what
more can a general do
When his troops are on review—
When his troops are on review?

[*General Snookfield marches to the reviewing stand. The U.S. Army enters and performs a military drill*]

"The Double Dummy Drill" (Instrumental)

[*Bugler enters, then blue-shirted army*]

"On and On and On" (Reprise)

BLUE SHIRTS:
[*approaching from offstage*]
On and on and on!
Hither and thither—and yon!
It seems to be the thing
For marching men to sing:
"On and on and on!"
So—
On and on and on!
Hither and thither—and yon!
For movements military,
There's no itinerary
Like
"On and on and on!"
On and on and on!

"The General's Gone to a Party?"

TWEEDLEDEE: What's this? What *is* this? What's
this?*

---

*Alternate (script) version of beginning of this section:

TWEEDLEDEE: What's this? What *is* this? What's
this?
WINTERGREEN: John P. Tweedledee, I call upon you
to surrender the government of
these United States!
TWEEDLEDEE: By whose authority?
WINTERGREEN: By the authority of the American
people!
TWEEDLEDEE: We'll see about that.
WINTERGREEN: All right—we'll see. Where's General
Snookfield?
TWEEDLEDEE: Oh! So you were counting on the
General, were you? [*Laughs*]
WINTERGREEN: What's funny about that?
TWEEDLEDEE: I have a surprise

WINTERGREEN: John P. Tweedledee, I call upon
you to surrender the
government of these United
States.
TWEEDLEDEE: By whose authority?
WINTERGREEN: By the only real authority! The
authority of the American
people.
TWEEDLEDEE: We'll see about that! General,
arrest this man!
WINTERGREEN: General, arrest this man!
TWEEDLEDEE: Where's the General?
WINTERGREEN: Yes, where's the General? Have
you seen the General?
TWEEDLEDEE: He was here a minute ago.
BOTH: General Snookfield!
[*Lieutenant steps up*]

LIEUTENANT: I have a report
To make. In short:
The General's gone to a party!

WINTERGREEN
AND
TWEEDLEDEE: The General's gone to a party?
ARMY: The General's gone to a party?
LIEUTENANT: That's my report,
In short.

ARMY: We all approve
The General's move
If the lady is young and hearty.

LIEUTENANT: I'm positive she is hearty;
The general likes 'em tarty!

ARMY: Then we approve
His move.
ALL MEN: We *all* approve
His move.

WINTERGREEN
AND
TWEEDLEDEE: Alackaday, alackaday!
The General has been called away!
ALL: Adayalack, adayalack!
Oh, what'll they do till he gets
back?

In store for you—
The General's gone to a party.
WINTERGREEN: The General's gone to a party?
BLUE SHIRTS: The General's gone to a party?
TWEEDLEDEE: That's my surprise for you,
And all your Shirts of Blue.
WINTERGREEN: Alackaday, alackaday,
The General has been called away.
BLUE SHIRTS: Adayalack, adayalack,
Oh, what'll we do till he gets back?

WINTERGREEN
AND
TWEEDLEDEE: Now, what's to be suggested?
Now, what in the world to do?
For you want me arrested,
And that's what I want for you!
[*Both clap hands. They've got it*]
Let's leave it to the Army!
[*aside*]
(I know they're on my side.)
[*aloud*]
And by their decision
We'll abide.

ARMY:
[*worried*]
The General now may be in bed.
Oh dear, oh dear, oh dear!
We agreed to do what the General
said,
But the General isn't here!

WINTERGREEN: I know the General isn't here.
So it's *you* who must decide!
Think it over! Who's the boss to
be?
Tweedledee or me?
[*Mary rushes on*]
MARY: Soldiers, oh, soldiers, why should
you think twice?
Are you men or mice?

"All the Mothers of the Nation"

All the mothers of the nation
Can tell you who your leader
ought to be;
Ev'ry female heart will tremble
with elation,
My soldiers, if you choose the man
who married me—
A man who is a husband,
The father of two children—
And *not* that other man who is a
bach'lor!
A selfish, old bach'lor, he!

WIVES AND
GIRLS: All the mothers of the nation
Can tell you who your leader
ought to be;
Ev'ry female heart will tremble
with elation,
Oh, soldiers, if you choose her
man
And *not* that other man who is a
bach'lor!
A selfish, old bach'lor, he!

"Yes, He's a Bachelor"

WINTERGREEN: Yes, he's a bach'lor;
His father was a bach'lor;
His father was a bach'lor—

BLUE SHIRTS: His great-great-great-great-
Great-great-great-grandfather
Was a bach'lor in the—
LIEUTENANT: Stop! The fam'ly tree, sir,
The genealogy, sir,
Of President Tweedledee, sir,
Does not int'rest me!

SOLDIERS:
[*variously, down the line*]
Or me! Or me! Or me! Or me!
TWEEDLEDEE: Or me!

"There's Something We're Worried About"

LIEUTENANT: But—there's something we're
worried about!
There's something we're worried
about!
Before we go
Ahead with the show,
There's something we'd like to
find out!

ARMY: There's something we've got to
discuss!
WOMEN: There's something they've got to
discuss!

ARMY: The man we name
Gets fortune and fame,
But what is there in it for us?
Yes, what is there in it for us?

TWEEDLEDEE: The question's a fair one, I say,
And I offer a dollar a day—
A dollar a day
Which I may not pay;
Still, the offer's a dollar a day.

ARMY: A dollar a day isn't bad;
A dollar a day isn't bad;
A dollar a day
He may never pay;
Still, a dollar a day isn't bad.

WINTERGREEN:
[*spoken*]
Wait a minute! I'll tell you what
I'll do!
[*In dialogue, he promises to pay the war debts
of the army "if we collect 'em." The army
declares him dictator. Then:*]
KRUGER:
[*Sings*]
Down with Wintergreen the tyrant!
ARMY: He's no tyrant!

KRUGER: He's the man against whom I rant!
[*He is hustled off*]
WINTERGREEN:
[*spoken*]
John P. Tweedledee, you are now
deposed as President of the
United States, and we hereby
establish a dictatorship of the
proletariat!
[*All cheer*]

"What's the Proletariat?"

TWEEDLEDEE: Wait a minute! What's the
proletariat?
WINTERGREEN: The pro—? What's the proletariat?
MARY:
[*Sings*]
What's the proletariat?
WIVES: What's the proletariat?
COMMITTEE: What's the proletariat?
What's the proletariat?
ARMY: We're the proletariat!
We're the proletariat!
You're the proletariat!
You're the proletariat!
We're all the proletariat!
ALL: All the proletariat!
All the proletariat!
All the proletariat!
Ah!

"Let 'Em Eat Cake"

WINTERGREEN: Oh, comrades, you deserve your
daily bread;
That's what I have always said!
But I'll go further—You shall have
a break!
From now on you'll be eating
cake!
ALL: We've always wanted cake;
At last we get that break!
WINTERGREEN: I'm asking payment on an ancient
debt*
As promised by Marie Antoinette!

ALL: Comrades, it is clear—
The millennium is here!

WINTERGREEN: Let 'em eat cake!
The land of freedom
Is free once more!

---

*Alternate version of this and the next line:
With drums a-booming and our flag un-
furled,
This is what I'm telling the world:

ALL: Rum tee um tee um tee ay!
Ra ta ta ta tee um tee ay!

WINTERGREEN: Let 'em eat cake!
Let there be sunshine
From shore to shore!

ALL: Rum tee um tee um tee ay!
Ra ta ta ta tee um tee ay!

WINTERGREEN: Now is the time to be waking!
Come on, let's start!
Now is the time to be taking
Your part!

Let 'em eat cake!
Good times are coming;
The skies are clear!
Let it be known the whole world
over:
The new day is here!

Let 'em eat cake!
The land of freedom
Is free once more!

ALL: Clear the way for better times!
Brother, begin to spend those
dimes!

WINTERGREEN: Let 'em eat cake!
Let there be sunshine
From shore to shore!

ALL: Lend a hand! The party's on!
Open the door, the wolf is gone!

WINTERGREEN: Now is the time to be waking!
Come on, let's start!
Now is the time to be taking
Your part!

Let 'em eat cake!
Good times are coming,
The skies are clear!

ALL: One for all and all for one!
Living has just begun!
Let it be known the whole world
over—
The new day is here!

[*Curtain*]

Alternate Version of "There's Something We're Worried About" and "What's the Proletariat?"

LIEUTENANT: The army is somewhat in doubt!
The army is somewhat in doubt!
Before we go
Ahead with the show,
There's something we'd like to
find out!

ARMY: There's something we've got to
discuss!
There's something we've got to
discuss!
The man we name
Gets fortune and fame,
But what is there in it for us?
Yes, what is there in it for us?

TWEEDLEDEE: The question's a fair one, I say,
And I offer a dollar a day—
A dollar a day
Which I may not pay;
Still, I *offer* a dollar a day.

ARMY: A dollar a day isn't bad;
A dollar a day isn't bad;
A dollar a day
He may never pay;
Still, a dollar a day isn't bad.

WINTERGREEN:
[*spoken*]
Wait a minute, you fellows!
[*In dialogue, he promises to pay the war debts
of the army "if we collect 'em." The army
declares him dictator. Then:*]
KRUGER: Down with Wintergreen, the tyrant!
ARMY: He's no tyrant!
KRUGER: He's the man against whom I rant!
[*He is hustled off*]
WINTERGREEN:
[*spoken*]
John P. Tweedledee, you are now
deposed as President of the
United States, and we hereby
establish a dictatorship of the
proletariat!
[*Cheers*]
TWEEDLEDEE: Wait a minute! What's the
proletariat?
WINTERGREEN: The pro—? What's the proletariat?
MARY:
[*Sings*]
What's the proletariat?
What's the proletariat?

CROWD: What's the proletariat?
What's the proletariat?

MARY: *We're* the proletariat!

CROWD: Yes, we're the proletariat!
And *you're* the proletariat!
You're the proletariat!
We're *all* the proletariat!

ALL: All the proletariat!
All the proletariat!
All the proletariat!
Ah!

OPENING, ACT II, including BLUE, BLUE, BLUE and WHO'S THE GREATEST?

"Blue, Blue, Blue" (published October 1933) was introduced by ensemble. "Who's the Greatest?" was introduced by William Gaxton (Wintergreen) and ensemble.

"Blue, Blue, Blue"

WIVES: It's off with the old, on with the new;
That's why we're painting the White
House blue.

ALL: It's off with the old, on with the new;
That's why we're painting the White
House blue.

Blue, blue, blue—
Not pink or purple or yellow,
Not brown like Mr. Othello—
But blue, blue, blue!
The country clamored
For somebody new
And grew enamored
Of Wintergreen, who
Gave us blue, blue, blue—
The color heaven is painted;
What color could be more sainted
Than blue, blue, blue?
The U.S.A. is the blue S.A.
It's a dream come true!

[*Dance*]
TWO GIRLS: Comrades, comrades,
Wintergreen is coming!
To start the working day,
Wintergreen is on the way!

"Who's the Greatest?"

ALL: There is no one greater
On any scene
Than our Dictator—
Wintergreen!
[*This is sung in three rhythms*]
[*Enter Wintergreen*]
WINTERGREEN: Saluta!
ALL: Saluta!
WINTERGREEN: Saluta!
ALL: Saluta!
WINTERGREEN:
[*spoken*]
How do you like my new sword?
ALL: Wonderful, Your Dictatorship!

WINTERGREEN: And how do you like my new suit?
ALL: Wonderful, Your Dictatorship!
WINTERGREEN: And how do you like the new Dictator?
ALL: Hooray, Your Dictatorship!

WINTERGREEN:
[*Sings*]

Who's the greatest leader
That the world has ever known?
ALL: Napoléon?
WINTERGREEN: Wrong!
ALL: Wintergreen!
WINTERGREEN: Right!
And who's the greatest statesman,
One who'll always stand alone?
ALL: Disraeli?
WINTERGREEN: Wrong!
ALL: Wintergreen!
WINTERGREEN: Right!
Who is ready
To keep the foe at bay?
Fight like Teddy
And speak like Henry Clay?
Who has got a mind that works
Just like a brain machine?
ALL: Who's the man you mean?
Nobody else but Wintergreen!

WINTERGREEN: Who's the greatest dreamer,
But with two feet on the ground?
ALL: Henry Ford?
WINTERGREEN: Warm!
ALL: Wintergreen!
WINTERGREEN: Right!
And who's the greatest horse's neck
Historians have found?
ALL: Wintergreen!
WINTERGREEN: Wrong!
[*Starts to unsheath sword*]
ALL: Tweedledee!
WINTERGREEN: Right!
What commander
Has only just begun?—
Alexander
And Caesar rolled in one!
Who's the man could muscle in
On Mr. Mussolin'?
ALL: You're the man you mean!
Nobody else but Wintergreen!
[*All dance. Much saluting*]
WINTERGREEN: Who is always great or lousy—
Nothing in-between?
ALL: Who's the man you mean?
WINTERGREEN: Nobody else but Wintergreen!

LEAGUE OF NATIONS FINALE, including NO COMPRENEZ, NO CAPISH, NO VERSTEH! and WHY SPEAK OF MONEY? and WHO'S THE GREATEST? (REPRISE)

"No *Comprenez*, No *Capish*, No *Versteh!*" (listed in programs as "No *Comprenez*, No *Capish*") was introduced by ensemble. "Why Speak of Money?" (which is not listed in the opening-night New York program and may have been cut) was introduced by William Gaxton (Wintergreen), Lois Moran (Mary), and ensemble. The "Who's the Greatest?" reprise was sung by Gaxton and ensemble.

MARY:
[*Sings*]

Now that everybody's here,
Welcome them, my dear!
WINTERGREEN: The Dictator and Committee say initially
That they're very glad to welcome you officially.
[*Interpreters turn to League members*]
INTERPRETERS: They are telling all you gentlemen initially
That they're very glad to welcome you officially.

LEAGUE: Tell your leader we appreciate his attitude
And present him with our compliments and gratitude.
[*Interpreters turn to Wintergreen*]
INTERPRETERS: They are saying they appreciate your attitude,
And they offer you their compliments and gratitude.
[*China steps out of line*]
CHINA: Girls, don't bother translating anymore.
We find that we speak English, too.
ALL: Isn't it wonderful that we all speak English?
WINTERGREEN: Gentlemen, not only do I speak English,
But I talk *turkey!*
What about the war debts?

"No Comprenez, No Capish, No Versteh!"

LEAGUE: No *comprenez*, no *capish*, no *versteh!*
We don't understand a single word you say!
It is very, very funny,
But each time you mention money—
No *comprenez*, no *capish*, no *versteh!*

[*Kruger goes to Wintergreen*]
KRUGER: You *comprenez*, you *capish*, you *versteh*
That you've got a job ahead of you today!
To the Army it's not funny
If you don't collect the money!
WINTERGREEN: I *comprenez*, I *capish*, I *versteh!*

WINTERGREEN:
[*to League*]

When nations get together,
The stormy winds won't blow—
They'll always have fair weather
If they pay up what they owe!
ENSEMBLE: Yes, if they pay up what they owe!
LEAGUE: When nations get together
And meet in mutual trust,
They'll always have fair weather
If money is not discussed—
If money is not discussed!
WINTERGREEN: In *this* land there's a custom—
A funny one, I know—
But people, when you trust 'em,
Must pay up the debt they owe!
ENSEMBLE: So, pay back what you owe!

No *comprenez*, no *capish*, no *versteh!*
It must be that we are very dumb today!
Ev'ry time you mention dollars,
Ev'ry fiber in us hollers,
"No *comprenez*, no *capish*, no *versteh!*"

WINTERGREEN: Mary, I can't seem to do a thing.
Maybe they'll respond if *you* will sing!
MARY: Is this the gratitude you show us?
Why don't you pay back what you owe us?
LEAGUE: Ah, ze beautiful American maid!
You put all the other women in the shade!
MARY: What about the *war debts?*

"Why Speak of Money?"

LEAGUE: Why speak of money when there's
love, love, love?—
Loveliest of your gender!
You're just the type that we keep
dreaming of—
So sweetly tender—
We must surrender!
There's no one like you back in
Copenhagen,
London, or Paree,
So, why speak of money when
there's love, love, love?
Love is the thing for we!

INTERPRETERS:
[to Wintergreen]
Why speak of money when there's
love, love, love?—
Handsomest of your gender!
You're just the type that we keep
dreaming of—
Virile but tender—
We must surrender!
There's no one like you back in
Cincinnati,
Troy, or Kankakee,
So, why speak of money when
there's love, love, love?
Love is the thing for we!

KRUGER: This foolishness must stop,
Or else I'll call a cop!
Our money is at stake and we'll
protect it!
The Army wants to say
[to League]
That *you* had better pay,
[to Wintergreen]
And *you* are designated to collect
it!

WINTERGREEN: Did you hear that? Pay!

LEAGUE: No *comprenez*, no *capish*, no
versteh!
That's our theme song when
you're wanting us to pay.
Ev'ry time you mention lucre,
We must give you this rebuker:
"No *comprenez*, no *capish*, no
versteh!"

WINTERGREEN:
[spoken]
What happens if we *insist* on the
money?

LEAGUE: It means war!

WINTERGREEN: But how can you have a war if we
don't lend you the money?

LEAGUE: What?

FRANCE: Do you mean to say you would
not lend us the money to fight
you?

WINTERGREEN: Certainly!

[League hisses him]
Things have come to a pretty pass
when ten nations won't pay
what they owe!

[Kruger shows bag of money from Finland]
Well, *nine* nations. Nine nations!
One, two, three, four, five, six,
seven, eight, nine—
Say! Can you boys play baseball?

LEAGUE: You mean—the Great American
Pastime?

WINTERGREEN: Yes.

LEAGUE: No, but we're willing to try!

WINTERGREEN: Great! We'll have a ball game
between the American Blue
Shirts and the League of
Nations for the war
debts—double or nothing!

[A cheer from the crowd]

FRANCE: But suppose we lose?

WINTERGREEN: Well—Suppose you do lose?

FRANCE: If we lose, we insist on another
conference. Do we get it?

WINTERGREEN: Yes, sir! We'll even pay your
expenses over.

LEAGUE: It's a game! Play ball!

[Another cheer]

"Who's the Greatest?" (Reprise)

ALL:
[Sing]
Who's the greatest leader
That the world has ever known?

KRUGER: Napoléon!

ALL: Wrong!

WINTERGREEN: Wintergreen!

ALL: Right!
And who's the greatest
statesman—
One who'll always stand alone?

KRUGER: Disraeli!

ALL: Wrong!

WINTERGREEN: Wintergreen!

ALL: Right!
Who's the laddie
Has something on the ball?
Who's the daddy—
The daddy of them all?

WINTERGREEN: Who's is always great or lousy—
Nothing in-between?

ALL: Who's the man you mean?

Nobody else—
Oh, nobody else—
Oh, nobody else—
Oh, nobody, nobody,
Nobody else but Wintergreen!

BASEBALL SCENE, including PLAY BALL! and NINE SUPREME BALL PLAYERS and NO BETTER WAY TO START A CASE and THE WHOLE TRUTH and UP AND AT 'EM, ON TO VICTORY

Introduced by Ralph Riggs (Chief Justice) and ensemble. The entire Baseball Scene was listed in the Boston tryout programs as "No Better Way to Start a Case" and "Up and At 'Em." At the New York opening, "No Better Way . . ." was listed as "When the Judges Doff the Ermine" (although this line does not appear in any of the surviving lyrics).

"Play Ball!"

GIRLS: Play ball! Play ball!
We're waiting for the game to start.
Oh, when will they begin it?
We're hoping our heroes do their part;
They've simply got to win it!
Play ball! Play ball!
Of course, we're yelling for the Blues,
And so is all the nation;
But what we'll yell if they should lose
Is not for publication!
Three cheers! Three cheers!
Here comes our ball team!
Here comes our ball team!

[Enter the Supreme Court Judges in baseball uniforms]

"Nine Supreme Ball Players"

SUPREME
COURT: We're the one, two, three, four,
five, six, seven, eight, nine
Supreme ball players.
Pitcher, catcher, first, second,
third, short, left, center, right
Supreme ball players!

CHIEF JUSTICE: Gentlemen, a word with you!
JUDGES: Whereas:
CHIEF JUSTICE: A baseball game is about to be
played between the Official
American Nine and the League
of Nations Nine for the war
debts, double or nothing—
JUDGES: Whereas:
CHIEF JUSTICE: We who represent the American
side must be victorious or incur
the displeasure of 120 million
ardent patriots—
JUDGES: Whereas:
CHIEF JUSTICE: After due deliberation, for there is
no precedent, all previous
statutes being incompetent,
irrelevant, and immaterial—
JUDGES: Whereas:
CHIEF JUSTICE: Now, therefore, be it resolved that
the captain of the Official
American Nine give an official
pep talk!
Gentlemen, your decision!
[Fingers thrust forth as in "evens or odds"]

CHIEF JUSTICE: Five concur and four dissent;
That seems to be the sentiment.
JUDGES: Five concur and four dissent;
So let us have the pep talk!

"No Better Way to Start a Case"

CHIEF JUSTICE: To set the court a-tingle,
A judge should hit a single—
For there's no better way to start
a case!
JUDGES: No better way to start a case!

The jury won't make trouble
If you should hit a double,
And it's not criminal to steal a
base!
Not criminal to steal a base!

CHIEF JUSTICE: To prove you're not a cripple,
Go slam yourself a triple;
Don't swing like Casey in the
well-known pome!
JUDGES: Like Casey in the well-known
pome!

CHIEF JUSTICE: The thing to do is hit balls,
So even if they're spitballs,
Just sock 'em out and run like
hell for home!
JUDGES: We'll sock 'em out and run like
hell for home!

We'll sock 'em out and run like
hell for home!

CHIEF JUSTICE: And now—the official cheer:

"The Whole Truth"

ALL: The whole truth, the whole truth,
Nothing but the truth!
The whole truth, the whole truth,
Nothing but the truth!
Hear ye! Hear ye!
Status quo! Status quo! Siss boom bah!
Habeas corpus! Rah! Rah! Rah!

"Up and At 'Em, On to Victory"

JUDGES: Up and at 'em! On to vict'ry!
Give a cheer for team, team, team!
Up and at 'em! On to vict'ry!
Show 'em we're supreme—preme—
preme!
Yowski wowski, boola boola, status quo,
status quo!
Are we cripples? No! No! No!
So up and at 'em! On to vict'ry!
Give a cheer for team, team, team!

OYEZ, OYEZ, OYEZ!

Not listed in any programs. May have been cut before
the New York opening. A fragment of this number
is reprised in "The Trial of Throttlebottom" sequence,
following.

TWO
SOLDIERS: Oyez! Oyez! Oyez!
SPECTATORS: Oh no! Oh no! Oh no!
SOLDIERS: Oyez! Oyez! Oyez!
SPECTATORS: Oh no! Oh no! Oh no!

SOLDIERS:
[to each other]
We seem to be outnumbered;
We seem to be encumbered
With a lack of reinforcement;
Let's get some reinforcement!
[Whistle. Two more soldiers appear]

FOUR
SOLDIERS: Oyez! Oyez! Oyez!
SPECTATORS: Oh no! Oh no! Oh no!
SOLDIERS: Oyez! Oyez! Oyez!

SPECTATORS: Oh no! Oh no! Oh no!
SOLDIERS:
[among themselves]
It seems they still outshout us;
I wonder why they doubt us;
We need some reinforcement;
Let's get some reinforcement!
[Whistle. Four more soldiers appear]

EIGHT
SOLDIERS: Oyez! Oyez! Oyez!
SPECTATORS: OH NO! OH NO! OH NO!
[Soldiers pull out megaphones]
SOLDIERS: OYEZ! OYEZ! OYEZ!

SPECTATORS: Hearing such a blast,
We're convinced at last.
ALL: Oyez! Oyez! Oyez is O.K.!

THE TRIAL OF THROTTLEBOTTOM, including THAT'S WHAT HE DID! and I KNOW A FOUL BALL and THROTTLE THROTTLEBOTTOM

"That's What He Did!" was introduced by Philip Loeb
(Kruger), William Gaxton (Wintergreen), Victor Moore
(Throttlebottom), and ensemble. "I Know A Foul Ball"
was introduced by Moore and ensemble. "Throttle Thot-
tlebottom" was introduced by Loeb and ensemble.

"That's What He Did!"

KRUGER: Billions of dollars were lost us;
Billions of dollars it cost us—
Because this viper
double-crossed us!
[Indicates Throttlebottom]
SUPREME COURT: This dirty viper double-crossed
us!

WINTERGREEN: Stop calling names and let's get
down to cases.

KRUGER: The score was eight to eight,
[Points to Judges]
And they were going great,
[Points to Throttlebottom]
And what did he do?

THROTTLE: What did I do?
KRUGER: What did you *do?*

In inning number nine,
He showed he had no spine.
And what did he do?

THROTTLE: What did I do?
SUPREME COURT: What did you *do?*

KRUGER: The others were at bat,
When suddenly—like that—
He called a foul a fair.
It was a foul, I swear!

SUPREME COURT: He's called a foul a fair,
So *he's* a foul affair!

KRUGER: That's what he did!
That's what he did!
That's what he did!
ALL: That's what he did!

SUPREME COURT: Deny that, if you can,
You hypocritical man!
You son of a gun,
You gave the run
To the player from Japan!

ARMY: Deny that, if you can,
You hypocritical man!
You son of a gun,
You gave the run
To the player from Japan!

KRUGER: And so we lost the game,
Our fortune, and our name.
This son of a gun
Gave them the run,
And he's the one to blame!

ALL: Yes, he's the one to blame!
WINTERGREEN: Alexander Throttlebottom, what
have you to say to this?

"I Know a Foul Ball"

THROTTLE: I know a foul ball when I see
one;
I know the ball that's known as
fair.
So far as human eyes can
guarantee one,
The ball I saw was fair, I swear!

ALL: He knows a foul ball when he
sees one;
He knows the ball that's known
as fair.

KRUGER: Oh, if there ever was a crook,
then *he's* one!

GIRLS: *He's* one!

SUPREME COURT: The ball was foul!
THROTTLE: The ball was fair!
ARMY: The ball was foul!
THROTTLE: The ball was fair!
ALL: Foul!
THROTTLE: Fair!
ALL: Foul!
THROTTLE: Fair!

KRUGER: I say that he's a traitor
indescribable!
I say they gave him money and
he's bribable!
Besmirching all of us who feel
we're Aryan—
To kill him is an act
humanitarian!

ALL: Yes, kill the umpire! Kill 'im!
With lead we ought to fill 'im!
The son of a gun
Gave them the run—
So kill 'im, kill 'im, kill 'im!

WINTERGREEN: Order in the court! To me it
would seem
That taking his life is a little
extreme!

KRUGER: Comrades, to throttle
Throttlebottom or not to
throttle Throttlebottom? That
is the question!

"Throttle Throttlebottom"

KRUGER: Now that we have got 'im,
Shall we throttle Throttlebottom,
Shall we throttle Throttlebottom,
Shall we throttle him or not?

ALL: Now that we have got 'im,
Shall we throttle Throttlebottom,
Shall we throttle Throttlebottom,
Shall we throttle him or not?

KRUGER: I say throttle Throttlebottom!
SUPREME
COURT: We say throttle Throttlebottom!
ARMY: If you say throttle Throttlebottom,
Let's throttle Throttlebottom on
the spot!
[*They all rush at Throttlebottom*]

WINTERGREEN
AND
COMMITTEE: Oh no! Oh no! Oh no! Oh no!
SOLDIERS: Oyez! Oyez! Oyez!
[*Point guns at Wintergreen*]

WINTERGREEN: We've been thinking fast;
We're convinced at last:
Now that you have got 'im,
You can throttle Throttlebottom!
I'm afraid, old Throttlebottom,
They have got you on the spot!

ALL: Now that we have got 'im,
We can throttle Throttlebottom!
We're afraid, old Throttlebottom,
We have got you on the spot!

ALL: Alexander Thrott'
Is on the spot!

KRUGER: The persecution rests.

THE TRIAL OF WINTERGREEN, including A HELL OF A HOLE and DOWN WITH EVERYONE WHO'S UP (REPRISE) and IT ISN'T WHAT YOU DID and MINE (REPRISE)

"A Hell of a Hole" was introduced by William Gaxton (Wintergreen), Philip Loeb (Kruger), and ensemble. The reprise of "Down with Everyone Who's Up" was sung by Loeb and ensemble. "It Isn't What You Did" was introduced by Gaxton and ensemble. The reprise of "Mine" was sung by Gaxton, Lois Moran (Mary), and ensemble. (Just before the "Mine" reprise, a snatch of "I'm About to Be a Mother," from *Of Thee I Sing* [1931], is sung by Mary.)

"A Hell of a Hole"

KRUGER:
[*spoken*]
What we want to know is: When
are we going to be paid?

ARMY:
[*sings*]
Yes, when are we gonna be paid?
Oh, when are we gonna be paid?

KRUGER: Your I.O.U.
Is overdue—

ARMY: So when are we gonna be paid?

WINTERGREEN: Wait a minute, Kruger! You're
going too far!
Remember: I'm Dictator!

KRUGER: You're Dictator as long as the
Army says so and not one
second longer! The Army made
you, and the Army can break
you! And see that you don't
forget it!

ARMY: That's something you shouldn't
forget!
That's something you shouldn't
forget!
KRUGER: What the Army can make
The Army can break—
ARMY: That's something you shouldn't
forget!

WINTERGREEN: Oh, we're in a hell of a hole!
Oh, we're in a hell of a hole!
COMMITTEE: The Army can make us;
The Army can break us—
So, we're in a hell of a hole,
A hell of a, hell of a, hell of a, hell
of a, hell of a, hell of a hole!
A hell of a, hell of a, hell of a, hell
of a, hell of a, hell of a hole!

ARMY: So what are you going to do?
So what are you going to do?
KRUGER: You'd better come clean*
Or the guillotine
Is ready to cut you in two!

COMMITTEE: Oh, we're in a hell of a fix!
Oh, we're in a hell of a fix!
The guillotine—
Is that what you mean?
Oh, we're in a hell of a fix!
A hell of a, hell of a, hell of a, hell
of a, hell of a, hell of a fix!
A hell of a, hell of a, hell of a, hell
of a, hell of a, hell of a fix!

LIPPMAN: Make 'em an offer!
WINTERGREEN: Look here, you men! We'll give
you ten percent of the shirt
business!
KRUGER: Don't make us laugh!
ARMY: Oh, ha, ha, ha, ha, ha, ha, ha!
Oh, ha, ha, ha, ha, ha, ha, ha!
Your ten percent

*Script version of this and the next two lines:
Believe it or not,
What happened to Thrott'
Is likely to happen to you.

Is very well meant—
But ha, ha, ha, ha, ha, ha, ha!
WINTERGREEN: How about fifteen?
LIPPMAN: Try twelve and a half.
ARMY: Oh, ha, ha, ha, ha, ha, ha, ha!
Oh, ha, ha, ha, ha, ha, ha, ha!
Don't make us laugh
With twelve and a half—
Oh, ha, ha, ha, ha, ha, ha, ha!
KRUGER: We wouldn't take ninety-five!
We're going to take it all.
What do you say, men?

"Down with Everyone Who's Up" (Reprise)

KRUGER: Down with all these politicians!
ARMY: Politicians!
KRUGER: Down with present-day conditions!
ARMY: Day conditions!
[Wintergreen and crew are being led down from
bench]
KRUGER: Down with traitors! Make 'em
shiver!
ARMY: Make 'em shiver!
KRUGER: Down upon the Swanee River!
[All go into soft-shoe dance]
KRUGER: Down with all the upper classes!
ARMY: Upper classes!
KRUGER: Might as well include the masses!
[By this time, Kruger is on bench, wearing wig]
Happiness will fill our cup
When it's down with ev'ryone
who's up!

KRUGER: That's the torch we're going to get
the flame from!
If you don't like it, why don't you
go back where you came from?
ARMY: If you don't like it, why don't you
go back where you came from?
If you don't like it, why don't you
go back where you came from?

KRUGER: And now, John P. Wintergreen,
have you or any of your
henchmen anything to say
before we find you guilty?

WINTERGREEN: Impeach me, fine me, sue me, jail
me!
But reasons for this action fail me!
KRUGER:
[to soldiers]
Our comrade thinks he'd like a
reason.
[to Wintergreen]
Perhaps you never heard of treason!
Treason, treason, treason!

WINTERGREEN: But fellows, I tried to get you the
war debts.
I did everything I could!
KRUGER: It isn't what you did. It's what you
didn't do!

"It Isn't What You Did"

SOLDIERS: It isn't what you did—
It's what you didn't do!
It isn't what you did—
It's what you didn't do!
When you promised us milk and
honey!
It isn't what you did—
It's what you didn't do!
It isn't what you did—
It's what you didn't do!
And you just didn't get us the
money!

WINTERGREEN: When it isn't what you did, but
what you didn't—
There is little that a fellow can
do.
I tried my best to get you the
money!

SOLDIERS: But you didn't get it. Isn't that
true?

WINTERGREEN
AND
COMMITTEE: We tried our best to get you the
money!

SOLDIERS: But you didn't get it. Isn't that
true?

WINTERGREEN: When it isn't what you did, but
what you didn't—
When it isn't what you did, but
what you didn't—
And the court has a judge
Whose mind won't budge—
There's nothing that a fellow can
do!
COMMITTEE: There's nothing that a fellow can
do!

[Kruger opens large law book]
KRUGER: Well, here's something I can do.
The penalty for treason is
beheading. John P.
Wintergreen, Francis X.
Gilhooley, Louis Lippman,
Carver Crockett Jones, Robert
E. Lyons, and Matthew Arnold
Fulton, I sentence you all to be
beheaded!

WINTERGREEN
AND
COMMITTEE: Beheaded?
ALL: Beheaded!
WINTERGREEN
AND
COMMITTEE: Oh, we're in a hell of a jam!
Oh, we're in a hell of a jam!
The guillotine—
Is that what you mean?
ALL: Yes, you're in a hell of a jam!
A hell of a, hell of a, hell of a, hell
of a, hell of a, hell of a jam!
A hell of a, hell of a, hell of a, hell
of a—

[*Mary and five wives rush on*]
WIVES: Stop! Stop! Stop!
[*Mary whispers to Wintergreen*]
WINTERGREEN: Try it. It worked once.
[*Mary turns to bench*]
MARY: Before you go any further, with
your permission,
I must tell you of my husband's
delicate condition!

ALL: Delicate condition? What do you
mean?
MARY: I'm about to be a mother!
He's about to be a father!
We're about to have a baby!

KRUGER: Hold on, here! You can't get away
with that again! That was all
right four years ago, but it
doesn't go with the Army. What
is it—twins again?
[*Mary is defenseless*]
Well, it's *your* tough luck. Now, if
you want to say good-bye to
your husband, all right, but
make it snappy. Just one chorus!

"Mine" (Reprise)

WINTERGREEN: Mine, love is mine,
Whether it rain or storm or shine!
Mine, carry on!
Give me a thought when I am
gone!
For I am yours,
You know that I'm yours,
Even up there on heav'nly shores!
MARY AND
WINTERGREEN: Mine, though it's good-bye,
A love like ours will never die!
ALL: His, she is his;
When you're that way, that's how
it is!

Hers, he is hers;
There's no one else her heart
prefers.
True love is theirs;
Love will still be theirs
When he has left all earthly cares.
MARY AND
WINTERGREEN: Mine, though it's good-bye—
ALL: A love like ours (theirs) will never
die!

HANGING THROTTLEBOTTOM IN THE MORNING

Introduced by George Kirk (Lieutenant) and ensemble.

LIEUTENANT:
[*recitative*]
This morning, October the fifth,
Nineteen hundred and um-tee-um,
The second day of our new
government under the
leadership of Citizen Kruger,
We celebrate with the following
program:
Part A will consist of seven
beheadings.
Part B. There is no Part B.
Part C will consist of a sale of
autographed photographs of
Citizen Kruger,
The proceeds of which will go to
Citizen Kruger.
Open the gates and let the
customers in.

ENSEMBLE: Oh, they're hanging Throttlebottom
in the morning!
Oh, they're hanging Throttlebottom
in the morning!
Oh, nine o'clock's too soon—
They might have waited till noon,
But they're hanging Throttlebottom
in the morn!

Oh, they're hanging the Committee
in the morning!
Oh, they're hanging the Committee
in the morning!
We hope they've had their brunch,
For they'll be missing at lunch!

Oh, they're hanging the Committee
in the morn!

Sing hallelujah!
We hope Saint Peter treats 'em well!
Sing hallelujah!
Ring out that golden bell!
Sing hallelujah!
They'll soon be winging through the
sky!
Sing hallelujah!
And good-bye!

Oh, they're hanging the Dictator in
the morning!
Oh, they're hanging the Dictator in
the morning!
He's proved himself a bust,
So dust returns to dust!
And they're hanging the Dictator in
the morn!
Oh, they're hanging the Dictator in
the morn!

FIRST LADY AND FIRST GENT

Intended for Grace Worth (Trixie) and Philip Loeb (Kruger). Dropped before the Boston tryout. The music was mostly lost: Only eleven bars survived. Kay Swift, recalling what she could, reconstructed and completed the number. It has now been restored to the performing edition. A number titled "Let 'Em Eat Caviar," which was once intended to fill this spot, is now lost entirely.

VERSE

TRIXIE: Our future looks colossal and terrific.
KRUGER: Why not?
TRIXIE: If you can find the courage to be mine!
KRUGER: Why not?
TRIXIE: We'll rule from the Atlantic to Pacific.
KRUGER: Why not?
TRIXIE: If we get both our forces to combine!
KRUGER: Of course, you know your past is rather
shady!
TRIXIE: Why not?
But then we two have so much on the
ball!
KRUGER: We really ought to be First Gent and
Lady!
TRIXIE: The soldiers and the sailors all at our
beck and call!
BOTH: And so we've got the wherewithal!

REFRAIN

TRIXIE: If you'll tie up with me,
    Boy, we'll make history.
KRUGER: With no one stopping us,
    Believe you me, there's no topping us!
BOTH: We'll be First Lady and First Gent!
TRIXIE: We'll be the country's toast,
    And rule from coast to coast.
KRUGER: Without legality,
    But that's just a technicality!
BOTH: Let's be First Lady and First Gent!
    A new regime and combination,
    The greatest team in all creation!
    First Lady and First Gent:
    That suits our temp'rament!
    Life will be so grand
    When we both rule the land!

FASHION SHOW and FINALE ULTIMO

Mostly spoken dialogue over underscoring. Introduced by Lois Moran (Mary), Grace Worth (Trixie), Philip Loeb (Kruger), and entire company. Trixie's "Down with Kruger . . ." line, and those following, are set to the music of "Down with Everyone Who's Up."

MARY: Stop! Halt! Pause! Wait!

CROWD: What's your silly notion,
    In causing this commotion?
    Who are you to dally
    With Throtty's big finale?

MARY: Before you go any further
    With this passion show,
    I would like to introduce
    A fashion show.

TRIXIE: A fashion show!
[*A reaction from the girls; dialogue follows. Music for the fashion show: "Blue, Blue, Blue." The five wives enter, each wearing a lovely evening gown. They parade, like mannequins, to much admiration. Dialogue, during which Mary, Trixie, and girls turn on Kruger*]
TRIXIE:
[*Sings*]
    Down with Kruger, the Dictator!
    GIRLS: The Dictator!
TRIXIE: To our sex he will not cater!
    GIRLS: Will not cater!
[*With a roar, the soldiers seize Kruger; the republic is restored with Throttlebottom as President. Segue to "Finale Ultimo," which is a reprise of "Of Thee I Sing" or "Let 'Em Eat Cake"*]

OPPOSITE: *Ray Bolger, Luella Gear, Frances Williams, and Bert Lahr in* Life Begins at 8:40

LIFE BEGINS AT 8:40 | 1934
MISCELLANEOUS | 1930–1934

LIFE BEGINS AT 8:40, 1934

Tryout: Shubert Theatre, Boston. August 6, 1934. New York run: Winter Garden, opened August 27, 1934. 237 performances. Music by Harold Arlen. Lyrics by Ira Gershwin and E. Y. Harburg. Produced by the Messrs. Shubert (Lee and J.J.). Sketches by David Freedman, H. I. Phillips, Alan Baxter, Henry Clapp Smith, Frank Gabrielson, Ira Gershwin, and E. Y. Harburg. Staged by John Murray Anderson, Philip Loeb, Robert Alton, and Charles Weidman. Orchestra under the direction of Al Goodman, who replaced Max Meth after the Boston tryout. Orchestrations by Hans Spialek, Robert Russell Bennett, and Don Walker. Cast, starring Bert Lahr, Ray Bolger, Luella Gear, and Frances Williams, featured Brian Donlevy, Earl Oxford, Dixie Dunbar, Robert Wildhack, Bartlett Simmons, Ofelia and Pimento, Esther Junger, James MacColl, Josephine Houston, Walter Dare Wahl, Emmett Oldfield, Adrienne Matzenauer, Eugene Ashley, Jack Barrett, Eddie Wells, Kai Hansen, and the Weidman Dancers.

Since it took my brother, among other activities, some twenty months (eleven to compose, nine to orchestrate) to complete *Porgy and Bess*, my job as collaborator on the lyrics wasn't a continuous one. I was able to keep busy in that period on two other pieces: *Life Begins at 8:40* and *Ziegfeld Follies of 1936*.

One day Harburg, Arlen, and I were having lunch at director John Murray Anderson's apartment on Park Avenue. One of the matters under discussion was a title for the revue. There were many suggestions, but none we thought right. When we were leaving, I happened to notice a book on the table in the apartment's foyer. It was the then nonfiction best-seller, Walter Boughton Pitkin's *Life Begins at Forty*. I turned to the others and said, "How about *Life Begins at Eight-Forty*?"

Later, producer Lee Shubert wasn't sure of it (even after, he admitted, he tried the title out on the staff of a Boston ticket agency which he controlled and it had met with approval). So, one night after rehearsal at the Winter Garden he called a meeting onstage for a further title-discussion. There were a dozen of us under the arc light, including some Shubert staff men I didn't know. Several alternatives were suggested, among them one of mine; this one, *Calling All Stars*, I paraphrased from the police radio signal "Calling all cars."* But the earlier title stood the gaff and remained. I was amused a year or so later to learn that Lew Brown had bought a title for

*Another title considered was *Family Album*—Editor.

$100 from someone (I point no finger) for his new revue to be named *Calling All Stars*.

—Ira Gershwin
(intended for but not included in
Lyrics on Several Occasions)

LIFE BEGINS (AT EXACTLY 8:40 OR THEREABOUTS)

Introduced by Earl Oxford, Luella Gear, and ensemble. (Introduced during the tryout by Josephine Houston and ensemble.) The music of "Life Begins . . . ," with new, adapted lyrics not by Ira Gershwin, was published in 1943 by USO Camp Shows, Inc., as part of *At Ease, Vol. IV, Musical Opening Choruses, Finales and Production Numbers for Soldiers' Shows*.

As Performed

OXFORD: At exactly eight-forty or thereabouts—
Or even later—
This the-ay-ter comes to life—
ALL: Tra la la la la la la la la!
Tra la la la la la la!
This little play world—
Not of the day world—
Comes to life.
They've been sleeping all day;
Theatre folk are funny that way.
Art is art, you mustn't forget;
Actors are a privileged set.
They've been sleeping all day;
Theatre folk are funny that way.
But they wake at eight-forty because
Actors love to get your applause—
Actors love to get your applause.
Tra la la la la la la la la!
Tra la la la la la la!
This little play world—
Not of the day world—
Comes to life.

Come, you Sister Team,
Wake and rub your dreamy eyes!
"When the moon comes over the mountain."
Mr. Crooner,
Show people how you vocalize!
"Your time is your time."
Wake up, you Hoofer Man, come to life!
"With a hey-nonny-nonny and a ha-cha-cha, with a hey-hey-hey and a ho!"

Wake up, you Husband, Lover, and Wife!
"Love thy neighbor."
Little Ingenue,
Show them all how you can smile!
Little Ingenue,
Show them all how you can smile!

Funny Man,
Begin throwing people in the aisle!
Torch Singer,
Sing your tale of woe!
"Don't know why
There's no sun up in the sky,
Stormy Weather."
Bring the Chorus on, then on with the show!
[*Chorus appears*]
BOYS: They've been sleeping all day;
Dancing girls are funny that way.
Art is art, as ev'ryone knows,
Though it's only waving the toes.
They've been sleeping all day;
Dancing girls are funny that way;
But they wake up at eight-forty because
This step always gets your applause:
One, two, three, kick! Now it's eight-forty.
One, two, three at eight-forty.
These little lassies,
Wiggling their chassis,
Come to life.
[*Dance*]
ALL: And now make way
For the most important people of the play!
For the most important people of the play,
Make way!
[*Stagehands appear*]
They've been sleeping all day;
Stagehands all are funny that way.
But they wake at eight-forty because
Blackouts always get your applause.
They've been sleeping all day;
Stagehands all are funny that way.
At eight-forty they all lift up their heads
'Cause they have to make up the beds!
'Cause they have to make up the beds!
[*Stagehands bring out large bed for radio sketch*]
Tra la la la la la la la la!
Tra la la la la la la!
GEAR:
[*to stagehands*]
Gentlemen, back out!

Let the first blackout
Come to life!
[Into sketch]

Early Version

At Exactly 8:40 or Thereabouts

At exactly eight-forty or thereabouts,
This little play world—
Not of the day world—
Comes to life.

Tra la la la la la la la la!
Tra la la la la la la!
This little play world—
Not of the day world—
Comes to life.

They've been sleeping all day;
Theatre folk are funny that way.
Art is art, you musn't forget;
Actors are a privileged set.
They've been sleeping all day;
Theatre folk are funny that way.
But they wake at eight-forty because
Actors love to get your applause—
Actors love to get your applause.

Tra la la la la la la la la!
Tra la la la la la la!
This little play world—
Not of the day world—
Comes to life.

Little Sister Team,
Wake and rub your dreamy eyes!
Mr. Crooner,
Show people how you vocalize!
Wake up, you Hoofer Man, come to life!
Wake up, you Husband, Lover, and Wife!
Little Ingenue,
Show them all how you can smile!
Funny Man,
Begin throwing people in the aisle.
Torch Singer,
Sing your tale of woe!
Get the Chorus on, then on with the show!

At exactly eight-forty or thereabouts,
This little play world—
Not of the day world—
Comes to life.

8:50 or Thereabouts

GIRLS: We've been sleeping all day;
Dancing girls are funny that way.
Art is art, as ev'ryone knows,
Though it's only waving the toes.

We've been sleeping all day;
Dancing girls are funny that way.
But we wake at eight-fifty because
This step always gets your applause—
This step always gets your applause!

One, two, three, kick!
Now it's eight-fifty.
One, two, three at eight-fifty.

Dancers from Minsky
To Nijinsky
Come to life!

[Dance]

[Girls begin to exit]
At exactly eight-fifty or thereabouts,
This little play world—
Not of the day world—
Comes to life!

[After girls exit, a voice is heard shouting:]
VOICE: Eight-fifty! Eight-fifty! The Mae West
picture goes on at Eight-fifty!
[Into sketch]

SPRING FEVER

Introduced by Frances Williams; danced by the Weidman Dancers and ensemble.

VERSE

There's a crazy, lackadaisy sort of feeling in the
town—
Makes you sing, "Ding a derry, Ding a derry,
derry down."
Willy-nilly comes a silly, daffodilly kind of
glow—
Makes the city dweller carol, "Piminy miminy
miminy mo!"
Union Square agitators
Move to Central Park and join the roller skaters.
Pretty soon, ev'ryone'll
Go to see the tulips in the Holland Tunnel.
There are newly painted signs for all the pickets,
And the Penthouse Nudist gets a coat of brown;
Oh, the rivet drills are chirping like the crickets,
"Ding ding a derry, derry down."

REFRAIN

Tweet, Tweets . . .
Heartbeats . . .
It's that . . .
Spring Fever, Spring Fever, Spring Fever . . .

I've got it again!
Park bench . . .
Man, wench . . .
It's that . . .
Spring Fever . . .
I'm shoutin' "Amen!"
The Checker Cab is honking to the Parmalee;*
The Bronx Express is whistling to its mate;
And all the world is one big happy Farm-a-lee—
The Chrysler loves the Empire State!
S P R I N G,
Spring Fever . . .
Hot-cha-cha!

ALTERNATE VERSE

There's a crazy, lackadaisy sort of feeling in the
air—
Makes you sing, "Ding a derry, and away with
every care."
Willy-nilly comes a silly, daffodilly kind of
glow—
Makes the farmer in the dell sing, "Piminy
miminy miminy mo!"
Hark the lark! Hear him carol!
As the butterflies parade their spring apparel!
All the bees in the clover
Put their heads together and they talk it over.
Ivy's climbing up the chimneys of the houses;
It's the season for the village clown.
You can hear the mooing of contented cows-es—
"Ding ding a derry, derry down."

YOU'RE A BUILDER-UPPER

Published August 1934. Previously registered for copyright as an unpublished song May 1934. Introduced by Ray Bolger, Dixie Dunbar, and ensemble.

VERSE

When you want to, you are able
To make me feel that I'm Clark Gable;
Then, next minute, you make me feel
I'm something from the zoo.
First you warm up, then you're distant—
Never knew a girl so inconsistent—
I'm a big shot at half past one,

*Alternate version of refrain, lines 11–14:
The orange stands of Nedick's are in bloom again;
The Tamm'ny Tiger's cooing like a dove.
The pigeons come to glorify Grant's Tomb again;
And Reuben's named a sandwich after love.

A so-and-so by two.
Heaven forgive you for your sins—
Keeping me on needles and pins!

REFRAIN 1

You're a builder-upper,
A breaker-downer,
A holder-outer,
And I'm a giver-inner;
Sad but true,
I'm a saperoo, too,
Taking it from a taker-over like you.
Don't know where I'm at-a,
I'm just a this-a,
Then I'm a that-a,
A taker-on-the-chinner;
My, my, my!
What a weakie am I
To love you as I do.
Just when I'm ready to sob,
You hand me a throb,
And ev'rything is hunky-dory;
And that's my story:
Open your arms,
And I'm a stooge for your charms!
You're a builder-upper,
A breaker-downer,
A holder-outer,
And I'm a giver-inner;
Sad but true,
I love it, I do,
Being broken by a builder-upper like you!

TAG

Being broken by a builder-upper,
A builder-upper,
A breaker-downer,
A taker-inner,
A chaser-outer,
A goer-wither,
A pusher-frommer,
A clinger-toer,
A shaker-offer,
A smiler-atter,
A squeezer-outer like you!

MY PARAMOUNT-PUBLIX-
ROXY ROSE

Introduced by Earl Oxford and Luella Gear.

OXFORD:
[to group of girls posing as a rosebush]
    You're the sweetest flower that grows,
    My Paramount-Publix-Roxy Rose;
    Ev'ry single petal
    Puts me on my mettle—
    Darling, let us settle
    Where the Mohawk River flows.
    Your sweet perfume makes me feel
    Life with you would be ideal;
    You're the sweetest flower that grows,
    My Paramount-Publix-Roxy Rose.
[Oxford exits and Luella Gear steps out of
rosebush]
  GEAR: I spend hours and hours and hours
    Rehearsing and playing the
      goddamnedest flowers!
    Every week I make botanical changes—
    I've played everything from buttercups
      to hydrangeas!

    When the tenor with the apparatus
      known as vocal
    Starts to bore hell out of the front-row
      yokel,
    The art director uses his cranium,
    Gets a brainstorm . . . and I'm a
      geranium!

    I've blossomed out on the world's
      biggest stages . . .
    A poppy for Loew's, a pansy for
      Pantages'.
    Oh, I've been a tulip for Shubert, a
      bluebell on Rivoli hats,
    A daisy for Fanchon and Marco, a
      cactus for Balaban Katz.
    Yes, I was an orchid for Carroll, asleep
      in a garden of rocks,
    And awoke as poison ivy for
      Paramount, Publix, and Fox.

    To give the boys credit, it's really
      uncanny
    How they disguise my torso, my head,
      and my fanny;
    But whenever a crocus comes to life,
      there, right in the thick of it,
    Is little me. . . . And by God and by
      cracky, I'm sick of it!

    Years ago in the days of Annette
      Kellerman
    I *swam* to entertain my fellerman:
    In a one-piece suit I'd show a gorgeous
      flank
    Or float a lovely buttock in an all-glass
      tank.

    Then I became a pillar

    In the line of Mr. Tiller,
    And nightly with my sisters I'd get
      blisters on my toes.
    But I was myself, a personality . . . not
      a lousy rose!

    Today, where do scene designers park us?
    In lilac bushes! And what good is a
      lovely carcass?
    What chance have I as a drooping violet
    Of ever crashing a movie set
    Like Mae West or Sally Rand, who get
      along something phenomenal
    By featuring their muscles abdominal?

    By God and by cracky, I'd rather pose
      as Goonya-Goonya
    Than star as another Roxy petunia!

    Oh, the flowers that bloom on the stage,
      tra-la,*
    Someday I hope I'll be through with
      'em!
    Oh, the flowers that bloom on the stage,
      tra-la,
    You know what you can do with 'em!
[Steps back in rosebush as Oxford enters with
watering pot]

SHOEIN' THE MARE

Published August 1934. Previously registered for copyright as an unpublished song May 1934. Introduced by Adrienne Matzenauer; danced by Esther Junger, the Weidman Dancers, Ofelia and Pimento, and ensemble. (Introduced during the tryout by Frances Williams.)

VERSE

This is a dance from La Frita—
La Frita is in Havana—
(On account of which this music is Cuban).
It isn't like "Carioca"—
Nor is it like "Peanut Vendor"—
They call it "Shoein' the Mare."
You may like it—You may hate it—
Anyway, here's how we translate it:

  Alternate version of the number's conclusion:
    For the flowers that bloom on the stage,
      tra-la,
    Are simply driving me nuts!
    The flowers that bloom on the stage, tra-la,
    I hate their guts!
[Oxford appears with a hose; all sing last 8 bars of
"Paramount-Publix-Roxy Rose"]

REFRAIN

Shoein' the Mare!
The mare needs shoein',
Or else it's ruin.
She'll keep you all a-twitter
If you never get to shoe the critter;
That Cuban critter.

Shoein' the Mare!
Don't be too tender;
Forget her gender!
Don't let her kick the ground up,
Or you're headin' for a Cuban round-up;
Last Cuban round-up!

Woman is like a mare—
She'll boss you, toss you, double-cross you;
You'll never know where on earth you stand
Unless you get the upper hand.

Shoein' the Mare!
When wild *muchacha*
Begins to hot-cha,
You're on the road to ruin,
Brother, if you never get to shoein',
Shoein' the Mare!

QUARTET EROTICA

Introduced by James MacColl (Rabelais), Brian Donlevy (De Maupassant), Ray Bolger (Boccaccio), and Bert Lahr (Balzac). Alternate titles: "Rabelais" and "Rabelais, De Maupassant, Boccaccio, Balzac."

VERSE 1

We once won all the glories
For writing dirty stories—
Sophisticated people thought our bawdiness
    immense.
We once stopped all the traffic
With stories pornographic—
But we can see the handwriting on the fence.

REFRAIN 1

Rabelais, De Maupassant, Boccaccio, Balzac—*
Once we were quite the lads;
We thought that our erotica

*In most early versions of this song, this line (and as
repeated) is:
Rabelais, Balzac, De Maupassant, Boccaccio—

Was very, very hotica,
But now we're only four unsullied Galahads.
Rabelais, Balzac, De Maupassant, Boccaccio—
Babes in the wood are we.
The dirt we used to dish up,
Sad to say,
Wouldn't shock a bishop
Of today;
A volume like *Ulysses*
Makes us look like four big sissies—
Rabelais, De Maupassant, Boccaccio, Balzac—
Lost all our T.N.T.—
We're not what we used to be!

VERSE 2

When parents could contrive it,
They read our books in private,
But now we're sold in Liggett's and the kids
    think we're a bore;
Because it seems that latterly
They're reading *Lady Chatterly*
And the *Life and Loves of Evelyn Nesbit* they
    adore.

REFRAIN 2

Rabelais, De Maupassant, Boccaccio, Balzac—
We've reached the bitter end.
We've staged the final fade-out;
Those happy days are played out
When a Lesbian was an islander and not your
    wife's best friend.
Rabelais, Balzac, De Maupassant, Boccaccio—
Babes in the wood are we.
For even with the censors
And Mr. Hays,
The kids know all the enswers
Nowadays.
We'll go back to our rockers
For we're just four *alter kockers!*
Rabelais, De Maupassant, Boccaccio, Balzac—
Lost our virility—
We're not what we used to be!

FUN TO BE FOOLED

Published August 1934. Previously registered for copyright as an unpublished song May 1934. Introduced by Frances Williams and Bartlett Simmons.

VERSE

Spring is here! I'm a fool if I fall again;
And yet, I'm enthralled by its call again.
You say you love me;
I know from the past,
You mean to love me;
But these things don't last.
Fools rush in to begin new love affairs,
But tonight, tonight, my dear, who cares?

REFRAIN

Fun to be fooled,
Fun to pretend,
Fun to believe
Love is unending.
Thought I was done,
Still, it is fun
Being fooled again.
Nice when you tell
All that you feel;
Nice to be told
This is the real thing;
Fun to be kissed,
Fun to exist,
To be fooled again.
It's that Old Debbil Moon having his fling once
    more;
Selling me spring once more;
I'm afraid love is king once more!
Fun to be fooled,
Fun to pretend
This little dream won't end.

C'EST LA VIE

Prologue introduced by Adrienne Matzenauer, Earl Oxford, and Frances Comstock. Sketch and song introduced by Ray Bolger, Bert Lahr, and Luella Gear. (The sketch as well as the "C'est la Vie" lyric is by Ira Gershwin and E. Y. Harburg.)

Prologue

[*Music very Puccini*]
Ladies and gentlemen, you are about to witness
    a slice of life,
A story of three human beings who had too
    much zest for the spice of life—
Who knew the value but not the price of life.
The time: the present.
The place: the River Seine in Paris, France.

It is a tale running the gamut of human
  emotions from A to Z of life;
The story of three bits of driftwood tossed about
  by the tempestuous sea of life;
Three little branches broken from the eternal
  tree of life.
The time: the present.
The place: the River Seine in Paris, France.
This is the tale of a lovers' quarrel,
Of hearts no longer fancy-free.
This is a tale that points a moral;
This is the moral: C'est la vie.

Sketch

[*Paris. A bridge across the Seine. Man in
evening clothes and high hat. Takes off hat and
cape. Pins note on cape. From other side of
bridge another figure appears, also in evening
clothes. Same business. As they are about to
jump into the water, each sees the other*]

BOLGER: Monsieur, you too?
  LAHR: I am afraid that—yes.
BOLGER: Ah, monsieur, la depression?
  LAHR: Non, monsieur, la dame. And you,
      monsieur?
BOLGER: La same.
[*Both sigh*]
  BOTH: Cherchez la femme.
BOLGER: Betrayed?
  LAHR: Non, she does not love me. She loves
      only herself. And you?
BOLGER: She loves only herself. She does not
      love me.
[*Both sigh and reach into back pockets. Each
brings out a photograph to show the other*]
  BOTH: Her picture.
[*Each looks at the other's*]
      Mon Dieu! Dolores!
  LAHR: She have double-crossed us both. She
      does not love *you*. She does not love
      me. Fickle woman! It is well we are
      getting rid of her. You first.
[*bowing and pointing to river below*]
BOLGER: Non, monsieur, *you* first.
  LAHR: Monsieur, we must stop this
      dilly-dallying. Even now she reads my
      note telling her where to find the
      body.
BOLGER: Why not jump togezzer, then?
  LAHR: Togezzer!
[*They embrace and are about to jump when taxi
brakes are heard. Taxi door is slammed.
Woman rushes on*]
  GEAR: Pierre! Jacques! What is it that you do?
      But non! You must not do it!
  MEN: You do not love *me*. You do not love
      him!

GEAR: But you do not understand. I tell you I
      do not love you because I love you
      each so much and if I tell one, I hurt
      the other. But wait. I have solution.
      Tonight before I get your terreeble
      note I am in ze cinema. I see la talkie
      Design for Living.
BOLGER: Ah, yes. It is by Noël Coward, non?
  GEAR: But yes.
  LAHR: It is where the woman and the two men
      love each the other and the other
      each?
  GEAR: But yes. And they live happily together
      after, forevermore. And I think to
      myself—Pierre, Jacques, me—Why
      not *we* so?
[*It sounds like a great idea to them. All
embrace*]
  ALL: One for three and three for one!

"C'est la Vie"

VERSE

Life is gay, we agree,
When a heart, it is big enough for three.
Night and day, ma cherie,
Me for you and you, and you and you for me.
We're living in the smart upper sets!
Let other lovers sing their duets!
Duets are made by the bourgeoisie-o,
But only God can make a trio.

REFRAIN 1

C'est la vie!
C'est Paree!
In a cute little love nest for three.
Love will see us through
In a rendezvous
Where three can live cheaply as two.
Savoir faire
In the air—
If the neighbors should talk—do we care?
Ziss is fun!—
Three hearts beating as one!
C'est la vie!
C'est la vie!

REFRAIN 2

C'est la vie!
C'est Paree!
In a cute little love nest for three.
Breakfast will be set
Tête à tête à tête,
We'll awake and we'll have crêpes Suzettes.
C'est l'amour!

C'est la guerre!
C'est la vie!
C'est la vie!
Sailor beware!
Ziss is fun!—
Three hearts beating as one!
C'est Paree!
C'est la vie!

[*They dance about happily, embrace one
another. The two men kiss each other and seem
to like it very much. They kiss again and now
they are sure they like it. They pantomime to
each other and suddenly seize the woman and
drop her into the Seine as all three sing "C'est
la vie!"*]

WHAT CAN YOU SAY IN A LOVE SONG? (THAT HASN'T BEEN SAID BEFORE?)

Published August 1934. Introduced by Josephine Houston, Bartlett Simmons, and ensemble. Added to the score during the pre-Broadway tryout.

VERSE

Looking through the pages of the program,
We know what puts that wrinkle in your brow;
This question you are raising,
"Isn't it amazing
There hasn't been a love song up to now?"

It's only fair that you should have that love
  song,
And curiously, the writers thought so, too;
So they studied all the pages
Of music through the ages
Because they thought the best was none too
  good for you.

Oh, they studied all the pages
Of music through the ages,
And here's the song of songs they wrote for you:

REFRAIN

Mn, mn, mn, surrender,
Mn, mn, mn, so tender,
Mn, mn, mn, forevermore—
What can you say in a love song
That hasn't been said before?

Mn, mn, mn, so sweetly,
Mn, mn, mn, completely,
Mn, mn, mn, *je vous adore*—
What can you say in a love song
That hasn't been said before?

You are my true love,
Old and new love,
I live for you, love,
You are my guiding star.

Lovers long before us
Sang the same old chorus—
If it worked in days of yore,
Why should I say in a love song
What hasn't been said before?

PUBLISHED VERSE

Darling, here's that song you inspired
In a style I acquired
Living with songs of the past.
I've gone all through the pages
Of songs down through the ages,
So perhaps my phrases
Are a little aged in the wood.
They may not be original,
But, my darling, they are always good.

LET'S TAKE A WALK AROUND THE BLOCK

Published August 1934. Previously registered for copyright as an unpublished song May 1934. Introduced by Earl Oxford and Dixie Dunbar ("as two young people working in a New York travel agency"—I.G.), and ensemble.

VERSE

I've never traveled further north
Than old Van Cortlandt Park,
And never further south than the Aquarium.
I've seen the charm of Jersey City—
But first, let me remark—
I saw it from the Empire State Solarium.
Still, I've been putting nickels
In the Postal Savings Bank;
And when those nickels pile up,
We can toddle off in swank.
And I don't mean an ordinary Cook's tour;
I mean a cabin-de-luxe tour.

REFRAIN 1

Someday we'll go places—
New lands and new faces—
The day we quit punching the clock.
The future looks pleasant,
But, at present,
Let's take a walk around the block.
You're just the companion
I want at Grand Canyon,
For throwing old blades down the rock.
Whatever we have'll
Go for travel—
Meantime, let's walk around the block.
Gangway! We'll begin
When our ship comes in;
You'll sit on my lap
All over the map.
To London in Maytime,
To Venice in Playtime,
To Paris in time for a frock,
To Boston in Beantime—
Darling, meantime—
Let's take a walk around the block.

REFRAIN 2

In winter, at Christmas,
We'll visit the Isthmus
To see how they lock up a lock;
And then in Caracas,
On a jackass,
We'll sit and ride around the block.
I give you my promise:
We'll visit St. Thomas
And then at the Virgins we'll dock.
(The Virgins can wait, sir;
It grows late, sir;
Meantime, let's walk around the block.)
Onward to Cathay—
Then to Mandalay!
Then Vladivostok,
Where Bolsheviks flock!
We'll send the folks cables,
Accumulate labels,
Buy souvenirs till we're in hock.
But while we are flat in
Old Manhattan—
Gangway, let's walk around the block!

THINGS!

Registered for copyright as an unpublished composition September 1937. Introduced by Bert Lahr.

LAHR:
[*spoken*]
The first number of my second group was written while I was living in a little garret on the left bank . . . of the Gowanus Canal. It is a little roundelay of moods and fancies . . . a little thing written entirely under astrological influences. Though the song itself has no specific relationship with the signs of the Zodiac, the music lover will find especial interest in its polychromatic undulations, its rhythmic reverberations, and its purely American chi-chi based on legendary folklore. If you are one able to turn the dust of the city into the gold of the imagination, this little effort will, I am sure, both rapture and capture you. The title: "Things." T, H, I, N, G, S. "T" for toast, "H" for Horange Ice, "I" for India Relish, "N" for New Pickles, "G" for Graham Crackers, "S" for Sour Cream. Things!

VERSE

[*Sings*]
When I was but a little lad,
I used to think of Things;
The only joy I ever had
I had because of Things.
And now that I'm to manhood grown,
Fond memory always brings
The utter, utter, utter, utter
Loveliness of Things.
Let others sing of Mandalay,
Let others sing of Trees,
Let others sing of Mothers
And the busy, busy Bees,
But I'm happier far
Than a million kings are
When my soul sings of Things. . . .

REFRAIN

Ah, Things! Sweet Happiness of Things!
Things that ease the Rocky Way,
Things that look at God all day!
Things! Sweet Misery of Things!
From the birth bed to the grave,
Aren't we all of them a slave?
What makes all the oceans wave?
Things, ah! Things, ah!
When the frost is on the punkin,
When the clouds in the West are sunken,
Can't you hear the paddles chunkin'
Of Things, just Things!
Lickety-split and to beddy for Things!
Fit as a fiddle and ready for Things!
You can keep your diamond rings

And your Saratoga Springs—
Give me, give me, give me Things!

ALL THE ELKS AND MASONS

Introduced by Ray Bolger, Dixie Dunbar, and ensemble. During the Boston tryout, the number also featured Bert Lahr, Luella Gear, Frances Williams, Earl Oxford, and other members of the cast and ensemble. Alternate title: "The Elks and Masons."

VERSE

BOLGER: There's no organization that I'm not a
    member of,
So when you get me,
You're getting a man of high degree.
Joining up with my fellow men is a
    practice that I love;
I'm one of the headmen
In the Masons and the Redmen;
My dues I never dodge
In the Hetsky Petsky Lodge.
I've joined the Knights of Pythias,
And I've joined the Theatre Guild;
So when I ask you to be mine,
You really should be thrilled.

REFRAIN 1

All the Elks, the Masons, too—
Darling, they'll be there for you—
Think of all the company
If you join up with me.

All the Moose, the Woodmen all,
Will be at your beck and call—
Fifty million brethren who
Will be brothers to you.

Lady, what a chance to be the toast
Of ev'ry lodge from coast to coast.
We won't meet ordinary dubs—
Just members of the Kate Smith clubs!

All the Elks, the Masons, too—
Darling, what a break for you!
Think what a popular couple we'll be—
Join up with me!

REFRAIN 2

CHORUS: All the Elks, the Masons, too—
Lady, we'll be there for you—

BOLGER: Think of all the company
If you join up with me.

CHORUS: All the Moose, the Woodmen all,
We'll be at your beck and call—
Fifty million brethren who
Will be brothers to you.

BOLGER: Lady, what a chance to be the toast
Of ev'ry lodge from coast to coast.
You won't meet ordinary dubs—
Just members fo the Kate Smith clubs!

CHORUS: Greetings from the D.A.R.
And Sisters of the Eastern Star!
You can have happiness, vigor, and
    vim—
Join up with him!

PATTER

If they ever catch you speeding in
    Peoria, Peoria, Peoria—
If they catch you with a gal in
    Kalamazoo—
No matter what the distance,
Who will come to your assistance?
The Redmen, the Elks, the Masons, too.

If your wife is in the horspital with
    trip-a-lets, trip-a-lets, trip-a-lets—
Who sends up the presents wrapped in
    baby blue?
Oh, who's the first to shoot up
Just to help her eat the fruit up?
The Odd Fellows, Elks, and Masons,
    too.

If you need a swell procession for a
    funeral, a funeral, a funeral—
Who can you depend on to do right by
    you?
Yes, on that day of dayses
Who's the one to sing your praises?
The Moose, the Elks, the Masons, too.

I COULDN'T HOLD MY MAN

Introduced by Luella Gear.

[*Girl is discovered with rope around her neck; a revolver and bottles of poison are in evidence. Obviously, she is about to commit suicide*]

VERSE

I'm blue! I'm through!
Oh, life is bare and shoddy!
I gave him soul and body,
But I'm jilted all the time!
I tried to be alluring
To make our love enduring,
But I'm jilted all the time!
I followed ev'ry beauty ad in ev'ry magazine;
I bought the things endorsed by leading ladies
    of the screen;
I tried the things the radio spoke very highly
    of—
But it all meant nothing to the man I love!

[*Takes a swig of poison*]

REFRAIN

I'm through with yeast by Fleischmann;
I'm through with Kellogg's Bran;
I fell for Listerine and Zulac—
But I couldn't hold my man!

I used a ton of Lifebuoy
And Coty's Sun Burn Tan;
Massages by Elizabeth Arden—
But I couldn't hold my man!

I took Lydia Pinkham and followed each
    direction;
To Helena Rubinstein I went for my
    complexion.
I even bought the Five Foot Shelf,
But I'm still sleeping by myself!

And so good-bye, Lavoris—
And Chase and Sanborn's can!
Oh, I'm better off dead—
Even tried Simmons' bed—
But I couldn't hold my man!

A WEEKEND CRUISE

Registered for copyright as an unpublished song May 1934 under the title "Will You Love Me Monday Morning as You Did on Friday Night?" Introduced by Frances Williams, Earl Oxford, Bert Lahr, and ensemble. Dropped after the New York opening.

VERSE

WILLIAMS: Sailed away
    Yesterday—
    Didn't know you from the captain;

One day out,
And it's you I'm rapt in.
Love at last!
Love works fast
Out on a weekend cruise—
But will it bring me bliss or blues?

REFRAIN 1

The question in my heart today
Before the weekend flies away
Is: Will you love me Monday morning
As you did on Friday night?

Is that a love-light in your eyes?
Or is it just Bermuda skies?
And will it shine on Monday morning
As it did on Friday night?

This blue Atlantic
Has done things to me;
It's too romantic,
But when we land will I be still at sea?

You know how easily I bruise!
Is this another weekend cruise?
Or will you love me Monday morning
As you did on Friday night?

REFRAIN 2

OXFORD: On Thursday we were worlds apart,
And now you're nestled in my heart.
WILLIAMS: But will I nestle Monday morning
As I nestled Friday night?

OXFORD: I fell for you with just one look
As we were passing Sandy Hook.
WILLIAMS: But will you still be falling Monday
When we're passing Ambrose Light.

OXFORD: And will that statue—
I mean Liberty—
Be smiling at you
While she is carrying the torch for
me?

Since I met you, I'm not the same;
And by the way, what *is* your name?
And will you love me Monday
morning
As you did on Friday night?

REFRAIN 3

SAILOR You've got me all a-twitter now;
(LAHR): I'm all agog from stern to bow!
But will you shiver my timbers
Monday
As you did on Friday night?

For you I'd be a galley slave;
You swept me like a tidal wave!
But will you sweep me Monday
morning
As you swept me Friday night?

Without you, I'm driftwood;
Without you, I fail;
I'm flotsam and jetsam;
I mean, I'm just a ship without a sail.

But when we pass that Customs House
Will you be just a weekend louse?
Or will you love me Monday morning
As you did on Friday night?

IT WAS LONG AGO

Introduced by Josephine Houston and ensemble. Alternate title: "Long Ago, Far Away, Once Upon a Time."

VERSE (RECITED)

We sing of the charm of the Nineties
When the Goulds and the Astors held sway;
Oh, there was a charm to the Nineties
That you never can find today.

We sing of the days before talkies
And airplanes and radio mikes;
We sing of the days of corsets
And bustles and buggies and bikes.

REFRAIN (SUNG)

Weren't those the lovely days?*
Simple people . . . charming ways . . .
It was long ago,
It was far away,
Once upon a time.

Kissing was their only sin;
Virtue always seemed to win.
It was long ago,
It was far away,
Once upon a time.

A time of purple and lace,
A time sublime of manner and grace . . .
In this age we're telling of
People still believed in love.
It was long ago,

Alternate version of refrain, lines 1–2:
Wasn't that a lovely age?
Loveliness on every page.

It was far away,
Once upon a time.

I'M NOT MYSELF

Introduced by Ray Bolger and ensemble. According to the New York program, this number was "arranged by Mr. Bolger." The Boston program states that the number was "directed by Mr. Bolger."

VERSE

When I look in the mirror ev'ry morning as I
shave,
I say to me—I do—
"Is this the man I knew?
Is this the Casanova who made ev'ry girl his
slave?
The man who once made hay
Is not himself today."
Since you've been taking me for a ride—
Don't know if I'm Jeykll or Hyde.

REFRAIN 1

Haven't the gift of gab—I sputter;
All I can do is blab—and splutter;
Lady, it's time you knew:
I'm not myself when I'm with you.

Beautiful, take a bow—You've got me;
Feller who's talking now is not me;
Maybe I'm Fu Manchu—
I'm not myself when I'm with you.

I used to sing and give out;
My song was just like the lark's;
But now, when you are about,
I'm just as dumb—I'm just as dumb—as Harpo
Marx.

There was a time when I was brainy;
Now I'm another guy—a zany;
All I can do is moo—
I'm not myself; I can't find words;
I must be those two other birds
When I'm with you.

REFRAIN 2

Twenty-four hours a day I'm grievin';
Never can hit the hay—Can't even
Paddle my own canoe—
I'm not myself when I'm with you.

What do I have to start to win you?
How can I reach the heart that's in you?
What do I have to do?
I'm not myself when I'm with you.

I know my face and my hair;
I know the spots on my tie;
I know these clothes that I wear;
But is the chap—but is the sap—that's in
  them I?

General Grant took Lee—That's nothing;
Lady, when you took me is something—
Talk about Waterloo!
I'm not myself; I'm all a-twit;
I'm just a flop; to wit, to wit—
When I'm with you.

LIFE BEGINS AT CITY HALL

Introduced by Eugene Ashley, Jack Barrett, Eddie Wells, and Kai Hansen (the Messrs. Grover Whalen), Bert Lahr (Fiorello La Guardia), Luella Gear (Eleanor Roosevelt), Frances Williams and Ray Bolger (the stowaways—Betty Compton and Jimmy Walker), and ensemble. The sketch as well as the lyric is by Ira Gershwin and E. Y. Harburg. Fragments of "All the Elks and Masons," "Fun to Be Fooled," "Let's Take a Walk Around the Block," and "You're a Builder-Upper" are included. Typed versions of the lyric bear the title "Beautifying the City," while the Boston programs list the title as "To Beautify the Bay."

THE GROVER
  WHALENS: We are Grover Whalen, and we are
      here today
    To help the Great La Guardia
      beautify the bay.

ENSEMBLE: We're here, we're here, assembled
      here today
    To help the Great La Guardia
      beautify the bay.
    He's beautified Manhattan
    And the Bronx and Queens and
      Staten,
    And tonight this mighty Latin
    Wants to beautify the bay.

THE GROVER
  WHALENS: He gave the city class, oh!
    There's dancing on the Mall.
    He introduced Picasso
    To the boys at City Hall.
    Delancey Street has flowers
    The Bow'ry has no bums;

With chromium-plated showers,
He has beautified the slums.

ENSEMBLE: And now we're here, assembled
      here today
    To help the Great La Guardia
      beautify the bay.
[Trumpets sound. La Guardia enters, dressed as a Roman emperor except for a broad-brimmed Stetson. Two girls follow, carrying tiger skins. Then four men in brown derbies and mustaches. All march on to "All the Elks and Masons"]

    Hail, Dictator La Gua, ha ha, di ah!
    Hail, Dictator La Gua, ha ha, di ah!
    La Gua, ha ha, ha ha, di ah!
    La Gua, ha ha, ha ha, di ah!
    He makes all the other dictators
      look like so much blah!
    La Gua, ha ha, ho ho, ha ha, ho
      ho, ha ha, di ah!

[All cheer]
LA GUARDIA: I'm Dictator Fiorello;
    I'm a many-sided fellow.
    When you look at me, you almost
      see Napoleon!
    I love music, I'm artistic,
    I'm a statesman pugilistic—
    As a brain, I'd even take Professor
      Moley on!

  VOICE: Like Caesar, he's a Roman;
    Like Barnum, he's a showman;
    Like Stalin, he gets things done in
      a hurry.

LA GUARDIA: Tammany Hall is growing graver,
    For I never curry favor,
    And I never, never, never, favor
      Curry!

THE GROVER
  WHALENS: He never curries favor, and he
      never favors Curry!
    Fiorello, he gets things done in a
      hurry!*

---

*In an early version, the following lines were sung at this point:
LA GUARDIA: I am small,
    But one and all
    Admit I've got a hell of a fist.
    I'm the guy
    Who took the ti-
    Ger by the tail and gave it a twist!

ENSEMBLE: He is small,
    But one and all
    Admit he's got one hell of a fist.
    He's the guy
    Who took the ti-
    Ger by the tail and gave it a twist!

ENSEMBLE: Fee-hee, fee-hee, fee-ha-ho-orello!
    Fee-hee-orello! A many-sided
      fellow!
    Fee-hee-hee-hee-hee-orello!

LA GUARDIA:
[spoken]
    And now, citizens and citinesses, a
      vocal offering by the Civic
      Choral Society, which, as you all
      know, used to be the Board of
      Aldermen. They used to sell the
      city for a song, so now I've got
      them singing songs for the city.
[Indicates men in brown derbies]
    They will now give you the
      Taxpayers' Theme Song.

CIVIC CHORAL
  SOCIETY:
[Sings]
    Fun to be fooled!
    Fun to be fooled!
    Fun to be fooled!
    Fun to be fooled!
[Everybody cheers]

LA GUARDIA:
[spoken]
    And now to the business at hand. I
      want to make this city beautiful.
      Who gave you platinum
      incinerators? I did! Who gave
      you slot machines with a jackpot
      every time you hit two cherries?
      I did! And today—

ENSEMBLE:
[Sings]
    We're here, we're here, assembled
      here today
    To help the Great La Guardia
      beautify the bay.

LA GUARDIA:
[spoken]
    We want to put poetry and
      romance into transportation.
      Away with the ugly and prosaic
      ferryboat. We are here to
      christen the first gondola, the
      first gondola to ply between
      Manhattan and Staten.

[Gondola is brought on]
ENSEMBLE:
[Sings]
    A gondola, pretty gondola,
    For redhead, brunette, and
      blond-ola.
    We'll be fond-ola
    Of floating on a gondola

On that pond-ola
Called New York Bay.
And that's why we're all here today;
That's why we're all here today!

[*Whirring of an airplane is heard*]

LA GUARDIA:
[*spoken*]

Ah! Mrs. Roosevelt is here for the launching!

THE GROVER
WHALENS:
[*Sing*]

If there's a dedication,
No matter where it's planned,
First Lady of the nation
Is sure to be on hand.

ENSEMBLE: If there's a celebration
With speakers on a stand,
First Lady of the nation
Will positively be on hand.

[*Mrs. Roosevelt enters with female secretary; they carry handbags*]

MRS.
ROOSEVELT: At seven o'clock this morning in Poughkeepsie,
I spoke at the opening of a bridle path;
Had breakfast in Savannah;
Then flew to Indiana
To dedicate a woman's Turkish bath.

I christened a Ferris wheel in Chattanooga;
And then I unveiled a western barbecue;
A Warner Brothers' palace
I opened next in Dallas;
And here I am to launch a gondola for you.

ENSEMBLE: At seven o'clock this morning in Poughkeepsie,
She opened a bridle path, then took a bus,
A horse, a trolley, a boat, a train—
LA GUARDIA: A covered wagon, a hydroplane—
MRS.
ROOSEVELT: I rode, I walked, I flew, I swam,
I floated over the Boulder Dam—
ENSEMBLE: And here she is to launch a gondola for us!

LA GUARDIA:
[*spoken*]

Unveil the gondola!

[*As this is done, Mrs. R. opens her handbag and takes out a bottle of champagne*]

MRS.
ROOSEVELT:
[*turning to La Guardia*]
What are we calling it?
LA GUARDIA: The *Samuel Seabury.*
MRS.
ROOSEVELT: I hereby christen thee—

[*Her secretary stops her, points to wrist watch. Mrs. R. puts bottle back in bag*]

Awfully sorry, but I can just make the boat to Puerto Rico, where I am christening a boat that'll take me to Havana.

[*She and secretary go off as all shout: "Good luck! Bon Voyage!"*]

LA GUARDIA:
[*now at gondola with own bottle*]
I hereby christen thee—

[*The window shade of the gondola's little cabin snaps up*]

A GONDOLIER:
[*peering in*]
Hey, boss! A stowaway!
ALL: A stowaway!
GONDOLIER:
[*looking again*]
Hey, boss! There's two stowaways!
LA GUARDIA: Bring 'em out!

[*Enter the stowaways, a man and a woman*]

GONDOLIER: Hey, boss! It's Jimmy Walker and Betty Compton!

[*Excitement*]

LA GUARDIA: What are *you* doing here? Where's your passport?
WALKER: We couldn't stand it anymore. Three years away from the Casino. For three years, nothing but pâté de foie gras. Three years with no A. C. Blumenthal.
COMPTON: Put yourself in his place. You were a mayor once. Please pardon us. We're tired of traveling.

WALKER:
[*Sings*]

To London in Maytime,*
To Paris in Playtime,

------

*In the earlier version, the following was sung here:
WALKER AND
COMPTON: We couldn't stand it anymore
In London and in Nice;
And so your pardon we implore:
Let's smoke the pipe of peace!
The hatchet we bury
With *Samuel Seabury.*
Your pardon we implore—
Oh, make us New Yorkers once more!

But homesick wherever we dock.
We just had to go 'way—
Even stow'way!
Please let us walk around the block!

COMPTON:
[*indicating Walker*]
I knew him when
His dancing took the town by storm!

ENSEMBLE:
[*on knees*]

Oh, pardon them!
COMPTON: But oh, since then,
I know he's promised to reform!
ENSEMBLE: Oh, pardon them!

[*La Guardia has taken out his handkerchief and is visibly and audibly affected*]

LA GUARDIA:
[*spoken*]

Stop, you're breaking my heart!
COMPTON: Oh, please give Jimmy a job. We've suffered enough.
WALKER: Three years of pâté de foie gras.
LA GUARDIA: All right, but what can you do?
WALKER: I can still write songs.
LA GUARDIA: What can you say in a love song that hasn't been said before?
WALKER: I guess that's right. There's nothing new I can say.
COMPTON: Well, how about bringing back the *old* songs, then?
LA GUARDIA: That's it. I've got it! I'll make you Commissioner of Reprises.

[*All cheer*]

WALKER: When do I start?
LA GUARDIA: *Now!*
WALKER: Okay, Fiorello. I dedicate the first reprise to you because—

ENSEMBLE:
[*Sings*]

He's a builder-upper,
A breaker-downer,
A cleaner-outer,
A puncher-on-the-chinner!
My, my, my!
What a strong little guy!
Took the tiger by the tail and then made him cry!

I KNEW HIM WHEN

Registered for copyright as an unpublished song October 1964. Intended for *Life Begins at 8:40.* Dropped during rehearsals, but a few bars of the song appear in "Life Begins at City Hall."

VERSE

He's living high in Beverly;
Three butlers he employs.
He's worked his way up cleverly,
One of Hollywood's White-Haired Boys.
He's called the greatest lover
The screen has ever had;
And women can't recover
After seeing this romantic lad.
I've watched him in his love scenes;
His acting still is good.
And I see what once took me
Has taken Hollywood.

REFRAIN

I knew him when
He brought me violets now and then;
I knew him when
The rings he bought
Were purchased at the five-and-ten;
I knew him when
He used to sit on top of a bus
And dream of that someday flat,
Then keep our date for dinner at eight
At the Automat.
So that's the guy
Whose name is up in blazing lights.
(That's all there is!)
The boy made good,
But local girl is still in tights.
(There is no more!)
Together when the going was rough,
He recognized me then.
Sister, it's tough
When you knew them when.

I'M A COLLECTOR OF MOONBEAMS

Intended for *Life Begins at 8:40*. Unused. No music is known to survive.

I'm a collector of moonbeams, sunsets, rainbows;
I'm a hoarder of dreams.
Keep your collection of gold plate, china, silver;
Me for golden fields and silvery streams.
Of Chippendale I haven't one set,

But my view of the Hudson at sunset
Makes me rich as anyone I know.
So
Start a collection of moonbeams, sunsets,
    rainbows—
Go get your share;
You'll find it wherever you go.

MISCELLA-NEOUS, 1930–1934

ASK ME AGAIN

Written in the late 1920s or early 1930s. Published April 1991 in the song folio *Rediscovered Gershwin*. Previously registered for copyright as an unpublished song June 1983. Music by George Gershwin. No. 50 in the George and Ira Gershwin Special Numbered Song File. Michael Feinstein says that Ira Gershwin considered this song the best of the unpublished George and Ira Gershwin collaborations. Introduced on Broadway in David Merrick's 1990 revival of *Oh, Kay!* by Brian Mitchell (Jimmy) and in the "new" 1991 version of the Merrick *Oh, Kay!* by Ron Richardson.

REFRAIN 1

Ask me again
Who's the one I've begun to adore.
Ask me again
Who's the partner my heart pounded for.*
Who is the who has me tied in a bow knot†
So that I know not
Just where I'm at?
Who is it makes my friends all find
That I've a one-track heart and mind?
Oh, ask me again—
Let me tell how I fell from the start;

  Earlier version of refrain 1, line 4:
Who's the partner my heart clamors for.
  †*Alternate version of refrain 1, lines 5–7:*
Who is the who has a charm that surpasses
All other lasses
I've ever known?

One look and then
Couldn't govern the love in my heart.
Who is it I looked high and low for
Whom I will go for
My whole life through?
Please ask me again,
'Cause I just love to say it's you.

REFRAIN 2

Ask me again
Who's the girl I shall always adore.
Ask me again,
For I'd like to explain it some more.
Who thrills me more than the circus of
    Ringling?
Who keeps me tingling
From head to toe?
Who is it's in my heart to stay
At least forever and a day?
Oh, ask me again—
Who's the moon and the stars and the sun?
Ask me again—
Who's the why and the where and the one?
Who is it I looked ev'rywhere for
To care to care for
My whole life through?
Please ask me again—
Let me shout to the world: It's you.

THAT WELL-KNOWN SMILE

Written in March 1930. Possibly an early lyric for *Girl Crazy*. No music is known to survive; none may have been composed.

VERSE

I have learned from almost every song
When you smile you simply can't go wrong.
So why are you
So sad and blue,
So gloomy and so tearful?—
When you can be
(Now let me see)
I think the rhyme is "cheerful."
Life is tough but why should we be critical
When we can be Pollyanalytical?

REFRAIN

Oh, the usual clouds of gray
In the customary sky

Always fade away
When you smile.
The proverbial rainy day
Toddles off and says good-bye
Every month is May
When you smile.
Remember, anytime you're pining—
Think of the rainbow;
Think of the bluebird;
Find the silver lining.
Oh, the usual clouds of gray
In the customary sky
Fade before that well-known smile.

I AM ONLY HUMAN AFTER ALL

Published June 1930. Music by Vernon Duke. Lyrics by Ira Gershwin and E. Y. Harburg. Introduced by Sterling Holloway and Cynthia Rodgers in the third edition of the *Garrick Gaieties*, which opened in New York at the Guild Theatre on June 4, 1930. 158 performances.

VERSE

I know that I should be above
Acting this way with you.
But when my heart is filled with love,
What can a poor girl (boy) do?
Though there may be lots of glory in
Behaving like a saint,
I just can't be mid-Victorian;
With you I've no restraint.

REFRAIN 1

BOY: Things you tell me not to do
Are just the things I've got to do;
For I am only human after all!

Tell me, is it wrong to touch
The skin I simply long to touch?—
When I am only human after all!

I'm losing time, for I'm Platonic with you,
It's chronic with you, I fear.
I'd rather be completely smothered by you
Than mothered by you, my dear.

Talk is heavenly for two,
But I want T.N.T. for two,
For I am only human after all!

REFRAIN 2

GIRL: I'm a hot volcano, dear,
Yet you sit there and say, "No, dear!"
I wonder, Are you human after all?

It is wrong that Papa sit
So far away and opposite
When baby may be heading for a fall?

There's no excuse, no use delaying, my
dear,
You're playing, my dear, with fate.
You know, you could and should be living
true love,
Not giving true love the gate.

Warm up, I'm beseeching you;
You'll find out while I'm teaching you
It's worthwhile being human after all!

REFRAIN 3

In my nice environment,
Say—Who knew what a siren meant?
But I've learnt that I'm human after all!

This is where a flapper owns
She's getting tired of chaperones,
'Cause something says I'm human after all.

There's no excuse, no use delaying, I
know,
I'm playing, I know, with fate.
Although I could and should be living true
love,
I'm giving true love the gate.

Till now I've been walked about;
From now on I'll be talked about;
'Cause I am only human after all!

CHEERFUL LITTLE EARFUL

Published November 1930. Music by Harry Warren. Lyrics by Ira Gershwin and Billy Rose. Introduced by Hannah Williams in the revue *Sweet and Low*, which opened in New York at the 46th Street Theatre on November 17, 1930. 184 performances. During the Philadelphia tryout, when the show was titled *Corned Beef and Roses*, the program credited a song titled "Cheerful Little Earful" to Ned Lehak (music) and Billy Rose and Allen Boretz (lyrics). Either the program was in error or the Warren-Gershwin-Rose song replaced the Lehak-Rose-Boretz version.

VERSE

I'm growing tired of lovey-dove theme songs
That fifty million pianos pound.
And in an age where those radios scream songs,
I only want one phrase around
Me.

REFRAIN

There's a cheerful little earful;
Gosh, I miss it something fearful!
And this cheerful little earful
Is the well-known "I love you."

Stocks can go down, business slow down,
But the milk and honey flow down
With a cheerful little earful
Of the well-known "I love you."

In ev'ry play, it's a set phrase,
What-the-public-get phrase,
But as a pet phrase,
It'll do do do.

Poopa roo-it soft and cu-it;
Make me happy you can do it;
With a cheerful little earful
Of the well-known "I love you."

IN THE MERRY MONTH OF MAYBE

Published May 1931. Music by Harry Warren. Lyrics by Ira Gershwin and Billy Rose. Introduced by Ethel Norris and Tom Monroe and danced by Gomez and Winona and ensemble in the revue *Crazy Quilt*, which opened in New York at the 44th Street Theatre on May 19, 1931. 67 performances.

VERSE

If I should call on you tomorrow,
And take you down to City Hall,
There'd be an end to sorrow;
But where's the wherewithall?
And yet I know the social pages
Will all announce the place and time;
It may be soon, it may be ages;
But someday, wedding bells will chime.

REFRAIN

In the very merry month of Maybe,
Off we'll go!

Should you ask when will that day be—
I don't know.

We won't get to Paris or Sahara—
We should care!
Rockaway's the Riviera
If you're there.

In a little two by four with you by,
We'll say goo-bye to the blues;
Sharing, ever sharing,
Never caring who's is who's.

There will be a happy ending, baby,
Someday soon;
In the merry month of Maybe—
Maybe June!

THE KEY TO MY HEART

Published October 1931. Music by Louis Alter. Introduced by Lenore Ulric in the play *The Social Register*, which opened in New York at the Fulton Theatre on November 9, 1931. 97 performances.

VERSE

Love was something that meant nothing to me
Till I met the man for whom I fell.
What's this passion that goes racing through
    me?
It's a bit of heaven mixed with hell.
I keep finding now that I have met love,
I may regret love
But can't forget love.

REFRAIN

I sang my song,
I got along,
My sun was shining, there was nothing wrong.
Why did I start
Giving away the key to my heart?

Once I was free
As I could be,
There wasn't a man who meant a thing to
    me.
Why did I start
Giving away the key to my heart?

Love keeps thrilling me when he's holding me
    tight,
But it's killing me when he leaves.
He can use me, abuse me, refuse me, but I
Know my love for him will never die.

If he should stray
And go away,
I'd wait for him forever and a day.
Why did I start
Giving away the key to my heart?

TILL THEN

Published October 1933. Music by George Gershwin.

VERSE

"Forever and a day is a long time."
I've heard it said, but is it true?
Forever and a day is a song time
If I can share it just with you.
I'm captured, heart and hand,
A slave in wonderland—
Your ev'ry wish is my command.

REFRAIN

Till black is white,
Till day is night,
Till moon stops shining
And wrong is right—
Till then I'm yours
To do with as you will.

Till East is West,
Till birds won't nest,
Till dreams and dreamers
Are all at rest—
Till then, till then,
It's you who'll make me thrill.

I don't know just what it is about you,
But where you go—
There my heart belongs.
Don't know why I could never doubt you—
Only know
You're my Song of Songs!

Till earth is sky,
No sun on high,
Till all the oceans
Are high and dry—
Till then I'm yours
To do with as you will.

OPPOSITE: *Crap game on Catfish Row. Standing, arms outstretched, Warren Coleman (Crown); behind him, Anne Brown (Bess); to his left, on the ground, John W. Bubbles (Sportin' Life) and Todd Duncan (Porgy)*

PORGY AND BESS | 1935

Tryout: Colonial Theatre, Boston, September 30, 1935. New York run: Alvin Theatre, opened October 10, 1935. 124 performances. Music by George Gershwin. Lyrics by DuBose Heyward and Ira Gershwin. Produced by The Theatre Guild. Libretto by DuBose Heyward, founded on the play *Porgy*, by DuBose and Dorothy Heyward, which had been adapted from the novel *Porgy*, by DuBose Heyward. Staged by Rouben Mamoulian. Orchestra under the direction of Alexander Smallens. Orchestrations by George Gershwin. Cast headed by Todd Duncan (Porgy), Anne Brown (Bess), John W. Bubbles (Sportin' Life), Ruby Elzy (Serena), Warren Coleman (Crown), Abbie Mitchell (Clara), Edward Matthews (Jake), Georgette Harvey (Maria), J. Rosamond Johnson (Frazier), Helen Dowdy (Lily), Ford L. Buck (Mingo), and the Eva Jessye Choir.

I GOT PLENTY O' NUTHIN'

Published separately and in the complete piano-vocal score September 1935. Lyrics by Ira Gershwin and DuBose Heyward. Per Ira Gershwin, *Lyrics on Several Occasions:* " '*Moderato con gioja*—Banjo Song.' . . . Act II, scene i: Todd Duncan as 'Porgy—at window—happily.' " The song was also introduced by Ruby Elzy (Serena), Georgette Harvey (Maria), and ensemble.

From a letter to Frank Durham, published in his *DuBose Heyward* (University of South Carolina Press, 1954):

"DuBose and I were in George's workroom. George felt there was a spot where Porgy might sing something lighter and gayer than the melodies and recitatives he had been given in Act I. He went to the piano and began to improvise. A few preliminary chords and in less than a minute a well-rounded, cheerful melody. 'Something like that,' he said. Both DuBose and I had the same reaction: 'That's it! Don't look any further.' 'You really think so?' and, luckily, he recaptured it and played it again. A title popped into my mind. (This was one out of only three or four times in my career that a possible title hit me on first hearing a tune. Usually I sweat for days.) ' "I got plenty o' nuthin'," ' I said tentatively. [And a moment later the obvious balance line, 'An' nuthin's plenty for me.'] Both George and DuBose seemed delighted with it, so with this assurance I said, 'Fine. I'll get to work on it later.' DuBose: 'Ira, would you mind if I tried my hand at it? So far everything I've done has been set by George and I've never written words to music. If it's all right with you I'd love to take the tune along with me to Charleston.' I think we discussed generally the mood and even arrived at a couple of lines. Two weeks later DuBose sent me a version that

had many useable lines; many, however, looked good on paper but were awkward when sung. This is no reflection on DuBose's ability. It takes years and years of experience to know that such a note cannot take such a syllable, that many a poetic line can be unsingable, that many an ordinary line fitted into the proper musical phrase can sound like a million. So on this song I did have to do a bit of 'polishing.' All in all, I'd consider this a 50-50 collaborative effort."

This, as the letter tells, is the only instance wherein DuBose tried working to a tune. All his fine and poetic lyrics were set to music by George with scarcely a syllable being changed—an aspect of this composer's versatility not generally recognized. These many years . . . and I can still shake my head in wonder at the reservoir of musical inventiveness, resourcefulness, and craftsmanship George could dip into. And no fraternal entrancement, my wonderment. He takes two simple quatrains of DuBose's, studies the lines, and in a little while a lullaby called "Summertime" emerges—delicate and wistful, yet destined to be sung over and over again. Out of the libretto's dialogue he takes Bess's straight, unrhymed speech which starts: "What you want wid Bess? She's gettin' old now," and it becomes a rhythmic aria; then he superimposes Crown's lines, "What I wants wid another woman? I gots a woman," amd now is heard at once a moving and exultant duet. Not a syllable of DuBose's poignant "My Man's Gone Now" is changed as the composer sets it to waltz time, adds the widow's heart-rending wail between stanzas, and climaxes the tragic lament with an ascending glissando—resulting in one of the most memorable moments in the American musical theater.

If I have stumbled into the field of the musicologist without being a musician, all I'm trying to say is that George could be as original and distinctive when musicalizing words (as in the above examples, plus "A Woman Is a Sometime Thing," "The Buzzard Song," and others) as when composing music which later would require words ("It Ain't Necessarily So," "There's a Boat Dat's Leavin' Soon for New York," "Bess, You Is My Woman Now," and others). Regardless of which procedure was used, the resultant compositions sang so naturally that I doubt if any listener, lacking the mentions in this note, could tell which came first—the words or the music.

—from *Lyrics on Several Occasions*

PORGY: Oh, I got plenty o' nuthin',
An' nuthin's plenty for me.
I got no car, got no mule, I got no
    misery.
De folks wid plenty o' plenty
Got a lock on dey door,
'Fraid somebody's a-goin' to rob 'em
While dey's out a-makin' more.

What for?
I got no lock on de door,
(Dat's no way to be).
Dey can steal de rug from the floor,
Dat's O.K. wid me,
'Cause de things dat I prize,
Like de stars in de skies,
All are free.
Oh, I got plenty o' nuthin',
An' nuthin's plenty for me.
I got my gal, got my song,
Got Hebben de whole day long.
(No use complainin'!)
Got my gal, got my Lawd, got my song.

WOMEN: Porgy change since dat woman come to
    live with he.
SERENA: How he change?
ALL: He ain' cross with chillen no more,
An' ain' you hear how
He an' Bess all de time singin' in their
    room?
MARIA: I tells you dat cripple's happy now.*
ALL: Happy.

PORGY: I got plenty o' nuthin',
An' nuthin's plenty fo' me.
I got de sun, got de moon, got de deep
    blue sea.
De folks wid plenty o' plenty,
Got to pray all de day.
Seems wid plenty you sure got to worry
How to keep the Debble away,
A-way.
I ain't a-frettin' 'bout Hell
Till de time arrive.
Never worry long as I'm well,
Never one to strive
To be good, to be bad—
What the hell! I is glad
I's alive.
Oh, I got plenty o' nuthin'
An nuthin's plenty fo' me.
I got my gal, got my song,
Got Hebben de whole day long.
(No use complainin'!)
Got my gal.
ALL: Got his gal.
PORGY: Got my Lawd.
ALL: Got his Lawd.
PORGY: Got my song!

*Ira Gershwin himself excised many instances of the word "nigger" years after the opera's premiere (see his note on page 241). The earlier version of this line is:
I tells you dat nigger's happy now.

BESS, YOU IS MY WOMAN NOW

Published separately and in the complete piano-vocal score September 1935. Lyrics by DuBose Heyward and Ira Gershwin. Introduced by Todd Duncan (Porgy) and Anne Brown (Bess).

PORGY: Bess, you is my woman now,
   You is, you is!
   An' you mus' laugh an' sing an' dance
      for two instead of one.
   Want no wrinkle on yo' brow,
   Nohow,
   Because de sorrow of de past is all done
      done.
   Oh, Bess, my Bess!
   De real happiness is jes' begun.

BESS: Porgy, I's yo' woman now,
   I is, I is!
   An' I ain' never goin' nowhere 'less you
      shares de fun.
   Dere's no wrinkle on my brow,
   Nohow,
   But I ain't goin'! You hear me sayin',
   If you ain' goin', wid you I'm stayin'!

   Porgy, I's yo' woman now!
   I's yours forever—
   Mornin' time an' ev'nin' time an'
      summer time an' winter time.
PORGY: Mornin' time an' ev'nin' time an'
      summer time an' winter time.
   Bess, you got yo' man.

   Bess, you is my woman now and
      forever.*
   Dis life is jes' begun,
   Bess, we two is one
   Now an' forever.
   Oh, Bess, don' min' dose women.
   You got yo' Porgy,
   You loves yo' Porgy.
   I knows you means it,
   I seen it in yo' eyes, Bess.
   We'll go swingin'
   Through de years a-singin'.

BESS: Mornin' time an' ev'nin' time an'
      summer time an' winter time.
PORGY: Mornin' time an' ev'nin' time an'
      summer time an' winter time.
BESS: Oh, my Porgy, my man, Porgy.

*Sung as Bess repeats her part from "Porgy, I's yo' woman now . . ." through "I's yours forever—"

PORGY: [simultaneously] My Bess, my Bess.
BESS: From dis minute I'm tellin' you, I keep
      dis vow:
   Porgy, I's yo' woman now.
PORGY: [simultaneously] From dis minute I'm
      tellin' you, I keep dis vow:
   Oh, my Bessie, we's happy now,
   We is one now.

OH, I CAN'T SIT DOWN!

Published in the complete piano-vocal score September 1935. Lyrics by Ira Gershwin. Introduced by ensemble. The stage direction reads: "Residents of the row pour from the doorways singing and dancing with the band." When he was preparing this lyric for possible inclusion in *Lyrics on Several Occasions*, Ira Gershwin changed "I's," "de," "dis," and "dat" to "I'm," "the," "this," and "that," respectively.

Written for the residents of Catfish Row and the Orphan Band on their way to the Kittiwah Island picnic, and sung more or less *unisono* in the stage versions, this song created a gay minute or two of rhythm and excitement before Porgy is left alone on stage to reprise "I Got Plenty o' Nuthin'." In the Goldwyn film production, it was decided to give a touch more importance to the role of Maria by having her start this number solo.

   The lyric change was a simple one requiring merely [the alteration of] "her sunny smile" to "his sunny smile," and substituting for the section "Sho' is dandy,/Got the licker handy;/Me an' Mandy,/We is on the way" the lines: "Hey there, Andy!/Be my sugar candy./Life is dandy!/Let's be on our way." This gave Maria an escort (Andy); also it cut out the word "licker" (a proper ousting as Maria's rectitude would probably have made her a teetotaler). And since the role of Maria in the film was played by accomplished and personable Pearl Bailey, her introducing this ensemble number naturally gave it more consequence.

—Ira Gershwin
(written for but not included in
Lyrics on Several Occasions)

Oh, I can't sit down!
Got to keep a-goin' like the flowin'
Of a song.
Oh, I can't sit down!
Guess I'll take my honey an' her sunny
Smile along!
Today I is gay an' I's free;
Jes' a-bubblin', nothin' troublin' me.

Oh, I'm gwine to town.
I can't sit down.

Happy feelin'
In my bones a-stealin',
No concealin'
Dat it's picnic day.
Sho' is dandy,
Got de licker handy;
Me an' Mandy,
We is on de way
'Cause dis is picnic day.

Oh, I can't sit down!
Got to keep a-jumpin' to de thumpin'
Of de drum.
Oh, I can't sit down!
Full of locomotion like an ocean
Full of rum!
Today I is gay an' I's free,
Jes' a-bubblin', nothin' troublin' me.
Oh, I'm gwine to town.
I can't, jes' can't, sit down!

IT AIN'T NECESSARILY SO

Published separately and in the complete piano-vocal score September 1935. Lyrics by Ira Gershwin. Introduced by John W. Bubbles (Sportin' Life) and ensemble.

Dummy Title. After my brother played me a sixteen-bar tune which he thought might be the start of something for Sportin' Life in the Picnic Scene, I asked for a lead sheet (the simple vocal line); and to remember the rhythm and accents better, I wrote across the top a dummy title—the first words that came to my mind: "It ain't necessarily so." (I could just as well have written "An order of bacon and eggs," "Tomorrow's the 4th of July," "Don't ever sell Telephone short"—anything—the sense didn't matter. All I required was a phrase which accented the second, fifth, and eighth syllables to help me remember the rhythm.)

   Struggling for two days with the tune, I came up with no eurekan notion. Then I remembered I had once written a dummy title to a Vincent Youmans melody when we were working on *Two Little Girls in Blue*, and a couple of days later when Youmans asked if I had finished the song, I told him I hadn't as yet got a title. Youmans: "What do you mean? It's called 'Oh, Me, Oh, My, Oh, You.'" Me: "But that was only my dummy title." Nevertheless, Youmans insisted that he was crazy about that particular title—which was fine with me, because I couldn't think of anything else—and the song turned out to be the most popular in the show.

237

So I began to explore the possibilities of *this* dummy title. At one point I decided that troublemaker Sportin' Life, being among a group of religious Sons-and-Daughters-of-Repent-Ye-Saith-the-Lord picnickers, might try to startle them with a cynical and irreligious attitude. And what would certainly horrify his auditors would be his saying that some accounts in the Bible weren't necessarily so. Once I had the rhymes "Bible—li'ble" and "Goliath—dieth," I felt I was probably on the right track. George agreed. He then improvised the scat sounds, "Wadoo, Zim bam boddle-oo." Together, in a week or so, we worked out the rather unusual construction of this piece, with its limerick musical theme, the crowd responses, the lush melodic middle, and the "ain't nessa, ain't nessa" coda. Happily, in all the years that the song has been around, I have received only one letter remarking on its possible irreverance.

"Resistance Hymn." During World War II *Porgy and Bess* was somehow permitted by the Nazis to be produced at the Royal Opera House in Copenhagen. This song came "to be something like a resistance hymn in Nazi-occupied Denmark—ever since the evening when, after the grimly boastful routine broadcast of the German army's usual victory communiqué, the secret Danish underground radio had cheerfully cut in with a significant 'It Ain't Necessarily So.' . . ." (Cf. Fred M. Hechinger: "American Goods Preferred," *Harper's*, December 1950, page 81.)

—from *Lyrics on Several Occasions*

SPORTIN' LIFE: It ain't necessarily so.
ALL: It ain't necessarily so.
SPORTIN' LIFE: De t'ings dat yo li'ble
To read in de Bible—
It ain't necessarily so.

Li'l David was small, but—oh my!
ALL: Li'l David was small, but—oh my!
SPORTIN' LIFE: He fought Big Goliath
Who lay down and dieth—
Li'l David was small, but—oh my!

Wadoo!
ENSEMBLE: Wadoo!
SPORTIN' LIFE: Zim bam boddle-oo!
ENSEMBLE: Zim bam boddle-oo!
SPORTIN' LIFE: Hoodle ah da wah da!
ENSEMBLE: Hoodle ah da wah da!
SPORTIN' LIFE: Scatty wah!
ENSEMBLE: Scatty wah!
SPORTIN' LIFE: Yeah!

Oh, Jonah, he lived in de whale.
ALL: Oh, Jonah, he lived in de whale.
SPORTIN' LIFE: Fo' he made his home in

Dat fish's abdomen—
Oh Jonah, he lived in de whale.

Li'l Moses was found in a stream.
ALL: Li'l Moses was found in a stream.
SPORTIN' LIFE: He floated on water
Till Ole Pharaoh's daughter
She fished him, she *says*, from dat stream.

Wadoo!
ENSEMBLE: Wadoo!
SPORTIN' LIFE: Zim bam boddle-oo!
ENSEMBLE: Zim bam boddle-oo!
SPORTIN' LIFE: Hoodle ah da wah da!
ENSEMBLE: Hoodle ah da wah da!
SPORTIN' LIFE: Scatty wah!
ENSEMBLE: Scatty wah!
SPORTIN' LIFE: Yeah!

SPORTIN' LIFE: It ain't necessarily so,
ALL: It ain't necessarily so.
SPORTIN' LIFE: Dey tell all you chillun
De Debble's a villun
But 'tain't necessarily so.

To get into Hebben
Don't snap fo' a sebben—
Live clean! Don' have no fault!
Oh, I takes dat gospel
Whenever it's pos'ple—
But wid a grain of salt!

Methus'lah lived nine hundred years.
ALL: Methus'lah lived nine hundred years.
SPORTIN' LIFE: But who calls dat livin'
When no gal'll give in
To no man what's nine hundred years?

I'm preachin' dis sermon to show
It ain't nessa, ain't nessa,
Ain't nessa, ain't nessa—
ALL: Ain't necessarily so!

Encore Limerick

'Way back in five thousand B.C.
Ole Adam an' Eve had to flee.
Sure, dey did dat deed in
De Garden of Eden—
But why chasterize you an' me?

New Version for Adlai Stevenson (1952)

During the 1952 presidential campaign, Ira Gershwin wrote a new lyric to the music of "It Ain't Necessarily

So" in support of Adlai Stevenson's unsuccessful run for the Oval Office. (See also the special pro-Stevenson version of "Love Is Sweeping the Country" in *Of Thee I Sing* [1931].)

It ain't necessarily so,
It ain't necessarily so—
They say Ike's arranging
For things to be changing,
But 'tain't necessarily so.

Unless I am barmy and daft
He still has McCarthy and Taft
And Jenner and others
He has to call brothers—
Unless I am barmy and daft.

Wadoo! Wadoo!
Zim bam boddle-oo! Zim bam boddle-oo!
Hoodle ah da wah da! Hoodle ah da wah da!
Stevenson! Stevenson!
Yeah!

The Gen'ral was living a dream
With sweetness and light as the theme;
No troubles to mix in—
Till they gave him Nixon
An' woke up the Gen. from that dream.

Li'l Nixon was small, but—oh my!
His office expenses were high,
Till Santa Claus flew in
With funds that he threw in—
And Santa was sweet, but—oh my!
Alas and alack and oh my!

Wadoo! Wadoo!
Zim bam boddle-oo! Zim bam boddle-oo!
Hoodle ah da wah da! Hoodle ah da wah da!
Stevenson! Stevenson!
Yeah!

It ain't necessarily so,
It ain't necessarily so—
The elephant's grunting,
"How happy the hunting!"
But 'tain't necessarily so.

Oh, we can be partial
To Ike when he's martial;
His five stars we will sing!
But guarding the millions
Of U.S. civilians
Is quite another thing.

The papers put Ike in the lead
And Stevenson better take heed—
But in that connection
I say—come election
We know what the headlines will read.

The papers and TV will show
That Adlai's respected
And he'll be elected—
And that's necessarily so!

I LOVES YOU, PORGY

Published in the complete piano-vocal score September 1935. Lyrics by Ira Gershwin and DuBose Heyward. Introduced by Anne Brown (Bess) and Todd Duncan (Porgy).

BESS: I wants to stay here, but I ain't worthy,
You is too decent to understan',
For when I see him, he hypnotize me,
When he take hol' of me with his hot han'.

Someday, I know he's comin' back to call me,
He's goin' to handle me an hol' me so.
It's goin' to be like dyin', Porgy, deep inside me.
But when he calls, I know I have to go.

PORGY: If dere warn't no Crown, Bess,
If dere was only jus' you an' Porgy,
What den?

BESS: I loves you, Porgy, don' let him take me,
Don' let him handle me an' drive me mad.
If you kin keep me, I wants to stay here
Wid you forever, an' I'd be glad.

PORGY: There, there, Bess, you don' need to be afraid no mo'.
You's picked up happiness an' laid yo' worries down.
You goin' to live easy, you goin' to live high.
You goin' to outshine ev'ry woman in dis town.
An' remember, when Crown come—That's my business. Bess!

[Bess and Porgy sing together:]
BESS: I loves you, Porgy, don' let him take me,
Don' let him handle me with his hot han'.
If you kin keep me, I wants to stay here
Wid you forever
I got my man.

PORGY: What you think I is anyway,
To let dat dirty houn' dog steal my woman?

If you wants to stay wid Porgy, you goin' stay.
You got a home now, Honey, an' you got love.
So no mo' cryin', can't you understan'?
You goin' to go about yo' business, singin',
'Cause you got Porgy, you got a man.

A REDHEADED WOMAN

Published in the complete piano-vocal score September 1935. Lyrics by Ira Gershwin. Introduced by Warren Coleman (Crown) and ensemble.

CROWN: A redheaded woman makes a choo-choo jump its track.
A redheaded woman she can make it jump right back.
Oh, she's jus' nature's child,
She's got somethin' dat drives men wild.
A redheaded woman's gonna take you
Wedder you're white, yellow, or black.

But show me the redhead that kin make a fool of me!
Oh, she ain' existin' on de lan' or on de sea.
Oh, you kin knock me down,
If they don't fall for Brudder Crown.
Oh, show me a redhead that kin make a goddam fool of me!

[Chorus sings prayer against Crown's jazz]
Oh, show me a redhead dat kin make a fool of me!
Oh, she ain' existin' on de lan' or on de sea.
Oh, you kin knock me down,
If they don' fall for Brudder Crown.
Oh, show me a redhead dat can make a goddam fool of—
I said a fool out o' me!

CHORUS: Lawd, Lawd, save us, don't listen to dat Crown.
Lawd Jesus, oh, pay no min' to Crown,
Oh Lawd, strike him down, strike down.
Oh Lawd, don't listen to dat Crown.

OH, HEAV'NLY FATHER

Published in the complete piano-vocal score September 1935. Lyrics by Ira Gershwin and DuBose Heyward. Introduced by principals and ensemble. (This sequence was titled "Oh, Heav'nly Father" to distinguish it from the earlier "Oh, Doctor Jesus" prayer [lyrics by Heyward], also titled "Time and Time Again.") Alternate title: "Six Prayers."

One of the most exciting sequences of sounds I ever heard was the singing of six different prayers going on at the same time during the storm scene in *Porgy and Bess*. Using the title of DuBose Heyward's "Doctor Jesus" prayer, I set words to five additional ones: "Oh, Heav'nly Father," "Professor Jesus," "Oh, Lawd Above," "Oh, Captain Jesus," and "Oh, Father What Die on Calbery." Each strain here was *ad libitum*, therefore musically not contrapuntal as are countermelodies. Outside of a shrieked "Doctor Jesus" or "Heav'nly Father" one couldn't catch a word of the prayers but one wasn't supposed to. What was striven for came off: an effect with almost shock-treatment impact. I can describe it only as a hi-fi recording, full volume, of musical bedlam at the Tower of Babel (set to music) in one of the most exciting musical moments anyone ever heard. This, however, was heard only in Carnegie Hall, which had been hired for a three-day rehearsal of the orchestra, with the cast singing at the footlights. Unfortunately, the opera being too long, this bit of musical pandemonium was one of the cuts before the Boston opening.

—Ira Gershwin
(written for but not included in
Lyrics on Several Occasions)

"Oh, Doctor Jesus"

2ND SOPRANO: Oh, Doctor Jesus, look down on me wit' pity.
Put Yo' lovin' arms through de roof of dis house
An lif' me to Yo' bosom till de storm is over.
Oh, Doctor Jesus, look down on me.
Why is You angry wit' dis po' sinner?
Why is You cryin' dose tears,
An' mumblin' dat thunder
When I ain' got nuthin' but
Rev'rence in my heart for You, Lawd.
Oh, Doctor Jesus, look down on me.
If You is lookin' down on me wit' disfavor

I ain' know what to do,
'Cause if worshipin' You
Ain' stoppin' dose tears an' dat
    thunder,
Lawd, I ain' know jes' what to do,
    Lawd.
Oh, Doctor Jesus, look down on
    me.
I's beseechin' You to look down on
    me wit' pity
An I's hopin' Yo's about to put
    Yo' lovin' arms
Through de roof of dis house an'
    lif' me to Yo' bosom,
Amen!

"Oh, Lawd Above"

TENOR: Oh, Lawd above, we knows You can
    destroy,
But we also knows You can raise,
An' we's beseechin' You to raise Yo'
    fallen chillen.
Oh, Lawd above, You got de pow'r to
    feed us,
You got de pow'r to clothe us,
An' You can lead us out of de
    wilderness.
Yes, Lawd, but we's not hungry now, an'
    we's got clo'es.
But we is askin' You to lead us out of de
    wilderness,
Oh, Lawd above, lead us out of de
    wilderness,
Into de golden meadows an' de silvery
    streams.
Oh, Lawd above, we know You can
    destroy,
But we knows You can raise, too,
An' we's askin' You for Yo' assistance
In dis time of storm an' thunder an'
    lightnin'.
Oh, Lawd above, we warrants Yo'
    assistance
An' we's beseechin' You to raise Yo'
    fallen chillen,
Amen!

"Oh, Heav'nly Father"

1ST SOPRANO: Oh, Heav'nly Father, hab mercy on
    we,
Look down wit' grace an'
    sympathy,
You whose po' chillen we is, show
    we how
You can protect Yo' chillen when
    dey is deserving.

Oh, Heav'nly Father, hab mercy on
    we
When de clouds an' de storms start
    raisin' hell upon dis earth.
We knows dat You can fix 'em,
'Cause You is de great fixer.
Oh my Father, fix dat Satan,
Tie up his hands an' his feet
An' t'row him back where he
    belong.
Oh, Heav'nly Father, hab mercy on
    we,
'Cause we is Yo' deservin' chillen,
    Amen.
Oh, Heav'nly Father, hab mercy on
    we,
Wit' grace an' sympathy an'
    understandin'
Of which we knows You got
    plenty.
Oh, my Lawd,
Amen!

"Professor Jesus"

ALTO: Professor Jesus, teach Yo' ignorant chillen
How to combat de fires an' torments
Of dat black visitation from below.
We leans on You, Professor Jesus, what
    die on Calbery.
Dispense Yo' blessings on
Yo' needful an' Yo' grateful followers.
Cast away dose black clouds an' de
    darkness
An' show we de golden sunshine gleaming
    once again.
Professor Jesus, teach Yo' ignorant
    chillen.
Cast away dose black clouds an' de
    darkness,
An' show we de golden sunshine gleamin'
    once again.
Professor Jesus, cast away dose black
    clouds an' de darkness
An' show we de golden sunshine
Shinin' on de fields an' de meadows
An' de mountains an' de plains,
Amen!

"Oh, Captain Jesus"

1ST BASS: Oh, Captain Jesus, find it in Yo' heart
    to save us.
I's given You six chillen to add to Yo'
    legions.
My po' wife is now wid You three year
    dis October.
Oh, Captain Jesus, but we is seven left

To tell dat Satan man where he get off
    at.
We has all lived sweetly
An' sweetly we is willin' to die for You.
Oh, Captain Jesus, we knows how
    sweetly You treats
Yo' soldiers when You opens de gates
    for dem.
Oh, Captain Jesus, find it in Yo' heart
    to save us worshipers
'Cause there is no truer followers of de
    Lawd
Den what's prayin' to You now.
Oh, Captain Jesus, we has all lived
    sweetly
An' sweetly we is willin' to die for You,
Amen!

"Oh, Father What Die on Calberry"

2ND BASS: Oh, Father what die on Calbery, we's
    dependin' on You.
We's leanin' on You to ease the rocky
    way.
We's been trabblin' de straight an'
    narrow path
Dat ends in glory.
Oh, Father what die on Calbery,
    darkness has descended,
We all knows it's temporary, Lawd,
But de sooner it disappears,
De sooner we gets goin' to You, Lawd.
Oh, Father what die on Calbery,
Maybe we is po', mis'able sinners,
But we certainly tries all de livelong
    day
To follow Yo' teachin's, Lawd.
Oh, Father, if we ain' been doin'
Jus' what You is wishin' us to do,
It ain' because we ain' been tryin',
'Cause we is been tryin' to follow Yo'
    sacred teachin's
All de livelong day,
Amen!

THERE'S A BOAT DAT'S LEAVIN' SOON FOR NEW YORK

Published separately and in the complete piano-vocal score September 1935. Lyrics by Ira Gershwin. Introduced by John W. Bubbles (Sportin' Life).

Spelling "there" as such in one spot and as "dere" in another wasn't an oversight. It didn't matter too much if dialect was exact or not, considering the stylized and characteristic music. All that was required was a suggestion of regional flavor; and if the artist preferred—for personal literacy or racial righteousness—to enunciate any words formally rather than colloquially, that was all right.

Some years ago when Goddard Lieberson of Columbia Records informed me he had decided to issue a six-side LP of the opera, I asked to be allowed to change some opprobrious terms in the recitatives—there were about twenty—to substitutes inoffensive to the ear of today. Lieberson heartily concurred, and I spent two days going through the 559 pages of the vocal score to make the changes. (Little by little, words like "wop," "kike," and "nigger" are disappearing from print and speech—but I do believe that a few recording artists and other well-intentioned persons are nice-nellying it a bit when they at times insist on elevating dialect grammar to Johnsonian heights.)

I was in my brother's apartment when the team of Buck and Bubbles (Ford L. Buck played Mingo) was chosen for *Porgy and Bess*. They were to go on a vaudeville tour for several months before rehearsals started. George asked their agent where they would be playing in about six weeks from that afternoon. On learning the itineraried city, George told them the vocal score would be printed by that time and he would forward a copy to the theater there so they could study up on their roles. When they returned to New York, George asked if they now had a good idea of their parts. "No, sir!" "Didn't you get a copy of the score?" "Yes, sir," said Bubbles, "I handed it to Buck and said: 'Can we learn this?'" The pages were flipped, the score hefted; then it was ruefully decided they couldn't. They thought the entire 559 pages were their parts.

George loved the telegram (I still have it) this talented team sent him opening night: "MAY THE CURTAIN FALL WITH THE BANG OF SUCCESS FOR YOU AS THE SUN RISES IN THE SUNSHINE OF YOUR SMILE   BUCK AND BUBBLES."
—from *Lyrics on Several Occasions*

There's a boat dat's leavin' soon for New York.
Come wid me, dat's where we belong, sister.
You an' me kin live dat high life in New York.
Come wid me, dere you can't go wrong, sister.

I'll buy you de swellest mansion
Up on upper Fi'th Avenue,
An' through Harlem we'll go struttin',
We'll go a-struttin',
An' dere'll be nuttin'
Too good for you.
I'll dress you in silks and satins
In de latest Paris styles.
All de blues you'll be forgettin',
You'll be forgettin',
There'll be no frettin'—
Jes' nothin' but smiles.

Come along wid me, dat's de place,
Don't be a fool, come along, come along!
There's a boat dat's leavin' soon for New York,
Come wid me, dat's where we belong, sister,
Dat's where we belong!

OH, BESS, OH WHERE'S MY BESS?

Published separately and in the complete piano-vocal score September 1935. The music and lyrics for Porgy's portion of the trio alone were printed in the separately published edition. Lyrics by Ira Gershwin. Introduced by Todd Duncan (Porgy), Georgette Harvey (Maria), and Ruby Elzy (Serena).

PORGY: Oh, Bess, oh where's my Bess,
Won't somebody tell me where?
I ain' care what she say,
I ain' care what she done,
Won't somebody tell me where's my Bess?
Bess, oh Lawd,
[*Maria and Serena sing their parts against the following:*]
My Bess! I want her now,
Widout her I can't go on.
I counted de days dat I was gone
Till I got home to see her face.
Won't somebody tell me where's my Bess?
I want her so, my gal, my Bess, where is she?
Oh Gawd, in Yo' big Heav'n,
Please show me where I mus' go.
Oh give me de strength, show me de way!
Tell me de truth, where is she, where is my gal,
Where is my Bess?

MARIA: Dat dirty dog Sportin' Life make believe
Dat you lock up forever.
He tol' her dat you would be gone
For de rest of yo' days.
Yo' woman been very low in her mind,
She believe ev'rything Sportin' Life say to her;
Dat's how it was.
She been very low, yo' woman, misunderstand,
She t'ink you never come back to her;
Sportin' Life fool her, fool yo' Bess.
She is gone.
Man, don't you let it break yo' heart 'bout dat gal.
We told you all along dat dat woman ain' worthy of you.
She was no good, Porgy, or she'd never go 'way.
Try forget 'bout Bess.

SERENA: She gone, but you very lucky;
She gone back to de happy dus'.
She done throw Jesus out of her heart.
Bess dat kin' of gal,
I told you dat all along.
Porgy, you is better off
Widout dat woman hangin' 'roun' an' makin' trouble.
She give herself away to de Debbil.
Porgy, you is better off
Widout dat woman hangin' 'roun';
There's plenty better gals than Bess.
Bess is gone.
She worse than dead, Porgy,
She gone back to de happy dus',
She gone back to de red-eye wid him
An she's headin' fo' Hell.
Thank God she's out of yo' way.
Try forget 'bout Bess.

OVERLEAF: *Fannie Brice as Baby Snooks. Inset: Eve Arden and Bob Hope in "I Can't Get Started"*

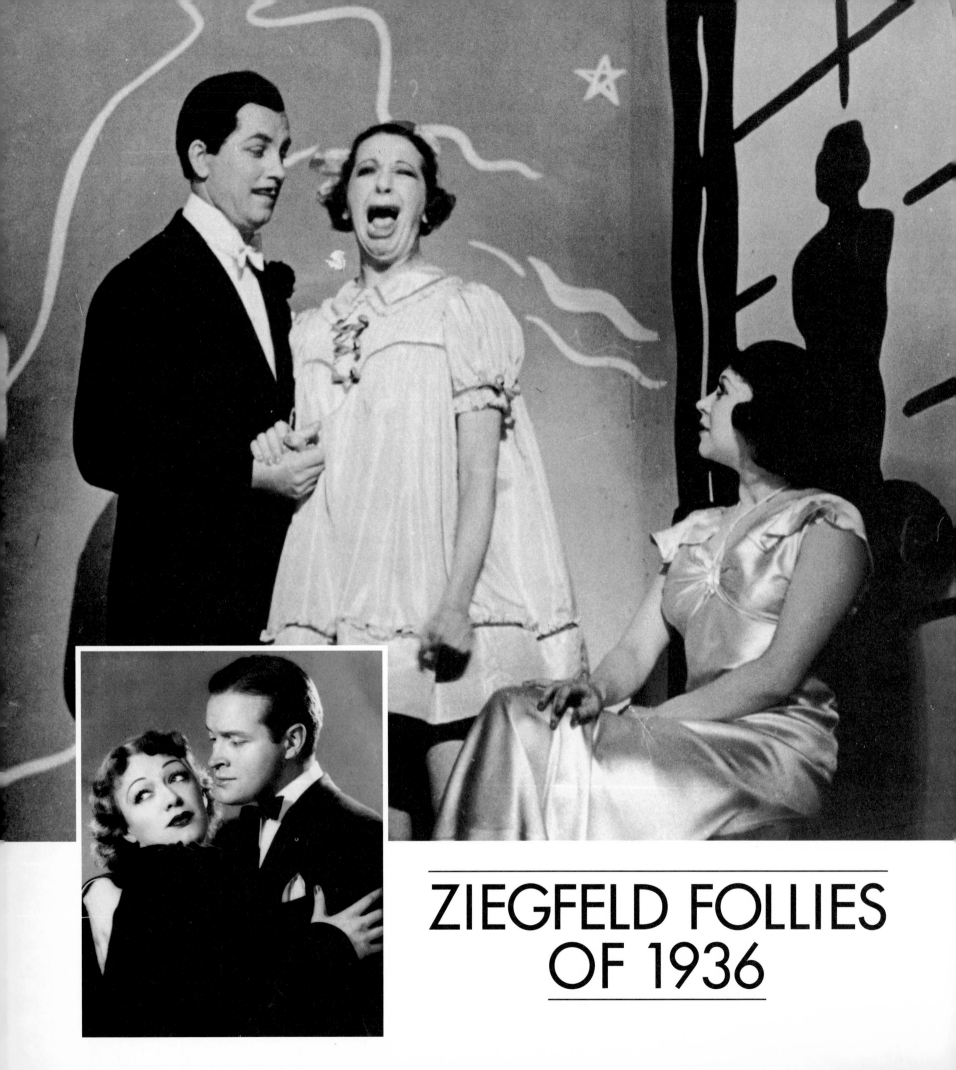

ZIEGFELD FOLLIES
OF 1936

Tryout: Boston Opera House, December 30, 1935; Forrest Theatre, Philadelphia, January 14, 1936. New York run: Winter Garden, opened January 30, 1936. 115 performances. Music by Vernon Duke. Lyrics almost entirely by Ira Gershwin. Produced by Mrs. Florenz Ziegfeld (Billie Burke) and the Messrs. Shubert (Lee and J.J.). Sketches by David Freedman. Staged by John Murray Anderson, Robert Alton, and George Balanchine. Orchestra under the direction of John McManus. Orchestrations largely by Hans Spialek. Additional orchestrations by Conrad Salinger, Robert Russell Bennett, and Don Walker. Cast, starring Fannie Brice, Bob Hope, Gertrude Niesen, Hugh O'Connell, Harriet Hoctor, Eve Arden, Judy Canova, Cherry and June Preisser, John Hoysradt, and Josephine Baker, featured the Nicholas Brothers (Harold and Fayard), Duke McHale, Rodney McLennan, Stan Kavanagh, Ben Yost's California Varsity Eight, George Church, Gene Ashley, Milton Barnett, and Willen van Loon.

A second edition of this production, with many cast changes and with several of the Vernon Duke–Ira Gershwin songs deleted, opened at the Winter Garden on September 14, 1936. 112 performances. Combined run of the two editions: 227 performances.

The music of "Time Marches On!," "He Hasn't a Thing Except Me," "The Economic Situation," "Fancy! Fancy!," and "Dancing to the Score," with new titles and new adapted lyrics not by Ira Gershwin, was published in 1943 by USO Camp Shows, Inc., as part of *At Ease, Vol. IV, Musical Opening Choruses, Finales and Production Numbers for Soldier's Shows.*

TIME MARCHES ON!

There are two versions of this number. The first was sung by Bob Hope and Ben Yost's California Varsity Eight (George Enz, Thomas Gleason, Paul Nelson, William Quentmeyer, Riques Tanzi, Everett West, Irving West, and Ben Yost) during the Boston and Philadelphia tryouts. Revised version reintroduced during the initial New York run by Rodney McLennan and Ben Yost's California Varsity Eight. Performed in the second (1936–37) edition by James Farrell and Ben Yost's (the "California" was dropped) Varsity Eight (six of whose original members had been replaced).

Original Version

BOB HOPE: Ladies and gentlemen,
Just because you don't see me surrounded by a bevy of beautiful squaws,
Don't get the impression this isn't the *Ziegfeld Follies* because

It's the *Follies* all right, but on a basis entirely new:
We feel that the day of the girly-girly show is definitely through.
In fact, we even have a song about it. Sing, boys.

BOYS: Gone is the day of the show girl Whose charms captivate the Don Juan;
This year we cater to no girl—
Time marches on.

HOPE: That's enough.
True, since the first *Follies* the girls have always brought home the bacon,
But if you imagine this is *that* kind of show, you're sadly mistaken.
We feel, for instance, that the day of the *tableau vivant* is through.
And about time, too.
Beautiful to look at, no doubt—
But something 1936 can do without.
[*Tableau lights up*]
Remember? Here we have "The Spirit of the Round Table."
That's Guinevere looking for Sir Lancelot.
[*Indicates girl on unicorn*]
And here—"Orgies at the Court of Louis the Fifteenth"—
Where they used to romance a lot.
[*Indicates girl in white wig*]
And that, I believe, was "The Spirit of the American Merchant Marine."
[*Indicates girl on swing*]
And *those*, so help me, "Venus Arising from the Waves at Quarantine."
[*Indicates remainder of tableau*]
Well, that's the sort of thing you've been seeing since the *Follies* of 1907.
And what did it all amount to? A show girl's idea of heaven.
We say, A pox on girls who are merely pulchritudinous,
Who keep arousing only the animal or the lewd in us.
Away with those undulating Amazons whose voices are like static,
Who merely clutter up the witty, the humorous, the epigrammatic.
Again, boys.

BOYS: Beauty is fleeting and flimsy.
Though she have the neck of the swan—

This year we're featuring whimsy—
Time marches on!

HOPE: That's enough.
Girls in sequins, in dimity, in organdy, in spangles,
Or any one of a thousand other costume designer's angles.
Of course, to help fill the stage we have a few who are ornamental.
But as you'll see later, we use them sparingly; they're only incidental.

HOPE
AND BOYS: Our girls may be quite ornamental,
But now that the pendulum swings,
Ladies are merely incidental
In our scheme of things.
So, on with the ultra in *Follies*—
The sex-ridden angle is gone!
Gangway, ye platinum dollies—
Time marches on!

HOPE: Very good, boys.
[*Boys exit*]
I am second to none in my admiration of Gladys Glad, Peggy Joyce, Justine Johnstone, Anastasia Reilly—
All thought of by the photographers very highly—
Bestrewn with honors the public has flung them—
But not a belly laugh among them.
[*Girls are advancing downstage*]
We feel that one deathless gag is worth a dozen adorable fannies.
We feel that one deathless gag is worth—
We feel that one—
[*Getting nowhere, shoved about, he gives up*]
Aw! The hell with it!
[*Girls dance*]

Revised Version

BOYS: Gone is the day of the show girl Whose charms captivate the Don Juan;
This year we cater to no girl—
Time marches on.

MCLENNAN: Ladies and gentlemen,
Just because you don't see me surrounded by a bevy of beautiful squaws,
Please don't get the impression this isn't the *Ziegfeld Follies* because
It's the *Follies* all right, but on a basis entirely new:

We feel that the day of the girly-girly
show is definitely through.
In fact, we even have a song about it.
Sing, boys.

BOYS: Beauty is fleeting and flimsy.
Though she may have the neck of the
swan—

MCLENNAN: This year we're featuring whimsy—

BOYS: Time marches on!

MCLENNAN: Of course, to help fill the stage we
have a few who are ornamental.
But as you'll see later, we use them
sparingly; they're only incidental.

MCLENNAN
AND BOYS: Our girls may be quite ornamental,
But now that the pendulum swings,
Ladies are merely incidental
In our scheme of things.
So, on with the ultra in *Follies*—
The sex-ridden angle is gone!
Gangway, ye platinum dollies—
Time marches on!

MCLENNAN: True, since the first *Follies* the girls
have always brought home the
bacon,
But if you imagine this is *that* kind
of show, you're sadly mistaken.
We feel, for instance, that the day of
the *tableau vivant* is through.
And about time, too.
Beautiful to look at, no doubt—
But something 1936 can do without.
That, I believe, was "The Spirit of
the American Merchant Marine."

[*Indicates girl on swing*]
Or "Venus Arising from the Waves at
Quarantine."

[*Indicates rest of tableau*]
Well, that's the sort of thing you've
been seeing since the *Follies* of
1907.
And what does it all amount to? A
show girl's idea of heaven.
We say, A pox on girls who are
merely pulchritudinous,
Who keep arousing only the animal
or the lewd in us.
Away with those undulating Amazons
whose voices are like static,
Who merely clutter up the witty, the
humorous, the epigrammatic.

MCLENNAN
AND BOYS: Our girls may be quite ornamental,
But now that the pendulum swings,
Ladies are merely incidental

In our scheme of things.
So, on with the ultra in *Follies*—
The sex-ridden angle is gone!
Gangway, ye platinum dollies—
Time marches on!

MCLENNAN: We feel that one good gag is worth a
dozen adorable—
We feel that one good gag is worth—
We feel that one—
[*getting nowhere, shoved about, he gives up*]
Aw! The hell with it!
[*Girls dance*]
Time marches on!

HE HASN'T A THING
EXCEPT ME

Lyrics first published in Ira Gershwin's *Lyrics on Several Occasions* (1959). Per that publication: "Leaning against a lamppost and looking forlorn, the one and only Fanny* Brice is discovered. The lamppost walks off and Fanny begins:"

Fanny was one of the most versatile and accomplished personalities in our musical theater. In this particular *Follies*, for example, she put over this torch song, and did a wonderful burlesque of modern dancing, following her singing of "Modernistic Moe." In the skits she played Baby Snooks; then a tough Tenth Avenue girl; then the most elegant English drawing-room matron in "Fawncy, Fawncy"; then a Bronx housewife who has misplaced her winning Sweepstakes ticket; then a starlet in a satire on Hollywood musicals—all exquisitely and incomparably executed.

—from *Lyrics on Several Occasions*

VERSE

Let me introduce a gentleman
High-class people call a louse;
Not a very sentimental man—
And he's nothing you'd want 'round the house.
Yet he twists me 'round his finger—
Funny that it's a rat I adore.
Oh, I really can't tell
Why I'm under his spell;
The chances are slim
I'll ever see what I see in him.

*Brice flirted with two spellings of her first name: "Fanny" and "Fannie." Though I.G.'s spelling here is the more widely used, in the '36 *Follies* she was Fannie.

REFRAIN 1

I give you His Highness,
A pain worse than sinus.
Though I felt all hopped up
The minute he popped up,
It's easy to see
He hasn't a thing except me.

The one thing he's mastered
Is just getting plastered;
Of money he's got less
Than someone who's potless;
It's clear as can be
He hasn't a thing except me.

What a guy!
What a man to save my dough for!
(Betcha somewhere there's a wife.)
Ask me why
He should be the one I go for,
I can only say "That's life!"

The future looks stormy;*
It's all too much for me.
But he is the soul with
Whom I'd share the dole with
If he'd guarantee
He hasn't a thing except me.

REFRAIN 2

I help out his brother,
Pay rent for his mother;
Feel when I took him in
I carry his women.
He's living for free,
He hasn't a thing except me.

His talk isn't flow'ry—
It's straight from the Bow'ry.
Yet something tremendous
Just happens to blend us.
I'm glad as can be
He hasn't a thing except me.

[*spoken*]
Well, you get the idea. You know, I've been
singing about this kind of bum for twenty-five
years. Sometimes he's called "Oh My Gawd, I
Love Him So!" Or "He's Just My Bill." Or

Version of this stanza in Lyrics on Several Occasions:
Though I brought this on me,
How long can he con me?
Still, it's not too late for
The day that I wait for:
The day he'll agree
He hasn't a thing except me.

"You Made Me What I Am Today." Once he was even called "The Curse of an Aching Heart." But he's always the same lowlife and he's always doing me dirt and I just keep on loving him. Can you imagine if I really ever *met* a guy like that, what I would do to him? Why, I'd . . . It's no use talkin'. That's my type.

[*Conductor raps impatiently. Fannie gets back into character*]

[*Sings*]
He's *mon homme;*
He can take my heart and break it—
Mend it when he starts to clown.
Just a bum—
But the guy can make me take it
When he ups and lets me down.

His actions, they slay me;*
But managers pay me;
So he is the soul with
Whom I'd share the dole with
If he'd guarantee
He hasn't a thing except me.

MY RED-LETTER DAY

Published February 1936. Introduced by Cherry and June Preisser, Duke McHale, and ensemble. Written during the pre-Broadway tryout and, apparently, first presented in the show at the New York opening. Replaced "Does a Duck Love Water?" Not included in the second (1936–37) edition.

VERSE

Why am I happy as the well-known lark
Singing in the well-known tree?

Earlier version and alternate version of this refrain:
For I've made my mind up
That though life may wind up
A hazard—a stymie—
Say, that's all right by me—
The day he'll agree
He hasn't a thing except me.

But as I'm directed,
It seems I'm expected
In movies and show life
To sing of a lowlife.
I'm singing, you see:
He hasn't a thing except me.

It's because I'm no longer in the dark
'Bout my sweetie and me.
We had a spat
And we hadn't spoken;
Life was flat
And my heart was broken.
But today the sun will shine again:
We've made up—She is mine again!

REFRAIN

Through with trouble! Watch me bubble!
My December turned to May!
Let me tell it! Let me yell it!
This is my red-letter day!

See the sunbeams! Ev'ry one beams
As I go my merry way!
Four-leaf clover, look me over:
This is my red-letter day!

Don't need rose-colored glasses,
Getting ready for shoes and rice.
I've just been given passes
To the gates of paradise.

Hear me sing it! See me swing it!
King of all that I survey!
Made a treaty with my sweetie
So it's my red-letter day!

ISLAND IN THE WEST INDIES

Published December 1935. Introduced by Gertrude Niesen and Ben Yost's California Varsity Eight; danced as "The Conga" by Josephine Baker, the Nicholas Brothers, and dancing ensemble, with Jilberto Sastere and Juanito Ramos, drummers. Sung in the second (1936–37) edition by Jane Pickens and Ben Yost's Varsity Eight. In that edition, "The Conga" was danced by Ruth Harrison, Alex Fisher, and dancing ensemble. The song's alternate titles are "West Indies," "Isle in the West Indies," and "There's an Island in the West Indies."

---

*L*ike I say. Since so many writers and speakers these days like "like" as a conjunction, it looks like "like" is being kicked upstairs not only to share the job with "as," but eventually to take over. And, like I say, if that's O.K. with the professors, O.K. by me. And if some used-car salesmen on TV got there because they pronounced "vehicle" "ve-*HICK*-l," I don't take that too serious too.

But if the many who believe that "Car-ib-*BE*-an" should be pronounced "Ca-*RIB*-be-an" become many more, drastic measures will have to be undertaken against the distorters by the composer and me. Why? Because "me an'" and "ca-*RIB*-be-an" don't rhyme. So, to all "Ca-*RIB*-be-an" lovers: please lay off and give "Car-ib-*BE*-an" and "Island in the West Indies" a chance, as the song is just beginning to get a play. If you must "Ca-*RIB*," at least hold out until 1992, when the song goes public domain.*

—from *Lyrics on Several Occasions*

VERSE

Let's both of us pack up,
Sail far from it all;
Tired having to back up
To the wall.
I know of a place where
Life really is fun—
Where days are golden
And you're beholden
To none.
Let's take passage and run!

REFRAIN

Oh, there's an island down in the West Indies
Ten dollars can buy;
Away from Reuben's and from Lindy's—
'Neath a tropic,
Kaleidoscopical sky.

We'll lie around all day and just be lazy—
The world far behind;
(If that's not heaven then I'm crazy)
With no taxes
And with no axes to grind.

No traffic jams
Under the palm trees by the sea;
With breadfruit and yams
We'll never need the A & P.

In that romantic isle in the West Indies—
No airplanes above—
We'll watch the turtles at their shindies,
You an' me an'
The Caribbean
And love.

Second Ending

We'll watch the turtles at their shindies;
Learn the lingos

---

*Revisions in the law extend the life of a copyright nineteen years beyond the original fifty-six. "Island in the West Indies" is protected until 2011—Editor.

Of pink flamingos;
Where nothing's immoral
'Way out on the coral;
All day we'll ramble
Where starfish gambol;
Just you an' me an'
The Caribbean
And love.

WORDS WITHOUT MUSIC

Published December 1935. Introduced by Gertrude Niesen, danced by Harriet Hoctor and dancing ensemble ("A Surrealist Ballet . . . setting by Vincente Minnelli, choreography by George Balanchine"—I.G.). Sung in the second (1936–37) edition by Jane Pickens, danced by Ruth Harrison, Alex Fisher, and dancing ensemble.

You can count on the fingers of one hand, and perhaps the thumb and index finger of the other, the number of our theater composers whose melodic line and harmonies are highly individual. There is no question but that Vernon Duke must be considered one of these. Although "Words Without Music" is scarcely known—and therefore not in the class of "April in Paris," "Autumn in New York," "I Can't Get Started," "What Is There to Say?" and many others—it is an excellent example of Duke's distinctive style.
—from *Lyrics on Several Occasions*

VERSE

It's an old, old, old variation
On the very oldest of themes:
It's the one that starts as flirtation
And that ends in broken dreams;
It's the feeling when he enfolds you,
He'll forget you soon as he's gone—
But, what can you do?
You're in love and you
Hold on.

REFRAIN

Words without music,
Smoke without flame—
Charming phrases
That sing your praises
And call your name.

Nights without magic,
Days without end—

Same old story,
The empty glory
Of Let's Pretend.

Had I had an inkling
That he could not be true,
These blues of mine could never start;
But stars above were twinkling,
And then before I knew—
He was locked up in my heart.

I'll hear words without music
All my life long—
Hoping, praying
That what he's saying
Will turn to song.

THE ECONOMIC SITUATION

Introduced by Eve Arden and twelve showgirls billed as "the *Ziegfeld Follies* Economists." Performed in the second (1936–37) edition by Gypsy Rose Lee and "the *Ziegfeld Follies* Economists." Alternate title: "Aren't You Wonderful! (or, The Economic Situation)."

VERSE

I'm tired of keeping up with the economic
   trends
And the universal problems that perplex;
Oh, tell me where can I find a man who
   condescends
To show an int'rest in sex.
Affairs of Heart mean nothing to men, of late;*
It seems they only go for Affairs of State.

REFRAIN 1

It used to be that a girl could get away
With "Aren't you wonderful!"—
But the economic situation has changed all that.

It used to be all you'd ever have to say
Was "Aren't you wonderful!"—
And a man would show his adoration—and you
   sat pat.

But today if you want to panic a
Guy without using a gun,

Earlier version of verse, lines 5–6:
Oh, things were very different before the Crash.
It wasn't only Wall Street that went to smash.

You've got to be a *Britannica*
And an almanac rolled into one.

It used to be a girl could get away
With "Aren't you wonderful!"—
But the economic situation has changed all that.

RECITED INTERLUDE

You're sitting with a man on a moonlit
   veranda—
You've got stars and music and other
   propaganda—
And what happens? Does he make love? No! We
   have a discussion
About the Effects of the Dynamo on the
   Russian.

You're looking your best, but he hasn't
   noticed,
For you're up to your neck in the Taxpayers'
   Protest.
Your perfume's thirty dollars an ounce and your
   makeup is fresh—
But not for *him* the lure of the flesh.

Discussing Germanism,
And Economic Determinism,
And H. G. Wells' latest Utopia,
And Mr. Borah on Ethiopia,
And Morgenthau on the Surtax,
And Jaeckel on the Fur Tax,
And what about Brooklyn—Will Roosevelt carry
   it?
And the Effect of Eccles and Ickes on the
   Proletariat.
With glittering eyes we get to the Underplowing
   of Cotton,
And Man Forgotten . . .
Forgotten Man, hell!
What about the Forgotten Gel?
But no! He throws you the Supreme Court's
   Latest Decisions,
And you retaliate with Franco-Polish Treaty
   Revisions,
And he Five-Five-Threes you about Japan,
And you knock him down with the Townsend
   Plan,
And he gives you Wallace and Tugwell until it
   hurts,
And by the time he leaves you're screaming,
   "Nerts! Nerts! Nerts!"

REFRAIN 2

It used to be that a girl could get away
With "Aren't you wonderful!"—
But the economic situation has changed all that.

It used to be all you'd ever have to say
Was "Aren't you wonderful!"—
There was never need in conversation of tit for
    tat.

But today we are mediocrities
If we can't get an A plus
On questions that Plato and Socrates
And Disraeli wouldn't dare discuss.

Oh, turn again to the day when baby chatter was
    effectual,
And you didn't have to be a goddamned
    highbrowed intellectual
With the men!

Earlier Version of Recited Interlude*

You're sitting with a man on a moonlit
    veranda—
You've got stars and music and other
    propaganda—
And what happens? Does he make love? No! We
    have a discussion
About the Effects of the Dynamo on the
    Russian.

You're looking your best, but he hasn't
    noticed
'Cause you're up to your ears in the Philippine
    Protest . . .
And Germanism . . .
And Economic Determinism . . .
And Fascism . . .
And Ogden Nashism . . .
And Borah on Abyssinia . . .
And the Sponge Trade of Sardinia . . .
And the President's Veto . . .
And the Books of Pareto . . .
And the Payment of the Debts . . .
And the Bonus for the Vets . . .
And what about Texas—Will Huey Long carry
    it?
And will the Irving Fisher Dollar help the
    Proletariat?

The thing that rankles
Is that he never notices your ankles.
Do we *have* to keep swallowing the *Tribune* and
    the *Masses*
Hoping a guy'll get wise to himself and maybe
    make passes?

With glittering eyes we get to the Underplowing
    of Cotton
And the Man Forgotten . . .

---

*The assassination of Huey Long on September 8,
1935, was a major reason why the recited interlude was
revised.

Forgotten Man, hell!
What about the Forgotten Gel?
But no! We carry on with the Panama Canal . . .
And he tosses you the Supreme Court's Latest
    Decisions . . .
And you retaliate with the Franco-Polish Treaty
    Revisions . . .
And he Five-Five-Threes you about Japan . . .
And you knock him down with the Townsend
    Plan . . .
And he gives you Wallace and Tugwell until it
    hurts . . .
And by the time he leaves you're screaming,
    "Nerts! Nerts! Nerts!"

FANCY! FANCY!

Introduced by Fannie Brice (Zuleika), Bob Hope (Sir
Robert), and John Hoysradt (Sir Henry). Performed in
the second (1936–37) edition by Brice, Bobby Clark (Sir
Robert), and Hugh Cameron (Sir Henry). Earlier titles:
"Fawncy! Fawncy!," "Fancy Fancy! And All That!,"
and "Fancy! Fancy! Fancy!"

[*An English drawing room. Zuleika and Sir
Robert are seated on sofa tightly embraced.
Seated in wing chair is Zuleika's husband, Sir
Henry. Sir Henry is reading* Punch. *All in
evening clothes.*]

SIR HENRY: I say, listen to this: "What's the
    difference between a premiere
    danseuse and a duck? Answer:
    One goes quick on her beautiful
    legs, the other goes quack on her
    beautiful eggs." Haw!*
[*Continues reading*]
SIR ROBERT:
[*to Zuleika*]
    Your kisses grow more enchanting
    every day, what, what!
ZULEIKA: Yes, quate lafelike, aren't they?
SIR ROBERT: Too, too ravishing for words!
    Darling, darling Zuleika, see what
    I have brought you for tonight's
    little gift.

---

*Alternate version:
    I say, listen to this: "What's the
    difference between the Prince of
    Wales and water in a fountain?
    Answer: One is heir to the throne, the
    other is thrown to the air." Haw!

[*Shows her large diamond bracelet*]
    Sheer heaven, isn't it?
ZULEIKA: How re'lly quate too far more than
    most awf'lly delicious! I adore
    them.
SIR ROBERT: And I adore you. My cup of tea.
    Will you merry me?
ZULEIKA: No, Sir Robert, not thet. Anything
    but marriage. It'll be too much
    trouble divorcing Henry. I'll be
    your mistress, though. We could
    have frightful fun and all thet,
    and whetnot.
SIR ROBERT: But demmit, gel, I already *have* a
    mistress. Your cousin, you know.
    What I want's a wife. Opposite
    ends of the dinner table, what ho,
    all thet, not, not?
ZULEIKA: How too tiresome decent of you, old
    platter of kipper—but I couldn't
    think of it. After all, darling,
    darling, you're only an Australian,
    a colonial.
SIR ROBERT: Oh, I'm not fawncy enough for you!
    A bit of egg on the old weskit,
    eh?
[*He rises. Sir Henry looks up from his* Punch]
SIR HENRY: Don't tiff, Sir Robert. No tiffing,
    please. Not crumpet, you know.
    I'm quate sure Zuleika means
    well.
[*He goes back to his reading. Sir Robert is
somewhat mollified. Looks at wrist watch*]
    Nine o'clock. Think I'll take a bit of
    a stroll on the moor and shoot a
    few poachers. Well, toodle-oo, old
    things.
[*Puts on Sherlock Holmes cap and exits*]
ZULEIKA:
[*to Sir Robert*]
    Come on. You're being difficult, old
    Yorkshire pudding.
[*She looks disapprovingly at his white tie, pulls
it in place. Looks him over. Goes into number*]

VERSE 1

ZULEIKA: I say, old tin of fruit,
    I find you awf'lly cute—
    But you could stand a bit of
        touching up.
    We two might make a pair,
    If you were, as it ware,
    More of the orchid than the
        buttercup.

REFRAIN 1

If you could wear top hats like
Buchanan—*
And do the rhumba like Fred
Astaire—
Be witty, but not like Julius Tannen—
If you'd the figure of Maxie Baer—
If you could speak like Ramsay
MacDonald—
And had that Cecil Beaton savoir
faire—
And charm like Noël Coward does
When he says, "How've you bean?"—
Make love as Leslie Howard does
When he is on the screen—
If you were like the fancies I
fawncy,
I fancy I could fency fawncy you.

VERSE 2

SIR ROBERT: Look here, old plate of fish,
Your notions are delish.
ZULEIKA: They'd make you tops when
strolling the Strand.
SIR ROBERT: They fascinate me quite.
ZULEIKA: A bit of quite all right.
SIR ROBERT: But then, old tidbit, on the other
hand:

REFRAIN 2

If you could warble like Ilona
Massey—†
And dressed as Lady Mountbatten
dressed—
If you possessed that Joan Crawford
chassis—
And had the dimples of Edna
Best—
If you had legs like Marlene
Dietrich—

---

*Earlier version of refrain 1, lines 1–4:
If you'd the style of Anthony Eden—
And did the rhumba like Fred Astaire—
If you played tennis like the king of
Sweden—
And had the figure of Maxie Baer—
†Earlier version of refrain 2, lines 1–4:
If you could sing like Miss Frieda
Hempel—
And dressed as Lady Mountbatten
dressed—
And earned the sal'ry paid Shirley
Temple—
And had the dimples of Edna Best—

And those alluring curves of Mae
West—
If stories you'd be telling like
Miss Parker—Too divine!—
If you could just be smelling like
Helena Rubinstein—
If you were like the fancies I
fawncy—
ZULEIKA: Then what the hell would I want
with you?

[*They go into a Jack Buchanan–Gertrude
Lawrence-ish dance, stopping every now and
then to tap a cigarette and ask conundrums*]
Q.: Why did Mother Eve have no fear of
the measles?
A.: Because she'd Adam!
(I say, I say, I say!)

Q.: Why is a lady's chin in the winter
like a certain fur?
A.: Because it's chin-chilly.
(Well bowled, my dear, well
bowled.)

Q.: What is the best way of making a
coat last?
A.: Why, you make the trousers and
waistcoat, first, of course.
(Touché, touché, touché, touché!)

Q.: What sort of cold ensures your
getting on well in the world?
A.: Influence—sir!

Q.: When is a blow from a lady
welcome?
A.: When she strikes you—agreeably.

Q.: Why is a piano like an onion?
A.: Because it'smellodious.

Q.: Cold cream and chaperones—Why
are they alike?
A.: Because they're both meant to keep
the chaps off.
(Quite, quite, quite, quite jolly
good!)

MARAHANEE

MAHARANEE

Introduced by Josephine Baker, with Rodney McLennan
and ensemble. Tryout programs listed Ben Yost's California Varsity Eight and the Nicholas Brothers as participants in this number. Not included in the second
(1936–37) edition. Program listing: "Maharanee (At the
Night Races in Paris)."

BEAUX: Who brings glamour to cafés,
To the Ritz and Zelli's,
In her Schiaparellis?
It's the Maharanee.
All the Paris boulevardiers
Seek the lady's favor.
She brings romance
To ze land of France.

[*Maharanee appears*]
MAHARANEE: Bon soir, mes amis. J'suis enchantée
de vous voir; J'suis un peu en
retard, mais vous m'excusez, car
j'ai été chez la princesse de
Marigny. Tout Paris était là: Jean
Cocteau, Bébé, Colette, Coco, et
cetera. . . . And I sink zat my
'orse Bouillabaisse is going to win
tonight. . . .

[*Beaux write down the name eagerly*]

REFRAIN

BEAUX: Maharanee, brighter than the bird of
paradise—
Show your smile—Prove that you're
a Maharanee.
Maharanee—Oh, the gay exotic
charm of you—
Oh, that leg, oh, that arm of you
Thrills Paree through and through.

Though each horse you race
Never wins a place
And our money goes for a fall,
Just a smile from you
Brightens up the view
And we find we don't mind our
losses at all.

Maharanee—Even if you were just
half as sweet,
It would still be like heaven to meet
Such a gay Maharanee—
Paree is at your feet!

MAHARANEE: When I leave my native land
And start going places,
Give me Paris races!
World of grace and fashion,
Everyone keeps askin' me
Who will be the winner.
Though it may slip,
Here's a tip for you. . . .

"Maharanee!" I'm enchanted by the
boulevardiers,
Especially when they praise
Maharanee. . . .

BEAUX: Maharanee!

MAHARANEE: Ev'ry time my horses race at night,
I know there's no place at night
Quite so charming to see;
Although I was meant for the
Orient,
Seems your town does something for
me.
Though I've never won
When my horses run,
How can anyone not be gay in
Paree?

BEAUX: Maharanee, even if you were just
half as sweet,
It would still be like heaven to meet
Such a gay Maharanee—
Paree is at your feet!

TRAILER FOR *THE 1936 BROADWAY GOLD MELODY DIGGERS* and THE GAZOOKA (sketch and song) and IT'S A DIFFERENT WORLD

"Trailer for *The 1936 Broadway Gold Melody Diggers*" (text by David Freedman and Ira Gershwin) replaced "Announcement for *Broadway Gold Melody Diggers of 42nd Street*" during rehearsals. "The Gazooka" (sketch by David Freedman and Ira Gershwin; song by Vernon Duke and Ira Gershwin) introduced by Fannie Brice (Ruby Blondell), Bob Hope (Bing Powell), and ensemble. Bobby Clark replaced Hope in the second (1936–37) *Follies* edition. Earlier titles of "The Gazooka": "The Kazooka" and "The Bazooka." The Duke-Gershwin song "It's a Different World" (contained within the "Gazooka" sketch) introduced by Brice, Hope, and quartet (Ben Yost, Paul Nelson, Riques Tanzi, and William Quentmeyer).

Following are the original eight-scene version of the "Gazooka" sketch and the four-scene version presented in New York.

"Announcement for Broadway Gold Melody Diggers of 42nd Street" (Unused)

CHORUS: Ladies and gentlemen, may we present
to you
A Hollywood musical, absolutely new!

We are certain you'll agree that it's the
greatest of all hits—
It's terrific, it's colossal, it'll tear you
into bits!
Metro, Fox, and Warner Brothers have
combined to make this film—
It's an epic, it's a panic, it'll slay 'em,
it'll kill'm!
It has dancing; it has music that will
thrill you to the core—
It's tremendous, it's stupendous, with a
story you'll adore!
For this latest super special from the
mills of Hollywood
Tells you all about a boy and girl on
Broadway who make good;
With a Technicolor sequence that's a
super, super thrill—
If this picture doesn't gross three
million, we don't know what will!

"Trailer for The 1936 Broadway Gold Melody Diggers"

[*The following titles are projected:*]
1ST TITLE: PRESENTING THE WORLD
PREMIERE OF
2ND TITLE: *THE 1936 BROADWAY GOLD
MELODY DIGGERS*
3RD TITLE: SOMETHING NEW! A STORY
WITH MUSIC!
4TH TITLE: IT'S COLOSSAL! IT'S
SENSATIONAL! IT'S
GIGANTIC! IT'S ALMOST
MEDIOCRE!
5TH TITLE: A HEART-SEARING,
SOUL-CURDLING MUSICAL
COMEDY!
6TH TITLE: SEE BING POWELL AS THE BOY
WHO MAKES GOOD!
7TH TITLE: SEE RUBY BLONDELL AS THE
GIRL WHO MAKES THE BOY
WHO MAKES GOOD!
8TH TITLE: SEE DOLORES DEL MORGAN AS
THE SIREN WHO LURES THE
BOY WHO MAKES GOOD TO
MAKE WHOOPEE!
9TH TITLE: A BIGGER CAST THAN *THE BIG
BROADCAST*!
MORE LOVE THAN *ONE NIGHT
OF LOVE*!
NAUGHTIER THAN *NAUGHTY
MARIETTA*!
MORE SCANDALOUS THAN
GEORGE WHITE'S SCANDALS!
10TH TITLE: IT'S SOMETHING NEW!
GIRLS! GIRLS! GIRLS!

11TH TITLE: STORY AND DIALOGUE
WRITTEN BY . . .
[*A list of names that covers the entire screen
and that is printed so fine it is impossible to
read. It looks like a page from the telephone
directory*]
12TH TITLE: ADDITIONAL DIALOGUE BY . . .
[*Same type of list of names as previous title*]
13TH TITLE: EXOTIC! ROMANTIC!
ENCHANTING! GLAMOROUS!
14TH TITLE: DIRECTED BY DARRYL
LIPSCHITZ!
[*The name "Darryl Lipschitz" should flash on
the screen the way the emblem of the Warner
Brothers appears before each of their pictures*]
15TH TITLE: *NEW!
UNPARALLELED!
TERRIFIC!
STUPENDOUS!*
16TH TITLE:
[*The words are wiped away, leaving only the
initial letters:*]
NUTS!
17TH TITLE: *THE 1937 BROADWAY GOLD
MELODY DIGGERS.*

"The Gazooka" (Original Version)

SCENE 1: A COUNTRY RAILROAD STATION

[*At rise, Train Conductor, Mother, Father, and
Bing are in stylized poses, saying good-bye.
Bing has a traveling bag*]
[*Train whistle*]
CONDUCTOR: All aboard! All aboard! Train leaves
immediately!
FATHER: Bing, my boy—I know you'll make
good in the big city.
BING: I know I will, Dad.
MOTHER: My boy! My boy!
BING: Don't cry, Mother. I know I'll make
good in the big city.
MOTHER: I know you'll make good in the big
city.
BING: Of course I'll make good in the big
city.
[*Train whistle*]
CONDUCTOR: All aboard! All aboard! Train leaves
immediately!
FATHER: Bing, you know how it is in the big
city. It's a different world.
BING: Yes. It's a different world. Say,
that's a great title for a song: "It's
a Different World."
[*Train whistle*]
CONDUCTOR: All aboard! All aboard! Train leaves
immediately!
[*Mother sobs*]

BING: Good-bye, Dad. Good-bye, Mom!

FATHER:

[*Takes out pocketbook and opens it*]

        Bing, I have a little surprise for you.

[*Takes money out of pocketbook*]

    BING: Gee, Dad—a surprise?

[*Looks at money Father has taken out of purse*]

        I can't imagine what it can be.

    FATHER: Mother and I have decided to give
        you our life's savings—two
        hundred and twelve dollars!

    BING: Gosh, Dad—two hundred dollars!

    FATHER: Two hundred and twelve dollars!

    BING:

[*Takes money and puts it in his pocket*]

        Gee, Dad—I haven't the heart to
        take it. Shucks, I'm a millionaire.
        Nothing can stop me from being
        another Cole Porter or Irving
        Berlin.

[*Train whistle*]

CONDUCTOR: All aboard! All aboard! Train leaves
        immediately!

    MOTHER: My boy! My boy!

    BING: Good-bye, Mom! Good-bye, Dad!

MOTHER

    AND

FATHER: Good-bye!

[*Bing rushes off. Then rushes back and
embraces Mother. Father and Conductor both
take out large handkerchiefs and wipe away a
tear*]

[*Blackout*]

SCENE 2: A CASTING OFFICE

[*At rise, Man at desk with derby on back of
head, toothpick in mouth, reading* Variety.
*Hillbilly quartet harmonizing. Girl doing
cartwheels*]

[*Enter Ruby*]

    RUBY: Something doing?

    MAN: Naw—No casting today!

[*Resumes picking his teeth and reading* Variety.
Puts feet on desk]

    RUBY: I've been to fifteen casting offices
        today. Oh, my feet! But I'm
        cheerful. Good fortune will smile
        on me. Oh, my feet!

    MAN: Beat it!

    RUBY: Someday I'll be a big star on
        Broadway, and you'll be hanging
        outside my dressing room begging
        me to go into your show and I'll
        say—Oh, my feet!

[*Bing enters. Ruby looks at him*]

    RUBY: Aha, a country bumpkin! In the big
        city to make good?

    BING: Yes. Say, how did you know?

    RUBY: A little birdie told me!

    BING: Say, you're different!

    RUBY: You're different too!

    BING: You mean you could care?

    RUBY: Ever since I first met you I cared
        only for you ever since I met you
        first!

    BING: Imagine someone like you caring for
        someone like me! Nothing can
        stop me now!

[*Music. They sing:*]

"It's a Different World"

    BING: It's a different world since I met you
        And you met up with me.

    RUBY: Boo hoo hoo hoo hoo.

    BING: It's a different world—The skies are
        blue—
        No clouds above I see.

    RUBY: Boo hoo hoo hoo hoo.
        Birdies in the trees
        Sing rhapsodies—
        They're happy as can be.

    BOTH: Boo hoo hoo hoo hoo.
        'Cause it's a different world since I
        met you
        And you met up with me.

[*They sing it again. A window shade is raised
to reveal a revolving globe of the world. Then
the desk opens, and girls come out of it dressed
in costumes of different nations. At finish of
song, everything is as it was before it started.
Ruby and Bing are in embrace*]

    RUBY:

[*spoken*]

        By the way, my name is Ruby.

    BING: And my name is Bing.

    RUBY: Glad to meet you.

[*Ruby and Bing go into a Garbo-Gable
embrace*]

[*Two men enter excitedly*]

    1ST MAN: I'm putting on a
        hundred-thousand-dollar
        production. I haven't paid for the
        scenery! I haven't paid for the
        costumes! Unless I get the money
        by four o'clock—

[*Looks at clock; it reads five to five*]

        By five o'clock—I can't open the
        show tomorrow night.

    2ND MAN: How can you ever get the money to
        pay for all that scenery and
        costumes by five o'clock?

    BING: I have some money.

    1ST MAN: How much?

    BING: Two hundred and twelve dollars!

    1ST MAN: Saved! Brother, you've saved the
        show!

    BING: I'll give you the money on one
        condition.

    1ST MAN: What's that?

    BING: That you give this little girl a job in
        the show.

    1ST MAN: Well, okay!

[*Counts out money that Bing has given him*]

    RUBY: And another condition. Give them
        only two hundred. That's enough.
        We need the other twelve.

    BING: What do you want the twelve for,
        Ruby?

    RUBY: For the little one when it arrives.

    BING: Darling! I didn't know!

    RUBY: Of course! And if your first song is a
        hit, we'll have a dozen!

    BING: Nothing can stop me now!

    RUBY: Oh, my feet!

[*Blackout*]

SCENE 3: DOLORES DEL MORGAN'S APARTMENT

[*At rise, Dolores is reclining on a chaise
longue*]

    DOLORES: Bing, my dear. What are you doing
        in there, Bing?

[*Bing enters. He wears a lounging robe, carries
a cigarette in a long holder and a highball
glass. He speaks with a Park Avenue accent*]

    BING: I've been trying to compose, but it's
        no use. Something has gone out of
        my life.

    DOLORES: Ah, you're thinking of that silly
        little girl you met in the casting
        office today.

    BING: You're right. I must find Ruby—my
        inspiration!

    DOLORES: No! No! Stay here! I'll make you
        forget!

[*Bing puts down cigarette and glass very
methodically. He embraces Dolores
passionately. After embrace he calmly picks up
cigarette and glass*]

    BING: Good heavens! I must go to the
        dress rehearsal. The show is
        opening tonight.

    DOLORES: No! No! Stay here! I'll make you
        forget!

[*The same embrace business. During the
embrace, Ruby enters. She coughs. Bing and
Dolores separate*]

    RUBY: Bing!

    BING: Who are you?

    RUBY: So soon you forgot? Don't you
        remember your little Ruby? They
        turned your head with all this

high life. Only at five o'clock today you were a clean kid, and now a quarter to six you're a dirty cad!

BING: Ruby!

RUBY: Let me finish my speech! Will you let silks and satins rob you of that heavenly gift you have to knock off hits?

BING: Ruby!

DOLORES: Leave us alone, Bing, I'll handle this little hussy!

BING: No! You can never separate me from my little Ruby!

DOLORES: Go mix me a cocktail!

BING: How can I refuse?

[Exits]

DOLORES: You see—He loves me.

RUBY: That isn't love. You're just a snake charmer and he's a poor innocent little snake.

DOLORES: Very well. Let him choose between us. I'll show you whom he loves.

BING:

[Enters with cocktail glass]

Here's your cocktail.

[Dolores takes glass]

RUBY: Bing, are you coming? The show is waiting.

DOLORES: Bing, I am waiting. Will you share this drink with me?

BING: Good God! What shall I do?

DOLORES:

[Drinks part of cocktail]

Here.

[Offers Bing rest of drink]

BING:

[Hesitates. Turns to Ruby]

Shall I?

RUBY: Wipe it off first!

[Bing drinks and immediately reels as if drunk. Dolores kisses him]

BING: Ohhhh! You've seduced me—you temptress!

[Dolores pulls Bing over to chaise longue with her]

RUBY: Did you forget me, Bing? Bing! Bing!

[Dolores and Bing are in embrace]

Bing!

[Sings]

It's a different world since I met you
And you met up with me.
Boo hoo hoo hoo hoo.
Sadness is unfurled; his heart so true
Is now so fancy-free.
Boo hoo hoo hoo hoo.

Smiling through my tears,
I hope, my dears,
That happy you will be.
Boo hoo hoo hoo hoo.
But it's a different world since I met him
And he met up with me.

[Blackout]

SCENE 4: BACKSTAGE

[At rise, Producer on stage. Girls are rehearsing. Ruby is among them. She is out of step]

PRODUCER: What's the matter, Ruby?

RUBY: Nothing!

PRODUCER: Don't worry about Bing; he'll be back.

RUBY: No, never! Never! He'll never come back!

[Bing rushes on]

BING: Ruby!

RUBY: I knew he'd come!

BING: Ruby, will you forgive me?

RUBY: What for?

BING: Don't you remember? I was unfaithful to you. I drank the cocktail.

RUBY: I know. But the show must go on.

PRODUCER: No show tonight. The leading lady just broke her ankle. It's no use. You can all go home.

BING: Just a minute. This little chorus girl knows the part perfectly. She's been understudying since dinner time. Let her go on.

[Cheer from all]

[Assistant Manager rushes on]

ASS'T MGR.: The leading man just left for the Coast!

PRODUCER: Good heavens! No show tonight. You can all go home.

RUBY: Just a minute! Bing knows the part. He understudied with me.

PRODUCER: Can you do it?

BING: I don't know.

RUBY: Darling!

BING: Of course! Nothing can stop me now!

[Cheers from all]

[Orchestra leader rushes on]

LEADER: The hit song is missing! "The Humpty-Dumpty"!

PRODUCER: "The Humpty-Dumpty"?

LEADER: Yes, the song that you gave Irving Berlin ten thousand dollars to write for this show. It's missing!

PRODUCER: Good God! No show tonight! You can all go home.

RUBY: Just a minute! Here's a new song that Bing wrote while you were talking. It's another "Carioca"! It's another "Continental"! It's another "Piccolino"! It's called—"The Gazooka"!

[Pulls manuscript from her dress]

PRODUCER: Let's hear it!

[Bing goes to piano, plays. Ruby sings and dances]

PRODUCER: It's great! Quick! Have copies of the song made and teach it to the whole cast! The show starts in five minutes!

[Everybody but Ruby and Bing exit]

BING: What a break! I wonder what happened to "The Humpty-Dumpty"?

RUBY: Look!

[Pulls manuscript from her bosom]*

Here's "The Humpty-Dumpty"!

[Blackout]

SCENE 5: IN FRONT OF THE THEATRE

[At rise, swanky people entering theatre. Father, Mother, Train Conductor dressed as in Scene 1 mingle with crowd]

1ST MAN: I hear it's a wonderful show. I paid a hundred dollars for these two tickets!

MOTHER: My boy! My boy!

2ND MAN: They say a young country lad wrote the songs.

WOMAN: I understand that he financed the show and produced it.

FATHER: Yes! And that boy is none other than my son!

CONDUCTOR: And I brought him on the train to the big city!

MAN: You ought to be proud of your boy. This production cost more than Jubilee.†

FATHER: And to think that he did it all for two hundred and twelve dollars!

[Blackout]

---

*Or from piano or bass tuba—I.G.

†Originally:

... This production cost more than The Miracle.

SCENE 6: ONSTAGE

"The Gazooka"

VERSE

CHORUS: What's the lastest rage
On radio, screen, and stage?
It's nothing else than the dance they
call "Gazooka"!

It'll be the hit
Of ev'ry orchestral pit—
I'm talking 'bout that new dance
they call "Gazooka"!

Ev'ry day its popularity grows;
Grab your partner now and learn
how it goes:

REFRAIN

First you take a step,
And then you take another,
And then you take another,
And then you take,
And then you take,
And then you,
And then you,
And then you,
And that's "The Gazooka"!

Next you take a step,
And you follow with another,
And follow with another,
And follow with,
And follow with,
And follow,
And follow,
And follow,
And that's "The Gazooka"!

It's terrific! It's colossal! Lifts you to
the sky!
Sweet and sloppy! It's thirty cents a
copy! One you ought to buy!*

'Cause first you take a step,
And then you take another,
And then you take another,
And then you take,
And then you take,
And then you,
And then you,
And then you and I—
We have both done "The Gazooka"!
[In the middle of the number, everything stops,
the stage darkens, and lights come up on:]

---

*Originally:

It's tremendous! Better than stupendous!
It's the song to buy!

SCENE 7: BACKSTAGE

[Dolores enters with two gangsters, who carry
machine guns]
DOLORES: There's Bing Powell! He jilted me!
I'll show him he can't make a fool
of Dolores Del Morgan. Quick
boys—Hide!
[They hide behind set piece]
[Call boy rushes on]
CALL BOY: Mr. Bing Powell—your cue! On stage
for "The Gazooka"!
[Bing rushes on]
BING: Okay!
[Two gangsters step out, shoot Bing, rush off]
DOLORES:
[stepping out from set piece]
So you thought you'd get away with
it?
BING: You!
[Takes out gun and shoots Dolores]
DOLORES: Ohhh!
RUBY:
[rushing on]
Quick, Bing! On stage! Darling!
What's happened?
DOLORES: If I can't have him—you can't!
[Shoots Ruby]
RUBY: Ohhh!
PRODUCER:
[rushing on]
Quick! Quick! The show must go on!
RUBY: If I can't do "The
Gazooka"—nobody'll do it!
[Shoots Producer]
[Lights rise on "The Gazooka," still in
progress. The number continues. Then, again,
everything stops, the stage darkens, and lights
come up on:]

SCENE 8: A HOSPITAL

[One large bed in which Dolores, Producer,
Bing, and Ruby lie. A doctor is with them]
[Assistant Manager rushes on]
ASS'T MGR.: Oh, so here's where all of you are!
I've been looking everywhere for
you!
RUBY: Ohhh! How's the show?
ASS'T MGR.: "The Gazooka" is going over great!
It's a sensation! If you could only
come back in time to finish the
number.
BING: Is the show a hit?
ASS'T MGR.: We're sold out for the next sixty-nine
weeks!
BING: Ruby, now that the show is a hit, will
you marry me?

RUBY: Who could marry us?
DOCTOR: I used to be a Justice of the Peace!
BING: That's great! Ruby, I've always loved
you!
[Everybody throws off sheet and stands up.
They are all in evening clothes]
PRODUCER:
[to Dolores]
And I've always loved you too,
Dolores.
ASS'T MGR.: I might as well tell you. I have a
little girl in the show.
RUBY: That's great! We'll all get married!
[Girl walks on. Couples pair off]
DOCTOR: Does everybody here take everybody
else . . .
[Blackout. Resume production of "The
Gazooka" to finish]

"The Gazooka" (Broadway Version)

[In the dark we hear:]
VOICE: It's terrific! The greatest musical
picture of all time! Don't fail to see
it at your neighborhood theatre:
*The Twenty-Million Gold-Melody
Scandal Diggers of 1936.* The most
fabulous of all Metro-Warner
productions. What a title! What a
cast! Watch Bing Powell as the boy
who makes good! See Ruby
Blondell as the girl who loves the
boy who makes good! See Warren
Warrens as the rounder who wants
the girl who loves the boy who
makes good! What a title! What
music! What a cast!

SCENE 1: A COUNTRY RAILROAD STATION

[Enter hick Boy, Father, and Mother. Sound of
train whistle in distance]
MOTHER: God bless you, son, and keep you safe
in the big city.
BOY: Don't worry about me, Maw. It'll be a
different world, but I'm sure to
make good. Say, that's a good title.
"It's a Different World Since I Met
You."
[Jots it down]
FATHER: I got a little surprise for you, son.
BOY: A surprise for me, Dad? Say!
FATHER: I just underplowed a hundred and
thirty-six chickens, and here's a
hundred eighty dollars from Uncle
Sam.
BOY: A hundred eighty dollars! Gosh, I'm a
millionaire! Nothing can stop me

now from being another Cole
Porter or Irving Berlin!
[*Train whistle, loud now. Frantic embraces*]

SCENE 2: CASTING OFFICE

[*Girls doing cartweels. Hillbilly quartet
harmonizing, etc. Man behind desk. Derby on
back of head. Enter Fannie, golden curls.
Typical ingenue*]

FANNIE:
[*coyly*]
Something doing?

MAN: Naw!
[*Continues picking teeth and reading* Variety]
No casting today.

FANNIE: I don't know what I'll do. I'm down
to my last can of pork and beans.
[*Boy enters. Looks about diffidently*]

FANNIE: In the big city to make good?

BOY: Yes. Say, how'd you know?

FANNIE: A little birdie told me.

BOY: Say, you're different!

FANNIE: So are you!

BOY: You mean you could care?

FANNIE: Who knows?

BOY: Imagine someone like you caring for
someone like me! Nothing can stop
me now.
[*They sing "It's a Different World." All join in
second chorus as Fannie and Boy embrace*]
[*Two men, cigar chewers, enter, talking
excitedly*]

1ST MAN: I need more money. Otherwise we
can't open tomorrow night.

2ND MAN: Where are we going to get it?
[*Boy steps up*]

BOY: I have some money.

1ST MAN: How much?

BOY: A hundred eighty dollars.
[*Men fall on him enthusiastically*]

1ST MAN: Brother, you've saved the show.

BOY: On one condition.

1ST MAN: What's that?

BOY: That little girl gets a job in the show.

1ST MAN:
[*grudgingly*]
Okay.

FANNIE: And a second condition.
[*Turns to Boy*]
Only a hundred sixty dollars. That's
plenty. We need that twenty.
[*Men rush off with the $160*]

BOY: What's the twenty for?

FANNIE: For the little one when it arrives.

BOY: Darling! I didn't know! Nothing can
stop me now!
[*Reprise—"It's a Different World"*]

SCENE 3: BACKSTAGE

[*Next evening. Orchestra tuning up. Girls
rushing to and fro in elaborate costumes from
the Shubert warehouse. Dance director giving
last-minute touches to an eight-girl group that
includes Fannie. Boy appears in faultless
evening clothes. Manager runs on frantically*]

MANAGER: No show tonight! The leading lady
broke her ankle! It's no use! You
can all go home!

BOY: Just a minute. This little lady
[*indicating Fannie*] knows the part perfectly.
She's been understudying all day.
Let her go on.
[*Cheer from all*]
[*Assistant rushes on*]

ASSISTANT: The leading man just left for the
Coast.

MANAGER: Good God! No show tonight! You can
all go home!

FANNIE: Just a minute.
[*Points to boy*]
He knows the part. He understudied
it with me.

MANAGER: Can you do it?

BOY: Nothing can stop me.
[*Cheers from all*]
[*Orchestra leader rushes on*]

LEADER: The hit song is missing. "The
Humpty-Dumpty." We've looked
everywhere for the orchestration.

MANAGER: Good God! No show tonight! You can
all go home! No
"Humpty-Dumpty"!

FANNIE: Just a minute. Here's a new song he
wrote last night. It's another
"Carioca." It's another
"Continental." It's another
"Piccolino." It's called "The
Gazooka"!
[*She pulls manuscript from under her dress*]
[*All cheer*]

MANAGER
[*to Assistant*]
Hurry up. Have copies made and
teach it to them.
[*All exit but Boy and Fannie*]

BOY: What a break! I wonder what
happened to "The
Humpty-Dumpty"?

FANNIE: Look in my bathroom.
[*Blackout*]

[*We go into Scene 4, an elaborate production of
"The Gazooka" à la Busby Berkeley. In middle
of final chorus, Mother, Father, and minister
run on amid cheers. Boy and Fannie are
married in one sentence. We fade as:*]

VOICE: It's overwhelming. The greatest
picture of all time. Coming next
week. *The Twenty-Million
Gold-Melody Diggers of 1937.* See
Bing Powell as the boy who makes
good. See . . .
[*The voice dies down*]

THAT MOMENT OF MOMENTS

Published 1935. Introduced by Gertrude Niesen, Rodney McLennan, and Ben Yost's California Varsity Eight. Danced by Harriet Hoctor, Herman Belmont, and dancing ensemble. Sung in the second (1936–37) edition by Jane Pickens, James Farrell, and Ben Yost's Varsity Eight, and danced by Ruth Harrison, Alex Fisher, and dancing ensemble.

Show Version

VERSE

What was there to do?
The opera was getting dull;
I found the setting dull;
So I looked around
The lobby aimlessly
And suddenly found
You staring shamelessly.
I felt a thrill,
And all the world stood still!

REFRAIN

That moment of moments!
That flash from the blue!
My moment of moments
Finding you!
I stood there in wonder
With never a word;
And that wasn't thunder,
That was my heart you heard.
Never was there any moment quite so
momentous,
For in that moment heaven was sent us.
Our moment of moments—
Two fond hearts in rhyme;
Here's hoping that moment
Lives until the end of time.

PUBLISHED VERSE

It was time to go.
The party was getting dull;

I found the setting dull;
So I got my hat
And I went to the door.
When just like that!—
A dream came through the door;
And as I stared—
I cared and cared and cared!

SENTIMENTAL WEATHER

Introduced by Cherry and June Preisser and Duke McHale. Performed in the second (1936–37) edition by Cherry and June Preisser and Marvin Lawler.

VERSE

Funny thing that
Poets sing that
Spring alone is mating time.
I beg to differ.
Lose my reason
Ev'ry season—
Swimming time or skating time;
I'm yours, my dear,
Twelve months in ev'ry year.

REFRAIN 1

Sentimental weather—
Whether it's fall or spring—
Long as we're together,
The calendar will never mean a thing.
When the weather's zero
Or ninety-nine above,
Columbine and Pierrot
Will love and love and love and love and love.
Oysters only show up in the months with "R";
Love beats that by far!
My cap wears a feather
In June or Janu'ree:
Long as we're together,
It's sentimental weather for me.

REFRAIN 2

Sentimental weather—
Three hundred sixty-five
Days to be together—
Three sixty-six when leap year will arrive.
Love should favor no time—
Darling, you must allow,
Swimming time or snow time,
There really isn't any time like now.
Spring, they tell us, is the only time to coo;

That's one quarter true.
Blizzards may be blizzing,
Blustering winds may bluss—
Long as we're together,
It's sentimental weather for us.

FIVE A.M.

Introduced by Josephine Baker, with Gene Ashley, Milton Barnett, George Church, and Willen van Loon as "The Shadows." Not included in the second (1936–37) edition. No music is known to survive.

Five A.M. And I am alone again. Five A.M.
Five A.M. My time is my own again. Five A.M.
Through with the night I slave in,
I'm in my haven at last.
Through with the smile that is deceiving,*
The make-believing is past.
Home again. No white tie is facing me. Home
again.†
Home again. No Don Juan embracing me. Home
again.
Soon enough the masquerade starts again—
Soon enough I'm playing with hearts again—
Five A.M.
I live in a world of my own.

I CAN'T GET STARTED

Published December 1935. Introduced by Bob Hope, with Eve Arden and ensemble. (During the pre-Broadway tryout it had been performed by Hope, Judy Canova, and ensemble.) Performed in the second (1936–37) edition by Bobby Clark, Gypsy Rose Lee, the Glorified Ziegfeld Show Girls, and Ben Yost's Varsity Eight.

Vernon played me this tune and told me it had had a lyric called "Face the Music with Me"; that noth-

---

*Earlier version of lines 5–6:
Through with cafés where I paraded,
To drink [or dance, or flirt] with jaded old men.
†Alternate version of lines 7–8:
Home again. No jazz rhythm pounding me. Home
again.
Home again. No Don Juan is hounding me. Home
again.

ing had happened to that version; that the tune was free and I could write it up if I liked it. I liked it and wrote it up. However, there is seemingly no end of lines for "I Can't Get Started." Besides the original version for Hope and Arden . . . a radio version avoiding proper names was requested by my publisher. After that, I was asked to write a version for a possible recording by Bing Crosby, here again avoiding wherever possible the proper noun. Then there was a request for a female version to be recorded by Nancy Walker. All in all, I have fooled around with many, many lines for this piece. The sheet-music sale of the song never amounted to much (I would say that in more than twenty years it has totaled less than forty thousand copies), but an early recording by Bunny Berigan—considered by jazz devotees a sort of classic in its field—may have been a challenge (or incentive) for the great number of recordings that have followed. Not a year has gone by, in the past fifteen or so, that up to a dozen or more new recordings haven't been issued.

—from *Lyrics on Several Occasions*

Ziegfeld Follies of 1936 Version

INTRODUCTION

HOPE:
[*spoken*]
    Wasn't it a wonderful dinner?
ARDEN: Oh, all right. I've had better. Well, good
    night.
[*Starts to leave*]
HOPE: Wasn't it funny how the customers
    recognized me? You know, I had to
    sign forty autographs.
ARDEN: So what? Well, good night. Here, taxi!
HOPE: Gosh, I can't seem to get to first base
    with you. Never a smile, never a kind
    word. Good God, what would I have to
    give you for a kiss?
ARDEN: Ronald Colman.
HOPE: You know, we were in the same class at
    Oxford.
ARDEN: Well, you're not in his class now.
HOPE: Listen, on six continents and seven
    oceans, I'm tops. Everybody is crazy
    about me. And I'm crazy about you. I
    love you so. I want you so.
ARDEN: So what? Well—
BOTH: Good night.

VERSE

HOPE: I'm a glum one; it's explainable:
I met someone unattainable;
Life's a bore,
The world is my oyster no more.
All the papers, where I led the news

With my capers, now will spread the
  news:
"Superman
Turns Out to Be Flash in the Pan."

REFRAIN 1

I've flown around the world in a plane;
I won the race from Newport to Maine;
The North Pole I have charted,
But can't get started with you.

Around a golf course I'm under par,
The Theatre Guilders want me to star;
I've got a house—a showplace—
But I get no place with you.

You're so supreme,
Lyrics I write of you;
Scheme
Just for a sight of you;
Dream
Both day and night of you,
And what good does it do?

I've been consulted by Franklin D.
And Greta Garbo's asked me to tea,
And yet I'm brokenhearted
'Cause I can't get started with you.

REFRAIN 2

I do a hundred yards in ten flat;
The Duke of Kent has copied my hat;
With queens I've à la carted,
But can't get started with you.

When Democrats are all in a mess,
I hear Jim Farley's call of distress,
And I help him maneuver,
But I'm just Hoover to you.

When first we met—
How you elated me!
Pet!
You devastated me!
Yet,
Now you've deflated me
Till you're my Waterloo.

When J. P. Morgan bows, I just nod;
Green Pastures wanted me to play God.
The Siamese Twins I've parted,
But I can't get started with you.

REFRAIN 3

The Himalaya Mountains I climb;
I'm written up in *Fortune* and *Time*.
New Yorker did my profile ["*pro-feel*"]
But I've had no feel from you.

There's always "Best regards and much
  love"
From Mr. Lehman—you know, the Gov;
I go to ev'ry state ball,
But I'm just behind the eight ball with
  you.

Oh, tell me why
Am I no kick to you?
I,
Who'd always stick to you?
Fly
Through thin and thick to you?
Tell me why I'm taboo!

Oh, what a man you're keeping at bay;
I use a pound of Lifebuoy each day;
But you've got me downhearted
'Cause I can't, I can't, I can't, I can't,
I can't get started with you.

ARDEN:
[*spoken*]
    Oh well, what can I lose?
[*She turns resignedly and permits him to
embrace her. A long kiss follows. Her lack of
interest becomes ardent cooperation. Never has
she met his equal. She holds him at arm's
length*]
    My God! You're wonderful! You're
      marvelous!
HOPE: That's all I wanted to know! Well, good
      night!
[*Jauntily he walks off, leaving her
flabbergasted*]
[*Blackout*]

Tryout Version sung by Judy Canova

REFRAIN 4

I've sold my kisses at a bazaar,
And after me they've named a cigar.
But lately, how I've smarted—
I can't get started with you.

Why, Lucius Beebe quotes me on styles,
And Pepsodent used one of my smiles.
The Vanderbilts I visit,
But say, what *is* it with you?

Oh, tell me why
Am I no kick to you?
I,
Who'd always stick to you?
Fly
Though thin and thick to you?
Tell me why I'm taboo!

In 1929, I sold short;

In England, I'm presented at court,
But you've got me downhearted,
'Cause I can't, I can't, I can't, I can't, I
  can't,
I can't get started with you.

Published Version

VERSE
[as in *Follies* version]

REFRAIN 1

I've flown around the world in a plane;
I've settled revolutions in Spain;
The North Pole I have charted,
But can't get started with you.

Around a golf course I'm under par,
And all the movies want me to star;
I've got a house, a showplace—
But I get no place with you.

You're so supreme,
Lyrics I write of you;
Scheme
Just for a sight of you;
Dream
Both day and night of you,
And what good does it do?

In 1929, I sold short;
In England, I'm presented at court,
But you've got me downhearted
'Cause I can't get started with you.

REFRAIN 2

I do a hundred yards in ten flat;
The Prince of Wales has copied my hat;
With queens I've à la carted,
But can't get started with you.

The leading tailors follow my styles.
And toothpaste ads all feature my smiles.
The Astorbilts I visit,
But say, what *is* it with you?

When first we met—
How you elated me!
Pet!
You devastated me!
Yet,
Now you've deflated me
Till you're my Waterloo.

I've sold my kisses at a bazaar,
And after me they've named a cigar.
But lately, how I've smarted—
'Cause I can't get started with you.

Female Version

Recorded by Nancy Walker in 1953. Lyrics first published in Ira Gershwin's *Lyrics on Several Occasions* (1959).

VERSE

I'm a glum one; it's explainable:
I met someone unattainable.
Life's a bore,
The world is my oyster no more.
All the papers, where I led the news
With my capers, now will spread the news:
"Super Gal
Is Punchy and Losing Morale!"

REFRAIN 1

I've flown around the world in a plane;
I'm known from California to Maine;
With kings I've à la carted—
But can't get started with you.

Around a golf course I'm under par,
And all the movies want me to star;
I've got a house—a showplace—
But I get no place with you.

You're so supreme,
Lyrics I write of you;
Scheme
Just for a sight of you;
Dream
Both day and night of you.
And what good does it do?

The market trembles when I sell short;
In England, I'm presented at court.
But you've got me downhearted
'Cause I can't get started with you.

REFRAIN 2

When I sell kisses at a bazaar,
The wolves line up from nearby and far;
Their methods I have charted,
But I can't get started with you.

The millionaires that I have turned down*
Would stretch from London to New York Town;
The upper crust I visit,
But say, what *is* it—with you?

When first we met—
How you elated me!
Pet!

Alternate version of refrain 2, line 5:
The millionaires I've had to turn down

You devastated me!
Yet—
Now you've deflated me
Till you're my Waterloo.

Though beauty columns ask my advice,
Though I was "Miss America" twice,
Still, you've got me outsmarted
'Cause I can't get started with you.

REFRAIN 3

The Himalaya Mountains I climb;
I'm written up in *Fortune* and *Time.*
I dig the Fourth Dimension,
But no attention from you!

There's always "Best regards and much love"
From Mr. Dewey—you know, the Gov;
I'm there at ev'ry state ball
But behind the eight ball with you.

Oh, tell me why
Am I no kick to you?
I,
Who'd always stick to you?
Fly
Through thin and thick to you?
Tell me why I'm taboo!

Good grief! I'm not exactly a clod!
Green Pastures wanted me to play God!
The Siamese Twins I've parted—
But I can't get started with you.

Duet Version

In 1958, Ira Gershwin, in collaboration with Sammy Cahn, worked out a duet version of "I Can't Get Started" for Bing Crosby and Rosemary Clooney, which they recorded for their album *Fancy Meeting You Here.* There is also the Frank Sinatra "No One Cares" album from 1959, which includes such couplets as:

Each time I chanced to see Franklin D.
He always said "Hi Buddy" to me.
and
In Cincinnati or in Rangoon
I simply smile and all the girls swoon.

VERSE

CROSBY: I'm a glum one; it's explainable:
I met someone unattainable;
Life's a bore,
The world is my oyster no more.

CLOONEY: All the papers, where you led the news
With your capers, now will spread the news:

"Superman
Turns Out to Be Flash in the Pan."

REFRAIN 1

CROSBY: The Himalaya Mountains I climb;
CLOONEY: You're written up in *Fortune* and *Time.*
CROSBY: I dig the Fourth Dimension—
But no attention from you.
CROSBY: When I sell kisses at a bazaar,
CLOONEY: The gals line up from near and from far.
CROSBY: Their methods I have charted,
But can't get started with you.
CROSBY: Oh, tell me why
Am I no kick to you?
I,
Who'd always stick to you?
Fly
Through thin and thick to you?
Tell me why I'm taboo.
CLOONEY: The market trembles when you sell short.
CROSBY: In England, I'm presented at court.
CLOONEY: With kings you've à la carted—
CROSBY: Still, I can't get started with you.

REFRAIN 2 (HALF CHORUS)

CLOONEY: When first we met—
How you elated me!
Pet!
You devastated me!
CROSBY: Yet—
How you've deflated me
Till you're my Waterloo.
CROSBY: Good grief! I'm not exactly a clod.
When Elvis Presley bows, I just nod.
CLOONEY: You're asked to every state ball.
CROSBY: Still, I'm behind the eight ball.
CLOONEY: Your dad's a Wall Street banker.
CROSBY: Still, I'm just a tanker.
CLOONEY: You sum up what a gent is.
CROSBY: Still, I'm non compos mentis with you.
BOTH: No, I (you) just can't get started with you (me).

MODERNISTIC MOE

Lyrics by Ira Gershwin and Billy Rose. Introduced by Fannie Brice.

My feet are full of splinters;
There's water on my knee;
A broken-down expressionistic dancer—
That's me.

I used to work in a nightclub
For sixty bucks a week.
To please the chumps,
I did the bumps
And turned the other cheek.
It wasn't so artistic,
But at least it used to pay;
When I was truckin',
There's no use talkin',
I ate three times a day.

Then came along Moe, the modernistic man—
With a beaver hat
And a long black coat
And a Morris Gest tie
Around his throat. . . .

He gave me a rectangular smile
And whispered into my ear,
"My love, there's pigeons on the grass;
There's pigeons on the grass, alas!"
And that was the end of my nightclub career.

Since Modernistic Moe
Made me leave the show,
I'm interpreting the rhythm of the masses.
I crawl around the stage
Interpreting the age,
But the masses they won't even come on passes.
I got the harmony of the body
And the melody of the feet—
I got coordination—
But I ain't got to eat.
Staccato and dynamic—
The Movement That Revolts—
A future panoramic
Of nuts and screws and bolts.
The Movement of the Masses
On the Economic Scene—
Every Movement has a Meaning,
But what the hell does it mean?
Since Modernistic Moe
Has made me movement-wise,
I joined up with the New School of Dancing,
And I'm dancing with tears in my eyes.

DANCING TO THE SCORE

Introduced by Rodney McLennan, Eve Arden, Ben Yost's California Varsity Eight, and the entire company. (During the tryout, it had been presented by Rodney McLennan, Fannie Brice, and the entire company.) Not included in the second (1936–37) edition. Alternate titles: "Dancing to Our Score" and "We Hope You'll Soon Be Dancing to the Score."

VERSE

We will not sing you a love song,
A ballad, or moon-above song.
We are not explaining the plot;
We cannot explain what is not.
But, say, if you will lend an ear,
We'll tell you just why we're here.

REFRAIN

We hope you'll soon be dancing to the score
Out on the ballroom or on the nightclub floor;
We'd like you to dance to
The songs of the show,
Like "Words Without Music"
And "Moment of Moments";
We'd like to feel that after you have gone,
The show is through but the melody lingers on.
If we're not too persistent,
Let's stress it once more:
We hope you'll soon be dancing to the score.

Earlier Version

VERSE

Before you reach for your sables
To dash to the nightclub tables—
Before you rush to your car
To get to your favorite bar—
In fact, before the curtains fall,*
May we sing to one and all:

REFRAIN

We hope you'll soon be dancing to the score:
It seems that's what the writers would adore.
They'd like you to whistle
As homeward you go;
They'd like you to dance to
The songs of the show.
We hope you'll soon be dancing to the score;
It helps the sales at ev'ry music store.
As we start the finale,
Let's mention once more:
We hope you'll soon be dancing to the score.

Unused version of verse, lines 5–6:
In fact, before your leave you take,
We have a request to make:

DOES A DUCK LOVE WATER?

Introduced by Bob Hope, Judy Canova, and Ben Yost's California Varsity Eight (danced by Cherry and June Preisser, Duke McHale, and ensemble) during the tryout. Dropped before the New York opening. Replaced with "My Red-Letter Day."

VERSE

There's a query
You never weary
Asking ev'ry time we meet.
Do I love you?
Put none above you?
Do you make my life complete?
Here's your answer since you
Seem to want me to convince you;

REFRAIN 1

Does a duck love water?
Does an Englishman love tea?
Would you say Italians
Care for scallions?
South love Robert E. Lee?

Does a duck love water?
Do the kids love gingerbread?
Do the Spanish dollies
Love tamales?
Bolsheviki love red?

Do dogs love trees?
Does an old romancer
Love a bubble dancer?
Do Swiss love cheese?
Does an actor in a show
Love S.R.O.?

Oh, does a duck love water?
Do New Havenites love blue?
There's your answer, dearie,
To the query
As to whether I love you!

REFRAIN 2

Does a duck love water?
Are the Chinese fond of rice?
Does the land of Dante
Love Chianti?
Postmen love to ring twice?

Does a duck love water?
Fred Astaire a tap routine?

Do New Deal officials
Love initials?
Do the Irish love green?

Do fleas love dogs?
Do the Minsky mammas
Love to shed pajamas?
Paree love frogs?
Tell me, is Missouri keen
For Dizzy Dean?

Oh, does a duck love water?
Does a comic love a wow?
There you have from me a
Rough idea
As to whether I love you!

REFRAIN 3

Does a duck love water?
Calloway love "Hi-de-hi"?
Mr. Mussolini
Scallopini?
Harlem a fish fry?

Does a duck love water?
Does an Eskimo love whale?
Debutantes their photos
In the rotos?
Frenchmen go for a snail?

Does Kiss love Kiss?
And does Woollcott (Alex)
Love his name in italics?
Do Reds love *siss?*
And does Mr. Bernard Shaw
Love Bernard Shaw?

Oh, does a duck love water?
Jolson love his Mammy's knee?
There's your answer, dearie,
To the query
As to whether I love thee!

We've got lots more;
Sing this song for ages;
We've a thousand pages,
But, say, what for?
We're as certain as can be
You've got the idea.

THE LAST OF THE CABBIES

Introduced by Bob Hope during the pre-Broadway tryout. In Boston, sung late in Act I; in Philadelphia, sung in the middle of Act II. Dropped before the New York opening. Years later, Ira Gershwin considered

including it in *Lyrics on Several Occasions* and planned to introduce it as follows: "Bob Hope, as an old cabby stationed near Manhattan's Hotel Plaza, bemoans his fate in waltztime."

VERSE 1

My hansom once carried John Sullivan,
Lil' Russell, and Chauncey Depew;
And Diamond Jim Brady
Kissed many a lady
In my hansom when it was new.
Then one day there came Mr. Henry Ford—
Invented a horseless machine.
That gol-darned contraption
Has caused my collapsion
And left me with nary a bean.
If my chin has stubble,
The cause is the automobubble.

REFRAIN 1

Oh, sad is my story and hard is my lot:
Today people taxi—To beauty they're blind!
And you can't make a living when all you have
    got
Is a horse with a hansom,
A horse with a hansom,
A horse with a hansom behind.

VERSE 2

I married, and no one was happier.
Each day my wife starched my cravat;
And till I would rush off,
My Nellie would brush off
My beautiful silken high hat.
Then into our garden a serpent came—
A Frenchified man with mustache—
A louse and a loafer,
But he was a chauffeur,
And she fell for him in a flash.
If my heart is heavy,
The reason's the Ford and the Chevy.

REFRAIN 2

Oh, sad is my story, of wife I'm bereft;
She smelled gasoline and went out of her mind.
Oh, the auto's my ruin, and all I have left*
Is a horse with a hansom,
A horse with a hansom,
A horse with a hansom behind.

Earlier version of refrain 2, line 3:
Oh, the world's not your oyster when all you have left

REFRAIN 3

Young men, don't be cabbies! Please take my
    advice!
Today people taxi—To beauty they're blind.
If a fortune you're seeking, you'd better think
    twice—
For you'll never amass it,
If your only asset
Is a horse with a hansom behind.

Earlier Lyrics

VERSE 2

Each day, my poor horsie grows skinnier,
For she is as troubled as I,
For she who pulled Whitneys
Must give way to jitneys—
If I weren't here, she would die.
'Tis not like the splendor of long ago;
I kept her as smart as could be:
In her Easter bonnet
With ribbons upon it,
Oh, she was a sight for to see.
If our hearts are heavy,
It's caused by the Ford and the Chevy.

REFRAIN 2

Oh, sad is my story as time runs its course,
For people will taxi—To beauty they're blind;
Oh, there's no one who needs me today but my
    horse.
There's just one way to class it:
You're an old horse's asset
When you've got a hansom behind.

THE BALLAD OF BABY FACE McGINTY (WHO BIT OFF MORE THAN HE COULD CHEW)

Lyrics first published in Ira Gershwin's *Lyrics on Several Occasions* (1959). Introduced by Judy Canova (Maw) and William Quentmeyer, Thomas Gleason, and Everett West (Sons) during the tryout. Dropped before the New York opening. Dubbed by Ira Gershwin: "A Ballad with a Moral."

R.I.P. "B. F. McGinty." During the tryout of the *Follies* in Boston this combination hillbilly-gangster-T-Man song-ballet was staged one night; and as choreographed by Balanchine and costumed by [Vincente] Minnelli I thought it a stunner. And so did many others. But this *Follies* was rare in that although the customary out-of-town phrase "It needs work" applied, the problem here was one of wealth of material rather than lack. With a cast containing, among others, Fanny Brice, Bob Hope, Eve Arden, and Judy Canova, there was a more than usual amount of comedy; there were plenty of stageable songs and special material (because of production postponements Duke and I had been at it eight or nine months, and twenty-five numbers were available); there was high-spirited dancing directed by Robert Alton; and there were ballets by Balanchine: "5 a.m." for Josephine Baker, "Night Flight" for ballerina Harriet Hoctor, "Words Without Music" ("A Surrealist Ballet") and "McGinty."

In his autobiography, *Passport to Paris*, Vernon writes: "A fresh and novel 'Ballad of Baby Face McGinty,' imaginatively staged by Balanchine, was inexplicably dropped in Boston." Inexplicable, yes—if ousting depended on quality alone. But we had too much show with too many elaborate production numbers, and "McGinty" was one of the discarded.

The business of stage entertainment is precarious enough without the producer's having to worry about such matters as stagehands' extra pay and Suburbia's railroad schedules. So, unless you are Richard Wagner or Eugene O'Neill, overlength has to be considered. The Show Must Go On—but not too long after eleven p.m.
—from *Lyrics on Several Occasions*

SECTION 1

[*Setting: a Kentucky cabin*]

MAW: Oh, Baby Face McGinty—
His story I will tell.
At seven his heart was flinty,
Though he looked as cute as hell.
He stole his granny's false teeth
To buy himself some gin.
The games of the other kids he'd shelve;
He was a pappy when he was twelve.
Oh, Baby Face McGinty
Was not what he might 'a' been.

SONS: McGinty loved his gin.
At seven he learned to sin.
'Twas plain to see
Even then that he
Was not what he might 'a' been—
Was not what he might 'a' been.

[*The lights dim, blacking out the cabin interior. Lights up on ballet of gangsters and T-Men. Then, back to the cabin for:*]

SECTION 2

MAW: McGinty ruled St. Louie
When he was twenty-one.
To see the police go screwy
Was Baby's idee of fun.
Each day he'd hold a bank up;
He dealt in booze—and how!
Machine guns he owned filled forty
  trucks,
And he had hidden three million bucks.
Said Baby Face McGinty,
"Oh, I'm goin' places now!"

SONS: He dealt in booze—and how!
He never could keep a vow.
McGinty said,
As he raised Old Ned,
"Oh, I'm goin' places now;
Oh, I'm goin' places now!"

[*Ballet continues*]

SECTION 3

MAW: He won new territory
Each hour of the day.
Soon Baby was in his glory;
Ten gov'nors were in his pay.
He killed, he raped, he arsoned—
But never did he swing.
He put Jesse James right on the shelf;
The devil, he acted like God Hisself.*
Was none but feared McGinty,
And no one could do a thing.

SONS: McGinty, he was king
Of every goddamn thing;
He'd rape and kill
Night and day, but still,
No judge ever made him swing—
No judge ever made him swing.

[*Ballet continues*]

SECTION 4

MAW: "Get Baby Face McGinty!"
Said Mr. Morgenthau.
"He cheated on taxes, di'n't he?
That's one thing we can't allow!"
They got, they shot McGinty;
They never gave a damn.
For you're up against true ma-ni-acs,
When you don't pay up your income tax.

Original version of section 3, lines 8–10:
The tabloids thought he was God Himself.
The whole world feared McGinty,
And no one could do a thing.

The moral of McGinty*
Is: Don't cheat your Uncle Sam.

SONS: Oh, Baby Face McGinty—
On one thing he was lax;
The moral of McGinty
Is: Pay your income tax.

MAW: You may get away with murder—
ALL: But not on your income tax!
[*They wave flags*]
[*The lights go up on all participating as they wave American flags and sing:*]
So long, good-bye, McGinty—
On one thing you were lax:
You could get away with murder,
But not on your income tax.

PLEASE SEND MY DADDY BACK TO MOTHER

Introduced by Fannie Brice during the tryout. Dropped before the New York opening.

VERSE

Oh, Madame, please excuse me—†
But I hear you've a heart of gold;
I know you won't refuse me
When my story I have told.
I'm not here to preach a moral—
Though from you people turn away;
With your work I have no quarrel—
I am only here to say:

REFRAIN 1

Madame, please send my daddy back to Mother,
Away from this scarlet abode—
For to us he means more than any other,
While to you he's just a passing episode.
Oh, our home is gloomy and frightful
Since my daddy to you did roam;
Let your heart make you do what is rightful,
And please send my daddy back home.

Original version of section 4, lines 9–10:
The moral of McGinty
Is: Don't fool with Uncle Sam.
†*Earlier version of verse, lines 1–4:*
Please pardon this intrusion—
But I hear you've a heart of gold;
I'm covered with confusion,
But my story must be told.

RECITATION

There's no bread upon the table;
There's no rug down on the floor;
And our home is like a stable,
Which it wasn't, heretofore.

Oh, I know the great temptation
Which has led him to disgrace;
It's the fatal fascination
Of the music in this place.

For I've heard him tell my mother
That he loves the piano here—
That the tone is like no other,
And the notes are sweet and clear.

Though to him it is like magic
When your piano player plays,
Back at home our nights are tragic,
And it's been like that for days.

So I don't mean to distress you
But oh, Madame, can't you see
That the angels all will bless you
If you send him back to me?

I was once a child so cheerful
And my cheeks were rosy red,
But the future is so fearful
That I might as well be dead.

REFRAIN 2

Madame, please send my daddy back to Mother,
Away from this scarlet abode—
For to us he means more than any other,
While to you he's just a passing episode.
Oh, my mother really is worried,*
For it seems, if you must know the truth,
That it happened she first met my daddy
In a joint just like this in Duluth.

THE KNIFE THROWER'S WIFE

Introduced by Fannie Brice during the tryout. Dropped before the New York opening. Likely part of the David Freedman–Ira Gershwin sketch "The Knife Thrower."

Alternate version of refrain 2, lines 5–8:
Oh, our home is all in disorder
Since my daddy to you did roam—
For Mamma's taken up with the boarder
So please send my daddy back home!

VERSE

I'm sharpening knives for me husband
And I'm happy as I can be;
I'm sharpening knives for me husband
So he can throw them at me.
He throws 'em—but not 'cause he's angry—
We both earns our living that way.
I stand at the board
For me master and lord.
And he knifes me six times a day.

REFRAIN

From Brighton to Margate
I'm known as the target
Of the man who throws the knife.
They whiz by my gizzard,
My neck, and my arm—
But he's such a wizard,
It don't do much harm.
Though sometimes he'll clip off
A bit of my hip off,
There's no one to blame—
It's all in the game.
Of my luck there's no doubt, for
I find I'm cut out for
The life of a knife thrower's wife.

I'M SHARING MY WEALTH

Intended for *Ziegfeld Follies of 1936.* Unused. No music is known to survive.

[*Boys on soap boxes*]

BOYS: Oh, I'll share my final dollar;
I'll give in when people holler;
They want half my shirt and collar—
Sharing my wealth.

Why, I'll even share my liquor
To make this world happy quicker;
I'm just in no mood to dicker—
Sharing my wealth.

Share your smile
And just keep on giving;
They say that makes living
Worth the while.

But, dear, don't share any glances
With men who may make advances;
No, ma'am, I'm not taking chances—

There's a limit, dear,*
Let me make it clear:
I'm sharing no part of you.

Unused Lyric Fragments

Share and share alike;
Here's the note I strike;
Lead me to the mike

I'll share my coat when it's cold out
And help out those who are sold out,
But on one thing I must hold out:
Darling, I will share
Ev'rything I've got but you.

My platform
Takes that form
Which says, "Share the wealth!"
And that's why I'm here to specify.
I teach it—
I preach it—
I love to share the wealth.
It's ruining my health
But worth it.
So please come in reach if I
May make so bold—
Lady, listen and be told:

WISHING TREE OF HARLEM

Intended for *Ziegfeld Follies of 1936.* Unused. No music is known to survive.

I'm tired of hopeless hopin'—
Seekin', gropin',
[But] "No jobs open"—
Oh, Wishin' Tree of Harlem,
I'm depending on you.

Ill wind is blowin' 'round me—
Loves to hound me
Since he's found me—
Oh, Wishin' Tree of Harlem,
You just got to come through.

They tell me that with a touch
My luck is bound to change.
I really ain't askin' much;
Any old job that you can arrange.

Alternate version of this and the next line:
Money I won't miss,
Dear, but I know this:

Fed up with beggin', bummin'—
Start me hummin'
"Good Times Comin' "—
Oh, Wishin' Tree of Harlem,
Make that job come true—
Make that job come true.

Additional Lyric Fragments

He's gone, I dunno where to;
Didn't care to
Tell me where to—
Oh, Wishin' Tree of Harlem,
Show me what you can do.

Altho' he wasn't blameless—
Acted shameless—
Nights are aimless.

Oh, Wishin' Tree of Harlem,
You just got to come through.
Send that man back to me.

At 132nd Street and 7th Avenue—
Just touch it and make it a wish.

Up in Harlem there's a shrine
Where high yaller, black, and tan—
Even those who pass—
Come eager, hopeful.

All day I've been applyin'—
No denyin'—
I've been tryin'—
Oh, Wishin' Tree of Harlem,
I'm dependin' on you.

Tired of being turned down—
Weary of havin' my bridges burned down.

Bad luck is hangin' round me—
Loves to hound me
Since he's found me.

Things happen shouldn't happen—
Luck is nappin';
Dice keep crappin'.

WHY SAVE FOR THAT RAINY DAY?

Intended for *Ziegfeld Follies of 1936*. Unused. No music is known to survive.

VERSE

What's the use of saving for that rainy day
If the politicians take it all away?

Gets you nothing if you don't live while you
   may—
Up in heaven, you
Won't find a revenue
Man.
Fellow citizens, when I am pleasure-bent,
I can't bother with Ole Debble three percent.
And the charm of my act is
That I preach what I practice:

REFRAIN

Get my hatter! Call my tailor!
Let me spend like a drunken sailor!
It's insaney
To save for that rainy day.

Times are lovely! No more troubles
When you're drinking the wine that bubbles!
Get champagney!
Why save for that rainy day?

It's a short existence,
And you know we don't live twice;
Tell me—Are we men or mice?
Nothing but the high life
Need apply in my life.

Burning both ends of the candle,
Let's give parties till it's a scandal!
Play the zany!
To hell with that rainy day!

HOT NUMBER

Intended for *Ziegfeld Follies of 1936*, possibly for Josephine Baker. Unused. No music is known to survive.

VERSE

Last night I had a dream,
An' the game of policy was the theme.
The Good Lord spoke to me, he did state,
"Play eight hundred and eighty-eight!"

From my stockin' I pulled a buck,
An' I'm shootin' it all on Lady Luck;
An' when that number comes roun',
I'll be the number one gal in town.

REFRAIN

My money's on a hot number;
Heaven was good to me
An' picked me out a hot number
For the policy.

I know another hot number,
Handsome and tall and brown,
An' when I cash my hot number
Will we go to town!

No more sighin';
Blues defyin';
I'll get dressed up;
I'll show the rest up
When we go hi-de-hi-in'.

Professor, play a hot number!
Waiter, a quart of gin!
I'm gonna be a hot number
When my number comes in!

SUNDAY TAN

Intended for *Ziegfeld Follies of 1936*. Unused. No music is known to survive.

VERSE

When the city is sweltering,
The temp'rature high—
People go helter-skeltering
To Coney and Rye.
One and all,
Let them fall
For their Sunday at the beach.
If it's hot,
We've a spot
That is just in reach.
Really haven't far to go,
Climbing up three flights or so.

REFRAIN 1

In a chimney setting,
With you I'll be getting
My Sunday tan.

Through with daily labors,
Up there with the neighbors—
The rooftop clan.

Our records we will play—
Toscanini will serenade us—
We'll be okay
Every way,
For no heart is aloof
On the roof.

We can give the raspberry
To Newport and Asbury
The minute we plan

Parading in our undies—
Getting our Sund'y's tan.

REFRAIN 2

In a chimney setting,
With you I'll be getting
My Sunday tan.

Reading Sunday comics,
Exposing our stomics—
The rooftop clan.

We'll look quite recherché
In a setting of lovely clotheslines;
We'll be okay
Every way,
For no heart is aloof
On the roof.

Who needs Narragansett
When up here you can sit
Dressed up in a fan?
The deuce with Mrs. Grundy—
Let's get our Sunday tan.

There's Mr. Shepherd's place in Egypt—
That Negresco spot in Nice—
Where the tourists love to be gypped
Thirty bucks a day apiece.
You can keep that place in Montauk
Even though it's fireproof.
You can pay more
At the Ritz or the Traymore,
But we prefer our roof.
[Oh yeah?]

OH, BRING BACK THE BALLET AGAIN

Intended for *Ziegfeld Follies of 1936*. Unused. No music is known to survive.

Oh, bring back the old-fashioned ballet;
Oh, save us from rhythm of jazz!
Oh, bring back the old-fashioned ballet—
The charm that Pavlova's "Dying Swan" has.
The music of paintings by Degas—
Not discords by pigs in a pen.
The charm of Nijinsky
Minus Stravinsky—
Oh, bring back the ballet again!

THE BETTER HALF KNOWS BETTER

Intended for *Ziegfeld Follies of 1936*, likely for Fannie Brice. Unused. No music is known to survive.

VERSE

Listen to the man with the high silk hat,
Six-inch collar, and gray cravat—
A front-page name of worldwide fame—
Darned important and all of that—
He's a big man—a big man.
You read about him every day:
From Maine to Californ-i-a—a big man.
Half an hour later, when he's at home,
A hot-water bottle propped against his dome,
His wifie sees him sitting there
In his baggy, fleece-lined underwear.
He's a big shot in public life
But he's no big shot to his wife.

REFRAIN

Ev'ryone thinks he's aces—
A dynamo and go-getter—
Napoleon and Baruch in one—
But his better half knows better.

Posing in public places—
Political baby-petter—
Sadie Glutz thinks that he's the nuts—
But his better half knows better.

Crowds may think he's dynamite,
But get his wife's report:
When they're all alone at night,
She'd like to sell him short.

Ev'ryone thinks he's aces—
Popular East and West—
People feel he's a man of steel—
But it's just a laugh
To his better half,
For his better half knows best.

The instances are ample
In ev'ry sphere of life.
Let's listen, for example,
To a famous comic's wife:

INTERLUDE

My name is Mrs. Cantor. You've heard of me, no doubt:

I'm the well-known Ida that Eddie keeps talking about.
What's that? You don't like him on the radio?
What right have you to speak?
You only hear him on Sunday.
I get those gags all week.
All we've got is daughters—five of them—
After twenty years' communion.
The only way he can get a boy
Is to call the Western Union.
But I think he's great in pictures,
And I like the money it yields.
Who is my favorite comic?
Mr. W. C. Fields.
[*Voices:* "We want Cantor! We want Cantor!"]
You want him? You can have him.
I'll take a gin physic.

I USED TO BE ABOVE LOVE

Published May 1936. Possibly intended for *Ziegfeld Follies of 1936*. Unused.

VERSE

Once I used to keep love at a distance;
Now I know I made a sad mistake.
Thanks to you I found a new existence;
Thanks to you I'm now awake.

REFRAIN

I used to be above love;
No kiss ever made me thrill.
But since meeting you I love love
And I always will.

Dear one, when you embrace me,
My heart sounds like fire alarms.
From now on no one can chase me
Away from your arms.

Oh, oh, oh, oh! What I've been missing!
Oh, fool that I was!
There's heaven in kissing!
Kiss me and then
Let's try it again.

I used to be above love;
No chills up and down my spine.
But since meeting you I love love;
You've made it divine.

OPPOSITE: *Ginger Rogers and Fred Astaire*

SHALL WE
DANCE
1937

A film produced by Pandro S. Berman for RKO Pictures. Released in May 1937. Music by George Gershwin. Screenplay by Allan Scott and Ernest Pagano, based on the story "Watch Your Step" by Lee Loeb and Harold Buchman. Directed by Mark Sandrich. Dances by Hermes Pan and Harry Losee. Music conducted by Nathaniel Shilkret. Orchestrations by Nathaniel Shilkret and Robert Russell Bennett. Cast, starring Fred Astaire (Petroff) and Ginger Rogers (Linda Keene), featured Edward Everett Horton (Baird), Eric Blore (Cecil Flintridge), and Harriet Hoctor.

SLAP THAT BASS

Published February 1937. Previously registered for copyright as an unpublished song November 1936. Introduced by Fred Astaire (Petroff) and Dudley Dickerson, a member of the engine room crew, "against the background of a transatlantic-liner engine room, and to the cadence of its pulsating machinery" (Ira Gershwin—*Lyrics on Several Occasions*).

Embarrassing Moment. Sunday nights at the old Trocadero Club in Hollywood were a sort of showcase for new and generally unknown talent the various studios had just signed. I was there the night a little thirteen-year-old-girl singer from MGM, accompanied at the piano by her bespectacled mother, was cheered by the professional audience after each of three songs. Then came the announcement that Miss Judy Garland's next number would be "Slap That Bass." Startled, I turned to producer Pandro Berman with a look that could mean only: "What's *this?* Where'd she get *that?*" (All the work on the film *Shall We Dance* hadn't as yet been completed; "Slap That Bass" was in, but, other than those at our table, who knew it?)

Judy hadn't sung eight bars before we again gave one another looks of "What's *this?*" It wasn't our number at all. Soon one table companion grinned at me; another winked—intimating wasn't I the sly one trying to put over someone else's title. I was not only embarrassed but concerned; perhaps a new effort was in order, so I paid little attention to the rest of the program. By the time we left, however, reason had overcome fluster. You can't copyright titles, and other than the title the two songs had nothing whatever in common. So our "Slap That Bass" stayed put.

Over the years several million songs have been published; and since titles as such aren't copyrightable, identicals among them are bound to occur. Now and then there is a plagiarism suit, but these are usually based on the melodic line—scarcely ever on lyric line or title. (See note to "Shall We Dance.") But if damage or possible harm—not merely vanity or irritation—is at stake (e.g.,

if someone had the temerity to publish a new song called "Old Man River") it's more than likely the courts could estop the Johnny-come-lately.

—from *Lyrics on Several Occasions*

VERSE

Zoom—zoom, zoom—zoom,
The world is in a mess.
With politics and taxes
And people grinding axes,
There's no happiness.

Zoom—zoom, zoom—zoom,
Rhythm, lead your ace!
The future doesn't fret me
If I can only get me
Someone to slap that bass.

Happiness is not a riddle
When I'm list'ning to that big bass fiddle.

REFRAIN

Slap that bass—
Slap it till it's dizzy.
Slap that bass—
Keep the rhythm busy.
Zoom, zoom, zoom—
Misery—you got to go.

Slap that bass—
Use it like a tonic.
Slap that bass—
Keep your Philharmonic.
Zoom, zoom, zoom—
And the milk and honey'll flow!

Dictators would be better off
If they zoom-zoomed now and then;
Today you can see that the happiest men
All got rhythm.

In which case,
If you want to bubble—
Slap that bass;
Slap away your trouble.
Learn to zoom, zoom, zoom—
Slap that bass!

(I'VE GOT) BEGINNER'S LUCK

Published February 1937. Previously registered for copyright as an unpublished song November 1936. Introduced by Fred Astaire (Petroff).

VERSE

At any gambling casino
From Monte Carlo to Reno,
They tell you that a beginner
Comes out a winner.
Beginner fishing for flounder
Will catch a seventeen-pounder.
That's what I always heard
And always thought absurd,
But now I believe ev'ry word.
For—

REFRAIN

I've got beginner's luck:
The first time that I'm in love,
I'm in love with you.
(Gosh, I'm lucky!)
I've got beginner's luck:
There never was such a smile
Or such eyes of blue!*
(Gosh, I'm fortunate!)
This thing we've begun
Is much more than a pastime,
For this time is the one
Where the first time is the last time!
I've got beginner's luck,
Lucky through and through,
'Cause the first time that I'm in love,
I'm in love with you.

THEY ALL LAUGHED

Published February 1937. Previously registered for copyright as an unpublished song November 1936. Introduced by Ginger Rogers (Linda), danced by Rogers and Fred Astaire (Petroff).

In the Twenties not only the stock market but the self-improvement business boomed. One correspondence-school advertisement, for instance, featured "They all laughed when I sat down to play the piano." Along this line, I recall writing a postcard from Paris to Gilbert Gabriel, the drama critic, saying: "They all laughed at the Tour d'Argent last night when I said I would order in French." So the phrase "they all laughed" hibernated and estivated in the back of my

*On the Fred Astaire/Johnny Green recording there is a second refrain with the lines:
They tell me beginners win,
Now I know it's true.

mind for a dozen years until the right climate and tune popped it out as a title.

This lyric is an example of the left-field or circuitous approach to the subject preponderant in Songdom. I believe it was George S. Kaufman (in Hollywood at the time) who, when we played him this one, interrupted us after the lines,

> They told Marconi
> Wireless was a phony—
> It's the same old cry!

and wondered aloud: "Don't tell me this is going to be a love song!" We assured him that that was the intention; and on hearing the catalytic line, "They laughed at me wanting you," he shook his head resignedly and said: "Oh, well."

—from *Lyrics on Several Occasions*

VERSE

The odds were a hundred to one against me,
The world thought the heights were too high to climb.
But people from Missouri never incensed me:
Oh, I wasn't a bit concerned,
For from hist'ry I had learned
How many, many times the worm had turned.

REFRAIN 1

They all laughed at Christopher Columbus
When he said the world was round;
They all laughed when Edison recorded sound.

They all laughed at Wilbur and his brother
When they said that man could fly;
They told Marconi
Wireless was a phony—
It's the same old cry!

They laughed at me wanting you,
Said I was reaching for the moon;
But oh, you came through—
Now they'll have to change their tune.

They all said we never could be happy,
They laughed at us—and how!
But ho, ho, ho—
Who's got the last laugh now!

REFRAIN 2

They all laughed at Rockefeller Center—
Now they're fighting to get in;
They all laughed at Whitney and his cotton gin.

They all laughed at Fulton and his steamboat,
Hershey and his choc'late bar.
Ford and his Lizzie

Kept the laughers busy—
That's how people are!

They laughed at me wanting you—
Said it would be Hello! Good-bye!
But oh, you came through—
Now they're eating humble pie.

They all said we'd never get together—
Darling, let's take a bow,
For ho, ho, ho—
Who's got the last laugh—
He, he, he—
Let's at the past laugh—
Ha, ha, ha—
Who's got the last laugh now?

LET'S CALL THE WHOLE THING OFF

Published February 1937. Previously registered for copyright as an unpublished song November 1936. Introduced by Fred Astaire (Petroff) and Ginger Rogers (Linda).

Many years ago a friend of mine was in London, where, among other activities, he sat in on a couple of chorus-girl calls. At the first audition one of the young ladies gave a copy of this song to the pianist, then sang:

> You say eyether and I say eyether,
> You say nyther and I say nyther;
> Eyether, eyether, nyther, nyther—
> Let's call the whole thing off!

Apparently this sort of thing was quite pronounced that London season. At another audition he listened to a girl doing "Do, Do, Do," but in her pronunciation it became "Doe, Doe, Doe." Evidently she was insistently musical and believed that our repetitive "do" meant the first note of the scale.

Preoccupation with these particular pronunciations must go far back with me, because I still clearly remember the story our 6B teacher in P.S. 20, New York, told the class when she digressed for a moment in a spelling session. It concerned an American and an Englishman arguing about the correct pronunciation of "neither," with the American insisting on "neether," the Englishman on "nyther." They called on a bystander to settle the dispute: Was it "neether" or "nyther"? "Nayther!" said—who else?—the Irishman.

May I conclude with a note of phonic and marital tolerance on the parts of Mr. and Mrs. Ira Gershwin? We

have been married over thirty years, and the pronunciations taught us in our youth still persist: my wife still "eyethers" and "tomahtoes" me, while I "eether" and "tomato" her.

—from *Lyrics on Several Occasions*

VERSE

Things have come to a pretty pass—
Our romance is growing flat,
For you like this and the other,
While I go for this and that.
Goodness knows what the end will be;
Oh, I don't know where I'm at. . . .
It looks as if we two will never be one.
Something must be done.

REFRAIN 1

You say eether and I say eyether,
You say neether and I say nyther;
Eether, eyether, neether, nyther—
Let's call the whole thing off!

You like potato and I like po-tah-to;
You like tomato and I like to-mah-to;
Potato, po-tah-to, tomato, to-mah-to—
Let's call the whole thing off!

But oh, if we call the whole thing off, then we must part.
And oh, if we ever part, then that might break my heart.

So, if you like pajamas and I like pa-jah-mas,
I'll wear pajamas and give up pa-jah-mas.
For we know we
Need each other, so we
Better call the calling off off.
Let's call the whole thing off!

REFRAIN 2

You say laughter and I say lawfter,
You say after and I say awfter;
Laughter, lawfter, after, awfter—
Let's call the whole thing off!

You like vanilla and I like vanella,
You, sa's'parilla and I sa's'parella;
Vanilla, vanella, choc'late, strawb'ry—
Let's call the whole thing off!

But oh, if we call the whole thing off, then we must part.
And oh, if we ever part, then that might break my heart.

So, if you go for oysters and I go for ersters,
I'll order oysters and cancel the ersters.

For we know we
Need each other, so we
Better call the calling off off.
Let's call the whole thing off!

Refrain 3 was not in the film,* but was given to a young American song-and-dance team to use as an encore in their night-club act—if they had enough breath left:

3

I say father and you say pater,
I say mother and you say mater;
Father, mother, auntie, uncle—
Let's call the whole thing off!

I like banana and you like ba-nahn-ah,
I say Havana and I get Ha-vahn-ah;
Banana, ba-nahn-ah, Havana, Ha-vahn-ah—
Never a happy medium!

But oh, &c.

So, if I go for scallops and you go for lobster,
No more discussion—we both order lobster.
For we &c.

—from *Lyrics on Several Occasions*

THEY CAN'T TAKE THAT AWAY FROM ME

Published February 1937. Previously registered for copyright as an unpublished song November 1936. Sung by Fred Astaire (Petroff) "to Ginger Rogers [Linda] on the ferry to Hoboken" (Ira Gershwin—*Lyrics on Several Occasions*).

They Can't Take That Away from Me. After George had composed *Porgy and Bess* for eleven months and then orchestrated it for nine, the royalties from the original company brought him a sum just about equal to the cost of copying the parts for the pit musicians. (Incidentally, my contributions to *P&B* required nowhere near the time George needed, and I was able to work on two other properties during the twenty months.) With no new project around proving of interest, George felt Hollywood should be our next step, and he got in touch with an agent. After a couple of weeks the agent wired that, so far, there were no takers, that since George had just written an opera he was now considered a highbrow.

---

*Actually, I.G. misremembered. Ginger Rogers does sing the banana-Havana couplet in the film.

George wired back: "I have written hit songs in the past and I expect to do so in the future." And they couldn't take that away from him.

—from *The George and Ira Gershwin Song Book*

Studying this lyric, I see that the release could have been improved to:

We may never, never meet again
On the bumpy road to love,
Still I don't know when
I won't be thinking of—
The way you hold your knife . . .

which would rhyme "again" and "when" on important notes where no rhyme now exists; also, the sequence "I don't know when I won't" contains a double negative, a form of phrasing I sometimes find myself favoring over a simple affirmative.

Half an hour later. If the above had occurred to me originally, I'd have kept it. But now after some reflection—no dice. Despite the rhyme and the indirect affirmative, "always, always" following "never, never," plus all the "No, no!"'s make a better-balanced refrain. So, *stet!*

"They Can't Take That Away from Me" was a Best Song nominee in the Academy of Motion Picture Arts and Sciences "Oscar" awards. And since then, if I check correctly, only two others of mine have been nominated: "Long Ago and Far Away" and "The Man That Got Away." These three songs have two things in common: (1) in the final voting none won; and (2) the title of each contains the word "away." So? So—away with "away"?

—from *Lyrics on Several Occasions*

VERSE

Our romance won't end on a sorrowful note,
Though by tomorrow you're gone;
The song is ended, but as the songwriter
    wrote,
"The melody lingers on."
They may take you from me,
I'll miss your fond caress.
But though they take you from me,
I'll still possess:

REFRAIN

The way you wear your hat,
The way you sip your tea,
The mem'ry of all that—
No, no! They can't take that away from me!

The way your smile just beams,
The way you sing off key,

The way you haunt my dreams—
No, no! They can't take that away from me!

We may never, never meet again
On the bumpy road to love,
Still I'll always, always keep
The mem'ry of—

The way you hold your knife,
The way we danced till three,
The way you've changed my life—
No, no! They can't take that away from me!
No! They can't take that away from me!

SHALL WE DANCE?

Published March 1937. Introduced by Fred Astaire (Petroff). A late addition to the score, it replaced "Wake Up, Brother, and Dance."

This simple lyric reads as though it might be an exercise in Basic English; certainly not an emanation of the "time's a-fleeting" boys from Horace to Herrick. But the distinctive tune it was fitted to brings to the listener (me, anyway) an overtone of moody and urgent solicitude.

The Lady from Montana. When *Stepping Toes*, the original name for the script we were working from, was changed to *Shall We Dance*, the producer asked for a title song, and this one resulted. Five or six weeks later we were still at work at RKO when the legal department telephoned that there was trouble: a woman in Montana threatened to sue because she had written a waltz called "Shall We Dance," which hadn't been published but had been played once on a radio station in Butte. Legal departments of the studios worry a great deal—the film industry being particularly vulnerable to, and apprehensive of, nuisance litigation—so we got in touch with our publisher's lawyer in New York. Investigation through the Copyright Office showed registration over the years of at least half a dozen songs called "Shall We Dance." That fact did not stop the RKO legal department's head-shaking; they continued to worry.

I never did find out who worked it out, or how; but do recall that the settlement was a charming one: RKO would permit the publication of the Montanan "Shall We Dance" if its composer could find a publisher; also, on her next visit to her married daughter in Los Angeles, the studio would see that she got two admissions to any theater showing the film at the time.

—from *Lyrics on Several Occasions*

Drop that long face! Come on, have your fling!
Why keep nursing the blues?
If you want this old world on a string,
Put on your dancing shoes—
Stop wasting time!
Put on your dancing shoes—
Watch your spirits climb.

REFRAIN

Shall we dance, or keep on moping?
Shall we dance, and walk on air?
Shall we give in to despair—
Or shall we dance with never a care?

Life is short; we're growing older.
Don't you be an also-ran.
You'd better dance, little lady!
Dance, little man!
Dance whenever you can!

HI-HO!

Published December 1967. Previously registered for copyright as an unpublished song November 1936. Intended for Fred Astaire (Petroff). Dropped from the score before production. Alternate title: "Hi-Ho! I've Got It."

In August 1936 my brother and I flew to California to work for RKO-Radio Pictures on an Astaire-Rogers film called *Shall We Dance.* Before my wife found a suitable house for us, George had a piano installed in our suite at the Beverly-Wilshire Hotel in Beverly Hills. The first song we worked on was a piece not called for in the script but an idea we had for the opening of the picture: "Fred Astaire sees on a Paris kiosk the picture-poster of Ginger Rogers, an American girl then entertaining in Paris, and immediately feels: THIS IS SHE! He dances through the streets, extolling to everyone the beauty and virtues of this girl whom he has never met, but whose picture he sees pasted on walls and kiosks everywhere." When we submitted the completed song to Pandro Berman, the producer, and Mark Sandrich, the director, Mark said, "This is real $4.40 stuff and I'm crazy about it." ($4.40 was then the top price for most Broadway

musicals.) When it came time to figure production costs, however, the film's budget couldn't stand the cost of the sets for this number ($55,000 in those Depression years—somewhat more than my brother and I together received for the entire score), and reluctantly the management decided to forgo "Hi-Ho!" So the song has been unknown except to a few of our friends, like Oscar Levant, Harold Arlen, and S. N. Behrman, who were around at the time, and to a few others who in the years since have learned of its existence. Like them, I feel that it's about time the song was published.

—Ira Gershwin
(quoted in *The Gershwins*)

Hi-ho! Hi-ho!
At last it seems I've found her;
Now I won't be happy till my arms are around her.
Hi-ho! Ho-hi!
If a kiss she'd only throw me—Oh me! Oh my!
Her charm! Her smile so sweet and dimply!
I want them or I'll simply die!
Hi-ho! Hi-ho! Oh—
There's no one like her here on earth below.
Perhaps I'm reaching too high. Hi-ho!
Hi-ho!

Please pardon me, sir,
But I'm in love with her—
And if you knew her, sir,
Then so would you
Be in love with her, too!

I beg of you, ma'am—
Look at this honey lamb;
Now that you've seen her, ma'am,
Don't you agree
No one's lovely as she?

She's lovely!
No one lovelier,
No one lovelier
Than she.

Hi-ho! Hi-ho!
For me there's none can top her;
Even if you offered Venus I wouldn't swap her.
Hi-ho! Ho-hi!
Will I ever be her Romeo? Me oh my!
Her eyes! They thrill and then they mock you—
My heart they'll always occupy!
Hi-ho! Hi-ho! Oh—

There's no one like her here on earth below.
Perhaps I'm reaching too high. Hi-ho!
Hi-ho!
I've got it! She's got me!
Haven't met her yet.
But I hope to. Hi-ho!

WAKE UP, BROTHER, AND DANCE

Published February 1937—professional copies only. Previously registered for copyright as an unpublished song January 1937. Intended for Fred Astaire (Petroff). Dropped from the score before production and replaced with "Shall We Dance?" The music was later adapted for "Sophia" (*Kiss Me, Stupid*—1964).

VERSE

Crash those cymbals!
Blow those trumpets!
Mister Maestro, start your beat!
Give me action
And excitement—
Music, rhythm, dancing feet!
That's what it takes to lose those wrinkles.
Wake up! Why should we be a lot of Rip Van Winkles?

REFRAIN

If the goblins have got you
And you're feeling you're not you—
Take a tip that's the topper:
Wake up, brother, and dance!

Lady Luck may desert you;
Don't let that disconcert you—
Why should you come a cropper?
Wake up, brother, and dance!

Don't cry, don't be a mourner!
You find the minute that you go into your dance
You've turned the corner.

So I say in conclusion,
Don't give trouble a chance—
Wake up, brother, and dance!

OVERLEAF: *Fred Astaire, Gracie Allen, and George Burns*

A DAMSEL IN DISTRESS | 1937

A film produced by Pandro S. Berman for RKO Pictures. Released in November 1937. Music by George Gershwin. Screenplay by P. G. Wodehouse, Ernest Pagano, and S. K. Lauren, adapted from a Wodehouse story. Directed by George Stevens. Dances by Hermes Pan. Music conducted by Victor Baravalle. Orchestrations by Robert Russell Bennett. Vocal arrangements by Ray Noble and George Bassman. Cast, starring Fred Astaire (Jerry), George Burns (George), and Gracie Allen (Gracie), featured Joan Fontaine (Lady Alyce), Reginald Gardiner (Keggs), and Ray Noble (Reggie).

I CAN'T BE BOTHERED NOW

Published September 1937. Previously registered for copyright as an unpublished song May 1937. Introduced by Fred Astaire (Jerry).

VERSE

Music is the magic that makes everything
    sunshiny;
Dancing makes my troubles all seem tiny.
When I'm dancing I don't care if this old world
    stops turning,
Or if my bank is burning,
Or even if Roumania
Wants to fight Albania.
I'm not upset;
I refuse to fret.

REFRAIN

Bad news, go 'way!
Call 'round some day
In March or May—
I can't be bothered now.

My bonds and shares
May fall downstairs—
Who cares? Who cares?
I'm dancing and I can't be bothered now.

I'm up among the stars;
On earthly things I frown.
I'm throwing off the bars
That held me down.

I'll pay the piper
When times are riper.
Just now, I shan't—
Because you see I'm dancing and I can't—
Be bothered now.

THE JOLLY TAR AND THE MILKMAID

Published October 1937. Previously registered for copyright as an unpublished song May 1937. Introduced by Fred Astaire (Jerry) with Jan Duggan, Mary Dean, Pearl Amatore, Betty Rone (members of the Belpher Society for the Preservation of Traditional English Ballads, Madrigals, and Rounds), and ensemble. Alternate title: "The Mother of Three."

Without Appreciable Meaning." The introduction of a group of madrigal singers in *Damsel in Distress* permitted the writing of a couple of pieces in the style, and with the flavor, of several centuries ago. In "The Jolly Tar and the Milkmaid" we tried for the feel of an English eighteenth-century light ballad. The "With a hey and a nonny" and "With a down-a, down-a-derry" inclusions, though, are refrain phrases ordinarily associated with songs of an earlier period. These and similar sixteenth-century phrases were attached to the stanzas of many songs for jingle quality and singability. They made little or no sense otherwise. For, according to *The Oxford English Dictionary*, "derry" (the year 1553 its first appearance in print) was "a meaningless word in the refrains of popular songs"; "down," as an adverb (1598), "used in ballad refrains without appreciable meaning"; and "nonny-nonny" (1533) "a meaningless refrain often used to cover indelicate allusions."
—from *Lyrics on Several Occasions*

VERSE 1

There was a jolly British tar
Who met a milkmaid bonny.
He said, "How beautiful you are."
With a hey and a nonny,
With a hey and a nonny.
"Such golden hair I ne'er did see,
With lips to shame the cherry—
Oh, buxom milkmaid, marry me!"
With a down-a-derry,
With a down-a, down-a-derry.

REFRAIN 1

"Our hearts could rhyme," said she.
" 'Tis flattered I'm," said she,
"But oh, ah me,
You see, you see,
You see, you see
I happen to be,
I happen to be
The mother of three,

A wife already
And mother of three,
Of three, of three, of three, of three, of three—
The mother of three!"

VERSE 2

The jolly tar, he laughed a laugh.
" 'Tis for the best, my bonny,
That you won't be my better half."
With a hey and a nonny,
With a hey and a nonny.
"I near forgot on seeing you
That I've a wife in Kerry,
In Spain, and also Timbuktu."
With a down-a-derry,
With a down-a, down-a-derry.

REFRAIN 2

"You've got me thinkin' twice;
Good-bye to shoes and rice,
For oh, ah me,
Just now, you see,
Just now, you see
I happen to be,
I happen to be
The husband of three
A-spliced already
And husband of three,
Of three, of three, of three, of three, of three—
The husband of three!"

PUT ME TO THE TEST

Registered for copyright as an unpublished song May 1937. Danced to but not sung by Fred Astaire (Jerry), George Burns (George), and Gracie Allen (Gracie). No. 100 in George and Ira Gershwin Special Numbered Song File. The unused lyric (somewhat revised) was reset by Jerome Kern for the film *Cover Girl* (1944) and published February 1944.

VERSE

The days of the knights of old are gone,
But chivalry still carries on.
I wear no armor,
But oh, fair charmer,
I'm ready to give my all.
In other words, I'm at your beck and call.

REFRAIN 1

Put me to the test
And I'll climb you the highest mountain,
Or I'll swim you Radio City Fountain.
Put me to the test
And I'll bag you a Bengal tiger
Or a crocodile from the River Niger.
It'll be a trifle
To jump off the Eiffel
If that is what my lady adores.
Just make your request,
Lady, put me to the test
And anything that you desire is yours!

PATTER

Test me! Put me on my mettle!
How would you like a snowball from
    Popocatepetl!
How would you like me wearing Gandhi's apparel?
For you I'd even jump Niag'ra Falls in a barrel!
Put me to the test!
How would you like to have your relatives
    overpow'red
Or opening-night tickets for a show by Noël
    Coward?
If you'd like a blossom from the base of
    Fujiyama,
I'll get it if I have to swim from here to
    Yokohama.
Anything that you suggest is yours;
Anything that you request is yours.

REFRAIN 2

Put me to the test,
And I'll get you a queen's tiara,
Or a pyramid from the hot Sahara.
Put me to the test,
And I'll ride you the Derby winner,
Or I'll get you Greta Garbo for dinner.
If your fortunes are low
I'll break Monte Carlo!
(With me it never rains but it pours!)
Just make your request,
Lady, put me to the test
And anything that you desire is yours!

STIFF UPPER LIP

Published November 1937. Previously registered for
copyright as an unpublished song May 1937. Introduced
by Gracie Allen (Gracie).

Surprise. When I did this lyric twenty-two years ago
I remembered "muddle through" as a Briticism—
sometimes of criticism, sometimes of resolution—much
used at the time of World War I. (Almost as prevalent
as World War II's term of approval, "good show.")
Then, from various characters in Wodehouse, came
phrases like "pip-pip," "toodle-oo," and "stout fella."
And whether Englishmen actually greeted each other or
not with "old bean" or "old fluff" or "old tin of fruit"
didn't matter frightfully—we had been conditioned by
vaudevillians and comic weeklies to think they did.

Recently I had occasion (the occasion being this note)
to look up "muddle through" and "stiff upper lip." And
"muddle through" is all right: it goes back to England's
statesman and orator John Bright, who used it in a
speech in the 1860's. But as for my lyric's title, "Stiff
Upper Lip"—I find—big surprise to me—that it's an
Americanism. The *Oxford English Dictionary* has this
1833 quote from *The Down Easters*, by American novelist John Neal: "What's the use of boo-hooin'? Keep a
stiff upper lip. . . ." And *A Dictionary of Americanisms*
has an even earlier quote (1815) from a Boston newspaper called *Massachusetts Spy:* "I kept a stiff upper
lip. . . ." So my believing it a Briticism was wrong by the
better half of a century; for according to the research of
British philologist Eric Partridge, the phrase was
adopted by the English only about 1880.
            —from *Lyrics on Several Occasions*

VERSE

What made Good Queen Bess
Such a great success?
What made Wellington do
What he did at Waterloo?
What makes every Englishman
A fighter through and through?
It isn't roast beef or ale or home or mother;
It's just a little thing they sing to one another:

REFRAIN 1

Stiff upper lip! Stout fella!
Carry on, old fluff!
Chin up! Keep muddling through!
Stiff upper lip! Stout fella!
When the going's rough—
Pip-pip to Old Man Trouble—and a toodle-oo,
    too!

Carry on through thick and thin
If you feel you're in the right.
Does the fighting spirit win?
Quite, quite, quite, quite, quite!

Stiff upper lip! Stout fella!
When you're in a stew—
Sober or blotto,
This is your motto:
Keep muddling through!

REFRAIN 2

Stiff upper lip! Stout fella!
Carry on, old bean!
Chin up! Keep muddling through!
Stiff upper lip! Stout fella!
Dash it all—I mean
Pip-pip to Old Man Trouble—and a toodle-oo,
    too!

When a bounder starts to hiss,
You must give him blow for blow.
Make the blighter cry, "What's this?
'Ullo, 'ullo, 'ullo, 'ullo, 'ullo!"

Stiff upper lip! Stout fella!
With a derring-do!
Sober or blotto,
This is your motto:
Keep muddling through!

THINGS ARE LOOKING UP

Published September 1937. Previously registered for
copyright as an unpublished song May 1937. Introduced
by Fred Astaire (Jerry). "Sung . . . to Joan Fontaine
[Alyce] on the downs of Totleigh Castle, located in
Upper-Pelham-Grenville, Wodehouse, England" (Ira
Gershwin—*Lyrics on Several Occasions*).

Parental Note. Although this song never reached
anywhere near as many ears as, say, "A Foggy Day"
from the same film, it is based on a good title and a
graceful tune; and I like it. For that matter, I like the
majority of the songs I have been connected with. And
I can't conceive of any songwriter not feeling the same
way about his output. The marriage of words and music
gives birth over the years to a catalogful of progeny.
Many of the offspring turn out to be lame and halting, or
too frenetic, or over-sophisticated, or something. But the
parents manage generally to find some excuse for, even
some endearing quality in, these disappointers: *This* one
was ahead of its time; *that* one stammered a bit—true—
but did sing like an angel; *yonder* got into bad hands,
&c. Metaphorical excursion over, over to the over-all
point:

Next to the antecedence of words or music, the question most frequently asked is: "What's your own favorite
song?" And the favorite answer of some writers is: "The
latest one." But generally, and more truthful, is: "Most
of them."

Losing the Rhyme. The reader or reciter of rhymed poetry is of course more concerned with meaning than with rhyme, so naturally doesn't pause at the end of a run-on line to emphasize the rhyming. In entertainment song, though, I feel that rhyme, even in a run-on couplet, ought to be observed—or at least not negated—especially when the music calls for pause or breath. An example of this perhaps not too important point shows up in a recent recording of "Things Are Looking Up." The vocalist sings the vest thus:

And it seems that suddenly—
I've become the happiest man alive.

Personally I'd rather hear:

And it seems that suddenly I've—
Become the happiest man alive.
          —from *Lyrics on Several Occasions*

VERSE

If I should suddenly start to sing
Or stand on my head—or anything,
Don't think that I've lost my senses;
It's just that my happiness finally commences.
The long, long ages of dull despair
Are turning into thin air,
And it seems that suddenly I've
Become the happiest man alive.

REFRAIN

Things are looking up!
I've been looking the landscape over*
And it's covered with four-leaf clover.
Oh, things are looking up
Since love looked up at me.

Bitter was my cup—
But no more will I be the mourner,
For I've certainly turned the corner.
Oh, things are looking up
Since love looked up at me.

See the sunbeams—
Ev'ry one beams
Just because of you.
Love's in session,
And my depression
Is unmistakably through.

Things are looking up!
It's a great little world we live in!

Original version of refrain, lines 2–4:
And I don't mean my stocks are moving,
And I don't mean my health's improving,
But things are looking up

Oh, I'm happy as a pup
Since love looked up
At me.

SING OF SPRING

Registered for copyright as an unpublished song May 1937. Introduced by Jan Duggan (Madrigal Singer) and ensemble. Reworked from an unused piece: "Back to Bach."

---

*A*dditional Uttered Nonsense. I have just spent the afternoon leafing through the thousand or so songs in D'Urfey's six-volume collection, *Pills to Purge Melancholy* (published 1719–20), to see how frequently various meaningless but singable phrases occurred in that period. Well, most of the songs use the short refrain, but most of these are meaningful (far too much so—unless one is an Erotica buff). Fixing upon only the innocuous, I find that the Elizabethan "hey nonny" and such were by then on the wane. The most favored refrain in the collection—some twenty songs use it—seems to have been "with a fa la la . . ." (incid., "fal la la" was a favorite refrain with Gilbert and Sullivan). Other of the innocent burthens in D'Urfey are: "with a hey ding, hoe ding, derry, derry, ding," "with a fadariddle la . . . ," "fa la la, lanky downdilly," "hey troly loly lo," and "with a humbledum grumbledum hey." Not forgetting an exuberant "huggle duggle, ha! ha! ha!"

The use of the easily assimilable nonsense phrase in song is of course not limited to the British, Irish, and Scottish. Hundreds of examples can be found in nineteenth- and twentieth-century American song. Offhand: "doodah, doodah," "yip i addy i ay," "ja da, ja da, jing, jing, jing," all the variants of "ho de ho" and "hi de hi," &c., &c. These are not necessarily all used as refrains—they may be titles, interjections, responses, or whatever. A longish example of the phrase-for-sound-alone's-sake is "It Ain't Necessarily So" 's "Wadoo! Zim bam boddle-oo! Hoodle ah da wah da! Scatty wah!"

Dramatist Thomas D'Urfey (1653–1723) included a number of his own songs in *Pills to Purge Melancholy.* And I cannot take leave of the collection without quoting the charmingly informative heading to one of them: "Advice to the City, a famous Song, set to a tune of Signior Opdar, so remarkable, that I had the Honour to Sing it with King Charles at Windsor; He holding one part of the Paper with Me."
          —from *Lyrics on Several Occasions*

Spring is here;
Sing "Willy-wally-willo!"
Spring is here;
Sing "Tilly-tally-tillo!"
Winter's past—
Tra la li lo!
The shepherd, free at last,
Sings "Piminy mo!
Jug-a, jug-a, jug!"
Spring appears;
The plowboy starts to carol;
Spring appears;
We don our gay apparel
And fa la la—
We all rejoice!
Come, lift up every voice
And sing of spring!

A FOGGY DAY (IN LONDON TOWN)

Published September 1937. Previously registered for copyright as an unpublished song May 1937. Introduced by Fred Astaire (Jerry).

---

*F*rom an Album Jacket: "Early in 1937 . . . Beverly Hills . . . *A Damsel in Distress.* We had finished three or four songs. One night I was in the living room, reading. About 1 a.m. George returned from a party . . . took off his dinner jacket, sat down at the piano. . . . 'How about some work? Got any ideas?' 'Well, there's one spot we might do something about a fog . . . how about *a foggy day in London* or maybe *foggy day in London Town?*' 'Sounds good. . . . I like it better with *town*' and he was off immediately on the melody. We finished the refrain, words and music, in less than an hour. ('Do, Do, Do' is the only other . . . in so short a time.) Next day the song still sounded good so we started on a verse."

Re Next Day and the Verse: All I had to say was: "George, how about an Irish verse?" and he sensed instantly the degree of wistful loneliness I meant. Generally, whatever mood I thought was required, he, through his instinct and inventiveness, could bring my hazy musical vision into focus. Needless to say, this sort of affinity between composer and lyricist comes only after long association between the two.

There was a different kind of musical communication between George and his earliest Broadway producer. Alex Aarons was quite musical himself and had faith enough to sign George at nineteen for *La, La, Lucille.*

Alex was fond at the time of at least twenty of George's tunes which had not yet been written up lyrically, so he had no means of calling for any one of them by numeral or title. But he could request what he wanted to hear this way: Whisking his hand across George's shoulder, he would say: "Play me the one that goes like *that*." Or: "Play the tune that smells like an onion." Or: "*You* know, the one that reminds me of the Staten Island ferry." And so on. Though this mutual musical understanding didn't develop between them at their first meeting, it didn't take too long. I met Alex a few weeks after George did and in Aarons's apartment heard five or six requests in this oblique manner.

Later when George had many tunes on tap for me and I couldn't recall exactly the start of a particular one I wanted to discuss, I would visualize the vocal line and my forefinger would draw an approximation of its curves in the air. And more often than not he would know the tune I meant.

P.S. (months later): I have since been told that this requesting of a tune through the senses of touch or smell or sight may be a form of what the psychologists call *synesthesia*: "a process in which one type of stimulus produces a secondary subjective sensation, as when a specific color evokes a specific smell sensation." (Whether it applies or doesn't, *synesthesia* makes an interesting addition to my vocabulary. I doubt, though, that I'll ever have use for it again.)

—from *Lyrics on Several Occasions*

VERSE

I was a stranger in the city.
Out of town were the people I knew.
I had that feeling of self-pity:
What to do? What to do? What to do?
The outlook was decidedly blue.
But as I walked through the foggy streets alone,
It turned out to be the luckiest day I've known.

REFRAIN

A foggy day in London Town
Had me low and had me down.
I viewed the morning with alarm.
The British Museum had lost its charm.
How long, I wondered, could this thing last?
But the age of miracles hadn't passed,
For, suddenly, I saw you there—
And through foggy London Town
The sun was shining ev'rywhere.

NICE WORK IF YOU CAN GET IT

Published September 1937. Registered for copyright as an unpublished song May 1937. Introduced by Fred Astaire (Jerry) with Jan Duggan, Mary Dean, Pearl Amatore (Madrigal Singers), and ensemble.

Somewhere, long ago, I read an illustrated article about a number of cartoons rejected by the humorous weeklies—cartoons and drawings not for the family trade. One, submitted to *Punch*, I think, was—I'm pretty sure—by George Belcher, whose crayon specialized in delineating London's lowly. In this one, two charwomen are discussing the daughter of a third, and the first says she's heard that the discussee 'as become an 'ore. Whereat the second observes it's nice work if you can get it. And that's all I remember about this title. It's all pretty vague and, on further reflection, it could be that I'm all wrong and that the phrase was around before I ever saw the Belcher two-liner. Anyway—

As I See It: Q.E.D. It. In lyric-writing it's nice work when you get hold of a seemly title, for that's half the battle. But what follows must follow through in the verse and refrain, whether the development is direct or oblique. In brief:

> A title
> Is vital.
> Once you've it—
> *Prove* it.
> —from *Lyrics on Several Occasions*

VERSE

The man who lives for only making money
Lives a life that isn't necessarily sunny;
Likewise the man who works for fame—
There's no guarantee that time won't erase his
    name.
The fact is
The only work that really brings enjoyment
Is the kind that is for girl and boy meant.
Fall in love—you won't regret it.
That's the best work of all—if you can get it.

REFRAIN

Holding hands at midnight
'Neath a starry sky . . .
Nice work if you can get it,
And you can get it—if you try.

Strolling with the one girl,
Sighing sigh after sigh . . .

Nice work if you can get it,
And you can get it—if you try.

Just imagine someone
Waiting at the cottage door,
Where two hearts become one . . .
Who could ask for anything more?

Loving one who loves you,
And then taking that vow . . .
Nice work if you can get it,
And if you get it—Won't You Tell Me How?

PAY SOME ATTENTION TO ME

There are two songs with this title. The first version was probably written in 1928; as musical-theatre historian Tommy Krasker has noted, the lyrics of the verse are very similar to those of the verse of "What Causes That?," which was introduced in *Treasure Girl* (1928). The second version, written for *A Damsel in Distress*, was registered for copyright as an unpublished song in May 1937. Unused.

First Version

VERSE

You're so full of trickery;
Life is bitter as chicory!
Yes, bitter is my cup;
You never call me up.

Once I thought I'd search around
For the Little Church Around
The Corner, but now I see
It never was meant to be.

All I get of late
Is the well-known gate.

REFRAIN 1

I moon! I moan!
I swoon! I groan
When you pay no attention to me!

I burn! I sigh!
I yearn! I die
When you pay no attention to me!

My clothes I keep pressing;
My hair I keep dressing;
My face I'm cold-creaming—
Just dreaming.

I'd laugh, I'd shout,
They'd have to throw me out
If you'd pay some attention to me—
Some attention to me—
I said attention to me!

REFRAIN 2

I cried! I shrank!
I died! I drank!
But you paid no attention to me!

I'd loop-the-loop!
You'd boop-a-doop!
And you paid no attention to me!

My sal'ry I saved up;
My chin I kept shaved up;
But your love you'd pour on
Some moron.

Heigh ho! That's life!
You'll have to ask my wife
If you want some attention from me—
Some attention from me—
I said attention from me!

REFRAIN 3

Paris! London!
Palm Beach! Riviera!
If you'll pay some attention to me.

Flowers! Jewels!
[*Gives her Ingersoll watch*]
Candy! Leisure!
[*Gives her chewing gum, then roll of bills*]
If you'll pay some attention to me!

Refuse me—I'll bump off
This amorous chump off;
The river I'll splash in
For passion!

To be precise,
I'll even pay the price
If you'll pay some attention to me—
Some attention to me—
I said attention to me!

A Damsel in Distress Version

VERSE

SHE: When we met I thought we two were very
    well matched,
    But, you sap, you simply passed me by.*
    So I guess I counted my chickens before
    they were hatched;
    But I'm not giving up—I'm here to do or
    die.
    I may not get you but it won't be because I
    don't try.

REFRAIN 1

My clothes I keep pressing,
My hair I keep dressing,
My face I keep soaping,
Hoping
You'll pay some attention,
Some attention to me.

My waist I keep thinner,†
No starches at dinner,
New hats I keep buying,
Sighing,
"Please pay some attention,
Some attention to me."

Alternate version of verse, line 2:
    Nonetheless, you simply passed me by.
†*Alternate version of refrain 1, lines 7–8:*
    My dates I'll keep breaking,
    Massages I'm taking,

I'm doing my darndest to try to make you
    care;
I'm hoping my darndest is getting me
    somewhere.

My dates I keep breaking,*
Massages I'm taking,
My hands I keep clasping,
Gasping,
"Please pay some attention,
Some attention to me."

REFRAIN 2

HE: Each day I get haircuts,
    My tailor with care cuts,
    My bankroll I'm busting,
    Trusting
    You'll pay some attention,
    Some attention to me.

    My shape I keep trimmer,
    My ties I keep dimmer,
    My smile I keep cheerful,
    Fearful
    You'll pay no attention to me.

    I'm doing my utmost to try to make you
        care;
    I'm hoping my utmost is getting me
        somewhere.

    My teeth I keep brushing,
    To you I keep rushing,
    My bridges I'm burning,
    Yearning,
    Please pay some attention,
    Some attention to me!

Alternate version of refrain 1, lines 15–16:
    My clothes I keep pressing,
    My hair I keep dressing,

OVERLEAF: *Vera Zorina and ensemble in* The Goldwyn
Follies

THE GOLDWYN FOLLIES | 1938
MISCELLANEOUS | 1935–1939

THE GOLDWYN FOLLIES, 1938

A film produced by Samuel Goldwyn for United Artists. Released in February 1938. Music almost entirely by George Gershwin. Screenplay by Ben Hecht. Directed by George Marshall. Dances by George Balanchine. Music conducted by Alfred Newman. Orchestrations by Edward Powell. Cast featured Adolphe Menjou (Oliver Merlin), the Ritz Brothers (as themselves), Vera Zorina (Olga Samara), Kenny Baker (Danny Beecher), Andrea Leeds (Hazel Dawes), Helen Jepson (Leona Jerome), Phil Baker (Michael Day), Ella Logan (Glory Wood), Bobby Clark (A. Basil Crane, Jr.), Jerome Cowan (Lawrence), Nydia Westman (Ada), Charles Kullmann (Alfredo), Frank Shields (Assistant Director), and Edgar Bergen and "Charlie McCarthy" (as themselves).

LOVE WALKED IN

Published January 1938. Previously registered for copyright as an unpublished song July 1937. Introduced by Kenny Baker (Danny).

*H*igh Reception. In the late spring of '38 my wife and I were making a weekend California and Nevada automobile tour. Saturday at twilight we were rounding the top of nine-thousand-foot-high Donner Pass when we were sideswiped by an oncoming car whose driver was higher than the Pass. Fortunately, no one was hurt, and another car offered to send us help from Truckee, a matter of waiting a couple of hours for a tow truck. We had overcoats on, but it was getting very chilly, so I said to my wife: "Let's get in the car, where it'll be warmer." We got in, turned on the radio, listened to a local commercial for a few seconds, then tried for some music and happened to get the Hit Parade. "Love Walked In" had been one of ten songs on the show for some weeks; however, since the program had just a few minutes left to go, I supposed we had missed finding out if the song was still on the list or not. But then came the announcement: "And now, the Number One Song in the country: 'Love Walked In.'" Which more than made up for a badly busted fender.

Despite the fact that this song was one of the top ones that year, the tune, which my brother considered "Brahmsian," deserved a better lyric. There was no special plot situation for it in the *Follies* screenplay when he chose it from a number of reserve tunes kept in his notebooks. All that was required was something for the fine tenor voice of Kenny Baker. Wallowing in a swamp of vague generalities, I finally emerged with this lyric based on its ambulatory title. What particularly bothered me was the injection of "right" in "Love walked right in"—obviously a padding word. This I deleted from the title when the song was sent to the music-publisher. But my feeling about the lyric is evidently of indifference to those who like the song.

—from *Lyrics on Several Occasions*

VERSE

Nothing seemed to matter anymore;
Didn't care what I was headed for.
Time was standing still;
Nothing counted till
There came a knock-knock-knocking at the
     door.

REFRAIN

Love walked right in
And drove the shadows away;
Love walked right in
And brought my sunniest day.

One magic moment,
And my heart seemed to know
That love said "Hello!"—
Though not a word was spoken.

One look, and I
Forgot the gloom of the past;
One look, and I
Had found my future at last.

One look, and I*
Had found a world completely new,
When love walked in with you.

I WAS DOING ALL RIGHT

Published January 1938. Previously registered for copyright as an unpublished song July 1937. Introduced by Ella Logan (Glory). An additional refrain, intended for Edgar Bergen and "Charlie McCarthy," was unused.

*Original version of refrain, lines 13–14:
Oh, then and there
I found a world completely new,

VERSE

Used to lead a quiet existence,
Always had my peace of mind.
Kept Old Man Trouble at a distance;
My days were silver-lined.

Right on top of the world I sat,
But look at me now—I don't know where I'm
     at.

REFRAIN

I was doing all right—
Nothing but rainbows in my sky;
I was doing all right
Till you came by.

Had no cause to complain—
Life was as sweet as apple pie;
Never noticed the rain
Till you came by.

But now, whenever you're away,
Can't sleep nights and suffer all the day.
I just sit and wonder
If love isn't one big blunder.

Still, when you hold me tight,*
Tingling all through, I feel somehow
I was doing all right—
But I'm doing better than ever now!

Bergen–McCarthy Lyric

REFRAIN

CHARLIE: I was doing all right—
         I was a tree—Oh me, oh my!
         I was doing all right
         Till you came by.

         Ev'rything was okay—
         Never a worry or a frown;
         Things were fine till the day
         You cut me down.

BERGEN:
[*spoken*]
         But look how I dressed you up!

CHARLIE:
[*Sings*]
         I had no monocle, it's true—
         But there were a million things I *didn't*
              have to do;
         In peace I would slumber
         When I was a piece of lumber.

         So, when you made me speak,
         I was a worried soul—and how!

*In the published version, this line reads:
But when you hold me tight,

Still, at three grand a week,
Guess I'm doin' better than ever now!

LOVE IS HERE TO STAY

Published January 1938. Previously registered for copyright (without the verse) as an unpublished song as "It's Here to Stay" in July 1937. Introduced by Kenny Baker (Danny). Frequently mistitled "Our Love Is Here to Stay."

So little footage was given to "Love Is Here to Stay"—I think only one refrain—that it meant little in *The Goldwyn Follies*. Beautifully presented in the Academy Award–winning musical *An American in Paris*, it became better known.

When George and I were on *The Goldwyn Follies* we managed to finish five songs the first six weeks of our contract. (Vernon Duke and I fixed up a couple of missing verses later.) The five were: "I Love to Rhyme," "Love Walked In," "I Was Doing All Right," "Just Another Rhumba" (the longest and most ambitious, but not used), and "Love Is Here to Stay." The reason we worked this fast on the vocal contributions was to allow the composer to have the following six or eight weeks free to write a ballet for Zorina. As it turned out, our first six weeks were George's last six weeks of work; and "Love Is Here to Stay" the last song he composed.
　　　　　　　　　　　　　—from *Lyrics on Several Occasions*

VERSE

The more I read the papers,
The less I comprehend
The world and all its capers
And how it all will end.
Nothing seems to be lasting,
But that isn't our affair;
We've got something permanent—
I mean, in the way we care.

REFRAIN

It's very clear
Our love is here to stay;
Not for a year,
But ever and a day.

The radio and the telephone
And the movies that we know
May just be passing fancies—
And in time may go.

But oh, my dear,
Our love is here to stay.
Together we're
Going a long, long way.

In time the Rockies may crumble,
Gibraltar may tumble
(They're only made of clay),
But—our love is here to stay.

SPRING AGAIN

Published January 1938. Music by Vernon Duke. Introduced by Kenny Baker (Danny). As published, the song does not have a verse. The interlude that follows the refrain was originally the verse. Also see "Night of Nights."

REFRAIN

Spring again—
It's time for your heart to sing again—
It's time for laughter to ring again—
It's time to fall in love.
June again—
Look at that yellow balloon again—
Look at that silv'ry lagoon again—
It's time to fall in love.
Tonight magic is filling the air,
Making it thrilling to dare
Finding out whether
We two can dream together.*
Spring again—
It's time for couples to cling again—
To leave this world and to wing again
Up to the gates above—
It's time to fall in love.

INTERLUDE

Venice in June—The music has started—
Lanterns aglow—The mandolins play.
Happiness soon—So why be downhearted?
Love will enthrall you;
It's a call you
Must obey.

REPEAT REFRAIN

---

*Original version of this line:
Two hearts can dream together.

NIGHT OF NIGHTS

An earlier lyric set to the music eventually used for "Spring Again." Intended for *The Goldwyn Follies*. Unused.

VERSE

Venice in June—The gondolas gliding—
Shimmering waves of heavenly blue;
Let's be in tune—The whole world's abiding
By the love rule—
The above rule
Holds for you.

REFRAIN

Night of nights—
Tonight I'm singing my song of songs;
Oh, is it bringing that day of days?
The day that has to be.
Night of nights—
At last I'm viewing my star of stars;
I'll keep pursuing that smile of smiles
Until it smiles on me.
Tonight magic is filling the air,
Making it thrilling to dare
Finding out whether
We two can dream together.
Night of nights—
Tonight I'm singing my song of songs;
I hope it's bringing that day of days
That offers new delights.
Make this my night of nights!

I LOVE TO RHYME

Published January 1938. Previously registered for copyright as an unpublished song July 1937. Introduced by Phil Baker (Michael), and Edgar Bergen and "Charlie McCarthy." A revised version of the second refrain, intended for Bobby Clark (Crane) and Ella Logan (Glory), was unused.

VERSE

There are men who, in their leisure,
Love to play the horses;*
There are others who get pleasure

---

*Published version of verse, line 2:
Love to fish for salmon;

Cursing on golf courses.*
General Grant loved to smoke;
Mark Twain loved to joke;
Radio comics love to pun—
But the thing I do is much more fun.

REFRAIN 1

I love to rhyme—
Mountaineers love to climb—
Criminals love to crime—
But I love to rhyme.

What joy to croon:†
Spoon, June, prune, moon, soon;
Chuckle, knuckle, nickel, fickle, pickle!
I love to rhyme.

Variety, society, propriety . . .
There's no stopping when you've begun;
Capacity, veracity, audacity . . .
Did you ever know such fun?

I love to rhyme—
And wouldn't it be sublime
If one day it could be
That *you* rhyme with *me*?

REFRAIN 2

I love to rhyme—
Steeple bells love to chime—
Citrus fruit loves to lime—
But I love to rhyme.

Such pure delight—
Bite, sight, fight, quite, right;
Castle, tassel, muscle, tussle, Yussel!
I love to rhyme.

Algerian, Siberian, Shakespearean . . .
Tell me, how can you resist?
Amnesia, Rhodesia, Zambesia
Cannot lightly be dismissed.

I love to rhyme—
But here we are wasting time!
The day is overdue
When *I* rhyme with *you*!

Logan–Clark Lyric

LOGAN: I love to rhyme—
        Steeple bells love to chime—

*Published version of verse, line 4:
When they play backgammon.
†Published version of refrain, lines 5–6:
I love to say:
Gay, day, may, hey, hey!

Handicappers love to time—
But I love to rhyme.

Such pure delight:
Bite, slight, fight, quite right!
Muscle, tussle, tassel, castle, "rassle"—
I love to rhyme.

[*Clark now begins to challenge her*]
CLARK: Pedestrian!
LOGAN: Equestrian!
CLARK: [*pointing to his head*] My cranium!
LOGAN: [*belittlingly*] Geranium!
CLARK: [*embracing her*] Harmonious!
LOGAN: [*breaking away*] Erroneous!
CLARK: [*posing like Napoleon*] Indispensable!
LOGAN: [*indicating he is "tetched in the head"*]
        Insensible!
CLARK: [*pointing to his waistcoat*]
        Splendiferous!
LOGAN: Pestiferous!
CLARK: [*indicating the loud tie he is wearing*]
        Unmatchable!
LOGAN: [*snatching it off*] Detachable!
CLARK: [*He has her now—no rhyme for
        "orange"*] Orange!
LOGAN: [*Nothing stops her*] Tangerine!

BOTH: I love to rhyme—
       And wouldn't it be sublime
       If one day it could be
       That *you* rhyme with *me?*

JUST ANOTHER RHUMBA

Published October 1959 (after being recorded by Ella Fitzgerald). Previously registered for copyright as an unpublished song July 1937. Possibly intended for Ella Logan (Glory). Unused. A note in Ira Gershwin's files suggests that this number—originally conceived as "The Rhumba That Blighted My Life"—may once have been intended for Fred Astaire, possibly in *A Damsel in Distress* (1937).

VERSE

It happened to me
On a trip to the West Indies.
Oh, I'm all at sea
Since that trip to the West Indies.
I'm jittery;
I'm twittery;
I guess I'm done for;
I guess I'm through!
And it's something about which

There's nothing anyone can do.
It isn't love;
It isn't money trouble;
It's a very funny trouble:

REFRAIN

It's Just Another Rhum-ba,
But it certainly has my num-bah;
So much so that I can't eat or slum-bah!
Can you imagine anything dum-bah?

Why did I have to plan a
Vacation in Havana?
Why did I take that trip
That made me lose my grip?
Oh,
That piece of music laid me low!

There it goes again!
Just Another Rhum-ba,
Which I heard only last Septum-bah;
I'm a wreck—Why did I have to succum-bah?
Can you imagine anything dum-bah?
Why did I have to succum-bah
To that Rhum-ba?

TRIO

Ah, ah! I'm the cu-ca-ra-cha
Who just went blah
And gave up swing and hot-cha.
Ah, ah, ah!

Ah, ah! At first it was divine-ah,
But it turned out a Cuban Frankenstein-ah.

Ah, ah, ah! It's got me by the throat-ah!
Oh, what's the antidote-ah?

Ah, ah, ah! It brought me woe and strife-ah!
It made me lose my wife-ah!*
It's the Rhum-ba that blighted my life!

There it goes again!
Just Another Rhum-ba,
Which has got me under it's thum-bah;
So much so that I can't eat or slum-bah!
Can you imagine anything dum-bah?
Why did I have to succum-bah
To that Rhum-ba?

*Alternate version of this line:
Oh, where's a gun or knife-ah?

I'M NOT COMPLAINING

Music by Vernon Duke. Intended for *The Goldwyn Follies*. Unused.

VERSE

You know the story of the Capulets
Versus the Montagues;
That story fits us and it's bringing on the blues.

We'd never have a chance to sing duets
If our parents were to choose.

They want us above it,
But we have each other and we love it.

REFRAIN

I'm not complaining—
Nevertheless, it's hardly fair—
Living a night without a care
And then to have to part.

I'm not complaining—
But when I dream a dream with you,
Why does the morning sun have to
Upset our apple cart?

Daybreak appears—The world goes hurrying on;
The wheels are in motion—The magic is gone.

Oh, I'm not complaining—
It's been divine—Don't get me wrong—
Only why can't the night last all day long?

EXPOSITION

Proposed ballet by George Balanchine and Ira Gershwin, to have been scored by George Gershwin and designed by Richard Day. Unfinished. The scenario had been rough-drafted, but George Gershwin died before he was able to begin work on the score. On a few occasions over the years, Balanchine spoke to this writer of the piece and some of the ideas he had had for it; he said that he even had worked out a model for the setting. In 1972, for the book *The Gershwins*, Balanchine recalled his collaboration with George and Ira: "I went to California to make my first movie in America. Samuel Goldwyn was the boss, and he arranged a conference at which I met George and Ira. My English was poor then, and Goldwyn spoke English with such an accent that we could not communicate very easily. So George Gershwin tried to be the translator, and he spoke to me like this:

'Me Tarzan, you Jane.' It was such crazy English, who knew what he was saying? Finally, Ira said to his brother, 'George, why don't you speak a little real English?'

"When I first saw George he seemed all right. He was writing songs for the film *The Goldwyn Follies* and then we were going to do a ballet together. That would have been very enjoyable.

"We met a few times and then I heard George was sick. I went to visit him and found him lying in bed in a dark room with all the shades drawn. He had a towel against his head and he obviously was in great pain. In that dark room he said to me, 'It is difficult for me to work now, but I'll be all right.' He knew I was trained in music, so he also said, 'Do what you must. I know it will be good.' He had more confidence in me than Goldwyn did then. 'And when I'm all better, we'll do our ballet just the way you want it.' A week later he was dead. . . ."

Following is George Balanchine and Ira Gershwin's rough draft of the "Exposition" scenario:

We are at the main entrance of the Exposition. The city sponsoring the Exposition is not identified geographically. It might be London, Paris, New York, or San Francisco. It is night. Flags of all nations flying over the entrance. Beyond and above the flags we see, not too clearly, the illuminated towers of the various Exposition buildings. Occasionally, fireworks burst into colored clusters in the sky. Searchlights, moving back and forth, keep piercing the heavens.

A visiting Maharajah and his retinue walk in. A fat couple with a fat son walk out. A group of Boy Scouts walks in. Paul Draper, carrying many parcels and souvenirs, staggers out. He tries to hail a taxi. While he is so engaged, a group of twelve girls from a finishing school appears. The clothes they are wearing are identical in design. They are headed by a prim-looking schoolmistress. Every now and then the schoolmistress uses a certain rhythm in clapping her hands to call her pupils to order. (This hand-clapping should be done at least once in each of the two following scenes.) While the schoolmistress is busy buying the tickets, Draper sees Vera Zorina, who is one of the students. Immediately he loses interest in his taxi (especially after he has had a slightly flirtatious glance from Zorina), checks his packages, and follows the girls. He is stopped by the doorman and is forced to buy another ticket. A group of society people in evening dress follows him in.

We are now in a room devoted to horticulture. On a platform is seen a large glass case. A seed is put in the soil at the bottom of the case. A new light ray is put over the case for a second and immediately a long-stemmed green sunflower shoots up. The teacher is lecturing on this latest development in horticulture, the pupils, in rhythm, alternately looking at the phenomenon and then at the pamphlets they are reading. Draper is trying to draw Zorina's attention, but she will not meet his ad-

vances although we more than suspect she is quite flattered by them.

The group is now seen watching, in the Hall of Science, a highly intricate machine. While the others are being fascinated by the elaborate mechanism, Zorina has an opportunity to make an appointment to meet Draper later. She points off to where we can see a Ferris wheel through the glass wall. He nods. He will be waiting for her there. He dances out in great elation.

We now see him by the ticket booth of the Ferris wheel. He is waiting impatiently. He looks at his watch, and finally deciding she has misunderstood the trysting place, he starts to look for her frantically. Zorina appears the moment he leaves. Passersby look at her curiously. She takes out her guidebook and pretends to read.

We follow Draper. He rushes to a guide and gesticulates: Have you seen her? Guide shakes head—No. There is a Spanish rural scene painted on a curtain nearby. He runs to this and opens the curtain. The rhythm of the music changes immediately to Flamenco and we are in the Spanish Village. There is a wild dance in progress. [Draper] is paid no attention. He looks at the dancers and believes he sees Zorina as the veiled girl dancing in the center. He picks up a discarded scarf and native hat and enters the group, gradually getting to the girl, with whom he now dances. In a moment, when the music reaches a crescendo, he lifts the veil. It is not Zorina. He rushes out to continue his search.

He approaches an astrologer, who studies the skies, then points out on the chart of the Signs of the Zodiac Sagittarius and then Virgo, the Virgin.

He hurries to the planetarium. On the ledge of a great opening, silhouetted against the starry sky, are the dancing figures of William Dollar as Sagittarius, the Archer, and Zorina as Virgo, the Virgin. Draper tries to reach them, but cannot. He dances madly around the room while their dance is in progress and finally jumps so that his hands reach the edge of the ledge. Suddenly the lights go up and Dollar and Zorina disappear, as, of course, their dance was just a hallucination of Draper's. A lecturer and a group of tourists are in the room. They see Draper hanging by his hands, grab him. Thinking he is intoxicated, they put him out.

We now see [Draper] dejectedly sitting down at a table in the American Café. An orchestra is swinging, and we see, vaguely, figures doing modern American rhythms. Draper comes out of his daze, the figures become clearer, and off on the other side he spies Zorina. Their eyes meet. As though hypnotized, they are drawn to the center of the floor and to each other. The other figures gradually stop dancing to watch the couple. These spectators become so excited by Draper's tapping (if it *is* tap at this point) that they, to help the basic rhythm, start to clap hands in the style done in the small Negro churches in Florida and the Carolinas, where often there are two distinct rhythms going against each other. Here we can do three and possibly four. At a climax reached, there is a sudden dramatic stop in the music and clapping, and Zorina finds herself doing a step to the beat we have heard previously done by the schoolmistress, a single pair of hands in a familiar, sharp, accented sound. She almost stumbles as she is horrifiedly brought to her senses. She pushes through the crowd, Draper frantically after her.

We see a long shot of the teacher and the eleven girls, now very tired after their inspection of the various exhibitions, drooping out. Their movements convey such fatigue that they haven't even noticed Zorina's absence. Zorina is quickly in line, assumes the tired attitude of the others as they exit.

Draper, seeing his cause is hopeless, gets his parcels, walks out as the gates are closing. The Maharajah and his retinue are the last ones out. The Exposition lights are being turned off as Draper hails a taxi.

MISCELLA-NEOUS, 1935-1939

BY STRAUSS

Published December 1936. Introduced by Grace Barrie in the revue *The Show Is On*, which opened in New York at the Winter Garden on December 25, 1936. 237 performances.

In New York one night in the spring of '36, stage director Vincente Minnelli was present when my brother and I were musically kidding around by exaggerating the lifts and plunges and *luftpauses* of the Viennese waltz. We had written only about half of this piece when we dropped it for something more usable. In August of that year we checked in at the Beverly Wilshire Hotel in Beverly Hills to start work on *Shall We Dance*. We were there but a few days when a telegram arrived from Vincente. In it he stated he was preparing a new Broadway revue and asked us please to work on the Straussian take-off, which he felt he could use. So we took off a day from the film for the stage take-off, finished the waltz, and airmailed it. We never saw the show, but I understand the song was acceptably presented and received.

"Extra Long Verses." When "By Strauss" was being prepared for sheet-music publication, my brother received a letter from a concerned young woman in the editing department. She wrote that the verse was "unusually long" and "would take up at least three pages. . . . Is there anything you can suggest that would help us to get the number out in the usual amount of pages?" (Usually two.)

—from *Lyrics on Several Occasions*

On 12/4/36 my brother wrote:

Dear Selma,

I am very sorry that the verse to BY STRAUSS is so long that it requires perhaps an extra page in the publication copy, but then it's always been my policy to give the public a lot for their money; and I think it would be a good idea to put on the title page—"This song has an extra long verse so you are getting more notes per penny than in any other song this season." . . . And even if the song doesn't sell I would like my grandchildren (if I ever have any) to see the trouble that their grand-daddy took with verses. In other words, dear Selma, I would like the song printed as I wrote it, with no commas left out.

Love and kisses,
GEORGE

VERSE

Away with the music of Broadway!
Be off with your Irving Berlin!
Oh, I'd give no quarter
To Kern or Cole Porter,
And Gershwin keeps pounding on tin.
How can I be civil
When hearing this drivel?
It's only for nightclubbing souses.
Oh, give me the free'n'easy
Waltz that is Viennesey—
And, go tell the band
If they want a hand,
The waltz must be Strauss's.
Ya, ya, ya—
Give me Oom-pah-pah!

REFRAIN

When I want a melody
Lilting through the house,
Then I want a melody
By Strauss.
It laughs! It sings! The world is in rhyme,
Swinging to three-quarter time.
Let the Danube flow along,
And *The Fledermaus!*
Keep the wine and give me song
By Strauss.
By Jo, by Jing,
By Strauss is the thing!
So I say to Ha-cha-cha:

Heraus!
Just give me an Oom-pah-pah
By Strauss.

When the song was to be included in the score of *An American in Paris* (under Vincente Minnelli's movie direction this time), MGM's legal department said clearances would have to be secured from Berlin and Porter and the Kern estate for use of the names. Which probably could have been easily acquired, but it was less bothersome to write new lines.

I wrote several variants for the opening of the verse. This is the one that was chosen for the film:

The waltzes of Mittel Europa—
They're mellow and warm you within,
While each day discloses
What Broadway composes
Is emptiness pounding on tin.
How can I be civil &c.

—from *Lyrics on Several Occasions*

One discarded:

Beware of that popular music!
In dynamite danger must lurk.
You hear in an awed way
The music of Broadway
And suddenly you go berserk.
How can I be civil &c.

[Here's another discarded verse—Editor.]

The music they go for on Broadway
Has never a reason or rhyme.
Quite rhythmic, but silly—
It all leaves me chilly. . . .
It isn't in three-quarter time.
or
Believe me, you're wasting your time.
How can I be civil . . .

[*etc.*]

DAWN OF A NEW DAY

Published April 1938. Kay Swift, who was among those in charge of music for the 1939 New York World's Fair, asked Ira if he had a song by himself and George that might be an appropriate theme song for the Fair. Ira hadn't but looked through his late brother's unlyricized melodies and found something to which he could set a lyric. "Dawn of a New Day" was published as a "Song of the New York World's Fair." In 1960, Ira revised the lyric for inclusion in a new version of *Girl Crazy*.

VERSE

Leave those cares and furrows!
Come, come where Five Boroughs
Join to fulfill a dream!
Where all creeds and races
Meet with smiling faces,
Democracy reigns supreme!
Let the New York Fair proclaim the story!
Orange, blue, and white beside Old Glory!

REFRAIN

Sound the brass! Roll the drum!
To the world of tomorrow we come!
See the sun through the gray,
It's the Dawn of a New Day!

Here we come, young and old,
Come to watch all the wonders unfold!
And the tune that we play*
Is the Dawn of a New Day!

Tell the wolf†
At the door
That we don't want him 'round anymore!
Better times
Here to stay
As we live and laugh the American way.

Listen one, listen all!
There can be no resisting the call!
Come, hail the Dawn of a New Day!

Revised Verse (1960)

Hey there! Strike the band up!
We must clean this land up!
I must fulfill a dream!
Good-bye, crook and grifter—
When this here uplifter
Begins his reform regime.
Here's the verse and chapter in my hymnal!
We must do away with all that's crim'nal!

BABY, YOU'RE NEWS

Published April 1939. Music by Johnny Green. Lyrics by Ira Gershwin and E. Y. Harburg. Registered for copyright under the title "T'me, Baby, You're News."

*The 1960 version of this line is:
And the platform, I say,
†The 1960 version of this line is:
Tell the crook

REFRAIN 1

Extra! Extras ev'ry day.
Extra! What's the Big Hooray?
Quakes! Crimes! Hard times!
Phoo! On those hullabaloos!
T'me, baby, you're news!

England builds another ship!
Market takes another dip!
Clouds loom! Bombs boom!
Same old monotonous blues!
T'me, baby, you're news!

You're a bolt from the blue;
You're a real scooperoo;
You're the flash of the year—
It's "Love Walks In as Thousands Cheer!"

Who cares what the paper cries
Long as I can read your eyes?
World scares! Who cares?
You are the headline I choose;
T'me, baby, you're news!

REFRAIN 2

Congress primes another pump!
Pump stocks take another slump!
Pump! Slump! Nerves jump!
Read me no current reviews—
T'me, baby, you're news!

Screen star buys another horse!
Screen star gets a new divorce!
Hearts crash! Rehash!
Read 'em and weep if you choose—
T'me, baby, you're news!

You're a bolt from the blue;
You're a real scooperoo.
You're the flash of the year—
It's "Love Walks In As Thousands Cheer!"

Yes, sir! You're the big event!
Headlines full of sentiment:
"Love Calls! Girl Falls!"
Those are the thrills I can use—
T'me, baby, you're news!

NO QUESTION IN MY HEART

Published March 1968. Music by Jerome Kern. Registered for copyright December 1938 as an unpublished song titled "No Question in My Mind, You're in My Heart."

VERSE

I often wonder
Why in thunder
You care to care,
And why I should share
A treasure so rare.

To find an answer,
This romancer
Never will dare.
Perhaps up in the blue
A reason is provided;
But on the theme of you
I'm not so undecided.

REFRAIN

No question in my mind
That you alone are in my heart;
No question in my heart,
You're on my mind.

I found the one who's all to me,
And blues no longer call to me;
I've but to see
You smile at me,
And cares are far behind.

No shadow of a doubt—
You made the shadows all depart;
You were my happy ending
From the start.

No question who's the one for me—
The moon, the stars, the sun for me;
No question in my mind,
You're in my heart.

ONCE THERE WERE TWO OF US

Published March 1968 with "Now that We Are One." Music by Jerome Kern. Registered for copyright December 1938 as an unpublished song.

VERSE

If you believe that a miracle can occur,
Pray for the one that pertains to a him and her.

That's the best of all—and I'll always say
I'm the one can prove that it's true:
All I have to do is recall the day
That united me with you.

REFRAIN

Once there were two of us,
And life was not much fun;
But heaven knew of us—
And made us one.

Once there were two of us—
Each day was one long sigh—
When you were you of us,
And I was I.

The moment we were together,
Skies were all aglow;
My urge to sing a dirge
Passed away
And the day
Grew rosy.

And this is true of us:
We'll see no setting sun—
Long as the two of us
Are always one.

Always one,
Never two;
Always one—
Thanks to you!

NOW THAT WE ARE ONE

Published March 1968 with "Once There Were Two of Us." Music by Jerome Kern. I.G. described it as "the sequel song to 'Once There Were Two of Us.'"

REFRAIN 1

Now that we are one,
Which one shall we be?
Shall we be you?
Shall we be me?

F'rinstance, where'll we live?
What's to be home base?
I'm all for the West Side;
You're for Sutton Place.

Shall we have our hamburgers rare or medium?
You like double features—I call them tedium.

So—

Now that we are one,
Which one shall we try?
Shall we be you of us?
Shall we be I?

Always one,
Never two;

But which one
Is up to you!

REFRAIN 2

Now that we are one,
Which one shall we be?
Shall we be you?
Shall we be me?

Let's be fair and square:
Who's to be the boss?
Seems to me, this moment,
We are at a loss.

Let's not argue about an Irish terrier.
Let's go in for children—The more the merrier!

So—

Now that we are one,
Which one shall we try?
Shall we be you of us?
Shall we be I?

Always one,
Never two;
But which one
Is up to you!

PEOPLE FROM MISSOURI

Written in 1938. Music by Jerome Kern. Registered for copyright as an unpublished song July 1956. A piano-vocal transcription was located by musical-theatre historian Tommy Krasker in the Music Division of the Library of Congress's Jerome Kern song file.

REFRAIN
CYNICS, TO YOU—
SAY WE TWO
WON'T COME THROUGH;
WE'LL SHOW THOSE PEOPLE FROM MISSOURI!

Let the judge and jury
Feel what they feel—
This is real.
We know we'll
Show up those people from Missouri!

If this is just a preview,
Dear, that we view,
Breathless, here, and now;
We've no equal*

On the copyright deposit copy at the Library of Congress, Jerome Kern, in his own distinctive hand, has

In the sequel
When we officially take that vow.

If skeptics from Missouri—
Lacking in charm—
Show alarm,
What's the harm?

Their little whimsy,
So petty and flimsy,
We'll put to rout—
Poor little people—
When up in the steeple
The chimes ring out.

I'VE TURNED THE CORNER

Written in 1938. Music by Jerome Kern. The verse was only roughed in by Ira Gershwin.

REFRAIN

I've turned the corner—
There's blue in the sky.
Each day is Fourth of July.
I'm turning nip-ups,
Turning somersaults, too.
If I'm acting like a crackpot—
I just hit the jackpot.
Gone are wrinkles that furrowed my brow;
The world is my oyster now.
My love's beside me and am I holding fast!
I've turned the corner at last!

VERSE* (IN SKETCH FORM)

Spirits were low.
One day last week the chart (of my heart)
    showed the lowest point in my depression.
The next day the line went upwards. It reached
    new heights.
The gain was recorded
Because you were what the doctor ordered.
My spirits were low. Don't sell me short.
I hadn't smiled for ages.
I kept sinking by easy stages.

changed the music of bar 20 and altered the lyric of this line to read "We'll surely have no equal."
  **An earlier idea for the verse reads:*
I wasn't in the red financially;
But oh, I had the blues substantially.
If I played an instrument, I beat the doldrums . . .

I WAS NAÏVE

Written in late 1938. Music by Jerome Kern. Registered for copyright as an unpublished song November 1938. The version included here is drawn from Ira Gershwin's lyric sketches.

REFRAIN

I was once so naïve,
So naïve in believing,
I was nothing if not blasé.
Truth to tell—being so blasé*
Was a sign of my naïveté.
But how was I to know
That with one glance I'd go
Completely shaken from head to toe?
Into heaven I'm hurled,
Wondering what in the world
Made me think I could be blasé—
I was just naïve that way.

SOMETHING'S WRONG

Written in late 1938. Music by Jerome Kern. Registered for copyright as an unpublished song December 1977. The version included here is drawn from Ira Gershwin's lyric sketches.

REFRAIN

Something's wrong—
I dream a dream with every hopeful song,
But I have yet to find those well-known flowers
April showers
Bring
Each spring.

I can't find
A cloud that's silver-lined;
Nor can I ever remember
Meeting Maytime in December.

Something's wrong—
I've seen no rainbow shine for oh! so long.
And troubles may be bubbles
But I've yet to hear the bluebird sing.

Though they say
It's always darkest just before the day,

Alternate version of lines 4–5:
So blasé that the field I'd play,
But no heart would I give away.

Something's wrong*
With every song
That kicks the gong
Or something's wrong with me!

HARD TO REPLACE

Written in 1938. Unfinished. Music by Jerome Kern. The melody of the refrain, set with an entirely new Ira Gershwin lyric, became the melody of the refrain of "Sure Thing" in the film *Cover Girl* (1944). Ira Gershwin developed the title and idea of this lyric into "You'd Be Hard to Replace" (music by Harry Warren) for the film *The Barkleys of Broadway* (1949).

REFRAIN

Lady, you'd be awf'ly hard to replace—
One might as soon
Climb to the moon.
So much loveliness and oh! so much grace!
Each time and ev'ry time your eyes look
That prize look
At me,
I seem to go into a stupor
Of super
Degree.
You are mine or I've no future to face—
I'm afraid that you'd be hard to replace.

I'LL SUPPLY THE TITLE (YOU'LL SUPPLY THE TUNE)

According to Edward Jablonski, biographer of the Gershwins and of Harold Arlen, this song (music by Arlen, lyrics by Ira Gershwin) was written in 1939.

REFRAIN

I'll supply the title,
You'll supply the tune.
But it's oh! so vital
That we get together soon.

Look at time advancing,
Why should music wait?
What a song we can sing
If we two collaborate

Alternate version of lines 17–20:
Something's wrong
With every happy song
Or else there's
Something wrong with me!

Wintertime or Maytime
Nighttime—Daytime
We'll reach the stars*
On our thirty-two bars.

What a tune and title!—
Gets me more and more.
Never was a song like this before.

LET IT RAIN! LET IT POUR!

Music by Harold Arlen. Written c. 1939. No music manuscripts or lyric sheets survive. The song is preserved on an acetate (private) recording by Harold Arlen—piano and vocal. Arlen's biographer Edward Jablonski called it to the attention of Ira Gershwin archivist Tommy Krasker.

REFRAIN

Let it rain! Let it pour!
With a song in my heart,
Who cares if there's rain at my door?
With your smile lighting my way,
How can anything ever darken up my day?
All is fair here in your eyes
And I don't give a care
What happens up there
In the skies.
Let it rain! Let it pour!
Oh, I'm out of the shadows now
Forevermore.
No more dreading cold December—
Now December is July.
Things are growing,†
Buds are blooming,
Hearts are booming,
Because why?
Found the one I adore.
Let it rain! Let it pour!

Alternate versions of this and the next line:
Sunshine or rain,
We can sing our refrain.
or
Toddling along
On an outburst of song.
or
Love sounds her A,
And we're both on our way.
†*Alternate version of lines 15–18:*
Stormy weather
Out of season
Is the reason
For the change.

OPPOSITE: *Donald Randolph and Gertrude Lawrence*

LADY IN THE DARK | 1941

Tryout: Colonial Theatre, Boston, December 30, 1940. New York run: Alvin Theatre, opened January 23, 1941. 467 performances. Music by Kurt Weill. Produced by Sam H. Harris. Book by Moss Hart. Book staged by Moss Hart and Hassard Short. Dances staged by Albertina Rasch. Orchestra under the direction of Maurice Abravanel. Orchestrations by Kurt Weill. Cast, starring Gertrude Lawrence (Liza Elliott), featured Evelyn Wyckoff (Miss Foster and Sutton), Danny Kaye (Russell Paxton, Beekman, and Ringmaster), Macdonald Carey (Charley Johnson and Marine), Victor Mature (Randy Curtis), Bert Lytell (Kendall Nesbitt and Pierre), Natalie Schafer (Alison Du Bois), Margaret Dale (Maggie Grant), Eleanor Eberle (Barbara), Dan Harden (Ben), and Donald Randolph (Dr. Brooks).

A film version was released by Paramount in 1944. Screenplay by Frances Goodrich and Albert Hackett. Produced by Dick Blumenthal. Directed by Mitchell Leisen. Cast, starring Ginger Rogers (Liza Elliott), featured Ray Milland, Warner Baxter, Jon Hall, and Mischa Auer. Most of the Weill-Gershwin score was dropped; a few new songs (by others) were added. The principal character of *Lady in the Dark* is Liza Elliott, a hard-driving magazine editor who has agreed to marry a much older man but is having second thoughts. In her indecision she consults a psychoanalyst, who asks her to describe her dreams. These, dramatized, were the show's musical sequences, alternating with dialogue scenes in the doctor's office, and included persons close to Liza—her publisher (and intended husband), her secretary, the magazine's chief photographer, a movie star, an art director, et al.—in a variety of roles. As her dreams portray her hopes and fears, through them runs a melody that she is unable to identify until the end, when she recognizes it as the expression of her long-repressed but deepest wish: to find true love.

GLAMOUR DREAM, including OH, FABULOUS ONE, and HUXLEY, and ONE LIFE TO LIVE, and GIRL OF THE MOMENT, and IT LOOKS LIKE LIZA, and GIRL OF THE MOMENT (REPRISE)

Published in the piano-vocal score and with the complete text of the play April 1941. ("One Life to Live" and "Girl of the Moment" published separately January 1941.) Introduced by Gertrude Lawrence (Liza Elliott), Evelyn Wyckoff (Sutton), Danny Kaye (Beekman), Bert Lytell (Pierre), Macdonald Carey (Marine), and ensemble. Alternate title of "Glamour Dream": "First Dream Sequence." Alternate title of "Oh, Fabulous One": "Oh, Fabulous One in Your Ivory Tower." Alternate title of "Huxley": "The World's Inamorata." Alternate title of "Girl of the Moment": "The Girl of the Moment."

About "One Life to Live"

I am Ungallant. Kurt's style direction for this song is "*Allegretto commodo.*" In Scholes's *Oxford Companion to Music*, "*Allegretto*" is defined as "Pretty lively," and "*Commodo*" as " 'Convenient,' i.e., without any suspicion of strain." Which gives me a fairly lively and convenient lead to say there was no suspicion of strain in Miss Lawrence's fondness for, and acceptance of, not only the dramatic but also the musical portion of her role. And after we opened, there were no reservations in the tremendous acclaim this gifted actress received from the critics and the public for her performance—whether in any of her dramatic scenes or in any of her numbers. Yet, after a while—although "One Life to Live" got over as well as ever on stage—off stage, Gertie found some suspicion of strain in it, much discussion *allegretto* resulting.

Some four months after the opening, Kurt wrote me, May 28, '41: "Gertie asked me if there is any possibility that we write her a new song instead of 'One life to live.' . . . I dismissed it the first few times she talked about it, but she keeps nagging and I finally told her I would get in touch with you. . . . The funny thing is that she is doing 'One life to live' much better now and that it gets the biggest hand next to 'Jenny' and 'Tschaikowsky.' " Kurt was willing to oblige; but collaboration by mail would have been unsatisfactory; and I didn't fancy going to New York for three weeks or more to work on replacing a number which was doing all right, and which perhaps we couldn't better. There was further correspondence until the show closed for the summer, when Gertie and "One Life to Live" took vacations.

Then, rehearsals again, and *Lady* reopened. Kurt, Sept. 9: "She keeps on kicking about 'One life to live' (which, by the way, gets a very good hand every night). She says it is just an ice-breaker [indeed!] and she has to work hard to get anything out of it, and what she needs at this moment is a funny song . . . because that would make the whole act easier for her. . . . I thought she had forgotten it, but she started again and in one rehearsal she got a fit and said, any other actress in her place would just demand a new song and it is not her fault that I cannot get together with the lyric writer etc. etc. Last week she said she would be perfectly happy if you could write a new lyric to the tune of 'Bats about you' [a discarded number]. . . . She suggested to keep the same verse we have now for 'One life to live' and then go into the new song. Well, Moss and I promised her to get in touch with you. . . ."

From me to Kurt, Sept. 29: "I figured the longer I took answering you—or rather, not answering you—the more louse I would be and the more you would blame me. . . . Of all the thankless jobs in show business—to be asked to write a new song for a hit which is in its second season. . . . If, as you say, the show makes too many demands on her physically mightn't it be a good idea to lighten her burden somewhat and cut the number down or even cut the whole number out. . . . [Then, a switch:] If she is still adamant and kicking, I suppose something will have to be done. Next week I'll start thinking about the problem [mine, mostly]. I'm hoping, though, you write me that she has entirely forgotten the issue." And apparently she had, because on Oct. 22 I was able to write: "The news is good especially about Gertie seemingly having forgotten that she wanted a song to replace 'One Life to Live.' "

Two years later, in the fall of '43, when *Lady* played Los Angeles (with Gertie as enchanting as ever and "One Life to Live" still getting a good hand), I went backstage to say hello. Since the days of *Oh, Kay!* Gertie had always been pleasantly cordial to me and was being so to a dozen visitors when I entered her dressing room. But my hello received so reluctant and lukewarm a response that about a minute and a half later I found myself taxiing back to Beverly Hills and wondering if Kurt and I were right about her "seemingly having forgotten."

—from *Lyrics on Several Occasions*

"Oh, Fabulous One"

LIZA'S
ADMIRERS: We come to serenade the lovely
lady we adore.
She occupies the seventeenth to
twenty-second floor.
Our lady so seraphic
May not be very near us,
And with the sound of traffic
She may not even hear us—
But love is wrong without a song,
So, now as heretofore,
We come to serenade the lovely
lady we adore.

TENOR: Oh, Fabulous One in your Ivory
Tower—
Your radiance I fain would see!
What Mélisande was to Pelléas
Are you to me. . . .

ANOTHER: Oh, Fabulous One in your Ivory
Tower—
My heart and I, they both agree:
What Juliet was to Romeo
Are you to me. . . .

FIRST
VOICE: What Beatrice was to Dante . . .
What Guinevere was to Lancelot . . .

What Brünnhilde was to
   Siegfried . . .
What Pocahontas was to Captain
   Smith . . .

SECOND
   VOICE: What Martha was to
      Washington . . .
      What Butterfly was to
         Pinkerton . . .
      What Calamity Jane was to Buffalo
         Bill . . .
      What Carmen was to Don José
      Are you to me. . . .

SIX MEN: Oh, Fabulous One in your Ivory
      Tower—
      Oh, Sweet! This is no potpourri!
      What Mélisande was to Pelléas
      Are you to me!

[*The music continues as Sutton, a maid, later
to be identified as Miss Foster, Liza's secretary,
appears*]

   SUTTON: I'm Miss Elliott's maid.
      Gentlemen, I'm afraid
      Your loyalty we must be testing.
      She cannot be seen. She's resting.
      But she wishes to thank you all for
         the serenade.

   MEN: Give the lady above
      Salutations and love.
      Advise her we leave in sweet
         sorrow
      But that we return on the morrow
      With our nightly serenade.

[*Leaving, they wave to the apartment above*]
      Each night we serenade the lovely
         lady we adore
      Who occupies the seventeenth to
         twenty-second floor.

[*"Glamour" theme as apartment projection
fades out and we fade in on boudoir projection*]

[*Sutton is getting Liza's clothes ready. The
color theme is blue. Doorbell rings*]
   SUTTON: Come in.
[*Boy enters, carries package*]
   BOY: A package for Miss Elliott.
   SUTTON: Put it on the table.
[*She points upstage*]
      What is it?
   BOY: A coat of sable.
[*He dances upstage and disappears. Bell rings*]
   SUTTON: Come in.
[*A tall, distinguished man, top hat and
beribboned stiff shirt, enters followed by a
Zouave carrying an enormous rose whose
cellophaned stem is at least fifteen feet long*]

MAN: A flower for Miss Elliott—
      Tribute to her splendor—
      From His Royal Highness,
      The French Pretender!

[*They salute as Sutton curtsies; then she points
upstage in which direction they both dance off,
to same step as the boy, and disappear. Bell
rings*]
   SUTTON: Yes?
[*Beekman, later to be identified as Russell
Paxton, the photographer of Allure, now
appears as a chauffeur in a bright yellow
uniform*]
      Good evening, Beekman.
   BEEKMAN: Good evening, Sutton.
[*Looks at clothes strewn about*]
      Ah, I see a touch of blue.
      She wears it as it's worn by few.

[*They march downstage, then sing ecstatically:*]
   BOTH: When as in silks our Liza goes
      Then, then, methinks how sweetly
         flows
      The liquefaction of her clothes—
      The liquefaction of her
         clothes. . . .
[*Sutton hums while countermelody is sung by:*]
   BEEKMAN: A delicate poem by Herrick—
      But, surely, heavier than a derrick
      Compared to our Miss Liza—She's
         so glamorous,
      She makes all other women appear
      Hammacher Schlammorous.
[*He looks at his wrist watch*]
      A thousand pardons—I must quit
         the scene.
      I must be off to perfume the
         gasoline.
[*He dances off.*]*

[*"Glamour" theme. Liza comes on to dress. Her
hair is now red*]
   LIZA: Good evening, Sutton.
   SUTTON: Good evening, Miss Elliott.

---

*The following, intended for this point in the score,
was dropped during rehearsals.
[*Bell rings*]
   SUTTON: Come in.
[*Truckdriver enters*]
TRUCKDRIVER: Got something for Miss Elliott.
      Got a warehouse handy?
   SUTTON: What's it this time?
TRUCKDRIVER: Two tons of candy.
   SUTTON: That makes eight tons of candy—
      What a bore!
      Pretty soon we'll have to take
      The twenty-third floor.

   LIZA: Are there any messages?
   SUTTON: Quite a number.
[*From dressing table Sutton takes an assortment
of letters, cables, telegrams, etc.*]

"Huxley"

   SUTTON: Huxley wants to dedicate his book to
         you—
      And Stravinsky, his latest sonata.
      Seven thousand students say they
         look to you
      To be at the Yale-Harvard Regatta.
      Epstein says you simply have to pose
         for him.
      Here's the key to the Island of Tobago.
      Du Pont wants you wearing the new
         hose for him.
      Can you christen a battleship in San
         Diego?

   LIZA: [*dreamily*] Huxley wants to dedicate
         his book to me.
[*Sutton finds another cable*]
   SUTTON: Shostakovitch his latest cantata.
   LIZA: Seven thousand students say they
         look to me
      To be at the Yale-Harvard Regatta.
   SUTTON: Oh, how lovely to be you!
   LIZA: How splendid!
   SUTTON: But it only is your due.
   LIZA: This must never be ended!

      Epstein says I simply have to pose for
         him. . . .
      No refusing these artistic ultimata!
      Du Pont wants me wearing the new
         hose for him. . . .
      Oh, how thrilling to be the world's
         inamorata!
      Oh, how thrilling to be the world's
         inamorata!

   SUTTON: You never looked lovelier, Miss
         Elliott.
   LIZA: Thank you, Sutton.
[*Miss Forsythe, the secretary, enters*]*
      And what are my engagements, Miss
         Forsythe?

[*The "Huxley" melody now becomes a Viennese
waltz. Following is spoken but in rhythm to the
waltz*]
   MISS
FORSYTHE:
[*from notebook*]
      Dinner at the Seventh Heaven.

---

*No "Miss Forsythe" is listed in *Lady in the Dark*
programs. It seems the part was cut prior to opening
night.

LIZA: With the Maharajah and those two
handsome men from Texas.

MISS
FORSYTHE: Toscanini broadcast.

LIZA: I told the Maestro I'd drop in for half
an hour or so.

MISS
FORSYTHE: Party at the Harrimans'.

LIZA: Saroyan promises to write a play in
front of us.

MISS
FORSYTHE: Skyscraper Room.

LIZA: Ah, yes. Sacheveral and I are reviving
the cakewalk.

MISS
FORSYTHE: That's all I have here.

LIZA: I'll probably motor to Bear Mountain
to see the sun rise. You needn't
wait up. Good night.

SUTTON
AND MISS
FORSYTHE: Good night, Miss Elliott.

[As lights dim down, waltz emerges fortissimo.
Liza is seen waltzing Grace La Rueishly in
spotlight until Beekman is discovered. He is in
a blue uniform, standing at attention, eyes
directly front. Music stops]

BEEKMAN: I learned it would be blue tonight. So
I'm driving the blue Duesenberg
with the blue license plates and I've
put the blue Picasso in the car.

LIZA: Very thoughtful, Beekman.

BEEKMAN: Where to, Miss Elliott?

LIZA: That new nightclub, the Seventh
Heaven.

[Beekman starts car. Green light. Then red
light. Brakes]

Where are we, Beekman?

BEEKMAN: Columbus Circle.

LIZA: Would you get me my blue soap box,
please? I want to make a speech.

[Beekman jumps out of car, opens door for her.
Liza gets on soap box. Beekman at attention
throughout]

"One Life to Live"

VERSE

LIZA: There are many minds in
circulation
Believing in reincarnation.
In me you see
One who doesn't agree.
Challenging possible affronts,
I believe I'll only live once,
And I want to make the most of it;

If there's a party, I want to be the
host of it;
If there's a haunted house, I want
to be the ghost of it;
If I'm in town, I want to be the
toast of it.

REFRAIN 1

I say to me ev'ry morning:
You've only one life to live,
So why be done in?
Let's let the sun in,
And gloom can jump in the riv'!

No use to beat on the doldrums;
Let's be imaginative.
Each day is numbered—
No good when slumbered—
With only one life to live.

Why let the goblins upset you?
One smile and see how they run!
And what does worrying net you?
Nothing!
The thing
Is to have fun!

All this may sound kind of
hackneyed,
But it's the best I can give.
Soon comes December,
So, please remember
You've only one life to live—
Just one life to live.

REFRAIN 2

BEEKMAN: She says to her ev'ry morning:
She's only one life to live;
No time like Now-time*
For that big Wow-time,
And gloom can jump in the riv'!

LIZA: What you collect at the grindstone
Becomes a millstone in time.
This is my thesis:
Why go to pieces?
Step out while you're in your
prime.

They may say I'm an escapist,
But I would rather, by far,
Be that than be a red tape-ist.
Lead me,

---

*In the script, score, and lyric sheets, lines 3 and 4 of
refrain 2 are:

So why be done in?
Let's let the sun in,

Speed me
Straight to the bar!

Just laugh at Old Man Repression
He'll fade out into obliv'—
And you're the winner!

[Beekman points to his wristwatch]
I'm off to dinner!
I've only one life to live—
Just one life to live.

[Short dance and back into car. Green traffic
light. Suddenly the Seventh Heaven appears.
Couples are dancing. Liza makes an entrance,
Beekman in attendance carrying her coat.
Pierre, the headwaiter, later to be identified as
Kendall Nesbitt, rushes to Liza]

PIERRE: Words fail me. My little
establishment which, I flatter
myself, is the world's most
exclusive nightclub since Louis
the Fourteenth ran Le Petit
Trianon, is only in the smallest
degree worthy of your presence.

LIZA: You are sweet, Pierre.

PIERRE: [clapping for attention] Miss Liza
Elliott!

ENSEMBLE: Darling! How nice of you to come.
Darling! How are you?

A MAN
FROM TEXAS: Gentlemen—a toast! The toast! The
toast of toasts! Liza Elliott!

ENSEMBLE: Hip, hip! Hip, hip! Liza Elliott!

"Girl of the Moment"

MEN: Oh, girl of the moment
With the smile of the day
And the charm of the week
And the grace of the month
And the looks of the year—
Oh, girl of the moment,
You're my moment ev'ry moment of
the time.

BEEKMAN: Oh, girl of the moment
With the light in your eyes
And the sun in your hair
And the rose in your cheeks
And the laugh in your voice—
Oh, girl of the moment,
In a moment you could make my life
sublime.

In all my flights of fancy
Your image I drew—
I look at you and can see
That fancy come true.

ENSEMBLE: Oh, girl of the moment
With the smile of the day

And the charm of the week
And the grace of the month
And the looks of the year—
Oh, girl of the moment,
You're my moment all the time!

[*On march a Soldier, Sailor, and a Marine. The Marine is later to be identified as Charley Johnson, advertising manager of* Allure]

ENSEMBLE: Oh, goodness, oh, gracious!
Our minds are capacious,
But what in the world does this
mean?
Although we are partial
To men that are martial,
What reason brings you on the scene?

MARINE: I bring a message for Miss Elliott.
LIZA: From?
MARINE: The President of the United States.

ENSEMBLE: Oh, goodness, oh, gracious!
Our minds are capacious,
But what in the world does this
mean?
Direct from the White House
He calls at this night house!
One cannot say this is routine!

LIZA: And?
MARINE: The President requests . . .
LIZA: Yes?
MARINE: That for the national unity . . .
LIZA: Yes?
MARINE: For the furtherance of goodwill . . .
LIZA: Yes?
MARINE: And for the advancement of cultural
and artistic achievement . . .
ENSEMBLE: Yes?
MARINE: Your portrait be painted and your
likeness used on the new two-cent
stamp.
LIZA: How really lovely!
[*"Glamour" theme*]

ENSEMBLE: Oh, how thrilled she ought to be!
At that, there's none so fair as she.

LIZA: Who is to paint me—and where?
MARINE: I am to paint you—and here.
[*Liza acquiesces. The soldiers' guns become legs of an easel. A thronelike chair is brought on for Liza. Marine poses her. Starts to paint her. All this to the first half of "Girl of the Moment" which from the instant Liza has nodded her acceptance to pose has become an oratorio with Bach-like harmonies as if we are in a Greek Catholic cathedral*]

"It Looks Like Liza"

MARINE: It's finished. The portrait is
painted!

ENSEMBLE: Of beauty untainted
The portrait is painted—
The portrait the nation awaits.
Oh, please, sir—unveil it!
And when can we mail it
To friends in the forty-eight states?

LIZA: Is It Impressionistic?
Or is it American Primitive?
This work of art he's done . . .
Is it Pointillistic?
Is it Surrealistic?
Or is it a W.P.A.-ish one?

[*The two themes are sung against each other:*]
LIZA,
SOPRANOS,
TENORS: Is it Impressionistic?
Or is it American Primitive?
This work of art he's done.
This work he's done.

CONTRALTOS,
BASSES: Of beauty untainted
The portrait is painted—
The portrait the nation awaits.
Oh, please, sir, unveil it,
And when can we mail it,
And when can we mail it,
And when can we mail it,
And when can we mail it,
And when can we mail it
To friends in the forty-eight states?
ENSEMBLE: Oh how thrilled she ought to be!
At that, there's none so fair as she.
[*The portrait is unveiled. It is not flattering. It is Liza as she appeared in the doctor's office—austere, somewhat forbidding, entirely without glamour. She looks at it for a few tense seconds, screams, slaps the face of its creator, throws herself onto the thronelike chair, and hides her face. The crowd is at first perplexed, then becomes cynical*]
WOMAN: It looks like Liza!
MAN: But it is Liza?
ANOTHER
WOMAN: The looks of Liza—
ANOTHER
MAN: The size o' Liza—
ENSEMBLE: But if it's Liza
Why is Liza
So un-Liza-like?

MARINE: I painted Liza!
It must be Liza!

The looks of Liza—
The size o' Liza—

ENSEMBLE: If *she* is Liza—
[*pointing to portrait*]
And *she* is Liza—
[*pointing to Liza*]
What is Liza really like?
What is Liza really like?
What is Liza really like?
What is Liza really like?

[*Imperceptibly this rhythm becomes that of "Girl of the Moment," which now is traced orchestrally as a wild bolero. All sing accusingly, and later, in the wild semiballet formations encircling Liza, they point at her scornfully and laugh mockingly*]

"Girl of the Moment" (Reprise)

ENSEMBLE: Oh, girl of the moment
With the smile of the day
And the charm of the week
And the grace of the month
And the looks of the year—
Oh, girl of the moment,
Ev'ry moment
Was a waste of precious time!

Oh, girl of the moment
With the light in your eyes
And the sun in your hair
And the rose in your cheeks
And the laugh in your voice—
Oh, girl of the moment,
From this moment
To the heights no more you'll climb.

My dreams are torn asunder.
Your image I drew.
I see you now and wonder
What I saw in you.

Oh, girl of the moment
With the smile of the day
And the charm of the week
And the grace of the month
And the looks of the year—
Oh, girl of the moment,
Where's the girl
That was sublime?

[*At end of dance, all sing, in a slower tempo:*]
Oh, girl of the moment,
Where's the girl
That was sublime?

END OF GLAMOUR DREAM

WEDDING DREAM, including MAPLETON HIGH CHORALE and THIS IS NEW and THE PRINCESS OF PURE DELIGHT and THE WOMAN AT THE ALTAR

Published in the piano-vocal score and with the complete text of the play April 1941. ("This Is New" published separately January 1941; "The Princess of Pure Delight" published separately February 1941.) Introduced by Bert Lytell (Kendall Nesbitt), Gertrude Lawrence (Liza Elliott), Macdonald Carey (Charley Johnson), Victor Mature (Randy Curtis), Evelyn Wyckoff (Miss Foster), Margaret Dale (Maggie Grant), Natalie Schafer (Alison Du Bois), Danny Kaye (Russell Paxton), and ensemble. Alternate title of "Wedding Dream": "Second Dream Sequence." Alternate title of "Mapleton High Chorale": "Mapleton High."

About "This Is New"

Several actors read for the role of Randy Curtis, movie star, in *Lady in the Dark*, but none had been found satisfactory. About a week before rehearsals were to start, a friend of mine, Gene Solow, just in from California, popped in to see me at the Essex House. When I told him of our casting problem, he said that a likely prospect, Victor Mature, had been on the plane with him, but he didn't know where Victor was to stay. I was busy shaving and asked: "Would you mind calling the Hotel Pierre? Maybe he's just registered there." No Mature. "Try the Algonquin." No Mature. "21" was phoned, with the same result. "It's probably crazy—but try the hotel desk here." "Crazy, eh?" said Gene a few seconds later—"He's registering right now."

Although . . . "This Is New" [was to have been] sung by Gertrude Lawrence and Victor Mature, actually it was finally done by Gertie alone. When handsome "hunk of man" Mature sang, his heart and the correct key weren't in it. By cutting out the verse with its "luckiest of men," we were able to give the song to Gertie and have it remain in the score.

—from *Lyrics on Several Occasions*

About "The Princess of Pure Delight"

Fairy Tale from Left Field. During the writing of *Lady in the Dark* Kurt Weill and I spent a couple of weekends with Moss Hart at his charming summer place in Bucks County. The food was excellent, the guestrooms cozy; there were a large swimming pool and thousands of trees and any amount of huge and overwhelmingly friendly, woolly dogs; there was even that rarity for those days (1940), a TV set; but the show was ever on our minds and mostly we were at it, discussing the score in progress and what lay ahead. Dinner, though, usually brought additional guests; and one Sunday night Richard Rodgers, who had been weekending at nearby George Kaufman's, offered us a ride back to the city (we had come by train), a convenience gladly accepted. We were to leave about nine p.m., but it was decided to wait until city-bound traffic died down a bit. To pass the time, Dick picked up an old quiz-and-conundrum book of the Twenties from Moss's shelves; and all present spent an hour or so answering quiz questions, correcting twisted quotations, solving riddles, &c. End of Part One.

Some weeks later when Kurt and I were in the Second Dream Sequence we came to a spot where Liza and some children were alone on the stage. I suggested—and Kurt liked the notion—that here a sung fairy tale might be incorporated. So next day I got hold of some Andersen and the Brothers Grimm, and leafed through for something not too well known to base a narrative on—any short one that could be transformed into a song. In my anxiousness to find something quickly, probably much possible was overlooked; my hurried impressions pictured mainly young princes turning into frogs and vice versa. Which form of corporeal alchemy seemed too complicated and farfetched. Metamorphosis out, I began thinking of other legendary magical gimmicks and concluded that the kind used so frequently in *The Arabian Nights' Entertainment* might do the trick: one where an in-a-spot young man answers brilliantly one or several loaded questions, and reaps, from an amazed and delighted potentate, rewards of non-decapitation, bushels of diamonds and rubies, a harem, and other desiderata. It was then that I remembered the Sunday night mentioned above and *my* brilliant answer to a conundrum Dick put: "What word of five letters is never spelled right?" This seemed short, sweet, and possible for a device; so, having something to head for, I started.

I had a rough idea of what I wanted to say, but none about the number of lines it would take. I finally decided on a title and came up with an opening stanza, which I gave to Kurt for tentative setting. Tentative because I was prepared to change the approach if he felt that a longish lyric with regular, confining stanzas might make for musical monotony. Soon after, he played me a setting I liked; then said there'd be no problem—that, no matter how many stanzas were required, the musical end would be reasonably cohesive. With this assurance I kept furthering and tickling up the narrative, with Kurt never more than a stanza behind me; and in a few days this section of the dream was completed.

Because several of my friends were being analyzed at twenty dollars a session, I couldn't resist "That will be twenty gulden, please."

—from *Lyrics on Several Occasions*

"Mapleton High Chorale"

[*Through the darkness the name "Liza" is heard, weirdly sung. The lights come up and we discover the singing is being done by a group of boys and girls dressed as high school graduates of a generation ago. Mostly their lines are sung—a few are spoken*]

CHORALE: There's a girl—Liza Elliott.
We all knew her. We went to high school together.
We graduated with her.

A BOY: She was cheer leader in the third year.

CHORALE: Mapleton High, Mapleton High,
For you we will do and for you we will die!
Rah, rah, rah!

A GIRL: I remember Liza well.
We read *Les Misérables* in her room on rainy days.
And *A Tale of Two Cities*, too.

ANOTHER GIRL: I liked her a lot.

ANOTHER GIRL: *I* thought she was stuck up.

A BOY: I remember the house she used to live in
And the tree in the garden where she used to swing.

ANOTHER BOY: I might as well tell it now.
On Graduation Day when Liza delivered the Valedictory
I asked her if she'd wait for me.
She smiled. She didn't take me seriously.

A GIRL: I never quite understood her. She had a pretty voice, though.

CHORALE: We sing the praise of Mapleton High;
Each heart is filled with loyalty.
And for our school we'll do or we'll die
And reach the goal of victory.

Oh, Alma Mater, Mapleton High—
Your bounty is on every hand;
And while we live we'll never deny
No finer school is in the land.

A BOY: She was a wiz at tennis. One time I had her five–two, point set. She beat me, nine–seven.

ANOTHER
BOY: Remember that caricature she drew of Monsieur D'Albert, the French teacher? Instead of getting sore at her, he took it home to show to his wife.

CHORALE: Le, la, les!
Parlez-vous français?
Ouvrez la fenêtre,
S'il vous plaît!

[to the tune of "Clair de lune":]
La la la la la la la, la la la la la,
La la la lala la, la lala la la.

A BOY: Happy, happy days.

CHORALE: Oh, Alma Mater, Mapleton High—
Your bounty is on every hand;
And while we live we'll never deny
No finer school is in the land.

[They split into two groups—opposite sides of the stage]

And now a Mapleton High girl is to be married.
[Bolero rhythm starts]
Liza Elliott is marrying Kendall Nesbitt.
[Kendall is spotlighted. He looks about expectantly]

A GIRL: Kendall Nesbitt is forty-eight years old. He loves Liza and Liza loves him. They get along beautifully.

CHORALE: It's quite idyllic.

A BOY: He started the magazine for her. It's been most successful.

CHORALE: They should be very happy.
[Liza appears in a white gown. Kendall goes to her]

And now they are buying the ring. But why is Liza hesitant?
[A salesman with a tray of rings appears. It is Charley Johnson]
Shall it be with emeralds
Or shall it be with diamonds?
[Liza finally decides, points. Johnson bows and instead of giving her the ring proffers a small golden dagger. Liza recoils as both men disappear and Randy is spotlighted]

MEN'S
VOICES: Randy Curtis.
Flame of the celluloid.
A precious amalgam of Frank Merriwell,
Anthony Eden,

And Lancelot!
Randy Curtis!

WOMEN'S
VOICES: Forty million women see him every week.

MEN'S
VOICES: Randy Curtis!

WOMEN'S
VOICES: And forty million women love him.
In Kansas, in Patagonia, in Hollywood itself,
He is a man every woman wants.
[Randy sees Liza, whose face is covered by her hands]

RANDY: Darling. At last.
[He turns her to face him. Slowly her expression changes. Finally she smiles, looks up at him trustingly]

"This Is New"

VERSE*

RANDY: With you I used to roam
Through The Pleasure Dome
Of Kubla Khan.
I held you tight, my love,
In the gardens of
Old Babylon.
I lost you through the centuries.
I find you once again,
And find myself the luckiest of men.

REFRAIN

RANDY
AND LIZA: This is new—
I was merely existing.
This is new
And I'm living at last.
Head to toe,
You've got me so I'm spellbound;
I don't know
If I am heaven- or hell-bound.

This is new—
Is it Venus insisting
That I'm through
With the shadowy past?
I am hurled
Up to another world
Where life is bliss,
And this
Is new.

---

*In the original production, this verse was deleted, and all lyrics or song cues hereafter assigned to Randy were reassigned or deleted. See I.G.'s note, following.

[A second refrain is sung by the chorale. Liza leaves Randy's arms, finds herself in Johnson's. They dance. Six girls in red wigs, with dresses exactly like Liza's, come on. Johnson disappears. Randy is again discovered. He sings to the six. As they dance, Liza merely watches. Finally Liza is alone on the stage. Reflectively she hums the beginning of the elusive tune,* stops]

CHORALE: Go on.

LIZA: I can't remember any more.

CHORALE: What's worrying you, Liza?

LIZA: I don't know.

CHORALE: What are you afraid of?
You should be happy.
Every woman wants to be married.
And this is the eve of your wedding day.
What are you thinking of?

VOICE OF
DR. BROOKS: Take all the time you want, Miss Elliott.

LIZA: How curious! How very curious! Of all the things I could be thinking of at the moment, a little school play I acted in when I was a child keeps running through my mind.

CHORALE: We are listening.

LIZA: It was called—
"The Princess of Pure Delight."
[The children appear in costume. They bow, then proceed to enact Liza's narrative. This should be done with an economy of motion—rigid poses, possibly, at the end of each stanza]

"The Princess of Pure Delight"

LIZA: The Prince in Orange and the Prince in Blue,
And the Prince whose raiment was of Lavender hue—
They sighed and they suffered and they tossed at night
For the neighboring Princess of Pure Delight . . .
(Who was secretly in love with a Minstrel).

Her father, the King, didn't know which to choose;
There were two charming suitors he'd have to refuse.†

---

*The "elusive tune" is "My Ship," following.
†In the piano-vocal score, this line is:
There were two charming Princes he'd have to refuse.

So he called for the Dean of his Sorcerers and
Inquired which one was to win her hand
(Which they always did in those days).

"My King, here's a riddle—you test them
 tonight:
'What word of five letters is never spelled
 right?
What word of five letters is always spelled
 wrong?'
The one who can answer will be wedded
 ere long.
(That will be twenty gulden, please!)"

The King called the three and he told
 them the test,
The while his fair daughter kept beating
 her breast.
He put them the riddle. They failed (as he
 feared).
Then all of a sudden the Minstrel
 appeared!
(Quite out of breath.)

"I'll answer that riddle," cried the Singer
 of Song.
"What's never spelled 'right' in five letters
 is 'wrong';
And it's right to spell 'wrong'—w-r-o-n-g!
Your Highness, the Princess belongeth to
 me!
(And I love her, anyway!)"

"Be off with you, villain!" the King cried
 in rage,
"For my Princess a Prince—not a man
 from the stage!"
"But, Sire!" said the Minstrel, " 'tis love
 makes me say,
No King who's a real King treats lovers
 this way!
(It isn't sporting.)

"And if you're no real King, no Princess is
 she—
And if she's no Princess then she can wed
 me!"
"By gad," cried His Highness, "you
 handsome young knave,
I fear me you're right!" And his blessing
 he gave
(As a trumpeter began to trumpet).

The Princess then quickly came out of her
 swoon
And she looked at her swain and her world
 was in tune.
And the castle soon rang with cheer and
 with laughter.
(And of course they lived happily ever
 after.)

"The Woman at the Altar"

[*All bow as orchestra music grows louder and
children gradually disappear. Suddenly
wedding bells fill the air. Liza looks
wonderingly about and slowly walks to other
side of stage where she discovers her office desk.
As though under a spell she goes to the desk
and presses a buzzer. Miss Foster appears*]

LIZA: Miss Foster, where *is* everybody?
 Where's Miss Grant,
 Miss Du Bois, Mr. Paxton, Mr.
 Johnson?

[*Miss Foster just looks at her and slowly backs
away. Liza frantically pushes all the buttons on
the desk*]

 Maggie! Alison! Russell! Johnson!
 Where are you?

[*Slowly they appear*]

 Maggie, where are the proofs?
 Johnson, where's your layout?
 Alison, where's your column?*
 What's the matter with you?
 What's the matter with everybody?

JOHNSON: Why, don't you know what day this
 is, Boss Lady?
 This is your wedding day.

ALISON
AND MAGGIE: Your wedding day. You must hurry,
 Liza. This is your wedding day.

[*Again the wedding bells ring out. As Johnson
backs away, Maggie and Alison go to Liza and
lead her upstage. Paxton appears in morning
coat, high hat, striped trousers. In back of him
are boys and girls as bridesmaids and ushers,
and as they proceed to dress Liza as a bride,
the stage turns into a church. In the back, a
huge stained-glass window with a grotesque
bride and groom as the motif, and for the altar
a huge wedding cake. The wedding procession
starts*]

CHORALE: And now Liza Elliott is going to be
 married.
 At last Liza Elliott is going to be
 married.

 Let music fill the air!
 We hail the happy pair!
 Lift every voice in praise!
 This is their day of days!

GUESTS: What a lovely day for a lovely
 wedding.
 What a lucky man to win himself
 such a bride.
 To the gates of paradise both are
 heading

---

*In the piano-vocal score, the "Johnson" line follows
the "Alison" line.

 With love and loy'lty acting as their
 guide.

[*Nesbitt appears, goes to Liza, offers his arm.
The children now act as flower boys and girls.
Randy sings "This Is New" as though it were
"Oh, Promise Me." The procession marches
towards the altar. During the second half of
"This Is New," Charley, who is now the
minister, starts murmuring the marriage service.
It becomes audible*]

CHARLEY: If there be any who know why these
 two should not be joined in holy
 wedlock let him speak now or
 forever hold his peace.

SEPULCHRAL
VOICE IN
CHORALE: The murmurings of conscience do
 increase.
 And conscience can no longer hold
 its peace.
 This twain should ne'er be joined in
 holy wedlock
 Or e'en in secular board and
 bed-lock.
 This is no part of heaven's marriage
 plan.
 This woman knows she does not
 love this man.

CHORALE: This woman knows she does not
 love this man.

LIZA: No, no! No, no! That isn't true!
 I do! I do! I do! I do!

CHORALE: This woman at the altar
 Is not the true Liza Elliott.
 Tell them about yourself, Liza
 Elliott.
 Tell them about the woman you
 really want to be—
 Longing to be beautiful
 And yet rejecting beauty.
 Tell them the truth.
 Tell them the truth.
 This is no part of heaven's marriage
 plan.

LIZA: No, no! It isn't true!
CHORALE: This woman knows she does not
 love this man.
LIZA: I do! I do! I do! I do!

[*Liza, who has been backing away slowly, her
hands pressing against her ears to shut out the
accusing voices, soon disappears. Randy starts
intoning "This Is New" as the guests sing the
countermelody "What a Lovely Day." It all
becomes a bizarre combination of oratorio and*

mysterious and ominous movement based on different melodies of the dream thrown together at first contrapuntally and winding up in a wild, cacophonous musical nightmare]

END OF WEDDING DREAM

CIRCUS DREAM, including THE GREATEST SHOW ON EARTH and THE BEST YEARS OF HIS LIFE and TCHAIKOWSKY (AND OTHER RUSSIANS) and THE SAGA OF JENNY

Published in the piano-vocal score and with the complete text of the play April 1941. ("Tchaikowsky" and "The Saga of Jenny" published separately February 1941.) Introduced by Danny Kaye (Ringmaster), Gertrude Lawrence (Liza Elliott), Macdonald Carey (Charley Johnson), Victor Mature (Randy Curtis), Bert Lytell (Kendall Nesbitt), and ensemble. Alternate title of "Circus Dream": "Third Dream Sequence." Alternate title of "Tchaikowsky (and Other Russians)": "Tchaikowsky." Alternate titles of "The Saga of Jenny": "Jenny" and "Poor Jenny."

About "Tchaikowsky (and Other Russians)"

This lyric, proper noun for proper noun, is based almost entirely on a bit of light verse called "The Music Hour," by Arthur Francis, in the then pre-pictorial, humorous weekly *Life*, June 12, 1924; and for which Mr. Francis received a check of twelve dollars from the editors. I have waited hopefully—but in vain—these many years for someone to accuse me of plagiarism, so that I could respond with the fact that for four years or so I was the pseudonymous Arthur Francis. The names of most of the forty-nine composers mentioned I compiled from advertisements on the back covers of piano music and orchestral scores in my brother's collection.

Not all of the forty-nine, however, have been necessarily merely names to me. *Rumshinsky*, who wrote many musical-comedy scores for the Yiddish theater, I met several times when I lived on Second Avenue in New York; he was a pinochle-playing companion of my father's. Dimitri *Tiomkin*, now one of the topflight Hollywood film composers (rich also in the possession of one of the topmost Russian accents extant), I have known

since the Twenties. With ballet and oratorio composer *Dukelsky*, whom I first knew as Vladimir Dukelsky, later as Vernon Duke (a name suggested to him by my brother), I collaborated on the *Ziegfeld Follies of 1936*. And through Vernon I met both *Stravinsky* (at the Met, 1935, during intermission of *Lady Macbeth of Mtsensk*) and *Prokofieff* (at my publisher's, New York, 1938. He was on his way back to Russia from Hollywood and I got him a copy of *Porgy and Bess*, which he wanted to take along). *Godowsky* I'd met in Paris on several occasions—this two years before his son Leo, musician and inventor, married my sister. And in January 1956, during a two-week stay in Moscow (I flew there for the opening of *Porgy and Bess*) I met Reinhold Moritzovich *Glière*, composer of "The Red Poppy" and some five hundred other works. This was at a luncheon given by the cultural organization called VOKS. At another table my wife, through an interpreter, told the affable and charming octogenarian that I had mentioned him in a song about Russian composers. Afterwards I was introduced to Glière and was somewhat embarrassed by his profuse thanks, since he didn't know there were forty-eight other mentions—all put together for comedic effect of names generally strange to American ears. I never met *Rachmaninoff*—but my brother knew him quite well. Rachmaninoff? I really have to stop—the subject has been dwelt upon enough.

New World Record. . . . I [have noted] that Danny Kaye rattled off "Tchaikowsky" in thirty-nine seconds. However, during a world-wide tour for the UN International Children's Emergency Fund he announced on the stage in Barcelona he would try for a world record in the delivery of this song—and was timed in thirty-six seconds. But this went by the wayside when in Madrid he was clocked in thirty-one.

—from *Lyrics on Several Occasions*

About "The Saga of Jenny"

The third musical dream sequence in *Lady in the Dark*, a mixture of Court Trial and Minstrel Show, was practically completed when it was decided that minstrel costume and background weren't novel enough. Agreeing that a circus setting seemed preferable—there could be more riotous color and regalia—we changed the opening, the jury patters, and most of the recitatives, from an environment of burnt cork and sanded floor to putty nose and tanbark.

One section of this sequence, however, remained unchanged: Liza Elliott's defense of her actions. It was a six- or seven-minute pseudo-metaphysical dissertation based on the signs of the Zodiac and their influences, all pretty fatalistic; in short, she'd done what she did because she couldn't help doing whatever she did do. We were quite proud of this bizarre and *Three Penny Opera*–like effort and felt it could be the play's musical highlight. (We wrote a fourth dream sequence, but this

one was not for her analyst. It was a rather extravagant daydream—following a marriage proposal by the Western movie star—in which Liza envisions her possible Hollywood life: an enormous ranch in the San Fernando Valley with a palatial home furnished from the Hearst Collection, butlers galore, private golf course, Chinese cooks, fifty-thousand-barrel gushers on the property, &c. But this twenty-minute daydream—not to be heard by the analyst—was also unheard and unseen by the audience, as the show was already about fifteen or more minutes too long.) Anyway, after some four months of hard work—twelve to sixteen hours a day, and through one of the hottest summers New York had ever known—our contributions to *Lady in the Dark* were completed; and Kurt could now remain in New City across the Hudson to orchestrate, and I return home until the start of rehearsals.

I had been back in California only about a week when producer Sam Harris telephoned me. After long and careful consideration he and Moss Hart felt that the Zodiac number, impressive as it was, might prove too dour and oppressive; something lighter and perhaps gayer was required. I telephoned Kurt. His feeling was, right or wrong, we owed them a go at it, since generally, everything else we'd done had been found so acceptable. So, a few days later I was again in New York. At one conference Moss had a suggestion that we do a number about a woman who couldn't make up her mind. That sounded possible; and after a week or so of experimenting with style, format, and complete change of melodic mood from the Zodiac song, we started "Jenny," and finished Liza's new defense about ten days later.

All through rehearsals Miss Lawrence did "Jenny" most acceptably. But I kept wondering whether it would be as effective as the Zodiac song. This is what happened opening night in Boston: We were playing to a packed house, and the show was holding the audience tensely. It was working out. I was among the standees at the back of the house; next to me was one of the Sam Harris staff. In the circus scene when Danny Kaye completed the last note of "Tschaikowsky," thunderous applause rocked the theater for at least a solid minute. The staff member clutched my arm, muttered: "Christ, we've lost our star!" couldn't take it, and rushed for the lobby. Obviously he felt that nothing could top Danny's rendition, that "Jenny" couldn't compete with it, and that either Miss Lawrence would leave the show or that Danny Kaye would have to be cut down to size.

But he should have waited. The next few lines of dialogue weren't heard because of the continuing applause. Then, as Danny deferred to Miss Lawrence, it ended; and "Jenny" began. She hadn't been singing more than a few lines when I realized an interpretation we'd never seen in rehearsal was materializing. Not only were there new nuances and approaches, but on top of this she "bumped" it and "ground" it, to the complete devastation of the audience. At the conclusion, there was an ovation which lasted twice as long as that for "Tchaikowsky." "Tchaikowsky" had shown us the emergence of a new star in Danny Kaye. But "Jenny" revealed to us that we didn't have to worry about losing our brighter-than-ever star.

It is easier to predict correctly what will happen to the stock market than what show numbers will do. One hopes for the best, but one best remains noncommittal. Not everyone does, though. Three or four nights after the Boston opening, with *Lady* looking like a big hit, Kurt told me he hadn't wanted to worry me but this is what occurred after the dress rehearsal. Hassard Short, a top revue man of excellent taste, in charge of the show's physical production and lighting, took Kurt aside and said: "If you'll take my advice, you boys had better get two new numbers ready in a hurry. You'll find that 'Jenny' and the Russian number won't make it."

—from *Lyrics on Several Occasions*

"The Greatest Show on Earth"

[*While voices are saying "Easter cover or circus cover?" we faintly hear circus parade music. It quickly grows louder and louder and paraders march on*]

PARADERS: Ta ra ra, tszing, tszing, tszing—
Ta ra ra, tszing, tszing, tszing—
Ta ra ra, tszing, tszing, tszing—
Ta ra ra ra!
Ta ra ra, tszing, tszing, tszing—
Ta ra ra, tszing, tszing, tszing—
Ta ra ra, tszing, tszing, tszing—
Ta ra ra ra!

The Greatest Show on Earth!
It's Full of Thrills and Mirth!
You Get Your Money's Worth!
Come one, come all!

Come see the Midgets and the
Bushman from Australia;
Come see the Cossacks in Their
Dazz-l-ing Regalia!

The Flower of Womankind
Who Can't Make Up Her Mind
Is a Feature You Will Always
Recall!

You Get Your Money's Worth!
It's Full of Thrills and Mirth!
The Greatest Show on Earth!
Come one, come all!

[*The Ringmaster appears. He is Russell Paxton*]
RINGMASTER:
[*very operatic*]
Ladies and Gentlemen, I Take Pride
in Introducing
The Greatest Show on Earth!

Liza Elliott's Gargantuan
Three-Ring Circus
Featuring for the First Time
The Captivating and Tantalizing
Liza Elliott . . .
The Woman Who Cannot Make Up
Her Mind!
In Addition, We Bring You an
Assortment
Of Other Scintillating Stars of the
Tanbark Ring
And a Galaxy of Clowns and
Neuroses
In a Modern Miracle of
Melodramatic Buffoonery
And Mental Tightrope Walking!
The Greatest Show on Earth!

ENSEMBLE: The Flower of Womankind
Who Can't Make Up Her Mind
Is a Feature You Will Always
Recall!

ENSEMBLE: You Get Your Money's Worth!
It's Full of Thrills and Mirth!
The Greatest Show on Earth!
Come one, come all!

RINGMASTER: Order in the arena!*
[*Drum rolls as a page somersaults on. Presents parchment*]
PAGE: The charges against Liza Elliott.
RINGMASTER: Thank you, my dear.
[*As a photographer rushes on, taking flashlight of Liza*]
LIZA:
[*bewildered*]
What is all this? Charges against
me? What for? What is all this?
RINGMASTER:
[*reading from parchment*]
Whereas—
ENSEMBLE: Whereas—
RINGMASTER: Liza Elliott cannot make up her
mind about the Easter cover or
the circus cover—
Secundus—
ENSEMBLE: Secundus—
RINGMASTER: Liza Elliott cannot make up her
mind whether she is marrying
Kendall Nesbitt or not—
ENSEMBLE: Moreover—
RINGMASTER: Liza Elliott cannot make up her
mind as to the kind of woman
she wants to be—the executive or
the enchantress—
And, inasmuchas—

In the piano-vocal score, this line is: "Order in the courtroom!"

ENSEMBLE: Inasmuchas—
RINGMASTER: In a world where tumult and
turmoil reign, these indecisions of
Liza Elliott only add to the
confusions of an already, as
indicated, confused world—
Therefore, be it resolved—
ENSEMBLE: Be it resolved—
RINGMASTER: That Liza Elliott be brought to trial
and be made to make up her
mind.
[*A cheer*]
Introducing That Death-Defying
Trapeze Artist and Prosecuting
Attorney, Charley Johnson!
[*Fanfare as Johnson marches on*]
CHARLEY: I'm the attorney for prosecution—
Can't be bought or sold!
For the jam she's in there's no
solution,
Once the story's told!

ENSEMBLE: He's the attorney for prosecution—
Flying into space!
Will there be an electrocution
If he wins the case?

RINGMASTER: Introducing That Thrilling
Bareback Rider and Attorney for
the Defense—Randy Curtis!
[*Fanfare as Randy marches on*]
RANDY: I'm the lawyer for the defendant—
Can't be sold or bought!
Miss Elliott's star is in the
ascendant—
This will come to naught!

ENSEMBLE: He's the lawyer for the defendant—
Bareback rider, too!
Miss Elliott's star is in the
ascendant—
'Cording to his view!
[*Fanfare as Jury gets up*]
RINGMASTER: Introducing Those Merry Madcaps
and Prankish Pantaloonatics—the
Jury!

JURY: Our object all sublime
We shall achieve in time:
To let the melody fit the rhyme—
The melody fit the rhyme!

[*Ringmaster bangs gavel*]
RINGMASTER: This is all immaterial and
irrelevant—
What do you think this is—Gilbert
and Sellivant?

JURY: Gilbert and Sellivant! Ha ha ha ha
ha ha ha ha ha!
If this is just a sample,

[*Goes to Liza*]

You're afraid. You're hiding
something. You're afraid of that
music, aren't you? Just as you're
afraid to compete as a woman—
afraid to marry Kendall Nesbitt—
afraid to be the woman you want to
be—afraid—afraid—afraid!*

[*Flutter in the orchestra. Ensemble turns on
Liza and laughs tauntingly and accusingly.
Immediately the original circus music starts as
all march, whispering in rhythm, "Make up
your mind, make up your mind, make up your
mind." As the lights dim, Liza is left standing
in the office exactly as she stood at the start of
the dream*]

END OF CIRCUS DREAM

MY SHIP

Published separately January 1941. Published in the
piano-vocal score with the complete text of the play,
April 1941. Introduced by Gertrude Lawrence (Liza El-
liott). "Supposedly a turn-of-the-century song known to
Liza Elliott in her childhood" (Ira Gershwin—*Lyrics on
Several Occasions*).

Missing Song. "My Ship" loomed significantly in
the unconscious of successful—but unhappy—
magazine editor Liza Elliott. It was important to the
analysis that Liza recall completely this song and what
happened in her childhood when last she sang it. Although the lyric itself was a mental block to her until
well into the second act, the haunting tune—orchestrated by Kurt to sound sweet and simple at times,
mysterious and menacing at others—heightened the sus-
pense of many moments in the play.

Later, when *Lady in the Dark* was filmed, the script
necessarily had many references to the song. But for
some unfathomable reason the song itself—as essential
to this musical drama as a stolen necklace or a missing
will to a melodrama—was omitted. Although the film
was successful financially, audiences evidently were puzzled or felt thwarted or something, because items began
to appear in movie-news columns mentioning that the
song frequently referred to in *Lady in the Dark* was "My
Ship." I hold a brief for Hollywood, having been more
or less a movie-goer since I was nine; but there are times.

**The piano-vocal score has four "afraids" after
"want to be."*

During the writing of a song, it is sung repeatedly, word
by word and line by line, by lyricist and/or composer, be
their voices fetching, raucous, or even nonexistent. This
is done to keep testing the singability and clarity in sense
and sound. Careful as one tries to be, however, occasionally an aural ambiguity is overlooked. For two weeks of
rehearsals, Miss Lawrence sang "My Ship" with its original release:

> I can wait for years
> Till it appears,
> One fine day one spring.

Then, one afternoon session, she sang these lines as she
had done previously, stopped, fixed me with a look (I
was in the fourth or fifth row), and demanded: "Why
four years, why not five or six?" She was quite right, and
I quickly told her to change "*for* years" to "*the* years."
Somehow neither Kurt nor I had noticed that preposi-
tion "for" received the same musical value as "wait" and
"years."

—from *Lyrics on Several Occasions*

My ship has sails that are made of silk—
The decks are trimmed with gold—
And of jam and spice
There's a paradise
In the hold.

My ship's aglow with a million pearls,
And rubies fill each bin;
The sun sits high
In a sapphire sky
When my ship comes in.

I can wait the years
Till it appears—
One fine day one spring.
But the pearls and such,
They won't mean much
If there's missing just one thing:

I do not care if that day arrives—
That dream need never be—
If the ship I sing
Doesn't also bring
My own true love to me—
If the ship I sing
Doesn't also bring
My own true love to me.

IT'S NEVER TOO LATE TO MENDELSSOHN

Introduced during the Boston tryout by Evelyn Wyckoff
(Miss Foster) and ensemble. Placed in the "Wedding

Dream" after "The Princess of Pure Delight" and
before "The Woman at the Altar." Originally intended
for Danny Kaye (Russell Paxton), Macdonald Carey
(Charley Johnson), and ensemble. Dropped before the
New York opening, although Charley's quatrain near the
end was retained as a spoken passage. The "Mendelssohn—Journey's Endelssohn" and "Lohengrin and bear
it" lines derive from "Bride and Groom," a song in *Oh,
Kay!* (1926). The "poached egg" and "Philadelphia"
lines had earlier been placed in "You Know How It Is,"
intended for but not used in *Rosalie* (1928). (The "egg"
line was finally placed in "I'm a Poached Egg" for the
1964 film *Kiss Me, Stupid*.) Danny Kaye liked "Mendelssohn" enough to include it among the six *Lady in
the Dark* songs he recorded in 1941 for Columbia
Records.

VERSE

PAXTON: A man without a woman
Or a woman without a man
Was never part of paradise's plan.

OTHERS: A man without a woman
Or a woman without a man.

PAXTON: It's like a poached egg without a piece
of toast. . . .
Philadelphia without the *Saturday
Evening Post*. . . .
George Jean Nathan without a play to
roast. . . .
And to make a man and woman
rhyme,
The wedding bell must chime.

REFRAIN

It's never too late to Mendelssohn!
Ding dong, ding dong dell!
Two hearts are at Journey's Endelssohn
When the people hear that steeple bell.
Without the strains of Lohengrin,
Love is Mischa or Jascha without a
violin.
It's never too late to Mendelssohn!
Dinga donga, dinga donga dell!

A man without a woman
Or a woman without a man
Is what the form sheet calls an
"also-ran."

OTHERS: A man without a woman
Or a woman without a man.

PAXTON: It's like an oyster without a month in
"R" . . .
A play by Bernstein that's not
triangular . . .

A notice by Mantle with only half a
        star . . .
And to make a man and woman rhyme
The wedding bell must chime.

[*All sing a refrain. Dance. At end of dance,
Liza is revealed dressed as a bride. The
wedding bells ring out again. Suddenly we are
in a church. The wedding procession starts*]

CHARLEY: It's never too late to Mendelssohn.
        Two hearts are at Journey's
            Endelssohn.
        Whate'er their future, they must share
            it.
        I trust they Lohengrin and bear it.
[*He repeats this in a loud tone, then, even
louder:*]
        If there be any who know why these
            two should not be joined in holy
            wedlock, let him speak now or
            forever hold his peace.

BATS ABOUT YOU

"This was written," recalled Ira Gershwin, "for a flashback scene and supposedly was a song of the late Twenties, from a show called *Nay, Nay, Nellie*, sung at a
Mapleton High School Graduation Dance." Introduced
in the final scene during the Boston tryout by Eleanor
Eberle (Barbara) and Dan Harden (Ben). Dropped
before the New York opening. Nearly revised and restored during the Broadway run when Gertrude Lawrence was seeking an additional song.

BEN: I don't know if I'm coming or going—
        My mind is one big hullabaloo!
        I hope nobody finds I can't remember
        If this month is April or September.
        I don't know if it's raining or snowing
        Or if my socks are yellow or blue;
        I don't know why or when or how
        Or wherefore or who—
        I only know I'm bats about you.

BARBARA: I don't know if I'm coming or going—
        Am I in Brooklyn or Timbuktu?
        I do my homework—What do I
            discover?
        All I write is "Lover! Lover! Lover!"
        I don't know if my petticoat's showing
        And if it is—don't know what to do!
        Of all the things I should know
        There's just one coming through,

And that is that I'm bats about you;
And that is that I'm bats about you.

UNFORGETTABLE

Intended for Danny Kaye (Russell Paxton) in the "Wed-
ding Dream," directly following "The Princess of Pure
Delight." Dropped during rehearsals. Alternate title:
"You Are Unforgettable."

[*Liza, the Minstrel, the King, the Princess, the
Sorcerer, and the three Princes all bow as the
chorale applauds softly and murmurs, "Encore,
encore!" Liza repeats the last stanza. During
this encore, a grotesque thing happens. The
Minstrel, instead of caressing his bride-to-be,
takes hold of her tresses and strangles her, as
fright is written on the faces of the other
participants. Liza, also reacting, watches, as the
lights dim down; once more she is alone. The
oboe is heard playing the start of the elusive
song. This is soon lost as we hear a piano
vamping, then the voice of Paxton. Gradually,
as the lights come up, we find that Paxton is
now a movie director. A sound camera is rolled
on; a few movie canvas-backed chairs with
names on them—"Mr. Paxton," "Miss Elliott,"
"Mr. Curtis"—are shoved on. Paxton is singing
for the edification of a group that contains
Randy and three or four girls in dance-hall
costume*]

PAXTON: You are unforgettable;
        You're the rainbow shining through.
        None so sweet and pettable
        As you.

        It was unforgettable
        When I found out with a start
        That I had so upsettable
        A heart.

        I'll always remember
        That unforgettable night:
        Love was no ember
        But still burns bright.

        You are unforgettable—
        Heaven here on earth below.
        Isn't it regrettable
        That we didn't meet years ago?

[*As he finishes, all nod understandingly*]
        Now, that's the way I'd like it done,
            Randy.

[*Dialogue follows*]
[*Lights dim down and bolero rhythm starts
again*]
CHORALE: And now Liza Elliott is going to be
            married.
        At last Liza Elliott is going to be
            married.

        Let the music fill the air!
        We hail the happy pair!
        Lift every voice in praise!
        This is their day of days!
        Let every church bell chime:
        Two hearts will ever rhyme!

[*Kendall Nesbitt appears and goes to Liza,
offering her his arm. Alison brings Liza a
bridal bouquet made of magazines, and
Maggie puts a bridal veil on Liza. In back of
them a procession forms. The children now act
as flower boys and girls. Randy, on some
elevation, if possible, begins singing "This Is
New" in the manner of "Oh, Promise Me" as
the procession reaches the altar. During second
half of chorus Charley, who is now the
minister, starts murmuring the marriage service.
Then it becomes audible*]
CHARLEY: It's never too late to Mendelssohn.
        Two hearts are at Journey's
            Endelssohn.
        Whate'er their future, they must share
            it.
        I trust they Lohengrin and bear it.
[*These four lines repeated; then, louder:*]
        If there be any who know why these
            two should not be joined in holy
            wedlock, let him speak now or
            forever hold his peace.

MINSTREL DREAM

Unfinished. Alternate title: "The Minstrel Show." According to Ira Gershwin, this is the "first draft of beginning of 3rd dream called at the time the 'Minstrel
Dream.' Because minstrel costumes weren't varied
enough for the Liza Elliott trial, Hassard Short, in charge
of scenery and costumes, decided the 3rd dream would
be more spectacular-looking if we changed the background to a circus trial. All agreed; hence Kurt and I
rewrote the opening." See also note for "The Saga of
Jenny."

[*Liza is reading. She is restless. Maid enters*]

MAID: Mr. Nesbitt to see you.

LIZA: Here? Well, ask him in.

[*A crash in the orchestra as entire company marches on in minstrel outfit*]

ALL: Hello, hello, hello.
We're ready to start the show.
We're ready to start the minstrel
show—
Hello, hello, hello.
The name of the show is *A Breach
of Promise.*
Hello, hello, hello.
We're ready to start the show.
We're ready to start, fortissimo—
Hello! Hello! Hello!

With song and dance and chatter
And legalistic patter,
We'll show where judge and jury
Will show they're from Missouri,
And prove to Doubting Thomas
That in this breach of promise
They promise not to breach
The law entitling each
To say his say,
Whatever he may,
And have his day
In court;
In short—
We're ready to start and set to go—
Hello, hello, hello.
A breach-of-promise-and-minstrel
show—
Hello! Hello! Hello!

ATTENDANT: Order in the courtroom. The next
case is that of Kendall Nesbitt
versus Liza Elliott.
Attention, please! Hats off!
Attention! Nobody budge!
Here comes the Interlocutor, His
Honor, the Judge!

[*Dr. Brooks marches on*]

BROOKS: Your vices get paralysis
When into them I pry—
For in the last analysis,
An analyst am I.

ALL: His mind a golden palace is
Where wisdom is the key—
For in the last analysis
An analyst is he!

Hello, hello, hello.
He's ready to start the show.
His Honor, the Interlocutor,
Is ready to start the show.

ATTENDANT: Introducing the Silvery Voiced End
Man and Prosecuting Attorney.

[*Fanfare*]

JOHNSON: I'm the prosecuting attorney—
Can't be bought or sold.
To prison Miss Elliott makes a
journey
Once the story's told.

ALL: He's the prosecuting attorney.
He's the end man, too.
To prison Miss Elliott takes a
journey
If the boy comes through.

Hello, hello, hello.
He's ready to start the show.
A prosecutor from head to toe—
Hello, hello, hello.

ATTENDANT: Introducing the Golden-Voiced End
Man and Lawyer for the
Defendant.

[*Fanfare*]

RANDY: I'm the lawyer for the defendant—
Can't be sold or bought.
Miss Elliott's star is in the
ascendant—
This will come to naught.

ALL: He's the lawyer for the defendant—
He's an end man, too.
Miss Elliott's star is in the ascendant
'Cording to his view.

Hello, hello again.
(We vary this now and then.)
But status quo says no and so—
Hello, hello, hello.
Hello, hello, hello.

RANDY: Your Honor, Mr. Interlocutor.

JUDGE: Yes, Mr. Bones?

RANDY: Why is the prosecuting attorney like
a man who didn't buy a ticket for
a raffle?

JUDGE: Why, Mr. Bones, is the prosecuting
attorney like a man who didn't
buy a ticket for a raffle?

RANDY: Because he hasn't got a chance.

ALL: Ha, ha, ha, ha, ha, ha, ha, ha, ha, ha,
ha, ha, ha!
If this is just a sample,
Then evidence is ample
That this is going to be
A hell of a show to see.

JOHNSON: Your Honor, Mr. Interlocutor.

JUDGE: Yes, Mr. Tambo?

JOHNSON: Why is the lawyer for the defense
like a man—

[*Judge strikes gavel*]

JUDGE: This is all immaterial and
irrelevant—
What do you think this is—Gilbert
and Sellivant?

ALL: Gilbert and Sellivant! Ha, ha, ha, ha,
ha, ha, ha, ha, ha!
You've heard another sample!
The evidence is ample
That this is going to be
A hell of a show to see.

JUDGE: At this moment it wouldn't be amiss
To get down to cases—especially
this!

A TRIAL COMBINED WITH CIRCUS and THE UNSPOKEN LAW and NO MATTER UNDER WHAT STAR YOU'RE BORN and SONG OF THE ZODIAC

A late, unused draft of the "Circus Dream." "No Matter Under What Star You're Born" and "Song of the Zodiac" (alternate title: "The Zodiac Song") were replaced with "The Saga of Jenny"; both these discarded songs were incorporated into *The Firebrand of Florence* (1945) under the title "You Have to Do What You Do Do." See also note for "The Saga of Jenny." Also included are earlier versions of "The Greatest Show on Earth" and "The Best Years of His Life."

BARKER: Ladies and Gentlemen, I Take Pride
in Introducing
The Greatest Show on Earth!
Kendall Nesbitt's Gargantuan
Three-Ring Circus
Featuring for the First Time
The Captivating and Tantalizing Liza
Elliott
Who Will Be Brought to Trial for
Breach of Promise
Right Before Your Very Eyes!
In Addition, We Bring You an
Assortment of
Other Scintillating Stars of the
Tanbark Ring
And a Galaxy of Clowns and
Witnesses

In a Modern Miracle of Melodramatic
    Buffoonery
And Acrobatic Jurisprudence!
The Greatest Show on Earth!

[*The magazine cover comes to life. Parade
starts, headed by Barker*]

PARADERS: Ta ra ra, tzing, tzing, tzing—
    Ta ra ra, tzing, tzing, tzing—
    Ta ra ra, tzing, tzing, tzing—
    Ta ra ra ra!

"The Greatest Show on Earth"

PARADERS: The Greatest Show on Earth!
    It's Full of Thrills and Mirth!
    You Get Your Money's Worth!
    Come one, come all!
    Come see the Bushman from Australia
      in His Fury—
    Come see the Acrobats, the Midgets,
      and the Jury.
    Come see the Trial for Life
    Of Her Who'd Be No Wife—
    Watch Her Fighting with Her Back to
      the Wall.
    You Get Your Money's Worth!
    It's Full of Thrills and Mirth!
    The Greatest Show on Earth!
    Come one, come all!

"A Trial Combined with Circus"

PARADERS: A trial combined with circus
    You'd think would overwork us;
    But really it's no trouble—
    In brass we love to double.
    And so with dance and chatter
    And legalistic patter,
    We'll show where judge and jury
    Will show they're from Missouri
    And prove to Doubting Thomas
    That in this Breach of Promise
    They promise not to breach
    The law entitling each
    To say his say,
    Whatever he may,
    And have his day
    In court.

    In short:
    This Breach of Promise Case
    Which Now Is Taking Place
    Is a Show That You Will Always
      Recall.
    You Get Your Money's Worth!
    It's Full of Thrills and Mirth!
    The Greatest Show on Earth!
    Come one, come all!

BARKER: Order in the arena!
    Attention, please! Attention, please!
    Nobody budge!
    Here comes the Ringmaster—His
      Honor, the Judge!

[*Nesbitt enters as ringmaster and judge*]

NESBITT: As owner of this outfit,
    The ringmaster am I;
    As such, I am no doubt fit
    The Elliott case to try.

ENSEMBLE: He's owner of the outfit,
    So nobody can deny
    As such, he is no doubt fit
    The Elliott case to try—
    As he gives himself the finest
      berth
    In The Greatest Show on Earth.

BARKER: Introducing That Death-Defying
    Trapeze Artist and Prosecuting
    Attorney, Charley Johnson!

[*Fanfare*]

CHARLEY: I'm the prosecuting attorney—
    Can't be bought or sold.
    To the altar Miss Elliott takes a
      journey,
    Once the story's told.

ENSEMBLE: He's the prosecuting attorney—
    Flying into space.
    To the altar Miss Elliott takes a
      journey
    If he wins the case.

BARKER: Introducing That Thrilling Bareback
    Rider and Attorney for the
    Defense, Randy Curtis!

[*Fanfare*]

RANDY: I'm the lawyer for the defendant—
    Can't be sold or bought.
    Miss Elliott's star is in the
      ascendant—
    This will come to naught.

ENSEMBLE: He's the lawyer for the defendant—
    Bareback rider, too.
    Miss Elliott's star is in the
      ascendant—
    'Cording to his view.

BARKER: Introducing Those Merry Madcaps
    and Prankish Pantaloonatics—the
    Jury!

JURY: Our object all sublime
    We shall achieve in time:
    To let the melody fit the rhyme—
    The melody fit the rhyme.

[*Nesbitt beats gavel*]

NESBITT: This is all immaterial and irrelevant!
    What do you think this is—Gilbert
    and Sellivant?

JURY: Gilbert and Sellivant! Ha ha ha ha ha
    ha ha ha ha!
    If this is just a sample,
    Then evidence is ample,
    You get your money's worth
    At The Greatest Show on Earth.

[*Everybody, including judge, dances*]

CHARLEY: Stop!
    The jury's getting clownish.
    They must be more sit-downish.
    This is no time for mirth
    At The Greatest Show on Earth.

NESBITT: Right!
    At this time it wouldn't be amiss
    To get down to cases—especially this!

BARKER:
[*Reading legal-looking document*]
    The next number on the program is
      the feature attraction—
    A breach of promise action,
    In which the plaintiff Kendall Nesbitt
      does assert
    That the defendant, Liza Elliott, did
      him dirt.

CHARLEY: Your Honor, Mr. Ringmaster, will
    you take the witness stand?
[*which Nesbitt does*]
    You divorced your wife so you could
      be free to marry the defendant,
      isn't that so?
NESBITT: Yes, sir.
CHARLEY: And you thought she would?
NESBITT: Yes, sir.
CHARLEY: But she hasn't.
NESBITT: No, sir.
CHARLEY: And, as of today, won't.
NESBITT: No, sir.
CHARLEY: Although you know no reason why
    she couldn't or shouldn't?
NESBITT: No, sir.

"The Best Years of His Life"

CHARLEY: You gave her the best years of your
    life
    And yet she refuses to be your wife!
BARKER: What a show! What a situation! Can
    you conceive it?
    If you saw it on the stage you
      wouldn't believe it.

He gave her the best years of his life.
She was—shall we call it—his
    mistress?
'Twas only for her he divorced his
    wife
And now the man's in *distress*.

The mister who once was the master
    of two
Would make of his mistress his Mrs.
But he's missed out on Mrs. for the
    mistress is through—
What a mess of a mish mash this is!

[*All repeat this. Some waltz to it, including
Liza*]

CHARLEY: His Honor's honor is at stake.
    Besides, His Honor is ready to break.
[*pointing*]
    She said she was his when she
        bewitched him.
    He bought the ring and then she
        ditched him.
[*to Jury*]
    For His Honor's honor we must not
        falter.
    We've got to sentence her to the altar.
    For His Honor's honor you must not
        falter.
    You've got to send her to the altar.

JURY: For His Honor's honor we must not
        falter.
    We've got to sentence her to the altar.

RANDY: Your Honor, Mr. Ringmaster.
NESBITT: Yes, Mr. Bareback Rider.
RANDY: May I call the defendant now?
NESBITT: You may call her anything you like.

JURY:
[*jumping up again*]
    Ha ha ha ha ha ha ha ha ha ha ha ha
        ha!
    That's just another sample,
    And evidence is ample
    You get your money's worth
    At The Greatest Show on Earth!

RANDY:
[*to Liza*]
    As regards marrying the plaintiff, you
        haven't, have you?
    LIZA: No, sir.
    RANDY: That being the case—*will* you?
    LIZA: No, sir.
    RANDY: Might you have?
    LIZA: Possibly.
    RANDY: But did you ever promise to?
    LIZA: No, sir.

[*One of the jury, a "rube," hand cupped to ear,
gets up*]
    RUBE: I can't hear a word, Mr. Ringmaster.
    RANDY:
[*to Liza*]
    Would you mind taking it a tone
        higher so that the last man in the
        jury can hear you?
    LIZA: Not at all.

    I gave him my heart but not my
        word—
    This case, therefore, is so much
        deadwood.
    My promise to wed he never heard,
    For I never promised I wed would.

    It's just that a change of heart occurred,
    So, gentlemen, won't you persuade him
    When a maid gives her heart but does
        not give her word,
    How on earth can that maid have
        betrayed him?

[*All sing this softly, swaying from side to side
as Liza comes downstage to sing the
countermelody*]
    Tra la—I never gave my word.
    Tra la—This action is absurd.
    Tra la—I loved him at the start
    And then I had a change of heart.
    Tra la—The rights of womankind—
    Tra la—permit a change of mind.
    When a maid gives her heart but does
        not give her word,
    How on earth can that maid have
        betrayed him?

ENSEMBLE: When a maid gives her heart but does
        not give her word,
    How on earth can that maid have
        betrayed him?

    BARKER: What a show! What a situation! At
        this juncture,
    The wheels of justice get a puncture!
[*Nesbitt pounds gavel*]
    NESBITT: This case isn't going to my satisfaction;
        It's more of a circus than a legal
            action.
        And, ladies and gentlemen, in
            addition,
        I'm hungry—so I call an intermission.

[*Immediately the irrepressible jury starts to
stretch, kick one another, etc. An Oriental
dancer appears and wiggles to the
accompaniment of a bass drum and "Persian
March." An attendant appears with lunch for
Nesbitt—an enormous mass of that fluffy candy
that, eaten by the handful, immediately*]

dissolves. Charley confers with him. From
offstage comes the sound of animals being fed.
A boy rushes on shouting: "Get your programs!
Get your programs! Liza Elliott in three colors!
Peanuts, popcorn, pink lemonade—the Elixir of
Life!" A photographer rushes on and takes
several flashlights of Liza, who shows more and
more of her legs with each snap. This goes on
for a minute or so. Then Nesbitt pounds gavel*]

NESBITT: Intermission over! I feel much better,
    by the way.
CHARLEY: Your Ringmastership. I call on one
    very close to the defendant.
[*Maggie comes on*]
    BARKER: Introducing That Sterling Witness
        and Sensational Lion Tamer,
        Maggie Grant. That Female Atlas
        Who, Whipless and Gatless,
        Entered the Arena—
[*Fanfare interrupts him. He looks disgusted,
whispers end of his sentence to one of the jury*]
    CHARLEY: At six-thirty P.M., October fifth
        last—did or didn't Miss Elliott
        intimate she was going to marry
        His Honor, the plaintiff?
    MAGGIE: Yes, sir—and no, sir!
    CHARLEY: No equivocating, please. I want a
        one-word answer. Is it yes or no?
    MAGGIE: I really can't say.

"The Unspoken Law"

    She felt quite warmly toward him,
    In fact, I think, adored him,
    And meant in her *mind* to marry him
    But never *signed* to marry him.

CHARLEY: Meant in her mind, eh? You may
    withdraw.
[*to Jury*]
    Gentlemen, it's a case of The
        Unspoken Law.

RANDY: Her word she hasn't broken.
    There was no promise spoken.
    And, anyway, womankind
    Has the right to change her mind.

CHARLEY: Her word she hasn't broken—
    But it's The Law Unspoken—
    And in that case, womankind
    Has no right to change her mind.
[*Then, to Nesbitt*]
    Regarding The Unspoken Law, I refer
        the plaintiff to McGillicuddy versus
        McGonigle, Illinois, Third District,
        Lot 5, Section 183, Opus 7, Part B,
        Line 12.

JURY:
[*accusingly, at Liza*]

There's no dismissing The Law
Unspoken,
And if it's true that the law you've
broken,
For His Honor's honor we must not
falter;
We've got to sentence you to the altar.

CHARLEY:
[*to Barker*]

The next witness, please.

BARKER: Introducing That Witness
Extraordinary and Snake Charmer
Second-to-None, Alison Du Bois! In
1917 at the Battle of the Marne,
Miss Du Bois, Single-Handed and
with Only Three Cobras—

[*Fanfare interrupts him. Same business*]

CHARLEY: Miss Du Bois, as a woman of the
world—

ALISON:
[*her hands weaving as flute plays in orchestra*]

Why not get it over with quickly?
Why not, for a quick moment, tell
the truth? Why not concede Miss
Elliott promised to marry him?
Why not admit all this never would
have happened if only she'd been
guided by the stars?
It wouldn't have been a question of
neurology
If only she had taken up astrology.

CHARLEY: Thank you, Miss Du Bois.
[*Liza snaps her fingers. An idea. She beckons to
Randy, whispers to him. He nods in agreement,
pats her hand*]

RANDY: We thank you also, Miss Du Bois.
[*Alison looks at him blankly as she leaves*]
Miss Elliott, will you return to the
witness stand, please?
[*She does so*]
You are, I take it, conversant with the
Signs of the Zodiac?
[*Liza nods*]
Are you a child of Aries, of
Sagittarius, of Pisces?

CHARLEY: I object. This is incompetent,
immaterial, irrelevant, and probably
dangerous! What has the Zodiac to
do with this case, or with anything
for that matter?

RANDY: Your Ringmastership, what we have
to disclose is competent, material,
and relevant. We are now prepared
to admit that the defendant
promised to marry the plaintiff.

ENSEMBLE:
[*to one another*]

Do *you* hear what *I* hear?
Do you hear what I hear?

RANDY: And she is undoubtedly guilty of The
Unspoken Law.

ENSEMBLE: Does he know what he's saying?
Does he know what he's saying?

RANDY: We admit everything and anything!

ENSEMBLE: Are they going crazy?
Are they going crazy?

RANDY: But we are going to prove that
whatever she promised whenever
she promised it, she was not
responsible for what she promised
and therefore innocent.

NESBITT: If you can prove that, I'm
Barnum—*and* Bailey. Proceed.

[*Randy waves for Liza to go ahead*]

"No Matter Under What Star You're Born"

LIZA: No matter under what star you're
born,
Your days are dark and your life
forlorn;
And till Mr. Gabriel blows his horn,
You go from bad to worse.
No matter under what star you're
starred,
The going's rough and the road is
hard—
You're always hoist on your own
petard
And wind up in a hearse.
With trouble always beckoning,
Who cares about the reckoning?
And who's to judge or blame anyone
For what anyone has done?
No matter under what star you're
born,
It works out just the same!
We're all in a stew,
So, whatever we do—
We are not to blame.

ENSEMBLE: No matter under what star you're
born,
It works out just the same!
We're all in a stew,
So, whatever we do—
We are not to blame.

[*The Jury stands up, quite carried away by this
philosophy that condones everything*]

JURY:
[*with gestures*]

I am not to blame,
Thou art not to blame,

He is not to blame,
We are not to blame,

[*to Liza*]

You are not to blame,
Nobody is to blame!
This lady's testimony
Is not so very phony!
With joy we all proclaim
That nobody is to blame.

BARKER: This is The Newer Freedom—and
they love it!
This is the existence they covet:
Where, whatever happens, you rise
above it,
And, whatever you do—"What *of* it?"

JURY:
[*They still like it*]

I am not to blame,
Thou art not to blame,
She is not to blame—

CHARLEY:
[*interrupting furiously*]

This is outrageous! What is this
romantic fiddle-faddle about the
stars—this hocus-pocus about the
Zodiac? Who can prove this
whim-wham about no one being
responsible?

LIZA: I can.

RANDY: Exhibit Sixteen, please.

[*This consists of any device to be agreed on to
show each Sign of the Zodiac, to be displayed
as its couplet is sung. Randy motions to Liza to
continue*]

"Song of the Zodiac"

LIZA: In Budapest one night, a Gypsy
Who drank too much Tokay grew
tipsy
And showed me her secret almanac—
And I learned the truth about the
Zodiac.

BARKER: I don't know where this is going to
go—
But a tipsy Gypsy told her so.

LIZA: Aries' children
Find life bewild'rin'.

RANDY:
[*to jury*]

There's no doubt that to Aries'
children
Life's bewild'rin'.

LIZA: Taurus' descendants
Become dependents.

RANDY: Never independent
Is the Taurus descendant.

LIZA: Gemini's duffer
Is born to suffer.

RANDY: Life is sour and lemon-y
Under Gemini.

LIZA: Next is Cancer—
You know the answer.

BARKER: Seems she wants it understood:
It's not so good.

LIZA: To be born under Leo
Is no panaceo.

Nothing burgeons
For Virgo's virgins.

Libra's progeny
Make for misogyny.

Scorpio's litter
Must turn out bitter.

Sagittarius
Makes life malarious.

JURY: What makes living so precarious?
Sagittarius!

LIZA: Not even a maybe
For Capricorn's baby.

JURY: There's frustration
Under any constellation.

LIZA: Under Aquarius,
All is nefarious.

JURY: There's no doubt that under
Aquarius,
All's nefarious.

LIZA: Under Pisces
You'll drown on the high seas.
So, there's no blaming anyone
For what he's done.

ENSEMBLE: There's no blaming anyone
For what he's done.

No matter under what star you're
born,
Your days are dark and your life
forlorn;
And till Mr. Gabriel blows his horn,
No happiness you claim.
No matter under what star you're
born,
It works out just the same!

[to Liza]

Oh, innocent one,
Whatever you've done,

You are not to blame!
Oh, innocent one,
Whatever you've done,
You are not to—

[A revolver shot startles everyone. It is from a
gun shot off into the air by Nesbitt. All cower
as a green light is played on him]

NESBITT: I can stand no more!
Liza Elliott, through her Machiavellian
machinations, has so swayed you
that I cannot sentence her.
But I know she is guilty and should
be made to suffer.
This case is not over.
This trial will go on as long as she
lives—every matinée and
evening—fourteen times a week for
the rest of her natural life.
Fourteen times a week she is doomed
to suffer humiliation in public.
Fourteen times a week on trial!

ENSEMBLE:
[Frightened by Nesbitt, they take it out on
Liza]

Fourteen times a week on trial!
Fourteen times a week on trial!
[Mockingly, they point at her]
Ha ha ha ha ha ha ha ha ha ha ha ha
ha!

[The parade re-forms, much as in the
beginning; Randy and the Barker remain
behind to comfort Liza]

This Breach of Promise Case
Which Now Is Taking Place
Is a Show That You Will Always
Recall!
You Get Your Money's Worth!
It's Full of Thrills and Mirth!
The Greatest Show on Earth!
Come one, come all!

[They march back to their original positions in
the Allure cover. If it is not practical to have
Randy and the Barker disappear at this point
(which is what should happen), then of course
Randy should not remain to comfort Liza and
probably the Barker should lead the parade.
Anyway, the cover starts slowly to fade. Liza
reaches for the telephone, dials a number]
LIZA: Dr. Brooks, please.

HOLLYWOOD DAYDREAM, including THE BOSS IS BRINGING HOME A BRIDE and HOME IN SAN FERNANDO VALLEY and PARTY PARLANDO

Lyrics from the unfinished "Fourth Dream Sequence"
(followed by director Moss Hart's outline of the dream's
conclusion). Alternate titles of "Home in San Fernando
Valley": "Our Little San Fernando Home" and "Our
Little San Fernando House." Alternate title of "Party
Parlando": "Hollywood Party." See also note for "The
Saga of Jenny."

"The Boss Is Bringing Home a Bride"

STAFF: The boss is bringing home a bride!
Yippee, yippee, yippee, ki-yi!
From far across the Great Divide!
Yippee, yippee, yip, ki-yi!
Where hills are high and space is wide!
Yippee, yippee, yippee, ki-yi!
We hail the boss and blushing bride!
Yippee, yippee, yip, ki-yi!

We've washed and filled the
swimming pool;
We've put in television;
We're air-conditioned, so it's cool,
And the gardens are Elysian.

The yellow orchids are in bloom;
The golf course is perfection;
The murals in the music room
Deserve your genuflection—
Are from the Hearst Collection.

[No. 1 Boy, a Chinaman with pigtail and
coolie outfit, appears]

NO. 1 BOY: Me hope my missy like it here—
My cooking my religion.
Tonight we have a soup that's clear
And caviar-fed pigeon.

STAFF: We've put in three more tennis courts
For him and his chiquita—
A ticker for the stock reports
And results from Sant' Anita.

The boss is bringing home a bride!
Yippee, yippee, yippee, ki-yi!
From far across the Great Divide!
Yippee, yippee, yip, ki-yi!

"Home in San Fernando Valley"

VERSE

RANDY: There's no spot on any map of Rand
McNally
As romantic as our San Fernando Valley.
Oh, grapefruit trees, oh, walnut trees, oh,
mountains!
Oh, nutburger stands and all you soda
fountains—
You are part of an earthly paradise with
charms
Second only to the angel in my arms!

REFRAIN

Alone at last in San Fernando Valley,
Where love lives on and there's no finale.
If it once was a thrill just facing you,
dear,
Imagine what it means embracing you,
dear.
A little home—a thousand acres of
clover—
At last, the endless journey is over!
And what fools we would be ever to
roam
From our heavenly San Fernando
home.

"Party Parlando"

GUESTS: Hello, how-de-do? Hello, how-de-do?
Hello, I'm fine! How are you? How are
you?

Did you see the preview last night?
We're having so much trouble with
the servants.

Did you see the preview last night?
We're building an addition to the
house.
And we're changing the garage—
Victorian, you know—
And adopting three more children.

What about the Academy Awards?
I think I'll have to get another agent.
But let's not talk about pictures for a
while.
We're building an addition to the
house.
And we're changing the garage—
Victorian, you know—
And there's trouble with the servants.

Let's not talk about pictures for a
while.
Did you see the preview last night?
Good-bye, what a lovely party!
Good-bye, what a lovely party!
Had a most wonderful time!
Had a most wonderful time!
[Orchestra crash. Footman enters]

FOOTMAN: I regret to announce there's been a
flood. The entire valley is under
water and two bridges have been
swept away.

GIRLS: Oh dear, what a nuisance!
Oh dear, what a bore!
[They zip off gowns and stand in bathing suits]
Oh dear, what a nuisance!
Now we'll have to swim to shore.
[Another crash]
ANOTHER
FOOTMAN: I regret to announce there's been a
forest fire. Everything is burning

west of Bel-Air and all the way to
Malibu.

BASS: Get the fire axes!
Damn it, what a bore!
What do we pay taxes
For?
[Men put on fire hats]
ALL: Good-bye, what a lovely party!
Had a most wonderful time!
Good-bye, what a lovely party!
Had a most wonderful time!
Good-bye, good-bye, [etc.]

LIZA: Was that a Hollywood party?
RANDY: Yes, my darling, and a very good one,
too.
[Reprise of "Home in San Fernando Valley"]

Conclusion of Hollywood Daydream (Moss Hart's Outline)

As is up to butler's announcement of fire. The guests are
about to go when another butler announces an earthquake is approaching. The earthquake arrives. Liza is
reassured by Randy—it's nothing, just unusual weather
they're having. The guests ask Liza whether she likes
Hollywood. For reply, she goes into number: "I Love
Hollywood." This is done finaletto fashion, à la *Of Thee
I Sing* or *Strike Up the Band*, with replies from the
guests: Liza: "And Mayer & Schenck" The Guests:
"Gott sei Dank!" etc. At the end of her song, the guests
depart, singing, "It's been a wonderful party," as before.
Liza goes to Randy's arms for a reprise of the San Fernando Valley song, but this time with new lyric covering
lapse of years. The stage is growing darker as they sing,
and blends into the trick of Christmas tree and children
at the end.

OPPOSITE: *Farley Granger and Anne Baxter*

THE NORTH STAR | 1943

A film produced by Samuel Goldwyn for RKO Pictures. Released in October 1943. Music almost entirely by Aaron Copland. Screenplay by Lillian Hellman. Directed by Lewis Milestone. Cast featured Anne Baxter (Marina), Dana Andrews (Kolya), Walter Huston (Dr. Kurin), Walter Brennan (Karp), Ann Harding (Sophia), Jane Withers (Clavdia), Farley Granger (Damion), Erich von Stroheim (Dr. von Harden), Dean Jagger (Rodion), Eric Roberts (Grisha), Carl Benton Reid (Boris), Ann Carter (Olga), and Esther Dale (Anna).

NO VILLAGE LIKE MINE

Published November 1943. Music based on a traditional Russian folk tune. Introduced by Dana Andrews (Kolya), Walter Brennan (Karp), other principals, and ensemble.

Published Version

VERSE

Stranger on the dusty highway,
If you're weary, come and travel my way
To a little village—
Peaceful night and day.

You, who've been to other places,
Once you see the happy, smiling faces
In our little village—
You have come to stay.

REFRAIN

Sing me not of other towns,
Of towns that twinkle and shine—
Excuse me, but there's no village like mine.

Dressed up in her greens and browns,
She's milk and honey and wine—
Excuse me, but there's no village like mine.

Such farmland, such pastures,
Such apple trees, and then,
Such schoolrooms, such children,
Such women and such men.

Though she has her ups and downs,
To argue I must decline—
Excuse me, but there's no village like mine.

Film Version

CHORUS: Sing me not of other towns,
Of towns that twinkle and shine;

Excuse me, but there's no village like mine.
KOLYA: Dressed up in her greens and browns,
She's milk and honey and wine.
KOLYA
AND CHORUS: Excuse me, but there's no village like mine.
Luli, luli, luli,
Luli, luli, luli-lu.
Luli, luli, luli.

Summer, winter, spring or fall,
Yes, any season at all—
KOLYA: In all the Ukraine, no village like mine.
CHORUS: Small is she on map and chart,
But oh, how big is her heart.
KOLYA: In all the Ukraine, no village like mine.
CHORUS: Luli, luli, luli,
Luli, luli, luli-lu.
Luli, luli, luli.
KARP: Though she has her ups and downs,
To argue I must decline.
KARP
AND CHORUS: Excuse me, but there's no village like mine.
YOUNG
FARMER: Stay with us and lose your frowns,
Your cares are sure to resign.
YOUNG
FARMER
AND CHORUS: Excuse me, but there's no village like mine.
Luli, luli, luli,
Luli, luli, luli-lu.
Luli, luli, luli.

CHORUS: Sing me not of other towns,
Of towns that twinkle and shine—
Excuse me, but there's no village like mine.

Earlier Version of Verse

Once they called me peasant;
Now I'm Comrade Farmer.
Life is far more pleasant;
Freedom is the charmer.
But one thing Mother Earth arranged
That Father Time has never changed—
It's old but always new;
It isn't well-to-do—
The village I've lived in my whole life through.

VILLAGE SCENE JINGLES

Introduced by Dana Andrews (Kolya), Esther Dale (Anna), other principals, and ensemble. Alternate title: "Loading Time at Last Is Over."

ALL: Chari, vari, rastabari,
Chari, vari, rastabari,
[etc.]

Loading time at last is over,
Loading time at last is over,
Loading time at last is over—
Let the workers mingle!
Let the locomotive labor
While we dance and join our neighbor
In a jingle,
In a jingle.

[*A group sees Clavdia looking at Kolya. Adoration, however, doesn't prevent her from stuffing herself*]
Milka, mulka, makabulka,
Milka, mulka, makabulka,
[etc.]

GROUP: Clavdia, Clavdia, take it easy—
Kolya likes 'em thinner.
If to him you want to live up,
Ev'ry day you've got to give up
Lunch and dinner,
Lunch and dinner.
[*Clavdia indignant*]

[*Group sees Damion and Marina*]
Chari, vari, rastabari,
Chari, vari, rastabari,
[etc.]

Damion and his Marina—
Love has got them floored yet!
Sixteen years of fond attention
Is beyond our comprehension!
Aren't you bored yet?
Aren't you bored yet?

[*Damion and Marina smile, shake their heads no. Kolya appears, sings:*]
KOLYA: Damion and his Marina—
Romeo and Jul-iet!
Cupid seems to have them leaping,
But their teacher should be keeping
Them in school yet—
Them in school yet!

[*Damion throws a hunk of bread at Kolya*]
[*The store manager comes to sit with a group that includes a fat lady. On seeing her he sniffs, moves away*]

GROUP: Bravo, bravo, Comrade Vanya,
On your stand unflinching.
[*They point at fat lady*]
Spoiling food that you examine,
Someday you will cause a famine
With your pinching,
With your pinching.

YOUNGER GENERATION

Published November 1943. Music adapted from a traditional Russian melody. Introduced by Eric Roberts (Grisha), Anne Baxter (Marina), Jane Withers (Clavdia), Dana Andrews (Kolya), and ensemble. Earlier title: "How Young I Am."

GRISHA: If I eat too much jam,
Mother, look how young I am;
Father dear, please recall
That at one time you were small.
If I'm hard on my clothes
And I do not wipe my nose,
Parents dear, please recall
That at one time you were small.

ALL: Tiddle-ee-um, tiddle-ee-um,
Tiddle-ee-um, tum, tum, tum, tum.
We're the younger generation
And the future of the nation.

MARINA: If I look, as I pass,
Into every looking glass,
Parents mine, have no fears,
Just go back some twenty years.
If I play out of doors
And don't help with kitchen chores,
Parents mine, have no fears,
Just go back some twenty years.

ALL: Tiddle-ee-um,
[*etc.*]

CLAVDIA: If to school I am late,
Please don't scold and agitate;
Parents dear, isn't it true,
One time you were that way too?
If I make too much noise
And I hit back at the boys,
Parents dear, isn't it true,
One time you were that way too?

ALL: Tiddle-ee-um,
[*etc.*]

KOLYA: Parents dear, use your tact.
If you don't like how we act,

Do not fret, do not mourn—
Is it our fault we were born?
Please forgive all we do
For someday we'll suffer, too,
When in turn we shall groan
At some children of our own.

ALL: Tiddle-ee-um,
[*etc.*]

SONG OF THE GUERRILLAS

Published November 1943. Introduced by ensemble (men).

VERSE

Rally round! Come and take your stand!
Rise up! There's a threat to our land!
Now's the time man can prove his worth,
Fighting for the land of his birth. . . .
Smashing those who would conquer the earth.

REFRAIN

From field and tower,
In snow or shower,
Through day, through night,
Guerrillas fight
The butcher's bloody power.

His guns keep drilling;
Our graves he's filling;
But men grow brave
Who fight to save
The land that they were tilling.

From forest, from river,
With rifle, hatchet, and stone,
Our land we'll deliver
Back to its own.

The dreams we cherish
Can never perish!
The Red Star will shine as before*
And we'll be free men once more!

Our banners will fly as before
And we'll know Victory once more!

In the published version, the last four lines become two:
Our banners will fly as before
And we'll know freedom once more!

SONG OF THE FATHERLAND

Music by I. Dunayevsky; transcribed by Aaron Copland. Text by V. Lebedev-Kumach; adapted by Ira Gershwin. Introduced by ensemble (schoolchildren). Alternate title: "Soviet Land."

From great Moscow to the farthest border,
From the Black Sea to the Sea of White,
There is peace where once there was disorder—
There is dawn where once was blackest night.
There is peace where once there was disorder—
There is dawn where once was blackest night.

Not a voice but sings in exultation,
Not a heart but beats for liberty—
Side by side, the peoples of our nation
Build a world where man is ever free.
Side by side, the peoples of our nation
Build a world where man is ever free.

Soviet Land, so dear to us forever,
We pledge loyalty in peace or strife;
To be worthy is our one endeavor
As we live the new and glorious life.

To be worthy is our one endeavor
As we live the new and glorious life.

COLLECTIVE LOADING-TIME SONG

Music adapted from traditional Russian melody. Alternate titles: "Loading Song" and "From the Baltic to the Pacific." Unused.

Work! Get going!*
Let's make a showing!
There's only one directive:
All out for your collective.

Bread means laughter
For now and after;
So, quickly fill the cars up
Before the evening star's up.

Alternate version of lines 1–2:
Work, you workers!
Let's have no shirkers.

Yes, from the Baltic to the Pacific,
Dreams alone won't butter the bread—
From the Baltic to the Pacific
Every worker has to be fed.

Work! Get going!
Let's make a showing!
Let everybody pitch in
To fill the country's kitchen.

Do your measure
And earn your leisure.
Let's prove on hist'ry's pages
We're not just making wages.

Yes, from the Baltic to the Pacific,
Dreams alone won't butter the bread—
From the Baltic to the Pacific,
Every worker has to be fed.

WAGON SONG

Intended for Dana Andrews (Kolya), Jane Withers (Clavdia), Walter Brennan (Karp), and ensemble. Unused.

VOICE: All the day is filled with song—
    Yes, Comrade, nothing is wrong
ALL: When I'm in my wagon, jogging along.

VOICE: Nature paints the earth and sky
    As time goes peacefully by—
    When I'm in a wagon, jogging along.
    Luli, luli, luli,
    Luli, luli, la, la, la—
    Luli, luli, luli.

KOLYA: Going on a walking spree,
    The best part, I guarantee,
    Is joining a wagon, jogging along.

CLAVDIA: Walking trips may be a treat,
    But they're not hurting my feet
    When I'm in a wagon, jogging along.
    Luli, luli, luli,
    [etc.]

KARP: Wheels fall off and axles break—
    It's not all honey and cake
    When I'm in my wagon, jogging along.

Roads go bad, and then, of course,
A horse can eat like a horse
When I'm in my wagon, jogging along.

VOICE: Some there are who fly by plane,
    And some who travel by train—
    But give me a wagon, jogging along.

Let the sailor sail the sea—
The good earth satisfies me
When I'm in my wagon, jogging along.

UNITE, YOU WORKERS OF ALL NATIONS

Intended for *The North Star*. Lyric apparently unfinished. No music is known to survive. (Other unfinished *North Star* lyrics, even less developed, include "Can I Help It?" "I'll Always Have a Roving Eye," "Love Is a Potato," and "Nature Blooms and Lovers Sigh.")

Unite, you workers of all nations.
Unite and fight for liberty.
Tear down the tottering foundations
And build a world where man is free.
Stand firm, you workers, be defiant;
Our dreams they'll never overthrow.
The common man becomes a giant
When standing off the common foe.

Fellow workers, give battle
For a future that's bright;
No man can be a chattel
If workers all unite.
Fellow workers, give battle
For a future that's bright;
Eternally, the race of man is free
If workers all unite.

Stand firm, you peoples of all nations,
Unite and fight for liberty.
Destroy the Vandal's aggregations
And build a world where man is free.

OPPOSITE: *Gene Kelly, Rita Hayworth, and Phil Silvers in* Cover Girl

COVER GIRL | 1944
MISCELLANEOUS | 1940–1944

COVER GIRL, 1944

A film produced by Arthur Schwartz for Columbia Pictures. Released in April 1944. Music by Jerome Kern. Screenplay by Virginia Van Upp. Adapted by Marion Parsonnet and Paul Gangelin from a story by Erwin Gelsey. Directed by Charles Vidor. Music conducted by Morris W. Stoloff. Cast, starring Rita Hayworth (Rusty Parker and Maribelle) and Gene Kelly (Danny McGuire), featured Lee Bowman (Noel Wheaton), Phil Silvers (Genius), Jinx Falkenburg (Jinx), Leslie Brooks (Maurine Martin), Eve Arden (Cornelia Jackson), Otto Kruger (John Coudair), Jess Barker (John Coudair as a young man), and Anita Colby (Anita). Rita Hayworth's songs were dubbed by Martha Mears. One number in the film is not by Kern and Gershwin: "Poor John" (Fred W. Leigh, Harry E. Pether).

THE SHOW MUST GO ON

Introduced by Rita Hayworth (Rusty), Leslie Brooks (Maurine), and ensemble.

Original Version

The show must go on!
The show must go on
To answer all the clamor
For oomph and glamour
And so on!

To captivate Tom, Dick, and Harry,
Each Matilda, Kate, and Carrie,
Cleopatra and Du Barry
Puts her show on.

What dough we blow on
The styles that go on!
And it ain't hay or chowder
The paint and powder we throw on!

We've got to feature frills and flounces
That the fashion page announces;
We must diet to take ounces off
That flow on!

'Way back in history,
Old Adam didn't give a care;
There was no mystery!—
A rag, a bone, a hank of hair.

But since humanity
Discovered vanity,
We only know the show must go on!

The pace is killing,
But flesh is willing!

There is no layoff—
No night or day off.

No intermission
In our tradition.

From when we get up
There is no letup—
Our show goes on!

This clever lyrical endeavor
Could probably go on forever.
But all we're saying is what you know:
That glamour is a woman's show.

The show most people like to view
Is evident in bur-le-que.

[*They sing and dance like a line of burlesque girls*]
The show must go on!
The show must go on!
The show must go on
To answer all the clamor
For oomph and glamour
And so on!

But since humanity
Discovered vanity,
We only know the show must go on! Whoop!

[*Girls now act like show girls*]
Now that's just a presentation
Of the physical type of show;
Here's a demonstration
Of the Ziegfeld girl you know.

[*Show-girl walk*]
But the show *we* show doesn't require

[*They swing their hips*]
This elementary sort of thing for you to admire;
Nor do we need *this* to set the world on fire.
Those we dismiss
With *this*—

[*and into dance*]

Film Version

The show must go on!
The show must go on
To answer all the clamor
For oomph and glamour
And so on!

To captivate Tom, Dick, and Harry,
Each Matilda, Kate, and Carrie,

Cleopatra and Du Barry
Puts her show on.

'Way back in history,
Old Adam didn't give a care;
There was no mystery!—
A rag, a bone, a hank of hair.

But since humanity
Discovered vanity
We only know the show must go on!
We only know the show must go on!

This clever lyrical endeavor
Could probably go on forever.
But all we're saying is what you know:
That glamour is a woman's show.

The show most people like to view
Is evident in bur-le-que.

[*They sing and dance like a line of burlesque girls*]
The show must go on!
The show must go on!
The show must go on
To answer all the clamor
For oomph and glamour
And so on!

But since humanity
Discovered vanity,
We only know the show must go on!

But the show *we* show is different because
We don't depend on *this* nor *this* for applause.

[*They swing their hips*]
That sort of thing we scornfully dismiss
For . . . *this!*

[*They dance*]
We only know the show must go on!

WHO'S COMPLAINING?

Lyrics first published in Ira Gershwin's *Lyrics on Several Occasions* (1959). Registered for copyright as an unpublished song May 1943. "Sung by Phil Silvers as 'Genius,' Master of Ceremonies in McGuire's Brooklyn Night Club. Time: Period of comparative civilian austerity during World War II" (Ira Gershwin—*Lyrics on Several Occasions*). Also present were Rita Hayworth (Rusty), Leslie Brooks (Maurine), and ensemble.

*U*pdating. Lyrics like this one, written in, and for, a special period and using topical allusions, inevitably become dated in a matter of years. For instance, few of the younger generation today would know that OPA stands for Office of Price Administration, a vital government agency during World War II. Sometimes an allusive-of-the-period lyric can be updated in later years, but this is a dangerous proceeding if the original is well known. A New York production of *The Mikado* once updated many of the references in "They'll None of 'Em Be Missed," a revision roundly denounced by the drama critics.

—from *Lyrics on Several Occasions*

VERSE

GENIUS: My butcher shop, my grocery,
Can keep on saying, "No sir-ee!"
But lack of this or that
Doesn't knock me flat;
For in times like these
Life's no life of ease.
Although I'm no saint,
I have no complaint.
We must do that task!
And it's little enough they ask.

REFRAIN 1

Who's complaining?
I'm not complaining;
You'll see we'll see the thing through.
Because of Axis trickery
My coffee now is chicory,
And I can rarely purloin
A sirloin.

But—no complaining
Through the campaigning;
Who cares if carrots are few?
I'll feed myself on artichokes
Until that Nazi party chokes—
So long as they don't ration
My passion
For you.

REFRAIN 2*

Who's complaining?
I'm not complaining;
That's one thing we mustn't do.
I go to work by bicycle,
My house is like an icicle,
And oh, my lack of butter
Is utter.

But—no complaining
Through the campaigning;
Don't ask what's in the ragout.
All rationing by OPA

*Not performed in film.

Is heaven and U-toe-pee-a—
So long as they don't ration
My passion
For you.

REFRAIN 3

GIRLS: Who's complaining?
I'm not complaining,
When taking on is taboo.*
My vanity may wonder where
To get new clothes and underwear;
My legs may be forgotten
In cotton.

But—no complaining
Through the campaigning;
I'll raise no hullabaloo.
My nails may lose their brilliancy,
But who cares what civilians see—
So long as they don't ration
My passion
For you.

PATTER

GENIUS: If things keep on at the rate they're going,
And if goods flow out at the rate they're flowing,
The time isn't very far away
When this will be my typical day:
[*Maid appears*]
At breakfast time after I first get up,
If there's very little on the breakfast setup,
For the little I'm served I'm well repaid
By the little that's on the serving maid.
[*Woman driver appears*]
The trip downtown that was unexciting†
Is a journey now that I'm underwriting.
Oh, a man is a dope who yells and storms
At the lack of drivers' uniforms.
[*Stenographer appears*]
From office work I want no vacation.‡

Refrain 3, lines 3–5, as performed:
The sacrifices are few.
My shoes may not be leathery;
My pillow not so feathery;
†*This and the next line, as performed:*
The trip downtown which once was boring
Now is a journey I keep adoring.
‡*This and the next three lines, as performed:*
And at the office during the duration,
What a pleasure giving dictation!
It ain't so bad
Being a dictator like me.

It's a pleasure now when I give dictation.
Oh, it's not so bad in the land of the free
When you get to be a dictator like me.
[*Girl in evening clothes—or lack of them—appears*]
And when my lady and I go dining—
Though the menu's cloudy, there's a silver lining—
A fellow just looks around the floor . . .
Who could ask for anything more?
Who could ask for anything more?

SURE THING

Published January 1944. Previously registered for copyright as an unpublished song May 1943. "A pre–World War I music-hall number with a race-track background and backdrop. Sung by Rita Hayworth [Maribelle] and Ensemble" (Ira Gershwin—*Lyrics on Several Occasions*).

Forgotten Melody. In 1939 when Kern was between assignments, I wrote nine or ten songs with him. Nothing ever happened to them, although both of us liked several. During this period he played me many other tunes I liked but just didn't get around to. Some four years later, *Cover Girl* period, I tried to remind him of a lovely tune of the earlier period by humming a snatch of it. But he had never put it on paper, and couldn't recall it. I told him his daughter Betty had been very fond of this melody, so he called her in and between us and our snatches, it came back to him. "Good tune," he said. "What about it?" I told him it had begun haunting me that morning, and if he could split the opening note into two notes, I had a two-word on-the-nose title for the flashback number in the film—one which had a production idea for the choreographer and the designer. When he heard the title, "Sure Thing," with its race-track background, he said: "Of course—nothing to it— in fact, the two notes make a better announcement."

In working on the song, however, it turned out that the on-the-nose title could be more advantageously placed within the first line, rather than at the start of it; and the double notes made place for the words "somehow" and "somewhere" (I.G. probably meant "something").

Burthen. Since the days of the Greeks, the word "Chorus" has had, and still has, many usages. Its special use as the heading for the body of a song (following the introductory portion, or "Verse") goes back about a hundred and fifty years and is still the prevalent one in popular song. "Refrain," some centuries old, was the term for a phrase recurring at intervals, especially at the end of stanzas—but around the turn of this century it began to be substituted for "Chorus" in the publication of musical-comedy and operetta songs. "Burthen," a variant of "Burden," was the term Kern always preferred to "Refrain" or "Chorus" in his published output. (I notice, though, that in the memorial *The Jerome Kern Song Book* his editors have seen fit to drop "Burthen" for the more usual "Refrain.")

—from *Lyrics on Several Occasions*

VERSE

The favorite doesn't always win,
No matter what the odds.
Since nobody knows how they'll
   come in—
I leave it to the gods.
So wish me luck—
Because I'm going to bet on
A sentimental hunch
I'm somehow suddenly set on.*

REFRAIN 1

Somehow I'm sure I've found a sure
   thing in you.
Something within
Tells me we'll win.
Somehow my heart has picked you
   out of the blue;
And since I'm only a beginner,
A winner
I'll be.
But, win or lose, whatever comes up,
You're thumbs up
With me.
One thing I'm sure I'm sure of
All my life through:
If love can figure out a sure thing,
That sure thing is you.

INTERLUDE

MEN: After the races are over,
After the races are run—
Loser or winner,
Let's go out to dinner—
And let's have a little,
Let's have a little fun.

Let's go to Rector's or Shanley's.
Champagne and duck are divine.

In the film and the published version of the song, this line is:

My heart is suddenly set on.

Let's lose our troubles
Imbibing some bubbles—
Oh, let's have a little,
Let's have a little wine.

Then, when we're mellow and feeling
   alive,
Let's take a drive along Riverside
   Drive.

MARIBELLE: No drive in the country for me after
   dark;
My limit is just once around Central
   Park.

MEN: After the races are over,
Being with you will be bliss.
P'raps you'll surrender
When gentlemen tender
Say, "Let's have a little,
Let's have a little kiss."

MARIBELLE: Though you are tender
I cannot surrender

ALL: To "Let's have a little,
Let's have a little kiss!"

REFRAIN 2

Somehow I'm sure I've found a sure
   thing in you.
Taking romance
I take no chance.
Somehow my heart has picked you
   out of the blue;
But if it turns out that my long shot
A wrong shot
Should be,
And all my castles come
   a-tumbling—
No grumbling
From me.
Long shot, one thing I'm sure of
All my life through:
If love can figure out a sure thing,
That sure thing is you.

MAKE WAY FOR TOMORROW

Lyrics by Ira Gershwin and E. Y. Harburg. Published February 1944. Introduced by Rita Hayworth (Rusty), Gene Kelly (Danny), and Phil Silvers (Genius). Earlier title: "Today's the Day (to Make Way for Tomorrow)."

Film Version

REFRAIN

RUSTY,
DANNY,
GENIUS: Let's keep on singing! Make way for
   tomorrow!
The sun is bringing a new day
   tomorrow!
Don't let the clouds get you down!
Show me a smile, not a frown!
Stand up and win! Turn about!
Don't give in! Let's give out!
To the blues just refuse to surrender;
One smile and you are a true solid
   sender.
What if it rains and it pours?
It only rains out of doors!
Let every frown disappear
And you'll find that tomorrow's here.

INTERLUDE

GENIUS: Listen, all, this is Genius calling:
   "Hear ye!"
RUSTY
AND DANNY: Hear ye!
GENIUS: Why not gather rainbows while ye
   may?
RUSTY
AND DANNY: While ye may?
GENIUS: You can lose the gremlins, the
   goblins, the glooms—
Laugh: Ha ha! And they're back in
   their tombs.

REFRAIN

[*Repeat first ten lines, then:*]
Let all the frowns disappear
And you'll find that tomorrow's here.

Published Version

VERSE

Listen, all, this is Vict'ry calling, "Make way!
Make way for that better day ahead!"
Let the echoes wake up and take up the cry
Till it rolls like the thunder on high!

REFRAIN

Today's the day to make way for tomorrow!
Strike up the band for a brand-new tomorrow!
Out of the blue comes the call—
Let there be music for all;
Let's have an end to despair—
Over here, over there!

Night is through and a new dawn is breaking;
We're on the beam with a dream in the making.
Let every heart be a drum
Beating for great days to come;
Let there be song everywhere
In a world that the world can share!

Unused Versions

VERSE

Listen, chum, take a lesson from the bluebird.
What's a bluebird got that you have not?
He just keeps on singing while winging along.
I'll translate what he says in his song.

REFRAIN

Today's the day to make way for tomorrow!
Let's pave the way for a brave new tomorrow!
Out of the night comes the call—
Let's have a new life for all!
Let's have an end to despair
Over here, over there!
On we go as the foe is retreating. . . .
A billion hearts are the drums that are beating!
Let there be freedom from want!
Let there be freedom from fear!
Let us prepare everywhere
For a world that the world can share!

INTERLUDE

Make way! Make way!
Why are nations all uniting?
Hey, Old Timer, read the writing!
It's a better world we're fighting for!
Tie the ties that none can sever!
Join up in that great endeavor:
Peace and happiness for evermore.

Reap the harvest! Share the harvest!
There is enough for all here!
Win the freedom! Share the freedom!
Brother, we rise or fall here!

Let's go! Fellow men, let's go!
Let the trumpets blow!
Let the music flow
Here on earth below!

REFRAIN

Today's the day to make way for tomorrow!
Make way today for that brave new tomorrow!
Out of the storm and the strife
Let's have a new way of life—
Let's have an end to despair
And a song everywhere.

On we go as the foe is retreating!
A billion hearts are the drums that are beating:
Beating for freedom from want,
Beating for freedom from fear,
Beating for all to prepare
For a world that the world can share!

REFRAIN

Today's the day to make way for tomorrow!
Out of the way, yesterday, with your sorrow!
The Newer Freedom is here:
Freedom from want and from fear,
Freedom for all everywhere,
Over here, over there.
On we go as the foe is retreating!
A billion hearts are the drums that are beating,
Beating through storm and through strife:
Let's have a new way of life—
Let's all unite to prepare
For a world that the world can share!

PUT ME TO THE TEST

Published February 1944. "Gene Kelly [Danny] tries out part of the number on a dummy in a dress shop; then, with courage up, addresses it to Rita Hayworth [Rusty]" (Ira Gershwin, *Lyrics on Several Occasions*). Lyric revised from version intended for *A Damsel in Distress* (music by George Gershwin). See also "Put Me to the Test" in *A Damsel in Distress* (1937).

VERSE

The days of the good old knights are gone.
But chivalry still carries on.
I wear no armor,
But to my charmer
I hereby pledge my all.
In other words, I'm at your beck and call.

REFRAIN 1

Put me to the test
And I'll climb you the highest mountain
Or swim you Radio City Fountain.
Put me to the test
And I'll get you a queen's tiara
Or a pyramid from the hot Sahara.
You can dress in sables
At nightclub front tables—
If that is what my lady adores.
Put me to the test, lady—
Just make your request
And anything that you desire is yours.

REFRAIN 2

Put me to the test
And I'll bag you a mountain puma
Or I'll dig you the treasure of Montezuma.
Put me to the test
And I'll ride you the Derby winner,
Then surprise you with tenderloin for
    dinner.
I'll be your Flash Gordon.
Red Ryder, Vic Jordan—
If that is what my lady adores.
Put me to the test, lady—
Just make your request
And anything that you desire is yours.

ADDITIONAL REFRAIN (UNUSED)

GIRL: Put me to the test—
How can you do any better
When I promise never to wear a sweater?
Put me to the test—
I'll put off my Keats and Shelley
And keep putting up corn and beans and
    jelly.
I don't want a villa
Or coat of chinchilla—
For you I'll even do kitchen chores.
Put me to the test, mister—
Just make your request
And anything in reason, mister, is yours.

LONG AGO (AND FAR AWAY)

Published January 1944. Introduced by Rita Hayworth (Rusty) and Gene Kelly (Danny).

Disregarding the verse (a last-minute rush job), this one took a lot of experimenting. (I have before me a dozen crowded worksheets; there must have been thirty or forty others I tore up at the time.) The smooth, meditative, melodic line brought the problem of where to embed the title. A one-syllable title like "Who?" or "Soon" was possible on the first note of the burthen; one like "Night and Day" or "All Alone" would suit the first three notes; and there were other possibilities—as, observably, the song was finally performed with a five-word seven-syllable title.

In all, I worked on four, maybe five, different lyrics. . . . But no one felt that any of the settings for this tune was a must; nothing was disliked, but no this-is-it enthusiasm was engendered. I seem to remember that the only advice I received at conferences was "Keep it simple, keep it simple."

One day Arthur Schwartz—our composer friend was *Cover Girl*'s producer—telephoned from the studio that this tune had to be recorded in a couple of days. Did I have anything? I mentioned the latest I'd been wrestling with: "Long Ago and Far Away." "Fine. Let's have it." "Now? On the telephone?" "Sure." So I read it to him; he wrote it down, and that was that. I heaved an enormous sigh of relief at not having to go down to the studio to face anyone with this lyric. Although Kern—and now Schwartz—had found it acceptable, I, by this time, was so mentally pooped that I felt it was just a collection of words adding up to very little. But, since it was over with, perhaps I could now get some sleep. (I realized some weeks later that I had come through, as requested, with a good, simple lyric—but if Schwartz hadn't told me of the imminent recording session I probably would have started on a fifth or sixth notion for the tune. Doubtless what had been throwing me was a feeling that the other *Cover Girl* lyrics were so much richer in rhyme and reference that they made this Miss Simplicity look like a wan wallflower.)

Dept. of You Never Can Tell, Who Knows?, That's Life, &c.: It turned out that this number was the biggest hit I'd had in any one year, with sheet-music sales of over six hundred thousand.

—from *Lyrics on Several Occasions*

VERSE

Dreary days are over,
Life's a four-leaf clover.
Sessions of depressions are through:
Ev'ry hope I longed for long ago comes true.

REFRAIN

Long ago and far away
I dreamed a dream one day—
And now that dream is here beside me.
Long the skies were overcast,
But now the clouds have passed:
You're here at last!
Chills run up and down my spine,
Aladdin's lamp is mine:
The dream I dreamed was not denied me.
Just one look and then I knew
That all I longed for long ago was you.

MIDNIGHT MUSIC

Registered for copyright as an unpublished song May 1943. One of the earlier settings of the melody that was eventually used for "Long Ago (and Far Away)." "The second [lyric], which used a two-word four-syllable title, wasn't too bad, and Kern liked it a great deal, especially the alliterative last line. It was called "Midnight Music" (Ira Gershwin, *Lyrics on Several Occasions*). Following are two versions of the refrain.

REFRAIN

Just a whisper, soft and low,
And midnight was aglow.
For oh, your words made midnight music—
Words that brought me such a thrill
The echoes haunt me still—
And always will.
In that midnight rendezvous
You said, "There's only you."
And oh, there never was such music!
Darkened streets began to shine
The moment midnight music made you mine.

REFRAIN

Midnight shadows, dark and weird,
Completely disappeared
The moment we heard midnight music—
And no roaring of the "El,"
No taxi horn, no bell,
Could break the spell.
Through that midnight ballyhoo
You said, "There's only you!"
And oh, there never was such music!
Darkened streets began to shine
The moment midnight music made you mine.

MIDNIGHT MADNESS

Another unused lyric for the "Long Ago (and Far Away)" melody.

Midnight shadows brought the fear:
The witching hour is here. . . .
And love may just be midnight madness.
But I threw aside alarms
To kiss the witching charms
Within my arms.
Midnight bells began to ring
And nightingales to sing:
"It's love, not merely midnight madness!"
Pierrot found his Columbine
The moment midnight madness made you mine.

ANY MOMENT NOW

Yet another early setting of the "Long Ago (and Far Away)" melody.

Any moment now I'll wake—*
It's all one big mistake,
This dream that I'm the one you care
    for.
Any moment now I'll feel
Those looks and that appeal
Just can't be real.
Is it true or is it trance—
My arms enfold romance
To have, to hold, to do and dare for?
This alone I know is true:
There's heaven any moment I'm with
    you.†

COVER GIRL

Published February 1944. Previously registered for copyright as an unpublished song May 1943 as "That Girl on the Cover." Introduced by ensemble. Danced by Rita Hayworth (Rusty) and ensemble. Alternate title: "That Girl on the Cover."

VERSE

Soldiers and civilians,
People by the millions,
Want to see the perfect Cover Girl.
So I've taken lots of
Candid cam'ra shots of
Beauty
On duty.
There's nothing like perfection—
So, in that connection,
I present my perfect Cover Girl.
Number one, I list her.
How can I resist her?

Alternate version of lines 1–2:
Any moment now I'll sigh
And kiss a dream good-bye,

†*Alternate version of line 11:*
It's heaven any moment now with you.

REFRAIN 1

I've seen the one I go for,*
One I've looked high and low for—
Life's not complete
Till I meet
That Girl on the Cover.

My problem has me sighing;
She keeps electrifying
Me—
But is she
Fancy-free?

We'd make a team
That could be supreme,
With love that's everlasting.
It wouldn't be extreme
To call us perfect casting.

Love, help a helpless lover,
Love, come and help uncover
That Girl on the Cover for me!

VERSE 2†

History can name us
Beauties that were famous,
But they'll never top my Cover Girl.
More than Mona Lisa
Let me tell you she's a
Vision
Elysian.
Oh, Helen of the Greek days—
Cleo in her peak days—
Aren't in it with my Cover Girl.
Number one, I list her.
How can I resist her?

REFRAIN 2‡

I've seen the one I go for,
One I've looked high and low for—
Life's not complete
Till I meet
That Girl on the Cover.

My problem has me sighing;
She keeps electrifying
Me—
But is she
Fancy-free?

This world below
Has a wealth of woe

*Earlier version of refrain, lines 1–2:
I've seen the one I care for,
One I've looked everywhere for—
†Published; unused in film.
‡Published; unused in film.

To make a fellow suffer;
She comes along, and oh!
A tough world's even tougher.

Days, I'm awake but dreaming—
Nights, I'm awake but scheming—
How I can bring it to be
To bring that Girl on the Cover to me?

*Lyric for Countermelody to Verse**

Screen or show girl,
There is no girl
Like the likes of you.
Cover girl, you're simply top-er-oo!
You've a glamour that no camera does justice to.
You're the nation's loveliest creation!

TIME: THE PRESENT

Registered for copyright as an unpublished song July 1956. Intended for *Cover Girl*. Unused.

VERSE

I want you to know
I've written a show.
There's a hit in it
As I've written it
And it's bound to go.
Shakespeare is a piker,
Ibsen is a pup,
Compared with The Great American Play
That I've dreamed up.

REFRAIN

Time: The present;
The place: Right here;
The characters: You and I.

That's the program of my show—
Something I dreamed up long ago.

Time: The present;
The place: Right here;
You're the girl; I'm the guy.

The plot is as simple as A B C:
I crave you; you crave me.
Action as brilliant as it can be:
You keep sitting on my knee.

Time: The present—
To make our bow,
To knock 'em all cold—and how!

*Unused in film.

Don't let the billing bother you;
You'll get the billing and the cooing, too.

Years I've been nursing it;
Let's start rehearsing it—
Time: The present means now!

THAT'S THE BEST OF ALL

Intended for Rita Hayworth (Rusty) and ensemble. Unused. Lyric is probably unfinished. Earlier title: "What I Love to Hear."

VERSE

The city's roar
Is often a bore—
With taxis and trolleys that clatter;

And rivets that
Go rat-tat-tat-tat
Can make me as mad as a hatter.

There are sounds that can drive me to tears,
But there are others that are music to my ears.

REFRAIN 1

Love to hear the bumblebee
Buzz, buzz, buzz away,
And the birdies in the tree
Tweet, tweet, tweet all day.

Love to hear the cows that go
"Moo, moo, moo, moo, moo."
And the rooster crow
"Cock-a-doodle doo!"

Love the crooner crooning love:
"Boo, boo, boo, boo, boo, boo."
And the choo-choo whistle of
"Whoo, whoo, whoo, whoo, whoo."

But the sound that has the rest
Backed up to the wall
Is when you make with "Kiss, kiss, kiss"—
That's the best of all.

REFRAIN 2

Love to hear that lamb that goes
"Baa, baa, baa, baa, baa."
And the goat sing through his nose:
"Ma, ma, ma, ma, ma."

Donald Duck, that maniac—
"Quack, quack, quack, quack, quack!"

And the doves that coo
"Coo, coo, coo, coo, coo."

What is Texas noted for?
[*Clap hands*]
And the kids who play at war?
[*Imitation of machine guns*]

But the sound that has the rest
Backed up to the wall
Is when you make with "Kiss, kiss, kiss"—
That's the best of all.

Additional Unused Stanzas

Listen to the ice-cream man:
"Ting a ling a ling!"
And the cowboy clan:
"Jingle, jangle, jing."

But the sound my heart adores,
Just my cup of tea,
Is to hear that heart of yours
"Boom, boom, boom" for me.

But the thrill that's most complete,*
Bringing ecstasy
Is to hear the beat, beat, beat
Of your heart for me.

TROPICAL NIGHT

Intended for *Cover Girl*. Unused.

Tropical night, tropical moon,
Why must you end so soon?
Tropical breeze, tropical sky,
Why does love say good-bye?
Seven heavens belong to me
When he's singing his song to me. . . .
Comes the daybreak and then
Comes that heartbreak once again. . . .
Tropical night, dreaming is gone—
Why did you lead me on?
Why must my heart turn into clay?
Why can't the night last all day?

**Next to this line on Ira Gershwin's lyric sheet,
Jerome Kern wrote:*
But the sound that thrills me through,

MISCELLA-NEOUS, 1940–1944

HONORABLE MOON

Published June 1941. Music by Arthur Schwartz. Lyrics by Ira Gershwin and E. Y. Harburg. The "Honorable Moon" lyric Ira wrote in 1923 (see Miscellaneous, 1921–1923, page 32) is somewhat similar in theme.

VERSE

Where the pomegranates used to grow,
Nothing blooms anymore;
No one smiles anymore.
When the China moon begins to glow,
No one sings anymore—
No one but a lonely little maid,
Trembling and yet somehow unafraid.

REFRAIN 1

Honorable Moon, each night I sing a song of
    sorrow;
Honorable Moon, how soon before that new
    tomorrow?
When will come an end to weeping
And to broken lullabies?
When will come an end to flaming dragons
Over China skies?
Honorable Moon, smile on my man where he is
    fighting,
Fighting through the endless night to keep the
    good earth free!
And then when life's worth living,
Send him home,
Send him home.
May Honorable Day come soon,
Honorable Moon.

REFRAIN 2

Honorable Moon, each night I sing a song of
    sorrow;
Honorable Moon, how soon before that new
    tomorrow?
When will come an end to weeping
And to broken lullabies?

When will come an end to flaming dragons
Over China skies?
Honorable Moon, smile on my man where he is
    dreaming,
Dreaming of the day when we will see the good
    earth free!
And then when life's worth living,
Send him home,
Send him home.
May Honorable Day come soon,
Honorable Moon.

IF THAT'S PROPAGANDA

Published December 1941. Music by Harold Arlen. Alternate title: "If This Be Propaganda."

VERSE

The whole wide world is in danger
As the Axis hacks away.
There's a mad dog in the manger
And he must be brought to bay!
Shall we who still know Freedom
Just stand by and be dumb?
Or shall we help to save the world
From those who would enslave the world?
Let's get out of the woods!
Let's deliver the goods!

REFRAIN

Put the pressure on Prussia!
Get the goods off to Russia!
If that's propaganda,
Make the most of it!

Bigger bundles for Britain
With no question of quittin'!
If that's propaganda,
We boast of it!

Take the chains off the Danes!
Clutch off the Dutch!
The curbs off the Serbs!
Save the souls
Of the Greeks and the Poles
And the legions of Norwegians.

If we still stand for Freedom,
Let them know it across the sea!
Let's have more and more
Propaganda for humanity!

314

WOMEN OF AMERICA

Music by Ted Grouya. Registered for copyright as an unpublished song March 1942. Twenty years later, when queried about this song by the Marlen Music Company in Beverly Hills, California, Ira Gershwin did not recall having written the lyric.

VERSE

In the urgency
Of the emergency,
We are ready, one and all,
To answer freedom's call—
Ready for any task
Uncle Sam may ask!

REFRAIN

We're here to help to see it through—
All out for Red and White and Blue!
Yes sir, the women of America are in it, too!
At any hour or anywhere,
Right here at home, or over there,
Yes sir, the women of America will do their
    share.
Ready to obey
The orders of the day!
No complaining,
Except you'll find
We've an Axis to grind!
Join up!
There's work that must be done!
Fall in!
And finish what's begun!
Yes sir! The women of America
Will help to win this war that must be won!

DON'T LET'S BE BEASTLY TO THE GERMANS

On November 12, 1943, author Rex Stout, chairman of the Writers' War Board in New York, asked Ira Gershwin to write an additional refrain, "with an American bite to it," to Noël Coward's song "Don't Let's Be Beastly to the Germans." On November 18, Ira supplied the following, which was performed by Celeste Holm (at the time, "Ado Annie" in Rodgers and Hammerstein's *Oklahoma!*) on a WOR (Mutual Network) broadcast.

Don't let's be beastly to the Germans,
For it isn't cricket or Amerikun!
When we've got 'em yelling "Uncle," don't put
    Fritzie on the fritz;
Lend them plenty so in twenty years they'll start
    another Blitz.
Let our policy
Be "Deutschland Über Alles"-y;
We mustn't destroy the dreams that they have
    spun.
Don't treat them too ignobally—
They just were thinking globally,
So why be provincial to the Hun?

1021 NRoxbury
Nov.18.43

Dear Mr. Stout,
    Here's a quick chorus. Quick because your letter didn't arrive until yesterday. Not knowing the tune I may be all wrong on accents but since it's a Coward topical I take for granted it's in 6/8. I don't know if the attached is what you want but whether or not, "Policy—Alles-y" ain't bad. The first line of the chorus, by the way, can be changed to

Don't Make a Patsy of the Nazi

unless you pronounce Nazi the way Churchill does. Me, obviously, I pronounce Nazi to rhyme with patsy.

    All the best to you and your good work.
    [*signed*] Ira Gershwin

LET'S SHOW 'EM HOW THIS COUNTRY GOES TO TOWN

Recitation verses (no music) written in 1943 or 1944 for the War Bond Drive at the request of Secretary of the Treasury Henry Morgenthau.

The battle won't be finished
If effort is diminished.
The Jap and Brownshirt must be done up
    brown.

With us it's V for Vict'ry
And nothing contradict'ry!
LET'S SHOW 'EM HOW THIS COUNTRY
    GOES TO TOWN!

We've got another War Drive.
It's *my* drive and it's *your* drive!
We're helping when we plunk those dollars
    down!

What's wrong will soon be righted
If we are not shortsighted!
LET'S SHOW 'EM HOW THIS COUNTRY
    GOES TO TOWN!

Through profitable savings
You stop the Nazi ravings
And help to topple Hirohito's crown.

Don't leave it to your neighbor!
Hey, Capital! Hey, Labor!
LET'S SHOW 'EM HOW THIS COUNTRY
    GOES TO TOWN!

OVERLEAF: *Top: June Haver (center). Bottom: Joan Leslie and Fred MacMurray*

WHERE DO WE GO FROM HERE? | 1945

A film produced by William Perlberg for 20th Century–Fox. Released in May 1945. Music by Kurt Weill. Screenplay by Morrie Ryskind, adapted from a story by Ryskind and Sig Herzig. Directed by Gregory Ratoff. Music conducted by Emil Newman. Orchestrations by Charles Henderson, David Raksin, Maurice B. De Packh, and others. Cast, starring Fred MacMurray (Bill), Joan Leslie (Sally), and June Haver (Lucilla), featured Gene Sheldon (Genie-Ali), Anthony Quinn (Indian Chief), Carlos Ramirez (Benito), Alan Mowbray (George Washington), Fortunio Bonanova (Christopher Columbus), Herman Bing (Hessian Colonel), and Howard Freeman (Kreiger).

ALL AT ONCE

Published March 1945. "Sung by Fred MacMurray [Bill] to his inamorata; the second [refrain] when a genie abracadabras him back to seventeenth-century Dutch New Amsterdam" (Ira Gershwin).

VERSE*

I kept hoping, hoping, hoping,
Had my fingers crossed for years;
But from now there'll be no moping,
Ev'ry shadow disappears.
Each day once was twenty-four hours of night,
Then suddenly you smiled
And suddenly I saw the light.

REFRAIN 1

All at once,
My lucky star was glowing;
All at once,
I knew I'd met my Once-for-All.
For I found
When I heard you helloing
That my heart
Somehow was answering your call.
Once or twice,
I thought I'd met That Someone;
Once or twice,†
That Someone somehow just wouldn't do.
Felt I never would fall,
I'd given up my hoping, when all
At once, my Once-for-All was you.

---

*Published; unused in film.
†Refrain 1, lines 11–12, sung in film and published as:
But I soon found that
That Someone never would do.

REFRAIN 2

All at once,
Mine lucky star aglow was;
All at once,
Mine Once-for-All I met I knew.
All a-thrill
Soon I from head to toe was—
Was enraptured
Mine heart when came you in view.
Twice or once,
Was meeting I Some Someone;
Twice or once,*
Was finding quick that wouldn't she do.
Never I felt would fall,
Mine hoping up I'd given, when all
For once and Once-for-All was you.

MORALE and DANCING WITH LUCILLA

Introduced by June Haver (Lucilla) and ensemble. Edited from a longer sequence that included "That's How It Is" and "Telephone Passage" (following).

"Morale"

SOLDIERS:
[*to girls*]
Don't ask me, dear,
Where do we go from here.
I don't know,
So couldn't tell you;
If I knew,
I wouldn't tell you.
Don't ask me, dear,
Where do we go from here.
When you are near,
Why should I go from here?

LUCILLA: Morale is the gal that you're fond of;
Morale is the pal at your side.
It's the smile you are wearing—
The buck you are sharing.
It's your hometown filled with pride.
ALL: You said it!
LUCILLA: Morale isn't fireworks and speeches;
Morale has to start at the start.
ALL: It's here, it's there,
It's everywhere
But nowhere—

---

*Refrain 2, lines 11–12, sung in film as:
But was finding quick
Some Someone wouldn't she do.

LUCILLA: Unless it's in your heart.
ALL: What a gal!

Morale is the gal that you're fond of;
Morale is the pal at your side.
It's the ride you are thumbing,
The tune you are humming,
Ham and eggs, yes, and french-fried.
Morale isn't only hooraying;
Morale has to start at the start.
It's here, it's there,
It's everywhere
But nowhere—unless it's in your heart.

GIRLS: Your U.S.O. Committee
Has picked a charming ditty!
SOLDIERS: So, isn't it a pity
It doesn't tell us anything
We didn't know before?

We like the way you sing it—
If there's a bell, you ring it—
But we are here to swing it—
ALL: Our promised land
Contains a band,
A girl, a dancing floor.
SOLDIERS: What we demand
Is right at hand:
A girl, a band, a dancing floor.
In other words, you G.I. birds,
Don't need a song to keep morale up;
And if there's any doubt about it,
Ask Doctor Gallup.

MEN: We got morale, we got morale,
We want a chance to dance.
We're wasting time and that's a crime
When there's a chance to dance.

And we want to dance with Lucilla—
Lucilla's the gal we adore.
ALL: Morale has to start at the start.
It's here, it's there,
It's everywhere
But nowhere—unless it's in your heart.

It's there, it's here. Ah,
But it's nowhere
Unless, unless morale is in your heart—
Unless it's in your heart. H'ray!

"Dancing with Lucilla"

SOLDIERS: And we want to dance with Lucilla—
Lucilla's the girl we adore.
[*to Lucilla*]
With your beauty so blinding,
We're sure to be finding

317

Heaven on the dancing floor.
We don't care to waltz with Matilda—
There's only one girl we can see.

LUCILLA: You boys are sweet,
And I'm complete-
Ly flattered, but
You can't all dance with me.

SOLDIERS:
[*crestfallen*]
She's just one girl, says she.
LUCILLA: You can't all dance with me. But—
SOLDIERS:
[*eagerly*]
Yes?
LUCILLA: There are many other girls available—
Whose characters, I can assure you,
are unassailable.
SOLDIERS: Where?
LUCILLA: There!
[*Soldiers look, decide they don't care about character*]

BIG
SOLDIER: No, we want to dance with Lucilla—
Lucilla's the girl we adore.
SOLDIERS: With your beauty so blinding,
We're sure to be finding
Heaven on the dancing floor.

ONE GIRL: How do you like that? How do you
like that?
Thought this was a People's War!
ANOTHER: How do you like that? How do you
like that?
What do they think we're fighting for?
[*Lucilla and the boys dance*]

IF LOVE REMAINS

Published June 1945. Introduced by Fred MacMurray
(Bill) and June Haver (Lucilla).

VERSE

BILL: Excuse it if I'm lyrical,
But the past is just passé;
The future is the miracle—
The future's here to stay!
Electric light by Edison!
Marconi's wireless wave!
The sulfa drugs in medicine!
The safety-razor shave!

LUCILLA: It all sounds so mechanical,
This dream that you adore;
Machines can be tyrannical,
And what's more—
The thing that seems to bother me
Is how much happiness will there
be. . . .

REFRAIN

BILL: Think of trains with the speed of
lightning!
LUCILLA: Oh, it all sounds rather fright'ning,
But I shall not mind those trains
If love remains. . . .

BILL: Think of planes and the horseless
carriage!
LUCILLA: Will there still be love and marriage?
I won't mind those cars and planes
If love remains. . . .

Oh, the future looks bewild'rin'—
All the shapes of things to be!
But so long as there are homes and
flowers and children,
The future is all right with me.

BILL: Think of talkies and television!
LUCILLA: In my heart there's one decision:
I don't care what the future contains
If love remains. . . .
If there's someone to love
And love remains!

TAG

SOLDIERS: But who cares about the future?
GIRLS: And who cares about the past?
BOTH: There is nothing like the present
When your heart beats fast.
There is nothing like the present
When your heart beats fast!

SONG OF THE RHINELAND

Published June 1945. Introduced by ensemble. Originally intended for Herman Bing (Colonel), June Haver
(Lucilla), and ensemble, as this version demonstrates.

HESSIANS: Drink, drink! *Donnervetter!*
Vot is better?
Drink, drink! Fill the seidel;
Don't be idle!

Drink, drink! Drink it all down
Till you fall down!

Drink day and night
To *gemütlichkeit.*

Clink, clink! *Mit a prosit!*
Down it goes it!
Clink, clink! Fill the stein up—
Yours and mine up!
Clink, clink! Life is cheery
When you're beery!

All else above,
Drink the drink you love!

Jawohl, skoal!
Jawohl, skoal!
Drink to the drink we love!

LUCILLA: A drinking song is fine—
About the pleasures of the stein;
But what about a song about the
Rhine?

COLONEL: *Gut! Gut! Fräulein!*
[*to soldiers*]
I command a song about the Rhine!

HESSIANS: We sing you the Song of the
Rhineland—
Europa's beauty spot.
Oh, never was there such a fine
land—
Each man's a fighter,
A lover—*und so weiter!*
That wonderful pretzel-and-stein
land
Can never be forgot!
And so, on that basis,
We say to your faces:
On earth there no place is
Like dot!
[*to one another, belligerently*]
Ja, Ja! On that basis,
We say to your faces:
On earth there no place is
Like dot!

LUCILLA: Life is milk-and-honey-er
Where the sun is sunnier
And the rain is rainier
And the brains is brainier!

COLONEL: Where the heart is mellower
And the hair is yellower
And the girls is juicier
And the goose-step goosier!

QUARTET: Where the stork is storkier
And the pig is porkier
And the beer is beerier
And the soup superior!

ENSEMBLE: Where the wine is winier
And the Rhine is Rhinier
And the Heinie's Heinier
And what's yours is minier!

Ve zing you no more of the
Rhineland—
Vot more is to discuss?
Oh, Fatherland,
Motherland,
Sisterland,
Brotherland—
No other land
Is for us!

THE *NINA*, THE *PINTA*, THE *SANTA MARIA*

Published in an abridged version July 1954. Previously registered for copyright as an unpublished song September 1946. Introduced by Carlos Ramirez (Benito), Fortunio Bonanova (Columbus), Fred MacMurray (Bill), and ensemble. Private recording by Ira Gershwin and Kurt Weill, vocals, with Weill at the piano, issued in 1975 on the Mark 56 album "Ira Gershwin Loves to Rhyme." Alternate titles: "Columbus" and "Mutiny Routine."

BENITO: This is a mutiny!
COLUMBUS: A what?
BENITO: A mutiny!
1ST SAILOR: A nautical rebellion!
2ND SAILOR: A washout that is tidal—
3RD SAILOR: Where you give way
Without delay
Unless you're suicidal!
[*Slitting-throat gesture*]
COLUMBUS: But why? By all the saints!
What are your complaints?
BENITO: We offer for your mental scrutiny
The reasons for the mutiny.
[*Green-light gesture to sailors*]
SAILORS:
[*to Columbus*]
Your believing that the world is
round
Is a belief that we believe unsound!
Our feet are on the ground,
And so far, we have found
The world is flat—like that!
Like that, like that, like that!
[*demonstrating*]
You believe that we believe you
know

There is a land to land on where we
go.
There's no land Westward Ho,
But *you* believe it—so
We believe that *you* should be
below!
Below, below, below!

COOK: On me the men are venting all their
passions;
They're tired of eating biscuit and
K rations.

COOK'S
ASSISTANTS: Yes, Commodore, their stomachs
Are in an ugly mood;
On top of getting nowhere,
They're fed up with the food.

SAILORS: On top of getting nowhere,
We are fed up with the food!
Day and night we brood,
Fed up with the food.

BENITO:
[*to mandolin accompaniment*]
Every night we are in tears
When we think of macaroni.
And it seems like forty years
Since we tasted minestrone.
Long to drink again the vino
With the wife and bambino!
So we're going to force
You to change the course
And we sail the foam
Back home!

[*As Benito and sailors repeat the above sequence, one of them, a terrific tenor, sings the contrapuntal aria*]
TENOR: If I'm in tears,
It seems like years
Since I have known the art
Of eating à la carte.
I miss my bambino,
My vino,
And "Sole Mia,"
And the Sextet from *Lucia*,
Across the foam
Back home!

A GROUP
ABOVE:
[*on a spar—obviously the claque*]
Bravo! Bis! Encore! Bravissimo!
[*Columbus looks up—then hears a loud "Psst!" It is the prompter, whose shell has suddenly opened in the deck just in front of Columbus. Prompter points at him frantically. Shell closes as:*]

COLUMBUS: I'll bravissimo you!
You fools!
You sons of sea-dogs!
You bilge-watery barnacles!
Have you no honor?
Is nothing sacred to you?
Have you no loyalty
To royalty?

SAILORS: Loyalty to royalty! What do you
mean?
COLUMBUS: I mean the Queen! The lovely
Isabella!
SAILORS: Isabella! What about Queen
Isabella?

COLUMBUS:
[*very Puccini*]
Don't you know that sailing west
meant
A terrific'ly expensive investment?
And who do you suppose supplied
the means
But—Isabella, Queen of Queens!
SAILORS:
[*awed*]
The Queen of Queens
Supplied the means!

COLUMBUS: Isabella, volunteering,
Hocked her every bracelet and
earring!
And if this journey adjourns,
We return with no returns;
Isabella, Queen of Queens,
Will be without any means—
Isabella will be flat
Like that, like that, like that!
[*Same gesture as sailors, earlier*]

SAILORS:
[*to one another*]
Who'd have thought that sailing
west meant
A terrific'ly expensive investment?
And who do you suppose supplied
the means
But—Isabella, Queen of Queens?

BENITO: Enough, enough!
Have you forgotten your vino?
Your wife and bambino?
Your "Sole Mia"?
TENOR: And the Sextet from *Lucia!*
BENITO: Right!
Are we mice or men?
Lock him up and then
We can sail the foam
Back home!

SAILORS: Very good advice!
Are we men or mice?
Let us have no more
Of the Commodore!
And we sail the foam
Back home!

[Sailors now advance menacingly on Columbus]
Your believing that the world is
round
Is a belief that we believe unsound,
And so we're sailing east—
And you are full of yeast!
The world is flat!

COLUMBUS: It's round!
SAILORS: It's flat!
COLUMBUS: It's round!
SAILORS: Flat!
COLUMBUS: Round!
SAILORS: Flat!

[As music reaches crescendo and sailors are
about to seize Columbus, Bill jumps on
elevation of some sort]
BILL: Stop! What do you think you're
doing? Stop! Stop!*
BENITO: Why should we stop? What's eating
you, you crackpot?—
When we're about to cash in on the
jackpot?
BILL: When all the world is vocal,
This is my point of view:
I'd feel just like a yokel
If I didn't sing along, too.
ALL:
[resignedly]
What is there to do
But hear the fellow through?

[tarantella]

BILL: This trouble you're brewing
You should be undoing—
You fellows don't get the idea!
The future you're failing
If you don't keep sailing
The Nina, the Pinta, the Santa
Maria.

You're just being dumb to
Not know that you'll come to
A land that's the world's panacea.
No laurels you'll rest on
If you don't keep west on
The Nina, the Pinta, the Santa
Maria.
SAILORS: The Nina, the Pinta, the Santa
Maria!
Let's not argue with 'im—

_____
*The published piano-vocal version begins here.

We like the waltz rhythm:
The Nina, the Pinta, the Santa
Maria!
BILL: What traffic terrific
From Maine to Pacific—
What hustle and bustle you'll
see-ah!
What rivers, what valleys—
If nobody dallies
On Nina and Pinta and Santa
Maria!

The girls are delightful,
Their sweaters are quite full,
[pointing to Benito]
So he's barking up the wrong
tree-ah.
What pictures you'll pin up,
If you keep your chin up
On Nina and Pinta and Santa
Maria!

SAILORS: If we keep our chin up,
What pictures we'll pin up
On Nina and Pinta and Santa
Maria!

THE CLAQUE: More, more! Encore!

BILL: There'll be forty-eight states and a
hundred thirty-five million*
residents
And George Washington will be the
first of many presidents. . . .
There'll be cities like Chicago, New
York, New Haven, and Hartford
and Minneapolis,
Not to mention Hollywood, the
global cinematrapolis. . . .
And when this land brings heaven
here on earth below,
Of glorious times there'll be no
dearth below:
Eastern Standard, Rocky Mountain,
Daylight Saving, and Pacific
Coast times,
But when you hear the sound of the
signal, you will know what time it
is, at least, most times.

And oh, my hearties,
What fun and what parties:
The Democratic party and the
G.O.P.,
The Prohibition party and the
Boston Tea. . . .

_____
*In 1954, when Ira Gershwin prepared this piece for
publication, he increased this figure to "a hundred
fifty-five million."

What a wonderful land in which to
be living—
Where you celebrate the Fourth of
July, Saint Patrick's Day, and
Thanksgiving.
And if you want an extra day off,
What you're doing to Columbus is
away off.
For the man you want to betray
Can give you not only Columbus
Circle and Columbus, Ohio, but
also Columbus Day!
So think twice, my friends, before
you doubt Columbus:
Just imagine what happens to
posterity without Columbus:

No New York for Fiorello,*
No Abbott for Costello,
No Automat nickels,
No Heinz and his pickles.
No land of the brave and the
free-ah!
Just think what you're losing
If west you're not cruising
The Nina, the Pinta, the Santa
Maria!

No Radio City,
And who'll feed the kitty
At Belmont Park and Hialeah?
But you'll be unveiling
A New World by sailing
The Nina, the Pinta, the Santa
Maria!

GROUP OF
SAILORS: You've certainly sold us
On all you have told us.
ANOTHER
GROUP: It's more than romantic
Across the Atlantic.
A THIRD
GROUP: The New World we're failing
If we don't keep sailing
ALL: The Nina, the Pinta, the Santa
Maria!†

TENOR: Three cheers for Columbusland!
Hip, hip—
BILL: Wait a minute, fellers! Not
Columbusland! The name is
America!

_____
*In 1954, this and the next line were changed to:
No New York and no skyscrapers,
No funnies in the papers,
†The published piano-vocal version ends here, as did
the number as filmed.

COLUMBUS: America! AMERICA!
You mean that it will be named
    after that second-rate explorer,
    Amerigo Vespucci?
Forget the whole thing!
This is too much!
I want no part of it!
We've been tricked, tricked!
My discovery
Won't be named for me,
So we'll sail the foam
Back home!

[*Benito rushes up and kisses Columbus on both cheeks*]

SAILORS:
[*advancing on Bill, same movement as the advance on Columbus, earlier*]
Your believing that the world is
    round
Is a belief that we believe unsound.
And you are full of yeast—
COLUMBUS: And I am sailing east!
To me the world is flat!
BILL: It's round!
COLUMBUS: It's flat!
BILL: Round!
SAILORS: Flat!
BILL: Round!
SAILORS: Flat!
BILL: Round!
SAILORS: Flat!
[*Over the tumult, a voice from above:*]
LOOKOUT: LAND HO!
LAND HO!

THAT'S HOW IT IS and TELEPHONE PASSAGE

Originally, part of the "Morale"/"Dancing with Lucilla" sequence. Intended for Fred MacMurray (Bill) and ensemble. Unused.

"That's How It Is"

BILL: Bring those pans and pots up!
Join the Salvage Drive!
Show the foe just what's up:
Liberty is alive!
Got to have that rubber mat,
Got to have that grease and fat,

And that silk and lisle—
For the salvage pile!

Throw in that old kettle
And that tennis cup;
Prove your mettle by the metal
You give up!

There's no law compelling you to—
Just your conscience telling you to!
That's how it is
In My Country 'Tis!
MAN: Here's a busted fender.
ANOTHER: Take this bumper, too.
WOMAN: Make the foe surrender
With this barbecue.

[*An old man appears; his chauffeur carries a statue*]
OLD MAN: Cast my eye around the lawn—
Found this old cast-iron faun.

WOMAN: Here's a garbage can.
MAN:
[*from the street*]
Here's an old sedan!

BILL: There's a hash to settle!
There's a war to win!
Prove your mettle by the metal
You turn in!

There's no law compelling you to—
Just your conscience telling you to!
That's how it is
In My Country 'Tis!

CHILDREN: Der Führer tells us not to,
So we have simply got to—
That's how it is
In My Country 'Tis.
With us it's V for Vict'ry
And nothing contradict'ry—
That's how it is
In My Country 'Tis.
[*Telephone in booth near stand rings*]

"Telephone Passage"

BILL: Excuse me for a minute!
You kids carry on
While I'm gone. . . .
[*very businesslike*]
Hello, hello!
[*softly*]
Oh! Lucilla! Hello, hello!
How nice of you to want to know.

Well, what happened this morning
    was I went to the draft board again.
And I don't know why or how or
    where or when,

But my draft board wants no part of
    me;
They don't want me on land or sea,
Or in the air,
Or anywhere.

But oh, you know, Lucilla, when this
    country goes to town,
You really never can keep a good man
    down!
And every door I'm going to storm
Until I get in uniform!
Lucilla, you can bet
You'll be proud of me yet!

[*spoken*]
What's that? Will I meet you tonight
    at the U.S.O.? Are you kiddin'?
    Baby, I'll be there with bells on!

[*Sings*]
There's no law compelling me to—
Just my heart that's telling me to. . . .

[*As Bill is hanging up, we hear:*]
CHILDREN: That's how it is
In My Country 'Tis!

IT COULD HAVE HAPPENED TO ANYONE

Earlier title: "It Happened to Happen to Me." Intended for *Where Do We Go from Here?* Unused. Private recording by Ira Gershwin, vocal, and Kurt Weill, piano, issued in 1975 on the Mark 56 album "Ira Gershwin Loves to Rhyme."

VERSE

He's no collection
Of manly perfection—
Other girls find him expendable.
Of love I'm a victim,
For my heart has picked him
And my heart is dependable.
When I look at that dope and his apparel,
I know I'm scraping the bottom of the barrel.

REFRAIN

It could have happened to anyone,
But it happened to happen to me.
When there's a heart to let these days,
You take what you can get these days—
But what I saw in him I cannot see.

I may be sorry for what I've done:
Locked him in my heart and threw away the
   key.
Oh, I dreamed a dream up,
Of old shoes and rice—
But he doesn't steam up—
He's cooking with ice.
He could have happened to anyone—
Why did he have to happen to me?

WOO, WOO, WOO, WOO, MANHATTAN

Alternate title: "Manhattan." Intended for *Where Do We Go from Here?* Unused. Private recording by Ira Gershwin, vocal, and Kurt Weill, piano, issued in 1975 on the Mark 56 album "Ira Gershwin Loves to Rhyme."

VERSE

We understand
That in this land

There is a tribe in Texas
That has no room
For care or gloom
Or a problem that perplexes.
Their medicine man says,
   "Give!"
And brother, as I live,
This icky folk,
They sing and joke
With curious reflexes.
It's not their glands!
They clap their hands—
[*Clap, clap, clap, clap*]
Deep in the heart of Texas.
Now, this here tribe,
We don't subscribe
To Texas tribe conniptions.
Our local medicine man
Worked out for this here clan
The best of all prescriptions:

REFRAIN

When troubles are too frightful,
What makes the day delightful?
Woo, woo, woo, woo—Manhattan!

When skies are gray and weepy,
What brightens up the teepee?
Woo, woo, woo, woo—Manhattan!

It always run-um
Number one-um,
Injun Hit Parade-um;
The squaws all say
No other way
Can Injun serenade-um!

More fun than tomahawking
It is to go a-squawking:
Woo, woo, woo, woo,
Woo, woo, woo, woo,
Woo, woo, woo, woo—
Manhattan!

TAG

It has a million uses—
It puts to sleep papooses!
Sinatra, Bing, or Dinah
Can dig you nothing finah!

On slightest provocation,
We give out to the nation:
Woo, woo, woo, woo—
Manhattan!

OPPOSITE: *Seated Center: Lotte Lenya and Melville Cooper. Inset: Beverly Tyler, Earl Wrightson (top) and Melville Cooper*

THE FIREBRAND OF
FLORENCE | 1945

Tryout, under the title *Much Ado About Love*, Colonial Theatre, Boston, February 23, 1945. New York run: Alvin Theatre, opened March 22, 1945, as *The Firebrand of Florence*. 43 performances. Music by Kurt Weill. Lyrics by Ira Gershwin. Produced by Max Gordon. Book by Edwin Justus Mayer, based on his play *The Firebrand*. Book staged by John Murray Anderson. Dances staged by Catherine Littlefield. Orchestra under the direction of Maurice Abravanel. Orchestrations by Kurt Weill and Ted Royal. Cast, starring Earl Wrightson (Cellini), Beverly Tyler (Angela), Melville Cooper (Duke), featured Lotte Lenya (Duchess), Randolph Symonette (Hangman), Gloria Story (Emilia), Paul Best (Marquis), Ferdi Hoffman (Ottaviano), Marion Green (Magistrate), Charles Sheldon (Captain of the Guard), Boyd Heathen (Maffio), Don Marshall (Tartman), James Dobson (Ascanio), Billy Williams* (Page), Jean Guelis (Arlecchino), and Norma Gentner (Columbina).

SONG OF THE HANGMAN and CIVIC SONG—"COME TO FLORENCE" and ARIA—"MY LORDS AND LADIES" and FAREWELL SONG—"THERE WAS LIFE, THERE WAS LOVE, THERE WAS LAUGHTER"

Contained, with vendors' street cries and recitatives, in the opening sequence of *The Firebrand of Florence*. "Song of the Hangman" introduced by Randolph Symonette (Hangman) and assistants. "Civic Song—'Come to Florence' " (lyrics first published in Ira Gershwin's *Lyrics on Several Occasions* [1959]) introduced by Symonette, Jean Guelis (Arlecchino), Norma Gentner (Columbina), and ensemble. "Aria—'My Lords and Ladies' " introduced by Earl Wrightson (Cellini), John Cassidy, Lynn Alden, Walter Rinner, and Frank Stevens (Apprentices), and ensemble. "Farewell Song—'There Was Life, There Was Love, There Was Laughter' " introduced by Wrightson and ensemble. (Music of the "Farewell Song" refrain is reprised in "Love Song—'There'll Be Life, Love, and Laughter.' ") Alternate title of "Song of the Hangman": "The Bell of Doom Is Clanging." Alternate titles of "Civic Song—'Come to Florence' ": "Florence" and "Florence (It.)." The entire opening sequence was recorded privately by Ira Gersh-

Now known as Billy Dee Williams.

win and Kurt Weill, vocals, and Kurt Weill, piano, issued in 1975 on the Mark 56 album "Ira Gershwin Loves to Rhyme."

[*A public square in Florence in the Spring of 1535, early morning. The only persons discovered are a Hangman and his three assistants. The gallows they are erecting is practically completed. Cathedral bells heard.*]

"Song of the Hangman"

HANGMAN: When the bell of doom is clanging
For the man awaiting hanging,
Let's face the fact with no misgiving:
One man's death is another man's living!

GALLOWS
BUILDERS: One man's death is another man's living
Under the gallows tree.
With union pay,
We sing all day,
The while our hammers bang.
If the world doesn't like it
The world can go hang—
Under the gallows tree!
Oh, riddle dee diddle dee dee!
Oh, under the gallows tree!

HANGMAN: There are those who have me baffled.
They refuse to choose the scaffold.
To die in bed than hang they'd ruther.

[*Shrugs*]
Six of one, half a dozen of t'other.

GALLOWS
BUILDERS: One man's death is another man's living
Under the gallows tree.
We earn our fee
Philosophically,
The while the hammers bang.
If the world doesn't like it
The world can go hang!
Under the gallows tree!
Oh, riddle dee diddle dee dee!
Oh, under the gallows tree!

[*A couple of street vendors enter carrying their stands. First Vendor's stand has cakes and candy. Second Vendor's stand shows a dozen small clay or wax busts, and from the sides dangle a dozen small nooses, various colors*]

FIRST
VENDOR: Sweets and tarts!
Get your sweets and tarts!
Fill your stomachs

And warm the cockles of your hearts!
Sweets and tarts!

SECOND
VENDOR: Hey, tartman! What's the idea?
There's nobody here yet!

FIRST
VENDOR: I was just warming up.

SECOND
VENDOR: By Saint Veronica! Not a bad notion!
Souvenirs! Hurry, hurry, hurry, get your souvenirs!
Souvenirs of the hanging of Cellini—
The greatest hanging of the season.
Get your likeness of Benvenuto Cellini—
The occasion isn't complete without one!
Souvenirs! Hurry, hurry, hurry, get your souvenirs!

[*Maffio enters*]
MAFFIO: How goes it, hangman?
HANGMAN: Almost ready, Count Maffio. Soon he'll bother you no more.
[*Maffio throws him a coin bag*]
HANGMAN
AND
GALLOWS
BUILDERS:
[*bowing low*]
Thank you, sir!
MAFFIO: Are you sure it'll hold?
HANGMAN: I've never had a rope break on me yet, sir.
MAFFIO: I want no slipups.
[*Sings*]
It was only by a stroke of Providence that I survived his murderous attack. And now I want to see him dangling there and I won't feel safe on this earth until I do.
HANGMAN: It's a great day for me, too, sir. The most famous neck of Florence. But 'tis pity that with that neck passes a great talent.
MAFFIO: Bah! Of sympathy I haven't any! He's tried to kill one man too many!
[*The vendors now sing simultaneously as the crowd by twos and threes strolls on*]
FIRST
VENDOR: Sweets and tarts!
SECOND
VENDOR: Souvenirs!
FIRST
VENDOR: Get your sweets and tarts!
SECOND
VENDOR: Hurry, hurry, hurry, get your souvenirs!

FIRST
VENDOR: Fill your stomachs!

SECOND
VENDOR: Souvenirs of the hanging of Cellini.

FIRST
VENDOR: Warm your hearts.

SECOND
VENDOR: The greatest hanging of the season.

HANGMAN: What a day! What a turnout!

SOMEONE: What a turnout! What a hanging!

SOMEONE
ELSE: What a hanging! What a city!

CROWD: What a city! What a city!

"Civic Song—'Come to Florence'"

OFFICIALS: With nothing but pity
The folk we dismiss
Who live in a city
That's other than this.

ONE GROUP: If you're bent on viewing
Something doing,
Come to Florence!
Where is life more active
And attractive
Than in Florence?
Where are people singing
At a swinging—
But in Florence?

ALL: Everything warrants
Our singing of Florence—
So, Florence we're singing of you.
Everything warrants
Our singing of Florence—
So, Florence we're singing of you.

ANOTHER
GROUP: There's artistic treasure
None can measure
Here in Florence:
Great is every statue
Looking at you*
Here in Florence;
And we've gotta lotta
Terra-cotta
Here in Florence.

ALL: Praises in torrents
We shower on Florence!
Oh, Florence, you always come
through!

GIRLS: In all of Italy—
No brighter star.

---

*For *Lyrics on Several Occasions*, *Ira Gershwin al-*
tered this line (and a few subsequently):
Great is ev'ry statue glowing at you

We're sitting prettily
Right where we are.

MEN: Don't mention Napoli,
Venice, or Rome!
Florence sings happily:*
No place like home!

THIRD
GROUP: If you're spending ducats
By the buckets—
You're in Florence.
All the girls are busty.
(Life is lusty†
Here in Florence.)
And did you know that Dante
And Chianti
Come from Florence?

ALL: Everything warrants‡
Our singing of Florence—
So, Florence, we're singing of you.
Everything warrants
Our singing of Florence—
So, Florence, we're singing of you.

[*Short dance follows. It is interrupted by the
sound of muffled drum*]

ALL: Hear the drum, hear the drum,
Beating out his fate.
Here they come! Here they come!

HANGMAN: I can hardly wait.

ALL: Hear the drum!
Here they come!

MAFFIO: At this point no angel or devil or
genie
Can possibly save the neck of
Cellini.

ALL: Here they come! Time to yell
Hail, Cellini, and farewell!

[*Apprentices, models, a lawyer, and Cellini
march on. Cellini and lawyer continue to the
platform, where they are joined by the
magistrate or other dignitary in charge*]

APPRENTICES: Our master
Has met disaster!
Our sculptor will sculp no more.
But high up
[*pointing to the sky*]
He'll find a tie-up
Redesigning heaven's golden door.

---

*Altered to:
Sing out (and happily):
†"Life" *altered to* "Love"
‡*This and the next three lines altered to:*
Naught but abhorrence
For cities not Florence;
Her equal this earth never knew.

ALL: He will make completer
The portals of Saint Peter.

MODELS: The models of Florence—
Disciples of grace—
All view with abhorrence
What's now taking place.

ALL: Oh, models of Florence,
Your master is through.
Your tears fall in torrents,
But what can you do?
The fatal bell has rung.
The trap will soon be spring!

MAGISTRATE: Benvenuto Cellini, have you a final
say to say? We allow three
minutes.

[*He takes out a sand clock and starts it afresh*]

"Aria—'My Lords and Ladies'"

CELLINI: My lords and ladies, foes and
friends—
In a moment, everything ends.
I call upon you all to witness
My true heroic and artistic fitness
To die as bravely and as full of
glory
As ever was known in Florence's
story.

I have sailed the deeps and
shallows;
Now I reach that sorry shore—the
gallows.
But for the life of me, I cannot see
Why death should be the death of
me.
My work will bud and blossom and
bloom
When Maffio yonder rots in his
tomb.

APPRENTICES: Our master says the chances are
slim
That death will be the death of
him.

"Farewell Song—'There Was Life, There Was Love, There Was Laughter'"

CELLINI: As I stand here, ready for eternity, I
have a thousand joys to look back
on—and only three regrets:
One—that I die without having slit
yon Maffio's throat.
Two—that the statue of my nymph,
my masterpiece, remains
unfinished.

325

Three—that I leave this earth
without ever having kissed the
lips of Angela—that divine
Angela whose fair form and spirit
inspired my unfinished
masterpiece.
Beyond these three regrets, I have
no regrets.

There was life, there was love, there
was laughter. . . .
These I've known, so I know no
despair.
Heaven or hell, who can tell what
comes after?
This I know: Of joys I've had my
share.
And so, unflinching I face the
shadows,
And if the future sings this glad
refrain:
"He lived life, he loved love, he
laughed laughter"—
I've not lived or loved or laughed in
vain.

ALL: And so, unflinching he'll face the
shadows,
And if the future sings this glad
refrain:
"He lived life, he loved love, he
laughed laughter"—
He's not lived or loved or laughed
in vain.

MAGISTRATE:
[Nods approvingly]
Very nice, Cellini.
[Takes out and looks at sand clock]
One minute left.
CELLINI: In this last moment, you see before
you a true son of Florence. I have
here my will, written only a few
minutes ago, and when you hear
it you will learn how great my
love is for my native city and
you, my brothers.
[Motions to lawyer to read]

LAWYER: I, Benvenuto Cellini, goldsmith,
sculptor, jewel-setter,
Craftsman to kings and
queens—and better—
Bequeath ten thousand ducats to the
citizenry
[A cheer from the crowd]
To erect in the Palazzo Vecchio—a
statue of me.
The balance of my estate I bequeath
to the Committee

For Perpetuating the Beauty of Our
City
To maintain a Cellini Foundation
that will keep alive
My memory for the generations yet
to arrive.
Signed, Benvenuto Cellini.

CELLINI: These monuments to Florence's
greatest son
Will make our city a city second to
none.
[A great cheer from the crowd]
MAGISTRATE:
[Looks at sand glass]
Time's up.
[The Hangman starts to put noose around
Cellini's neck]

ALL: There was life, there was love, there
was laughter. . . .
These he's known, so why should he
despair?
CELLINI:
[noose around his neck]
When I rot, matters not what comes
after. . . .
This I know: Of joys I've had my
share.

ALL: And so, unflinching he'll face the
shadows,
And if the future sings this glad
refrain:
"He lived life, he loved love, he
laughed laughter"—
[During last line, a commotion is heard and on
rushes Ottaviano]
OTTAVIANO: Stop! Stop! Halt the halter!
MAFFIO: What is this? Why halt the halter
For this murderous assaulter?
OTTAVIANO:
[Waves document]
A pardon! A pardon from the Duke!
ALL: A pardon! A pardon! A pardon!
[They are quite happy about it]

OTTAVIANO:
[Reads]
"I, Alessandro the Wise, Duke of
Florence, having suddenly been
reminded that the nymph
designed for me by Cellini is
unfinished, although practically
paid for in full, do hereby pardon
him until such time as the statue
is completed. Signed, Alessandro
the Wise, Duke of Florence."
[Another cheer from the crowd]

CELLINI: Oh lucky world, I live to create!
Saint Peter's portals will have to
wait.
ALL: Our happiness we cannot contain.
What's heaven's loss is Florence's
gain!

VENDOR: Souvenirs, hurry, hurry, hurry, get
your souvenirs!
Souvenirs of the pardon of Cellini!
The greatest pardon of the season!

[music—"Florence"—starts as Cellini walks
from the gallows, taking bows and
congratulations. Suddenly his eye lights on
Maffio. Maffio starts to back away but draws
sword. Cellini snatches a sword from someone
nearby and rushes after Maffio. The clatter and
clang of the swords is heard for a second as the
crowd stands frozen, looking in the direction of
the flight and fight. With strained expressions
they stand rigid for a few seconds, then they
wheel as one, beaming, their palms
outstretched, as if to say, "Didn't we tell you?"
They come downstage and sing]
ALL: If you're bent on viewing
Something doing,
Come to Florence.
Highly temp'ramental
Are the gentle-
Men of Florence.
Blood is always spilling,
Life is thrilling
Here in Florence.

Everything warrants
Our singing of Florence—
So, Florence, we're singing of you.
Everything warrants
Our singing of Florence—
So, Florence, we're singing of you.

DUET—"OUR MASTER IS FREE AGAIN"

Introduced by Gloria Story (Emilia) and James Dobson (Ascanio). Not listed in Boston tryout or New York programs, but unmistakably part of the score. Alternate title: "Master Is Free Again."

The master is free again!
Gaily we sing!

Master is free again!
He didn't swing!

There'll be no gloom again—
Happy are we!
Right in this room again,
Genius will bloom again,
Business will boom again—
Master is free!

ARIETTA—"I HAD JUST BEEN PARDONED"

Introduced during the Boston tryout by Earl Wrightson (Cellini). Not listed in New York program; may have been dropped.

A

I had just been pardoned and peacefully
Was pushing my way through the crowd
When I saw three villainous fellows
Glaring, dark, and beetle-browed.
There was Maffio on one side,
His henchmen on the other—
But being of those who love repose
My rage I had to smother.

B

Well, sure enough, the boys got rough—
At me the three of 'em sprang.
But Cellini's sword is a noted one,
And when it started to clang,
I quickly got rid of the henchmen
And the murder they tried to promote.
And as for Mister Maffio . . .
I drove my sword through his throat.

[*Emilia squeals*]

What else could I do?
Three of them attacked me, and three of them
    are gory.
And there they lie and here am I—and that's
    the story.

[*When Cellini reprises the arietta to Angela,
the A section is the same but for the
substitution of "six villainous fellows" for
"three"*]

B

Well, sure enough, the boys got rough—
At me the six of 'em sprang.
But Cellini's sword is a noted one,
And when it started to clang,
I quickly got rid of the henchmen
And the murder they tried to promote.
And as for Mister Maffio . . .
I drove my sword through his throat.
It's still there, I've no doubt.
I strove and strained with all my strength
But couldn't pull it out.

[*Angela registers*]

What else could I do?
Eight of them attacked me, and eight of them
    are gory.
And there they lie and here am I—and that's
    the story.

LOVE SONG—"YOU'RE FAR TOO NEAR ME"

Published February 1945. Introduced by Earl Wright-son (Cellini) and Beverly Tyler (Angela). Private record-ing by Ira Gershwin, vocal, and Kurt Weill, piano, issued in 1975 on the Mark 56 album "Ira Gershwin Loves to Rhyme."

CELLINI: I think you very beautiful.
ANGELA: I think you very handsome.

VERSE

CELLINI: I never heard you so bold before.
ANGELA: The words came out. They're now
        beyond recall.
CELLINI: I always found you so cold before.
ANGELA: I didn't think you thought of me at
        all.
CELLINI: I'm mad about your smile, your eyes,
        your hair;
    Your every wish I'm eager to obey.
    In all your loveliness I see you sitting
        there,
    So near, so near—yet miles and miles
        away,
    Miles and miles away.
ANGELA: I'm afraid that's near enough.
    When you talk to me like that,
    I don't know where I am at.

REFRAIN 1

ANGELA: I'm afraid, afraid you're far too near
        me!
    So I pray you, stay you where you are,
    For, oh dear me, I fear me
    Should you come too near me
    My heart may go too far.
    But to think, to think that you might
        leave me
    Makes me feel I have to have you know:
    I'm afraid, afraid you're far too near me
    To ever, ever let you go.
    I'm afraid, afraid you're far too near
        me
    To ever let you go.

REFRAIN 2

CELLINI: You can never, never be too near me!
    From today you stay you where you
        are.
    When from heaven you descended,
    'Twas never intended
    I worship from afar.
    If you ever, ever dare to leave me,
    No excuse for living would I know.
    I'm afraid, afraid you're far too near
        me
    To ever, ever let you go.
    I'm afraid, afraid you're far too near
        me
    To ever let you go.

THE DUKE'S SONG—"ALESSANDRO THE WISE"

Lyrics first published in Ira Gershwin's *Lyrics on Several Occasions* (1959). "Act I, scene iii. Cellini's studio. En-trance of the Duke of Florence, who wastes no time in listing his virtues. Melville Cooper and Soldiers." (Ira Gershwin—*Lyrics on Several Occasions*). Alternate title: "The Duke's Entry Song—'Alessandro the Wise.'" Private recording by Ira Gershwin, vocal, and Kurt Weill, piano, issued in 1975 on the Mark 56 album "Ira Gershwin Loves to Rhyme."

SOLDIERS: Make way for the noblest of nobility!
    Make way or suffer his rebuke.
    Bow low to show humility.

Bow, you peasants
In the presence
Of the Duke!
Sing his praises to the skies—
Alessandro the Wise!
Hail the man you subsidize—
Alessandro the Wise!

DUKE: A hundred years ago or so, the
Medici—
That's my family—began to win
renown—
When lovely Florence—be it to her
credit—she
Got Grandpapa's papa to rule the
town.

ALL: Sing out! Sing out! Or have it played
orchestrally!
Sing out the while you worship at his
shrine!

DUKE: There never was a fellow who,
ancestrally,
Could boast a genealogy like mine!
Lorenzo the Magnificent and
What's-His-Name? the Wondrous,
And many and many another whose
deeds were great and thund'rous!*
We've many blossoms in our
pedigree—
But I'm the flower of the family.
ALL: He's the flower of the family.

REFRAIN 1

DUKE: I'm aesthetic, poetic,
To beauty I'm sympathetic.
ALL: A patron of the arts—is Alessandro.
DUKE: My weakness is chicness—
If the lady has no antiqueness.
ALL: The ladies lose their hearts to
Alessandro.

DUKE: My art collection features Botticelli
and Da Vinci,
But also I collect young women who
are plump and pinchy.
I sponsor the celestial,
But I don't run down the bestial—

*For Lyrics on Several Occasions, *this and the next two lines were altered to:*
Plus Other Great who lie in state, and
whose acclaim Was thund'rous!
Though all were blossoms on the fam'ly
tree,
The flower in full bloom you see in me.

That combination makes 'em idolize*
Alessandro the Wise!
ALL: Alessandro the Wise!

REFRAIN 2

DUKE: I've a yearning for learning
To which I am always returning.
ALL: It's Women, Wine, and Song for
Alessandro!
DUKE: Patrician musician,
And a bit of a mathematician.
ALL: It's figures all day long with
Alessandro!

DUKE: I try to raise the public taste whene'er
I can contrive it.
So paintings pornographic I will only
show in private.
By action I embellish
Both the heavenly and the hellish—
That combination makes 'em idolize
Alessandro the Wise!
ALL: Alessandro the Wise!

REFRAIN 2 (REVISED)

DUKE: I've a yearning for learning—
To which I am always returning.
ALL: He's learned a great amount, has
Alessandro.
DUKE: Patrician musician,
And a bit of a mathematician.
ALL: It figures that figures count—with
Alessandro.

DUKE: I educate the female mind, the which I
do in private.
No matter what erotica their shelves
are lacking—I've it.
With doctrines that embellish
Both the heavenly and the hellish,
I make the population idolize
Alessandro the Wise!
ALL: Alessandro the Wise!

FINALETTO—"I AM HAPPY HERE"

Introduced by Melville Cooper (Duke), Ferdi Hoffman (Ottaviano), Earl Wrightson (Cellini), Beverly Tyler

Line changed in Lyrics on Several Occasions *to:*
A combination makes 'em idolize

(Angela), Paul Best (Marquis), Gloria Story (Emilia), and ensemble. Alternate title: "Finaletto, Act I, Scene 3."

DUKE: And now everything is arranged.
Let us be off.
[*Trumpet call*]
SOLDIERS: Make way for the noblest of nobility!
Make way or suffer his rebuke.
Bow low to show humility.
Bow, you peasants in the presence of
the Duke!
OTTAVIANO: But my lord, you forget about
Cellini!
DUKE: Of course, of course! Cellini, I
command you not to leave
Florence—in fact—you do not
leave this house until judgment is
rendered.
CELLINI: You are very good, my lord.
DUKE: Not at all. I shall probably hang you
yet. Come along, my children.

[*Angela's triolet (1) is sung first. Then (1) and (2) are sung together. Then the quartet follows. Duke busy with Ottaviano during (1) and (2)*]

1

ANGELA: I am happy here.
Why then must I go?
Life is very queer.
I am happy here.
Fate comes from the rear,
Floors me with a blow.
I am happy here.
Why then must I go?

2

CELLINI: Every moment will be gloomy
Once my Angela is gone.
What is this they're doing to me?
How am I to carry on?
Body, heart and soul, I own her—
But the Duke I must obey.
Heaven, heaven have I shown her—
Yet they're taking her away.

3

EMILIA: She is happy here.
Why then must she go?
Life is very queer.
She is happy here.
Fate comes from the rear,

Floors her with a blow.
She is happy here.
Why then must she go?

4

DUKE: You will be happy there, my
    child. . . .
By all the pleasures there beguiled.
You'll know an evening of romance.
The tarantella we shall dance.
You will be happy there, my pet.
You'll meet a most bohemian set.
Why the waiting,
Hesitating?
I'm impatient, so—
Let's go!

[*Duke takes Angela by the hand as she waves good-bye sadly with her free hand to Cellini, who stands glaring at the procession as it leaves*]

SOLDIERS: Make way for the noblest of nobility!
Make way or suffer his rebuke.
Bow low to show humility.
Bow, you peasants in the presence of
    the Duke.
Sing his praises to the skies—
Alessandro the Wise!

[*They are off now. We hear from offstage Angela's voice*]

ANGELA: I was happy there.

SOLDIERS: Alessandro the Wise!

[*Cellini, with narrowed eyes, turns head slowly to look at soldier guarding him*]

DUCHESS'S ENTRANCE

Introduced by Billy Williams (Page). Alternate title: "Make Way for the Duchess." Private recording by Ira Gershwin, vocal, and Kurt Weill, piano, issued in 1975 on the Mark 56 album "Ira Gershwin Loves to Rhyme."

Make way for the Duchess,
For Her Grace, the Duchess!
Make way for the Duchess,
For the regal, legal Duchess!

THE DUCHESS'S SONG— "SING ME NOT A BALLAD"

Published February 1945. Introduced (from a sedan chair) by Lotte Lenya (Duchess) and four courtiers. Earlier title: "Spare Me Your Advances." Private recording by Ira Gershwin, vocal, and Kurt Weill, piano, issued in 1975 on the Mark 56 album "Ira Gershwin Loves to Rhyme."

For the first entrance of the Duchess, we had a little page walk across the stage intoning to a rather bizarre melody:

> Make way for the Duchess—
> For Her Grace, the Duchess—
> Make way for the Duchess—
> For the regal, legal Duchess!

When we had to face the writing of a solo song for the Duchess, Kurt wondered what sort of melodic mood should be striven for. The page's little sing-song had echoed many times in my mind, and I suggested that its first line of ascending notes seemed a theme that could be developed into a refrain. Kurt thought this a good idea and, using the six notes of the first line, evolved this full and distinctive melody.

"I Suggested." Whether to Kurt or George or others, there must be, without counting, at least half a dozen uses of "I suggested" among my "informative annotations." These aren't put in for any credit-claiming purposes. If, once in a great while in deliberations with the composer, a short musical phrase came to me as a possibility and was found acceptable to my collaborator, that didn't make me a composer. More often than not, as in "Sing Me Not a Ballad," my suggestion arose from some musical phrase of the composer's own, which he had overlooked or whose potentiality he was unaware of. Example 2:

Sometime in the middle Twenties my brother and I spent three weeks or so with librettist Herbert Fields on a musical to be called *The Big Charade*. I forget now why this project was dropped. Anyhow, we did some work on it, including a pseudo-medieval march called "Trumpets of Belgravia." Years later, when *Of Thee I Sing* was being written, my brother was dissatisfied with several starts he had made for the opening—a political-campaign marching theme which inevitably had to be titled "Wintergreen for President." One day, out of the blue, I found myself humming these seven syllables to the exact rhythm and tune of the cast-behind "Trumpets of Belgravia, / Sing ta-ra, ta-ra, ta-ra. . . ." When I suggested this tune to its composer, his approval was non-verbal but physical. He immediately went to the piano

and "Trumpets of Belgravia" became the serendipitous musical start of "Wintergreen for President."

Conclusion? The lyricist needn't be a musician, but if he is musically inclined he can sometimes be of help to the composer. (Not that the composer can't be of help with suggestions to the lyricist, but, in my experience, alas, rarely. Really.)

—from *Lyrics on Several Occasions*

VERSE

I am not like Circe,
Who showed men no mercy;
Men are most important in my life.
Venus, Cleo, Psyche,
Are melodies in my key;
They knew how to live the high life.
Gallantry I find archaic,
Poetry I find prosaic.
Give me the man who's strong and silent:
Inarticulate—but vi'lent.

REFRAIN

Sing me not a ballad,
Send me not a sonnet.
I require no ballad:
Rhyme and time are wasted on it.

Save your books and flowers;
They're not necessaries.
Oh, the precious hours
Lost in grim preliminaries!

Deck me not in jewels;
Sigh me not your sighs;
Duel me no duels;
And—please don't vocalize.

Romance me no romances;
Treasure not my glove.
Spare me your advances—
Just, oh just make love!
Spare me your advances—
Just, oh just make love!

MADRIGAL—"WHEN THE DUCHESS IS AWAY"

Introduced by Charles Sheldon (Captain of the Guard), Melville Cooper (Duke), Gloria Story (Emilia), and ensemble. Private recording by Ira Gershwin, vocal, and Kurt Weill, piano, issued in 1975 on the Mark 56 album "Ira Gershwin Loves to Rhyme."

SOLO: When the Duchess is away, tra la la,
Just like the mice, the Duke will play,
    tra la la.
All the world is now in tune, tra la la.
Duchess away—
Let's make hay
'Neath the moon.
[Repeated by guests]

EMILIA: All convention scorning,
Let's, until the morning,
All our cares remove
And all the pleasures prove!
[Repeated by guests]

ALL: When the duchess is away,
    [etc.]
[Round. When completed, Duke appears with Angela]

DUKE: Your study in counterpoint really is
    clever,
But oh, I'm afraid it could go on
    forever.
Tonight's not for vocal or mental
    excursion.
Tonight is an evening for fleshly
    diversion.
So, off to the fleshpots, dear friends!

LOVE SONG—"THERE'LL BE LIFE, LOVE, AND LAUGHTER"

Published February 1945. Introduced by Earl Wrightson (Cellini) and Beverly Tyler (Angela). Private recording by Ira Gershwin, vocal, and Kurt Weill, piano, issued in 1975 on the Mark 56 album "Ira Gershwin Loves to Rhyme."

VERSE

Although by black misfortune we're surrounded,
Although by fallen angels we are hounded,
We'll manage yet to thwart their base designs.
Before the dawn, we'll shatter these confines
And shelter where the sun ever shines.

REFRAIN

There'll be life, there'll be love, there'll be
    laughter. . . .
Hearts aglow, we'll never know despair.
From this day, come what may, ever after—

Brass or gold, what joys untold we'll share.
We'll face the future alone, together . . .
Away from all the world and its alarms.
There'll be life, there'll be love, there'll be
    laughter. . . .
Forever in each other's arms.

TRIO—"I KNOW WHERE THERE'S A COZY NOOK"

Lyrics first published in Ira Gershwin's *Lyrics on Several Occasions* (1959). "The *palazzo* garden in moonlight. Duke Alessandro is making a play for Cellini's model, Angela. But his passes are fraught with apprehension, as he senses that Cellini lurks in the background. At times the sardonic latter sneaks a glance over a hedge. Duke, Melville Cooper; Angela, Beverly Tyler; Cellini, Earl Wrightson" (Ira Gershwin, *Lyrics on Several Occasions*). Alternate titles: "The Cozy Nook Song," "Trio—'The Nosy Cook,'" and "The Cozy Nook Trio." Private recording by Ira Gershwin, vocal, and Kurt Weill, piano, issued in 1975 on the Mark 56 album "Ira Gershwin Loves to Rhyme."

More than thirty years ago, in *Lady, Be Good!*, I tried for a number based on spoonerisms, but it never made rehearsal. This later attempt, "The Cozy Nook Trio," was, I think, not unagreeably accepted by the few who paid to see *The Firebrand of Florence*, and by the few more who came in on passes.

Gratuitous Cultural Note. "Spoonerism" (a form of what the professors call "metathesis") is defined as "the accidental transposition of initial letter or syllables of two or more adjacent words." These inadvertent verbal lapses are of course named after the Rev. W. A. Spooner (1844–1930) of New College, Oxford, who was given to transpositions like "Will nobody pat my hiccup?" for "Will nobody pick my hat up?"; "our queer old dean" for "our dear old queen," &c. But, although named after the good Dr., this sort of unintentional juxtaposition must have occurred countless times in the thousands of languages ever since primitive speech. Verbal speech, that is—as I can't conceive of a spoonerism in Grunt Communication. (Nor, for that matter, in African Drum, Indian Smoke Signal, Wigwag, Mirror Flash, Footsie, or any of the numerous other nonverbal languages.)

Two days after I wrote the above note I happened across No. 20 of the quarterly *Gentry*. An article in it, coincidentally enough, pertains to "Spoonerisms, that little trick of transposing word beginnings that was a popular

form of humor in frontier days." This definition introduces the reproduction of a hitherto unpublished manuscript "kept in deliberate oblivion for a hundred years." The author (a Midwest lawyer at the time) began his one-page piece of playful syllable-juggling with: "He said he was riding *bass-ackwards* on a *jass-ack* through a *patton-cotch* . . ." and there follow a dozen other examples of the twisted term—all in the handwriting of Abraham Lincoln. But it was another President, our thirty-first, who, through no slip of his own, was connected with the most-publicized syllable-switch: when radio announcer Von Zell introduced him across the country as "Hoobert Heever."

To revert—a year later—to Spooner: I can't resist this one, thanks to a new edition of *Brewer's Dictionary:* "Yes, indeed; the Lord *is* a shoving leopard."
    —from *Lyrics on Several Occasions*

VERSE 1

DUKE: Dear young woman, when I'm
    gazing
Fondly at you, it's amazing
How much love I'd love to vow.
But though I've had a lot of practice
At this sort of thing, the fact is
I am not myself just now.
ANGELA: Dear my lord, I fear you're scoffing.
DUKE: With Cellini in the offing,
I'm as nervous as can be.
ANGELA: Your Highness—
DUKE: Call me Bumpy.
ANGELA: You do seem rather jumpy.
DUKE: I beg you bear with me.

REFRAIN 1

I know where there's a nosy cook—
ANGELA: My lord, you mean a cozy nook.
DUKE: Yes, yes! Of course! A cozy nook for
    two.
And there we two can kill and boo.
ANGELA: My lord, you mean we'll bill and
    coo.
[Cellini's head appears]
CELLINI: It seems to me that killing and booing
    should do.
DUKE: I cannot promise you bedding wells.*
ANGELA: My thoughts, they weren't on wedding
    bells.

*For *Lyrics on Several Occasions,* *Ira Gershwin changed this and the next three lines to:*
DUKE: I cannot promise bedding wells.
ANGELA: My thoughts were not on wedding bells.
DUKE: Whatever I do is for the fatherland.
And so I love your sturgeon vile.

DUKE: Whatever you do is for the fatherland.*
I love you for your sturgeon vile.
ANGELA: My lord, you mean my virgin style?
DUKE: It's wonderful how love can understand!
[*He beams*]
ALL: It's wonderful how love can understand!

VERSE 2

[*after interruptions*]

DUKE: Listen, loveliest of your gender:
Somehow phrases soft and tender
Do not sound their best tonight.
ANGELA: It seems you get the words all twisted—
DUKE: But the way that you assisted
Thrills me through with sheer delight.
ANGELA: When the ducal throat is vocal,
Women from afar, or local,
Always know what's on his mind.
CELLINI: The situation vexes,
I'm finding out that sex is
The curse of humankind.

REFRAIN 2

DUKE: I know where there's a booden wench—
ANGELA: My lord, you mean a wooden bench.
DUKE: Yes, yes! Of course! A wooden bench
for two.
And there we two can biss a kit.
ANGELA: My lord, you mean we'll kiss a bit.
[*Cellini steps forward*]
CELLINI: He may be biting more biss-a-kit than
he can chew!
ANGELA: I like the way that you stress your
puit.†
[*Waves Cellini back*]
I mean the way that you press your
suit.
I sense it from the way you press my
hand.
DUKE: And so I offer wedless bliss.
ANGELA: I'd rather it were bedless wiss!
DUKE: It's wonderful how love can understand!
[*Emilia and other guests are heard from behind hedges*]
ALL: It's wonderful how love can understand!

*In both the vocal score and the Ira Gershwin–Kurt Weill recording, this line is:
But what a happy future I have planned.
†For Lyrics on Several Occasions, Ira Gershwin changed this line to:
How masterf'ly you stress your puit.

NIGHT MUSIC—"THE NIGHTTIME IS NO TIME FOR THINKING" and TARANTELLA—"DIZZILY, BUSILY" and THIS NIGHT IN FLORENCE

These linked numbers comprise the finale of Act I. (In Weill's score the numbers are collectively titled "Finale alla Tarantella.") "Night Music: 'The Nighttime Is No Time for Thinking' " was introduced by Gloria Story (Emilia), Melville Cooper (Duke), Beverly Tyler (Angela), and ensemble. "Tarantella—'Dizzily, Busily' " was introduced by Story, Jean Guelis (Arlecchino), Norma Gentner (Columbina), and ensemble. "This Night in Florence" was introduced by ensemble.

The Act I finale privately recorded by Ira Gershwin, vocal, and Kurt Weill, piano, was issued in 1975 on the Mark 56 album "Ira Gershwin Loves to Rhyme."

DUKE: Help, help! Guards! Help!
[*Guests rush on*]

GUESTS: All a-tremble,
We assemble,
Shouting, "What's the matter?"
All that yelling,
So compelling,
Sets our teeth a-chatter.
All was quiet.
What's the riot?
Shall we stay or scatter?
[*Ottaviano and a couple of his soldiers rush on*]

OTTAVIANO: Are you all right, cousin?
DUKE: [*Gestures. Can barely speak*]
Cellini! He threatened me!
OTTAVIANO: Which way did he go?
DUKE: That way.
OTTAVIANO: Here's the warrant. Sign it and we
get rid of him right away.
[*He rushes off; soldiers follow*]
DUKE:
[*holding warrant in shaking hand*]
Get me a quill! Why aren't there any
quills here?
[*Page runs on with writing materials. Duke is just about to sign on the page's back when Angela steps between and sings seductively*]
ANGELA: Bumpy, you have promised that this
night belongs to Venus.
All the stars are winking and I'm
thinking that they mean us.

You're a meanie if you let Cellini
come between us.
Nighttime in Florence
Is not for death warrants
When there is a bright moon above.
[*The models also start working on him*]

ANGELA,
EMILIA,
MODELS: Nighttime in Florence
Is not for death warrants
Where fond hearts are beating with
love.
[*During which Angela has taken warrant from Duke and hidden it in her bosom*]
DUKE:
[*still a little groggy*]
But I was thinking—
EMILIA: Thinking! On a night like this!

"Night Music—'The Nighttime Is No Time for Thinking' "

EMILIA: The nighttime is no time for thinking!
The night is for loving and drinking!
So, revel and frolic
And get alcoholic
And never mind if you get stinking.

ALL: The nighttime is no time for thinking!
The night is the time to get stinking!

DUKE: The nighttime is meant for caresses.
You look in your book of addresses
And find a fair pigeon
Who makes a religion
Of giving out nothing but yesses.

ALL: The nighttime is meant for caresses,
For giving out nothing but yesses.

ANGELA,
DUKE,
EMILIA: The nighttime is also for dancing,
For rhythm exciting, entrancing!
And what can excel a
Good hot tarantella
For keeping an orgy advancing.

ALL: The nighttime is also for dancing—
For keeping an orgy advancing!
Oh———oh!

"Tarantella—'Dizzily, Busily' "

ALL: Dizzily, dizzily, moments go busily,
Heaven you quickly discover. . . .
Dreamily, dreamily, peaches and
creamily
Lost in a rhythmical spell . . .
Lustily, lustily, gustily, gustily,

Never too far from your lover . . .
Merrily, merrily, verily, verily,
Dancing the gay tarantel!

Dizzily, dizzily, busily, busily,
Dreamily, dreamily, peaches and
creamily,
Lustily, lustily, gustily, gustily,
Merrily, merrily, verily, verily,
[*etc.*]

[*When tarantella is at its dizziest, trumpet in pit sounds Duchess's music. All stop, petrified. From the distance we hear the Duchess's page boy: "Make way for the Duchess—for Her Grace, the Duchess"*]

DUKE: I will be on crutches if the Duchess now should face us!

ANGELA: I feel faint!

DUKE: If we're in the clutches of the Duchess, she'll erase us!

ANGELA: I FEEL FAINT!

[*Faints in Duke's arms. He and Emilia try to revive her as guests tiptoe out singing sotto voce*]

"This Night in Florence"

GUESTS: This night in Florence
We view with abhorrence:
We all thought the Duchess away!

This night in Florence
We view with abhorrence:
The moon shines but we can't make hay!

[*Curtain*]

CAVATINA—"THE LITTLE NAKED BOY"

Introduced by Beverly Tyler (Angela) and female ensemble. Followed a reprise of "You're Far Too Near Me." In the original sequence of the score and in the Boston tryout, it also was preceded by the "Letter Song—'My Dear Benvenuto.' "

VERSE

The little god of love
Is the one I'm fondest of
And the one that I am scared the most of.

When, right out of the blue,
He aims his dart at you,
A chance you haven't got the ghost of.

Of all the gods the Romans and the Greeks
invented,
He's the one who keeps us most tormented.

REFRAIN

The little naked boy
With golden bow and arrow
Can bring you endless joy
Or chill you to the marrow.

With love he loves to toy:
You burn and then you shiver
Through the magic quiver
Of the little naked boy.

Many's the time he wrinkles your brow,
Unstrings the strings of your heart;
Many's the time you say, "From now,
I'll dodge whenever he aims his dart!"

Next day the tender sigh
You're longing to recapture. . . .
Life would lose its rapture
If the little naked boy should pass me by.

LETTER SONG—"MY DEAR BENVENUTO"

Introduced by Earl Wrightson (Cellini) and Beverly Tyler (Angela). Preceded "Cavatina—'The Little Naked Boy' " in the original sequence and in the Boston tryout.

ANGELA: My dear Benvenuto,
Somehow I can't bear you any malice.
That I'm still your friend I guarantee
you.
Hurry! Meet me at the Summer Palace,*
But be sure that no one see you.
Study this epistle.
Follow each detail:
When you get there, whistle
Just like the nightingale.
Near the second bed of yellow roses,
Almost hidden by a lemon tree,
A secret door discloses nobody but me;
A secret door discloses nobody but me.

In the vocal score, this line reads:
Hurry! Meet me at the City Palace,

MARCH OF THE SOLDIERS OF THE DUCHY—"JUST IN CASE"

Introduced by Charles Sheldon (Captain of the Guard) and male ensemble. Alternate title: "March Chorus—'We're Soldiers of the Duchy.' " Private recording by Ira Gershwin, vocal, and Kurt Weill, piano, issued in 1975 on the Mark 56 album "Ira Gershwin Loves to Rhyme."

VERSE

We're soldiers of a duchy
Whose Duke is very touchy,
Exploding on the slightest provocation.
The ducal front we back up,
And we're supposed to hack up
The enemies who cause him aggravation.
Night and day we have to drill—
He doesn't like us standing still.

REFRAIN 1

On to Pisa! On to Verona!
On to Venice! On to Bologna!
On to, on to, on to, on to, on to!
We don't want to, want to, want to, want to,
want to!
But on to Roma! On to Ravenna!*
On to Naples! On to Sienna!
We don't want to—We're not mad at anyone—
But he feels he may need more space.
Our teeth we're gnashing,
Our swords we're flashing—
Just in case!

REFRAIN 2

On to Pisa! On to Verona!
On to Venice! On to Bologna!
On to, on to, on to, on to, on to!
We don't want to, want to, want to, want to,
want to!
But on to vict'ry! On, on to glory!
Missing home-made chicken cacciatore!
We don't want to—We've enough of
everything—
But he feels we mustn't lose face!
And so we swagger
With gun and dagger—
Just in case!

On the recording, Ira Gershwin sings:
But on to Parma! On to Ravenna!

ODE—"A RHYME FOR ANGELA"

Published February 1945. Introduced by Melville Cooper (Duke) and ensemble. " 'Lively and graceful.' Library of the Palazzo. Duke Alessandro, never having failed to win a coveted maid by lyricizing her, attempts again the tactic, this time hoping to intrigue Cellini's model, Angela. He tries his poetic effort out on a group of Ladies-in-Waiting, who listen well but, more entertainingly, dance with him after the second refrain" (Ira Gershwin—*Lyrics on Several Occasions*).

Rhyming feminine given names presents little difficulty, there being so many to choose from. (Withycombe's interesting *The Oxford Dictionary of English Christian Names* lists about six hundred female; and many new ones, I'm sure, continue to be bestowed at christenings by imaginative and/or reckless parents.) Had "Angela" required an encore, these were some of the leftovers:

If only her name were Mercedes,
She'd bring me both Heaven and Hades.

Among other graces, Hermione
Would feature an ankle that's ti-o-ny.

(fill in) . . . . Amy,
I'm jelly when her eyes survey me.

(fill in) . . . . Cora,
A lovely from Sodom and Gomorrah.

(fill in) . . . . Charlotte,
A mixture of angel and harlot.

&c., &c.

Rhyme and Time. It was fitting that Alessandro try his hand at rhyming, as by his time the Italians had been making use of this verbal or syllabic harmonization for some centuries. (Petrarch declared the Italians learned the device from the Sicilians; the Sicilians stated they acquired it from the Provençals; the Provençals felt they'd inherited the chiming effect from their erstwhile masters, the Arabians, while the Germans maintained they had adopted it from the Scandinavians. And so on.) In his *Amenities of Literature*, erudite Isaac D'Israeli (father of brilliant "Dizzy") has an essay on the origin of rhyme and is rather severe with those antiquarians who believe that the invention of rhyme arose among the above-mentioned European peoples. He backs up only the scholars who state that rhyme was known to, and practiced by, the ancients, especially "in the Hebrew, in the Sanscrit, . . . and in the Chinese poetry. . . ." (He is not quite certain about the Greeks and Romans.) He concludes: "We might as well inquire the origin of danc-ing as that of rhyming: the rudest society as well as the most polished practiced these arts at every era. And thus it has happened . . . that the origin of rhyme was everywhere sought for, and everywhere found."

Some authorities today still state that rhyme was known and used by the ancients (always excluding the Greeks and the Romans). But most of the articles I've looked up feel that exact rhyme came into use in late Latin about the third century A.D. when, in the Catholic Church ritual, priests of the African Coptic Church found it not only pleasing to the ear but also a mnemonic aid.

Rhyme and "Time." To give the correct pronunciation of proper nouns, the popular newsweekly *Time* has for many years used the phrase "rhymes with." Thus, for example: "Donizetti (rhymes with jetty)" or "Truman (rhymes with human)," &c.—and O.K. But in many other instances, "rhymes with" shouldn't appear, for when one reads "Orwell (rhymes with doorbell)" or "Longstreet (rhymes with wrong beat)," &c., these aren't being rhymed correctly. What is being done is that *Time* is rhyming each syllable perpendicularly instead of double-rhyming the name horizontally.

A Short Refresher Course. In double, or triple, or rhymes of more than three syllables, one rhymes *only* the accented syllable, and the syllables that follow must be identical in sound. For instance: (double) LONGstreet, WRONG street; JIFfy, IF he; (triple) vaRIety, improPRIety; VAcancy, THEY can see; (quadruple) LYRically, saTIRically; MORE if I love, GLORify love.

From the second set of rhymes in each example one will notice the spelling is not a determinant in rhyme, since (again): rhyme is based solely on the pronunciation and harmonization of accented syllables.

(Most modern poets find "perfect" or "full" or "exact" rhyme too limiting, and favor sound devices called "visual rhyme," "suspended rhyme," "historical rhyme," "dissonance-consonance," and other literary and intellectual varieties. These are not, I feel, for the lyricist, whose output in the field of entertainment must be easily assimilable and whose work depends a good deal on perfect rhyme's jingle.)

—from *Lyrics on Several Occasions*

VERSE

It's always been a pleasure
To dedicate a measure
To the lady who intrigues me at the time.
Diana and Roxana
And Lana and Susannah
Were names I sang in rhythm and in rhyme.
Cornelia and Aurelia,
Cecelia and Ophelia,
Inspired lovely lyrics from my pen—
But Angela is something else again.

REFRAIN 1

I can find a rhyme for Lucy—
For instance, her kiss is juicy.
But I must confess
I'm lost, more or less,
With Angela, Angela.

I can find a rhyme for Chloe—*
For instance, her breast is snowy.
But rhyming is lame
When you get a name
Like Angela, Angela.

If only her name were Olivia,†
She could be a cute bit of trivia;
If she were tagged Maria,
Or even Dorothea,
She'd be my Sole Mia
Divine.

I can find a rhyme for Irma:
She's Heaven on Terra Firma.
But Angela has no patter—
And yet, what does it matter
If Angela's heart rhymes with mine!

REFRAIN 2

I can find a rhyme for Margot:
On her favors there's no embargo.
But rhyming is tough
When one's bit of fluff
Is Angela, Angela.

What a joy to rhyme Amanda:
Each movement is pure propaganda.
(The heights I can climb—
Till I seek a rhyme
For Angela, Angela.)

If only her name were Titania,
I'd star her in my miscellanea;
If she were called Marcella
Or even Isabella
This most poetic fella
Could shine.

I can find a rhyme for Edith
She possesses what Everyman needeth.
But Angela has no patter—
And yet, what does it matter
If Angela's heart rhymes with mine!

*For Lyrics on Several Occasions, *Ira Gershwin* changed this line to:
Takes no time to rhyme, say, Chloe—

†*For Lyrics on Several Occasions, *Ira Gershwin* changed this line to:
If only they called her Olivia,

PROCESSION—"SOUVE- NIRS," "HEAR YE! HEAR YE!" and CHANT OF LAW AND ORDER—"THE WORLD IS FULL OF VILLAINS" and TRIAL BY MUSIC—"YOU HAVE TO DO WHAT YOU DO DO"

"Procession—'Souvenirs'; 'Hear Ye, Hear Ye' " intro- duced by Randolph Symonette (Hangman) and ensem- ble. "Chant of Law and Order—'The World Is Full of Villains' " introduced by Melville Cooper (Duke) and ensemble. "Trial by Music: 'You Have to Do What You Do Do' " introduced by Cooper, Earl Wrightson (Cel- lini), Paul Best (Marquis), Lotte Lenya (Duchess), Ferdi Hoffman (Ottaviano), Marion Green (Magistrate), and ensemble. "Trial by Music: 'You Have to Do What You Do Do' " was adapted from "No Matter Under What Star You're Born" and "Song of the Zodiac," both de- leted from *Lady in the Dark* (1941).

"Procession—'Souvenirs' "

TWO VENDORS: Souvenirs! Hurry, hurry, hurry,
get your souvenirs!
Souvenirs of the trial of Cellini—
The greatest trial of the season.
Get your likeness of Benvenuto
Cellini—
The occasion isn't complete
without our
Souvenirs! Hurry, hurry, hurry,
get your souvenirs!

HANGMAN: When the bell of doom is clanging
For the man awaiting hanging,
Let's face the fact with no misgiving:
One man's death is another man's
living!

MODELS AND
APPRENTICES: Our master
Has met disaster!
Our sculptor will sculp no more.
But high up
He'll find a tie-up
Redesigning heaven's golden door.

"Hear Ye! Hear Ye!"

CLERK: Hear ye, hear ye, hear ye!
If you are guilty, fear ye!

If innocent, we clear ye!
Hear ye, hear ye, hear ye!

"Chant of Law and Order—'The World Is Full of Villains' "

MAGISTRATE,
DUKE, CLERK: Oh, the world is full of villains
Whose crimes we all bewail.
Oh, the world is full of villains
And justice must prevail.

ALL: Oh, the world is full of villains
And justice must prevail.

2ND CLERK: The Duchy of Florence versus
Benvenuto Cellini.

CLERK: Whereas it is alleged that you,
Benvenuto Cellini,
Allegedly assaulted an alleged
Count Maffio
And were because of your alleged
artistic ability
Pardoned by our alleged Duke—

DUKE: *Alleged* Duke!

CLERK: A calligraphical error, my lord.

DUKE: Make that "our blessed, benign,
and benevolent Duke"!

[*Explains to crowd*]
It's more alliterative.

CLERK: Pardoned by our blessed, benign,
and benevolent Duke;
And likewise, therefore and as
aforementioned, you showed
your alleged gratitude
By allegedly making another
murderous assault,
It is the alleged wish of our
blessed, benign, and benevolent
Duke that you
Pay with your life for these alleged
allegations.

ALL: Oh, the world is full of villains
And justice must prevail.

DUKE: What do I do now?

MAGISTRATE: You must examine the defendant.

DUKE: I do that sort of thing very well.
Where shall I begin, Benvenuto?

CELLINI: With the fact, my lord, that I am
not to blame.

DUKE: But you drew your sword on
Maffio!

CELLINI: My lord, was it my fault that he
happened to be there at the
time?

DUKE: You mean if he hadn't been there
he'd still be alive? So he's really
to blame for getting himself

killed? There's a great deal in
that.

CELLINI: No, my lord, he's not to blame
either.

DUKE: But damn it all, someone is.

CELLINI: No, no, my lord. Let me tell you
all about it.

DUKE: Very well. We allow three minutes.
[*Takes out the same sand clock we saw in
Act I, scene 1*]

"Trial by Music—'You Have to Do What You Do Do' "

CELLINI: In Naples one night a wandering
Gypsy
After three or four bottles too many
grew tipsy:
On the Secret of Secrets she let
down the bars
And told me what really is written
in the stars.

DUKE: [*to crowd*]
I don't know where this is going to
go,
But a tipsy Gypsy told him so.

ALL: A Gypsy let down the bars
And told him what's really in the
stars.

CELLINI: You will offer your apology
When you hear the New Astrology.

CROWD: The New Astrology!
[*whispering*]

CELLINI: No matter under what sign you're
born—
If Leo, Virgo, or Capricorn—
Whatever you do from morn to
morn,
You have to do what you do do!

No matter under what star you're
starred,
It doesn't help you to be on guard.
You're always hoist on your own
petard
And have to do what you do do!

CROWD: What does he mean
With this routine
That comes like bolts from the blue
do?

CELLINI: You have to do what you do do!
'Tisn't up to you at all.
We all live under a hoodoo
Till you hear the trumpet call.
In this life, what else can you do?

In this life, we're pawns in a game!
If you have to do what you do do,
Whatever you do, you're not to
blame.

[*Cellini and crowd sing simultaneously*]

CELLINI: In this life, what else can you do?
In this life, we're pawns in a game!

CROWD: What does he mean
With this routine?

CELLINI AND
CROWD: If you have to do what you do do,
Whatever you do, you're not to
blame.

CELLINI: Was Plato to blame for being
Platonic?
Or Babylon for being Babylonic?
Was Caesar to blame for being
Cesarean?
Or the people for being proletarian?
Was Nero to blame for being
destructive?
Or the Queen of Sheba for being
seductive?
Was Helen of Troy to blame for the
Trojan Horse?
No, no! My friends, 'twas a greater
force!
And so by the shades of Pluto,
Am I to blame for acting like
Benvenuto?

You have to do what you do do!

ALL: 'Tisn't up to you at all.
We all live under a hoodoo
Till you hear the trumpet call.
In this life, what else can you do?
In this life, we're pawns in a game!
If you have to do what you do do,
Whatever, whatever, whatever,
whatever you do,
You're not to blame!

DUKE:
[*Jumps up*]
I like it! No one's to blame for
anything!
I am not to blame,
Thou art not to blame,
[*pointing to Cellini*]
He is not to blame,
We are not to blame,
You are not to blame,
They are not to blame,
Nobody, nobody, nobody, nobody,
Nobody is to blame!

You have to do what you do do—
'Tisn't up to you at all.

ALL: We all live under a hoodoo
Till you hear the trumpet call.

CELLINI: Whatever your station, whatever
your name,
Whatever you do do, you're never to
blame.

ALL: You have to do what you do do
Is the fact that we proclaim.

DUKE: You may think that you do
Whatever you do do,
But there is a hoodoo
That's running the game.

CELLINI: No matter whatever
You do do endeavor,
I'm here to assever
That—

ALL: Nobody, nobody, nobody, nobody,
Nobody is to blame!

ARIETTA—"HOW WONDERFULLY FORTUNATE" and DUET—"LOVE IS MY ENEMY" and REPRISE—"THE LITTLE NAKED BOY"

Contained in the conclusion of the trial scene. "Arietta—'How Wonderfully Fortunate' " introduced by Beverly Tyler (Angela) during the Boston tryout. Not listed in the New York program; may have been dropped. "Duet—'Love Is My Enemy' " introduced by Tyler and Earl Wrightson (Cellini). Reprise of "The Little Naked Boy" sung by Tyler and Lotte Lenya (Duchess).

DUKE: Too bad. You should always have a
witness. They often come in handy.

ENSEMBLE: Oh, it pays to have a witness
When you run afoul the state.
Oh, it pays to have a witness—
That's a thing to cultivate!

HANGMAN: But he hasn't got a witness—
And I can hardly wait!

[*Angela pushes her way through group*]

ANGELA: Please make way! Make way!

[*Cellini, surprised, and Duke, delighted, exclaim:*]

CELLINI
AND DUKE: Angela!

"Arietta—'How Wonderfully Fortunate' "

ANGELA: How wonderfully fortunate! How
splendidly sublime
That I arrive at the moment known as
the nick of time
To save an innocent soul accused of a
dastardly crime!
How wonderfully fortunate! How
sublime!
We live in a world where knavery
Is often ascribed to those imbued with
loyalty and bravery,
But happily for the innocent pawn,
'Tis frequently darkest before the
dawn.
How wonderfully fortunate! How
splendidly sublime
That I'm here just in time!

ENSEMBLE: She seems to be importunate
About Cellini's crime!

DUKE: Very interesting. But Cellini still has
no witness.

ANGELA: Don't leave me, Benvenuto. You
know you love me.

[*Cellini looks helplessly from one to the other*]

"Duet—'Love Is My Enemy' "

CELLINI: Love is my enemy, my beloved enemy,
And you, my love, are love.

Work is my destiny, my relentless
destiny,
Urging me onward, ever onward.

Love and life are fleeting . . .
A wonderful but momentary song;
While to the ages my work and I
belong.

Love is my enemy, my beloved enemy,
And you, my love, are love.

ANGELA:
[*bowing to the inevitable*]
Love is my destiny; work is my enemy,
Urging you onward, ever onward.

CELLINI: Love and life are fleeting . . .
A wonderful but momentary song;
While to the ages my work and I
belong.

BOTH: Love is my (your) enemy, my (your)
beloved enemy.

ANGELA: My love, if love can cast no spell,
Farewell, my love. . . .

CELLINI: Farewell, my love. . . .

BOTH: Farewell.

[*Cellini moves toward her. She turns. He makes a gesture of helplessness and goes off with the Marquis, singing a snatch of "You Have to Do What You Do Do." Angela sinks into a chair, cries a little. Duchess enters, raging*]

DUCHESS: Then it's true! It's true what I hear!
　　　　　He's gone!

　ANGELA:
[*heartbrokenly*]
　　　　　What do you care? I love him!

"Reprise—'The Little Naked Boy'"

DUCHESS:
[*gently*]
　　　　My poor child, he isn't worth one of
　　　　　your tears!

[*Sings softly*]
　　　　The little naked boy
　　　　Whose realm is the romantic
　　　　Can bring you endless joy
　　　　And then can drive you frantic.
　　　　With love he loves to toy;
　　　　You burn and then you shiver
　　　　Through the magic quiver
　　　　Of the little naked boy.

　　BOTH:
[*Angela singing through her tears*]
　　　　Many's the time he wrinkles your
　　　　　brow,
　　　　Unstrings the strings of your heart;
　　　　Many's the time you say, "From now,
　　　　I'll dodge whenever he aims his
　　　　　dart. . . ."

CIVIC SONG—"COME TO PARIS"

Lyrics first published in Ira Gershwin's *Lyrics on Several Occasions* (1959). Introduced by Paul Best (Marquis) and ensemble. Alternate title: "Paris (Fr.)." "Naturally, Cellini couldn't hang in the Prologue of *The Firebrand of Florence*, or we'd have had no show—not that we had. Anyway, toward the end of Act II, he is hired by France's Francis I, and—to the same music and rhythms as "Florence"—now Francophiles take over" (Ira Gershwin—*Lyrics on Several Occasions*).

Two *Ensemble Numbers, Same Music.* The prologue to *The Firebrand of Florence* included Song of the Hangman: "One Man's Death Is Another Man's Living";

Civic Song: "Come to Florence"; Cellini's Farewell Song: "Life, Love, and Laughter"; vendors' sales cries; plus recitatives carrying the story line.

Since Chamber of Commerce propaganda wasn't limited to Florentines extolling that city's virtues, we decided to use the music and rhythms of "Florence" late in the second act for similar civic pride by Parisians. Which is why both numbers have the same form in print, although most of the lines are different.

Reprising a song, usually a ballad (sometimes with lines changed to suit the later situation), is standard procedure. (I recall that in 1920's *Mary* the big song hit, "Love Nest," was sung at least six times during the evening by Jack McGowan, not counting a couple of other renditions, one as a duet, the other by the entire company. And who is to say that this was too much of a good thing when the song sold over a million copies?) Technically, however, I wouldn't call "Paris" a reprise of "Florence," even though the same music was listened to in both. I would say the intention was to effect a sort of counterbalance, especially as the longish entities were not in customary song form.
　　　　　　　—from *Lyrics on Several Occasions*

OFFICIALS: With nothing but pity
　　　　　The folk we dismiss
　　　　　Who live in a city
　　　　　That's other than this.

　ONE
GROUP: If you're bent on viewing
　　　　Something doing,
　　　　Come to Paris!
　　　　Music, art, and passion*
　　　　Set the fashion
　　　　Here in Paris.
　　　　Literary gentry
　　　　Make their entry†
　　　　Here in Paris.

　ALL: Paris, oh Paris,
　　　　Your riches embarrass!
　　　　So, Paris, we're singing of you.

Piano-vocal score version of this and the next five lines:
　　　　Where is life more active
　　　　And attractive
　　　　Than in Paris?
　　　　Music, art, and passion
　　　　Set the fashion
　　　　Here in Paris.
†*For* Lyrics on Several Occasions, *Ira Gershwin changed this and the next line to:*
　　　　Have you naught but loathing for your
　　　　　clothing?
　　　　Come to Paris.

ANOTHER
GROUP: Bottles full of bubbles*
　　　　For your troubles
　　　　Tickle Paris.†
　　　　Paradise is when you
　　　　Read a menu
　　　　Off in Paris.‡
　　　　(There's no overlooking
　　　　What is cooking
　　　　Here in Paris.)

　ALL: Liver with truffle
　　　　Makes gourmets unruffle;
　　　　Oh, Paris, you always come through.

　GIRLS: Cities in Italy,
　　　　Sweden, or Spain
　　　　(Quite noncommittally)
　　　　Give us a pain.

　MEN: Don't mention Tripoli,
　　　　London, or Rome!
　　　　We sing hip-hippily:§
　　　　No place like home!

　THIRD
GROUP: Where have men more talent
　　　　For what's gallant
　　　　Than in Paris?
　　　　Where do girls wear bodices
　　　　Like goddesses—
　　　　But Paris?
　　　　(Bodies delightful
　　　　All are quite full
　　　　Here in Paris.)

　ALL: Paris, oh Paris—
　　　　Where nothing can harass—
　　　　Your equal this earth never knew.
　　　　Paris, oh Paris,
　　　　Your riches embarrass!
　　　　So, Paris, we're singing of you.

Piano-vocal score version of this and the next five lines:
　　　　Bottles full of bubbles
　　　　For our troubles
　　　　Here in Paris.
　　　　Paradise is when you
　　　　Read a menu
　　　　Here in Paris.
†*For* Lyrics on Several Occasions, *Ira Gershwin changed this line to:*
　　　　Pop in Paris.
‡*For* Lyrics on Several Occasions, *Ira Gershwin changed this line to:*
　　　　Here in Paris.
§*For* Lyrics on Several Occasions, *Ira Gershwin changed this line to:*
　　　　Sing out hip-hippily:

PARK AVENUE | 1946

Tryout: Colonial Theatre, Boston, September 23, 1946; Shubert Theatre, Philadelphia, October 7, 1946; Shubert Theatre, New Haven, October 21, 1946. New York run: Shubert Theatre, opened November 4, 1946. 72 performances. Music by Arthur Schwartz. Produced by Max Gordon. Book by Nunnally Johnson and George S. Kaufman, based on a short story by Nunnally Johnson. Book staged by George S. Kaufman. Dances staged by Helen Tamiris, who replaced Eugene Loring during the tryout. Orchestra under the direction of Charles Sanford. Orchestrations by Don Walker. Cast, starring Leonora Corbett (Sybil) and Arthur Margetson (Oggie), featured Raymond Walburn (Richard), Martha Stewart (Madge), Ray McDonald (Ned), Mary Wickes (Betty), Ruth Matteson (Myra), David Wayne (Mr. Meachem), Robert Chisholm (Charles), Martha Errolle (Elsa), Charles Purcell (Reggie), William Skipper (James), Harold Mattox (Ted), Dorothy Bird (Laura), and Joan Mann (Beverly).

In *Park Avenue*, George S. Kaufman, Nunnally Johnson, Arthur Schwartz, and I thought we would have a novelty show—a so-called "smart" show—if only for the reason that it pertained to the upper-bracket-income-and-black-tie set as against four or five years of nothing but costume and period operettas on Broadway. Novelty or not, there were two reasons for our flopping: (A) charm wasn't enough to sustain the second act; (B) evidently divorce is a ticklish subject to be funny about for an entire show. In Boston during the first week of our tryout, Arthur Schwartz told me that a friend of his, whom he had invited to see the show, cried through most of it. She had recently been divorced and just couldn't take it.

—from Lyrics on Several Occasions

TOMORROW IS THE TIME

Introduced by twelve bridesmaids, all named "Brenda": Adele Rasey, Sherry Shadbourne, Carol Chandler, Betty Ann Lynn, Kyle MacDonnell, Eileen Coffman, June Graham, Betty Low, Virginia Morris, Judi Blacque, Gloria Anderson, and Margaret Gibson.

[*Part 1 solo. Parts 2 and 3 by all excepting the lines that start with "Hail," which should be done by an especially enthusiastic bridesmaid*]

1

We live in an age that's the pinnacle
Of the cynical,

Where those who are brittle belittle true
romance.
To us, however, it's conceivable
That this garden can be Adam and Eveable;
And frequently it is fated
That two hearts were born to be mated.
Tomorrow, for instance, right here, at this time,
Wedding bells will chime.

2

The wedding bell will chime.
Hail the bell,
Hail the chime!
Two happy hearts will rhyme.
Hail the rhyme!
We are the bridesmaids:
We'll be marching in
When they begin *Lohengrin.*
We'll hear them say, "I do!"
Hail "I do!"
Hail "I do!"
The magic words that make one out of two.
Here on Long Island tomorrow
Is the time,
Is the time,
Wedding bells will chime.

3

They'll need a number of cops
To guard the gifts from the shops;
As weddings go, this'll be tops!
They will be unified by the bishop;
Oh, what a ceremony he'll dish up!
And now that ev'rything's plain,
We wind up with a refrain
That Gilbert and Sullivan once wrote,
Quote:
"Hail the bridegroom, hail the bride!
Let the nuptial knot be tied!"
Not be tied too lightly,
But secure and tightly.

[*All sigh*]
In short, tomorrow's the day
True love is having its way.
What more can a bevy of bridesmaids say?

Revised Version of Part 1

1

When happy boy and girl decide
To take a chance as groom and bride,
The impulse they obey is universal.
But weddings, you must understand,
Do not just happen—they are planned—
And all of us need oodles of rehearsal.

We went through it this morning;
We're at it once again—
Against that moment when:

FOR THE LIFE OF ME

Published September 1946. Introduced by Ray McDonald (Ned), Martha Stewart (Madge), and bridesmaids. Danced by McDonald, Stewart, William Skipper (James), Harold Mattox (Ted), and bridesmaids.

VERSE 1

NED: Look me up in the *Social Register,*
Just look up "Ned Scott" there,
And of all the names they've got
there,
You will find that I am not there.

Then look up *Who's Who in
America,*
And though it would be pleasant
To be among those present,
I've no claim
To fame.
Of me they'll have none
In Bradstreet and Dun.

Your choosing me was a bolt from
the blue;
I'm not exactly the type I would
choose for you.

REFRAIN 1

I don't know how I won you—
For the life of me!
Can't understand how you could
care to care.

I can't get over it yet.
Of all the many I'd met,
You were so unlike—
Not anyone like
You anywhere.

How did I ever win you
For the wife of me?
How did the likes of you and me
combine?

I look at you and then
I pinch myself again
To realize that
For the life of me—
You're mine.

VERSE 2

MADGE: At my finishing school in
    Switzerland,
Never met a Swiss there
That I ever cared to kiss there
(Or, when I left, I would miss
    there).

When I got me back to America,
All through my Junior Leaguing,
There was no one intriguing
With that real
Appeal.
So don't go to town
To build yourself down.

If you're a headhunter straight
    from Peru,
I'm still exactly the type I would
    choose for you.

REFRAIN 2

MADGE: Don't get the point you're making—
For the life of me!
How can you ask how could I care
    to care?

Although my taste may be queer
I want to make myself clear:
Don't want Van Johnson
Or John L. Lewis
Or Fred Astaire.

NED: Just tell the world from now on:
"Here's the wife of me!"
That's all I ask and all you have to
    do.

Historians will agree
In my biography
The only reason
For the life of me
Is you.

INTERLUDE

BRIDESMAIDS: If you only heard
An occasional word,
This is what they
Are trying to say:

For the life of him and the life of
    her,
They will both be happier than
    they ever were.

They will really tingle
When they're no longer single.

Oh, the life of her and the life of
    him
Will be like a fairy tale from the
    Brothers Grimm.

And a wedding ring'll
Make it come true.

He is very modest, he wishes to
    state:
He is not Thomas Jefferson or
    Peter the Great.

She says that in spite of her
    vitamin shots
She is not Ingrid Bergman or Mary,
    Queen of Scots.

They're only themselves
And that's what they prefer
For the life of him and her.

REFRAIN 3

MADGE: I don't know how I won you—
For the life of me!
I only thought I'd worship
From afar.

I can't get over it yet.
The very first time we met,
I had no inkling
My star was twinkling—
But here we are!

NED: I'll tell the world from now on:
"Here's the wife of me!"
MADGE: That's all I ask and all you have to
    do.

NED: Historians will agree
In my biography
BOTH: The only reason
For the life of me—
You're mine.

COUNTERMELODY

CHORUS: For all the life of him
And the life of her,
They will both be happier
Than they ever were.
They will really tingle
When they're no longer single.
They can't get over it yet.
The very first time they met,
They didn't think
Their star would twink—
But here they are together!
And so the life of her
And the life of him

Will be like a fairy tale
From the Brothers Grimm.
When no longer single,
That's when they'll
Really tingle.

For the life of him
And the life of her,
She's his—
He's hers—
They're theirs!

THE DEW WAS ON THE ROSE

Introduced by Leonora Corbett (Sybil), Arthur Marget-son (Oggie), and Charles Purcell, Raymond Walburn, and Robert Chisholm (Reggie, Richard, and Charles, three ex-husbands). Reprised twice by Corbett and Margetson.

VERSE 1

SYBIL: This reunion brings a glow that's
    rapturous,
Husbands that were mine.
Matrimonial boredom couldn't capture
    us—
The grape was on the vine.
3 EXES: Like sparkling Burgundy we bubbled;
Our waters never were troubled.
REGGIE: Gallantly we played the game
To keep alive the flame.

REFRAIN 1

CHARLES: We didn't wait to separate the usual
    way. . . .
SYBIL: We parted while the dew was on the
    rose—
RICHARD: With friendship never wilting.
SYBIL: We differed from the throng—
REGGIE: Our madrigal is lilting—
3 EXES: And life a perennial song.
SYBIL: We said good-bye before the sky grew
    gray above—
3 EXES: That's why the sunlight of our love still
    glows.
SYBIL: How splendid that we drifted
Before we rifted—
3 EXES: And parted while the dew was on the
    rose.

INTERLUDE 1

OGGIE: How sensitive the spirit!
How intelligent the heart!
Before they ever rifted,
They drifted
Apart!

VERSE 2

SYBIL: Ev'ry mating can be happy-endable—
Here's the recipe:
Always make your marriages
expendable
To camaraderie.
3 EXES: We laughed, we traveled, we
frolicked. . . .
And mostly, we alcoholicked.
SYBIL: But the moment super fine
Was the moment you made me mine.

REFRAIN 2

CHARLES: It's very plain why we remain the best
of friends:
SYBIL: We parted while the dew was on the
rose.
CHARLES: The stars were shining brightly;
The crest was on the wave.
REGGIE: We did the right thing rightly—
OGGIE: The civilized way to behave.
ALL: We said good-bye before the twilight of
our love;
We gave romance no chance to
decompose.
SYBIL: Before dull care could find us,
We uncombined us—
ALL: And parted while the dew was on the
rose.

INTERLUDE 2

SYBIL: I recollect with gratitude
Your most attentive attitude;
Your clothes and manners were
supreme.
3 EXES: Our castle was a haven
Where chins were never unshaven.
SYBIL: I never let it get to where
The face that I was set to wear
Could show the slightest trace of cold
cream.
OGGIE: Though they led a turtledove life
With an eighteen-karat love life.

REFRAIN 3

3 EXES: How most sublime to know the time to
separate—
To part them while the dew is on the
rose!
SYBIL: When joy was at the greatest
And ev'ry month was May,
That night I told my latest:
"Dear darling, let's call it a day."
OGGIE: How very smart of us to part the way
we did.
SYBIL: How lucky I, in all the men I chose.
Love never was diminished—
3 EXES: Nor friendship finished—
By parting while the dew was on the
rose.

INTERLUDE 3

OGGIE: How sensitive the spirit!
How intelligent the heart!
Before their love diminished,
They finished
Apart!

TAG

ALL: No sorrowful finale—
We're all still pally—
We're/They're all still pally—
By parting while the dew was on the
rose.

Act I Reprise

SYBIL: How most unique, how ultra chic our
attitude!
SYBIL
AND OGGIE: We're parting while the dew is on the
rose.
SYBIL: The way that we've been fashioned,
Unpleasantness one scorns.
With words quite unimpassioned—
BOTH: We're taking the bull by the horns.
Now here's your hat and that is that
and off you go:
The mortgage on our dreams they
can't foreclose.
SYBIL: Before an eye can flicker—
OGGIE: And even quicker—
BOTH: We're parting while the dew is on the
rose.

Act II Reprise

SYBIL: Why must we part and have to start
With someone else?
Let's try to keep the dew upon the rose!
OGGIE: As I look in your eyes now,
I see that I was blind;
I look and realize now,
Your equal I never shall find.
SYBIL: So come what may,
Why don't we stay
The way we are?
BOTH: By standing pat,
We'll keep our stat-
Us quos.
SYBIL: As blushing bride and groom again—
OGGIE: We'll share one room again—
BOTH: And always keep the dew upon the rose!

DON'T BE A WOMAN IF YOU CAN

Published November 1950. "An Upper-Bracket Litany sung by Mary Wickes [Betty], Martha Errolle [Elsa], and Ruth Matteson [Myra]. (Naturally the lines were divided among them; *unisono*, they'd soon have been out of breath in the patters)" (Ira Gershwin—*Lyrics on Several Occasions*).

The title "Don't Be a Woman If You Can" is a paraphrase of an oft-quoted remark by a turn-of-the-century songwriter. I met Dave Clark in the early Twenties at the billiard-and-pool parlor on 52nd Street—a hangout frequented nightly by songwriters. Clark was always neatly dressed, clean-shaven, and soft-spoken, even though over the years the poor chap's brain had become disordered. He was supported by contributions from the boys and a publisher or two, but he had his dignity and definite notions on quotas, so wouldn't accept more than what he considered correct. Once when I tried offering him a dollar—others gave him more—he shook his head and took only the usual quarter. (I like to think this sum was not his measure of me as a songwriter, but that either I was a newcomer or wasn't doing too well financially.)

Despite his mental handicap, every once in a great while Dave would turn out a new song—with words somewhat Gertrude Stein-ish to 1905-ish music—for a show he intended calling *The All-Set Waltzette Revue*. Harry Warren still remembers several of them. One, "Lazy Lou," began its verse with:

Cotton time in Georgia
Is the name he knew the place . . .

and the chorus ended with:

The echo from the valley moon
Sounds its voice like tender tune—
[*a sequence of chime chords, then:*]
He was known as Lazy Lou.

Sometimes Harry, to please Dave, would play one of the songs, and would invariably be complimented with: "You played it better than Paderewski meant it." A publisher Dave didn't take to was "a faint little man"; of another annoyer he said: "I never liked him and I always will." Once when I greeted him on 47th Street he told me he was going down to 23rd Street to see what time it is." (All I could make of this was that the four big clocks on the Metropolitan Life Insurance tower were the ones to trust.)

Even before I knew Dave I'd heard of his liking a Broadway show and recommending it to many with: "Don't miss it if you can." Had he been around in the Forties, I doubt that he would have been displeased by my adapting his most-quoted line for use as a song title. Perhaps he might even have elevated me to the dollar-donor class.

—from *Lyrics on Several Occasions*

VERSE

In this vale of tears you're either baby boy
Or baby girl when you come on the scene.
Whichever you are you find that all is not
    serene.
It's tough enough to be male—
But if you're born a female
You're headed for a hideous routine.

REFRAIN

If you're born that way you have to be a
    woman,
But we often wonder—is it worth the while?
Your neck you break
On decisions you must make
To be beguilingly in style.

If you have a choice, don't ever be a woman,
For you'll spend your life just catering to man.
You're better off a zombie,
Or Fitch and Abercrombie—
But Don't Be a Woman If You Can!
Take our advice,
Don't pay the price.
Don't Be a Woman If You Can!

[*They get into a huddle, come out of it with:*]

PATTER A

F'rinstance—NAIL POLISH!
You must have the gift of vision
Making ev'ry day's decision
On the color of the polish of your nails.
Tangerine or Peach or Henna,
Moscow Red or Burnt Sienna,
Bismarck Herring, Apricot, or Peacock Tails;
Danube Blue or maybe Hudson River
Or that new tone called Chopped Liver;
Colors pure or those immoral,
Yellow Jaundice, Pink, or Coral;
Ham and Eggs or Flaming Scarlet
Make a lady or a harlot;
Ev'ry day they put out new ones,
Brown and green and gray and blue ones;
Kidney Pie or Peanut Brittle,
One cannot be noncommittal;
London Fog or Purple Daisy—
Any wonder we go crazy?
AND THAT'S JUST NAIL POLISH!
Take our advice,
Don't pay the price!
Don't Be a Woman If You Can!
Till your arteries all harden,
All your dough goes to Elizabeth Arden.
Don't Be a Woman If You Can!

[*Another huddle—then:*]

PATTER B

F'rinstance—PERFUME!
Ev'ry woman using perfume
Has to worry whether her fume
Will attract the men or chase 'em off instead.
Shall it be Chanel or Flattery,
Sexy or Assault-and-Battery,
Innuendo, Radiant, or Dash-of-Bed?
Who knows on what adventure you're
    embarking
Should you use It's-Better-When-
    You're-Parking?
Bottles by the score unveiling,
All day long you keep inhaling—
Glamorous or Stolen Heaven*
Or a sniff of Ernie Bevan;
Jezebel or Farmer's Daughter—
Which one leads them to the slaughter?
Call-Me-Later† or Narcissus,

---

*For Lyrics on Several Occasions, *Ira Gershwin changed this and the next line to:*
Wond'ring which will make love burgeon:
Courtesan or Vestal Virgin,
    †*Alternate version:*
See-Me-Later

Midnight Passion, Morning Kisses?
Worried which one will beguile 'um
Till you're fit for the asylum. . . .
AND THAT'S JUST PERFUME!
Take our advice,
Don't pay the price!
Don't Be a Woman If You Can!
When you take an inventory,
You'd be better off being Peter Lorre.
Don't Be a Woman If You Can!
If you have a choice, don't ever be a woman,
For you'll spend your life just catering to men.
You're better off a zombie,
Or Fitch and Abercrombie—
But Never a Woman If You Can!

[*Another huddle—then:*]

PATTER C

F'rinstance—HAIRDO!
As to woman's crowning glory,
It's the same old gruesome story:
How and why and where and when to do your
    hair?
When at last they do a hairdo,
They do everything they dare do—
As they weave and wave you, you get mal de
    mer.
Up-swept, down-swept, would you like it
    broom-swept?
Side-swept, swept-swept, maybe
    powder-room-swept?
With so many styles invented,
Any wonder you're demented?
Tint it purple,
Try it blonder,
Till your mind begins to wander.
Paris Knot or Grecian Knot
Or try the new Venetian Knot—
Or Girlish Bob or Mannish Bob
Or Hi-Ya, Bob! or Spanish Bob—
Or Virgin Bun or Brazen Bun
Or Cinnamon Bun or Raisin Bun. . . .
AND THAT'S JUST HAIRDO!
Take our advice,
Don't pay the price!
To the analyst you're driven.
It's a hell of a sex that we've been given!
Don't Be a Woman If You Can!

PATTER D

F'rinstance—FUR COATS!
Anybody is nobody,
Just a body that is shoddy,
If she hasn't got a dozen furs to wear.
Which will sell the propaganda,

Skunk or wolf or baby panda,
Elephant or chimpanzee or polar bear?
Maybe soon you'll see advertising splashes
For a coat made of *Life with Father*'s old
    mustaches.
Bring them on, the more the merrier—
Belgian Donkey, Irish Terrier.
Soon they'll have a killer-diller
Made of unborn caterpillar.
Shall the coats that top-to-bottom us
Be giraffe or hippopotamus?
Persian Lamb is very festive.
(Leg of lamb is more digestive!)
Looking for a skin that's wearable
Makes the livelong day unbearable. . . .
AND THAT'S JUST FUR COATS!
Take our advice,
Don't pay the price!
Oh, the problems are inhuman;
You'd be better off being President Truman.
Don't Be a Woman If You Can!

SWEET NEVADA

Lyrics first published in Ira Gershwin's *Lyrics on Several Occasions* (1959). Introduced by Leonora Corbett (Sybil) and David Wayne (Mr. Meachem). The role of "Mr. Meachem" was originated during the tryout by Ralph Riggs and subsequently played by Jed Prouty, David Wayne (who had the role at the opening), and George Keane. See Ira Gershwin's note, following, on the evolution of the number and its associated dance— "In the Courtroom"—which was performed by Dorothy Bird (Laura), Joan Mann (Beverly), and Betty Low (Brenda Cathcart-Cartcath) as Plaintiffs, David Wayne as the Judge, William Skipper (James) and Harold Mattox (Ted) as the Court Attendants, and the other bridesmaids.

A rthur Schwartz and I thought we would be different and do a song about Nevada in an ultra-Viennesy style. And through three weeks of rehearsal our leading lady gave us the elegance we hoped for. But the constant strain on a voice unused to the demands of musical comedy proved too taxing, and opening night in New Haven she could barely project vocally beyond the first few rows. By the time the show reached Philadelphia the song had been completely rewritten. It was no longer a solo but a number with several participants plus a satirical courtroom ballet; and the undulating Blue Danube-ish three-quarter-time rip-roared to a clop-clop, plunk-plunk, bang-bang rowdy-dow. "Sweet Nevada" 's migration to a more natural musical habitat

was happily welcomed by the audience; unhappily, though, after nine weeks in New York, there were no longer any audiences.

        —from *Lyrics on Several Occasions*

Waltz Version

VERSE 1

When lady fair
Is deep in despair
And needs a new elixir—
One magical place can fix'er.
Young woman, go West,
Unfeather your nest!
By car, by train,
Or—better—by plane,
One rushes to arrive there.
Your girlish glands revive there.
Oh, how one feels alive there!

REFRAIN 1

A bill of divorcement
At one time, of course, meant
A lady was dragged in the dust—
Till Nevada saved the day;
Sweet Nevada led the way.
The judge (there's no jury)*
Is not from Missouri—
A lady is taken on trust.
In Nevada, hearts are free;
Sweet Nevada—for me!

VERSE 2

Some states have laws
Quite wretched, because
To claim, let's say, insanity
Might hurt your husband's vanity.
Oh, so many grounds
Are way out of bounds.
Your days you spend,
Embarrassed no end
To prove he took a shot at you
Or—panting and looking hot at you—
Much too frequently got at you.

REFRAIN 2

I give you Montana,
Vermont, Indiana—
They still aren't wired for sound.

Earlier version of refrain 1, lines 5–6:
The judge and the jury
Are not from Missouri—

Sweet Nevada, tried and true—
My Nevada, I love you.
Although you may seek well,
The like and the equal
On this earth can never be found.
Hail Nevada—Arcadee!
Sweet Nevada—for me!

INTERLUDE

The stars in the desert give out a brighter glow
Just because they know
Life is easy-go . . .
In Nevada—
When birds sing, they sing fortissimo.
They sing on the basis
That in this oasis
The courthouse erases
All traces of despair.
Every lovely little breeze
Blowing through the yucca trees
Murmurs to you, soft and low,
"Go get your decrees."
Morning sun is singing, "Wake up!
What a lovely day to break up!"
There in Las Vegas
No husbands to plague us—
You go out on horseback
And come with divorce back—
In Nevada, in Nevada,
In the land I've learned to love!

VERSE 3

I'm on my way
Where, yippee aye ay!
They glorify the credo:
Be true to your libido—
Where freedom can glow
In six weeks or so.
One's in the groove
Not having to prove
By statutory doses
He's heading for cirrhosis,
You're heading for psychosis.

REFRAIN 3

I give you my quota
Of Maine and Dakota,
Wisconsin and Michigan, too.
Oh Nevada, I am thine.
Sweet Nevada, thou art mine.
What spot transatlantic
Is half so romantic?
Who cares if the Danube is blue?
Keep Granada! Keep Paree!
Save Nevada—for me!

Western Version

VERSE

Among the forty-eight states,
There are some very great states,
But I can do without some forty-seven.
If marriage you have tackled
And want to be unshackled,
There's one state this side of Heaven.
When on the great decision you've decided—
Just cross the Great Divide and get divided!

REFRAIN 1

Out there, out there in Sweet Nevada!
From top to toe you tingle:
In six weeks you'll be single!
Out there, out there in Sweet Nevada!
You're riding high, it's yippee-aye all day long.
'Neath the desert moonlight
Heavy hearts are soon light
For tomorrow they're free—
When the birds sing: "Wake up!
What a day to break up!
Git along—get your decree!"
No state, no state like Sweet Nevada!
They've got a way that's painless
To make you ball-and-chainless,
There's no state like Nevada for me!
Yippee-aye, Yippee-o,
There's only one place to go.

REFRAIN 2

Out there, out there in Sweet Nevada!
That tumbleweed oasis
Where you kick off the traces!
Out there, out there in Sweet Nevada!
You're riding high, it's yippee-aye all day long.
Where the judge and jury
Aren't from Missouri,
They don't question your plea—
Any grounds you make up,
They'll be glad to take up—
Git along—get your decree!
No state, no state like Sweet Nevada!
When love is in its gloaming,
I won't be in Wyoming,
There's no state like Nevada for me!
Yippee-aye, Yippee-o
There's only one place to go.

PATTER

In New York and Pennsylvania,
All the judges are aloof.
They all seem to have a mania
For that nonsense known as proof.

Proof is what they want in Connecticut!
Evidence they ask in Maine!
Is this decent? Is this etiquette?
Was the Bill of Rights in vain?
You can have my quota
Of Utah and Dakota—
Michigan and Arkansas
With their antiquated law—
In Reno and Las Vegas
No Puritans to plague us—
Nevada's the Land that I Love!

ALTERNATE ENDING

You just go out on horseback
And gallop with divorce back,
There's no state like Nevada for me!
Yippee-aye, Yippee-o,
There's only one place to go.

THERE'S NO HOLDING ME

Published September 1946. Introduced by Martha Stewart (Madge) and Ray McDonald (Ned). Alternate title: "There's No Holding Me (If I Can Keep On Holding You)."

VERSE 1

NED: What can stop us?
Who can top us
Now?
We'll make the world kowtow!

That's my story
Just make your re-
Quest.
Just say the word; Put me to the test!

I feel that I can
Out-super Superman
When you stand by me—
Try me!

REFRAIN 1

Name your heart's desire—
Presto! It's done!
I'll turn on the starlight,
Turn off the sun.
There's no holding me
If I can keep on holding you.

Want us to be rich?
Or don't you care?

Either way, I'll have us
Walking on air.
Just give me the cue
And there's no magic I can't do.

All our days, our nights,
There's nothing that you'll be denied.
We can climb the heights—
But you've got to be at my side.

We can conquer all—*
Country or town.
Got yourself a partner—
Won't let you down.
There's no holding me
If I can keep on holding you.

VERSE 2

MADGE: Silas Marner
Loved to garner
Gold
Which he would only hold.

Alexander
Had a grander
Dream:
Collecting more and more lands was the
    theme.

Something about you
Makes me a miser, too.
But I'm a wiser
Miser.

REFRAIN 2

Not concerned about
Your pocketbook.
I'll be maid and butler,
Also the cook.
There's no holding me
If I can keep on holding you.

Anybody else
Never will count.
Do you care for children?
[Ned nods eagerly]
Any amount!
There's no holding me
If I can keep on holding you.

All our days, our nights,
There's nothing that you'll be denied.

*Earlier version of refrain 1, lines 17–20:
    On Manhattan Isle
    Or in South Bend,
    I'll be in there pitching
    Right till the end.

We can climb the heights—
But you've got to be at my side.

Name your heart's desire
On land or sea.
But each time you name her—
Better name me.
There's no holding you
Unless it's I,
Unless it's I who's holding you!

Act II Reprise (Unused)

MADGE: Want my heart's desire—
Funny that way;
Want to be beside him
Hearing him say:
"There's no holding me
If I can keep on holding you."

If he disappears,
What's to be done?
Who'll turn on the starlight,
Turn off the sun?
I'm out on a limb
If I can't keep on holding him.

All my days, my nights,
Are hopeless if I'm not his bride.
I can climb the heights
But only if he's by my side.

Anybody else
Never will do;
He's the one I wanted
All my life through.
There's no holding me
Unless it's he,
Unless it's he who's holding me.

THERE'S NOTHING LIKE MARRIAGE FOR PEOPLE

Lyrics first published in Ira Gershwin's *Lyrics on Several Occasions* (1959). Introduced by entire company. "Finale, Act I, sung at Mrs. Ogden Bennett's house, Long Island, by an octet of the much-married-and-divorced set. . . . Husbands and wives, having just announced the newest matrimonial permutation possible among themselves, enthusiastically endorse (for the third or fourth time in their years) Marriage and True-Happiness-At-Last" (Ira Gershwin—*Lyrics on Several Occasions*).

INTRODUCTION

SYBIL:
[*recitative*]
You've heard of spontaneous
combustion, Mr. Meachem.
Well, something like that has happened
here, Mr. Meachem.
Hearts that were a-smolder
Suddenly grew bolder.
How wonderful to realize
You can finally possess the wonderful
one you idealize.
ALL: Mr. Meachem:
[*Lines and/or couplets from here on to be split among appropriate voices and characters, solo and in combinations*]

VERSE 1

Imagine living with someone
Who's longing to live with you!

Imagine signing a lease together
And hanging a Matisse together!

Oh, what felicity
In domesticity!

Let no one disparage
Marriage!

Being alone and breaking bread
together—
Reading *The New Yorker* in bed together.

What else are we living for?

Growing old together—
Sharing a cold together—
Starting a family tree together—
Voting for the G.O.P. together—

REFRAIN 1

There's nothing, oh nothing, like
marriage for people—
It means you're living at last!
Carry me over the threshold!*
When you her flesh hold,
On life you get a fresh hold.
How can we miss? There'll be bliss
unsurpassed!
Give me the kingdom
Of wedding ringdom!
Let there be ding-a-dong up there in the
steeple
And thousands of old shoes to throw!

*Alternate version for refrain 1,
line 3: "Carry us over the threshold!"*

There's nothing as wonderful as marriage
for people
And we are the people who know!

VERSE 2

Imagine signing a license
And finally settling down.

Of music growing fond together,*
Sleeping† through *Pelléas and
Mélisande* together.

No more philandering
When on my hand a ring.

Oh, living is lifeless‡
Wifeless!

Palm Beach in the very late fall
together—
Getting coats of tan in the altogether—

What more can life hold in store?

Shopping at Cartier's together—
Giving dinner partiers together—

Finishing a magnum of Lanson
together—
Making application at Groton for our
gran'son together—

REFRAIN 2

There's nothing, oh nothing, like
marriage for people.
It means you're living at last!
Hurry, let's call up the minister!
Why be a sinister
Old bachelor or spinister?
Give me the feast, not the fast of the past.
If there's misogyny
You can't have progeny.
Let there be ding-a-dong up there in the
steeple
And heaven on earth here below;§
There's nothing as wonderful as marriage
for people—
And we are the people who know.

Alternate version of verse 2, lines 3–4:
Vowing always to be true together,
Paddling your own canoe together.
†*Alternately:*
Dozing
‡*Alternately:*
This life, it is lifeless
or
Existence is lifeless
§*Early version of refrain 2, line 10:*
And thousands of old shoes to throw;

HOPE FOR THE BEST

Opening, Act II. Combines material adapted from "Tomorrow Is the Time," "For the Life of Me," and "Don't Be a Woman If You Can." Introduced by the twelve bridesmaids, Martha Stewart (Madge), Martha Errolle (Elsa), Mary Wickes (Betty), and Ruth Matteson (Myra). The "Lohengrin and bear it" line had been used by Ira Gershwin twice already, most recently in *Lady in the Dark* (1941).

1

    We told you this age was the
       pinnacle
    Of the cynical,
    Where those who are brittle belittle
       true romance.
    We thought we were making a jest
       of it,
    But just now the skeptics seem to
       have the best of it.
    Fate played us a trick that's scurvy,
    And ev'rything is topsy-turvy.
    Tomorrow, for instance, could be, at
       this time,
    Wedding bells won't chime.

2

    The bells may never chime.
    Drat the bell,
    Drat the chime!
    Two hearts may never rhyme.
    Drat the rhyme!
    Unhappy bridesmaids!—
    Sadly we declare it.
    We'll have to Lohengrin and bear it.
    Unless a change occurs,
    Not unless a change occurs,
    She never will be his, he won't be
       hers.
    Here on Long Island tomorrow is the
       time,
    Is the time,
    Bells may never chime.

3

    This pretty kettle of fish
    Is just the prettiest dish
    For which a columnist could wish.
    Was ever anything more excuseless?
    The lovely dresses we brought are
       useless.
    And furthermore, it is plain

We have to change the refrain
That Gilbert and Sullivan once
   wrote,
Quote:
"Where's the bridegroom for the
   bride?
Will the nuptial knot be tied?"
That's the problem, chiefly:
And to sum up briefly:

[*All sigh*]

The air is full of unrest
And we are deeply depressed . . .
But cross our fingers and hope for
   the best.

4

MADGE: It doesn't look so good.
GIRLS: Not so good,
       Not so good.
MADGE: There's little likelihood
       Two hearts will rhyme.
ALL: Here on Long Island
     Tomorrow is the time,
     Is the time,
     Bells may never chime.

5

MADGE: Can't understand what's happened—
       For the life of me!
       I know I'll never, ever be the same.
       This afternoon I thought I'd
       Become tomorrow's June Bride,
       Yet now it's farewell—
       We didn't wear well—
       And who's to blame?

       I'll never hear him saying, "Here's
        the wife of me!"
       He'll never boast that I never
        burned his toast.
       In my biography,
       The saddest page will be
       The page that says I've lost him
       For the life of me.

6

BETTY,
MYRA, ELSA: If you're born that way, you have to
       be a woman,
       But we often wonder—is it worth
        the while?
       Tomorrow you
       Are prepared to say "I do!"
       Tomorrow you'll walk down the
        aisle.

But a man is full of something called
   misgiving—
If he thinks it over, you're an
   also-ran.
The groom you would be tied to
Is much too petrified to—
So Don't Be a Woman If You Can!
To be sure of board and bedlock
On the groom you had better get a
   headlock.
Don't Be a Woman If You Can!

The outlook doesn't look so good
Though we did everything we could
To make us letter-perfect in
   rehearsal.
Though our performance was
   sublime,
It proved to be a waste of time.
The wedding plans have gone into
   reversal.

MY SON-IN-LAW

Lyrics first published in Ira Gershwin's *Lyrics on Several Occasions* (1959). "Mrs. Sybil Bennett and one of her early husbands, Mr. Richard Nelson, are co-parents of a daughter engaged to a young man who is not in Dun and Bradstreet. This is not their idea of a son-in-law. Sung by Leonora Corbett and Raymond Walburn" (Ira Gershwin—*Lyrics on Several Occasions*). During the tryout, Martha Stewart (Madge) also performed in this number.

The musical trick in the last line to emphasize the lyrical twist was brought about by an acceleration of tempo for the phrase "nothing's too good for a daughter of mine." (Frequently, on the other hand, special emphasis can be obtained by a deceleration, as, say, in slowing up the last line, "Won't you tell me how?" of "Nice Work If You Can Get It" to "Won't—You—Tell—Me—How?")

It will be noticed that the third refrain—the one in which Sybil apostrophizes—is longer than the others. This ten-line amplification of wistful wishing is an example of extension which occasionally can be done to build up the exit refrain; actually it is a sort of incorporated patter. But of course there is no rule about this device: you either feel it or don't.

                —from *Lyrics on Several Occasions*

VERSE

SYBIL: Ever since my little girl was a little
       girl,

I've dreamed of the man of her dreams—
Not merely one who'd love her*
But also be worthy of her:
The sort of Prince Charming the world
   esteems.†
Let me draw
My picture of the perfect son-in-law.

REFRAIN 1

He will be six foot two,
My son-in-law;
His haircut will be crew,
My son-in-law.
At Princeton he was crowned the hero
   of the gridiron;
He once beat Bobby Jones and only
   used a midiron.
He'll take me out to dance,‡
My daughter's groom;
Our rumba will entrance
The Persian Room.
I'll be the envy of all women who'll
   find him divine,
For—nothing's too good for a daughter
   of mine.

REFRAIN 2

RICHARD: Someday he'll come along,
My son-in-law;
His strongbox will be strong,
My son-in-law.
His oil and lumber lands so great they
   can't be mapped in;§
So loaded he need never tip a
   nightclub captain.
I'll travel on his yacht—
Belay, below!
For music he'll be hot—
And back a show;
And I'll be meeting all the lovelies in
   the chorus line,
For—nothing's too good for a daughter
   of mine.

Earlier version of verse, line 3:
   Not only one who'd love her.
†*Earlier version of verse, line 5:*
   The kind of Prince Charming the world
      esteems.
‡*Earlier version of refrain 1, line 7:*
   He'll take us out to dance,
§*Earlier version of refrain 2, lines 5–6:*
   We'll wear the same-sized shirts; from
      heaven he'll be manna;
   We'll smoke cigars from his own fact'ry in
      Havana.

REFRAIN 3

SYBIL:
[apostrophizing]
   So, join our entourage,*
   Dear son-in-law;
   She's meant for your menage,
   Dear son-in-law.
   The one she yearns for now is really an
      absurd one;
   But bide your time—you'll be the
      second or the third one.
   She's bound to come around—
   You'll have your nest.
   Meanwhile, keep on compound-
   Ing interest.
   The style of living she's accustomed to
      I'll not resign,
   With minks and chinchillas
   And mansions and villas . . .
   And how she rejoices
   In yachts and Rolls-Royces,
   And portraits by Dalí,
   Green orchids from Bali;†
   Then, parting divinely,
   You treat her benignly
   With trust funds bewild'rin'
   And the custody of the children.
   You'll do the proper thing—no
      sacrifices you'll decline,
   For—nothing's too good for a daughter
      of mine.

Trio Version

LEAD-IN

MADGE: I don't want to impose, but since he's
      going to be
   My husband, may I pass just a few
      remarks?
SYBIL: Why, certainly!

REFRAIN 2

MADGE: He may look good to you,
   Your son-in-law;
   To me he's just snafu,
   Your son-in-law.

Early version of refrain 3, lines 1–4:
   Don't fade away, don't go,
   Dear son-in-law;
   She's much too young to know,
   Dear son-in-law.
†*A couplet was deleted here:*
   Her own Constellation
   For quick transportation.

SYBIL: So debonair that clouds of glamour
      he'll be wrapt in.
RICHARD: So rich that he need never tip a
      nightclub captain.
MADGE: He's made of gingerbread,
   Your son-in-law;
   He's not a bit like Ned,
   Your son-in-law.
   Why can't I have the one and only one
      my heart adores
   If nothing's too good for a daughter of
      yours?

THE LAND OF OPPORTUNITEE

Lyrics first published in Ira Gershwin's *Lyrics on Several Occasions* (1959). Introduced by Arthur Margetson (Oggie), Raymond Walburn (Richard), Charles Purcell (Reggie), and Robert Chisholm (Charles). "A calypso about the stock market, the race track, and quiz programs. Sung in Trinidadian rhythms and dialect by four dinner-jacketed, well-heeled Park Avenue gentlemen. *N.B.*: No phonetic spelling is attempted. Many vowels, though, vary in their vocal values. Thus, "land" should be pronounced *"lond"*; "immigrants," *"immigrahnts"*; "told," *"tulled"*; "gold," *"gulled"*; "man," *"mahn,"* &c." (Ira Gershwin—*Lyrics on Several Occasions*).

Although calypso music generally hasn't as much variety in rhythm and melody as has, say, Brazilian popular song, no song form anywhere is more all-inclusive in subject matter than the Trinidadian. The improvised calypso, with its odd syllabic stress and loose rhyme, can narrate, advise, philosophize, fulminate, use this morning's headlines—and any theme goes, including the political and sexual. Thanks to subject matter and Schwartz's varied rhythms, our longish "Land of Opportunitee" sat well with the audience.
   —from *Lyrics on Several Occasions*

INTRODUCTION

All the immigrants came to the U.S.A.
Because they had been told
That in ev'ry cit*ee* of the U.S.A.
The streets were paved with gold.

They dug themselves a pile,
Then went back to Italy and the Emerald Isle.

In the U.S.A. not all the gold is gone—
The pioneer spirit will carry on.

For example and to wit—
We give you a sample of it:

VERSE 1

You take the subway to the street called Wall;
On a dignified broker's man you call.
He shows you a ticker goes tick, tick, tick—
And helps you a stock to pick pick, pick.

Fascinating names you have from which to choose,
Biggest corporations which cannot lose:
Delaware and Lackawanna,
United Fruit and Banana—
Or you buy Nash Kelvinator,
Maybe Otis Elevator.
Oh boy, can't miss!
Anaconda Copper Mining,
'Merican Smelting and Refining;
Biggest bargains ever wuz,
Like Paramount and Warner Bros.
Oh boy, some class!
With a thousand corporations to pick from—
You clean up, my friend, or else you're dumb.

REFRAIN 1

You buy a block of stock, say, American Tel;
Goes up a hundred points, then quickly you sell.
Making a fortune is A B C,
In the Grand Land of Opportunitee.
Making a fortune is A B C,
In the Grand Land of Opportunitee.
It's so simple, anyone can do it.
Just open an account and nothing to it.

VERSE 2

By now you have piled up such a bundle of jack
You take a taxi to the nearest racetrack.
Is easy to take the racetrack by storm—
A pencil, a program, a "Racing Form."

Then you handicap the possibilities*
By the Past Performances of all the gee-gees:

---

*Earlier version of verse 2, lines 5–16:
Handicapping all the possibilities
By the Past Performances of all the gee-gees:
In the first race—Roman Toga;
Second race—Ticonderoga.
In the third race, Tom the Peeper—
(Looks to me like he's a sleeper.)
Oh boy, some tips!
In the fourth, I like Disraeli,
Also I like Ukulele,
Also I like Countess Rhoda,
Also I like Lemon Soda.
Oh boy, sure things!

Man-o'-War, Sun Beau, and Stymie—
They have not done badly by me.
Good-bye, Care!—and also, Trouble!
(Compliments of Daily Double)
Oh boy, some tips!
In the first, I like Disraeli;
In the second race, Rose Bailey.
In the big race, Tom the Peeper—
(Looks to me like he's a sleeper.)
Oh boy, sure things!
So you study and study all the dope you got,
And at the window you bet a long *shot*.

REFRAIN 2

They're at the gate—and off! The race she is
    run.
Your horse comes in and pays a hundred to one.
Making a fortune is A B C,
In the Grand Land of Opportunitee.
Making a fortune is A B C,
In the Grand Land of Opportunitee.
It's so simple, anyone can do it.
Take a taxi to the racetrack—nothing to it.

VERSE 3

Though now you have got of money quite a
    store,
After all you're only human, so you want more.
So you go to a radio show which is
A question-and-answer program known as quiz.

When you face the mike you make no faux pas;
All night long you studied the Britann*i*ca:
What's the color of red roses?
On your feet how many toes is?
Name the month after September.
What's on Twenty-fifth December?
Oh boy, oh boy!
In one day how many hours?
Oranges are fruits or flowers?
Which is more, ten or eleven?
Just what year was Nineteen-Seven?
Oh boy, quiz kid!
Your answers have put the man in his place,
But now the big moment you must face.

REFRAIN 3

The questioner he ask you, "What is your
    name?"
You get a hundred thousand dollars if you tell
    him the same.
Making a fortune is A B C,
In the Grand Land of Opportunitee.
And—
If you know what flag is Red, White, and Blue,

He will throw in the sponsor's daughter too.
Making a fortune is A B C,
In the Grand Land of Opportunitee.
It's so simple, anyone can do it.
Just visit a quiz program—nothing to it!

ENCORE

You buy a block of stock, American Tel;
Goes up a hundred points, then quickly you sell.
They're at the gate—they're off! The race she is
    run.
Your horse comes in and pays a hundred to one.
The questioner he ask you, "What is your name?"
You get a hundred thousand dollars if you tell
    him the same.
Making a fortune is A B C,
In the Grand Land of Opportunitee!

GOOD-BYE TO ALL THAT

Published September 1946. Introduced by Martha
Stewart (Madge) and Ray McDonald (Ned). Dance—
"Echo"—performed by Harold Mattox (Ted), Dorothy
Bird (Laura), William Skipper (James), Joan Mann (Bev-
erly), and bridesmaids.

VERSE

NED: Don't look now, but summer's over;
    The North Wind is here.
    The red rose, the four-leaf clover,
    Disappear.

    The shadows start to fall;
    The writing's on the wall.
    You can't, you can't fight City Hall.

REFRAIN 1

MADGE: The things we planned—
    Good-bye to all that!
    We built on sand—
    Good-bye to all that!

    Whoever called a parting sweet sorrow
    Never knew
    What I'm going through.

    The years ahead
    We never will share;
    Our golden anniversary
    Melts into thin air.
    The paradise we could have known
        tomorrow,
    Good-bye, good-bye to all that!

REFRAIN 2

NED: Those gay hellos—
Good-bye to all that!
The book we close—
Good-bye to all that!

Why do they call a parting sweet sorrow?
This farewell
Is hurting like hell.

MADGE: So long, my own,
Can't blame you at all.
NED: Our bright and sunny future
We'll never recall.
MADGE: The years for which I'd steal or beg or
borrow . . .
BOTH: Good-bye, good-bye to all that.

INTERLUDE

NED: If you and I and love weren't in a spin,
What a world this old world might have
been!
Up on a rainbow we would find us,
All of our lonesome nights behind us.
MADGE: You were about to take me to far-off
places.
We were about to meet new friends and
faces.
Oh, what a lovely picture you had
painted!
Off in a world where we could really get
acquainted!
NED: This moment is the one I've been living
for:
Being one with the one I adore.

REPEAT REFRAIN 2

STAY AS WE ARE

Introduced by Leonora Corbett (Sybil) and Arthur Margetson (Oggie) during the tryout. Dropped before the New York opening.

VERSE 1

OGGIE: Darling, when the dew is on the rose
And the love-light is ablaze,
It's custom'ry for couples to be parting.
SYBIL: I'm so happy with you, I suppose
We should go our sep'rate ways.
OGGIE: But this is the time that something new
I'm starting;

I'm weary of questing;
I can't keep up the pace.
And so I'm suggesting
A future we might face:

REFRAIN 1

Why don't we stay as we are,
The livelong day as we are?
Why look for a new love to love?
It's so gemütlich with you,
Not bittersweet-lich with you.
You're comf'table as an old glove.
And of late I find it something of a
bother
To request permission of another father.
It would be splendid, old girl,
I'd feel befriended, old girl,
If you should say
We can stay
As we are.

VERSE 2

SYBIL: Darling, though the crest is on the wave
And the sun still in the West.
My heart is astir. The future I'm
surveying.
OGGIE: Though it's not tradition to behave
In the manner I suggest . . .
SYBIL: What matter to me what people will be
saying?
The notion enchants me:
To share the years with you.
What comfort it grants me!
Besides, it's something new.

REFRAIN 2

What fun to stay as we are,
As blithe and gay as we are!
We've nothing, but nothing! to lose.
At Narragansett with you,
At bridge I can sit with you,
Or go to bed when I choose.
And another reason that I'll cling to you
so
Is that Mainbocher's too busy to make
my trousseau.
It's everlasting this time,
It's perfect casting this time,
So from today,
Dear, let's stay
As we are!

REVISED VERSE*

OGGIE: Imagine not having to cope with
somebody new,
Someone you needn't send tons of candy
to.
SYBIL: Someone you don't have to wrestle in
taxis with,
Nor cater to his collection of kin and
kith.
OGGIE: Not going to El Morocco each night to
cavort;
No future brother-in-law to have to
support.
SYBIL: No telephone, telephone ringing and
ringing all day
And finding he loves you is all that he
wishes to say.
BOTH: When I think of the torture that I would
have to go through,
I cannot consider not being devoted to
you.
No, no, no, no,
I cannot consider not being devoted to
you.

REMIND ME NOT TO LEAVE THE TOWN

Intended for Raymond Walburn (Richard) and girls. Unused. A forerunner of "Weekend in the Country" in the film, *The Barkleys of Broadway* (1949).

VERSE

GIRLS: Come out, come out, you
stick-in-the-mud
And leave the marble halls.
Let's jump the garden walls,
For Mother Nature calls.
Come where the cow is chewing the
cud
And trees are all abud.
Let's frolic to where the berries are
ripe for picking
And grasshoppers hop and hop and
crickets are cricking.
RICHARD: I never cared for Vitamin A,
So get you another Queen of the
May.

Seems to have replaced verses 1 and 2.

GIRLS: Let's be parking
Where the lark is larking.
RICHARD: From this day on, my whole life
through,
I'm parking only on Park Avenue!

REFRAIN

So please remind me never to leave the
town;
Remind me not to find me in the
country,
For Mother Nature always gets me
down
With even one tree.

The bosky dell and greenery poets
praise
Are only stinkweed making me allergic;
One little whiff and I am out for
days—
My type is more blue-serge-ic.

Sing tra-la-la-la-la! Spring is here
With mossy bank and thicket;
Hark, the chirpetty chirp of the
cricket!
With a hey-nonny you can stick it!

The very next individual I shall crown
Who bids me visit where the vistas are
bucolic.
Into his highball I shall pour carbolic.
So keep your ozone!
To me there's no zone
Like the town!

HEAVENLY DAY

Conceived either as a duet for Martha Errolle (Elsa) and
Arthur Margetson (Oggie) or as a quartet for Errolle,
Margetson, Ruth Matteson (Myra), and Raymond Walburn (Richard) (this version is the duet). Unused. According to a note by Ira Gershwin, Arthur Schwartz's
tune for this number was used later in *Inside U.S.A.*
(1948).

VERSE 1

ELSA: Obviously
You can't have me
Here below, here below. . . .
But there'll be no frustration
In our very next reincarnation.
OGGIE: We must wait—
It's much too late
Here below, here below.
ELSA: In this life
I can't be your wife,
But there's millions of years to go.

REFRAIN

We'll meet some heavenly day,
The day that I fly to the gates above
And find me the true love who waits
above.
How we'll cling,
Wing to wing!
Be sure you're not lost on the way.
Don't turn you up
Where they can burn you up.
What heaven we'll share
That heavenly day 'way up there.

INTERLUDE

Going through my previous lives,
When I lay them end to end,
I find I was never one of your wives
Or even a lady friend.
I'm afraid you weren't Paris
When I was Helen of Troy.
OGGIE: What a shame you weren't Juliet
When I was the Montague boy.
When I ruled as Henry the Eighth,
At my palace you never dropped off.
ELSA: I was not in the mood
To have my noodle chopped off.
BOTH: But why reminisce of the missing bliss of
the past
When at present we're facing our future
at last?

VERSE 2

I'll take care
Of you up there,
Look ahead, look ahead. . . .

When your feathers need pruning
Or the strings of your harp need tuning,
We will get
Together yet.
Look ahead, look ahead. . . .
OGGIE: When I see
What's waiting for me,
I keep wishing that I were dead.

REFRAIN 2

We'll meet some heavenly day
Where life on a cloud is unmatchable.
I'll latch on to you, you're so latchable,
And we'll glide
Side by side.
Till then, let us live while we may;
Don't kill yourself
Now just to thrill yourself.
What heaven we'll share
That heavenly day 'way up there.

It's a date, it's a date
Sharp at eight, at the gate,
Don't be late, I can't wait. . . .
It's a date!

THE FUTURE MRS. COLEMAN

An unfinished song intended for *Park Avenue*.

REFRAIN

The future Mrs. Coleman
Will make you a wonderful wife;
She'll give you the very best months of her life.
The future Mrs. Coleman—
Her penthouse is simply sublime.
Her lease has a long way to go—
Five years' time.
To London, she flies for a week;
To Capri, she's off with a Greek
(Don't fret—He'll be awfully chic)—
Everything based on excellent taste.
The future Mrs. Coleman—
Her outlook isn't small;
You'll hardly have to live with her at all.

OVERLEAF: *Betty Grable. Dick Haymes is fourth from left.*

THE SHOCKING MISS PILGRIM
1947

A film produced by William Perlberg for 20th Century–Fox. Released in January 1947. Music adapted from George Gershwin manuscripts by Kay Swift and Ira Gershwin. Screenplay by George Seaton, adapted from a story by Ernest and Frederica Maas. Directed by George Seaton. Dances by Hermes Pan. Music conducted by Alfred Newman. Orchestrations by Herbert Spencer and Edward Powell. Cast, starring Betty Grable (Cynthia Pilgrim) and Dick Haymes (John Pritchard), featured Anne Revere (Alice Pritchard), Allyn Joslyn (Leander Woolsey), Gene Lockhart (Saxon), Elizabeth Patterson (Catherine Dennison), Elisabeth Risdon (Mrs. Pritchard), Arthur Shields (Michael Michael), Lillian Bronson (Viola Simmons), and Charles Kemper (Herbert Jothan).

P *osthumous Score.* When Producer William Perlberg wanted me for *The Shocking Miss Pilgrim* he mentioned two composers, either of whom I'd have been happy to work with. But, approached, each had already contracted for another project. Asked if I had any suggestions, I told Bill that my brother had left much unused musical material; and if the studio would take a chance, I was pretty sure a satisfactory score could be evolved. Perlberg was more than favorably inclined and sold the studio on the idea. So, contracts were drawn up for the Gershwin Estate and for me.

Being no musician, I needed the services of one, and called on Kay Swift. Kay, a composer-musician in her own right, a close friend of George's and mine, was ideal for the job. She knew almost everything George had ever written, had frequently taken down sketches as he composed in his New York apartment, and had total musical recall. (At one time she could play from memory the entire *Porgy and Bess* vocal score of 559 pages.)

We spent ten weeks going carefully through all my brother's notebooks and manuscripts; from them she played and then copied for me well over a hundred possibilities—forty or fifty complete tunes (several of which, such as "Aren't You Kind of Glad We Did?," I had started setting lyrics to in George's lifetime), plus verses, plus themes for arias, openings, &c. During this time I worked also on the lyrics and continued on them for approximately ten more weeks after Kay's work was done. I wound up with a score which pleased Perlberg, screenwriter-director George Seaton, and—just as important to me—me, with: "For You, For Me, For Evermore," a ballad; "One, Two, Three," a waltz; a suffragette number; a Temperance Society theme song, "Demon Rum"; "The Back Bay Polka"; "Changing My Tune"; "Aren't You Kind of Glad We Did?"; and three or four incidental pieces, including a musical montage, "Tour of the Town," which sang the landmarks and historic buildings of then Boston (the 1870's). The music, outside of a few grace notes which I had to add for extra syllables, was all my brother's. So, thanks to Perlberg's trust in the notebooks, manuscripts, and me,

a score materialized—the first posthumous one, I believe, for a film musical.

—from *Lyrics on Several Occasions*

SWEET PACKARD

The graduation song of Packard's Business College. Introduced by Betty Grable (Cynthia) and ensemble.

REFRAIN 1

Enhance your resources
By taking the courses
At Packard's Business College on Broadway.

On life's mighty ocean
We sail with devotion
From Packard's on Graduation Day.

From her shores departed,
Sailing seas uncharted,
We go valiant-hearted to the fray.

Sweet Packard!
You'll have a section
In our recollection
Wherever we're working, come what may—
Packard's Business College at Twenty-Second
    and Broadway.

REFRAIN 2

For days that were golden
We all are beholden
To Packard's Business College on Broadway.

So let us be voicing
Our praises, rejoicing
For Packard's on Graduation Day.

From her shores departed,
Sailing seas uncharted,
We go valiant-hearted to the fray.

Sweet Packard!
You'll have a section
In our recollection
Wherever we're working, come what may—
Packard's Business College at Twenty-Second
    and Broadway.

CHANGING MY TUNE

Published August 1946. "Verse: 'Conversationally'; refrain: 'With a rocking rhythm.' Betty Grable as Cynthia Pilgrim, the first female typist in Boston (1874), has finally found a broad-minded landlady whose boarding house will accept a working girl neither teacher, nurse, nor governess" (Ira Gershwin).

Q *ualm Calmed.* This charming tune was another must for *Miss Pilgrim* from the dozens of hitherto unlyricized ones in my brother's notebooks. After I fitted the words to it I liked the "permit—hermit" stanza but suddenly felt uneasy about the "sailor—whaler—typhoon" one. I figured that Antarctica whaling was too recent a development to be known in 1874, so a whaler probably had to be in the Arctic; and "typhoon" somehow sounded Oriental, even tropical. My problem was geographical—could one meet the other? So, to the encyclopedia—and relief in fifteen minutes. There had been a good deal of American whaling off Japan and typhoons weren't unknown there. Nothing like checking.

—intended for but not included in
Lyrics on Several Occasions

VERSE

Yesterday the sky was black
And I was blue.
Yesterday—Alas, alack!—
I thought I was through.
But knock on wood!
My job looks good,
And having found a dwelling,
My happiness is beyond the telling.

REFRAIN 1

Castles were crumbling
And daydreams were tumbling—
December was battling with June—
But on this bright afternoon
Guess I'll be changing my tune.

Kept on despairing,
Beyond any caring
If I jumped out of a balloon—
But I'm arranging
From now to be changing my tune.

At last the skies are bright and shiny;
It's a human world once more.
Yesterday's troubles are tiny—
What was I worried for?

Wanted a permit
To make me a hermit,
To grumble and glare at the moon—
But I'm arranging
From now to be changing my tune.

REFRAIN 2

No more the feeling
That my world is reeling—
No fearing I'll fall in a swoon.
Problems are all picayune—
That's why I'm changing my tune.

Felt like a sailor
Adrift on a whaler
A-sailing into a typhoon—
But I'm arranging
From now to be changing my tune.

At last the skies are bright and shiny;
It's a human world once more.
Yesterday's troubles are tiny—
What was I worried for?

No more resentment,
I'm full of contentment—
Afloat on a dreamy lagoon;
And I'm arranging
From now to be changing my tune.

STAND UP AND FIGHT

Introduced by Anne Revere (Alice), Betty Grable (Cynthia), Dick Haymes (John), and ensemble. Alternate title: "March of the Suffragettes."

A

Stand up and fight!
We're in the right!
March out of the darkness
Into the light!

We've been fed too long on sugarcoating;
There's no reason why we can't be voting!

Land of the free,
You've got to see,
We're only requesting
Equality!

Like it or not,
Men have got
To take the view
That women are people, too!

B

Why can't we be judges judging evildoers?
Why can't we be engineers and book reviewers?
Why can't we be Chief Commissioners of
    Sewers?
Butchers? Bakers?
Undertakers?
Next November's
Cabinet members?
Aren't women human beings?

MARCH OF THE SUFFRAGETTES

Intended for *The Shocking Miss Pilgrim.* Unused. Alternate title: "Women Can Be People, Too." Some of the lines were incorporated into "Stand Up and Fight."

Taking care of children, house, and crockery
May be jobs on which we women dote.
But Man has made equality a mockery
If we women cannot have the vote.

"Equal rights for all"
Is our battle call.

Freedom's torches are flaming!
Tyranny we'll be taming!
Fight on, sister, proclaiming:
Women can be people, too!

Marching, shoulder to shoulder,
We are Freedom's upholder!
Sing out, bolder and bolder!
Women can be people, too!

We want to be judges judging evildoers;
We want to be engineers and book reviewers;
We want to be Chief Commissioners of Sewers;
Butchers, bakers,
Undertakers;
Next November's
Cabinet Members!

Too long tied to a tether—
Sister, show no white feather!
If we fight on together,
Man has got to take the view
Women can be people, too!

AREN'T YOU KIND OF GLAD WE DID?

Published August 1946. " 'Moderato—in conversational style.' On an afternoon off, Cynthia Pilgrim of New York (Betty Grable), Boston's first typist (1874), is shown the city's sights by her employer, John Pritchard (Dick Haymes). Subsequently, they take supper at a most respectable restaurant. Then, as he is seeing her home in a cab, both suddenly realize the enormity of their social crime: no chaperone. Momentarily, though, they aren't bothered" (Ira Gershwin—*Lyrics on Several Occasions*).

This song was written in the early Thirties with no particular show in mind, but intended for the following spot if ever it came up: a young couple in love takes a chance and gets married, despite the fact that they are practically penniless. The words of the refrain began exactly as is, but the release and last section were:

Socially, I'm rather hazy;
Financially, I've not a dime.
Realistically, we're both ka-ra-zy—
But we'll have one hell of a time.
Though creditors may try to floor us,
Though relatives will carp and bore us—
For us no anvil chorus!
Whatever we did we're glad we did.

Since no libretto ever called for the situation, this nuptial notion gathered dust for a dozen years. But I liked the tune; and, for *The Shocking Miss Pilgrim,* was able to rework the lyric, changing it from an Epithalamium of the Depression to a Mid-Victorian Colloquy.

The innocent and innocuous "Aren't You Kind of Glad We Did?" was filmed most charmingly. I realized, though, that without visual viewing the song would be considered improper by those who didn't listen too well. So, for the printed sheet music I changed the "vest" from:

What's done, is done.
But wasn't—and isn't—it fun?

to:

With just one kiss,
What heaven, what rapture, what bliss!

thus making all morally impeccable. To no avail, however. A few recordings were pressed, but the song was banned from the air by the networks.

—from *Lyrics on Several Occasions*

VERSE

JOHN: Oh, it really wasn't my intention
To disregard convention;
It was just an impulse that had to be
obeyed.

Beacon Hill behavior we've been
scorning,
CYNTHIA: But I'll not go in mourning—
Though my reputation is blemished,
I'm afraid.

What's done, is done.
JOHN: But wasn't—and isn't—it fun?

REFRAIN 1

Honestly, I thought you wouldn't;
Naturally, you thought you couldn't.
And probably we shouldn't—
But aren't you kind of glad we did?
Actually, it all was blameless;
Nevertheless, they'll call it shameless.
So the lady shall be nameless,
But aren't you kind of glad we did?
CYNTHIA: Socially, I'll be an outcast:
Obviously we dined alone.
On my good name there will be doubt
cast—
With never a sign of any chaperone.
JOHN: No matter how they may construe it—
Whether or not we have to rue it—
Whatever made us do it—
Say, aren't you kind of glad we did?

REFRAIN 2

CYNTHIA: Honestly, I thought I wouldn't;
Naturally, I thought I couldn't.
And probably I shouldn't—
JOHN: But aren't you kind of glad we did?
The community will call me viper.
CYNTHIA: The opportunity should have been
riper.
BOTH: We'll have to pay the piper—
But what we did we're glad we did.
CYNTHIA: Supper was quite above suspicion;
Milk in the glasses when they'd
clink.
JOHN: Listening to a tired musician—
CYNTHIA: But what is it Mrs. Grundy's going to
think?
JOHN: I'm a rounder, a bounder, a cad, a
Boston blighter—
CYNTHIA: You shouldn't be seen alone with your
typewriter.
BOTH: Let's turn to something brighter:
Whatever we did, we're glad we did.

Refrain 2 (Published Version)

CYNTHIA: Honestly, I thought I wouldn't;
Naturally, I thought I couldn't.
And probably I shouldn't—
JOHN: But aren't you kind of glad we did?
The community will call me viper.

HE: People we know will call me viper.
Maybe the time could have been
riper.
HE AND SHE: We'll have to pay the piper—
But what we did we're glad we did.

HE: Heaven is mine, at last I kissed
you!
Yesterday's world seems far away.
SHE: Truthfully I could not resist you,
But what is it Mrs. Grundy's going
to say?
HE: That I'm a cad, a Boston blighter,
Running around with my typewriter.
HE AND SHE: Let's turn to something brighter:
Whatever we did, we're glad we
did.

Tag

JOHN: Unfortunately, we had to break up.
CYNTHIA: Eventually I knew you'd wake up.
BOTH: Now true love makes us make up,
And aren't you kind of glad we
did?

THE BACK BAY POLKA

Published September 1946. " 'With humorous emphasis.' A boardinghouse—Boston, 1874—run by an emphatic landlady. A quartet of roomers—a painter, a
female lexicographer, a composer, and a poet—calling
themselves The Outcasts, carol their sentiments about
the city" (Ira Gershwin—*Lyrics on Several Occasions*).
Introduced in fact by a group somewhat larger than
I.G.'s "quartet": Allyn Joslyn (Leander), Charles
Kemper (Herbert), Elizabeth Patterson (Catherine), Lillian Bronson (Viola), Arthur Shields (Michael), and
Betty Grable (Cynthia). Alternate titles: "Boston" and
"But Not in Boston."

REFRAIN 1

Give up the fond embrace,
Pass up that pretty face;
You're of the human race—
But not in Boston.

Think as your neighbors think,
Make lemonade your drink;
You'll be the Missing Link—
If you don't wear spats in Boston.

Painters who paint the nude
We keep repressing.
We take the attitude
Even a salad must have dressing.

New York or Philadelph'
Won't put you on the shelf
If you would be yourself—
But you can't be yourself in Boston.

You can't be yourself,
You can't be yourself,
You can't be yourself in Boston.

REFRAIN 2

Don't speak the naked truth—
What's naked is uncouth;
It may go in Duluth—
But not in Boston.

Keep up the cultured pose;
Keep looking down your nose;
Keep up the status quos—
Or they keep you out of Boston.

Books that are out of key
We quickly bury;
You will find liberty
In Mr. Webster's dictionary.

Laughter goes up the flue;
Life is one big taboo;
No matter what you do—
It isn't being done in Boston.

It isn't being done,
It isn't being done,
It isn't being done in Boston.

REFRAIN 3

Somewhere the fairer sex
Has curves that are convex,
And girls don't all wear "specs"—
But not in Boston.

One day it's much too hot,
Then cold as you-know-what;
In all the world there's not
Weather anywhere like Boston.

At natural history
We are colossal.
That is because, you see,
At first hand we study the fossil.

Strangers are all dismissed—
(Not that we're prejudiced)
You simply don't exist—
If you haven't been born in Boston.

You haven't been born,
You haven't been born,
If you haven't been born in Boston.

REFRAIN 4

On Boston beans you dine,
Then go to bed at nine.
You mustn't undermine
The town of Boston.

No song except a hymn—
And keep your language prim:
You call a leg a "limb"
Or they boot you out of Boston.

You're of the bourgeoisie
And no one bothers—
Not if your fam'ly tree
Doesn't date from the Pilgrim Fathers.

Therefore, when all is said,
Life is so limited,
You find, unless you're dead,
You never get ahead in Boston.

You never get ahead,
You never get ahead,
You never get ahead in Boston.

ONE, TWO, THREE

Published September 1946. Introduced by Dick Haymes
(John), Betty Grable (Cynthia), and ensemble. Alternate
title: "Waltzing Is Better Sitting Down."

VERSE

ENSEMBLE: One, two, three,
One, two, three,
One, two, three!

JOHN: The latest of dances
Enhances romances,
So you're taking chances
When dancing the waltz.

This pleasure we're sharing
Is really quite daring—
But let's not be caring
Till the band halts.

If I have my way I'd endeavor
To keep waltzing forever.

One, two, three,
One, two, three,
One, two, three!

REFRAIN 1

When we go waltzing—
One, two, three,
One, two, three,
One, two, three—
Entering heaven is A B C—
Magical music the key.
This modern dance may be new to
    you—
But oh, what I hope it will do to you!
How can my heart be fancy-free
When you go one, two, three, dear?
When you go one, two, three, dear?
When you go one, two, three, with me?

REFRAIN 2

Waltzing is better
Sitting down—
One, two, three,
One, two, three—
Waltzing is better sitting down,
Gazing in your eyes of brown.*
Wonderful waltzes I've known with
    you—
But oh, what a thrill here alone with
    you!
You'll have me singing over town:
"Waltzing is better sitting,
Waltzing is better sitting,
Waltzing is better sitting down!"

REFRAIN 3

CYNTHIA: Waltz me no waltzes
Sitting down—
One, two, three,
One, two, three—
Waltz me no waltzes sitting down;
All Massachusetts will frown.
Who knows what moonlight may
    bring about?
It's probably safer to swing about.
Why start them singing over town?
Waltzing is rather risky;
Partners can get too frisky;
Waltz me no waltzes sitting down.

*Since Betty Grable's eyes were blue, this couplet had
to be changed.

DEMON RUM

Introduced by ensemble. Before Ira Gershwin wrote a
lyric for it, the music was Gershwin melody No. 48 in the
George and Ira Gershwin Special Numbered Song File.

Demon Rum,
We'll efface you!
Demon Rum,
You disgrace, you!
You're an evil too many men crave!

Devil's Brew!
Satan's Nectar!
Soon shall you
Be a specter!
For we're digging your liquory grave!

Down with Sin!
Alcohol we'll throttle
When we win
The Battle of the Bottle!

Demon Rum
You're a goner!
Demon Rum,
On my honor—
Lips that taste of wine
Shall never touch mine!

FOR YOU, FOR ME, FOR EVERMORE

Published August 1946. Introduced by Dick Haymes
(John) and Betty Grable (Cynthia). The melody for this
number, at one time Numbers 51 and 52 of the George
and Ira Gershwin Special Numbered Song File, was
dubbed by Ira Gershwin and Kay Swift a "gold mine"
long before Ira wrote the lyric for it. They saw it as
arguably the standout of all the previously unlyricized
George Gershwin melodies.

*N*ote for One Singer. Possibly my lyric to this posthumous tune may be variation #4,708,903½, Series E, on the Three-Little-Words theme—but the song
was considered good enough to be the principal ballad in
The Shocking Miss Pilgrim. However, this is written
neither to criticize nor to defend the words. The point:
if a song is thought good enough and/or commercial
enough or whatever enough to be recorded for public
sale, why don't some singers check the lyric?

A recent album was called *For You, For Me, For Evermore,* so I bought it. The young lady who sang the title song had a pleasing voice, and the orchestral background, too, was good. But what happened to:

> What a lovely world this world will be
> With a world of love in store—
> For you, for me, for evermore

I cannot quite make the best of. She sings this as:

> What a lovely world this world *would* be
> With a *love that can endure*—
> For you, for me, for evermore.

Which changes tense and sense, and suddenly rhyme doesn't chime. On the album jacket the vocalist is quoted: "No, I don't read music . . . and all my own training was by ear." Good girl—but how about reading the words?

Once a musical composition is licensed to a recording organization, it becomes available for license to, and issuance by, any other company in the field. And, except for rare cases, neither publisher nor creators have any monitoring rights on the resultant performance. Still, even if given the privilege, it would be quite a job getting around to O.K.ing or N.G.ing songs like "Tea for Two," "Star Dust," "Night and Day," "Always," and others which become standards and eventually receive dozens, even hundreds, of recordings.

> —from *Lyrics on Several Occasions*

VERSE

Paradise cannot refuse us—
Never such a happy pair!
Ev'rybody must excuse us
If we walk on air.
All the shadows now will lose us;
Lucky stars are ev'rywhere.
As a happy being,
Here's what I'm foreseeing:

REFRAIN

For you, for me, for evermore—
It's bound to be for evermore.
It's plain to see
We found, by finding each other,
The love we waited for.

I'm yours, you're mine, and in our hearts
The happy ending starts.
What a lovely world this world will be
With a world of love in store—
For you, for me, for evermore.

TOUR OF THE TOWN

Intended for Dick Haymes (John) and Betty Grable (Cynthia). Unused.

The Common

JOHN: Let me show you the town—
All the places of great renown.
Come with me on a tour of Boston Town.

Faneuil Hall

In this hall, with words undying,
Patriots were heard.
Men like Washington defying
England's George the Third.
Here they planned and here they plotted,
Answ'ring Freedom's call.
Meet a building that's unspotted—
This is Faneuil Hall.

Old North Church

Ev'ry good American salutes the Old
North Church;
One of hist'ry's highlights happened here
When a lantern signal in that ivy-towered
perch
Started the midnight ride of Paul Revere.

The Constitution

Here's the warship *Constitution,*
Peaceful as can be,
But she fought with resolution
When she sailed the sea.
Finally the junkman craved her—
But she rides the tides:
'Twas a famous poem saved her—
Famous "Old Ironsides."

Public Library

Here's the Public Library—'twas built in
'fifty-eight;
Hundred thousand volumes 'neath her
roof.
There's another fact about her that we
celebrate:
Top to bottom, she is fireproof.

The Elm Tree at Cambridge

There's a tree that's monumental—
Precious ev'ry leaf.

Here the ragged Continental
Hailed his brand-new chief.
Famous in our nation's hist'ry
Is this giant elm;
Underneath the shade of this tree,
Washington took the helm.

Harvard

As a loyal son of Harvard, let me
introduce
The oldest college in the U.S.A.
Here I learned about the square of the
hypotenuse
And to wear my clothes the Princeton
way.

The House

That, Miss Pilgrim, is the one house
We do not have to peep in.
That's the one George Washington
Did not sleep in.

Bunker Hill

This is where the musket rattled
And the bullet sped.
Here the volunteer, embattled,
Fought the coat of red.
Here the British Lion swallowed
His first bitter pill.
Quite a bit of trouble followed
After Bunker Hill.

The Common*

Comes the end of the day.
Soon the sun will be going down.
Comes the end of the tour of Boston
Town.

WELCOME SONG

Intended for Betty Grable (Cynthia), Dick Haymes (John), and ensemble. Unused.

---

*Earlier version of ending:
JOHN: I have shown you the town—
CYNTHIA: With a bit of it upside down—
JOHN: You can say now you've seen our Boston
Town.
or
'Twas a pleasure to show you Boston Town.

ENSEMBLE: One and all, we bid you welcome to
the office,
And we're hoping you'll be very
happy here.
Though we never, never worked with
a New Yorker,
We will wage as a worker you're a
corker.

JOHN: We're sure to get on capitally
together;
Our policy is a family atmosphere.

ENSEMBLE: Right! Once again we bid you
welcome to the office,
And we're hoping you'll be very
happy here!

CYNTHIA: From my heart, I thank you kindly
for your welcome,
And I'm sure that I'll be very happy
here.

[*She is escorted to the machine, sits down,
types. Each letter is punctuated musically.
Music is synchronized with typing*]

[*The Office Force, crowded about her, reads her
typing. Having learned the line, they sing,
blissfully:*]

OFFICE
FORCE: The quick brown fox jumps over the
lazy dog.
The quick brown fox jumps over the
lazy dog.
The quick brown fox jumps over the
lazy dog.

OPPOSITE: *Ginger Rogers and Fred Astaire*

356

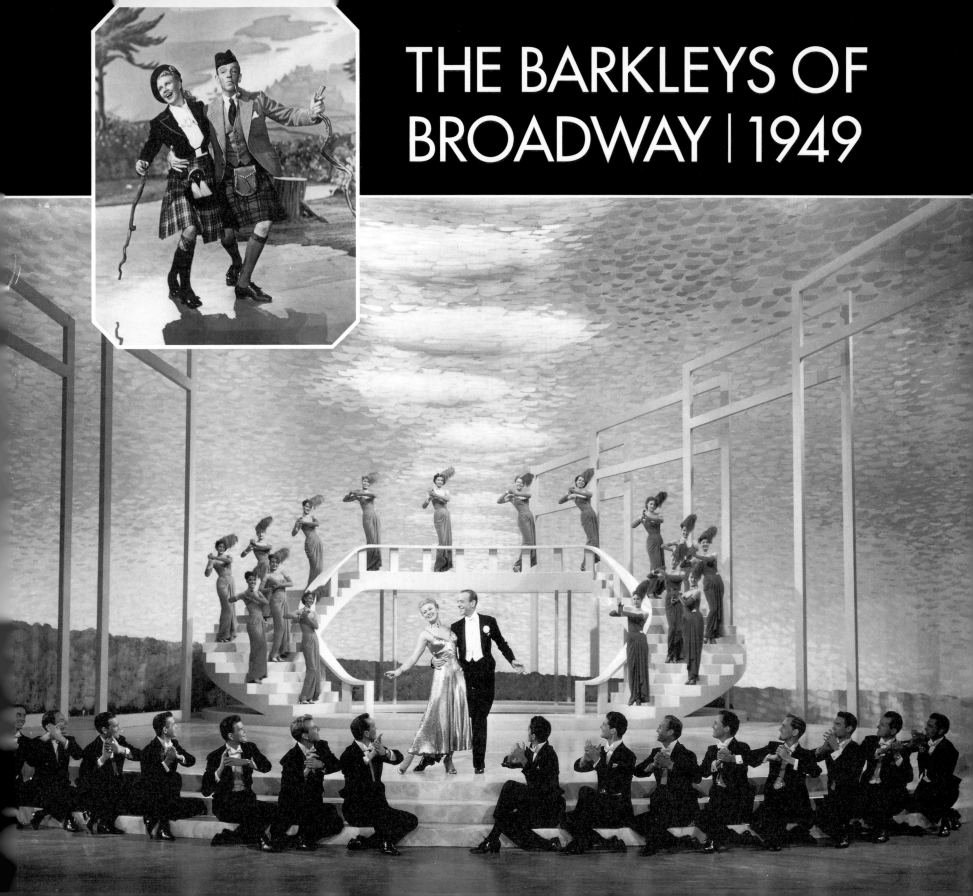

A film produced by Arthur Freed for Metro-Goldwyn-Mayer. Released in May 1949. Music by Harry Warren.* Screenplay by Betty Comden and Adolph Green. Directed by Charles Walters. Dances by Robert Alton. Fred Astaire's dances by Hermes Pan. Music conducted by Lennie Hayton. Orchestrations by Conrad Salinger. Vocal arrangements by Robert Tucker. Cast, starring Fred Astaire (Josh Barkley) and Ginger Rogers (Dinah Barkley), featured Oscar Levant (Ezra Miller), Billie Burke (Mrs. Livingston Belney), Jacques François (Jacques-Pierre Barredout), and Gale Robbins (Shirlene May).

SWING TROT

Published October 1949. Previously registered for copyright as an unpublished song October 1948, the last song written for the film. Introduced by ensemble. Danced by Fred Astaire (Josh) and Ginger Rogers (Dinah) during the opening credits.

VERSE

Take a step in the right direction
And step that step with me.
Never in my recollection
Did I dream such a step could be.
It's the latest;
That makes it the greatest.
Sweeping ev'ry section
Of My Country 'Tis of Thee.

REFRAIN

You'll adore
The step that ev'ryone's been waiting for;
You'll find a crowd on ev'ry dancing floor
Because of something called
The Swing Trot! Remember: Swing Trot!

It's a deal
That's very simple with terrif' appeal.
You grab a partner when you hear a band
And you're the greatest dancer in the land.

It's bill and coo-y,
Tea for two-y;
Just watch your partner's
Eyes grow dewy.
Entre nous-y,
You're slightly screwy
But—irresistible!

*George and Ira Gershwin's "They Can't Take That Away from Me" (see *Shall We Dance*—1937) was reprised in *The Barkleys of Broadway*.

On and on!
Oh, what a natural they've hit upon!
It gets you going till you're really gone—
And you will never rue the day,
The day you realize the Swing Trot is here to stay.

Optional Ending

Near or far—
Look through the telescope at Palomar,
And all the way from Rome to Zanzibar,
What is the picture that you view?
You find the whole world is swinging the Swing Trot, too.

YOU'D BE HARD TO REPLACE

Published March 1949. Previously registered for copyright as an unpublished song June 1948 and August 1948. Introduced by Fred Astaire (Josh). In the film, Astaire sings the first refrain only. Originally intended as a duet for Astaire and Ginger Rogers (Dinah), which version follows.

VERSE

JOSH: Frequently we bicker,
But you know that there's no one but you.
DINAH: Don't we make up quicker
Even when love looks black-and-blue?
JOSH: Oh, happiness seems hopeless
When peace flies up the flue.
DINAH: Let the plot grow thicker;
Always there'll be a happy ending in view.

REFRAIN 1

JOSH: All that I know is you'd be hard to replace.
Where else in all the world such loveliness and such grace?
With charm so all-embracing*
And laughter in those eyes,

*Refrain 1, lines 3–6, as performed in the film:
The poet often chanted
The love he found divine,
But never was he granted
A ladylove like mine.

It's easier replacing
The moon and starry skies.
Deep down, deep down inside, my secret heart knows
The more that I'm with you, the more and more my rapture grows.
Without you at my side, I fear no future could I face,
For you'd be oh, so hard to replace.

REFRAIN 2

DINAH: All that I know is you'd be hard to replace.
Who else in all this world could thrill me with his embrace?
No happiness denied me,
No cloud is in my sky;
With you to hold and guide me,
No others need apply.
Deep down, deep down inside, each night there's a plea:
The two of us remain as one for all the days to be.
Without you, all those days would be just empty time and space.
For you'd be oh, so hard to replace.

MY ONE AND ONLY HIGHLAND FLING

Published March 1949. Previously registered for copyright as an unpublished song May 1948. "Entertainingly burred by Fred Astaire [Josh] and Ginger Rogers [Dinah] in kilts and tams" (Ira Gershwin—*Lyrics on Several Occasions*). Earlier title: "You're My Highland Fling."

During the first conference on *The Barkleys*, producer Arthur Freed thought a Scottish number for Astaire might be interesting. Neither Harry Warren nor I knew much about Scottish dialect; but, like the girl in the Harbach lyric, we didn't say yes, we didn't say no. After the conference, on our way to inspect the work-cottage the studio had assigned us, I thought of the title with its play on the word "fling." We spent only half an hour in the cottage—it was merely a perfunctory visit because both Warren and I preferred working at home. But while we were there Harry made several tentative attempts at a main theme, one of which we felt good about; and this was the start of the song.

Perhaps the compromise dialect I finally wound up

with wouldn't be approved by the student of Scottish lore, but it served its entertainment purpose. For the Scottish surnames in the patter I went through all the Mac's and Mc's in *Who's Who*; also those in the L.A. telephone book. Careful to avoid rhyming "McTavish" and "lavish" because this pairing belonged to Ogden Nash, I went for "MacDougal" and "frugal."

When one does a stage show the published songs have to be ready before the opening, and the authors are usually in New York and can proofread them. But in Hollywood, when one finishes a score it then takes many months before the picture is filmed; and the song proofs and the writers are seldom in touch with one another. To my dismay, when the first published copies of this song reached me in California I found that someone in the New York publishing house had undialected the lyric. A letter of complaint brought an answer from the studio's music-publisher that no sheet-music buyer (if any) would understand the original.

So, another letter of protest. Excerpt:

When practically every English-speaking child in the world sings "Where early fa's the dew" and "Gie'd me her promise true" in "Annie Laurie" I cannot see—even for commercial reasons—why our song had to be emasculated, and "Na' one would do" became "Not one would do" and "hame" became "home" &c. How in the world idiomatic Brooklynese like "spoke real soft" got into the song where "spoke me soft" was indicated is something I'll never understand.

This brought results. A new edition, with the lyric as is, followed.

—from *Lyrics on Several Occasions*

VERSE

JOSH: Though we're called a people of serious
    mind,
    'Tis often we dance and 'tis often we
    sing;
DINAH: And bein' as human as all humankind,
    We aren't superior to havin' a fling.
JOSH: I'm takin' the fling of a lifetime—
DINAH: The fling of a husband-and-wifetime.

REFRAIN

JOSH: When I went romancin'
    I gied no thought to any weddin' ring;
    Ev'ry bonny lassie was my highland fling.
    No chance was I chancin';
    I'm not the mon you dangle on a string.
    I was canny, waitin' for the real, real
    thing.
    Though I danced each girl
    In the twist and twirl,
    Nae one would do.

An' I went my way
Till the fatal day
In the fling I was flung with you.
Oh, now my heart is prancin',
Drunk as a lord and happy as a king.*
The years I'll weather
In the hame or on the heather
With my one and only highland fling.

PATTER

JOSH: I thought you were fallin' for Andy
    McPherson.
DINAH: Nae, nae, he became an impossible
    person.
    But what about you and that Connie
    MacKenzie?
JOSH: She talked when I putted and drove me
    to frenzy.
    But what of the lad known as Bobbie
    MacDougal?
DINAH: It pays to be thrifty, but he was too
    frugal.
    An' weren't you daft about Maggie
    McDermott?
JOSH: I tasted her cookin'—'Twould make me a
    hermit.
    How jealous I was of MacDonald
    McCutcheon!
DINAH: His neck had a head on, but there wasn't
    much in.
JOSH: And what about Sandy?
DINAH: His hands were too handy.
    And wasn't there Jenny?
JOSH: I'm nae wantin' any—
    I'm nae wantin' any but you.

REFRAIN 2

DINAH: When I went a-dancin'
    No special lad I was encouragin';
    Ev'ry likely laddie was my highland fling.
    No glance was I glancin';
    Well, nothin' really worth the
    mentionin'—
    Hopin', watchin', waitin' for the real, real
    thing.
    Though they spoke me soft
    In the moonlicht oft,
    Nae one would do—
    Till it came to pass
    To this lucky lass
    In the fling I was flung with you.
    Oh, now my heart is prancin';
    Nothin' about you I'd be alterin'.

This line sung in the film as:
Gay as a lark and happy as a king.

The years I'll weather
In the hame or on the heather
With my one and only highland fling.

WEEKEND IN THE COUNTRY

Lyrics first published in Ira Gershwin's *Lyrics on Several Occasions* (1959). Registered for copyright as an unpublished song June 1948. Introduced by Fred Astaire (Josh), Ginger Rogers (Dinah), and Oscar Levant (Ezra), "striding down a country lane" (Ira Gershwin—*Lyrics on Several Occasions*).

Lyric." A recent book on American usage (by Bergen and Cornelia Evans) is excellent and comprehensive. But under "lyric": "The use of the noun *lyric* for the words of a song . . . is slang." I have just given a couple of hours to half a dozen books about the theater. There have been few writers as precise as Max Beerbohm; and in *Around Theatres*, in a review written in 1904, he uses "lyrics" for the words of songs. And the year 1900 saw the publication of Harry B. Smith's compilation, *Stage Lyrics*. (Incidentally, it's hard to believe that Harry B. Smith or anyone else could be librettist and lyricist of three hundred operettas and musicals, but I have read this was so. One reference book lists seventy-seven—probably grew tired—and added "&c.") And in an early book on Gilbert and Sullivan, Gilbert, explaining his working methods, is quoted using the word. True, these references happen to be to musical-comedy songs. But all my life I have heard the words of any song referred to, mostly, as "the lyric" (sometimes "the words," and on rare, flossy occasions, "the poem" or "the verses"). It would seem to me that "lyric" in connection with any song these days has gained such recognition that the term is no longer limited to shoptalk or jargon.

—from *Lyrics on Several Occasions*

Film Version

VERSE

JOSH: With golf and tennis 'round you
    And no cares to hound you—
DINAH: When Mother Nature beckons, who
    can decline?
EZRA: Till Mother Nature vetos
    The bees and mosquitoes,
    Mother Nature is no mother of mine.
JOSH
AND DINAH: From Saturday night to Monday
    morn there's always joy ahead.

EZRA: From Saturday night to Monday
morn I wish that I were dead.

REFRAIN 1

JOSH
AND DINAH: A weekend in the country
Never will let you down.
EZRA: You'll pardon my effront'ry—
I'd rather spend it in town.

JOSH
AND DINAH: A weekend in the country—
Healthy and full of sport—*
DINAH: And then it isn't small potatoes
JOSH: When you get those fresh tomatoes—
EZRA: I've a list of fresh tomatoes
Sueing me now in court.

DINAH: Oh, give me the milk from the
moo-cow!
JOSH: Of corn right from the field I'm fond.
EZRA: In town I'd be splurgin'
On venison and sturgeon
Beside a beautiful blonde.

JOSH
AND DINAH: A weekend gets you sunburnt—
Vitamin A you win.
EZRA: I'd rather get back unburnt
With my original skin.

JOSH
AND DINAH: A weekend in the country—
Glorious, there's no doubt!
EZRA: A weekend in the country?
What's the next train out?

REFRAIN 2

JOSH
AND DINAH: A weekend in the country—
Trees in the orchard call.
EZRA: When you've examined one tree,
Then you've examined them all.

JOSH
AND DINAH: A weekend in the country—
Happily we endorse.
DINAH: Come, get your share of nature's
bounty!
JOSH: Ride the trail around the county.

Earlier version of refrain 1, lines 6–10:
JOSH
AND DINAH: Keeping your health at par—
DINAH: As on the grassy green we frolic—
JOSH: Mid the fields of rye we rollick—
EZRA: Give me a rye that's alcoholic
Frolicking at a bar.

EZRA: I am no Canadian Mountie—
Why do I need a horse?
JOSH
AND DINAH: Hark, hark to the song of the
bullfrog—
JOSH: At dawn you rise up with the lark.
EZRA: When roosters run riot
I much prefer the quiet
Of Forty-second and Park.

JOSH
AND DINAH: Get peppy and alive-y—
Don't be a city poke.
EZRA: I once got poison ivy.
DINAH: Will you try for poison oak?

JOSH
AND DINAH: A weekend in the country
Dickeybirds overhead!
EZRA: A weekend in the country
I should 'a' stood in bed!

Lyrics on Several Occasions Version

VERSE

JOSH
AND DINAH: With golf and tennis 'round you
And no cares to hound you—
When Mother Nature beckons, who
can decline?
EZRA: Till Mother Nature vetoes
The bees and mosquitoes,
Mother Nature is no mother of mine.

REFRAIN

JOSH
AND DINAH: A weekend in the country—
Trees in the orchard call.
EZRA: When you've examined one tree
Then you've examined them all.

JOSH
AND DINAH: A weekend in the country,
Keeping your health at par,
As on the grassy green we frolic,
'Mid the fields of rye we rollick . . .
EZRA: Give me rye that's alcoholic
Frolicking at a bar.

JOSH: Hark, hark to the song of the
bullfrog!
DINAH: At dawn you rise up with the lark.
EZRA: When roosters run riot
I much prefer the quiet
Of Forty-second and Park.

JOSH: Get peppy and alive-y—
DINAH: Don't be a city poke.

EZRA: I once got poison ivy.
Shall I try for poison oak?
JOSH
AND DINAH: A weekend in the country—
Glorious, there's no doubt!
EZRA: A weekend in the country?
What's the next train out?

SHOES WITH WINGS ON

Published April 1949. Previously registered for copyright as an unpublished song May 1948. Introduced by Fred Astaire as part of his "one-man ballet in a shoe shop" (Ira Gershwin—*Lyrics on Several Occasions*).

It's tough to get a title for a song about a dance. By which rhythmic remark I mean that unless you're bent on inventing a new stage or ballroom frisk to be called "Do the Hoopla Poopla" of "The Whatchamacallit Ha Cha Cha," you're usually limited to titles like "Dancing Shoes" or "May I Have the Next Dance, Please, Madame?" and such. So, when looking up something else in Bulfinch a picture of Mercury with his winged cap and winged sandals brought the notion of "Shoes with Wings On" for an Astaire solo, I thought: "Well, even if just the least bit, it's at least a little bit different for a dance title." But leaden rather than mercurial were the time and effort spent on the lyric to fit Warren's tricky tune. There was much juggling and switching and throwing out of line and phrase and rhyme—maybe ten days' worth—before the words made some singable sort of sense. Wodehouse once told me that the greatest challenge (and greatest worry) to him in lyric-writing was to come across a section of a tune requiring three double rhymes. And I well realized what this special torture was when I tackled "wings on." When I finally wound up with "wings on—strings on—things on," that was *that*, and I felt like a suddenly unburdened Atlas.

—from *Lyrics on Several Occasions*

VERSE

Aladdin had a wonderful lamp;
King Midas had the touch of gold;
In magic they had many a champ
'Way back in days of old.
But magic was in its infancy;
Today they'd ring no bell.
Today they'd mimic
Me and my gimmick
To cast a spell.

REFRAIN

When I've got shoes with wings on—
The winter's gone, the spring's on.
When I've got shoes with wings on—
The town is full of rhythm and the world's in
    rhyme.

The Neon City glows up;
My pretty Pretty shows up.
We'll dance until they close up—
(Got my Guardian Angel working overtime.)

I give Aladdin the lamp,
Midas the gold.
Who needs a wizard or magician
In the old tradition?
That's not competition—
I've got 'em beat a thousandfold!
Why?

'Cause I've got shoes with wings on—
And living has no strings on.
I put those magic things on,
And I go flying with 'em—
And the town is full of rhythm
And the world's in rhyme.

TAG

Happens ev'ry time;
Put my shoes with wings on—
Yes, siree! The world's in rhyme!

MANHATTAN DOWNBEAT

Registered for copyright as an unpublished song August
1948. Introduced by Fred Astaire (Josh); danced by Astaire, Ginger Rogers (Dinah), and ensemble.

VERSE

From Battery Park to Spuyten Duyvil
In the time when Peter Stuyvesant held sway,
For peacefulness this island had no rival—
But it's just a little bit different today.

If you should ask if I've nostalgic yearning
For the charm and quaintness of the long ago,
And would—if I could—to those days be
    returning,
The answer, emphatically, is "No!"

REFRAIN

Just give me that Manhattan Downbeat
That beats a tempo of its own!*
You've got to shout, "This *is* it!"
The day you visit
The jumpin'est town was ever known.

Keep your Paree and London Town Beat;
Pop Knickerbocker stands alone.
Drive up any avenue,
Swing down any street—
There's no beat has Manhattan Downbeat beat!

PATTER

Listen to that bebop orchestration
In a symphony of cosmic sound!
Taxi horns and tintinnabulation . . .
Planes above and subways underground . . .
Glamour, glitter—
Sweet and bitter—
How you laugh and cry!
Faster, faster,
To disaster
Or a goal up high!
Listen to those seven million voices!
The Tower of Babel merely was a toot!
Listen—and your beating heart rejoices,
Getting that electrifying boot!
Right from the minute
You get in it,
Got to follow suit!

TAG

Keep your Paree and London Town Beat;
Pop Knickerbocker stands alone.
Drive up any avenue,
Swing down any street—
There's no beat has Manhattan Downbeat beat!

There's no beat has Manhattan Downbeat beat!
Battery Park to Spuyten Duyvil,
Manhattan has no rival—
No beat has Manhattan Downbeat beat!

NATCHEZ ON THE MISSISSIP'

Registered for copyright as an unpublished song May
1948. One of four songs intended for Judy Garland, who

Original version of refrain 1, line 2:
That beats a tempo all its own!

was to have played "Dinah" (illness caused her with-
drawal from the film). Unused. Earlier titles: "97,704"
and "Natchez."

JUDY: There are ninety-seven thousand seven
    hundred and three
    Songs about the South and its
    hospitality—
    Songs of ev'ry river, ev'ry state, and ev'ry
    town—
    You can hardly find an acre that hasn't
    won renown.

MEN: Alabama, Lou'siana, Georgia, Tennessee,
    Chattanooga, Tallahassee . . . there I want
    to be!

JUDY: Brother, how they write 'em—
    Ad infinitum!
MEN: That's Greek to us!
JUDY: But it's Latin to me.
    "Ad infinitum" means they write 'em
    endlessly.

    But I've studied all the maps and there is
    one town overlooked.
MEN: You really mean there is a town the
    songsters haven't booked?
    You mean you studied all the maps of
    Rand McNally
    And found a spot that yet has not been
    done by Tin Pan Alley?
JUDY: To all the songs about the South you
    please will add one more.
MEN: That makes ninety-seven thousand seven
    hundred and four!
JUDY: Ninety-seven thousand seven hundred and
    four!
    No use, you see, opposing me; I'm on a
    vocal trip
    To a certain town in the state of
    Mississip'!

REFRAIN

JUDY: I've got to go
    Back to Natchez,
    Where there are no*
    Doors with latches.
    Howdy! Hello,

Alternate version of refrain, lines 3–7:
    Livin' where no
    Doors have latches.
    Where it's "Hello,
    Friends in batches!"
    And the sun shines for me.

361

Friends in batches
Where the sun shines for me.

Guess I was wrong
Leavin' Natchez;
I got along
Dressed in patches;
Life was a song
Singin' snatches—
Snatches of songs like "The Robert E.
    Lee."

Trouble hatches out of Natchez;
Got the Big-Town Blues, so I'm
Thumbin' any truck I catches
Headin' for that sunny clime.

I'll hitch and hike
Back to Natchez.
And when I strike,
I attaches!
Say what you like—
Boy! I scratches.
Take my tip
That no town matches,
No town matches
Natchez,
Mississip'!

THE COURTIN' OF ELMER AND ELLA

Registered for copyright as an unpublished song April 1948. Intended for Fred Astaire and Judy Garland. Unused.

PROLOGUE

We sing you a tale of a man and a maid.
It's one that the jukeboxes yet haven't played:
Where Elmer was willin' but Ella afraid . . .
A love tale
That just wouldn't dovetail.

VERSE 1

Elmer came around one day in his new store
    clothes;
Thought a lovin' look from Ella he would get.
She said, "In the village I saw your clothes,
But the goldarn dummy in them is there yet."

REFRAIN 1

Oh, the courtin' of Elmer and Ella,
I reckon, wasn't what it should be;
She hit with broom and bottle,
But his love she couldn't throttle
In the mountains of Old Kentuckee.

VERSE 2

Elmer found that Ella had a tooth for
    gumdrops.
"Here's a nickel's worth," he said. "What good
    is pelf?"
When she opens up the bag, he plumb drops—
He's forgotten that he ate them all himself.

REFRAIN 2

Oh, the courtin' of Elmer and Ella
Was somethin' like a dog with a flea;
His eye she up and blackened,
But his sparkin' never slackened
In the mountains of Old Kentuckee.

VERSE 3

Elmer stood outside one night to serenade her,
Moanin' through a piece of paper and a comb.
Till the dawn a thousand songs he played her—
But he didn't know that night she wasn't home.

REFRAIN 3

Oh, the courtin' of Elmer and Ella
Was pretty one-sided, you'll agree;
He should have learned his lesson,
But his suit he kept a-pressin'
In the mountains of Old Kentuckee.

VERSE 4

Elmer found her one day feelin' in good humor;
She said, "Name the day. Could be that I was
    wrong."
Weddin' day he pulled his final bloomer:
Seems he brought his wife and seven kids along.

REFRAIN 4

Oh, the courtin' of Elmer and Ella
Is now a matter of history.
There was a blast like thunder—
Now he's lyin' six foot under
In the mountains of Old Kentuckee.

EPILOGUE

We've sung you a tale of a maid and a man.
Should you like a moral, to give one we can:
Where there is no fire, no flame can you fan;*
Your love tale
Just never will dovetail.

THE WELL-KNOWN SKIES OF BLUE

Intended for Judy Garland and Fred Astaire. Unused. No music is known to survive.

VERSE

FRED: 'Neath the old magnolia,
    Why the melancholia,
    Annabelle, my own?

JUDY: Things are looking dismal;
    I've the most abysmal
    Blues I've ever known.

FRED: Life is more beguiling
    When I see you smiling,
    Annabelle, my own.

REFRAIN

    Oh, the well-known skies of blue—
JUDY: Fwoo, fwoo, fwoo—
FRED: Will be shinin', shinin', through—
JUDY: Fwoo, fwoo, fwoo—
FRED: When my girly
    Shows me that pearly
    Ever-, ever-lovin' smile.†

JUDY: And the usual clouds of gray—
FRED: Whah, whah, whay—
JUDY: Will they drift and fade away?
FRED: Whah, whah, whay—
    Nothing to it!
    One smile can do it!‡
    And your cares will run a mile!

*Alternate of epilogue, line 3:
If you are born Elmer, you're not Dapper Dan—
†Alternate version of refrain, line 7:
    Customary lovin' smile.
‡Alternate version of refrain, lines 13–14:
    You'll never rue it!
    Smile and make this earth worthwhile!

JUDY: When the weather storms and thunders,
How do I go working wonders?
FRED: Very simple:
You show your dimple.
JUDY: Will the sky be rainbow-tinted?
FRED: Like no picture ever printed!
JUDY: And the bluebird?
FRED: Sings like a new bird!

The proverbial rainy day—
JUDY: Whah, whah, whay—
FRED: Can become the month of May.
JUDY: Whah, whah, whay—
BOTH: Late and early,
Show me that pearly
Smile and make this earth worthwhile!*

FRED: By stars above
JUDY: I'm dreamin' of
FRED: That smile I love
JUDY: From you,
FRED: So, honeybunch—
JUDY: You funnybunch—
FRED: You funnybunch—
BOTH: Come through!

THE POETRY OF MOTION

Registered for copyright as an unpublished song June 1948. According to *The World of Entertainment*, Hugh Fordin's history of MGM's Freed Unit, this "comic ballet" was dropped from the *Barkleys of Broadway* score when Judy Garland withdrew from the film. Earlier title: "Since the Ballet Swept the Town."

VERSE

All the traffic cops are pirouetting;
Bus conductors leap in the air for dimes.
Congressmen say, "Ha-da-do?"
As they do a pas de deux;
Ballet is the spirit of the times.

Waitresses are budding ballerinas;
With each course you get a classic pose.
Thanks to choreographers,
Even the stenographers
Take dictation standing on their toes.

Alternate version of refrain, line 29:
Customary lovin' smile.

REFRAIN

Ev'rything's the poetry of motion
Since the bally ballet swept the town.
What goes on they dance in terms artistic,
Surrealistic,
And upside down.

Through the air they leap and prance and whiz,
Interpreting the spirit of whatever-it-is.

Oh, bravo for the poetry of motion!
Choreography is king today!
Though the goings-on may seem erratic,
You grow ecstatic
Or you're considered passé.

Brother, better be a ballet maniac
Since ballet mania has hit Broadway!

TAKING NO CHANCES ON YOU

Intended for Fred Astaire (Josh) and Ginger Rogers (Dinah). Unused. No music survives.

VERSE 1

JOSH: As a kid I used to revel
In being called a young daredevil—
Climbing trees and swimming out of sight.
In a life of do-and-daring—
Taking chances—never caring—
Suddenly it seems I've seen the light.
I've found the one that I find indispensable,
And believe it or not, I'm growing much more sensible.

REFRAIN 1

Though I'm known as one who's always taking chances—
Here-today-and-gone-tomorrow point of view—
Though I'd bet my final dollar
Like a gentleman and scholar,
Still, I'm taking no chances on you.

I have hunted and confronted charging tigers;
I fought City Hall and boxed a kangaroo;
I've canoed on Congo rivers
Where you really get the shivers,
But I'm taking no chances on you.

So starting now and all the time,
I'm keeping you in sight;
I'd be lost if I should lose you—That's why I'm
Holding on day and night.

In the past I picked the petals of a daisy;
If the lady loved or loved me not, I knew;
But in this case I'm not crazy,
I'm not asking any daisy,
'Cause I'm taking no chances on you.

VERSE 2

DINAH: As a child I acted likewise:
I was tricycle and bikewise,
And I roller-skated just like mad.
As I grew up, it was needless
Saying I was rash and heedless—
Till I came across a certain lad.
The tomboy who did everything capriciously
Is now turning a leaf and acting more judiciously.

REFRAIN 2

If the calendar says Thirteen and it's Friday
And I see the blackest cat, I don't say boo;
Spilling salt upon the table
Finds me relatively stable,
But I'm taking no chances on you.

When the breezes bring the sneezes of the springtime,
Should you give out with the tiniest "Kachoo!"
At a speed that's supersonic
I'll be rushing with a tonic,
Simply taking no chances on you.

Through thick and thin, through cold and hot,
I'm holding tight, don't fear,
So the fellow featured in my dreams will not
Suddenly disappear.

I have nonchalantly walked beneath a ladder;
Should I break a mirror I'm not in a stew;
I'm not scared by any mobster;
I'll eat ice cream after lobster—
But I'm taking no chances on you.

THERE IS NO MUSIC

Registered for copyright as an unpublished song August 1948. Intended for *The Barkleys of Broadway*. Unused.

REFRAIN

Stars without glitter,
Sun without gold;
Nightfall is bitter,
Endless, and cold.
Silent the city,
Silent the sea—
There is no music for me.

Gone the charms
Of his arms,
Gone the spell that dispelled all alarms.
Gone the bright,
Twinkling light
That beguiled
As he smiled
And enfolded me tight.

Gone is the singer,
Lost is the song
That I longed for all my life long.

Once there was music,
Joyous and free;
Now salty tears glisten;
All night I listen,
But there's no music for me.

THESE DAYS

Registered for copyright as an unpublished song April 1948. Intended for *The Barkleys of Broadway*. Unused.

REFRAIN 1

Though the traffic's overflowing,
No one knows just where he's going
These days, these days.

Buildings keep on growing taller;
Dollars keep on getting smaller
These days, these days.

Who knows what this little old
World is coming to?
He doesn't know and she doesn't know
And we don't know, do you?

Shopping at a store or market,
You've a car but try and park it*
These days, these days.

So the world grows daft and dafter,
But tonight it's fun and laughter
That we're after—
Quite, quite, quite!

So let's forget these days tonight—
Let's forget these days tonight.

REFRAIN 2

Junior's chewing gum that bubbles;
Grandma's on the daily doubles
These days, these days.

Sister goes with fourteen steadies;
Uncle's on the floor at Eddie's
These days, these days.

If things aren't what they were—
Future looking bleak,
Don't shed a tear, for that's what we're here for
Seven shows a week.

It's a short but merry lifey;
That's no lady, that's your wifey
These days, these days.

But an end to melancholy!
From the curtain to finale
Let's be jolly!
Right? Right? RIGHT!

And we'll forget these days tonight.
We'll forget these days tonight!

CALL ON US AGAIN

Registered for copyright as an unpublished song June 1948. Intended for *The Barkleys of Broadway*. Unused.

Hate to see you go, but it's the final curtain.
As an audience you've been immense—and how!
From the footlights here
We give you a cheer,
For we're certain
Ev'ryone out front deserves a bow!

Hate to see you go, but it's the final curtain.
Thank you one and all, ladies and gentlemen.

*In November 1980, Ira Gershwin reexamined this lyric and changed refrain 1, line 12, from the original:
You've a car but you can't park it.

If we're feeling proud—
You're the greatest crowd
Since we don't know when.
We needn't think it over twice,
If you have got the time and price,
We call on you to call on us again!

SECOND FIDDLE TO A HARP

Intended for *The Barkleys of Broadway*. Unused. No music is known to survive.

PRELUDIO, INTRODUZIONE, AND VERSE

Though she plays the harp in the
    symphony,*
She plucks at my heartstrings to boot.
She's lovely, *animato*,
And built so *delicato*—
She's *dolce, differente*, she's cute.

I wait after all the performances;
For one of her smiles I would die.
I'd sing my *obbligato*
Con molto passionato,
But she turns up her nose and goes by.
In a melancholy key—
The angel at the harp
Plays the devil with me.

BURDEN, REFRAIN, AND CHORUS

I'm in love *fortissimo*,
But she takes me *pianissimo*.
Though I'm all *amoroso*,
She gives me, "No, no, no!" So
That's why I'm, head to toe, so
Furioso!
Dreams of love *crescendo*ing
Are now *diminuendo*ing,
So, "Ha, ha, ha, ha, ha!" *alla Pagliaccio*
With cyanide down the old hatch*io*.
No "Kiss Me Again" or "Il Bacio"—
Staccato, agitato!
Oh, the pain is sharp
Playing second fiddle to a harp!

CODA, PARLANDO

By love I've been treated so shabbily,
I'm giving up—lost all my starch—

*Alternately:
Though she plays the harp in the orchestra,

Tchaikowsky's *"Andante Cantabile"*
For Chopin's "Funeral March."

BURDEN, REFRAIN, AND CHORUS, *SECONDO*

SOLO: I'm in love—
ALL: *Fortissimo!*
SOLO: But she takes me—
ALL: *Pianissimo!*
SOLO: Whenever she *glissandos*
My heart *accelerandos*
But my life still is oh, so
Doloroso.
Dreams of love—
ALL: *Crescendo*ing!
SOLO: Are now—
ALL: *Diminuendo*ing.
SOLO: So, "Ha, ha, ha, ha!" Just like that clown
I laugh.

With tears running down till I drown, I
laugh.
I'm certain that were she introduced to
me,
In four or five years she'd get used to
me.
Staccato, agitato!
Oh, the pain is sharp
Playing second fiddle to a harp!

MINSTRELS ON PARADE

Intended for *The Barkleys of Broadway*. Unused. No
music is known to survive.

Here, here come the minstrels!
Minstrels on parade!

We are the blokes
Who've got oodles of jokes,
And we've oodles of noodles
To sing in raggy ragtime.

Laugh, laugh with the minstrels!
Frowns for smiles we will trade!

Presenting dances and jingles,
Doubles and singles,
Till your heart tingles!

Funsters, punsters,
Charming son-of-a-gunsters—
Minstrels on parade!

OVERLEAF: *Marge Champion, Debbie Reynolds, and Helen Wood*

GIVE A GIRL A BREAK | 1953

A film produced by Jack Cummings for Metro-Goldwyn-Mayer. Released in December 1953. Music by Burton Lane. Screenplay by Albert Hackett and Frances Goodrich, based on a story by Vera Caspary. Directed by Stanley Donen. Musical numbers staged by Stanley Donen and Gower Champion. Music conducted by André Previn. Music supervised by Saul Chaplin. Cast, starring Marge Champion (Madelyn Corlane), Gower Champion (Ted Sturgis), and Debbie Reynolds (Suzy Doolittle), featured Helen Wood (Joanna Moss), Bob Fosse (Bob Dowdy), Kurt Kasznar (Leo Belney), and Richard Anderson (Burton Bradshaw).

GIVE A GIRL A BREAK

Registered for copyright as an unpublished song September 1951. Introduced by Debbie Reynolds (Suzy), Marge Champion (Madelyn), Helen Wood (Joanna), and five women of the ensemble. Originally intended for Gower Champion (Ted) and female ensemble. Private recording by Ira Gershwin, vocal, and Burton Lane, vocal and piano, issued in 1975 on the Mark 56 album "Ira Gershwin Loves to Rhyme."

Original Version (Unused)

VERSE

SHE: The pursuit of happiness
In a woman's plan
Obviously is—
The pursuit of man.

So with vim and scrappiness,
I'll get you if I can!
Call it unladylike—
But who wants to be old-maidylike?

REFRAIN 1

Hey, stunning,
Cute and cunning—
What does it take?
You've won me;
Please don't shun me—
Give a girl a break!

Hey, single!
If we mingle—
Things will be jake.
Yes, sir! To my uttermost,
You're the man I'd butter most—
Give a girl a break!

Why back up?
Don't I stack up?
Do I have to draw a chart?
Oh, give a girl a break,
Or you're going to break my heart!
Give a girl a break or else you'll break my
heart!

INTERLUDE

Heaven only helps a girl who helps
herself—
Otherwise you end up on the back-room
shelf.
HE: I don't know why you should waste your
time;
Ev'ryone who knows me knows I haven't
got a dime.
You deserve a string of horses and a yacht.
Lady, if you think I'm loaded, I am not.
SHE: You don't have to buy me cars and furs—
Can't you see that I'm a gal who only wants
what's hers?

REFRAIN 2

Hey, dreamy!
Can't you see me?
Are you awake?
Just latch on
And you'll catch on!
Give a girl a break!

Take over!
Live on clover!
And no mistake!
Let's call up a minister,
Or I'll be a spinister
Jumping in a lake.

Hey, gorgeous!
Yes, sir! You're jus'
What I ordered from the start!
So give a girl a break,
Or you're going to break my heart!
Give a girl a break or else you'll break my
heart!

Film Version

REFRAIN 1

1ST GIRL: My singing
Has 'em winging;
Not hard to take.
2ND GIRL: In school, yet,
I played Juliet—
Give a girl a break!

3RD GIRL: Sioux City
Says I'm pretty;
That's no mistake.
4TH GIRL: Look at me, I'm comical,
And I'm anatomical—
Nothing is a fake!
5TH GIRL: He'll back it
With a packet
(If they sign me for the part).
ALL FIVE: So give a girl a break,
Or you're going to break my heart!

REFRAIN 2 (Unused)

No gyppin'
When I'm strippin'—
They stay awake.
Yes, this'll
Make 'em whistle—
Give a girl a break!

My tapping
Starts them clapping
Till theatres shake.
If they want ability,
I got versatility
That should take the cake!

Played *Show Boat*—
That's no rowboat—
And I tore the house apart!
So, give this girl a break,
Or you're going to break her heart!

NOTHING IS IMPOSSIBLE

Registered for copyright as an unpublished song September 1952. Introduced by Gower Champion (Ted), Bob Fosse (Bob), and Kurt Kasznar (Leo). As filmed, the lyric is edited somewhat.

VERSE

TED AND BOB: There's no other way—
Beginning today,
You're going to work under
pressure.
LEO: With pressure I will not know
where I'm at.
TED AND BOB: You've got to come through;
And isn't it true,
The new stuff you write may be
fresher?

LEO: Yes, I've a thesis;
Masterpieces
Often happen like that!
If I work with might and main,
TED AND BOB: We have ev'rything to gain.

REFRAIN 1

Nothing is impossible!
Put your shoulder to the wheel!
Nothing is impossible—
That's the way you've got to feel!
They said it couldn't be built;
Our country said, "It shall!"
We struggled hard and we built
The Panama Canal!
Napoleon was a corporal
And he had a tiny frame.
But he became the emperor
Just the same!
Oh, nothing is impossible
If a goal is to be won,
But you are impossible
If you say it can't be done!

REFRAIN 2

Nothing is impossible
Though the future may look dim;
Nothing is impossible
If you tackle it with vim!
The desert, it was burned up
Till good old Uncle Sam,
He sweated and he turned up
With Boulder Dam!
King George of England thought
  he'd throw
George Washington for a loss,
But Washington at the Delaware
Came across!
Oh, nothing is impossible
If you work and dig and strive,
Or else it is possible
You will not stay alive!

REFRAIN 3

Nothing is impossible
If you're full of pep and zest!
Nothing is impossible!
I can stand the acid test!
When Samson was in prison,
They felt his hopes were dashed,
But fortitude was his 'n'
The temple crashed!
When Monte Cristo jumped the
  sea,

They thought that he was sunk,
But it didn't turn out the way
The thinkers thunk!
Oh, nothing is impossible!
Sound the trumpets! Kick the
  gongs!
By twelve o'clock tomorrow,
I will write you sixty songs!

IN OUR UNITED STATE

Published August 1953. Registered for copyright as an unpublished song September 1951. "Nighttime in Manhattan. Boy and Girl out for a stroll see the lighted windows in the distant UN Building, where evidently an important night session is in progress." (Ira Gershwin—*Lyrics on Several Occasions*). Introduced by Bob Fosse (Bob); danced by Fosse and Debbie Reynolds (Suzy). As filmed, the lyric was considerably edited. The full version, following, may have been intended as a duet.

---

*T*echnical Note. In the refrain the third lines in stanzas A, B, and D end in dactyls, a set-up which could call for a trio of triple rhymes. But "foreign entanglements," "unconstitutional," and "Representatives" are words importantly germane to the theme; also, with the rest of the refrain closely rhymed—e.g., "*Great* will be our united *state*"—they give an unexpected tickle to the ear; they may dangle but do not jangle (I think). Too, even if triple rhymes were arrived at, they'd be lost in the shuffle, since the lines they'd belong to are so far apart. (If this isn't clear, skip it; the song sold less than a hundred copies.)

Reading a Lyric without Benefit of the Tune. One who reads the verse of this song without knowing the melody will accent certain words thus:

> The *state* of the *world* is such
> That the *world* is in *quite* a *state*, &c.

and one will, as the quiz-masters have it, be absolutely correct. Correct because the music here happens to accent the same words.

But when it comes to the refrain, the reader isn't aware that the unknown melody has emphasized unexpected syllables and words. For instance, the reading will probably be:

> Out-*side*-rs will not rate
> In *our* united state.

And

> I *won't* investigate
> In *our* united state.

Whereas one learns, when hearing the song sung, that the melody has shifted the accents to stress:

> *Out*-siders will not rate
> *In* our united state.

And, in the same fashion, "I" and "In" are on notes getting the downbeat—not "won't" and "our." Sidney Lanier (1842–1881) and others have written formidable books given mostly to the thesis that the laws governing music and verse are identical; but, say what you will (even—it shouldn't happen to a doggerel), where *song* is involved, music frequently makes for prosodic perversion—and no contest. This is why some songwriters, when demonstrating a new song to a publisher or some possible performer, do not bother with exact punctuation in the typewritten lyric they hand the listener; they merely use capital letters throughout.

Thus an old-time lyricist might or might not today submit:

> WHO IS SYLVIA WHAT IS SHE
> THAT ALL OUR SWAINS COMMEND HER
> HOLY FAIR AND WISE IS SHE
> THE HEAVEN SUCH GRACE DID LEND HER
> THAT SHE MIGHT ADMIRED BE, &c.

—from *Lyrics on Several Occasions*

VERSE

The state of the world is such
That the world is in quite a state.
But let's not worry too much;
Let the rest of the world debate.
Right now the thing to discuss
Is the wonderful status of us.

REFRAIN 1

The state of our union,
Hearts in communion,
Never will know any foreign entanglements;
Outsiders will not rate
In our united state!

We'll make the altar
Strong as Gibraltar—
Fooling around will be unconstitutional.
Great will be our united state!

With nothing but true love in the ascendance,
We'll always sign and renew
A Declaration of Dependence—
Where you depend on me
And I depend on you.

Peaceful and cozy,
We'll have a rosy
Future with a House of cute Representatives;

So, I can hardly wait,
Darling, for our united state!

REFRAIN 2

Our annual budget?
I'll let you judge it—
You do what you will with what's in our
    treasury;
I won't investigate
In our united state.

This is my platform:
That face and that form!
You will find out that's a permanent policy
Slated for our united state.

But there will be changes I'll be unfolding:
Withholding taxes are through—
For when it's you, dear, that I'm holding,
You can't withhold on me—
I can't withhold on you.

We'll have a White House,
Small, but a bright house,
Built on the Pursuit of Star-Spangled Happiness.
Hurry, let's name the date,
Darling, for our united state!

The following, "State of Our Union," was written while
Ira Gershwin worked on *Park Avenue* (1946) with composer Arthur Schwartz. It seems to have been intended
for Ray McDonald (Ned), Martha Stewart (Madge), and
bridesmaids; it may have been replaced with "For the
Life of Me," which it resembles structurally.

VERSE

The state of the world today is such
Ev'ry country is in quite a state.
But at the moment we can't do much;
We can take that up at a later date.
Right now the thing to discuss
Is the wonderful status of us.

REFRAIN

The state of our union
Will be stronger than Gibraltar,
The state of our union
(Two hearts in communion)
When I meet you at the altar.
Though world conditions
May puzzle politicians,
No question that
We know what we're at.
As Mr. and Mrs.,
We'll make it everlasting.

No doubt of it, this is
What they call perfect casting.
I'm so romantic-
Ly frantic
That I can hardly wait
To live in our united state.

[*After this—or a second refrain—Madge's
friends sneak on*]
GIRLS: If you only heard
An occasional word,
This is what they
Are trying to say:

Till the Guaranty Trust
Goes up in dust,
Love will last.
Till you hunt for a flat
And find it like that!
They'll hold fast.

Yes, together they will stick,
Holding on through thin and thick.
They will be one
Till *Oklahoma!* ends its run.

Till commercials all go
From radio,
Love will glow!

And Einstein's theory
Is relatively A B C.
[*Lyric breaks off here*]

IT HAPPENS EV'RY TIME

Published August 1953. Registered for copyright as an
unpublished song November 1952. Introduced by
Gower Champion (Ted); danced by him and Marge
Champion (Madelyn).

REFRAIN

I look and see the stormy skies,
You look at me with laughing eyes—
December days are like July's;
It happens every time!

When trouble brings a tale of woe,
The phone bell rings—it's your hello;
The room I'm in begins to glow;
It happens every time!

Life is good;
Without you days were sunless.
I just could
Not settle for anyone less.

Each time I fold you in my arms,
Lo and behold! A million charms—
And gone are all the world's alarms!

You make it happen—
It happens every time!

APPLAUSE, APPLAUSE

Lyrics first published in Ira Gershwin's *Lyrics on Several
Occasions* (1959). Registered for copyright as an unpublished song November 1952. Introduced by Debbie
Reynolds (Suzy) and Gower Champion (Ted). Private
recording by Ira Gershwin, vocal, and Burton Lane,
vocal and piano, issued in 1975 on the Mark 56 album
"Ira Gershwin Loves to Rhyme."

Constructive Criticism. Although this lyric makes a
plea for handmade appreciation from an audience,
it evoked little, if any. Unhappily, the backstage film
musical *Give a Girl a Break* got few breaks from the
press. True, the picture was nowhere near Academy
Award nomination, but it wasn't this bad: On leaving the
studio projection room after seeing a rough cut of the
film, my wife asked me if I owned any stock in the film
company. I told her I had bought several hundred shares
the previous year. "Sell it," she said. Being a dutiful
husband and California a community-property state, I
called my broker next morning and sold. (I lost five
hundred dollars by this acquiescence—a month later
there could have been a profit—but my action demonstrates (A) that I am a dutiful husband; (B) that something more effective than verbal criticism can be
accomplished through the facilities of the New York
Stock Exchange.)

Giving Girls (and Other Females) Titular Breaks. One
of the first shows to be labeled "musical comedy" (a
term which emerged in London in the 1890's) was the
successful *A Gaiety Girl.* Should anyone interest himself in a study of musical-comedy titles from that time on
(why anyone would is beyond me), I'm sure he could
prove that the uses of Girl, Lady, Miss, and other female
classifications (plus given names like Sally, Irene, Nanette, &c.) vastly outnumber the male variations and
prenames. Obviously the entitled female is not Kipling's
"a rag and a bone and a hank of hair," but an attractive
and potential box-office come-on. No world-shaking thesis this; it's just a sudden awareness of the major number
of such uses even in the entertainments I've contributed
to: *Two Little Girls in Blue, A Dangerous Maid, The
Shocking Miss Pilgrim, Oh, Kay!, Rosalie, Damsel in
Distress, Treasure Girl, Cover Girl, Country Girl, Show
Girl, That's a Good Girl, Girl Crazy, Lady, Be Good!,*

Lady in the Dark, *My Fair Lady* (this last, of course, not the enormously successful Lerner-Loewe *My Fair Lady*, but the original title on the road and on sheet music of a 1925 musical which for Broadway we renamed *Tell Me More*). The lone marqueed male I've worked for is Porgy and he had to share billing fifty-fifty with Bess.
—from *Lyrics on Several Occasions*

VERSE

When the voodoo drum is drumming
Or the hummingbird is humming,
Does it thrill you? Does it fill you with delight?
To continue with our jingle:
Are you one of those who tingle
To your shoes-ies at the blues-ies in the night?
Oh, the sounds of bugles calling
Or Niag'ra Falls a-falling
May enchant you—We will grant you that they
    might;
But for us on the stage, oh brother!
There's just one sound and no other:

REFRAIN 1

Applause, applause!
We like applause because
It means when it is striking us
The audience is liking us.

Our work demands
You don't sit on your hands—
And if the hand's tremendous,
You send us!

We live, we thrive,
You keep us all alive
With *"Bravo!"* and *"Bravissimo!"*
We're dead if it's *pianissimo*.

Our quirk is work,
Is work we never shirk
In a happyland of tinsel and gauze,
Because—we like applause!

PATTER VERSE

Whether you're a Swiss bell ringer
Or a crooner or a singer
Or monologist, ventriloquist, or what—
Or a dog act or magician
Or a musical-saw musician
Or an ingenue or pianist who is hot—
Whether you play Punchinello,
Little Eva, or Othello—
Having heard the call, you've given all you've
    got.
And what better reward for a trouper
Than the sound we consider super?

REFRAIN 2

Applause, applause!
Vociferous applause
From orchestra to gallery
Could mean a raise in salary.

Give out, give in!—
Be noisy, make a din!
(The manager, he audits
Our plaudits.)

We won renown
When opening out of town;
(In Boston and in Rockaway
They heard applause a block away)—

If we've come through,
Give credit where it's due,
And obey the theatre's unwritten laws,
Because—we like applause!

DREAMWORLD

Registered for copyright as an unpublished song September 1951. Intended for Helen Wood (Joanna), Kurt Kasznar (Leo), and ensemble. Unused, though a few bars of the melody are heard as background. Private recording by Burton Lane, piano and vocal, issued in 1975 on the Mark 56 album "Ira Gershwin Loves to Rhyme."

VERSE

JOANNA: This mundane life of Mondays
Is suddenly looking up—
With a calendar full of Sundays
And joy brimming my cup.

My favorite flight of fancy
Was getting me nowhere fast. . . .
But the glorious goal I can see
At last, at last!

REFRAIN 1

Dreamworld, how was I to know
My little dreamworld was no dream?
You were just a theme
When the stars were all agleam.

Dreamworld, you were locked up in
    my heart—
A dreamworld none could see—
But I found the key;
Suddenly we're free!

How can, how can words reveal
The wondrous feeling that I feel?
What a dream of a world is
    unfurled—
My dreamworld is real!

INTERLUDE

The reviews were ecstatic;
All the critics were terribly sweet!
It's all so dramatic—
The city is fanatic!
Oh, how thrilling when you sweep a
    city off its feet!

LEO: See that line at the wicket!
Though a fortune they're willing to
    pay,
They'll probably picket
The theatre, for no ticket
Is available until the middle of next
    May.

AUTOGRAPH
SEEKERS: Just see how the marquee is
    blazing—
Her name flashing nineteen feet high!

JOANNA: Each night in the entr'acte,
I'm offered a new contract
But I'm concertizing in Europe in
    July. . . .

Tra la la, tra la la la—
In the kingdom of stardom I shine!
And all else means nothing—
It's talent that is the thing,
And I'm talented and Paradise is
    mine!

REFRAIN 2

ALL: Dreamworld, how was she to know
Her little dreamworld was no dream?
You were just a theme
When the stars were all agleam.

Dreamworld, you were locked up in
    her heart—
A dreamworld none could see—
But she found the key;
Suddenly you're free!

JOANNA: How can, how can words reveal
The wondrous feeling that I feel?
What a dream of a world is
    unfurled—

ALL: Her dreamworld is really, really real!

ACH, DU LIEBER OOM-PAH-PAH

Registered for copyright as an unpublished song September 1952. Private recording by Ira Gershwin, vocal, and Burton Lane, piano, issued in 1975 on the Mark 56 album "Ira Gershwin Loves to Rhyme."

VERSE 1

Ve do not play to crowded concert houses,
But ve is musikers from tip to toe!
To join our band you must be men, not mouses;
Till in the face you're blue you got to blow.

Ve blow you something sad or something
    gayer;
For schmaltziness our band cannot be matched.
Ve string along without a fiddle player—
Ve are a band that has no strings attached!
No strings attached! Holy smoke!
Dot's a joke!

REFRAIN 1

Ach, du lieber oom-pah-pah! Ven the band
    commences—
Ach, du lieber oom-pah-pah! Makes you lose the
    senses!
Ve don't finger *Meistersinger*
But our Straussian valtzes
Makes the people longer linger—
Und the traffic halts-es!
On the lovely oom-pah-pah, ve are standing
    pat!
Listen how sublime it is—
Rhythm und rhyme it is!
But for us now time it is
To pass the hat!

VERSE 2

Vere no policeman is, is our locations,
Und so ve mostly in backyards appear.
Ve oom-pah you not only Strauss creations
But Offenbach und often Meyerbeer.

So do not ask for ragtime—Dot is futile;
Mit only high-class music do ve fuss.
Ve have no harp but ven we blow und tootle

Vidout a harp you cannot harp on us!
Can't harp on us! Holy smoke!
Anudder joke!

REFRAIN 2

Ach, du lieber oom-pah-pah! Ven the band
    commences—
Ach, du lieber oom-pah-pah! Makes you lose the
    senses!
Ve keep standing all day handing
You the polkas und marches,
Notwithstanding dot with standing
Ve got fallen arches!
Ach, du lieber oom-pah-pah! Fills you full of
    cheer!
But by now ve played enough;
Yah! Ve have stayed enough—
For, you see, ve made enough
To buy a beer!

EXIT

Though ve sooner
Drink a schooner,
Ve're not idle
Mit a seidel;
Ve say "Prosit!
Down it goes it!"
Oom-pah-pah!

WOMAN, THERE IS NO LIVING WITH YOU

Registered for copyright as an unpublished song September 1951. Intended for *Give a Girl a Break*. Unused. (Two other intended titles—"Whizzin' Thru Space" and "Outline"—were never developed into finished songs.)

VERSE

BOY: Woman, you are of the opposite sex—
    So to fall in love was not too complex;
    But man and woman though we are—
    Lately the opposition go too far.

REFRAIN 1

Seem no matter what I say
You interpret it a diff'rent way;
You, you're driving me cuckoo!
Woman, there is no living with you!

I go hither, you go yon—
Never know if you are pro or con!
First you ha-ha, then boo-hoo—
Woman, there is no living with you!

When from work I have turned up
And for supper I am waiting—
It's all burned up—
And this can be exasperating!

You are dumber than a goose—
Dumb but beautiful—so what's the use?
There's no living with you, no doubt—
But you're the woman I cannot live
    without—
Not live without—
Woman, you're the woman that I cannot
    live without!

REFRAIN 2

GIRL: Life with you is not a cinch;
    Comes to money and you penny-pinch.
    It is time the coop I flew—
    Mister, there is no living with you.

At the movies you get mad
If I say the actor is not bad.
Out of nothing, much ado—
Mister, there is no living with you.

When my hair, it is messed up,
Then you tell me I'm untidy;
I get dressed up—
You think I've got men on the side-y.

I could holler, I could shriek—
Then I take one look at that physique . . .
There's no living with you, no doubt—
But you're the mister I cannot live
    without—
Not live without—
Mister, you're the master that I cannot live
    without!

OVERLEAF: *Judy Garland sings "The Man That Got Away."*

A STAR IS BORN | 1954

A film produced by Sidney Luft for Warner Bros. Released in September 1954. Music by Harold Arlen.* Screenplay by Moss Hart based on an earlier screenplay by Dorothy Parker, Alan Campbell, and Robert Carson, from a story by William A. Wellman and Robert Carson. Directed by George Cukor. Dances staged by Richard Barstow; additional choreography by Eugene Loring. Music conducted by Ray Heindorf. Orchestral arrangements by Skip Martin. Vocal arrangements by Jack Cathcart. Cast, starring Judy Garland (Esther Blodgett) and James Mason (Norman Maine), featured Jack Carson (Libby), Charles Bickford (Oliver Niles), Tom Noonan (Danny McGuire), and Lucy Marlow (Lola Lavery).

Shortly after the film's release, Warner Bros. cut twenty-seven minutes from the negative and all existing prints. Three of the film's musical numbers ("The TV Commercial," "Here's What I'm Here For," and "Lose That Long Face") were deleted. Much of the cut footage, including the three musical numbers, was rediscovered and restored in the early 1980s.

GOTTA HAVE ME GO WITH YOU

Published in the vocal selections November 1954. Registered for copyright as an unpublished song April 1954. "Sung by Judy Garland as girl vocalist Esther Blodgett (later movie star Vicki Lester) at a benefit in the Shrine Auditorium, Los Angeles" (Ira Gershwin—*Lyrics on Several Occasions*). Garland was joined in the number by band singers Don McKay and Jack Harmon.

Composer Arlen is no thirty-two-bar man. As one of the most individual of American show-composers he is distinctive in melodic line and unusual construction ("Black Magic," seventy-two bars; "One for My Baby," forty-eight bars; "The Man That Got Away," sixty-two bars). "Gotta" is unusual not only in its twenty-four-bar verse and forty-eight-bar refrain but also in that the first eight bars of the verse music are introduced twice in the refrain.

When inspiration or something else worth-while hits Arlen, it is rarely a complete tune. It may be a fragment of only two bars or twelve—but it is the beginning of something at some time worth mulling over, and onto an envelope or into a notebook it goes. These snatches or possible themes he calls "jots." Frequently when col-

*The "Born in a Trunk" sequence, added to the film late in production, incorporates a number of standards (including the George Gershwin–Irving Caesar song "Swanee") and new music and lyrics by Leonard Gershe.

laborating with him the lyricist—whether Koehler or Mercer or Harburg or myself—finds himself wondering if a resultant song isn't too long or too difficult or too mannered for popular consumption. But there's no cause for worry. Many Arlen songs do take time to catch on, but when they do they join his impressive and lasting catalogue.

—from *Lyrics on Several Occasions*

VERSE

What a spot, this—
Not so hot, this!
Hey, there—shy one,
Come be my one!
Please don't rush off—
Want no brush-off.
I can't compel you
To buy what I'd sell you . . .
But I've got to tell you
Like so:

REFRAIN

You wanna have bells that'll ring?
You wanna have songs that'll sing?
You want your sky a baby blue?
You gotta have me go with you!

Hey, you fool, you—
Why so cool, you,
When I'm ready
To go steady?

You wanna have eyes that'll shine?
You wanna have grapes on the vine?
You want a love that's truly true?
You gotta have me go with you!

Why the holdout?
Have you sold out?
Time you woke up,
Time you spoke up!

This line I'm handing you is not a handout;
As a team we'd be a standout.

You wanna live high on a dime?
You wanna have two hearts in rhyme?
Gotta have me go with you all the time!

THE MAN THAT GOT AWAY

Published June 1954 and in the vocal selections November 1954. Previously registered for copyright as an un-

published song April 1954. "Judy Garland as Esther Blodgett, girl singer with a band, in a Sunset Strip musicians' hangout, after hours" (Ira Gershwin—*Lyrics on Several Occasions*).

Some movie-reviewers, in noticing this number, called it "The Man Who Got Away"—a whodunit title I wouldn't have considered a lyric possibility. The change, whether deliberate or unwitting, was made by those who obviously prefer "who" to "that" when the relative pronoun refers to Homo sapiens, or any reasonable facsimile thereof. Generally, of course, my syntactical course would follow theirs. But this had to be "The Man *That* Got Away" because, actually, the title hit me as a paraphrase of the angler's "You should have seen the one that got away."

The word "man" in a title ("My Man," "A Good Man Is Hard to Find"—hundreds of others) usually limits the rendition of a song to female vocalists. There would be much contracting-of-brow and looking-askance if a male singer attempted: "Some day he'll come along / The man I love. . . . " And if he tried mere gender-changing, some undesirable attributes could emerge—Amazonian here, for instance:

> Some day she'll come along,
> The girl I love;
> And she'll be big and strong. . . .

Opposite-sex versions of such lyrics being rare, it was consequently a surprise when Frank Sinatra telephoned me he wanted to do a recording called "The *Gal* That Got Away." He pointed out that, outside of the concluding lines, the lyric required only a change of pronoun: "No more his eager call" to "her eager call," &c. That sounding likely, I improvised this ending:

> Ever since this world began
> There is nothing sadder than
> A lost, lost loser looking for
> The gal that got away.

Which alliterative line he liked and wrote down. His excellent recording resulted, and "The Gal That Got Away" got away with it. But, again: a sex transilience of this sort is unusual.

When the composer of this song visited me a year ago and found I'd actually started working on this book, he insisted on having something of his included among the notes. I said: "O.K., Harold. What'll you write about?" He said: "I'll think of something."

Recently he sent me a piece, dictated by him in New York. I find it charming. The characters, in the order of their appearance, are:

> Ira—lyricist of the film *A Star Is Born*.
> Moss—Moss Hart, screenwriter of ditto.
> Judy—Judy Garland, star of ditto.

Sid—Sid Luft, Judy's husband and producer of the film.
Kitty—Kitty Carlisle, Mrs. Hart.

Somehow my contributor overlooked dictating a title. I'll call it:

MY BROKEN PROMISE
by Harold Arlen

WE had been working about two weeks on *A Star Is Born* and—luckily—somehow or other we'd got the first two songs done. (That was "Gotta Have Me Go with You" and "The Man That Got Away.") We were at it every afternoon, and I wanted to go away for the weekend. "Ira, I want to go to Palm Springs." "Don't." "Why not?" "Well, Moss is there, and Judy is there, and you'll be playing the songs for them and it's much too early." And he was as vehement as Ira can get. He said: "You'll spoil things." I said: "Ira, I promise you. I'm not going there to see Moss and Judy; I just want a break."

I went up to that golf course where Ben Hogan was the pro—the Tamarisk—and I went out that Saturday morning. Because I wasn't feeling too well, I wasn't supposed to play. But I saw Judy and Sid, large as life, just teeing off. I said: "I'll walk around with you." Nobody said anything about the picture. Then about the middle of the round (I'd be trailing them, and then be ahead of them, and they'd catch up, and then I'd trail them again) I started to whistle, very softly. I don't know what tempted me. She was about twenty yards away—it was a kind of tease and I couldn't stand it. I love Ira and I love Judy, and, well, I just whistled the main phrase of "The Man That Got Away." Suddenly, third or fourth whistle, Judy turned around. "Harold, what are you whistling?" "Nothing. I don't know." This continued. "Harold, what *are* you whistling? Don't tell me it's something from the picture." I said no. "Harold, I've got an idea it *must* be from the picture—don't hold out on me." Finally, on the eighteenth hole, Sid hit the ball 320 yards into the sand trap, and while he dug it out, Judy insisted: "Harold, there's a piano in the clubhouse, and you've *got* to play it." I kept playing it down: "It's just something we've been working on. I don't know how well you'll like it." So I played both songs, and—well—they were the first songs, the script wasn't finished, it was their first picture—and they went wild with joy. "Ira, Smira, he'll be happy about it," I thought. So I went to see Moss and Kitty. Same thing. They wanted to call Ira. I said: "Oh, don't! I've promised him not to play them." But they insisted and phoned Ira and said how wonderful it was, and he was delighted. And when I came back he was beaming and never said a word about my broken promise.

—from *Lyrics on Several Occasions*

The night is bitter,
The stars have lost their glitter;

The winds grow colder
And suddenly you're older—
And all because of the man that got away.

No more his eager call,
The writing's on the wall;
The dreams you've dreamed have all
Gone astray.

The man that won you
Has run off and undone you.
That great beginning
Has seen the final inning.
Don't know what happened. It's all a crazy game.

No more that all-time thrill,
For you've been through the mill—
And never a new love will
Be the same.

Good riddance, good-bye!
Ev'ry trick of his you're on to.
But, fools will be fools—
And where's he gone to?

The road gets rougher,
It's lonelier and tougher.
With hope you burn up—
Tomorrow he may turn up.
There's just no letup the livelong night and day.

Ever since this world began
There is nothing sadder than
A one-man woman looking for
The man that got away . . .
The man that got away.

THE TV COMMERCIAL

Registered for copyright as an unpublished composition April 1954. Introduced by Judy Garland (Esther). Alternate title: "The Commercial (Calypso)."

If you are a woman who is a wife
And you want to keep your husband for all your life,
There is one inevitable thing you must do:
Use Trinidad Coconut Oil Shampoo.

It's very nice!
It's a bargain at double the price!

Try it and you find as long as you live
Your crowning glory will be most attractive.
If you want to be a girl that the men run to—
Use Trinidad Coconut Oil Shampoo.

Take my advice!
It's a bargain at double the price!

HERE'S WHAT I'M HERE FOR

Published in the vocal selections November 1954. Previously registered for copyright as an unpublished song April 1954. Introduced by Judy Garland (Esther) and ensemble.

REFRAIN

What am I here for?
It's time you knew.
Here's what I'm here for;
I'm here for you.

Can you forgive me? Am I too late?
All the years that I wandered
And pondered
Were squandered.

My heart insisted
I seek you out.
That you existed
My heart had no doubt.

To share a journey that leads to heaven's door,
You'll find is what I'm here for.

IT'S A NEW WORLD

Published October 1954 and in the vocal selections November 1954. Previously registered for copyright as an unpublished song April 1954. Introduced by Judy Garland (Esther). In the summer of 1963, Ira Gershwin wrote a new lyric for Lena Horne to sing at a September 1963 Carnegie Hall concert dedicated to the "March on Washington for Jobs and Freedom."

Original Version

VERSE

How wonderful that I'm beholding
A Never-Never Land unfolding—
Where we polish up the stars
And mountains we move
In a life where all the pleasures
We will prove.

REFRAIN

It's a new world I see—
A new world for me!

The tears have rolled off my cheek,
And fears fade away ev'ry time you speak . . .

A new world, though we're in a tiny room—
What a vision of joy and blossom and bloom!

A newfound promise, one that will last—
So I'm holding on and I'm holding fast!

You've brought a new world to me,
And that it'll always, always be!

1963 Version

VERSE

How wonderful that I'm beholding
A vision of a world unfolding—
Where we reach up to the stars
As mountains we move
In a life where all the pleasures
We will prove.

REFRAIN

It's a new world I see—
A new world for me!

The tears have rolled off my cheek,
And fears fade away, seeing all I seek:

A new world—though it once was just a
dream—
Full of love, full of faith and self-esteem.

A newfound promise, one that will last—
So I'm holding on and I'm holding fast!

Hope brings a new world to me;
Let's hope it's a world that'll always be!

WESTERN UNION
TELEGRAM
325P PDT SEP 12 63 LB250
L NA360 PD NEW YORK NY 12 606P EDT
IRA GERSHWIN
    1021 NORTH ROXBURY DR BEVERLY HILLS CALIF
DEAR IRA I CANT TELL YOU HOW BEAUTIFUL AND HOW
INSPIRING THE LYRICS ARE TO ME I WILL BE SO PROUD
TO SING THEM I AM VERY GRATEFUL LOVE
    LENA HORNE
(12).

SOMEONE AT LAST

Published in the vocal selections November 1954. Previously registered for copyright as an unpublished song April 1954. Music by Harold Arlen. Introduced by Judy Garland (Esther).

Somewhere there's a someone who's the
    someone for me;*
Someday there will come one and my lover he
    will be.
Somehow I shall know him from the moment
    he's in view,†
And he'll know affection he's never known
    hitherto.

I pay no mind to the waiting—
Let the clock ticktock away.
The dream I'm contemplating
Will be here to stay.

Oh, somewhere in the sometime when the
    humdrum days have passed,
With my someone I'll be someone at last,
With my someone I'll be someone at last.

LOSE THAT LONG FACE

Published in the vocal selections November 1954. Previously registered for copyright as an unpublished song April 1954. "Judy Garland as an irrepressibly cheerful little newsboy, unstoppably bent on making euphoric those in the scene and in the audience" (Ira Gershwin, *Lyrics on Several Occasions*). Earlier title: "Get That Long Face Lost." I.G.'s first attempts at this lyric looked back at an old theme:

> The proverbial skies of gray
> On that customary rainy day
> Disappear in their usual style
> When you give 'em that well-known smile.

An earlier title of the song was "Somewhere in the Sometime." The earlier opening line was:
Somewhere in the sometime, there's a someone for
    me;
†*Alternate version of lines 3–4:*
Somehow I shall meet him on some fifty-second floor
Or perhaps at the crossroad in some cracker-barrel
    store.

INTRODUCTION

If, as, and when you've got a long face
Rearrange it.
Don't be contented with the wrong face;
There's a way to change it.

VERSE

Does the day look painful,
The future glum?
Does the sky look rainful?
Hey, there! Say, there:
Are you in a vacuum?
All that stuff and nonsense
You can overcome.
A long face gets you nowhere—
You lose that Month of May.
Like Peter Pan, the sweeter pan
Wins the day.

REFRAIN 1

Go lose that long face, that long face—
Go 'long and get that long face lost.
The blues black out when they can see
A smile that says, "Move on. No vacancy!"
This panacea idea
I'm handing you without any cost.
There isn't any tax on it,
So just relax on it—
If you want trouble double-crossed.
Don't give in to a frown;
Turn that frown upside down,
And get yourself that long face lost!

REFRAIN 2 (UNUSED)

Go lose that long face, that long face—
Go 'long and get that long face lost.
Let Gloomy Gus be critical,
But we'll be Pollyannalytical.
Take my suggestion—
Don't question
The smile that gets you out of the frost.
You don't need a psychologist
Or numerologist
If you want trouble double-crossed.
With a face full of fun,
Take your place in the sun,
And get yourself that long face lost!

I'M OFF THE DOWNBEAT

Registered for copyright as an unpublished song April 1954. "Blue verse, spirited refrain. Written for Judy Garland [Esther]. Considered but not used" (Ira Gershwin).

Downbeat" is one of three songs—all unproduced—(the other two: "Green Light Ahead" and "Dancing Partner") Arlen and I wrote for a spot in *A Star Is Born*. The situation in the film was the sneak-previewing of Vicki Lester's first movie—a showing which makes her a star overnight. All that was necessary was to put Vicki in a good number for four or five minutes, then show the audience's enthusiastic acceptance of a new star (as preview cards are signed in the lobby.) Instead it was finally deemed necessary to top everything with a fifteen-minute musical (mélange) sequence using special material to introduce seven or so standards. This sequence, "Born in a Trunk," based on Miss Garland's act at the Palace Theatre, was excellent for its original purpose—vaudeville and nightclubs—and as Judy can do no wrong received a good hand. But it added fifteen minutes to a three-hour film, held up the show, and cost $300,000. Big mistake (but all none of my business).

—intended for but not included in
Lyrics on Several Occasions

VERSE

Too long, too long, too long
Have I been dejected.
I heard me the same old tune;
I mean I moaned through too many a moon.
The life I led, I fear me,
Has been misdirected.
No more those defenses;
I've come to my senses;
And I'll take me the consequences.

REFRAIN 1

I'm off the downbeat—
Out of the haze;
I've seen the error
Of my ways.

From now I'm flying
To brighter skies.
Why be earthbound?
Shine and rise!

I've got the town beat—
From now I rate.
Look, look, I'm dancing
And feel great.

Hey, broken downbeat,*
You're just a noun!
I'm off you, downbeat—
I'm on the town.

REFRAIN 2

I'm off the downbeat—
Out of the haze;
I've seen the error
Of my ways.

From now I'm flying
On wings of song.
Why be earthbound?
Fly along!

I've got the town beat—
Queen of the Prom.
No looking back where
I came from.

Ta-ta! You downbeat—
You're just a noun!
I'm off the downbeat—
I'm on the town.

GREEN LIGHT AHEAD

Registered for copyright as an unpublished song April 1954. Intended for Judy Garland (Esther). Unused.

VERSE

The puritanical bluenose
Is a man with red-light stops—
"You mustn't do this! You mustn't do that!" he pops.

Lend an ear to one who knows
Those negative minds are 'way off;
Brimmin' the cup and livin' it up pay off.

If, as, and when you haven't seen light,
You must learn to
Light up the shadows with the green light;
That's the one to turn to.

Alternate version of refrain 1, lines 13–16:
That broken downbeat
Won't get me down
I'm off the downbeat—
I'm on the town.

REFRAIN

Go have yourself a time—
Spinnin' like a top;
No reason and no rhyme
For a red-light stop;
Don't be misled!
Green light ahead!

Go have your fill of fun—
It's all on the cuff;
When all is said and done—
Life is short enough.
I done done said,
"Green light ahead!"

So then—whether you are seventeen
Or sittin' on three-score ten or more—
Age means nothin',
Livin' is somethin'!
That's what the shoutin's for.

The best is yet to be—
Why be limited?
Come, hit the road with me—
But I mean
Hit the scene
With that green
Light ahead!

DANCING PARTNER

Intended for Judy Garland (Esther). Unused.

VERSE

So Columbus discovered America
And Balboa found the Pacific.
Centuries pass,
And I'm not in their class—
But I'm not a dumb thing;
I, too, have found something,
Something—

[*spoken*]
For me, anyway—

[*sung*]
Terrific.

REFRAIN

I found me a dancing partner
For both the night and day;
Forever I'll follow my dancing partner
As he leads me all the way.

We'll trip it beside the Hudson,
We'll cakewalk the Mississip'—
Beats ev'rything hollow
To follow
My dancing Apollo—
Solid, the partnership!

We'll go whirling and twirling, sliding and
    gliding;
We'll hop it for all we're worth.
From Rome to Cucamonga, we'll rumba and
    we'll conga
The far-flung corners of the earth.

I found me a dancing partner
Who needs no drumbeat to start—
For, when I am with 'im,
Existence is rhythm
And the music's in my heart!

OVERLEAF: *Bing Crosby*

THE COUNTRY GIRL | 1954

A film produced by William Perlberg for Paramount. Released in December 1954. Music by Harold Arlen. Screenplay by George Seaton, adapted from the play by Clifford Odets. Directed by George Seaton. Music conducted by Joseph J. Lilley. Cast, starring Bing Crosby (Frank Elgin), Grace Kelly (Georgie Elgin), and William Holden (Bernie Dodd), included Anthony Ross (Phil Cook), Gene Reynolds (Larry), and Jacqueline Fontaine (Singer-Actress).

THE PITCHMAN and IT'S MINE, IT'S YOURS

Introduced by Bing Crosby (Frank).

"The Pitchman"

FRANK:

[on stage]

> Well, I just wanted to say I was carrying an imaginary valise—you know, one of those pitchman's outfits.

[Walk-on music]

> Then a crowd began to gather round.

[He attempts mannerisms and voice of pitchman]

> Hurry, hurry, hurry, and do away with worry, worry, worry.
> Step right up, folks, et cetera, et cetera, et cetera, et cetera.
> Nothin' like pitchin' into a pitch with a pitch,
> With a pitch pipe makes a pitch a pipe.
> Hurry, hurry, hurry, and do away with worry, worry, worry.

> Sometime or other, brother,
> Ev'ryone has his back to the wall.
> Hist'ry discloses
> Life's no bed of roses;
> Kings topple and nations fall.
> Rich man, poor man, Indian chief,
> I include you all.

> Get away from me, son, you bother me, et cetera, et cetera.
> (She may be hard of hearing.)

> Simpletons, noodleheads, you're all—
> If you don't take advantage of my cure-all.

> Tell you what I'm gonna do, Tell you what I'm here for, et cetera, et cetera, et cetera.

> Listen, friend, believin' only what you see, that's nothin'.
> The trick is believin' only things you can't see.
> Visualize the indiscernible.
> For instance:

[Sings]

> Here's a mirrorlike lake to go fishin' in.
> Here's the gold at the break of day.
> Here's a moss-covered well to go wishin' in
> And stars from the Milky Way.

[spoken]

> What's that, lady? Et cetera, et cetera, et cetera.
> Madam, what that does for you?
> Try some of the rest of the merchandise.

[Sings]

> Here's a moonbeam that wants to go peepin' in.
> Here's a lilt that the bluebird shares.
> Here's a tropical night to go sleepin' in—
> Step up and sample my wares.

[spoken]

> What's that, small fry? Et cetera, et cetera, et cetera.
> Every single article in this valise belongs to you as well as it does to me.

"It's Mine, It's Yours"

REFRAIN 1

Here's the silver moon from the sky up there
And the em'rald meadow outdoors.
What a wealth of treasure there is to share.
It's mine, it's yours.

If you'd live a dream, oh, how precious is
An imagination that soars.
It can make the world we're in hers and his
And mine and yours.

If you want blue skies about
Year in, year out,
All you ever need in the last analysis
Is this:

Try a cheerful song and a valentine
And a sense of humor that scores.
You're no longer in a spin.
It's a great world we're in—
And it's mine, it's yours.

[spoken]
What's that, officer? Et cetera, et cetera, et cetera.
Well, we'll take care of him.

REFRAIN 2*

Oh, you make your fortune and win your place
And the banks all open their doors;
Then the green stuff leads you a merry chase—
It's mine, it's yours.

All your hopes are high as you play the game;
Oh, how sweet the bows and encores!
Then they cut you down—That's the way with fame—
It's mine, it's yours.

Year in, year out—
You're in, you're out;
You may be high man on the totem pole—
Or not.
So what?

With a cheerful song and a valentine
And a sense of humor that scores,
You're no longer in a spin.
It's a great world we're in—
And it's mine, it's yours.

COMMERCIALS

Registered for copyright as an unpublished song March 1954. The music of the "Liebermeyer Beer" commercial is by Harold Arlen; the rest are set to the tune of "London Bridge." Introduced by Bing Crosby (Frank).

"Liebermeyer Beer"

VERSE

They met in a garden years ago;
It was not just one of those things—
For he knew right then
He'd be happiest of men,
And he was—and he is—as he sings:

REFRAIN

[in German accent]

Drink! Clink!

Liebermeyer Beer for me!
Faithful I was and I will always be.
If you want to feeling fit,
Just uncan a can of it.
Liebermeyer Beer is best

*Only the last five lines of this refrain are sung in the film.

From North to South and from the East to
  West!

"Jamaica Chewing Gum"

Try Jamaica Chewing Gum;
It's a gum
Flavorsome,
And it gives you freedom from
In-di-ges-tion!

"Honey-Sweet Peanut Brittle"

When your ladylove you meet,
Here's a treat
Can't be beat!
Bring a box of Honey-Sweet
Peanut Brittle!

"Ups-a-Daisy Shaving Cream"

Would you like to live a dream?
Feel supreme?
On the beam?
Ups-a-Daisy Shaving Cream
Is the answer!

"Boston Ballpoint"

Here's a pen you ought to know—
Easy flow—
It'll go
Hundred thousand words or so:
Boston Ballpoint!

"Dr. Brett Dog and Cat Food"

Get the right food for your pet—
Meat or fish—
Both delish!
Yes, siree! Get Dr. Brett
Dog and Cat Food.

THE SEARCH IS THROUGH

Published December 1954. "Verse: 'Tenderly'; chorus:
'With a slow steady pulse.' Bing Crosby plays Frank
Elgin, a onetime musical-comedy star attempting a
comeback. In a flashback we are at a recording session.
The star is at the height of his career and is making a
record (78 RPM) of a presumable hit song of the period"
(Ira Gershwin—*Lyrics on Several Occasions*). Earlier
title: "You've Got What It Takes."

In the film a flashback to the Thirties showed Crosby
dubbing an imagined hit song of that period, but
"The Search Is Through" was no hit in the period in
which it was written—the middle Fifties. As Arlen
might put it: it didn't make any noise. "Noise" in this
connection is Arlen's term and has nothing to do with
decibels. A "noisy" song is one that gets around, sells
copies, and is recorded a good many times.
　　　　　　　　　—from *Lyrics on Several Occasions*

VERSE

The flaxen hair,
The tender voice,
The laughing eyes . . .
Gave me no choice.

No more the doubt
I used to face;
No more the doubt—
No more the chase.

REFRAIN

The search is through—
You've got what it takes;
There was no passing you by.

In my *Who's Who*
You've got what it takes:
The Who, the Where, the When, the Why.

One look, and oh!
No painting I know
Can equal your loveliness—
Head to toe.

At last the breaks!
You've got what it takes;
So easy to see
For all time to be—
You've got what it takes
To take me.

THE LAND AROUND US

Registered for copyright as an unpublished song February 1954. Prepared for publication in late 1954 but remains unpublished. Introduced by Bing Crosby (Frank)
and chorus.

VERSE

FRANK: We hardly ever faced land
　　　　That looks like so much wasteland;

But here our journey ends,
And here we stay.

With wealth the soil is bursting;
We've but to quench its thirsting,
And there's a river
Not too far away.

Here we'll settle and prove our mettle.

GROUP:
[*softly*]
　　　Here we'll settle and prove our mettle.

REFRAIN 1

FRANK: The land around us
　　　　Will be in bloom
　　　　With song and laughter
　　　　And elbow room.

A town will blossom here
With all serene,
With houses white
And with gardens green.

The lanes are shady;
The streets are wide.
You and your lady
Are full of pride.

I can hear children's voices;
I can hear Sunday chimes.
All across the valley:
Better times.

On land we found us,
One thing I know.
The land around us
Will grow and grow.

REFRAIN 2

The land around us
Is now in bloom
With song and laughter
And elbow room.

A town has blossomed here
With all serene,
[*Lines 7–21 as in refrain 1*]

PATTER

We'll put the post office here
And the high school there.
Then if we fail to put up a jail,
We hope you don't mind.
Round here, we'll have no galoot
Who totes a six-shooter shoot.
For in our plan, each citizen
Will be the respectable kind.

Railroad station here—
Op'ry house will be there;
We'll do our best the uncivilized West
To conquer and tame.
We'll settle for not less
Than a town that's pure and spotless,
Or mud will be our name.

DISSERTATION ON THE STATE OF BLISS or LOVE AND LEARN BLUES

Published December 1954. "Sung at a bar by Mistress of Ceremonies Jacqueline Fontaine, assisted by a somewhat swacked customer, played by Bing Crosby [Frank]" (Ira Gershwin—*Lyrics on Several Occasions*).

This blues was written and titled as "Love and Learn." I subsequently learned that there had been at least three songs so named, and when the creators of one of them objected, it was a simple matter to make the phrase the subtitle and to decorate the number with the rather impressive "Dissertation on the State of Bliss."
—from *Lyrics on Several Occasions*

Love and learn, love and learn.
It's a breeze, then a burn.
You retreat, then return.
You may have climbed the Tree of Knowledge,
But when you love you *really* learn.

Love and learn. Learn a lot.
It's the be-and-end-all, then it's not.
It's a dream, it's a plot.
It's something out of Seventh Heaven—
Then Something Misbegot.

Each morning when I count my blessings,
They tally up to none.

I've arrived at this:
What some call bliss
Is somewhat overdone.

Love and learn. Weep and sing
Till the final day of reckoning.
But when arms start to cling,
With the thrills kisses bring—
What you have learned is,
Is:
You haven't learned a thing.

CODA

It's a dream and it's a plot;
What you thought it was, was not.
But when arms begin to cling,
And angels start to sing—
What you have learned is,
Is:
You haven't learned a thing.

OVERLEAF: *Ray Walston and Kim Novak*

KISS ME,
STUPID
1964

A film produced by Billy Wilder for United Artists. Released in December 1964. Music by George Gershwin (posthumous). Screenplay by Billy Wilder and I.A.L. Diamond from the play *"L'Ora della Fantasia"* by Anna Bonacci. Directed by Billy Wilder. Music conducted by Andre Previn. Cast, starring Dean Martin (Dino), Kim Novak (Polly), Ray Walston (Orville J. Spooner), Felicia Farr (Zelda Spooner), and Cliff Osmond (Barney Millsap), featured Barbara Pepper (Big Bertha), James Ward (Milkman), Doro Merande (Mrs. Pettibone), Howard McNear (Mr. Pettibone), Bobo Lewis (Waitress), Tommy Nolan (Johnny Mulligan), John Fiedler (Rev. Carruthers), Bern Hoffman (Bartender), and Henry Berkman (Truck driver).

SOPHIA

Published September 1964. Introduced by Ray Walston (Orville); reprised by Dean Martin (Dino) and ensemble. The music for this number was adapted from "Wake Up, Brother, and Dance," intended for but not used in *Shall We Dance* (1937).

VERSE

Ev'ry day I
Sit and pray I
Win you over soon.

Say yes, won't you?
Do you, don't you
Want this world in tune?

What does it take to persuade you?
And how much more must I serenade you?

REFRAIN 1

Listen to me, Sophia—
Have you any idea
How much you mean to me-a?
How much you'll never know!

If I'm all *agitato*,
Ev'ry heartstring *vibrato*,
Ev'ry look *passionato*—
Who but you made me so?

It's love, it's love *crescendo*—
Never ever *diminuendo*.

Say the word, sweet Sophia—
Or from earth I resign.
Oh, Sophia, be mine!

REFRAIN 2

Listen to me, Sophia—
Have you any idea
How much you mean to me-a?
Ev'ry day more and more!

All the others were so-so,
Not a one *amoroso*—
But with you I'm aglow, so
Only you I adore.

You're sweeter than spumone;*
Sweeter even than zabaglione.

Say the word, sweet Sophia—
Let our hearts intertwine.
Oh, Sophia, be mine!
Oh, Sophia, be mine!

CODAS (UNUSED)

Sweet Sophia, be mine!
Let that honeymoon shine!
Let our hearts intertwine!
Put your love on the line
Or from earth I resign!

Sweet Sophia, be mine!
Put the grape on the vine!
With your love on the line,
Let that honeymoon shine
Or from earth I resign!

Sweet Sophia, be mine!
Put your love on the line!
Let that honeymoon shine
Through a future divine!
Sweet Sophia, be mine!

Put your heart on the line!
Let that honeymoon shine!
On ambrosia we'll dine—
Milk and honey and wine.
What a future divine
When, Sophia, you're mine!

Sweet Sophia, be mine!
Let that honeymoon shine!
Pluck the grape from the vine!
Let our hearts intertwine!
Put your love on the line
Or from earth I resign!
Oh, Sophia, be mine!

Earlier version of refrain 2, lines 9–10:
Be my inamorata—
Hot-like, not like a Lysistrata.

I'M A POACHED EGG

Published September 1964. Previously registered for copyright as an unpublished song February 1964. Introduced by Cliff Osmond (Barney) and Ray Walston (Orville). Earlier title: "When I'm Without You."

The music for the verse was derived from No. 105 of the George and Ira Gershwin Special Numbered Song File and had once been intended for "I Can't Be Bothered Now" in *A Damsel in Distress* (1937). The music to the release was derived from the release of "Are You Dancing?," intended for *Girl Crazy* (1930). When Ira Gershwin prepared worksheets of this song for donation to the Library of Congress, he wrote the following explanatory note (August 19, 1969):

When I signed to do three songs to Gershwin music for a Billy Wilder film called *Kiss Me, Stupid,* I was told one of the numbers was to be a rather "nutty" one. I recalled that my brother and I had once written (for no particular show or reason) something called "I'm a Poached Egg."

I sang Billy the first 8 bars which went:

I'm a poached egg without a piece of toast;
Philadelphia without the *Sat. Eve. Post*;
George Jean Nathan without a play to roast—
When I'm without you.

Naturally these lines and others were of the early Thirties,* but of course they could be changed and updated. Wilder liked the idea. . . .

1930s Version (Unfinished Worksheet)

I'm a Poached Egg
I Without You
I'm a poached egg without a piece of toast
I'm a newstand without the Sat. Eve. Post
George Jean Nathan without a play to roast
When I'm without you. (Cal. golden coast)
Am I'm without you'm
I'm the Yankees without Bambino Ruth
I'm a cocktail with no gin or vermouth
Douglas Fairbanks without a single tooth
When I'm without you
I'm a Gilbert without a triple rhyme
Rockefeller without a silver dime
Cal. without that golden clime
Greenwich Village without a bottle of gin
Jascha Heifetz without a violin
I'm a headache without an aspirin
English—how have you been (bean)

*In fact, the lyric's origins are even older than Ira recalled. See *Rosalie* (1928): "You Know How It Is."

Summer resort without a man
Russia without a 5 year plan

I'm a dipso
I'm a klepto without a thing to steal
I'm a nympho without a man to feel

Cyril without a who or whom

Highball without the real McCoy
Collar that doesn't come from Troy

I'm Chicago without a racketeer
I'm Milwaukee without a glass of beer
Rudy Vallee *with* a megaphone

I'm "How are you?" without "How have you
    been?"
I am Kipling without a Gunga Din
Andy Gump without Oh Min!

If I can't make a showing
With the hints that I am throwing
I'm going astray
I need you to complete me
But like dirt you seem to treat me—
Oh, meet me halfway.

Al Jolson without a Mammy's knee
Fanny Brice without Billy Rose

Kiss Me, *Stupid* Version

VERSE

'Way back in Noah's Ark,
When couples came to park,
It is stated
They were fated
To be truly mated.

And so I dreamed a dream:
Like them we'd be a team—
The tightest twosome hist'ry could reveal.
But the way you act of late has made me feel
That

REFRAIN 1

I'm a poached egg
Without a piece of toast,
Yorkshire pudding
Without a beef to roast,
A haunted house
That hasn't got a ghost—
When I'm without you.

I'm a mousetrap
Without a piece of cheese,
I'm Vienna
Without the Viennese,
I'm Da Vinci

Without the Mona Lis'—
I'm skies without blue.

When you don't hang a-
Round I'm a kanga-
Roo without a hop.
When will you show me
That as Ro-me-
O I'm not a flop?

I'm a Western
Without a hitching post,
I'm a network
Without a Coast to Coast,
Just a poached egg
Without a piece of toast—
Each time I'm without you.

REFRAIN 2

I'm Las Vegas
Without a slot machine,
I'm a Gypsy
Without a tambourine,
I'm Napoleon
Without a Josephine—
When I'm without you.

I'm a letter
Without the right address,
I'm a sandwich
With only watercress,
I'm a tenant,
The kind they dispossess,
I'm bill without coo.

There comes a time I
Don't know if I'm I
Or a wrestling match.
The way you treat me,
Soon they'll greet me
At the booby hatch.

I'm a lawyer
Who never won a case,
I'm a missile
That can't get into space,
Just a poached egg
With egg upon its face—
Each time I'm without you.

REFRAIN 3*

I am Venice
Without a gondolier,
Or Milwaukee
Without a glass of beer,
Could be Switzerland

Written especially for Ella Fitzgerald.

Without a mountaineer—
When I'm without you.

Like Columbus
Without Queen Isabel',
Neiman-Marcus
Without a thing to sell,
Mr. Hilton
With only one hotel—
I'm "What can I do?"

Each time you wander
Hither and yonder,
Don't know where I'm at.
I only know I'm
Lonely, so I'm
Here to tell you that.

I'm a girlfriend
Without a thing to boast—*
Any egghead
Would have me diagnosed
As a poached egg
Without a piece of toast—
Each time I'm without you.

Additional Lyrics (Unused)

I am Tarzan
Without his lady Jane,
Sadie Thompson
Without a drop of rain,
or
My Fair Lady
Without the rain in Spain,
I'm a dentist
Without his novocaine—
When I'm without you.
or
I'm a bullfight
Without a matador,
Casanova
The night he didn't score,
Just a poached egg
That's fallen on the floor—
When I'm without you.

I'm a Frenchman
Who never tasted tripe,
I'm a newscast
Without a teletype,
I'm a zebra
Without a single stripe—
I'm beer without brew.
or
I am Groucho

The male version of refrain 3, lines 21–22, is:
As a loser,
I'm just about the most—

Without a single brother,
I'm a Whistler
Who never had a mother,
I'm Othello
When you look at another—
But what can I do?

When you don't show up
I just blow up
And become a grouch!
Our love was thriving—
Now you're driving
Me back to the couch.

I'm a Pierrot
Without a Columbine,
I'm the New Year
Without the "Auld Lang Syne,"
Manischewitz
Without a bottle of wine—
Each time I'm without you.

I'm a missile
That can't get into space,
Monte Carlo
Without a Princess Grace,
Perry Mason
The time he lost a case—
When I'm without you.

I'm a Porgy
Who'll never find his Bess,
A sinking ship
Without an SOS,
I'm a tenant,
The kind they dispossess—
Can't sleep the night through.

ALL THE LIVELONG DAY (AND THE LONG, LONG NIGHT)

Published September 1964. Previously registered for copyright as an unpublished song February 1964. Intro-duced by Ray Walston (Orville). The music of the verse is the same as the music of the verse of the song "Phoebe" (1921) and is part of No. 89 of the George and Ira Gershwin Special Numbered Song File. The music of the refrain was taken from No. 57 of the George and Ira Gershwin Special Numbered Song File.

VERSE

You've really got me—
I find I'm not me—
The me I'd known in the past.

You simply stun me—
Love has undone me
At last.

From the beginning,
You had me spinning—
Around your finger I'm twirled.

But who's rebelling?
From now I'm telling*
The world:

REFRAIN 1

All the livelong day and the long, long night—
What do I do-oo-oo?
Dream about you-oo-oo!

Felt this way the first time you came in
   sight;
Suddenly my gloomy old sky
Turned magic'ly bright.

You'll find I'm perfect casting†
Opposite you.
You'll find love everlasting:

Published version of verse, lines 11–12:
You've got me telling
The world.
†*Earlier version of refrain 1, lines 7–11:*
You'll find we're perfect casting
You-oo and I.
With love that's everlasting—
Will I leave you ever?
Never-never-never!

Summer, spring, and falltime,
You're my One and All-Time.

All I live for now is to hold you tight—
All the livelong day and the long, long night.

REFRAIN 2

All the livelong day and the long, long night—
What do I do-oo-oo?
Dream about you-oo-oo!

Felt this way the first time you came in sight;
Suddenly my gloomy old sky
Turned magic'ly bright.

No chance you're taking chances
Taking me on.
Believe me when this man says:*
You're the Why and Wherefore
I am here to care for.

All I live for now is to hold you tight—
All the livelong day and the long, long night.

Ira Gershwin's Dummy Lyric

REFRAIN

When it's wintertime, many flowers droop.
There is a saying old:
"Summer is not so cold."

Some love turtle better than onion soup.
Alagazam! How's your wife, Sam?
I'm what I am.

If we can smile at trouble—
Ha-ha, ha-ha—
Then trouble is a bubble
Even in Nebraska,
Hong Kong, or Alaska.

So let's go outside and sit on the stoop.
When it's wintertime, many flowers droop.

Refrain 2, lines 9–11, as revised for Ella Fitzgerald:
No doubt my lifelong plan says:
You're the Why and Wherefore
I was born to care for.

OVERLEAF: *Clockwise from top left: Rehearsal of* Park Avenue: *Ira and Arthur Schwartz at the piano; Ira and Jerome Kern; Ira and Vincent Youmans; Vernon Duke and Ira; Rehearsal of* Rosalie: *Jack Donahue, Marilyn Miller, George, Sigmund Romberg, and Florenz Ziegfeld; Kurt Weill and Ira*

EPILOGUE

From time to time, as the years passed, Ira Gershwin returned to the manuscripts and musical fragments left by his brother George. He drew upon them when, working with composer Kay Swift, he wrote lyrics to George's melodies for the 1947 film *The Shocking Miss Pilgrim*. Seventeen years later he turned to them again for three more posthumous collaborations with George; the *Kiss Me, Stupid* songs were the last "new" songs he offered the public.

Yet many more Gershwin melodies remained in the trunk. Ira offered some to André Kostelanetz and George Balanchine, but Balanchine decided that his Gershwin ballet, *Who Cares?*, would be a realization of George's piano transcriptions from his 1932 song book—all previously published songs. Gene Kelly also worked with the unlyricized Gershwin music, but he, too, could not find a suitable way to bring them to a larger audience. Ira Gershwin, however, kept returning to an idea of his own: creating a suite inspired by locations in New York City. Among the melodies he considered for a Gotham travelogue was one (No. 59 in the George and Ira Gershwin Special Numbered Song File) he called "Sutton Place"; another (No. 77) he titled "The Cloisters," a third (No. 24) simply "52nd Floor." Yet he never carried these ideas to fruition.

One musician whom he encouraged was noted conductor-pianist Michael Tilson Thomas. In 1985 Thomas recorded "Sleepless Night" (No. 17), "Violin Piece" (No. 40), and "For Lily Pons" (No. 79). Ira had tried to write a lyric for "Sleepless Night," which George had composed in California in 1936, but was never convinced that his words would be able to enhance George's melody. Thomas, who had access to all of George's unlyricized melodies, has been planning to record others under the title of one of them: "Blue Parade" (No. 46).

While most of the music in the Gershwin trunk is unlyricized, more than forty of the pieces in the Numbered Song File are complete songs or piano pieces, and the lyrics for almost all of these were written specifically for shows or films. They can be found in this volume with the other lyrics for those productions. One of the others, "Ask Me Again" (No. 50), was recorded by Rosemary Clooney and Michael Feinstein; another, No. 99, "A Corner of Heaven with You," later reset by Ira as "The Hurdy-Gurdy Man," was recorded by Maureen McGovern. Of the others, arguably only three remain to be printed, and they appear here in the epilogue to this compilation.

DOUBTING THOMAS

No. 35 in the George and Ira Gershwin Special Numbered Song File.

REFRAIN 1

There was a time
You said you'd always love me.
You promised very faithfully.
Now I'm a Doubting Thomas
Since you broke your promise to me.

I used to think
The stork brought all the babies,
But now I'm thinking diff'rently.
I'm such a Doubting Thomas
Since you broke your promise to me.

Now I'm a cynic,
A Philadelphia lawyer,
A destroyer of every myth.
Since you told my kin and kith
To set the wedding day
And then you ran away.

In every cloud
I saw a silver lining.
But now it's more than I can see,
'Cause I'm a Doubting Thomas
Since you broke your promise to me.

REFRAIN 2

I used to think
That Georgie told his father
The truth about that Cherry Tree.
But I'm a Doubting Thomas
Since you broke your promise to me.

Once I believed
That kindly Mr. Kringle
Would mingle with the family.
But I'm a Doubting Thomas
Since you broke your promise to me.

Now I'm a cynic,
A Philadelphia lawyer,
A destroyer of every myth.
Since you told my kin and kith
To set the wedding day
And then you ran away.

I used to say
That love could last forever.
But now I know it's T.N.T.
'Cause I'm a Doubting Thomas
Since you broke your promise to me.

REFRAIN 3

I used to call
The country that we live in
"The Land of Opportunity."

But I'm a Doubting Thomas
Since you broke your promise to me.

I used to say
"A barking dog won't bite you.
He wouldn't even hurt a flea!"
But I'm a Doubting Thomas
Since you broke your promise to me

Now I'm a cynic,
A Philadelphia lawyer,
A destroyer of every myth.
Since you told my kin and kith
To set the wedding day.
And then you ran away

I used to think
That if you watched a kettle
You'd have to wait all night for tea.
But I'm a Doubting Thomas
Since you broke your promise—
Forgot about your promise to me.

I WON'T GIVE UP

No. 25 in the George and Ira Gershwin Special Numbered Song File. Alternate title: "The Happy News." On one piano-vocal score someone has, incorrectly, attributed this lyric to Al Stillman.

REFRAIN

Oh, just imagine the thrill,
A little house on a hill
Where Jack is happy with Jill.
I won't give up
Till you give in
And we give out the happy
    news.

The starry heavens may fall,
My caddy may find the ball,
It's not important at all.
I won't give up
Till you give in
And we give out the happy
    news.

I've met ladies who
Mother thought would do.
Pretty ones and clever,
But I never fell somehow.
Won't you understand?
I just waited and
Here you are now.

There's no use answering no.
I'm under thirty and so
With fifty more years to go
I won't give up Till you give in
And we give out the happy
   news.

SAYING MY SAY

No. 19 in the George and Ira Gershwin Special Numbered Song File. Ira Gershwin and Michael Feinstein did some editorial work on this song to prepare it for possible publication.

REFRAIN

There's no stopping me.*
I've come here to say my say.
Don't try topping me,

Alternate version, lines 1–4:
There's no holding me.
I've come here to say my say.
No use scolding me,
Simply have to say my say.

I've just got to say my say.
So, say what you will,
This Jack gets a thrill,
He's needing a Jill,
You fill the bill,
Say what you will
With impunity.
Once again I'll say my say.
Opportunity
Now to change your name, I say,
I say you can bring heaven in view
By saying one day you'll say, "I do!"*

Alternate version, line 15:
Just say that one day you'll say, "I do!"

INDEX

Reversionary Territories; New World Music Company (Ltd.) administered by WB Music Corp. and Warner Bros. Inc. for all other countries.

[33] © New World Music Company (Ltd.), assigned to George Gershwin Music and Ira Gershwin Music both administered by WB Music Corp. and Gilbert Keyes Music for the United States and all other countries.

[34] © Ira Gershwin Music administered by WB Music Corp. and Gilbert Keyes Music for the United States and all other countries.

[35] © (Renewed) New World Music Corp. assigned to WB Music Corp. and Gilbert Keyes Music for the United States; Chappell & Co. and New World Music Company (Ltd.) administered by WB Music Corp. for all British Reversionary Territories; New World Music Company (Ltd.) administered by WB Music Corp., for all other countries.

[36] © George Gershwin Music and Ira Gershwin Music both administered by WB Music Corp. for the United States and all other countries. Additional material © New World Music Corp. (Renewed) assigned to WB Music Corp. for the United States; Chappell & Co. and New World Music Company (Ltd.) administered by WB Music Corp. for all British Reversionary Territories; New World Music Company (Ltd.) administered by WB Music Corp., for all other countries.

[37] © (Renewed) New World Music Corp. assigned to WB Music Corp. for the United States; Chappell & Co. and New World Music Company (Ltd.) administered by WB Music Corp. for all British Reversionary Territories; New World Music Company (Ltd.) administered by WB Music Corp., for all other countries. Additional material © George Gershwin Music and Ira Gershwin Music both administered by Warner Bros Music for the United States and all other countries.

[38] © George Gershwin Music administered by WB Music Corp. for the United States and all other countries.

[39] © Ira Gershwin Music administered by WB Music Corp. and Glocca Morra Music for the United States and all other countries.

[40] © (Renewed) Harms, Inc., assigned to Harwin Music Co., administered by MPL Communications, Warner Bros Music, and Glocca Morra Music for the United States; Warner Bros. Inc. for all other countries.

[41] © (Renewed) New World Music Corp. assigned to New World Music Company (Ltd.), administered by WB Music Corp. and Harwin Music administered by MPL Communications for the United States; New World Music Company (Ltd.), administered by WB Music Corp. for all other countries.

[42] © (Renewed) Harms, Inc., assigned to WB Music Corp., Warner Bros. Inc., and Vernon Duke

Publishing Co. for the United States; New World Music Company (Ltd.) administered by WB Music Corp., and Warner Bros. Inc. for all other countries.

[43] © (Renewed) Remick Music Corp. assigned to WB Music Corp. and Warner Bros. Inc. for the United States; New World Music Company (Ltd.) administered by WB Music Corp., and Warner Bros. Inc. for all other countries.

[44] © (Renewed) Harms, Inc., assigned to WB Music Corp. and Louis Alter Publishing Descendants for the United States; New World Music Company (Ltd.) administered by WB Music Corp., and Warner Bros. Inc. for all other countries.

[45] © (Renewed) Gershwin Publishing Corp. (Renewed) by Chappell & Co. assigned to George Gershwin Music, Ira Gershwin Music, and Dubose and Dorothy Heyward Memorial Fund Publishing (all administered by WB Music Corp.) for the United States; Chappell & Co. for all other countries.

[46] © Chappell & Co. assigned to Chappell & Co. and Ira Gershwin Music administered by WB Music Corp. for the United States and all other countries.

[47] © (Renewed) Chappell & Co. assigned to Chappell & Co. and Ira Gershwin Music administered by WB Music Corp. for the United States; Chappell & Co. for all other countries.

[48] © (Renewed) Gershwin Publishing Corp. administered by Chappell & Co. assigned to George Gershwin Music and Ira Gershwin Music both administered by WB Music Corp. for the United States; Chappell & Co. for all other countries.

[49] © (Renewed) George Gershwin and Ira Gershwin assigned to George Gershwin Music and Ira Gershwin Music both administered by WB Music Corp. for the United States and all other countries.

[50] © (Renewed) Chappell & Co. assigned to George Gershwin Music and Ira Gershwin Music both administered by WB Music Corp. for the United States; Chappell & Co. for all other countries.

[51] © (Renewed) Chappell & Co. for the United States and all other countries.

[52] © (Renewed) Jerome Kern and Ira Gershwin assigned to T. B. Harms, Inc., administered by PolyGram International Publishing as successor-in-interest for the United States and all other countries.

[53] © T. B. Harms, Inc., assigned to PolyGram International Publishing, Inc., as successor-in-interest for the United States and all other countries.

[54] (Renewed) Jerome Kern and Ira Gershwin assigned to Betty Kern Miller and Ira Gershwin Music administered by WB Music Corp. as successors-in-

interest for the United States and all other countries.

[55] © (Renewed) Chappell & Co. assigned to Chappell & Co. and Hampshire House Publishing Corp. for the United States; Chappell & Co. for all other countries.

[56] © (Renewed) Jerome Kern, Ira Gershwin, and E. Y. Harburg assigned to T. B. Harms, Inc., administered by PolyGram International Publishing Corp. as successor-in-interest for the United States and all other countries.

[57] © (Renewed) Putnam Music, Inc., administered by PolyGram International Publishing, Inc., as successor-in-interest for the United States and all other countries.

[58] © (Renewed) Gershwin Publishing Corp. assigned to Chappell & Co. for the United States and all other countries.

[59] © (Renewed) Harry Warren Music and Loews, Inc., assigned to Chappell & Co. and Four Jays Music Company for the United States and all other countries.

[60] © (Renewed) Loews, Inc., assigned to Ira Gershwin Music administered by WB Music Corp. and Four Jays Music Company for the United States; Chappell & Co. and Four Jays Music Company for all other countries.

[61] © (Renewed) Loews, Inc., assigned to Ira Gershwin Music administered by WB Music Corp. and Chappell & Co. for the United States and all other countries.

[62] © (Renewed) Loews, Inc., assigned to EMI Feist Catalog Inc. as successor-in-interest for the United States and all other countries.

[63] © (Renewed) Harwin Music Co. assigned to Harwin Music Co. administered by MPL Communications and New World Music Company (Ltd.) administered by WB Music Corp. for the United States; Harwin Music Co. administered by MPL Communications for all other countries.

[64] © (Renewed) Harwin Music Corp. assigned to Harwin Music Co. administered by MPL Communications and Ira Gershwin Music administered by WB Music Corp. for the United States and all other countries.

[65] © (Renewed) Famous Music Corp. and Edwin H. Morris & Co., Inc., assigned to Harwin Music Corp. administered by MPL Communications and Ira Gershwin Music administered by WB Music Corp. for the United States and all other countries.

[66] © (Renewed) Famous Music Corp. and Edwin H. Morris & Co., Inc., assigned to Harwin Music Corp. administered by MPL Communications and New World Company, Ltd., administered by WB Music Corp. for the United States and all other countries.

Excerpts from *Lyrics on Several Occasions:*

© 1959 (Renewed) Ira Gershwin assigned to the Ira and Leonore Gershwin Trusts for the United States and all other countries. All rights reserved. International copyright secured. Used by permission.

A Babbitt met a Bromide on the avenue one day, 107

A bill of divorcement, 342

A charity bazaar, 61

A foggy day (in London Town), 271

A man without a woman, 295

A rhyming dictionary isn't all that it should be, 7

A sunny disposish, 76

A weekend in the country, 360

ACCORDING TO MR. GRIMES, 129 © 1993 Ira Gershwin Music.[1]

ACH, DU LIEBER OOM-PAH-PAH, 371 © 1952 (Renewed) Ira Gershwin Music and Chappell & Co.[61]

ACROBATS, 111 © 1993 Ira Gershwin Music.[1]

ADLAI'S SWEEPING THE COUNTRY, 179 © 1993 Ira Gershwin Music.[1]

ADORED ONE, 146 © 1987 George Gershwin Music, Ira Gershwin Music, and Gilbert Keyes Music.[33]

After all is said and done, 38

After the races are over, 310

Age was creeping on me, 90

Ah, ah! I'm the cu-ca-ra-cha, 277

Ah—, Ah— / Wintergreen for President!, 206

Ah, Things! Sweet Happiness of Things!, 227

A-HUNTING WE WILL GO, 129 © 1993 Ira Gershwin Music.[1]

AIN'T IT ROMANTIC?, 86 © 1993 Ira Gershwin Music.[1]

Aladdin had a wonderful lamp, 360

ALESSANDRO THE WISE, *See* DUKE'S SONG, THE—"ALESSANDRO THE WISE"

All aboard! All aboard! Train leaves immediately!, 249

ALL AT ONCE, 317 © 1945 (Renewed) Chappell & Co. and Hampshire House Publishing Corp.[55]

All a-tremble / We assemble, 331

All gloom and sorrow ended, 12

All hands are aboard, 15

All night long I've waited, 59

ALL OF THEM WAS FRIENDS OF MINE, 39 Lyric © 1993 Ira Gershwin Music.[1]

All that I know is you'd be hard to replace, 358

All the crooks that I am after—, 197

All the day is filled with song—, 306

ALL THE ELKS AND MASONS, 228 Lyric © 1993 Ira Gershwin Music and Glocca Morra Music.[39]

All the Elks, the Masons, too—, 228

All the flowers are in bloom, back home, 7

All the immigrants came to the U.S.A., 346

ALL THE LIVELONG DAY (AND THE LONG, LONG NIGHT), 385 © 1964 (Renewed) Chappell & Co.[58]

ALL THE MOTHERS OF THE NATION, 211 © 1987 George Gershwin Music and Ira Gershwin Music.[12]

All the town is falling, 24

All the traffic cops are pirouetting, 363

All you preachers, 27

Alone at last in San Fernando Valley, 302

Although by black misfortune we're surrounded, 330

Although I should know better, 126

Although we're only the chorus, 144

Always find you at the Ritz or Plaza, 44

Always I'll recall the night, 118

Am I happy? Am I proud? Tra-la-la!, 25

Amid the ice, amid the snow, 28

Among the forty-eight states, 343

An American in Paris—, 143

AND I HAVE YOU, 168 Lyric © 1993 Ira Gershwin Music.[1]

And now everything is arranged, 328

And we want to dance with Lucilla—, 317

ANNOUNCEMENT FOR *BROADWAY GOLD MELODY DIGGERS OF 42ND STREET*, 249 Lyric © 1993 Ira Gershwin Music.[1]

Any man who would appeal to me, 43

ANY MOMENT NOW, 312 Lyric © 1993 Ira Gershwin Music.[1]

ANYTHING FOR YOU, 12 © 1993 Ira Gershwin Music.[1]

Anytime the thunder starts to rumble down, 76

APPLAUSE, APPLAUSE, 369 © 1952 (Renewed) Ira Gershwin Music and Chappell & Co.[61]

ARE YOU DANCING?, 169 © 1993 Ira Gershwin Music.[1]

AREN'T YOU KIND OF GLAD WE DID?, 352 © 1946 (Renewed) Chappell & Co.[58]

AREN'T YOU WONDERFUL! (OR, THE ECONOMIC SITUATION), *See* ECONOMIC SITUATION, THE

ARIA—"MY LORDS AND LADIES," 324 Lyric © 1993 Ira Gershwin Music.[1]

Aries' children, 300

ARIETTA—"HOW WONDERFULLY FORTUNATE," 335 Lyric © 1993 Ira Gershwin Music.[1]

ARIETTA—"I HAD JUST BEEN PARDONED," 327 Lyric © 1993 Ira Gershwin Music.[1]

As a kid I used to revel, 363

As a prestidigitator, 21

As a tot, 109

As I stand here, ready for eternity . . . , 325

As soon as I have saved a little nest egg, 198

AS THE CHAIRMAN OF THE COMMITTEE, 177 © 1932 (Renewed) WB Music Corp.[28]

ASK ME AGAIN, 232 © 1983 George Gershwin Music and Ira Gershwin Music.[29]

At a very early age I decided, 84

At any gambling casino, 264

AT 11 P.M., 41 Lyric © 1993 Ira Gershwin Music.[1]

At exactly eight-forty or thereabouts—, 222

AT MRS. SIMPKIN'S FINISHING SCHOOL, 146 © 1993 Ira Gershwin Music and Gilbert Keyes Music.[34]

At seven o'clock this morning in Poughkeepsie, 231

AT THE EX-KINGS' CLUB, 118 © 1993 Ira Gershwin Music.[1]

'ATTA GIRL!, 40 Lyric © 1993 Ira Gershwin Music.[1]

AVIATOR, 108 © 1987 George Gershwin Music and Ira Gershwin Music.[18]

AWAKE, CHILDREN, AWAKE, 139 Lyric © 1993 Ira Gershwin Music.[1]

Away with the music of Broadway!, 279

BABBITT AND THE BROMIDE, THE, 107 © 1927 (Renewed) WB Music Corp.[28]

BABY!, 64 © 1925 (Renewed) WB Music Corp., Warner Bros. Inc., and Stephen Ballentine Music.[16]

Baby, heed me, 64

BABY ME BLUES, 33 Lyric © 1993 Ira Gershwin Music.[1]

BABY, YOU'RE NEWS, 280 © 1939 (Renewed) Chappell & Co.[51]

BACK BAY POLKA, THE, 353 © 1946 (Renewed) Chappell & Co.[58]

BACK HOME, 7 © 1993 Ira Gershwin Music.[1]

Back in the days of knights in armor, 194

Back in the land where Buddha is all supreme, 34

BAD, BAD MEN, THE, 56 Lyric © 1993 Ira Gershwin Music.[1]

Bad news, go 'way!, 269

BALLAD OF BABY FACE MCGINTY (WHO BIT OFF MORE THAN HE COULD CHEW), THE, 258 Lyric © 1959 (Renewed) Ira Gershwin; © 1993 Ira Gershwin Music.[1]

BAMBINO, 10 Lyric © 1993 Ira Gershwin Music.[1]

BARBARY COAST, 163 © 1954 (Renewed) WB Music Corp.[28]

BASEBALL SCENE, *See* PLAY BALL!, et al.

BATS ABOUT YOU, 296 Lyric © 1993 Ira Gershwin Music.[1]

BAZOOKA, THE, *See* GAZOOKA, THE

BEAUTIFUL BIRD, 4 © 1993 Ira Gershwin Music.[1]

BEAUTIFUL GYPSY, 118 © 1927 (Renewed) WB Music Corp.[28]

BEAUTIFYING THE CITY, *See* LIFE BEGINS AT CITY HALL

BECAUSE, BECAUSE, 176, 183 © 1931 (Renewed) WB Music Corp.[28]

Before Dan Cupid knew of us, 42

BEFORE WE WERE MARRIED, 125 Lyric © 1993 Ira Gershwin Music.[1]

Before you reach for your sables, 257

BEGINNER'S LUCK, (I'VE GOT), 264 © 1936 George Gershwin Music and Ira Gershwin Music.[48]

Being somewhat older, 38

BELL OF DOOM IS CLANGING, THE, *See* SONG OF THE HANGMAN

BESS, YOU IS MY WOMAN NOW, 237 © 1935 (Renewed) George Gershwin Music, Ira Gershwin Music, and DuBose and Dorothy Heyward Memorial Fund Publishing.[45]

BEST YEARS OF HIS LIFE, THE, 291 © 1941 (Renewed) Chappell & Co. and Hampshire House Publishing Corp.[55]

BETTER HALF KNOWS BETTER, THE, 262 Lyric © 1993 Ira Gershwin Music.[1]

Beware of that popular music!, 279

BIDIN' MY TIME, 161 © 1930 (Renewed) WB Music Corp.[28]

Billions of dollars were lost us, 216

BIRTHDAY PARTY, 102 © 1977 George Gershwin Music and Ira Gershwin Music.[12]

BITTERSWEET, 30 Lyric © 1993 Ira Gershwin Music.[1]

BLAH, BLAH, BLAH, 173 © 1931 (Renewed) WB Music Corp.[28]

BLOW THAT SWEET AND LOW-DOWN, *See* SWEET AND LOW-DOWN

BLOWIN' THE BLUES AWAY, *See* BLOWING THE BLUES AWAY

BLOWING THE BLUES AWAY, 77 © 1926 (Renewed) WB Music Corp. and Warner Bros. Inc.[10]

BLUEBEARD, 111 © 1993 Ira Gershwin Music.[1]

BLUE, BLUE, BLUE, 213 © 1933 (Renewed) WB Music Corp.[28]

BLUE HULLABALOO, 107 © 1993 Ira Gershwin Music.[1]

Born on the thirteenth, on a Friday—, 131

BOSS IS BRINGING HOME A BRIDE, THE, 301 Lyric © 1993 Ira Gershwin Music.[1]

BOSTON, *See* BACK BAY POLKA, THE

Boy! But it's grand when you're single—, 108

Boy! It's simply grand to have the gang around, 85

BOY WANTED, 12 © 1921 (Renewed) WB Music Corp.[7]; © 1924 (Renewed) WB Music Corp.[8]

BOY! WHAT LOVE HAS DONE TO ME!, 167 © 1930 (Renewed) WB Music Corp.[28]

BRIDE AND GROOM (OH, KAY! VERSION), 83 © 1958 (Renewed) New World Music Company (Ltd.)[24]

BRIDE AND GROOM (PARDON MY ENGLISH VERSION), *See* HAIL THE HAPPY COUPLE

BRING ON THE DING DONG DELL, 86 © 1993 Ira Gershwin Music.[1]

Bring on the rice and shoes, 19

Bring those pans and pots up!, 321

BRONCO BUSTERS, 163 © 1954 (Renewed) WB Music Corp.[28]

BUT NOT FOR ME, 166 © 1930 (Renewed) WB Music Corp.[28]

But on this glorious day I find, 180

But—there's something we're worried about!, 212

But they don't make 'em that way anymore, 39

BY STRAUSS, 279 © 1936 (Renewed) George Gershwin Music and Ira Gershwin Music.[50]

CACTUS TIME IN ARIZONA, 168 © 1954 (Renewed) WB Music Corp.[28]

CADET SONG, 122 © 1993 Ira Gershwin Music.[1]

CADETS ON PARADE, *See* WHEN CADETS PARADE

Call me whate'er you will—, 182

CALL ON US AGAIN, 364 © 1948 (Renewed) Ira Gershwin Music and Four Jays Music Company.[60]

Cares of day will fade away, 10

CASANOVA, ROMEO, AND DON JUAN, 148 © 1993 Ira Gershwin Music and Gilbert Keyes Music.[34]

Castles were crumbling, 351

CAVATINA—"THE LITTLE NAKED BOY," 332, 335 Lyric © 1993 Ira Gershwin Music.[1]

C'EST LA VIE, 225 Lyric © 1993 Ira Gershwin Music and Glocca Morra Music.[39]

CHANGING MY TUNE, 351 © 1946 (Renewed) Chappell & Co.[58]

CHANT OF LAW AND ORDER—"THE WORLD IS FULL OF VILLAINS," 334 Lyric © 1993 Ira Gershwin Music.[1]

Chari, vari, rastabari, 304

CHEERFUL LITTLE EARFUL, 233 © 1930 (Renewed) WB Music Corp. and Warner Bros. Inc.[43]

CHEERIO!, 40 Lyric © 1993 Ira Gershwin Music.[1]

CHIRP-CHIRP, 123 © 1928 (Renewed) WB Music Corp., Warner Bros. Inc., and Joro Music.[32]

CIRCUS DREAM, THE, *See* GREATEST SHOW ON EARTH, THE, et al.

CIVIC SONG—"COME TO FLORENCE," 324 Lyric © 1959 (Renewed) Ira Gershwin; 1993 Ira Gershwin Music.[1]

CIVIC SONG—"COME TO PARIS," 336 Lyric © 1959 (Renewed) Ira Gershwin; 1993 Ira Gershwin Music.[1]

Civilization is improving—, 100

CLAP YO' HANDS, 81 © 1926 (Renewed) WB Music Corp.[21]

Clap-a yo' hand! Slap-a yo' thigh!, 81

CLIMB UP THE SOCIAL LADDER, 209 © 1987 George Gershwin Music and Ira Gershwin Music.[12]

CLOISTERED FROM THE NOISY CITY, *See* UNION LEAGUE, THE

COLLECTIVE LOADING-TIME SONG, 305 Lyric © 1993 Ira Gershwin Music.[1]

COLUMBUS, *See* NINA, THE *PINTA*, THE *SANTA MARIA*, THE

COME ALONG, LET'S GAMBLE, *See* FUNNY FACE—FINALE, ACT I

COME! COME! COME CLOSER!, 105 © 1993 Ira Gershwin Music.[1]

COME-LOOK-AT-THE-WAR CHORAL SOCIETY, 100 © 1993 Ira Gershwin Music.[1]

Come on along! You can't go wrong!, 62

Come on and do what you do!, 142

Come on and listen, think what you're missin, 77

Come on, get in it—,122

Come on, there, sister!, 143

Come on, you children, gather around—, 81

Come out, come out, you stick-in-the-mud, 348

COME TO FLORENCE, *See* CIVIC SONG—"COME TO FLORENCE"

COME TO PARIS, *See* CIVIC SONG—"COME TO PARIS"

Comes a time in ev'ry life when love starts calling, 121

COMES THE REVOLUTION, 208, 210 © 1987 George Gershwin Music and Ira Gershwin Music.[12]

COMMERCIAL (CALYPSO), THE, *See* TV COMMERCIAL, THE

COMMERCIALS, 379 © 1954 Famous Music Corp. Lyric © 1993 Ira Gershwin Music.[1]

Commissioner Bauer! Commissioner Bauer! The wedding presents—, 198

Conditions as they are, 207

COULD YOU USE ME?, 162 © 1930 (Renewed) WB Music Corp.[28]

COURTIN' OF ELMER AND ELLA, THE, 362 © 1948 (Renewed) Ira Gershwin Music and Four Jays Music Company.[60]

COVER GIRL, 312 © 1943, 1944 (Renewed) PolyGram International Publishing, Inc.[52]

COZY NOOK SONG, THE, *See* TRIO—"I KNOW WHERE THERE'S A COZY NOOK"

COZY NOOK TRIO, THE, *See* TRIO—"I KNOW WHERE THERE'S A COZY NOOK"

Crash those cymbals!, 267

CRAZY QUILT, OPENING, *See* OPENING—CRAZY QUILT

Crooks and dips, you'd better beware!, 111

DANCE ALONE WITH YOU, 111 © 1927 (Renewed) WB Music Corp.[28]

Dance along with me, 32

DANCING IN THE STREETS, 195 © 1993 George Gershwin Music and Ira Gershwin Music.[12]

DANCING PARTNER, 376 © 1954 (Renewed) Harwin Music Corp. and Ira Gershwin Music.[64]

DANCING SHOES, 14 © 1921 (Renewed) WB Music Corp.[6]

DANCING TO OUR SCORE, *See* DANCING TO THE SCORE

DANCING TO THE SCORE, 257 Lyric © 1993 Ira Gershwin Music.[1]

DANCING WITH LUCILLA, 317 Lyric © 1993 Ira Gershwin Music.[1]

Darling, here's that song you inspired, 227

Darling, when the dew is on the rose, 348

Dat dirty dog Sportin' Life make believe, 241

DAWN OF A NEW DAY, 279 © 1938 (Renewed) George Gershwin Music and Ira Gershwin Music.[48]

DAY AFTER DAY, 126 Lyric © 1993 Ira Gershwin Music.[1]

Day is done and the sun descends in red splendor, 45

Days can be sunny, 166

DEAD MEN TELL NO TALES, 135 © 1993 Ira Gershwin Music.[1]

Dear lady, / My silk-and-lace-able you, 164

DEAR LITTLE GIRL, 80 © 1958 (Renewed) New World Music Company (Ltd.)[24]

Dear old correspondence alma mater, 42

DEAR OLD CORRESPONDENCE SCHOOL, 42 Lyric © 1993 Ira Gershwin Music.[1]

Dear one, it was fated, 199

Dear young woman, when I'm gazing, 330

Deep in the heart of me, 200

Delilah was a floozy, 165

DELISHIOUS, 172 © 1931 (Renewed) WB Music Corp.[28]

DEMON RUM, 354 © 1993 Ira Gershwin Music.[1]

DEW WAS ON THE ROSE, THE, 339 Lyric © 1993 Ira Gershwin Music.[1]

DIMPLE ON MY KNEE, THE, 176 © 1932 (Renewed) WB Music Corp.[28]

Ding a derry, ching a roo!, 169

DING-DONG, *See* RING-A-DING-A-DING-DONG DELL

DING-DONG-DELL, *See* BRING ON THE DING DONG DELL

DISSERTATION ON THE STATE OF BLISS (LOVE AND LEARN BLUES), 381 © 1954 (Renewed) Harwin Music Corp. and New World Music Company (Ltd.)[66]

DIZZILY, BUSILY, *See* TARANTELLA—"DIZZILY, BUSILY"

Dizzily, dizzily, moments go busily, 331

DO, DO, DO, 81 © 1926 (Renewed) WB Music Corp.[21]

DO WHAT YOU DO!, 142 © 1929 (Renewed) WB Music Corp. and Gilbert Keyes Music.[35]

Doctor Freud and Jung and Adler, Adler and Jung and Freud—, 202

DOES A DUCK LOVE WATER?, 257 Lyric © 1993 Ira Gershwin Music.[1]

Does the day look painful, 375

DOLLY, 18 © 1921 (Renewed) WB Music Corp. and Schuyler Greene Publishing Descendants.[9]

DON'T ASK!, 79 © 1958 (Renewed) New World Music Company (Ltd.)[24]

Don't ask me, dear, 317

DON'T BE A WOMAN IF YOU CAN, 340 © 1950 (Renewed) PolyGram International Publishing, Inc.[57]

DON'T LET'S BE BEASTLY TO THE GERMANS, 315 Lyric © 1993 Ira Gershwin Music.[1]

Don't look now, but summer's over, 347

Don't mind telling you, 104

Don't worry, little girl, 176

DON'T YOU REMEMBER?, 40 Lyric © 1993 Ira Gershwin Music.[1]

DOUBTING THOMAS, 388 © 1993 Ira Gershwin Music.[1]

Down with all these politicians!, 218

DOWN WITH EVERYONE WHO'S UP, 207, 217 © 1933 (Renewed) WB Music Corp. Additional material © 1987 George Gershwin Music and Ira Gershwin Music.[37]

Down with Kruger, the Dictator!, 220

Down with one and one make two!, 207

Dozens of girls would storm up, 164

DREAM SEQUENCE, 172 © 1993 Ira Gershwin Music.[1]

DREAMWORLD, 370 © 1951 (Renewed) Ira Gershwin Music and Chappell & Co.[61]

Dreary days are over, 312

DRESDEN NORTHWEST MOUNTED, THE, 197 © 1993 George Gershwin Music and Ira Gershwin Music.[12]

Drink! Clink!, 379

Drink, drink! *Donnervetter!*, 318

DRINK, DRINK, DRINK, *See* FATHERLAND, MOTHER OF THE BAND

Drop that long face! Come on, have your fling!, 267

DUCHESS'S ENTRANCE, 329 Lyric © 1993 Ira Gershwin Music.[1]

DUCHESS'S SONG, THE—"SING ME NOT A BALLAD," 329 © 1945 (Renewed) Chappell & Co. and Hampshire House Publishing Corp.[55]

DUET—"LOVE IS MY ENEMY," 335 Lyric © 1993 Ira Gershwin Music.[1]

DUET—"OUR MASTER IS FREE AGAIN," 326 Lyric © 1993 Ira Gershwin Music.[1]

DUKE'S ENTRY SONG, THE—"ALESSANDRO THE WISE," *See* DUKE'S SONG, THE—"ALESSANDRO THE WISE"

DUKE'S SONG, THE—"ALESSANDRO THE WISE," 327 Lyric © 1993 Ira Gershwin Music.[1]

Each time you trill a song with Bill, 52

EAST IS WEST, 140 © 1993 Ira Gershwin Music.[1]

ECONOMIC SITUATION, THE, 246 Lyric © 1993 Ira Gershwin Music.[1]

ELKS AND MASONS, THE, *See* ALL THE ELKS AND MASONS

Elmer came around one day in his new store clothes, 362

Embrace me, 164

EMBRACEABLE YOU, 164 © 1930 (Renewed) WB Music Corp.[28]

END OF A STRING, 47 © 1977 George Gershwin Music and Ira Gershwin Music.[12]

Enhance your resources, 351

ENJOY TODAY, 121 © 1993 Ira Gershwin Music.[1]

ENTRANCE OF COLONEL HOLMES, *See* MAN OF HIGH DEGREE, A

ENTRANCE OF FRENCH AMBASSADOR, 183 © 1932 (Renewed) WB Music Corp.[28]

ENTRANCE OF PHOTOGRAPHERS, *See* DIMPLE ON MY KNEE, THE

ENTRANCE OF SUPREME COURT JUDGES, 180 © 1932 (Renewed) WB Music Corp.[28]

ENTRANCE OF WINTERGREEN AND MARY, 189 © 1993 Ira Gershwin Music.[1]

Even though the wind is roaring, 32

EVENING STAR, 57 © 1987 George Gershwin Music and Ira Gershwin Music.[18]

Ever since my little girl was a little girl, 345

Ever since the world began, 30

EVERY GIRL HAS A METHOD OF HER OWN, 15 © 1993 Ira Gershwin Music.[1]

EVERY GIRL HAS A WAY, *See* EVERY GIRL HAS A METHOD OF HER OWN

Everything warrants, 325

Ev'ry day I, 383

Ev'ry day my love keeps grow-, 8

Ev'ry girl is dressed, 100

Ev'ry highball has its morning after, 168

Ev'ry jokesmith 'neath the sun, 8

Ev'ry man can find some consolation, 36

Ev'ry poached egg needs a piece of toast, 121

Ev'ry single time I hear your name, 29

Ev'ry Sunday, 141

Ev'ry time the Lorelei of long ago would play, 64

Ev'ry widow is a flirt, they say, 27

EV'RYBODY KNOWS I LOVE SOMEBODY, 117 © 1927 (Renewed) WB Music Corp.[28]

Ev'ryone thinks he's aces—, 262

Ev'ryone's asleep by nine o'clock since I have been here, 114

Ev'rything's the poetry of motion, 363

Excuse it if I'm lyrical, 318

Excuse me for a minute!, 321

EXIT, ATLANTIC CITY SCENE, 177 © 1932 (Renewed) WB Music Corp.[28]

EX-KINGS' NUMBER, *See* AT THE EX-KINGS' CLUB

EXPOSITION, 278 © 1993 Ira and Leonore Gershwin Trusts and George Balanchine Trust.

Extra! Extras ev'ry day, 280

FABRIC OF DREAMS, 34 © 1923 (Renewed) WB Music Corp., Warner Bros. Inc., and Stephen Ballentine Music.[16]

FANCY! FANCY!, 247 Lyric © 1993 Ira Gershwin Music.[1]

Far away in old Japan, a little maid is sad, 32

FAREWELL SONG—"THERE WAS LIFE, THERE WAS LOVE, THERE WAS LAUGHTER," 324 Lyric © 1993 Ira Gershwin Music.[1]

FASCINATING RHYTHM, 48 © 1924 (Renewed) WB Music Corp.[21]

Fascinating wedding, 49

FASCINATION, 26 Lyric © 1993 Ira Gershwin Music and Schuyler Greene Publishing Descendants.[15]

FASHION SHOW, 220 © 1931, 1933 (Renewed) WB Music Corp. Additional material © 1992 George Gershwin Music and Ira Gershwin Music.[37]

FATHERLAND, MOTHER OF THE BAND, 202 © 1987 George Gershwin Music and Ira Gershwin Music.[18]

FAWNCY! FAWNCY!, See FANCY! FANCY!

FEELING I'M FALLING, 132 © 1928 (Renewed) WB Music Corp.[28]

FEELING SENTIMENTAL, 144 © 1929 (Renewed) WB Music Corp. and Gilbert Keyes Music.[35]

FIDGETY FEET, 84 © 1926 (Renewed) WB Music Corp.[21]

FINALE ALLA TARANTELLA, See NIGHT MUSIC—"THE NIGHTTIME IS NO TIME FOR THINKING," et al.

FINALETTO—ATLANTIC CITY HOTEL SCENE, See AS THE CHAIRMAN OF THE COMMITTEE, et al.

FINALETTO—ACT I, SCENE 3, See FINALETTO—"I AM HAPPY HERE"

FINALETTO—"I AM HAPPY HERE," 328 Lyric © 1993 Ira Gershwin Music.[1]

FINEST OF THE FINEST, 110 © 1993 Ira Gershwin Music.[1]

FIRST LADY AND FIRST GENT, 219 © 1987 George Gershwin Music and Ira Gershwin Music.[12]

First you take a step, 252

FIVE A.M., 254 Lyric © 1993 Ira Gershwin Music.[1]

Five concur and four dissent, 216

FLETCHER'S AMERICAN CHEESE CHORAL SOCIETY, 90 © 1930 (Renewed) WB Music Corp. Additional material © 1991 George Gershwin Music and Ira Gershwin Music.[26]

FLETCHER'S AMERICAN CHOCOLATE CHORAL SOCIETY, 150 © 1930 (Renewed) WB Music Corp.[28]

FLORENCE, See CIVIC SONG—"COME TO FLORENCE"

FLORIDA, See WAITING FOR THE TRAIN

FLYING FETE, See AVIATOR

FOGGY DAY (IN LONDON TOWN), A, 271 © 1937 (Renewed) George Gershwin Music and Ira Gershwin Music.[48]

Folks, I was born, 94, 154

FOLLOW THE DRUM, 117 © 1977 George Gershwin Music and Ira Gershwin Music.[12]

FOLLOW THE MINSTREL BAND, 143 © 1993 Ira Gershwin Music and Gilbert Keyes Music.[34]

For I'm at my prime with the girls, 16

For it is "Steward, here, steward, I say," 18

FOR NO REASON AT ALL, 7 © Ira Gershwin Music and Stephen Ballentine Music.[3]

FOR THE LIFE OF ME, 338 © 1946 (Renewed) PolyGram International Publishing Corp.[57]

For there is magic in the air, 6

For when they hear the war drum sound, 114

FOR YOU, FOR ME, FOR EVERMORE, 354 © 1946 (Renewed) Chappell & Co.[58]

"Forever and a day is a long time," 234

Four little sirens, we, 14

Frankie, dear, your birthday gift reveals to me, 102

FRENCH PASTRY WALK, 26 © 1922 WB Music Corp. and Warner Bros. Inc.[10]

Frequently we bicker, 358

FREUD AND JUNG AND ADLER, 202 © 1993 George Gershwin Music and Ira Gershwin Music.[12]

Friends, Romans, and fellow men, 107

F'rinstance—FUR COATS!, 341

F'rinstance—HAIRDO!, 341

F'rinstance—NAIL POLISH!, 341

F'rinstance—PERFUME, 341

From Battery Park to Spuyten Duyvil, 361

From Brighton to Margate, 260

From field and tower, 305

From great Moscow to the farthest border, 305

From nine to five, half-alive, 60

FROM THE BALTIC TO THE PACIFIC, See COLLECTIVE LOADING-TIME SONG

From the Congo jungle it came, 143

From the Island of Manhattan to the Coast of Gold, 179

From the very first I made my mind up, 37

FUN TO BE FOOLED, 225 © 1934 (Renewed) Harwin Music Co., WB Music Corp., and Glocca Morra Music.[40]

FUNNY FACE, 102 © 1927 (Renewed) WB Music Corp.[28]

FUNNY FACE—FINALE, ACT I, 105 © 1977 George Gershwin Music and Ira Gershwin Music.[12]

FUNNY FACE—OPENING, ACT I, See AVIATOR

FUNNY FACE—OPENING, ACT II, See IN THE SWIM

Funny thing that, 254

FUTURE MRS. COLEMAN, THE, 349 Lyric © 1993 Ira Gershwin Music.[1]

GABRIEL, GABRIEL, BLOW YOUR GOLDEN HORN, See TRUMPETER, BLOW YOUR GOLDEN HORN

GAMBLER OF THE WEST, THE, 169 © 1993 Ira Gershwin Music.[1]

GARÇON, S'IL VOUS PLAÎT, 183, 185 © 1932 (Renewed) WB Music Corp.[28]

GATHER YE ROSEBUDS, 75 © 1987 George Gershwin Music and Ira Gershwin Music.[18]

GAZOOKA, THE, 249 © 1936 (Renewed) Chappell & Co. and Ira Gershwin Music.[47]

GAZOOKA, THE (sketch), 249 © 1993 Ira and Leonore Gershwin Trusts and David Freedman Publishing Descendants.

Gee! But it's great to get up in the morning, 99

Gee! It's simply grand to have the gang around, 85

GENERAL'S GONE TO A PARTY, THE, 211 © 1987 George Gershwin Music and Ira Gershwin Music.[12]

Gentlemen, duty calls. . . . , 188

Get my hatter! Call my tailor!, 261

GET THAT LONG FACE LOST, See LOSE THAT LONG FACE

Get the right food for your pet—, 380

GIRL CRAZY—ENTR'ACTE, 166 © 1954 (Renewed) WB Music Corp.[28]

GIRL CRAZY—FINALE, ACT I, 166 © 1954 (Renewed) WB Music Corp.[28]

GIRL CRAZY—FINALETTO, ACT I, See GOLDFARB, THAT'S I'M!

GIRL CRAZY—OPENING, ACT I, SCENE 3, See BRONCO BUSTERS

GIRL CRAZY—OPENING, ACT II, See LAND OF THE GAY CABALLERO

GIRL I LOVE, THE, See MAN I LOVE, THE

GIRL OF THE MOMENT, 284 © 1941 (Renewed) Chappell & Co. and Hampshire House Publishing Corp.[55]

Girlie, late and early, 112

Girls and boys, come and try it, 108

Girls, I've studied osculation, 42

Give a cheer for Alma Mater!, 122

GIVE A GIRL A BREAK, 367 © 1951 (Renewed) Ira Gershwin Music and Chappell & Co.[61]

Give in!, 73

Give up the fond embrace, 353

GLAD TIDINGS IN THE AIR, 120 © 1993 Ira Gershwin Music.[1]

GLAMOUR DREAM, See OH, FABULOUS ONE, et al.

Go have yourself a time—, 376

Go lose that long face, that long face—, 375

Going through my previous lives, 349

GOLDFARB, THAT'S I'M!, 165 © 1954 (Renewed) WB Music Corp.[28]

GONDOLIER, 10 Lyric © 1993 Ira Gershwin Music.[1]

Gone is the day of the show girl, 243

GOOD-BYE TO ALL THAT, 347 © 1946 (Renewed) PolyGram International Publishing, Inc.[57]

GOOD-BYE TO THE OLD LOVE, 135 © 1993 Ira Gershwin Music.[1]

Good evening, ladies fair and fellow pirates!, 129

Good little Susan stays at home—, 126

Got a little rhythm, a rhythm, a rhythm, 48

GOT A RAINBOW, 131 © 1928 (Renewed) WB Music Corp.[28]

GOTTA HAVE ME GO WITH YOU, 373 © 1954 (Renewed) Harwin Music Corp. and New World Music Company (Ltd.)[63]

Grab a cab and go down, 72

GREATEST SHOW ON EARTH, THE, 291 © 1941 (Renewed) Chappell & Co. and Hampshire House Publishing Corp.[55]

GREEN LIGHT AHEAD, 376 © 1954 (Renewed) Harwin Music Corp. and Ira Gershwin Music.[64]

GUESS WHO?, 79 © 1993 Ira Gershwin Music.[1]

GUSH-GUSH-GUSHING, See GUSHING

GUSHING, 65 © 1993 Ira Gershwin Music.[1]

Hail! Hail! The ruler of our gov'ment!, 180

Hail! Hail! The rulers of our gov'ment!, 189

HAIL THE HAPPY COUPLE, 197 © 1993 George Gershwin Music and Ira Gershwin Music.[12]

HALF OF IT, DEARIE, BLUES, THE, 52 © 1924 (Renewed) WB Music Corp.[21]

HANG ON TO ME, 47 © 1924 (Renewed) WB Music Corp.[21]

HANGIN' AROUND WITH YOU, 154 © 1929 (Renewed) WB Music Corp.[28]

HANGING THROTTLEBOTTOM IN THE MORNING, 219 © 1987 George Gershwin Music and Ira Gershwin Music.[12]

HAPPY BIRTHDAY, 140 © 1993 Ira Gershwin Music and Gilbert Keyes Music.[34]

HAPPY ENDING, 21 Lyric © 1993 Ira Gershwin Music.[1]

Happy, happy workers, we, 90, 150

Happy hearts, happy hearts mingling—, 119

HAPPY NEWS, THE, See I WON'T GIVE UP

HARBOR OF DREAMS, 75 © 1993 Ira Gershwin Music.[1]

HARD TO REPLACE, 282 Lyric © 1993 Ira Gershwin Music.[1]

Hark, fairest maid, 45

Hark to the song of the lover, 146

HARLEM RIVER CHANTY, 74 Lyric © 1959 (Renewed) Ira Gershwin; © 1968 New World Music Company (Ltd.)[23]

HARLEM SERENADE, 143 © 1929 (Renewed) WB Music Corp. and Gilbert Keyes Music.[35]

Hate to see you go, but it's the final curtain, 364

Have some pity on an Easterner, 162

Haven't the gift of gab—I sputter, 229

Haven't you a lot of things to say to me?, 150

HE HASN'T A THING EXCEPT ME, 244 © 1971 Chappell & Co. and Ira Gershwin Music.[46]

He is a typical self-made American!, 151

He is stubborn—We must teach him, 184

He is toodle-ooing all his lady loves, 180

HE KNOWS MILK, 154 © 1930 (Renewed) WB Music Corp.[28]

HE LOVES AND SHE LOVES, 106 © 1927 (Renewed) WB Music Corp.[28]

HE-MAN, THE, 65 © 1993 Ira Gershwin Music and Stephen Ballentine Music.[3]

He must be able to dance, 12, 13

He will be six foot two, 346

Hear me, ev'ryone, 123

Hear the bells in the belfry go ding-dong, 158

HEAR YE! HEAR YE!, 334 Lyric © 1993 Ira Gershwin Music.[1]

HEAVEN ON EARTH, 84 © 1926 (Renewed) WB Music Corp. and Warner Bros. Inc.[25]

HEAVENLY DAY, 349 Lyric © 1993 Ira Gershwin Music.[1]

HELL OF A HOLE, A, 217 © 1992 George Gershwin Music and Ira Gershwin Music. Additional material © 1933 (Renewed) WB Music Corp.[36]

HELLO, GOOD MORNING, 182 © 1932 (Renewed) WB Music Corp.[28]

Hello, hello, hello, 297

Hello! How are you?, 107

Hello, how-de-do? Hello, how-de-do?, 302

Here comes our little captain!, 72

Here, here come the minstrels!, 365

HERE, STEWARD, 18 Lyric © 1993 Ira Gershwin Music.[1]

Here's a bit of all right, 102

HERE'S A KISS FOR CINDERELLA, See KISS FOR CINDERELLA, A

Here's a pen you ought to know—, 380

Here's some information, 182

Here's the silver moon from the sky up there, 379

HERE'S WHAT I'M HERE FOR, 374 © 1954 (Renewed) Harwin Music Corp. and New World Music Company (Ltd.)[63]

He's a bronco buster, 166

He's living high in Beverly, 232

He's no collection, 321

HE'S NOT HIMSELF, 201 © 1993 George Gershwin Music and Ira Gershwin Music.[12]

HE'S OVERSEXED!, 202 © 1993 George Gershwin Music and Ira Gershwin Music.[12]

He's the only man, 196

Hey, folks! Say, folks!, 143

Hey! How about a dance?, 86, 114

Hey, stunning, 367

Hey there! Strike the band up!, 280

HIGH HAT, 103 © 1927 WB Music Corp.[28]

HI-HO!, 267 © 1936 (Renewed) George Gershwin Music and Ira Gershwin Music.[48]

Hist'ry discloses, 125

Holding hands at midnight, 272

HOLLYWOOD DAYDREAM, See BOSS IS BRINGING HOME A BRIDE, THE, et al.

HOLLYWOOD PARTY, See PARTY PARLANDO

Home— / That's where the sunshine learned to shine, 143

HOME BLUES, 143 © 1990, 1993 Ira Gershwin Music and Gilbert Keyes Music.[34]

HOME IN SAN FERNANDO VALLEY, 301 Lyric © 1993 Ira Gershwin Music.[1]

HOME-LOVIN' GAL, 147 © 1993 Ira Gershwin Music and Gilbert Keyes Music.[34]

HOME-LOVIN' MAN, 147 © 1993 Ira Gershwin Music and Gilbert Keyes Music.[34]

HOMEWARD BOUND, 99 © 1991 George Gershwin Music and Ira Gershwin Music.[12]

Honestly, I thought you wouldn't, 353

HONEYMOON, 20 © 1921 (Renewed) WB Music Corp.[7]

HONORABLE MOON (1923), 32 Lyric © 1993 Ira Gershwin Music and Stephen Ballentine Music.[3]

HONORABLE MOON (1941), 314 © 1941 (Renewed) Chappell & Co.[51]

HOPE FOR THE BEST, 345 Lyric © 1993 Ira Gershwin Music.[1]

HOPING THAT SOMEDAY YOU'D CARE, 97 © 1987 George Gershwin Music and Ira Gershwin Music.[18]

HOT HINDOO, 34 © 1923 (Renewed) WB Music Corp.[19]

HOT NUMBER, 261 Lyric © 1993 Ira Gershwin Music.[1]

Hotsy-totsy! Heebie-jeebie! Ev'rything is jake!, 140

HOW ABOUT A BOY?, 156 © 1930 (Renewed) WB Music Corp.[28]

HOW ABOUT A MAN?, 98 © 1991 George Gershwin Music and Ira Gershwin Music.[12]

HOW BEAUTIFUL, 177 © 1932 (Renewed) WB Music Corp.[28]

HOW CAN I WIN YOU NOW?, 62 © 1993 Ira Gershwin Music and Stephen Ballentine Music.[3]

HOW COULD I FORGET?, 141 © 1993 Ira Gershwin Music and Gilbert Keyes Music.[34]

How dry I am!, 136

How glad the many millions, 128

HOW LONG HAS THIS BEEN GOING ON?, 109 © 1927 (Renewed) WB Music Corp.[28]

How most unique, how ultra chic our attitude!, 340

How sad it is to be a Sing-Song Girl, 139
How sensitive the spirit!, 340
How wonderful that I'm beholding, 374
HOW WONDERFULLY FORTUNATE, *See*
    ARIETTA—"HOW WONDERFULLY FORTUNATE"
HOW YOUNG I AM, *See* YOUNGER GENERATION
Howda do, Papa—Howda do, Mamma—, 41
HUBBY, 31 Lyric © 1993 Ira Gershwin Music.[1]
Hum a little tune, 64
HURDY-GURDY MAN, THE, 34 © 1993 Ira
    Gershwin Music.[1]
Hush! Hush! Hush!, 112
HUSSAR MARCH, 114 © 1927 (Renewed) WB
    Music Corp.[8]
HUXLEY, 284 © 1941 (Renewed) Chappell & Co.
    and Hampshire House Publishing Corp.[55]

I am a typical self-made American, 91, 151
I AM HAPPY HERE, *See* FINALETTO—"I AM HAPPY
    HERE"
I am just a little girl, 69
I am looking forward to the day, 5
I am not like Circe, 329
I AM ONLY HUMAN AFTER ALL, 233 © 1930
    (Renewed) WB Music Corp., Warner Bros.
    Inc., and Vernon Duke Publishing Co.[42]
I am the Ambassador of France, 183
I CAME HERE, 36 © 1924 (Renewed) WB Music
    Corp. and Warner Bros. Inc.[10]
I came here; I saw you, 36
I came here, saw, like, love, tell—yours, 37
I came in—thought I'd been here before, 59
I can dance the old gavotte, 26
I can find a rhyme for Lucy—, 333
I can tell you where the jewels are, 20
I CAN'T BE BOTHERED NOW, 269 © 1937
    (Renewed) George Gershwin Music and Ira
    Gershwin Music.[48]
I CAN'T GET STARTED, 254 © 1935 (Renewed)
    Chappell & Co. and Ira Gershwin Music.[47]
I come from the bargain basement—, 124
I come highly recommended, 124
I could cry / Salty tears, 110
I COULDN'T HOLD MY MAN, 228 Lyric © 1993 Ira
    Gershwin Music and Glocca Morra Music.[39]
I didn't mean to, 104
I don't know how I won you—, 338
I don't know if I'm coming or going—, 296
I DON'T THINK I'LL FALL IN LOVE TODAY, 130 ©
    1928 (Renewed) WB Music Corp.[28]
I fetch his slippers, 168
I find you so attractive!, 194
I FORGOT WHAT I STARTED TO SAY, 119 © 1993
    Ira Gershwin Music.[1]
I found me a dancing partner, 376
I give you His Highness, 244
I got a cousin in Milwaukee, 196

I GOT PLENTY O' NUTHIN', 236 © 1935
    (Renewed) George Gershwin Music, Ira
    Gershwin Music, and DuBose and Dorothy
    Heyward Memorial Fund Publishing.[45]
I GOT RHYTHM, 165 © 1930 (Renewed) WB
    Music Corp.[28]
I grow all excited and tinglish, 158
I HAD JUST BEEN PARDONED, *See* ARIETTA—"I
    HAD JUST BEEN PARDONED"
I had to wait till I was seventeen, 91
I have a report, 211
I have been haunted by a sound that I heard, 4
I have definite ideas about the deficit, 180
I have definite ideas about the Philippines, 180
I have found my little girl, 69
I have learned from almost every song, 232
I have seen a movie show without a theme song,
    169
I HAVE YOU, *See* AND I HAVE YOU
I hear the rustle of the trees, 92
I hope you've missed me as I missed you, 80
I just heard a spiritual, 62
I JUST LOOKED AT YOU, 144 © 1993 Ira
    Gershwin Music and Gilbert Keyes Music.[34]
I kept hoping, hoping, hoping, 317
I KNEW HIM WHEN, 231 © 1964 (Renewed) New
    World Music Company (Ltd.) and Harwin
    Music Co.[41]
I knew, my dear, from the moment that we met,
    125
I know a boy who is very much in love, 66
I KNOW A FOUL BALL, 216 © 1987 George
    Gershwin Music and Ira Gershwin Music.[12]
I know just how I got this way, 174
I KNOW SOMEBODY (WHO LOVES YOU), 66 Lyric ©
    1993 Ira Gershwin Music.[1]
I know that I should be above, 233
I know the way, 42
I KNOW WHERE THERE'S A COZY NOOK, *See*
    TRIO—"I KNOW WHERE THERE'S A COZY
    NOOK"
I know where there's a nosy cook—, 330
I lead a regiment bold, 114
I left my mademoiselle in New Rochelle, 156
I look and see the stormy skies, 369
I love the simple life, 14
I LOVE TO RHYME, 276 © 1937 (Renewed)
    George Gershwin Music and Ira Gershwin
    Music.[48]
I love to stroll along with Molly on the shore, 24
I love your funny face, 102
I LOVES YOU, PORGY, 239 © 1935 (Renewed)
    George Gershwin Music, Ira Gershwin Music,
    and DuBose and Dorothy Heyward Memorial
    Fund Publishing.[45]
I may be nothin' on Fift' Avenue, 65
I MEAN TO SAY, 150 © 1929 (Renewed) WB
    Music Corp.[28]

I met him and he met me—, 86
I moon! I moan!, 272
I MUST BE HOME BY TWELVE O'CLOCK, 142 ©
    1929 (Renewed) WB Music Corp. and Gilbert
    Keyes Music.[35]
I never heard you so bold before, 327
I never knew love was so nice, 142
I never stayed up late, 147
I often feel I'd like to get away, 21
I often wonder, 280
I once had a father, 195
I place my faith, 135
I recited once when I was small, 15
I remember the bliss, 82
I sang my song, 234
I say, listen to this, 247
I say, old tin of fruit, 247
I say to me ev'ry morning, 286
I should feel oh, so flurried—, 146
I sing of a dress for my lady, 34
I sing the praise of good old days, 111
I SPEAK ENGLISH NOW, 140 © 1993 Ira Gershwin
    Music.[1]
I think you very beautiful, 327
I thought you were fallin' for Andy McPherson,
    359
I traveled hither, 174
I trust no man but a dead man, 135
I USED TO BE ABOVE LOVE, 262 © 1936
    (Renewed) Chappell & Co. and Ira Gershwin
    Music.[47]
I used to laugh at—, 10
I WANT A YES-MAN, 66 © 1925 (Renewed) WB
    Music Corp., Irving Caesar Music Corp., and
    Mirose Music.[22]
I WANT TO BE A WAR BRIDE, 158 © 1993 Ira
    Gershwin Music.[1]
I want to be like that gal on the river, 194
I want to dally in a valley, 126
I want to learn a new step ev'ry day, 26
I want to make my getaway, 126
I WANT TO MARRY A MARIONETTE, 135 © 1987
    George Gershwin Music and Ira Gershwin
    Music.[29]
I want to sing of that gal on the river, 194
I want you to know, 313
I wants to stay here, but I ain't worthy, 239
I was a stranger in the city, 272
I was above love, 134
I WAS DOING ALL RIGHT, 275 © 1937 (Renewed)
    George Gershwin Music and Ira Gershwin
    Music.[48]
I WAS NAÏVE, 282 © 1938 (Renewed) Betty Kern
    Miller and Ira Gershwin Music.[54]
I was once so naïve, 282
I WAS THE MOST BEAUTIFUL BLOSSOM, 180 ©
    1932 (Renewed) WB Music Corp.[28]
I wasn't in the red financially, 281

I wish that I were young again, 199

I WON'T GIVE UP, 388 © 1987 George Gershwin Music and Ira Gershwin Music.[18]

I WON'T SAY I WILL, BUT I WON'T SAY I WON'T, 33 © 1923 (Renewed) WB Music Corp., Warner Bros. Inc., and Stephen Ballentine Music.[16]

I'd do a lot for / Your eyes! Your smile!, 109

I'd have no roughneck taxi drivers there, 21

If a maid I chance to dandle, 116

If a person starts to quiver, 202

If, as, and when you've got a long face, 375

If ever fortune had an unlucky victim, 97

If ever you could get in trouble, 115

If happiness is failing you—Tell the doc!, 106

IF I BECAME THE PRESIDENT, 153 © 1930 (Renewed) WB Music Corp.[28]

If I eat too much jam—, 305

If I had my way, 61

If I made you the ruler, 153

If I say so, I was rather eligible, 158

If I should call on you tomorrow, 233

If I should suddenly start to sing, 271

If I'm a guy who doesn't seem so merry, 119

If it's true that love affairs, 69

IF LOVE REMAINS, 318 © 1945 (Renewed) Chappell & Co. and Hampshire House Publishing Corp.[55]

If someone like you, 25

IF THAT'S PROPAGANDA, 314 © 1941 (Renewed) Chappell & Co.[51]

If the goblins have got you, 267

If they ever catch you speeding in Peoria, Peoria, Peoria—, 228

If things keep going at the rate they're going, 309

IF THIS BE PROPAGANDA, See IF THAT'S PROPAGANDA

If we girls all should 'fess up why, 65

If we were Mr. and Mrs., 8

If you are a woman who is a wife, 374

If you ask me what place, 164

If you believe that a miracle can occur, 280

If you could wear top hats like Buchanan—, 248

If you ever take a trip, 57

If you hang on to me, 47

IF YOU ONLY KNEW, 6 © 1993 Ira Gershwin Music.[1]

If you want a girl who's sentimental, 44

If you want to know what's what, here's the spot, 52

IF YOU WILL TAKE OUR TIP, See IN THE SWIM

If you wonder why I am dressed up in my best, 161

If you'd the style of Anthony Eden—, 248

If you'll tie up with me, 220

If your mate, you find, is out of date, 32

If you're bent on viewing / Something doing, 325, 336

If you're born that way you have to be a woman, 341

If you're looking for a playmate, 79

If you've wondered where the good songs go, 34

I'll build a Stairway to Paradise, 27

(I'LL BUILD A) STAIRWAY TO PARADISE, See STAIRWAY TO PARADISE, (I'LL BUILD A)

I'll buy me some plottage, 139

I'll call round about, 61

I'll never have the fame of Mussolini, 197

I'll say I'm having a hot time, 142

I'll say Piccadilly's not a bit like Broadway, 9

I'LL SUPPLY THE TITLE (YOU'LL SUPPLY THE TUNE), 282 Lyric © 1993 Ira Gershwin Music.[1]

ILLEGITIMATE DAUGHTER, THE, 183, 185 © 1932 (Renewed) WB Music Corp.[28]

I'M A COLLECTOR OF MOONBEAMS, 232 Lyric © 1993 Ira Gershwin Music and Glocca Morra Music.[39]

I'm a glum one; it's explainable, 254, 256

I'm a little jazz bird, 53

I'm a physician whose mission you know—, 106

I'M A POACHED EGG, 383 © 1964 (Renewed) Chappell & Co.[58]

I'm about the luckiest girl in the world, 198

I'm about the luckiest man in the world—, 198

I'M ABOUT TO BE A MOTHER, 185, 186 © 1932 (Renewed) WB Music Corp.[28]

I'm aesthetic, poetic, 328

I'm afraid, afraid you're far too near me!, 327

I'm after the crooks, 193

I'm Bidin' My Time, 161

I'm blue! I'm through!, 228

I'm fed up with discussions, 70

I'm five feet nowt, my eyes are brown, 124

I'm growing tired of lovey-dove theme songs, 233

I'm in love fortissimo, 364

I'M JUST A BUNDLE OF SUNSHINE, 146 © 1993 Ira Gershwin Music and Gilbert Keyes Music.[34]

I'm just a home-lovin' gal, 147

I'm just a home-lovin' man, 147

I'm lonesome all through the day, 33

I'm looking for that lost barber shop chord—, 77

I'm making up for all the years, 152

I'm no Apollo, I'm granting you that, 86

I'm not as rich as Henry Ford is, 110

I'M NOT COMPLAINING, 278 Lyric © 1993 Ira Gershwin Music.[1]

I'M NOT MYSELF, 229 Lyric © 1993 Ira Gershwin Music and Glocca Morra Music.[39]

I'm not what you'd call irresistibly handsome, 19

I'M OFF THE DOWNBEAT, 376 © 1954 (Renewed) Harwin Music Corp. and Ira Gershwin Music.[64]

I'M OUT FOR NO GOOD REASON TONIGHT, 147 © 1993 Ira Gershwin Music and Gilbert Keyes Music.[34]

I'M SHARING MY WEALTH, 260 Lyric © 1993 Ira Gershwin Music.[1]

I'm sharpening knives for me husband, 260

I'm six foot tall, my eyes are blue, 124

I'm so elated, 18

I'm so tired of going places, doing things, 147

I'M SOMETHIN' ON AVENUE A, 65 © 1993 Ira Gershwin Music and Stephen Ballentine Music.[3]

I'm the Gambler of the West, 169

I'm the unofficial, unofficial, 93, 152

I'm through with yeast by Fleischmann, 228

I'M TICKLED SILLY, 20 Lyric © 1993 Ira Gershwin Music.[1]

I'm tired of hopeless hopin'—, 260

I'm tired of keeping up with the economic trends, 246

Imagine living with someone, 344

IMAGINE ME WITHOUT MY YOU, 36 © 1924 (Renewed) WB Music Corp. and Warner Bros. Inc.[10]

Imagine not having to cope with somebody new, 348

IMPEACHMENT PROCEEDING, 185 © 1932 (Renewed) WB Music Corp.[28]

IMPROMPTU IN TWO KEYS, See YELLOW BLUES

In a chimney setting, 261

In Budapest one night, a Gypsy, 300

In my dreams you've always played the leading part, 119

In Naples one night a wandering Gypsy, 334

IN OUR UNITED STATE, 368 © 1951, 1953 (Renewed) EMI Feist Catalog Inc.[62]

In Peacock Alley, 24

In reading my Britannica, 56

IN SARDINIA, 63 © 1987 George Gershwin Music and Ira Gershwin Music.[18]

IN THE MANDARIN'S ORCHID GARDEN, 138 © 1930 (Renewed) WB Music Corp.[28]

IN THE MERRY MONTH OF MAYBE, 233 © 1931 (Renewed) WB Music Corp. and Warner Bros. Inc.[10]

IN THE RATTLE OF THE BATTLE, 155 © 1930 (Renewed) WB Music Corp.[28]

In the springtime you discover, 17

IN THE SWIM, 105 © 1983, 1984 George Gershwin Music and Ira Gershwin Music.[29]

In the urgency / Of the emergency, 315

In the very first dream that I ever had, 64

In the very merry month of Maybe, 233

In this vale of tears you're either baby boy, 341

IN THREE-QUARTER TIME, 193 Lyric © (Renewed) Ira Gershwin; © 1993 George Gershwin Music and Ira Gershwin Music.[12]

In town we used to fret away, 163

In your eyes I see, 30

Into a cabaret, one fatal day, 53

Into the center, 30

INVALID ENTRANCE, 112 © 1993 Ira Gershwin Music.[1]

ISLAND IN THE WEST INDIES, 245 © 1935 (Renewed) Chappell & Co. and Ira Gershwin Music.[47]

ISLE IN THE WEST INDIES, *See* ISLAND IN THE WEST INDIES

ISN'T IT A PITY?, 195 © 1932 (Renewed) WB Music Corp.[28]

ISN'T IT GRAND, *See* OH, KAY!—FINALE, ACT I

ISN'T IT WONDERFUL, 42 © 1924 (Renewed) WB Music Corp.[8]

IT AIN'T NECESSARILY SO, 237 © 1935 (Renewed) George Gershwin Music, Ira Gershwin Music, and DuBose and Dorothy Heyward Memorial Fund Publishing.[45]

IT COULD HAVE HAPPENED TO ANYONE, 321 Lyric © 1993 Ira Gershwin Music.[1]

It gave me joy to be a Boy Scout many years ago, 109

It happened down at the Golden Gate, 168

IT HAPPENED TO HAPPEN TO ME, *See* IT COULD HAVE HAPPENED TO ANYONE

It happened to me, 277

IT HAPPENS EV'RY TIME, 369 © 1952, 1953 (Renewed) EMI Feist Catalog Inc.[62]

It is never too late for man to mend, 43

It isn't good for one to stay up late, and so, 73

IT ISN'T WHAT YOU DID, 217 © 1987 George Gershwin Music and Ira Gershwin Music.[12]

IT LOOKS LIKE LIZA, 284 © 1941 (Renewed) Chappell & Co. and Hampshire House Publishing Corp.[55]

It makes no difference who you are—, 147

It makes no diff'rence if I roam, 16

It seems as if this trip, 17

It seems to be the right thing now, 31

It sets me all aglow—, 9

It used to be that a girl could get away, 246

IT WAS LONG AGO, 229 Lyric © 1993 Ira Gershwin Music and Glocca Morra Music.[39]

It was time to go, 253

IT'S A DIFFERENT WORLD, 249 Lyric © 1993 Ira Gershwin Music.[1]

It's a funny thing, 196

IT'S A GREAT LITTLE WORLD!, 72 © 1926 (Renewed) WB Music Corp.[21]

IT'S A NEW WORLD, 374 © 1954 (Renewed) Harwin Music Corp. and New World Music Company (Ltd.)[63]

It's always been a pleasure, 333

It's always "Uh-uh! uh-uh! uh-uh! uh-uh!" when I come closer, 38

It's an old, old, old variation, 246

It's finished. The portrait is painted!, 287

It's good to see familiar faces—, 80

It's great to be a sailor, 74

IT'S HERE TO STAY, *See* LOVE IS HERE TO STAY

It's Just Another Rhum-ba, 277

IT'S MINE, IT'S YOURS, 379 Lyric © 1993 Ira Gershwin Music.[1]

IT'S NEVER TOO LATE TO MENDELSSOHN, 295 Lyric © 1993 Ira Gershwin Music.[1]

It's never too late to Mendelssohn, 83, 295

It's off with the old, on with the new, 213

It's rumored by neighbors who have seen us, 125

It's terrific! The greatest musical picture of all time!, 252

It's time for little boys like you to be in bed, 73

It's very clear, 276

I've an i-de-a, 158

I've been all along the Gay White Way, 14

I'VE BRUSHED MY TEETH, 211 © 1987 George Gershwin Music and Ira Gershwin Music.[12] (Includes lyrics © 1959 [Renewed] Ira Gershwin)

I've flown around the world in a plane, 255, 256

I'VE GOT A CRUSH ON YOU, 128 © 1930 (Renewed) WB Music Corp.[28]

I'VE GOT A RAINBOW, *See* GOT A RAINBOW

I've got a rhythm—a raggedy rhythm—and oh!, 31

I've got a secret that I can conceal no longer, 170

(I'VE GOT) BEGINNER'S LUCK, *See* BEGINNER'S LUCK (I'VE GOT)

I've got beginner's luck, 264

I've got fidgety feet, fidgety feet, fidgety feet!, 84

I've got the You-Don't-Know-the-Half-of-It-Dearie Blues, 52

I'VE GOT TO BE THERE, 200 © 1933 (Renewed) WB Music Corp.[28]

I've got to go, 361

I've just finished writing an advertisement, 12, 13

I've just got a feeling, 146

I've met the one and only one, 19

I've never traveled further north, 227

I've not been entangled in romances, 18

I've often been a best man, 108

I've often wanted a class reunion, 42

I've one aim in life, 12

I've seen the one I care for, 313

I've seen the one I go for, 313

I've taken a fancy to the U.S.A., 16

I'VE TURNED THE CORNER, 281 Lyric © 1993 Ira Gershwin Music.[1]

I've written you a song, 173

JENNY, *See* SAGA OF JENNY, THE

Jenny made up her mind when she was three, 294

JILTED, 185 © 1932 (Renewed) WB Music Corp.[28]

JIM, CONSIDER WHAT YOU ARE DOING!, 98 © 1930 (Renewed) WB Music Corp.[28]

Jim, how could you do such a thing?, 95, 155

John, the names they call you mean nothing—, 182

JOLLY TAR AND THE MILKMAID, THE, 269 © 1937 (Renewed) George Gershwin Music and Ira Gershwin Music.[48]

JUANITA, 53 © 1977 George Gershwin Music and Ira Gershwin Music.[12]

Just a little block of U.S. Steel, 38

Just a little while ago, 132

Just a whisper, soft and low, 312

JUST ANOTHER RHUMBA, 277 © 1937 (Renewed) George Gershwin Music and Ira Gershwin Music.[48]

Just before Dan Cupid knew of us, 42

Just before I go, I'd like to know, 49

Just give me that Manhattan Downbeat, 361

JUST IN CASE, *See* MARCH OF THE SOLDIERS OF THE DUCHY—"JUST IN CASE"

Just learn this little song, 25

JUST LIKE YOU, 19 © 1921 (Renewed) WB Music Corp. and Warner Bros. Inc.[10]

Just take a word like "hubby," 7

Just tell me what to do, 12

Just think of what love leads to, 131

Just to know that you are mine, 12

JUST TO KNOW YOU ARE MINE, 12 © 1921 (Renewed) WB Music Corp.[6]

KATINKITSCHKA, 172 © 1931 (Renewed) WB Music Corp.[28]

KAZOOKA, THE, *See* GAZOOKA, THE

Keep the trumpeter blowing, 158

KENNETH WON THE YACHTING RACE, *See* TELL ME MORE—FINALETTO, ACT II, SCENE 1

KEY TO MY HEART, THE, 234 © 1931 (Renewed) WB Music Corp. and Louis Alter Publishing Descendants.[44]

KICKIN' THE CLOUDS AWAY, 62 © 1925 (Renewed) WB Music Corp., Warner Bros. Inc., and Stephen Ballentine Music.[16]

KIND OF FRIEND, THE, *See* LET ME BE A FRIEND TO YOU

KING CAN DO NO WRONG, THE, 116 © 1977 Ira Gershwin Music, Sigmund Romberg Publishing Descendants, and P. G. Wodehouse Publishing Descendants.[31]

KISS FOR CINDERELLA, A, 180 © 1931 (Renewed) WB Music Corp.[28]

KISS ME, THAT'S ALL, 42 Lyric © 1993 Ira Gershwin Music.[1]

KITCHENETTE, 5 Lyric © 1993 Ira Gershwin Music and Stephen Ballentine Music.[3]

Knew it from the start—, 71
KNIFE THROWER'S WIFE, THE, 260 Lyric © 1993 Ira Gershwin Music.[1]
KNITTING SONG, THE, *See* OH, THIS IS SUCH A LOVELY WAR
K-RA-ZY FOR YOU, 130 © 1928 (Renewed) WB Music Corp.[28]

La, la, singing ev'ry morning, 150
LADDIE DADDIE (lyrics missing), 47
Ladies and Gentlemen, I Take Pride in Introducing, 292, 297
Ladies and gentlemen, / Just because you don't see me . . . , 243
Ladies and gentlemen, ladies and gentlemen, 145
Ladies and gentlemen, may we present to you, 249
Ladies and gentlemen, you are about to witness a slice of life, 225
LADY, BE GOOD!—FINALE ACT I, 51 © 1977 George Gershwin Music and Ira Gershwin Music.[12]
LADY, BE GOOD!—OPENING, ACT II, *See* LINGER IN THE LOBBY
LADY, BE GOOD!—OPENING, ACT II (ORIGINAL), *See* WEATHERMAN *and* RAINY-AFTERNOON GIRLS
LADY FAIR, *See* MY FAIR LADY
Lady, I was always classed, 51
LADY IN THE DARK—FIRST DREAM SEQUENCE, *See* OH, FABULOUS ONE, et al.
LADY IN THE DARK—SECOND DREAM SEQUENCE, *See* MAPLETON HIGH CHORALE, et al.
LADY IN THE DARK—THIRD DREAM SEQUENCE, *See* GREATEST SHOW ON EARTH, THE, et al.
LADY IN THE DARK—FOURTH DREAM SEQUENCE, *See* BOSS IS BRINGING HOME A BRIDE, THE, et al.
Lady, Lady Bountiful, 98
Lady, let me go!, 200
Lady, look at me, 156
LADY LUCK, 69 © 1977 George Gershwin Music and Ira Gershwin Music.[12]
LADY OF THE MOON, 138 © 1993 Ira Gershwin Music.[1]
Lady, you'd be awf'ly hard to replace—, 282
LAND AROUND US, THE, 380 © 1954 (Renewed) Harwin Music Corp. and Ira Gershwin Music.[64]
LAND OF OPPORTUNITEE, THE, 346 Lyric © 1959 (Renewed) Ira Gershwin; © 1993 Ira Gershwin Music.[1]
LAND OF THE GAY CABALLERO, 166 © 1954 (Renewed) WB Music Corp.[28]
Land of Washington and Lincoln, Henry Ford and Morris Gest, 93, 153
Last January—It was February . . . , 120
Last night I had a dream, 261

LAST OF THE CABBIES, THE, 258 Lyric © 1993 Ira Gershwin Music.[1]
Leading lady, I have an improvement, 57
LEAVE IT TO LOVE (lyrics missing), 47
Leave those cares and furrows!, 280
Leaving you— / Me oh my! I am blue—, 49
Left! Right! Left! Right!, 210
Lena, go see who's making that din, 203
LET 'EM EAT CAKE, 211 © 1933 (Renewed) WB Music Corp.[28]
LET 'EM EAT CAKE—FINALE, ACT I, *See* I'VE BRUSHED MY TEETH, et al.
LET 'EM EAT CAKE—FINALE ULTIMO, 220 © 1931, 1933 (Renewed) WB Music Corp. Additional material © 1992 George Gershwin Music and Ira Gershwin Music.[26]
LET 'EM EAT CAKE—LEAGUE OF NATIONS FINALE, *See* NO COMPRENEZ, NO CAPISH, NO VERSTEH!, et al.
LET 'EM EAT CAKE—OPENING, ACT II, *See* BLUE, BLUE, BLUE, et al.
LET 'EM EAT CAVIAR (lyrics missing), 206, 219
Let it rain and thunder!, 183
LET IT RAIN! LET IT POUR!, 282 Lyric © 1993 Ira Gershwin Music.[1]
LET ME BE A FRIEND TO YOU, 115 © 1993 Ira Gershwin Music.[1]
Let me give you the lowdown, 130
Let me introduce a gentleman, 244
Let me introduce you to Tra-la-la, 25
Let me show you the town, 355
Let the drums roll out!, 96
Let the wedding bells ring on!, 86
LET YOURSELF GO!, 122 © 1928 (Renewed) WB Music Corp., Warner Bros. Inc., and Joro Music.[32]
Let's be seasoning, 76
Let's both of us pack up, 245
LET'S CALL THE WHOLE THING OFF, 265 © 1936 (Renewed) George Gershwin Music and Ira Gershwin Music.[48]
Let's keep on singing! Make way for tomorrow!, 310
LET'S KISS AND MAKE UP, 104 © 1927 (Renewed) WB Music Corp.[28]
Let's kiss and make up, 104, 105
Let's pretend that I'm in love with you and you with me, 170
LET'S SHOW 'EM HOW THIS COUNTRY GOES TO TOWN, 315 Lyric © 1993 Ira Gershwin Music.[1]
LET'S TAKE A WALK AROUND THE BLOCK, 227 © 1934 (Renewed) Harwin Music Co., WB Music Corp., and Glocca Morra Music.[40]
Let's tear down the House of Morgan!, 207
LETTER SONG—"MY DEAR BENVENUTO," 332 Lyric © 1993 Ira Gershwin Music.[1]
Life as it goes is no bed of red roses, 30

LIFE BEGINS AT CITY HALL, 230 Lyric © 1993 Ira Gershwin Music and Glocca Morra Music.[39]
LIFE BEGINS (AT EXACTLY 8:40 OR THEREABOUTS), 222 Lyric © 1993 Ira Gershwin Music and Glocca Morra Music.[39]
Life has just begun, 103
Life is gay, we agree, 226
Life is never mellow, 138
LIFE'S TOO SHORT TO BE BLUE, 75 © 1993 Ira Gershwin Music.[1]
Like a hero in an Alger novel, 151
Like Mother Goose's Mary, 38
Like the hero in an Alger novel, 91
LINGER IN THE LOBBY, 52 © 1977 George Gershwin Music and Ira Gershwin Music.[12]
Liquor flows and worry goes, 136
Listen, all of you, 122
Listen, all, this is Genius calling: "Hear ye!", 310
Listen, all, this is Vict'ry calling, "Make way!," 310
Listen, chum, take a lesson from the bluebird, 311
Listen, fair one, I'm in love!, 63
Listen to a dream—, 86
Listen to me, Sophia—, 383
Listen to my tale of woe, 51
Listen to that bebop orchestration, 361
Listen to the man with the high silk hat—, 262
LITTLE BAG OF TRICKS, 21 Lyric © 1993 Ira Gershwin Music.[1]
Little girly, 17
LITTLE JAZZ BIRD, 53 © 1924 (Renewed) WB Music Corp.[21]
Little lady, as you stand before me, 156
Little lady of my dreams, 18
LITTLE NAKED BOY, THE, *See* CAVATINA—"THE LITTLE NAKED BOY"
LITTLE RHYTHM, GO 'WAY, 31 Lyric © 1993 Ira Gershwin Music.[1]
LITTLE THEATRE, 57 © 1993 Ira Gershwin Music.[1]
LIZA, 143 © 1929 (Renewed) Warner Bros. Inc. and Gilbert Keyes Music.[35]
LOADING SONG, *See* COLLECTIVE LOADING-TIME SONG
LOADING TIME AT LAST IS OVER, *See* VILLAGE SCENE JINGLES
LOLITA, MY LOVE, 141 © 1993 Ira Gershwin Music and Gilbert Keyes Music.[34]
LONESOME COWBOY, THE, 161 © 1954 (Renewed) WB Music Corp.[28]
LONG AGO (AND FAR AWAY), 311 © 1944 (Renewed) PolyGram International Publishing, Inc.[52]
LONG AGO, FAR AWAY, ONCE UPON A TIME, *See* IT WAS LONG AGO

Look me up in the *Social Register*, 338

LOOK WHAT LOVE HAS DONE FOR ME, *See* BOY! WHAT LOVE HAS DONE TO ME!

LOOKING FOR A BOY, 69 © 1925 (Renewed) WB Music Corp.[8]

Looking for a good time, I've come here to get some action, 114

Looking through the pages of the program, 226

LORELEI, THE, 194 © 1932 (Renewed) WB Music Corp.[28]

LOSE THAT LONG FACE, 375 © 1954 (Renewed) Harwin Music Corp. and New World Music Company (Ltd.)[63]

LOST BARBER SHOP CHORD, *See* THAT LOST BARBER SHOP CHORD

Love and learn, love and learn, 381

"Love comes once to ev'ryone"—, 144

Love is a gamble, 47

Love is at its highlight, 22

LOVE IS HERE TO STAY, 276 © (Renewed) 1937, 1938 George Gershwin Music and Ira Gershwin Music.[48]

LOVE IS IN THE AIR, 62 Lyric © 1993 Ira Gershwin Music and Stephen Ballentine Music.[3]

LOVE IS MY ENEMY, *See* DUET—"LOVE IS MY ENEMY"

LOVE IS SWEEPING THE COUNTRY, 178 © 1931 (Renewed) WB Music Corp.[28]

Love, let us go flying, 30

LOVE SONG—"THERE'LL BE LIFE, LOVE, AND LAUGHTER," 330 © 1945 (Renewed) Chappell & Co. and Hampshire House Publishing Corp.[55]

LOVE SONG—"YOU'RE FAR TOO NEAR ME," 327 © 1945 (Renewed) Chappell & Co. and Hampshire House Publishing Corp.[55]

Love to hear the bumblebee, 313

LOVE WALKED IN, 275 © 1937 (Renewed) George Gershwin Music and Ira Gershwin Music.[48]

Love walked right in, 275

Love was something that meant nothing to me, 234

Love your funny smile, 196

LUCKIEST BOY IN THE WORLD, *See* LUCKIEST MAN IN THE WORLD

LUCKIEST MAN IN THE WORLD, 197 © 1933 (Renewed) WB Music Corp.[28]

Madame, please send my daddy back to Mother, 259

MADEMOISELLE FROM NEW ROCHELLE, *See* MADEMOISELLE IN NEW ROCHELLE

MADEMOISELLE IN NEW ROCHELLE, 156 © 1930 (Renewed) WB Music Corp.[28]

MADRIGAL—"WHEN THE DUCHESS IS AWAY," 329 Lyric © 1993 Ira Gershwin Music.[1]

MAGNOLIA FINALE, 141 © 1993 Ira Gershwin Music and Gilbert Keyes Music.[34]

MAHARANEE, 248 Lyric © 1993 Ira Gershwin Music.[1]

MAKE THE BEST OF IT, 21 Lyric © 1993 Ira Gershwin Music.[1]

Make way! Make way!, 311

MAKE WAY FOR THE DUCHESS, *See* DUCHESS'S ENTRANCE

Make way for the noblest of nobility!, 328

MAKE WAY FOR TOMORROW, 310 © 1944 (Renewed) PolyGram International Publishing, Inc.[56]

MAN I LOVE, THE, 54, 94 © 1924 (Renewed) WB Music Corp.[21]

MAN OF HIGH DEGREE, A, 152 © 1930 (Renewed) WB Music Corp.[28]

MAN THAT GOT AWAY, THE, 373 © 1954 (Renewed) Harwin Music Corp. and New World Music Company (Ltd.)[63]

MAN, THE MASTER, 30 Lyric © 1993 Ira Gershwin Music.[1]

MAN WHO GOT AWAY, THE, *See* MAN THAT GOT AWAY, THE

MANHATTAN, *See* WOO, WOO, WOO, WOO, MANHATTAN

MANHATTAN DOWNBEAT, 361 © 1948 (Renewed) Ira Gershwin Music and Four Jays Music Company.[60]

MAPLETON HIGH CHORALE, 288 © 1941 (Renewed) Chappell & Co. and Hampshire House Publishing Corp.[55]

MARCH CHORUS—"WE'RE SOLDIERS OF THE DUCHY," *See* MARCH OF THE SOLDIERS OF THE DUCHY—"JUST IN CASE"

MARCH OF THE SOLDIERS OF THE DUCHY—"JUST IN CASE," 332 Lyric © 1993 Ira Gershwin Music.[1]

MARCH OF THE SUFFRAGETTES, 352 © 1993 Ira Gershwin Music.[1] *See also* STAND UP AND FIGHT

MARY-LOUISE, 29 Lyric © 1993 Ira Gershwin Music.[1]

MASTER IS FREE AGAIN, *See* DUET—"OUR MASTER IS FREE AGAIN"

MAYBE, 80 © 1926 (Renewed) WB Music Corp.[21]

Maybe in the face of stormy weather, 36

MEADOW SERENADE, 92 © 1986 George Gershwin Music and Ira Gershwin Music. Additional material © 1991 George Gershwin Music, Ira Gershwin Music, and Chappell & Co.[27]

MEMBERS OF THE UNION LEAGUE, *See* UNION LEAGUE, THE

Men are so difficult to handle!, 135

MIDNIGHT MADNESS, 312 Lyric © 1993 Ira Gershwin Music.[1]

MIDNIGHT MUSIC, 312 © 1943 (Renewed) PolyGram International Publishing, Inc.[52]

Midnight shadows brought the fear, 312

Midnight shadows, dark and weird, 312

MILITARY DANCING DRILL (1927 VERSION), 98 © 1927 (Renewed) WB Music Corp.[28]

MILITARY DANCING DRILL (1930 VERSION), 155 © 1930 (Renewed) WB Music Corp.[28]

MINE, 208, 217 © 1933 (Renewed) WB Music Corp.[28]

MINSTREL DREAM, 296 Lyric © 1993 Ira Gershwin Music.[1]

MINSTREL SHOW, THE (LADY IN THE DARK VERSION), *See* MINSTREL DREAM

MINSTREL SHOW (SHOW GIRL VERSION), 145 © 1993 Ira Gershwin Music and Gilbert Keyes Music.[34]

MINSTRELS ON PARADE, 365 Lyric © 1993 Ira Gershwin Music.[1]

MISCHA, JASCHA, TOSCHA, SASCHA, 28 © 1922 (Renewed) WB Music Corp.[8]

Miss Foster, where *is* everybody?, 290

Mn, mn, mn, surrender, 226

MODERNISTIC MOE, 256 Lyric © 1993 Ira Gershwin Music.[1]

MOLLY ON THE SHORE, 24 © 1987 George Gershwin Music and Ira Gershwin Music.[12]

MONEY DOESN'T MEAN A THING, 38 Lyric © 1993 Ira Gershwin Music.[1]

Monsieur, you too?, 226

MONTY! THEIR ONLY CHILD!, *See* MR. AND MRS. SIPKIN

MOON IS ON THE SEA, THE, 85 Lyric © 1993 Ira Gershwin Music.[1]

Moon shinin' on the river—, 144

MORALE, 317 Lyric © 1993 Ira Gershwin Music.[1]

More important than a photograph of Parliament, 176

MOTHER OF THREE, THE, *See* JOLLY TAR AND THE MILKMAID, THE

MOTHERS OF THE NATION, *See* ALL THE MOTHERS OF THE NATION

MR. AND MRS., 8 Lyric © 1993 Ira Gershwin Music.[1]

MR. AND MRS. SIPKIN, 60 © 1993 Ira Gershwin Music and Stephen Ballentine Music.[3]

Mr. Nesbitt to see you, 297

Mr. Porter and Mr. Ferguson, 39

Music is the magic makes a gloomy day sunshiny, 269

MUTINY ROUTINE, *See* NINA, THE *PINTA*, THE *SANTA MARIA*, THE

MY ALL, 30 Lyric © 1993 Ira Gershwin Music.[1]

My butcher shop, my grocery, 309

My clothes I keep pressing, 273

MY COUSIN IN MILWAUKEE, 196 © 1932 (Renewed) WB Music Corp.[28]

MY DEAR BENVENUTO, *See* LETTER SONG—"MY DEAR BENVENUTO"

MY FAIR LADY, 63 © 1925 (Renewed) WB Music Corp., Warner Bros. Inc., and Stephen Ballentine Music.[16]

My feet are full of splinters, 256

My good friends, don't praise *me*!, 209

My hansom once carried John Sullivan, 258

MY HEART IS YOURS, 37 Lyric © 1993 Ira Gershwin Music.[1]

MY LORDS AND LADIES, *See* ARIA—"MY LORDS AND LADIES"

My lords and ladies, foes and friends—, 325

My money's on a hot number, 261

My name is Mrs. Cantor . . . , 262

MY ONE AND ONLY, 106 © 1927 (Renewed) WB Music Corp.[28]

MY ONE AND ONLY HIGHLAND FLING, 358 © 1948, 1949 (Renewed) Chappell & Co. and Four Jays Music Company.[59]

MY PARAMOUNT-PUBLIX-ROXY ROSE, 224 Lyric © 1993 Ira Gershwin Music and Glocca Morra Music.[39]

My poor child, he isn't worth one of your tears!, 336

MY RED-LETTER DAY, 245 © 1936 (Renewed) Chappell & Co. and Ira Gershwin Music.[47]

My Rosie knows the places where, 81

MY SHIP, 295 © 1941 (Renewed) Chappell & Co. and Hampshire House Publishing Corp.[55]

My simple notions will cause no commotions, 40

My singing / Has 'em winging, 367

MY SON-IN-LAW, 345 Lyric © 1959 (Renewed) Ira Gershwin; © 1993 Ira Gershwin Music.[1]

MY SUNDAY FELLA, 141 © 1993 Ira Gershwin Music and Gilbert Keyes Music.[34]

Name your heart's desire—, 343

NATCHEZ ON THE MISSISSIP', 361 © 1948 (Renewed) Ira Gershwin Music and Four Jays Music Company.[60]

NAUGHTY BABY, 44 © 1924 WB Music Corp. and Warner Bros. Inc.[10]

Near Barcelona the peasant croons, 5

Near Michael Arlen's Armenia, 63

'Neath the old magnolia, 362

NEVADA, THE, 32 Lyric © 1993 Ira Gershwin Music.[1]

Never drink, never smoke, 145

Never thought I'd ever meet, 134

NEVER TOO LATE TO MENDELSSOHN, *See* BRIDE AND GROOM (OH, KAY! VERSION)

NEVER WAS THERE A GIRL SO FAIR, 177 © 1932 (Renewed) WB Music Corp.[28]

NEW BLUE D.A.R., THE, *See* CLIMB UP THE SOCIAL LADDER

New Mexico, I love you, 168

NEW STEP EVERY DAY, A, 26 © 1993 Ira Gershwin Music.[1]

New York may have its Plaza and Ambassador and Ritz, 52

NEW YORK SERENADE, 116 © 1977 George Gershwin Music and Ira Gershwin Music.[12]

NICE BABY, 68 © 1925 (Renewed) WB Music Corp.[8]

NICE WORK IF YOU CAN GET IT, 272 © 1937 (Renewed) George Gershwin Music and Ira Gershwin Music.[48]

NIGHT MUSIC—"THE NIGHTTIME IS NO TIME FOR THINKING," 331 Lyric © 1993 Ira Gershwin Music.[1]

NIGHT OF NIGHTS, 276 Lyric © 1993 Ira Gershwin Music.[1]

NIGHTIE-NIGHT!, 73 © 1925 (Renewed) WB Music Corp.[21]

NIGHTTIME IS NO TIME FOR THINKING, THE, *See* NIGHT MUSIC—"THE NIGHTTIME IS NO TIME FOR THINKING"

NIGHTY-NIGHT!, *See* NIGHTIE-NIGHT!

NINA, THE *PINTA*, THE *SANTA MARIA*, THE, 319 © 1946, 1954 (Renewed) Chappell & Co. and Hampshire House Publishing Corp.[55]

NINE SUPREME BALL PLAYERS, 215 © 1993 Ira Gershwin Music.[1]

NINE SUPREME COURT JUDGES, *See* OF THEE I SING—FINALE, ACT I

97,704, *See* NATCHEZ ON THE MISSISSIP'

NO BETTER WAY TO START A CASE, 215 © 1993 Ira Gershwin Music.[1]

NO *COMPRENEZ*, NO *CAPISH*, NO *VERSTEH!*, 214 © 1987 George Gershwin Music and Ira Gershwin Music.[12]

No fooling, I'm feeling I'm falling, dear, 132

NO MATTER UNDER WHAT STAR YOU'RE BORN, 297 Lyric © 1993 Ira Gershwin Music.[1]

NO QUESTION IN MY HEART, 280 © 1938 (Renewed), 1968 PolyGram International Publishing, Inc.[52]

No question in my mind, 280

NO TICKEE, NO WASHEE, *See* PARDON MY ENGLISH—OPENING, ACT II (ORIGINAL)

NO VILLAGE LIKE MINE, 304 © 1943 (Renewed) Chappell & Co.[51]

Nobody knows how happy I'd be to find someone—, 66

NOSY COOK, THE, *See* TRIO—"I KNOW WHERE THERE'S A COZY NOOK"

NOT FOR ME, *See* BUT NOT FOR ME

Not long ago, wine used to flow, 9

Not many miles from Armenia, 63

NOT SO LONG AGO, 40 Lyric © 1993 Ira Gershwin Music.[1]

NOTHING IS IMPOSSIBLE, 367 © 1952 (Renewed) Ira Gershwin Music and Chappell & Co.[61]

Nothing seemed to matter anymore, 275

Now that everybody's here, 214

Now that I am starting, 57

Now that I have found you, 106

Now that the dance is near, 120

NOW THAT THE DANCE IS OVER, 120 Lyric © 1993 Ira Gershwin Music.[1]

NOW THAT WE ARE ONE, 281 © 1968 PolyGram International Publishing, Inc.[53]

Now that we have got 'im, 217

NOW THAT WE'RE MR. AND MRS., *See* MR. AND MRS.

Now that we've finished dining, 123

NURSIE, NURSIE, 100 Lyric © 1991 Ira Gershwin Music.[1]

Obviously / You can't have me, 349

ODE—"A RHYME FOR ANGELA," 333 © 1945 (Renewed) Chappell & Co. and Hampshire House Publishing Corp.[55]

Of beauty untainted, 287

OF THEE I SING, 179, 180 © 1931 (Renewed) WB Music Corp.[28]

OF THEE I SING—FINALE, ACT I, 180 © 1932 (Renewed) WB Music Corp.[28]

OF THEE I SING—FINALE ULTIMO, *See* ON THAT MATTER, NO ONE BUDGES

OF THEE I SING—FINALETTO, ACT I, SCENE 4, *See* AS THE CHAIRMAN OF THE COMMITTEE, et al.

OF THEE I SING—FINALETTO, ACT II, SCENE 1, *See* GARÇON, S'IL VOUS PLAÎT, et al.

OF THEE I SING—FINALETTO, ACT II, SCENE 3, *See* IMPEACHMENT PROCEEDING, et al.

OF THEE I SING—FINALETTO, ATLANTIC CITY HOTEL SCENE (SCENE 5), *See* AS THE CHAIRMAN OF THE COMMITTEE, et al.

OF THEE I SING—OPENING, ACT I, SCENE 3, *See* WHO IS THE LUCKY GIRL TO BE?, et al.

OF THEE I SING—OPENING ACT II, *See* HELLO, GOOD MORNING

OF THEE I SING—OPENING ACT III, SCENE 3, *See* SENATORIAL ROLL CALL, THE

OFFICIAL RÉSUMÉ, 157 © 1930 (Renewed) WB Music Corp.[28]

Oh, Baby Face McGinty—, 259

OH, BESS, OH WHERE'S MY BESS?, 241 © 1935 (Renewed) George Gershwin Music, Ira Gershwin Music, and DuBose and Dorothy Heyward Memorial Fund Publishing.[45]

OH, BRING BACK THE BALLET AGAIN, 262 Lyric © 1993 Ira Gershwin Music.[1]

Oh, bring back the old-fashioned ballet, 262

Oh, Captain Jesus, find it in Yo' heart to save us, 240

Oh, comrades, you deserve your daily bread, 212

Oh, Doctor Jesus, look down on me wit' pity, 239

Oh, east is west, 140

OH, FABULOUS ONE, 284 © 1941 (Renewed) Chappell & Co. and Hampshire House Publishing Corp.[55]

Oh, Father what die on Calbery, we's dependin' on You, 240

Oh, gather 'round me, ladies, 158

OH GEE! OH JOY!, 115 © 1928 (Renewed) WB Music Corp. and Warner Bros. Inc.[30]

Oh, girl of the moment, 286, 287

Oh, happy wedding day, 141

OH, HEAV'NLY FATHER, 239 © 1935 (Renewed) George Gershwin Music, Ira Gershwin Music, and DuBose and Dorothy Heyward Memorial Fund Publishing.[45]

Oh, how I love you—, 24

Oh, how I need cheering up, 51

OH, I CAN'T SIT DOWN!, 237 © 1935 (Renewed) George Gershwin Music, Ira Gershwin Music, and DuBose and Dorothy Heyward Memorial Fund Publishing.[45]

Oh, I got plenty o' nuthin', 236

Oh, I think I'd love to lead a life of crime, 56

Oh, I'll share my final dollar, 260

Oh, I'm afraid, 40

Oh, I'm the chappie, 162

Oh, isn't that thrilling!, 82

Oh, it pays to have a witness, 335

Oh, it really wasn't my intention, 353

Oh, it's great to be a secret'ry, 182

Oh, I've met your fine lassies in Dublin, 24

Oh, just imagine the thrill, 388

OH, KAY!, 85 © 1926 (Renewed) WB Music Corp. and Warner Bros. Inc.[25]

OH, KAY!—FINALE, ACT I, 82 © 1977 George Gershwin Music and Ira Gershwin Music.[12]

OH, KAY!—FINALETTO, ACT II, SCENE 1, 84 © 1993 Ira Gershwin Music.[1]

OH, KAY!—OPENING, ACT II, See BRIDE AND GROOM

OH, LADY, BE GOOD!, 50 © 1924 (Renewed) WB Music Corp.[21]

Oh, Lawd above, we knows You can destroy, 240

Oh, let me be a friend to you—, 115

Oh, Madame, please excuse me—, 259

OH ME! OH MY!, 17 © 1921 (Renewed) WB Music Corp.[5]

OH ME, OH MY, OH YOU, See OH ME! OH MY!

Oh, my goodness! What a mess this place is!, 79

Oh! Rhythm, slow rhythm, 31

Oh, sad is my story and hard is my lot, 258

Oh, say that you love me, Bambino, 10

OH, SO NICE!, 134 © 1928 (Renewed) WB Music Corp.[28]

Oh, sweet and lovely lady, be good, 50

Oh, the country's unafraid, 122

Oh, the courtin' of Elmer and Ella, 362

Oh, the gay trombone, 118

Oh, the lonesome cowboy won't be lonesome now, 162

Oh, the minute that you strike it, 164

Oh, the usual clouds of gray, 232

Oh, the well-known skies of blue—, 362

Oh, the world is full of villains, 334

Oh, there's an island down in the West Indies, 245

Oh, they're hanging Throttlebottom in the morning!, 219

OH, THIS IS SUCH A LOVELY WAR, 97 © 1991 George Gershwin Music and Ira Gershwin Music.[12]

Oh, trumpeter, trumpeter, blow your golden horn!, 187

Oh, what a lovely party, 47

Oh, what sort of wedding is this?, 198

Oh, what was that noise?, 72

Oh, when it starts to blow, 68

Oh, when it's nighttime here at West Point, 116

Oh, when we get our little kitchenette, 5

Old Man Sunshine—listen, you!, 167

On Alligator Island there is light, 132

ON AND ON AND ON, 210, 211 © 1933 (Renewed) WB Music Corp.[28]

On Monday—happy as a lark, 27

On single life today, 84

ON THAT MATTER, NO ONE BUDGES, 188 © 1932 (Renewed) WB Music Corp.[28]

ON THE WINGS OF ROMANCE, 30 Lyric © 1993 Ira Gershwin Music.[1]

On to Pisa! On to Verona!, 332

ONCE, 64 © 1987 George Gershwin Music and Ira Gershwin Music.[18]

Once again the golden sun is shining, 99

Once I cared for women, wine, and song, 168

Once I used to keep love at a distance, 262

Once I visited my cousin, 196

Once I was so willing, 61

Once in a music hall, 9

Once Rockefeller didn't have a nickel, 65

Once the highbrows, when they heard the blues, 41

ONCE THERE WERE TWO OF US, 280 © 1938 (Renewed), 1968 PolyGram International Publishing, Inc.[52]

ONCE THERE WERE TWO OF US (NOW WE'RE ONLY ONE), See ISN'T IT WONDERFUL

Once they called me peasant, 304

Once upon a time they called me Little Boy Blue, 158

Once you would hang around me, 154

One and all, we bid you welcome to the office, 355

ONE I'M LOOKING FOR, THE, 124 © 1928 (Renewed) WB Music Corp., Warner Bros. Inc., and Joro Music.[32]

ONE LIFE TO LIVE, 284 © 1941 (Renewed) Chappell & Co. and Hampshire House Publishing Corp.[55]

ONE MAN, 142 © 1993 Ira Gershwin Music and Gilbert Keyes Music.[34]

One man's death is another man's living, 324

One time I was as gay as a king, 144

ONE, TWO, THREE, 354 © 1946 (Renewed) Chappell & Co.[58]

Open in the name of the law!, 200

OPENING—CRAZY QUILT, 41 © 1993 Ira Gershwin Music and Morrie Ryskind Publishing Descendants.[20]

OPPORTUNITY HAS BECKONED, 189 © 1993 Ira Gershwin Music.[1]

ORDERS, ORDERS!, See SHIRTS BY MILLIONS

Orders, orders, orders by the thousands!, 208

Our future looks colossal and terrific, 219

Our hearts are in communion, 207

"Our hearts could rhyme," said she, 269

OUR LITTLE CAPTAIN, 72 © 1977 George Gershwin Music and Ira Gershwin Music.[12]

OUR LITTLE KITCHENETTE, See KITCHENETTE

OUR LITTLE SAN FERNANDO HOME, See HOME IN SAN FERNANDO VALLEY

OUR LITTLE SAN FERNANDO HOUSE, See HOME IN SAN FERNANDO VALLEY

OUR LOVE IS HERE TO STAY, See LOVE IS HERE TO STAY

OUR MASTER IS FREE AGAIN, See DUET—"OUR MASTER IS FREE AGAIN"

Our romance won't end on a sorrowful note, 266

Out there, out there in Sweet Nevada!, 343

Over in Paris they show, 26

OYEZ, OYEZ, OYEZ!, 216 © 1993 Ira Gershwin Music.[1]

Paradise cannot refuse us—, 355

PARDON MY ENGLISH, 194 © 1993 Ira Gershwin Music.[1]

PARDON MY ENGLISH—FINALE, ACT I, See WHAT SORT OF WEDDING IS THIS?

PARDON MY ENGLISH—FINALE, ACT II, See HE'S NOT HIMSELF

PARDON MY ENGLISH—FINALETTO, ACT II, SCENE 4, 200 © 1993 George Gershwin Music and Ira Gershwin Music.[12]

PARDON MY ENGLISH—OPENING, GARDEN SCENE, See HAIL THE HAPPY COUPLE

PARDON MY ENGLISH—OPENING, ACT II (ORIGINAL), 203 © 1993 George Gershwin Music and Ira Gershwin Music.[12]

PARIS (FR.), See CIVIC SONG—"COME TO PARIS"

PARK AVENUE—OPENING, ACT II, See HOPE FOR THE BEST

PARTY PARLANDO, 301 Lyric © 1993 Ira Gershwin Music.[1]

PATRIOTIC RALLY (1927 VERSION), 93 © 1930 (Renewed) WB Music Corp. Additional material © 1991 George Gershwin Music and Ira Gershwin Music.[26]

PATRIOTIC RALLY (1930 VERSION), *See* THREE CHEERS FOR THE UNION (1930 VERSION) *and* THIS COULD GO ON FOR YEARS (1930 VERSION)

PAY SOME ATTENTION TO ME (DAMSEL IN DISTRESS VERSION), 272 © 1937 (Renewed) George Gershwin Music and Ira Gershwin Music.[49]

PAY SOME ATTENTION TO ME (FIRST VERSION), 272 © 1993 Ira Gershwin Music.[1]

PEACOCK ALLEY, 24 Lyric © 1993 Ira Gershwin Music.

PEOPLE FROM MISSOURI, 281 © 1956 (Renewed) PolyGram International Publishing, Inc.[4]

People! People! I'm here to state, 76

People say the lover today, 148

Philosophers the whole world over often put this query, 48

PHOEBE, 24 © 1993 Ira Gershwin Music.[1]

PICCADILLY WALK, THE, 24 Lyric © 1992, 1993 Ira Gershwin Music and Arthur Riscoe Publishing Descendants.[13]

PICCADILLY'S NOT A BIT LIKE BROADWAY, 9 Lyric © 1993 Ira Gershwin Music.[1]

PICK YO' PARTNER! (GET READY FOR THE RAGGY BLUES), 9 Lyric © 1993 Ira Gershwin Music.[1]

PIDGIE WOO (lyrics missing), 12

PITCHMAN, THE, 379 © 1954 (Renewed) Harwin Music Corp. and Ira Gershwin Music.[65]

PLACE IN THE COUNTRY, 129 © 1993 Ira Gershwin Music.[1]

PLAY BALL!, 215 © 1993 Ira Gershwin Music.[1]

Please pardon this intrusion—, 259

PLEASE SEND MY DADDY BACK TO MOTHER, 259 Lyric © 1993 Ira Gershwin Music.[1]

POETRY OF MOTION, THE, 363 © 1948 (Renewed) Ira Gershwin Music and Four Jays Music Company.[60]

POOR JENNY, *See* SAGA OF JENNY, THE

POSTERITY IS JUST AROUND THE CORNER, 185 © 1932 (Renewed) WB Music Corp.[28]

Pray tell me how much longer must my poor heart suffer, 29

Presenting the world premiere of, 249

PRESIDENT'S FUTURE WIFE, THE, *See* WHO IS THE LUCKY GIRL TO BE?

Presto! The rest, oh! You never will detect, 21

PRINCESS OF PURE DELIGHT, THE, 288 © 1941 (Renewed) Chappell & Co. and Hampshire House Publishing Corp.[55]

PROCESSION—"SOUVENIRS," 334 Lyric © 1993 Ira Gershwin Music.[1]

Professor Jesus, teach Yo' ignorant chillen, 240

Puritans often say, 75

Puritans there are who say, 75

PUT ME TO THE TEST (A DAMSEL IN DISTRESS VERSION), 269 © 1937 (Renewed) George Gershwin Music and Ira Gershwin Music.[49]

PUT ME TO THE TEST (COVER GIRL VERSION), 311 © 1944 (Renewed) PolyGram International Publishing, Inc.[52]

Put the pressure on Prussia!, 314

QUARTET EROTICA, 225 Lyric © 1993 Ira Gershwin Music and Glocca Morra Music.[39]

RABELAIS, *See* QUARTET EROTICA

Rabelais, Balzac, De Maupassant, Boccaccio—, 225

Rabelais, De Maupassant, Boccaccio, Balzac—, 225

RAINY-AFTERNOON GIRLS, 55 © 1993 Ira Gershwin Music.[1]

Rally round! Come and take your stand!, 305

Reach up high—Pull down the sky—, 84

REAL AMERICAN FOLK SONG (IS A RAG), THE, 4 © 1959 (Renewed) Chappell & Co.[2]

Really, I'm not trying to be flirtatious, 40

REDHEADED WOMAN, A, 239 © 1935 (Renewed) George Gershwin Music, Ira Gershwin Music, and DuBose and Dorothy Heyward Memorial Fund Publishing.[45]

REMIND ME NOT TO LEAVE THE TOWN, 348 Lyric © 1993 Ira Gershwin Music.[1]

RHUMBA THAT BLIGHTED MY LIFE, THE, *See* JUST ANOTHER RHUMBA

RHYME FOR ANGELA, A, *See* ODE—"A RHYME FOR ANGELA"

RICE AND SHOES, 19 © 1921 (Renewed) WB Music Corp. and Schuyler Greene Publishing Descendants.[9]

RING-A-DING-A-DING-DONG DELL, 157 © 1930 (Renewed) WB Music Corp.[28]

Rolling along, 54

Romantic land of the gay caballero, 166

RONDEAU TO ROSIE, 81 © 1993 Ira Gershwin Music.[1]

ROSALIE, 119 © 1927 (Renewed) WB Music Corp.[28]

ROSALIE—FINALE, ACT I, 116 Lyric © 1993 Ira Gershwin Music.[1] *See also* NOW THAT THE DANCE IS OVER

Rosalie, Rosalie, hear us, 119

Rough and ready buccaneers are we!—, 128

SAGA OF JENNY, THE, 291 © 1941 (Renewed) Chappell & Co. and Hampshire House Publishing Corp.[55]

Sailed away / Yesterday—, 228

SAM AND DELILAH, 165 © 1930 (Renewed) WB Music Corp.[28]

Sat'day, Sunday—, 124

SAY SO!, 115 © 1928 (Renewed) WB Music Corp. and Warner Bros. Inc.[30]

SAYING MY SAY, 389 © 1987 George Gershwin Music and Ira Gershwin Music.[18]

Screen or show girl, 313

SEARCH IS THROUGH, THE, 380 © 1954 (Renewed) Harwin Music Corp. and New World Music Company (Ltd.)[63]

Seated one day at the barber's, 77

SECOND FIDDLE TO A HARP, 364 Lyric © 1993 Ira Gershwin Music.[1]

SEEING DICKIE HOME, 54 © 1993 Ira Gershwin Music.[1]

Seem no matter what I say, 371

SENATE, THE, *See* IMPEACHMENT PROCEEDING, et al.

SENATORIAL ROLL CALL, THE, 185 © 1932 (Renewed) WB Music Corp.[28]

SENTIMENTAL WEATHER, 254 Lyric © 1993 Ira Gershwin Music.[1]

17 AND 21, 90 © 1927 (Renewed) WB Music Corp.[28]

SHALL WE DANCE?, 266 © 1936 (Renewed) George Gershwin Music and Ira Gershwin Music.[48]

She felt quite warmly toward him, 299

She gone, but you very lucky, 241

She had the *You*-must-come-over, You-*must*-come-over, 45

SHE'S INNOCENT, *See* TWO LITTLE GIRLS IN BLUE—FINALE, ACT II

She's the illegitimate daughter, 184, 186

SHIRTS BY MILLIONS, 208 © 1987 George Gershwin Music and Ira Gershwin Music.[12]

SHOEIN' THE MARE, 224 © 1934 (Renewed) Harwin Music Co., WB Music Corp., and Glocca Morra Music.[40]

SHOES WITH WINGS ON, 360 © 1948, 1949 (Renewed) Chappell & Co. and Four Jays Music Company.[59]

SHOPGIRLS AND MANNEQUINS, 60 © 1993 Ira Gershwin Music and Stephen Ballentine Music.[3]

SHOW GIRL—FINALETTO, ACT I, SCENE 1, 141 © 1993 Ira Gershwin Music and Gilbert Keyes Music.[34]

SHOW ME THE TOWN (OH, KAY! VERSION), 85 © 1926 (Renewed) WB Music Corp.[21]

SHOW ME THE TOWN (ROSALIE VERSION), 114 © 1977 George Gershwin Music and Ira Gershwin Music.[18]

SHOW MUST GO ON, THE, 308 Lyric © 1993 Ira Gershwin Music.[1]

SILLY SEASON, THE, 17 Lyric © 1993 Ira Gershwin Music.[1]

SIMPLE LIFE, THE, 13 © 1921 (Renewed) WB Music Corp.[6]

Since I came from Romanza, 116

Since Modernistic Moe, 257

SINCE THE BALLET SWEPT THE TOWN, *See* POETRY OF MOTION, THE

Since the world began, 62

SING ME NOT A BALLAD, *See* DUCHESS'S SONG, THE—"SING ME NOT A BALLAD"

Sing me not of other towns, 304

SING OF SPRING, 271 © 1937 (Renewed) George Gershwin Music and Ira Gershwin Music.[48]

SING-SONG GIRL, 139 © 1993 Ira Gershwin Music.[1]

SINGIN' PETE, 57 © 1993 Ira Gershwin Music.[1]

SINGING IN THE RAIN, 32 © 1987 George Gershwin Music and Ira Gershwin Music.[18]

Singing, singing ev'ry morning, 90

Singing, singing in the rain, 32

SIRENS, THE, 14 © 1993 Ira Gershwin Music.[1]

Sitting, sitting, 97

Six little rainy-afternoon girls, 55

SIX PRAYERS, *See* OH, HEAV'NLY FATHER

SKULL AND BONES, 128 © 1993 Ira Gershwin Music.[1]

SLAP THAT BASS, 264 © 1936 (Renewed) George Gershwin Music and Ira Gershwin Music.[48]

SLAPSTICK, *See* I'M TICKLED SILLY

SO AM I, 49 © 1925 (Renewed) WB Music Corp.[21]

SO ARE YOU!, 142 © 1929 (Renewed) WB Music Corp. and Gilbert Keyes Music.[35]

So Columbus discovered America, 376

So please remind me never to leave the town, 349

SO WHAT?, 195 © 1932 (Renewed) WB Music Corp.[28]

So why be a good girl—, 126

Soldier, advance!, 98, 156

Soldier, soldier!, 156

Soldiers and civilians, 312

SOLDIERS FINE OF MINE, *See* HUSSAR MARCH

Some day he'll come along, 55, 94

Some day she'll come along, 94

SOME FARAWAY SOMEONE, 43 © 1924 (Renewed) WB Music Corp.[8]

Some fellers love to Tip-Toe Through The Tulips, 161

SOME GIRLS CAN BAKE A PIE, 177, 180 © 1932 (Renewed) WB Music Corp.[28]

Some girls woo you with a smile, 15

SOME RAIN MUST FALL, 15 © 1921 (Renewed) WB Music Corp.[6]

SOME SWEET FARAWAY SOMEONE, *See* SOME FARAWAY SOMEONE

SOMEBODY FROM SOMEWHERE, 172 © 1931 (Renewed) WB Music Corp.[28]

SOMEBODY STOLE MY HEART AWAY, 146 © 1993 Ira Gershwin Music and Gilbert Keyes Music.[34]

Someday, someday you'll realize, 29

Someday we'll go places—, 227

SOMEDAY YOU'LL REALIZE, 29 Lyric © 1993 Ira Gershwin Music.[1]

Somehow by fate misguided, 138

Somehow I feel much more sentimental, 139

Somehow I feel there's bound to be, 21

SOMEHOW I KNEW, 10 Lyric © 1993 Ira Gershwin Music.[1]

Somehow I'm sure I've found a sure thing in you, 310

Somehow—somehow I knew, 10

SOMEONE, 25 © 1922 (Renewed) WB Music Corp.[7]

SOMEONE AT LAST, 375 © 1954 (Renewed) Harwin Music Corp. and New World Music Company (Ltd.)[63]

Someone I can care for, 19

SOMEONE TO WATCH OVER ME, 83 © 1926 (Renewed) WB Music Corp.[21]

Someone waits for me, / Wonder who he (she) will be, 47

SOMEONE'S ALWAYS CALLING A REHEARSAL, 147 Lyric © 1993 Ira Gershwin Music and Gilbert Keyes Music.[34]

Something is the matter with me, 84

SOMETHING PECULIAR, 9 © 1993 Ira Gershwin Music.[1]

SOMETHING'S WRONG, 282 © 1977 PolyGram International Publishing, Inc.[53]

SOMEWHERE IN THE SOMETIME, *See* SOMEONE AT LAST

Somewhere there's a someone who's the someone for me, 375

SONG OF THE FATHERLAND, 305 Lyric © 1993 Ira Gershwin Music.[1]

SONG OF THE GUERRILLAS, 305 © 1943 (Renewed) Chappell & Co.[51]

SONG OF THE HANGMAN, 324 Lyric © 1993 Ira Gershwin Music.[1]

SONG OF THE NEW YORK WORLD'S FAIR, *See* DAWN OF A NEW DAY

SONG OF THE RHINELAND, 318 © 1945 (Renewed) Chappell & Co. and Hampshire House Publishing Corp.[55]

SONG OF THE ZODIAC, 297 Lyric © 1993 Ira Gershwin Music.[1]

SOON, 151 © 1929 (Renewed) WB Music Corp.[28]

Soon or late—maybe—, 80

Soon the bells away up in the belfry will be ringing—, 197

Soon—the lonely nights will be ended, 152

SOPHIA, 383 © 1964 (Renewed) Chappell & Co.[58]

Sound the brass! Roll the drum!, 280

SOUVENIRS, *See* PROCESSION—"SOUVENIRS"

Souvenirs! Hurry, hurry, hurry . . . , 334

SOVIET LAND, *See* SONG OF THE FATHERLAND

SPARE ME YOUR ADVANCES, *See* DUCHESS'S SONG, THE—"SING ME NOT A BALLAD"

Spirits were low, 281

SPRING AGAIN, 276 © 1938 (Renewed) Chappell & Co. and Ira Gershwin Music.[47]

SPRING FEVER, 223 Lyric © 1993 Ira Gershwin Music and Glocca Morra Music.[39]

Spring is here! I'm a fool if I fall again, 225

Spring is here / Sing willy-wally-willo!, 271

Spring is in the air—, 179

STAGE DOOR SCENE, 144 Lyric © 1993 Ira Gershwin Music and Gilbert Keyes Music.[34]

STAIRWAY TO PARADISE (I'LL BUILD A), 26 © 1922 (Renewed) WB Music Corp., Warner Bros. Inc., and Stephen Ballentine Music.[16]

STAND UP AND FIGHT, 352 © 1993 Ira Gershwin Music.[1]

Stars without glitter, 364

Start it with a little bit of ginger, 26

STATE OF OUR UNION, *See* IN OUR UNITED STATE

STAY AS WE ARE, 348 Lyric © 1993 Ira Gershwin Music.[1]

STEPPING WITH BABY, 86 © 1993 Ira Gershwin Music.[1]

STEWARDS, *See* HERE, STEWARD

STIFF UPPER LIP, 270 © 1937 (Renewed) George Gershwin Music and Ira Gershwin Music.[48]

Still, the king can do no wrong!, 117

Stop! Halt! Pause! Wait!, 220

Stop, put that stick down!, 166

Stop! We want a little attention!, 157

Stop! What is this mischief you're brewing?, 159

Stop! What is this mischief you're doing?, 94, 154

STORE SCENE, *See* SHIRTS BY MILLIONS, et al.

Stranger on the dusty highway—, 304

STRIKE THE LOUD-RESOUNDING ZITHER, 189 © 1993 Ira Gershwin Music.[1]

STRIKE UP THE BAND, 96 © 1927 (Renewed) WB Music Corp.[28]

STRIKE UP THE BAND ('27)—ENSEMBLE, *See* STRIKE UP THE BAND ('27)—FINALETTO, ACT I

STRIKE UP THE BAND ('27)—FINALETTO, ACT I, 94 © 1930 (Renewed) WB Music Corp. Additional material © 1991 George Gershwin Music and Ira Gershwin Music.[26]

STRIKE UP THE BAND ('27)—FINALETTO, ACT II, *See* JIM, CONSIDER WHAT YOU ARE DOING!

STRIKE UP THE BAND ('27)—FINALETTO, ACT II, SCENE 1, *See* JIM, CONSIDER WHAT YOU ARE DOING!

STRIKE UP THE BAND ('30)—FINALETTO, ACT II, SCENE 1, 159 © 1993 Ira Gershwin Music.[1]

STRIKE UP THE BAND ('27)—OPENING, ACT II, *See* OH, THIS IS SUCH A LOVELY WAR

STRIKE UP THE BAND ('27)—OPENING, ACT II, SCENE THREE, *See* WAR THAT ENDED WAR, THE

STRIKE UP THE BAND ('30)—OPENING, ACT I, *See* FLETCHER'S AMERICAN CHOCOLATE CHORAL SOCIETY

STRIKE UP THE BAND ('30)—OPENING, ACT I, SCENE THREE, *See* THREE CHEERS FOR THE UNION (1930 VERSION) *and* THIS COULD GO ON FOR YEARS (1930 VERSION)

STRIKE UP THE BAND ('30)—OPENING, ACT II, *See* IN THE RATTLE OF THE BATTLE *and* MILITARY DANCING DRILL (1930 VERSION)

STRIKE UP THE BAND FOR U.C.L.A., 96, © 1936 (Renewed) WB Music Corp.[28]

Strike up the music and turn on the pep, 147

Strolling underneath my new umbrella—, 141

Success has only made me more lonely, 33

Summer is the season, 62

SUMMERTIME, 22 Lyric © 1993 Ira Gershwin Music.[1]

SUN IS ON THE SEA, THE, *See* MOON IS ON THE SEA, THE

SUNDAY TAN, 261 Lyric © 1993 Ira Gershwin Music.[1]

SUNNY DISPOSISH, 76 © 1926 (Renewed) WB Music Corp. and Warner Bros. Inc.[10]

SUNSHINE TRAIL, THE, 31 © 1923 (Renewed) WB Music Corp.[8]

SURE THING, 309 © 1943, 1944 (Renewed), 1975 PolyGram International Publishing, Inc.[52]

Susie wasn't mad about, 44

SWEET AND LOW-DOWN, 72 © 1925 (Renewed) WB Music Corp.[21]

SWEET NEVADA, 342 Lyric © 1959 (Renewed) Ira Gershwin; © 1993 Ira Gershwin Music.[1]

SWEET PACKARD, 351 © 1993 Ira Gershwin Music.[1]

SWEET SO-AND-SO, 125 © 1927, 1928, 1931 (Renewed) WB Music Corp., Warner Bros. Inc., and Joro Music.[32]

SWEETEST GIRL, *See* RICE AND SHOES

Sweets and tarts!, 324

SWING TROT, 358 © 1948, 1949 (Renewed) Chappell & Co. and Four Jays Music Company.[59]

SWISS MISS, 53 © 1977 George Gershwin Music and Ira Gershwin Music.[12]

'S WONDERFUL, 103 © 1927 (Renewed) WB Music Corp.[28]

SYNCOPATED CITY, *See* FASCINATING RHYTHM

Take a step in the right direction, 358

Take a taxi and go there, 143

Take me, take me, 40

Taking care of children, house, and crockery, 352

TAKING NO CHANCES ON YOU, 363 Lyric © 1993 Ira Gershwin Music.[1]

Talk about the music of the Sirens, 94

TALLY HO, *See* A-HUNTING WE WILL GO

Ta ra ra, tszing, tszing, tszing—, 292

TARANTELLA—"DIZZILY, BUSILY," 331 Lyric © 1993 Ira Gershwin Music.[1]

TCHAIKOWSKY (AND OTHER RUSSIANS), 291 © 1941 (Renewed) Chappell & Co. and Hampshire House Publishing Corp.[55]

TELEPHONE PASSAGE, 321 Lyric © 1993 Ira Gershwin Music.[1]

TELL ME IN THE GLOAMING, 32 Lyric © 1993 Ira Gershwin Music and Irving Caesar.[17]

TELL ME MORE, 59 © 1925 (Renewed) WB Music Corp., Warner Bros. Inc., and Stephen Ballentine Music.[16]

TELL ME MORE—FINALETTO, ACT II, SCENE 1, 64 © 1993 Ira Gershwin Music and Stephen Ballentine Music.[3]

TELL ME MORE—OPENING, ACT I, *See* SHOPGIRLS AND MANNEQUINS

TELL ME MORE—OPENING, ACT II, *See* LOVE IS IN THE AIR

TELL ME MORE—OPENING ENSEMBLE, *See* SHOPGIRLS AND MANNEQUINS

Tell me, tell me, do!—my Evening Star, 57

Tell me, what has happened?, 141

TELL THE DOC, 106 © 1928 (Renewed) WB Music Corp.[28]

Tell us, señorita, do they grow, 53

Temp'ramental Oriental Gentlemen are we, 28

Ten thousand steamboats hootin'—, 116

Test me! Put me on my mettle!, 270

THANKS TO YOU, 158 © 1993 Ira Gershwin Music.[1]

THAT CERTAIN FEELING, 71 © 1925 (Renewed) Warner Bros. Inc.[21]

THAT GIRL ON THE COVER, *See* COVER GIRL

That I'm the talk of Broadway isn't doubtful, 60

THAT LOST BARBER SHOP CHORD, 77 © 1926 (Renewed) WB Music Corp.[21]

THAT MOMENT OF MOMENTS, 253 © 1935 (Renewed) Chappell & Co. and Ira Gershwin Music.[47]

THAT WELL-KNOWN SMILE, 232 Lyric © 1993 Ira Gershwin Music.[1]

THAT'S HOW IT IS, 321 Lyric © 1993 Ira Gershwin Music.[1]

THAT'S THE BEST OF ALL, 313 Lyric © 1993 Ira Gershwin Music.[1]

THAT'S WHAT HE DID! 216 © 1987 George Gershwin Music and Ira Gershwin Music.[12]

The army is somewhat in doubt!, 213

The battle won't be finished, 315

The ceremony was over, 4

The city's roar, 313

The country thinks it's got depression, 185

The days of the good old knights are gone, 311

The days of the knights of old are gone, 269

The Dictator and Committee say initially, 214

The favorite doesn't always win, 310

The first number of my second group, 227

The flaxen hair, 380

The future of this nation, with the present generation, 39

The Great American Folk Song is a rag—, 5

The he-man ain't the man he used to be, 65

The Himalaya Mountains I climb, 256

The little god of love, 332

The maid of long ago, 15

The man who lives for only making money, 272

The man you are about to see, 92

The master is free again!, 326

The military man, 98

The more I read the papers, 276

The music they go for on Broadway, 279

The next business before the Senate . . . , 185

The night is bitter, 374

The odds were a hundred to one against me, 265

The people think they've got taxation, 185

The point they're making in the song, 209

The Prince in Orange and the Prince in Blue, 289

The puritanical bluenose, 376

The pursuit of happiness, 367

The question in my heart today, 229

The reviews were ecstatic, 370

The rose is red, 142

The score was eight to eight, 216

The sea is bright blue, 133

The Senator from Minnesota?, 185, 186

The state of our union, 368, 369

The state of the world is such, 368

The state of the world today is such, 369

The thing to do from ev'ry Monday to Sunday, 75

The things we planned—, 347

The waltzes of Mittel Europa—, 279

The way we respond to the 3/4, 193

The way you wear your hat, 266

The whole wide world is in danger, 314

The whole world's always building, 28

The world is full of trouble—, 146

The world is so full of a number of things, 73

The world runs on, 139

There are lots of fellows at ev'ry dance, 111

There are many minds in circulation, 286

There are men who, in their leisure, 276

There are ninety-seven thousand seven hundred and three, 361

There are some dames who, lamping men, 45

THERE I'D SETTLE DOWN, 126 Lyric © 1993 Ira Gershwin Music.[1]

There is no doubt, 134

THERE IS NO MUSIC, 364 © 1948 (Renewed) Ira Gershwin Music and Four Jays Music Company.[60]

There is no one greater, 213

There is one at ev'ry party, 142

There is something peculiar, 9

There isn't a jokesmith 'neath the sun, 8

THERE NEVER WAS SUCH A CHARMING WAR, 158 © 1993 Ira Gershwin Music.[1]

There once was a girl named Jenny, 294

There should be dancing in the streets!, 195

There was a jolly British tar, 269

There was a time, 388

THERE WAS LIFE, THERE WAS LOVE, THERE WAS LAUGHTER, See FAREWELL SONG—"THERE WAS LIFE, THERE WAS LOVE, THERE WAS LAUGHTER"

There we were, way up in an Alp!, 99

THERE'LL BE LIFE, LOVE, AND LAUGHTER, See LOVE SONG—"THERE'LL BE LIFE, LOVE, AND LAUGHTER"

There'll be life, there'll be love, there'll be laughter . . . , 330

THERE'S A BOAT DAT'S LEAVIN' SOON FOR NEW YORK, 240 © 1935 (Renewed) George Gershwin Music, Ira Gershwin Music, and DuBose and Dorothy Heyward Memorial Fund Publishing.[45]

There's a cabaret in this city, 72

There's a cheerful little earful, 233

There's a crazy, lackadaisy sort of feeling in the air—, 223

There's a crazy, lackadaisy sort of feeling in the town—, 223

There's a girl—Liza Elliott, 288

There's a haven meant for you and me, 75

There's a part of Manhattan, 65

There's a place that never knows dull care, 24

There's a query, 257

There's a saying old, 83

There's a somebody I'm longing to see, 84

There's a somebody I've wanted to see, 84

There's a southern spiritual, 62

There's a treat in store for you, 74

There's a wondrous fascination, 26

There's always something doing, 118

There's an aggregation down South, 77

THERE'S AN ISLAND IN THE WEST INDIES, See ISLAND IN THE WEST INDIES

There's just one thing about a king that makes his job worth trying, 117

THERE'S MAGIC IN THE AIR, 6 © 1993 Ira Gershwin Music.[1]

There's Malichevsky, Rubinstein, Arensky, and Tschaikowsky, 293

There's no bread upon the table, 260

THERE'S NO HOLDING ME, 343 © 1946 (Renewed) PolyGram International Publishing, Inc.[57]

There's no holding me, 389

There's no organization that I'm not a member of, 228

There's no other way—, 367

There's no spot on any map of Rand McNally, 302

There's no stopping me, 389

There's no use sighing, 28

There's nothing can attain the charms, 121

THERE'S NOTHING LIKE MARRIAGE FOR PEOPLE, 344 Lyric © 1959 (Renewed) Ira Gershwin; © 1993 Ira Gershwin Music.[1]

There's nothing, oh nothing, like marriage for people—, 344

There's one hour of the night, 41

There's some sweet faraway someone, 43

THERE'S SOMETHING ABOUT ME THEY LIKE, 19 Lyric © 1993 Ira Gershwin Music and Fred Jackson Publishing Descendants.[11]

THERE'S SOMETHING WE'RE WORRIED ABOUT, 211, 213 © 1993 Ira Gershwin Music.[1]

THESE CHARMING PEOPLE, 70 © 1925 (Renewed) WB Music Corp.[8]

THESE DAYS, 364 © 1948 (Renewed) Ira Gershwin Music and Four Jays Music Company.[60]

THEY ALL LAUGHED, 264 © 1936 George Gershwin Music and Ira Gershwin Music.[48]

THEY CAN'T TAKE THAT AWAY FROM ME, 266 © 1936 (Renewed) George Gershwin Music and Ira Gershwin Music.[48]

THEY DON'T MAKE 'EM THAT WAY ANYMORE, 39 Lyric © 1993 Ira Gershwin Music.[1]

They met in a garden years ago, 379

They needed a man who was brave and strong, 165

They're writing songs of love, 167

THINGS!, 227 © 1937 (Renewed) Harwin Music Co., WB Music Corp., and Glocca Morra Music.[40]

THINGS ARE LOOKING UP, 270 © 1937 (Renewed) George Gershwin Music and Ira Gershwin Music.[48]

Things have come to a pretty pass—, 265

Things you tell me not to do, 233

Think of trains with the speed of lightning!, 318

THIS COULD GO ON FOR YEARS (1927 VERSION), See PATRIOTIC RALLY (1927 VERSION)

THIS COULD GO ON FOR YEARS (1930 VERSION), 152 © 1930 (Renewed) WB Music Corp.[28]

This is a dance from La Frita—, 224

This is a mutiny!, 319

THIS IS NEW, 288 © 1941 (Renewed) Chappell & Co. and Hampshire House Publishing Corp.[55]

This morning, October the fifth, 219

This mundane life of Mondays, 370

THIS NIGHT IN FLORENCE, 331 Lyric © 1993 Ira Gershwin Music.[1]

THIS PARTICULAR PARTY, 135 © 1993 Ira Gershwin Music.[1]

This reunion brings a glow that's rapturous, 339

This time it's really love, 25

Tho' I always laugh and frolic, 37

Tho' I'm not the least bit willful, 37

THOSE EYES, See YOUR EYES! YOUR SMILE!

Though I'm known as one who's always taking chances—, 363

Though life to me just seems to be, 26

Though my clothes from London are imported—, 151

Though my voice is just a singsong, 92

Though our troubles may to us seem endless, 21

Though she plays the harp in the orchestra, 364

Though she plays the harp in the symphony, 364

Though the cares of state are ever so troublesome, 116

Though the old Bartenders' Union don't come 'round no more for dues, 39

Though the traffic's overflowing, 364

Though they say love is blind, 19

Though today is a blue day, 80

Though we're called a people of serious mind, 359

Though you have gentility, 209

Though you know I'm rather British, 80

Though you've read about Old King Cole, 40

THREE CHEERS FOR THE UNION (1927 VERSION), See PATRIOTIC RALLY (1927 VERSION)

THREE CHEERS FOR THE UNION (1930 VERSION), 152 © 1930 (Renewed) WB Music Corp.[28]

THREE-QUARTER TIME, See IN THREE-QUARTER TIME

THREE TIMES A DAY, 61 © 1925 (Renewed) WB Music Corp., Warner Bros. Inc., and Stephen Ballentine Music.[16]

THROTTLE THROTTLEBOTTOM, 216 © 1987 George Gershwin Music and Ira Gershwin Music.[12]

Through with trouble! Watch me bubble!, 245

Till black is white, 234

TILL THEN, 234 © 1933 (Renewed) PolyGram International Publishing, Inc.[4]

TIME MARCHES ON!, 243 Lyric © 1993 Ira Gershwin Music.[1]

TIME: THE PRESENT, 313 © 1956 (Renewed) PolyGram International Publishing, Inc.[4]

Ting-a-ling, the wedding bells will jing-a-ling-a-ling, 51

TIP-TOES, 74 © 1977 George Gershwin Music and Ira Gershwin Music.[12]

TIP-TOES—FINALE, ACT I, 72 © 1977 George Gershwin Music and Ira Gershwin Music.[12]

TIP-TOES—OPENING, ACT I, See WAITING FOR THE TRAIN

TIP-TOES—OPENING, ACT I, SCENE 2, See LADY LUCK

T'ME, BABY, YOU'RE NEWS, See BABY, YOU'RE NEWS

TO BEAUTIFY THE BAY, See LIFE BEGINS AT CITY HALL

To have a ghost of a chance, 13

To set the court a-tingle, 216

To show affection, 106

Today I was true to the one girl, 121

TODAY'S THE DAY (TO MAKE WAY FOR TOMORROW), *See* MAKE WAY FOR TOMORROW

TODDLIN' ALONG, *See* WORLD IS MINE, THE

Toddling along, 110

TOGETHER AT LAST, 203 © 1993 Ira Gershwin Music.[1]

Tolstoy, Pushkin—, 173

TOMORROW IS THE TIME, 338 Lyric © 1993 Ira Gershwin Music.[1]

TONIGHT, 199 © 1993 George Gershwin Music and Ira Gershwin Music.[12]

Tonight, July the fourth, 211

TONIGHT'S THE NIGHT, 145 © 1992 George Gershwin Music, Ira Gershwin Music, and Gilbert Keyes Music.[33]

Too bad. You should always have a witness . . . , 335

True sweethearts are again united 41

Too long, too long, too long, 376

TOUR OF THE TOWN, 355 © 1993 Ira Gershwin Music.[1]

TRAILER FOR *THE 1936 BROADWAY GOLD MELODY DIGGERS*, 249 © 1993 Ira and Leonore Gershwin Trusts and David Freedman Publishing Descendants.

TRA-LA-LA, 25 © 1922 (Renewed) WB Music Corp.[7] Additional lyrics © 1951 (Renewed) WB Music Corp.[14]

Tra la la la, Good morning, Mr. Colonel!, 92, 152

TREASURE GIRL—FINALE, ACT I, 132 © 1993 Ira Gershwin Music.[1]

TREASURE GIRL—OPENING, ACT I, SCENE 3, *See* PLACE IN THE COUNTRY

TREASURE GIRL—OPENING, ACT II, *See* TREASURE ISLAND

TREASURE ISLAND, 133 © 1993 Ira Gershwin Music.[1]

TREAT ME ROUGH, 167 © 1944 (Renewed) WB Music Corp.[28]

TRIAL BY MUSIC—"YOU HAVE TO DO WHAT YOU DO DO," 334 © 1945 (Renewed) Chappell & Co. and Hampshire House Publishing Corp.[55]

TRIAL COMBINED WITH CIRCUS, A, 297 Lyric © 1993 Ira Gershwin Music.[1]

TRIAL OF THROTTLEBOTTOM, THE, *See* THAT'S WHAT HE DID!, et al.

TRIAL OF WINTERGREEN, THE, *See* HELL OF A HOLE, A, et al.

TRIO—"I KNOW WHERE THERE'S A COZY NOOK," 330 Lyric © 1959 (Renewed) Ira Gershwin; 1993 Ira Gershwin Music.[1]

TRIO—"THE NOSY COOK," *See* TRIO—"I KNOW WHERE THERE'S A COZY NOOK"

TROPICAL NIGHT, 314 Lyric © 1993 Ira Gershwin Music.[1]

Trouble may hound us, 47

TRUE LOVE (missing), 12

True sweethearts are again united 41

TRUE TO THEM ALL, 121 © 1993 Ira Gershwin Music.[1]

TRUMPETER, BLOW YOUR GOLDEN HORN, 187 © 1932 (Renewed) WB Music Corp.[28]

Try Jamaica Chewing Gum, 380

TURN TO THE DREAMS AHEAD, 36 Lyric © 1993 Ira Gershwin Music.[1]

Turn to the dreams that are lying before you, 36

TV COMMERCIAL, THE, 374 © 1954 (Renewed) Harwin Music Corp. and Ira Gershwin Music.[64]

'Twas a silver summer night, 141

TWEEDLEDEE, *See* WINTERGREEN V. TWEEDLEDEE

TWEEDLEDEE FOR PRESIDENT, 206 © 1987 George Gershwin Music and Ira Gershwin Music. Additional material © 1931 (Renewed) WB Music Corp.[36]

Tweedledee! Tweedledee!, 206

Tweet, Tweets, 223

TWO HEARTS WILL BLEND AS ONE, 120 © 1993 Ira Gershwin Music.[1]

TWO LITTLE GIRLS IN BLUE, 16 Lyric © 1993 Ira Gershwin Music.[1]

TWO LITTLE GIRLS IN BLUE—FINALE, ACT I, *See* WE'RE OFF TO INDIA

TWO LITTLE GIRLS IN BLUE—FINALE, ACT II, 20 Lyric © 1993 Ira Gershwin Music.[1]

TWO LITTLE GIRLS IN BLUE—OPENING, ACT I, *See* WE'RE OFF ON A WONDERFUL TRIP

TWO LITTLE GIRLS IN BLUE—OPENING, ACT II, *See* HERE, STEWARD

TWO WALTZES IN C, *See* TONIGHT

TYPICAL SELF-MADE AMERICAN (1927 VERSION), 91 © 1930 (Renewed) WB Music Corp. Additional material © 1991 George Gershwin Music and Ira Gershwin Music.[26]

TYPICAL SELF-MADE AMERICAN (1930 VERSION), 151 © 1930 (Renewed) WB Music Corp.[28]

UH-UH, 37 © 1924 (Renewed) WB Music Corp. and Warner Bros. Inc.[10]

UKULELE LORELEI, 64 © 1993 Ira Gershwin Music and Stephen Ballentine Music.[3]

UNDER THE CINNAMON TREE, 138 © 1993 Ira Gershwin Music.[1]

UNDER THE FURLOUGH MOON, 121 © 1993 Ira Gershwin Music.[1]

UNFORGETTABLE, 296 Lyric © 1993 Ira Gershwin Music.[1]

UNION LEAGUE, THE, 210 Lyric © 1959 (Renewed) Ira Gershwin; © 1987 George Gershwin Music and Ira Gershwin Music.[12]

UNION SQUARE, 207 © 1933 (Renewed) WB Music Corp. Additional material © 1987 George Gershwin Music and Ira Gershwin Music.[37]

UNITE, YOU WORKERS OF ALL NATIONS, 306 Lyric © 1993 Ira Gershwin Music.[1]

UNOFFICIAL SPOKESMAN, THE (1927 VERSION), 92 © 1930 (Renewed) WB Music Corp. Additional material © 1991 George Gershwin Music and Ira Gershwin Music.[26]

UNOFFICIAL SPOKESMAN, THE (1930 VERSION), 152 © 1930 (Renewed) WB Music Corp.[28]

UNSPOKEN LAW, THE, 297 Lyric © 1993 Ira Gershwin Music.[1]

UP AND AT 'EM, ON TO VICTORY, 215 © 1987 George Gershwin Music and Ira Gershwin Music.[12]

Up on the top of a snow-covered mountain, 54

Used to lead a quiet existence, 275

UTOPIA, 21 Lyric © 1993 Ira Gershwin Music.[1]

Ve do not play to crowded concert houses, 371

Venice in June—The gondolas gliding—, 276

Venice in June—The music has started—, 276

Very soon my troubles will be over, 65

VIENNESE SEXTET, *See* FREUD AND JUNG AND ADLER *and* HE'S OVERSEXED!

VILLAGE SCENE JINGLES, 304 Lyric © 1993 Ira Gershwin Music.[1]

VOICE OF LOVE (CELLINI'S LOVE SONG), THE, 45 © 1924 (Renewed) WB Music Corp. and Warner Bros. Inc.[10]

Voices are singing—sorrow is winging, 36

WAGON SONG, 306 Lyric © 1993 Ira Gershwin Music.[1]

WAIT A BIT, SUSIE, 44 © 1924 (Renewed) WB Music Corp. and Warner Bros. Inc.[10]

Wait a minute! What's the proletariat?, 212

WAITING FOR THE SUN TO COME OUT, 6 © 1920 (Renewed) WB Music Corp.[6]

WAITING FOR THE TRAIN, 68 © 1977 George Gershwin Music and Ira Gershwin Music.[12]

WAKE UP, BROTHER, AND DANCE, 267 © 1937 (Renewed) George Gershwin Music and Ira Gershwin Music.[48]

WALTZING IS BETTER SITTING DOWN, *See* ONE, TWO, THREE

Want my heart's desire—, 344

WAR THAT ENDED WAR, THE, 100 © 1991 George Gershwin Music and Ira Gershwin Music.[12]

Wasn't it a wonderful dinner?, 254

Wasn't that a lovely age?, 229

Watch the little wheel spin, 69

WATCH YOUR HEAD, 203 © 1993 George Gershwin Music and Ira Gershwin Music.[12]

'Way back in Noah's Ark, 384

WE, 76 © 1993 Ira Gershwin Music.[1]

We all are yearning back home, 7

We always make a scramble for, 69

We are all in this together, 184

We are Fletcher's Come-Look-at-the-War Choral Society, 100

We are Fletcher's Get-Ready-for-War Choral Society, 93

We are Grover Whalen, and we are here today, 230

We are members, 210

We are pupils, 146

We are taught to walk with downcast eye, 146

WE ARE THE DEBS, *See* WHEN THE DEBBIES GO BY

We are the red, white, and blue nurses—, 100

WE ARE VISITORS HERE, 139 © 1993 Ira Gershwin Music.[1]

We can't conceal, 124

We come to serenade the lovely lady we adore, 284

We didn't wait to separate the usual way . . . , 339

We don't want to know about the moratorium, 182

We fought in 1917, 96

We hardly ever faced land, 380

We have to serve six meals a day, 18

We heard the rustle of the trees, 92

We hope you'll soon be dancing to the score, 257

We laugh and we sing, Oom-pah-pah, 193

We live in an age that's the pinnacle, 338

We must make it our ambition, 70

We must make the best of it, 22

We must try to make the best of it, 21

We never seem to realize, 87

We once won all the glories, 225

We really think you ought to know, 28

We sing of the charm of the Nineties, 229

We sing the praise of Mapleton High, 288

We sing you a tale of a man and a maid, 362

We—spelt W E—, 76

We stand undaunted in the fray, 96

We told you this age was the pinnacle, 345

We understand / That in this land, 322

We want to tell you to your face, 202

We will not sing you a love song, 257

WEAKEN A BIT, 75 © 1993 Ira Gershwin Music.[1]

Weary are the flowers, 6

WEATHERMAN, 55 © 1993 Ira Gershwin Music.[1]

Weaving a dress for my lady, 34

We'd love / To take a picture of, 83

The wedding bell will chime, 338

WEDDING DREAM, *See* MAPLETON HIGH CHORALE, et al.

WEEKEND, 124 Lyric © 1993 Ira Gershwin Music.[1]

WEEKEND CRUISE, A, 228 © 1934 (Renewed) Harwin Music Co., WB Music Corp., and Glocca Morra Music.[40]

WEEKEND IN THE COUNTRY, 359 © 1948 (Renewed) Ira Gershwin Music and Four Jays Music Company.[60]

WELCOME SONG, 355 Lyric © 1993 Ira Gershwin Music.[1]

WELCOME TO THE MELTING POT, *See* DREAM SEQUENCE

Well, I just wanted to say . . . , 379

WELL-KNOWN SKIES OF BLUE, THE, 362 Lyric © 1993 Ira Gershwin Music.[1]

We'll be like These Charming People, 70

We'll build a little theatre of our own, 57

WE'LL IMPEACH HIM, 183 © 1932 (Renewed) WB Music Corp.[28]

We'll meet some heavenly day, 349

WE'RE ALL A-WORRY, ALL AGOG, *See* AVIATOR

We're all here for a rally, 93, 152

We're bronco busters; we bust the broncos, 163

We're from the *Journal*, the *Wahrheit*, the *Telegram*, the *Times*, 172

WE'RE HERE BECAUSE, 48 © 1977 George Gershwin Music and Ira Gershwin Music.[12]

We're here to help to see it through—, 315

We're here to see the fighting—, 100

We're here, we're here, we're here because, 48

We're in Atlantic City, 176

We're looking for a place, 129

We're looking for the treasure, 132

We're not going to start our minstrel show, 145

WE'RE OFF ON A WONDERFUL TRIP, 15 Lyric © 1993 Ira Gershwin Music.[1]

WE'RE OFF TO INDIA, 18 Lyric © 1993 Ira Gershwin Music.[1]

We're soldiers of a duchy, 332

"WE'RE SOLDIERS OF THE DUCHY," *See* MARCH OF THE SOLDIERS OF THE DUCHY—"JUST IN CASE"

We're the Dresden Northwest Mounted, 197

We're the finest of the finest of the finest, 111

We're the one, two, three, four, five, six, seven, eight, nine Supreme ball players, 216

We're the one, two, three, four, five, six, seven, eight, nine Supreme Court Judges, 180

Weren't those the lovely days?, 229

WEST INDIES, *See* ISLAND IN THE WEST INDIES

West Point—, / You will ever be calling me, 122

WEST POINT BUGLE, *See* ROSALIE—FINALE, ACT I

We've been sleeping all day, 223

We've come down to meet the train, 68

We've got a bottle of rum—, 128

We've traveled far, 124

What a killing we could make, 50

What a lovely day for a lovely wedding, 290

What a spot, this—, 373

WHAT AM I GONNA DO?, *See* MY ONE AND ONLY

What am I here for?, 374

WHAT ARE WE HERE FOR?, 133 © 1928 (Renewed) WB Music Corp.[28]

WHAT CAN I DO?, 27 Lyric © 1993 Ira Gershwin Music and Schuyler Greene Publishing Descendants.[15]

What can I say, 172

What can stop us?, 343

WHAT CAN YOU SAY IN A LOVE SONG? (THAT HASN'T BEEN SAID BEFORE?), 226 © 1934 (Renewed) Harwin Music Co., WB Music Corp., and Glocca Morra Music.[40]

WHAT CAUSES THAT?, 133 © 1987 George Gershwin Music and Ira Gershwin Music.[29]

WHAT COULD I DO?, 115 © 1993 Ira Gershwin Music.[1]

WHAT I CARE!, 26 Lyric © 1993 Ira Gershwin Music and Schuyler Greene Publishing Descendants.[15]

WHAT I LOVE TO HEAR, *See* THAT'S THE BEST OF ALL

WHAT I STARTED TO STAY, *See* I FORGOT WHAT I STARTED TO SAY

What made Good Queen Bess, 270

What makes my misery fly, 131

WHAT MORE CAN A GENERAL DO, *See* I'VE BRUSHED MY TEETH

WHAT OF IT?, 38 Lyric © 1993 Ira Gershwin Music.[1]

WHAT SORT OF WEDDING IS THIS?, 198 © 1993 Ira Gershwin Music.[1]

WHAT TO DO?, *See* WHOOPEE

What was there to do?, 253

What we want to know is: When are we going to be paid?, 217

What's the latest rage, 252

WHAT'S THE PROLETARIAT?, 211, 213 © 1993 Ira Gershwin Music.[1]

WHAT'S THE USE?, 87 © 1993 Ira Gershwin Music.[1]

WHAT'S THE USE OF HANGIN' AROUND WITH YOU?, *See* HANGIN' AROUND WITH YOU

What's the use of saving for that rainy day, 261

What's this? What *is* this? What's this?, 211

When a body knows nobody, 172

When a child is ushered into, 189

When a fella / Tries to tell a, 142

When a fellow feels he's got to win a girlie's handie, 103

When a guy like Byron, 130

When a heart is bruised a bit, 38

WHEN ALL YOUR CASTLES COME TUMBLING DOWN, 28 © 1922 (Renewed) WB Music Corp. and Warner Bros. Inc.[10]

When cadets are on parade, 117

WHEN CADETS PARADE, 122 © 1993 Ira Gershwin Music.[1]

WHEN DO WE DANCE?, 70 © 1925 (Renewed) WB Music Corp.[8]

When flowers are blooming, perfuming the air, 22

When Fred'rick the Great was at Potsdam, 193

When happy boy and girl decide, 338

When I am sad and grave, 26

When I crossed the ocean, 119

When I go my way, 57

When I keep seeing things and going places, 200

When I look at a girl, at a girl like you, 40

When I look at you, I have to own up, 68

When I look in the mirror ev'ry morning as I shave, 229

When I marry, if I marry, 142

When I take a husband, I shall want one that will last, 25

When I want a melody, 279

When I was born into this universe, 93, 152

When I was born, they found a silver spoon in my mouth, 167

When I was but a little lad, 227

When I went romancin', 359

When I'm away from you, I start despairing—, 133

When I'm stepping with baby—, 86

WHEN I'M WITH THE GIRLS, 16 Lyric © 1993 Ira Gershwin Music.[1]

WHEN I'M WITHOUT YOU, See I'M A POACHED EGG

When it's cactus time in Arizona, 168

When it's wintertime, many flowers droop, 385

When I've got shoes with wings on—, 361

When lady fair, 342

When music is playing, 200

When my oil well starts gush-gush-gushing, 65

When nations get together, 214

When night is falling, 20

WHEN OUR SHIP COMES SAILING IN, 87 © 1993 Ira Gershwin Music.[1]

When our supply of pieces of eight, 74

When Spring puts on her gay apparel, 123

When the bell of doom is clanging, 324

When the bells in the belfry go ding-dong, 86

When the city is sweltering, 261

When the clouds, the skies, are filling, 6

WHEN THE DEBBIES GO BY, 61 © 1993 Ira Gershwin Music and Stephen Ballentine Music.[3]

WHEN THE DUCHESS IS AWAY, See MADRIGAL—"WHEN THE DUCHESS IS AWAY"

When the hurdy-gurdy man is here, 34

WHEN THE JUDGES DOFF THE ERMINE, See NO BETTER WAY TO START A CASE

When the latest film by Sennett, 20

When the little pinholes start peeping through the blue, 57

When the mellow moon begins to beam, 55, 94

WHEN THE RIGHT ONE COMES ALONG, 112 © 1993 Ira Gershwin Music.[1]

When the voodoo drum is drumming, 370

When there's a chance for me to dance, 6

WHEN THERE'S A CHANCE TO DANCE, 6 © 1993 Ira Gershwin Music.[1]

When troubles are too frightful, 322

When two arms steal around me, 27

When we get a furlough, do we rush away?, 121

When we go waltzing—, 354

When we met I thought we two were very well matched, 273

When we were little tots, our brains would always go a-tingling, 111

When you and me first meet-a, 10

When you find your friends have tricked you, 87

When you kiss your dad, I've nothing to say, 117

When you lend a helping hand to others, 31

When you meet girls most attractive, 26

When you roam, 122

When you want to, you are able, 223

When your eyes look into mine, 115

When your ladylove you meet, 380

WHEN YOU'RE SINGLE, 108 © 1993 Ira Gershwin Music.[1]

WHERE THE DELICATESSEN FLOWS, See IN SARDINIA

Where the pomegranates used to grow, 314

WHERE YOU GO, I GO, 200 © 1933 (Renewed) WB Music Corp.[28]

WHERE'S THE BOY? HERE'S THE GIRL!, 134 © 1928 (Renewed) WB Music Corp.[28]

Whether you're a Swiss bell ringer, 370

While other lads were trying out the bicycle, 91, 151

While the silver furlough moon, 115

WHILE WE'RE WAITING FOR THE BABY, 189 © 1993 Ira Gershwin Music.[1]

Who brings glamour to cafés, 248

WHO CARES?, 182, 183 © 1931 (Renewed) WB Music Corp.[28]

WHO COULD ASK FOR ANYTHING MORE?, See I'M ABOUT TO BE A MOTHER

Who is the chap—, 80

Who is the guy—, 79

WHO IS THE LUCKY GIRL TO BE?, 176 © 1932 (Renewed) WB Music Corp.[28]

Who is the lucky girl to be?, 176, 177

Who knows if we'd agree?, 131

WHOLE TRUTH, THE, 215 © 1991 Ira Gershwin Music.[1]

WHOLE WORLD'S TURNING BLUE, THE, 41 Lyric © 1993 Ira Gershwin Music and Morrie Ryskind Publishing Descendants.[20]

WHOOPEE, 123 Lyric © 1993 Ira Gershwin Music.[1]

WHO'S COMPLAINING?, 308 © 1943 (Renewed) PolyGram International Publishing, Inc.[52]

WHO'S THE GREATEST?, 213, 214 © 1987 George Gershwin Music and Ira Gershwin Music.[12]

Who's the greatest leader, 214, 215

WHO'S WHO WITH YOU?, 7 © 1921 (Renewed) WB Music Corp.[5]

Why am I happy as the well-known lark, 245

Why are people gay, 178

WHY BE GOOD?, 126 Lyric © 1993 Ira Gershwin Music.[1]

Why can't we be judges judging evildoers?, 352

Why did I wander, 195

WHY DO I LOVE YOU?, 61 © 1925 (Renewed) WB Music Corp., Warner Bros. Inc., and Stephen Ballentine Music.[16]

Why do I love you, love you, love you?, 61, 64

WHY DOES EV'RYBODY HAVE TO CUT IN?, See DANCE ALONE WITH YOU

Why don't we stay as we are, 348

Why must we part and have to start, 340

WHY SAVE FOR THAT RAINY DAY?, 261 Lyric © 1993 Ira Gershwin Music.[1]

Why should worry bother, 195

WHY SPEAK OF MONEY?, 214 © 1987 George Gershwin Music and Ira Gershwin Music.[12]

WILL YOU LOVE ME MONDAY MORNING AS YOU DID ON FRIDAY NIGHT?, See WEEKEND CRUISE, A

WILL YOU REMEMBER ME?, 57 © 1987 George Gershwin Music and Ira Gershwin Music.[18]

WIN SOME WINSOME GIRL (lyrics missing), 16

Window gazing, nothing rankles, 210

WINTERGREEN FOR PRESIDENT, 176 © 1932 (Renewed) New World Music.[28]

WINTERGREEN V. TWEEDLEDEE, See TWEEDLEDEE FOR PRESIDENT

Wise men all have come to this conclusion, 6

WISHING TREE OF HARLEM, 260 Lyric © 1993 Ira Gershwin Music.[1]

With a heart as light as the thistledown, 92

With an Irish cook and a wild-man crew, 17

With golf and tennis 'round you, 359

With nothing but pity, 325, 336

With you I used to roam, 289

Without the least excuse, 293

WIZARD OF THE AGE, THE, See UNOFFICIAL SPOKESMAN, THE

WOMAN AT THE ALTAR, THE, 288 © 1941 (Renewed) Chappell & Co. and Hampshire House Publishing Corp.[55]

WOMAN, THERE IS NO LIVING WITH YOU, 371 © 1951 (Renewed) Ira Gershwin Music and Chappell & Co.[61]

Woman, you are of the opposite sex—, 371

WOMAN'S TOUCH, THE, 79 © 1958 (Renewed) New World Music Company (Ltd.)

WOMEN CAN BE PEOPLE, TOO, See MARCH OF THE SUFFRAGETTES

WOMEN OF AMERICA, 315 © 1942 Ted Grouya and Ira Gershwin.

Wonderful Juanita, 53

Wonderful maid, I can't evade, 6

WONDERFUL PARTY, A, 47 © 1977 George Gershwin Music and Ira Gershwin Music.[12]

WONDERFUL TRIP, A, *See* WE'RE OFF ON A WONDERFUL TRIP

WONDERFUL U.S.A., 16 Lyric © 1993 Ira Gershwin Music.[1]

Wondering whether this thundering weather will clear up soon—, 55

WOO, WOO, WOO, WOO, MANHATTAN, 322 Lyric © 1993 Ira Gershwin Music.[1]

WORDS WITHOUT MUSIC, 246 © 1935 (Renewed) Chappell & Co. and Ira Gershwin Music.[47]

Work! Get going!, 305

Work, you workers!, 305

WORLD IS FULL OF VILLAINS, THE, *See* CHANT OF LAW AND ORDER—"THE WORLD IS FULL OF VILLAINS"

WORLD IS MINE, THE, 110 © 1927 (Renewed) WB Music Corp.[28]

WORLD'S INAMORATA, THE, *See* HUXLEY

Would you like to live a dream?, 380

WRONG THING AT THE RIGHT TIME, THE, 37 © 1925 (Renewed) WB Music Corp. and Warner Bros. Inc.[10]

Yankee doo doodle-oo doodle-oo, 155

YANKEE DOODLE RHYTHM, 94 © 1927 (Renewed) WB Music Corp.[28]

Yea bo, but isn't love great! Gee whiz!, 115

YELLOW BLUES, 138 © 1993 Ira Gershwin Music.[1]

YES, HE'S A BACHELOR, 211 © 1993 Ira Gershwin Music.[1]

Yes, when are we gonna be paid?, 217

Yesterday the sky was black, 351

You are my all, 30

YOU ARE NOT THE GIRL (lyrics missing), 4

YOU ARE UNFORGETTABLE, *See* UNFORGETTABLE

You buy a block of stock, say, American Tel, 347

"You can lose your heart, but better watch your head!," 203

YOU CAN'T UNSCRAMBLE SCRAMBLED EGGS, 169 © 1993 Ira Gershwin Music.[1]

You dare assert that you were hurt, 53

You darling, you ducky, you sweet so-and-so!, 125

You fall in love with the modern Galahad, 125

You gave her the best years of your life, 293

YOU GO WHERE I GO, *See* WHERE YOU GO, I GO

You have got that certain something, 194

YOU HAVE TO DO WHAT YOU DO DO, *See* TRIAL BY MUSIC—"YOU HAVE TO DO WHAT YOU DO DO"

YOU KNOW HOW IT IS, 121 © 1993 Ira Gershwin Music.[1]

You know the story of the Capulets, 278

You lose your heart, and you start, 87

YOU MAY THROW ALL THE RICE YOU DESIRE, 4 Lyric © 1973, 1993 Ira Gershwin Music.[1]

YOU MUST COME OVER BLUES, 45 Lyric © 1925 (Renewed) WB Music Corp. and Warner Bros. Inc.[10]

You say eether and I say eyether, 265

You sigh, 195

YOU STARTED IT, 173 © 1987 George Gershwin Music and Ira Gershwin Music.[18]

YOU STARTED SOMETHING, 18 © 1921 (Renewed) WB Music Corp.[5]

You take the subway to the street called Wall, 347

You wanna have bells that'll ring?, 373

You were enthralling, how could I help falling, 97

You will find, / That it's a great life only, 75

YOU'D BE HARD TO REPLACE, 358 © 1948, 1949 (Renewed) Chappell & Co. and Four Jays Music Company.[59]

You'd think a little more of me, 6

You'll adore / The step that ev'ryone's been waiting for, 358

You'll find the bluebird, the rainbow, the silver lining, too, 75

You'll find the whole world's turning blue, 41

You'll find true happiness along, 31

YOU'LL PARDON ME IF I REVEAL, 189 © 1993 Ira Gershwin Music.[1]

You'll pardon me if I / Should sigh a manly sigh, 203

You'll start to sway in a gay sort of way, 15

YOUNGER GENERATION, 305 © 1943 (Renewed) Chappell & Co.[51]

YOUR EYES! YOUR SMILE!, 109 © 1987 George Gershwin Music and Ira Gershwin Music.[18]

Your institutions all are meritorious, 16

YOUR WONDERFUL U.S.A., *See* WONDERFUL U.S.A.

YOU'RE A BUILDER-UPPER, 223 © 1934 (Renewed) Harwin Music Co., WB Music Corp., and Glocca Morra Music.[40]

You're a very naughty boy, 33

You're as cute as you can be, Baby!, 64

You're as fair as you can be—, 63

You're each of you a dumb thing, 123

YOU'RE FAR TOO NEAR ME, *See* LOVE SONG—"YOU'RE FAR TOO NEAR ME"

You're gonna start a-reeling, 9

YOU'RE MY HIGHLAND FLING, *See* MY ONE AND ONLY HIGHLAND FLING

You're sitting with a man on a moonlit veranda—, 246, 247

You're so delishious, 172

You're so full of trickery—, 133, 272

You're the girl / I've been waiting for, 134

You're the sweetest flower that grows, 224

You've a charm that is all your own—, 85

YOU'VE GOT WHAT GETS ME, 170 © 1932 (Renewed) WB Music Corp.[28]

YOU'VE GOT WHAT IT TAKES, *See* SEARCH IS THROUGH, THE

You've heard of spontaneous combustion, Mr. Meachem, 344

You've really got me—, 385

ZODIAC SONG, THE, *See* SONG OF THE ZODIAC

Zoom—zoom, zoom—zoom, 264

ZWEI HERTZEN, 180 © 1993 Ira Gershwin Music.[1]

A NOTE ON THE TYPE

This book was set in Bodoni Book, named after
Giambattista Bodoni (1740–1813), son of a printer of
Piedmont. After gaining experience and fame as
superintendent of the Press of the Propaganda in
Rome, Bodoni became, in 1766, the head of the ducal
printing house at Parma, which he soon made the
foremost of its kind in Europe. In type designing he
was an innovator, making his new faces rounder,
wider, and lighter, with greater openness and delicacy.
His types were rather too rigidly perfect in detail, the
thick lines contrasting sharply with the thin wiry
lines. It was doubtless this feature that caused
William Morris to condemn the Bodoni types as
"swelteringly hideous." Bodoni Book, as originally
reproduced by the Linotype Company, is a modern
version based not on any one of Bodoni's fonts, but
on a composite conception of the Bodoni manner,
designed to avoid the details stigmatized as "bad"
by typographical experts and to secure the pleasing
and effective results of which the Bodoni types
are capable.

Composed by The Haddon Craftsmen, Inc.,
Scranton, Pennsylvania

Printed and bound by Kingsport Press,
Kingsport, Tennessee

Designed by Cassandra J. Pappas,
following an original design by Holly McNeely